W9-BCN-445

BUSINESS & SOCIETY

Ethics and
Stakeholder Management
FOURTH EDITION

Archie B. Carroll
University of Georgia

Ann K. Buchholtz
University of Georgia

South-Western College Publishing
Thomson Learning™

Australia • Canada • Denmark • Japan • Mexico • New Zealand • Philippines
Puerto Rico • Singapore • South Africa • Spain • United Kingdom • United States

Business & Society: Ethics and Stakeholder Management, 4e,
by Archie B. Carroll & Ann K. Buchholtz

Publisher: Dave Shaut
Executive Editor: John Szilagyi
Developmental Editors: Judith O'Neill and Mardell Toomey
Marketing Manager: Rob Bloom
Production Editor: Elizabeth A. Shipp
Manufacturing Coordinator: Dana Began Schwartz
Internal Design: Michael H. Stratton
Cover Design: Matulionis Design
Cover Image: ©1999/PhotoDisc, Inc.
Production House: Stratford Publishing Services
Printer: R.R. Donnelley & Sons Company—Crawfordsville Manufacturing Division

COPYRIGHT ©2000 by South-Western College Publishing, a division of Thomson Learning.
The Thomson Learning logo is a registered trademark used herein under license.

All Rights Reserved. No part of this work covered by the copyright hereon may be reproduced or used in any form or by any means—graphic, electronic, or mechanical, including photocopying, recording, taping, or information storage and retrieval systems—without the written permission of the publisher.

Printed in the United States of America
1 2 3 4 5 02 01 00 99

For more information contact South-Western College Publishing, 5101 Madison Road, Cincinnati, Ohio, 45227 or find us on the Internet at http://www.swcollege.com

For permission to use material from this text or product, contact us by
- **telephone: 1-800-730-2214**
- **fax: 1-800-730-2215**
- **web: http://www.thomsonrights.com**

Library of Congress Cataloging-in-Publication Data
Carroll, Archie B.
    Business & society : ethics and stakeholder management / Archie B.
Carroll, Ann K. Buchholtz — 4th ed.
        p.   cm.
    Includes bibliographical references.
    ISBN 0-324-00102-9
    1. Business ethics. 2. Social responsibility of business—United
States.   I. Buchholtz, Ann K.   II. Title.
HF5387.C35 1999   99-58739
658.4'08—dc20

This book is printed on acid-free paper.

Contents

CASES

Preface

Business & Society: Ethics and Stakeholder Management, Fourth Edition, employs a stakeholder management framework, emphasizing business's social and ethical responsibilities to both external and internal stakeholder groups. A managerial perspective is embedded within this book's dual themes of business ethics and stakeholder management. The ethics dimension is essential because it is becoming increasingly clear that ethical or moral considerations are woven into the fabric of the public issues that organizations face. Economic and legal issues are inevitably present, too. However, these aspects are typically treated thoroughly in other business administration courses.

The stakeholder management perspective is essential because it requires managers to (1) identify the various groups or individuals who have stakes in the firm or its actions and decisions, and (2) incorporate the stakeholders' concerns into the firm's strategic plans and operations. Stakeholder management is an approach that increases the likelihood that decision makers will integrate ethical wisdom with management wisdom in all that they do.

COURSE DESCRIPTION

This text is intended for college and university courses that are variously titled *Business and Society; Business and Its Environment; Business and Public Policy; Social Issues in Business; Business, Government, and Society;* and *Business Ethics.* This book is appropriate for either an elective or a *required* course that fulfills the American Assembly of Collegiate Schools of Business (AACSB) requirement for a coverage of social, ethical, and political influences. It is intended for undergraduate courses, but if supplemented with other materials it could be appropriate for a graduate course.

COURSE OBJECTIVES

Depending on the placement of a course in the curriculum or the individual instructor's philosophy, this book could be used for a variety of objectives. The courses for which it is intended include several legitimate objectives, such as the following:

1. Students should be made aware of the demands emanating from stakeholders that are placed on business firms.

2. As prospective managers, students need to understand appropriate business responses and management approaches for dealing with social issues and stakeholders.

3. An appreciation of ethical issues and the influence these issues have on management decision making is important.

4. The entire question of business's legitimacy as an institution in society is at stake and must be addressed.

5. The increasing extent to which social, ethical, and public issues must be considered from a strategic perspective is critical in such courses.

NEW TO THE FOURTH EDITION

This Fourth Edition has been updated and revised to reflect the most recent research, laws, cases, and examples. Material new to this edition includes:

- A new co-author experienced in social issues related to management, corporate governance, strategic management, and nonprofit organizations

- Sixteen new cases

- Revised and updated cases from the previous edition

- A new section on the topic of feminist ethics

- A new section on "America's Promise" and corporate commitment to volunteerism

- Updated coverage of the EEOC and OSHA

- New research on PACs, corporate lobbying, and the issue of "soft money"

- Expanded coverage of the influence of new technologies on workplace privacy

- New research throughout the chapters

ETHICS IN PRACTICE FEATURE

Continuing in this Fourth Edition are features titled "Ethics in Practice." Interspersed throughout the text, these features represent actual ethical situations or dilemmas faced personally in the work experiences of our former students. These were originally written for class discussion and are real-life situations actually confronted by college students in their part-time and full-time work experiences. The students contributed these experiences on a voluntary basis, and we are pleased to acknowledge them for their contributions to the book. Instructors may wish to use these as mini-cases for class discussion.

SEARCH THE WEB FEATURE

New to the Fourth Edition is a special "Search the Web" feature in each chapter. The "Search the Web" inserts in each chapter highlight an important and relevant web page or pages that augment each chapter's text material. The "Search the Web" feature may highlight a pertinent organization and its activities or special topics covered in the chapter. These features will permit students to explore topics in depth.

STRUCTURE OF THE BOOK

Part 1 provides an introductory coverage of pertinent topics and issues. Because most courses for which this book is intended evolved from the issue of corporate social responsibility, this concept is treated early on. Part 1 documents and discusses how corporate social responsiveness evolved from social responsibility and how these two matured into a concern for corporate social performance. Also given early coverage is the stakeholder management concept.

Part 2 addresses business ethics specifically. In real life, business ethics cannot be separated from the full range of external and internal stakeholder concerns. For discussion purposes, Part 2 focuses on a variety of business ethics fundamentals, personal and organizational ethics, and the all-important global arena. Ethical issues in the international sphere are among the most complex. Although we cannot resolve these issues, an early treatment of them will help to keep them fresh in our minds throughout the study of this book.

External stakeholder issues are the subject of Part 3. Vital topics here include business's relations with government, consumers, the environment, and the community.

The theme of Part 4 is internal stakeholder issues. Here we consider employees and the related issues of employee rights, employment discrimination, and affirmative action. Owner stakeholders are also treated in Part 4. The topic of corporate governance captures most owner stakeholder concerns.

Part 5 addresses strategic management for social responsiveness. The purpose of this section is to discuss management considerations for dealing with the issues developed in Parts 1 to 4. A strategic management perspective is vital because these issues have impacts on the total organization and have become all-consuming to many upper-level managers. Special treatment is given to corporate public policy, issues and crisis management, and public affairs management. Some instructors may elect to cover Part 5 earlier in their courses. Part 5 could easily be covered after Part 1 or Part 2. This option would be most appropriate for those who desire to emphasize the strategic management perspective.

CASE STUDIES

The 37 cases at the end of the book address a wide range of topics and decision situations. The cases are of varying length. More than 40 percent of the cases are new to the Fourth Edition. Many of the cases have been updated. All the cases are intended to provide instructors and students with real-life contexts within which to further analyze course issues and topics covered throughout the book. The cases have intentionally been placed at the end of the text material so that instructors will feel freer to use them as they desire.

Many of the cases in this book carry ramifications that spill over into several areas. Almost all of them may be used for different chapters. Also provided is a set of guidelines for case analysis that the instructor may wish to use in place of or in addition to the questions that appear at the end of each case. The Instructor's Manual provides suggestions regarding which cases to use with each chapter.

SUPPORT FOR THE INSTRUCTOR

Instructor's Manual with Test Bank (ISBN 0-324-00103-7). Prepared by David A. Vance, Southern Illinois University, the Instructor's Manual includes teaching suggestions, complete chapter outlines, highlighted key terms, answers to discussion questions, and recommended cases. The test bank for each chapter includes true/false and multiple choice questions.

PowerPoint Slides (0-324-00104-5). There are more than 200 slides. The PowerPoint 4.0 presentation is colorful and varied, designed to hold students' interest and reinforce all of each chapter's main points. The slides include a "Search the Web" feature, inducating web sites pertinent to each chapter, as well as key terms.

Videos (0-324-01666-2). A set of five videos, one for each part, is available in VHS format. Also appropriate for use with the text is a CNN Legal Issues video update (ISBN 0-538-88833-4), which brings the latest legal issues into the classroom. All videos are designed to elicit lively classroom discussion.

Thomson Learning Testing Tools™ (0-324-00105-3). The test bank cited above is also available electronically. Included are approximately 20 true/false and 20 multiple choice questions per chapter.

Web Site. Visit our web site at **http://carroll.swcollege.com**, where you will find a complete listing of URLs found in the text, cases from prior editions, and current cases, along with sidebars found in the text and Microsoft Word files of all ancillaries except the test bank. The presentation slides in PowerPoint TM 97, in a higher version, (9.0), are available there as well.

ACKNOWLEDGMENTS

There are many people to acknowledge for their contributions to and support of this book. First, we would like to express gratitude to our professional colleagues in the Social Issues in Management Division of the National Academy of Management, the International Association for Business and Society (IABS), and the Society for Business Ethics. Over the years these individuals have meant a lot to us and have helped provide a stimulating environment in which we could intellectually pursue these topics in which we have a common interest. Many of these individuals are cited in this book quite liberally, and their work is appreciated.

Second, we would like to thank the many adopters of the first, second, and third editions who took the time to provide us with helpful critiques. Many of their ideas and suggestions have been used for this Fourth Edition. We give particular thanks to the reviewers of this edition for their input and direction:

Steven C. Alber, Hawaii Pacific University

Douglas M. McCabe, Georgetown University

Harvey Nussbaum, Wayne State University

E. Leroy Plumlee, Western Washington University

William Rupp, Robert Morris College

George E. Weber, Whitworth College

A special note of appreciation goes to Professor Mark Starik of George Washington University for his contribution and revisions of Chapters 11 and 12.

We would also like to express gratitude to our students, who not only have provided comments on a regular basis but have also made this Fourth Edition unique with the ethical dilemmas they have personally contributed, which are highlighted in the Ethics in Practice features that accompany many of the chapters. In addition to those students who are named in the Ethics in Practice features and have given permission for their materials to be used, we would like to thank the following students: Edward Bashuk, Adrienne Brown, Luis Delgado, Henry DeLoach, Chris Fain, Kristen Nessmith, and Angela Sanders.

We would like to thank especially Arthur Andersen & Co., SC for granting us permission to use several case studies that were originally prepared for their Business Ethics Program. These cases were written by faculty members from around the country. In addition, we express appreciation to the authors of the other cases that appear in the final section of the text.

At the University of Georgia, we especially want to thank our departmental staff without whose support we would not have been able to finish the book on time. This group includes Michelle Doster, Sebrena Mason, Nada Morris, and Billie Najour.

Finally, we wish to express appreciation to our family members for their patience, understanding, and support when work on the book altered the family's plans.

Archie B. Carroll
Ann K. Buchholtz

About the Authors

Archie B. Carroll is professor of management and holder of the Robert W. Scherer Chair of Management and Corporate Public Affairs in the Terry College of Business at the University of Georgia. He has served on the faculty of the University of Georgia since 1972. Dr. Carroll received his three academic degrees from The Florida State University in Tallahassee.

Professor Carroll has published numerous books and articles. His research has appeared in the *Academy of Management Journal, Academy of Management Review, Business and Society, Journal of Business Ethics, California Management Review, Sloan Management Review,* and many others. His 1981 book, *Business & Society: Managing Corporate Social Performance,* was chosen in 1984 by *The Good Book Guide for Business* (from the publishers of *The Economist* in Great Britain) to be among their Top 20 Books on Strategy and Planning.

His teaching, research, and consulting interests are in business and society, business ethics, corporate social performance, and strategic management. He has served on the editorial review boards of the *Academy of Management Review, Business and Society: The Journal of the International Association for Business and Society (IABS),* and *Business Ethics Quarterly.* He is former division chair of the Social Issues in Management (SIM) Division of the Academy of Management and a founding board member of IABS, and he has served on the board of the Southern Management Association.

In 1992, Dr. Carroll was awarded the Sumner Marcus Award for Distinguished Service by the SIM Division of the Academy of Management; and in 1993, he was awarded the Terry College of Business, University of Georgia, Distinguished Research Award for his 20 years of work in corporate social performance, business ethics, and strategic planning. In 1995, he was named chairman of the Department of Management at the University of Georgia. In 1998–1999, he served as president of the Society for Business Ethics.

Ann K. Buchholtz is a faculty member in the Terry College of Business at the University of Georgia. She has served on the faculty of the University of Georgia since 1997. Dr. Buchholtz received her Ph.D. from the Leonard N. Stern School of Business at New York University.

Professor Buchholtz's teaching, research and consulting interests are in business ethics, social issues, strategic management, and corporate governance. Her work has been published in *Business and Society, Academy of Management Journal, Academy of Management Review, Journal of Management, Business Horizons,* and *Journal of General Management.* She has served as a reviewer for the *Academy of Management Journal,*

Academy of Management Review, Journal of Management, Journal of Management Inquiry, Academy of Management Executive, and numerous national and international conferences. Prior to entering academe, Dr. Buchholtz's work focused on the educational, vocational, and residential needs of individuals with disabilities. She has worked in a variety of organizations, in both managerial and consultative capacities, and has consulted with numerous public and private firms.

P A R T

1

Business, Society, and Stakeholders

1   The Business/Society Relationship

CHAPTER OBJECTIVES

After studying this chapter, you should be able to:

1   Define business and society and their interrelationship.

2   Explain pluralism and identify its strengths and weaknesses.

3   Explain how our pluralistic society has become a special-interest society.

4   Discuss the major criticisms of business and characterize business's general response.

5   Identify the major themes of this book: the managerial approach, ethics, and stakeholder management.

Over the past decade, many news stories have brought to the attention of the public numerous social and ethical issues that have framed the business/society relationship. Because the news media have a flair for the dramatic, it is not surprising that the reporting of these issues has been characterized by criticisms of various actions, decisions, and behaviors on the part of business management. Visible examples of these criticisms have included accusations against H.B. Fuller Co. that it has been selling glue in Honduras that is being indiscriminately used for "sniffing" by Honduran street children, an exposé of Beech-Nut Nutrition Company's practice of selling adulterated apple juice and passing it off to the public as "100% fruit juices," lawsuits against Dow Corning for its sale of defective silicone breast implants, allegations that Sears Roebuck & Co. engaged in sales abuses at its auto centers by pressuring customers to purchase unneeded or unwanted services, and accusations and lawsuits against the tobacco industry for manufacturing and marketing what an increasing number of people consider to be an inherently dangerous product. The litany of such issues could go on and on, but these examples will serve to illustrate the continuing tensions between business and society, which can be traced to specific incidents or events.

In addition to these specific incidents, many general issues that carry social or ethical implications have arisen within the relationship between business and society. Some of these general issues have included sexual harassment in the workplace, toxic waste disposal crises, use of lie detectors, minority rights, AIDS in the workplace, smoking in the workplace, drug testing, insider trading, whistle blowing, product liability crises, fetal protection issues, and use of political action committees by business to influence the outcome of legislation.

This sampling of both specific corporate incidents and general issues typifies the kinds of stories about business and society that one finds today in newspapers and magazines and on television. We offer these issues as illustrations of the widespread interactions between business and society that occur on an almost daily basis.

Most of these corporate episodes are situations in which the public or some segment of the public believes that a firm has done wrong or treated some individual or group unfairly. Indeed, in some cases major laws have been broken. In any event, all of these episodes have involved questions of whether or not business firms have behaved properly. Thus, ethical questions typically reside in these kinds of situations. In today's socially aware environment, a business firm frequently finds itself on the defensive— that is, it finds itself being criticized for some action it has taken or failed to take. Whether a business is right or wrong sometimes does not matter. Powerful groups of individuals can frequently exert enormous pressure on businesses and wield significant influence on public opinion, causing firms to take particular courses of action.

In other cases, such as the general issues mentioned earlier, businesses are attempting to deal with broad societal concerns (such as the "rights" movement, smoking in the workplace, and AIDS in the workplace), on which there are no positions that are clearly acceptable to everyone involved. Nevertheless, businesses must weigh the pros and cons of these issues and adopt the best postures, given the many and conflicting points of view that are being expressed. Although the correct responses are not easy to identify, businesses must respond and be willing to live with the consequences.

At a broad level, we are discussing the role of business in society. Abstract debates on this issue have taken place. In this book we will address some of these concerns— the role of business versus government in our socioeconomic system, what a firm must do to be considered socially responsible, and what managers must do to be thought of as ethical. The issues we mentioned earlier are anything but abstract. They require immediate attention and definite courses of action, which quite often become the next subject of debate on the roles and responsibilities of business in society.

As we reach the millennium, many economic, legal, ethical, and social questions and issues about business and society are under debate. This period is turbulent in the sense that it has been characterized by significant changes in the economy, in society, in technology, and in global relationships. Against this continuing turbulence in the business/society relationship, we want to develop some ideas that are fundamental to an understanding of where we are and how we got here.

BUSINESS AND SOCIETY

This chapter will discuss certain concepts that are important in the continuing business/society discussion. Among these concepts are pluralism, our special-interest society, business criticism, and corporate social response. But let us first define and explain two key terms: *business* and *society*.

Business: Defined

Business is the collection of private, commercially oriented (profit-oriented) organizations, ranging in size from one-person proprietorships (such as The Grill Restaurant, Chastain's Office Supplies, and Zim's Bagels) to corporate giants (such as

Microsoft, BellSouth, Coca-Cola, and Hewlett-Packard). Between these extremes, of course, are many medium-sized proprietorships, partnerships, and corporations.

When we speak of business in this comprehensive sense, we refer to businesses of all sizes and in all types of industries. But as we embark on our discussion of business and society, we will, for a variety of reasons, doubtless find ourselves speaking more of *big* business in *selected* industries. Why? For one thing, big business is highly visible. Its products and advertising are more widely disseminated. Consequently, it is more frequently in the critical public eye. In addition, people in our society often associate size with power, and the powerful are given closer scrutiny. Although it is well known that small businesses in our society far outnumber large ones, the impact, pervasiveness, power, and visibility of large firms keep them on the front page much more of the time.

With respect to different industries, some are simply more conducive to the creation of visible social problems than are others. For example, many manufacturing firms by nature cause air and water pollution. Such firms, therefore, are more likely to be subject to criticism than, say, a life insurance company, which emits no obvious pollution. The auto industry is a particular case in point. Much of the criticism against General Motors (GM) and the other automakers is raised because of their high visibility as manufacturers, the products they make (which are the largest single source of air pollution), and the popularity of their products (nearly every family owns one or more cars). In the case of the auto industry, we have not yet worked out an ideal solution to the product-disposal problem, so we see unsightly remnants of metal and plastic on every roadside.

Some industries are highly visible because of the advertising-intensive nature of their products (for example, Miller Brewing, General Mills, Toyota, and Procter & Gamble). Other industries (for example, the cigarette, toy, and food products industries) are scrutinized because of the possible effects of their products on health or because of their roles in providing health-related products (pharmaceutical firms).

When we refer to business in its relationship with society, therefore, we may focus our attention too much on large businesses in particular industries. But we should not lose sight of the fact that small- and medium-sized companies also are important. In fact, over the past decade, problems have arisen for small businesses because they have been subjected to many of the same regulations and demands as those imposed by government on large organizations. In many instances, however, smaller businesses do not have the resources to meet the requirements for increased accountability on many of the social fronts that we will discuss.

Society: Defined

Society may be defined as a community, a nation, or a broad grouping of people having common traditions, values, institutions, and collective activities and interests. As such, when we speak of business/society relationships, we may in fact mean business and the local community (business and Cincinnati), business and the United States as a whole, or business and a specific group of people (consumers, minorities, stockholders).

When we refer to business and the entire society, we think of society as being composed of numerous interest groups, more or less formalized organizations, and a variety of institutions. Each of these groups, organizations, and institutions is a purposeful aggregation of people who have banded together because they represent a common cause or share a set of common beliefs about a particular issue. Examples of interest groups or purposeful organizations are numerous: Friends of the Earth, Common Cause, chambers of commerce, National Association of Manufacturers, Mothers Against Drunk Driving, and Ralph Nader's consumer activists.

THE MACROENVIRONMENT

The environment is a key concept in understanding business/society relationships. At its broadest level, the environment might be thought of in terms of a macroenvironment, which includes the total environment outside the firm. The macroenvironment is the total societal context in which the organization resides. In a sense, the idea of the macroenvironment is just another way of thinking about society. In fact, early courses on business and society in business schools were sometimes (and some still are) entitled "Business and Its Environment." The concept of the macroenvironment, however, evokes different images or ways of thinking about business/society relationships and is therefore useful in terms of framing or understanding the total business context.

The view of the macroenvironment as developed by Liam Fahey and V.K. Narayanan is useful for our purposes. They see the macroenvironment as being composed of four segments: social, economic, political, and technological.[1]

The *social* segment (or environment) focuses on demographics, lifestyles, and social values of the society. Of particular interest here is the manner in which shifts in these factors affect the organization and its functioning. The *economic* segment focuses on the nature and direction of the economy in which business operates. Variables of interest might include such indices as gross national product, inflation, interest rates, unemployment rates, foreign-exchange fluctuations, and various other aspects of economic activity. In the past decade, the global economy has dominated the economic segment of the environment.

The *political* segment focuses on the processes by which laws get passed and officials get elected and all other aspects of the interaction between the firm, political processes, and government. Of particular interest to business in this segment are the regulatory process and the changes that occur over time in business regulation, various industries, and various issues. Finally, the *technological* segment represents the total set of technology-based advancements or progress taking place in society. Pertinent aspects of this segment include new products, processes, and materials, as well as the states of knowledge and scientific advancement in both theoretical and applied senses. The process of technological change is of special importance here.[2]

Thinking of business/society relationships in terms of the macroenvironment provides us with a different but useful way of understanding the kinds of issues that constitute the broad milieu in which business functions. Throughout this book we will see evidence of these environmental segments in a state of turbulence and will come to appreciate what challenges managers face as they strive to develop effective organizations. Each of the many specific groups and organizations that make up our pluralistic society can typically be traced to one of these four environmental segments; therefore, it is helpful to appreciate at a conceptual level what these segments are.

ROLE OF PLURALISM

Our society's pluralistic nature makes for business/society relationships that are more interesting and novel than those in some other societies. *Pluralism* is a condition in which there is diffusion of power among the society's many groups and organizations. Joseph W. McGuire's straightforward definition of a pluralistic society is useful for our purposes: "A pluralistic society is one in which there is wide decentralization and diversity of power concentration."[3]

The key descriptive terms in this definition are *decentralization* and *diversity.* In other words, power is dispersed. Power is not in the hands of any single institution (such as business, government, labor, or the military) or a small number of groups. Many years ago, in *The Federalist Papers,* James Madison speculated that pluralism was a virtuous scheme. He correctly anticipated the rise of numerous organizations in our society as a consequence of it. Some of the virtues of a pluralistic society are summarized in Figure 1–1.

Weaknesses and Strengths of Pluralism

All societal systems have their weaknesses, and pluralism is no exception. One weakness in a pluralistic system is that it creates an environment in which the diverse institutions pursue their own self-interests, with the result that there is no central direction to unify individual pursuits. Another weakness is that groups and institutions proliferate to the extent that their goals tend to overlap, thus causing confusion as to which organizations best serve which functions. Pluralism forces conflict onto center stage because of its emphasis on autonomous groups, each pursuing its own objectives. In light of these concerns, a pluralistic system does not appear to be very efficient.

History and experience have demonstrated, however, that the merits of pluralism are considerable and that most people in our society prefer the situation that has resulted from it. Indeed, pluralism has worked to achieve equilibrium in the balance of power of the dominant institutions that constitute the American way of life.

Business versus Multiple Publics and Systems

Knowing that society is composed of so many different semiautonomous and autonomous groups might cause one to question whether we can realistically speak of society in a broad sense that has any generally agreed-upon meaning. Nevertheless, we do speak in such terms, knowing that, unless we specify a particular societal subgroup or subsystem, we are referring to all those persons, groups, and institutions that constitute our society. This situation raises an important point: When we speak of business/society relationships, we usually refer either to particular segments or subgroups of society (consumerists, women, minorities, environmentalists, youth) or to business and some system in our society (politics, law, custom, religion, economics). These groups of people or systems may also be referred to in an institutional form (business and the courts, business and Common Cause, business and the church, business and the AFL-CIO, business and the Federal Trade Commission).

Figure 1–2 displays in pictorial form the points of interface between business and some of these multiple publics, or stakeholders, with which business has social relationships. Stakeholders are those groups or individuals with whom an organization interacts or has interdependencies. We will develop the stakeholder concept further

FIGURE 1–1   The Virtues of a Pluralistic Society

- A pluralistic society prevents power from being concentrated in the hands of a few.

- A pluralistic society maximizes freedom of expression and action and strikes a balance between monism (social organization into one institution) on the one hand and anarchy (social organization into an infinite number of persons) on the other.[a]

- In a pluralistic society, the allegiance of individuals to groups is dispersed.

- Pluralism creates a wildly diversified set of loyalties to many organizations and minimizes the danger that a leader of any one organization will be left uncontrolled.[b]

- Pluralism provides a built-in set of checks and balances, in that groups can exert power over one another with no single organization (business, government) dominating and becoming overly influential.

SOURCES: [a]Keith Davis and Robert L. Blomstrom, *Business and Society: Environment and Responsibility,* 3d ed. (New York: McGraw-Hill, 1975), 63. [b]Joseph W. McGuire, *Business and Society* (New York: McGraw-Hill, 1963), 132.

in Chapter 3. Note that each of the stakeholder groups may be further divided into more specific subgroups.

If sheer numbers of relationships are an indicator of complexity, we could easily argue that business's current relationships with different segments of society constitute a truly complex environment. And if we had the capacity to draw a diagram similar to Figure 1–2 that noted all the detail composing each of those points of interface, it would be too overwhelming to comprehend. Today, business management cannot sidestep this problem, because management must live with these interfaces on a daily basis.

FIGURE 1–2   Business and Selected Stakeholder Relationships

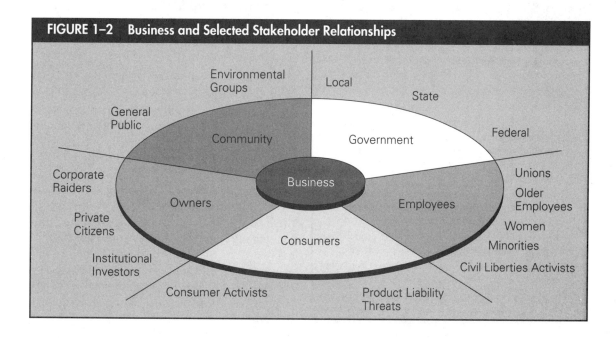

OUR SPECIAL-INTEREST SOCIETY

One could well argue that our pluralistic society has become a *special-interest society*. That is, we have carried the idea of pluralism to an extreme position in which we have literally tens of thousands of special-interest groups, each pursuing its own limited agenda. General-purpose interest organizations, such as Common Cause and the United States Chamber of Commerce, still exist. However, the past two decades have been characterized by increasing specialization on the part of interest groups representing all sectors of society—consumers, employees, communities, the environment, government, and business itself. One recent newspaper headline noted that "there is a group for every cause." Special-interest groups not only have grown in number at an accelerated pace but also have become increasingly activist, intense, diverse, and focused on single issues. Such groups are increasingly committed to their causes.

The consequence of such specialization is that each of these groups has been able to attract a significant following that is dedicated to the group's goals. Increased memberships have meant increased revenues and a clearer focus as each of these groups has aggressively sought its limited purposes. The likelihood of these groups working at cross-purposes and with no unified set of goals has made life immensely more complex for the major institutions, such as business, that have to deal with them.

SEARCH THE WEB

One of the most interesting and demanding pressures on the business/society relationship is that exerted by special-interest groups. Many of these groups focus on specific topics, then direct their concerns or demands to companies they wish to influence. Special-interest groups have become more numerous and increasingly activist, diverse, and focused on single issues. Unique companies, such as Good Money, Inc., which specialize in socially responsible and ethical investing, consuming, and business practices, have reason to catalog and monitor these interest groups. One of Good Money's Web pages, "Social Investing and Consuming Activist Groups and Organizations," found at **www.goodmoney.com/directry_active.htm**, lists and briefly describes a few of the special-interest groups with which business must contend. Good Money's Web page contains more information about the following special-interest groups, but it catalogs many more.

- *20/20 Vision*—An advocacy organization dedicated to protecting the environment and promoting peace through grassroots action.
- *EarthWINS*—An organization dedicated to supporting activism for the environment, peace, justice, human rights, and Native Americans.
- *Environmental Defense Fund*—A group that reports and acts on a broad range of regional, national, and international environmental issues.
- *International Fund for Animal Welfare*—An organization that promotes the just and kind treatment of animals.
- *Public Interest Research Group (The PIRGs)*—Groups that promote social action to safeguard the public interest.
- *Rainforest Action Network*—An organization whose mission is to save the world's rainforests from destruction.

BUSINESS CRITICISM AND CORPORATE RESPONSE

It is inevitable in a pluralistic, special-interest society that the major institutions that make up that society, such as business and government, will become the subjects of considerable criticism. Our purpose here is not so much to focus on the negative as to illustrate how the process of business criticism has shaped the major issues in the evolution of the business/society relationship today. Were it not for the fact that individuals and groups have been critical of business, we would not be dealing with this subject in a book, and no changes would occur in the business/society relationship over time. But such changes *have* taken place, and it is helpful to see the role that business criticism has assumed. The idea of business response to criticism will be developed more completely in Chapter 2, where we present the business criticism/response cycle.

Figure 1–3 illustrates how selected factors that have arisen in the societal environment have created an atmosphere in which business criticism has taken place. In this chapter, we see response on the part of business as entailing an *increased concern for the social environment* and a *changed social contract* (relationship) between business and society.

Factors in the Social Environment

Many factors in the social environment have created a climate in which criticism of business has taken place and flourished. Some of these factors are relatively independent, and some are interrelated with others. In other words, they occur and grow hand in hand.

Affluence and Education

Two factors that have developed side by side are *affluence* and *education.* As a society becomes more affluent and better educated, higher expectations for its major institutions, such as business, naturally follow.

Affluence refers to the level of wealth, disposable income, and standard of living of the society. Measures of our country's standard of living indicate that it has been rising for decades. Although some Americans perceive that U.S. living standards have stopped rising, data from the Conference Board indicate that life is better for most

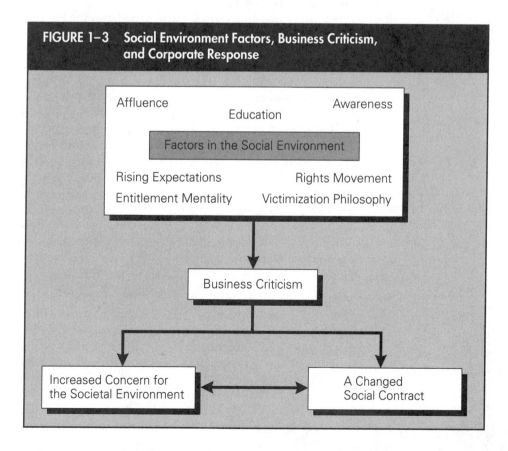

FIGURE 1–3   Social Environment Factors, Business Criticism, and Corporate Response

of us now than in the past and continues to be so in spite of the recent state of the economy, which has been mixed over the past few years. The Conference Board concludes: "All told, the period 1970–1990 represents an era of substantial economic expansion and a marked improvement in the living standards of the average American." Although the expansion has subsided somewhat in the 1990s, the Conference Board further observes that today's young adults are living nearly twice as well as their parents and that this improvement in American living standards will continue throughout this final decade of the twentieth century.[4] When asked in a 1997 *Wall Street Journal*/NBC News poll if they were satisfied with their financial situations, 71 percent of Americans indicated they were, and this was a new high over previous years.[5]

Alongside an increased standard of living has been a growth in the average formal education of the populace. The Census Bureau reported that between 1970 and 1995, the percentage of American adults who were high school graduates grew from 55 to 81, and the percentage who were college graduates increased from 11 to 22. As people continue to become more highly educated, their expectations of life generally rise. The combination of affluence and education forms the underpinning for a climate in which societal criticism of major institutions, such as business, naturally arises.

Awareness Through Television

Closely related to formal education is the high and growing level of public *awareness* in our society. Although newspapers and magazines are still read by only a fraction of our population, a more powerful medium—television—is accessed by virtually our entire society. Through television, the citizenry gets a variety of information that contributes to a climate of business criticism.

First, let us establish the power and prevalence of TV. Several statistics document the extent to which our society is dependent on TV for information. According to data compiled by the A. C. Nielsen Company, the average daily time spent viewing television per household rose from 4½ hours in 1950 to a little over 7 hours in 1983. Recent data suggests that this figure is still valid today. As one writer put it: "Think about it. A typical day for an American household now divides into three nearly equal parts: eight hours of sleep, seven hours of TV, and nine hours of work or school, including getting there and back."[6] Other statistics indicate that there were 2.3 TVs in the average home in 1990, that over 98 percent of American homes have at least one TV,[7] and that from ages 2 to 18 the average American spends 11,000 hours in school but more than 20,000 hours in front of the TV.[8] These statistics continue to be valid. Television is indeed a powerful medium in our society.

Straight News and Investigative News Programs.   There are at least three ways in which information that leads to criticism of business appears on television. First, there are *straight news shows*, such as the evening news on the major networks, and *investigative news programs*. It is debatable whether or not the major news programs are treating business fairly, but in one major study, an overwhelming 73 percent of the business executives surveyed indicated that business and financial coverage on TV news was prejudiced against business. TV pollster Lou Harris suggests that TV news has to deal with subjects too briefly and that, whenever a company makes the evening news, it is usually because the story is unfavorable.[9]

In another major study, chief executive officers of companies of all sizes reported overwhelmingly that newspapers and magazines report business and economic news with a negative bias. Of the total number of CEOs surveyed, 19 percent thought such coverage was *very negative,* 46 percent thought it was *negative,* 27 percent thought it was *neutral,* and only 7 percent thought it was *positive.*[10] This negativism in reporting both business news and political news led James Fallows to write a book titled *Breaking the News: How the Media Undermine American Democracy.* Fallows skewers what media writer Howard Kurtz calls "drive-by journalism," which tends to take down all institutions in its sights.[11]

Although many business leaders believe that the news media are out to get them by exaggerating the facts and overplaying the issues, journalists see it differently. They counter that business executives try to avoid them, are evasive when questioned about major issues, and try to downplay problems that might reflect negatively on their companies. The consequence is an adversarial relationship that perhaps helps to explain some of the unfavorable coverage.

Business has to deal not only with the problems of straight news coverage but also with a growing number of investigative news programs, such as "60 Minutes," "20/20," "Dateline NBC," and "Primetime Live," that seem to thrive on exposés of business wrongdoings or questionable practices. Whereas the straight news programs make some effort to be objective, the investigative shows are tougher on business. These shows are enormously popular and influential, and many companies squirm when reporters show up on their premises complete with camera crews.

What is behind this apparent antagonism between business and the news media? There are many answers. One fundamental reason is that business executives and journalists differ considerably in their basic political ideologies and attitudes concerning the major business and economic issues of the day. With respect to political ideology, studies show that journalists are much more liberal than either CEOs of major corporations or the general public. Journalists overwhelmingly vote Democratic, whereas CEOs tend to vote Republican. Although journalists say that they do not oppose the basic institutions of capitalism, they are much less likely than business executives to think that unregulated markets are consistent with the public interest, and they are considerably more likely to think that regulation is needed to protect the public.[12] Furthermore, it should be noted that some businesses do indeed engage in questionable practices that the news legitimately must cover.

Prime-Time Television Programs.   The second way in which criticisms of business appear on TV is through *prime-time television programs.* Television's depiction of businesspeople brings to mind the scheming J.R. Ewing of "Dallas," whose backstabbing shenanigans dominated prime-time TV for over a decade (1978–1991) before it went off the air. In most cases, the businessperson is portrayed across the nation's television screens as a smirking, scheming, cheating, and conniving "bad guy." A vice president of the Chamber of Commerce of the United States put it this way: "There is a tendency in entertainment television to depict many businesspeople as wealthy, unscrupulous, and succeeding through less-than-honorable dealings. This is totally incorrect."[13]

A major research study on this issue concluded that most businesspeople depicted in television programs and serious literature have been characterized as greedy, unethical, and immoral (or amoral). Another researcher has argued that there is a much higher ratio of "bad guys" among businesspeople than among doctors or police officers.[14]

Another major study conducted over an 8-week period analyzed portrayals of businesspeople on major prime-time shows. Businesspeople proved to be the major staple of prime-time shows, appearing in about half the shows studied. In this study, not one businessperson was of the working class or poor. Many resided in beautifully furnished estates, were pampered by servants, and sported expensive jewelry and clothing. How were they portrayed? Sixty percent were portrayed negatively. Of the 60 percent who were "bad guys," 35 percent did something illegal; 32 percent were greedy or otherwise self-interested; 21 percent "played the fool," mainly in sitcoms; and the remaining 12 percent were malevolent. In general, big-business people fared worse than small-business people. Businesspeople were also shown to be at their worst when performing purely business functions, more so than when they were performing under purely personal circumstances.[15]

Any redeeming social values that business and businesspeople may have rarely show up on prime-time television. Rather, businesspeople are cast as evil and greedy social parasites whose efforts to get more for themselves are justly condemned and usually thwarted.[16] There are many views as to why this portrayal has occurred. Some would argue that business is being characterized accurately. Others say that the television writers are dissatisfied with the direction our nation has taken and believe they have an important role in reforming American society.[17] Apparently they think that this treatment of business will bring about change.

Commercials.   The third way in which television contributes to business criticism is through *commercials.* To the extent that business does not honestly and fairly portray its products on TV, it undercuts its own credibility. Commercials are a two-edged sword. On the one hand, they may sell more products in the short run. On the other hand, they may damage business's long-term credibility if they promote products deceptively.

One major study hints at how this occurs. In an investigation of how television commercials were reviewed by children, Harvard Business School researchers found considerable skepticism, tension, and anger among children because of misleading advertising. By age 11, the study concluded, "Most children have already become cynical—ready to believe that like advertising, business and other institutions are riddled with hypocrisy." About three-fourths of the 11- and 12-year-olds studied thought that advertising is sometimes designed to "trick" the consumer.[18]

Thus, we see three specific settings—news coverage, prime-time programming, and commercials—in which a strained environment is being created and fostered by this "awareness" factor made available through the power and pervasiveness of television. We should make it clear that the media are not to blame for business's problems. If it were not for the fact that the behavior of some businesses is questionable, the media would not be able to create this kind of environment. The media, therefore, should be seen as only one major factor that contributes to the environment in which business now finds itself.

Revolution of Rising Expectations
In addition to affluence, formal education, and awareness through television, there are other societal developments that have fostered the climate in which business criticism has occurred. Growing out of these factors has been a *revolution of rising*

expectations. This might be defined as an attitude or a belief that each succeeding generation ought to have a standard of living higher than that of its predecessor and that its expectations of major institutions, such as business, should be greater also. Building on this line of thinking, one could argue that business is criticized today because society's expectations of its performance have outpaced business's ability to meet these growing expectations. To the extent that this has occurred over the past 20 to 30 years, business finds itself with a larger problem.[19]

A *social problem* has been described as a gap between society's expectations of social conditions and the present social realities.[20] From the viewpoint of a business firm, the social problem is the gap between society's expectations of the firm's social performance and its actual social performance. The nature of rising expectations is such that they typically outpace the responsiveness of institutions such as business, thus creating a constant condition that it is conducive to criticism. Figure 1–4 illustrates the larger "social problem" that business faces today.

Although the general trend of rising expectations continues, there are signs that the revolution may have moderated in spite of citizens' beliefs that their job situations, health, family lives, and overall quality of life have been better in the 1990s. The emergence or exacerbation of social problems such as crime, poverty, homelessness, AIDS, environmental pollution, and alcohol and drug abuse threaten to worsen and to moderate rising expectations.[21]

Entitlement Mentality

One outgrowth of the revolution of rising expectations has been an *entitlement mentality.* Several years ago, the Public Relations Society conducted a study of public expectations, with particular focus on public attitudes toward the *philosophy of entitlement.* This philosophy is the general belief that someone is owed something (for

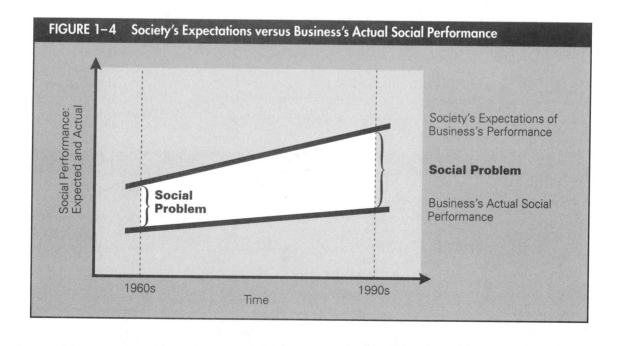

FIGURE 1–4   Society's Expectations versus Business's Actual Social Performance

example, a job) just because she or he is a member of society. The survey was conducted on a nationwide basis, and respondents were asked to categorize items they thought people (1) were entitled to have and (2) have now. A sampling of the findings, shown in Figure 1–5, illustrates some interesting perspectives on what people think are due them.[22] In the mid-1990s, the implicit assumption underlying the health care debate was that health care is a right or an entitlement of the citizenry. If such health care legislation is ever passed, it is estimated that health care would instantly become the largest entitlement program in U.S. history, exceeding Social Security and Medicare.

For each of the items studied, as shown in Figure 1–5, there was a yawning gap between those who thought that the public was entitled to a particular benefit and those who thought that the public already had it. The sizes of the differences boldly underscored what pollsters had been telling business and government for years—that society is not satisfied with the performance of these institutions.

Rights Movement

The revolution of rising expectations, the entitlement mentality, and all of the factors discussed so far have contributed somewhat to what might be termed the *rights movement* that is present in our country today. The Bill of Rights was attached to the U.S. Constitution almost as an afterthought and was virtually unused for more than a century. But in the past several decades, and at an accelerating pace, the U.S. Supreme Court has heard large numbers of cases aimed at establishing for some groups various rights that perhaps never occurred to the founders of our nation.[23]

Some of these rights, such as the right to privacy and the right to due process, have been perceived as generic for all citizens. However, in addition to these generalized rights, there has been pressure for rights for particular groups in our society. This modern movement began with the civil rights cases of the 1950s. Many groups have been inspired by the success of African Americans and have sought success by similar means. Thus, we have seen the protected status of minorities grow to include Hispanic Americans, Asian Americans, Native Americans, women, the handicapped, the aged, and other groups. At various levels—federal, state, and local—we have seen claims for the rights of homosexuals, smokers, nonsmokers, obese persons, and AIDS victims, just to mention a few.

There seem to be no limits to the numbers of groups and individuals seeking "rights" in our society. And business, as one of society's major institutions, has been

FIGURE 1–5   Findings on the Entitlement Mentality

Item	Entitled to Have (Percent)	Have It Now (Percent)
1. Steadily improving standard of living	88	39
2. A guaranteed job for all those willing and able to work	85	34
3. Products certified as safe and not hazardous to one's health if properly used	90	54

hit with an ever-expanding array of constraints and expectations as to how people want to be treated and dealt with, not only as employees but also as owners, consumers, and members of the community. The "rights" movement is interrelated with the special-interest society we discussed earlier and sometimes follows an "entitlement" mentality among some people and within some sectors of society.

John Leo, a columnist for *U.S. News & World Report,* has argued for a moratorium on new rights.[24] He has argued that freshly "minted" rights are so common these days that they even appear on cereal boxes. He cites as an example Post Alpha-Bits® boxes, which recently carried a seven-point "Kids Bill of Rights" that included one right concerning world citizenship ("you have the right to be seen, heard, and respected as a citizen of the world") and one right entitling each cereal buyer to world peace ("you have the right to a world that is peaceful and an environment that is not spoiled"). One cannot help but speculate what challenges business will face when every "goal, need, wish, or itch" is framed as a right.[25]

Victimization Philosophy

It became apparent to several observers during the early 1990s that there are growing numbers of individuals and groups who see themselves as having been victimized by society. In 1991, *New York* magazine featured a cover story on "The New Culture of Victimization," with the title "Don't Blame Me!"[26] *Esquire* magazine probed what it called "A Confederacy of Complainers."[27] Charles Sykes published *A Nation of Victims: The Decay of the American Character.*[28] Sykes' thesis, with which these other observers would agree, is that the United States is fast becoming a "society of victims."

What is particularly interesting about the new philosophy of victimization is the widespread extent to which it is infecting the population. According to these writers, the victim mentality is just as likely to be seen among all groups in society—regardless of race, gender, age, or any other classification. Sykes observed that previous movements may have been seen as a "revolution of rising expectations," whereas the current movement might be called a "revolution of rising sensitivities" in which grievance begets grievance. In the society of victims, feelings rather than reason prevail and people start perceiving that they are being unfairly "hurt" by society's institutions—government, business, and education. One example is worthy of note. In Chicago, a man complained to the Minority Rights Division of the U.S. Attorney's office that McDonald's was violating equal-protection laws because its restaurants' seats were not wide enough for his unusually large backside. As Sykes observes, "The new culture reflects a readiness not merely to feel sorry for oneself but to wield one's resentments as weapons of social advantage and to regard deficiencies as entitlements to society's deference."[29]

As the example above illustrates, the philosophy of victimization is intimately related to and sometimes inseparable from the rights movement and the entitlement mentality. Taken together, these new ways of viewing one's plight—as someone else's unfairness—may pose special challenges for business managers in the future.

In summary, affluence and education, awareness through television, the revolution of rising expectations, an entitlement mentality, the rights movement, and the victimization philosophy have formed a backdrop against which criticism of business has grown. To be sure, this list does not summarize all issues and trends that are present in the social environment. However, it does help to explain why we have an environment that is so conducive to criticism of business. In the next two subsections, we will see what some of the criticisms of business have been, and we will discuss some of the general results of such criticisms.

Criticisms: Use and Abuse of Power

Many criticisms have been leveled at business over the years: It's too big, it's too powerful, it pollutes the environment and exploits people for its own gain, it takes advantage of workers and consumers, it does not tell the truth, and so on. A catalog of business criticisms would occupy too much space to be presented here. If one were to identify a common thread that seems to run through all the complaints, it seems to be business's use and abuse of power. Before discussing business power in more detail, we should note that the major criticism seems to be that business often engages in questionable or unethical behavior with respect to its stakeholders.

Now, what is power? *Power* refers to the ability or capacity to produce an effect or to bring influence to bear on a situation. Power, in and of itself, may be either positive or negative. In the context of business criticism, however, power typically is perceived as being abused. Business certainly does have enormous power, but whether it abuses power is an issue that needs to be carefully examined. We will not settle this issue here, but the criticism that business abuses power remains.

Levels of Power

To understand corporate power, one must recognize that it resides at several levels. Edwin M. Epstein identified four such levels: the macro level, the intermediate level, the micro level, and the individual level.[30] The *macro level* refers to the corporate system—the totality of business organizations. Power here emanates from the sheer size and dominance of the corporate system. The *intermediate level* refers to groups of corporations acting in concert in an effort to produce a desired effect—to raise prices, control markets, dominate purchasers, promote an issue, or pass or defeat legislation. Prime examples are office equipment leaders, banks, OPEC, defense contractors, and the Conference Board, pursuing interests they have in common. The *micro level* of power is the level of the individual firm. This might refer to the exertion of power by any major corporation—GM, IBM, Procter & Gamble, or Wal-Mart, for example. The final level is the *individual level*. This refers to the individual corporate leader—Ted Turner, Donald Trump, Michael Eisner (Disney), Jill Barad (Mattel), Bill Gates (Microsoft), or Anita Roddick (The Body Shop).

The important point here is that as one analyzes corporate power, one should think in terms of the different levels at which that power is manifested. When this is done, it is not easy to conclude whether corporate power is excessive or has been abused.

Spheres of Power

There are not only *levels* of power to examine but also many different *spheres* in which this power resides. Figure 1–6 briefly portrays one way of looking at the levels Epstein identified and some of the spheres of power to which he was referring. Economic power and political power are two spheres that are referred to often, but business has other, more subtle forms of power as well. These other spheres include social and cultural power, power over the individual, technological power, and environmental power.

FIGURE 1–6   Levels and Spheres of Corporate Power

Spheres \ Levels	Macro Level (the business system)	Intermediate Level (several firms)	Micro Level (single firm)	Individual Level (executive)
Economic				
Social / Cultural				
Individual				
Technological				
Environmental				
Political				

Is the power of business excessive? Does business abuse its power? Obviously, many people think so. To provide reasonable and fair answers to these questions, however, one must very carefully stipulate which level of power is being referred to and in which sphere the power is being employed. When this is done, it is not simple to arrive at clear or fair answers.

Furthermore, the nature of power is such that it is sometimes wielded unintentionally. Sometimes it is consequential; that is, it is not wielded intentionally but nevertheless exerts its influence even though no attempt is made to exercise it.[31] An example of this might be a large firm such as IBM purchasing huge parcels of land in cities all across the United States to keep in its real estate inventory for possible future use. Even if IBM comes right out and says that it has no definite plans to move to any of these cities—that is, even if it makes an attempt *not* to wield power—it still has enormous power with the various city councils and county commissions in the areas in which it has purchased land.

Balance of Power and Responsibility

Whether or not business abuses its power or allows its use of power to get out of hand is a central issue that cuts through all the topics we will be discussing in this book. But power cannot be viewed in isolation from responsibility, and this power/responsibility relationship is the foundation of calls for corporate social responsibility. Davis and Blomstrom articulated this major concern in what they called the ***Iron Law of Responsibility:*** "In the long run, those who do not use power in a manner which society considers responsible will tend to lose it."[32] Stated another way, whenever power and responsibility become substantially out of balance, forces will be generated to bring them into closer balance.

When power gets out of balance, a variety of forces come to bear on business to be more responsible and more responsive to the criticisms being made against it.

Some of these more obvious forces include governmental actions, such as increased regulations and new laws. The investigative news media become interested in what is going on, and a whole host of special-interest groups bring pressure to bear.

The tobacco industry is an excellent example of an industry that is feeling the brunt of efforts to address allegations of abuse of power. Complaints that the industry produces a dangerous, addictive product and markets that product to young people have been escalating for years. The U.S. Food and Drug Administration (FDA) has asserted jurisdiction over cigarettes and is trying to rein in tobacco companies through aggressive regulation. One major outcome of this effort to bring the tobacco industry under control was a proposed $368 billion settlement over 25 years in which the tobacco firms settle lawsuits against them, submit to new regulations, and meet strict goals for reducing smoking in the United States. Although the industry continues to fight these measures, as it always has, it is expected that by the year 2022 tobacco's role in American society will be forever reduced.[33]

Response: A Changing Social Environment and Social Contract

Growing out of criticisms of business and the idea of the power/responsibility equation has been an increased concern for the social environment on the part of business and a changed social contract. We previously indicated that the *social environment* was composed of such factors as demographics, lifestyles, and social values of the society. It may also be seen as a collection of conditions, events, and trends that reflect how people think and behave and what they value. As firms have sensed that the social environment and the expectations of business are changing, they have realized that they have to change, too. The *social contract* is a set of two-way understandings that characterize the relationship between major institutions—in our case, business and society. The social contract is changing, and this change is a direct outgrowth of the increased importance of the social environment.

The social contract between business and society, as illustrated in Figure 1–7, is partially articulated through:

1. *Laws and regulations* that society has established as the framework within which business must operate.

2. *Shared understandings* that prevail as to each group's expectations of the other.

It is clear how laws and regulations spell out the "rules of the game" for business. Shared understandings, on the other hand, create more confusion and room for misunderstandings. In a sense, these shared understandings reflect mutual expectations regarding each other's roles, responsibilities, and ethics. These unspoken components of the social contract represent what Donaldson and Dunfee refer to as the normative perspective on the relationship (that is, what "ought" to be done by each party to the contract).[34]

A parallel to the business/society relationship may be seen in the relationship between a professor and the students in his or her class. University regulations and the syllabus for the course spell out the formal aspects of this relationship. The shared understandings address those expectations that are generally understood but not necessarily spelled out formally. An example might be "fairness." The student expects the professor to be "fair" in making assignments, in the level of work

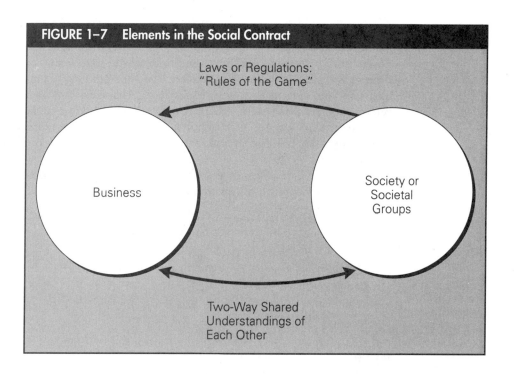

FIGURE 1–7   Elements in the Social Contract

Laws or Regulations:
"Rules of the Game"

Business

Society or
Societal
Groups

Two-Way Shared
Understandings of
Each Other

expected, in grading, and so on. Likewise, the professor expects the student to be fair in evaluating him or her on teaching evaluation forms, to be fair by not passing off someone else's work as his or her own, and so on.

An editorial from *Business Week* magazine on the subject of the social contract summarizes well the modern era of business/society relationships: "Today it is clear that the terms of the contract between society and business are, in fact, changing in substantial and important ways. Business is being asked to assume broader responsibilities to society than ever before, and to serve a wider range of human values. . . . Inasmuch as business exists to serve society, its future will depend on the quality of management's response to the changing expectations of the public."[35] More recently, a *Business Week* editorial commented on how the role of the corporation in society is continuing to be challenged. The writer made it clear that citizens today want corporations to do more for society than boost their stock prices. The editorial concluded with this observation: "U.S. corporations may have to strike a new balance between the need to cut costs to be globally competitive and the need to be more responsible corporate citizens."[36] Such a statement suggests that we will continue to witness changes in the social contract between business and society.

FOCUS OF THE BOOK

This book takes a managerial approach to the business/society relationship. The managerial approach emphasizes two major themes that are important today: business ethics and stakeholder management. First, let us discuss the managerial focus.

Managerial Approach

Managers are practical, and they have begun to deal with social and ethical concerns in ways similar to those they have used to deal with traditional business functions—production, marketing, finance, and so forth—in a rational, systematic, and administratively sound fashion. By viewing issues of social concern from a managerial frame of reference, managers have been able to reduce seemingly unmanageable social concerns to ones that can be dealt with in a rational fashion. Yet, at the same time, managers have had to integrate traditional economic considerations with ethical or moral considerations.

A managerial approach to the business/society relationship confronts the individual manager continuously with questions such as:

- What changes are occurring or will occur in society's expectations of business that mandate business's taking the initiative with respect to particular societal or ethical problems?

- Did business in general or our firm in particular have a role in creating these problems?

- What impact is social change having on the organization, and how should we best respond to it?

- Can we reduce broad social problems to a size that can be effectively addressed from a managerial point of view?

- With which social and ethical problems can we act most effectively?

- What are the specific problems, alternatives for solving these problems, and implications for management's approach to dealing with social issues?

- How can we best plan and organize for responsiveness to socially related business problems?

Two Broad Classes of Social Issues

From the standpoint of urgency in managerial response, management is concerned with two broad classes of social issues. First, there are those issues or *crises* that arise on the spur of the moment and for which management formulates relatively quick responses. These may be either issues that management has never faced before or issues it has faced but does not have time to deal with, except on a short-term basis. A typical example might be a protest group that shows up on management's doorstep one day, arguing vehemently that the company should withdraw its sponsorship of a violent television show scheduled to air the next week.

Second, there are issues or problems that management has time to deal with on a more long-term basis. These issues include environmental pollution, employment discrimination, product safety, and occupational safety and health. In other words, these are *enduring* issues that will be of concern to society for a long time and for which management must develop a reasonably thoughtful organizational response. It is true that issues of this type could also appear in the form of ad hoc problems necessitating immediate responses, but they should suffice to illustrate areas that have matured somewhat. Management must thus be concerned with both short-term and long-term capabilities for dealing with social problems and the organization's social performance.

Our managerial approach, then, will be one that (1) clarifies the nature of the social or ethical issues that affect organizations and (2) suggests alternative managerial responses to these issues in a rational and systematic fashion. The test of success will be the extent to which we can improve an organization's social performance by taking a managerial approach rather than dealing with the issues on an ad hoc basis.

The Ethics Theme

As hard as one might try to extricate business from the major ethical issues of the day, it just cannot be done. The managerial focus attempts to take a practical look at the social issues and expectations business faces, but ethical questions inevitably come into play. *Ethics* basically refers to issues of right, wrong, fairness, and justice, and *business ethics* focuses on ethical issues that arise in the commercial realm. Ethical threads run throughout our discussion because questions of right, wrong, fairness, and justice, no matter how slippery they are to deal with, permeate business's activities as it attempts to interact effectively with major stakeholder groups: employees, customers, owners, government, and the community.

The inevitable task of management is not only to deal with the various stakeholder groups in an ethical fashion but also to reconcile the conflicts of interest that occur between the organization and the stakeholder groups. Implicit in this challenge is the ethical dimension present in practically all business decision making where stakeholders are concerned. In addition to the challenge of treating fairly the groups with which business interacts, management faces the equally important task of creating an organizational climate in which all employees make decisions with the interests of the public, as well as those of the organization, in mind. At stake is not only the firm's reputation but also the reputation of the business community in general.

The Stakeholder Management Theme

As we have indicated throughout this chapter, *stakeholders* are individuals or groups with which business interacts who have a "stake," or vested interest, in the firm. They could be called "publics," but this term may imply that they are outside the business sphere and should be dealt with as external players rather than as integral components of the business/society relationship. As a matter of fact, stakeholders actually constitute the most important elements of that broad grouping known as *society*.

We deal with two broad groups of stakeholders in this book. First, we consider *external stakeholders*, which include government, consumers, and community members. We treat government first because it represents the public. It is helpful to understand the role and workings of government in order to best appreciate business's relationships with other groups. Consumers may be business's most important stakeholders. Members of the community are crucial, too, and they are concerned about a variety of issues. One of the most important is the natural environment. Two other major community issues include business giving (or corporate philanthropy) and plant closings (including downsizing). All these issues have direct effects on the community. Social activist groups representing external stakeholders also must be considered to be a part of this classification.

The second broad grouping of stakeholders is composed of *internal stakeholders*. Business owners and employees are the principal groups of internal stakeholders. We

---

ETHICS IN PRACTICE

The Boss

A few years ago, I worked for a health and fitness store in Queens, New York. We sold vitamins, weights, health food, exercise equipment, and clothing. I worked for a manager who showed a tendency to be lazy by always leaving work early. She would leave work early and ask the employees to cover for her if any of the upper managers called.

The manager was in charge of recording the hours we worked and always gave herself 40 hours. Most of the time she worked only about 30 hours a week and often left one of us in charge of the store. My hours were always set, so it did not matter if I stayed later, because I was credited only for the hours on her time sheet. The dilemma here was that she was actually getting paid for time that she was spending away from the store. I was not sure if I was supposed to tell anyone or just look the other way, since she was my boss. I thought that her behavior was wrong, especially for a manager, and that it was very unethical of her to ask us to lie in order to keep her out of trouble.

1. Are there any ethical issues involved in this case? What are they?

2. Should upper management be notified about the manager's actions? Why or why not?

3. What would you do if you were in my place?

Contributed by Terence O'Brien

---

live in an organizational society, and many people think that their roles as employees are just as important as their roles as investors or owners. Both of these groups have legitimate claims on the organization, and management's task is to address their needs and balance these needs against those of the firm and of other stakeholder groups. We will develop the idea of stakeholder management more fully in Chapter 3.

STRUCTURE OF THE BOOK

The structure of this book is illustrated in Figure 1–8.

Part 1 provides an overview of the business/society relationship (Chapter 1); corporate social responsibility, responsiveness, and performance (Chapter 2); and the stakeholder management concept (Chapter 3). These chapters provide a crucial basis for understanding all of the discussions that follow. They provide the *context* for the business/society relationship.

Part 2 focuses exclusively on business ethics. Business ethics fundamentals are established in Chapter 4, and the management of business ethics is discussed in Chapter 5. Chapter 6 treats business ethics in the global or international sphere. Although ethical issues cut through and permeate many of the discussions in this book, this special treatment of business ethics is warranted by a need to explore in some detail what is meant by the ethical dimension in management.

Part 3 addresses the major external stakeholders of business. First (in Chapter 7), because government is an active player in all the groups to follow, we consider

FIGURE 1–8   The Structure and Flow of the Book

BUSINESS, SOCIETY, AND STAKEHOLDERS

PART ONE

1. The Business/Society Relationship
2. Corporate Social Responsibility, Responsiveness, and Performance
3. The Stakeholder Management Concept

BUSINESS ETHICS AND MANAGEMENT

PART TWO

4. Business Ethics Fundamentals
5. Personal and Organizational Ethics
6. Ethical Issues in the Global Arena

EXTERNAL STAKEHOLDER ISSUES

PART THREE

7. Business, Government, and Regulation
8. Business's Influence on Government and Public Policy
9. Consumer Stakeholders: Information Issues and Responses
10. Consumer Stakeholders: Product and Service Issues
11. The Natural Environment as Stakeholder: Issues and Challenges
12. Business and Stakeholder Responses to Environmental Challenges
13. Business and Community Stakeholders

INTERNAL STAKEHOLDER ISSUES

PART FOUR

14. Employee Stakeholders and Workplace Issues
15. Employee Stakeholders: Privacy, Safety, and Health
16. Employment Discrimination and Affirmative Action
17. Owner Stakeholders and Corporate Governance

STRATEGIC MANAGEMENT FOR SOCIAL RESPONSIVENESS

PART FIVE

18. Strategic Management and Corporate Public Policy
19. Issues Management and Crisis Management
20. Public Affairs Management

business/government relationships and government regulations. Next (in Chapter 8), we discuss how business endeavors to shape and influence public policy. Consumer stakeholders (Chapters 9 and 10), environmental issues (Chapters 11 and 12), and community issues (Chapter 13) are then dealt with in turn.

In Part 4, internal stakeholders, which include employees and owners, are addressed. We first deal with the growing employee rights movement (Chapters 14 and 15) and then focus on the special case of employment discrimination (Chapter 16). Part 4 concludes with a discussion of corporate governance and the management/ shareholder relationship (Chapter 17).

In Part 5, we place our managerial and stakeholder perspective within the context of strategic management. We assume a knowledge and an awareness of the issues at this point and focus on the more enduring management responses that are essential to a well-conceived managerial approach. In addition to conceptual materials on strategic management and social issues (Chapter 18), we examine issues management and crisis management (Chapter 19) and public affairs management (Chapter 20). Here we are concerned with generalizable management and organizational response patterns that are proving to be effective in dealing with social issues. Part 5 contains chapters and materials that could easily be covered after Part 1 or Part 2, should an even stronger strategic management perspective be desired.

Taken as a whole, this book strives (1) to take the reader through basic concepts and ideas that are vital to the business/society relationship and (2) to explore the nature of social and ethical issues and stakeholder groups with which management must interact. It considers the external and internal stakeholder groups in some depth and closes with a treatment of management issues and approaches to making the firm more responsive to the full range of societal expectations that are placed on it.

SUMMARY

The pluralistic business system in the United States has several advantages and some disadvantages. Within this context, business firms must deal with a multitude of stakeholders and an increasingly special-interest society. A major force that shapes the public's view of business is the criticism that business receives from a variety of sources. Factors in the social environment that have contributed to an atmosphere in which business criticism thrives include affluence, education, public awareness developed through the media (especially TV), the revolution of rising expectations, a growing entitlement mentality, the rights movement, and a philosophy of victimization. In addition, actual questionable practices on the part of business have made it a natural target. Not all firms are guilty, but the guilty attract negative attention to the entire business community.

A major criticism of business is that it has abused its power. To understand power, you need to recognize that it may operate at four different levels: the entire business system, groups of companies acting in concert, the individual firm, and the individual corporate executive. Moreover, business power may be manifested in several different spheres: economic, political, technological, environmental, social, and individual. It is difficult to assess whether business is actually abusing its power, but it is clear that business has enormous power. Power evokes responsibility, and this is the central reason that calls for corporate responsiveness have been prevalent in recent years. These concerns have led to a changing social environment for business and a changed social contract.

KEY TERMS

affluence (page 9)

business (page 3)

business ethics (page 21)

ethics (page 21)

Iron Law of Responsibility (page 17)

philosophy of entitlement (page 13)

pluralism (page 6)

revolution of rising expectations (page 13)

rights movement (page 14)

social contract (page 18)

social environment (page 18)

social problem (page 13)

society (page 4)

special-interest society (page 8)

stakeholders (page 21)

DISCUSSION QUESTIONS

1. In discussions of business and society, why is there a tendency to focus on large rather than small- or medium-sized firms?
2. What are the one greatest strength and the one greatest weakness of a pluralistic society? Do these characteristics work for or against business?
3. Identify and explain the major factors in the social environment that create an atmosphere in which business criticism takes place and prospers.
4. Give an example of each of the four levels of power discussed in this chapter. Also, give an example of each of the spheres of business power.
5. Explain in your own words the social contract. Give an example of a shared understanding between you as a consumer or an employee and a firm with which you do business or for which you work.

ENDNOTES

1. Liam Fahey and V.K. Narayanan, *Macroenvironmental Analysis for Strategic Management* (St. Paul: West, 1986), 28–30.
2. *Ibid.*
3. Joseph W. McGuire, *Business and Society* (New York: McGraw-Hill, 1963), 130.
4. Fabian Linden, "The American Dream," *Across the Board* (May, 1991), 7–10.
5. Jackie Calmes, "Economic Satisfaction Sets Records, With Senior Citizens Most Content," *Wall Street Journal* (December 12, 1997), R2.
6. "Average American Family Watches TV 7 Hours Each Day," *Athens Banner Herald* (January 25, 1984), 23.
7. George Gallup, Jr., and Frank Newport, "Americans Have Love-Hate Relationship With Their TV Sets," *The Gallup Poll Monthly* (October, 1990), 5.
8. "Observations," *San Jose Mercury Times* (July 19, 1981), 19.
9. "Business Thinks TV Distorts Its Image," *Business Week* (October 18, 1982), 26.
10. "CEOs: Biz News Is Negative," *USA Today* (February 27, 1987), 1B.

11. James Fallows, *Breaking the News: How the Media Undermine American Democracy* (Pantheon Press, 1996). See also Howard Kurtz, *Hot Air: All Talk, All the Time* (Basic Books, 1997).
12. Fred J. Evans, "Management and the Media: Is Accord in Sight? View Four: The Conflict Surveyed," *Business Forum* (Spring, 1984), 16–23.
13. Eric Pace, "On TV Novels, the Bad Guy Sells," *The New York Times* (April 15, 1984).
14. *Ibid.*
15. Linda S. Lichter, S. Robert Lichter, and Stanley Rothman, "How Show Business Shows Business," *Public Opinion* (November, 1982), 10–12.
16. *Ibid.*, 12.
17. Nedra West, "Business and the Soaps," *Business Forum* (Spring, 1983), 4.
18. Morton C. Paulson, "What Youngsters Learn on TV," *National Observer* (May 19, 1976), 10.
19. Robert J. Samuelson, *The Good Life and Its Discontents: The American Dream in the Age of Entitlement, 1945–1995* (Times Books, 1996).
20. Neil H. Jacoby, *Corporate Power and Social Responsibility* (New York: Macmillan, 1973), 186–188.
21. Linda DeStefano, "Looking Ahead to the Year 2000: No Utopia, but Most Expect a Better Life," *The Gallup Poll Monthly* (January, 1990), 21.
22. Joseph Nolan, "Business Beware: Early Warning Signs for the Eighties," *Public Opinion* (April/May, 1981), 16.
23. Charlotte Low, "Someone's Rights, Another's Wrongs," *Insight* (January 26, 1987), 8.
24. John Leo, "No More Rights Turns," *U.S. News & World Report* (October 23, 1995), 34.
25. John Leo, "A Man's Got a Right to Rights," *U.S. News & World Report* (August 4, 1997), 15.
26. John Taylor, "Don't Blame Me!" *New York* (June 3, 1991).
27. Pete Hamill, "A Confederacy of Complainers," *Esquire* (July, 1991).
28. Charles J. Sykes, *A Nation of Victims: The Decay of the American Character* (New York: St. Martin's Press, 1991).
29. *Ibid.*, 12.
30. Edwin M. Epstein, "Dimensions of Corporate Power: Part I," *California Management Review* (Winter, 1973), 11.
31. *Ibid.*
32. Keith Davis and Robert L. Blomstrom, *Business and Its Environment* (New York: McGraw-Hill, 1966), 174–175.
33. John Carey, "The Tobacco Deal: Not So Fast," *Business Week* (July 7, 1997), 34–37; Richard Lacayo, "Smoke Gets in Your Aye," *Time* (January 26, 1998), 50; Jeffrey H. Birnbaum, "Tobacco's Can of Worms," *Fortune* (July 21, 1997), 58–60; Dwight R. Lee, "Will Government's Crusade Against Tobacco Work?" (July, 1997, Center for The Study of American Business).
34. Thomas Donaldson and Thomas W. Dunfee, "Toward a Unified Conception of Business Ethics: Integrative Social Contracts Theory," *Academy of Management Review* (April, 1994), 252–253.
35. "The New 'Social Contract,'" *Business Week* (July 3, 1971).
36. "The Backlash Building Against Business" (editorial), *Business Week* (February 19, 1996), 102.

2

Corporate Social Responsibility, Responsiveness, and Performance

---

CHAPTER OBJECTIVES

After studying this chapter, you should be able to:

1 Explain how corporate social responsibility (CSR) encompasses economic, legal, ethical, and philanthropic components.

2 Outline the pros and cons of the CSR issue.

3 Differentiate between social responsibility and responsiveness.

4 Elaborate on the concept of corporate social performance (CSP).

5 Provide an overview of studies relating social performance to financial performance.

6 Describe the socially conscious investing movement.

For the past three decades, business has been undergoing the most intense scrutiny it has ever received from the public. As a result of the many charges being leveled at it—charges that it has little concern for the consumer, cares nothing about the deteriorating social order, has no notion of acceptable ethical behavior, and is indifferent to the problems of minorities and the environment—concern is increasingly being expressed as to what responsibilities business has to the society in which it resides. These concerns have generated an unprecedented number of pleas for corporate social responsibility (CSR).

The basic issue can be framed in terms of two key questions: Does business have a social responsibility? If so, how much and what kinds? Although these questions seem simple and straightforward, answers to them must be phrased carefully. What is particularly paradoxical is that large numbers of businesspeople have enthusiastically embraced the concept of corporate social responsibility during the past three decades, but only limited consensus has emerged about what corporate social responsibility really means.

That CSR continues to be a "front-burner" issue within the business community is highlighted by the formation in 1992 of a new organization called *Business for Social Responsibility (BSR)*. According to BSR, it was formed to fill an urgent need for a national business alliance that fosters socially responsible corporate policies. By 1994, BSR had over 700 business member firms and included among its membership such recognizable names as Levi Strauss & Co., Stride Rite, Hasbro, Reebok, Honeywell, Lotus Development Corp., The Timberland Co., and hundreds of others.

In this chapter, therefore, we intend to explore several different facets of the CSR question and to provide some insights into the questions raised above. We say "insights" because the dynamics of social change preclude our obtaining conclusive agreement on answers to these questions for any extended period. We are dedicating an entire chapter to the CSR issue and concepts that have devolved from it because it is a core idea that underlies most of our discussions in this book.

THE CORPORATE SOCIAL RESPONSIBILITY CONCEPT

In Chapter 1, we traced how criticisms of business have led to increased concern for the social environment and a changed social contract. Out of these ideas has grown the notion of corporate social responsibility, or CSR. Before treating this topic in some depth and providing some historical perspective, let us provide an initial view of what corporate social responsibility means.

Raymond Bauer presented an early view as follows: "Corporate social responsibility is seriously considering the impact of the company's actions on society."[1] Another definition that may be helpful is "The idea of social responsibility . . . requires the individual to consider his [or her] acts in terms of a whole social system, and holds him [or her] responsible for the effects of his [or her] acts anywhere in that system."[2]

Both of these definitions provide preliminary insights into the idea of business responsibility that will help us appreciate some brief evolutionary history. Figure 2–1 illustrates how the concept of CSR grew out of the ideas introduced in Chapter 1— the increased concern for the social environment and the changed social contract. We see further in Figure 2–1 that the assumption of social responsibility by businesses has led to increased corporate responsiveness and improved social performance—ideas that are developed more fully in this chapter. All of this has resulted in a more satisfied society. However, this satisfaction, although it has reduced the number of factors leading to business criticism, has at the same time led to increased expectations that perhaps will result in more criticism. The net result is that the overall levels of business performance and societal satisfaction should increase with time in spite of this interplay of positive and negative factors. Should business not be responsive to societal expectations, it could conceivably enter a downward spiral, resulting in significant changes in the business/society relationship.

Historical Perspective on CSR

The concept of business responsibility that prevailed in the United States during most of our history was fashioned after the traditional, or *classical*, economic model. Adam Smith's concept of the "invisible hand" was its major point of departure. The classical view held that a society could best determine its needs and wants through the marketplace. If business simply responds to these demands, society will get what it wants. If business is rewarded on the basis of its ability to respond to the demands of the market, the self-interested pursuit of that reward will result in society getting what it wants. Thus, the "invisible hand" of the market transforms self-interest into societal interest. Unfortunately, although the marketplace did a reasonably good

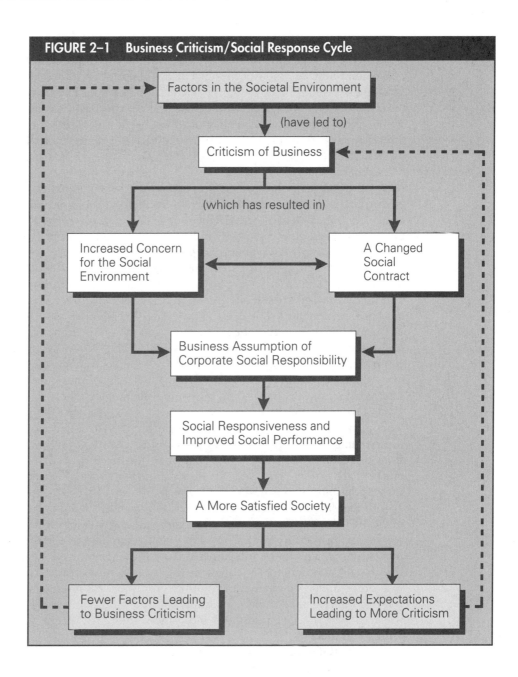

FIGURE 2–1   Business Criticism/Social Response Cycle

Factors in the Societal Environment

(have led to)

Criticism of Business

(which has resulted in)

Increased Concern for the Social Environment

A Changed Social Contract

Business Assumption of Corporate Social Responsibility

Social Responsiveness and Improved Social Performance

A More Satisfied Society

Fewer Factors Leading to Business Criticism

Increased Expectations Leading to More Criticism

job in deciding what goods and services should be produced, it did not fare as well in ensuring that business always acted fairly and ethically.

Somewhat later, when laws constraining business behavior began to proliferate, it might be said that a *legal model* prevailed. Society's expectations of business changed from being strictly economic in nature to encompassing aspects that had been previously at business's discretion.

In practice, although business early subscribed to the economic emphasis and was willing to be subjected to an increasing number of laws imposed by society, the business community later did not fully live by the tenets of even these early conceptions of business responsibility. As James W. McKie observed, "The business community never has adhered with perfect fidelity to an ideologically pure version of its responsibilities, drawn from the classical conception of the enterprise in economic society, though many businessmen have firmly believed in the main tenets of the creed."[3]

Modification of the Classical Economic Model

A modification of the classical economic model was seen in practice in at least three areas: philanthropy, community obligations, and paternalism.[4] History shows that businesspeople did engage in *philanthropy*—contributions to charity and other worthy causes—even during periods characterized by the traditional view. In addition, voluntary *community obligations* to improve, beautify, and uplift were evident. One early example of this was the cooperative effort between the railroads and the YMCA immediately after the Civil War to provide community services in areas served by the railroads. Although these services economically benefited the railroads, they were at the same time philanthropic.[5]

During the latter part of the nineteenth century and even into the twentieth century, *paternalism* appeared in many forms. One of the most visible examples was the company town. Although business's motives for beginning company towns (for example, the Pullman/Illinois experiment) were mixed, business had to do a considerable amount of the work in governing them. Thus, the company accepted a form of social responsibility.[6]

The emergence of large corporations during the late 1800s played a major role in hastening movement away from the classical economic view. As society evolved from the economic structure of small, powerless firms governed primarily by the marketplace to large corporations in which power was concentrated, questions of the responsibility of business to society surfaced.[7]

Although the idea of corporate social responsibility had not yet fully developed in the 1920s, managers even then had a more positive view of their role. Community service was in the forefront. The most visible example was the Community Chest movement, which received its impetus from business. Morrell Heald suggests that this was the first large-scale endeavor in which business leaders became involved with other nongovernmental community groups for a common, nonbusiness purpose that necessitated their contribution of time and money to community welfare projects.[8] The social responsibility of business, then, had received a further broadening of its meaning.

The 1930s signaled a transition from a predominantly laissez-faire economy to a mixed economy in which business found itself one of the constituencies monitored by a more activist government. From this time well into the 1950s, business's social responsibilities grew to include employee welfare (pension and insurance plans), safety, medical care, retirement programs, and so on. McKie has suggested that these new developments were spurred both by governmental compulsion and by an enlarged concept of business responsibility.[9]

Neil J. Mitchell, in his book *The Generous Corporation,* presents an interesting thesis regarding how CSR evolved.[10] Mitchell's view is that the ideology of corporate social responsibility, particularly philanthropy, was developed by American business leaders as a strategic response to the antibusiness fervor that was beginning in the late 1800s and early 1900s. The antibusiness reaction was the result of specific business actions, such as railroad price gouging, and public resentment of the emerging gigantic fortunes being made by late nineteenth-century moguls, such as Andrew Carnegie and John D. Rockefeller.[11]

As business leaders came to realize that the government had the power to intervene in the economy and, in fact, was being encouraged to do so by public opinion, there was a need for an ideology that promoted large corporations as a force for social good. Thus, Mitchell argued, business leaders attempted to persuade those affected by business power that such power was being used appropriately. An example of this early progressive business ideology was reflected in Carnegie's 1889 essay, "The Gospel of Wealth," which asserted that business must pursue profits but that business wealth should be used for the benefit of the community. Philanthropy, therefore, became the most efficient means of using corporate wealth for public benefit. A prime example of this was Carnegie's funding and building of more than 2,500 libraries.

In a discussion of little-known history, Mitchell documents by way of specific examples how business developed this idea of the generous corporation and how it had distinct advantages: It helped business gain support from national and local governments, and it helped to achieve in America a social stability that was unknown in Europe during that period. In Ronald Berenbeim's review of Mitchell's book, he argues that the main motive for corporate generosity in the early 1900s was essentially the same as it has been in the 1990s—to keep government at arm's length.[12]

Acceptance and Broadening of Meaning

The period from the 1950s to the present may be considered part of the modern era in which the concept of corporate social responsibility gained considerable acceptance and broadening of meaning. During this time, the emphasis has moved from little more than a general awareness of social and moral concerns to a period in which specific issues, such as product safety, honesty in advertising, employee rights, affirmative action, environmental protection, and ethical behavior, have been emphasized. The issue orientation eventually gave way to the more recent focus on social responsiveness and social performance, which we will discuss later in this chapter. First, however, we can expand the modern view of CSR by examining various definitions or understandings of this term that have prevailed in recent years.

Corporate Social Responsibility: Several Viewpoints

Let's now return to the basic question: What does corporate social responsibility really mean? Up to this point we have been operating with Bauer's definition of social responsibility: "Corporate social responsibility is seriously considering the impact of the company's actions on society." Although this definition has inherent frailties, we will find that most of the definitions presented by others also have limitations. Part of the difficulty in deriving a definition on which we might get consensus is the problem of determining, operationally, what the definition implies for management. This poses an almost insurmountable problem because organizations vary in size, in the types of products they produce, in their profitability and resources, in

S E A R C H   T H E   W E B

Businesses are very interested in CSR. One leading organization that companies join to learn more about CSR is Business for Social Responsibility (BSR). BSR is a national business association that helps companies seeking to implement policies and practices that contribute to the companies' sustained and responsible success. BSR also operates the Business for Social Responsibility Education Fund, a nonprofit research, education, and advocacy organization that promotes more responsible business practices in the broad business community and in society. BSR runs programs on a range of social responsibility and stakeholders issues, including business ethics, the workplace, the marketplace, the community, the environment, and the global economy. To learn more about what business is doing in the realm of social responsibility, visit BSR's Web site at **www.bsr.org/**.

their impact on society, and so on. Because this is the case, the ways in which they embrace and practice social responsibility also vary.

One might ask: Why is this so? Are there not absolutes, areas in which all firms must be responsible? Yes, there are, and these are expressed by those expectations society has translated into legal aspects of the social contract. But as we will suggest here, CSR goes beyond simply abiding by the law (although abiding by the law is not always simple). In the realm of activities above and beyond abiding by the law, the variables (size of the firm, types of products produced, and so on) become more relevant.

A second definition is worth considering. Keith Davis and Robert Blomstrom defined corporate social responsibility as follows: "Social responsibility is the obligation of decision makers to take actions which protect and improve the welfare of society as a whole along with their own interests."[13] This definition is somewhat more pointed. It suggests two *active* aspects of social responsibility—protecting and improving. To *protect* the welfare of society implies the avoidance of negative impacts on society. To *improve* the welfare of society implies the creation of positive benefits for society.

Like the first definition, the second contains several words that are perhaps unavoidably vague. For example, words from these definitions that might permit managers wide latitude in interpretation include *seriously, considering, protect, improve,* and *welfare* (of society). The intention here is not to be critical of these good, general definitions but rather to illustrate how businesspeople and others become quite legitimately confused when they try to translate the concept of CSR into practice.

A third definition, by Joseph McGuire, is also quite general. But, unlike the previous two, it places social responsibilities in context vis-à-vis economic and legal objectives. McGuire asserts: "The idea of social responsibility supposes that the corporation has not only economic and legal obligations, but also certain responsibilities to society which extend beyond these obligations."[14] Although this statement is not fully operational either, its attractiveness is that it acknowledges the primacy of economic objectives side by side with legal obligations while also encompassing a broader conception of the firm's responsibilities.

A fourth definition, set forth by Edwin Epstein, relates CSR to business management's growing concern with stakeholders and ethics. He asserts: "Corporate social responsibility relates primarily to achieving outcomes from organizational decisions concerning specific issues or problems which (by some normative standard) have beneficial rather than adverse effects upon pertinent corporate stakeholders. The normative correctness of the products of corporate action have been the main focus of corporate social responsibility."[15] Epstein's definition is useful because it concentrates on the outcomes, products, or results of corporate actions for stakeholders.

A Four-Part Definition of CSR

Each of the aforementioned definitions of corporate social responsibility has value. At this point, we would like to present Archie Carroll's four-part definition that focuses on the types of social responsibilities it might be argued that business has. This four-part definition attempts to place economic and legal expectations of business in perspective by relating them to more socially oriented concerns.[16] These social concerns include ethical responsibilities and voluntary/discretionary (philanthropic) responsibilities. In a sense, this definition, which includes four kinds of responsibilities, elaborates and builds on the definition proposed by McGuire.

Economic Responsibilities

First, there are business's *economic* responsibilities. It may seem odd to call an economic responsibility a social responsibility, but, in effect, that is what it is. First and foremost, the American social system calls for business to be an economic institution. That is, it should be an institution whose orientation is to produce goods and services that society wants and to sell them at fair prices—prices that society thinks represent the true values of the goods and services delivered and that provide business with profits adequate to ensure its perpetuation and growth and to reward its investors.

Legal Responsibilities

Second, there are business's *legal* responsibilities. Just as society has sanctioned our economic system by permitting business to assume the productive role mentioned above, as a partial fulfillment of the social contract, it has also laid down the ground rules—the laws—under which business is expected to operate. Legal responsibilities reflect a view of "codified ethics" in the sense that they embody basic notions of fairness as established by our lawmakers. It is business's responsibility to society to comply with these laws. If business does not agree with laws that have been passed or are about to be passed, our society has provided a mechanism by which dissenters can be heard through the political process.

Ethical Responsibilities

Ethical responsibilities embrace those activities and practices that are expected or prohibited by societal members even though they are not codified into law. Ethical responsibilities embody the range of norms, standards, and expectations that reflect a concern for what consumers, employees, shareholders, and the community regard as fair, just, or in keeping with the respect for or protection of stakeholders' moral rights.[17]

In one sense, changes in ethics or values precede the establishment of laws because they become the driving forces behind the very creation of laws and regulations. For example, the civil rights, environmental, and consumer movements reflect basic alterations in societal values and thus may be seen as ethical bellwethers foreshadowing and leading to later legislation. In another sense, ethical responsibilities may be seen as embracing and reflecting newly emerging values and norms that society expects business to meet, even though they may reflect a higher standard of performance than that currently required by law. Ethical responsibilities in this sense are often ill defined or continually under public scrutiny and debate as to their legitimacy and thus are frequently difficult for business to agree upon.

ETHICS IN PRACTICE

A Fish Story

During a few of the years I spent at college, I worked as a sales associate at a local fish company that sold fish both to other retailers and to customers who came into the store. At the fish company, we sold many different types of fresh fish. The ethical dilemma that I faced on a few occasions was that when we ran out of fresh fish for retail sale, we would get frozen fish out of the freezer, defrost it, and sell it as fresh. If the fish had not been in storage for a long period, it often looked, felt, and tasted like fresh fish. But sometimes the fish was so bad that it fell apart as it was cut open and smelled like rotten sewage.

I felt terrible when I knew that the fish that someone wanted was not fresh and, because of this, I tried to pick the nicest looking and firmest fish to give to the customer. I spoke to my boss about this, but he never gave me much advice. All he ever told me was that I should not concern myself because the people buying the fish could not tell the difference. I knew that this could not be ethical behavior, because it was not being honest with the customer. Most of the time the fish was not so bad, but should I have done something for the few times that it was? How could I have kept my job while still being ethical?

1. Is this a socially responsible fish company? Why or why not?

2. Which of the four kinds of social responsibility (economic, legal, ethical, or philanthropic) comes into play here? Where are the greatest tensions between or among the different types of CSR?

Contributed by Edward Bashuk

Superimposed on these ethical expectations emanating from societal and stakeholder groups are the implied levels of ethical performance suggested by a consideration of the great ethical principles of moral philosophy, such as justice, rights, and utilitarianism.[18]

Because ethical responsibilities are so important, we devote three chapters to the subject (Chapters 4, 5, and 6). For the moment, let us think of ethical responsibilities as encompassing those areas in which society expects certain levels of performance but for which it has not yet been able or willing to articulate and codify those levels into law.

Philanthropic Responsibilities

Fourth, there are business's *voluntary/discretionary,* or *philanthropic,* responsibilities. Perhaps it is a misnomer to call these "responsibilities," because they are guided primarily by business's discretion—its choice or desire. These activities are purely voluntary, guided only by business's desire to engage in social activities that are not mandated, not required by law, and not generally expected of business in an ethical sense. Such activities might include establishing loaned executive programs in the community, giving to charitable causes, providing day-care centers for working parents, initiating adopt-a-school programs, and conducting in-house programs for drug abusers.

The distinction between ethical responsibilities and voluntary/discretionary or philanthropic responsibilities is that the latter typically are not expected in a moral or an ethical sense. Communities desire business to contribute its money, facilities, and employee time to humanitarian programs or purposes, but they do not regard firms as unethical if they do not provide these services at the desired levels. Therefore, these responsibilities are more discretionary, or voluntary, on business's part, although the societal expectation that they be provided is always present. This category of responsibilities might be deemed "corporate citizenship."

The Four-Part CSR Model

In essence, then, our definition forms a four-part conceptualization of corporate social responsibility that may be summarized as follows: The social responsibility of business encompasses the economic, legal, ethical, and philanthropic expectations placed on organizations by society at a given point in time.

It is suggested that this four-part definition provides us with categories within which to place the various expectations that society has of business. With each of these categories considered as one facet of the total social responsibility of business, we have a conceptual model that more completely describes what society expects of business. One advantage of this model is that it can accommodate those who have argued against CSR by characterizing an economic emphasis as separate from a social emphasis. This model offers these two facets along with others that collectively make up corporate social responsibility. Figure 2–2 depicts the model as it might appear when superimposed on a scale denoting all of the social responsibilities of business.

Another helpful way of graphically depicting the four-part model is envisioning a pyramid composed of four layers. This Pyramid of Corporate Social Responsibility is shown in Figure 2–3.[19]

The pyramid portrays the four components of CSR, beginning with the basic building block of economic performance. At the same time, business is expected to obey the law, because the law is society's codification of acceptable and unacceptable behavior. Next is business's responsibility to be ethical. At its most fundamental level, this is the obligation to do what is right, just, and fair and to avoid or minimize harm to stakeholders (employees, consumers, the environment, and others). Finally, business is expected to be a good corporate citizen—to fulfill its voluntary/discretionary or philanthropic responsibility to contribute financial and human resources to the community and to improve the quality of life.

No metaphor is perfect, and the Pyramid of CSR is no exception. It is intended to illustrate that the total social responsibility of business is composed of distinct components that, taken together, make up the whole. Although the components have been treated as separate concepts for discussion purposes, they are not mutually exclusive and are not intended to juxtapose a firm's economic responsibilities with its other responsibilities. At the same time, a consideration of the separate components helps the manager to see that the different types of obligations are in constant but dynamic tension with one another.

The most critical tensions, of course, are those between economic and legal, economic and ethical, and economic and philanthropic. The traditionalist might see this as a conflict between a firm's "concern for profits" and its "concern for society," but it is suggested here that this is an oversimplification. A CSR or stakeholder perspective would recognize these tensions as organizational realities but would focus

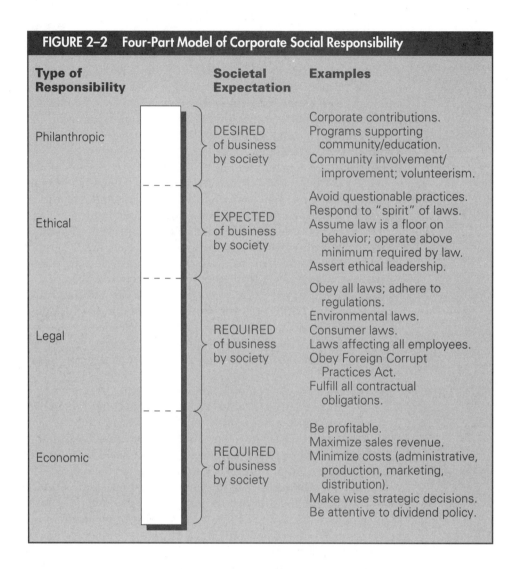

FIGURE 2–2   Four-Part Model of Corporate Social Responsibility

Type of Responsibility	Societal Expectation	Examples
Philanthropic	DESIRED of business by society	Corporate contributions. Programs supporting community/education. Community involvement/ improvement; volunteerism.
Ethical	EXPECTED of business by society	Avoid questionable practices. Respond to "spirit" of laws. Assume law is a floor on behavior; operate above minimum required by law. Assert ethical leadership.
Legal	REQUIRED of business by society	Obey all laws; adhere to regulations. Environmental laws. Consumer laws. Laws affecting all employees. Obey Foreign Corrupt Practices Act. Fulfill all contractual obligations.
Economic	REQUIRED of business by society	Be profitable. Maximize sales revenue. Minimize costs (administrative, production, marketing, distribution). Make wise strategic decisions. Be attentive to dividend policy.

on the total pyramid as a unified whole and on how the firm might engage in decisions, actions, and programs that simultaneously fulfill all its component parts.

In summary, the total social responsibility of business entails the simultaneous fulfillment of the firm's economic, legal, ethical, and philanthropic responsibilities. In equation form, this might be expressed as follows:

Economic Responsibilities + Legal Responsibilities + Ethical Responsibilities

+ Philanthropic Responsibilities

= Total Corporate Social Responsibility

Stated in more pragmatic and managerial terms, the socially responsible firm should strive to:

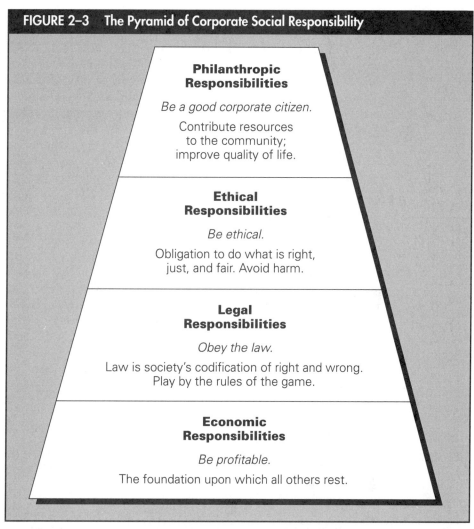

FIGURE 2–3   The Pyramid of Corporate Social Responsibility

Philanthropic Responsibilities

Be a good corporate citizen.

Contribute resources to the community; improve quality of life.

Ethical Responsibilities

Be ethical.

Obligation to do what is right, just, and fair. Avoid harm.

Legal Responsibilities

Obey the law.

Law is society's codification of right and wrong. Play by the rules of the game.

Economic Responsibilities

Be profitable.

The foundation upon which all others rest.

SOURCE: Archie B. Carroll, "The Pyramid of Corporate Social Responsibility: Toward the Moral Management of Organizational Stakeholders," *Business Horizons* (July–August, 1991), 42. Copyright © 1991 by the Foundation for the School of Business at Indiana University. Used with permission.

- Make a profit.
- Obey the law.
- Be ethical.
- Be a good corporate citizen.

What is especially important to note about the four-part CSR model is that it is really a stakeholder model. That is, each of the four components of responsibility addresses different stakeholders in terms of the varying priorities in which the stakeholders are affected. Thus, economic responsibilities most dramatically impact owners and employees (because if the business is not economically viable, owners and employees will be directly affected). Legal responsibilities are certainly crucial with respect to owners, but in today's society the threat of litigation against businesses emanates largely from employee and consumer stakeholders. Ethical responsibilities affect all stakeholder groups, but an examination of the ethical issues business faces today suggests that they involve consumers and employees most frequently. Finally, philanthropic responsibilities most affect the community, but it could be argued that employees are next affected because some research has suggested that a company's philanthropic performance significantly affects its employees' morale. Figure 2–4 presents this stakeholder view of CSR, along with a priority scheme in which the stakeholder groups are addressed/affected by the companies' actions in that realm. The numbers in the cells are not based on empirical evidence but are only suggestive. Other priority schemes could easily be argued.

As we study the evolution of business's major areas of social concern, as presented in various chapters in Parts 2 and 3, we will see how our model's four facets (economic, legal, ethical, and philanthropic) provide us with a useful framework for conceptualizing the issue of corporate social responsibility. The social contract between business and society is to a large extent formulated from mutual understandings that exist in each area of our basic model. But, it should be noted that the ethical and philanthropic categories, taken together, more nearly capture the essence of what people generally mean today when they speak of the social responsibility of business. Situating these two categories relative to the legal and economic obligations, however, keeps them in proper perspective.

ARGUMENTS AGAINST AND FOR CORPORATE SOCIAL RESPONSIBILITY

In an effort to provide a balanced view of the CSR issue, we will consider the arguments that have been raised against and for it. We should state clearly at the outset, however, that those who argue against corporate social responsibility are not using in their considerations the comprehensive CSR model presented above. Rather, it

FIGURE 2–4	A Stakeholder View of Corporate Social Responsibility				
	Stakeholder Group Addressed and Affected				
CSR Component	**Owners**	**Consumers**	**Employees**	**Community**	**Others**
Economic	1	4	2	3	5
Legal	3	2	1	4	5
Ethical	4	1	2	3	5
Philanthropic	3	4	2	1	5

Numbers in cells suggest the prioritization of stakeholders addressed and affected within each CSR component. Numbers are illustrative only.

appears that the critics are viewing CSR more narrowly—as only the efforts of the organization to pursue social, noneconomic/nonlegal goals (our ethical and philanthropic categories). Some critics equate CSR with only the philanthropic category. We should also state that only a few businesspeople and academics argue against the fundamental notion of CSR today. The debate among businesspeople more often centers on the kinds and degrees of CSR and on subtle ethical questions, rather than on the basic question of whether or not business should be socially responsible. Among academics, economists are probably the easiest group to single out as being against the pursuit of corporate social goals. But even some economists no longer resist CSR on the grounds of economic theory.

Arguments Against CSR

Let us first look at the arguments that have surfaced over the years from the anti-CSR school of thought. Most notable has been the classical economic argument. This traditional view holds that management has one responsibility: to maximize the profits of its owners or shareholders. This classical economic school, led by economist Milton Friedman, argues that social issues are not the concern of businesspeople and that these problems should be resolved by the unfettered workings of the free market system.[20] Further, this view holds that if the free market cannot solve the social problem, then it falls upon government and legislation to do the job. Friedman softens his argument somewhat by his assertion that management is "to make as much money as possible *while conforming to the basic rules of society, both those embodied in the law and those embodied in ethical customs.*"[21] When Friedman's entire statement is considered, it appears that he accepts three of the four categories of the four-part model—economic, legal, and ethical. The only item not specifically embraced is the voluntary or philanthropic category. In any event, it is clear that the economic argument views corporate social responsibility more narrowly than we have in our conceptual model.

A second major objection to CSR is that business is not equipped to handle social activities. This position holds that managers are oriented toward finance and operations and do not have the necessary expertise (social skills) to make social decisions.[22] While this may have been true at one point in time, it is less true today. Closely related to this argument is a third: If managers were to pursue corporate social responsibility vigorously, it would tend to dilute the business's primary purpose.[23] The objection here is that CSR would put business into fields not related, as F.A. Hayek has stated, to their "proper aim."[24]

A fourth argument against CSR is that business already has enough power—economic, environmental, and technological—and so why should we place in its hands the opportunity to wield additional power?[25] As it is, the influence of business permeates society. By giving decision-making opportunities in the social domain to business, would we not be aggravating the balance-of-power problem that already exists in our society? This view tends to ignore the potential use of business power for public good.

One other argument that merits mention is that by encouraging business to assume social responsibilities we might be placing it in a deleterious position in terms of the international balance of payments. One consequence of being socially responsible is that business must internalize costs that it formerly passed on to society in the form of dirty air, unsafe products, consequences of discrimination, and so on. The increase in the costs of products caused by including social considerations in the price structure would necessitate raising the prices of products, making them less competitive in international markets. The net effect might be to dissipate the country's advantages gained previously through technological advances. This argument weakens somewhat when one considers that social responsibility is quickly becoming a global concern, not one restricted to U.S. firms and operations.

The arguments we have discussed constitute the principal claims made by those who oppose the CSR concept. Many of the reasons given appear quite rational. Value choices as to the type of society the citizenry would like to have, at some point become part of the total social responsibility question. Whereas some of these objections might have had validity at one point in time, it is doubtful that they do today. Let us now examine some of the main arguments in favor of CSR.

Arguments for CSR

It is worthwhile summarizing Thomas Petit's perspective as our point of departure in discussing support of the CSR doctrine. Petit synthesizes the thoughts of such intellectuals as Elton Mayo, Peter Drucker, Adolph Berle, and John Maynard Keynes. He asserts that although their ideas on this matter vary considerably, they agree on two fundamental points: "(1) Industrial society faces serious human and social problems brought on largely by the rise of the large corporations, and (2) managers must conduct the affairs of the corporation in ways to solve or at least ameliorate these problems."[26]

This generalized justification of corporate social responsibility is appealing. It actually comes close to what we might suggest as a first argument for CSR—namely, that it is in business's long-range self-interest to be socially responsible. This argument provides an additional dimension by suggesting that it was partially business's fault that many of today's social problems arose in the first place and, consequently, that business should assume a role in remedying these problems. It might be inferred from this that deterioration of the social condition must be halted if business is to survive and prosper in the future.

The long-range self-interest view is basically that if business is to have a healthy climate in which to exist in the future, it must take actions now that will ensure its long-term viability. Perhaps the reasoning behind this view is that society's expectations are such that if business does not respond on its own, its role in society may be altered by the public—for example, through government regulation or, more dramatically, through alternative systems for the production and distribution of goods and services.

It is frequently difficult for managers who have a short-range orientation to appreciate that their rights and roles in the economic system are determined by society. Business must be responsive to society's expectations over the long term if it is to survive in its present form or in a less restrained form.

One of the most pragmatic reasons for business to be socially responsible is to ward off future government intervention and regulation. Today there are numerous areas in which government intrudes with an expensive, elaborate regulatory apparatus to fill a void left by business's inaction. To the extent that business polices itself with self-disciplined standards and guidelines, future government intervention can be somewhat forestalled. Later, we will discuss some areas in which business could have prevented intervention and simultaneously ensured greater freedom in decision making had it imposed higher standards of behavior on itself.

Keith Davis presents two additional arguments that deserve mention together: "Business has the resources" and "Let business try."[27] These two views maintain that because business has a reservoir of management talent, functional expertise, and capital, and because so many others have tried and failed to solve general social problems, business should be given a chance. These arguments have some merit, because there are some social problems that can be handled, in the final analysis, only by business. Examples include avoiding discrimination, providing safe products, and engaging in fair advertising. Admittedly, government can and does assume a role in these areas, but business must make the final decisions.

Another view is that "proacting is better than reacting." This position holds that *proacting* (anticipating and initiating) is more practical and less costly than simply reacting to problems once they have developed. Environmental pollution is a good example, particularly business's experience with attempting to clean up rivers, lakes, and other waterways that were neglected for years. In the long run, it would have been wiser to have prevented the environmental deterioration from occurring in the first place.

A final argument in favor of CSR is that the public strongly supports it. A *Business Week*/Harris poll revealed that, with a stunning 95 percent majority, the public believes that companies should not only focus on profits for shareholders but that companies should be responsible to their workers and communities, even if making things better for workers and communities requires companies to sacrifice some profits.[28]

CORPORATE SOCIAL RESPONSIVENESS

We have discussed the evolution of corporate social responsibility, a model for viewing social responsibility, and the arguments for and against it. It is now important to address a concern that has arisen in recent years over the use of the terms *responsibility* and *responsiveness*. We will consider the views of several writers to make our point.

Ackerman and Bauer's Action-Oriented View

A general argument that has generated much discussion over the past 20 years holds that the term *responsibility* is too suggestive of efforts to pinpoint accountability or obligation. Therefore, it is not dynamic enough to fully describe business's willingness—apart from obligation—to respond to social demands. For example, Robert Ackerman and Raymond Bauer criticized the term by stating, "The connotation of 'responsibility' is that of the process of assuming an obligation. It places an emphasis on motivation rather than on performance." They go on to say, "Responding to social demands is much more than deciding what to do. There remains the management task of doing what one has decided to do, and this task is far from trivial."[29] As the title of their book suggests, they then argue that "social responsiveness" is a more apt description of what is essential.

Their point is well made. **Responsibility**, taken quite literally, does imply more of a state or condition of having assumed an obligation, whereas **responsiveness** connotes a dynamic, action-oriented condition. We should not overlook, however, that much of what business has done and is doing has resulted from a particular motivation—an assumption of obligation—whether assigned by government, forced by special-interest groups, or voluntarily assumed. Perhaps business, in some instances, has failed to accept and internalize the obligation, and thus it may seem odd to refer to it as a responsibility. Nevertheless, some motivation that led to social responsiveness had to be there, even though in some cases it was not admitted to be a responsibility or an obligation.

Sethi's Three-Stage Schema

S. Prakash Sethi takes a slightly different, but related, path in getting from social responsibility to social responsiveness. He proposes a three-stage schema for classifying corporate behavior in responding to social or societal needs: social obligation, social responsibility, and social responsiveness.

Social obligation, Sethi argues, is corporate behavior in response to market forces or legal constraints. Corporate legitimacy is very narrow here and is based on legal and economic criteria only. *Social responsibility*, Sethi suggests, "implies bringing corporate behavior up to a level where it is congruent with the prevailing social norms, values, and expectations."[30] He argues that whereas the concept of social obligation is proscriptive in nature, social responsibility is prescriptive in nature. *Social responsiveness*, the third stage in his schema, suggests that what is important is "not how corporations should respond to social pressure but what should be their long-run role in a dynamic social system."[31] He suggests that here business is expected to be "anticipatory" and "preventive." Note that his *obligation* and *responsibility* categories embody essentially the same message we were attempting to convey with our four-part conceptual model.

Frederick's CSR_1 and CSR_2

William Frederick has distinguished between corporate social responsibility, which he calls CSR_1, and corporate social responsiveness, which he terms CSR_2, in the following way:

> *Corporate social* responsiveness *refers to the capacity of a corporation to respond to social pressures. The literal act of responding, or of achieving a generally responsive posture, to society is the focus. . . . One searches the organization for mechanisms, procedures, arrangements, and behavioral patterns that, taken collectively, would mark the organization as more or less capable of responding to social pressures.*[32]

Frederick further argued that advocates of social responsiveness (CSR_2) "have urged corporations to eschew philosophic questions of social responsibility and to concentrate on the more pragmatic matter of responding effectively to environmental pressures." He later articulated an idea known as CSR_3—corporate social rectitude—which addressed the moral correctness of actions taken and policies formulated.[33] However, we would argue that the moral dimension is implicit in CSR, as we included it in our basic four-part definition.

Epstein's Process View

Edwin Epstein discusses corporate social responsiveness within the context of a broader concept that he calls the corporate social policy process. In this context,

Epstein emphasizes the *process* aspect of social responsiveness. He asserts that corporate social responsiveness focuses on the individual and organizational processes "for determining, implementing, and evaluating the firm's capacity to anticipate, respond to, and manage the issues and problems arising from the diverse claims and expectations of internal and external stakeholders."[34]

Other Views

Several other writers have provided conceptual schemes that describe the responsiveness facet. Ian Wilson, for example, asserts that there are four possible business strategies: *reaction, defense, accommodation,* and *proaction.*[35] Terry McAdam has likewise described four social responsibility philosophies that mesh well with Wilson's and describe the managerial approach that would characterize the range of the responsiveness dimension: "Fight all the way," "Do only what is required," "Be progressive," and "Lead the industry."[36] Davis and Blomstrom describe alternative responses to societal pressures as follows: *withdrawal, public relations approach, legal approach, bargaining,* and *problem solving.*[37] Finally, James Post has articulated three major social responsiveness categories: *adaptive, proactive,* and *interactive.*[38]

Thus, the corporate social responsiveness dimension that has been discussed by some as an alternative focus to that of social responsibility is, in actuality, the action phase of management's response in the social sphere. In a sense, the responsiveness orientation enables organizations to rationalize and operationalize their social responsibilities without getting bogged down in the quagmire of definition problems, which can so easily occur if organizations try to get an exact determination of what their true responsibilities are before they act.

In an interesting study of social responsiveness among Canadian and Finnish forestry firms, researchers concluded that the social responsiveness of a corporation will proceed through a predictable series of phases and that managers will tend to respond to the most powerful stakeholders.[39] This study demonstrates that social responsiveness *is* a process and that stakeholder power, rather than a sense of responsibility, may sometimes drive the process.

CORPORATE SOCIAL PERFORMANCE

For the past few decades, there has been a trend toward making the concern for social and ethical issues more and more pragmatic. The responsiveness thrust that we just discussed was a part of this trend. It is possible to integrate some of the concerns into a model of corporate social *performance* (CSP). The performance focus is intended to suggest that what really matters is what companies are able to accomplish—the results of their acceptance of social responsibility and adoption of a responsiveness philosophy. In developing a conceptual framework for CSP, we not only have to specify the nature (economic, legal, ethical, philanthropic) of the responsibility, but we also need to identify a particular philosophy, pattern, or mode of responsiveness. Finally, we need to identify the stakeholder issues or topical areas to which these responsibilities are tied. One need not ponder the stakeholder issues that have evolved under the rubric of social responsibility to recognize how they have changed over time. The issues, and especially the degree of organizational interest in the issues, are always in a state of flux. As the times change, so does the emphasis on the range of social issues that business must address.

Also of interest is the fact that particular issues are of varying concern to businesses, depending on the industry in which they exist as well as other factors. A bank, for example, is not as pressed on environmental issues as a manufacturer. Likewise, a manufacturer is considerably more absorbed with the issue of environmental protection than is an insurance company.

Carroll's Corporate Social Performance Model

Figure 2–5 illustrates Carroll's *corporate social performance model*, which brings together the three central dimensions we have discussed:

1. *Social responsibility categories*—economic, legal, ethical, and discretionary (philanthropic)

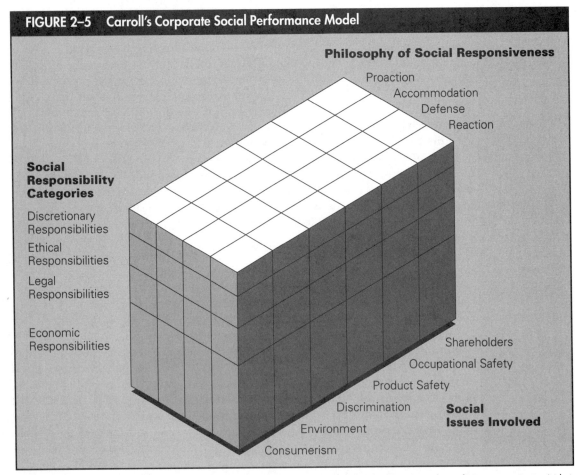

FIGURE 2–5   Carroll's Corporate Social Performance Model

SOURCE: Archie B. Carroll, "A Three-Dimensional Conceptual Model of Corporate Social Performance," *Academy of Management Review* (Vol. 4, No. 4, 1979), 503. Reproduced with permission.

2. *Philosophy (or mode) of social responsiveness*—reaction, defense, accommodation, and proaction

3. *Social (or stakeholder) issues involved*—consumerism, environment, discrimination, etc.)[40]

One dimension of this model pertains to all that is included in our definition of social responsibility—the economic, legal, ethical, and discretionary (philanthropic) components. Second, there is a social responsiveness continuum. Although some writers have suggested that this is the preferable focus when one considers social responsibility, the model suggests that responsiveness is but one additional aspect to be addressed if CSP is to be achieved. The third dimension concerns the range of social or stakeholder issues (for example, consumerism, environment, and discrimination) that management must address.

Usefulness of the Model to Academics and Managers

The corporate social performance conceptual model is intended to be useful for both academics and managers. For *academics*, the model is primarily an aid to perceiving the distinction among the definitions of corporate social responsibility that have appeared in the literature. What heretofore have been regarded as separate definitions of CSR are treated here as three separate aspects pertaining to CSP. The model's major use to the academic, therefore, is in helping to systematize the important issues that must be taught and understood in an effort to clarify the CSR concept. The model is not the ultimate conceptualization. It is, rather, a modest but necessary step toward understanding the major facets of CSP.

The conceptual model can assist *managers* in understanding that social responsibility is not separate and distinct from economic performance. The model integrates economic concerns into a social performance framework. In addition, it places ethical and philanthropic expectations into a rational economic and legal framework. The model can help the manager systematically think through major stakeholder issues. Although it does not provide the answer to how far the organization should go, it does provide a conceptualization that could lead to better-managed social performance. Moreover, the model could be used as a planning tool and as a diagnostic problem-solving tool. The model can assist the manager by identifying categories within which the organization can be situated.

The following example may help show how an organization may position its actions using the CSP model (see the segments in Figure 2–5). The major pharmaceutical firm Merck & Co. discovered a drug (Mectizan) it later concluded could cure a disease known as "river blindness." Merck learned that this disease was common in tiny villages in Africa and in parts of the Middle East and Latin America. Initially, Merck wanted to market the drug at a profit. It learned, however, that there was no viable market for the drug because its potential customers were too poor, lived in isolated locations, and had no access to pharmacies or routine medical care. Merck then hoped a group like the World Health Organization (WHO) or a foundation would volunteer to fund a distribution program for the drug, which could cost as much as $20 million a year.

When no funder came forward, Merck decided to supply Mectizan to everyone who needed it, indefinitely, and at no charge. By 1995, more than 6 million people in 21 countries had received at least one dose of Mectizan, and many others were receiving annual doses. Mectizan distribution received a significant boost in 1996 when the WHO and World Bank announced an ambitious 12-year project to wipe out river blindness. Former President Jimmy Carter agreed to coordinate the $124 million project through the Carter Center in Atlanta.[41]

According to the social performance model in Figure 2–5, Merck saw itself moving from the economic category to the ethical or philanthropic one. On the social issues dimension, the firm initially focused on potential consumers who became consumer-recipients of the firm's socially responsible commitment. On the philosophy of social responsiveness continuum, Merck was at the proaction end. Given Merck's leadership on this issue, it is not surprising to note that the company was voted the "most admired" corporation from 1986–1992 in *Fortune* magazine's annual survey of corporate reputations. As recently as 1998, Merck was still ranked as one of *Fortune*'s top ten most admired companies in America.[42]

This example shows how a business's response can be positioned in the social performance model. The average business firm faces many such controversial issues and might use the conceptual model to analyze its stance on these issues and perhaps to help determine its motivations, actions, and response strategies. Managers would have a systematic framework for thinking through not only the social issues they face but also the managerial response patterns they should contemplate. The model could serve as a guide in formulating criteria to assist the organization in developing its posture on various stakeholder issues. The net result could be an increase in the amount of systematic attention being given to the entire realm of corporate social performance.

Wartick and Cochran's Extensions

Before leaving our discussion of the CSP model, it is important to examine extensions of the model. The initial version of the model employed "social issues" as the third aspect or dimension, which embraced such issues as consumerism, environment, and discrimination. That dimension is now referred to as stakeholder issues, to place it within our current framework. While it was still being framed as social issues, however, Steven Wartick and Philip Cochran proposed that the dimension of social issues had, in fact, matured from simply an identification of the social issue categories in which companies must take action to a whole new management field, known as *social issues management*. Issues management, which we will treat more fully in Chapter 19, entails such activities as issues identification, issues analysis, and response development. Whether the third dimension is perceived as social issues or stakeholder issues, the issues management approach is equally useful.

Wartick and Cochran extended the social performance model even further by proposing that the three dimensions be thought of as depicting *principles* (corporate social responsibilities, reflecting a philosophical orientation), *processes* (corporate social responsiveness, reflecting an institutional orientation), and *policies* (social issues management, reflecting an organizational orientation). These extensions are extremely useful because they help us to more fully appreciate complementary aspects that were neglected in the original model. Figure 2–6 summarizes Wartick and Cochran's extensions to the model.[43]

FIGURE 2-6 Wartick and Cochran's Corporate Social Performance Model Extensions		
Principles	*Processes*	*Policies*
Corporate Social Responsibilities	**Corporate Social Responsiveness**	**Social Issues Management**
(1) Economic	(1) Reactive	(1) Issues Identification
(2) Legal	(2) Defensive	(2) Issues Analysis
(3) Ethical	(3) Accommodative	(3) Response Development
(4) Discretionary	(4) Proactive	
Directed at:	*Directed at:*	*Directed at:*
(1) The Social Contract of Business	(1) The Capacity to Respond to Changing Societal Conditions	(1) Minimizing "Surprises"
(2) Business as a Moral Agent	(2) Managerial Approaches to Developing Responses	(2) Determining Effective Corporate Social Policies
Philosophical Orientation	*Institutional Orientation*	*Organizational Orientation*

SOURCE: Steven L. Wartick and Philip L. Cochran, "The Evolution of the Corporate Social Performance Model," *Academy of Management Review* (Vol. 10, 1985), 767.

Wood's Reformulated Model

More recently, Donna Wood has elaborated and reformulated Carroll's model and Wartick and Cochran's extensions. Using Wartick and Cochran's extensions, she has produced a useful definition of corporate social performance:

> *A business organization's configuration of principles of social responsibility, processes of social responsiveness, and policies, programs, and other observable outcomes as they relate to the firm's societal relationships.*[44]

Wood's proposal is (1) to think of social responsiveness as a *set* of processes rather than as a single process and (2) to think of Wartick and Cochran's policies as entailing *observable outcomes* of corporate and managerial actions. Wood takes this definition further by proposing that each of the three components—principles, processes, and outcomes—is composed of specific elements. Figure 2–7 presents Wood's corporate social performance model.

These extensions and reformulations of Carroll's corporate social performance model add significantly to our appreciation of what is involved as we strive to think of CSP as a dynamic and multifaceted managerial concept.

After this discussion of CSP, one might ask whether people really care about CSP. In the next section, we will examine nonacademic research into CSP. We will close this section, however, by reporting a major study of whether U.S. consumers really care about CSP. In this study, Karen Paul and other researchers developed a scale to measure consumers' sensitivity to CSP. Among the researchers' findings were that CSP does matter, that women were more sensitive than men to CSP, and that those identifying themselves as Democrats were more sensitive to CSP than Republicans.[45]

FIGURE 2-7   Wood's Corporate Social Performance Model

Principles of corporate social responsibility:
- Institutional principle: legitimacy
- Organizational principle: public responsibility
- Individual principle: managerial discretion

Processes of corporate social responsiveness:
- Environmental assessment
- Stakeholder management
- Issues management

Outcomes of corporate behavior:
- Social impacts
- Social programs
- Social policies

SOURCE: Donna J. Wood, "Corporate Social Performance Revisited," *Academy of Management Review* (October, 1991), 694.

Nonacademic Research on Corporate Social Performance

Although there has been considerable academic research on the subject of corporate social performance over the past decade, we should stress that academics are not the only ones who are interested in this topic. Prominent organizations and periodicals that report on social performance include *Fortune* magazine, the Council on Economic Priorities (CEP), the Business Enterprise Trust, WalkerInformation, Business for Social Responsibility, *Business and Society Review* magazine, *Business Ethics* magazine, and Kinder, Lydenberg, Domini, and Co., Inc. (KLD). We will discuss several of these.

Fortune's Rankings of "Most Admired" and "Least Admired" Companies

For several years now, *Fortune* magazine has conducted rankings of "America's Most Admired Companies" and has included among their "Eight Key Attributes of Reputation" the category titled "Social Responsibility." The rankings are the result of a poll of more than 12,600 senior executives, outside directors, and financial analysts. In the social responsibility category, the most admired firms for 1998 were Herman Miller, Coca-Cola, and DuPont.[46] It is not clear what impact, if any, the *Fortune* rankings have for these businesses, but surely they have some impact on the firms' general reputations. The important point to note here, however, is that the social responsibility category is one indicator of corporate social performance and that it was included as a criterion of admired companies by one of our country's leading business magazines.

CEP's Rating of America's Corporate Conscience

Another indication of the public's interest in corporate social performance was the 1986 publication of a volume entitled *Rating America's Corporate Conscience*, which was compiled by the Council on Economic Priorities. The book rated various companies and their products (food products, health care products, hotels, automobiles, appliances, and dozens of other consumer goods) according to several categories of social performance. The CEP issued what it called the first comprehensive shopping guide for the socially conscious consumer, with the goal of "enhancing corporate performance as it affects society in critically important areas. . . ."[47] "This book," the authors wrote, "will help you cast an economic vote on corporate social responsibility when you shop—whether you're buying toothpaste, a typewriter, or an airline ticket."[48]

This 500-page volume rated corporate social performance by analyzing comparable data and presenting it in a practical format. The authors chose seven issues on which to base their judgments of CSP:[49]

1. Charitable contributions
2. Representation of women on boards of directors and among top corporate officers
3. Representation of minorities on boards of directors and among top corporate officers
4. Disclosure of social information
5. Involvement in South Africa
6. Conventional-weapons–related contracting
7. Nuclear-weapons–related contracting

Included in the book were product charts and company profiles that assessed the firms and their products using the criteria presented above. Figure 2–8 presents an example of their product charts (in this case, the chart for soft drinks).

Many could debate whether or not the criteria CEP chose were appropriate measures of CSP and whether or not they were accurately applied. The important point, however, is that such a volume was produced in the first place and was made commercially available to the public in bookstores. It demonstrated further the public's interest in the social performance of business. When the book came out, it certainly got noticed by the business press, although some of the reviews were somewhat tongue-in-cheek.[50] On the whole, however, the reviews were quite positive, and many consumers have found the book to be a useful layperson's guide to corporate social performance.

The latest volume of the CEP was titled *Shopping for a Better World: The Quick and Easy Guide to ALL Your Socially Responsible Shopping* (1994). The CEP updated its social criteria to the following key areas, and these areas were still being used as recently as 1998:

• Environment
• Charitable giving
• Community outreach
• Women's advancement
• Advancement of minorities
• Family benefits
• Workplace issues
• Disclosure of information

The CEP also evaluated the companies in specific industries. In 1996, for example, CEP issued a special report on the airline industry in which it rated each of the major airlines on the eight criteria listed above.[51]

FIGURE 2–8   Product Chart for Soft Drinks

Beverages   **Soft Drinks**

Size of Charitable Contributions	Women Directors and Officers	Minority Directors and Officers	Social Disclosure	Brand Name	Company (Profile Page)	Involvement in South Africa	Conv. Weapons–Related Contracts	Nuclear Weapons–Related Contracts	Authors' Company of Choice
$	♀♀	♦♦	✍ ✍ ✍	Coca-Cola Fanta Fresca Mello Yello Ramblin' Root Beer Sprite Tab	Coca-Cola	Yes B	No	No	
$ $	No	♦	✍ ✍ ✍	Mountain Dew Pepsi Slice	PepsiCo	No	No	No	
$ $	♦	♦♦♦	✍ ✍ ✍	7-Up	Philip Morris	No	No	No	
$ $ $	♦	♦♦♦	✍ ✍ ✍	Crush Hires Root Beer	Procter & Gamble	No	No	No	✓
$ $	♀♀	♦	✍ ✍	Gatorade	Quaker Oats	No	No	No	

* = See company profile
? = No information available
Single figure ($, ♦) = Minimal
Double figure ($$, ♦♦, ✍✍) = Moderate
Triple figure ($$$, ♦♦♦, ✍✍✍) = Substantial

No = No involvement or participation
Yes = Involvement or participation, A, B, C in the South African column reflect the degree of compliance with Sullivan Principles and/or involvement in strategic industries.

SOURCE: Steven D. Lydenberg, Alice Tepper Marlin, Sean O'Brien Strub, and the Council on Economic Priorities, *Rating America's Corporate Conscience: A Provocative Guide to the Companies Behind the Products You Buy Every Day* (Reading, MA: Addison-Wesley Publishing Co., 1986), 67.

Business Enterprise Trust Awards

The Business Enterprise Trust was founded in 1989 to stimulate a national debate on responsible business behavior in the complex economy of the 1990s and beyond. The Trust was created by 17 prominent business leaders, including such notables as Warren Buffett (Berkshire Hathaway, Inc.), Norman Lear (Act III Communications), and James Burke (Partnership for a Drug-Free America). One of the major activities of the Trust is an annual awards program that seeks to identify and promote acts of courage, integrity, and social vision in business. The Trust's board of directors hopes that the Business Enterprise Awards will become a kind of Pulitzer Prize for business. The Trust presented its first awards in 1991. James E. Burke, chairman of the Trust, provides a useful summary of the awards' purpose:

> *The Business Enterprise Awards will stimulate and inspire businesspeople to the kind of behavior which reflects the simple truth—that business institutions have a responsibility to all of those in society who are dependent upon them—and that following this simple moral imperative turns out to be very good business.*[52]

The types of individuals and actions honored by the Business Enterprise Trust Awards include entrepreneurs who demonstrate social vision by creating new products, services, or forms of corporate organization that address important social needs; managers who show moral thoughtfulness, commitment to principle, and sensitivity to the needs of businesses' many stakeholders; business leaders who resist pressures for short-term performance in serving the genuine long-term interests of both shareholders and society; and any businessperson who struggles productively with the natural tension between corporate profitability and social needs.

WalkerInformation

A major comprehensive study designed to measure the impact of corporate social responsibility was conducted in 1994 by Walker Group (now WalkerInformation), the twelfth largest research organization in the United States. Employing a 14-page questionnaire, responses were received from 1,037 heads of U.S. households (43 percent male and 57 percent female). Respondents were asked to answer questions as potential consumers, employees, or investors depending on the nature of the question. The WalkerInformation study painted a detailed account of the impact of corporate social responsibility on business firms' reputations and its relationship to stakeholder decisions to purchase from, become employed by, or invest in a particular company.[53]

In one of its questions, WalkerInformation sought to discover what the general public perceived to be the activities or characteristics of socially responsible companies. Figure 2–9 summarizes what the sample said were the top 20 activities/characteristics of socially responsible companies. The items in this listing are quite compatible with our discussion of CSR earlier in this chapter. It should be noted that most of these characteristics would be representative of the legal, ethical, and philanthropic/discretionary components of our four-part CSR definition.

Another issue of interest in the WalkerInformation study was the question of corporate reputation and the impact on reputation of both traditional purchase drivers (such as product quality, price, convenience, and service) and citizenship or social responsibility drivers (such as community support, business practices, employee treatment, and environmental concern). The research disclosed that the significant majority of respondents are still concerned with price, quality, and service, but they are also concerned with how a company practices business, treats employees, invests in the community, and cares for the environment. Figure 2–10 demonstrates how the respondents ranked the importance of the various factors in terms of their impact on company reputation.

FIGURE 2-9　Top 20 Activities/Characteristics of Socially Responsible Companies

- Makes products that are safe
- Does not pollute air or water
- Obeys the law in all aspects of business
- Promotes honest/ethical employee behavior
- Commits to safe workplace ethics
- Does not use misleading/deceptive advertising
- Upholds stated policy banning discrimination
- Utilizes "environmentally friendly" packaging
- Protects employees against sexual harassment
- Recycles within company
- Shows no past record of questionable activity
- Responds quickly to customer problems
- Maintains waste reduction program
- Provides/pays portion of medical
- Promotes energy-conservation program
- Helps displaced workers with placement
- Gives money to charitable/educational causes
- Utilizes only biodegradable/recycling materials
- Employs friendly/courteous/responsive personnel
- Tries continually to improve quality

SOURCE: WalkerInformation, 1994. Used with permission.

Although quality, service, and price dominated the top five, it is important to note the roles played by business practices, employee treatment, and the other social responsibility factors. WalkerInformation's conclusion was that the public thinks CSR factors impact a company's reputation just as do traditional factors, such as quality, service, and price. A related question pertains to the impact of social irresponsibility on firm reputation. The WalkerInformation study found that companies that are ethical and obey the law can reap rewards from CSR activities and enjoy enhanced reputations. However, those that are perceived to be unethical or that do not obey the law can do little in the way of CSR activities to correct their images. Thus, the penalties for disobeying the law are greater than the rewards for helping society. Later in the book we will examine some of the other findings of the Walker-Information study.

SOCIAL PERFORMANCE AND FINANCIAL PERFORMANCE

One issue that comes up frequently in considerations of corporate social performance is whether or not there is a demonstrable relationship between a firm's social

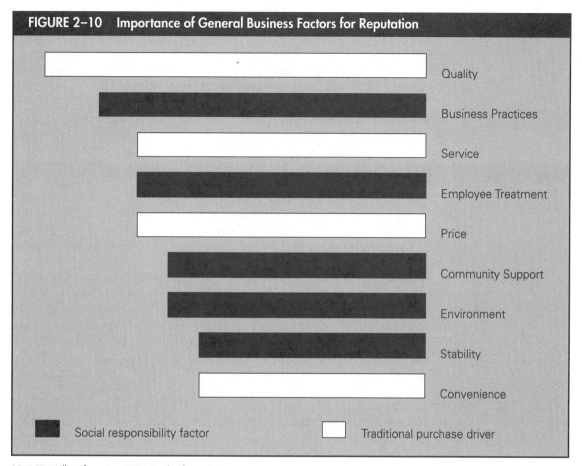

FIGURE 2–10   Importance of General Business Factors for Reputation

Quality

Business Practices

Service

Employee Treatment

Price

Community Support

Environment

Stability

Convenience

■ Social responsibility factor   □ Traditional purchase driver

SOURCE: WalkerInforamtion, 1994. Used with permission.

responsibility or performance and its financial performance. Unfortunately, attempts to measure this relationship are typically hampered by measurement problems. The appropriate performance criteria for measuring financial performance and social responsibility are subject to debate. Furthermore, the measurement of social responsibility is fraught with definitional problems. Even if a definition of CSR could be agreed on, there still would remain the complex task of operationalizing the definition.

Over the years, studies on the social responsibility–financial performance relationship have produced varying results.[54] In one of the more recent studies of this relationship, Lee Preston and Douglas O'Bannon examined data from 67 large U.S. corporations covering the years 1982–1992. They concluded that "there is a *positive* association between social and financial performance in large U.S. corporations."[55]

It is important to note that there have been at least three different views, hypotheses, or perspectives that have dominated these discussions and research. Perhaps the most popular view, which we shall call Perspective 1, is built on the belief that socially responsible firms are more financially profitable. To those who advocate the concept of social performance, it is apparent why they would like to think that social performance is a driver of financial performance and, ultimately, a corporation's reputation. If it could be demonstrated that socially responsible firms, in general, are more financially successful and have better reputations, this would significantly bolster the CSP view, even in the eyes of its critics.

Over the past two decades, Perspective 1 has been studied extensively. Unfortunately, the findings of most of the studies that have sought to demonstrate this relationship have been either flawed in their methodology or inconclusive. Numerous studies have been done well, but even these have failed to produce conclusive results. In spite of this, some studies have claimed to have successfully established this linkage. For example, a study by Covenant Investment Management, a Chicago investment firm, concluded that social concern pays. This study found that 200 companies ranking highest on Covenant's overall social responsibility scale had outperformed the Standard & Poor's 500-stock index during the 5 years (1988–1992) studied.[56] To be considered a valid finding, however, the Covenant research would have to be subjected to careful scrutiny.

Perspective 2, which has not been studied as extensively, argues that a firm's financial performance is a driver of its social performance. This perspective is built somewhat on the notion that social responsibility is a "fair weather" concept; that is, when times are good and companies are enjoying financial success, we witness higher levels of social performance. In their study, Preston and O'Bannon found the strongest evidence that financial performance either precedes, or is contemporaneous with, social performance. This evidence supports the view that social-financial performance correlations are best explained by positive synergies or by "available funding."[57]

Perspective 3 argues that there is an interactive relationship among social performance, financial performance, and corporate reputation. In this symbiotic view, the three major factors influence each other, and, because they are so interrelated, it is not easy to identify which factor is driving the process. Regardless of the perspective taken, each view advocates a significant role for CSP, and it is expected that researchers will continue to explore these perspectives for years to come. Figure 2–11 depicts the essentials of each of these views.

A basic premise of all these perspectives is that there is only one "bottom line"—a corporate bottom line that addresses primarily the stockholders', or owners', investments in the firm. An alternative view is that the firm has "multiple bottom lines" that benefit from corporate social performance. This *stakeholder-bottom-line* perspective argues that the impacts or benefits of CSP cannot be fully measured or appreciated by considering *only* the impact of the firm's financial bottom line.

To truly operate with a stakeholder perspective, companies need to accept the multiple-bottom-line view. Thus, CSP cannot be fully comprehended unless we also consider that its impacts on stakeholders, such as consumers, employees, the community, and other stakeholder groups, are noted, measured, and considered. Research may never conclusively demonstrate a relationship between CSP and financial performance. If a stakeholder perspective is taken, however, it may be more straightforward to assess the impact of CSP on multiple stakeholders' bottom lines. This model of CSP and stakeholders' bottom lines might be depicted as shown in Figure 2–12.

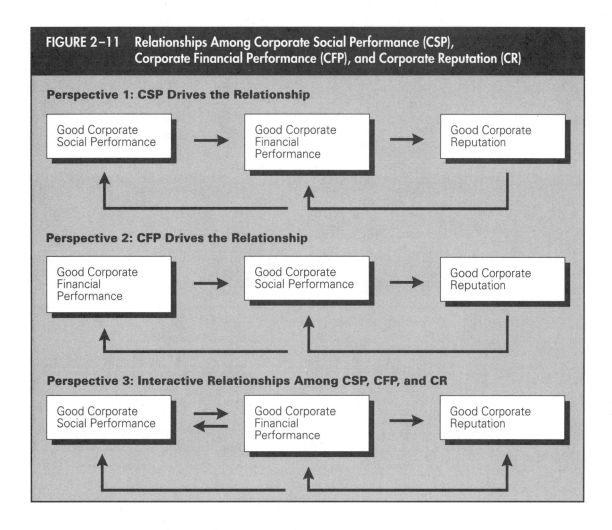

FIGURE 2–11   Relationships Among Corporate Social Performance (CSP), Corporate Financial Performance (CFP), and Corporate Reputation (CR)

Perspective 1: CSP Drives the Relationship

Good Corporate Social Performance → Good Corporate Financial Performance → Good Corporate Reputation

Perspective 2: CFP Drives the Relationship

Good Corporate Financial Performance → Good Corporate Social Performance → Good Corporate Reputation

Perspective 3: Interactive Relationships Among CSP, CFP, and CR

Good Corporate Social Performance ⇄ Good Corporate Financial Performance → Good Corporate Reputation

SOCIALLY CONSCIOUS OR ETHICAL INVESTING

The media, academics, and special-interest groups are not alone in their interest in business's social performance. Investors are also interested. The *socially conscious or ethical investing* movement arrived on the scene in the 1970s and has continued to grow and prosper.

Historically, social responsibility investing dates back to the early 1900s, when church endowments refused to buy "sin" stocks—then defined as shares in tobacco, alcohol, and gambling companies. During the Vietnam War era of the 1960s and early 1970s, antiwar investors refused to invest in defense contracting firms. In the early 1980s, universities, municipalities, and foundations sold off their shares of companies that had operations in South Africa to protest apartheid. In the 1990s, self-styled socially responsible investing has come into its own.[58]

Socially conscious investments in pension funds, mutual funds, and municipal and private portfolios exceed $1 trillion. However, managers of socially conscious

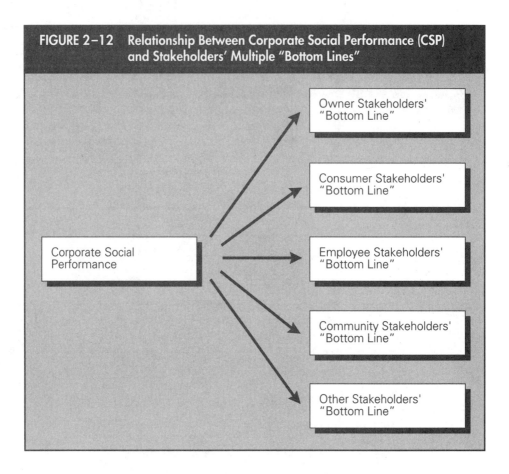

FIGURE 2-12   Relationship Between Corporate Social Performance (CSP) and Stakeholders' Multiple "Bottom Lines"

funds do not use only ethical or social responsibility criteria to decide which companies to invest in. They typically consider a company's financial health before all else. Moreover, a growing corps of brokers, financial planners, and portfolio managers are available to help people evaluate investments for their social impacts.[59]

The concept of "social screening" is the backbone of the socially conscious investing movement. Investors seeking to put their money into socially responsible firms want to screen out those firms they consider to be socially irresponsible or to actively invest in those firms they think of as being socially responsible. Thus, there are negative social screens and positive social screens. Some of the negative social screens that have been used in recent years include the avoidance of investing in tobacco manufacturers, gambling casino operators, defense or weapons contractors, and firms doing business in South Africa.[60] In 1994, however, with the elimination of the official system of apartheid in South Africa, this was eliminated as a negative screen by many.

It is more difficult, and thus more challenging, to implement positive social screens, because they require the potential investor to make judgment calls as to what constitutes an acceptable or a good level of social performance on social investment criteria. Criteria that may be used as either positive or negative screens, depending on the firm's performance, might include the firm's record on issues such as equal employment opportunity and affirmative action, environmental protection, treatment of employees, corporate citizenship (community-minded behavior), and treatment of animals.

The financial performance of socially conscious funds shows that investors do not have to sacrifice profitability for principles. For example, the Domini 400 Social Index, which measures the performance of stocks in "socially responsible" mutual funds, outperformed Standard and Poor's 500-stock index for 3 consecutive years (1995–1997). The gains in the Domini Index show that investors can find financial performance *and* social accountability.[61]

It should be added, however, that there is no clear and consistent evidence that returns from socially conscious funds will equal or exceed the returns from funds that are not so carefully screened. Therefore, socially conscious funds are valued most highly by those investors who really care about the social performance of their investments and are willing to put their money at some risk. A recent study concluded that there is no penalty for improved CSP in terms of institutional ownership and that high CSP tends in fact to lead to an increase in the number of institutional investors holding a given stock.[62]

The Council on Economic Priorities indicates that there are at least four reasons why there has been an upsurge in social or ethical investing:[63]

1. There is more reliable and sophisticated research on CSP than in the past.

2. Investment firms using social criteria have established a solid track record, and investors do not have to sacrifice gains for principles.

3. The socially conscious 1960s generation is now making investment decisions.

4. The Reagan administration's cutbacks on social service programs and regulation have brought an increased public awareness of the need for new and innovative corporate initiatives.

In recent years, several different guides for socially responsible investing have been published. For example, the Council on Economic Priorities published *The Better World Investment Guide.*[64] This volume discusses the history of ethical investing and the many different social screens that have been used for evaluating the social performance of companies. A significant portion of this volume is dedicated to an analysis of companies and their records on 12 criteria, including charitable contributions, advancement of women, minority advancement, military contracts, animal testing, and the environment. Another book, *Investing from the Heart,* provides A-to-Z coverage of topics of interest to socially conscious investors.[65] Finally, *The Social Investment Almanac: A Comprehensive Guide to Socially Responsible Investing* deserves special mention. A unique part of this volume is its treatment of social investing outside the United States.[66] With the advent of the World Wide Web, social investors can now receive up-to-date guidelines and data on social investing. For example, the Social Investment Forum has its own Web site dedicated to the topic, with insights into social and financial performance data.[67]

Socially conscious funds continue to be debated in the investment community. The fact that they exist, have grown, and have prospered, however, provides evidence that the idea is a serious one and that there truly are investors in the real world who take the social performance issue quite seriously.

SUMMARY

The corporate social responsibility concept has a rich history. It has grown out of many diverse views and even today does not enjoy a consensus of definition. A four-part conceptualization was presented that broadly conceives CSR as encompassing economic, legal, ethical, and philanthropic components. The four parts were also presented as part of the Pyramid of CSR.

The concern for corporate social responsibility has been expanded to include a concern for social responsiveness. The responsiveness focus suggests more of an action-oriented theme by which firms not only must address their basic obligations but also must decide on basic modes of responding to these obligations. A CSP model was presented that brought the responsibility and responsiveness dimensions together into a framework that also identified realms of social or stakeholder issues that must be considered. The identification of social issues has blossomed into a field now called "issues management" or "stakeholder management."

The interest in corporate social responsibility extends beyond the academic community. On an annual basis, *Fortune* magazine polls executives on various dimensions of corporate performance; one major dimension is called "Social Responsibility." The Council on Economic Priorities published a landmark volume entitled *Rating America's Corporate Conscience,* which further heightened public interest in the social and ethical domains of business performance. The Business Enterprise Trust now gives awards for exceptional social performance. A new organization, Business for Social Responsibility, promises to be on the cutting edge of CSR practice. Walker-Information has investigated how the general consuming public regards social responsibility issues.

Finally, the socially conscious or ethical investing movement seems to be flourishing. This indicates that there is a growing body of investors who are sensitive to business's social and ethical (as well as financial) performance. Studies of the relationship between social responsibility and economic performance do not yield consistent results, but social efforts are nevertheless expected and are of value to both the firm and the business community.

KEY TERMS

Business for Social Responsibility (BSR) (page 27)

community obligations (page 30)

corporate social performance model (page 44)

legal model (page 29)

paternalism (page 30)

philanthropy (page 30)

Pyramid of CSR (page 37)

responsibility (page 41)

responsiveness (page 41)

social obligation (page 42)

social responsibility (page 42)

social responsiveness (page 42)

socially conscious or ethical investing (page 55)

DISCUSSION QUESTIONS

1. Identify and explain the four-part definition of corporate social responsibility. Provide several examples of each component of the definition. Identify and discuss some of the tensions among the definition's components.
2. In your view, what is the single strongest argument against the idea of corporate social responsibility? What is the single strongest argument in support of corporate social responsibility? Briefly explain.
3. Differentiate corporate social responsibility from corporate social responsiveness. Give an example of each.
4. Of the social responsiveness categories mentioned in the text, which set of categories do you find most useful in describing the responsiveness dimension? Explain.
5. Based on your understanding of corporate social responsibility as developed in this chapter, classify each of the seven criteria used by the Council on Economic

ENDNOTES

Priorities in its book, *Rating America's Corporate Conscience,* into one of the four CSR categories: economic, legal, ethical, or philanthropic.

1. John L. Paluszek, *Business and Society: 1976–2000* (New York: AMACOM, 1976), 1.
2. Keith Davis, "Understanding the Social Responsibility Puzzle," *Business Horizon* (Winter, 1967), 45–50.
3. James W. McKie, "Changing Views," in *Social Responsibility and the Business Predicament* (Washington, DC: The Brookings Institute, 1974), 22.
4. *Ibid.*
5. See Morrell Heald, *The Social Responsibilities of Business: Company and Community, 1900–1960* (Cleveland: Case Western Reserve University Press, 1970), 12–14.
6. McKie, 23.
7. *Ibid.,* 25.
8. Heald, 119.
9. McKie, 27–28.
10. Neil J. Mitchell, *The Generous Corporation: A Political Analysis of Economic Power* (New Haven, CT: Yale University Press, 1989).
11. Ronald E. Berenbeim, "When the Corporate Conscience Was Born" [A review of Mitchell's book], *Across the Board* (October, 1989), 60–62.
12. *Ibid.,* 62.
13. Keith Davis and Robert L. Blomstrom, *Business and Society: Environment and Responsibility,* 3rd ed. (New York: McGraw-Hill, 1975), 39.
14. Joseph W. McGuire, *Business and Society* (New York: McGraw-Hill, 1963), 144.
15. Edwin M. Epstein, "The Corporate Social Policy Process: Beyond Business Ethics, Corporate Social Responsibility and Corporate Social Responsiveness," *California Management Review* (Vol. XXIX, No. 3, 1987), 104.
16. Archie B. Carroll, "A Three-Dimensional Conceptual Model of Corporate Social Performance," *Academy of Management Review* (Vol. 4, No. 4, 1979), 497–505.

17. Archie B. Carroll, "The Pyramid of Corporate Social Responsibility: Toward the Moral Management of Organizational Stakeholders," *Business Horizons* (July–August, 1991), 39–48. Also see Archie B. Carroll, "The Four Faces of Corporate Citizenship," *Business and Society Review* (Vol. 100–101, 1998), 1–7.

18. *Ibid.*

19. *Ibid.*

20. Milton Friedman, "The Social Responsibility of Business Is to Increase Its Profits," *New York Times* (September, 1962), 126.

21. *Ibid.*, 33 (italics added).

22. Christopher D. Stone, *Where the Law Ends* (New York: Harper Colophon Books, 1975), 77.

23. Keith Davis, "The Case For and Against Business Assumption of Social Responsibilities," *Academy of Management Journal* (June, 1973), 312–322.

24. F. A. Hayek, "The Corporation in a Democratic Society: In Whose Interest Ought It and Will It Be Run?" in H. Ansoff (ed.), *Business Strategy* (Middlesex: Penguin, 1969), 225.

25. Davis, 320.

26. Thomas A. Petit, *The Moral Crisis in Management* (New York: McGraw-Hill, 1967), 58.

27. Davis, 316.

28. "Business Week/Harris Poll: America, Land of the Shaken," *Business Week* (March 11, 1996), 65.

29. Robert Ackerman and Raymond Bauer, *Corporate Social Responsiveness: The Modern Dilemma* (Reston, VA: Reston Publishing Company, 1976), 6.

30. S. Prakash Sethi, "Dimensions of Corporate Social Performance: An Analytical Framework," *California Management Review* (Spring, 1975), 58–64.

31. *Ibid.*, 62–63.

32. William C. Frederick, "From CSR_1 to CSR_2: The Maturing of Business-and-Society Thought," Working Paper No. 279 (Graduate School of Business, University of Pittsburgh, 1978), 6. See also *Business and Society* (Vol. 33, No. 2, August, 1994), 150–164.

33. William C. Frederick, "Toward CSR_3: Why Ethical Analysis is Indispensable and Unavoidable in Corporate Affairs," *California Management Review* (Winter, 1986), 131.

34. Epstein, 107.

35. Ian Wilson, "What One Company Is Doing About Today's Demands on Business," in G.A. Steiner (ed.), *Changing Business-Society Interrelationships* (UCLA, 1975).

36. T.W. McAdam, "How to Put Corporate Responsibility into Practice," *Business and Society Review/Innovation* (Summer, 1973), 8–16.

37. Davis and Blomstrom, 85–86.

38. James E. Post, *Corporate Behavior and Social Change* (Reston, VA: Reston Publishing Co., 1978), 39.

39. Juha Näsi, Salme Näsi, Nelson Phillips, and Stelios Zyglidopoulos, "The Evolution of Corporate Responsiveness," *Business and Society* (Vol. 36, No. 3, September, 1997), 296–321.

40. Carroll, 1979, 502–504.

41. David Bollier and the Business Enterprise Trust, *Aiming Higher* (New York: AMA-COM, 1996), 280–293.

42. "America's Most Admired Companies," *Fortune* (March 2, 1998), 70.

43. Steven L. Wartick and Philip L. Cochran, "The Evolution of the Corporate Social Performance Model," *Academy of Management Review* (Vol. 10, 1985), 765–766.

44. Donna J. Wood, "Corporate Social Performance Revisited," *Academy of Management Review* (October, 1991), 691–718.

45. Karen Paul, Lori Zalka, Meredith Downes, Susan Perry, and Shawnta Perry, "U.S. Consumer Sensitivity to Corporate Social Performance," *Business and Society* (Vol. 36, No. 4, December 1997), 408–418.

46. Edward A. Robinson, "The Ups and Downs of the Industry Leaders," *Fortune* (March 2, 1998), 86–87.

47. Steven D. Lydenberg, Alice Tepper Marlin, Sean O'Brien Strub, and the Council on Economic Priorities, *Rating America's Corporate Conscience: A Provocative Guide to the Companies Behind the Products You Buy Every Day* (Reading, MA: Addison-Wesley, 1986). Also see updated volume: Benjamin Hollister, Rosalyn Will, and Alice Tepper Marlin, *Shopping for a Better World: The Quick and Easy Guide to ALL Your Socially Responsible Shopping* (CEP, 1994).

48. *Ibid.*, vii, 3.

49. *Ibid.*, 17.

50. Daniel Seligman, "The Case of the Ethical Ketchup," *Fortune* (February 16, 1987), 28; and Alan Murray, "New Book Rates Consumer Firms on Social Issues," *The Wall Street Journal* (January 16, 1987), 25.

51. Council on Economic Priorities, *Airline Corporate Responsibility: Grounded or Flying High?* (CEP, June, 1996).

52. *The Business Enterprise Awards for Courage, Integrity and Social Vision in Business: Request for Nominations*, 1990.

53. Walker Group, *Corporate Character: It's Driving Competitive Companies: Where's It Driving Yours?* 1994. See WalkerInformation's Web page: *www.walkerinfo.com/*.

54. See, for example, Mark Starik and Archie B. Carroll, "In Search of Beneficence: Reflections on the Connections Between Firm Social and Financial Performance," in Karen Paul (ed.), *Contemporary Issues in Business and Society in the United States and Abroad* (Lewiston, NY: The Edwin Mellen Press, 1991), 79–108; and I.M. Herremans, P. Akathaporn, and M. McInnes, "An Investigation of Corporate Social Responsibility, Reputation, and Economic Performance," *Accounting, Organizations, and Society* (Vol. 18, No. 7/8, 1993), 587–604.

55. Lee E. Preston and Douglas P. O'Bannon, "The Corporate Social-Financial Performance Relationship: A Typology and Analysis," *Business and Society* (Vol. 36, No. 4, December 1997), 419–429.

56. Chicago Tribune, "Social Concern Pays, Study Suggests," *The Atlanta Journal* (June 7, 1993), E4.

57. Preston and O'Bannon, 428.

58. See, for example, Lawrence A. Armour, "Who Says Virtue Is Its Own Reward?" *Fortune* (February 16, 1998), 186–189; Thomas D. Saler, "Money & Morals," *Mutual Funds* (August 1997), 55–60; and Keith H. Hammonds, "A Portfolio with a Heart Still Needs a Brain," *Business Week* (January 26, 1998), 100.

59. See Jack A. Brill and Alan Reder, *Investing from the Heart* (New York: Crown Publishers, 1992); and Patrick McVeigh, "The Best Socially Screened Mutual Funds for 1998," *Business Ethics* (January–February, 1998), 15–21.

60. William A. Sodeman, "Social Investing: The Role of Corporate Social Performance in Investment Decisions," Unpublished Ph.D. dissertation, University of Georgia, 1993. See also William A. Sodeman and Archie B. Carroll, "Social Investment Firms: Their Purposes, Principles, and Investment Criteria," in *International Association for Business and Society 1994 Proceedings,* edited by Steven Wartick and Denis Collins, 339–344.

61. "Good Works and Great Profits," *Business Week* (February 16, 1998), 8.

62. Samuel B. Graves and Sandra A. Waddock, "Institutional Owners and Corporate Social Performance," *Academy of Management Journal* (Vol. 37, No. 4, August, 1994), 1034–1046.

63. *Ibid.*

64. Council on Economic Priorities, *The Better World Investment Guide* (New York: Prentice Hall Press, 1991).

65. Jack A. Brill and Alan Reder, *Investing from the Heart* (New York: Crown Publishers, 1992).

66. Peter D. Kinder, Steven D. Lydenberg, and Amy L. Domini, *The Social Investment Almanac: A Comprehensive Guide to Socially Responsible Investing* (New York: Henry Holt & Co., 1992).

67. The Social Investment Forum's Web address is *http://www.socialinvest.org/*.

3

The Stakeholder Management Concept

CHAPTER OBJECTIVES

After studying this chapter, you should be able to:

1 Define *stake* and *stakeholder* and describe the origins of these concepts.

2 Differentiate among the production, managerial, and stakeholder views of the firm.

3 Differentiate among the three values of the stakeholder model.

4 Discuss the concept of stakeholder management.

5 Identify and discuss the five major questions that capture the essence of stakeholder management.

6 Identify and discuss the concept of stakeholder management capability (SMC).

At one time, life in business organizations was simpler. First, there were the investors who put up the money to get the business started. Of course, this was in the pre-corporate period, so there was only one person, or a few at most, financing the business. Next, the owners needed employees to do the productive work of the firm. Because the owners themselves were frequently the managers, another group—the employees—was needed to get the business going. Then the owners needed suppliers to make raw materials available for production and customers to purchase the products or services they were providing. All in all, it was a less complex period, with minimal expectations among the various parties.

It would take many books to describe how and why we got from that relatively simple period to the complex situation we face in today's society. Many of the factors we discussed in the first two chapters were driving forces behind this societal transformation. The principal factor, however, has been the recognition by the public, or society, that the business organization has evolved to the point where it is no longer the sole property of the founder, the founder's family, or even a group of owner-investors.

The business organization today, especially the modern corporation, is the institutional centerpiece of a complex society. Our society today consists of many people with a multitude of interests, expectations, and demands as to what major organizations ought to provide to accommodate people's lifestyles. We have seen business respond to the many expectations placed on it. We have seen an ever-changing social contract. We have seen many assorted legal, ethical, and philanthropic expectations and demands being met by organizations willing to change as long as the economic incentive was still there. What was once viewed as a specialized means of providing profit through the manufacture and distribution of goods and services has become a multipurpose social institution that many people and groups depend on for their livelihood and prosperity.

In a society conscious of an always-improving lifestyle, with more groups every day laying claims to their pieces of the good life, business organizations today need to be responsive to individuals and groups they once viewed as powerless and unable to make such claims on them. We call these individuals and groups *stakeholders*.

The growing importance of the stakeholder concept to business was highlighted by several important conferences on stakeholder theory and thinking in the 1990s. Max Clarkson of the University of Toronto convened two conferences in 1993 and 1994 on stakeholder theory.[1] In 1994, Juha Näsi convened a conference on stakeholder thinking in Finland.[2] These conferences were predicated on the basic notion that the stakeholder approach to management was an idea poised for further development, especially in the business/society arena. In the academic community, advances in stakeholder theory illustrate the crucial need for further work on the stakeholder concept.[3]

The stakeholder view was advanced even further in 1996 when Britain's then Labour Party Leader Tony Blair called for an economy characterized by stakeholder capitalism as opposed to traditional shareholder capitalism. All over the world, people began rediscussing an age-old question: Who do companies belong to and in whose interests should they be run? These discussions sharply contrasted the traditional American and British view, wherein a public company has the overriding goal of maximizing shareholder returns, with the view held by the Japanese and much of continental Europe, wherein firms accept broader obligations that seek to balance the interests of shareholders with those of other stakeholders, notably employees, suppliers, customers, and the wider "community."[4]

Within the context of stakeholder capitalism, David Wheeler and Maria Sillanpää have proposed a model for the "stakeholder corporation," which is discussed later in this chapter. For now it suffices to state that Wheeler and Sillanpää believe stakeholder inclusion to be the key to company success in the twenty-first century.[5]

An outgrowth of these discussions is that it is becoming apparent that business organizations must address the legitimate needs and expectations of stakeholders if they want to be successful in the long run. Business must also address stakeholders because it is the ethical course of action to pursue. Stakeholders have claims, rights, and expectations that should be honored, and the stakeholder approach encourages that pursuit. It is for these reasons that the stakeholder concept and orientation are useful in the arena of business, society, and ethics.

ORIGINS OF THE STAKEHOLDER CONCEPT

The stakeholder concept has become a central idea in understanding business/society relationships. The term grew out of the more familiar and traditional idea of *stockholders*—the investors in or owners of businesses. Just as a private individual might own his or her house, automobile, or video recorder, a stockholder owns a portion or a share of one or more businesses. Thus, a stockholder is also called a stakeholder.

What Is a Stake?

To appreciate the concept of stakeholders, it helps to understand the idea of a stake. A *stake* is an interest or a share in an undertaking. If a group is planning to go out to dinner and a show for the evening, each person in the group has a stake, or interest, in the group's decision. No money has yet been invested, but each member sees his or her interest (preference, taste, priority) in the decision. A stake is also a claim. A *claim* is an assertion to a title or a *right* to something. A claim is a demand for something due or believed to be due. We can see clearly that an owner or a stockholder has an interest in and an ownership of a share of a business.

The idea of a stake, therefore, can range from simply an interest in an undertaking at one extreme to a legal claim of ownership at the other extreme. In between these two extremes is a right to something. This right might be a *legal* right to certain treatment rather than a legal claim of ownership, such as that of a shareholder. Legal rights might include the right of due process (to get an impartial hearing) or the right to privacy (not to have one's privacy invaded or abridged). The right might be thought of as a *moral* right, such as that expressed by an employee: "I've got a right not to be fired because I've worked here 30 years, and I've given this firm the best years of my life." Or a consumer might say, "I've got a right to a safe product after all I've paid for this."

As we have seen, there are several different types of stakes. Figure 3–1 summarizes various categories or types of stakes.

What Is a Stakeholder?

A *stakeholder,* then, is an individual or a group that has one or more of the various kinds of stakes in a business. Just as stakeholders *may be affected* by the actions, decisions,

FIGURE 3–1 Types of Stakes		
An Interest	*A Right*	*Ownership*
When a person or group will be affected by a decision, it has an interest in that decision.	*Legal Right:* When a person or group has a legal claim to be treated in a certain way or to have a particular right protected.	When a person or group has a legal title to an asset or a property.
Examples: This plant closing will affect the community. This TV commercial demeans women, and I'm a woman.	*Examples:* Employees expect due process, privacy; customers or creditors have certain legal rights.	*Examples:* "This company is mine, I founded it, and I own it," or, "I own 1,000 shares of this corporation."
	Moral Right: When a person or group thinks it has a moral right to be treated in a certain way or to have a particular right protected.	
	Examples: Fairness, justice, equity.	

policies, or practices of the business firm, these stakeholders also *may affect* the organization's actions, decisions, policies, or practices. With stakeholders, therefore, there is a potential two-way interaction or exchange of influence. In short, a stakeholder may be thought of as "any individual or group who can affect or is affected by the actions, decisions, policies, practices, or goals of the organization."[6]

WHO ARE BUSINESS'S STAKEHOLDERS?

In today's business environment, there are many individuals and groups who are business's stakeholders. From the business point of view, there are certain individuals and groups that have legitimacy in the eyes of management. That is, they have a legitimate interest in, or claim on, the operations of the firm. The most obvious of these groups are stockholders, employees, and customers. From the point of view of a highly pluralistic society, stakeholders might include not only these groups, but other groups as well. These other groups might include competitors, suppliers, the community, special-interest groups, and society or the public at large. It has also been strongly argued that the natural environment should be considered as one of business's key stakeholders.[7]

Production, Managerial, and Stakeholder Views

The growth of the stakeholder concept parallels the evolution of the business enterprise. In what has been termed the traditional *production view of the firm*, owners thought of stakeholders as only those individuals or groups who supplied resources or bought products or services.[8] As time passed and we witnessed the growth of corporations and the resulting separation of ownership from control, business firms began to see the need for interaction with major constituent groups if they were to be managed successfully. Thus, we witnessed the evolution of the *managerial view of the firm*. Finally, as major internal and external changes occurred in business, managers were required to undergo a major conceptual shift in how they saw the firm and its multilateral relationships with constituent or stakeholder groups. The result was the *stakeholder view of the firm*.[9] In actual practice, however, many managers have not yet come to appreciate the need for the stakeholder view. Figure 3–2 depicts the evolution from the production view to the managerial view of the firm, and Figure 3–3 illustrates the stakeholder view.

In the stakeholder view of the firm, management must perceive its stakeholders as not only those groups that management thinks have some stake in the firm but also as those groups that themselves think they have a stake in the firm. This must be the perspective that management takes at the outset, at least until it has had a chance to weigh very carefully the legitimacy of the claims and the power of the various stakeholders. We should note here that each stakeholder group is composed of subgroups. For example, the government stakeholder group includes federal, state, and local government stakeholders.

Primary and Secondary Stakeholders

Wheeler and Sillanpää have presented a useful way to categorize stakeholders. Using such categories as primary and secondary and social and nonsocial, they propose defining stakeholders as follows:[10]

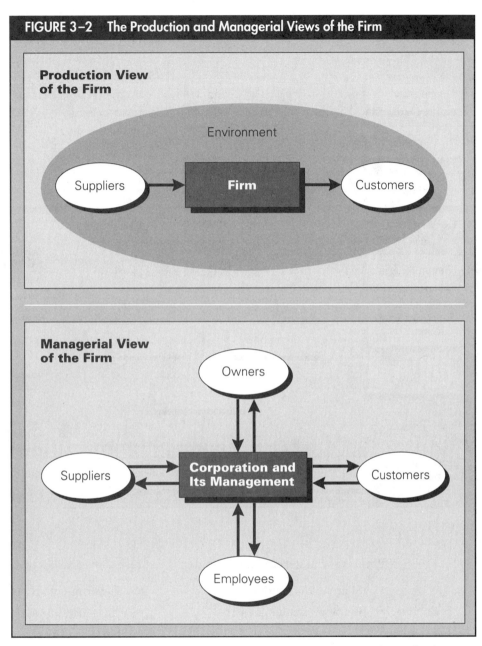

FIGURE 3–2   The Production and Managerial Views of the Firm

Production View of the Firm

Environment

Suppliers → **Firm** → Customers

Managerial View of the Firm

Owners

Suppliers ↔ **Corporation and Its Management** ↔ Customers

Employees

SOURCE: Freeman's *Strategic Management: A Stakeholder Approach*. Copyright © 1984 by R. Edward Freeman. Reprinted with permission from Pitman Publishing Company.

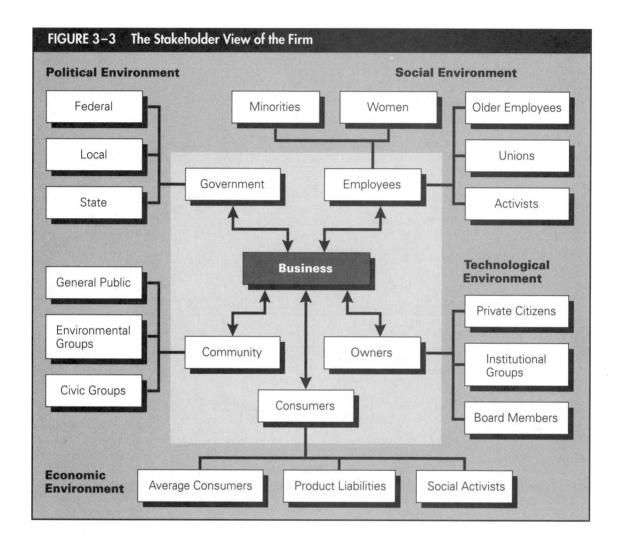

FIGURE 3–3   The Stakeholder View of the Firm

Primary social stakeholders include:

- Shareholders and investors
- Employees and managers
- Customers
- Local communities
- Suppliers and other business partners

Secondary social stakeholders include:

- Government and regulators.
- Civic institutions
- Social pressure groups
- Media and academic commentators
- Trade bodies
- Competitors

Primary social stakeholders have a direct stake in the organization and its success and therefore are influential. Secondary social stakeholders may be extremely influential as well, especially in affecting reputation and public standing, but their stake in the organization is more representational than direct. Therefore, the level of moral accountability to a secondary stakeholder tends to be lower.

Primary nonsocial stakeholders include:

- The natural environment
- Future generations
- Nonhuman species

Secondary nonsocial stakeholders include:

- Environmental pressure groups
- Animal welfare organizations[11]

It should be kept in mind that secondary stakeholders can quickly become primary ones. This often occurs with the media or special-interest groups when the urgency of a claim (as in a boycott or demonstration) takes precedence over the legitimacy of that claim. In today's business environment, the media have the power to instantaneously transform a stakeholder's status with coverage on the evening news. Thus, it may be useful to think of primary and secondary classes of stakeholders for discussion purposes, but we should understand how easily and quickly those categories can shift.

SEARCH THE WEB

Considerable information on stakeholder theory and stakeholder management may be found in the programs and work of the Clarkson Centre for Business Ethics, Faculty of Management, University of Toronto. The Clarkson Centre has sponsored a number of special conferences on stakeholder theory and facilitates the project known as "Redefining the Corporation: An International Colloquy," which is funded by the Alfred P. Sloan Foundation. One project theme is the stakeholder perspective, as the following excerpt suggests: "Principal emphasis will be placed on stakeholder theory, including both supportive and critical perspectives and emphasizing both its conflicts and compatibility with other theories."

Professor Max Clarkson, the Centre's major project leader, died in 1998, but the Centre's work on stakeholder theory continues. For more information, visit the Centre's Web site at **www.mgmt.utoronto.ca/~stake/**. On this Web site, you may find project descriptions, ongoing research grants, other Web sites of interest, and a comprehensive bibliography on stakeholder theory.

Core, Strategic, and Environmental Stakeholders

There are other ways to categorize stakeholders. At the 1994 Second Toronto Conference on Stakeholder Theory, for example, a working group came up with an alternative scheme for classifying stakeholders. In this scheme, stakeholders were thought of as being core, strategic, or environmental. *Core stakeholders* are a specific subset of strategic stakeholders that are essential for the survival of the organization. *Strategic stakeholders* are those stakeholder groups that are vital to the organization and the particular set of threats and opportunities it faces at a particular point in time. *Environmental stakeholders* are all others in the organization's environment that are not core or strategic. One could conceptualize the relationship among these three groups of stakeholders by thinking of a series of concentric circles with core stakeholders in the middle and with strategic and environmental stakeholders moving out from the middle.[12]

The working group went on to assert that whether stakeholders were core, strategic, or environmental would depend on their characteristics or attributes, such as legitimacy, power, or urgency. Thus, stakeholders could move from category to category in a dynamic, fluid, and time-dependent fashion. It was thought that this set of terms for describing stakeholders would be useful because it captured, to some degree, the contingencies and dynamics that must be considered in an actual situation.

A Typology of Stakeholders

Expanding on the idea that stakeholders have such attributes as legitimacy, power, and urgency, Mitchell, Agle, and Wood generated a typology of stakeholders based on these three attributes.[13] When these three attributes are superimposed, as depicted in Figure 3–4, seven stakeholder categories result.

A brief look at the three attributes of legitimacy, power, and urgency helps us to see how stakeholders may be thought of in these terms. *Legitimacy* refers to the perceived validity or appropriateness of a stakeholder's claim to a stake. Therefore, owners, employees, and customers represent a high degree of legitimacy due to their explicit, formal relationships with a company. Stakeholders who are more distant from the firm, such as social activist groups, competitors, or the media, might be thought to have less legitimacy. *Power* refers to the ability or capacity to produce an effect. Therefore, whether one has legitimacy or not, power means that the stakeholder could affect the business. For example, with the help of the media, a large, vocal, social activist group could wield extraordinary power over a business firm. *Urgency* refers to the degree to which the stakeholder claim on the business calls for the business's immediate attention or response. A management group may perceive a union strike, a consumer boycott, or a social activist group picketing outside headquarters as urgent.

Mitchell, Agle, and Wood take the position that managers must attend to stakeholders based on their assessment of the extent to which competing stakeholder claims are characterized by legitimacy, power, and urgency. Using the categories in Figure 3–4, therefore, the stakeholder groups represented by overlapping circles (for example, those with two or three attributes, such as Categories 4, 5, 6, and 7) are highly "salient" to management and would likely receive priority attention.

STRATEGIC, MULTIFIDUCIARY, AND SYNTHESIS VIEWS

One challenge embedded in the stakeholder approach is to determine whether it should be perceived primarily as a way to *manage* better those groups known as stakeholders or as a way to treat more *ethically* those groups known as stakeholders. Kenneth Goodpaster has addressed this issue by distinguishing among the strategic approach, the multifiduciary approach, and the stakeholder synthesis approach.[14] Goodpaster uses the term "strategic" in a sense slightly different from that in which it was used in the previous discussion.

The *strategic approach* views stakeholders primarily as factors to be taken into consideration and managed while the firm is pursuing profits for its shareholders. In this view, managers might take stakeholders into account because offended stakeholders might resist or retaliate (for example, through political action, protest, or boycott). This approach sees stakeholders as instruments that may facilitate or impede the firm's pursuit of its strategic objectives.

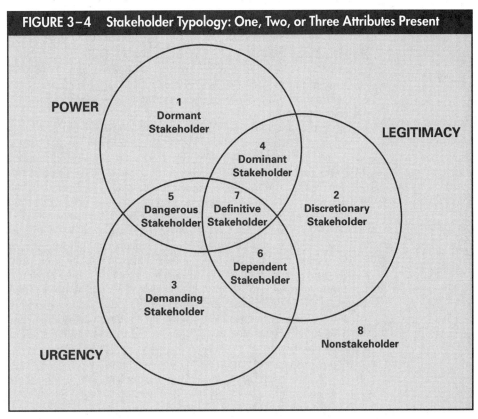

FIGURE 3–4   Stakeholder Typology: One, Two, or Three Attributes Present

Reprinted with permission of Academy of Management, PO Box 3020, Briar Cliff Manor, NY 10510–8020. *Stakeholder Typology: One, Two, or Three Attributes Present* (Figure), R. K. Mitchell, B. R. Agle & D. J. Wood, *Academy of Management Review,* October 1997. Reproduced by permission of the publisher via Copyright Clearance Center, Inc.

The *multifiduciary approach* views stakeholders as more than just individuals or groups who can wield economic or legal power. This view holds that management has a fiduciary responsibility to stakeholders just as it has this responsibility to shareholders. Here, management's traditional fiduciary, or trust, duty is expanded to embrace stakeholders on roughly equal footing with shareholders. Thus, shareholders are no longer of exclusive importance as they would be under the strategic approach.

Goodpaster recommends that business organizations take neither of these extreme postures but rather pursue a new *stakeholder synthesis.* This new view holds that business does have moral responsibilities to stakeholders but they they should not be seen as part of a fiduciary obligation. Thus, management's basic fiduciary responsibility to shareholders is kept intact, but it is also expected to be implemented within a context of ethical responsibility. This ethical responsibility is its duty not to harm, coerce, lie, cheat, steal, and so on.[15]

As we continue our discussion of stakeholder management, it should be clear that we are pursuing it from a balanced perspective. This balanced perspective suggests that we are integrating the strategic view with the multifiduciary view such that they are compatible. We should be managing strategically and morally at the same

---

ETHICS IN PRACTICE

Health Care Ethics

I am the president and business manager of MedClaim, Inc. We do billing and accounting for medical doctors. In 1992, we were approached by a group of doctors. They owned seven mobile diagnostic testing centers in five different states and were interested in using our service.

We started with this group and immediately began receiving dozens and sometimes hundreds of tests per month to bill to health, automobile, and worker's compensation insurance. The nerve testing they were performing was a common medical test, but they were charging almost twice the normal rate, usually $2,600 per test. While this rate surprised us, there is no law against doctors charging whatever they want for services, so we processed the claims normally.

As the number of tests we were processing for them increased, we began to notice strange circumstances surrounding their cases. Often, we would be unable to reach their patients at home to get additional information, because the phone numbers were completely wrong. When we could reach patients, they were very surprised and angry at the cost of the test and refused to cooperate. The referring physicians were sometimes unable to provide us data on cases, as if the patients had never existed, and they were always very evasive in dealing with us. Also, insurance companies began to watch these cases very carefully, at times rejecting fully half of the claims on grounds that either the patient's condition did not support this expensive test or the license of the doctor prescribing it was invalid.

After about a year of working with them, we discovered from some of their referring physicians that these clients of ours were paying $600 per patient to doctors for referrals. They had this kickback structured as an office rental fee to stay legal, but they were clearly violating the spirit of the law.

This doctors' group had grown to be our largest client, generating over $10,000 per month in revenue and submitting over $200,000 per month in bills. However, I decided to terminate our service to them immediately after discovering the true nature of their business. Even though we needed the revenue and referrals from this large client, I decided that I was not interested in building our business on corrupt health care providers.

1. Who are the stakeholders in this case, and what are their stakes?

2. Are there any ethical issues embedded in this situation? What are they?

3. Should MedClaim, Inc., scrutinize the claims as described or simply "do the paperwork" and mind its own business? What would you do?

Contributed by Todd D. Stewart

---

time. The stakeholder approach should not be just a better way to manage, it should be an ethical way to manage.

THREE VALUES OF THE STAKEHOLDER MODEL

In a vein related to Goodpaster's strategic, multifiduciary, and stakeholder synthesis views, Donaldson and Preston articulate three aspects or values of the stakeholder model of the firm. These three aspects, although interrelated, are distinct. They differentiate among the descriptive, instrumental, and normative aspects of stakeholder theory or the stakeholder model.[16]

First, the stakeholder model is *descriptive*. That is, it describes the corporation or organization. The corporation is a constellation of cooperative and competitive interests possessing intrinsic value. Understanding organizations in this way allows us to have a fuller description or explanation of how they function. Second, the stakeholder model is *instrumental*. It is useful in establishing the connections between the practice of stakeholder management and the resulting achievement of corporate performance goals. The fundamental premise here is that practicing effective stakeholder management should lead to the achievement of traditional goals, such as profitability, stability, and growth. Third, the stakeholder model is *normative*. In the normative perspective, stakeholders are identified by their interest in the organization whether or not the organization has any corresponding interest in them. Thus, the interests of all stakeholders are of *intrinsic* value. Stakeholders are seen as possessing value irrespective of their instrumental use to management.

In summary, Donaldson and Preston assert that stakeholder theory is *managerial* in the broad sense of the term. It is managerial in the sense that it does not simply describe or predict but also recommends attitudes, structures, and practices that constitute stakeholder management. Such management necessitates the simultaneous attention to the legitimate interests of all appropriate stakeholders in the creation of organizational structures and policies.[17]

STAKEHOLDER MANAGEMENT

The managers of a business firm have the responsibilities of establishing the firm's overall direction (its goals, policies, and strategies) and seeing to it that these plans are carried out. As a consequence, managers have some long-term responsibilities and many that are of more immediate concern. Before the social environment became as turbulent and rapidly changing as it now is, the managerial task was relatively straightforward and the external environment was stable. As we have evolved to the stakeholder view of the firm, however, we see the managerial task as an inevitable consequence of the trends and developments we described in our first two chapters.

Stakeholder management has become important as managers have discovered the many groups that have to be relatively satisfied for the firm to meet its objectives. Without question, we still recognize the primacy and necessity of profits as a return on the stockholders' investments, but we also see the growing claims of other stakeholder groups and the success they have had in getting what they want.

The challenge of stakeholder management, therefore, is to see to it that the firm's primary stakeholders achieve their objectives and that other stakeholders are dealt with ethically and are also satisfied. This is the classic "win-win" situation. It does not always occur, but it is a legitimate goal for management to pursue to protect its long-term self-interests. Management's second-best alternative is to meet the goals of its primary stakeholders, keeping in mind the important role of its owner-investors. Without economic viability, all other stakeholders' interests are lost.

With these perspectives in mind, let us approach stakeholder management with the idea that managers can become successful stewards of their stakeholders' resources by gaining knowledge about stakeholders and using this knowledge to predict and deal with their behavior and actions. Ultimately, we should manage the situation in such a way that we achieve our objectives ethically and effectively. Thus, the important functions of stakeholder management are to describe, to understand, to analyze, and, finally, to manage.

Five major questions must be asked if we are to capture the essential information we need for stakeholder management:

1. Who are our stakeholders?

2. What are our stakeholders' stakes?

3. What opportunities and challenges do our stakeholders present to our firm?

4. What responsibilities (economic, legal, ethical, and philanthropic) does our firm have to its stakeholders?

5. What strategies or actions should our firm take to best manage stakeholder challenges and opportunities?[18]

Who Are Our Stakeholders?

To this point, we have described the likely primary and secondary stakeholder groups of a business organization. To manage them effectively, each firm must ask and answer this question for itself: Who are our stakeholders? To answer this question fully, management must identify not only generic stakeholder groups but also the specific groups. A *generic stakeholder group* is simply a broad grouping, such as employees, shareholders, environmental groups, or consumers. Within each of these generic categories there may be a few or many specific groups. Figure 3–5 illustrates some of the generic and specific stakeholder groups of a very large organization.

To illustrate the process of stakeholder identification, we will look at two classic cases of companies that experienced stakeholder issues. The first case is that of Nestlé, S.A., and its marketing of infant formula in less-developed countries. The second case is that of Hooker Chemical Co. and its experience at Love Canal.

Stakeholder Identification: The Case of Nestlé

Nestlé, S. A., is the Swiss conglomerate that at one time dominated the marketing of infant formula in the Third World, or less-developed countries (LDCs). Other companies also marketed infant formula in LDCs, but Nestlé was the major company.

Beginning in about 1970, Nestlé became involved in a controversy over the morality of selling any infant formula in the Third World and of using specific promotional and marketing techniques considered immoral by some. The basic allegation against Nestlé and the others was that in these Third World countries, infant formula was likely to be misused and therefore might lead to malnutrition, diarrhea, and death. Also, it was claimed that Nestlé's aggressive marketing tactics encouraged women to choose bottle feeding, thus resulting in a decline in breast feeding, which is safer and more healthful, particularly in the Third World. Poor sanitation, impure water, inadequacy of water supplies, and inability to read, comprehend, and follow directions resulted in disease and malnutrition. Mothers who were poor (and most are in these countries) tried to save money and thus overdiluted the infant formula to make it go further.

FIGURE 3–5 Some Generic and Specific Stakeholders of a Large Firm			
Owners	*Employees*	*Governments*	*Customers*
Trusts	Young employees	Federal	Business
Foundations	Middle-aged	• EPA	purchasers
Mutual funds	employees	• FTC	Government
Board members	Older employees	• OSHA	purchasers
Management	Women	• CPSC	Educational
owners	Minority groups	State	institutions
Employee pension	Handicapped	Local	Special-interest
funds	Special-interest		groups
Individual owners	groups		
	Unions		
		Social Activist	
Community	*Competitors*	*Groups*	
General fund-	Firm A	People United to	
raising	Firm B	Save Humanity	
United Way	Firm C	(PUSH)	
YMCA/YWCA		Friends of the	
Middle schools		Earth	
Elementary		Mothers Against	
schools		Drunk Driving	
Residents who		(MADD)	
live close by		American Civil	
All other residents		Liberties Union	
Neighborhood		Consumers Union	
associations			
Local media			
Chamber of Commerce			

The complete controversy over the marketing of infant formula in the Third World requires a longer discussion, and we will consider it in more depth in Chapter 6. Suffice it to say, however, that Nestlé fought its critics for years, and its array of stakeholder groups became numerous. Picture, if you can, what the stakeholder map of Nestlé might have looked like before the infant formula controversy arose. Most likely it was similar to the relatively simple managerial view of the firm shown in Figure 3–2. When Third World governments, social activist groups, and United Nations agencies got involved, the stakeholder map grew considerably. Figure 3–6 illustrates what Nestlé's stakeholder map might have looked like after all these various groups got involved.

Do you think Nestlé had any idea that its persistence in wanting to sell infant formula would have resulted in such a complex situation? Perhaps if Nestlé had taken a stakeholder view before it got embroiled in this controversy, it would have saved itself years of grief and lost reputation.

Stakeholder Identification: The Case of Hooker Chemical Company
The second example worth considering is the case of Hooker Chemical Company and Love Canal.[19] Love Canal was really just a partially dug canal in the southeast corner of the city of Niagara Falls, New York, in the late 1800s. Originally the canal was to be used for generating and transmitting hydroelectric power from the falls to the businesses in the city, but the project was abandoned.

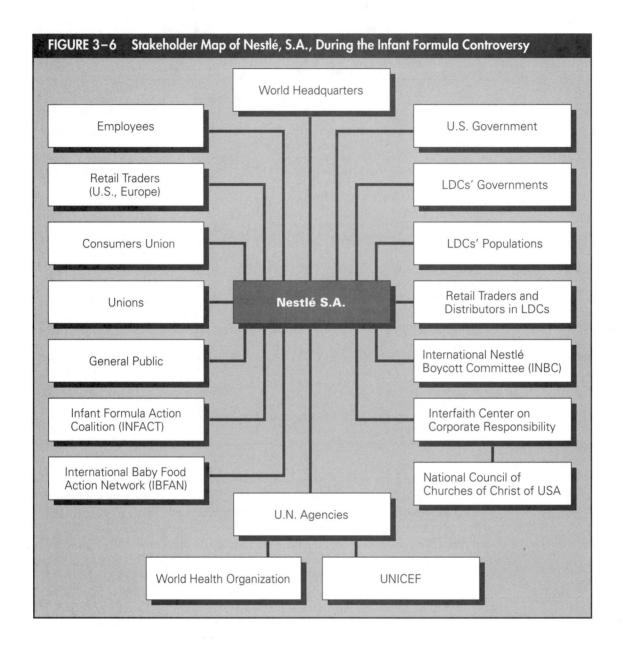

FIGURE 3–6   Stakeholder Map of Nestlé, S.A., During the Infant Formula Controversy

Hooker Chemical Company, later a subsidiary of Occidental Petroleum Company, built its first plant in the area in 1905. In the 1940s, the abandoned section of Love Canal became a toxic waste dump for several chemical companies. In 1942, Hooker received permission to use the site for chemical dumping. In 1947, Hooker purchased the Love Canal site from Niagara Power and Development Company. In 1953, the canal, filled with years of toxic waste accumulation, was closed and sealed with an impermeable clay top. Figure 3–7 shows what Hooker Chemical's stakeholder map

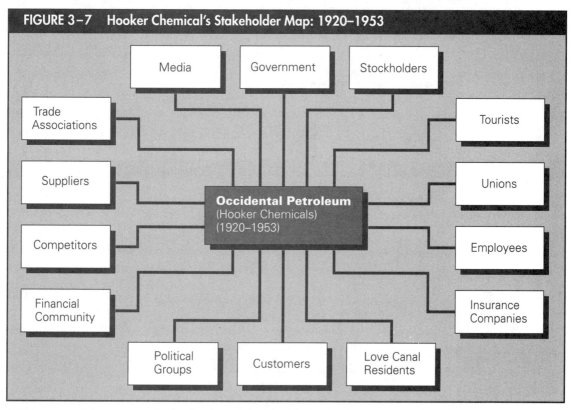

FIGURE 3–7   Hooker Chemical's Stakeholder Map: 1920–1953

SOURCE: Steven Michalove, "Love Canal and Hooker Chemical: The Stakeholder Dilemma" (unpublished paper, March 6, 1985). Used with permission.

might have looked like in the period from 1920 to 1953—the time spanning the active operation of the dump.

Subsequently, the land encompassing and surrounding Love Canal was purchased by the Niagara Falls School Board, even though Hooker Chemical advised against it. The board built a school adjacent to the dump site and sold some of the property to developers, who then built a tract of homes. During the construction of the homes, thousands of cubic yards of soil were removed from the surface of the sealed canal. Figure 3–8 represents what Hooker's stakeholder map might have looked like during the period 1953 to 1971, which corresponds to the active settlement of the Love Canal area. Note that the first and second stakeholder maps indicate only slight changes of stakeholder interests in the Love Canal situation.

Apparently, the construction work damaged the seal on the Love Canal dump. This, combined with water from heavy rains and snow, resulted in seepage of water into the clay-lined basin, which eventually overflowed, causing seepage of toxic waste into the homes and basements of nearby residents. By 1978, evidence of toxic chemicals was found in the living areas of many homes. After lengthy investigations, a variety of health problems, such as liver damage, miscarriages, birth defects, and other

FIGURE 3-8   Hooker Chemical's Stakeholder Map: 1953–1971

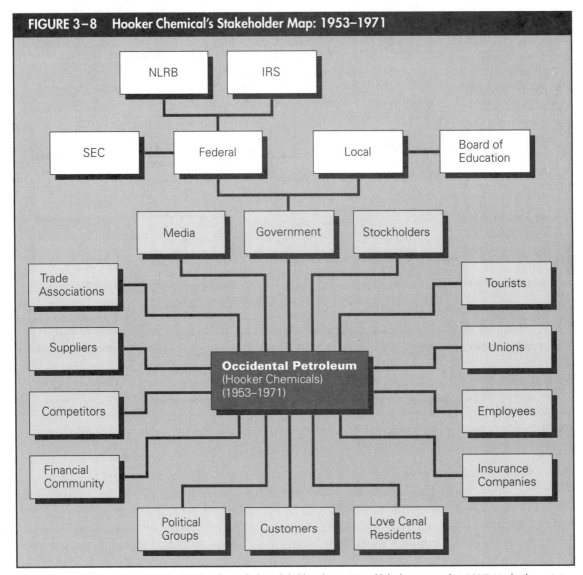

SOURCE: Steven Michalove, "Love Canal and Hooker Chemical: The Stakeholder Dilemma" (unpublished paper, March 6, 1985). Used with permission.

ills, began showing up. The following description of the area in 1979 illustrates why the Love Canal incident became a national crisis and disgrace.

Today the Love Canal area of Niagara Falls looks like a war zone. The 235 houses nearest the landfill are boarded up and empty, surrounded by an 8-foot-high cyclone fence that keeps tourists and looters away. Still other houses outside the fenced area are also boarded up and deserted, their owners having fled the unknown. Here and there throughout the neighborhood, newly erected green signs mark the pickup points for emergency evacuation in case there is a sudden release of toxins. An ambulance and a fire truck stand by in the area as workers struggle to seal off the flow of chemicals and render the area once again safe—if not exactly habitable.[20]

It is little wonder that the Love Canal incident now stands in the annals of environmental history as the crisis that awoke the United States to the problems of toxic waste disposal and was the impetus behind the national Superfund clean-up legislation.

Without question, Hooker Chemical was not exclusively responsible for what happened at Love Canal. Others, such as the school board, the developers, and the health department, must shoulder part of the blame. As is so often the case, however, the business firm bore the brunt of the responsibility, especially in the media. Figure 3–9 illustrates what the stakeholder map of Hooker Chemical might have become during the period 1971 to 1982, during which the Love Canal issue became a national problem.

The purpose of this discussion has been to illustrate the evolving nature of the question, "Who are our stakeholders?" In actuality, stakeholder identification is an unfolding process over time. However, by recognizing early the potential of failure if one does not think in stakeholder terms, the value and usefulness of stakeholder thinking can be readily seen.

Many businesses do not carefully identify their generic stakeholder groups, much less their specific stakeholder groups. This must be done, however, if management is to be in a position to answer the second major question, "What are our stakeholders' stakes?"

What Are Our Stakeholders' Stakes?

Once stakeholders have been identified, the next step is to determine the stakes of the various groups. Even groups in the same generic category frequently have different specific interests, concerns, perceptions of rights, and expectations. Management's challenge here is to identify the *nature/legitimacy* of a group's stake(s) and the group's *power* to affect the organization. As we discussed earlier, *urgency* is another critical factor.

Identifying the Nature/Legitimacy of a Group's Stakes

Let's consider an example of stakeholders who possess varying stakes. Assume that we are considering corporate owners as a generic group of stakeholders and that the corporation is large, with several million shares of stock outstanding. Among the ownership population are these more specific groups:

1. Institutional owners (trusts, foundations, churches, universities)

2. Large mutual fund organizations

3. Board of director members who own shares

4. Members of management who own shares

5. Thousands of small, individual shareholders

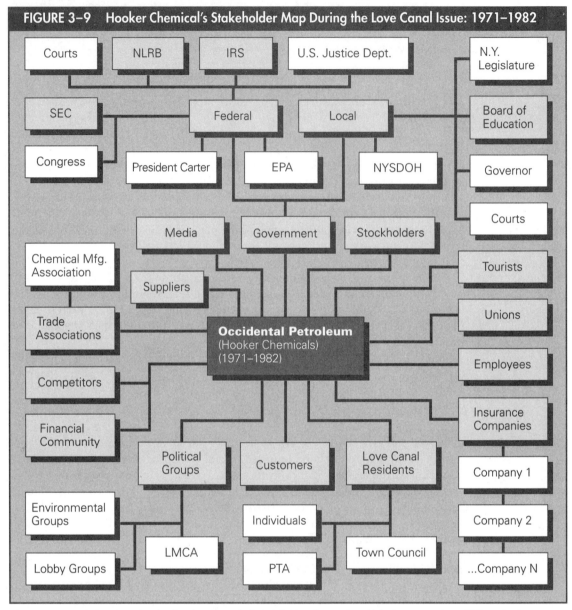

FIGURE 3-9   Hooker Chemical's Stakeholder Map During the Love Canal Issue: 1971-1982

SOURCE: Steven Michalove, "Love Canal and Hooker Chemical: The Stakeholder Dilemma" (unpublished paper, March 6, 1985). Used with permission.

For all these groups, the nature of stakeholder claims on this corporation is owner-ship. All these groups have legitimate claims—They are all owners.

Identifying the Power of a Group's Stakes

When we examine power, we see significant differences. Which of the groups in the list above are the most powerful? Certainly not the thousands of small, individual investors, unless they have found a way to organize and thus wield considerable power. The powerful stakeholders in this case are (1) the institutional owners and mutual fund organizations, because of the sheer magnitude of their investments, and (2) the board and management shareholders, because of their dual roles of ownership and management (control).

However, if the individual shareholders could somehow form a coalition based on some interest they have in common, they could exert significant influence on management decisions. This is the day and age of dissident shareholder groups filing stockholder suits and proposing shareholder resolutions. These shareholder resolutions address issues ranging from complaints of excessive executive compensation to demands that firms improve their environmental protection policies or cease making illegal campaign contributions.

Identifying Specific Groups within a Generic Group

Let us now look at a manufacturing firm in an old-line industry in Pennsylvania that is faced with a generic group of environmental stakeholders. Within the generic group of environmental stakeholders might be the following specific groups:

1. Residents who live within a 10-mile radius of the plant
2. Other residents in the city
3. Residents who live in the path of the jet stream hundreds of miles away (some in Canada) who are getting acid rain
4. Environmental Protection Agency (federal)
5. Pennsylvania Environmental Protection Division (state)
6. Friends of the Earth (social activist group)
7. The Wilderness Society (social activist group)
8. Pennsylvanians Against Smokestack Emissions (PASE)

It would require some degree of care to identify the nature, legitimacy, power, and urgency of each of these specific groups. However, it could and should be done if the firm wants to get a handle on its environmental stakeholders. Furthermore, we should stress that companies have an ethical responsibility to be sensitive to legitimate stakeholder claims even if the stakeholders have no power or leverage with management.

What Opportunities and Challenges Do Our Stakeholders Present to Our Firm?

In many respects, opportunities and challenges represent opposite sides of the coin when it comes to stakeholders. Essentially, the opportunities are to build good, productive working relationships with the stakeholders. Challenges, on the other hand, usually present themselves in such a way that the firm must handle the stakeholders well or be hurt in some way—financially (short term or long term) or in terms of its public image or reputation in the community. Therefore, it is understandable why our emphasis is on challenges rather than on opportunities posed by stakeholders.

These challenges typically take the form of varying degrees of expectations or demands. In most instances, they arise because stakeholders think or feel that their needs are not being met adequately. The challenges also arise when stakeholder groups think that any crisis that occurs is the responsibility of the firm or that the firm caused the crisis in some way. In addition to the Nestlé and Hooker Chemical crises described earlier, examples of other stakeholder crises from the 1990s include:[21]

- *Texaco.* Taped evidence of executive-level race discrimination set off national protests against the company in 1996. A lawsuit settlement for $176 million was one result.

- *W. R. Grace.* Allegations of sexual harassment cost the CEO his job. Directors of the firm organized and ousted the CEO in 1995 because of evidence of sexual misconduct.

- *Banker's Trust.* Evidence in 1995 that the bank deliberately misled and deceived its customers resulted in an enormous lawsuit and a significantly damaged reputation. *Business Week* revealed this in an explosive cover story.

If one looks at the business experiences of the past couple of decades, including the crises mentioned above, it is evident that there is a need to think in stakeholder terms to fully understand the potential threats that businesses of all kinds face on a daily basis.

Opportunities and challenges might also be viewed in terms of potential for cooperation and potential for threat. Savage et al. have argued that such assessments of cooperation and threat are necessary so that managers might identify strategies for dealing with stakeholders.[22] In terms of potential for threat, Savage et al. assert that managers need to consider the stakeholder's relative power and its relevance to a particular issue confronting the organization. In terms of potential for cooperation, the firm needs to be sensitive to the possibility of joining forces with other stakeholders for the advantage of all parties involved.

Savage et al. cite how Ross Laboratories, a division of Abbott Laboratories, was able to develop a cooperative relationship with some critics of its sales of infant formula in Third World countries. Ross and Abbott convinced these stakeholder groups (UNICEF and the World Health Organization) to join them in a program to promote infant health. Other firms, such as Nestlé, did not develop the potential to cooperate and suffered from consumer boycotts.[23]

Figure 3–10 presents a list of the factors that Savage et al. claim will increase or decrease a stakeholder's potential for threat or cooperation. By carefully analyzing these factors, managers should be able to better assess such potentials.

What Responsibilities Does Our Firm Have to Its Stakeholders?

Once threats and opportunities of stakeholders have been identified and understood, the next logical question is, "What responsibilities does our firm have in its relationships with all stakeholders?" Responsibilities here could be thought of in terms of the concepts presented in Chapter 2. What economic, legal, ethical, and philanthropic responsibilities does management have to each stakeholder? Because most of the firm's economic responsibilities are principally to itself, the analysis really begins to focus on legal, ethical, and philanthropic questions. The most pressing threats present themselves as legal and ethical questions.

We should stress, however, that the firm itself has an economic stake in the legal and ethical issues it faces. For example, when J&J was faced with the Tylenol poisoning incident, it had to decide what legal and ethical actions to take and what actions were

FIGURE 3–10 Factors Affecting Potential for Stakeholder Threat and Cooperation		
	Increases or Decreases Stakeholder's Potential for Threat?	Increases or Decreases Stakeholder's Potential for Cooperation?
Stakeholder controls key resources (needed by organization)	Increases	Increases
Stakeholder does not control key resources	Decreases	Either
Stakeholder more powerful than organization	Increases	Either
Stakeholder as powerful as organization	Either	Either
Stakeholder less powerful than organization	Decreases	Increases
Stakeholder likely to take action (supportive of the organization)	Decreases	Increases
Stakeholder likely to take nonsupportive action	Increases	Decreases
Stakeholder unlikely to take any action	Decreases	Decreases
Stakeholder likely to form coalition with other stakeholders	Increases	Either
Stakeholder likely to form coalition with organization	Decreases	Increases
Stakeholder unlikely to form any coalition	Decreases	Decreases

SOURCE: Grant T. Savage, Timothy W. Nix, Carlton J. Whitehead, and John D. Blair, "Strategies for Assessing and Managing Organizational Stakeholders," *Academy of Management Executive* (Vol. V, No. 2, May, 1991), 64. Reprinted with permission.

in the firm's best economic interests. J&J probably judged that recalling the Tylenol products was not only the ethical action to take but also would ensure its reputation for being concerned about consumers' health and well-being. Figure 3–11 illustrates the stakeholder/responsibility matrix that management faces when assessing the firm's responsibilities to stakeholders.

What Strategies or Actions Should Management Take?

Once responsibilities have been assessed, a business must contemplate strategies and actions for dealing with its stakeholders. In every decision situation, a multitude of alternative courses of action are available, and management must choose one or several that seem best. MacMillan and Jones state that management has before it a number of basic strategies or approaches in dealing with stakeholders. Important questions or decision choices include:

- Do we deal *directly* or *indirectly* with stakeholders?

- Do we take the *offense* or the *defense* in dealing with stakeholders?

- Do we *accommodate, negotiate, manipulate,* or *resist* stakeholder overtures?

- Do we employ a *combination* of the above strategies or pursue a *singular* course of action?[24]

FIGURE 3-11   Stakeholder/Responsibility Matrix

Stakeholders	Types of Responsibilities			
	Economic	Legal	Ethical	Philanthropic
Owners				
Customers				
Employees				
Community				
Public at Large				
Social Activist Groups				
Others				

Savage et al. argue that development of specific strategies may be based on a classification of stakeholders according to the concepts of the potentials for cooperation and threat. If we use these two dimensions, four stakeholder types and resultant strategies emerge.[25] These stakeholder types and corresponding strategies are shown in Figure 3–12.

Stakeholder Type 1—the supportive stakeholder—is high on potential for cooperation and low on potential for threat. This is the ideal stakeholder. To a well-managed organization, supportive stakeholders might include its board, managers, employees, and customers. Others might be suppliers and service providers. The strategy here is one of involvement. An example of this might be the strategy of involving employee stakeholders through participative management or decentralization of authority.

Stakeholder Type 2—the marginal stakeholder—is low on both potential for threat and potential for cooperation. For large organizations, these stakeholders might include professional associations of employees, consumer interest groups, or stockholders—especially those who are not organized. The strategy here is for the organization to monitor the marginal stakeholder. Monitoring is especially called for to make sure circumstances do not change. Careful monitoring could avert later problems.

Stakeholder Type 3—the nonsupportive stakeholder—is high on potential for threat but low on potential for cooperation. Examples of this group could include competing organizations, unions, federal or other levels of government, and the media. The authors' recommended strategy here is to defend against the nonsupportive stakeholder.

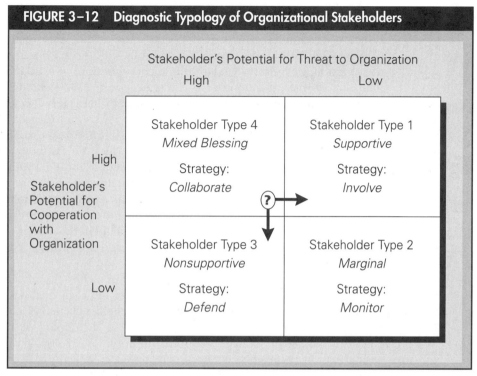

FIGURE 3–12   Diagnostic Typology of Organizational Stakeholders

Stakeholder's Potential for Threat to Organization

High — Low

Stakeholder's Potential for Cooperation with Organization

High

| Stakeholder Type 4
Mixed Blessing

Strategy:
Collaborate | Stakeholder Type 1
Supportive

Strategy:
Involve |

Low

| Stakeholder Type 3
Nonsupportive

Strategy:
Defend | Stakeholder Type 2
Marginal

Strategy:
Monitor |

SOURCE: Grant T. Savage, Timothy W. Nix, Carlton J. Whitehead, and John D. Blair, "Strategies for Assessing and Managing Organizational Stakeholders," *Academy of Management Executive* (Vol. V, No. 2, May, 1991), 65. Reprinted with permission.

Stakeholder Type 4—the mixed blessing stakeholder—is high on both potential for threat and potential for cooperation. Examples of this group, in a well-managed organization, might include employees who are in short supply, clients, or customers. A mixed blessing stakeholder could become a supportive or a nonsupportive stakeholder. The recommended strategy here is to collaborate with the mixed blessing stakeholder. By maximizing collaboration, the likelihood is enhanced that this stakeholder will remain supportive.

The authors summarize their position regarding these four stakeholder types as follows:

> *. . . managers should attempt to satisfy minimally the needs of marginal stakeholders and to satisfy maximally the needs of supportive and mixed blessing stakeholders, enhancing the latter's support for the organization.*[26]

The four stakeholder types and recommended strategies are what was referred to earlier in this chapter as the "strategic" view of stakeholders. By taking stakeholders' needs and concerns into consideration, we are improving our ethics. We must go beyond just considering them, however. Management still has an ethical responsibility to stakeholders that extends beyond the strategic view. We will develop a fuller appreciation of what this responsibility is in Chapters 4, 5, and 6.

EFFECTIVE STAKEHOLDER MANAGEMENT

Effective stakeholder management requires the careful assessment of the five core questions we have posed. To deal successfully with those who assert claims on the organization, we must understand these core questions at least at a basic level. It is tempting to wish that none of this was necessary. However, such wishing would require management to accept the production or managerial view of the firm, and these views are no longer tenable. Business today cannot turn back the clock to a simpler period. Business has been and will continue to be subjected to careful scrutiny of its actions, practices, policies, and ethics. This is the real world in which management lives, and management must accept it and deal with it. Criticisms of business and cries for corporate social responsibility have been the consequences of the changes in the business/society relationship, and the stakeholder management approach to viewing the organization has become one needed response. To do less is to refuse to accept the realities of business's plight in the modern world and to fail to see the kinds of adaptations that are essential if businesses are to prosper in the present and in the future.

In fairness, we should also note that there are criticisms and limitations of the stakeholder management approach. One major criticism relates to the complexity of identifying, assessing, and responding to stakeholder claims, which constitute an extremely difficult and time-consuming process. Also, the ranking of stakeholder claims is no easy task. Some managers continue to think in *stockholder* terms because this is easier. To think in stakeholder terms increases the complexity of decision making, and it is overly taxing for some managers to determine which stakeholders' claims take priority in a given situation. Despite its complexity, however, the stakeholder management view is most consistent with the environment that business faces today.

STAKEHOLDER MANAGEMENT CAPABILITY

Another way of thinking about effective stakeholder management is in terms of the extent to which the organization has developed its *stakeholder management capability (SMC)*.[27] Stakeholder management capability, as described by Freeman, may reside at one of three levels of increasing sophistication. Level 1—the *rational level*—simply entails the company identifying who their stakeholders are and what their stakes happen to be. This is the level of stakeholder maps. This level is descriptive and somewhat analytical, because the nature of stakes, the stakeholders' power, and urgency are identified. This actually represents a low level of SMC. Most organizations have at least identified who their stakeholders are, but not all have analyzed the nature of the stakes or the stakeholders' power. Starik has referred to Freeman's first level as the component of *familiarization* and *comprehensiveness*, because management operating at Level 1 is seeking to become familiar with their stakeholders and to develop a comprehensive assessment as to their identification and stakes.[28]

Level 2 of SMC is the *process level*. At the process level, organizations go a step further than Level 1 and actually develop and implement organizational processes by which the firm may scan the environment and receive relevant information about stakeholders, which is then used for decision-making purposes. Typical approaches at this level include portfolio analysis processes, strategic review processes, and environmental scanning processes, which are used to assist managers in their strategic management processes.[29] Other approaches, such as issues management or crisis management, might also be considered examples of Level 2 SMC. This second level has been described by Starik as *planning integrativeness,* because management does focus on planning processes for stakeholders and integrating a consideration for stakeholders into organizational decision making.[30]

Level 3, the highest level of SMC, is the ***transactional level.*** This is in a sense the bottom line for stakeholder management—the extent to which managers actually engage in transactions (relationships) with stakeholders.[31] At this highest level of SMC, management must take the initiative in meeting stakeholders face to face and attempting to be responsive to their needs. Starik refers to this as the *communication* level, which is characterized by communication proactiveness, interactiveness, genuineness, frequency, satisfaction, and resource adequacy. Resource adequacy refers to management actually spending resources on stakeholder transactions.[32]

An example of Level 3—the transactional level—is provided in the 1998 agreement between the Mitsubishi group and an environmentalist organization, the Rainforest Action Network (RAN), based in San Francisco. Mitsubishi agreed to curb its pollution and protect the rain forest in an agreement that was the result of 5 years of negotiations and meetings with RAN. The agreement would never have been possible if the two groups had not been willing to establish a relationship in which each side made certain concessions.[33]

THE STAKEHOLDER CORPORATION

Perhaps the ultimate form of the stakeholder approach or stakeholder management is the "stakeholder corporation," a concept argued strongly by Wheeler and Sillanpää. The primary element of this concept is ***stakeholder inclusiveness.*** The authors argue this position as follows:

> *In the future, development of loyal relationships with customers, employees, shareholders, and other stakeholders will become one of the most important determinants of commercial viability and business success. Increasing shareholder value will be best served if your company cultivates the support of all who may influence its importance.*[34]

Advocates of the stakeholder corporation would doubtless believe in "stakeholder symbiosis," which has been discussed widely by a consortium of organizations in their inaugural year activities of the Best Practices for Global Competitiveness Initiative (BPI), created and launched in 1997 by the American Productivity and Quality Center, the European Foundation for Quality Management, Arthur Andersen, and Fortune Custom Projects. ***Stakeholder symbiosis*** is an idea that recognizes that all stakeholders depend on each other for their success and financial well-being.[35] Executives who have a problem with this concept would probably also have trouble becoming parts of stakeholder corporations.

SUMMARY

A stakeholder is an individual or a group that claims to have one or more stakes in an organization. Stakeholders may affect the organization and, in turn, be affected by the organization's actions and decisions. The stakeholder approach extends beyond the traditional production and managerial views of the firm and warrants a much broader conception of the parties involved in the organization's functioning and success. Both primary and secondary social and nonsocial stakeholders assume important roles in the eyes of management. A typology of stakeholders suggests that three attributes are important: legitimacy, power, and urgency.

Strategic, multifidiciary, and stakeholder synthesis views help us appreciate the perspectives that may be adopted with regard to stakeholders. The stakeholder synthesis perspective is recommended because it highlights the ethical responsibility business has to its stakeholders. The stakeholder model of the firm has three values: it is descriptive, instrumental, and normative.

Five key questions aid managers in stakeholder management: (1) Who are our stakeholders? (2) What are our stakeholders' stakes? (3) What challenges or opportunities are presented to our firm by our stakeholders? (4) What responsibilities does our firm have to its stakeholders? (5) What strategies or actions should our firm take with respect to our stakeholders? The concept of stakeholder management capability (SMC) illustrates how firms can grow and mature in their approach to stakeholder management. Although the stakeholder management approach is quite complex and time consuming, it is a way of managing that is in tune with the complex environment that business organizations face today. The stakeholder corporation is a model that represents stakeholder thinking in its most advanced form.

KEY TERMS

generic stakeholder group (page 74)

managerial view of the firm (page 66)

process level (page 86)

production view of the firm (page 66)

rational level (page 86)

stake (page 65)

stakeholders (page 64)

stakeholder inclusiveness (page 87)

stakeholder management capability (SMC) (page 86)

stakeholder symbiosis (page 87)

stakeholder view of the firm (page 66)

transactional level (page 87)

DISCUSSION QUESTIONS

1. Explain the concepts of *stake* and *stakeholder* from your perspective as an individual. What kinds of stakes and stakeholders do you have? Discuss.
2. Differentiate between primary and secondary social and nonsocial stakeholders in a corporate situation.
3. Define the terms *core stakeholders, strategic stakeholders,* and *environmental stakeholders.* What factors affect into which of these groups stakeholders are categorized?

4. Explain in your own words the differences among the production, managerial, and stakeholder views of the firm.

5. Choose any group of stakeholders listed in the stakeholder/responsibility matrix in Figure 3–11 and identify the four types of responsibilities the firm has to that stakeholder group.

6. Is the stakeholder corporation a realistic model for business firms? Will stakeholder corporations become more prevalent in the twenty-first century? Why or why not?

ENDNOTES

1. For an overview of the first conference, see "The Toronto Conference: Reflections on Stakeholder Theory," *Business and Society* (Vol. 33, No. 1, April, 1994), 82–131.

2. Juha Näsi, "A Scandinavian Approach to Stakeholder Thinking," presented at the Understanding Stakeholder Thinking Conference, Jyäskylä, Finland, June 21–23, 1994. Also see Archie B. Carroll and Juha Näsi, "Understanding Stakeholder Thinking: Themes from a Finnish Conference," *Business Ethics: A European Review* (Vol. 6, No. 1, January, 1997), 46–51.

3. See, for example, Steven N. Brenner and Philip Cochran, "The Stakeholder Theory of the Firm: Implications for Business and Society Theory and Research," *International Association for Business and Society (IABS) 1991 Proceedings,* 449–467; Steven N. Brenner, "The Stakeholder Theory of the Firm and Organizational Decision Making," *International Association for Business and Society (IABS) 1993 Proceedings,* 205–210; Lee Preston and H.J. Sapienza, "Stakeholder Management and Corporate Performance," *The Journal of Behavioral Economics,* (Vol. 19, No. 4, 1990), 361–375; Robert A. Phillips, "Stakeholder Theory and a Principle of Fairness," *Business Ethics Quarterly* (Vol. 7, No. 1, January 1997), 51–66; and Sandra A. Waddock and Samuel B. Graves, "Quality of Management and Quality of Stakeholder Relations," *Business and Society* (Vol. 36, No. 3, September 1997), 250–279.

4. "Stakeholder Capitalism," *The Economist* (February 10, 1996), 23–25. See also "Shareholder Values," *The Economist* (February 10, 1996), 15–16; and John Plender, *A Stake in the Future: The Stakeholding Society* (Nicholas Brealey, 1997).

5. David Wheeler and Maria Sillanpää (1997). *The Stakeholder Corporation: A Blueprint for Maximizing Stakeholder Value.* London: Pitman Publishing.

6. This definition is similar to that of R. Edward Freeman in *Strategic Management: A Stakeholder Approach* (Boston: Pitman, 1984), 25.

7. Mark Starik, "Is the Environment an Organizational Stakeholder? Naturally!" *International Association for Business and Society (IABS) 1993 Proceedings,* 466–471.

8. Freeman, 5.

9. Freeman, 24–25.

10. Wheeler and Sillanpää (1997), 167.

11. *Ibid.*, 168.

12. Max B.E. Clarkson (ed.), *Proceedings of the Second Toronto Conference on Stakeholder Theory* (Toronto: The Centre for Corporate Social Performance and Ethics, University of Toronto, 1994).

13. Ronald K. Mitchell, Bradley R. Agle, and Donna J. Wood, "Toward a Theory of Stakeholder Identification and Salience: Defining the Principle of Who and What Really Counts," *Academy of Management Review* (October, 1997), 853–886.

14. Kenneth E. Goodpaster, "Business Ethics and Stakeholder Analysis," *Business Ethics Quarterly* (Vol. 1, No. 1, January, 1991), 53–73.

15. *Ibid.*

16. Thomas Donaldson and Lee Preston, "The Stakeholder Theory of the Corporation: Concepts, Evidence, Implications," *Academy of Management Review* (Vol. 20, No. 1, 1995), 65–91.

17. *Ibid.*

18. Similar questions are posed by Ian C. MacMillan and Patricia E. Jones, *Strategy Formulation: Power and Politics* (St. Paul, MN: West, 1986), 66.

19. The description of this incident comes from Martha W. Elliott and Tom L. Beauchamp, "Hooker Chemical and Love Canal," in Tom L. Beauchamp, *Case Studies in Business, Society and Ethics* (Englewood Cliffs, NJ: Prentice Hall, 1983), 107–115; and Steven Michalove, "Love Canal and Hooker Chemical: The Stakeholder Dilemma," unpublished paper (March 6, 1985).

20. Thomas H. Maugh II, "Toxic Waste Disposal a Growing Problem," *Science* (Vol. 204, May 25, 1979), 820.

21. "Does It Pay to Be Ethical? *Business Ethics* (March/April 1997), 14.

22. Grant T. Savage, Timothy W. Nix, Carlton J. Whitehead, and John D. Blair, "Strategies for Assessing and Managing Organizational Stakeholders," *Academy of Management Executive* (Vol. V, No. 2, May, 1991), 61–75.

23. *Ibid.*, 64.

24. MacMillan and Jones, 66–70.

25. Savage, Nix, Whitehead, and Blair, 65.

26. *Ibid.*, 72.

27. Freeman, 53.

28. Mark Starik, "Stakeholder Management and Firm Performance: Reputation and Financial Relationships to U.S. Electric Utility Consumer-Related Strategies," unpublished Ph.D. dissertation, University of Georgia, 1990, 34.

29. Freeman, 64.

30. Starik, 1990, 36.

31. Freeman, 69–70.

32. Starik, 1990, 36–42.

33. Charles McCoy, "Two Members of Mitsubishi Group and Environmental Activists Reach Pact," *Wall Street Journal* (February 11, 1998), A8.

34. Wheeler and Sillanpää (1997), book cover.

35. "Stakeholder Symbiosis," *Fortune* (March 30, 1998), S2–S4, special advertising section.

P A R T 2

Business Ethics and Management

Business Ethics Fundamentals

CHAPTER OBJECTIVES

After studying this chapter, you should be able to:

1 Describe how the public regards business ethics.

2 Provide a definition of business ethics and appreciate the complexities of making ethical judgments.

3 Explain the conventional approach to business ethics.

4 Enumerate and discuss the four important ethics questions.

5 Identify and explain three models of management ethics.

6 Recognize the challenges in making moral management actionable.

7 Describe Kohlberg's three levels of developing moral judgment.

8 Identify and discuss the elements of moral judgment.

In regard to public interest in business ethics during the modern business period—approximately the past 30 years—two conclusions may be drawn. First, interest in business ethics has heightened during each of the past three decades. Second, the interest in business ethics seems to have been spurred by major headline-grabbing scandals. Certainly, there has been an ebb and flow of interest on society's part, but lately this interest has grown to a preoccupation or, as some might say, an obsession.

In the modern period, public interest in business ethics was stimulated by several cases in 1960 in which electrical equipment manufacturers were indicted for allegedly conspiring to fix prices and restrict competition. The following year, the U.S. Secretary of Commerce formed a Business Ethics Advisory Council, which had as its objective the voluntary improvement of business conduct.

In 1961, Raymond Baumhart published his now-classic work, "How Ethical Are Businessmen?"[1] Although his survey of 1,700 *Harvard Business Review* readers did not indicate a prevalence of unethical practices in the private sector, business executives did admit and point out that there were numerous generally accepted practices in their industries that they considered unethical.

Several books and articles on the subject of business ethics were published in the middle and late 1960s, but public preoccupation with ethical behavior did not set in again until 1974, with the Watergate scandal and its aftermath. Since that time, a profusion of headline stories has suggested an exploding interest in the ethical behavior of businesspeople.

In 1982, *U.S. News & World Report* published two important findings that caught the public eye. First, it found that of the 500 largest corporations in the United States, 115 had been convicted in the past decade of at least one major crime or had paid civil penalties for serious misbehavior. Second, it found that among the 25 biggest firms—with annual sales running from 15 to 108 billion dollars—the rate of documented misbehavior had been even greater.[2] The "who's who" of firms with convictions or civil penalties included the backbone of the American business system: Exxon, Mobil, GM, AT&T, IBM, Gulf, Sears, GE, K Mart, Bank of America, and others.[3]

Numerous ethical scandals occurred in the mid-1980s. In 1985, E.F. Hutton pleaded guilty to federal charges stemming from an elaborate check-kiting scheme, and General Dynamics, the second-largest U.S. defense contractor, was the target of a barrage of embarrassing revelations, including a criminal indictment for conspiracy to defraud the Pentagon. Following the 1986 *Challenger* disaster, Morton Thiokol, manufacturer of the booster rocket that exploded, was implicated for going along with NASA's decision to launch the shuttle even though it knew that the weather conditions were not appropriate. The famed 1986 Ivan Boesky insider-trading scandal called into question the fundamental integrity of the entire financial system in the United States.

The megascandal of the late 1980s that spilled over into the 1990s was the Savings and Loan (S&L) industry debacle. The S&L scandal has been referred to as the nation's largest fiscal scandal and resulted not only in the indictment and conviction of hundreds of S&L executives for fraud but the destruction of the industry as well. The most noteworthy figure in the S&L scandal was Charles Keating, former chairman of Lincoln Savings and Loan in Irvine, California. It is estimated that the S&L debacle could eventually cost Americans as much as $1 trillion, because the U.S. government had to absorb the cost of the S&L failures. By 1990, the Justice Department had convicted and sentenced over 300 S&L felons, well over half of whom were jailed.

In the 1990s, business ethics scandals continued. Several notable examples are worth mentioning. The Salomon Brothers bond-buying scandal helped to usher in the 1990s. Salomon, the world's fourth-largest underwriter of securities, admitted in 1991 to repeatedly violating Treasury rules against buying more than 35 percent of a Treasury issue of securities at auction. The scandal led to three top officials resigning, among other consequences.[4] It should come as no surprise that the U.S. Sentencing Commission in 1991 created new Federal Sentencing Guidelines designed to deter corporate crime by creating incentives for corporations to report and accept responsibility for unlawful behavior.

One of the most visible examples of questionable behavior occurred in 1993. The NBC News show "Dateline NBC" aired a supposed exposé of exploding gas tanks in GM trucks, but NBC officials later admitted that toy rocket engines had been used as "igniters" to ensure that the staged crashes resulted in explosions. NBC, a unit of General Electric Co., eventually apologized for the misrepresentation and agreed to reimburse GM the roughly $2 million it had incurred investigating the NBC report. In exchange, GM agreed to drop its defamation suit against NBC.[5] To add to GE's troubles, the big story in 1994 concerned its Kidder, Peabody & Co. unit, which got embroiled in a bond-trading scandal. Kidder's government bond chief, Joseph Jett, was accused of creating $350 million in fake profits to mask losses over a several-year period. Kidder fired Mr. Jett, who denied the accusations. Jett claimed that Kidder knew about his trades and was trying to make him the fall guy. One major fallout from the scandal was the exodus of some of the firm's most successful brokers, who took with them about $2 billion in client accounts.[6]

To be sure, business ethics scandals have continued well into the 1990s. One noticeable change during this time, however, has been the significant extent to which ethics, morals, and values have come to characterize the general public debate concerning business in the United States. Examples of this elevated discussion include the 1992 *Newsweek* cover story entitled "Whose Values?"[7] One of the most popular national best-sellers has been William J. Bennett's 1993 anthology entitled *The Book of Virtues: A Treasury of Great Moral Stories.*[8] In 1994, *Newsweek* featured a cover story entitled "The Politics of Virtue: The Crusade Against America's Moral Decline." In this story, *Newsweek* reported the response to its poll question: "Do you think the U.S. is in a moral and spiritual decline?" Seventy-six percent of those responding to this national poll said "yes," whereas only 20 percent said "no."[9] Also in 1994, *U.S. News & World Report* featured the special report "America's New Crusade," in which we learned of politicians of all stripes who are now painting themselves as guardians of old-fashioned values as Americans seek a way out of the cultural recession.[10]

In the summer of 1994, "Forrest Gump" became a movie phenomenon. Gump, played by Tom Hanks, was a figure of some moral force—the simple guy who always does the right thing. Gump's success portrayed the inherent message that there is no need to choose between virtuous living and the accumulation of great wealth as he got richer and richer simply by being decent.[11]

In the second half of the 1990s, many of the ethical scandals found in business involved massive charges of racial discrimination and sexual harassment. Among the well-known companies that experienced such allegations were Home Depot, Mitsubishi, and Texaco. The Texaco case involved a $196 million settlement in a class-action race discrimination lawsuit brought by employees fighting for equal pay and a chance for promotions. Bari-Ellen Roberts, lead plaintiff in the case against the oil company, revealed a dark side of corporate America in her 1998 book, *Roberts vs. Texaco: A True Story of Race and Corporate America.*[12]

Another industry that attracted widespread criticism in the late 1990s was the tobacco industry. The Food and Drug Administration's (FDA's) crackdown on tobacco, along with Congress's 1998 attempts to draft and pass landmark tobacco legislation, caused tobacco executives to begin thinking in settlement terms that would have been unthinkable in years past.[13]

It appears that the American society of the late 1990s is clamoring for a renewed emphasis on values, morals, and ethics and that the business ethics debate of this period is but a subset of this larger societal concern. Whether the business community will be able to respond remains to be seen. One thing is sure: There is a renewed interest in business ethics, and the proliferation of business ethics courses in colleges and universities, along with the revitalized interest on the part of the business community, is encouraging.

To gain an appreciation of the kinds of issues that are important under the rubric of business ethics, Figure 4–1 presents an inventory of business ethics issues compiled by the Josephson Institute of Ethics. Here we see business ethics issues categorized on

FIGURE 4–1   Inventory of Ethical Issues in Business

*This checklist is designed to stimulate thought and discussion on important
ethical concerns in your company and the larger business community.*

For each of the following issues indicate whether ethical problems are:
5 = Very serious; 4 = Serious; 3 = Not very serious;
2 = Not a problem; 1 = No opinion.

Column I = In the business world in general   Column II = In your company

Employee–Employer Relations

_____ _____ 1. Work ethic—giving a full day's work for a full day's pay
_____ _____ 2. Petty theft (i.e., supplies, telephone, photocopying, etc.)
_____ _____ 3. Cheating on expense accounts
_____ _____ 4. Employee acceptance of gifts or favors from vendors
_____ _____ 5. Distortion or falsification of internal reports
_____ _____ 6. Cheating or overreaching on benefits (sick days, insurance, etc.)

Employer–Employee Relations

_____ _____ 7. Sexual or racial discrimination in hiring, promotion, or pay
_____ _____ 8. Sexual harassment
_____ _____ 9. Invasions of employee privacy
_____ _____ 10. Unsafe or unhealthy working conditions
_____ _____ 11. Discouragement of internal criticism re: unfair, illegal, or improper
                activities
_____ _____ 12. Unfair or insensitive handling of assignment changes or major
                reorganizations
_____ _____ 13. Improper dealing with persons with AIDS
_____ _____ 14. Failure to give honest, fair, and timely work appraisals
_____ _____ 15. Recruiting for employee's replacement without telling employee being
                replaced
_____ _____ 16. Using strategies or technical justifications to deny employees earned
                benefits
_____ _____ 17. Dealing peremptorily or unfairly with employee complaints
_____ _____ 18. Misleading employees about the likelihood of layoffs, terminations, or job
                changes
_____ _____ 19. Inadequate training or supervision to ensure employee's success
_____ _____ 20. Inadequate participation by qualified staff in major policy decisions
_____ _____ 21. Unfair demands on or expectations of paid staff
_____ _____ 22. Inadequate compensation
_____ _____ 23. Inadequate recognition, appreciation, or other psychic rewards
                to staff
_____ _____ 24. Inappropriate blame-shifting or credit-taking to protect or advance personal
                careers
_____ _____ 25. Unhealthy competition among employees about "turf," assignments, budget,
                etc.
_____ _____ 26. Inadequate communication among departments and divisions for the wrong
                reasons
_____ _____ 27. Inadequate mutual support and teamwork; individuals focus primarily on
                their own narrow jobs

(continued)

FIGURE 4–1 *(continued)*

Company–Customer Relations

___	___	28. Unfair product pricing
___	___	29. Deceptive marketing/advertising
___	___	30. Unsafe or unhealthy products
___	___	31. Unfair and/or legalistic handling of customer complaints
___	___	32. Discourtesy or arrogance toward customers

Company–Shareholder Relations

___	___	33. Excessive compensation for top management
___	___	34. Self-protective management policies (golden parachutes, poison pills, greenmail)
___	___	35. Mismanagement of corporate assets or opportunities
___	___	36. Public reports and/or financial statements that distort actual performance

Company–Community/Public Interest

___	___	37. Injury to the environment
___	___	38. Undue influence on the political process through lobbying, PACs, etc.
___	___	39. Payoffs, "grease," or bribes to union or public officials
___	___	40. Payoffs, "grease," or bribes in foreign countries
___	___	41. Doing business in countries with inhumane or anti-American policies (e.g., South Africa, Iran)
___	___	42. Inadequate corporate philanthropy
___	___	43. Inadequate community involvement

SOURCE: Reprinted with permission © Josephson Institute of Ethics, *Ethics: Easier Said Than Done,* Vol. 2, No. 1, 1989.

the basis of stakeholder relationships. Against this backdrop, we plan to discuss business ethics, specifically in this chapter and the next two. In this chapter we will introduce business ethics fundamentals. In Chapter 5 we will consider personal and organizational ethics. In Chapter 6 our attention will turn to the international sphere as we discuss ethical issues in the global arena.

BUSINESS ETHICS AND PUBLIC OPINION

The public's view of business's ethics has never been very high. Anecdotal evidence suggests that many people see business ethics as essentially a contradiction in terms and feel that there is only a fine line between a business executive and a crook. It is useful for our discussion here, however, to look at some of the surveys of business ethics that have been taken over the years.

The Gallup Poll

Perhaps the most reliable expression of public attitudes on business ethics may be found in the Gallup Poll, which regularly surveys public opinion of social and political issues. Gallup periodically quizzes the public on its feelings about the ethics of business executives and other professionals. Survey data from the 1997 Gallup Poll, the latest data available, reveals that the honesty and ethics of business executives are thought to be "very high" or "high" by only 20 percent of those surveyed. Over the period from 1991 to 1997, this percentage has fluctuated between a low of 17 percent in 1996 and a high of 22 percent in 1994. Specific groups of businesspeople rank even lower than the general category of business executives. Among those specific groups are real estate agents, stockbrokers, advertising practitioners, insurance salespeople, and car salespeople. Pharmacists and bankers rank higher than business executives, generally.

It is useful to compare the public's perception of business executives' ethics with its perception of the ethics of other professionals. Such a comparison finds that business ranks about in the middle of the pack of those considered. Although business executives do not achieve the high rankings of such groups as pharmacists, clergy, doctors, college teachers, and dentists, they do rank higher than newspaper reporters, lawyers, senators, congressmen, and state officeholders.[14] Such a contrast reveals some possible ethical problems in the political arena.

It is difficult to pinpoint the exact public sentiment on business ethics today. In general, however, it is safe to conclude that the public thinks business ethics is at least somewhat suspect and that it would like to see improvements. There is sentiment that business is only one of the major institutions that have questionable ethics today; however, business is the focus of our attention here.

If we were to make judgments about the current state of business ethics by reading the daily newspapers or news magazines or watching "60 Minutes," "20/20," or "Primetime Live" on television, we might quickly reach the conclusion that it is in a shambles and that behind every business door an evil-minded individual is lurking. To help us understand the public sentiment, we must ask three intriguing questions: (1) Has business ethics really deteriorated? (2) Are the media reporting ethical problems more frequently and vigorously? (3) Is it actually society that is changing so that once-accepted practices are now considered unacceptable by the public?

Has Business Ethics Really Deteriorated?

Unfortunately, there is no scientific way to determine whether or not business ethics has really deteriorated. Max Ways's description of a statistical analysis (the twentieth century's favorite kind of investigation) aimed at answering the question, "How widespread is corporate misconduct?" is enlightening. He says that to describe such a project would demonstrate its impossibility. He argues that the researcher would have to count the transgressions publicly exposed in a certain period of time. Then the total number of known misdeeds would have to be correlated with the trillions and trillions of business transactions that occur daily. He concludes:

> *If we assume (recklessly) that a believable estimate of total transactions could be made, then the sum of the publicly known malfeasances almost certainly would be a minute fraction of the whole. At this point the investigator would have to abandon the conclusion that the incidence of business misconduct is so low as to be insignificant.*[15]

In fact, no such study has ever been attempted. Public opinion polls might be our best way to gather data about the current state of business ethics, but such polls are hardly definitive.

Are the Media Reporting Ethical Problems More Vigorously?

There is no doubt that the media are reporting ethical problems more frequently and fervently. Spurred on by the Watergate event in 1974 and the post-Watergate moral climate, the media have found business ethics and, indeed, ethics questions among all institutions to be subjects of sustaining interest during the past two decades.

Of particular interest in recent years has been the in-depth investigative reporting of business scandals on such TV shows as "60 Minutes," "20/20," "Dateline NBC," and "Primetime Live," as well as the growing number of such programs. Such investigations keep business scandals in the public eye and make it difficult to assess whether public opinion polls are reflecting the actual business ethics of the day or simply the reactions to the latest scandals.

Is It Society That Is Actually Changing?

We would definitely make this argument here, as we did in Chapter 1. Many business managers subscribe to this belief. W. Michael Blumenthal, former U.S. Secretary of the Treasury and chief executive officer of the Bendix Corporation, has been one of the leading advocates of this view. He argued:

> *It seems to me that the root causes of the questionable and illegal corporate activities that have come to light recently . . . can be traced to the sweeping changes that have taken place in our society and throughout the world and to the unwillingness of many in business to adjust to these changes.*[16]

He goes on to say, "People in business have not suddenly become immoral. What has changed are the contexts in which corporate decisions are made, the demands that are being made on business, and the nature of what is considered proper corporate conduct."[17]

Although it would be difficult to prove Blumenthal's thesis, it is an attractive one. You do not have to make a lengthy investigation of some of today's business practices to realize that a good number of what are now called unethical practices are ones that were at one time considered acceptable. Or it may be that the practices never really were acceptable to the public but that, because they were not known, they were tolerated, thus causing no moral dilemma for the public.

Figure 4–2 illustrates how the ethical problem may be more severe today than it once was, as a result of the public's expectations of business ethical behavior rising more rapidly than actual business ethics. Note that actual business ethics is assumed to be improving slightly but not as quickly as public expectations are rising. The magnitude of the current ethical problem, therefore, is seen here partially to be a function of rapidly rising societal expectations.

WHAT DOES BUSINESS ETHICS MEAN?

In Chapter 2 we discussed the ethical responsibilities of business as if we all knew exactly what that meant. To be sure, we all have a general idea of what business ethics means, but here we would like to probe the topic more deeply. To understand business ethics, we need to appreciate the relationship between ethics and morality.

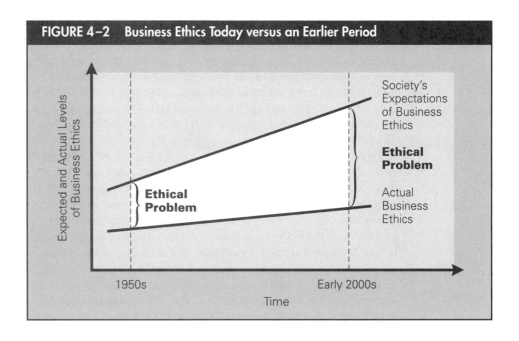

FIGURE 4–2   Business Ethics Today versus an Earlier Period

Ethics is the discipline that deals with what is good and bad and with moral duty and obligation. Ethics can also be regarded as a set of moral principles or values. *Morality* is a doctrine or system of moral conduct. Moral conduct refers to that which relates to principles of right and wrong in behavior. In a sense, then, we can think of ethics and morality as being so similar to one another that we may use them interchangeably to refer to the study of right and wrong behavior in business.

Business ethics, therefore, is concerned with good and bad or right and wrong behavior that takes place within a business context. Concepts of right and wrong are increasingly being interpreted today to include the more difficult and subtle questions of fairness, justice, and equity.

Two key branches of moral philosophy, or ethics, are descriptive ethics and normative ethics. It is important to distinguish between the two because they each take a different perspective. *Descriptive ethics* is concerned with describing, characterizing, and studying the morality of a people, a culture, or a society. It also compares and contrasts different moral codes, systems, practices, beliefs, and values.[18] In descriptive business ethics, therefore, our focus is on learning what is occurring in the realm of behavior, actions, decisions, policies, and practices of business firms, managers, or, perhaps, specific industries. Descriptive ethics focuses on "what is" the prevailing set of ethical standards in the business community.

SEARCH THE WEB

What is going on in the world of business ethics as it relates to the world of enterprises? Two interesting Web sites offer useful insights. First, visit the Ethics Officer Association (EOA) Web site, located at **www.eoa.org/**. The EOA is the professional association for managers of corporate ethics and compliance programs. Its Web site has a considerable amount of interesting information about what the practitioners of business ethics are doing. It also has links to other useful Web pages. For additional insights, visit **www.kpmg.net/ library/97/january/story2.asp**, the Web site of KPMG, a major, global consulting firm. This site illustrates KPMG's work in the areas of social and ethical auditing and includes "The Age of Ethics," an essay on the history of business ethics from Aristotle to the present.

By contrast, **normative ethics** is concerned with supplying and justifying a coherent moral system. Normative ethics seeks to uncover, develop, and justify basic moral principles that are intended to guide behavior, actions, and decisions.[19] Normative business ethics, therefore, seeks to propose some principle or principles for distinguishing right from wrong in the business context. It deals more with "what ought to be" or "what ought *not* to be" in terms of business practices. Normative ethics is concerned with establishing norms or standards by which business practices might be guided or judged.

In our study of business ethics, we need to be ever mindful of this distinction between descriptive and normative perspectives. It is tempting to observe the prevalence of a particular practice in business (for example, padding expense accounts or deceptive advertising) and conclude that because so many are doing it (descriptive ethics), it must be acceptable behavior. Normative ethics would insist that a practice be justified on the basis of some ethical principle, argument, or rationale before being considered acceptable. Normative ethics demands a more meaningful moral anchor than just "everyone is doing it."

In this chapter and the next, we will discuss three major approaches to determining what ethical business conduct is: (1) the conventional approach, (2) the principles approach, and (3) the ethical tests approach. We will discuss the conventional approach to business ethics in this chapter and the other two approaches in Chapter 5.

The Conventional Approach to Business Ethics

The **conventional approach to business ethics** is essentially an approach whereby we compare an act, a decision, or a behavior with prevailing norms of acceptability. We call it the conventional approach because it is believed that this is the way the conventional or general society thinks. The major challenge of this approach is answering the questions "Whose norms do we use?" and "What norms are prevailing?" There is considerable room for variability on both of these issues. With respect to whose norms are used as the basis for ethical judgments, the conventional approach would consider as legitimate those norms emanating from family, friends, the local community, one's employer, and so on. In addition, one's conscience, or the individual, would be seen by many as a legitimate source of ethical norms. A classic "Frank and Ernest" cartoon pokes fun at the use of conscience. A sign on the wall reads "Tonight's Lecture: Moral Philosophy." Then it shows Frank saying to Ernest, "I'd let my conscience be my guide, but I'm in enough trouble already!" Figure 4–3 illustrates some of the sources of norms that come to bear on the individual and that might be used in various circumstances under the conventional approach.

In many circumstances, the conventional approach to ethics is useful and applicable. What does a person do, however, if norms from one source conflict with norms from another source? Also, how can we be sure that societal norms are really right or defensible? Culture in our society sends us many and often conflicting messages about what is appropriate behavior. We get these messages from television, movies, music, and other sources. An interesting example of the kind of message television sends occurred one night on "Dallas" when J. R. Ewing blurted out to a colleague this sage advice: "Once you give up integrity, the rest is a piece of cake!" We might call this tidbit of wisdom "J. R.'s Rule of Ethics." At first blush, this appears to most of us as humorous. It is just possible, however, that an impressionable young person

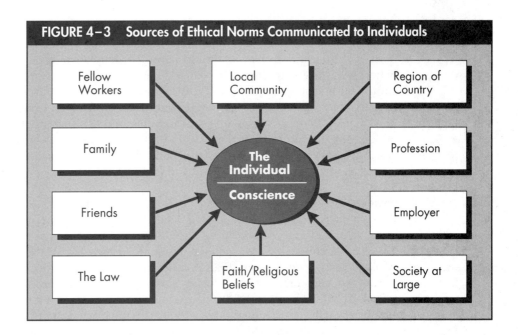

FIGURE 4–3   Sources of Ethical Norms Communicated to Individuals

might see this and hundreds of other references like it and conclude that dishonesty is really the standard in business.

Another example of the conflicting messages people get today from society occurs in the realm of sexual harassment in the workplace. On the one hand, today's television, movies, advertisements, and music are replete with sexual innuendo and the treatment of women as sex objects. This would suggest that such behavior is normal. On the other hand, the law and the courts are stringently prohibiting any kind of sexual gesture or innuendo in the workplace. As we will see in a later chapter, it does not take much sexual innuendo to constitute a "hostile work environment" and a sex discrimination charge under Title VII of the Civil Rights Act. In this example, we see a norm arising from culture and society clashing with a norm evolving from employment law.

Ethics and the Law

We have made various references to ethics and the law. In Chapter 2, we said that ethical behavior resides above behavior required by the law. This is the generally accepted view of ethics. We should make it clear, however, that in many respects the law and ethics overlap. To appreciate this, you need to recognize that the law embodies notions of ethics. That is, the law may be seen as a reflection of what society thinks are minimal standards of conduct and behavior. Both law and ethics have to do with what is deemed right or wrong, but law reflects society's *codified* ethics. Therefore, if a person breaks a law or violates a regulation, she or he is also behaving unethically. In spite of this overlap, we continue to talk about desirable ethical behavior as behavior that extends beyond what is required by law. Viewed from the standpoint of minimums, we would certainly say that obedience to the law is a minimum standard of behavior.

In addition, we should make note of the fact that the law does not address all realms in which ethical questions might be raised. Thus, there are clear roles for both law and ethics to play. It should be noted that research on illegal corporate behavior has been conducted for some time. Illegal corporate behavior, of course, comprises business practices that are in direct defiance of law or public policy. Research has focused on two dominant questions: (1) Why do firms behave illegally or what leads them to engage in illegal activities, and (2) what are the consequences of behaving illegally?[20] We will not deal with these studies of lawbreaking in this discussion; however, we should view this body of studies and investigations as being closely aligned with our interest in business ethics.

Making Ethical Judgments

When a decision is made about what is ethical (right, just, fair) using the conventional approach, there is room for variability on several counts (see Figure 4–4). Three key elements go into such a decision. First, we observe the behavior, act, or practice that has been committed. Second, we compare the practice with prevailing norms of acceptability—that is, society's or some other standard of what is right or wrong. Third, we must recognize that value judgments are being made by someone as to what really occurred (the actual behavior) and what the prevailing norms of acceptability really are. This means that two different people could look at the same behavior, compare it with their concepts of what the prevailing norms are, and reach different conclusions as to whether the behavior was ethical or not. This becomes quite complex as perceptions of what is ethical inevitably lead to the difficult task of ranking different values against one another.

If we can put aside for a moment the fact that perceptual differences about an incident do exist, and the fact that we differ among ourselves because of our personal values and philosophies of right and wrong, we are still left with the problematical task of determining society's prevailing norms of acceptability of business behavior. As a whole, members of society generally agree at a very high level of abstraction that certain behaviors are wrong. However, the consensus tends to disintegrate as we move from the abstract to specific situations.

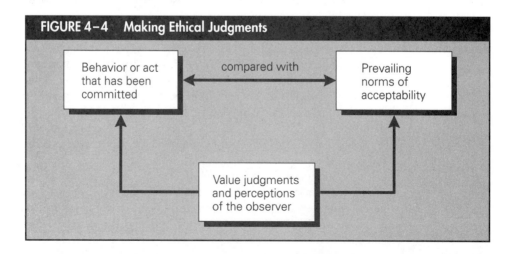

FIGURE 4–4   Making Ethical Judgments

ETHICS IN PRACTICE

To Steal or Not to Steal, That Is the Question

A very good friend of mine worked for a large department store in a nearby large city. The store is known for its quality and name-brand products. A position with the inventory staff became available and my friend suggested that I apply. I did and later received the job.

As part of the inventory staff, I was placed in the back of the store, where inventory came to be checked in. The inventory staff members were left pretty much on their own to do their own jobs, because the supervisors were very busy with various other duties. The system of inventory was set up so that it was difficult for the store to know exactly what it had ordered before it was stocked. This was readily apparent to my colleagues. On several occasions I noticed thefts by my co-workers and, unfortunately, thefts by my close friend. This activity didn't sit well with me, so I asked my friend about it. He dismissed my concern in a joking fashion, and even bragged about his great employee "five-finger discount." I did not want to be a part of this type of activity, and I had only worked for the store for a few days. I decided that staying too long in that environment would not be the best idea, and so I left the store without notice.

1. Is this an example of deteriorating ethics in society, or has this kind of behavior gone on all along in business?

2. What would the conventional approach to business ethics say about this practice of employees helping themselves?

3. Was quitting the correct course of action, or should I have done something different?

Contributed by David W. Jeffrey

Let us illustrate with a business example. We might all agree with the general dictum that "You should not steal someone else's property." At a high level of abstraction (as a general precept), we probably would have consensus on this. But as we look at specific situations, our consensus may tend to disappear. Is it acceptable to take home from work such things as pencils, pens, paper clips, paper, staplers, adding machines, and calculators? Is it acceptable to use the company telephone for personal long-distance calls? Is it acceptable to use company gasoline for private use or to pad expense accounts? What if everyone else is doing it?

What is interesting in this example is that we are more likely to reach consensus in principle than in practice. Some people who would say these practices are not acceptable might privately engage in them. Furthermore, a person who would not think of shoplifting even the smallest item from a local store might take pencils and paper home from work on a regular basis. A cartoon depicting the "Born Loser" is related to this discussion. In the first panel the father admonishes his son Wilberforce in the following way: "You know how I feel about stealing. Now tomorrow I want you to return every one of those pencils to school." In the second panel, Father says to Wilberforce, "I'll bring you all the pencils you need from work." This is an example of the classic double standard.

Thus, in the conventional approach to business ethics, determinations of what is ethical and what is not require judgments to be made on three counts:

1.   What is the true *nature* of the practice, behavior, or decision that occurred?

2.   What are society's (or business's) *prevailing norms* of acceptability?

3.   What *value judgments* are being made by someone about the practice or behavior, and what are that person's perceptions of applicable norms?

The human factor in the situation thus introduces the problem of perception and values.

The conventional approach to business ethics can be valuable, because we all need to be aware of and sensitive to the total environment in which we exist. It has limitations, however, and we need to be cognizant of these as well. The most serious danger is that of falling into an **ethical relativism** where we pick and choose which source of norms we wish to use based on what will justify our current actions or maximize our freedom. In the next chapter we will argue that a principles approach is needed to augment the conventional approach. The principles approach looks to the general guides to ethical decision making that come from moral philosophy. We will also present the ethical tests approach, which is more of a practical approach, in the next chapter.

FOUR IMPORTANT ETHICS QUESTIONS

It is hard to do justice to ethics discussions in such a short space, but we ought to provide some "big picture" perspective that could legitimately be asked of ethics, in general, or of business ethics, in particular. Philosophers have concepts and terminology that are more academic, but let us approach this broad perspective, as Otto Bremer has done,[21] by starting with four apparently simple but really different kinds of questions:

1.   What is?

2.   What ought to be?

3.   How do we get from what is to what ought to be?

4.   What is our motivation in all this?

These four questions capture the core of what ethics is all about. They force an examination of what *really is,* what *ought to be,* how we close the gap between what *is* and what *ought to be,* and what our *motivation* is for doing all this.

Before we discuss each question briefly, let us suggest that these four questions may be asked at four different levels: the level of the individual (the personal level), the level of the organization, the level of the industry or profession, and, finally, the societal level.

What Is?

This question forces us to face the reality of what is actually going on in an ethical sense in business. Ideally it is a factual, scientific, or descriptive question. Its purpose is to help us understand the reality of the ethical behavior we find before us. As we discussed earlier when we were describing the nature of making ethical judgments, it is not always simple to state exactly what the "real" situation is. This is because we are humans and thus make mistakes when we "sense" what is happening. Also, we are conditioned by our personal beliefs, values, and biases, and these factors affect what we see or sense. Or, we may perceive real conditions for what they are but fail to think in terms of alternatives or in terms of "what ought to be." Think of the difficulty you might have in attempting to describe "what is" with respect to business ethics at the personal, organizational, industry/professional, and societal levels. The questions then become:

- What *are* your personal ethics?
- What *are* your organization's ethics?
- What *are* the ethics of your industry or profession?
- What *are* society's ethics?

What Ought to Be?

This second question is quite different from the first question. It is normative rather than descriptive. It is certainly not a scientific question. It is a question that seldom gets answered directly, particularly in a managerial setting. Managers are used to identifying alternatives and choosing the best one, but seldom is this done with questions that entail moral content or the "rightness" of a decision. The "ought to be" question is often viewed in terms of what management *should* do in a given situation. Examples of this question in a business setting might be:

- How *ought* we treat our aging employees whose productivity is declining?
- How safe *ought* we make this product, knowing full well we cannot pass all the costs on to the consumer?
- How clean an environment *should* we aim for?
- How *should* we treat long-time employees when the company is downsizing or moving the plant to a foreign country?

At a corporate planning seminar several years ago, the leader suggested that if you are the president of a large corporation the place to start planning is with a vision of society, not with where you want to be 5 or 10 years into the future. What kind of world do you want to have? How does your industry or your firm fit into that world? An executive cannot just walk into the office one day and say, "I had a vision last night," and expect many adherents.[22] But this does not make the question or the vision invalid. It simply suggests that we must approach the "What ought to be?" question at a more practical level. There are plenty of issues to which this question can be applied in the everyday life of a manager. Therefore, such lofty, visionary exercises are not necessary.

How Do We Get from What Is to What Ought to Be?

This third question represents the challenge of bridging the gap between where we are and where we ought to be with respect to ethical practices. Therefore, it represents an action dimension. We may discuss endlessly where we "ought" to be in terms of our own personal ethics or the ethics of our firm, of our industry, or of society. And as we move further away from the individual level, we have less control or influence over the "ought to be" question.

When faced with these ideas as depicted by our "ought to be" questions, we may find that from a practical point of view we cannot achieve our ideals. This does not mean we should not have asked the question in the first place. Our "ought to be" questions become goals or objectives for our ethical practices. They form the normative core of business ethics. They become moral benchmarks that help us to measure progress.

In all managerial situations, we are faced with this challenge of balancing what we ought to do with what we must or can do. The notions of Leslie Weatherhead in his book, *The Will of God,* could be adapted to our discussion here. He refers to God's intentional will, circumstantial will, and ultimate will. Looking at these concepts from a managerial or an ethics point of view, we might think in terms of what we intend to accomplish, what circumstances permit us to accomplish, and what we ultimately are able to accomplish. These ideas interject a measure of realism into our efforts to close the gap between where we are and where we want to be.

This is also the stage at which managerial decision making and strategy come into play. The first step in managerial problem solving is identifying the problem (what "is"). Next comes identifying where we want to be (the "ought" question). Then comes the managerial challenge of closing the gap. "Gap analysis" sets the stage for concrete business action.

What Is Our Motivation in All This?

Pragmatic businesspeople do not like to dwell on this fourth question, which addresses the motivation for being ethical, because so often it reveals some manipulative or self-centered motive. At one level, is it perhaps not desirable to discuss motivation, because it is really *actions* that count? If someone makes a $100 contribution to a charitable cause, is it fair to ask whether the person did it (1) because she or he really believes in the cause (altruistic motivation) or (2) because she or he just wanted a tax deduction (selfish motive)? Most of us would agree that it is better for a person to make a contribution rather than not make it, regardless of the motive.

Ideally, we would hope that people would be ethical because they intrinsically see that being ethical is a better way to live or manage. What kind of world (or organization) would you prefer: one in which people behave ethically because they have selfish or instrumental reasons for doing so, or one in which they behave ethically because they really believe in what they are doing? We will accept the former, but the latter is more desirable. We will be better off in the long run if "right" managerial practices are motivated by the knowledge that there is inherent value in ethical behavior.

This can be compared to the organizational situation in which managers are attempting to motivate their workers. If a manager is interested only in greater productivity and sees that being "concerned" about employees' welfare will achieve this goal, she or he had better be prepared for the fact that employees may see through the "game playing" and eventually rebel against the manager's effort. On the other hand, employees can see when management is genuinely concerned about their welfare, and they will be responsive to such well-motivated efforts. This is borne out in practice. You can examine two companies that on the surface appear to have identical personnel policies. In one company the employees know and feel they are being manipulated, and in the other company there is confidence that management really does care.[23]

Although we would like to believe that managers are appropriately motivated in their quest for ethical business behavior and that motivations are important, we must continue to understand and accept Andrew Stark's observation that we live in a "messy world of mixed motives." Therefore, managers do not typically have the luxury of making abstract distinctions between altruism and self-interest but must get on with the task of designing structures, systems, incentives, and processes that accommodate the "whole" employee, regardless of motivations.[24]

THREE MODELS OF MANAGEMENT ETHICS

In attempting to understand the basic concepts of business ethics, it is useful to think in terms of key ethical models that might describe different types of management ethics.[25] These models should provide some useful base points for discussion and comparison. The media have focused so much on immoral or unethical business behavior that it is easy to forget or not think about the possibility of other ethical styles or types. For example, scant attention has been given to the distinction that may be made between those activities that are *immoral* and those that are *amoral;* similarly, little attention has been given to contrasting these two forms of behavior with ethical or *moral* management.

Believing that there is value in developing descriptive models for purposes of clearer understanding, here we will describe, compare, and contrast three models or types of ethical management:

1.   Immoral management

2.   Moral management

3.   Amoral management

A major goal is to develop a clearer understanding of the full gamut of management styles in which ethics or morality is a major dimension. By seeing these styles come to life through description and example, managers are expected to be in an improved position to assess their own ethical approaches and those of other organizational members (supervisors, subordinates, and peers).

Another central objective is to identify more completely the *amoral* management model, which often is overlooked in the human rush to classify things as good or bad, moral or immoral. In a later section we will discuss the elements of moral judgment that must be developed if the transition to moral management is to succeed. Figure 4–5 portrays these three models of management ethics.

A more detailed development of each management model is valuable in coming to understand the range of ethics that leaders may intentionally or unintentionally

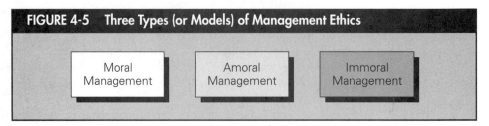

FIGURE 4-5　Three Types (or Models) of Management Ethics

Moral Management　　Amoral Management　　Immoral Management

SOURCE: Archie B. Carroll, "In Search of the Moral Manager," *Business Horizons* (March/April, 1987), 8. Copyright © 1987 by the Foundation for the School of Business at Indiana University. Used with permission.

display. Let us consider the two extremes first—immoral and moral management—and then amoral management.

Immoral Management

Using *immoral* and *unethical* as synonyms, we can define **immoral management** as a posture that not only is devoid of ethical principles or precepts but also implies a positive and active opposition to what is ethical. Immoral management decisions, behaviors, actions, and practices are discordant with ethical principles. This view holds that management's motives are selfish and that it cares only or principally about its own or its company's gains. If management's activity is actively opposed to what is regarded as ethical, this implies that management knows right from wrong and yet chooses to do wrong. Thus, its motives are deemed greedy or selfish. According to this model, management's goals are profitability and organizational success at almost any price. Management does not care about others' claims to be treated fairly or justly.

What about management's orientation toward the law, considering that law is often regarded as an embodiment of minimal ethics? Immoral management regards legal standards as barriers that management must overcome in order to accomplish what it wants. Immoral management would just as soon engage in illegal activity as in immoral or unethical activity.

Operating Strategy

The operating strategy of immoral management is focused on exploiting opportunities for corporate or personal gain. An active opposition to what is moral would suggest that managers cut corners anywhere and everywhere it appears useful. Thus, the key operating question guiding immoral management is, *"Can we make money with this action, decision, or behavior, regardless of what it takes?"* Implicit in this question is that nothing else matters, at least not very much.

Illustrative Cases

Examples of immoral management abound. The Frigitemp Corporation, a manufacturer of refrigerated mortuary boxes, provides an example of immoral management at the highest levels of corporate hierarchy. In litigation, criminal trials, and federal investigations, corporate officials, including the president and chairman, admitted to having made millions of dollars in payoffs to get business. They admitted taking kickbacks from suppliers, embezzling corporate funds, exaggerating earnings in reports to shareholders, and providing prostitutes to customers. One corporate official said that greed was their undoing. They were so busy stealing that they got caught. Records indicate that Frigitemp's executives permitted a corporate culture of chicanery to flourish. The company eventually went bankrupt because of management's misconduct.[26]

Federal prosecutors unraveled a long-running fraud scheme in which a group of U.S. Honda Motor Co. executives had pocketed in excess of $10 million in bribes and kickbacks paid them by car dealers. In exchange, the executives gave dealers permission to open lucrative dealerships, and they also received Honda automobiles, which were in short supply at the time. Eight executives pleaded guilty, and many others were indicted. American Honda, the parent company, maintained that it was a victim in the case and had plans to sue the guilty executives.[27]

Blind ambition led Bausch & Lomb (B&L) to experience numerous cases of immoral management during the past decade. Former executives of the billion-dollar company with 13,000 employees say that, under former CEO Dan Gill, maintaining B&L's double-digit sales and earnings growth was all-important, creating pressures that led to unethical behavior throughout the company. Several examples illustrate. Under pressure to beat sales targets in 1993, contact-lens managers shipped products that doctors never ordered and forced distributors to take up to 2 years of unwanted inventories. Forced to meet inflated sales goals, many U.S., Asian, and Latin American B&L managers knowingly sold contact lenses and Ray-Ban sunglasses to gray-market distributors, in violation of company policy. B&L's Hong Kong unit allegedly inflated revenues by faking sales of Ray-Bans to real customers. Some of the sunglasses were then allegedly sold at cut-rate prices to gray-market dealers.[28]

Archer-Daniels-Midland (ADM), whose advertising slogan is "Supermarket to the World," paid a $100 million fine in 1996 for price fixing. After years of denying any wrongdoing, the agribusiness giant pleaded guilty to conspiring to fix prices for the livestock food supplement lysine and for citric acid. An acting assistant attorney general for antitrust said, "In essence, greed, simple greed, replaced any sense of corporate decency or integrity" at ADM.[29]

All of the above are examples of immoral management where executives' decisions or actions were self-centered, actively opposed to what is right, focused on achieving organizational success at whatever the cost, and cutting corners where it was useful. These decisions were made without regard to the possible consequences of such concerns as honesty or fairness to others.

Moral Management

At the opposite extreme from immoral management is moral management. ***Moral management*** conforms to high standards of ethical behavior or professional standards of conduct. Although it is not always crystal clear what ethical standards prevail, moral management strives to be ethical in terms of its focus on high ethical norms and professional standards of conduct, motives, goals, orientation toward the law, and general operating strategy.

In contrast to the selfish motives in immoral management, moral management aspires to succeed, but only within the confines of sound ethical precepts—that is, standards predicated on such norms as fairness, justice, and due process. Moral management's motives, therefore, might be termed fair, balanced, or unselfish.

Organizational goals continue to stress profitability, but only within the confines of legal obedience and sensitivity to ethical standards. Moral management, therefore, pursues its objectives of profitability, legality, and ethics as both required and desirable. Moral management would not pursue profits at the expense of the law and sound ethics. Indeed, the focus here would be not only on the letter of the law but on the spirit of the law as well. The law would be viewed as a minimal standard of ethical behavior, because moral management strives to operate at a level above what the law mandates.

Operating Strategy

The operating strategy of moral management is to live by sound ethical standards, seeking out only those economic opportunities that the organization or management can pursue within the confines of ethical behavior. The organization assumes a leadership position when ethical dilemmas arise. The central question guiding moral management's actions, decisions, and behaviors is, *"Will this action, decision, behavior, or practice be fair to all stakeholders involved as well as to the organization?"*

Lynn Sharp Paine has set forth what she calls an "integrity strategy" that closely resembles the moral management model.[30] The integrity strategy is characterized by a conception of ethics as the driving force of an organization. Ethical values shape management's search for opportunities, the design of organizational systems, and the decision-making process. Ethical values in the integrity strategy provide a common frame of reference and serve to unify different functions, lines of business, and employee groups. Organizational ethics, in this view, helps to define what an organization is and what it stands for. Some common features of an integrity strategy include the following,[31] which are all consistent with the moral management model:

- Guiding values and commitments make sense and are clearly communicated.

- Company leaders are personally committed, credible, and willing to take action on the values they espouse.

- Espoused values are integrated into the normal channels of management decision making.

- The organization's systems and structures support and reinforce its values.

- All managers have the skills, knowledge, and competencies to make ethically sound decisions on a daily basis.

Each year, *Business Ethics* magazine gives its Annual Business Ethics Awards. Considering the criteria for these awards is useful, because these criteria are consistent with moral management as we have been describing it. *Business Ethics'* award criteria require a company to meet many, although not necessarily all, of the following criteria:[32]

- Be a leader in the company's field, showing the way ethically.

- Sponsor programs or initiatives in responsibility that demonstrate sincerity and ongoing vibrancy, and reach deep into the company.

- Be a significant presence on the national scene, so the company's ethical behavior sends a loud signal.

- Stand out in at least one area; a company need not be perfect, nor even exemplary, in all areas.

- Demonstrate the ability to face a recent challenge and overcome it with integrity.

Note that *Business Ethics* does not expect companies to be perfect in all their actions. Likewise, the moral management model acknowledges that a firm may exhibit moral management by overcoming a challenge with integrity.

Illustrative Cases

Moral management may be illustrated by one of the 1997 Business Ethics Award winners—Medtronic, a Minneapolis-based company that makes medical devices and technologies, from pain-blocking neurostimulators and implantable drug-delivery systems to the world's most-prescribed cardiac pacemakers. Medtronic is a highly successful, highly profitable health care company. At the heart of Medtronic's success is the unwavering devotion of its 13,000 employees, working in more than 120 countries, to the highest possible legal, moral, and ethical standards.[33]

One example of Medtronic's leadership is its Compliance Program. This program is designed to ensure that every Medtronic employee lives up to the company's Key Corporate Policies, which are the company's legal and ethical standards of conduct. Each of the 4,000 employees who comes into contact with Medtronic customers directly is annually required to fill out a 12-page questionnaire and sign the company's code of conduct. Medtronic also has a telephone hotline that enables its employees to report ethics problems anonymously. One of the company's newest initiatives, which it is working on with other medical technology companies, is to establish uniform codes of conduct for doing business in foreign countries.

One story from the company's lore about ethics involved a former president of Medtronic Europe. The president had approved "promotional funds" that found their way into the Swiss bank account of a key customer. The president pleaded with his CEO to "let us do business the way the Europeans do." Instead, the president was fired.

Another excellent example of moral management taking the initiative in displaying ethical leadership was provided by McCulloch Corporation, a manufacturer of chain saws. Chain saws are notoriously dangerous. The Consumer Product Safety Commission one year estimated that there were 123,000 medically attended injuries involving chain saws, up from 71,000 5 years earlier. In spite of these statistics, the Chain Saw Manufacturers Association fought mandatory safety standards. The association claimed that the accident statistics were inflated and did not offer any justification for mandatory regulations. Manufacturers support voluntary standards, although some of them say that when chain brakes, major safety devices, are offered as an option, they do not sell. Apparently, consumers do not have adequate knowledge of the risks inherent in using chain saws.

McCulloch became dissatisfied with the Chain Saw Manufacturers Association's refusal to support higher standards of safety and withdrew from it. Chain brakes have been standard on McCulloch saws since 1975 and are mandatory for most saws produced in Finland, Britain, and Australia. A Swedish Company, Husqvarna, Inc., now installs chain brakes on saws it sells in the United States. Statistics from the Quebec

Logging Association and from Sweden demonstrate that kickback-related accidents were reduced by about 80 percent after the mandatory installation of safety standards, including chain brakes.[34]

McCulloch is an example of moral management. After attempting and failing to persuade its association to adopt a higher ethical standard that would greatly reduce injuries, it took a courageous action and withdrew from the association. This is a prime example of moral leadership.

Another well-known case of moral management occurred when Merck & Co., the pharmaceutical firm, invested millions of dollars to develop a drug for treating "river blindness," a Third World disease that was affecting almost 18 million people. Seeing that no government or aid organization was agreeing to buy the drug, Merck pledged to supply the drug for free forever. Merck's recognition that no effective mechanism existed to distribute the drug led to its decision to go far beyond industry practice and organize a committee to oversee the drug's distribution.[35]

We should stress at this time that not all organizations now engaging in moral management have done so all along. These companies sometimes arrived at this posture after years or decades of rising consumer expectations, increased government regulations, lawsuits, and pressure from social and consumer activists. We must think of moral management, therefore, as a desirable posture that in many instances has evolved over periods of several years. If we hold management to an idealistic 100 percent historical moral purity test, no management will fill the bill. Rather, we should consider moral those managements that now see the enlightened self-interest of responding in accordance with the moral management model.

Amoral Management

Amoral management is not just a middle position on a continuum between immoral and moral management. Conceptually it has been positioned between the other two, but it is different in kind from both. There are two kinds of amoral management. First, there is *intentional amoral management*. Amoral managers of this type do not factor ethical considerations into their decisions, actions, and behaviors because they believe business activity resides outside the sphere to which moral judgments apply. These managers are neither moral nor immoral. They simply think that different rules apply in business than in other realms of life. Intentionally amoral managers are in a distinct minority today. At one time, however, as managers first began to think about reconciling business practices with sound ethics, some managers adopted this stance. A few intentionally amoral managers are still around, but they are a vanishing breed in today's ethically conscious world.

Second, there is *unintentional amoral management*. Like intentionally amoral managers, unintentionally amoral managers do not think about business activity in ethical terms. These managers simply are casual about, careless about, or inattentive to the fact that their decisions and actions may have negative or deleterious effects on others. These managers lack ethical perception and moral awareness; that is, they blithely go through their organizational lives not thinking that what they are doing has an ethical dimension. These managers are well intentioned but are either too insensitive or too self-absorbed to consider the effects of their behavior on others.

Amoral management pursues profitability as its goal but does not cognitively attend to moral issues that may be intertwined with that pursuit. If there is an ethical guide to amoral management, it would be the marketplace as constrained by law—the letter of the law, not the spirit. The amoral manager sees the law as the parameters within which business pursuits take place.

Operating Strategy
The operating strategy of amoral management is not to bridle managers with excessive ethical structure but to permit free rein within the unspoken but understood tenets of the free enterprise system. Personal ethics may periodically or unintentionally enter into managerial decisions, but it does not preoccupy management. Furthermore, the impact of decisions on others is an afterthought, if it ever gets considered at all. Amoral management represents a model of decision making in which the managers' ethical mental gears, to the extent that they are present, are placed in neutral. The key management question guiding decision making is, *"Can we make money with this action, decision, or behavior?"* Note that the question does not imply an active or implicit intent to be either moral or immoral.

Paine has articulated a "compliance strategy" that is consistent with amoral management. The compliance strategy, as contrasted with her earlier discussed integrity strategy, is more focused on obedience to the law as its driving force. The compliance strategy is lawyer driven and is oriented not toward ethics or integrity but more toward compliance with existing regulatory and criminal law. The compliance approach uses deterrence as its underlying assumption. This approach envisions managers as rational maximizers of self-interest, responsive to the personal costs and benefits of their choices, yet indifferent to the moral legitimacy of those choices.[36]

Figure 4–6 provides a summary of the major characteristics of amoral management and the other two models that have been identified and discussed.

Illustrative Cases
There are perhaps more examples of amoral management than any other kind. When police departments stipulated that recruits must be at least 5'10" tall and weigh at least 180 pounds, they were making an amoral decision, because they were not considering the deleterious exclusion this would impose on women and other groups who do not, on average, attain that height and weight. When companies decided to use scantily clad young women to advertise autos, men's cologne, and other products, these companies were not thinking of the degrading and demeaning characterization that would result from their ethically neutral decision. When firms decided to do business in South Africa years ago, their decisions were neither moral nor immoral, but a major, unanticipated consequence of these decisions was the appearance of capitalistic (or United States) approval of apartheid.

Nestlé's *original* decision to market infant formula in Third World countries (see Chapter 3) could have initially been an amoral decision. Nestlé may not have considered the detrimental effects such a seemingly innocent business decision would have on mothers and babies in a land of impure water, poverty, and illiteracy.

It could be argued that the video-game industry has been amoral because it has developed games that glorify extreme violence, sexism, and aggression, with little attention to how these games impact the young people who become addicted to them. In *Mortal Kombat,* for example, players rip out an opponent's still-beating heart or bloody spinal cord. In *Night Trap,* Ninja-like vampires stalk minimally dressed, cowering coeds and drill through their necks with power tools. These "games" have

FIGURE 4–6   Three Approaches to Management Ethics

Organizational Characteristics		Immoral Management	Amoral Management	Moral Management
	Ethical Norms	Management decisions, actions, and behavior imply a positive and active opposition to what is moral (ethical). Decisions are discordant with accepted ethical principles. An active negation of what is moral is implied.	Management is neither moral nor immoral, but decisions lie outside the sphere to which moral judgments apply. Management activity is outside or beyond the moral order of a particular code. May imply a lack of ethical perception and moral awareness.	Management activity conforms to a standard of ethical, or right, behavior. Conforms to accepted professional standards of conduct. Ethical leadership is commonplace on the part of management.
	Motives	Selfish. Management cares only about its or the company's gains.	Well-intentioned but selfish in the sense that impact on others is not considered.	Good. Management wants to succeed but only within the confines of sound ethical precepts (fairness, justice, due process).
	Goals	Profitability and organizational success at any price.	Profitability. Other goals are not considered.	Profitability within the confines of legal obedience and ethical standards.
	Orientation Toward Law	Legal standards are barriers that management must overcome to accomplish what it wants.	Law is the ethical guide, preferably the letter of the law. The central question is what we can do legally.	Obedience toward letter and spirit of the law. Law is a minimal ethical behavior. Prefer to operate well above what law mandates.
	Strategy	Exploit opportunities for corporate gain. Cut corners when it appears useful.	Give managers free rein. Personal ethics may apply but only if managers choose. Respond to legal mandates if caught and required to do so.	Live by sound ethical standards. Assume leadership position when ethical dilemmas arise. Enlightened self-interest.

SOURCE: Archie B. Carroll, "In Search of the Moral Manager," *Business Horizons* (March/April, 1987), 12. Copyright © 1987 by the Foundation for the School of Business at Indiana University. Used with permission.

changed significantly since Atari introduced the popular video game "Pong" in 1972, a digital version of Ping-Pong consisting of a square ball and two rectangular paddles.[37]

Today's video games have plenty of critics—educators, psychologists, politicians—who worry about the multitude of themes that are bloodthirsty and sexist and have foul language. About the only response from the game makers has been to introduce an age-based rating system similar to that now used in the movie industry. The game makers' view seems to be that their games are legal and harmless and that little else is left to say.

A final useful illustration of amoral management involves the 1992 case of Sears Roebuck & Co. and its automotive service business. Paine describes how consumers and attorney generals in 40 states accused the company of misleading consumers and selling them unneeded parts and services.[38] In the face of declining revenues and a shrinking market share, Sears' executives put into place new goals, quotas, and incentives for auto-center service personnel. Service employees were told to meet product-specific and service-specific quotas—sell so many brake jobs, batteries, and front-end alignments—or face consequences such as reduced working hours or transfers. Some employees spoke of the "pressure" they felt to generate business. Although Sears' executives did not set out to defraud customers, they put into place a commission system that led to Sears' employees feeling pressure to sell products and services that consumers did not need. Soon after the complaints against Sears occurred, CEO Edward Brennan acknowledged that management had created an environment in which mistakes were made, although no intent to deceive consumers had existed. Fortunately, Sears eliminated its quota system as a partial remedy to the problem.[39]

The Sears case is a classic example of amoral management—a well-intentioned company slipping into questionable practices because it just did not think ethically. The company simply did not think through the impacts that its strategic decisions would have on important stakeholders.

Two Hypotheses

There are numerous other examples of amoral management, but the ones presented above should suffice to illustrate the point. A thorough study has not been conducted to ascertain precisely what proportions of managers each model represents in the total management population. One hypothesis is that the distribution might approximate a normal curve, with the amoral group occupying the large middle part of the curve and the moral and immoral categories occupying the smaller tails of the curve. A limited survey of managers, however, revealed findings contrary to this hypothesis. In this study, managers estimated that among other managers, about 70 percent were moral, 20 percent were amoral, and 10 percent were immoral.[40] Because this limited study polled just under 50 managers in a specific industry, we should not generalize the results.

Equally disturbing as the belief that the amoral management style is common among managers today is an alternative hypothesis that, within the average manager, these three models may operate at various times and under various circumstances. That is, the average manager may be amoral most of the time but may slip into a moral or an immoral mode on occasion, based on a variety of impinging factors. This view cannot be empirically supported at this time, but it does provide an interesting perspective for managers to think about. This perspective would be somewhat similar to the situational ethics argument that has been around for some time.

The more serious social problem in organizations today seems to be this group of well-intended managers who for one reason or another subscribe to or live out the amoral ethic. These are managers who are driven primarily by the profitability or

ETHICS IN PRACTICE

The Cook Did It

For the past 5 years I have worked at a restaurant in my hometown. During my span with the restaurant, I have become very loyal to them, our store in particular, and many times I find myself obligated to protect it. One night last summer, as I was cleaning up out front, I noticed that one of the cooks had several cans of the bug spray that we use at night. He came up to my area through the kitchen and set down three or four cans out of sight of the manager. He asked me to hand him the cans when he came around to the front. I asked him what he was doing with the cans, and he said he was taking them home to use them. I couldn't believe it. So I said, "No, if you are going to steal from this store then I'm certainly not helping you!"

1. Did I have an ethical obligation to step in and take action when it was not my place to do so?

2. Would it have been amoral or immoral to do nothing?

3. Should I have told management and looked like a tattletale in front of my peers? What should I have done in this situation?

Contributed by Ann Winstead

bottom-line ethos, which regards economic success as the exclusive barometer of organizational and personal achievement. They are basically good people, but they essentially see the competitive business world as ethically neutral. Until this group of managers moves toward the moral ethic, we will continue to see American business and other organizations criticized as they have been in the past two decades.

To connect the three models of management morality with concepts introduced earlier, we show in Figure 4–7 how the components of corporate social responsibility (Chapter 2) would likely be viewed by managers using each of the three models of management morality, and we illustrate in Figure 4–8 how managers using the three

FIGURE 4–7   Three Models of Management Morality and Their Views on CSR

Models of Management Morality	Components of the CSR Definition			
	Economic Responsibility	*Legal Responsibility*	*Ethical Responsibility*	*Philanthropic Responsibility*
Immoral Management	✓✓✓	✓		✓
Amoral Management	✓✓✓	✓✓	✓	✓
Moral Management	✓✓✓	✓✓✓	✓✓✓	✓✓✓

Weighting code:
√ = token consideration (appearances only)
√√ = moderate consideration
√√√ = significant consideration

FIGURE 4–8 The Moral Management Models and Acceptance of Stakeholder Thinking (SHT)		
Moral Management Model	**Acceptance of Stakeholder Thinking (SHT)**	**Stakeholder Thinking Posture Embraced**
Immoral Management	SHT rejected: management is self-absorbed.	SHT rejected, not deemed useful. Accepts profit maximization model but does not really pursue it.
Amoral Management	SHT accepted: narrow view (minimum number of stakeholders considered).	Instrumental view of SHT prevails. How will it help management?
Moral Management	SHT enthusiastically embraced: wider view (maximum number of stakeholders considered).	Normative view of SHT prevails. SHT is fully embraced in all decision making.

models would probably embrace or reject the stakeholder concept or stakeholder thinking (Chapter 3). It is hoped that these depictions of the interrelationships among these concepts will make them easier to understand and appreciate.

MAKING MORAL MANAGEMENT ACTIONABLE

The characteristics of immoral, moral, and amoral management discussed in this chapter should provide some useful benchmarks for managerial self-analysis, because self-analysis and introspection will ultimately be the way in which managers will recognize the need to move from the immoral or amoral ethic to the moral ethic. Numerous others have suggested management training for business ethics; therefore, this prescription will not be further developed here, although it has great potential. However, until senior management fully embraces the concepts of moral management, the transformation in organizational culture that is so essential for moral management to blossom, thrive, and flourish will not take place. Ultimately, senior management has the leadership responsibility to show the way to an ethical organizational climate by leading the transition from amoral to moral management, whether this is done by business ethics training and workshops, codes of conduct, corporate ombudspeople, tighter financial controls, more ethically sensitive decision-making processes, or leadership by example.

Underlying all these efforts, however, needs to be the fundamental recognition that amoral management exists and that it is an undesirable condition that can be certainly, if not easily, remedied. Most notably, organizational leaders must acknowledge that amoral management is a morally vacuous condition that can be quite easily disguised as just an innocent, practical, bottom-line philosophy—something to take pride in. Amoral management is, however, and will continue to be, the bane of American management until it is recognized for what it really is and until managers take steps to overcome it. American managers are not all "bad guys," as they so frequently are portrayed, but the idea that managerial decision making can be ethically neutral is bankrupt and no longer tenable in the society of the new millennium.[41]

DEVELOPING MORAL JUDGMENT

It is helpful to know something about how individuals, whether they are managers or employees, develop moral (or ethical) judgment. Perhaps if we knew more about this process we could better understand our own behavior and the behavior of those around us and those we manage. A good starting point is to come to appreciate what psychologists have to say about how we as individuals develop morally. The major research on this point is Kohlberg's levels of moral development.[42] After this discussion, we will consider other sources of a manager's values.

Levels of Moral Development

An American psychologist, Lawrence Kohlberg has done extensive research into the topic of *moral development.* He has concluded, on the basis of 20 years of research, that there is a general sequence of three levels (each with two stages) through which people evolve in learning to think morally. Although his theory is not universally accepted, there is widespread practical usage of his levels of moral development, and this suggests a broad if not unanimous consensus. Figure 4–9 illustrates Kohlberg's three levels and six stages.

Level 1: Preconventional Level

At the *preconventional level of moral development,* which is typically descriptive of how people behave as infants and children, the focus is mainly on *self.* As an infant starts to grow, his or her main behavioral reactions are in response to punishments and rewards. Stage 1 is the reaction-to-punishment stage. If you want a child to do something (such as stay out of the street) at a very early age, spanking or scolding is typically needed. The orientation at this stage is toward avoidance of pain.

As the child gets a bit older, rewards start working. Stage 2 is the seeking-of-rewards stage. The child begins to see some connection between being "good" (that is, doing what Mom or Dad wants the child to do) and some reward that may be forthcoming. The reward may be parental praise or something tangible, such as candy, extra TV time, or a trip to the movies. At this preconventional level, children do not really understand the moral idea of "right" and "wrong" but rather learn to behave according to the consequences—punishment or reward—that are likely to follow. Like children, adults frequently learn to behave in appropriate ways in response to threats of punishment or promises of reward.

Level 2: Conventional Level

As the child gets older, she or he learns that there are *others* whose ideas or welfare ought to be considered. Initially, these others include family and friends. At the *conventional level of moral development,* the individual learns the importance of conforming to the conventional norms of society.

The conventional level is composed of two stages. Stage 3 has been called the "good boy/nice girl" morality stage. The child learns that there are some rewards (such as feelings of loyalty, warmth, acceptance, or trust) for living up to what is expected by family and peers, so the individual begins to conform to what is generally expected of a good son, daughter, sister, brother, friend, and so on.

Stage 4 is the law-and-order morality stage. Not only does the individual learn to respond to family, friends, the school, and the church, as in Stage 3, but the individual

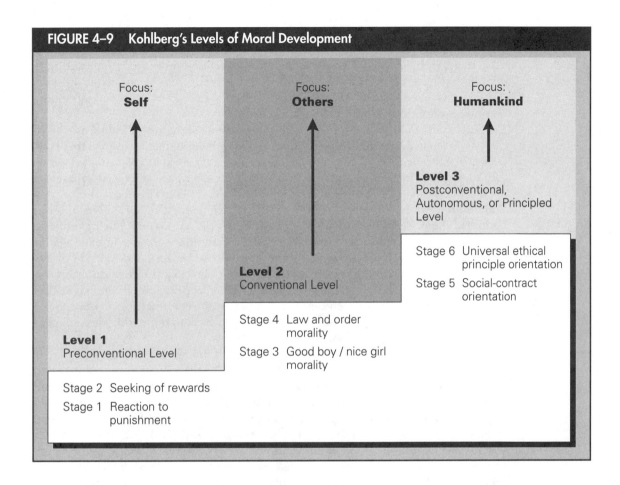

FIGURE 4–9   Kohlberg's Levels of Moral Development

Focus: **Self**

Focus: **Others**

Focus: **Humankind**

Level 3
Postconventional,
Autonomous, or Principled
Level

Stage 6 Universal ethical
principle orientation

Stage 5 Social-contract
orientation

Level 2
Conventional Level

Stage 4 Law and order
morality

Stage 3 Good boy / nice girl
morality

Level 1
Preconventional Level

Stage 2 Seeking of rewards

Stage 1 Reaction to
punishment

now recognizes that there are certain norms in society (in school, in the theater, in the mall, in stores, in the car) that are expected or needed if society is to function in an orderly fashion. Thus, the individual becomes socialized or acculturated into what being a good citizen means. These rules for living include not only the actual laws (don't run a red light, don't walk until the "Walk" light comes on) but also other, less official norms (don't smoke in the classroom, don't break into line, be sure to tip the server). At Stage 4 the individual sees that she or he is part of a larger social system and that to function in and be accepted by this social system requires a considerable degree of acceptance of and conformity to the norms and standards of society.

Level 3: Postconventional, Autonomous, or Principled Level

At this third level, which Kohlberg argues few people reach (and those who do reach it have trouble staying there), the focus moves beyond those "others" who are of immediate importance to the individual to *humankind* as a whole. At the *postconventional level of moral development*, the individual develops a notion of right and wrong that is more mature than the conventionally articulated notion. Thus, it is sometimes called the level at which moral principles become self-accepted, not because they are held by society but because the individual now perceives and embraces them as "right."

Kohlberg's third level seems to be easier to understand as a whole than when its two individual stages are considered. Stage 5 is the social-contract orientation. At this stage, right action is thought of in terms of general individual rights and standards that have been critically examined and agreed upon by society as a whole. There is a clear awareness of the relativism of personal values and a corresponding emphasis on processes for reaching consensus.

Stage 6 is the universal-ethical-principle orientation. Here the individual uses his or her conscience in accord with self-chosen ethical principles that are hoped to be universal, comprehensive, and consistent. These universal principles (such as the Golden Rule) might be focused on such ideals as justice, human rights, and social welfare.

Kohlberg suggests that at Level 3 the individual is able to rise above the conventional level where "rightness" and "wrongness" are defined by societal institutions and that she or he is able to defend or justify her or his actions on some higher basis. For example, in our society the law tells us we should not discriminate against minorities. A Level 2 manager might not discriminate because to do so is to violate the law. A Level 3 manager would not discriminate but might offer a different reason—for example, it is wrong *not* to consider universal principles of human justice. Part of the difference between Levels 2 and 3, therefore, is traceable to our motivation for the course of action we take. This takes us back to our earlier discussion of motivation as one of the important ethics questions.

Our discussion to this point may have suggested that we are at Level 1 as infants, at Level 2 as youths, and, finally, at Level 3 as adults. There is some approximate correspondence between chronological age and Levels 1 and 2, but the important point should be made again that Kohlberg thinks many of us as adults never get beyond Level 2. The idea of getting to Level 3 as managers is desirable, because it would require us to think about people, products, and markets at a level higher than that generally attained by conventional society. However, even if we never get there, Level 3 urges us to continually ask "What ought to be?" And the first two levels tell us a lot about moral development that should be useful to us as managers. If we state the issue in terms of the question, "Why do managers behave ethically?" we might infer conclusions from Kohlberg that look like those in Figure 4–10.

Feminist Views

One of the major criticisms of Kohlberg's research was set forth by Carol Gilligan. Gilligan argued that Kohlberg's conclusions may accurately depict the stages of moral development among men, whom he used as his research subjects, but that his findings are not generalizable to women.[43] According to Gilligan's view, men tend to deal with moral issues in terms that are impersonal, impartial, and abstract. Examples might include the principles of justice and rights that Kohlberg argues are relevant at the postconventional level. Women, on the other hand, perceive themselves to be part of a network of relationships with family and friends and thus are more focused on relationship maintenance and hurt avoidance when they confront moral issues. For women, then, morality is more a matter of caring and showing responsibility toward those involved in their relationships than in adhering to abstract or impersonal principles, such as justice.

According to Gilligan, women move in and out of three moral levels.[44] At the first level, the *self* is the sole object of concern. At the second level, the chief desire is to

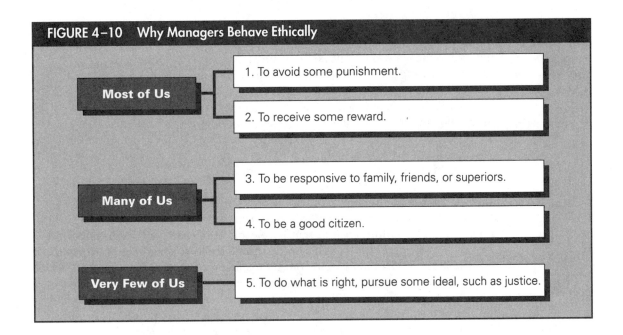

FIGURE 4–10   Why Managers Behave Ethically

Most of Us
1. To avoid some punishment.
2. To receive some reward.

Many of Us
3. To be responsive to family, friends, or superiors.
4. To be a good citizen.

Very Few of Us
5. To do what is right, pursue some ideal, such as justice.

establish *connections* and *participate* in social life. In other words, maintaining relationships or directing one's thoughts toward others becomes dominant. Gilligan says that this is the conventional notion of women. At the third level, women recognize their *own* needs and the needs of *others*—those with whom they have relationships. Gilligan goes on to say that women never settle completely at one level. As they attain moral maturity, they do more of their thinking and make more of their decisions at the third level. This level requires care for others as well as care for oneself. In this view, morality moves away from the legalistic, self-centered approach that feminists say characterizes traditional ethics.

Some recent research does not show that moral development varies by gender in the fashion described by Gilligan. However, it does support Gilligan's claim that a different perspective toward moral issues is sometimes used. Apparently, both men and women sometimes employ an impartial or impersonal moral-rules perspective and sometimes they employ a care-and-responsibility perspective. This "care perspective" is still at an early stage of research, but it is useful to know that perspectives other than those found by Kohlberg are being considered.[45] More will be said about feminist theory in the next chapter.

Sources of a Manager's Values

In addition to considering the levels of moral development as an explanation of how and why people behave ethically, it is also useful to look at the sources of a manager's values. Ethics and values are intimately related. We referred earlier to ethics as the rightness or wrongness of behavior. More precisely, ethics is the set of moral principles or values that drives behavior. Thus, the rightness or wrongness of behavior really turns out to be a manifestation of the ethical beliefs held by the individual. *Values,* on the other hand, are the individual's concepts of the relative worth, utility, or importance of certain ideas. Values reflect what the individual considers important in the larger scheme of things. One's values, therefore, shape one's ethics. Because this is so, it is important to understand the many different value-shaping forces that influence managers.

The increasing pluralism of the society in which we live has exposed managers to a great number of values of many different kinds, and this has resulted in ethical diversity. We can examine the sources of a manager's values by considering both forces that come from outside the organization to shape or influence the manager and those that emanate from within the organization. This, unfortunately, is not as simply done as we would like, because some sources are difficult to pinpoint. It should lend some order to our discussion, however.

Sources External to the Organization

When we talk about the *external sources* of a manager's values, we are referring to those broad sociocultural values that have evolved in society over a long period of time. Although current events (kickbacks, fraud, bribery cases) seem to affect these historic values by bringing specific ones into clearer focus at a given time, these values are rather enduring and change slowly.

George Steiner has stated that "every executive is at the center of a web of values" and that there are five principal repositories of values influencing businesspeople. These five include *religious, philosophical, cultural, legal,* and *professional values.*[46]

Religion has long been a basic source of morality in American society, as in most societies. Religion and morality are so intertwined that William Barclay relates them for definitional purposes: "Ethics is the bit of religion that tells us how we ought to behave."[47] The biblical tradition of Judeo-Christian theology forms the core for much of what we believe today about the importance of work, the concept of fairness, and the dignity of the individual.

Philosophy and various philosophical systems are also external sources of the manager's values. Beginning with preachments of the ancient Greeks, philosophers have claimed to demonstrate that reason can provide us with principles or morals in the same way it gives us the principles of mathematics. John Locke argued that morals are mathematically demonstrable, although he never explained how.[48] Aristotle with his Golden Rule and his doctrine of the mean, Kant with his categorical imperative, Bentham with his pain and pleasure calculus, and modern-day existentialists have shown us time and again the influence of various kinds of reasons for ethical choice.

Culture, that broad synthesis of societal norms and values emanating from everyday living, has also had an impact on the manager's thinking. Modern examples of culture include music, movies, and television. The melting-pot culture of the United States is a potpourri of norms, customs, and rules that defy summarization.

The *legal system* has been and continues to be one of the most powerful forces defining what is ethical and what is not for managers. This is true even though ethical behavior generally is that which occurs over and above legal dictates. As stated earlier, the law represents the codification of what the society considers right and wrong. Although we as members of society do not completely agree with every law in existence, there is typically more consensus for law than for ethics. Law, then, "mirrors the ideas of the entire society."[49] Law represents a minimum ethic of behavior but does not encompass all the ethical standards of behavior. Law addresses only the grossest violations of society's sense of right and wrong and thus is not adequate to describe completely all that is acceptable or unacceptable. Because it represents our official consensus ethic, however, its influence is pervasive and widely accepted.

Professional values are those emanating, for the most part, from professional organizations and societies that represent various jobs and positions. As such, they presumably articulate the ethical consensus of the leaders of those professions. For example, the Public Relations Society of America has a code of ethics that public relations executives have imposed on themselves as their own guide to behavior. The National Association of Realtors adopted its "Rules of Conduct" in 1913. Compliance with the code was first recommended for voluntary adoption and then made a condition of membership in 1924.[50] Professional values thus exert a more particularized impact on the manager than the four broader values discussed earlier.

In sum, several sources of values that are external to the organization come to bear on the manager. In addition to those mentioned, the manager is influenced by family, friends, acquaintances, and social events of the day. The manager thus comes to the workplace with a personal philosophy that is truly a composite of numerous interacting values that have shaped her or his views of the world, of life, and of business.

Sources Internal to the Organization

The external forces described above constitute the broad background or milieu against which a manager or an employee behaves or acts. They affect a person's personal views of the world and of business and help the person to formulate what is acceptable and unacceptable. There are, however, a number of less remote factors that help to channel the individual's behavior, and these grow out of the specific organizational experience itself. These *internal sources* of a manager's values (within the business organization) constitute more immediate and direct influences on one's behavior and decisions.

When an individual goes to work for an organization, a socialization process takes place in which the individual assumes the predominant values of that organization. The individual learns rather quickly that, to survive and to succeed, certain norms must be perpetuated and revered. There are several norms that are prevalent in business organizations, including *respect for the authority structure, loyalty, conformity, performance,* and *results.* Each of these norms may assume a major role in a person who subordinates her or his own standard of ethics to those of the organization. In fact, research suggests that these internal sources play a much more significant role in shaping business ethics than do the host of external sources we considered first.

Respect for the authority structure, loyalty, conformity, performance, and results have been historically almost synonymous with survival and success in business. When these influences are operating together, they form a composite ethic that is extremely persuasive in its impact on individual and group behavior. These values form the central motif of organizational activity and direction.

Underlying the first three norms is the focus on *performance* and *results.* Carl Madden referred to this as the "calculus of the bottom line."[51] One does not need to study business organizations for long to recognize that the bottom line—profits—is the sacred value that seems to take precedence over all others. "Profits now" rather than later seems to be the orientation that spells success for managers and employees alike. Respect for authority, loyalty, and conformity become means to an end, although one could certainly find organizations and people who see these as legitimate ends in themselves. We will examine these internal sources in more detail in the next chapter.

ELEMENTS OF MORAL JUDGMENT

Managers must come to appreciate the key elements in making moral judgments. This is a notion central to the transition from the amoral management condition to the moral management condition. According to Charles Powers and David Vogel, there are six major elements or capacities that are essential to making moral judgments: (1) moral imagination, (2) moral identification and ordering, (3) moral evaluation, (4) tolerance of moral disagreement and ambiguity, (5) integration of managerial and moral competence, and (6) a sense of moral obligation.[52]

Moral Imagination

Moral imagination refers to the ability to perceive that a web of competing economic relationships is, at the same time, a web of moral or ethical relationships. Developing moral imagination means not only becoming sensitive to ethical issues in business decision making but also developing the perspective of searching out subtle places where people are likely to be detrimentally affected by decision making or behaviors of managers. This is a necessary first step but is extremely challenging because of prevailing methods of evaluating managers on bottom-line results. It is essential before anything else can happen, however.

Moral Identification and Ordering

Moral identification and ordering refers to the ability to discern the relevance or non-relevance of moral factors that are introduced into a decision-making situation. Are the moral issues real or just rhetorical? The ability to see moral issues as issues that can be dealt with is at stake here. Once moral issues have been identified, they must be ranked, or ordered, just as economic or technological issues are ranked during the decision-making process. A manager must not only develop this skill through experience but also finely hone it through repetition. And it is only through repetition that this skill can be developed.

Several decision environments in which moral identification and ordering have become important in recent years include the issue of business or plant closings, the future of affirmative action programs, the status of employees' "right to know" what toxic chemicals they are being exposed to, and the question of how to deal with whistle-blowers. In each of these instances, the ability to identify and order moral issues is a key to their effective handling. To decide wrongly opens the firm up to extensive public criticism and the threat of endless lawsuits. Moral identification and ordering are vital skills that need to be developed in order to practice stakeholder management.

Moral Evaluation

Once issues have been identified and ordered, evaluations must be made. *Moral evaluation* is the practical phase of moral judgment and entails essential skills, such as coherence and consistency, that have proved to be effective principles in other contexts. What managers need to do here is to understand the importance of clear principles, develop processes for weighing ethical factors, and develop the ability to identify what the likely moral as well as economic outcomes of a decision will be.

The real challenge in moral evaluation is to integrate the concern for others into organizational goals, purposes, and legitimacy. In the final analysis, though, the manager may not know the "right" answer or solution, although moral sensitivity has been introduced into the process. The important point is that amorality has not prevailed or driven the decision process.

Tolerance of Moral Disagreement and Ambiguity

An objection managers often have to ethics discussions is the amount of disagreement generated and the volume of ambiguity that must be tolerated in thinking ethically. This must be accepted, however, for there is no other way. To be sure, managers need closure and precision in their decisions. But the situation is never clear in moral discussions, any more than it is in many traditional but more familiar decision contexts of managers, such as introducing a new product based on limited test marketing, choosing a new executive for a key position, deciding which of a number of excellent computer systems to install, or making a strategic decision based on instincts. All of these are precarious decisions, but managers have become accustomed to making them in spite of the disagreements and ambiguity that prevail among those involved in the decision or within the individual.

In a real sense, the *tolerance of moral disagreement and ambiguity* is simply an extension of a managerial talent or facility that is present in practically all decision-making situations managers face. But managers are more unfamiliar with this special kind of decision making because of a lack of practice.

Integration of Managerial and Moral Competence

The *integration of managerial and moral competence* underlies all that we have been discussing. Moral issues in management do not arise in isolation from traditional business decision making but right smack in the middle of it. The scandals that major corporations face today did not occur independently of the companies' economic activities but were embedded in a series of decisions that were made at various points in time and culminated from those earlier decisions. Therefore, moral competence is an integral part of managerial competence. And managers are learning—some the hard way—that there is a significant corporate, and in many instances personal, price to pay for their amorality. The amoral manager sees ethical decisions as isolated and independent of managerial decisions and competence, but the moral manager sees every evolving decision as one in which an ethical perspective must be integrated. This kind of future-looking view is an essential executive skill.

A Sense of Moral Obligation

The foundation for all the capacities we have discussed is a *sense of moral obligation* and integrity. This sense is the key to the process but is the most difficult to acquire. This sense requires the intuitive or learned understanding that moral fibers—a concern for fairness, justice, and due process to people, groups, and communities—are woven into the fabric of managerial decision making and are the integral components that hold systems together.

These qualities are perfectly consistent with, and indeed are essential prerequisites to, the free enterprise system as we know it today. One can go all the way back to Adam Smith and the foundation tenets of the free enterprise system and not find references to immoral or unethical practices as being elements that are needed for the system to work. Milton Friedman, our modern-day Adam Smith, even alluded to the importance of ethics when he stated that the purpose of business is "to make as much money as possible while conforming to the basic rules of society, both those embodied in the law and *those embodied in ethical custom.*"[53] The moral manager, then, has a sense of moral obligation and integrity that is the glue that holds together the decision-making process in which human welfare is inevitably at stake.

Figure 4–11 summarizes the six elements of moral judgment identified by Powers and Vogel as they might be seen by amoral and moral managers.

FIGURE 4–11   Elements of Moral Judgment in Amoral and Moral Managers

Amoral Managers	Moral Managers
Moral Imagination	
See a web of competing economic claims as just that and nothing more. Are insensitive to and unaware of the hidden dimensions of where people are likely to get hurt.	Perceive that a web of competing economic claims is simultaneously a web of moral relationships. Are sensitive to and hunt out the hidden dimensions of where people are likely to get hurt.
Moral Identification and Ordering	
See moral claims as squishy and not definite enough to order into hierarchies with other claims.	See which moral claims being made are relevant or irrelevant; order moral factors just as economic factors are ordered.
Moral Evaluation	
Are erratic in their application of ethics if it gets applied at all.	Are coherent and consistent in their normative reasoning.
Tolerance of Moral Disagreement and Ambiguity	
Cite ethical disagreement and ambiguity as reasons for forgetting ethics altogether.	Tolerate ethical disagreement and ambiguity while honestly acknowledging that decisions are not precise like mathematics but must finally be made nevertheless.
Integration of Managerial and Moral Competence	
See ethical decisions as isolated and independent of managerial decisions and managerial competence.	See every evolving decision as one in which a moral perspective must be integrated with a managerial one.
A Sense of Moral Obligation	
Have no sense of moral obligation and integrity that extends beyond managerial responsibility.	Have a sense of moral obligation and integrity that holds together the decision-making process in which human welfare is at stake.

SOURCE: Archie B. Carroll, "In Search of the Moral Manager," *Business Horizons* (March/April, 1987), 15. Copyright © 1987 by the Foundation for the School of Business at Indiana University. Used with permission.

SUMMARY

Business ethics has become a serious problem for the business community over the past several decades. Polls indicate that the public does not have a high regard for the ethics of managers. It is not easy to say whether business's ethics have declined or just seem to have done so because of increased media coverage and rising public expectations. Business ethics concerns the rightness or wrongness of managerial behavior, and these are not easy judgments to make. Multiple norms compete to determine which standards business behavior should be compared with. The conventional approach to business ethics was introduced as an initial way in which managers might think about ethical judgments. One major problem with this approach is that it is not clear which standards or norms should be used, and thus the conventional approach is susceptible to ethical relativism. Four important ethics questions are: (1) What is? (2) What ought to be? (3) How can we get from what is to what ought to be? and (4) What is our motivation in this transition?

Three models of management ethics are (1) immoral management, (2) moral management, and (3) amoral management. Amoral management is further classified into intentional and unintentional categories. A generally accepted view is that moral judgment develops according to the pattern described by Lawrence Kohlberg. His three levels of moral development are (1) preconventional, (2) conventional, and (3) postconventional, autonomous, or principled. Some research, however, suggests that there are gender differences between the perspectives taken by men and by women as they perceive and deal with moral issues. Managers' ethics are affected by sources of values external to the organization and sources from within the organization. The latter category includes respect for the authority structure, loyalty, conformity, and a concern for financial performance and results. Finally, six elements in developing moral judgment were presented. If the moral management model is to be realized, these six elements need to be developed.

KEY TERMS

amoral management
(page 112)

business ethics
(page 99)

conventional approach
to business ethics
(page 100)

descriptive ethics
(page 99)

ethical relativism
(page 104)

immoral management
(page 108)

moral development
(page 118)

moral management
(page 109)

normative ethics
(page 100)

DISCUSSION QUESTIONS

1. Give a definition of ethical business behavior, explain the components involved in making ethical decisions, and give an example from your personal experience of the difficulties involved in making these determinations.
2. To demonstrate that you understand the three models of management ethics— moral, immoral, and amoral—give an example, from your personal experience, of each type. Do you agree that amorality is a serious problem? Explain.

3. Give examples, from your personal experience, of Kohlberg's Levels 1, 2, and 3. If you do not think you have ever gotten to Level 3, give an example of what it might be like.

4. Compare your motivations to behave ethically with those listed in Figure 4–10. Do the reasons given in that figure agree with your personal assessment? Discuss the similarities and differences between Figure 4–10 and your personal assessment.

5. From your personal experience, give an example of a situation you have faced that would require one of the six elements of moral judgment.

ENDNOTES

1. Raymond C. Baumhart, "How Ethical Are Businessmen?" *Harvard Business Review* (July/August, 1961), 6ff.

2. Orr Kelly, "Corporate Crime: The Untold Story," *U.S. News & World Report* (September 6, 1982), 25–29.

3. *Ibid.*, 26–27.

4. David R. Francis, "Have Wall Street Ethics Slipped?" *The Christian Science Monitor* (August 21, 1991).

5. "Tale of the Tape: How GM One-Upped an Embarrassed NBC on Staged News Event," *The Wall Street Journal* (February 11, 1993), A1.

6. Michael Siconolfi, "Kidder Brokers Defect Amid Scandal, Taking $2 Billion in Client Accounts," *The Wall Street Journal* (August 30, 1994), C1. See also Terence P. Paré, "Jack Welch's Nightmare on Wall Street," *Fortune* (September 5, 1994), 40–48.

7. "Whose Values?" *Newsweek* (June 8, 1992), 19–22.

8. William J. Bennett (ed.), *The Book of Virtues: A Treasury of Great Moral Stories* (New York: Simon & Schuster, 1993).

9. "The Politics of Virtue: The Crusade Against America's Moral Decline," *Newsweek* (June 13, 1994), 30–39.

10. "America's New Crusade," *U.S. News & World Report* (August 1, 1994).

11. John Leo, "A Gump in Our Throat," *U.S. News & World Report* (August 8, 1994), 22.

12. Bari-Ellen Roberts, with Jack E. White, *Roberts vs. Texaco: A True Story of Race and Corporate America* (New York: Avon Books, 1998).

13. Matthew Cooper, "Tobacco: Turning Up the Heat," *Newsweek* (April 13, 1998), 50–51.

14. You may search the Gallup Organization, Gallup Poll Archives to study rankings of the ethics of various professional groups: *http://www.gallup.com/archive.htm.*

15. Max Ways, "A Plea for Perspective," in Clarence C. Walton (ed.), *The Ethics of Corporate Conduct* (Englewood Cliffs, NJ: Prentice Hall, 1977), 108.

16. Michael Blumenthal, "Business Morality Has Not Deteriorated—Society Has Changed," *The New York Times* (January 9, 1977).

17. *Ibid.*

18. Richard T. DeGeorge, *Business Ethics*, 4th ed. (New York: Prentice Hall, 1995), 20–21. Also see Rogene A. Buchholz and Sandra B. Rosenthal, *Business Ethics* (Upper Saddle River, NJ: Prentice Hall, 1998), 3.

19. *Ibid.*, DeGeorge, 15.

20. See, for example, Melissa Baucus and Janet Near, "Can Illegal Corporate Behavior Be Predicted? An Event History Analysis," *Academy of Management Journal* (Vol. 34, No. 1, 1991), 9–36; and P.L. Cochran and D. Nigh, "Illegal Corporate Behavior and the Question of Moral Agency," in William C. Frederick (ed.), *Research in Corporate Social Performance and Policy,* Vol. 9 (Greenwich, CT: JAI Press, 1987), 73–91.

21. Otto A. Bremer, "An Approach to Questions of Ethics in Business," Audenshaw Document No. 116 (North Hinksey, Oxford: The Hinksey Centre, Westminster College, 1983), 1–12.

22. *Ibid.*, 7.

23. *Ibid.*, 10–11.

24. Andrew Stark, "What's the Matter with Business Ethics?" *Harvard Business Review* (May–June, 1993), 7.

25. Most of the material in this section comes from Archie B. Carroll, "In Search of the Moral Manager," *Business Horizons* (March/April, 1987), 7–15.

26. Edward T. Pound and Bruce Ingersoll, "How Frigitemp Sank After It Was Looted by Top Management," *The Wall Street Journal* (September 20, 1984), 1.

27. "Honda Bribery Case Brings Guilty Pleas," *The Atlanta Journal* (March 15, 1994), D5.

28. Mark Maremont, "Blind Ambition: How the Pursuit of Results Got Out of Hand at Bausch & Lomb," *Business Week* (October 23, 1995), 78–92.

29. John Greenwald, "The Fix Was in at ADM," *Time* (October 28, 1996), 64.

30. Lynn Sharp Paine, "Managing for Organizational Integrity," *Harvard Business Review* (March–April, 1994), 106–117.

31. *Ibid.*, 111–112.

32. "Business Ethics Award Criteria," *Business Ethics* (November/December, 1997), 8.

33. Joel Makower, "Medtronic: Award for Excellence in Ethics," *Business Ethics* (November/December, 1997), 9.

34. Ray Vicker, "Rise in Chain-Saw Injuries Spurs Demand for Safety Standards, But Industry Resists," *The Wall Street Journal* (August 23, 1982), 17.

35. Business Enterprise Trust, 1994, "The Business Enterprise Trust Awards—1991 Recipients," unpublished announcement.

36. Paine, 109–113.

37. "Video-game Systems," *Consumer Reports* (December, 1996), 38–41.

38. Paine, 107–108.

39. *Ibid.*

40. Archie B. Carroll, "Management Ethics in the Workplace: An Investigation," *Management Quarterly* (Fall, 1989), 40–44.

41. Carroll, 1987, 7–15.

42. Lawrence Kohlberg, "The Claim to Moral Adequacy of a Highest Stage of Moral Judgment," *The Journal of Philosophy* (Vol. LXX, 1973), 630–646.

43. Carol Gilligan, *In a Different Voice: Psychological Theory and Women's Development* (Cambridge, MA: Harvard University Press, 1982).

44. Manuel G. Velasquez, *Business Ethics,* 3rd ed. (Englewood Cliffs, NJ: Prentice Hall, 1992), 30. Also see Brian K. Burton and Craig P. Dunn, "Feminist Ethics as Moral Grounding for Stakeholder Theory," *Business Ethics Quarterly* (Vol. 6, No. 2, 1996), 136–137.

45. See, for example, Robbin Derry, "Moral Reasoning in Work Related Conflicts," in William C. Frederick (ed.), *Research in Corporate Social Performance and Policy,* Vol. 9 (Greenwich, CT: JAI Press, 1987), 25–49. See also Velasquez, 30–31.

46. George A. Steiner, *Business and Society* (New York: Random House, 1975), 226.

47. William Barclay, *Ethics in a Permissive Society* (New York: Harper & Row, 1971), 13.

48. Marvin Fox, "The Theistic Bases of Ethics," in Robert Bartels (ed.), *Ethics in Business* (Columbus, OH: Bureau of Business Research, Ohio State University, 1963), 86–87.

49. Carl D. Fulda, "The Legal Basis of Ethics," in Bartels, 43–50.

50. H. Jackson Pontius, "Commentary on Code of Ethics of National Association of Realtors," in Ivan Hill (ed.), *The Ethical Basis of Economic Freedom* (Chapel Hill, NC: American Viewpoint, 1976), 353.

51. Carl Madden, "Forces Which Influence Ethical Behavior," in Clarence C. Walton (ed.), *The Ethics of Corporate Conduct* (Englewood Cliffs, NJ: Prentice Hall, 1977), 31–78.

52. Charles W. Powers and David Vogel, *Ethics in the Education of Business Managers* (Hastings-on-Hudson, NY: The Hastings Center, 1980), 40–45.

53. Milton Friedman, "The Social Responsibility of Business Is to Increase Its Profits," *The New York Times* (September, 1962), 126 (italics added).

5

Personal and Organizational Ethics

CHAPTER OBJECTIVES

After studying this chapter, you should be able to:

1 Understand the different levels at which business ethics may be addressed.

2 Enumerate and discuss principles of personal ethical decision making and ethical tests.

3 Identify the factors affecting an organization's moral climate and provide examples of these factors at work.

4 Describe and explain actions or strategies that management may take to improve an organization's ethical climate.

The ethical issues on which managers must make decisions are numerous and varied. The news media tend to focus on the major ethical scandals involving well-known corporate names. Therefore, Texaco, Dow Corning, Union Carbide, Prudential, and other such high-visibility firms attract considerable attention. The consequence of this is that many of the everyday, routine ethical dilemmas that managers face in medium-sized and small organizations are often overlooked.

A more typical situation for managers is to encounter day-to-day ethical dilemmas in such arenas as conflicts of interest, sexual harassment, inappropriate gifts to corporate personnel, unauthorized payments, affirmative action, customer dealings, and evaluation of personnel.

Unfortunately, many managers face these ethical quandaries on a daily basis but have no background or training in business ethics or ethical decision making to help them. A recent training program conducted by one of the authors illustrates this point well. The training session was in a continuing-education program, and the topic was business ethics. The 62 managers in attendance were asked how many of them had had formal business ethics training before—in college or in a company-sponsored program. Not one hand went up.

The ethics problem in business is, indeed, a serious one, but what is a manager to do? A relevant poll indicated that 71 percent of the managers surveyed responded that integrity was a major trait leading to success.[1] But how does one get personal integrity and, as a manager, how do you instill it in your organization and create an ethical organizational climate? Indeed, these are significant challenges. How, for example, do you keep your own personal ethics focused in such a way that you avoid immorality and amorality? What principles or guidelines are available to help you to be ethical? What specific strategies or approaches might be emphasized to bring about an ethical culture in your company or organization?

LEVELS AT WHICH ETHICAL ISSUES MAY BE ADDRESSED

As individuals and as managers we experience ethical pressures or dilemmas in a variety of settings. These pressures or dilemmas occur on different levels. These levels include the individual or personal level, the organizational level, the industry level, the societal level, and the international level. These levels cascade out from the individual to the global.

Personal Level

First, we experience *personal level* ethical challenges. These include situations we face in our personal lives that are generally outside the work context. Questions or dilemmas that we might face at the personal level include:

- Should I cheat on my income tax return by overinflating my charitable contributions?
- Should I return this extra pair of socks that the department store sent me by accident?
- Should I help my son with his research report when I know he is supposed to be working on his own?
- Should I notify my bank that it credited someone else's $500 to my checking account?
- Should I tell the cashier that she gave me change for a $20 bill when all I gave her was a $10 bill?

Organizational Level

We also confront ethical issues at the *organizational level* in our roles as managers or employees. Certainly, many of these issues are similar to those we face personally. However, these issues may carry consequences for the company's reputation and success in the community and also for the kind of ethical environment or culture that will prevail on a day-to-day basis at the office. The kinds of issues posed at the organizational level might include:

- Should I set high production goals for my subordinates to benefit the organization, even though I know it may cause them to cut corners to achieve such goals?
- Should I overlook the wrongdoings of my colleagues and subordinates in the interest of harmony in the company?
- Should I authorize a subordinate to violate company policy so that we can close the deal and both be rewarded?
- Should I make this product safer than I'm required to by law, because I know the legal standard is grossly inadequate?
- Should I accept this gift or bribe that is being given to me to close a big deal for the firm?
- What kinds of values am I communicating to my peers and subordinates by my behavior?

- Should I blow the whistle on the vice president of purchasing for the shady practices I think she or he is employing?

A survey on corporate ethics by The Conference Board found widespread agreement that the following represented current ethical issues at the organizational level for business: employee conflicts of interest, inappropriate gifts to corporate personnel, sexual harassment, unauthorized payments, affirmative action, employee privacy, and environmental issues.

Industry Level

A third level at which a manager might influence business ethics is the *industry level.* The industry might be stock brokerage, real estate, insurance, manufactured homes, financial services, telemarketing, automobiles, or a host of others. Related to the industry might be the *profession* of which an individual is a member—accounting, engineering, pharmacy, medicine, or law. Examples of questions that might pose ethical dilemmas at this level include the following:

- Is this practice that we stockbrokers have been using for years with prospective clients really fair and in their best interests?

- Is this safety standard we electrical engineers have passed really adequate for protecting the consumer in this age of do-it-yourselfers?

- Is this standard contract we mobile home sellers have adopted really in keeping with the financial disclosure laws that have recently been strengthened?

- As an accountant, is my profession really being honest with this new "generally accepted" principle, or are we just making it easy on ourselves and really neglecting the best interests of our clients?

Societal and International Levels

At the *societal and international levels* it becomes very difficult for the individual manager to have any *direct* effect on business ethics. However, managers acting in concert through their companies and trade and professional associations can definitely bring about high standards and constructive changes. Because the industry, societal, and international levels are quite removed from the actual practicing manager, we will focus our attention in this chapter primarily on the personal and organizational levels. The manager's greatest impact can be felt through what he or she does personally or as a member of the management team.

We should also note that managers have an important role to play as *ethical role models* for society. To the extent that they successfully convey to the general public that they believe in the importance of integrity in business and throughout society, managers may have a significant impact on society's general level of ethics and on the future course of the free enterprise system. In Chapter 6, we will deal with global ethics—a crucial topic that is increasing in importance with each passing year.

PERSONAL AND MANAGERIAL ETHICS

The point of departure for discussing personal and managerial ethics is the assumption that the individual wants to behave ethically or to improve his or her ethical behavior in personal or managerial situations. Keep in mind that each individual is a stakeholder of someone else. Someone else—a friend, a family member, an associate, or a businessperson—has a stake in your behavior; therefore, your ethics are important to them also. What we discuss here is aimed at those who desire to be ethical and are looking for help in doing so. All the difficulties with making ethical judgments that we discussed in the previous chapter are applicable.

Personal and managerial ethics, for the most part, entails making decisions. It typically confronts the individual with a conflict-of-interest situation. A conflict of interest is usually present when the individual has to choose between her or his interests and the interests of someone else or some other group (stakeholders). What it boils down to in the final analysis is answering the question, *"What shall I do in this situation?"*

In answering this question, more often than not it seems that individuals think about the situation briefly and then go with their instincts. There are, however, guides to ethical decision making that one could turn to if she or he really wanted to make the best ethical decision. What are some of these guides?

In Chapter 4 we indicated that there are three major approaches to ethics or ethical decision making we would like to discuss: (1) the conventional approach, (2) the principles approach, and (3) the ethical tests approach. In Chapter 4 we discussed the conventional approach, which entailed a comparison of an act, a decision, a behavior, or a practice with prevailing norms of acceptability. In this chapter, we discuss the other two approaches and other ethical principles and concepts as well.

Principles Approach to Ethics

The principles approach to ethics or ethical decision making is based on the idea that managers may desire to anchor their decisions on a more solid foundation than was present in our discussion of the conventional approach to ethics. Several principles of ethics have evolved over the centuries as moral philosophers and ethicists have attempted to organize and codify their thinking. This raises the question of what constitutes a principle of business ethics and how it might be applied. A principle of business ethics is a concept, guideline, or rule that, if applied when you are faced with an ethical dilemma, will assist you in making an ethical decision.[2]

There are many different principles of ethics, but we must limit our discussion to those that have been deemed most useful in business settings. Therefore, we will concentrate on three major principles: utilitarianism, rights, and justice. In addition, we will consider the ethics of care and virtue ethics, views that are gaining popularity today, as well as a few other key ethical principles. The basic idea behind the principles approach is that managers may improve their ethical decision making if they factor into their proposed actions, decisions, behaviors, and practices a consideration of certain principles or concepts of ethics. We will conclude this section with a brief consideration of how we might reconcile ethical conflicts that might arise in the use of these principles.

Principle of Utilitarianism

Many have held that the rightness or fairness of an action can be determined by looking at its results or consequences. If the consequences are good, the action or decision is considered good. If the consequences are bad, the action or decision is considered wrong. Utilitarianism is, therefore, a consequential principle. In its simplest form, *utilitarianism* asserts that "we should always act so as to produce the greatest ratio of good to evil for everyone."[3] Two of the most influential philosophers who advocated this consequential view were Jeremy Bentham (1748–1832) and John Stuart Mill (1806–1873).

The attractiveness of utilitarianism is that it forces us to think about the general welfare. It proposes a standard outside of self-interest by which to judge the value of a course of action. It also forces us to think in stakeholder terms: What would produce the greatest good in our decision, considering stakeholders such as owners, employees, customers, and others, as well as ourselves? Finally, it provides for latitude in decision making in that it does not recognize specific actions as inherently good or bad but rather allows us to fit our personal decisions to the complexities of the situation.

A weakness of utilitarianism is that it ignores actions that may be inherently wrong. By focusing on the *ends* (consequences) of a decision or an action, the *means* (the decision or action itself) may be ignored. Thus, we have the problematic situation where one may argue that the end justifies the means. Therefore, the action or decision is considered objectionable only if it leads to a lesser ratio of good to evil. Another problem with the principle of utilitarianism is that it may come into conflict with the idea of justice. Critics of this principle say that the mere increase in *total* good is not good in and of itself because it ignores the *distribution* of good, which is also an important issue. Another stated weakness is that, when using this principle, it is very difficult to formulate satisfactory rules for decision making. Therefore, utilitarianism, like most ethical principles, has its advantages and disadvantages.[4]

Principle of Rights

One major problem with utilitarianism is that it does not handle the issue of *rights* very well. That is, utilitarianism implies that certain actions are morally right when in fact they may violate another person's rights.[5] Moral rights are important, justifiable claims or entitlements. The right to life or the right not to be killed by others is a justifiable claim in our society. The Declaration of Independence referred to the rights to life, liberty, and the pursuit of happiness. John Locke earlier had spoken of the right to property. Today we speak of human rights. Some of these are legal rights and some are moral rights.

The basic idea behind the *principle of rights* is that rights cannot simply be overridden by utility. A right can be overridden only by another, more basic right. Let us consider the problem if we apply the utilitarian principle. For example, if we accept the basic right to human life, we are precluded from considering whether killing someone might produce the greatest good for the greatest number. To use a business example, if a person has a right to equal treatment (not to be discriminated against), we could not argue for discriminating against that person so as to produce more good for others.[6] However, some people would say that this is precisely what we do when we advocate affirmative action.

The rights principle expresses morality from the point of view of the *individual* or *group of individuals,* whereas the utilitarian principle expresses morality in terms of the *group or society as a whole.* The rights view forces us in our decision making to ask what is due each individual and to promote individual welfare. The rights view also limits the validity of appeals to numbers and to society's aggregate benefit.[7] However, a central question that is not always easy to answer is: "What constitutes a right, and what rights or whose rights take precedence over others?"

Figure 5–1 provides an overview of the types of rights that are being claimed in our society today. Some of these rights are legally protected, whereas others are claimed as moral rights but are not legally protected. Managers are expected to be attentive to both legal and moral rights, but there are no clear guidelines available to help one sort out which claimed rights should be protected, to what extent they should be protected, and which rights take precedence over others.

In recent years, some have argued that we are in the midst of a rights revolution in which too many individuals and groups are attempting to urge society to accept their wishes or demands as rights. The proliferation of rights claims has the potential to dilute or diminish the power of more legitimate rights. If everyone's claim for special consideration is perceived as a legitimate right, the rights approach may lose its power to help management concentrate on the morally justified rights. A related problem has been the politicization of rights in recent years. As our lawmakers bestow legal or protected status upon rights claims for political reasons rather than moral reasons, managers may become blinded to which rights or whose rights really should be honored in a decision-making situation. As rights claims expand, the common core of morality may diminish, and decision makers may find it more and more difficult to balance individuals' interests with the public interest.[8]

Principle of Justice

Just as the utilitarian principle does not handle well the idea of rights, it does not deal well with *justice* either. One way to look at justice involves the fair treatment of each person. But how do you decide what is fair to each person? How do you decide what each person is due? People might be given what they are due according to their work, their effort, their merit, their need, and so on. Each of these criteria

---

FIGURE 5–1   Legal Rights and Claimed Moral Rights in Society Today

Civil rights	Smokers' rights
Minorities' rights	Nonsmokers' rights
Women's rights	AIDS victims' rights
Disabled people's rights	Children's rights
Older people's rights	Fetal rights
Religious affiliation rights	Embryo rights
Employee rights	Animals' rights
Consumer rights	Right to burn the American flag
Shareholder rights	Right of due process
Privacy rights	Gay rights
Right to life	Victims' rights
Criminals' rights	

might be appropriate in different situations. At one time, the view prevailed that married heads of households ought to be paid more than single males or women. Today, however, the social structure is different. Women have entered the work force in greater numbers, some families are structured differently, and a revised concept of what is due people has evolved. The just action now is to pay everyone more on the basis of equality than needs.[9]

To use the principle of justice, we must ask, *"What do we mean by justice?"* There are several kinds of justice. *Distributive justice* refers to the distribution of benefits and burdens. *Compensatory justice* involves compensating someone for a past injustice. *Procedural justice* refers to fair decision-making procedures, practices, or agreements.[10]

John Rawls provides what some have referred to as a comprehensive *principle of justice*.[11] His theory is based on the idea that what we need first is a fair method by which we may choose the principles through which conflicts will be resolved. The two principles of justice that underlie his theory[12] are as follows:

1. Each person has an equal right to the most extensive basic liberties compatible with similar liberties for all others.

2. Social and economic inequalities are arranged so that they are both (a) reasonably expected to be to everyone's advantage and (b) attached to positions and offices open to all.

Under Rawls's first principle, each person is to be treated equally. The second principle is more controversial. It is criticized by both those who argue that the principle is too strong and those who think the principle is too weak. The former think that, as long as we have equal opportunity, there is no injustice when some people benefit from their own work, skill, ingenuity, or assumed risks. Therefore, such people deserve more and should not be required to produce benefits for the least advantaged. The latter group thinks that the inequalities that may result may be so great as to be clearly unjust. Therefore, the rich get richer and the poor get only a little less poor.[13]

Supporters of the principle of justice claim that it preserves the basic values—freedom, equality of opportunity, and a concern for the disadvantaged—that have become embedded in our moral beliefs. Critics object to various parts of the theory and would not subscribe to Rawls's principles at all. Utilitarians, for example, think the greatest good for the greatest number should reign supreme.

Principle of Caring

It is useful to introduce the ethics of care or *principle of caring* right after our discussion of utilitarianism, rights, and justice, because the theory, frequently referred to as feminist theory, is critical of these traditional views. These views, it has been argued, embrace a masculine approach to perceiving the world. The feminist or "care" perspective builds on the work of Carol Gilligan, whose criticisms of Kohlberg's theory of moral development were discussed in the previous chapter.

The care perspective holds that traditional ethics like the principles of utilitarianism and rights focus too much on the individual self and on rational thought processes. In the traditional view, "others" may be seen as threats, so rights become important. Resulting moral theories then tend to be legalistic or contractual.

Feminist theory is founded on wholly different assumptions. Feminist philosophers, for example, view the person as essentially relational, not individualistic. These philosophers do not deny the existence of the self but hold that the self has relationships that cannot be separated from the self's existence. This view emphasizes the relationships' moral worth and, by extension, the responsibilities inherent in those relationships, rather than in rights, as in traditional ethics.[13a]

Feminist moral theory, therefore, emphasizes caring as opposed to justice or rights. Several writers have argued that this is consistent with stakeholder theory, or the stakeholder approach, in that the focus is on a more cooperative, caring type of relationship. In this view, firms should seek to make decisions that satisfy stakeholders, leading to situations in which all parties in the relationship gain.

Jeanne Liedtka has questioned whether organizations can care in the sense in which feminist moral theory proposes. Liedtka contends that to care in this sense, an organization would have to care in a way that is:

- Focused entirely on *people,* not quality, profits, or other such ideas that today use "care talk"

- Undertaken with caring as an *end,* not merely as a means to an end (such as quality or profits)

- Essentially *personal,* in that the caring reflects caring for other individuals

- Growth enhancing for the cared-for, in that the caring moves the cared-for toward the development and use of their capacities

Liedtka takes the position that caring people could lead to a caring organization that offers new possibilities for simultaneously enhancing the effectiveness and the moral quality of organizations.[14] The principle of caring has weaknesses, but it offers a different perspective to guide ethical decision making—a perspective that clearly is thought provoking and valuable.

Virtue Ethics

The major principles just discussed have been more action oriented. That is, they were designed to guide our actions and decisions. Another ethical tradition, often referred to as **virtue ethics,** merits consideration even though it is not a principle per se. Virtue ethics, rooted in the thinking of Plato and Aristotle, focuses on the individual becoming imbued with virtues (e.g., honesty, fairness, truthfulness, benevolence, nonmalfeasance).[15]

Virtue ethics is a system of thought that is centered in the heart of the person—in our case, the manager. This is in contrast to the principles we have discussed, which see the heart of ethics in actions or duties. Action-oriented principles focus on *doing.* Virtue ethics emphasizes *being.* The assumption, of course, is that the actions of a virtuous person will also be virtuous. Traditional ethical principles such as utilitarianism, rights, and justice focus on the question, "What should I do?" Virtue ethics focuses on the question, "What sort of person should I be or become?"[16]

Programs that have developed from the notion of virtue ethics have sometimes been called *character education,* because this particular theory emphasizes character development. Many observers think that one reason we have moral decline in business and society today is because we have failed to teach our children universal principles of good character. As a consequence, both the U.S. Congress and the White House have responded by launching initiatives to address America's ethical decline with character education programs for youth. A White House Conference on Character Building was held in 1994, and a U.S. Senate resolution designated October 16–22, 1994, as "National Character Counts Week."[17] VF Corporation, the Josephson Institute of Ethics, and the Ethics Resource Center in Washington all launched character education programs in 1994. Esther Schaeffer, executive director of the Character Education Partnership, has argued that character education is needed not only in schools, but in corporations as well. She holds that corporate well-being demands character and that business leaders are a vital and necessary force for putting character back into education.[18]

Virtue ethicists have brought back to the public debate the idea that virtues are important whether they be in the education of the young or in management training programs. Virtues such as honesty, integrity, loyalty, promise keeping, fairness, and respect for others are perfectly compatible with the major principles we have been discussing. The principles, combined with the virtues, form the foundation for effective ethical action and decision making. Whether the virtues are seen as character traits or as principles of decision making is not our major concern at this point. That they be used, whatever the motivation, is our central concern here. Business ethicists Oliver Williams and Patrick Murphy have strongly argued that the ethics of virtue in business is an idea whose time has arrived.[19]

Other Principles

In addition to the ethical principles and theories that we have chosen to discuss in some detail, Figure 5–2 provides a brief sketch of several ethical principles that have evolved over the years.

The *Golden Rule* merits brief discussion because of its popularity as a basic principle of ethical living and decision making. A number of studies have found it to be the most powerful and useful to managers.[20] The Golden Rule—"Do unto others as you would have them do unto you"—is a fairly straightforward, easy-to-understand principle. Further, it guides the individual decision maker to behavior, actions, or decisions that she or he should be able to express as acceptable or not based on some direct comparisons with what she or he would consider ethical or fair.

The Golden Rule simply argues that, if you want to be treated fairly, treat others fairly; if you want your privacy protected, respect the privacy of others. The key is impartiality. According to this principle, we are not to make an exception of ourselves. In essence, the Golden Rule personalizes business relations and brings the ideal of fairness into business deliberations.[21]

Perhaps the reason the Golden Rule is so popular is that it is rooted in history and religious tradition and is among the oldest of the principles of living. Further, it is universal in the sense that it requires no specific religious belief or faith. Almost since time began, religious leaders and philosophers have advocated the Golden Rule in one form or another. It is easy to see, therefore, why Martin Luther could say that the Golden Rule is a part of the "natural law," because it is a moral rule that

FIGURE 5–2   A Brief Sketch of Ethical Principles

- THE *CATEGORICAL IMPERATIVE:* Act only according to that maxim by which you can at the same time "will" that it should become a universal law. In other words, one should not adopt principles of action unless they can, without inconsistency, be adopted by everyone else.

- THE *CONVENTIONALIST ETHIC:* Individuals should act to further their self-interests so long as they do not violate the law. It is allowed, under this principle, to bluff (lie) and to take advantage of all legal opportunities and widespread practices and customs.

- THE *DISCLOSURE RULE:* If the full glare of examination by associates, friends, family, newspapers, television, etc., were to focus on your decision, would you remain comfortable with it? If you think you would, it probably is the right decision.

- THE *GOLDEN RULE:* Do unto others as you would have them do unto you. It includes not knowingly doing harm to others.

- THE *HEDONISTIC ETHIC:* Virtue is embodied in what each individual finds meaningful. There are no universal or absolute moral principles. If it feels good, do it.

- THE *INTUITION ETHIC:* People are endowed with a kind of moral sense with which they can apprehend right and wrong. The solution to moral problems lies simply in what you feel or understand to be right in a given situation. You have a "gut feeling" and "fly by the seat of your pants."

- THE *MARKET ETHIC:* Selfish actions in the marketplace are virtuous because they contribute to efficient operation of the economy. Decision makers may take selfish actions and be motivated by personal gain in their business dealings. They should ask whether their actions in the market further financial self-interest. If so, the actions are ethical.

- THE *MEANS-ENDS ETHIC:* Worthwhile ends justify efficient means—i.e., when ends are of overriding importance or virtue, unscrupulous means may be employed to reach them.

- THE *MIGHT-EQUALS-RIGHT ETHIC:* Justice is defined as the interest of the stronger. What is ethical is what an individual has the strength and power to accomplish. Seize what advantage you are strong enough to take without respect to ordinary social conventions and laws.

- THE *ORGANIZATION ETHIC:* The wills and needs of individuals should be subordinated to the greater good of the organization (be it church, state, business, military, or university). An individual should ask whether actions are consistent with organizational goals and what is good for the organization.

- THE *PROFESSIONAL ETHIC:* You should do only that which can be explained before a committee of your peers.

- THE *PROPORTIONALITY PRINCIPLE:* I am responsible for whatever I "will" as a means or an end. If both the means and the end are good in and of themselves, I may ethically permit or risk the foreseen but unwilled side effects if, and only if, I have a proportionate reason for doing so.

- THE *REVELATION ETHIC:* Through prayer or other appeal to transcendent beings and forces, answers are given to individual minds. The decision makers pray, meditate, or otherwise commune with a superior force or being. They are then apprised of which actions are just and unjust.

- THE *UTILITARIAN ETHIC:* The greatest good for the greatest number. Determine whether the harm in an action is outweighed by the good. If the action maximizes benefit, it is the optimum course to take among alternatives that provide less benefit.

SOURCE: T. K. Das, "Ethical Preferences Among Business Students: A Comparative Study of Fourteen Ethical Principles," Southern Management Association (November 13–16, 1985), 11–12. For further discussion, see T. K. Das, "Ethical Principles in Business: An Empirical Study of Preferential Rankings," *International Journal of Management* (Vol. 9, No. 4, December, 1992), 462–472.

anyone can recognize and embrace without any particular religious teaching. In three different studies, when managers or respondents were asked to rank ethical principles according to their value to them, the Golden Rule was ranked first.[22]

Figure 5–3 presents another list of ethical principles as developed by the Josephson Institute of Ethics. This list of principles identifies those generic characteristics, virtues, and values most people associate with ethical behavior.

FIGURE 5–3   Ethical Principles for Business Executives

This list of principles incorporates the characteristics and values most people associate with ethical behavior. Ethical decision making systematically considers these principles.

I. HONESTY. Ethical executives are honest and truthful in all their dealings and they do not deliberately mislead or deceive others by misrepresentations, overstatements, partial truths, selective omissions, or any other means.

II. INTEGRITY. Ethical executives demonstrate personal integrity and the courage of their convictions by doing what they think is right even when there is great pressure to do otherwise; they are principled, honorable, and upright; they will fight for their beliefs. They will not sacrifice principle for expediency, be hypocritical, or be unscrupulous.

III. PROMISE-KEEPING AND TRUSTWORTHINESS. Ethical executives are worthy of trust, they are candid and forthcoming in supplying relevant information and correcting misapprehensions of fact, and they make every reasonable effort to fulfill the letter and spirit of their promises and commitments. They do not interpret agreements in an unreasonably technical or legalistic manner in order to rationalize noncompliance or create justifications for escaping their commitments.

IV. LOYALTY. Ethical executives are worthy of trust, and demonstrate fidelity and loyalty to persons and institutions by friendship in adversity, support, and devotion to duty; they do not use or disclose information learned in confidence for personal advantage. They safeguard the ability to make independent professional judgments by scrupulously avoiding undue influences and conflicts of interest. They are loyal to their companies and colleagues and if they decide to accept other employment, they provide reasonable notice, respect the proprietary information of their former employer, and refuse to engage in any activities that take undue advantage of their previous position.

V. FAIRNESS. Ethical executives are fair and just in all dealings; they do not exercise power arbitrarily, and they do not use overreaching or indecent means to gain or maintain any advantage or take undue advantage of another's mistakes or difficulties. Fair persons manifest a commitment to justice, the equal treatment of individuals, and tolerance for and acceptance of diversity, and they are open-minded; they are willing to admit they are wrong and, where appropriate, change their positions and beliefs.

VI. CONCERN FOR OTHERS. Ethical executives are caring, compassionate, benevolent, and kind; they live the Golden Rule, they help those in need, and they seek to accomplish their business objectives in a manner that causes the least harm and the greatest positive good.

VII. RESPECT FOR OTHERS. Ethical executives demonstrate respect for the human dignity, autonomy, privacy, rights, and interests of all those who have a stake in their decisions; they are courteous and treat all people with equal respect and dignity regardless of sex, race, or national origin.

VIII. LAW ABIDING. Ethical executives abide by laws, rules, and regulations relating to their business activities.

IX. COMMITMENT TO EXCELLENCE. Ethical executives pursue excellence in performing their duties, are well informed and prepared, and constantly endeavor to increase their proficiency in all areas of responsibility.

X. LEADERSHIP. Ethical executives are conscious of the responsibilities and opportunities of their positions of leadership and seek to be positive ethical role models by their own conduct and by helping to create an environment in which principled reasoning and ethical decision making are highly prized.

XI. REPUTATION AND MORALE. Ethical executives seek to protect and build the company's good reputation and the morale of its employees by engaging in no conduct that might undermine respect, and by taking whatever actions are necessary to correct or prevent inappropriate conduct of others.

XII. ACCOUNTABILITY. Ethical executives acknowledge and accept personal accountability for the ethical quality of their decisions and omissions to themselves, their colleagues, their companies, and their communities.

SOURCE: Reprinted with permission © Josephson Institute of Ethics, *Ethics: Easier Said Than Done*, Vol. 2, No. 1, 1989.

There is no single principle we should recommend. As one gets into each principle, one encounters numerous problems with definitions, with measurement, and with generalizability. The more one gets into each principle, the more one realizes how difficult it would be for a person to use each principle consistently as a guide to decision making. On the other hand, to say that an ethical principle is imperfect is not to say that it has not raised important issues that must be addressed in personal or business decision making. The major principles we have discussed, as well as a consideration of the ethics of care and virtue ethics and other principles, have raised to our consciousness the importance of the collective good, individual rights, caring, character, and fairness.

Reconciling Ethical Conflicts

What does a manager do when using some of the ethical principles and guidelines we have been discussing and she or he finds that there are conflicts between and among the principles? For example, what if the manager perceives that one employee's right to safety conflicts with another's right to privacy? How should this conflict be resolved? There is no absolute way to reconcile ethical principles; however, some brief discussion may be helpful. Shaw and Barry have argued, following the ideas introduced by V.R. Ruggiero, that three common concerns must be addressed: obligations, ideals, and effects.[23] We will tie these concepts into our current discussion.

First, we enter into *obligations* as a part of our daily organizational lives. An example might be a verbal or written contract to which we have agreed. Principles of justice, rights, and virtue would hold that we should honor obligations. Second, as managers we might hold certain *ideals*. Such an ideal may be some morally important goal, principle, virtue, or notion of excellence worth striving for. A quest for justice, protection of rights, and balancing of individual versus group goals might be examples. Third, we are interested in the *effects*, or consequences, on stakeholders of our decisions or actions.[24] Hopefully, we can see how obligations, goals, and effects are all aspects of the ethical principles we have been discussing.

The question now arises as to how we might handle a situation wherein our obligations, goals, and effects conflict or produce mixed effects. Three rough guidelines have been proposed by Shaw and Barry:[25]

1. When two or more moral obligations conflict, choose the stronger one.

2. When two or more ideals conflict, or when ideals conflict with obligations, honor the more important one.

3. When the effects are mixed, choose the action that produces the greater good or less harm.

These guidelines are rough because they do not precisely answer the question of which obligations or ideals should take precedence over others. However, they do give us a general approach to raising the issue of how such conflicts might be resolved. In the final analysis, the manager will need to consider carefully which values or obligations are more important than others.

In summary, the principles approach to ethics focuses on guidelines, ideas, or concepts that have been created to help people and organizations make wise, ethical decisions. In our discussion, we have treated the following as important components of the principles approach: utilitarianism, rights, justice, caring, virtue, and other principles, like the Golden Rule. Such principles should cause us to think deeply and to reflect carefully on the ethical decisions we face in our personal and organizational lives. For the most part, these principles are rooted in moral philosophy. On a more pragmatic level, we turn now to a series of ethical tests that constitute our third major approach to ethics.

Ethical Tests Approach

In addition to the ethical principles approach to guiding personal and managerial decision making, a number of practical *ethical tests* might be set forth, too. Whereas the principles have almost exclusively been generated by philosophers, the tests we discuss here are more practical in orientation and do not require the depth of moral thinking that the principles do. No single test is recommended as a universal answer to the question, "What action or decision should I take in this situation?" However, each person may find one or more tests that will be useful in helping to clarify the appropriate course of action in a decision situation. To most students, the notion of a test invokes the thought of questions posed that need to be answered. And, indeed, each of these tests for personal ethical decision making requires the thoughtful deliberation of a central question that gets to the heart of the matter.

Test of Common Sense

With this first test, the individual simply asks, *"Does the action I am getting ready to take really make sense?"* When you think of behavior that might have ethical implications, it is logical to consider the practical consequences. If, for example, you would surely get caught engaging in a questionable practice, the action does not pass this test. Many unethical practices have come to light where one is led to ask whether a person really used her or his common sense at all. This test has severe limitations. For example, if you conclude that you would not get caught engaging in a questionable practice, this test might lead you to think that the questionable practice is an acceptable course of action, when in fact it is not. In addition, there may be other common-sense aspects of the situation that you have overlooked.

Test of One's Best Self

Each person has a self-concept. Most people could construct a scenario of themselves at their best. This test requires the individual to pose the question, *"Is this action or decision I'm getting ready to take compatible with my concept of myself at my best?"* This test addresses the notion of the esteem in which we hold ourselves and the kind of person we want to be known as. Naturally, this test would not be of much value to those who do not hold themselves in high esteem.

Test of Making Something Public

This is one of the most powerful tests.[26] It is similar to the disclosure rule defined in Figure 5–2. If you are about to engage in a questionable practice or action, you might pose the following questions: *"How would I feel if others knew I was doing this? How would I feel if I knew that my decisions or actions were going to be featured on the national evening news tonight for all the world to see?"* This test addresses the issue of whether your action or decision can withstand public disclosure and scrutiny. How would you feel if all your friends, family, and colleagues knew you were engaging in this action? If you feel comfortable with this thought, you are probably on solid footing. If you feel uncomfortable with this thought, you ought to rethink your position.

The concept of public exposure is quite powerful. Several years ago, a poll of managers was taken asking whether the Foreign Corrupt Practices Act would stop

ETHICS IN PRACTICE

Promise versus Lie

During the spring, I worked in the billing department of a large organization as a student worker. All of the secretaries who worked in the billing department were close and would talk to each other about almost anything. One of the topics we enjoyed talking about the most was the office manager of the billing department and how much we would like to find another job to get away from her, because we did not like working with her. While I was working in the department, I became very close friends with the senior secretary, who worked with me in the front office.

During the same spring, my friend was offered a very prestigious job at the company. She told a few of us about having applied for the job, but she did not want us to let the office manager know that she was applying for it in case she did not get it. I was her friend, so I was not going to say anything about the situation. After a few weeks of waiting to find out if she got the job or not, she was offered the job and took it immediately. After she knew she had the new job, she told the office manager that she had been offered another job and was giving her 2 weeks' notice. All was well until the office manager came up to me one day and asked me if I had known anything about the secretary planning to leave. I was not sure what to say. I did not want to lie to the office manager, but I also did not want to break a promise I made to a good friend. What was I to do?

1. Is this ethical dilemma at the personal level or the organizational level?

2. What ethical principles are at stake in this situation?

3. What should the person who faces this ethical situation do?

Contributed by Erika Carlson-Durham

bribes abroad. Many of the managers said it would not. When asked what would stop bribes, most managers thought that public exposure would be most effective. "If the public knew we were accepting bribes, this knowledge would have the best chance of being effective," they replied.

Test of Ventilation

The idea of ventilation is to expose your proposed action to others and get their thoughts on it. This test works best if you get opinions from people who you know might not see things your way. The important point here is that you do not isolate yourself with your dilemma but seek others' views. After you have subjected your proposed course of action to other opinions, you may find that you have not been thinking clearly.

Test of the Purified Idea

An idea or action may be thought to be "purified"—that is, made right—when a person with authority says it is appropriate. Such a person might be a supervisor, an accountant, or a lawyer. The central question here is, *"Am I thinking this action or decision is right just because someone with appropriate authority or knowledge says it is right?"* If you look hard enough, you can find a lawyer or an accountant to endorse almost any idea if it is phrased right.[27] However, neither of them is the final arbiter of what is right or wrong. Similarly, just because a superior says an action or a decision is ethical does not make it so. The decision or course of action may still be questionable or wrong even though someone else has sanctioned it with her or his approval. This is one of the most common ethical errors people make, and they must constantly be reminded that they themselves ultimately will be held accountable if the action is indefensible.

Gag Test

This test was provided by a judge on the Louisiana Court of Appeals. He argued that a manager's clearest signal that a dubious decision or action is going too far is when you simply gag at the prospect of carrying it out.[28] Admittedly, this test can only capture the grossest of unethical behaviors, but there are some managers who may need such a general kind of test. Actually, this test is intended to be more humorous than serious, but a few might be helped by it.

None of the above-mentioned tests alone offers a perfect way to question the ethicalness of a decision or an act. If several tests are used together, especially the more powerful ones, they do provide a means of examining proposed actions before engaging in them. To repeat, this assumes that the individual really wants to do what is right and is looking for assistance. To the fundamentally unethical person, however, these tests would not be of much value.

Phillip V. Lewis conducted a 5-year study of ethical principles and ethical tests. Based on his findings, he asserted that there is high agreement on how a decision maker should behave when faced with a moral choice. He concludes:

> *In fact, there is almost a step-by-step sequence. Notice: one should (1) look at the problem from the position of the other person(s) affected by a decision; (2) try to determine what virtuous response is expected; (3) ask (a) how it would feel for the decision to be disclosed to a wide audience and (b) whether the decision is consistent with organizational goals; and (4) act in a way that is (a) right and just for any other person in a similar situation and (b) good for the organization.*[29]

Implicit in Lewis's conclusion is evidence of the Golden Rule, the disclosure rule, and Rawls's principle of justice.

MANAGING ORGANIZATIONAL ETHICS

To this point, our discussion has centered on personal or managerial decision making. Clearly, ethical decision making is at the heart of business ethics, and we cannot stress enough the need to sharpen decision-making skills if amorality is to be avoided and moral management is to be achieved. Now we shift our attention somewhat to the organizational level, where we find the context in which decision making occurs. The organization and its environment, culture, or climate are just as vital as decision making in bringing about ethical business practices and results.

To manage ethics in an organization, a manager must appreciate that the organization's ethical climate is just one part of its overall corporate culture. When McNeil Laboratories, a subsidiary of Johnson & Johnson, voluntarily withdrew Tylenol from the market immediately after the 1982 and 1986 reports of tainted, poisoned products, some people wondered why they made this decision as they did. An often cited response was, "It's the J & J way."[30] This statement conveys a significant message about the firm's ethical climate. It also raises the question of how organizations and managers should deal with, understand, and shape business ethics through actions taken, policies established, and examples set. The organization's moral climate is a complex entity, and we can discuss only some facets of it in this section.[31]

Figure 5–4 illustrates several levels of moral climate and the factors that may come to bear on the manager as she or he makes decisions. Our focus in this section is on the organization's moral climate. Two major questions that need to be considered are: (1) What factors contribute to unethical behavior in the organization? and (2) What actions or strategies might management employ to improve the organization's ethical climate?

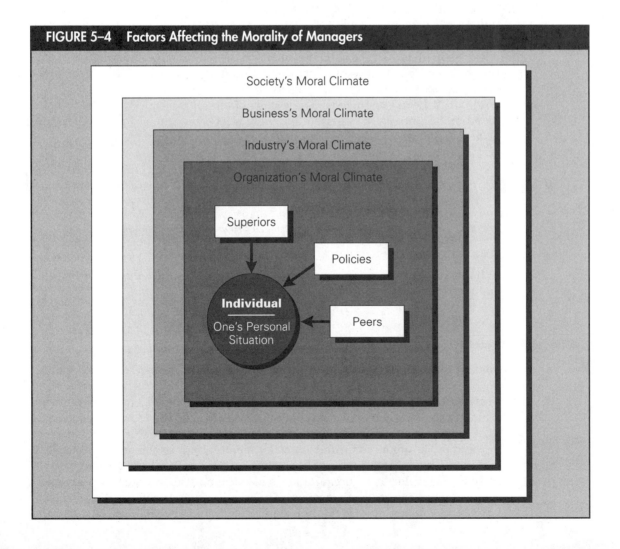

FIGURE 5–4   Factors Affecting the Morality of Managers

Society's Moral Climate

Business's Moral Climate

Industry's Moral Climate

Organization's Moral Climate

Superiors

Policies

Individual
One's Personal
Situation

Peers

Factors Affecting the Organization's Moral Climate

For managers to be in a position to create an ethical climate, they must first understand the factors at work in the organization that influence whether or not managers or employees behave ethically. Over the past 30 years or so, several studies have been conducted that have sought to identify and to rank the sources of ethical problems in organizations.

Baumhart conducted one of the earliest studies, in which he surveyed over 1,500 *Harvard Business Review* readers (executives, managers).[32] One of the questions asked was to rank several factors that the managers thought influenced or contributed to unethical behaviors or actions. The factors found in his study, in descending order of frequency of mention, were:

1. Behavior of superiors
2. The ethical practices of one's industry or profession
3. Behavior of one's peers in the organization
4. Formal organizational policy (or lack thereof)
5. Personal financial need

Brenner and Molander later replicated the Baumhart study using over 1,200 *Harvard Business Review* readers. They added one additional factor to the list: society's moral climate.[33] Posner and Schmidt surveyed over 1,400 managers, again asking them to rank the list of six factors in terms of their influence or contribution to unethical behavior.[34] Figure 5–5 presents the findings of these three landmark studies.

Although there is variation in the rankings of the three studies, several findings are worthy of note:

1. *Behavior of superiors* was ranked as the number one influence on unethical behavior in all three studies.
2. *Behavior of one's peers* was ranked high in two of the three studies.
3. *Industry or professional ethical practices* ranked in the upper half in all three studies.
4. *Personal financial need* ranked *last* in all three studies.

What stands out here from an organizational perspective is the influence of the behavior of one's superiors and peers. Also notable about these findings is that quite often it is assumed that society's moral climate has a lot to do with managers' morality, but this factor was ranked low in the two studies in which it was considered. Apparently, society's moral climate is a background factor that does not have a direct bearing on organizational ethics. Furthermore, it is interesting that personal financial need ranked so low.

Pressures Exerted on Subordinates by Superiors

One major consequence of the behavior of superiors and peers is that pressure is placed on subordinates and/or other organizational members. In a national study conducted by one of the authors of this text, managers were asked to what extent they agreed with the following proposition: "Managers today feel under pressure to compromise personal standards to achieve company goals."[35] It is insightful to

FIGURE 5–5   Factors Influencing Unethical Behavior Question: "Listed below are the factors that many believe influence unethical behavior. Rank them in order of their influence or contribution to unethical behaviors or actions by managers."[a]

Factor	1984 Study[b] (N = 1443)	1977 Study[c] (N = 1227)	1961 Study[d] (N = 1531)
Behavior of superiors	2.17(1)	2.15(1)	1.9(1)
Behavior of one's organizational peer	3.30(2)	3.37(4)	3.1(3)
Ethical practices of one's industry or profession	3.57(3)	3.34(3)	2.6(2)
Society's moral climate	3.79(4)	4.22(5)	[e]
Formal organizational policy (or lack thereof)	3.84(5)	3.27(2)	3.3(4)
Personal financial need	4.09(6)	4.46(6)	4.1(5)

[a]Ranking is based on a scale of 1 (most influential) to 6 (least influential).
SOURCES: [b]Barry Z. Posner and Warren H. Schmidt, "Values and the American Manager: An Update," *California Management Review* (Spring, 1984), 202–216.
[c]Steve Brenner and Earl Molander, "Is the Ethics of Business Changing?" *Harvard Business Review* (January/February, 1977).
[d]Raymond C. Baumhart, "How Ethical Are Businessmen?" *Harvard Business Review* (July/August, 1961), 6ff.
[e]This item not included in 1961 study.

consider the management levels of the 64.4 percent of the respondents who agreed with the proposition. The results were:

Top management: 50 percent agreed

Middle management: 65 percent agreed

Lower management: 85 percent agreed

This study revealed that the perceived pressure to compromise seems to be felt most by those in lower management, followed by those in middle management. In their subsequent study, Posner and Schmidt also asked managers whether they sometimes had to compromise their personal principles to conform to organizational expectations.[36] Twenty percent of the top executives agreed, 27 percent of the middle managers agreed, and 41 percent of the lower managers agreed. In other words, the same pattern prevailed.

This co-author's study posed another proposition: "I can conceive of a situation where you have sound ethics running from top to bottom, but because of pressures from the top to achieve results, the person down the line compromises." The pattern of findings on this proposition was similar to that of the other two findings.[37]

What is particularly troublesome about these findings is the pattern of response. It seems that the lower a manager is in the hierarchy, the more that manager perceives pressures toward unethical conduct. Although there are several plausible explanations for this phenomenon, one explanation seems particularly attractive because of its agreement with conversations this co-author has had with various managers. This interpretation is that top-level managers do not know how strongly their subordinates perceive pressures to go along with their bosses. These varying perceptions at different levels in the managerial hierarchy suggest that higher-level managers may not be tuned in to how pressure is received at lower levels. There seems to be a gap in the understanding of higher managers and lower managers regarding the pressures toward unethical behavior that exist, especially in the lower echelons. This breakdown in understanding, or lack of sensitivity by top management to how far subordinates will go to please them, can be conducive to lower-level subordinates behaving unethically out of a real or perceived fear of reprisal, a misguided sense of loyalty, or a distorted concept of their jobs.

A study of the sources and consequences of workplace pressure was conducted in 1997 by the American Society of Chartered Life Underwriters & Chartered Financial Consultants and the Ethics Officer Association.[38] The findings of this study were consistent with the studies reported above and provided additional insights into the detrimental consequences of workplace pressure. Among the key findings of this study were the following:

- The majority of workers (60 percent) felt a substantial amount of pressure on the job. More than one out of four (27 percent) felt a "great deal" of pressure.

- The amount of workplace pressure has increased significantly from 5 years previously and 1 year previously. Of workers surveyed, 57 percent felt more pressure than 5 years ago, and 40 percent felt that pressure had increased in the past year.

- Nearly half of all workers (48 percent) reported that, due to pressure, they had engaged in one or more unethical and/or illegal actions during the past year. The most frequently cited misbehavior was cutting corners on quality control.

- The top five types of unethical/illegal behavior that workers reported they had engaged in over the past year in response to pressure were cutting corners on quality, covering up incidents, abusing or lying about sick days, lying or deceiving customers, and putting inappropriate pressure on others.

- The sources most commonly cited as contributing to workplace pressure were "balancing work and family" (52 percent), "poor internal communications" (51 percent), "work hours/work load" (51 percent), and "poor leadership" (51 percent).

In addition to the studies that document the extent to which managers feel pressure to perform, even if it leads to questionable activities, several actual business cases demonstrate the reality of cutting corners to achieve high production goals. In a glass container plant in Gulfport, Mississippi, for example, the plant manager began to fear that top management might close the aging facility because its output was falling behind those of other plants. So, the plant manager secretly started altering records and eventually inflated the value of the plant's production by 33 percent. Top management learned of this when a janitor acquired documents and reported this bogus information to company auditors. The plant manager was fired. He was not willing to discuss the matter, but his wife said her husband was under "constant pressure" to raise the plant's production and that he believed he and the other employees would have jobs as long as he was able to do so. The company's president said he had no intention of firing the plant manager for failing to meet the production goal.[39]

Another interesting case involved a big Chevrolet truck plant in Flint, Michigan. Here, three plant managers installed a secret control box in a supervisor's office so that they could override the control panel that governed the speed of the assembly line. The plant managers claimed they felt pressure to do this because top management did not understand that high absenteeism, conveyor breakdowns, and other problems were preventing them from reaching their goals. Once they began using the hidden controls, they began meeting their production goals and winning praise from their superiors. The plant managers claimed they thought top management knew that the plant managers were speeding up the line and that what the plant managers were doing was unethical. However, top management never said anything and therefore it was thought that the practice was accepted. The executives denied any knowledge of the secret box. The speed-up was in violation of GM's contract with the United Auto Workers' union. Once it was exposed, the company had to pay $1 million in back pay to the affected UAW members.[40]

The motive behind managers putting pressure on subordinates to perform, even at the sacrifice of their ethical standards, seems to be driven by the "bottom-line" mentality that places economic success above all other goals. Employees frequently find themselves making compromises as a result of the pressure coupled with the socialization process that emphasizes compliance with the authority structure, the need to conform to their superiors' wishes, and the expectation of loyalty.

Other Behaviors of Superiors and/or Peers

Other behaviors of one's superiors and/or peers that create a questionable organizational atmosphere include:

1. *Amoral decision making.* This includes managers who themselves fail to factor ethical considerations into their actions, decisions, and behaviors. The result of this is a vacuous leadership environment.

2. *Unethical acts, behaviors, or practices.* Some managers simply are not ethical themselves, and this influence wears off on others. Employees watch their superiors' behavior carefully and take cues from them as to what is acceptable.

3. *Acceptance of legality as a standard of behavior.* Some managers think that if they are strictly abiding by the law they are doing the most they ought to do.

4. *"Bottom-line" mentality and expectations of loyalty and conformity.* This focus places little value on doing what is right and on being sensitive to other stakeholders.

5. *Absence of ethical leadership.* This is a global indicator of sorts that includes some of the other points already mentioned. In addition, management never steps out ahead of the pack and assumes a leadership role in doing what is right. This reflects an absence of moral management.

6. *Objectives and evaluation systems that overemphasize profits.* If management sets unrealistic goals or does not take ethics into consideration in evaluating employees, it is creating a potentially destructive environment.

7. *Insensitivity toward how subordinates perceive pressure to meet goals.* This is related to several of the previous points. Management must be constantly vigilant of the directives and expectations it is making on employees. The manager might always ask, "How might this goal, directive, or expectation be misread or misunderstood in terms of how far I want people to go to achieve it?"

8. *Inadequate formal policies.* Problems here might include inadequate management controls for monitoring and compliance, unreasonable reimbursement/expense policies, and the absence of a clear code of conduct.

Improving the Organization's Ethical Climate

Because the behavior of managers has been identified as the most important influence on the ethical behavior of organization members, it should come as no surprise that most actions and strategies for improving the organization's ethical climate must emanate from top management and other management levels as well. The process by which these kinds of initiatives have taken place is often referred to as "institutionalizing ethics" into the organization.[41] In this section, we will consider some of the best practices that managers have taken to improve their organizations' ethical climate. Figure 5–6 depicts a number of best practices for creating an ethical organization climate or culture. Top management leadership is at the hub of these initiatives, actions, or practices.

Top Management Leadership (Moral Management)

It has become almost a cliché, but this premise must be established at the outset: *The moral tone of an organization is set by top management.* This is because all managers

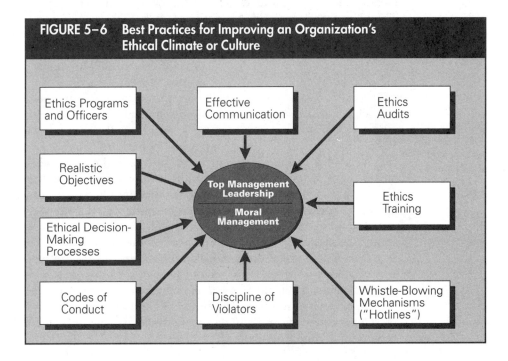

FIGURE 5–6   Best Practices for Improving an Organization's Ethical Climate or Culture

and employees look to the highest level for their cues as to what is acceptable. A former chairman of Bethlehem Steel Corporation stated it well: "Starting at the top, management has to set an example for all the others to follow."[42] Top management, through its capacity to set a personal example and to shape policy, is in the ideal position to provide a highly visible role model. The authority and ability to shape policy, both formal and implied, forms one of the vital aspects of the job of any leader in any organization.

An example of bad ethical leadership and one of good ethical leadership make these points clear. In one of his consulting experiences, one of the authors encountered a situation in a small company where a long-time employee was identified as having embezzled about $20,000 over a 15-year period. When the employee was approached and questioned as to why she had done this, she explained that she thought it was all right because the president had led her to believe it was. She further explained that any time during the fall, when the leaves had fallen in his yard and he needed them raked, he would simply get company personnel to do it. When the president needed cash, he would take it out of the company's petty cash box or get the key to the soft drink machine and raid its coin box. When he needed stamps to mail his personal Christmas cards, he would take them out of the company stamp box. The woman's perception was that it was all right for her to take the money because the president did it frequently. Therefore, she thought it was an acceptable practice for her as well.

An example of positive ethical leadership may be seen in the case of a firm that was manufacturing vacuum tubes. One day the plant manager called a hurried meeting to announce that a sample of the tubes had failed a critical safety test. This meant that the 10,000 tubes were of highly questionable safety and performance. The plant manager wondered out loud, "What are we going to do now?" Ethical leadership was shown by the vice president for technical operations, who looked around the room at each person and then declared in a low voice, "Scrap them!" According to a person who worked for this vice president, that act set the tone for the corporation for years, because every person present knew of situations in which faulty products had been shipped under pressures of time and budget.[43]

Each of these cases provides a vivid example of how a leader's actions and behavior communicated important messages to others in the organization. In the absence of knowing what to do, many employees look to the behavior of leaders for their cues as to what conduct is acceptable. In the second case, another crucial point is illustrated. When we speak of management providing ethical leadership, it is not just restricted to top management. Vice presidents, plant managers, and, indeed, all managerial personnel carry the responsibility for ethical leadership.

In a period in which the importance of a sound corporate culture has been strongly advocated, management must stress the primacy of integrity and morality as vital components of the organization's culture. There are many different ways and situations in which management needs to do this. In general, management needs to create a climate of *moral consciousness*. In everything it does, it must stress the importance of sound ethical principles and practices. A former president and chief operating officer for Caterpillar Tractor Company suggested four specific actions for accomplishing this:[44]

1. Create clear and concise policies that define the company's business ethics and conduct.

2. Select for employment only those people and firms whose characters and ethics appear to be in keeping with corporate standards.

3. Promote people on the basis of performance and ethical conduct and beliefs.

4. Company employees must feel the obligation and the opportunity to report perceived irregularities in ethics or in accounting transactions.

Mark Pastin has recommended a set of four principles that high-ethics firms employ to help develop a climate of moral consciousness. Figure 5–7 summarizes these four principles, which provide organizational guidelines that focus on (1) stakeholders, (2) fairness, (3) individual responsibility, and (4) purpose. They are based on his research of 25 firms recognized for both ethical and economic performance.[45]

We should also note that the leader must infuse the organization's climate with values and ethical consciousness, not just run a one-person show. This point is made vividly clear by Steven Brenner, who concludes: "Ethics programs which are seen as part of one manager's management system, and not as a part of the general organizational process, will be less likely to have a lasting role in the organization."[46]

Effective Communication

Management also carries a heavy burden in terms of providing ethical leadership in the area of *effective communication*. We have seen the importance of communicating through acts, principles, and organizational climate. We will discuss further the communication aspects of setting realistic objectives, codes of conduct, and the decision-making process. Here, however, we want to stress the importance of communication principles, techniques, and practices.

Conveying the importance of ethics through communication includes both written and verbal forms of communication. In each of these settings, management

---

FIGURE 5–7   Principles for High-Ethics Firms

Principle 1 High-ethics firms are at ease *interacting with diverse internal and external stakeholder groups.* The ground rules of these firms make the good of these stakeholder groups part of the firm's own good.

Principle 2 High-ethics firms are *obsessed with fairness.* Their ground rules emphasize that the other person's interests count as much as their own.

Principle 3 In high-ethics firms, *responsibility is individual* rather than collective, with individuals assuming personal responsibility for actions of the firm. These firms' ground rules mandate that individuals are responsible to themselves.

Principle 4 The high-ethics firm sees its activities in terms of a *purpose.* This purpose is a way of operating that members of the firm value. And purpose ties the firm to its environment.

SOURCE: Mark Pastin, *The Hard Problems of Management: Gaining the Ethics Edge* (San Francisco: Jossey-Bass, 1986), 221–225. Reproduced with permission.

SEARCH THE WEB

One of the best ways to appreciate all the ethics issues a major company faces and to see how that company addresses those issues from a policy perspective is to review the company's set of core values and code of conduct. Unlike other companies, Northern Telecom (Nortel) has posted this vital information on the Web. Visit Nortel's Web site at **www.nortel.com/cool/ethics/** to review its conduct code, entitled "Acting with Integrity." This code provides a quick reference to such topics of interest as bribes and kickbacks, conflicts of interest, discrimination, facilitation payments, gifts and gratuities, purchasing decisions, and privacy issues. The standards and expectations outlined in Nortel's Code of Business Conduct were designed to guide the company's managers and employees as they seek to make the right choices. As Nortel president and CEO John A. Roth stated on the Web site in 1999, "At Nortel we recognize the importance of credibility, integrity, and trustworthiness to our success as a business."

should operate according to certain key ethical principles. *Candor* is one very important principle. Candor requires that a manager be forthright, sincere, and honest in communication transactions. In addition, it requires the manager to be fair and free from prejudice and malice in the communication. Related to this is the principle of fidelity. *Fidelity* in communication means that the communicator should be faithful to detail, should be accurate, and should avoid deception or exaggeration. *Confidentiality* is a final principle that ought to be stressed. The ethical manager must exercise care in deciding what information she or he discloses to others. Trust can be easily shattered if the manager does not have a keen sense of what is confidential in a communication.

Ethics Programs and Ethics Officers

In recent years, many companies have begun creating ethics programs. These programs are often headed up by an *ethics officer* who is in charge of implementing the array of ethics initiatives of the organization. In some cases, the creation of ethics programs and designation of ethics officers have been in response to the 1991 Federal Sentencing Guidelines, which reduced penalties to those companies with ethics programs that were found guilty of ethics violations.[47] Other companies started ethics programs as an effort to centralize the coordination of ethics initiatives in those companies. Typical initiatives of companies include codes of conduct (or ethics), ethics hotlines, ethics training, and ethics audits, which we will discuss later.

An illustration of an ethics program is the one created in 1990 by NYNEX, the $13 billion Baby Bell, which is now one of the country's most impressive ethics programs. At NYNEX, Chairman and CEO William Ferguson initiated the program partially in anticipation of stiffer government penalties for white collar crime and partially in response to a troubling pattern of ethical problems the company had faced in prior years. Historically, the company had decades of culture building and a durable set of corporate values. When AT&T broke up in 1984, however, the new company was thrown into chaos and, in the late 1980s, allegations of illegal gifts to suppliers and other questionable transactions led to federal investigators probing into company activities. This was when Ferguson tapped a 30-year executive to head up the new ethics program and to provide new leadership. The program at NYNEX eventually included ethics training initiatives, a company code of conduct, and an Ethics Policy Committee. An ethics hotline was also installed whereby company employees could phone in their ethics questions and concerns.[48]

Other major companies with ethics programs include Texas Instruments, Xerox, Boeing, McDonnell Douglas, and Sears.

Just as ethics programs have proliferated in companies, the number of *ethics officers* occupying important positions in major firms has grown significantly. In fact, in

1992, ethics officers created the Ethics Officer Association (EOA) to help define their profession and its possibilities. The three major objectives of the EOA, which are consistent with the quest to improve organizations' ethical climates, are to:[49]

- Provide multiple opportunities for wider acquaintance, understanding, and cooperation among ethics officers

- Provide a structure for sharing practical approaches to specific issues of common concern

- Foster the general advancement of research, learning, teaching, sharing, and practice in the field of business ethics

Ethics officers in major companies provide ethics programs the best chance of succeeding and continuing to be integral parts of top management programs.

Setting Realistic Objectives

Closely related to all ethics initiatives and programs being implemented by top management is the necessity that managers at all levels set realistic objectives or goals. A manager may quite innocently and inadvertently create a condition leading to unethical behavior on a subordinate's part. Take the case of a marketing manager setting a sales goal of a 25 percent increase for the next year when a 15 percent increase is all that could be realistically expected, even with outstanding performance. In the absence of clearly established and communicated ethical norms, it is easy to see how a subordinate might feel that she or he should go to any lengths to achieve the 25 percent goal. With the goal having been set too high, the salesperson faces a situation that is conducive to unethical behavior in order to please the superior.

Fred T. Allen, a former executive, reinforces this point:

> *Top management must establish sales and profit goals that are realistic—goals that can be achieved with current business practices. Under the pressure of unrealistic goals, otherwise responsible subordinates will often take the attitude that "anything goes" in order to comply with the chief executive's target.[50]*

The point here is that there are ethical implications to even the most routine managerial decisions, such as goal setting. Managers must be keenly sensitive to the possibility of innocently creating situations in which others may perceive a need or an incentive to do the wrong thing.

Ethical Decision-Making Processes

Decision making is at the heart of the management process. If there is any practice or process that is synonymous with management, it is decision making. Decision making usually entails a process of stating the problem, analyzing the problem, identifying the possible courses of action that might be taken, evaluating these courses of action, deciding on the best alternative, and then implementing the chosen course of action.

Decision making at best is a challenge for management. Many decisions management faces turn out to be ethical decisions or to have ethical implications or consequences. Once we leave the realm of relatively ethics-free decisions (such as which production method to use for a particular product), decisions quickly become complex, and many carry with them an ethical dimension.

According to LaRue Hosmer, five important points should be made about the character and nature of ethics and decision making:[51]

1. Most ethical decisions have extended consequences. First-level consequences are followed by a multitude of effects having impacts both within and outside the organization that should be considered when decisions are made.

2. Most ethical decisions have multiple alternatives. Such decisions do not present themselves in simple yes-or-no form, such as "Do we pay a bribe or not?" The simple dichotomy makes for sharp contrasts but does not always capture the real complex alternatives presented.

3. Most ethical decisions have mixed outcomes. Like alternatives, outcomes are mixed and complex rather than occurring in any clear, unambiguous fashion.

4. Most ethical decisions have uncertain consequences. Some consequences may occur that were not anticipated. Thus, it is not always clear what consequences will follow a decision.

5. Most ethical decisions have personal implications. The ethical issues that management faces are not all impersonal but often have very real individual benefits and costs for the decision makers.

Ethical decision making is not a simple process but rather a multifaceted process that is complicated by the characteristics just described. It would be nice if a set of ethical principles were readily available for the manager to "plug in" and walk away from, with a decision to be forthcoming. However, such was not the case when we discussed principles that help personal decision making, and it is not the case when we think of organizational decision making. The ethical principles we discussed earlier are useful here, as are the principles for high-ethics firms that we presented in Figure 5–7. But there are no simple formulas.

Although it is difficult to portray graphically the process of ethical decision making, it is possible as long as we recognize that such an effort cannot totally capture reality. Figure 5–8 presents one conception of the ethical decision-making process. In this model, the individual is asked to identify the action, decision, or behavior that is being considered and then to articulate all dimensions of the proposed course of action. Next, the individual is asked to subject the course of action to what we call an *ethics screen*. An ethics screen consists of several select standards against which the proposed course of action is to be compared. In the illustrated ethics screen, we reference our earlier discussion of the conventional approach (embodying standards/norms), the principles approach, and the ethical tests approach to ethical decision making.

In this model, it is left up to the individual to determine what mix of guidelines to use as the ethics screen. Normally, some combination of the guidelines contained in the screen would be helpful to the individual who truly is attempting to make an ethical decision. If the proposed course of action fails the ethics screen, the decision maker should not engage in the course of action but should consider a new decision, behavior, or action and submit it to this same process. If the proposed course

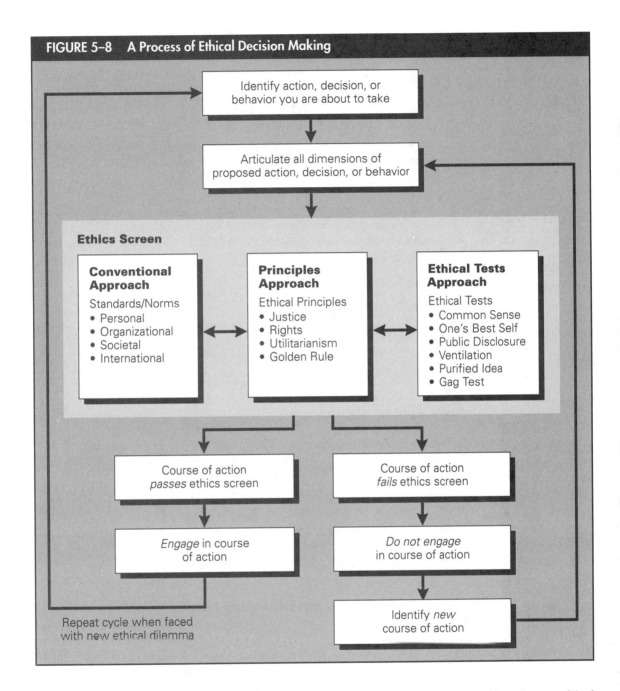

FIGURE 5–8   A Process of Ethical Decision Making

Identify action, decision, or behavior you are about to take

Articulate all dimensions of proposed action, decision, or behavior

Ethics Screen

Conventional Approach

Standards/Norms
• Personal
• Organizational
• Societal
• International

Principles Approach

Ethical Principles
• Justice
• Rights
• Utilitarianism
• Golden Rule

Ethical Tests Approach

Ethical Tests
• Common Sense
• One's Best Self
• Public Disclosure
• Ventilation
• Purified Idea
• Gag Test

Course of action *passes* ethics screen

Course of action *fails* ethics screen

Engage in course of action

Do not engage in course of action

Repeat cycle when faced with new ethical dilemma

Identify *new* course of action

of action passes the screen (the decision maker has determined it to be an ethical course of action), she or he should engage in the action, decision, or behavior and then repeat the cycle only when faced with a new ethical dilemma.

Another useful approach to making ethical decisions is to systematically ask and answer a series of simple questions. One well-known set of questions merits mention here because of its popularity in the book *The Power of Ethical Management.*[52]

Kenneth Blanchard and Norman Vincent Peale proposed the "ethics check" questions as follows:

1. *Is it legal?* Will I be violating either civil law or company policy?

2. *Is it balanced?* Is it fair to all concerned in the short term as well as the long term? Does it promote win-win relationships?

3. *How will it make me feel about myself?* Will it make me proud? Would I feel good if my decision was published in the newspaper? Would I feel good if my family knew about it?

Using a brief set of questions to make ethical decisions has become popular in business. For example, Texas Instruments has printed its seven-part "Ethics Quick Test" on a wallet card its employees may carry. The test's seven questions and reminders are as follows:[53]

- Is the action *legal*?

- Does it comply with our *values*?

- If you do it, will you feel *bad*?

- How will it look in the *newspaper*?

- If you know it's *wrong*, don't do it.

- If you're not sure, *ask*.

- Keep asking until you get an *answer*.

In its Code of Business Conduct, Sears, Roebuck and Co. presents its five "Guidelines for Making Ethical Decisions," which are:[54]

1. Is it legal?

2. Is it within Sears' shared beliefs and policies?

3. Is it right/fair/appropriate?

4. Would I want everyone to know about this?

5. How will I feel about myself?

The sets of questions posed above are intended to produce a process of ethical inquiry that is of immediate use and understanding to a group of employees and managers. Note that many of the items are similar to points raised earlier. These questions help ensure that ethical due process takes place. They cannot tell us whether our decisions are ethical or not, but they can help us be sure that we are raising the appropriate issues and genuinely attempting to be ethical.

Codes of Conduct

Top management has the responsibility for establishing standards of behavior and for effectively communicating those standards to all managers and employees in the organization. One of the classic ways by which companies and ethics officers have fulfilled this responsibility is through the use of *codes of ethics*, or *codes of conduct*. Codes of ethics are a phenomenon of the past 20 years. Over 95 percent of all major corporations have them today, and the central questions in their usefulness or effectiveness revolve around the managerial policies and attitudes associated with their use.[55]

A survey of corporate officers by the Ethics Resource Center, a nonprofit organization based in Washington, DC, revealed several of the values or benefits that business organizations received as a result of their codes of ethics. The results achieved and the percentages of executives citing the reasons give us insights into what companies really think they get from corporate ethics codes:[56]

1. Legal protection for the company (78 percent)

2. Increased company pride and loyalty (74 percent)

3. Increased consumer/public goodwill (66 percent)

4. Improved loss prevention (64 percent)

5. Reduced bribery and kickbacks (58 percent)

6. Improved product quality (14 percent)

7. Increased productivity (12 percent)

Through a code of conduct, management attempts to communicate to all organization members general precepts to guide decision making and actions. The *content* of codes of conduct is also a critical factor. A large-scale survey of ethical codes revealed that codes covered a number of different policy areas. These policy areas were found to be in two general categories: (1) conduct on behalf of the firm and (2) conduct against the firm.

A major observation about the policy areas covered in the codes should be made. There did not appear to be any consensus among the topics covered in the codes. Although over 15 areas were addressed in the codes, in only three areas were the items covered by at least two-thirds of the firms. These three areas were (1) relations with the U.S. Government, (2) relations with customers and suppliers, and (3) conflicts of interest. This diversity of focus suggests an attempt by the firms to tailor the codes to their individual concerns.[57]

In another major study of codes of ethics, Marilynn Cash Mathews found that her Fortune 500 respondents included the following issues at least 75 percent of the time: (1) relations with the U.S. Government, (2) customer/supplier relations, (3) political contributions, (4) conflicts of interest, and (5) honest books or records. She also found that companies tended not to address in their codes such issues as product safety, environmental affairs, product quality, and civic/community affairs.[58]

A study by the Ethics Resource Center of the content of corporate codes found the following to be among the most frequently addressed topics in corporate codes:[59]

1. Conflicts of interest

2. Receiving gifts, gratuities, entertainment

3. Protecting company proprietary information

4. Giving gifts, gratuities, entertainment

5. Discrimination

6. Sexual harassment

7. Kickbacks

8. General conduct

9. Employee theft

10. Proper use of company assets

Let us illustrate what might be involved in creating and administering a code of ethics by looking at the experience of a major firm—Motorola, Inc.[60] Motorola is a worthwhile company to highlight because it won one of the Business Enterprise Trust Awards for exemplary acts of socially concerned business leadership in 1996. At Motorola, a Business Ethics Compliance Committee was created as a subcommittee of the Board of Directors. The three-person committee was composed of the chairman of the board, the chief financial officer, and the senior vice president/general counsel. The committee was charged with the following responsibilities:

- Development, distribution, and periodic revision of a code of conduct

- Interpretation and clarification of the code to ensure that Motorola employees abide by these established principles

- Examination of specific cases of potential code violations with the authority to pass judgment and impose appropriate sanctions

In promulgating its code, the committee reached the conclusion that the company's general principles had to be converted to detailed guidelines. It also decided to clarify the guidelines by including specific examples of prohibited practices. For example:

- "Acceptance by Motorolans of presents from suppliers at Christmas as well as the acceptance by Motorolans of money, property, or services (e.g., free trips) from business associates is prohibited by the code."

- "Suppliers win Motorola business on the basis of product or service suitability, price, delivery, and quality. *There is no other basis.* Attempts to influence procurement decisions by any offers of any compensation, commission, kickback, paid vacation, special discount on a product or service, entertainment, or any form of gift or gratuity must be firmly rejected by all Motorolans."[61]

The committee also was responsible for *communicating* the code to over 100,000 Motorola employees. The code has been disseminated throughout the world and translated into most European and Asian languages. When new workers are hired, they are familiarized with the code. Periodic seminars are conducted to remind employees of the company's continuing commitment to high ethical standards, and videotapes have been produced and distributed to this end.

In addition to its educational function, the Business Ethics Compliance Committee has an active and ongoing role in *interpreting* the code. Hundreds of requests per year are handled. The committee meets on an ad hoc basis six to eight times a year and issues statements clarifying relevant code provisions. Finally, the committee serves a judicial function in cases requiring not only an interpretation of the code but also a ruling on an individual's conduct.

The adjudicatory actions of the committee range from mere advice giving to demotion and economic penalties, discharge, civil pursuit of restitution, and recommendation of prosecution to law enforcement officials. The committee monitors adherence to the code by asking key personnel, along with all personnel in audit or control functions, to sign specific acknowledgments of the code to ensure that they are integrating its precepts into their daily routines. Entering its second decade of activity, the committee is regarded by the chairman as a highly successful and integral element in Motorola's commitment to ethics.[62]

There have been both successes and failures reported with organizational codes of ethics, but the acid test seems to be whether or not such codes actually become "living documents," not just platitudinous public relations statements that are put into a file drawer on dissemination. Codes may not be a panacea for management, but, when properly developed and administered, they serve to raise the level of ethical behavior in the organization by clarifying what is meant by ethical conduct and encouraging moral behavior.

A 1996 study of the effectiveness of corporate codes found that there is a relationship between corporate codes and employee behavior in the workplace, particularly to the degree that employees perceive the codes to be implemented strongly and embedded in the organizational culture. Therefore, when codes are implemented forcefully and embedded strongly in the culture, reports of unethical employee behavior tend to be lower.[63] One example of a conduct code being implemented strongly took place at General Motors (GM), when the company strengthened its ethics code. GM's new policy, entitled "Policy on Gifts, Entertainment, and Other Gratuities" and introduced in 1996 in a 12-page document, outlined new, tougher standards that have become some of the toughest in America. For example, the new policy puts an end to employees enjoying stadium box seats, steak dinners, and weekend golf outings at the expense of their suppliers and vendors.

Another company with strong conduct code enforcement is Wal-Mart. There, employees who accept anything of monetary value face immediate dismissal. After revamping its code, NYNEX Corporation went so far as to prepare a brochure for its suppliers spelling out its restrictions. The company sends its vendors the brochure with its usual holiday-time reminder to send Nynex employees no presents.[64] As these examples illustrate, a number of companies are starting to take their codes of conduct more seriously.

Disciplining Violators of Ethics Standards

To bring about an ethical climate that all organizational members will believe in, management must discipline violators of its accepted ethical norms. A major reason the general public, and even employees in many organizations, have questioned business's sincerity in desiring a more ethical environment has been business's unwillingness to discipline violators. There are numerous cases of top management officers who behaved unethically and yet were retained in their positions. At lower levels there have been cases of top management overlooking or failing to punish unethical behavior of subordinates. These evidences of inaction on management's or the board's part represent implicit approval of the individual's behavior.

Fred Allen argues that an organization should respond forcefully to the individual who is guilty of deliberately or flagrantly violating its code of ethics: "From the pinnacle of the corporate pyramid to its base, there can only be one course of action: dismissal. And should actual criminality be involved, there should be total cooperation with law enforcement authorities."[65]

Phillip Blumberg supports this general line of reasoning with his assertion that "there should be effective sanctions for violations so that there is no doubt that the code really represents corporate policy and that the effort is more than a public relations charade."[66] The effort has to be complete in communicating to all, by way of disciplining offenders, that unethical behavior will not be tolerated in the organization. It is management's tacit approval of violations that has seriously undermined efforts to bring about a more ethical climate in many organizational situations.

Whistle-Blowing Mechanisms and "Hotlines"

One problem that frequently leads to the covering up of unethical acts by people in an organization is that they do not know how to react when they observe a questionable practice. An effective ethical climate is contingent on employees having a mechanism for (and top management support of) "blowing the whistle" on or reporting violators. Allen has summarized this point as follows: "Employees must know exactly what is expected of them in the moral arena and how to respond to warped ethics."[67]

It frequently occurs that unethical practices or crimes come to the attention of organization members several levels down in the organization's structure. John McCloy, who served as chairman of the Special Review Committee to study the use of corporate funds by Gulf Oil Corporation, found that some boards of directors of companies have "adopted and disseminated throughout their companies a policy which encourages any employee who observes a criminal act to report the incident to his or her superior. If the superior is not responsive, the employee then has direct access to the board, usually through its audit committee."[68] This would illustrate the functioning of a whistle-blowing mechanism. Extreme care should be exercised, however, in use of this approach, because there is considerable evidence of whistle-blowing that backfires.

Perhaps the whistle-blowing mechanism in most common use today is the ethics "hotline." At both NYNEX and Northrop, for example, hotlines are used whereby employees may phone in their inquiries about the company's ethics code or report suspected wrongdoing. In one recent year, Northrop reported that about 5 percent of the company's 32,000 employees used its hotline. NYNEX also receives thousands of calls per year. At NYNEX it was estimated that half the callers were seeking information or clarification about the corporate code, whereas only about 10 percent of the callers made allegations of wrongdoing. Ethics officers see this as a positive indication that employees are proacting and trying to head off potential problems before they occur.[69]

Hotlines can have a downside risk, however. Ethicist Barbara Ley Toffler argues that the hotlines may do a lot of harm. She suspects that many of the reported wrongdoings are false accusations and that if the company does not handle these issues carefully, it may do a lot of damage.[70]

Xerox Corporation has a complaint resolution process to handle reported wrongdoings. Xerox employs a four-step process.[71] First, the company receives and examines a complaint. The complaint, or allegation, may come from its hotline, from outside sources such as vendors, customers, or former employees, from whistle-blowers, or from law enforcement agencies. Second, the company conducts an investigation. This is completed by a team—a senior manager, legal counsel, and a human resources executive. Third, there is a management review of the team's report. Finally, step four involves the resolution. Part of the resolution is an attempt to determine why and how the reported incident occurred in the first place. Xerox thinks that the essential elements of the ethics investigation include adherence to a plan, good management communications, and a dedicated interest in ensuring a fair and impartial investigation.

In addition to hotlines for reporting wrongdoing, some companies employ toll-free numbers wherein employees may simply inquire about ethics matters. For example, the Sears Office of Ethics and Business Policy employs an "Ethics Assist" program in which employees may call about such topics as:[72]

- Interpretation of or guidance on company policy
- General ethics questions
- Code of conduct issues
- Workplace harassment/discrimination
- Selling practices
- Theft

Business Ethics Training

For several years there has been debate and controversy about whether managerial ethics can and should be taught. One school of thought assumes that ethics is personal, already embedded within the employee or manager and, hence, not alterable or teachable. A growing school of thought, on the other hand, argues that instruction in business ethics should be made a part of business school education, management training, executive development programs, and seminars.

Professor Kirk Hanson has been teaching business ethics at the Stanford Business School for many years. Whereas he agrees with some critics who say it is tough to infuse values in university students, he also thinks that there is a legitimate role for business ethics courses. Hanson believes that we can most help the fundamentally decent, well-intentioned student. He says:

> *If we teach techniques and strategies for handling a wide variety of business decisions, we can do the same for predictable ethical decisions or challenges. Among those situations are: finding a match between a person's values and those of his or her employer; managing the pushback point where one's values are tested by peers, subordinates, or superiors; handling an unethical directive from one's boss; and coping with a performance system that gives strong incentives to cut ethical corners.*[73]

In addition, in numerous organizations in the United States today, management training in business ethics is taking place. A survey by the Ethics Resource Center found a dramatic increase in the number of major firms teaching ethics to their employees over the past few years. In 1980, the center found seven companies doing on-site ethics training of managers. By the mid-1990s, close to half were providing ethics training on the job.[74] One specific, positive example is the ethics training conducted at Syntex by former vice chairman Hans A. Wolf. According to Wolf, "our ethics seminars have had a significant effect on Syntex managers. In a sense, part of the message was in the process. The fact that the vice chairman was willing to spend so much time on this issue has been a powerful testimony to the importance the company attaches to ethical behavior."[75]

What might be the purposes or objectives of such ethics training? Several purposes have been suggested:

1. To increase the manager's sensitivity to ethical problems
2. To encourage critical evaluation of value priorities
3. To increase awareness of organizational realities
4. To increase awareness of societal realities
5. To improve understanding of the importance of public image and public/society relations[76]

To this list we might add some other desirable goals:

6. To examine the ethical facets of business decision making
7. To bring about a greater degree of fairness and honesty in the workplace
8. To respond more completely to the organization's social responsibilities

Materials and formats typically used by firms in their ethics training include the following: ethics codes (as a training device), lectures, workshops/seminars, case studies, films/discussions, and articles/speeches.[77] One major firm, Lockheed Martin, introduced some humor into its ethics training in 1997 by introducing the Dilbert-inspired board game, "The Ethics Challenge," for company-wide ethics training. To play the game, players (employees) move around the board by answering "Case File" questions such as, "You've been selected for a training course in Florida, and you want to go only for the vacation." Among the answers and their respective points are: "Go, but skip the sessions" (0 points), "Ask your supervisor if it would be beneficial" (5 points), and, the Dogbert answer, "Wear mouse ears to work and hum 'It's a Small World After All' all day." Sessions for the company's 185,000 employees were led by supervisors, not ethics officers. Chairman of the company, Norm Augustine, kicked off the training by leading the training of those who reported to him directly.[78]

In terms of the effectiveness of ethics training, Thomas Jones discovered in his research that exposure to lengthy programs (for example, 10 weeks) resulted in significant improvements in moral development. Brief exposures to business ethics, however, yielded less encouraging results.[79] Questions remain, therefore, as to the ultimate and lasting value of superficial ethics education.

There will doubtless be difficulties in training managers in business ethics. These difficulties, however, should not preclude serious attempts and experimentation with case studies, incidents, role playing, games, and discussion of crucial ethical issues. With respect to the teaching of ethics, John Adair has asserted, "A good teacher can help managers to become generally aware of their values and to compare them with

ETHICS IN PRACTICE

Would You Make the Call?

I work at a little dress and jewelry store in Atlanta. Because my manager's grandfather fell gravely ill during my first week on the job, and because the store was severely understaffed, I was left to work alone one night. It was only my fifth time at the store, and I was somewhat frazzled by customers' questions and a computer that was not so user-friendly.

The phone rang at a quarter past five o'clock. The lady on the other end said that she was calling from an apartment complex in Atlanta and wanted to verify the employment and salary of Bradley Agle. My first thought was "Who?" I had never heard of that name, but I was new. I told her that she could call back in the morning to speak with my manager because I was unable to give her such information over the phone. She told me that she needed the information that night, because that was when Bradley and his roommates wanted to move in. Otherwise they would have to spend the night in a hotel. She also explained that the law allows shopkeepers to verify information with a simple "yes" or "no" when information is voluntarily given by the employee in question. But I still had never heard of this guy. I quickly grabbed the next week's schedule to see if he was on it. The lady had said that he should average about 40 hours a week, yet he was not on the schedule. I finally explained to the lady that I was new and had not yet met all of the employees, but I would try to reach my manager and call her back. She asked me to hurry because she would be leaving at 5:30.

I was very confused at this point. My manager is very laid back and many of the rules strictly enforced in all of my past retail jobs were never even mentioned here. Not only did we not "go by the book," but there was no book to go by. I had to call someone, but I didn't want to call my manager at the hospital. I decided to call Susan. Susan was my manager's best friend and the only other person I had ever worked with.

When Susan heard my dilemma, she started laughing. Now I was even more confused. Then she explained that Bradley was her boyfriend who had just moved to Atlanta. Bradley did not have a job, so he used our store as a reference, claiming he earned up to $500 per week. Then Susan asked me to please call the lady back and tell her that I had found out that Bradley was an assistant manager. When she asked for wage verification I should simply answer "yes" to whatever she provided. I agreed to do it as I hung up with Susan, because she can be highly intimidating, and, as she said, it could never hurt my store in any way. Besides, she said that Bradley had plenty of money and would not fall behind on his rent. He was also a lifelong friend of my manager, who knew all about this and, according to Susan, said it was fine.

What should I have done? Doing what Susan had asked me seemed harmless, and I didn't want to make these guys go to a hotel, or to get Susan on my bad side. Should I have called the lady back, and if so, what should I have told her? What would you have done?

1. Describe the ethical climate of this little dress and jewelry store.

2. What ethical principles or tests would have been helpful to the decision maker in this case?

3. What should I have done? Does it matter if you lie if nobody will be hurt, as in this case?

Contributed by Angie Briguccia

the consensus of value judgments in a particular company, industry, or profession."[80] We believe, therefore, that there is merit in management training and development in ethics as a viable aid to bringing about more ethical organizational behavior. Companies, in growing numbers, are turning to ethics training to help foster a sound organizational ethical climate.

Ethics Audits and Self-Assessments

In increasing numbers, companies today are beginning to appreciate the need to follow up on their ethics initiatives and programs. Ethics audits are mechanisms or approaches by which a company may assess or evaluate its ethical climate or programs. Ethical audits are intended to carefully review such ethics initiatives as ethics programs, codes of conduct, hotlines, and ethics training programs. In addition, they are intended to examine other management activities that may add to or subtract from the company's initiatives. This might include management's sincerity, communication efforts, incentive and reward systems, and other management activities. Ethics audits may employ written instruments, committees, and employee interviews.[81]

An experimental approach to ethics audits using a peer review process was recently conducted by Texas Instruments and Martin Marietta, both signatories to the Defense Industry Initiative, a group of companies that voluntarily joined together to enhance public confidence in the defense industry. The purpose of the peer review exchange was for the two companies to "audit" or review each other's ethics programs and initiatives. The focus of the reviews was on processes, training, communication, and budgets, not on individual cases of ethics issues.[82]

The reviews offered several advantages. The informality of the process permitted time to delve into the most important program aspects. On-site visits permitted direct observation of local operations. Finally, the companies were more candid with each other than might have been the case in a more formal meeting. Disadvantages identified were that the informality may have led to less information being exchanged than might have occurred in a more structured process, and that, because the companies were reviewing each other, there was always the risk of mutual "back scratching." Perhaps one of the clearest results of the process was that the companies got a chance to check on their peers and to see what worked for them.[83]

More and more companies will assess and attempt to improve their organizations' ethical climates as instruments, methods, and services are made available for conducting such programs. The resources now available include the "Business Integrity Assessment" program offered by Walker Information, a company with headquarters in Indianapolis, Indiana, and offices around the world. With the methodology and instruments developed by Walker Information, companies may assess their ethical cultures and measure their ethics or compliance programs' effectiveness. Companies may then compare their results with national benchmark data established by Walker.[84]

Figure 5–9 summarizes what the Ethics Resource Center has concluded about improving the ethical climate of organizations. These conclusions are based on its surveys of the actual practices of 2,000 U.S. corporations. This statement is not the definitive word on the subject, but it does give us keen insights into what major companies are doing today in actual practice.

Although we have not touched on all that can be done at the organizational level to improve or manage business ethics, the actions suggested represent best practices

---

FIGURE 5–9   Improving the Organization's Ethical Climate

Executives and managers seeking to improve the ethical climate of their organizations should consider the following conclusions from the present survey report:

Companies that see their ethics monitoring and enforcement methods as very effective share these characteristics:

- Written codes, policies, or guidelines;

- Distribution of policies to all employees, not just management;

- Reinforcement through communications, including videotapes, articles, posters, and public talks by company executives;

- Additional training geared toward application of policies to everyday work situations;

- Sources of information and advice, such as ombudspersons and hotlines; and

- Monitoring and enforcement through a Corporate Ethics Office and a Board of Directors Ethics Committee.

If companies' perceptions correlate with actual effectiveness, then companies that do not have the above elements are risking greater amounts of unethical conduct than companies that do.

SOURCE: *Ethics Policies and Programs in American Business* (Washington, DC: Ethics Resource Center and Behavior Research Center, 1990). Used with permission.

that can move management a long way toward improving the organization's ethical climate. If management takes specific steps as suggested, many behaviors or decisions that might otherwise have been questionable have a greater chance of being in line with leadership's ethical standards. Thus, ethics can be managed, and managers do not have to treat value concerns as matters totally out of their control. On the contrary, managers can intercede and improve the organization's ethical climate.[85]

SUMMARY

The subject of business ethics may be addressed at several different levels: personal, organizational, industry, societal, and international. This chapter focuses on the personal and organizational levels.

A number of different ethical principles serve as guides to personal decision making. Major philosophical principles include utilitarianism, rights, and justice. The Golden Rule was singled out as a particularly powerful ethical principle among various groups studied. Virtue ethics was identified as an increasingly popular concept. A general method for reconciling ethical conflicts was introduced. Six practical tests were proposed to assist the individual in making ethical decisions: the test of common sense, the test of one's best self, the test of making something public, the test of ventilation, the test of the purified idea, and the gag test.

At the organizational level, factors were discussed that affect the organization's moral climate. It was argued that the behavior of one's superiors and peers and industry ethical practices were the most important influences on a firm's ethical climate. Society's moral climate and personal needs were considered to be less important. Best practices for improving the firm's ethical climate include providing leadership from management, ethics programs and ethics officers, setting realistic objectives, infusing the decision-making process with ethical considerations, employing codes of conduct, disciplining violators, creating whistle-blowing mechanisms or hotlines, training managers in business ethics, and using ethics audits.

KEY TERMS

codes of conduct (page 158)

codes of ethics (page 158)

compensatory justice (page 137)

distributive justice (page 137)

ethical tests (page 143)

Golden Rule (page 139)

personal and managerial ethics (page 134)

principle of caring (page 137)

principle of justice (page 137)

principle of rights (page 135)

procedural justice (page 137)

utilitarianism (page 135)

virtue ethics (page 137)

DISCUSSION QUESTIONS

1. From your personal experience, give two examples of ethical dilemmas in your personal life. Give two examples of ethical dilemmas you have experienced as a member of an organization.
2. Using the examples you provided for Question 1, identify one or more of the guides to personal decision making or ethical tests that you think would have helped you resolve your dilemmas. Describe how it would have helped.
3. Assume that you are in your first real managerial position. Identify five ways in which you might provide ethical leadership. Rank them in terms of importance, and be prepared to explain your ranking.
4. What do you think about the idea of codes of conduct? Give three reasons why an organization ought to have a code of conduct, and give three reasons why an organization should not have a code of conduct. On balance, how do you regard codes of conduct?
5. A lively debate is going on in this country over the question of whether business ethics can or should be taught in business schools. Do you think business ethics can and should be taught? Be prepared to explain your reasons carefully.

ENDNOTES

1. Lisa Crowe, "Typical Top Exec: He's White, Male and Republican," *Atlanta Journal and Constitution* (February 2, 1987), 13-C.
2. Archie B. Carroll, "Principles of Business Ethics: Their Role in Decision Making and an Initial Consensus," *Management Decision* (Vol. 28, No. 28, 1990), 20–24.
3. Vincent Barry, *Moral Issues in Business* (Belmont, CA: Wadsworth, 1979), 43.
4. *Ibid.*, 45–46.

5. Manuel C. Velasquez, *Business Ethics: Concepts and Cases,* 3rd ed. (Englewood Cliffs, NJ: Prentice Hall, 1992), 72–73.

6. Richard T. DeGeorge, *Business Ethics,* 5th ed. (Upper Saddle River, NJ: Prentice Hall, 1999), 69–72.

7. Velasquez, 73.

8. See the following sources for a discussion of these points: David Luban, "Judicial Activism and the Concept of Rights," *Report from the Institute for Philosophy & Public Policy* (College Park, MD: University of Maryland, Winter/Spring, 1994), 12–17; George F. Will, "Our Expanding Menu of Rights," *Newsweek* (December 14, 1992), 90; John Leo, "The Spread of Rights Babble," *U.S. News & World Report* (June 28, 1993), 17; and William Raspberry, "Blind Pursuit of Rights Can Endanger Civility," *The Atlanta Journal* (September 14, 1994), A14.

9. DeGeorge, 69–72.

10. *Ibid.*

11. John Rawls, *A Theory of Justice* (Cambridge, MA: Harvard University Press, 1971).

12. DeGeorge, 69–72.

13. *Ibid.,* 72.

13a. Brian K. Burton and Craig P. Dunn, "Feminist Ethics as Moral Grounding for Stakeholder Theory," *Business Ethics Quarterly* (Vol. 6, No. 2, 1996), 133–147. Also see A. C. Wicks, D. R. Gilbert, and R. E. Freeman, "A Feminist Reinterpretation of the Stakeholder Concept," *Business Ethics Quarterly* (Vol. 4, 1994), 475–497.

14. Jeanne M. Liedtka, "Feminist Morality and Competitive Reality: A Role for an Ethic of Care?" *Business Ethics Quarterly* (Vol. 6, 1996), 179–200. Also see John Dobson and Judith White, "Toward the Feminine Firm," *Business Ethics Quarterly* (Vol. 5, 1995), 463–478.

15. Alasdair MacIntyre, *After Virtue* (University of Notre Dame Press), 1981. Also see Louis P. Pojman, *Ethics: Discovering Right and Wrong,* 2nd ed. (Belmont, CA: Wadsworth, 1995), 160–185.

16. Pojman, 161. Also see Bill Shaw, "Sources of Virtue: The Market and the Community," *Business Ethics Quarterly* (Vol. 7, 1997), 33–50; and Dennis Moberg, "Virtuous Peers in Work Organizations," *Business Ethics Quarterly* (Vol. 7, 1997), 67–85.

17. Lawton Bloom, "Character Education Movement Garners National Attention," *Ethics Journal* (Summer/Fall, 1994), 4–5.

18. Esther F. Schaeffer, "Character Education: A Prerequisite for Corporate Ethics," *Ethics Today* (Summer, 1997), 5.

19. Oliver F. Williams and Patrick E. Murphy, "The Ethics of Virtue: A Moral Theory for Business," in Oliver F. Williams and John W. Houck (eds.), *A Virtuous Life in Business* (Lanham, MD: Rowman & Littlefield Publishers, Inc., 1992), 9–27.

20. Carroll, 22.

21. Barry, 50–51.

22. Carroll, 22.

23. William Shaw and Vincent Barry, *Moral Issues in Business* (Belmont, CA: Wadsworth, 1989), 77–78; and Vincent R. Ruggiero, *The Moral Imperative* (Port Washington, NY: Alfred Publishers, 1973).

24. Shaw and Barry, 77.

25. *Ibid.*, 78.

26. Gordon L. Lippett, *The Leader Looks at Ethics,* 12–13.

27. "Stiffer Rules for Business Ethics," *Business Week* (March 30, 1974), 88.

28. Frederick Andrews, "Corporate Ethics: Talks with a Trace of Robber Baron," *The New York Times* (April 18, 1977), C49–52.

29. Phillip V. Lewis, "Ethical Principles for Decision Makers: A Longitudinal Study," *Journal of Business Ethics* (Vol. 8, 1989), 275.

30. Cited in John B. Cullen, Bart Victor, and Carroll Stephens, "An Ethical Weather Report: Assessing the Organization's Ethical Climate," *Organizational Dynamics* (Autumn, 1989), 50.

31. For an excellent discussion, see Deborah Vidaver Cohen, "Creating and Maintaining Ethical Work Climates: Anomie in the Workplace and Implications for Managing Change," *Business Ethics Quarterly* (Vol. 3, No. 4, October, 1993), 343–355. Also see B. Victor and J. Cullen, "The Organizational Bases of Ethical Work Climates," *Administrative Science Quarterly* (Vol. 33, 1988), 101–125; and H.R. Smith and A.B. Carroll, "Organizational Ethics: A Stacked Deck," *Journal of Business Ethics* (Vol. 3, 1984), 95–100.

32. Raymond C. Baumhart, "How Ethical Are Businessmen?" *Harvard Business Review* (July/August, 1961), 6ff.

33. Steve Brenner and Earl Molander, "Is the Ethics of Business Changing?" *Harvard Business Review* (January/February, 1977).

34. Barry Z. Posner and Warren H. Schmidt, "Values and the American Manager: An Update," *California Management Review* (Spring, 1984), 202–216.

35. Archie B. Carroll, "Managerial Ethics: A Post-Watergate View," *Business Horizons* (April, 1975), 75–80.

36. Posner and Schmidt, 211.

37. Carroll, 75–80.

38. American Society of Chartered Life Underwriters & Chartered Financial Consultants and Ethics Officer Association, "Sources and Consequences of Workplace Pressure: A Landmark Study," unpublished report (1997). Also see Del Jones, "48% of Workers Admit to Unethical or Illegal Acts," *USA Today* (April 4–6, 1997), 1A–2A.

39. George Getschow, "Some Middle Managers Cut Corners to Achieve High Corporate Goals," *The Wall Street Journal* (November 8, 1979), 1, 34.

40. *Ibid.*, 34.

41. T.V. Purcell and James Weber, *Institutionalizing Corporate Ethics: A Case History,* Special Study No. 71 (New York: The President's Association, American Management Association, 1979); also see James Weber, "Institutionalizing Ethics into Business Organizations: A Model and Research Agenda," *Business Ethics Quarterly* (Vol. 3, No. 4, October, 1993), 419–436.

42. L. W. Foy, "Business Ethics: A Reappraisal," Distinguished Lecture Series, Columbia Graduate School of Business (January 30, 1975), 2.

43. Harvey Gittler, "Listen to the Whistle Blowers Before It's Too Late," *The Wall Street Journal* (March 10, 1986), 16.

44. Lee L. Morgan, "Business Ethics Starts with the Individual," *Management Accounting* (March, 1977), 14, 60.

45. Mark Pastin, *The Hard Problems of Management: Gaining the Ethics Edge* (San Francisco: Jossey-Bass, 1986), 221–225.

46. Steven N. Brenner, "Influences on Corporate Ethics Programs" (San Diego, CA: International Association for Business and Society, March 16–18, 1990), 7.

47. Susan Gaines, "Handing Out Halos," *Business Ethics* (March/April, 1994), 20–24.

48. *Ibid.*, 20–24. Also see Stephen J. Garone (ed.), *Business Ethics: Generating Trust in the 1990s and Beyond* (New York: The Conference Board, 1994).

49. "Ethics Officer Association: Overview and Benefits" (1996), 2. The EOA office is in the Bentley College Center for Business Ethics (Waltham, MA 02154).

50. Fred T. Allen, "Corporate Morality: Is the Price Too High?" *The Wall Street Journal* (October 17, 1975), 16.

51. LaRue T. Hosmer, *The Ethics of Management* (Homewood, IL: Richard D. Irwin, 1987), 12–14.

52. Kenneth Blanchard and Norman Vincent Peale, *The Power of Ethical Management* (New York: Fawcett Crest, 1988), 20.

53. Texas Instruments, "Ethics Quick Test" (Texas Instruments Ethics Office), wallet card.

54. Sears, Roebuck and Co., *Code of Business Conduct* (1997), 2.

55. Gary Edwards, "And the Survey Said . . . ," in Garone (ed.), 1994, 25.

56. *Creating a Workable Company Code of Ethics* (Washington, DC: Ethics Resource Center, 1990), VIII–1.

57. Donald R. Cressey and Charles R. Moore, "Managerial Values and Corporate Codes of Ethics," *California Management Review* (Summer, 1983), 57–58. Also see Patrick E. Murphy, "Improving Your Ethics Code," *Business Ethics* (March/April, 1994), 23; and James Krohe, Jr., "Ethics Are Nice, But Business Is Business," *Across the Board* (April, 1997), 16–22.

58. Cited in Rick Wartzman, "Nature or Nurture? Study Blames Ethical Lapses on Corporate Goals," *The Wall Street Journal* (October 9, 1987), 31.

59. *Ethics Policies and Programs in American Business* (Washington, DC: Ethics Resource Center, 1990), 23–24. Also see W. F. Edmondson, *A Code of Ethics: Do Corporate Executives and Employees Need It?* (Itawamba Community College Press, 1990).

60. "Motorola's Ethics Committee: Adding Teeth to the Corporate Code," *Ethics Resource Center Report* (Summer, 1986), 4–6.

61. *Ibid.*

62. *Ibid.*

63. Donald L. McCabe, Linda Klebe Trevino, and Kenneth D. Butterfield, "The Influence of Collegiate and Corporate Codes of Conduct on Ethics-Related Behavior in the Workplace," *Business Ethics Quarterly* (Vol. 6, October 1996), 473.

64. Gabriella Stern and Joann Lublin, "New GM Rules Curb Wining and Dining," *Wall Street Journal* (June 5, 1996), B1.

65. Allen, 16.

66. Phillip I. Blumberg, "Corporate Morality and the Crisis of Confidence in American Business," *Beta Gamma Sigma Invited Essay* (St. Louis: Beta Gamma Sigma, January, 1977), 7.

67. Allen, 16.

68. Myles L. Mace, "John J. McCloy on Corporate Payoffs," *Harvard Business Review* (July–August, 1976), 28.

69. Cited in Gaines, 22.

70. *Ibid.*, 22–23.

71. Brian R. Hollstein, "From Complaint to Resolution," in Garone (ed.), 1994, 21–22.

72. Sears Code of Business Conduct, 1997.

73. Kirk O. Hanson, "What Good Are Ethics Courses?" *Across the Board* (September, 1987), 10–11.

74. Edwards, in Garone (ed.), 1994, 25.

75. Hans A. Wolf, "Ethics by Example," in Garone (ed.), 1994, 17–18.

76. Ron Zemke, "Ethics Training: Can We Really Teach People Right from Wrong?" *Training HRD* (May, 1977), 39.

77. *Ethics Policies and Programs in American Business,* 34.

78. "At Last: Humor in Ethics Training," *Business Ethics* (May/June 1997), 10.

79. Thomas M. Jones, "Can Business Ethics Be Taught? Empirical Evidence," *Business & Professional Ethics Journal* (Vol. 8, 1989), 86.

80. John E. Adair, *Management and Morality: The Problems and Opportunities of Social Capitalism* (London: David & Charles, 1974), 143.

81. Michael Metzger, Dan R. Dalton, and John W. Hill, "The Organization of Ethics and the Ethics of Organizations: The Case for Expanded Organizational Ethics Audits," *Business Ethics Quarterly* (Vol. 3, No. 1, January, 1993), 27–43. Also see S. Andrew Ostapski, "The Moral Audit," *Business and Economic Review* (Vol. 38, No. 2, January–March, 1992), 17–20; and Thomas Petzinger, Jr., "This Auditing Team Wants You to Create a Moral Organization," *Wall Street Journal* (January 19, 1996), B1.

82. Carl M. Skooglund, "Using Peer Companies to Audit Ethics Programs," in Garone (ed.), 1994, 19–20.

83. *Ibid.*

84. Walker Information, "Assessing and Measuring Business Integrity" (Indianapolis, IN).

85. W. Edward Stead, Dan L. Worrell, and Jean Garner Stead, "An Integrative Model for Understanding and Managing Ethical Behavior in Business Organizations," *Journal of Business Ethics* (Vol. 9, 1990), 223–242. Also see Robert D. Gatewood and Archie B. Carroll, "Assessment of Ethical Performance of Organization Members: A Conceptual Framework," *Academy of Management Review* (Vol. 16, No. 4, 1991), 667–690.

6

Ethical Issues in the Global Arena

CHAPTER OBJECTIVES

After studying this chapter, you should be able to:

1 Identify and describe the four eras in the trend toward the internationalization of business.

2 Explain the evolving role of and problems with multinational corporations in the global environment.

3 Recognize the major ethical challenges of operating in the multinational environment.

4 Discuss strategies for improving global ethics.

5 Enumerate seven moral guidelines for improving multinational corporations' operations in the global sphere.

The rise of international business as a critical element in the world economy is one of the most significant developments of the past 40 years or more. This period has been characterized by the rapid growth of direct investment in foreign lands by the United States, by countries in Western Europe, by Japan, and by other industrialized countries as well. In the United States, domestic issues have been made immensely more complex by the rising international focus. At the same time, the internationalization of business has created unique problems of its own. It no longer appears that international markets can be seen as opportunities that may or may not be pursued. Rather, international markets should be seen as natural extensions of an ever-expanding marketplace that must be pursued if firms are to remain competitive.

Peter Drucker has termed this expanded marketplace the *transnational economy*. He goes on to say that, if business expects to establish and maintain leadership in one country, it must also strive to hold a leadership position in all developed markets worldwide. This apparent need helps explain the worldwide boom in transnational investments.[1] This transnational or global economy has been defined concretely as follows: trade in goods, a much smaller trade in services, the international movement of labor, and international flows of capital and information.[2]

The complexity introduced by the transnational economy and the internationalization of business is seen clearly in cases in which ethical issues arise. At best, business ethics is difficult when we are dealing with one culture. Once we bring two or possibly more cultures into consideration, it gets extremely complicated. Managers have to deal not only with differing customs, protocol, and ways of operating but also with differing concepts of law or notions of what is acceptable or unacceptable behavior in an ethical sense. All of this is then exacerbated by the fact that world political issues become intertwined. For example, what might be intended as a corporate attempt to simply bribe an official of a foreign government, in keeping with local custom, could explode into major international political tension between two countries.

International business is an extremely broad topic. We can expose only the tip of the iceberg here, and, because we must limit our discussion to ethical and social issues, we can examine only one small facet of that exposed tip. Nevertheless, we do need to briefly consider some of the challenges introduced in business ethics at an international level, and that will be our major purpose in this chapter. For a broader consideration of international business and society issues, see Wartick's and Wood's 1998 book, *International Business and Society*.[3]

ERAS IN THE INTERNATIONALIZATION OF BUSINESS

Depending on which international business expert you read, the period from 1945 to the present may be divided into three or four general eras in the growth of the international economy. We do not need to consider these eras in detail, but it is helpful to note some of the major changes that occurred during this time to help us appreciate the modern situation.

The Post World War II Decade (1945–1955)

Immediately after World War II, the United States was the dominant country as Western Europe and Japan underwent a period of reconstruction. According to Richard D. Robinson, this *postwar decade* is the first era in international development.[4]

The Growth Years (1955–1970)

By 1955, Japanese and European reconstruction was essentially completed and we entered the *growth years*. Both Japanese and European firms began to seek global markets more aggressively. Also during this time the United States got bogged down in Vietnam. As the United States built up massive balance-of-payments deficits, the dollar came under increasing pressure. A number of the larger U.S.-based international firms became multinational in that they moved toward globally integrated production and marketing systems that necessitated central control.

Because of the development of international communication systems and technology, jet air travel, and increased international expertise, such centralized control became possible.[5] It was one thing to sell products in a foreign land, but with the increasing prevalence of multinational corporations (MNCs)—first in the United States, then in Western Europe and Japan—the sensitivities of host governments became heightened. A ***multinational corporation*** is a firm that has extended its operations beyond the boundaries of its home country by having one or more subsidiaries in countries other than that in which it is chartered (its home country). Production and distribution systems are still significantly owned by the companies of a home country but are located in a host country, where they have become a vital element in that country's economy.

The 1955–1970 period witnessed a strong rise in MNCs, with U.S. firms dominating. The growth of U.S.-based MNCs was followed by rapid expansion of Western European MNCs, and then by expansion of Japanese MNCs, particularly during the 1970s. The United States felt the Japanese expansion as well. Practically everyone in the United States today recognizes such names as Sony, Toyota, Honda, and Mitsubishi as they would such U.S. names as GE, Ford, and General Motors.

The Troubled Years (1970–1980)

The 1970s—the *time of trouble*—is Robinson's third era in international business development.[6] During this time, the persistent balance-of-payments deficit forced the United States to drop the fixed exchange rate system, and the value of the dollar declined significantly, especially in relation to the Japanese yen and the German mark. During this time, the political power of the MNC was finally recognized. The worldwide oil crisis and the high visibility of OPEC also occurred during this period.

The New International Order (1980–Present)

The *new international order* (1980 and beyond) is Robinson's fourth era.[7] By the mid- to late 1970s, the entire sphere of international business was being heavily politicized, both at home and abroad. There was mounting government regulation in many countries as public concerns intensified with regard to pollution, natural resource allocation, income and wealth distribution, consumer protection, and energy. All this was made more complex by intranational conflict, lack of clear national policies, and the increasingly strong voices of special-interest groups. Some of these groups—whether they were religious, ethnic, political, economic, or professional–have been establishing international linkages and loyalties that are quite distinct from the traditional nation-state loyalties. Efforts to create new international agencies based on common interest (consumers, labor, the poor, conservationists, business) have become commonplace. Many of these groups wanted to create a new international order in their own image. The upshot of these developments has been a complex multiactor era.[8]

One of the most significant occurrences in international business over the past 20 years has been the diminishment of the United States as a world economic power. Whereas it once dominated global markets, this is no longer the case. The new international order, therefore, is one in which the United States no longer occupies the almost monopolistic position it once did. It is still a major actor, but it now shares the stage with Japan, Western Europe, Asia, and the developing countries. Perhaps it has been this diminishment of status in the world that has made the push toward better business ethics at the international level a bitter pill to swallow for many businesspeople. The United States has definitely lost some of its economic status and is scrambling to become competitive again. Yet, at the same time, it is under increasing pressures to be a world leader in the ethics arena.[9]

From the perspective of the United States as well as other countries, the passage of the North American Free Trade Agreement (NAFTA) in 1993 ushered in a new era of free trade that is expected to intensify the debate over which stakeholders U.S. MNCs should primarily serve. Will it be those American shareholders, workers, and communities to which they traditionally have been bound, or will it be the broader community of interests brought about by the global economy? As international business increases, there will be a whole set of issues, such as environmental protection, wage disparities, and the heightened insistence on the part of their new stakeholders that companies refocus their view of the world. It is little wonder that by the late 1990s international business has been identified as a highly explosive ethical land mine.[10] As we enter the new millennium, the MNC has become the focal point of global business ethics. Therefore, MNCs are worth considering more closely.

MNCs AND THE GLOBAL ENVIRONMENT

Not all problems of operating in a global environment are attributable to MNCs. However, MNCs have become the symbolic heart of the problem because they represent the prototypical international business. We will focus on U.S.-based MNCs, but we should remember that the MNCs of other countries experience these same environmental circumstances. In fact, the presence of MNCs from multiple countries makes for a complex operating environment for all firms.

Changed Scope and Nature of U.S.-Based MNCs

Over the years, both the scope and the nature of U.S.-based MNCs have changed. In the early 1900s, the United Fruit Company was growing bananas in Central America and achieving a degree of notoriety for its "invasion" of Honduras. Another wave of MNCs was in the extractive industries (oil, gas, gems). Today, financial institutions, chemical companies, pharmaceutical companies, manufacturers, and service firms represent the kinds of enterprises that may be found operating in the multinational environment.

The investment of U.S.-based MNCs has been phenomenal over the past three decades or more, growing from $20 billion to well over $250 billion.[11] We should also note that the most challenging situation for MNCs is when they are operating in so-called emerging nations, or *less-developed countries (LDCs)*, where charges of exploitation and abuse of power seem more plausible. These situations are ripe for charges of American imperialism in struggling economies.

Underlying Challenges of Operating in a Multinational Environment

It has been argued that there are at least two underlying and related challenges or problems as firms attempt to operate in a multinational environment. One problem is *corporate legitimacy* as the MNC seeks a role in a foreign society. The other problem is the fundamentally *different philosophies* that may exist between the firm's home country and the host country in which it seeks to operate.[12] These two challenges set the stage for understanding how ethical problems arise in the global environment.

Corporate Legitimacy

For an MNC to be perceived as legitimate in the eyes of a host country, it must fulfill its social responsibilities. As we discussed earlier, these include economic, legal, ethical, and philanthropic responsibilities. Larger firms, in particular, are seen as outsiders, and the expectations on them are greater than on smaller, less visible firms. Further, the similarities and differences between the cultures of the two countries affect the perceived legitimacy. For example, an American firm operating in Canada is not likely to experience major problems. An American or a Western firm operating in Iran, however, could be perceived as quite alien.[13] Differences between the values and lifestyles of managers who live in the two countries could pose serious legitimacy problems. If a host country finds the lifestyles or values repugnant—as many LDCs may well find the materialistic lifestyles and values of American managers—legitimacy may be difficult to achieve.

Another, perhaps more basic, barrier to achieving legitimacy is the inherent conflict that may exist between the *interests* of the MNC and those of the host country. The MNC is seeking to optimize globally, while host governments are seeking to optimize locally. This may pose little difficulty for an MNC operating in a developed country, where macroeconomic or regulatory policies are sophisticated and appropriate. But it may pose serious problems in the LDCs, where there is often the perception that MNCs are beyond the control of local governments. In these latter situations, especially, it is not uncommon to see the local government impose various control devices, such as *indigenization* laws requiring majority ownership by locals, exclusion of foreign firms from certain industries, restrictions on foreign personnel, or even expropriation.[14]

Part of the reason MNCs have difficulty achieving legitimacy is a reaction to the real or perceived conflicts between the interests of the firm and those of the host country or government that place the MNC in a "no-win" situation. If the MNC tries to bring in the latest labor-saving technology, this may conflict with the perceived need for labor-creating technology in high-unemployment-prone LDCs. If the MNC repatriates large parts of its profits, this may be seen as depriving the local economy of new wealth. If the MNC reinvests the profits locally, this may be perceived as furthering its control over the economy. If the MNC pays market rate wages, this may be seen as exploiting labor with low wage rates. If the MNC pays a premium for labor, this may be seen as skimming the cream of the local labor supply and thus hurting local businesses that cannot afford to pay a premium. Consequently, whatever it does, the MNC is a convenient target for criticism from some faction or stakeholders. In this sometimes hostile environment, legitimacy can be both elusive and fleeting—difficult to get and even harder to keep.[15]

Differing Philosophies

Closely related to the legitimacy issue is the dilemma of MNCs that have quite different philosophical perspectives from those of their host countries. The philosophy of Western industrialized nations, and thus their MNCs, focuses on economic growth, efficiency, specialization, free trade, and comparative advantage. By contrast, LDCs, for example, have quite different priorities. Other important objectives for them might include a more equitable income distribution or increased economic self-determination. In this context, the industrialized nations may appear to be inherently exploitative in that their presence may perpetuate the dependency of the poorer nation. This is evident in relations not only between Western-based MNCs and LDCs, but also between market-oriented Western-based MNCs and planning-oriented communist countries.[16]

These philosophical differences build in an environment of tension that sometimes results in stringent actions being unilaterally taken by the host country. During the 1970s, for example, the environment for MNCs investing in LDCs became much more harsh. Some of these harsh actions initiated by the host countries included outright expropriation (as occurred in the oil industry) and creeping expropriation (as occurred in the manufacturing industries when foreign subsidiaries were required to take on some local partners). Other restrictions included limits on profits repatriation.[17] As a result of the dilemmas that the MNCs face, it is easy to understand why philosopher Richard DeGeorge has argued that "First World MNCs are both the hope of the Third World and the *scourge* of the Third World."[18]

Thus, MNCs increasingly find themselves in situations where their very legitimacy is in question and their philosophical perspective is radically different than that of their host countries. Added to this are the normal problems of operating in a foreign culture with different types of governments, different languages, different legal systems, diverse stakeholders, and different social values. One could well argue that ethical problems are built into this environment. MNCs are attempting to bridge the cultural gaps between two peoples; yet, as they attempt to adapt to local customs and business practices, they are assailed at home for not adhering to the standards, practices, laws, or ethics of their home country. Indeed, there are ethical dilemmas for MNCs. Figure 6–1 portrays the dilemma of MNCs caught between the characteristics and expectations of a home country and those of one or more host countries.

MNC–Host Country Challenges

Globalization is "one of the most powerful and pervasive influences on nations, businesses, workplaces, communities, and lives at the end of the 20th century," according to Rosabeth Moss Kanter, in *World Class: Thriving Locally in a Global Economy*.[19] Recent research suggests that global issues are at the forefront of CEOs' agendas. According to Richard Cavanagh, president and CEO of The Conference Board, a hot topic has been "navigating the management maze of globalization."[20] As part

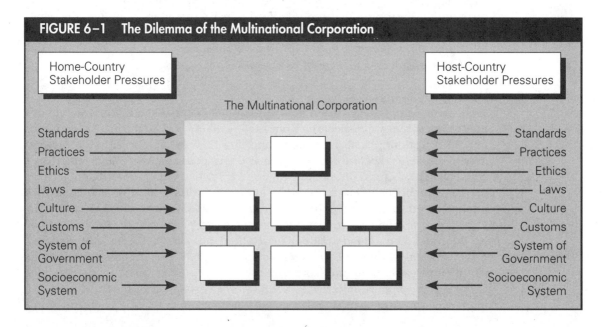

FIGURE 6–1   The Dilemma of the Multinational Corporation

of this, challenges facing business have been significant in the social values and ethics arenas.

There are so many issues characterizing the challenges between MNCs and host countries that it is almost impossible to draw limits on them. However, we must limit our focus in this chapter. Before discussing a few select ethical issues in the next section, we will first attempt at least to identify what some of these broader challenges are. The issues we will touch on include the cultural aspects of global business, business/government interactions in global operations, management and control of resources in global operations, and, finally, exploration of global markets.[21]

It has been argued that the most significant reason why MNC managers fail is their inability to cope with the foreign environment. Managers and companies experience culture shock when they are faced with cultures and languages that are significantly different from their own. Culture becomes one of the most critical make-or-break factors in successful multinational corporate operations. Culture, customs, language, attitudes, and institutions vary from country to country, and these differences pose sometimes insurmountable obstacles to success for MNCs.

Many humorous stories are told of how changing cultural contexts have created problems for MNCs. The following brief excerpt from Senator Paul Simon illustrates this point well:

> *Body by Fisher, describing a General Motors product, came out "Corpse by Fisher" in Flemish, and that did not help sales. . . . Come Alive with Pepsi almost appeared in the Chinese version of the Reader's Digest as "Pepsi brings your ancestors back from the grave." A major ad campaign in green did not sell in Malaysia, where green symbolizes death and disease. An airline operating out of Brazil advertised that it had plush "rendezvous" lounges on its jets, unaware that in Portuguese, "rendezvous" implied a room for making love.*[22]

If these kinds of problems arise because of language, customs, or symbols, it is interesting to speculate what issues are likely to result from contrasting ethical standards.

Beyond the differences that stem from cultural variables, the interaction of the business and government sectors poses challenges for MNC executives. Depending on the region of the world and industry under consideration, the extent of the business/government interactions may vary widely. In worldwide financial services, for example, heavy regulation was typical until the 1980s, when deregulation began in the United States and spread to other countries as well. Deregulation came fast to world banking, yet now some reregulation is occurring.

Government continues to be very important in some countries. "Japan, Inc.," for example, refers to the close-knit relationship between the Japanese government and the private sector. By contrast, government and business are more at arm's length in the United States. In Korea, government has always been influential, and only in recent years has the banking sector been privatized. In Europe, government has been intimately involved in business and banking from time to time. Many key industries have been nationalized in Great Britain, depending on which political party is in power.[23]

It is not uncommon for conflicts to arise between host country governments and MNCs. These conflicts typically relate to control over operations in the host country and the division of profits that accrue from the operations. Host governments are also typically interested in such issues as the regulation of technology transfer and transfer prices used by MNCs for conducting intrafirm trade.[24]

Two issues are worthy of mention under a consideration of the management and control of global operations. One issue is organizational structure and design, and the other issue is human resource management. MNCs must employ a multiplicity of organizational approaches in their markets. This is in significant part due to host government regulations. MNC management becomes complex when the firm licenses in Country A, has joint ventures in Country B, and countertrades in Country C. In each environment the firm faces different challenges. A second major topic that needs to be addressed is the proper use of human resources. In the arena of staffing, a question arises concerning the tactical use of home versus host country nationals. Use of each implies different costs and benefits for the firm. Other critical human resource issues include selection and training.[25]

A final topic in this section is the exploration of global markets as a vital MNC–host country challenge. Although U.S. MNCs dominated world markets for a period of time, this is no longer the case. Today, we have a world of intense competition among firms all over the globe. In the past 20 years there has been a remarkable resurgence, not only from Japan and the European economies but from some other countries as well (e.g., China, Korea, Latin America). One major issue in this general topic is the question of strategic alternatives that may be used by MNCs considering expansion into new foreign markets. Various strategies involving products and promotions are possible. Relevant factors in such strategic planning include the product function or need satisfied, conditions of product use, consumers' ability to buy, and communications strategy.[26]

Another major issue surrounds the pursuit of developing Third World markets. Marketing concepts for Asia, Africa, and some countries in Latin America may differ markedly from those we have become accustomed to in the United States. This category of issue is quite important in connection with our discussion of global ethics, because less developed countries pose significant temptations to MNCs to exploit and cut corners. International expert Richard D. Robinson suggests that we need to be sensitive to the long-run national interests of such countries. He advocates three levels of sensitivity. First, management of MNCs should be sensitive to the need to *modify or redesign products* so that they will be appropriate for their intended markets. An example of this was a truck manufacturer that modified its truck design to accommodate the rough roads, extreme heat, and high elevations found in Turkey. Second, management must be sensitive to the *impact of products,* especially in terms of their impacts on the long-term interests of non-Western markets. For example, luxury products and those of a fundamentally labor-saving nature would not necessarily be appealing under all circumstances to a development-conscious foreign government. Third, MNC managers should be sensitive to the extent to which their products are *politically vulnerable.* Products that are politically vulnerable may lead to labor agitation, public regulation (for example, price fixing and allocation quotas), nationalization, or political debates. Examples of products that in the past have led to political debates and action include sugar, salt, kerosene, gasoline, tires, and medicines.[27]

The need to be sensitive to marketing in other countries provides an appropriate transition to our discussion of ethical issues. It should be clear from this discussion that ethical issues or conflicts might easily arise from cultural conditions that are not anticipated by the MNCs. Further, even though we will examine in more detail quite interesting and highly visible issues such as marketing practices, plant safety, questionable payments, and sweatshops in cheap-labor factories in developing countries, we should be ever vigilant of the fact that such ethical dilemmas can also arise in such realms as production management, financial management, labor relations, and global strategic management.

ETHICAL ISSUES IN THE MULTINATIONAL ENVIRONMENT

For many companies, most of the ethical problems that arise in the international environment are the same as those that arise in their domestic environments. These ethical issues reside in all of the functional areas of business: production, marketing, finance, and management. These issues concern the fair treatment of stakeholders—employees, customers, the community, and competitors. These issues involve product safety, plant safety, advertising, human resource management, environmental problems, and so on.

The ethical problems seem to be somewhat fewer in developed countries, but they exist there as well. The ethical problems seem to be worse in underdeveloped countries or LDCs, because these countries are at a different stage of economic development. This situation creates an environment in which there is a temptation to adhere to lower standards, or perhaps no standards, because few government regulations or activist groups exist to protect the stakeholders' interests. In the LDCs, the opportunities for business exploitation and the engagement in questionable (by developed countries' standards) practices are abundant.

We will illustrate some prominent examples of ethical problems in the multinational sphere to provide some appreciation of the development of these kinds of issues for business. First, we will discuss two classic ethical issues that have arisen with regard to questionable marketing and safety practices. Second, we will discuss the issue of "sweatshops" (the use of cheap labor in developing countries)—a topic that has dominated international business in the 1990s and carries forward into the new millennium. Third, we will consider the special problems of bribery, corruption, and questionable payments, which have been ethical issues in the United States for over 20 years. From these examples we should be able to develop an appreciation of the ethical challenges that confront MNCs and others doing business abroad.

Questionable Marketing and Plant Safety Practices

A classic example of a questionable marketing practice is the now infamous infant formula controversy that spanned most of the 1970s and continued into the 1990s. The plant safety issue is best illustrated by examining the Union Carbide Bhopal crisis that began in late 1984 and continued into the 1990s.

The Infant Formula Controversy

The *infant formula controversy* is a classic in illustrating the ethical questions that can arise while doing business abroad. We will briefly refer to James Post's observations about this now-classic case. For decades, physicians working in tropical lands (many of which were LDCs) realized that there were severe health risks posed to infants from bottle feeding as opposed to breast feeding. Such countries typically had neither refrigeration nor sanitary conditions. Water supplies were not pure, and, therefore, infant formula mixed with this water contains bacteria that would likely lead to disease and diarrhea in the bottle-fed infant. Because these LDCs are typically poor, this condition encourages mothers to overdilute powdered formula, thus diminishing significantly the amount of nutrition the infant receives. Once a mother begins bottle feeding, her capacity for breast feeding quickly diminishes. Poverty also leads the mother to put in the bottle substitute products that are less expensive. These products, such as powdered whole milk and corn starch, are not acceptable substitutes— They are nutritionally inadequate and unsatisfactory for the baby's digestive system.

By the late 1960s, it was apparent that in the LDCs there was increased bottle feeding, decreased breast feeding, and a dramatic increase in the numbers of malnourished and sick babies. Bottle feeding was cited as one of the major reasons.[28] The ethical debate began when it was noted that several of the infant formula companies, aware of the environment just described, were promoting their products and, therefore, promoting bottle feeding in a very intense way. Such marketing practices as mass advertising, billboards, radio jingles, and free samples became commonplace. These promotional devices typically portrayed the infants who used their products as healthy and robust, in sharp contrast with the reality that was brought about by the conditions mentioned.

One of the worst marketing practices entailed the use of "milk nurses"—women dressed in nurses' uniforms who walked the halls of maternity wards urging mothers to get their babies started on formula. In reality, these women were sales representatives employed by the companies on a commission basis. Once the infants began bottle feeding, the mothers' capacity to breast feed diminished.[29]

Although several companies were engaging in these questionable marketing practices, the Swiss conglomerate Nestlé was singled out by a Swiss social activist group in an article published in 1974 entitled "Nestlé Kills Babies." At about the same time, an article appeared in Great Britain entitled "The Baby Killers."[30] From this point on, a protracted controversy developed with Nestlé and other infant formula manufacturers on one side and a host of organizations on the other side filing shareholder resolutions and lawsuits against the company. Among the groups that were actively involved in the controversy were church groups such as the National Council of Churches and its Interfaith Center on Corporate Responsibility (ICCR), UNICEF, the World Health Organization (WHO), and the Infant Formula Action Coalition (INFACT). Nestlé was singled out because it had the largest share of the world market and because it aggressively pushed sales of its infant formula in developing countries, even after the World Health Organization developed a sales code to the contrary.[31]

In 1977, INFACT and ICCR organized and led a national boycott against Nestlé that continued for almost 7 years. More than 70 American organizations representing churches, doctors, nurses, teachers, and other professionals participated in the boycott. These groups mounted an international campaign aimed at changing these objectionable marketing practices in the LDCs.[32] In 1984, after spending tens of millions of dollars resisting the boycott, Nestlé finally reached an accord with the protesters. The company agreed to four changes in its business practices:

1. It would restrict the distribution of free samples.

2. It would use Nestlé labels to identify the benefits of breast feeding and the hazards of bottle feeding.

3. It promised to help ensure that hospitals would use its products in accordance with the WHO code.

4. It agreed to drop its policy of giving gifts to health professionals to encourage them to promote infant formula.

The protesters, in return, agreed to end their boycott but to continue monitoring Nestlé's performance.[33]

The infant formula controversy continued through the 1980s and well into the 1990s. In 1991, Nestlé (which controls more than 40 percent of the worldwide market) and American Home Products (which controls about 15 percent of the worldwide market) announced that after decades of boycotts and controversy, they planned to discontinue the practice of providing free and low-cost formula to developing countries.

With this action—its most aggressive ever—Nestlé attempted to quell the protracted criticism that it had defied WHO's marketing restrictions by dumping huge quantities of baby formula on Third World hospitals. The distribution of supply had been a lingering concern in the infant formula controversy. Until this announcement, Nestlé had supplied formula on a request basis but over the next several years planned to distribute formula only on a request basis to children "in need," as outlined in the WHO guidelines. The pledges by Nestlé and American Home Products, the world's two biggest infant formula makers, were regarded as a watershed in the bitter infant formula controversy.[34]

The infant formula controversy is rich with examples of the actions and power of social activist groups and governments and the various strategies that might be employed by MNCs. For our purposes, however, it illustrates the character of questionable business practices by firms pursuing what might be called normal practices were it not for the fact that they were being pursued in foreign countries where circumstances made them questionable.[35] The infant formula controversy also illustrates the endurance of certain ethical issues, particularly in the global arena. A survey of the World Wide Web shows, for example, numerous Web sites that are devoted to the infant formula controversy and that document how the Nestlé boycott continues today.

The Bhopal Tragedy and Plant Safety

The Union Carbide *Bhopal tragedy* in late 1984 brings into sharp focus the dilemma of multinationals operating in a foreign, particularly less developed, environment. At this writing, the issues surrounding this event have not been totally resolved and may not be for years to come. On December 3, 1984, a leak of methyl isocyanate gas caused what many have termed the "worst industrial accident in history." The gas leak killed more than 2,000 people and injured 200,000 others. The tragedy has raised numerous legal, ethical, social, and technical questions for MNCs.[36]

Interviews with experts just after the accident revealed a belief that the responsibility for the accident had to be shared by the company and the Indian government. According to Union Carbide's own inspector, the Bhopal plant did not meet U.S.

ETHICS IN PRACTICE

Suppliers versus Buyers in the Turkish Market

Every summer since 1992, I have been working for a clothing manufacturing company in Istanbul, Turkey. Throughout this experience, I have learned the "ins and outs" of the business.

Last summer, I wanted to work in the buying department of the company so I could gain a better understanding of the relationship between the buyers and the suppliers. Everything went well until an increase in the price of cotton yarn was announced. Two weeks before this price increase, I recall my manager telling a particular supplier that the market was in need of the cotton fabric for 2 more months and then the market would lose its interest in the fabric. Therefore, this particular supplier had to make sure that the cotton fabric was available for the coming 2 months. I also recall the supplier saying, "We are aware of the market being in need of this cotton fabric. Do not worry, we already have our stocks for the next 3 months."

Two weeks later, the cotton yarn manufacturers increased their prices, claiming a higher cost for labor. During our next meeting with the suppliers, they informed us that they had to increase the price of the cotton fabric we were going to use for the next 2 months. The new pricing would start with the next order.

And there I was, asking myself: Is this ethical? What is my manager supposed to do—Buy the yarn at the new price?

1. What is the ethical dilemma in this situation? Is it unique to Turkey, or does this happen everywhere?

2. Is this clothing manufacturer being exploited? What are the suppliers' responsibilities to their buyers in this situation?

Contributed by Ethem Dogan

---

standards and had not been inspected in over 2 years. The Indian government allowed thousands of people to live very near the plant, and there were no evacuation procedures.[37]

Many different issues have been raised by the Bhopal disaster. Among the more important of these issues are:[38]

1. To what extent should MNCs maintain identical standards at home and abroad, regardless of how lax laws are in the host country?

2. How advisable is it to locate a complex and dangerous plant in an area where the entire work force is basically unskilled and where the populace is ignorant of the inherent risks posed by such plants?

3. How wise are laws that require plants to be staffed entirely by local employees?

4. What is the responsibility of corporations and governments in allowing the use of otherwise safe products that become dangerous because of local conditions? (This question applies to the infant formula controversy also.)

5. After reviewing all the problems, should certain kinds of plants be located in developing nations?

At the heart of these issues is the question of differing standards in different parts of the world. This dilemma arose in the 1970s, when American firms continued to export drugs and pesticides that had been restricted in the United States. Pesticides, such as DDT and others that had been associated with cancer, were shipped to and used in LDCs by farmers who did not understand the dangers or the cautions that were needed in the use of these products. Not surprisingly, poisonings occurred. In 1972, hundreds to thousands of Iraqis died from mercury-treated grain from the United States. In 1975, Egyptian farmers were killed and many made ill by a U.S.-made pesticide. Asbestos and pesticide manufacturing plants that violated American standards were built in several countries. These companies typically broke no laws, but many experts are now saying that the Bhopal tragedy has taught us that companies have a moral responsibility to enforce high standards, especially in developing countries not yet ready or able to regulate these firms.[39]

One major problem that some observers say contributed to the Bhopal explosion and, indeed, applies to MNCs generally, is the requirement that firms be significantly owned by investors in the host country. Union Carbide owned only 50.9 percent of the Bhopal, India, subsidiary. It has been observed that this situation may have reduced Union Carbide's motivation and/or capacity to ensure adequate industrial and environmental safety at its Bhopal plant, mainly by diluting the degree of parent control and reducing the flow of technical expertise into that plant. If developing countries continue to insist on a dilution of MNC control over manufacturing plants, this may also diminish the MNC's motivation and incentive to transfer environmental management and safety competence. As Gladwin and Walter conclude, "The painful realities of this tradeoff may turn out to be a key lesson of the world's worst industrial accident."[40] Other observers have said that this is a contrived excuse that firms use to obfuscate the issue and evade responsibility.

Another major problem highlighted by the Bhopal explosion was the fact that the people of developing countries are often unaware of the dangers of new technology. As one expert observed, countries such as India have not "internalized the technological culture."[41] On the one hand, the LDCs want technology because they see it as critical to their economic development, but their ability to understand and manage the new technology is in serious doubt.

The complexity and tragedy of the Bhopal explosion case for its victims, the Indian government, and Union Carbide are attested to by the fact that this issue is still unresolved well over a decade after it occurred. In 1989, Union Carbide extricated itself from relief efforts by agreeing to pay the Indian government $470 million to be divided among victims and their families. By 1993, courts had only distributed $3.1 million of this sum. The overburdened government relief programs in India have been mired in mismanagement and corruption. It has been observed that virtually every level of the relief bureaucracy in India is rife with corruption. Government officials have demanded bribes from illiterate victims trying to obtain documents required for the relief money, doctors have taken bribes from victims to testify in their court cases, and unscrupulous agents have fished for bribes by claiming they could get victims' cases expedited on the crowded docket. Claims courts that would determine final compensation for victims were not set up until 1992—eight years after the gas leak. Lawyers and officials say it could be another 20 years before this case is settled.[42] Current World Wide Web pages show that the Bhopal tragedy continues to be of deep concern, even as we transition to the twenty-first century.

The lessons from the Bhopal disaster are many and will continue to be debated. In companies around the globe, the Bhopal disaster has sparked new enthusiasm in the debate about operating abroad. To be sure, ethical and legal issues are central to the discussions. What is at stake, however, is not just the practices of businesses abroad but also the very question of the presence of businesses abroad. Depending on the final outcome of the Union Carbide debacle, MNCs may decide that the risk of doing business abroad is too great. As Professor Jack Behrman stated, "You aren't going to invest in situations that are going to jeopardize the whole company."[43]

Sweatshops and Labor Abuses

No issue has been more important in the 1990s global business ethics debate than MNCs' use and abuse of women and children in cheap-labor factories in developing countries. The major players in this controversy, large corporations, have highly recognizable names—Nike, Wal-Mart, K-Mart, Reebok, J. C. Penney, and Disney—to name a few. The countries and regions of the world that have been involved are also recognizable—Southeast Asia, Pakistan, Indonesia, Honduras, Dominican Republic, Thailand, the Philippines, and Vietnam. Sweatshops have not been eliminated in the United States either.[44]

Though *sweatshops*, characterized by child labor, low pay, poor working conditions, worker abuse, and health and safety violations, have existed for decades, they have grown in number in the past few years as global competition has heated up and corporations have gone to the far reaches of the world to lower their costs and increase their productivity. A landmark event that brought the sweatshop issue into sharp focus was the 1996 revelation by labor rights activists that part of Wal-Mart's Kathie Lee Collection, a line of clothes endorsed by prominent U.S. talk-show host Kathie Lee Gifford, was made in Honduras by seamstresses slaving 20 hours a day for 31 cents an hour. The revelation helped turn Gifford, who was unaware of where the clothes were being made or under what conditions, into an antisweatshop activist.[45] The Nike Corporation has also become a lightning rod for social activists concerned about overseas manufacturing conditions, standards, and ethics. A major reason for this is the company's high visibility, extensive advertising, and expensive shoes, as well as the stark contrast between the tens of millions of dollars Nike icon Michael Jordan earns and the $2.23 daily wage rate the company's subcontractors pay their Indonesian workers.[46]

Former ambassador to the United Nations Andrew Young calls the recent debate over child labor "the world's next moral crusade."[47] Young likens the sweatshop issue with the civil rights movement, a crusade for freedom against the injustices done to helpless children and poor women. To support his argument, Young invokes a 1997 UNICEF publication, "The State of the World's Children 1997," which documents the high level of suffering that millions of child laborers are forced to endure. Referring to India, the UNICEF report discloses:

> *Thousands of children in the carpet industry are kidnaped or lured away or pledged by their parents for paltry sums of money. Most of them are kept in captivity, tortured, and made to work for 20 hours a day without a break. Little children are made to crouch on their toes, from dawn to dusk every day, severely stunting their growth during formative years.*[48]

The International Labor Organization (ILO) reported that there is an unprecedented number of child laborers in the world—some 250 million. The ILO estimate, which is double previous estimates, documents almost 153 million child laborers in Asia, 80 million in Africa, and 17.5 million in Latin America. All these children are between ages 5 and 14, and nearly half work full time.

Critics of MNC labor practices, including social activist groups and grassroots organizations, are speaking out, criticizing business abusers and raising public awareness. These critics claim certain businesses are exploiting children and women by paying them poverty wages, working them to exhaustion, punishing them for minor violations, violating health and safety standards with them, and tearing apart their families. Many of these companies counter that they offer the children and women workers a superior alternative. They say that, while their wage rates are embarrassing by developed-world standards, those rates frequently equal or exceed local legal minimum wages, or average wages. They further say that, because so many workers in LDCs work in agriculture and farming, where they make less than the average wage, the low but legal minimums in many countries put sweatshop workers among the higher-paid workers in their areas.[49]

The sweatshop issue has been so prominent in the past few years that, to improve their situations or images, many criticized companies have begun working to improve working conditions, further joint initiatives, establish codes of conduct or standards for themselves and their subcontractors, conduct social or ethical audits, or take other steps. In 1996, President Clinton, with Kathie Lee Gifford, was instrumental in helping to establish the Apparel Industry Partnership, a task force of clothing firms, unions, and human-rights groups focused on the worldwide elimination of sweatshops. Its members, which include L. L. Bean, Nike, Liz Claiborne, Nicole Miller, and Reebok, were encouraged by a survey showing that three-quarters of America's shoppers would pay higher prices for clothes and shoes bearing "No Sweat" labels.

A new proposal should also help eliminate sweatshops. This proposal calls for clothing firms and their contractors to impose a code of conduct that would prohibit child labor, forced labor, and worker abuse; establish health and safety regulations; recognize workers' right to join a union; limit the work week to 60 hours (except in exceptional business circumstances); and insist that workers be paid at least the legal minimum wage (or the "prevailing industry wage") in every country in which garments are made. Under this proposal, the garment industry would also create an association to police the agreement.[50]

This proposal has some drawbacks, however. For example, the legal minimum wage in many developing countries is below the poverty line. In addition, the "prevailing industry wage" could prove to be a convenient escape clause. Some groups are also concerned that the task force has, in effect, sanctioned 60-hour working weeks and that it will still allow 14-year-olds to work if local laws do. Another big issue will be monitoring the agreement abroad. For example, Liz Claiborne alone has 200 contractors in over 25 countries. Furthermore, in some countries, like the Philippines, Malaysia, Thailand, and Vietnam, sweatshops go to great lengths to hide their business dealings by "fronting" businesses using false documents to "prove" they pay minimum wages and by intimidating workers to keep quiet.[51]

Another initiative to improve sweatshop conditions has been organized by the Council on Economic Priorities (CEP), a New York public-interest group. The CEP, with a group of influential companies, has introduced a new scheme called Social Accountability 8000, or SA8000, which is designed to piggyback on the ISO8000 quality-auditing system of the International Standards Organization (ISO), now used in 80 countries.[52]

The SA8000 initiative, launched in fall 1997, involves a broad spectrum of U.S. and foreign companies, such as Avon, Sainsbury, Toys 'R' Us, and Otto Versand, which owns Eddie Bauer, plus such labor and human rights groups as KPMG-Peat Marwick and SGS-ICS. The group approved an initial set of labor standards, which would then be monitored. The initial labor standards were as follows:[53]

- Do not use child or forced labor.
- Provide a safe working environment.
- Respect workers' right to unionize.
- Do not regularly require more than 48-hour work weeks.
- Pay wages sufficient to meet workers' basic needs.

Companies that want to comply with SA8000 standards can apply for certification by an outside auditor. CEP has set up an agency to accredit the auditors, and most are likely to be accounting firms. The CEP planned to have the system up and running by 1998, and it expected that companies would not meet every standard right away. Companies like Avon and Toys 'R' Us expect to get their plants certified and will expect that their suppliers get their plants certified. Skeptics of the CEP initiative include human rights and labor groups that think real change in sweatshops will not occur. Skeptics fear that companies will use the CEP monitoring process as a cover and that real changes will not occur. For its part, the CEP thinks the system will work and that millions of consumers will eventually insist on SA8000-approved products.[54]

Sweatshops and labor abuses sharply contrast the "haves" and the "have-nots" of the world's nations. Consumers in developed countries have benefited greatly by the lower prices made possible by cheap labor. It remains to be seen how supportive those consumers will be if prices rise because MNCs improve wage rates and conditions in LDCs. The MNCs face a new and volatile ethical issue that is not likely to go away. Their profits, public image, and reputations may hinge on how well they respond. The MNCs must handle a new dimension in their age-old quest to balance shareholder profits with the desires of expanded, global stakeholders who want better corporate social performance.

Bribery and Questionable Payments

Bribes and questionable payments occurred for decades prior to the 1970s. It was in the mid-1970s, however, that evidence of widespread questionable corporate payments to foreign government officials, political parties, and other influential persons became widely known. Such major corporations as Lockheed, Gulf Oil, Northrop, Carnation, and Goodyear were among those firms admitting to such payments. Huge sums of money were involved. Gulf, for example, admitted paying $4.2 million to the political party of Korean President Park. Gulf also created a subsidiary in the Bahamas that was then used as a conduit for unlawful political contributions. Lockheed acknowledged payments of $22 million, mostly to officials in the Middle East.[55]

One of the most notorious cases was that of Lockheed giving $12.5 million in bribes and commissions in connection with the sale of $430 million worth of TriStar airplanes to All Nippon Airways. The president of Lockheed defended the payments, claiming that it was common practice and it was expected to give bribes in Japan. The news of the payments rocked Japan more than it did the United States, because Prime Minister Kakuei Tanaka and four others were forced to resign and stand trial. Another important point made about this case was that Lockheed did not offer a bribe, but rather the Japanese negotiator demanded it. This point raises the continuing question in matters of this kind: "Are those who accede to bribery equal in guilt to those who demand bribes?"[56]

Corruption in international business continues to be a major problem. It starts with outright bribery of government officials and the giving of questionable political contributions. Beyond these there are many other activities that are corrupt: the misuse of company assets for political favors, kickbacks and protection money for police, free junkets for government officials, secret price-fixing agreements, and insider dealing, just to mention a few. All of these activities have one thing in common: They are attempts to influence the outcomes of decisions wherein the nature and extent of the influence are not made public. In essence, these activities are abuses of power.[57] Bribes, more than any other form of corruption, have been the subject of continuing debate, and they merit closer examination.

Arguments for and Against Bribery

Arguments typically given in favor of permitting bribery include the following: (1) It is necessary for profits in order to do business; (2) everybody does it—it will happen anyway; (3) it is accepted practice in many countries—it is normal and expected; and (4) bribes are forms of commissions, taxes, or compensation for conducting business between cultures.[58]

Arguments frequently cited against giving bribes include (1) bribes are inherently wrong and cannot be accepted under any circumstances; (2) bribes are illegal in the United States and, therefore, unfair elsewhere; (3) one should not compromise her or his own beliefs; (4) managers should not deal with corrupt governments; (5) such demands, once started, never stop; (6) one should take a stand for honesty, morality, and ethics; (7) those receiving bribes are the only ones who benefit; (8) bribes create dependence on corrupt individuals and countries; and (9) bribes deceive stockholders and pass on costs to customers.[59]

The costs of bribes and other forms of corruption are seldom fully understood or described. Several studies suggest the economic costs of such corrupt activities. When government officials accept "speed" money or "grease payments" to issue licenses, the economic cost is 3 to 10 percent above the licensing fee. When tax collectors permit underreporting of income in exchange for a bribe, income tax revenues may be reduced by up to 50 percent. When government officials take kickbacks, goods and services may be priced 20 to 100 percent higher to them. In addition to these direct economic costs, there are many indirect costs—demoralization and cynicism and moral revulsion against politicians and the political system. In recent years, politicians have been swept from office in Brazil, Italy, Japan, and Korea.[60]

The Foreign Corrupt Practices Act

Many of the payments and bribes made by U.S.-based MNCs were not illegal prior to the passage of the 1977 Foreign Corrupt Practices Act (FCPA). Even so, firms could have been engaging in illegal activities depending on whether and how the payments were reported to the IRS. With the passage of the FCPA, however, it became a criminal offense for a representative of an American corporation to offer or give payments to the officials of other governments for the purpose of getting or maintaining business. The FCPA specifies a series of fines and prison terms that can result if a company or management is found guilty of a violation.[61] The legislation was passed not only for ethical reasons but also out of a concern for the image of the United States abroad.

The FCPA has been controversial, to say the least. The law does not prohibit so-called grease payments, or minor payments to officials, for the primary purpose of getting them to do whatever they are supposed to do anyway. Such payments are commonplace in many countries. The real problem is that some forms of payments are prohibited (for example, bribes), but other payments (for example, grease payments) are not prohibited. The law is sometimes ambiguous on the distinctions between the two.[62] To violate the FCPA, payments (other than grease payments) must be made corruptly to obtain business. This suggests some kind of *quid pro quo*. The idea of a corrupt *quid pro quo* payment to a foreign official may seem clear in the abstract, but the circumstances of the payment may easily blur the distinction between what is acceptable "grease" (e.g., payments to expedite mail pickup or delivery, to obtain a work permit, to process paperwork) and what is illegal bribery. The safest strategy for managers to take is to be careful and to seek a legal opinion when questions arise.

Figure 6–2 presents a basic distinction between bribes (which are prohibited) and *grease payments* (which are not prohibited) based on the FCPA.

Impact of the FCPA

Since the passage of the FCPA, which prohibited bribery for U.S.-based MNCs, the major criticism against the act has been that it is unilateral; that is, it affects U.S. firms but not foreign competitors. U.S. firms have often claimed that they could not compete successfully if they were prohibited from giving bribes but others were not. The consequence, it has been argued, would be a decline in U.S. exports.

Over the years there have been many studies attempting to assess the impact of the FCPA on U.S. companies. Some studies have concluded that U.S. firms have been placed at a disadvantage, which caused them to lose money or be unable to compete. For example, a study by James Hinds, an economist, concluded that U.S. firms took a beating after the FCPA was passed. Hinds found that U.S. corporate direct investment and exports declined markedly in "corrupt" countries in the 5 years after the law was passed. By contrast, investment and export activities by America's foreign competitors in the same countries accelerated sharply.[63] Other studies, however, found that the impact of the FCPA has been negligible or minimal.[64]

Bribery Trends in the 1990s

As we reach the end of the 1990s and usher in the new millennium, corruption and bribery in international business continue to be current topics. With significant increases in global competition, free markets, and democracy over the past decade,

FIGURE 6–2   Bribes versus Grease Payments

Definitions	Examples
Grease Payments Relatively *small sums* of money given for the purpose of getting minor officials to: • Do what they are *supposed to be doing* • Do what they are supposed to be doing *faster or sooner.* • Do what they are supposed to be doing *better* than they would otherwise.	Money given to minor officials (clerks, attendants, customs inspectors) for the purpose of expediting. This form of payment helps get goods or services through red-tape or administrative bureaucracies.
Bribes Relatively *large amounts* of money given for the purpose of *influencing officials to make decisions or take actions* that they *otherwise* might not take. If the officials considered the merits of the situation only, they might take some other action.	Money given, often to high-ranking officials. Purpose is often to get these people to purchase goods or services from the bribing firm. May also be used to avoid taxes, forestall unfavorable government intervention, secure favorable treatment, and so on.

this comes as no surprise. Two developments in the past 5 years are worthy of mention. Both have contributed to what some have called a growing anticorruption movement. First, a new special-interest group was founded in Berlin in about 1993—*Transparency International (TI)*—modeled after the human rights group Amnesty International. TI has established itself as the world's foremost anticorruption lobby. It maintains over 70 national chapters run by local activists and compiles an annual corruption rating using surveys of businesspeople, political analysts, and the general public. Using various color shades to represent labels varying from "least corrupt" to "most corrupt" on a map of the world, TI's "Corruption Perception Index" depicts countries in various ways. Some of the findings of TI's 1997 survey illustrate: Companies from Belgium, France, and Italy are the most likely to pay bribes, while American and Swedish firms are among the least likely; Nigeria is ranked as the most corrupt country, while Denmark is ranked as the least corrupt.[65] Undoubtedly, TI hopes and expects that public exposure to its corruption ratings will bring pressure to bear on countries and companies.

A second development in the growing anticorruption movement is a new anti-bribery treaty that the 29 industrialized nations of the Organization for Economic Cooperation and Development (OECD) and five other countries agreed to in late 1997.[66] The OECD member nations agreed to ban international bribery and to ask each member to introduce laws patterned after the U.S. FCPA in its country. The main thrust of the treaty was to criminalize bribes to foreign officials who have sway over everything from government procurement contracts and infrastructure projects to privatization tenders. After heated debate, the OECD partners agreed to extend the ban to include bribes to executives at state-owned companies and to elect parliamentarians. The next step will be for the countries to get the agreement passed into national laws, which could take time. Many countries remain fearful of adopting the new agreement before competitor countries do. In addition, there is concern that countries might opt out of portions of the agreement as it works its way through national legislatures.[67]

The best way to deal with bribes seems to be to stem the practice before it starts. A major paradox is that the very people who often benefit from illicit payments—the politicians—are the ones who must pass the laws and set the standards against bribes and corruption in the first place. Another factor is that bribes and corruption, whenever possible, need to be exposed. Public exposure, more than anything else, has the potential to bring questionable payments under control. This means that practices and channels of accountability need to be made public.[68] The new Corruption Perception Index should help in this regard. Beyond these steps, managers need to be able to see that such activities are no longer in their best interests. Not only do bribes corrupt the economic system, but they corrupt business relationships as well and cause business decisions to be made on the basis of factors that ultimately destroy all the institutions involved. In a sense, the new OECD treaty indicates that member nations now understand this important point. It will not eliminate bribery, but it does represent a significant step toward reducing bribery and bringing it under control.

We have by no means covered all the areas in which ethical problems reside in the multinational environment. The topics treated have been major ones subjected to extensive public discussion. Examples of other issues that have become important recently and will probably increase in importance include the issues of international competitiveness, protectionism, industrial policy, and political risk analysis. These issues are of paramount significance in discussions of business's relations with international stakeholders. Other issues that include an ethical dimension are national security versus profit interests, the use of internal transfer prices to evade high taxes in a country, and mining of the ocean floor. Space does not permit us to discuss these issues in detail.

IMPROVING GLOBAL BUSINESS ETHICS

The most obvious observation to extract from the discussion up to this point is that business ethics is more complex at the global level than at the domestic level. The complexity arises from the fact that a wide variety of value systems, stakeholders, cultures, forms of government, socioeconomic conditions, and standards of ethical behavior exists throughout the world. Recognition of diverse standards of ethical behavior is important, but if we assume that U.S. firms should operate in closer accordance with U.S. standards than with foreign standards, the strategy of ethical leadership in the world is indeed a challenging one. Because the United States, and hence U.S.-based MNCs, have played such a leadership role in world affairs—usually espousing fairness and human rights—U.S. firms have a heavy responsibility, particularly in underdeveloped countries and LDCs. The power-responsibility equation also argues that U.S. firms have a serious ethical responsibility in global markets. That is, our larger sense of ethical behavior and social responsiveness derives from the enormous amount of power we have.

In this section, we will first discuss the challenge of honoring and balancing the ethical standards of a business's home country with those of its host country. Next, we will discuss Gene Laczniak and Jacob Naor's four recommended courses of action for conducting business in foreign environments: (1) develop worldwide codes of conduct, (2) factor ethics into global strategy, (3) suspend activities when faced with unbridgeable ethical gaps, and (4) develop periodic "ethical impact statements."[69]

Thomas Donaldson has set forth ten fundamental international rights that are based on the principle of rights discussed in the last chapter. These are worthy of consideration, as are Richard DeGeorge's seven "moral guidelines" that provide guidance for MNCs. Finally, we will consider the ethical guidelines for international corporations identified in a Vesper International-sponsored multistakeholder consultation. Figure 6–3 summarizes these guidelines for improving global business ethics.

Honoring and Balancing Ethics of Home and Host Countries

Perhaps one of the greatest challenges that face businesses operating in foreign countries is achieving some kind of balance in honoring both the cultural and moral standards of their home and host countries. Should a business adhere to its home country's ethical standards for business practices or to the host country's ethical standards? There is no simple answer to this question. The diagram presented in Figure 6–4 frames the extreme decision choices businesses face when they consider this issue.

At one extreme is a position some might call "ethical imperialism." This position argues that the MNC should continue to follow its home country's ethical standards even while operating in another country. Because U.S. standards for treating employees, consumers, and the natural environment are quite high relative to the standards in many other less-developed countries, it is easy to see how managers might find this posture appealing.

As reliance on foreign factories has soared in recent years and harsh conditions have been documented by the media, an increasing number of companies, such as Levi Strauss; Nordstrom, Inc.; Wal-Mart; and Reebok, have espoused higher standards for foreign factories that cover such issues as wages, safety, and workers' rights to organize.[70] These standards more nearly approximate U.S. views on how such stakeholders ought to be treated than some host country's views. Such higher standards could be seen by foreign countries, however, as the U.S. attempting to impose its standards on the host country—thus the name "ethical imperialism" for one end of the continuum.

FIGURE 6–3   Guidelines for Improving Global Business Ethics

- **Honoring and Balancing Ethics of Home and Host Countries**
- **Laczniak and Naor's Four Recommended Actions**
    - → **Global Codes of Conduct**
    - → **Ethics and Global Strategy**
    - → **Suspension of Activities**
    - → **Ethical Impact Statements**
- **Donaldson's Fundamental International Rights**
- **DeGeorge's Seven Moral Guidelines**
- **Vesper's International Guidelines**

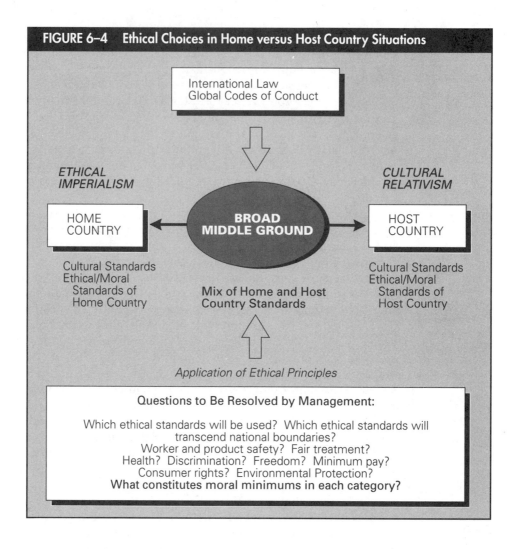

FIGURE 6–4   Ethical Choices in Home versus Host Country Situations

At the other extreme in Figure 6–4 is a position often called "cultural relativism." This position is characterized by foreign direct investors, such as MNCs following the host country's ethical standards. This is the posture reflected in the well-known saying, "When in Rome, do as the Romans." This position would argue that the investing MNC should set aside its home country's ethical standards and adopt the ethical standards of the host country. For example, if Saudi Arabia holds that it is illegal to hire women for most managerial positions, the investing MNC would accept and adopt this standard, even if it counters its home country's standards. Or, if the host country has no environmental protection laws, this position would argue that the MNC need not be sensitive to environmental standards.

As Tom Donaldson has argued, cultural relativism holds that no culture's ethics are better than any other's and that there are, therefore, no international rights or wrongs. If Thailand tolerates the bribery of government officials, then Thai toler-

ETHICS IN PRACTICE

An Innocent Revelation?

For a couple of years, I worked as an assistant manager at a gas station in my home town of Randers, Denmark. The location of the station was perfect, and this was proven every day by long lines and big sales. The way the job was scheduled was that the person on duty would always manage the station single-handedly, standing behind the desk, running the cash register. Every day, several thousand dollars was secured in the gas station's safe. Six people worked the gas station—all around the age of 18. The key to the safe was hidden in the back, and only the employees and the manager knew the hiding place. The manager would take the money stored in the safe and deposit it at the local bank every third day, but one week this action was postponed a couple of days because of a holiday. Therefore, a large sum of money was accumulating at the station. One employee was aware of this fact and revealed it to her friends. At the same time, she agreed to tell about the hiding place for the key, and within a few days her friends broke into the station, found the key, and stole $17,000 to $19,000.

The employee and her friends had figured that the insurance company would pay for my manager's loss and therefore all parties would be satisfied, except for the insurance company, whom, they thought, would not really be affected by the loss. They claimed, "Everybody knows how rich these insurance companies are."

The bottom line of this story was that the insurance company did *not* pay, because the key was hidden in the same room where the safe was kept.

The ethical question in this story is this. If you knew that no one would discover the employee's irresponsible decision to tell about the hidden key, and that the insurance company would reimburse the manager, would you also have done the same thing if you had received a fairly big portion of the money? In this case, I assume that the insurance company could easily afford the reimbursement, which means that all parties should be satisfied (and you would get a little richer).

1. What is the ethical dilemma in this story? Is it a situation unique to business in Denmark?

2. If the employee's decision to tell about the hidden key was never discovered, can her action somehow be justified as just an innocent revelation? Why or why not? Identify the ethical principles involved here.

3. Imagine that the employee's revelation was never discovered. Would you have chosen to do as she did if we assume that the manager got reimbursed? Many of us pay a lot of money in insurance premiums, so why not get a little back?

Contributed by Anders Braad

ance is no worse than Japanese or German intolerance. If Switzerland does not find insider trading morally repugnant, then Swiss liberality is no worse than American restrictiveness.[71] Most ethicists find cultural relativism to be a case of moral or ethical relativism and, therefore, an unacceptable posture for MNCs to take.

It may sound like a simplistic solution to say that the MNC needs to operate in the broad middle ground where a mix of home and host country ethical standards may be used. The challenge for managers will be to determine what mix of ethical standards should be used and how this decision should be made. Managers will need to ask themselves which moral standards are applicable in the situations they face. Use of ethical principles such as those articulated in the previous chapters—rights, justice, utilitarianism, and the Golden Rule—still apply. Managers will need to decide which ethical standards should transcend national boundaries—safety? health? discrimination? freedom? minimum pay? Managers will need to decide what will represent their moral minimums with respect to these and other issues. It would be nice to think that international laws and global codes of conduct will make these decisions easier. It is doubtful, however, that such guidelines will be readily forthcoming. In the interim, managers will need to be guided by the ethical concepts at their disposal, possibly with help from some of the approaches to which we now turn.

Four Actions for Conducting International Business

Laczniak and Naor have set forth four actions that would help MNCs conduct international business while maintaining an ethical sensitivity in their practices and decision making.

Global Codes of Conduct

In the previous chapter, we discussed codes of conduct, and that discussion applies in the global sphere as well. While operating in the global sphere, MNCs have been severely criticized for operating with divergent ethical standards in different countries, thus giving the impression that they are attempting to exploit local circumstances. When in doubt, the course of action that manifests ethical leadership is to adhere to higher rather than lower standards. A growing number of MNCs, such as Caterpillar Tractor, Allis Chalmers, Johnson's Wax, and Rexnord, have developed and used codes geared to worldwide operations.[72]

One of the first and most well known of the codes is that of Caterpillar Tractor Company, issued by the chairman of the board, entitled "A Code of Worldwide Business Conduct." The code goes into considerable detail and has major sections that cover the following vital areas: ownership and investment, corporate facilities, relationships with employees, product quality, sharing of technology, accounting and financial records, different business practices, competitive conduct, observance of local laws, business ethics, relationships with public officials, and international business. The purpose of the code is clearly set forth in its introduction:

SEARCH THE WEB

Over the years, various groups interested in international business ethics have developed a number of different guidelines or codes of conduct for conducting business in the global arena. "Principles & Codes for Socially Responsible Business Practices" at **www.goodmoney.com/directry_codes. htm**, the Web site developed by Good Money, a company focused on socially responsible investing, has an excellent listing of select global guidelines. These important and interesting guidelines include:

- *Caux Round Table: Principles for Business*—designed to set a world standard against which business behavior can be measured.
- *CERES Principles*—formerly the Valdez Principles, the CERES Principles are for environmentally sound global business practices.
- *Declaration Toward a Global Ethic*—a code to address the crises in the global economy, ecology, and politics.
- *The MacBride Principles*—a corporate code of conduct for U.S. companies doing business in Northern Ireland.
- *The Maquiladoras Standards of Conduct*—drafted for companies doing business in the Maquiladores of Mexico.
- *Principles for Global Corporate Responsibility*—drafted by three interfaith organizations from Canada, U.S., and U.K. for transnational corporations.

"Sweatshops" in developing or underdeveloped countries are another vital international business ethics topic. To review current activities in this arena, visit the Sweatshop Watch Web site at **www.sweatshopwatch.org/ swatch/headlines/**.

This revised "Code of Worldwide Business Conduct" is offered under the several headings that follow. Its purpose continues to be to guide us, in a broad and ethical sense, in all aspects of our worldwide business activities. Of course, this code isn't an attempt to prescribe actions for every business encounter. It is an attempt to capture basic, general principles to be observed by Caterpillar people everywhere.[73]

Other companies do not have comprehensive codes addressing their international operations but rather codes containing sections that address foreign practices. For example, in its "General Dynamics Standards of Business Ethics and Conduct," General Dynamics has a section entitled "International Business." One excerpt from this section is encouraging and illustrates the point we have been developing:

Our policy is to comply with all laws which apply in the countries where we do business. In countries where common practices might indicate acceptance of standards of conduct lower than those to which we aspire, we will follow our own Standards as outlined in this booklet.[74]

An example of a global code of conduct aimed at improving workplace standards and workers' standards of living was implemented in fall 1997 by Mattel, Inc., the $4.5 billion toy manufacturer. According to Jill E. Barad, Mattel chairman and CEO, "We are as concerned with the safety and fair treatment of the men and women who manufacture our products as we are with the safety and quality of the products themselves, and our new Global Manufacturing Principles demonstrate our strong commitment to that philosophy."[75] Topics covered in Mattel's new Global Manufacturing Principles include:

- Wages and hours
- Child labor
- Forced labor
- Discrimination
- Freedom of association
- Working conditions
- Legal and ethical business practices
- Product safety and quality
- Environment
- Customs
- Evaluation and monitoring
- Compliance

With offices in 36 countries and products being marketed in 150 nations around the world, Mattel is a classic example of the kind of MNC that needs, and can benefit from, a global code of conduct.

Ethics and Global Strategy
The major recommendation here is that the ethical dimensions of multinational corporate activity should be considered as significant inputs into top-level strategy

formulation and implementation.[76] Carroll, Hoy, and Hall have argued even more broadly that corporate social policy should be integrated into strategic management.[77] At the top level of decision making in the firm, corporate strategy is established. At this level, commitments are made that will define the underlying character and identity that the organization will have. The overall moral tone of the organization and all decision making and behaviors are set at the strategic level, and management needs to ensure that social and ethical factors do not get lost in the preoccupation with market opportunities and competitive factors.

If ethics does not get factored in at the strategic formulation level, it is doubtful that ethics will be considered at the level of operations where strategy is being implemented. Unfortunately, much current practice has tended to treat ethics and social responsibility as residual factors. We cannot overemphasize that a more proactive stance is needed for dealing with ethical issues at the global level. Strategic decisions that may be influenced by ethical considerations in the global sphere include, but are not limited to, product/service decisions, plant location, manufacturing policy, marketing policy and practices, and personnel or human resources management policies.

A useful illustration of ethics being factored into strategic decision making is provided by Levi Strauss & Co. Because Levi Strauss operates in many countries and diverse cultures, it reasoned that it must take special care in selecting its contractors and the countries where its goods are produced in order to ensure that its products are being made in a manner consistent with its values and reputation. In 1992, therefore, the company developed a set of global sourcing guidelines that established standards its contractors must meet. As examples, their guidelines banned the use of child and prison labor. They stipulated certain environmental standards. Wages must, at minimum, comply with the law and match prevailing local practice. By factoring these ethical considerations into its strategic decisions, Levi argues that it receives important short- and long-term commercial benefits.[78]

Another example of a company integrating ethical concerns into its corporate strategies is that of Starbucks Coffee Co., a Seattle-based firm. In an innovative pilot program announced in 1998, Starbucks plans to pay a premium above market price for coffee, with the bonus going to improve the lives of coffee workers. The initial payments would be made to farms and mills in Guatemala and Costa Rica, which would co-fund health care centers, farm schools, and scholarships for farm workers' children. Starbucks's incentive program was part of a larger "Framework for Action," its plan for implementing its code of conduct, created in 1995.[79]

Suspension of Activities

Laczniak and Naor note that an MNC may sometimes encounter unbridgeable gaps between the ethical values of its home country and those of its host country. When this occurs, and reconciliation does not appear to be in sight, the MNC should consider suspending activities in the host country. For example, IBM and Coca-Cola suspended their activities in India because of that country's position on the extent of national ownership and control.[80]

Also, Levi Strauss undertook a phased withdrawal from China, largely in response to human rights concerns, and suspended sourcing in Peru because of concerns about employee safety. It later lifted the suspension because conditions had improved.[81] More recently, companies have pulled out of Burma due to human rights violations.

Suspension of business in a foreign country is not a decision that can or should be taken precipitously, but it must be regarded as a viable option for those firms that desire to travel on the higher moral road. Each country is at liberty to have its own standards, but this does not mean that U.S. firms must do business in that country. What does ethical leadership mean if it is not backed up by a willingness and an ability to take a moral stand when the occasion merits?

Ethical Impact Statements

MNCs should be constantly aware of the impacts they are having on society, particularly foreign societies. One way to do this is to periodically assess the company's impacts. Companies have a variety of impacts on foreign cultures, and ethical impacts represent only a few of these. The impact statement idea probably derived, in part, from the practice of environmental impact statements that the U.S. Environmental Protection Agency pioneered in the early 1970s. These statements are similar to the corporate social audit, a concept we will discuss more fully in Chapter 18. Social auditing is "a systematic attempt to identify, analyze, measure (if possible), evaluate, and monitor the effect of an organization's operations on society (that is, specific social groups) and on the public well-being."[82] *Ethical impact statements* would be an attempt to assess the underlying moral justifications for corporate actions and the consequent results of those actions. The information derived from these actions would permit the MNCs to modify or change their business practices if the impact statement suggested that such changes would be necessary or desirable.

One form of ethical impact assessment is some firms' attempts to monitor their compliance with their companies' global ethics codes. For example, Mattel developed an independent audit and monitoring system for its code. Mattel's monitoring program is headed by an independent panel of commissioners who select a percentage of the company's manufacturing facilities for annual audits. In its 1997 audit, for example, Mattel terminated its relationship with three contractor facilities—one in Indonesia for its inability to confirm the age of its employees and two in China for refusing to meet company-mandated safety procedures.[83] Such audits conducted for monitoring compliance are not as comprehensive as ethical impact statements, but they serve similar purposes.

Fundamental International Rights

Thomas Donaldson has set forth ten fundamental international rights that he argues should be honored and respected by all international actors, including nation-states, individuals, and corporations. He argues that these rights serve to establish a moral minimum for the behavior of all international economic agents. Donaldson's ten fundamental rights are as follows:[84]

1. The right to freedom of physical movement
2. The right to ownership of property
3. The right to freedom from torture
4. The right to a fair trial

5. The right to nondiscriminatory treatment (freedom from discrimination on the basis of such characteristics as race and gender)

6. The right to physical security

7. The right to freedom of speech and association

8. The right to minimal education

9. The right to political participation

10. The right to subsistence

Such a list of rights is somewhat general and still leaves considerable room for interpretation. However, it serves to establish a beginning point for MNCs as they contemplate what responsibilities they have in international markets.

Seven Moral Guidelines

According to Richard DeGeorge, a business ethicist, MNCs should apply seven moral guidelines in their international operations.[85] Some of these are rather straightforward, but they do summarize a useful perspective that might well improve MNC operations in the global sphere.

1. MNCs should do no intentional, direct harm.

2. MNCs should produce more good than bad for the host country.

3. MNCs should contribute by their activities to the host country's development.

4. MNCs should respect the human rights of their employees.

5. MNCs should pay their fair share of taxes.

6. To the extent that local culture does not violate moral norms, MNCs should respect the local culture and work with it, not against it.

7. MNCs should cooperate with the local government in the development and enforcement of just background institutions (for example, the tax system and health and safety standards).

DeGeorge does not present these seven guidelines as a panacea. He does suggest that if they were brought to bear on the dilemmas that MNCs face, the companies could avoid the moral stings of their critics. The spirit of these seven guidelines, if adopted, would go a long way toward improving MNC–host country relations.

Guidelines for International Corporations

In 1990, Vesper International and the Hinksey Centre of Oxford, England, held a Conference in San Francisco entitled "Just Profits: Wending Our Way Through the Moral Maze." The conference was billed as a "multi-stakeholder consultation" because it was composed of representatives from many groups, such as management, labor, consumer groups, academics, and religious organizations. Both domestic and international representatives participated. The objective of the conference was to explore the relationship between values and decision making in MNCs. One major outcome of the 3-day conference was the creation of a set of guidelines designed to assist MNCs in their international decision making. The guidelines evolved into a format that specified the

---

FIGURE 6–5   Guidelines for International Corporations

International Corporations Have a Responsibility to:

- Commit to a long-term relationship when investing in a community and to operate in cooperation with the host community to seek beneficial impacts

- Act in ways that respect and protect fundamental human rights

- Make full and fair disclosure of all information relevant to the well-being of stakeholders and the general public

- Protect the ecosystem by specifically meeting identified environmental standards and conserving natural resources through efficient use

- Produce products and services which meet adequate standards of safety within a healthy workplace environment

- Recognize the rights of employees to organize and bargain collectively

- Seek to promote employee welfare through fair terms of employment, job security, a safe and non-discriminatory workplace, and a commitment to retraining in order to mitigate the impact of layoffs or a plant closure

- Seek long-term profitability by providing quality goods and services at a fair price

- Identify and involve stakeholders at appropriate levels and phases of the decision-making process

- Provide management leadership and resources to develop and implement internal ethical guidelines

- Respect local practices and customs or adhere to the corporation's own ethical guidelines, whichever is most beneficial for the local community

- Respect international law and support the development and implementation of codes of conduct for international business which achieve broad international consensus

SOURCES: Vesper International, 311 MacArthur Blvd., San Leandro, CA 94577, USA (1-510-633-0666). The Hinksey Centre, Westminster College, Oxford OX2 9AT, United Kingdom (44–865), 247–644. Reprinted with permission.

---

responsibilities of international corporations in 12 areas. Figure 6–5 presents the guidelines decided on by the group.

Like the other lists presented, these guidelines can serve only as general principles for managers who are aspiring to make ethical decisions in the global arena. They do, however, provide the consensus thinking of a host of stakeholder representatives as to the responsibilities of international corporations.

SUMMARY

Ethical dilemmas pose difficulties, in general, for businesses, and those arising in connection with doing business in foreign lands are among the most complex. A cursory examination of major issues that have arisen in global business ethics over the past two decades shows that they rank right up there with the most well-known news stories. The infant formula controversy, the Bhopal tragedy, the Lockheed payments to high-ranking Japanese government officials, and the continuing concern about sweatshops and the exploits of MNCs in Third World countries have all provided an opportunity for business critics to assail corporate ethics in the international sphere. These problems arise for a multiplicity of reasons, but differing cultures, value systems, forms of government, socioeconomic systems, and underhanded and ill-motivated business exploits have all been contributing factors.

The balancing of home and host country standards, global codes of conduct, the integration of ethical considerations into corporate strategy, the option of suspending activities, the use of ethical impact statements, and the adherence to international rights and moral guidelines offer some hope that conditions can be better managed. Current trends point to a growth in business activity in the transnational economy, and therefore these issues will become more rather than less important in the future. Indeed, it could easily be argued that business's greatest ethical challenges in the future will be at the global level.

KEY TERMS

Bhopal tragedy (page 183)

bribes (page 188)

ethical impact statements (page 199)

grease payments (page 190)

infant formula controversy (page 181)

less-developed countries (LDCs) (page 176)

multinational corporation (page 174)

sweatshops (page 186)

transnational economy (page 173)

DISCUSSION QUESTIONS

1. Drawing on the notions of moral, amoral, and immoral management introduced in Chapter 4, categorize your impressions of (a) Nestlé, in the infant formula controversy and (b) Union Carbide in the Bhopal tragedy.
2. As an MNC seeks to balance and honor the ethical standards of both the home and host countries, conflicts inevitably will arise. What criteria do you think managers should consider as they try to decide whether to use home or host country ethical standards?
3. Differentiate between a bribe and a grease payment. Give an example of each.
4. Using Donaldson's fundamental international rights, rank what you consider to be the top five of the ten rights. Explain your ranking.
5. Of DeGeorge's seven moral guidelines, identify which single guideline you think is of most practical value for an MNC. Give a brief explanation of your choice.

ENDNOTES

1. Peter F. Drucker, "The Transnational Economy," *The Wall Street Journal* (August 25, 1987), 38. Also see T.S. Pinkston and Archie B. Carroll, "Corporate Citizenship Perspectives and Foreign Direct Investment in the U.S.," *Journal of Business Ethics* (Vol. 13, 1994), 157–169.

2. Paul Krugman, cited in Alan Farnham, "Global—Or Just Globaloney?" *Fortune* (June 27, 1994), 97–98.

3. Steven L. Wartick and Donna J. Wood, *International Business and Society* (Malden, MA: Blackwell Publishers, 1998).

4. Richard D. Robinson, "Background Concepts and Philosophy of International Business from World War II to the Present," in William A. Dymsza and Robert G. Vambery (eds.), *International Business Knowledge: Managing International Functions in the 1990s* (New York: Praeger, 1987), 3–4.

5. *Ibid.*

6. *Ibid.*, 5–6.

7. *Ibid.*, 6.

8. *Ibid.*

9. For further discussion, see A.G. Kefalas, "The Global Corporation: Its Role in the New World Order," *Phi Kappa Phi Journal* (Fall, 1992), 26–30.

10. Craig Cox, "High Explosives: Ten Ethical Landmines to Avoid in 1994," *Business Ethics* (January–February, 1994), 33–35.

11. W. Michael Hoffman, Ann E. Lange, and David Fedo (eds.), *Ethics and the Multinational Enterprise* (Lanham, MD: University Press of America, 1986), xix.

12. John Garland and Richard N. Farmer, *International Dimensions of Business Policy and Strategy* (Boston: Kent Publishing Company, 1986), 166–173.

13. *Ibid.*, 167–168.

14. *Ibid.*, 169.

15. *Ibid.*, 170–171.

16. *Ibid.*, 172.

17. *Ibid.*

18. "Ethical Dilemmas of the Multinational Enterprise," *Business Ethics Report,* Highlights of Bentley College's Sixth National Conference of Business Ethics (Waltham, MA: The Center for Business Ethics at Bentley College, October 10 and 11, 1985), 3. Also see Richard T. DeGeorge, *Competing with Integrity in International Business* (New York: Oxford University Press, 1993).

19. Rosabeth Moss Kanter, *World Class: Thriving Locally in the Global Economy* (New York: Simon & Schuster, 1995).

20. Michael L. Wheeler, "Global Diversity: Reality, Opportunity, and Challenge," *Business Week* (December 1, 1997), special section.

21. James C. Baker, John C. Ryans, Jr., and Donald G. Howard, *International Business Classics* (Lexington, MA: Lexington Books, 1988), 73–367.

22. Paul Simon, *The Tongue Tied American* (New York: Continuum Press, 1980), 32.

23. Baker, Ryans, and Howard, 127–138.

24. Alan M. Rugman, Donald J. Lecraw, and Laurence D. Booth, *International Business: Firm and Environment* (New York: McGraw-Hill, 1985), 293.

25. Baker, Ryans, and Howard, 245–246.

26. *Ibid.*, 314–315.

27. Richard D. Robinson, "The Challenge of the Underdeveloped National Market," in Baker, Ryans, and Howard, 347–356.

28. James E. Post, "Assessing the Nestlé Boycott: Corporate Accountability and Human Rights," *California Management Review* (Winter, 1985), 115–116.

29. *Ibid.*, 116–117.

30. Rogene A. Buchholz, William D. Evans, and Robert Q. Wagley, *Management Response to Public Issues* (Englewood Cliffs, NJ: Prentice Hall, 1985), 80.

31. *Ibid.*, 81–82.

32. Oliver Williams, "Who Cast the First Stone?" *Harvard Business Review* (September–October, 1984), 155.

33. "Nestlé's Costly Accord," *Newsweek* (February 6, 1984), 52.

34. Alix M. Freedman, "Nestlé to Restrict Low-Cost Supplies of Baby Food to Developing Nations" and "American Home Infant-Formula Giveaway to End," *The Wall Street Journal* (February 4, 1991), B1.

35. For further discussion, see S. Prakash Sethi, *Multinational Corporations and the Impact of Public Advocacy on Corporate Strategy: Nestlé and the Infant Formula Case* (Boston: Kluwer Academic, 1994).

36. Stuart Diamond, "The Disaster in Bhopal: Lessons for the Future," *The New York Times* (February 5, 1985), 1. Also see Russell Mokhiber, "Bhopal," *Corporate Crime and Violence* (San Francisco: Sierra Club Books, 1988), 86–96.

37. Stuart Diamond, "Disaster in India Sharpens Debate on Doing Business in Third World," *The New York Times* (December 16, 1984), 1.

38. *Ibid.*, 1.

39. *Ibid.*

40. Thomas M. Gladwin and Ingo Walter, "Bhopal and the Multinational," *The Wall Street Journal* (January 16, 1985), 1.

41. Diamond, 1984, 1.

42. Molly Moore, "In Bhopal, A Relentless Cloud of Despair," *The Washington Post National Weekly Edition* (October 4–10, 1993), 17.

43. "For Multinationals, It Will Never Be the Same," *Business Week* (December 24, 1984), 57.

44. Mark Clifford, Michael Shari, and Linda Himelstein, "Pangs of Conscience: Sweatshops Haunt U.S. Consumers," *Business Week* (July 29, 1996), 46–47. Also see Keith B. Richburg and Anne Swardson, "Sweatshops or Economic Development?" *The Washington Post National Weekly Edition* (August 5–11, 1996), 19.

45. "Stamping out Sweatshops," *The Economist* (April 19, 1997), 28–29.

46. Clifford, Shari, and Himelstein, 46.

47. Andrew Young, "A Debate Over Child Labor: The World's Next Moral Crusade," *The Atlanta Journal* (March 9, 1997), R2.

48. *Ibid.*

49. *Ibid.*

50. *The Economist* (April 19, 1997), 28.

51. *Ibid.*

52. Aaron Bernstein, "Sweatshop Police: Business Backs an Initiative on Global Working Conditions," *Business Week* (October 20, 1997), 39.

53. *Ibid.*

54. *Ibid.*

55. Dwight R. Ladd, "The Bribery Business," in Tom L. Beauchamp (ed.), *Case Studies in Business, Society and Ethics* (Englewood Cliffs, NJ: Prentice Hall, 1983), 251.

56. Richard T. DeGeorge, *Business Ethics* (New York: Macmillan, 1982), 53.

57. Bruce Lloyd, "Bribery, Corruption and Accountability," *Insights on Global Ethics* (Vol. 4, No. 8, September, 1994), 5.

58. Ian I. Mitroff and Ralph H. Kilmann, "Teaching Managers to Do Policy Analysis: The Case of Corporate Bribery," *California Management Review* (Fall, 1977), 50–52.

59. *Ibid.*

60. "The Destructive Costs of Greasing Palms," *Business Week* (December 6, 1993), 133–138. Also see Paul Barrett, Robert McGough, and Maureen Kline, "Murky Italian Scandal Over Judicial Bribery Engulfs Fund Manager," *Wall Street Journal* (August 5, 1997), A1.

61. Ladd, 256.

62. Garland and Farmer, 183.

63. "Bribes Can Cost the U.S. an Edge," *Business Week* (April 15, 1996), 30.

64. Barry Richman, "Stopping Payments Under the Table," *Business Week* (May 22, 1978), 18; Thomas Goldwasser, "Don't Make Foreign Bribery by U.S. Firms Easier," *The Wall Street Journal* (October 1, 1986), 32; and Kate Gillespie, "The Middle East Response to the U.S. Foreign Corrupt Practices Act," *California Management Review* (Summer, 1987), 9–30.

65. "Who Will Listen to Mr. Clean?" *The Economist* (August 2, 1997), 52; Greg Steinmetz, "U.S. Firms Appear Among Least Likely to Bribe Overseas," *Wall Street Journal* (August 25, 1997), 9A; and Thomas Omestad, "Bye-bye to Bribes," *U.S. News & World Report* (December 22, 1997), 39–44.

66. Paul Deveney, "34 Nations Sign Accord to End Bribery in Deals," *Wall Street Journal* (December 18, 1997), A16.

67. Neil King, Jr., "Bribery Ban Is Approved by OECD," *Wall Street Journal* (November 24, 1997), A14; and William M. Davey, "The Battle Against Bribery," *Wall Street Journal* (December 17, 1997), A22.

68. Lloyd, 5.

69. Gene R. Laczniak and Jacob Naor, "Global Ethics: Wrestling with the Corporate Conscience," *Business* (July–September, 1985), 3–10.

70. G. Pascal Zachary, "Levi Tries to Make Sure Contract Plants in Asia Treat People Well," *The Wall Street Journal* (July 28, 1994), A1.

71. Tom Donaldson, "Global Business Must Mind Its Morals," *The New York Times* (February 13, 1994), F-11. Also see Tom Donaldson, "Ethics Away from Home," *Harvard Business Review* (September–October, 1996).

72. Laczniak and Naor, 7.

73. "A Code of Worldwide Business Conduct," in Frederick D. Sturdivant (ed.), *The Corporate Social Challenge: Cases and Commentaries* (Homewood, IL: Richard D. Irwin, 1985), 159–169.

74. "General Dynamics Standards of Business Ethics and Conduct" (August, 1985), 17.

75. "Mattel, Inc. Launches Global Code of Conduct" (November 20, 1997), unpublished press release. Also see "Global Manufacturing Principles" (1997), 1–11.

76. Laczniak and Naor, 7–8.

77. Archie B. Carroll, Frank Hoy, and John Hall, "The Integration of Corporate Social Policy into Strategic Management," in S. Prakash Sethi and Cecilia M. Falbe (eds.), *Business and Society: Dimensions of Conflict and Cooperation* (Lexington, MA: Lexington Books, 1987), 449–470.

78. Robert D. Haas, "Ethics in the Trenches," *Across the Board* (May, 1994), 12–13.

79. "Starbucks Pays Premium Price to Benefit Workers," *Business Ethics* (March/April 1998), 9.

80. Laczniak and Naor, 8.
81. Haas, 12.
82. David H. Blake, William C. Frederick, and Mildred S. Myers, *Social Auditing: Evaluating the Impact of Corporate Programs* (New York: Praeger, 1976), 3.
83. Mattel press release (November 20, 1997).
84. Thomas Donaldson, *The Ethics of International Business* (New York: Oxford University Press, 1989), 81.
85. Richard T. DeGeorge, "Ethical Dilemmas for Multinational Enterprise: A Philosophical Overview," in Hoffman, Lange, and Fedo (eds.), 39–46. Also see Richard T. DeGeorge, *Business Ethics,* 5th ed. (Englewood Cliffs, NJ: Prentice Hall, 1999), Chapters 18–20. Also see Richard T. DeGeorge, *Competing with Integrity in International Business* (New York: Oxford University Press, 1993).

PART 3

External Stakeholder Issues

7

Business, Government, and Regulation

CHAPTER OBJECTIVES

After studying this chapter, you should be able to:

1 Articulate a brief history of government's role in its relationship with business.

2 Appreciate the complex interactions among business, government, and the public.

3 Identify and describe government's nonregulatory influences, especially the concepts of industrial policy and privatization.

4 Explain government regulation and identify the major reasons for regulation, the types of regulation, and issues arising out of regulation.

5 Provide a perspective on regulation versus deregulation along with accompanying trends.

6 Describe major types of regulatory reform and their characteristics.

Few issues seem to excite businesspeople as much as government's role in society. This became especially true when government began playing a more active role in the 1960s and 1970s. Over the past 30 years, the depth, scope, and direction of government's involvement in business has made the business/government relationship one of the most hotly debated issues of modern times. In addition, government's role, particularly in the regulation of business, has ensured its place among the major stakeholders with which business must establish an effective working relationship if it is to survive and prosper.

Business has never been fond of government's increasingly activist role in establishing the ground rules under which it operates. Business has almost always been against an increased role for government, especially the federal government. In contrast, public interest has been cyclical, going through periods when it has thought that the federal government had too much power and other periods when it has thought that government should be more activist. President Ronald Reagan came into office in 1980, when the public was growing somewhat weary of an active federal role. President Reagan's favorite saying was that "government isn't the solution; it's the problem." He seemed to hit a responsive chord with the public at that particular point in time. In 1982, 38 percent of a Gallup Poll sample indicated the federal government had too much power. By 1986, this figure had fallen to 28 percent, with 41 percent of the public sample now indicating the federal government should use its power more vigorously.[1]

Throughout the decade of the 1980s, the federal government played less and less of a role, especially in terms of monitoring and regulating business. It was not without reason, therefore, that in late 1989 *Time* magazine ran a cover story entitled "Is Government Dead?"[2] This article was not limited to government's role vis-à-vis business but criticized government's lack of initiative and responsiveness on a host of problems facing the United States, such as the unprecedented opportunity to promote democracy in Eastern Europe, the spreading plague of drugs, the plight of the underclass, and the dire need for educational reform. In essence, the Reagan Revolution of an inactive federal government had left the public with a desire for government to become active again. It was against this backdrop that Republican candidate George Bush was elected president in 1988.

The George Bush administration turned out to be a one-term presidency. Bush was narrowly defeated by Democratic candidate Bill Clinton in 1992. During the Bush administration, the country witnessed a growth in the rate of federal government spending that exceeded that of the Reagan years. This trend continued with President Clinton. Ironically, these increases in government spending occurred during periods in which the administrations in office were simultaneously advocating the downsizing of government.

The midterm elections for Congress in 1994 ushered in conservative Republican majorities in both the Senate and the House of Representatives. This election was perceived by many as a significant message to President Clinton that the American people were displeased with the escalating role of the federal government in their lives. Some exit polls suggested that resentment of big government was a major factor in the political tide shifting.[3] The tide has continued to shift. A survey by the National Election Studies at the University of Michigan indicates that the public's faith in government is beginning to grow again.[4] However, another study by the American Enterprise Institute contends that Americans remain wary of their federal government.[5] While a strengthened economy has reassured some, many people remain skeptical of government's role in their lives.

In this chapter we will examine the relationship between business and government, although the general public will assume an important role in the discussion as well. A central concern in this chapter is the government's role in influencing business. Exploring this relationship carefully will provide an appreciation of the complexity of the issues surrounding business/government interactions. From the prospective manager's standpoint, one needs a rudimentary understanding of the forces and factors that are involved in these issues before one can begin to talk intelligently about strategies for dealing with them. Unfortunately, more is known about the nature of the problem than about the nature of solutions, as is common when dealing with complex social issues. In the next chapter, we will discuss how business attempts to influence government and public policy.

A BRIEF HISTORY OF GOVERNMENT'S ROLE

In the early days of the United States, the government supported business by imposing tariffs to protect our fledgling industries. In the second half of the 1800s, government gave large land grants as incentives for private business to build railroads. Several railroads had grown large and strong through mergers, and people began to use them because their service was faster, cheaper, and more efficient. This resulted in a decline in the use of alternative forms of transportation, such as highways, rivers, and canals. Many railroads began to abuse their favored positions. For example, a railroad that had a monopoly on service to a particular town might charge unfairly high rates for the service. Competitive railroads sometimes agreed among themselves to charge high but comparable rates. Higher rates were charged for shorter hauls, and preference was shown to large shippers over smaller shippers.

Public criticism of what were perceived as abusive practices led to the passage of the Interstate Commerce Act of 1887, which was intended to prevent discrimination and abuses by the railroads. This act marked the beginning of extensive federal government regulation of interstate commerce. The act created the Interstate Commerce Commission, which became the first federal regulatory agency and a model for future agencies.[6]

Many large manufacturing firms and mining firms also began to abuse consumers during the late 1800s. Typical actions included the elimination of competition and the charging of excessively high prices. During this period, several large firms formed organizations known as trusts. A trust was an organization that brought all or most competitors under a common control that then permitted them to eliminate most of the remaining competitors by price cutting, an act that forced the remaining competitors out of business. Then, the trusts would restrict production and raise prices. As a response, Congress passed the Sherman Antitrust Act in 1890, which became the first in a series of actions intended to control monopolies in various industries. The Sherman Act outlawed any contract, combination, or conspiracy in restraint of trade, and it also prohibited the monopolization of any market. In the early 1900s, the Sherman Act was used by the federal government to break up the Standard Oil Company, the American Tobacco Company, and several other large firms that had abused their economic power.[7]

The Clayton Antitrust Act was passed in 1914 to augment the Sherman Act. It addressed other abusive practices that had arisen. It outlawed price discrimination that gave favored buyers preference over others and forbade anticompetitive contracts whereby a company would agree to sell only to suppliers who agreed not to sell the products of a rival competitor. The act also prohibited an assortment of other anticompetitive practices. Also in 1914, Congress formed the Federal Trade Commission, which was intended to maintain free and fair competition and to protect consumers from unfair or misleading practices.[8]

Another great wave of regulation occurred during the Great Depression and the subsequent New Deal of the 1930s. Significant legislation included the Securities Act of 1933 and the Securities and Exchange Act of 1934. These laws were aimed at curbing abuses in the stock market, stabilizing markets, and restoring investor confidence. Significant labor legislation during this same period signaled government involvement in a new area. Several examples were the 1926 Railway Labor Act, the 1932 Norris–LaGuardia Act, and the 1935 Wagner Act.

During the New Deal period in the 1930s, government also took on a new dimension in its relationship with business, actively assuming responsibility for restoring prosperity and promoting economic growth through public works programs. In 1946, this new role of government was formalized with the passage of the Full Employment Act.

In the present period, government has passed considerable legislation, involving itself deeply in the affairs of business. Prior to the mid-1950s, most congressional legislation affecting business was economic in nature. Since that time, however, legislation has had social goals as well. Much legislation of the past three decades has been concerned with the quality of life.[9] Several illustrations of this include the Civil Rights Act of 1964, the Water Quality Act of 1965, the Occupational Safety and Health Act of 1970, the Consumer Product Safety Act of 1972, the Warranty Act of 1975, and the Americans with Disabilities Act of 1990.

Just as the areas in which government has chosen to initiate legislation have changed, the multiplicity of roles that government has assumed has increased the complexity of its relationship with business. Several of the varied roles that government has assumed in its relationship with business are worth looking at because they suggest the influence, interrelationships, and complexities that are present.[10] These roles indicate that government:

1. Prescribes the rules of the game for business.
2. Is a major purchaser of business's products and services.
3. Uses its contracting power to get business to do things it wants.
4. Is a major promoter and subsidizer of business.
5. Is the owner of vast quantities of productive equipment and wealth.
6. Is an architect of economic growth.
7. Is a financier.
8. Is the protector of various interests in society against business exploitation.
9. Directly manages large areas of private business.
10. Is the repository of the social conscience and redistributes resources to meet social objectives.

After examining and assessing these various roles, one can perhaps begin to appreciate the crucial interconnectedness between business and government and the difficulty both business and the public have in fully understanding (much less prescribing) what government's role ought to be in relation to business.

Near the end of the Clinton presidency, it was becoming apparent that government's role, as always, was not going to fade away but would continue to grow or decline in response to the political mood, as it has for decades, between laissez-faire and intervention. One view was that the pendulum was swinging over a narrower arc with a belief that the new role of government in the economy would emphasize pragmatism and modest, achieveable goals rather than idealism and great expectations, in order to provide a stable environment in which the economy could grow.[11] Because the public has learned that regulations bring advantages and disadvantages, it expects a careful cost-benefit analysis of proposed regulations.[12]

THE ROLES OF GOVERNMENT AND BUSINESS

We do not intend to philosophize in this chapter on the ideal role of government in relation to business, because this is outside our stakeholder frame of reference. However, we will strive for an understanding of current major issues as they pertain to this vital relationship. For effective management, government, as a stakeholder, must be understood.

The fundamental question underlying our entire discussion of business/government relationships is, *"What should be the respective roles of business and government in our socioeconomic system?"* This question is far easier to ask than to answer, but as we explore it, some important basic understandings begin to emerge.

The issue could be stated in a different fashion: Given all the tasks that must be accomplished to make our society work, which of these tasks should be handled by government and which should be handled by business? This poses the issue clearly, but there are other questions that remain to be answered. If we decide, for example, that it is best to let business handle the production and distribution roles in our society, the next question pertains to how much autonomy we are willing to allow business. If goals were simply the production and distribution of goods and services, we would not have to constrain business severely. In modern times, however, other goals have been added to the production and distribution functions: for example, a safe working environment for those engaging in production, equal employment opportunities, fair pay, clean air, safe products, employee rights, and so on. When these goals are superimposed on the basic economic goals, the task of business becomes much more complex and challenging.

Because these latter, more socially oriented goals are not automatically factored into business decision making and processes, it often falls on government to ensure that those goals that reflect concerns of the public interest be achieved. Thus, whereas the marketplace dictates economic production decisions, government becomes one of the citizenry's designated representatives charged with articulating and protecting the public interest.

A Clash of Ethical Belief Systems

A clash of emphases partially forms the crux of the antagonistic relationship that has evolved between business and government over the years. This problem has been termed "a clash of ethical systems." The two ethical systems (systems of belief) are the *individualistic* ethic of business and the *collectivistic* ethic of government. Figure 7–1 summarizes the characteristics of these two philosophies.[13]

The clash of these two ethical systems partially explains why the current business/government relationship is adversarial in nature. In elaborating on the adversarial nature of the business/government relationship, Jacoby offered the following comments:

> *Officials of government characteristically look upon themselves as probers, inspectors, taxers, regulators, and punishers of business transgressions. Businesspeople typically view government agencies as obstacles, constraints, delayers, and impediments to economic progress, having much power to stop and little to start.*[14]

The business/government relationship not only has become adversarial but also has been deteriorating. The goals and values of our pluralistic society have become more complex, more numerous, more interrelated, and, consequently, more difficult to reconcile. The result has been increasing conflicts among diverse interest

FIGURE 7–1 The Clash of Ethical Systems Between Business and Government	
Business Beliefs	**Government Beliefs**
• Individualistic ethic	• Collectivistic ethic
• Maximum concession to self-interest	• Subordination of individual goals and self-interest to group goals and group interests
• Minimizing the load of obligations society imposes on the individual (personal freedom)	• Maximizing the obligations assumed by the individual and discouraging self-interest
• Emphasizes inequalities of individuals	• Emphasizes equality of individuals

groups, with trade-off decisions becoming harder to make. In this process it has become more difficult to establish social priorities, and consensus has in many cases become impossible to achieve.[15]

Social, Technological, and Value Changes

As we attempt to understand why all this has happened, it is only natural to look to changes in the social and technological environments for some explanations. According to Daniel Bell, since World War II four major changes have had profound impacts on American society in general and on the business/government relationship in particular. First, out of local and regional societies a truly national one has arisen.[16] Second, we have seen a "communal society" arise, characterized by a great emphasis on public goods and the internalization of external costs. Third, the revolution of rising expectations has brought with it the demand for "entitlements"—good jobs, excellent housing, and other amenities. Fourth, a rising concern has emerged for an improved "quality of life."[17]

In addition to these, six other societal value changes have shaped the course of business/government relations. These are the youth movement, the consumer protection movement, the ecology movement, the civil rights movement, the women's liberation movement, and the egalitarian movement.[18]

In a sense, this last movement—the egalitarian movement—embraces all of the others, because it represents an effort to create an equitable balance of all facets of what is good in life in the United States. Thus, the value changes that have taken place "have multiplied the number of political decisions that have to be made relative to the number of decisions made in markets."[19] And to the extent that these political decisions affect business—and they do to a great extent—we can understand the basic conflict arising once again in a clash between individualist and collectivist belief systems. Government's responses to changes taking place in society have put it in direct opposition to business in terms of both philosophy and mode of operation. Although one might argue that this clash of belief systems is not as severe today as it once was, the basic differences still serve to frame the positions of the two groups.

INTERACTION OF BUSINESS, GOVERNMENT, AND THE PUBLIC

This section offers a brief overview of the influence relationships among business, government, and the public. This should be helpful in understanding both the nature of the process by which public policy decisions are made and the current problems that characterize the business/government relationship. Figure 7–2 illustrates the pattern of these influence relationships.

One might rightly ask at this point, "Why include the public? Isn't the public represented by government?" In an ideal world, perhaps this would be true. To help us appreciate that government functions somewhat apart from the public, it has been depicted separately in the diagram. In addition, the public has its methods of influence that need to be singled out.

Government/Business Relationship

Government influences business through regulation, taxation, and other forms of persuasion that we will consider in more detail in the next section. Business, likewise, has its approaches to influencing government, which we will deal with in Chapter 8. Lobbying, in one form or another, is business's primary means of influencing government.

Public/Government Relationship

The public uses the political processes of voting and electing officials (or removing them from office) to influence government. It also exerts its influence by forming special-interest groups (farmers, small-business owners, educators, senior citizens,

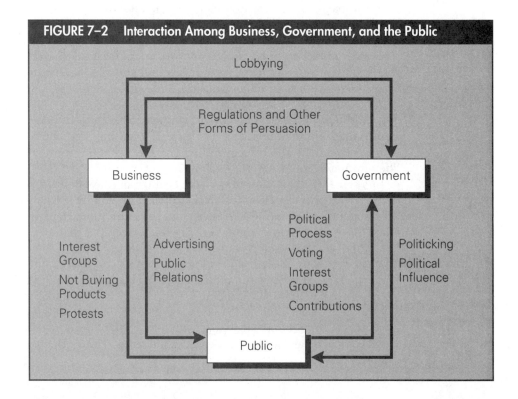

FIGURE 7–2   Interaction Among Business, Government, and the Public

truckers, manufacturers, etc.) to wield more targeted influence. Government, in turn, uses politicking, public policy formation, and other political influences to have an impact on the public.

Business/Public Relationship

Business influences the public through advertising, public relations, and other forms of communication. And the public influences business through the marketplace or by forming special-interest groups (for example, People United to Save Humanity, American Association of Retired Persons, Friends of the Earth, American Civil Liberties Union) and protest groups.

Earlier we raised the question of whether government really represents the public. This question may be stated another way: "Who determines what is in the public interest?" In our society, determining the public interest is not a simple matter. Whereas government may be the official representative of the public, we should not assume that representation occurs in a straightforward fashion. As we saw in Figure 7–2, the public takes its own initiatives both with business and with government. The three major groups, therefore, are involved in a dynamic interplay of influence processes that determines what is currently considered to be in the public interest.

Our central concern in this chapter is with government's role in influencing business, and we now turn our attention to that topic. Here we will begin to see more clearly how government is a major stakeholder of business. Government's official priority is in representing the public interest as it sees and interprets the public's wishes. But, like all large bureaucratic organizations, government also takes on a life of its own with its own goals and agenda.

GOVERNMENT'S NONREGULATORY INFLUENCE ON BUSINESS

Recognizing that in 1998 the federal government's budget went over the $1.5 trillion mark, approximately one-fifth of the U.S. gross domestic product, we can begin to appreciate the magnitude of the effect government has on all institutions in society. We will limit our treatment to the federal government's influence on business, but we must be repeatedly reminded of the presence and influence of state and local governments as well.

Broadly speaking, we may categorize the kinds of influence government has on business as *nonregulatory* and *regulatory*. In the next major section, we will focus on government regulation, but in this section let us consider the wide range of nonregulatory influences that government has on business.

Two major issues merit consideration before we examine some of the specific policy tools or mechanisms government uses to influence business. These two major issues are (1) industrial policy and (2) privatization. Industrial policy is concerned with the role that our government plays in the world of international trade, and privatization zeroes in on the question of whether current public functions (for example, public education, public transit, social security, fire service) should be turned over to the private (business) sector. Both of these issues have important implications for the business/government relationship. They are both important, because they seem to come into and out of popularity on a fairly regular basis.

Industrial Policy

Important initial questions include, *"What does industrial policy mean, and why has it become such a hotly debated issue?"* An **industrial policy** may be defined as follows: "Any selective government measure that prevents or promotes changes in the structure of an economy."[20]

This very broad definition by itself does not give us enough focus to understand the concept. Let us elaborate. One school of thought thinks of industrial policy as some variation of the British model, wherein government provides help for older, declining industries. Therefore, when steel company executives in the United States argue for tax breaks and tariffs that would enable them to survive and compete with foreign competition, they are asking for an industrial policy.[21]

Another school of thought is exemplified by Robert Reich in his book *The Next American Frontier,* wherein he argues for a national industrial policy that attempts to identify *winning* (or sunrise) industries and foster their growth. As for *losing* (or sunset) industries, industrial policy would have as its goal redirecting resources into growth fields.[22]

Variations on these themes could yield a variety of industrial policy schools of thought. Five schools of thought that give us insights into industrial policy include the following: the accelerationists, the adjusters, the targeters, the central planners, and the bankers.[23] The **accelerationists** would try to pinpoint industries that promise to become strong international competitors and position them to move rapidly into world markets. Their goal would be to accelerate changes already signaled by the marketplace. The **adjusters** would offer adjustment assistance to declining industries in return for commitments that they would slim down, modernize, and help their employees relocate and train for new skills and jobs.

The **targeters** would target a select group of sectors or industries (for example, high tech, agriculture, energy, finance, health care equipment) to be turned into engines for growth. The **central planners** would advocate growth-oriented macroeconomic policies that would come close to comprehensive planning. Finally, the **bankers** would advocate a federally backed industrial development bank that would provide "patient capital"—money that could be sunk into a high-risk venture for 5 to 10 years or longer.

The debate over industrial policy became more active upon publication of Reich's *The Next American Frontier* in 1983 and the realization of our drab economic performance during the 1979–1982 period, when the United States lost significant ground to Japan as the world leader in industrial expansion. Many experts saw the very survival of the U.S. economy at stake in the face of subsidized foreign competition from Japan and other industrialized countries. Indeed, in 1987 a trade confrontation arose between the United States and Japan over the significant trade imbalances arising out of these issues.

During the Reagan (1980–1988) and Bush (1988–1992) administrations, the notion of industrial policy was not looked upon with great favor. Both of these administrations advocated a free-market posture rather than government activism via industrial policy. President Clinton, however, has proposed several actions that typify an active industrial policy. Clinton-initiated U.S. industrial policies include supports (subsidies, tax breaks, contributions) for shipbuilding, information infrastructure, oil and gas tax breaks, and advanced technology.[24]

Some of the most recent policy initiatives center around global electronic commerce. Many analysts believe that the Internet could become the most active trade vehicle in the United States within a decade. However, businesses are often wary of becoming involved in Internet commerce because they are unsure of the legal environment and they fear government regulation and taxation will stifle Internet commerce. The Clinton administration has taken an activist stance in promoting the Internet by issuing a Framework for Global Electronic Commerce. This framework outlines key principles for supporting the evolution of electronic commerce, identifies where international efforts are needed, and designates the U.S. governmental agencies responsible for leading the effort.[25]

Even an issue as simple as naming domains has created controversy. Network Solutions (*www.networksolutions.com*), a private, Virginia-based company, had received an exclusive government contract for assigning and registering Internet domain names in the most popular top-level domains: .com, .net, .org, and .edu. In 1998, the Commerce Department proposed that the registration process be transferred to a newly developed, private nonprofit corporation, made up of representatives of various Internet stakeholder groups. The Department also recommended that up to five new top-level domains be added. Meanwhile, the Geneva-based Council of Registrars (*www.gtld-mou.org*) was planning to implement its own registering program while adding seven new top-level domains. Clearly, the worlds of business and politics often overlap, and the actions of one can profoundly impact the other. Up-to-date information about the government activity surrounding global electronic commerce is available at *www.ntia.doc.gov*,[26] Web site for the National Telecommunications & Information Administration.

Arguments for Industrial Policy

Proponents of an industrial policy (more active role of government in the business sector) cite a variety of reasons for supporting it. First, of course, is the declining or threatened competitiveness of the United States in world markets. A second argument is the use of industrial policy by other world governments, including Germany, Britain, France, and Italy. A third major argument is that the United States already has an industrial policy but it is the haphazard result of unplanned taxes, tariffs, regulatory policies, and research and development policies. Others have called our current system an ad hoc industrial policy because the United States has, in fact, intervened in many specific industries as emergencies have arisen. Protection schemes have been used in the apparel, auto, and steel industries to deal with foreign competition. The federal government's decision in 1979 to provide loan guarantees to Chrysler Corporation and Chrysler's early repaying of its $1.2 billion loan are cited by many advocates as an example of

---

SEARCH THE WEB

One of the Internet-related problems facing the administration is **cybersquatting**. Cybersquatters are people who register names that correspond to well-known brand names and trademarks in the hope they will receive a lucrative payoff when the real company goes to register that name. For protection, companies have been forced to pre-emptively register and maintain any names they might ever choose to use. Recently, moves to combat cybersquatting have occurred on several fronts. In April 1999, Network Solutions purged 18,000 registrations that were held by suspected cybersquatters. They said they had a legal right to reclaim those names because the registration fee, $70 for two years, had not been paid on time. At the same time, the World Intellectual Property Organization (WIPO), a United Nations agency, was drafting new domain name registration rules, designed to address the issue of cybersquatting. To learn about the range of cybersquatting issues and/or check to see if your name is registered as a domain, go to **www.igoldrush.com**.

how federal intervention can benefit companies, employees, and communities at no net cost to the United States Treasury.

Arguments Against Industrial Policy

Critics of industrial policy also have significant reasons for their views. Critics say that government interference reduces the market's efficiency. How do you keep politics out of what ought to be economic decisions? Some politicians, as well as experts, think the United States should focus on rescuing steel and other "sunset" industries. Others argue we ought to promote emerging "sunrise" industries, such as high-technology electronics.

Those who oppose industrial policy say that foreign success with it has been very overrated. It is argued that Japan, for example, has had as many failures as successes with its government's development agency, Ministry of International Trade and Industry (MITI). MITI is generally credited with helping to build Japan's computer, semiconductor, and steel industries, but efforts to promote the aluminum-refining, petrochemical, shipping, and commercial aircraft industries were viewed as failures.[27] One economist, Gary Saxonhouse, reports that Japanese support for research and development is less than that in the United States. He says that less than 2 percent of nondefense business research and development is financed by government in Japan, compared with 22 percent in the United States.[28] Further, Japan's favorable industrial policies (keiretsu), combined with lifetime employment, are ill suited to surviving economic recessions: The Japanese business system has produced too few entrepreneurial risk-takers.[29]

Finally, attempts at forming an industrial policy have been criticized as being irrational and uncoordinated and composed largely of "voluntary" restrictions on imports, occasional bail-outs for near-bankruptcy companies, and a wide array of subsidies, loan guarantees, and special tax benefits for particular firms and industries. Thus, such efforts have constituted an industrial policy by default.[30] One could argue that the United States is incapable of developing a successful and planned industrial policy, given its experience and the composition of the public policy process that has characterized past decision making.

There is an ebb and flow of interest in the concept of industrial policy depending on which administration is in office. And because many of the problems that initially started the current debate on industrial policy in the 1980s are still with us, it is easy to believe that it could continue to be a business/government debate for years to come. This is particularly true given the increasing importance of international competitiveness. Either way, industrial policy is a powerful nonregulating approach by government to influence business.

Privatization

Whereas industrial policy is a macro policy issue more oriented toward international trade and world markets, privatization is more focused on the domestic scene. Privatization threatens to displace "partnerships" as the primary buzzword when people talk about the contribution business can make to the solution of problems that beset the public and government. *Privatization*, generally speaking, refers to the process of "turning over to" the private sector (business) some function or service that was previously handled by some government body. To understand privatization, we need to differentiate two functions government might perform: (1) *producing* a service and (2) *providing* a service.[31]

Producing versus Providing a Service

A city government would be *providing* security if it employed a private firm to work at the coliseum during the state basketball playoffs. This same city government would be *producing* a service if its own police force provided security at the same basketball tournament. The federal government would be *providing* medical care to the aged with a national Medicare program. The "production" of medical care would be coming from private physicians. The government would be providing *and* producing medical care if it employed its own staff of doctors, as, for example, the military does. The terminology can be very confusing, but the distinction must be made, because sometimes government provides a service (has a program for and actually pays for a service) and at other times it also produces a service (has its own employees who do it).[32]

The Tennessee Valley Authority (TVA) was once widely regarded as a model for how electric power should be produced and distributed. Now there is talk of proposals to sell TVA to the private sector to increase its efficiency. Conrail, Amtrak, the postal service, public housing, and even public lands are federal enterprises that some are arguing should be sold to the private sector.

Private Firm versus Government-Provided Services

A study compared eight government services provided by local governments with those same services provided by private firms. The services were street sweeping, janitorial operations, refuse collection, payroll administration, traffic signal maintenance, asphalt surface repair, tree trimming, and lawn care. In seven out of eight services, the private firms showed a savings of 37 to 96 percent over the government-provided services.[33]

In the United States, the idea of free enterprise managing the public's affairs is catching on everywhere, even in Washington. To date, there is more evidence of actual privatization in cities, counties, and states than perhaps anywhere else. In Fairfax County, Virginia, officials signed an $11 million agreement for private fleet maintenance. Indianapolis signed an $87 million agreement to have a private company operate two of its wastewater treatment facilities.[34] School districts in Florida, Minnesota, Maryland, and Connecticut signed contracts with Education Alternatives, Inc. (EAI), to manage and administer their public schools.[35]

Privatization has become a worldwide movement, especially in Europe. Across the continent and in Great Britain, governments are selling off big, government-owned businesses to private investors. It has been estimated that nearly 100 government-owned industries in Western Europe are likely candidates for privatization during the next few years. It is projected that billions of dollars worth of government holdings are candidates for privatization by 1998: France ($81.3 billion), Italy ($34.6 billion), Germany ($23.9 billion), Spain ($20.7 billion), Britain ($13.4 billion), and Sweden ($10 billion).[36]

Proponents of privatization in both the United States and Europe suggest that the functions of entire bureaucracies need to be contracted out to the private sector. They maintain that government at all levels is involved in thousands of businesses in which it has no real comparative advantage and no basic reason for being involved.[37] Proponents also argue that publicly owned enterprises are less efficient and less flexible than competitive private firms. It should be acknowledged, however, that privatization is not always easy, cost efficient, and effective. For example, the Baltimore Board of School Commissioners canceled its contract with EAI citing low achievement scores and high costs. It then found success by obtaining a $400,000 grant from a private foundation and implementing a plan by a Baltimore school principal.[38] Therefore, care must be exercised as this approach is undertaken.

These two issues—industrial policy and privatization—are largely unresolved. They continue to be discussed and experimented with, however. They could have significant implications for the business/government relationship for years to come.

We should now return to our discussion of the ways in which government uses various policies and mechanisms for influencing business.

Other Nonregulatory Governmental Influences on Business

Government has a significant impact on business by virtue of the fact that it has a large payroll and is a *major employer* itself. At all levels, government employs millions of people who, as a consequence of being government employees, see things from the government's perspective. This influence is felt by business throughout society. Government is also in the position of being a standard-setter: The 8-hour work day began in the federal government. When the Reagan administration broke the air traffic controller's strike in 1981, it ushered in wage restraints in the private sector.

Government is one of the largest *purchasers* of goods and services produced in the private sector. Some key industries, such as aerospace, electronics, and shipbuilding, are very dependent on government purchasing. Government can exert significant influence over the private sector by its insistence that minorities be hired, depressed areas be favored, small businesses be favored, and so on. Changes in government policy can dramatically change a firm's business environment.[39] For some firms in narrow markets, such as defense, the government dominates and controls whether or not those firms have a good year—indeed, whether or not they survive at all.[40]

Government influences the behavior of business through the use of *subsidies* in a variety of ways. Generous subsidies are made available to industries such as agriculture, fishing, transportation, nuclear energy, and housing and to groups in special categories, such as minority-owned enterprises and businesses in depressed areas. Quite often these subsidies have special qualifications attached.

Government also influences business, albeit indirectly, by virtue of its *transfer payments*. Government provides money for social security, welfare, and other entitlement programs that total hundreds of billions of dollars every year. These impacts are indirect, but they do significantly affect the market for business's goods and services.[41]

Government is a major *competitor* of business. Organizations such as the TVA compete with private suppliers of electricity, the Government Printing Office competes with private commercial publishers and printing firms, and the United States Postal Service competes with private delivery services. In areas such as health, education, recreation, and security, the competition between government and private firms runs the gamut of levels—federal, state, and local.

Government loans and *loan guarantees* are sources of influence as well. Government lends money directly to small businesses, housing providers, farmers, and energy companies. Often such loans are made at lower interest rates than those of private competitors. Loan guarantee programs, such as the one provided to Chrysler, is another way in which government's influence is felt.[42]

Taxation, through the Internal Revenue Service, is another example of a government influence. Tax deductibility, tax incentives, depreciation policies, and tax credits are tools that are all at the disposal of the government. A critical example of the government's taxing power occurred when a "luxury tax" was added as a minor part of the government's deficit reduction package in the early 1990s. This new luxury tax ended up virtually crippling the boatbuilding industry. It led to massive layoffs and adversely affected dozens of related industries. Ironically, the luxury tax resulted in less tax revenues than it produced.[43]

Monetary policy, although it is administered through the Federal Reserve System, can have a profound effect on business. Although the Federal Reserve System is technically independent of the executive branch, it often responds to presidential leadership or initiatives.

Finally, *moral suasion* is a tool of government.[44] This refers to the government's attempts, usually through the president, to "persuade" business to act in the public interest by taking or not taking a particular course of action. These public-interest appeals might include a request to roll back a price hike, show restraint on wage and salary increases, or exercise "voluntary" restraints of one kind or another.

GOVERNMENT'S REGULATORY INFLUENCES ON BUSINESS

For more than two decades, government regulation has been the most controversial issue in the business/government relationship. Government regulation has affected virtually every aspect of how business functions. It has affected the terms and conditions under which firms have competed in their respective industries. It has touched almost every business decision ranging from the production of goods and services to packaging, distribution, marketing, and service. Most people agree that some degree of regulation has been necessary to ensure that consumers and employees are treated fairly and are not exposed to unreasonable hazards and that the environment is protected. However, they also think that government regulation has often been too extensive in scope, too costly, often unreasonable, and inevitably burdensome in terms of paperwork requirements and red tape.

Businesspeople, more than the general public, have felt these disadvantages and have borne the frustration of attempting to live up to government's expectations. An Arthur Andersen Enterprise Group study found that, among midsize companies, "government relations" represented its most significant challenge, exceeding the challenges of health care and insurance and turning a profit. The study revealed further that the companies estimate they spend 36 percent of their time on regulatory compliance.[45] In another survey of affluent business owners, 85 percent said that "government policies" most threaten their privately held companies. Government policies were seen as more of a threat than the difficulty of attracting and keeping skilled workers, rising interest rates/slow growth, and inflation.[46]

Regulation: What Does It Mean?

Generally, *regulation* refers to the act of governing, directing according to rule, or bringing under the control of law or constituted authority. Although there is no universally agreed-upon definition of federal regulation, we can look to the definition of a federal regulatory agency proposed years ago by the Senate Governmental Affairs Committee.[47] It described a federal regulatory agency as one that:

1. Has decision-making authority.

2. Establishes standards or guidelines conferring benefits and imposing restrictions on business conduct.

3. Operates principally in the sphere of domestic business activity.

4. Has its head and/or members appointed by the president (generally subject to Senate confirmation).

5. Has its legal procedures generally governed by the Administrative Procedures Act.

The commerce clause of the U.S. Constitution grants to the government the legal authority to regulate. Within the confines of a regulatory agency as outlined above, the composition and functioning of regulatory agencies differ. Some are headed by an administrator and are located within an executive department—for example, the Federal Aviation Administration (FAA). Others are independent commissions composed of a chairperson and several members located outside the executive and legislative branches—such as the Interstate Commerce Commission (ICC), the Federal Communications Commission (FCC), and the Securities and Exchange Commission (SEC).[48]

Reasons for Regulation

Regulations have come about over the years for a variety of reasons. Some managers probably think that government is just sitting on the sidelines looking for reasons to butt into their business. There are several legitimate reasons why government regulation has evolved, although these same businesspeople may not entirely agree with them. For the most part, however, government regulation has arisen because some kind of market defect or market failure has occurred and government, intending to represent the public interest, has chosen to take corrective action. We should make it clear that many regulations have been created primarily because of the efforts of special-interest groups that have lobbied successfully for them. The governmental decision-making process in the United States is characterized by congressional regulatory response to the pressures of special-interest groups as well as to perceived market failures.

Four major reasons or justifications for regulation are typically offered: (1) controlling natural monopolies, (2) controlling negative externalities, (3) achieving social goals, and (4) other reasons.

Controlling Natural Monopolies

One of the earliest circumstances in which government felt a need to regulate occurred when a natural monopoly existed. A *natural monopoly* exists in a market where the economics of scale are so great that the largest firm has the lowest costs and thus is able to drive out its competitors. Such a firm can supply the entire market more efficiently and cheaply than several smaller firms. Local telephone service is a good example, because parallel sets of telephone wires would involve waste and duplication that would be much more costly.

Monopolies such as this may seem "natural," but when left to their own devices could restrict output and raise prices. This potential abuse justifies the regulation of monopolies. As a consequence, we see public utilities, for example, regulated by a public utility commission. This commission determines the rates that the monopolist may charge its customers.[49]

Related to the control of natural monopolies is the government's desire to intervene when it thinks companies have engaged in anticompetitive practices. A recent example of this was the Justice Department's investigation of the Microsoft Corporation case in which the company was accused of anticompetitive trade practices. Some of Microsoft's competitors might have been happier if the Justice Department had explicitly prohibited Microsoft from using its dominance in computer operating systems to achieve an advantage for its own applications programs, but lesser sanctions were used instead. In July 1994, the company signed an agreement to stop some of its sales practices that the Justice Department said squelched competition and bullied competitors such as Novell, Apple, IBM, and Lotus.[50] Since then, however, the company's tactics for marketing Web browsers, its deals with Internet service providers, and its purchases of video technology companies have drawn the continued scrutiny of the Justice Department.[51]

Controlling Negative Externalities

Another important rationale for government regulation is that of controlling the *negative externalities* (or spillover effects) that result when the manufacture or use of a product gives rise to unplanned or unintended side effects on others (other than the producer or the consumer). Examples of these negative externalities are air pollution, water pollution, and improper disposal of toxic wastes. The consequence of such negative externalities is that neither the producer nor the consumer of the product directly "pays" for all the "costs" that are created by the manufacture of the product. The "costs" that must be borne by the public include an unpleasant or a foul atmosphere, illness, and the resulting health care costs. Some have called these "social" costs, because they are absorbed by society rather than being truly incorporated into the cost of making the product.

Preventing negative externalities is enormously expensive, and few firms are willing to pay for these added costs voluntarily. This is especially true in an industry that produces an essentially undifferentiated product, such as steel, where the millions of dollars needed to protect the environment would only add to the cost of the product and provide no benefit to the purchaser. In such situations, therefore, government regulation is seen as reasonable, because it requires all firms competing in a given industry to operate according to the same rules (costs).

Just as companies do not voluntarily take on huge expenditures for environmental protection, individuals often behave in the same fashion. For example, automobile emissions are one of the principal forms of air pollution. But how many private individuals would voluntarily request an emissions control system if it were offered as optional equipment? In situations such as this, a government standard that requires everyone to adhere to the regulation is much more likely to address the public's concern for air pollution.[52]

Achieving Social Goals

Government not only employs regulations to address market failures and negative externalities but also seeks to use regulations to help achieve certain social goals it deems to be in the public interest. Some of these social goals are related to negative externalities in the sense that government is attempting to correct problems that might also be viewed as negative externalities by particular groups. An example of this might be the harmful effects of a dangerous product or the unfair treatment of minorities resulting from employment discrimination. These externalities are not as obvious as air pollution, but they are just as real.

Another important social goal of government is to keep people informed. One could argue that *inadequate information* is a serious problem and that government should use its regulatory powers to require firms to reveal certain kinds of information to consumers. Thus, the Consumer Product Safety Commission requires firms to warn consumers of potential product hazards through labeling requirements. Other regulatory mandates that address the issue of inadequate information include grading standards, weight and size information, truth-in-advertising requirements, product safety standards, and so on. A prime example of recent labeling requirements can be seen on canned goods and other products at the grocery store. Most canned goods now carry a "Nutrition Facts" label that provides consumer information on calories, fat content, and quantities per serving of sodium, cholesterol, carbohydrates, proteins, and vitamins.

Other important social goals that have been addressed include preservation of national security (deregulation of oil prices to lessen dependence on imports), considerations of fairness or equity (employment discrimination laws), protection of those who provide essential services (farmers), allocation of scarce resources (gasoline rationing), and protection of consumers from excessively high price increases (natural gas regulation).[53]

Other Reasons

There are several other reasons for government regulation. One is to *control "excess profits."* The claim for regulation here would be aimed at transferring income for the purposes of economic fairness. For example, as a result of the Arab oil embargo between 1973 and 1980, oil stocks went up suddenly by a factor of 10. One argument is that the extra profits collected by these producers are somehow undeserved and the result of plain luck, not wise investment decisions. So, in situations such as this in which profits are drastically, suddenly, and perhaps undeservedly increased, an argument has been made for government regulation.[54]

Another commonly advanced rationale for regulation is to *deal with "excessive competition."* The basic idea behind this rationale is that excessive competition will lead to prices being set at unprofitably low levels. This action will force firms out of business and ultimately will result in products that are too costly because the remaining firm will raise its prices to excessive levels, leaving the public worse off than before.[55]

These "other" reasons for regulation are not cited much anymore, and arguments against them could be set forth. They are mentioned primarily to round out our discussion of the various rationales that have been given over the years for government regulation.

Types of Regulation

Broadly speaking, government regulations have been used for two central purposes: achieving certain *economic* goals and achieving certain *social* goals. Therefore, it has become customary to identify two different types of regulation: economic regulation and social regulation.

Economic Regulation

The classical or traditional form of regulation that dates back to the 1800s in the United States is *economic regulation.* This type of regulation is best exemplified by old-line regulatory bodies such as the Interstate Commerce Commission (ICC), which was created in 1887 by Congress to regulate the railroad industry; the Civil Aeronautics Board (CAB), which was created in 1940; and the Federal Communications Commission (FCC), which was established in 1934 to consolidate federal regulation of interstate communications and, later, radio, telephone, and telegraph.

These regulatory bodies were designed primarily along industry lines and were created for the purpose of regulating business behavior through the control of or influence over economic or market variables such as prices (maximum and minimum), entry to and exit from markets, and types of services that can be offered. It is estimated that the industries subject to economic regulations by federal and state agencies accounted for about 10 percent of the gross national product.[56]

In the federal regulatory budget today, the major costs of economic regulation are for (1) finance and banking (e.g., Federal Deposit Insurance Corporation and Comptroller of the Currency), (2) industry-specific regulation (e.g., Federal Communications Commission and Federal Energy Regulatory Commission), and (3) general business (e.g., Department of Commerce, Department of Justice, Securities and Exchange Commission, and Federal Trade Commission).[57]

Later we will discuss deregulation, a trend that significantly affected the old-line form of economic regulation that dominated business/government relations for the past 100 years.

Social Regulation

The 1960s ushered in a new form of regulation that for all practical purposes has become what regulation means to modern-day business managers. This new form of regulation has come to be known as *social regulation,* because it has had as its major thrust the furtherance of societal objectives quite different from the earlier focus on markets and economic variables. Whereas the older form of economic regulation focused on markets, the new social regulation focuses on business's *impacts on people.* The emphasis on people essentially addresses the needs of people in their roles as employees, consumers, and citizens.

Two major examples of social regulations having specific impacts on people as *employees* were (1) the Civil Rights Act of 1964, which created the Equal Employment Opportunity Commission (EEOC), and (2) the creation of the Occupational Safety and Health Administration (OSHA) in 1970. The goal of the EEOC is to provide protection against discrimination in all employment practices. The goal of OSHA is to ensure that the nation's workplaces are safe and healthful.

An example of major social regulation protecting people as *consumers* was the 1972 creation of the Consumer Product Safety Commission (CPSC). This body's goal is to protect the public against unreasonable risks of injury associated with consumer products. An example of a major social regulation to protect people as *citizens* and residents of communities was the 1970 creation of the Environmental Protection Agency (EPA). The goal of EPA is to coordinate a variety of environmental protection efforts and to develop a unified policy at the national level.

Figure 7–3 summarizes the nature of economic versus social regulations along with pertinent examples.

Whereas the older form of economic regulation was aimed primarily at companies competing in *specific* industries, the newer form of social regulation addresses business practices affecting *all* industries. In addition, there are social regulations that are industry specific, such as the National Highway Traffic Safety Administration (automobiles) and the Food and Drug Administration (food, drugs, medical devices, and cosmetics). The consequence of social regulations (beginning in the 1960s) has been a matrix effect whereby many firms get hit by industry-specific regulations and also the newer form of social regulations. Figure 7–4 summarizes the major U.S. independent regulatory agencies along with their dates of establishment. In addition to these, we should remember that there are several regulatory agencies that exist within executive departments of the government. Examples of this latter category include the following:

Agency	*Department*
Food and Health Administration	Health and Human Services
Antitrust Division	Justice
Drug Enforcement Administration	Justice
Occupational Safety and Health Administration	Labor
Federal Highway Administration	Transportation

FIGURE 7–3	Comparison of Economic and Social Regulations	
	Economic Regulations	*Social Regulations*
Focus	Market conditions, economic variables (entry, exit, prices, services)	People in their roles as employees, consumers, and citizens
Industries affected	Selected (railroads, aeronautics, communications)	Virtually all industries
Examples	Civil Aeronautics Board (CAB) Federal Communications Commission (FCC)	Equal Employment Opportunity Commission (EEOC) Occupational Safety and Health Administration (OSHA) Consumer Product Safety Commission (CPSC) Environmental Protection Agency (EPA)
Trend	From regulation to deregulation	Stable—No significant increase or decrease in agencies

FIGURE 7–4   Major U.S. Independent Regulatory Agencies

Agency	Year Established
Interstate Commerce Commission*	1887
Federal Reserve System (Board of Governors)	1913
Federal Trade Commission	1914
International Trade Commission	1916
Federal Home Loan Bank Board	1932
Federal Deposit Insurance Corporation	1933
Farm Credit Administration	1933
Federal Communications Commission	1934
Securities and Exchange Commission	1934
National Labor Relations Board	1935
Small Business Administration	1953
Federal Maritime Commission	1961
Council on Environmental Quality	1969
Cost Accounting Standards Board	1970
Environmental Protection Agency	1970
Equal Employment Opportunity Commission	1970
National Credit Union Administration	1970
Occupational Safety and Health Review Commission	1971
Consumer Product Safety Commission	1972
Commodity Futures Trading Commission	1974
Council on Wage and Price Stability	1974
Nuclear Regulatory Commission	1974
Federal Election Commission	1975
National Transportation Safety Board	1975
Federal Energy Regulatory Commission	1977
Office of the Federal Inspector for the Alaska Natural Gas Transportation System	1979

*Terminated in 1995. Replaced by the Surface Transportation Board.

The new wave of government regulation brought about in the past 30 years through use of the social regulatory model has had sweeping effects on society. It has signaled a new and seemingly increasing role for government in the affairs of business. As a consequence, no manager today, whether she or he operates a small neighborhood grocery store or manages a Fortune 500 firm, is exempt from the many and varied standards, guidelines, and restrictions that the government imposes. Close attention must be paid to these issues, just as close attention needs to be paid to making traditional managerial decisions. To better appreciate the impact that government regulation is having on business, it is helpful to consider some of the issues that have arisen as a direct outgrowth of government regulations.

ETHICS IN PRACTICE

To Comply or Not to Comply with the Government Regulation?

Every summer and Christmas vacation for the past 4 years I have worked in the mainte-nance department of Gilman Paper Company. Working there to help finance my col-lege education, I have been exposed to many questionable practices. One of the most prominent problems is the adherence to safety regulations.

OSHA (Occupational Safety and Health Administration) requires that a vessel-confined-space entry permit be filled out before a person enters the confined area, and that a "sniffer" (a device used to detect oxygen deficiencies and other harmful or com-bustible gases) be present and operational whenever a person is inside. A *confined space* is defined as any area without proper air ventilation and/or an area more than 5 feet deep. For example, tanks and pits are confined spaces.

Anytime a person enters or leaves a confined space, the person is required to place her or his initials on the entry permit. This is for the physical protection of the worker and the liability protection of the company. If workers are seen violating this policy, they can be reprimanded or fired on the spot.

In my many experiences with these confined spaces, I have observed on numerous occasions that these policies are not broken by the workers, but by the supervisors. It is their responsibility to obtain these permits and sign them, as well as obtain the use of a sniffer. Sometimes the supervisors and the workers will forget that we are working in a confined space, and thus forget the permit and sniffer. When someone has realized that we are in a confined space, however, the supervisors have often asked us to initial-ize the permit at various places as if the permit had been there all along.

When we are working for extended periods of time in these areas, the sniffer's bat-teries often go dead as well. Instead of following regulations and leaving the area until a new sniffer is obtained, the supervisors often tell employees to stay, declaring, "The air is fine. You don't need a sniffer!"

My problem is this: Should I sign these permits when I know it is dishonest, or should I do the "right" thing and let OSHA know that this regulation is being broken time and time again? After all, I'm not even a full-time employee, so who am I to cause trouble?

1. Does this sound like just one more example of a needless government regulation?

2. Who are the stakeholders in this case, and what are their stakes?

3. What should I have done in this situation? Is this regulation important, or is this just more government "red tape"? Should I have just "gone along to get along" with the supervisors?

Contributed by Dale Dyals

Issues Related to Regulation

It is important to consider some of the issues that have arisen out of the increased governmental role in regulating business. In general, managers have been con-cerned with what might be called "regulatory unreasonableness."[58] We could expect that business would just as soon not have to deal with these regulatory bodies. Therefore, some of business's reactions are simply related to the nuisance factor of having to deal with a complex array of restrictions. Other legitimate issues that have arisen over the past few years also need to be addressed.

Benefits of Regulation

To be certain, there are benefits of government regulation. Employees are treated more fairly and have safer work environments. Consumers are able to purchase safer products and receive more information about them. Citizens in all walks of life have cleaner air to breathe and cleaner water in lakes and rivers where they go for recreational purposes. These benefits are real, but their exact magnitudes are difficult to measure.

One study designed to determine the benefits of regulation was done by the Center for Policy Alternatives at MIT. This study claimed that billions of dollars were saved each year as a direct result of federal regulation. The study found that effective health, safety, and environmental regulations reduced rates of job-related deaths and injuries, resulted in increased productivity, fostered the development of new and better products and processes, and decreased environmental abuse.[59] The specific benefits identified included the following:

- Air pollution control benefits ($5 billion to $58 billion annually)

- Avoidance of lost-workday accidents and deaths during a 2-year period (cost reduction of $15 billion)

- Water pollution cleanup resulting in a $9 billion gain due to increased recreational use

- Crib safety standards resulting in reduced injuries to infants (44 percent injury reduction over 6 years)[60]

Of course, the benefits listed above are estimates, and the dollar amounts become quickly outdated, but they do serve to remind us of the relative magnitudes of the benefits that are derived from government regulations.

Costs of Regulation

Costs resulting from regulation also are difficult to measure. However, let us consider in more detail what some of these costs are. Weidenbaum has argued that the costs that result from government regulation may be grouped into three categories: direct, indirect, and induced.[61]

Direct Costs.   The ***direct costs of regulation*** are most visible when we look at the number of new agencies created, aggregate expenditures, and growth patterns of the budgets of federal agencies responsible for regulation. There were 14 major regulatory agencies prior to 1930, over two dozen in 1950, and 57 by the early 1980s. The most rapid expansion came in the 1970s.[62] Figure 7–5 illustrates the magnitude of the changes that occurred from 1970 to 1994. Figure 7–6 summarizes the costs of federal regulatory agencies in 1998.

Indirect Costs.   In addition to the direct costs of administering the regulatory agencies, there are ***indirect costs of regulation*** that need to be identified. The costs of government regulation get passed on to the consumer in the form of higher prices that

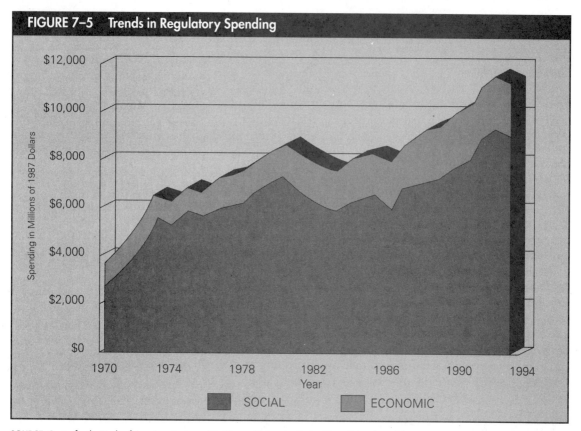

FIGURE 7–5   Trends in Regulatory Spending

SOURCE: Center for the Study of American Business, Washington University. Derived from the Budget of the U.S. Government and related documents, various fiscal years.

constitute a "hidden tax" of government. Each year, billions of dollars are added to the costs of goods and services because of regulation. One estimate is that, on average, each dollar Congress appropriates for regulation results in an additional $20 in costs imposed on the private sector.[63] One part of these added costs is the paperwork burden that business must absorb. There is an endless flow of forms, reports, and questionnaires that business must complete to satisfy the requirements of the regulatory agencies.

Induced Costs. The **induced effects of regulation** are diffuse and elusive, but they constitute some of the most powerful consequences of the regulatory process. In a real sense, then, these induced effects have to be thought of as costs. Three effects are worthy of elaboration:[64]

1. *Innovation is affected.* When corporate budgets must focus on "defensive research," certain types of innovation do not take place. To the extent that firms must devote more of their scientific resources to meeting government requirements, fewer resources are available to dedicate to new product and process research and development and innovation. One industry affected in this way is the drug industry. Economists estimate that stringent FDA regulations seriously

FIGURE 7–6   Costs of Federal Regulatory Agencies in Fiscal 1998

Social Regulation	
Agency Category	*Millions of Dollars*
Consumer Safety and Health	$ 5,906
Job Safety and Working Conditions	1,314
Environment	5,979
Energy	505
Total Social Regulation	$13,704

Economic Regulation	
Agency Category	*Millions of Dollars*
Finance and Banking	$ 1,623
Industry-Specific Regulation	484
General Business	1,364
Total Economic Regulation	$ 3,471
Grand Total (Social and Economic Regulations)	$17,175

Derived from the Budget of the U.S. Government and related documents.

hinder innovation in the drug industry. The consequences are a slowed pace and a decreased number of new drugs arriving on the marketplace for consumer use.

2. *New investments in plant and equipment are affected.* To the extent that corporate funds must be used for regulatory compliance purposes, these funds are diverted from more productive uses. One estimate is that environmental and job safety requirements diminish by one-fourth the potential annual increase in productivity. It should also be pointed out that uncertainty about future regulations has an adverse effect on the introduction of new products and processes.[65]

3. *Small business is adversely affected.* Although it is not intentional, most federal regulations have a disproportionately adverse effect on small firms. Large firms have more personnel and resources and are therefore better able to get the work of government done than are small firms. In one study of small-business owner-managers, responses were solicited as to what they expected of government. Out of a list of nine choices, tax breaks for small firms was listed first and relief from government regulation was a close second.[66] More than any other group, small business seems to feel keenly affected by government regulation.

The frustrations of many small-business owners and managers about government regulation are conveyed by Frank Cremeans's experience. On one single day, as owner of Cremeans Concrete & Supply Co. in Ohio, he was visited by officials from four separate federal and state regulatory agencies. They dropped in unannounced on his concrete business on the same day in January. The four agencies were the EPA, OSHA, the local health department, and the mine-inspection agency. Mr. Cremeans said he could not believe it. He had to drop everything and spend the entire day dealing with the officials' demands. Small-business people have always grumbled about government regulation, but their mood had turned especially sour after the Clinton administration strengthened regulatory programs and raised the possibility of mandated health care. Mr. Cremeans tried to turn the tables. In 1994, he was elected as a freshman member of the new Congress, swept in with a Republican landslide.[67] However, after 2 years, he lost his seat to Ted Strickland, the Democrat he had unseated in the previous race.

In addition to the induced effects described above, several others affect managers especially. These include stress on managers, modified decision processes, and alterations of corporate structure. To be sure, these kinds of effects are seen and experienced by managers as costs of government regulation, although they are typically overlooked in most calculations.

DEREGULATION

Quite frequently, trends and countertrends overlap with one another. Such is the case with regulation and its counterpart, deregulation. There are many reasons for this overlapping, but typically they include both the economic and the political. From an economic perspective, there is a continual striving for the balance of freedom and control for business that will be best for society. From a political perspective, there is an ongoing interplay of different societal goals and means for achieving those goals. The outcome is a mix of economic and political decisions that seem to be in a constant state of flux. Thus, in the economy at any point in time, trends that appear counter to one another can coexist simultaneously. These trends are the natural result of competing forces seeking some sort of balance or equilibrium.

This is how we can explain the trend toward deregulation that evolved in a highly regulated environment. Deregulation represents a counterforce aimed at keeping the economy in balance. It also represents a political philosophy that was prevailing during the period of its origin and growth.

Deregulation may be thought of as one kind of regulatory reform. But, because it is unique and quite unlike the regulatory reform measures discussed earlier, we will treat it separately. Deregulation has taken place primarily with respect to economic regulations, and this, too, helps to explain its separate treatment.

Purpose of Deregulation

The basic idea behind deregulation has been to remove certain industries from the old-line economic regulations of the past. The purpose of this deregulation, or at least a reduced level of regulation, has been to increase competition with the expected benefits of greater efficiency, lower prices, and enhanced innovation. These goals have not been uniformly received, and it is still undecided whether deregulation will work as a method of maximizing society's best interests.

Deregulation of certain industries has been basically a phenomenon of the past 20 years, although some big steps toward deregulation took place in the late 1960s and throughout the 1970s. Most of the landmark decisions in the move toward deregulation have occurred in the following fields: telecommunications (for example, the breakup of AT&T), finance (for example, phasing out of interest rate ceilings), energy (for example, decontrol of gas/petroleum products), and transportation (for example, deregulation of the trucking, railroad, and airline industries).

Trend Toward Deregulation

The trend toward deregulation, most notably exemplified in the financial industry, the telecommunications industry, and the transportation (trucking, airline, railroad) industry, represents business's first major redirection in 50 years.[68] The result seems to be a mixed bag of benefits and problems. On the benefits side, prices have fallen in many industries, and better service has appeared in some industries along with increased numbers of competitors and innovative products and services.

Several problems have arisen also. Although prices have fallen and many competitors have entered some of these industries, it appears more and more that these competitors are unable to compete with the dominant firms. Thus, they are failing, going bankrupt, or being absorbed by the larger firms. Experts are now seeing that entry barriers into some industries are enormous and have been greatly underestimated. This has been shown to be the case in airline, trucking, railroad, and long-distance telephone service.[69] In addition, many of the problems that arose with savings and loan associations and banks have been attributed to deregulation.

Concerns are being expressed about what may be growing anticompetitive side effects as key industries increasingly are dominated by a few firms. This trend is obvious in transportation, where the major railroad, airline, and trucking companies boosted their market shares considerably during the 1980s. The top six railroads went from about 56 percent of market share to about 90 percent during this time. The top six airlines went from about 75 percent of market share to about 85 percent. The top ten trucking firms went from about 38 percent of market share to about 58 percent. In long-distance telephone service, AT&T still enjoys about an 80 percent share of the domestic market and a virtual monopoly in the huge toll-free, big-business, and overseas markets.[70]

To guard against the growing concentration in these major industries, greater vigilance will be needed in the antitrust area. Many of the experts who advocated deregulation during the 1970s knew that anticompetitive side effects would be likely. However, they expected the regulatory agencies to do a better job of actively supervising the transition to free markets. If this close supervision does not take place, the regulatory pendulum could readily swing back in the other direction.[71]

Dilemma with Deregulation

The intent of deregulation was to deregulate the *industries*, thus allowing for freer competition. The intent was not to deregulate health and safety requirements. The dilemma with deregulation is how to enhance the competitive nature of the affected industries without sacrificing the applicable social regulations. This is the second major problem with deregulation that needs to be discussed. Unfortunately, the dog-eat-dog competition unleashed by economic deregulation can force many companies to cut corners in ways that endanger the health and/or safety of their customers. This pattern, which seems to occur in any deregulated industry, was apparent in the trucking and airline industries.[72]

Trucking Industry

To survive in a deregulated industry, many truckers delayed essential maintenance and spent too many hours behind the wheel. According to some industry experts, as many as one-third of the long-haul drivers turned to illegal drugs to help them cope with the grueling hours on the road. Others turned to alcohol. Statistics showed a sharp increase in the number of truck accidents from 1980 to 1986, and roadside inspections in one year turned up serious problems in 30 to 40 percent of the trucks inspected.[73]

Airline Industry

The changes in the airline industry also had various experts concerned. Numerous accidents in the 1980s have been traced to poor maintenance or increased congestion at airports. Although the major airlines have historically maintained safety and maintenance standards higher than the minimum prescribed by the FAA, continuous price wars forced the best and largest firms to cut costs by abandoning previous standards. FAA-imposed fines for safety violations increased 20-fold over a recent 3-year period. Other cost-cutting measures that compromised safety include the widespread use of unapproved parts and a reduction in the number of flight attendants.[74]

Almost two decades after the trucking and airline industries were deregulated, the outlook appears brighter. In the trucking industry, the Federal Highway Administration (FHWA) has turned up the heat on truck safety, with some evidence of success. For instance, the percentage of fatal accidents in which the drivers' blood level alcohol content exceeded legal limits dropped by 25 percent from 1984 to 1994.[75] In the airline industry, concerns over deregulation have also lessened. Since 1929, accidents have been on a downward trend that was unaffected by deregulation, and recent research has shown no correlation between airline profitability and air safety.[76] Nevertheless, concerns about "underserved" small communities and low-cost carrier survival have prompted members of Congress to consider legislation that would reregulate part of the industry by redistributing airport slots and limiting predatory behavior.[77]

Overall, the trend toward deregulation continues globally. Around the world, industries that were once considered public goods are now being opened to market forces. In the United States, attention is being devoted to deregulating the telecommunications industry and electric utilities.

Telecommunications Industry

Since the breakup of AT&T in 1984, telephone rates have been cut in half and aggressive competitors, such as MCI and Sprint, have moved quickly to adopt fiber optic cable and other service improvements.[78] The Telecommunications Act of 1996, however, has yet to achieve its promise of lower rates and better service. In fact, 2 years after the Act's inception, thousands of rural phone subscribers are without phone service. Before the Act, cross-subsidization (urban subscribers and major long-distance carriers paid extra) ensured universal service. Although the new law proposed a new subsidy system, legal battles have slowed its implementation.[79] In contrast, business and urban customers are expected to be the first beneficiaries of the new broadband services.[80]

Electric Utilities

Since 1996, various states have passed electric restructuring initiatives, and Congress has been considering a range of bills all geared to bring competition to the electric utilities. As has been true with telephone deregulation, consumers are likely to save money, but those savings have inherent trade-offs.[81] Power companies have traditionally provided special programs to aid the community and people in need. As was true of telephone companies, these programs were financed by spreading the cost over the customer base. Following deregulation, only those programs that can be used to enhance image or advertising are likely to remain.[82]

REGULATORY REFORM

The 1970s witnessed a surge of regulatory initiatives unprecedented in the history of the United States. Ironically, at almost the same time, or at least during the same decade, a surge of second thoughts about the wisdom of these initiatives occurred. Many questions began to be asked: Had we gone too far? Had our best intentions gotten the better of us? Had our idealism reached beyond the bounds of practicality?[83]

By the mid- to late 1970s, the calls for regulatory reform were begun by President Gerald Ford and were quickly embraced by President Jimmy Carter. President Ronald Reagan interpreted his 1980 election as a mandate to further the efforts at reform and to get the government off the backs of the people. President George Bush reactivated some of the attentiveness the regulatory agencies had given their missions. President Bill Clinton's record is somewhat more difficult to interpret. There is significant evidence of a resurgence in government regulation. At the same time, however, President Clinton and Vice President Al Gore have pledged to make the federal government more efficient through their "reinventing government" initiative.

Approaches to Regulatory Reform

Three broad kinds of regulatory reform proposals surfaced during the past 15 years. One approach was to *streamline the process* and to *review justifications* for existing and proposed rules. The idea here was that a rule should not be developed unless its benefits clearly outweighed its costs. President Carter promoted this idea with Executive Order 12044. This order requires agencies to justify new rules with cost-benefit analysis. President Reagan embraced the cost-benefit idea enthusiastically, as did many members of Congress. President Clinton and Vice President Gore have pushed the government agencies into developing streamlining plans, but it is too early to see the effects of this initiative.

A second approach to regulatory reform advocated that *regulators be more accountable* to Congress, the courts, and the executive branch. In this connection, the controversial legislative veto was proposed that would allow Congress to void proposed rules. The courts would be given power to review regulations under another proposal. The president's powers would be expanded under another proposal. Picking up on this, the Reagan administration sought and received from Congress the authority to enlarge the power of the Office of Management and Budget (OMB) to review independent regulatory commissions. Along these lines, President Clinton, in keeping with a previously announced Gore theme, has been encouraging agencies to measure program performance—getting the government focused on results so taxpayers can see what they are getting for their money.

A third approach to regulatory reform held that these procedural reforms were superficial and what was needed was a *broad-based attack on the regulations* themselves and the statutes that gave the agencies power. This approach was brought up during the lengthy controversy over renewal of the Clean Air Act and the reauthorization of several regulatory commissions.[84]

No single approach to regulatory reform is likely to cure all the problems we have with government regulations. The important consideration is that policy makers be sensitive to the problems that bring about regulatory failure and be prepared to address these problems when regulations are proposed and, later, when it is evident that reform is necessary. In some cases, generic reforms will be adequate. In other cases, a regulation-by-regulation examination may be necessary.

Regulatory Trends: A Decade of Experience

In late 1986 and in 1987, there was some evidence that a regulatory revival was beginning. A *Wall Street Journal*/NBC poll showed that 38 percent of the public still believed there was too much government regulation of the economy, 32 percent thought there was about the right amount, and 23 percent said there was not enough. These results indicated a major swing in public opinion in favor of regulation since polls taken in the early 1980s.[85]

Although President Reagan pursued a deregulation strategy during the period 1980 to 1985, in his second term he allowed modest growth in regulatory agencies' budgets and staffs. Similarly, President Bush was more inclined to allow the federal agencies to increase their budgets and staff levels. Economists from the Center for the Study of American Business at Washington University concluded that regulation was rebounding under the Bush administration. The 1991 budget, which was President Bush's first, showed spending levels at the federal regulatory agencies reaching record highs both in current dollars and in real terms. President Bush seemed to be less skeptical about the role of federal regulators in the economy, and his first budget suggested a growth trajectory similar to the budget trends from the Carter years, just prior to Reagan.[86]

In addition to stepping up enforcement of existing regulations and expanding budgets and staffing of the regulatory agencies, Congress passed costly laws in the early 1990s that will increase the focus on regulation. In 1990, Congress passed two significant pieces of legislation: the Clean Air Act amendments and the Americans with Disabilities Act. Some estimates suggest that the new air pollution laws may turn out to be the costliest regulations in the nation's history. Estimates of the annual costs of the law range from $25 billion to $40 billion. This sum would amount to an annual cost of about $300 to $400 for each U.S. household. Economists were alarmed because of the fear that these regulatory expenditures threaten needed U.S. economic expansion and could lead to a diminishment of productivity, an undermining of competitiveness, and significant numbers of lost jobs in the U.S. work force.[87]

Another significant factor that may have brought about public concern for more regulation was the stock market crash in October 1987. It is clear that the public was greatly unsettled by this event. Moreover, this event may have precipitated renewed interest in tighter government regulations. To this must be added the Savings and Loan Association bail-out by the federal government and the increasing numbers of bank failures, both of which are at least in part attributable to careless or inadequate government regulation.

In his book *Putting People First,* then Governor Clinton pledged to reduce the federal bureaucracy and budget.[88] Since entering office, his administration has reduced the federal work force by 332,000 people, presented the first balanced budget in 30 years, and reformed welfare. Yet, anecdotes of regulatory zeal suggest an increased level of activism by such agencies as OSHA, the FDA, and the EPA.[89] Only time will tell whether the Clinton administration will meet its goal of creating a government that works better while costing less.

Professional economists will continue to debate the pros and cons of government regulation, but in the final analysis the outcome of the political process will prevail. It can be readily seen by these trends, countertrends, and examples that the public does, indeed, see government as one major mediator of its relationship with business. This is how the system works, and the changes we continue to see and sense in the business/government/public relationship are constantly evolving; they cannot be pinned down for any significant period. The best judgment at this point is that there will be some moderate interest in social regulation but that the trend toward economic deregulation will not be reversed anytime soon. Part of the reason, of course, is that the economic decisions are of such a large magnitude and, once made, are not easily changed.

SUMMARY

Business cannot be discussed without considering the paramount role played by government. Although the two institutions have opposing systems of belief, they are intertwined in terms of their functioning in our socioeconomic system. In addition, the public assumes a major role in a complex pattern of interactions among business, government, and the public. Government exerts a host of nonregulatory influences on business. Two influences with a macro orientation include industrial policy and privatization. A more specific influence is the fact that government is a major employer, purchaser, subsidizer, competitor, financier, and persuader. These roles permit government to affect business significantly.

One of government's most controversial interventions in business is direct regulation. Government regulates business for several legitimate reasons, and in the past two decades social regulation has been more dominant than economic regulation. There are many benefits and various direct, indirect, and induced costs of government regulation.

A trend of the 1980s was deregulation. However, bad experiences in key industries, such as trucking, airlines, savings and loans, and banks, have caused many to wonder whether the government has gone too far in that direction. Although regulatory reform was a central issue throughout the 1980s, there has been some amount of talk about *reregulation.* This has occurred for a variety of reasons, but the stock market crash in October 1987 made the general public quite anxious about the private sector and its stability. Obviously, these perceptions of the business sector come and go, but they often assume much more weight in determining government's role than do theoretical economic arguments.

KEY TERMS

accelerationists (page 216)

adjusters (page 216)

bankers (page 216)

central planners (page 216)

cybersquatting (page 217)

deregulation (page 232)

direct costs of regulation (page 229)

economic regulation (page 225)

indirect costs of regulation (page 229)

induced effects of regulation (page 230)

industrial policy (page 216)

natural monopoly (page 222)

privatization (page 218)

regulation (page 222)

social regulation (page 225)

targeters (page 216)

DISCUSSION QUESTIONS

1. Briefly explain how business and government represent a clash of ethical systems (belief systems). Go through the list of characteristics of each belief system in Figure 7–1. With which do you find yourself identifying most? Explain. With which would most business students identify? Explain.
2. Explain why the public is treated as a separate group in the interactions among business, government, and the public. Doesn't government represent the public's interests? How should the public's interests be manifested?
3. What is regulation? Why does government see a need to regulate? Differentiate between economic and social regulation. What social regulations do you think are most important, and why? What social regulations ought to be eliminated? Explain.
4. Outline the major benefits and costs of government regulation. In general, do you think the benefits of government regulation exceed the costs? In what areas, if any, do you think the costs exceed the benefits?
5. The airline and trucking industries were cited as examples of problems with deregulation. What is the current mood of the country regarding deregulation? What evidence can you present to substantiate your opinion?

ENDNOTES

1. "Wanted: More Action," *Newsweek* (November 17, 1986), 7.
2. "Is Government Dead?" *Time* (October 23, 1989).
3. Arthur Schlesinger, Jr., "Election 94: Not Realignment but Dealignment," *The Wall Street Journal* (November 16, 1994), A28; and Howard Fineman, "Revenge of the Right," *Newsweek* (November 21, 1994), 37ff.
4. Anonymous, "He Believes in Government, So Why Doesn't America?," *The Economist* (January 24, 1998), 19–21.
5. Charles Murray, "Americans Remain Wary of Washington," *The Wall Street Journal* (December 23, 1997), A14.

6. "Antitrust Laws," *The World Book Encyclopedia* (Chicago: World Book, 1988), Vol. 1, 560; also see "The Interstate Commerce Act," Vol. 10, 352–353.

7. *Ibid.*

8. *Ibid.*

9. Alfred L. Seelye, "Societal Change and Business-Government Relationships," *MSU Business Topics* (Autumn, 1975), 5–6.

10. George A. Steiner, *Business and Society,* 2nd ed. (New York: Random House, 1975), 359–361.

11. Rob Norton, "Government Learns Humility," *Fortune* (June 27, 1994), 64.

12. Murray Weidenbaum, "Regulatory Process Reform: From Ford to Clinton," *Regulation* (Winter, 1997), 1–7.

13. L. Earle Birdsell, "Business and Government: The Walls Between," in Neil H. Jacoby (ed.), *The Business-Government Relationship: A Reassessment* (Santa Monica, CA: Goodyear, 1975), 32–34.

14. Jacoby, 167.

15. *Ibid.,* 168.

16. For a view somewhat counter to this, see Kevin Phillips, "The Balkanization of America," *Harper's* (May, 1978), 37–47.

17. Daniel Bell, "Too Much, Too Late: Reactions to Changing Social Values," in Jacoby, 17–19.

18. Seelye, 7–8.

19. Jacoby, 168.

20. Arthur T. Denzau, *"Will an 'Industrial Policy' Work for the United States?"* (St. Louis: Center for the Study of American Business, Washington University, September, 1983), 1.

21. *Ibid.,* 2.

22. Robert B. Reich, *The Next American Frontier* (New York: Penguin Books, 1983).

23. "Industrial Policy: Is It the Answer?" *Business Week* (July 4, 1983), 55–56.

24. John Carey and Douglas A. Harbrecht, "Bill's Recipe: How He Plans to Help U.S. Business Cream Rivals," *Business Week* (October 18, 1993), 30–31. See also Owen Ullman, "Remember Clinton's Industrial Policy? OK, Now Forget It," *Business Week* (December 12, 1994), 53.

25. Anonymous, "The Clinton Administration's Framework for Global Electronic Commerce: Executive Summary—July 1, 1997," *Business America* (Vol. 119, No. 1, January, 1998), 5–6.

26. Shirley Duglin Kennedy, "The Future of Internet Domain Names," *Information Today* (Vol. 15, No. 3, March, 1998), 40–41.

27. Monroe W. Karmin, "Industrial Policy: What Is It? Do We Need One?" *U.S. News & World Report* (October 3, 1983), 47.

28. Robert J. Samuelson, "The New (Old) Industrial Policy," *Newsweek* (May 23, 1994), 53.

29. Hiroyuki Tezuka, "Success as the Source of Failure? Competition and Cooperation in the Japanese Economy," *Sloan Management Review* (Vol. 38, No. 2, March, 1997), 83–93.

30. Ira C. Magaziner and Robert B. Reich, *Minding America's Business: The Decline and Rise of the American Economy* (New York: Vintage Books, 1983), 255.

31. Ted Kolderie, *"What Do We Mean by Privatization?"* (St. Louis: Center for the Study of American Business, Washington University, May, 1986), 2–5.

32. *Ibid.*, 3–5.

33. "Privatization Increases at Local, State and Federal Levels," *What's Next: A Newsletter of Emerging Issues and Trends* (Washington, DC: Congressional Clearinghouse on the Future, Summer, 1985), 1, 5.

34. Robert O'Harrow, Jr., "The Business of Government, Run by Business," *The Washington Post National Weekly Edition* (May 2–8, 1994), 32. See also "Privatization" (special issue), *Business Forum* (Vol. 19, Nos. 1 and 2, Winter/Spring, 1994), 1–52.

35. Ruth Eckdish Knack, "Schools 'R' Us," *Planning* (Vol. 59, No. 1, November, 1993), 22–28.

36. Steve Coll, "Retooling Europe," *The Washington Post National Weekly Edition* (August 22–28, 1994), 6–7.

37. *Ibid.*, 5.

38. Andrew Nikiforuk, "It Was the Best of Schools, It Was the Worst . . . ," *Canadian Business* (Vol. 70, No. 1, January, 1997), 91.

39. Richard Reed, David J. Lemak, and W. Andrew Hesser, "Cleaning Up After the Cold War: Management and Social Issues," *Academy of Management Review* (Vol. 22, No. 3, July, 1997), 614–642.

40. Murray L. Weidenbaum, *Business, Government and the Public*, 3rd ed. (Englewood Cliffs, NJ: Prentice Hall, 1986), 5–6.

41. *Ibid.*, 6–8.

42. *Ibid.*

43. Alan Keyes, "Why 'Good Government' Isn't Enough," *Imprimis* (Vol. 21, No. 10, October, 1992), 2.

44. *Ibid.*, 10–11.

45. Cited in "The Regulatory Chokehold," *Impact* (October, 1994), 1.

46. "The Big Picture," *Business Week* (December 5, 1994), 8.

47. *Congressional Quarterly's Federal Regulatory Directory*, 5th ed. (1985–1986), 2.

48. *Ibid.*, 2–3.

49. *Ibid.*, 9.

50. "Next Stop, Chicago," *Business Week* (August 1, 1994), 24–26; and "Antitrust, the Smart Way," *Business Week* (August 1, 1994), 88.

51. Don Clark, "Microsoft Is Unlikely to Be Hurt by Ruling," *Wall Street Journal* (December 15, 1997), B8.

52. *Congressional Quarterly's Federal Regulatory Directory*, 5th ed. (1985–1986), 10–11.

53. *Ibid.*, 12.

54. Stephen Breyer, *Regulation and Its Reform* (Cambridge, MA: Harvard University Press, 1982), 21–22.

55. *Ibid.*, 31–32.

56. Weidenbaum, 1986, 178–179.

57. Melinda Warren, "Mixed Message: An Analysis of the 1994 Federal Regulatory Budget" (St. Louis, Missouri: Center for the Study of American Business, August, 1993), 16–17 (derived from the Budget of the U.S. Government).

58. Graham K. Wilson, *Business and Politics: A Comparative Introduction* (Chatham, NJ: Chatham House, 1985), 39.

59. *Congressional Quarterly's Federal Regulatory Directory* (1985–1986), 30.
60. *Ibid.*
61. Murray L. Weidenbaum, *Costs of Regulation and Benefits of Reform* (St. Louis: Center for the Study of American Business, Washington University, November, 1980), 3. Also see Murray Weidenbaum and Melinda Warren, *It's Time to Cut Government Regulations* (St. Louis: Center for the Study of American Business, Washington University, February, 1995).
62. *Ibid.*, 3.
63. Weidenbaum, 1980, 6–11.
64. *Ibid.*, 12–14.
65. *Ibid.*, 12.
66. James J. Chrisman and Fred L. Fry, "How Government Regulation Affects Small Business," *Business Forum* (Spring, 1983), 25–28.
67. Brent Bowers and Udayan Gupta, "To Fight Big Government, Some Join It," *The Wall Street Journal* (November 11, 1994), B1. See also Robert Samuelson, "The Regulatory Juggernaut," *Newsweek* (November 7, 1994), 43.
68. "Deregulating America," *Business Week* (November 28, 1983), 80–89.
69. "Is Deregulation Working?" *Business Week* (December 22, 1986), 50–55.
70. *Ibid.*, 52.
71. *Ibid.*, 55.
72. Frederick C. Thayer, "The Emerging Dangers of Deregulation," *The New York Times* (February 23, 1986), 3.
73. Kenneth Labich, "The Scandal of Killer Trucks," *Fortune* (March 30, 1987), 85–87.
74. Thayer, 3.
75. David Cullen, "The Road Not Taken," *Fleet Owner* (Vol. 91, No. 12, December, 1996), 97.
76. Bahram Adrangi, "Airline Deregulation, Safety, and Profitability in the U.S.," *Transportation Journal* (Vol. 36, No. 4, Summer, 1997), 44–52.
77. Perry Flint, "Washington's Shadow of Doubt," *Air Transport World* (Vol. 35, No. 5, May, 1998), 47–50.
78. Robert J. Samuelson, "The Joy of Deregulation," *Newsweek* (February 3, 1997), 39.
79. Fred Vogelstein, "A Really Big Disconnect," *U.S. News & World Report* (February 2, 1998), 39–40.
80. Alex J. Mandl, "Telecom Competition Is Coming—Sooner Than You Think," *The Wall Street Journal* (January 26, 1998), A18.
81. Glenn Hodges, "Deregulating Electricity," *The Washington Post* (April 6, 1997), C1.
82. Patricia Irwin, "Why Deregulation Is Inevitable," *Electrical World* (Vol. 21, No. 7, July, 1997), 62–63.
83. Timothy B. Clark, Marvin H. Kosters, and James C. Miller III (eds.), *Reforming Regulation* (Washington, DC: American Enterprise Institute, 1980), 1.
84. *Congressional Quarterly's Federal Regulatory Directory*, 5th ed. (1985–1986), 59–60. Also see Ian Ayres and John Braithwaite, *Responsive Regulation* (New York: Oxford University Press, 1992).
85. Laurie McGinley, "Federal Regulation Rises Anew in Matters That Worry the Public," *The Wall Street Journal* (April 21, 1987), 1.

86. Melinda Warren and Kenneth Chilton, *Regulation's Rebound: Bush Budget Gives Regulation a Boost* (St. Louis: Center for the Study of American Business, May, 1990), 1–2.
87. Carolyn Lochhead, "Economists Say Federal Rules May Choke U.S. Productivity," *Insight* (November 19, 1990), 42–43.
88. Warren, 1993, 1–2.
89. Owen Ullman and Catherine Yang, "The Regulators Are Back in Business," *Business Week* (January 20, 1997), 41.

8

Business's Influence on Government and Public Policy

CHAPTER OBJECTIVES

After studying this chapter, you should be able to:

1 Identify the four major changes that have shaped the current political environment of business.

2 Describe the evolution of corporate political participation.

3 Differentiate among the different levels at which business lobbying occurs, and explain the lack of unity among the umbrella organizations.

4 Explain the phenomenon of political action committees (PACs) in terms of their historical growth, the magnitude of their activity, and the arguments for and against them.

5 Define coalitions and describe the critical role they now assume in corporate political involvement.

6 Outline the principal strategic approaches to political activism that firms are employing.

It is obvious from our discussion of business/government relationships and government regulation that government is a central stakeholder of business. Government's interest, or stake, in business is broad and multifaceted, and its power is derived from its legal and moral right to represent the public in its dealings with business.

Today, because of the multiple roles it plays in regulating and otherwise influencing business activity, government poses significant challenges for business owners and managers. Government not only establishes the rules of the game for business functions but also influences business in its roles as competitor, financier, purchaser, supplier, watchdog, and so on. Opportunities for business and government to cooperate in a mutual pursuit of common goals are present to some extent, but the major opportunity for business is in developing strategies for effectively working with government in such a way that business's own objectives are achieved. In doing this, business has the responsibility of obeying the laws of the land and of being ethical in its responses to government expectations and mandates. To do otherwise raises the specter of abuse of political power—a criticism that the corporate community has had enough of over the years. As the regulatory environment has become more intense and complex and as other changes have taken place in society, businesses have had little choice but to become more politically active.

It should be emphasized at the outset of this chapter that attempts by business to influence government are a major and accepted part of the public policy process in the United States. The U.S. political system is driven by the active participation of interest groups striving to achieve their own objectives. The business sector is, therefore, behaving in a normal and expected fashion when it assumes an advocacy role for its interests. Other groups, whether they be labor organizations, consumer groups, farmers' groups, doctors' organizations, real estate broker organizations, military groups, women's rights organizations, environmental groups, church groups, and so on, all strive to pursue their special interests with government. Today's new pluralism necessitates that all of these groups seek to influence government. The public interest in this special-interest-driven process is that some semblance of a balance of power be maintained and that the activities and practices of these organizations remain legal and ethical.

THE CURRENT POLITICAL ENVIRONMENT

In the early 1970s, business was at a low point as far as its political fortunes were concerned because of a hostile public mood that had arisen in the 1960s. In response to a set of perceived national crises, including product safety, employment discrimination, energy shortages, environmental problems, foreign bribery, and domestic political payoffs, business was hit with a wave of legislation that left it in an environment of reduced autonomy and sharply curtailed prerogatives.

By the 1980s it was becoming clear that, in four key areas, changes that had occurred over the past 25 years were shaping a political environment in which business's participation in the political process would be greatly affected. Gerald Keim defined these four major changes as follows: (1) a growth in the volume of government activity, (2) the democratization of Congress, (3) the rise of special-interest groups, and (4) a decline in voter participation in the United States.[1] The trends in these areas have continued through the 1990s and have significantly affected the current political environment.

Growth in Government Activity

In the last chapter we chronicled the growth of business-related government activity. Some other statistics that document this growth include increases in the numbers of recorded votes in the two houses of Congress and an increase in the number of regulatory acts that became law. In 1960, there were 310 recorded votes in both houses of Congress. This number grew to 861 in 1972 and jumped to 1,349 in 1976. It fell back to 683 in 1984. In the 1950s, fewer than 30 regulatory bills were passed. In the 1960s, there were fewer than 60. In the 1970s, more than 120 new regulations were passed. While all these increases have taken place, the number of elected officials handling this work has remained the same.[2] The pattern over the past two decades has reflected a continuation of this growth in government activity. As we enter the millennium, evidence of renewed regulatory zeal underscores the continued importance of the business/government relationship.[3]

Democratization of Congress

Another important change in the political environment has been the "democratization" of Congress. Beginning in about 1970, several incremental changes began altering the structure of Congress in ways that decentralized power in both houses, made the legislative process more open to public scrutiny, reduced the importance of seniority, and increased the opportunity for more junior members of Congress to have an impact on legislative proceedings.

In 1970, the Legislative Reorganization Act made roll-call votes in committees and votes on floor amendments matters of public record. The result was less secrecy. The influence of senior members was diluted as more subcommittees were created and given more autonomy. Junior members' opportunities to chair important subcommittees increased. Senior members were restricted in the number of leadership positions they could hold. The net result of these changes was to open up Congress, lessen party discipline, and increase member independence from traditional party lines. This independence was increased when many states moved from party caucuses to primary elections as the means to choose candidates for the general election. The party no longer provided all the financial and personnel backing. Organized special-interest groups began playing important roles in getting candidates elected. Contributions by political action committees (PACs) became significantly more important.[4]

Rise of Special-Interest Groups

Still another change was taking place in the realm of special-interest groups. They began to increase in number and in political activism. In fact, a nationwide outburst of public-interest group activity grew out of the 1960s. This growth was related to the social changes and events that produced significant protest movements that were at first dedicated to fostering African-American civil rights and opposing the Vietnam War. These movements stimulated the growth of related reform groups concerned with the environment, nuclear power and weaponry, feminism, gay rights, and other issues.[5] An important contribution these groups made to their members was low-cost information about current political issues, thus making it easier for group members to be informed about key issues. As we will discuss later, groups that are organized have more political power than those that are not organized.[6] Thus, the rise in special-interest groups constitutes a significant change in the political landscape.

The 1980s was a period in which politics was often defined in terms of special-interest groups, and this trend continued through the 1990s. During the Reagan years of the 1980s, conservative groups began appearing on the scene and joined the liberal interest groups as powerful actors in Washington. Formerly unorganized groups got together and began having a noticeable impact on American politics. Significantly, special-interest groups began to replace political parties as the dominant organizations of the American political system. This new era of sharply declining political party influence and a related rise in articulation of political demands by interest groups has continued unabated on the national and state levels.[7] It is not a surprising consequence, therefore, that the business sector has perceived a need for greater political participation.

Decline in Voter Participation

The rapid growth of special-interest groups occurred in tandem with a decline in voter participation in the United States, which fell from about two-thirds to less than one-half of the eligible voting population. In the 1996 election, only 49 percent of the voting age population cast a ballot.[8] As a result, it now seems that 25 percent is enough votes to determine who gets elected to Congress or the presidency.

Furthermore, voters who are members of organized groups tend to be the most knowledgeable about issues; therefore, candidates have to pay special attention to them. The rest of us have less information about specific issues and are likely to vote on the basis of more general information.[9] Consequently, as a decline in voter participation continues, organized special-interest groups are able to capture the attention of Senate and House members because these groups have specific, formalized expectations that must be addressed.

In summary, these four broad changes in the political environment have created a set of circumstances of which business must be aware when it interacts with government. First, the growth of regulations has created a need for business response. Second, the new openness of Congress has made it more approachable. Third, the rise and success of special-interest groups have made it clear that business, too, must get organized and more involved. Fourth, the decline in voter participation permits these interest groups to be more powerful. Against this backdrop, it is not surprising that we have witnessed increased and growing levels of corporate political participation.

CORPORATE POLITICAL PARTICIPATION

Political involvement is broadly defined as participation in the formulation and execution of public policy at various levels of government. As decisions about the current and future shape of society and the role of the private sector shift from the marketplace to the political arena, corporations, like all interest groups, find it imperative to increase their political involvement and activity.[10]

Historically, companies entered into debates in Washington only on an issue-by-issue basis and with no overall sense of a purpose, goal, or strategy. Furthermore, companies tended to be reactive; that is, they dealt with issues only after the issues had become threats. This approach became obsolete as the kinds of changes we have described began to occur. Today, in many industries, success in Washington is just as important as success in the marketplace. Just as business has learned that it must develop competitive strategies if it is to succeed, it has learned that political strategies are essential as well.[11]

Corporate political involvement greatly increased in the 1970s. Between 1968 and 1978, the number of corporations with offices in Washington quintupled to more than 500. Washington office staffs grew, and companies created or expanded public affairs/government relations units in their corporate staffs. Significant efforts were made by many companies to mobilize constituent groups, such as past and present stockholders and employees, into grassroots lobbying networks.

As campaign finance laws changed, the number of companies participating in federal elections through political action committees (PACs) increased dramatically. The increased political participation resulted in a number of important business victories in the 1970s, such as the defeat of a proposed consumer protection agency, reformed labor laws, and reduction in the capital gains tax rate. Business started to play a very significant role in the legislative process in Congress. By the mid-1980s, there were signs that business was working harder at lobbying Congress but enjoying it less. The easy victories had been won, and the problems remaining were proving to be intractable.[12]

By the end of the 1990s, it had become imperative for business to assume an extremely active political role in order to deal with government stakeholders. Special-interest politics had become the way in which all legislation was passed, and even a corporate giant like Microsoft had to learn to be an active and effective player. Microsoft opened its first lobbying office 20 years after the company was founded. The office had only one staff person, a 33-year-old lawyer with no real Washington experience and no secretary. It soon became clear that even a company as powerful as Microsoft must pay Washington heed.

In 1997, after the U.S. Justice Department brought an antitrust case against Microsoft, a federal district judge ordered the company to remove its Internet browser from the Windows operating systems bundle. Microsoft was quick to respond. In addition to increasing its political giving, the company retained a cadre of well-connected lobbyists and public relations officials to present its case to legislators and the public. By May 1998, the 88 registered lobbyists for Microsoft included four retired Congress members and dozens of former staff members.[13]

After Microsoft changed its approach to government relations, the pendulum began swinging back in its favor. In 1998, a federal appeals court ruled that Microsoft has the right to incorporate its browser, as well as any other software, into its operating system as long as doing so offers its customers certain advantages. As of this writing, the Justice Department's case against Microsoft has yet to be tried. Whatever the outcome, Microsoft's new approach to government relations has improved the company's position with the courts.

To appreciate more fully the participation of business in the process of public policy formation in the United States, it is necessary to understand the approaches that business uses to influence the government stakeholder. We will focus only on the following major approaches: (1) lobbying, (2) PACs, (3) coalition building, and (4) political strategy. At this point, our perspective will be largely descriptive as we seek to understand these approaches, their strengths and weaknesses, and business's successes and failures with them. At the same time, however, we must be constantly vigilant of possible abuses of power or violations of sound ethics.

BUSINESS LOBBYING

Lobbying is the process of influencing public officials to promote or secure the passage or defeat of legislation. Lobbying is also used to promote the election or defeat of candidates for public office. Lobbyists are intensely self-interested. Their goals are to promote legislation that is in their organizations' interests and to defeat legislation that runs counter to their organizations' interests. As the changes we described earlier have taken place, groups representing all kinds of special interests have increased their lobbying efforts. Today, business interests, labor interests, ethnic and racial groups, professional organizations, and those simply pursuing ideological goals they believe to be in the public interest are lobbying at the federal, state, and local levels. Our focus is on business lobbying at the federal level, although we must remember that this process is also occurring daily at the state and local levels.

H. R. Mahood defines lobbying as the professionalization of the art of persuasion.[14] Lobbying serves several purposes. It is not just a technique for gaining legislative support or institutional approval for some objective such as a policy shift, a judicial ruling, or the modification or passage of a law. Lobbying may also be directed toward the reinforcement of established policy or the defeat of proposed policy shifts. Lobbying also targets the election or defeat of national, state, and local legislators. A lobbyist may be a lawyer, a public relations specialist, a former head of a public agency, a former corporate executive, or a former elected official. In this sense, there is no typical lobbyist.[15] It is clear, however, that more and more businesses, as well as other special-interest groups, are turning to lobbyists to facilitate their involvement in the public policy process. A cartoon depicts the increasing stature of lobbyists. The teacher asks the class, "Who runs America?" She then gives her students the following choices: "the President, the Supreme Court, or Congress?" An astute class member responds, "Lobbies."[16]

Organizational Levels of Lobbying

The business community engages in lobbying at a variety of organizational levels. At the broadest level are *umbrella organizations*, which represent the collective business interests of the United States. The best examples of umbrella organizations are the Chamber of Commerce of the United States and the National Association of Manufacturers (NAM). Out of these have grown organizations that represent some subset of business in general, such as the Business Roundtable, which was organized to represent the largest firms in America, and the National Federation of Independent Businesses (NFIB), which represents smaller firms.

At the next level are *trade associations*, which are composed of many firms in a given industry or line of business. Examples include the National Automobile Dealers Association, the National Association of Home Builders, the National Association of Realtors, and the Tobacco Institute. Finally, there are individual *company lobbying* efforts. Here, firms such as IBM, BellSouth, Ford, and Delta Airlines lobby on their own behalf. Typically they use their own personnel, establish Washington offices for the sole purpose of lobbying, or hire professional lobbying firms or consultants located in Washington or a state capital. Figure 8–1 depicts examples of the broad range of lobbying and political-interest organizations used by businesses.

We will now consider these levels of lobbying in greater detail, beginning with the efforts of individual firms and the use of professional lobbyists.

Company Lobbying

Lobbyists, sometimes derisively referred to as "influence peddlers," operate under a variety of formal titles and come from a variety of backgrounds. Officially, they are lawyers, government affairs specialists, public relations consultants, or public affairs consultants. Some are on the staffs of large trade associations based in Washington. Others represent specific companies that have Washington offices dedicated to the sole purpose of representing those companies in the capitol city. Still others are professional lobbyists who work for large law firms or consulting firms in Washington that specialize in representing clients to the lawmakers.

FIGURE 8–1   Examples of the Range of Lobbying Organizations Used by Businesses

Broad Representation: Umbrella Organizations

- Chamber of Commerce of the United States
- National Association of Manufacturers (NAM)
- Business Roundtable
- National Federation of Independent Businesses (NFIB)
- State Chambers of Commerce
- City Chambers of Commerce

Midrange Representation: Trade and Professional Associations and Coalitions

- National Auto Dealers Association
- National Association of Realtors
- American Petroleum Institute
- American Trucking Association
- National Association of Medical Equipment Suppliers
- Tobacco Institute
- Coalitions: Coalition for the Advancement of Industrial Technology; National Clean Air Coalition; Coalition to Reduce High Effective Tax Rates; Basic Industries Coalition

Narrow/Specific Representation: Company-Level Lobbying

- Washington and State Capital Offices
- Law Firms Specializing in Lobbying
- Public Affairs Specialists
- Political Action Committees (PACs)
- Grassroots Lobbying
- Company-Based Coalitions
- Former Government Officials

The new breed of lobbying consultant in Washington frequently is a former government official. Some are ex-congressional staff members or ex-members of Congress. Others are former presidential staff assistants or other highly placed government officials. Many of these individuals are legally prohibited from discussing private business matters with anyone in the White House for 1 year after leaving office. However, 1 year is a relatively short apprenticeship for people who will likely increase their former salaries manyfold. Examples of former government officials who left positions to represent private interests include Michael Deaver (former Reagan deputy chief of staff), Richard Allen (former national security adviser), Jody Powell (former White House press secretary), and Robert Dole (former U.S. senator).

What do business lobbyists accomplish? Lobbyists offer a wide range of services that include drafting legislation, creating slick advertisements and direct-mail campaigns, consulting, and, most important, getting access to lawmakers. *Access,* or connections, seems to be the central product that the new breed of lobbyist is selling—the returned phone call, the tennis game with a key legislator, or the golf outing with the Speaker of the House. With so many competing interests in Washington today, the opportunity to get your point across in any format is a significant advantage. Lobbyists also play the important role of showing busy legislators the virtues and pitfalls of complex legislation.[17] Figure 8–2 summarizes some of the various activities that business lobbyists accomplish for their clients.

FIGURE 8–2   What Business Lobbyists Do for Their Clients

- Get access to key legislators (connections)
- Monitor legislation
- Establish communication channels with regulatory bodies
- Protect firms against surprise legislation
- Draft legislation, slick ad campaigns, direct-mail campaigns
- Provide issue papers on anticipated effects of legislative activity
- Communicate sentiments of association or company on key issues
- Influence outcome of legislation (promote helpful legislation, defeat harmful legislation)
- Assist companies in coalition building around issues that various groups may have in common
- Help members of Congress get reelected
- Organize grassroots efforts

Grassroots Lobbying

In addition to lobbying directly through the use of professional lobbyists, firms use what is called *grassroots lobbying*, which refers to the process of mobilizing the "grassroots"—individual citizens who might be most directly affected by legislative activity—to political action. Grassroots lobbying is also used actively by trade associations and the umbrella organizations. The better corporate grassroots lobbying programs usually arise in companies whose leaders recognize that people are a firm's most potent political resource. Although people cannot be directed or required to become politically involved, they can be persuaded and encouraged.

Trade associations often use grassroots support by asking their members to contact their representatives. They also organize rallies, target mail campaigns, develop instant advertisements, and use computerized phone banks.[18] However, the grassroots response must be genuine and sustained. The old techniques of phony "Astro-Turf lobbying" no longer hold much sway. Hundreds of phone calls or thousands of identical postcards that arrive on the same day are rarely effective.[19]

Grassroots lobbying has become one of the most frequently used and most effective techniques both for individual firms and for associations and coalitions. A few examples of successful grassroots lobbying efforts at the company level are helpful in understanding its power. During the debate over the North American Free Trade Agreement (NAFTA), Ford Motor Co. as well as other automakers tapped into a network of 32 top automobile suppliers and their employees to drum up letters and telephone calls to Capitol Hill in support of the trade pact. The company also called on its 5,000 dealers for grassroots lobbying support.[20] NAFTA was passed in 1994. In 1998, credit unions across the nation employed grassroots lobbying to urge congressional support of H. R. 1151—the Credit Union Membership Access Act, which relaxes credit union membership requirements. In addition to eliciting the traditional onslaught of petitions and personal letters, thousands of credit union members lobbied their lawmakers directly on Capitol Hill.[21] These efforts undoubtedly led to the landslide vote in which the House passed the bill.

Trade Association Lobbying

Most major companies are members of trade associations that lobby on their behalf. A trade association is an organization that represents firms in a *specific* industry. The association receives its funds from firms in the industry that join and pay dues.

According to the *Encyclopedia of Associations,* which lists all the registered national and international associations, there are over 23,000 registered in the United States today. Of these, nearly 4,000 are classified as "Trade, Business, and Commercial."[22]

A central issue facing trade associations today is the question of representing specific industry needs versus general business needs. Trade associations are best equipped to represent the narrow interests of their members, but by doing so they may enter into conflicts with other associations or fail to support broader business interests that are also important to them. This point is illustrated by the experience of the National Association of Wholesalers. Until the late 1970s, this group was a sleepy organization that focused on the narrow issues affecting its members. Then it broadened its outlook, and its power and influence grew. One member of the organization said, "We realized that we could do a masterful job on parochial issues, but unless the big problems were worked out it wouldn't make any difference."[23]

Grassroots lobbying at the industry or association level is frequent today. One successful experience worth noting was the pharmaceutical industry's success at defusing criticism leveled at it during the 1994 health care debate. The Clinton administration kicked off its health care debate in 1993 by attacking the drug industry for "shocking" prices and "unconscionable" profiteering. Soon the drug industry went to work with its lobbying efforts and convinced one key state legislator and then others that the drug cost controls being sought by the White House could destroy the drug firms' ability to perform research. The drug industry's 18-month lobbying campaign against President Clinton's depicting them as special-interest enemy number one had an interesting result: The industry, through grassroots lobbying, had recast itself as the good guys—researchers dedicated to improving health care.[24] The health care fight is far from over, however. In 1998, the Health Benefits Coalition, a Washington-based association of employers and insurance groups, launched a national grassroots campaign to block the proposed patient health care "Bill of Rights."[25]

Much to their dismay, trade associations sometimes find themselves in the undesirable role of battling with each other in their attempts to lobby Congress. An example of these types of battles occurred in 1998 between the credit union and the banking industries. Credit unions argue that they provide services to individuals and small businesses that are shunned by traditional banks. They contend that they should be able to expand the services they provide to this generally underserved population. Banks counter that credit unions enjoy an unfair competitive advantage by virtue of their exemptions from both taxes and the Community Reinvestment Act (CRA) obligations required of banks and thrifts. They believe that large, multiple-employer credit unions should be subject to the same taxes, CRA rules, and safety requirements as banks.

The battle rages on, as both sides take turns enjoying victory and suffering defeat. In February 1998, the U.S. Supreme Court ruled that membership in federally chartered multiemployer credit unions should be restricted but, later that year, the House passed H. R. 1151—the Credit Union Membership Access Act, which relaxes restrictions on credit union membership.[26] The war is likely to rage on for years, because the membership requirements for credit unions represent only one of a variety of issues. The central issues of tax exemption and community obligation have yet to be addressed.

Umbrella Organizations

The umbrella organizations are associations, too. But unlike a trade association, an umbrella organization has a broad base of membership that represents businesses in several different industries of various sizes. Historically, the two major umbrella organizations in the United States have been the Chamber of Commerce of the United States and the National Association of Manufacturers. Two other prominent organizations include the Business Roundtable and the National Federation of Independent Businesses. Each of these groups has political action as one of its central objectives.

Chamber of Commerce of the United States.   The national Chamber of Commerce was founded in 1912 as a federation of businesses and business organizations. In addition to firms, corporations, and professional members, the Chamber has thousands of local, state, and regional chambers of commerce; American chambers of commerce abroad; and several thousand trade and professional associations. Its diversity of membership indicates why it is referred to as an umbrella organization.

The U.S. Chamber of Commerce is the largest and most broadly represented business association in Washington. It has dozens of committees that study and initiate policy positions in such diverse areas as antitrust, taxation, environment, labor relations, agribusiness, governmental relations, and community affairs. The members of the committees are representatives of the member companies and organizations that belong to the Chamber, and they are assisted by a paid professional staff. The Chamber seeks to influence the legislative process by way of congressional testimony, by lobbying in conjunction with the Washington representatives of its member organizations, and through grassroots efforts of the local and state chambers.

The Chamber specializes in grassroots political action. Its grassroots lobbying involves frequent communication with members and others, urging them to write, phone, fax, or e-mail key legislators. One example of the Chamber's main techniques for mobilizing its membership on an issue is the distribution of what it terms an "action call." An **action call** is essentially a memorandum outlining the Chamber's position on an issue and urging members to contact their lawmakers. Action calls are typically sent to a district or state where the representative or senator is thought to hold a key vote on the pending legislation.[27]

Historically, the U.S. Chamber of Commerce has been a legislative powerhouse in its ability to influence public policy. Its power gradually waned over the years, but a recent loss on "fast-track" trade legislation gave it a wake-up call.[28] The Chamber responded by launching a multimillion dollar campaign to put restrictions on product liability lawsuits, class action litigation, and contingency fees.[29]

National Association of Manufacturers (NAM).   The NAM is organized similar to the U.S. Chamber of Commerce but represents a more specialized grouping of businesses. It was founded in 1895. The membership of the NAM has historically been tilted toward the larger smokestack industry firms, whereas the Chamber's membership includes small firms, retailers, service industries, and professionals. Today the NAM is more diverse, with large, small, old-line, and high-tech manufacturers.

Historically, the NAM has been thought of as staunchly conservative and dominated by Republicans, just like the Chamber. In fact, in 1922 the NAM withdrew from the Chamber because it disliked the Chamber's unwillingness to denounce all Democrats and all forms of government interference in the economy.[30]

Significant changes occurred in the NAM late in 1979, when two Democrats were installed in key positions. Alexander Trowbridge, who had been secretary of commerce during the Lyndon Johnson administration, was named president. He chose as the number two person Jerry Jasinowski, an assistant secretary of state in President Jimmy Carter's administration. When Trowbridge and Jasinowski took over the helm, the NAM took a decidedly different direction. Some of the new policy directions included an advocacy of industrial policy (arguing for a new federal program to subsidize robotics) and a movement toward protectionist trade policies. Both views had been traditionally opposed by business organizations.[31]

The NAM did not shift to the radical left as some feared but rather became more moderate. One CEO said, "Too moderate, if you ask me." However, this executive had to admit that he was generally impressed with the NAM's lobbying efforts.[32] On Capitol Hill, the NAM has gotten mixed ratings. One legislator said the NAM is far less effective and influential than it once was, but others praised the NAM for its more practical, accommodationist approach to politics. One top legislative aide argued, "Compared to the Chamber of Commerce, which is the Model T of the Washington scene, the NAM looks like a Ferrari." Others also say that of the two, the NAM is better.[33]

Not surprisingly, the changes at the NAM created a split within the Washington business community on a growing number of issues. This was a significant factor because the NAM and the Chamber have settled on opposite sides of some major issues, and members of Congress tend to write off the business community when it is divided.[34] Recently, however, the NAM and the Chamber of Commerce have worked together on a variety of issues, including trade with China, Medicare reform, and OSHA.[35]

Business Roundtable.   Formed in 1972, the Business Roundtable is often regarded as an umbrella organization, although, like the NAM, it has a restricted membership. It is composed of the chief executive officers (CEOs) of 200 major corporations. The Roundtable's success could be attributed to its two unique premises: (1) the CEOs themselves lobby in Washington, and (2) the group focuses on large public policy matters and not on narrow business interests.[36]

During the early years of the Business Roundtable, a handful of corporate CEOs came to dominate Washington's relationship with business. Especially prominent were Irving Shapiro (DuPont), Reginald Jones (GE), John deButts (AT&T), and Thomas Murphy (GM). These corporate superstars (as they were sometimes called) pioneered an unusual era of business involvement in government affairs, and they spoke in unison for the collective concerns of business. They were heard and listened to by everyone in Washington who counted, from the President on down.[37]

The decline of the Washington superstar era ended when these four leaders all retired between 1979 and 1981 and President Ronald Reagan arrived on the scene in 1980 with his probusiness philosophy and administration. The exodus of the four corporate giants left a vacuum in leadership atop U.S. businesses. But there was no real need for other leaders to emerge, because the Reagan administration seemed to embrace business's views wholeheartedly. No other set of corporate leaders has achieved the status and power of the four leaders mentioned above.

The broad issues of the 1970s on which the Business Roundtable was successful gave way to a whole new set of issues in the 1980s. With the Reagan administration dominating the 1980s, business was not involved in the general lobbying that characterized the Roundtable's efforts in the 1970s. The concerns of the 1980s—growth of global competition, trade policy, and the aftereffects of a worldwide recession—left businesspeople confused and often at odds with one another. For example, some of the troubled smokestack industries raised calls for protectionist measures, whereas those in high tech waved the flag for free trade. With this disunity, which continued into the 1990s, it had become difficult for anyone to speak clearly for the business community.[38] Now the Business Roundtable wields little power. Corporate giants like Microsoft and Intel are not even members.[39]

National Federation of Independent Businesses (NFIB).   During the 1980s and 1990s, the growth of small businesses came to dominate the business news. It should not be surprising, therefore, that the NFIB, as a small-business association, also came into a position of power. We might think of the NFIB as an umbrella organization for smaller businesses. One of the best ways to appreciate the NFIB's newfound power is to describe its recent success at grassroots lobbying.[40] In the wake of its success, it has become clear that such groups as the Chamber of Commerce, the NAM, and the Business Roundtable no longer exclusively call the shots on business and economic issues.

The NFIB made its mark by strong and successful lobbying in 1993 and 1994 against President Clinton's ambitious health care plan. The plan called for "employer mandates" requiring most employers to pay for their employees' health insurance. The NFIB and its 600,000 foot soldiers went to work in a grassroots lobbying campaign that eventually defeated the employer mandates proposal and helped stall the overall health care plan.

The NFIB's assault began with a study arguing that Clinton's plan would kill up to 1.5 million jobs. This study was then faxed to all 535 members of Congress. The NFIB strategically targeted its further efforts at legislators it thought were "gettable." As one example, it blitzed one key congressional committee chair's district and state with phone calls, faxes, and handwritten letters. In addition, the organization whipped its members into a panic by sending out 500,000 "action alerts" with warnings such as this: "Because a new plan would stick YOU with the bill for a new health care system, you need to contact Rep. X RIGHT AWAY!"

More than anything else, the small-business lobby showed that it had become a dominant player in the Washington public policy arena.[41] In a recent *Fortune* magazine survey of lobbyists' influence in Washington, the NFIB ranked fourth, while the NAM ranked thirteenth and the Chamber of Commerce lagged behind at fifteenth.[42]

Lack of Unity Among Umbrella Organizations

With the passage of the 1981 tax bill, a unified business community celebrated one of its most impressive legislative victories in decades. By 1987, the business alliance had shattered. The long, fierce debates over the 1986 tax reform bill produced deep divisions and much bitterness. According to Irving Shapiro, one of its former leaders, the leadership of the Roundtable split on the tax issue. Leaders in the business community have been trying to recover the unity they once had, but so far their efforts have been futile. It no longer seems possible to come up with an effective business consensus that all the diverse groups can support. The decline in effectiveness, ironically, comes at a time when business is investing more than it ever has in political campaigns.

Reasons for Lack of Unity

There are several reasons why business lobbying efforts have become splintered. First, the power of the large umbrella groups, such as the Chamber, the NAM, and the Roundtable, has diminished because of their inability to reach a consensus on important issues. Second, the traditional heavy industry clique that used to dominate has declined in power as service firms, high-technology firms, and midsize and smaller firms have become increasingly active. Third, the nature of business lobbying has changed. Business lobbyists could once cut deals with a few powerful legislators but, as power in Congress has become more dispersed, they have had to work with more and different people. According to Raymond Hoewing, formerly of the Public Affairs Council, "The old-boy network just doesn't work very well anymore."[43]

Different Needs of Specialized Groups

Business lobbying is changing as the call for increasingly specialized lobbying arises to meet the needs of specialized groups. Trade problems and the budget deficit are examples of two issues on which lobbying groups have come down on opposite sides of the fence. One example of the specialized kind of organization that has grown up and prospered in the new environment is the American Business Conference. Started in 1981, this group consists of 100 CEOs of medium-sized, fast-growing companies. Membership in this group requires double-digit growth each year.[44] The NFIB, discussed earlier, is another example of a group representing a special constituency—small business.

Need to Strengthen Business's Collective Interest

Some experts have expressed concern over the increasingly fragmented business community and dwindling power of the umbrella organizations. Ian Maitland, for example, has argued that the fragmented form of current political involvement by the business community has resulted in each business interest lobbying separately for its own parochial goals. The outcome has been a free-for-all in which business's collective interest has been the real loser. Maitland argues that if business is to avoid the self-defeating consequences of much of today's lobbying, it must find a way to strengthen its collective institutions, such as the Chamber of Commerce, the NAM, and the Business Roundtable.[45] There is evidence that the lobby groups have begun to realize the importance of forming coalitions around issues of joint concern. For example, in 1997, the presidents of the American Business Conference (ABC), the NAM, NFIB, and the U.S. Chamber of Commerce met for a roundtable discussion of the importance of working together to effect change in the second term of the Clinton presidency.[46]

As a summary of our discussion of business lobbying and as a transition to our consideration of political action committees, it is appropriate to note the observations of Mary Ann Pires of The Pires Group, Inc., a public relations/affairs firm that advises many of the Fortune 500 firms. She notes:

> *Lobbying in the U.S. has changed a great deal in recent years. Some of these changes are obvious. Others aren't. Among the former is the array of lobbying resources needed by an organization today versus twenty years ago. Then, all it took was one well-connected lobbyist who knew*

"The Hill." Today, a company often relies on multiple lobbies, in DC, and the state capitals, and often on a political action committee, a grassroots capability, opinion research, coalitions, targeted charitable contributions, a legislative tracking system, and more.[47]

In short, lobbying has become a complicated, multilayered process.

POLITICAL ACTION COMMITTEES

To this point, our discussion of lobbying has focused primarily on interpersonal contact and powers of persuasion. We now turn our attention to *political action committees (PACs)*, the principal instruments through which business uses financial resources to influence government. PACs should be thought of as one facet of lobbying. However, because they have become such an influential phenomenon, they deserve separate treatment in this text.

Evolution of PACs

PACs have been around for years, but their influence has been most profoundly felt in the past two decades. This is perhaps because the bottom line in politics, as well as in business, is most often measured in terms of money—who has it, how much they have, and how much power they are able to bring to bear as a result. This has often been referred to as the *Golden Rule of Politics*: "He who has the gold, rules."[48]

Business PACs appeared on the scene in the early 1970s as a direct result of the 1974 amendments to the Federal Election Campaign Act (FECA). Under this law, organizations of like-minded individuals (such as business, labor, and other special-interest groups) may form together and create a PAC for the purpose of raising money and donating it to candidates for public office. PACs may contribute $5,000 per candidate per election—primary, runoff, general, or special. There are no aggregate limits on how much a PAC may contribute to numerous candidates or on how much money a candidate may accept from all sources. The $5,000 limit is less restricting than that placed on individuals, who are limited to donating $1,000 per federal candidate per election and to donating an aggregate $25,000 in total annual contributions. Under the 1976 amendments to FECA, individuals may contribute up to $5,000 per year to PACs.[49]

The 1974 amendments to FECA grew out of an unprecedented number of companies being indicted for illegal campaign contributions in the 1972 presidential election campaign. In 1974, after Watergate, PACs offered corporations an organized, centralized, safe route for campaign participation. Labor organizations had managed to be politically active using PACs since the 1930s, but it was not until the 1970s that business PAC activity took off.

SEARCH THE WEB

Information about a specific corporate PAC or the contributions a particular candidate received from that PAC is now available online. The Web site of the Federal Election Commission (**www.fec.gov**) provides an opportunity to track the funds that committees, groups, and individuals have contributed to House, Senate, and presidential campaigns, parties, and PACs. For House and presidential campaigns, it is possible to view actual financial disclosure reports. The Senate, however, presently files its reports with the secretary of state. Contributions to Senate campaigns can be found by searching the Web site's disclosure database. This site also provides a variety of brochures and instructional information designed to help voters, candidates, parties, and PACs.

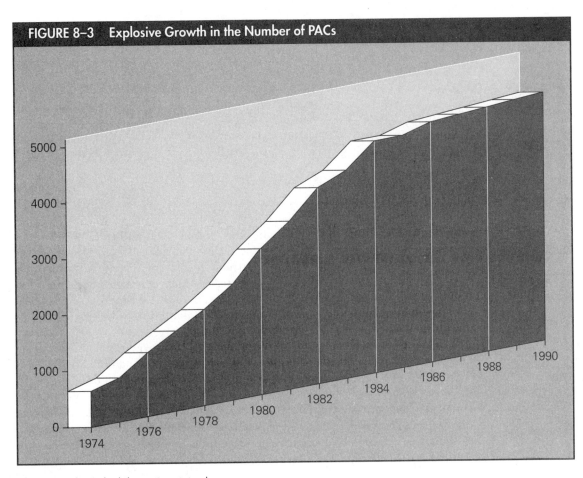

FIGURE 8-3   Explosive Growth in the Number of PACs

SOURCE: Based on Federal Election Commission data.

Figure 8–3 illustrates the explosive growth in numbers of PACs from 1974 to 1984. Since 1986, the number of PACs has remained relatively constant.

In 1975, the Federal Election Commission announced a landmark ruling involving Sun Oil Company's PAC: SunPAC. The company was given permission to solicit stockholders and employees for contributions, to establish a separate political giving program among employees using payroll deduction, and to use general treasury funds to create and administer the PAC and solicit contributions. Labor, displeased with the SunPAC decision, campaigned to have the rules amended in 1976, whereby corporate solicitation among employees was restricted to twice a year. In 1979, other amendments were passed, eliminating much of FECA's paperwork and red tape. The net effect was that political involvement through PACs was encouraged.[50]

Attitudes toward PACs may be grouped into opposing camps. Supporters of PACs laud the process as pluralism in action and point to the large numbers of people who are brought into the political process, thereby making government more responsive. Critics see PACs as powerful catalysts for corruption and favoritism.

They accuse candidates for office, as well as incumbents, of adjusting their positions on issues in order to maximize their own special-interest dollars.[51] We will discuss these two extreme positions more fully later.

Magnitude of PAC Activity

One reason PACs have drawn so much attention in recent years is the amount of money they control. Over 4,000 PACs were officially registered at the end of the 1996 election year (the last presidential election held as of this writing). Their total contributions to Senate and House of Representative candidates in 1996 were about $201 million.[52]

Arguments for PACs

Not surprisingly, those who support PACs are primarily those who collect and donate the money (for example, the business community) and those who receive the money (many members of Congress and candidates for office). Businesses see PACs as a positive and constructive way by which they can participate in the political process. They see PACs as a reasonable means by which business, labor, and other interest groups may organize their giving. They argue that business giving is offset by labor giving and by the multitude of other special-interest groups that also have formed PACs.

Many of the congressional recipients of the PAC contributions also advocate PACs. There is less uniformity of support among Congress than among the business community, however. One reaction from our elected officials is resentment at the suggestion that they can be bought. The larger problem seems to be the growing dependency of politicians on the PAC money to get elected. In general, members of Congress seem to support the idea of PAC contributions, because their campaign financing has become increasingly dependent on it. It may be that some Congress members are against the PACs or see the need for reform but just cannot bring themselves to do it. With each passing year, however, the need for reform of the PAC laws is becoming more apparent to many politicians.

Arguments Against PACs

Some of the most vocal opposition to PACs and the role they are playing comes from current and past members of Congress themselves. Veteran lawmakers like Paul Simon (D-Illinois) and Bill Bradley (D-New Jersey) have cited the perpetual need to chase money as a major factor in why they left office.[53] The frustrations of many members of Congress are summed up in the comments of former Senator Robert Dole (R-Kansas): "When these political action committees give money, they expect something in return other than good government. It is making it much more difficult to legislate. We may reach a point where if everybody is buying something with PAC money, we can't get anything done." He worries about differing treatment of the rich and the poor: "Poor people don't make campaign contributions. You might get a different result if there were a Poor-PAC up here."[54] Dole's point is borne out by a recent *Money* article. In it, Ann Reilly Dowd estimated the price that special-interest contributions exact on the average household. According to a Progressive Policy Institute study, U.S. taxpayers paid $47.7 billion for corporate tax breaks and subsidies in 1997, costing the average household about $483. Import quotas for sugar, textiles, and other goods totaled another $110 billion, according to the Progressive Policy Institute, with a total cost per household of $1,114. The average U.S. household was expected to pay $1,600 in 1997 for legislation that protects corporations and the wealthy.[55] While some of these tax breaks and subsidies are certain to be sound policy and would be implemented with or without financial motivation, Dowd raises an interesting point. Certainly many of those tax breaks, subsidies, and quotas can be traced back to the coffers of PACs.

Three principal criticisms come through in these comments and in criticisms of PACs by others. First, it is argued that PACs are buying votes with their contributions. Second, it is argued that members of Congress have become too dependent on PAC money for election and reelection. Third, many worry that the existence of PACs further disadvantages the poor and the disenfranchised.

PACs and the Vote-Buying Controversy

A serious allegation about PACs is that their contributions "buy" votes in Congress. Philip Stern's key book *Still the Best Congress Money Can Buy* documents this case.[56] Many studies have been done to calculate correlations between PAC giving and congressional voting. The major problem is that correlations do not necessarily prove causation. But many of the correlations do appear convincing and are used by PAC critics to fullest advantage.

Several political analysts have been able to conduct studies using more sophisticated statistical techniques than simple correlation. These studies have been able to control variables, such as party ideology and past voting records, to determine what independent effects the contributions have. W. P. Welch studied the effect of dairy PAC contributions on the following year's vote for milk price supports. His finding was that the PAC gifts had a relatively small effect on the vote. It seemed that voting for members of Congress was determined more by how important dairy production was in each legislator's home district than by ideology and party affiliation. However, Welch also established that dairy price support voting was clearly related to contributions made in the next election as the PACs offered "reward" money.[57]

Center for Public Integrity Study

A 1991 study released by the Washington-based Center for Public Integrity reported the results of tracking contributions from 1981 to 1990 and found that money appeared to be a factor in a number of votes. The center concluded that "patterns do emerge when votes are compared with campaign contributions."[58] The study's findings included the following:

- Eighty-five percent of the senators who received $15,000 or more from sugar interests voted against curtailing the sugar support program in 1990. The support program costs consumers $3 billion annually in higher prices.

- Insurance industry contributions averaged $44,030 to Judiciary Committee members who backed the industry on a key vote. Those who voted against the industry averaged $16,294.

- The auto industry gave $44,000 to key lawmakers in an 11-day period between two Senate procedural votes on a bill to raise auto mileage standards. Two of the senators who received contributions switched from opposing the industry position against raising the requirements to supporting it. The industry won by just three votes the second time and was able to kill the bill.[59]

This study cited several other specific examples where it appeared that contributions by PACs had influenced the outcome of voting.

The Tobacco Industry

In 1994, several articles appeared in the *Journal of the American Medical Association* documenting how campaign contributions from the tobacco industry hindered the passage of laws to tax tobacco or control smoking. Despite some well-publicized hearings that embarrassed tobacco company executives, Congress had not passed any major taxes or controls on tobacco for about 4 years prior to the appearance of these articles.[60]

Tobacco industry PACs contributed $2.4 million in 1991–1992 to the campaigns of members of Congress. Eighty-three percent of senators and 68 percent of House members were recipients of tobacco industry donations. One article observed, "The more tobacco money a member received, the less likely the member was to support tobacco-control legislation." Another article reported that researchers had found a similar linkage between tobacco donations and tobacco policy in the California legislature.[61] In the mid-1990s, however, things began to change. In 1996 and 1997, the tobacco industry spent $60 million on lobbying and millions more on campaign contributions. Nevertheless, in 1998 the industry found itself "with few friends and even less influence in a Congress that seems bent on penalizing cigarette makers."[62] Clearly, there are limits to the influence a lobbyist can buy.

What conclusion can we reach about the charge that PAC contributions buy votes? The opinion of Larry Sabato appears most balanced:

> The best answer based on the available evidence seems to be that PAC contributions do make a difference, at least on some occasions, in securing access and influencing the course of events on the House and Senate floors. But those occasions are not nearly as frequent as Anti-PAC spokesmen, even Congressmen themselves, often suggest.[63]

It has also been observed by Sabato that PAC contributions appear to be most effective when certain conditions prevail.[64] These conditions include the following:

1. *When the issue is less visible.* PAC funds are more likely to be effective while the issue being debated is less visible—that is, not yet in the full glare of public and media scrutiny.

2. *During the early stages of the legislative process.* When agenda setting and subcommittee work are being done, the public, the press, and "watchdog" groups are not as attentive.

3. *When the issue is narrow, specialized, or unopposed.* PAC contributions are more effective on specialized or unopposed issues than on broad national issues.

4. *When PACs are allied.* When "PACs travel in packs" and work together, they can wield considerable power.

5. *When PACs adapt lobbying techniques to their contribution strategies.* Successful PACs also employ grassroots lobbying with contributions.

PACs and Campaign Financing

Because PAC money is easy to come by, it is clear why PACs have so much influence with their contributions. When this fact is combined with the ever-escalating sums of money that legislators need to get and stay elected, the result is quite powerful. The increasing dependency on PAC contributions is driven partly by the rising costs of getting elected and partly by the ease of getting PAC money. In 1996, a Senate seat cost an average of $4.7 million, a 53 percent increase since 1986. Twenty-five percent of the $800 million raised by congressional candidates in 1996 came from PACs.[65]

Not only has the dependency on PAC money become a serious problem, but it is growing increasingly evident that the majority of the money is going to incumbents. Common Cause, a citizen's lobby, studied the giving patterns of PACs. In 1984, according to Common Cause research, PACs contributed $4.60 to incumbents for every $1 given to challengers. By 1986, the ratio had grown to $6 to $1. In 1986, the average incumbent received 44 percent of her or his campaign money from PACs.[66] By 1988, this percentage had grown to 46 percent.[67] In 1995–1996, 67 percent of PAC contributions went to incumbents, while only 15 percent went to challengers (the remaining 18 percent went to open seats).[68]

One problem with this continuing trend is that it indicates the extent to which congressional elections have become special-interest affairs. Another problem is that incumbents have an advantage over challengers that arises from their greater ability to raise PAC funds. In one election year, the average incumbent raised 44 percent of campaign funds from PACs. The corresponding figure for challengers was 22 percent. According to Common Cause, 98 percent of all challengers lost that year. Political analysts think that the ability of incumbents to amass huge sums of money has a "totem effect"—a tendency to scare off political challengers.[69]

Not only are citizen lobby groups and a growing number of legislators becoming alarmed at the effects of PACs, but the general public, too, distrusts PACs and considers them harmful to the nation's political process. S. Prakash Sethi and Nobuaki Namiki found that the negative reactions toward PACs were independent of socioeconomic and demographic factors, political ideology, and party affiliation. In a national survey, they found that (1) 17.6 percent of the respondents felt PACs were a good thing, (2) 43.1 percent felt PACs were a bad thing, (3) 35.6 percent believed PACs had a great deal of influence, and (4) 45.8 percent thought PACs had some influence. Sethi and Namiki concluded that "business must undertake substantive and communications-related measures to improve public perception of PAC activities if it is to maintain societal legitimacy in its involvement in the political process."[70]

Campaign Financing Reform Proposals

For several years, proposals to reform the method by which legislators raise funds have been surfacing. As far back as 1977, proposals were introduced and then defeated that sought to provide public funds for congressional campaigns and to restrict the amount candidates could accept from PACs. It is becoming more evident, however, that money is dominating the political process to such a degree that even supporters of PACs now think that reform is necessary.[71]

Ideas that have been suggested for campaign financing reform include federal funding, caps on campaign spending, routing campaign funds through political parties instead of directly to individuals, limiting the terms of legislators, and taxing

PACs. No action is expected to take place, however, until a stable and reasonable alternative source of campaign funds can be identified.[72]

President Clinton's campaign finance reform proposal, which was aimed at both reducing the cost of running for office and the candidates' dependence on special-interest money, was pronounced dead in the 1994 Congress when no action on it was taken. It is interesting to note one reason why no action was taken. In 1996, PAC contributions to federal candidates totaled over $218 million—an increase of 350 percent from 1980's contribution of $60 million.[73] Limiting PAC donations to candidates addresses only half the problem, however. The other half is the so-called "soft money" that special interests may donate on an unlimited basis for the purposes of educating and registering voters.

By law, PACs can only contribute $5,000 to a candidate for any given election. There are no limits on soft money, which is given directly to political parties. In the 1996 elections, soft money tripled to over $260 million, helping to make the 1996 elections the most expensive in history, in which more than $2 billion was spent on federal campaigns. According to Ann McBride, Common Cause president, "Ending the corrupt soft money system will not solve all of the problems with the current campaign finance system, but it is the most important step to curb huge special-interest money in the process."[74] If it passes the House, a bill sponsored by Christopher Shays (R-Connecticut) and Martin Meehan (D-Massachusetts) would ban soft money. However, House leadership has allowed debate on over 200 amendments to the bill, a move that is widely acknowledged as an effort to weaken the bill.[75]

ETHICS IN PRACTICE

Influencing Local Government

My friend runs a small Atlanta chemical company that produces alum. Alum is used for many purposes, including water purification, and the company had a contract with Fulton County for this use for many years. In all the years they had this contract, they received it through open bidding. This was the case every renewal year until this year, when they were again the low bidder. A larger company based in the North with a division in Georgia was awarded the contract, even though its bid was about 3 percent higher. This would have been acceptable if there had been a quality or delivery problem in the past, but this had never been the case.

My friend met with a former county commissioner to seek advice about, and reasons for, this situation. The commissioner believed that there was an under-the-table agreement and advised my friend to sue the county and its purchasing manager. The problem is that the contract is relatively small and the lawsuit would almost certainly cost more than the contract.

1. Is filing a lawsuit the best way for this chemical company to influence the county commission? What options does the company have?

2. Do companies now have to lobby local or other governments to get business? Do they need to make PAC contributions? Bribes or kickbacks?

3. What action should this small chemical company take?

Contributed by Jack Rood

Reform of the current system seems more likely than ever to take place. However, experience has shown the political process to be unpredictable, and such reform would require legislators to change a system under which many if not all of them have been beneficiaries. Still, there is growing public sentiment that the current PAC contributions–campaign funds system must be reformed if it is to survive. The relationship between business and government in this connection is coming under increased scrutiny.

COALITION BUILDING

A noteworthy and growing mechanism of political involvement in the public policy process is the creation and use of coalitions to influence government processes. A *coalition* is formed when distinct groups or parties realize they have something in common that might warrant their joining forces, at least temporarily, for joint action. More often than not, an issue that various groups feel similarly about creates the opportunity for a coalition.

Historically, businesses have been reluctant to form coalitions for the purpose of gaining political advantage, but this is changing. Coalition formation is becoming a standard practice for firms interested in accomplishing political goals or influencing public policy. If a company or an association wants to pass or defeat particular legislation, it needs to seek the support of any individual or organization that has a similar position on the issue.[76]

Because coalitions tend to form around issues, an astute political strategist could analyze past, present, and likely future coalitions so that coalitional behavior could be anticipated and managed. To do this, MacMillan and Jones[77] recommend the following steps:

1. Manage the sequence in which issues are addressed. This kind of control can dictate priorities and emphasis and result in the proper channeling of effort to suit the organization's interests.

2. Increase the visibility of certain issues. By doing this, the strategist can focus attention in such a way that her or his goals are met.

3. Unbundle issues into smaller subissues. The strategist may be able to successfully reach her or his goals by slowly but surely accomplishing one small step at a time. The net result may be more success for the entirety.

One recent example of coalition building around a specific issue is the Council for a Competitive Marketplace. Backers of this coalition include Netscape, Sun Microsystems, and Sabre Group (a firm that provides information services to the travel industry). The concern these backers share is that Microsoft will use its presence and power in the market to achieve an unfair advantage. The group's first order of business is to convince the legislature and the public that Microsoft's Internet browser should be unbundled from the Windows operating system. The coalition has enlisted the help of prominent Washington insiders Jody Powell (former press secretary) and Robert Dole (former senator).[78] They face an uphill battle for the public's opinion. In a June 1998 *New York Times*/CBS News poll, 55 percent of adults surveyed (and 78 percent of those who use computers) held a favorable opinion of Microsoft. Only 19 percent agreed that Microsoft uses illegal sales tactics.[79]

STRATEGIES FOR POLITICAL ACTIVISM

We have discussed some of the principal approaches by which business has become politically active—lobbying, PACs, and coalitions. To be sure, there are other approaches, but these are the major ones. In our discussion we have unavoidably made reference to the use of these approaches as part of a strategy. To develop the idea of strategy for political activism, it is important to understand that managers must not only identify useful approaches but also address when and under what conditions these various approaches should be used or would be most effective. We do not want to carry this idea too far, because it is beyond the scope of this book. On the other hand, some discussion of strategies for political activism is necessary to help us fulfill our stakeholder frame of reference. As managers devise and execute political strategies, it is useful to see their initiatives as factors in their development of stakeholder management capabilities.

John Mahon has argued that organizations, having experienced failures and surprises in the political and social arenas, are now expanding their strategic vision and action by developing strategies for coping with a rapidly changing social and political environment. Some of the classic cases cited as justifications for this new emphasis on political strategy include challenges such as the following: Procter & Gamble (Rely Tampons, satanism), Johnson & Johnson (Tylenol poisonings), Manville (asbestos and bankruptcy), A.H. Robins (Dalkon Shield and bankruptcy), and the chemical industry (Superfund, Bhopal, etc.).[80] It is useful to observe that these kinds of challenges are somewhat different from those discussed previously, wherein the emphasis was on influencing government directly. In these cases, the business/government relationship is more indirect and sometimes subtle.

Mahon asserts that the purpose of political strategy is "to secure a position of advantage regarding a given regulation or piece of legislation, to gain control of an idea or a movement and deflect it from the firm, or to deal with a local community group on an issue of importance."[81] Often such strategies are exercised in arenas beyond the regulatory/legislative scene. In pursuing political strategy, two major approaches or strategies are desirable: (1) keeping an issue off the public agenda and out of the limelight, and (2) helping to *define* the public issue. If the company cannot do the first, which is a strategy of containment, it should strive for the second, which allows the firm to exercise some control in shaping the issue. If both of these approaches fail, the company will need to pursue a coping strategy.[82]

At this point, it is useful to consider several other ideas about political strategy: the regulatory life cycle approach, contingency approaches, and corporate political entrepreneurship.

Regulatory Life Cycle Approach

Several fairly sophisticated attempts to link corporate political strategies with key issues or variables have been set forth. Arieh Ullman has developed a relationship between the *regulatory life cycle* and the *use of political strategies*. He argues that there are various stages in the *regulatory life cycle*—formation, formulation, implementation, administration, and modification—that require or demand that the firm adjust its political strategy contingent on the stage that an issue has reached. He concludes, for example, that capturing key bureaucrats is meaningful only in the later stages, whereas corporate grassroots campaigns are advantageous only during the early stages.[83]

Contingency Approaches

Similarly, Gerald Keim and Carl Zeithaml have developed a *contingency approach of corporate political strategy* and legislative decision making. Their model considers two major variables: (1) the number of salient issues in a legislative district and (2) the amount of information a legislator possesses concerning voter preferences on these issues. Keim and Zeithaml then argue that knowledge of these two contingencies is useful in the selection of effective corporate political strategies for specific issues. If the corporation can identify the set of legislators who will be the key to important decisions, then the task is (1) to determine the salience of the issue under consideration to each legislator's constituency and (2) to identify the expected position(s) of voters on the issue. This will permit a prediction of the probable position of each legislator and facilitate the company's selection of an appropriate political strategy (for example, lobbying, constituency building, or making campaign contributions through a PAC).[84]

S. Prakash Sethi proposes a more straightforward approach to developing political strategies. His approach takes the position that the political activities (campaign financing, direct lobbying, coalition building) of a company are contingent on (1) the various modes of corporate responses the firm determines are appropriate for the environment in which it finds itself, (2) its internal corporate conditions, and (3) its anticipated political risks.[85] The three modes a firm may find itself in are (1) the defensive mode, (2) the accommodative mode, and (3) positive activism.

The *defensive mode* is characterized by a situation in which a company sees its objectives as completely legitimate, thinks that anyone opposing these objectives is an adversary, and generally operates by itself in the political arena. The major company goal in this situation is to maintain the status quo in terms of political climate, legislative makeup, and regulatory environment. The strategies suggested are typically ad hoc and reactive. In this mode, of course, the firm would see the external environment and internal corporate conditions as conducive to such a defensive posture.[86]

The *accommodative mode* is one in which the firm thinks its political objectives are contingent on its ability to coopt other groups to its viewpoint. Here the firm is willing to form coalitions that are likely to become the norm. This mode does not require a radical departure from traditional goals and strategies but is more responsive and adaptive to a changing political environment and structure. The accommodative mode would appear to be minimally required in today's environment.

Positive activism is a mode in which the focus moves from responding to external pressures to the *initiation* and *development* of a national agenda and a more progressive role in the public policy process. Firms become active leaders for social and political change rather than just responding to external factors. This mode is proactive in nature, and its goal is to anticipate and shape future events.[87]

In today's environment, it could be argued that the politically successful firm needs at least to take an accommodative mode and ideally to adopt a positive activism mode. There may be situations in which the defensive mode would still be appropriate, but these situations are rapidly fading from the scene. For the firm or industry that finds itself in an increasingly competitive environment, positive activism should be the strategy of choice. Furthermore, it is the strategy that is most compatible with innovative, aggressive, and professional management that understands the broader role of business in society and what it takes to be successful today.

SUMMARY

The current political environment has been characterized by a growth in government activity, the democratization of Congress, the rise of special-interest groups, and a decline in voter participation. These factors have created an environment in which corporate political participation has flourished. Lobbying is the principal approach for influencing government and the public policy process. Lobbying is now done at the company level, at the trade association level, and through large umbrella organizations such as the U.S. Chamber of Commerce, the National Association of Manufacturers, and the National Federation of Independent Businesses. Lobbying has become increasingly specialized, and one major consequence of this trend has been the diminishment of power of the broad-based umbrella organizations. Grassroots lobbying has become one of the dominant ways of wielding influence.

Political action committees (PACs) are the major force in raising and distributing monies for congressional campaigns. There has been an explosion in the growth and power of PACs over the past decade, and their influence has caused a heated debate. Supporters claim that PACs represent pluralism in action. Critics claim that PACs buy votes and have assumed too large a role in campaign financing. Several campaign financing reform proposals are currently before Congress.

Coalition building is one of the most successful strategies for exercising influence over the public policy process. Corporate political strategy has become a vital topic for businesses. Important strategies for political activism include keeping issues off the public agenda, defining issues, coping, the regulatory life cycle approach, and contingency approaches.

KEY TERMS

accommodative mode (page 265)

action call (page 252)

coalition (page 263)

company lobbying (page 248)

contingency approach of corporate political strategy (page 265)

defensive mode (page 265)

Golden Rule of Politics (page 256)

grassroots lobbying (page 250)

lobbying (page 247)

political action committees (PACs) (page 256)

political involvement (page 246)

positive activism (page 265)

regulatory life cycle (page 265)

trade associations (page 248)

umbrella organizations (page 248)

DISCUSSION QUESTIONS

1. Of the four major business-related changes that have occurred in the political environment over the past 25 years, which in your opinion has been most significant, and why?
2. Explain *lobbying* in your own words. Describe the different levels at which lobbying takes place. Why is there a lack of unity among the umbrella organizations?
3. What is a PAC? What are the major arguments in favor of PACs? What are the major criticisms of PACs? In your opinion, are PACs a good way for business to influence the public policy process? What changes would you recommend for PACs?
4. Explain the regulatory life cycle approach to political activism. Differentiate it from contingency approaches.
5. What type of campaign financing reform would you recommend?

ENDNOTES

1. Gerald D. Keim, "Corporate Grassroots Programs in the 1980s," *California Management Review* (Fall, 1985), 111–116.
2. *Ibid.*, 111.
3. Owen Ullman and Catherine Yang, "The Regulators Are Back in Business," *Business Week* (January 20, 1997), 41.
4. Keim, 112–114.
5. Seymour Martin Lipset, "The Sources of Public Interest Activism," *Public Relations Quarterly* (Fall, 1986), 9–13.
6. Keim, 114–115.
7. Ronald J. Hrebenar and Ruth K. Scott, *Interest Group Politics in America*, 2nd ed. (Englewood Cliffs, NJ: Prentice Hall, 1990), vii–viii.
8. The U.S. Federal Elections Commission maintains a Web site with current and historical information about elections and voting. Its address is *http://www.fec.gov.*
9. Keim, 115–116.
10. S. Prakash Sethi, "Corporate Political Activism," *California Management Review* (Spring, 1982), 32.
11. David B. Yoffie and Sigrid Bergenstein, "Creating Political Advantage: The Rise of the Corporate Political Entrepreneur," *California Management Review* (Fall, 1985), 124. Also see John F. Mahon, "Corporate Political Strategy," *Business in the Contemporary World* (Autumn, 1989), 50–62.
12. Ian Maitland, "Self-Defeating Lobbying: How More Is Buying Less in Washington," *Journal of Business Strategy* (Fall, 1986), 67–68.
13. Hanna Rosin, "Mining Microsoft," *New Republic* (June 8, 1998), 12–13. See also Jeffrey H. Birnbaum, "Microsoft's Capital Offense," *Fortune* (February 2, 1998), 84–86.
14. H. R. Mahood, *Interest Group Politics in America* (Englewood Cliffs, NJ: Prentice Hall, 1990), 52.
15. *Ibid.*, 53–54.
16. Dick Lochner, Editorial Cartoon, *U.S. News & World Report* (September 19, 1983), 63.

17. Evan Thomas, "Peddling Influence," *Time* (March 3, 1986), 27.
18. Jane M. Keffer and Ronald Paul Hill, "An Ethical Approach to Lobbying Activities of Businesses in the United States," *Journal of Business Ethics* (September, 1997), 1371–1379.
19. Jeffrey H. Birnbaum, "Washington's Power 25," *Fortune* (December 8, 1997), 145–158.
20. Peter H. Stone, "Learning from Nader," *National Journal* (June 11, 1994), 1342–1344.
21. Kristin Gilpatrick, "Sound Your Horn," *Credit Union Management* (May, 1998), 10–11.
22. *Encyclopedia of Associations* (Detroit, MI: Gale Research , Inc., 1997).
23. Alan Murray, "Lobbyists for Business Are Deeply Divided, Reducing Their Clout," *The Wall Street Journal* (March 25, 1987), 1, 22.
24. Rick Wartzman, "Drug Firms' Lobbying to Defuse Criticism by Clinton Pays Off," *The Wall Street Journal* (August 16, 1994), A1.
25. Jill Wechsler, "Employers, Healthcare Industry Lash Back at White House, Congress," *Managed Healthcare* (February, 1998), 8.
26. Jeffrey Marshall, "Credit Union Battleground Shifts," *US Banker* (April, 1988), 10–11.
27. *The Washington Lobby,* 3rd ed. (Washington, DC: Congressional Quarterly, October, 1979), 113–117.
28. Nancy E. Roman, "Chamber of Commerce Hires New Lobbyists to Counter Unions," *Washington Times—National Weekly Edition* (January 11, 1998), 10.
29. Douglas Harbrecht, "Chamber of Commerce Battle Cry—Kill All the Lawyers," *Business Week* (March 2, 1998), 53.
30. Walter Olson, "A Malleable Manufacturer's Lobby," *The Wall Street Journal* (October 10, 1984), 32.
31. *Ibid.*
32. Marilyn Wilson, "The New Look at NAM," *Dun's Business Monthly* (April, 1984), 44.
33. *Ibid.,* 50.
34. Olson, 32.
35. For examples of collaboration, see the following articles: Anonymous, "Employers Seek Court Review of OSHA Compliance Program," *Business Insurance* (January 26, 1998), 1–2; John S. McClenahon, "The Dragon and the Bull(Market)," *Industry Week* (September 1, 1997), 82–86; Steven Brostoff, "Employers Back GOP Push for Medicare Market Reforms," *National Underwriter* (October 23, 1995), 33.
36. Leslie Wayne, "The New Face of Business Leadership," *The New York Times* (May 22, 1983), F3, F8, F9.
37. *Ibid.*
38. *Ibid.*
39. Birnbaum, 156.
40. Susan Headden, "The Little Lobby That Could," *U.S. News & World Report* (September 12, 1994), 45–48.
41. *Ibid.*
42. Birnbaum, 145.
43. Cited in Murray, 1.

44. *Ibid.*, 22.
45. Maitland, 67, 73.
46. William H. Miller, "Seize the Moment," *Industry Week* (January 20, 1997), 13–20.
47. Mary Ann Pires, "Lobbying: The Ethical Challenge," *Impact* (June, 1994), 1.
48. Larry J. Sabato, "PAC-Man Goes to Washington," *Across the Board* (October, 1984), 16.
49. Herbert E. Alexander and Mike Eberts, "Political Action Committees: A Practical Approach," *Business Forum* (Winter, 1984), 6.
50. Andria Sagedy, "Why We Have PACs," *Business Forum* (Winter, 1984), 8.
51. Alexander and Eberts, 6.
52. The U.S. Federal Elections Commission maintains a Web site with current and historical information about candidates, parties, and PACs. The address is *http://www.fec.gov.*
53. Ann Reilly Dowd, "Look Who's Cashing in on Congress," *Money* (December, 1997), 128–138.
54. Albert R. Hunt, "Special Interest Money Increasingly Influences What Congress Enacts," *The Wall Street Journal* (July 26, 1982), 1.
55. Dowd, 128–138.
56. Philip M. Stern, *Still the Best Congress Money Can Buy* (Washington, DC: Regnery Gateway, 1992).
57. Cited in Sabato, 21–22.
58. "Contributions from Special Interests Buy Attention in Congress, Study Finds" (The Associated Press), *The Atlanta Journal* (July 2, 1991), A3.
59. *Ibid.*
60. Andrew Mollison, "Tobacco Money Denounced," *The Atlanta Journal* (October 19, 1994), A8.
61. *Ibid.*
62. Jim Drinkard, "Tobacco Learns That Lobbying Has Limits," *USA Today* (April 20, 1998), 4A.
63. Sabato, 23.
64. *Ibid.*
65. Dowd, 128–138.
66. John J. Fialka, "House Incumbents Increasingly Depend on PAC Funds, Study Says," *The Wall Street Journal* (April 8, 1987), 70.
67. Larry Makinson, "Open Secrets: The Dollar Power of PACs in Congress," *Congressional Quarterly* (1990), 3.
68. The Federal Elections Commission Web site, *www.fec.gov.*
69. Makinson, 3.
70. S. Prakash Sethi and Nobuaki Namiki, "The Public Backlash Against PACs," *California Management Review* (Spring, 1983), 133.
71. David Shribman and Brooks Jackson, "Conservative Support Adds Momentum to a Move by Congress to Limit PACs' Influence in Elections," *The Wall Street Journal* (November 22, 1985), 64.
72. Norman Ornstein, "If They Can't Be Banned, Make Them Pay—Tax PACs!" *The Washington Post National Weekly Edition* (April 1–7, 1991), 24. See also Rick

Wartzman, "After Years of Scandal, Congress Makes a Show of Cleaning Up Its Act," *The Wall Street Journal* (August 11, 1994), A1.

73. The Federal Elections Commission Web site, *www.fec.gov.*

74. Common Cause Web site, *www.commoncause.org.*

75. James Dao, "An Uneasy Republican Maverick," *New York Times* (June 22, 1998), B1.

76. Gerald D. Keim, "Foundations of a Political Strategy for Business," *California Management Review* (Spring, 1981), 45.

77. Ian C. MacMillan and Patricia E. Jones, Strategy Formulation: Power and Politics, 2nd ed. (St. Paul, MN: West, 1986), 68.

78. Jeffrey H. Birnbaum, "D. C.'s Anti-Gates Lobby," *Fortune* (January 12, 1998), 135.

79. Steve Lohr and Marjorie Connelly, "Most Approve of Microsoft, A Poll Shows," *New York Times* (June 15, 1998), D1.

80. John F. Mahon, "Corporate Political Strategy," *Business in the Contemporary World* (Autumn, 1989), 50–62.

81. *Ibid.*

82. *Ibid.*

83. Arieh A. Ullman, "The Impact of the Regulatory Life Cycle on Corporate Political Strategies," *California Management Review* (Fall, 1985), 140–154.

84. Gerald D. Keim and Carl P. Zeithaml, "Corporate Political Strategy and Legislative Decision Making: A Review and Contingency Approach," *Academy of Management Review* (Vol. 11, No. 4, 1986), 828–843.

85. S. Prakash Sethi, "Corporate Political Activism," *California Management Review* (Spring, 1982), 41.

86. *Ibid.*

87. *Ibid.*

9

Consumer Stakeholders: Information Issues and Responses

CHAPTER OBJECTIVES

After studying this chapter, you should be able to:

1 Recite the consumer's Magna Carta and explain its meaning.

2 Chronicle the evolution of the consumer movement.

3 Identify the major abuses of advertising and discuss specific controversial advertising issues.

4 Enumerate and discuss other product information issues that present problems for consumer stakeholders.

5 Describe the role and functions of the FTC.

6 Discuss the strengths and weaknesses of regulation and self-regulation of advertising.

How important are consumers as stakeholders? An argument could be made that consumers, or customers, rank at or very near the top when it comes to stakeholder priorities. Their importance may be seen in a variety of ways. While discussing the fundamental question of business purpose, management expert Peter Drucker emphasized the centrality of consumers with his assertion that there is only one valid definition of business purpose: *to create a customer.* The customer is the foundation of a business and keeps it in existence.[1] When Steven Brenner and Earl Molander surveyed executives as to which stakeholder groups were owed the most by business; the results[2] were ranked as follows:

1. Customers (consumers)

2. Stockholders

3. Employees

4. Local community environment

Businesses cannot exist, much less survive and prosper, without customers. Customer satisfaction, therefore, is a central objective of all organizations, large and small alike. The business/consumer relationship is of utmost concern to all of us, because we are all consumers of the products and services provided by the business community.

Ironically, consumers seldom seem completely satisfied with their exchange relationships with business, in spite of the fact that business cannot exist without them.

In a 1997 survey, 90 percent of customers felt they paid enough to get the highest level of service, yet only 64 percent of those surveyed felt the service they received matched their expectations.[3] The results of a 1998 survey show the damage customer dissatisfaction can wreak. Of the 1,000 people surveyed, one in five would become disloyal after receiving poor value for their money, one in ten would become disloyal if they believed the company just did not listen, and over half (54 percent) would feel no loyalty after receiving rude or unhelpful service.[4] Although businesses are trying to get better at meeting consumer needs, consumer dissatisfaction remains a major issue managers face.

It is no surprise that the issue of business and the consumer stakeholder is at the forefront of discussions about business and its relationships with and responsibility to the society in which it exists. Products and services are the most visible manifestations of business in society. For this reason, the whole issue of business and its consumer stakeholders deserves a careful examination. We devote two chapters to it. In this chapter, we focus on the evolution and maturity of the consumer movement and product information issues—most notably, advertising. In Chapter 10 we consider product issues, especially product safety and liability, and business's response to its consumer stakeholders.

THE PARADOX OF THE CONSUMER ORIENTATION

If one studies the history of business in America, one sees how business has evolved through different eras in the evolution of marketing. It has been said that these changes in business practices could be characterized as a revolution in marketing.[5] Basically, this revolution stems from the idea that the customer, not the product or the company, is the focus of business. The focus, in other words, has shifted from problems of production to problems of marketing. The product business *can* make is no longer as important as the product the consumer *wants* business to make.

Robert Keith, using the Pillsbury Company as a model, asserts that this company went through four eras—which he suggests also typifies American business in general. The first era was that of manufacturing, in which the company philosophy was product oriented. In the second era, which was sales oriented, the focus was on having a first-rate sales organization that could dispose of all the products (in Pillsbury's case, flour) it could make. The third era was marketing oriented. During this era, the philosophy was, "We make and sell products for consumers." The fourth era followed a philosophy of marketing control, articulated as, "We are moving from a company that has the marketing concept to a marketing company."[6] This emphasis is confirmed by Regis McKenna in a recent article in which he argues that "marketing is everything."[7]

A *Fortune* magazine cover story featuring "the tough new consumer—demanding more and getting it"—captures in a nutshell the business/consumer stakeholder relationship of the 1990s. Thus, "know thy customer!" has become the watchword for companies in the newly competitive environment they face today. With the rise of developing nations and their rising incomes, the "new global consumer" has become a fixation as well.[8]

The consumer orientation, which prevails today, is at the heart of what has been termed the marketing concept.[9] However, the paradox of the marketing concept is that in a period when all marketing theorists and practitioners proclaim a consumer orientation, we continue to see a concomitant rise in the voice of the consumer exclaiming that business does not care enough about the consumer. Indeed, the consumer movement of the past two decades or so, marching under the banner of "consumerism," seems to contradict the marketing concept. *Business Week* magazine expressed this concern 30 years ago when it asserted, "In the very broadest sense, consumerism can be defined as the bankruptcy of what the business schools have been calling the 'marketing concept.'"[10]

We will return to the subject of consumerism later. At this point, however, we should look at the fundamental questions that have already emerged. The most important of these questions is, "What does business owe the consumer stakeholder?" Or, stated differently, "What does the consumer stakeholder have a right to expect from business?" This expectation not only embraces market considerations, but legal and ethical concerns as well.

THE CONSUMER MOVEMENT

Many marketing experts have chosen to suggest what business owes the consumer by reciting what Holloway and Hancock once termed the "consumer's Magna Carta," or the four basic consumer rights spelled out by President John F. Kennedy in his 1962 Special Message on Protecting the Consumer Interest.[11] Those rights included the right to safety, the right to be informed, the right to choose, and the right to be heard.

The *right to safety* is concerned with the fact that many products (insecticides, foods, drugs, automobiles, appliances) are dangerous. The *right to be informed* is intimately related to the marketing and advertising function. Here the consumer's right is to know what a product really is, how it is to be used, and what cautions must be exercised in using it. This right includes the whole array of marketing: advertising, warranties, labeling, and packaging. The *right to choose*, although perhaps not as great a concern today as the first two rights, refers to the assurance that competition is working effectively. The fourth right, the *right to be heard*, was proposed because of the belief of many consumers that they could not effectively communicate to business their desires and, especially, their grievances.[12]

Although these four basic rights do not embody all the responsibilities that business owes to consumer stakeholders, they do capture the fundamentals of business's social responsibilities to consumers. Consumers today want "fair value" for money spent, a product that will meet "reasonable" expectations, full disclosure of the product's (or service's) specifications, a product/service that has been truthfully advertised, and a product that is safe and has been subjected to appropriate product safety testing. Consumers also expect that if a product is too dangerous it will be removed from the market or some other appropriate action will be taken.

For decades, there have been outcries that business has failed in these responsibilities to consumers, leaving them often neglected or mistreated.[13] The roots of consumer activism date back to 1906, when Upton Sinclair published *The Jungle,* his famous exposé of unsanitary conditions in the meat-packing industry.[14] The contemporary wave of consumer activism, however, started to build in the late 1950s, took form in the 1960s, matured in the 1970s, and continues even today, although in a different form. The following definition of consumerism captures the essential nature of the consumer movement:

> **Consumerism** *is a social movement seeking to augment the rights and powers of buyers in relation to sellers.*[15]

Henry Assael elaborates by saying that consumerism is a "set of activities of independent consumer organizations and consumer activists designed to protect the consumer. Consumerism is concerned primarily with ensuring that the consumer's rights in the process of exchange are protected." He also clarifies that it is somewhat misleading to use the term "consumer movement" unless we understand it to mean the conglomeration of the efforts of many groups rather than the efforts of any single unified organization of consumers.[16]

Although the consumer movement is often said to have begun in 1965 with the publication of Ralph Nader's criticism of General Motors in *Unsafe at Any Speed*,[17] the impetus for the movement was actually a complex combination of circumstances. With respect to consumerism, Philip Kotler asserted:

> *The phenomenon was not due to any single cause. Consumerism was reborn because all of the conditions that normally combine to produce a successful social movement were present. These conditions are structural conduciveness, structural strains, growth of a generalized belief, precipitating factors, mobilization for action, and social control.*[18]

Ralph Nader's Consumerism

We cannot overstate the contribution that Ralph Nader made to the birth, growth, and nurturance of the consumer movement. It is now over 30 years since Nader arrived on the scene, but he is still the acknowledged father of the consumer movement. Figure 9–1 summarizes some interesting information on Nader.

Consumer complaints did not disappear with the advent of Ralph Nader's activism. On the contrary: They intensified. Someone once said that Nader made consumer complaints respectable. Indeed, consumer complaints about business proliferated. It is impossible to catalog them all, but Figure 9–2 lists examples of the major problems consumers worry about in terms of business's products and services.

Nader and the consumer movement were the impetus for consumer legislation being passed in the 1970s. The 1980s, however, did not turn out to be a consumer decade. One observer noted how uncontroversial Nader had become, not only because of the climate of the times but also because most of the significant gains that were to be made had been made.[19] In the late 1980s, however, Nader began what *Business Week* dubbed his "second coming." Nader successfully campaigned to roll back car insurance rates in California and to squelch a congressional pay raise. These victories vaulted him to a prominence he had not enjoyed in years. Other consumer issues he has pursued include air bags, an unsuccessful fight against the North American Free Trade Agreement (NAFTA), and new environmental protection regulations.[20] Nader's influence inside the beltway ebbs and flows, but his influence on the public remains strong.[21]

FIGURE 9–1   Ralph Nader: Father of the Consumer Movement

In 1985, friends and admirers of Ralph Nader gathered with him to celebrate the 20th anniversary of his auto safety exposé, *Unsafe at Any Speed.* If any book ever created a "movement," this one did—the consumer movement. His book not only gave rise to auto safety regulations and devices (safety belts, padded dashboards, stronger door latches, head restraints, air bags, and so on) but also created a new era—that of the consumer. Nader, personally, was thrust into national prominence.

Unsafe at Any Speed criticized the auto industry generally and General Motors specifically. Nader objected to the safety of the GM Corvair in particular. GM could not figure out what motivated Nader, so in 1966 it hired a couple of detectives to trail and discredit him. GM denied that it had used women as "sex lures" as part of its investigation. However, the company did apologize to Nader at a congressional hearing and paid him $480,000 for invasion of his privacy.

Nader put his money to work and built an enormous and far-reaching consumer protection empire. His legions of zealous activists became known as "Nader's Raiders." Today, Nader-operated nonprofit groups include the Public Interest Research Group, Center for Study of Responsive Law, and the Corporate Accountability Research Group. He initiated public interest research groups (PIRGs) in over 26 states, and he inspired numerous public citizen groups. His network has budgets running into millions of dollars and a staff exceeding 100 in Washington, DC.

One of Nader's landmark achievements was his recent victory in the California referendum that ordered an immediate 20 percent rollback of auto insurance rates and stringent future rate regulations. In recent years, Nader has expanded beyond consumer issues to attack corruption in government. Prominent Nader-led groups include Public Citizen and his Taxpayer Assets Project. Most recently, Nader has taken on Microsoft, accusing the company of unfair competition. He has also raised questions about the constitutionality of mediation as states increasingly adopt it.

What is Nader's current status? He is still very much hated by many businesspeople and legislators. Nader has an absolutist vision that has infuriated many and alienated some. One observer has commented, " . . . the impact of the Nader movement is greater than ever."

REFERENCES: UPI, "Raiders Gather to Honor Nader 20 years after Car Safety Exposé," *The Atlanta Constitution* (November 21, 1985); "The Second Coming of Ralph Nader," *Business Week* (March 6, 1989), 28; "Safe at This Speed?" *Business Week* (August 22, 1994), 40; Michelle Marchetti, "Why Nader Is Taking on Gates," *Sales and Marketing Management* (Vol. 750, No. 1, January, 1998), 82; and Jay W. Stein, "Mediation and the Constitution," *Dispute Resolution Journal* (Vol. 53, No. 2, May, 1998), 22–28.

Consumerism in the 1990s

Many groups make up the loose confederation known as the consumer movement. In the 1980s, these groups waged an essentially defensive struggle to hold on to earlier gains after a conservative Reagan administration opposed to regulation had come into power. In the 1990s, the record is mixed. On one hand, consumer groups still appear to have lost much of their influence in Washington. In a 1997 *Fortune* ranking of pressure group power, no consumer group made the top 25. Common Cause was strongest at 91. The Consumer Federation was ranked at 102, Consumer's Union at 113, and the Center for Science in the Public Interest was ranked last, at 120.[22] Still, the goals of consumer groups are increasingly being met with regulators enforcing old laws and enacting new ones.[23]

Although they were virtually ignored during the Reagan years (1980–1988), consumer groups have achieved some specific victories by returning to grassroots activism. Consumer victories were won over insurance underwriters, cigarette and

---

FIGURE 9–2   Examples of Consumer Problems with Business

- The high prices of many products
- The poor quality of many products
- The failure of many companies to live up to claims made in their advertising
- The poor quality of after-sales service
- Too many products breaking or going wrong after you bring them home
- Misleading packaging or labeling
- The feeling that it is a waste of time to complain about consumer problems because nothing substantial will be achieved
- Inadequate guarantees and warranties
- Failure of companies to handle complaints properly
- Too many products that are dangerous
- The absence of reliable information about various products and services
- Not knowing what to do if something is wrong with a product you have bought

---

food companies, and producers of racy television shows.[24] An interesting and specific example of 1990s-style consumerism occurred when a 66-year-old Omaha millionaire, Phil Sokolof, began a crusade against fat-laden tropical oils typically found in cookies, cereals, and many fast foods. He not only pleaded with food companies to eliminate these ingredients, which had been linked to heart disease, he then sent out 11,000 letters and bought a full-page, $200,000 ad in national newspapers with offending Hydrox cookies and Cracklin Oat Bran cereal depicted over the strong headline "The Poisoning of America." Kellogg's initial defense of its cereal was to label the ad as irresponsible. Within a month, however, the food-processing giant made the decision to eliminate coconut oil from its products. Soon thereafter, most of the food industry's major firms, as well as some fast-food chains, followed Kellogg's lead.[25]

Some have argued that the new wave of consumer protests, boycotts, and activism that we are witnessing in the 1990s represents a backlash against the 1980s deregulation of industries such as airlines and broadcasting and the budget cuts in the staffs of such agencies as the Federal Trade Commission and the Consumer Product Safety Commission. These protests should have been expected as a response to the greedy tendencies of corporate leaders and Wall Streeters during the 1980s. Specific corporate misdeeds are also likely to have eroded public confidence in business. Ivan Boesky and a ring of Wall Streeters traded on insider information. Managers at Beech-Nut attempted to pass off flavored water as apple juice. Uniroyal was using the suspected carcinogen Alar to ripen apples and keep them fresh, but finally took Alar off the market. Highly visible industrial accidents, such as the deadly chemical explosion in Bhopal, India; ground water contamination at Colorado's Rocky Flats nuclear weapons plant; and the oil slick from the Exxon *Valdez,* all suggested a lack of business sensitivity to safety.[26]

The consumer movement came somewhat as a shock to many businesspeople, for they believed that, because they had created the most advanced and productive economic machinery known, they were beyond consumer criticism. Some businesspeople still express disbelief that the movement continues despite all they have done for the consumer and the world. But the consumer movement has not gone away and neither have business's problems with consumer issues. The increased competitiveness brought about by the global economy has seen to that. Today, in fact, companies are increasingly becoming obsessed with a consumer orientation.

Technological advances have enabled consumers not only to demand what they want but also to expect to get it. Consumers have a wide range of choices and a great deal of information available to them. Mass customization, which allows companies to customize products or services to customers' needs, has evolved as a way for companies to serve customers on a one-to-one basis. Companies in industries as diverse as clothing, computers, software, and hotels have implemented the mass customization concept.[27] Paul Saffo, a director at the Institute for the Future, says that mass customization has brought new meaning to "the customer is king" nature of business:

> *The thing about yesterday's kings is they were very remote and they didn't bother you very often. Now I think the customer is an ever-more demanding partner. And, if you just blindly follow the old "customer is king" idea, you are going to miss opportunities.*[28]

According to Glover T. Ferguson, director of worldwide eCommerce programs for Andersen Consulting:

> *Yes, the customer is still king. But not it's not just a king who says "Bring me my costly raiments and a horse to ride." It's a king who says, "I want my raiments in this color, and I want them to fit. And this is the kind of horse I want. This is the saddle I want. This is the bridle I want. And here's where I want to go."*[29]

Still, it is clear they are more concerned with the "business" side of attracting and keeping customers than with the social and ethical facets of dealing with consumers.

Before we consider more closely the corporate response to the consumer movement and the consumer stakeholder, it is fruitful to look in more detail at some of the issues that have become prominent in the business/consumer relationship and the role that the major federal regulatory bodies have assumed in addressing these issues. Broadly, we may classify the major kinds of issues into two groups: *product information* and *the product itself.* As stated earlier, in this chapter we focus on product information issues such as advertising, warranties, packaging, and labeling. The next chapter will focus on the product itself. Throughout our discussion of products, the reader should keep in mind that we are referring to services also.

PRODUCT INFORMATION ISSUES

Why have questions been raised about business's social and ethical responsibilities in the area of product information? Most consumers know the answer. Consider, for a moment, the following actual cases:

- An ad for Lysol disinfectant spray carried a tempting inducement: "Buy one, get one free." The photo in the ad showed two same-sized cans of the stuff. But the small

---

SEARCH THE WEB

The Better Business Bureau (BBB) maintains a Web site that provides useful information for both business and individual consumers (**www.bbb.org**). Funded by member businesses, the purpose of the BBB is to "promote and foster the highest ethical relationship between businesses and the public." To further that goal, the BBB's Web site provides a variety of helpful resources, such as business and consumer alerts, consumer buying guidelines, and business publications. Web site visitors can file complaints online, obtain reports on businesses or charities, or locate the BBB serving their local communities. Although the BBB is best known for its work as a watchdog organization, it also acknowledges organizations that exemplify the best in marketplace ethics. Information about past and present BBB Torch Award winners is available on the BBB Web site.

print gave the details: You buy a 12- or 18-ounce can and get a coupon for a free 6-ounce can.[30]

- The "American Patriot Whistle" is sold in a red, white, and blue package that has a flag flying next to the name of the product. It is sold by the "American Whistle Corporation" and is described as being "crafted by pride in the USA." Only on closer examination of the whistle can a customer learn the whistle is made in Taiwan. When called by *Consumer Reports,* the company confirmed that the whistle is made in Taiwan and only packaged in the United States.[31]

- "Free waterbed" said the newspaper ad for Harry Smith Woodworking in Hellam, Pennsylvania. There *was* one catch: You had to buy a fill-and-drain kit ($3 value) for $159.[32]

- The Damark catalog ad said, "Elegantly light up your home this holiday season with your own Tree of Light." A 6-foot tree was priced at $39.99. There was only one problem: The tree had no lights. Customers could either drape their own lights over the plastic frame being sold or buy the lights from the company for an additional $29.99.[33]

- On the front of the package of Tyson Chick'n Quick patties, a highlighted message read, "Ideal for Microwaves," but the instructions on the back recommended using a conventional oven "for best results."[34]

These cases are actual examples of the questionable use of product information. It is estimated that the public is exposed to as many as 500 to 1,500 similar advertisements or product communications each day. It is not clear whether or not the firms that created the aforementioned communications were intending to deceive, but one might reasonably conclude that some effort to mislead might have been present. Whether the motive was there or not, business has a legal responsibility, and an ethical responsibility, to fairly and accurately provide information on its products or services.

The primary issue with product or service information falls in the realm of advertising. Other information-related areas include warranties or guarantees, packaging, labeling, instructions for use, and the sales techniques used by direct sellers.

Advertising Issues

The debate over the role of advertising in society has been going on for decades. Most observers have concentrated on the economic function of advertising in our market system, but opinions are diverse as to whether advertising is beneficial or detrimental as a business function. Critics charge that it is a wasteful and inefficient tool of business and that our present standard of living would be even higher if we could be freed from the negative influence of advertising. These critics argue that advertising raises the prices of products and services because it is an unnecessary business cost whose main effect is to circulate superfluous information that could better and more cheaply be provided on product information labels or by salespeople in stores. The result is that significant amounts of money are spent that produce no net consumer benefit.[35]

In response, others have claimed that advertising is a beneficial component of the market system and that the increases in the standard of living and consumer satisfaction may be attributed to it. They argue that, in general, advertising is an efficient

---

ETHICS IN PRACTICE

Where Are My Slippers?

For the past 6 months I have been working as a telesales accounts manager for a manufacturer of bedroom slippers. The firm had recently opened the telesales department, on a trial basis, to reach smaller retailers whose sales volumes were not large enough to attract the attention of the regional field representatives. Traditionally, the busiest time for the firm is the period from September to December, when retailers are ordering the inventories they want to have on hand for the Christmas shopping season. Last year, the number of orders coming in was unexpectedly heavy and the lead time needed to ship the orders was nearly a month. Unless the order was placed by the end of November, it was unlikely that the customer would have the merchandise on its shelves by Christmas.

However, the department manager encouraged us to take the late orders and promise delivery by Christmas, even though we knew that the merchandise wouldn't be delivered until early January. Most likely, the retailers wouldn't have wanted the merchandise if they had known the actual delivery date. Our manager's reasoning for this practice was that we needed to boost our department's sales revenue to ensure that upper management saw our department as a success at the end of the trial period. In other words, our jobs could be on the line. Also, each order that we may have lost meant a smaller commission check.

1. How would you characterize the practice our firm engaged in?

2. Were the jobs of all the people associated with the telesales department more important than ethical principles?

3. Should I have followed my manager's orders and gone along with what I thought was a deceptive marketing practice? Is the practice all that bad if there is some chance we could deliver on time?

Contributed by David Alan Ostendorff

---

means of distributing information because there is such an enormous and ever-changing array of products that consumers need to know about. Advertising is an effective and relatively inexpensive way to inform consumers of new and improved products.[36]

It has been argued that even uninformative advertising still tells consumers a lot. Two researchers have argued that advertising heavily, even if vaguely, helps attract shoppers to retail stores through a kind of they-must-be-doing-something-right logic. The increased traffic then enables the retailer to offer a wider selection of goods, raising the incentive to invest in cost-reduction technologies such as computerized inventory, modern warehouses, and quantity discounts, thus further lowering marginal costs. Thus, the advertising can promote efficiency, even if it provides no hard information, by signaling to consumers where the big-company, low-price, high-variety stores are. Economists have argued that retail juggernauts such as Wal-Mart, Home Depot, and Circuit City have taken advantage of this phenomenon. Viewed in this way, advertising is seen as a net plus for society because it tends to lower prices and increase variety.[37]

The debate over whether advertising is a productive or wasteful business practice will undoubtedly continue. As a practical matter, however, advertising has become the lifeblood of the free enterprise system. It stimulates competition and makes available information that consumers can use in comparison buying. It also provides competitors with information with which to respond in a competitive way and contains a mechanism for immediate feedback in the form of sales response. So, despite its criticisms, advertising does provide social and economic benefits to the American people.

With the thousands of products and their increasing complexity, the consumer today has a real need for information that is *clear, accurate,* and *adequate. **Clear information*** is that which is direct and straightforward and on which neither deception nor manipulation relies. ***Accurate information*** communicates truths, not half-truths. It avoids gross exaggeration and innuendo. ***Adequate information*** provides potential purchasers with enough information to make the best choice among the options available.[38]

Whereas providing information is one legitimate purpose of advertising in our society, another legitimate purpose is *persuasion.* Most consumers today expect that business advertises for the purpose of persuading them to buy their products or services, and they accept this as a part of the commercial system. Indeed, many people enjoy companies' attempts to come up with yet another interesting way to sell their products. It is commonplace for people to talk with one another about the latest interesting or clever advertisement they have seen. Thus, awards for outstanding or interesting advertisements have appeared on the scene. Awards for bad advertisements have become popular also.

Ethical issues in advertising usually arise as companies attempt to inform and persuade consumer stakeholders. The frequently heard phrase "the seamy side of advertising" alludes to the economic and social costs that derive from advertising abuses, such as those mentioned earlier in the chapter, and of which the reader is probably able to supply ample personal examples.

Advertising Abuses

William Shaw and Vincent Barry have identified four types of advertising abuses in which ethical issues reside. These include situations in which advertisers *are ambiguous, conceal facts, exaggerate,* or *employ psychological appeals.*[39] These four types cover most of the general criticisms leveled at advertising.

Ambiguous Advertising. One of the more gentle ways that companies deceive is through **ambiguous advertising**, in which something about the product or service is not made clear because it is stated in a way that may mean several different things.

There are several ways in which an ad can be made ambiguous. One way is to make a statement that leaves to the viewer the opportunity to *infer* the message by using **weasel words**. These are words that are inherently vague and for which the company could always claim it was not misleading the consumer. An example of a weasel word is "help." Once an advertiser uses the qualifier "help," almost anything could follow, and the company could claim that it was not intending to deceive. We see ads that claim to "help us keep young," "help prevent cavities," or "help keep our houses germ free." Think how many times you have seen expressions in advertising such as "helps stop," "helps prevent," "helps fight," "helps you feel," "helps you look," or "helps you become."[40] Other weasel words include "like," "virtually," and "up to" (for example, stops pain "up to" 8 hours). The use of such words makes ads clearly ambiguous. Other vague terms that are ambiguous include "big" savings, "low" prices, "mild" cigarettes, and "sporty" cars.

Concealed Facts.   A type of advertising abuse called ***concealing facts*** refers to the practice of not telling the whole truth or deliberately not communicating information the consumer ought to have access to in making an informed choice. Another way of stating this is to say that "a fact is concealed when its availability would probably make the desire, purchase, or use of the product less likely than its absence."[41] This is a difficult area, for few would argue that an advertiser is obligated to tell "everything," even if that were humanly possible. For example, a pain reliever company might claim the effectiveness of its product in superlative terms without stating that there are dozens of other products on the market that are just as effective. Or, an insurance company might promote all the forms of protection that a given policy would provide without enumerating all the situations for which the policy *does not* provide coverage.

Few of us honestly expect business to inform us of all the facts. As consumers, it is up to us to be informed about factors such as competitors' products, prices, and so on. Ethical issues arise when a firm, through its advertisements, presents facts in such a selective way that a false belief is created. Of course, judgment is required in determining which ads have and have not created false beliefs. This makes the entire realm of deceptive advertising difficult to deal with.

Three examples in which facts were clearly concealed so as to create inaccurate impressions were the Colgate-Palmolive ad for Rapid Shave, a Campbell Soup ad, and a Volvo ad. Colgate concealed that the "sandpaper" in an ad was actually Plexiglas and that real sandpaper had to be soaked in Rapid Shave for over an hour before it came off with a razor stroke. A Campbell ad showed a bowl of vegetable soup appearing to be rich and thick. It was later discovered that the company had placed clear glass marbles in the bottom of the bowl, thus lifting the vegetables and making the soup appear richer and thicker than it actually was.[42] Volvo Cars of North America admitted that it had reinforced the roof of a Volvo station wagon so that it could withstand the weight of a huge truck that was driven over it in an ad. With its rigged demonstration, Volvo put at risk its longstanding reputation as "a car you can believe in." The company was required to run corrective ads in 19 Texas newspapers where the ad had appeared. That we mention these examples here is proof that such advertising abuses are not quickly forgotten by consumers.

Exaggerated Claims.   Companies can also mislead consumers by exaggerating the benefits of their products and services. ***Exaggerated claims*** are claims that simply cannot be substantiated by any kind of evidence. An example of this would be a claim that a pain reliever is "50 percent stronger than aspirin" or "superior to any other on the market."

A frequent mistake made by advertisers is making claims that are too broad. This is what happened to Carnation, which promoted its New Breed dog food as better than all other brands. When a small competitor was able to demonstrate that its dog food was actually preferred by dogs to New Breed, Carnation was forced by the FTC to modify its ads. Its revised claim was that New Breed was the best of the "leading brands."[43]

ETHICS IN PRACTICE

Whose Sale Is It? Does It Matter to the Consumer?

One recent summer, I worked in sales at a shoe store. There were several salespeople on the floor at one time. Our pay system was minimum wage plus commission. A certain quota of sales had to be averaged per week in order for our commission to be paid. It did not take long before I realized that some people would go to great lengths to get a sale, even if it meant stealing other people's sales. One worker in particular would wait for me to help a customer. When I would leave temporarily to find a size or color she would walk over to the customer and pick up where I left off. When I would return, she would be there in a full conversation with the customer, getting them to try something else. I really wanted to yank her to the side and give her a piece of my mind, but I did not want the customer to witness a scene or think that all the workers cared about was getting commissions on sales.

This happened repeatedly, and our manager seemed oblivious to the situation. All she saw was this salesperson bringing the shoes up to the register and getting credit for the sale. After each pay period I would always hear how much commission she made and how she was the best salesperson this store had ever had. When I did complain to the manager she said, "Well, this is just a summer job for you," or "You don't really *need* the money anyway." I did not agree with my coworker's attitude on taking someone else's sale or my manager's attitude when I brought it to her attention. They all seemed to have chips on their shoulders because I was only working there for the summer and was the only person in the entire store who was continuing my education after high school. The district manager was the "token nephew" of the founder of the company and would never believe that there was any problem in this company. My ethical dilemma was how to deal with someone who is impossible to work with—i.e., takes legitimate sales from other people and plays them off as her own. I was reluctant to complain too much, because it was only a summer job and I needed to make as much money as possible before college. To me, it wasn't worth the hassle of going through a formal grievance procedure for another month, but I'm sure this won't be the only time I will be put in this situation.

1. What is the ethical dilemma in this situation? Was the coworker who was taking away the sales engaging in an ethical marketing practice?

2. Is what the coworker did really against the rules, even though she would often sell a different pair of shoes than the pair I was trying to sell the customer?

3. If high sales are the most important factor at this shoe store, should the manager really be concerned with *who* makes the sale to the customer?

Contributed by Mary Holmes Heilig

Another kind of exaggeration is known as *puffery*, a euphemism for hyperbole or exaggeration that usually refers to the use of general superlatives. Was Eastern Airlines truly "America's favorite way to fly"? Its bankruptcy in 1991 suggests that it was not. Does Ford Motor Company make "the best-built American cars and trucks"? Is Bud really the "King of Beers"? Is Wheaties the "Breakfast of Champions"? Is Dial soap "the most effective deodorant soap you can buy"? Is Buck's Barbecue the "best money can buy"? Most people are not too put off by puffery, because the claims are so general and so frequent that any consumer would know that the firm is exaggerating and simply doing what many do by claiming their product is the best. It has been argued, however, that such exaggerated product claims (1) induce people to buy things that do them no good, (2) result in loss of advertising efficiency as companies are forced to match puffery with puffery, (3) drive out good advertising, and (4) generally result in consumers losing faith in the system because they get so used to companies making claims that exceed their products' capabilities.[44]

Psychological Appeals.   In advertising, **psychological appeals** are those designed to persuade on the basis of human emotions and emotional needs rather than reason. There is perhaps as much reason to be concerned about ethics in this category as in any other category. One reason is that the products can seldom deliver what the ads promise. What they promise are power, prestige, sex, masculinity, femininity, approval, acceptance, and other such psychological satisfactions.[45] Throughout advertising today, there is an increasing emphasis on "emotional" commercials in which the consumer is exposed to an endless series of nonverbal gratification promises associated with the product only inferentially. Love, friendship, acceptance, sex, and the other promises cited above are routine.[46] Many other specific emotional appeals—fear, hope, flattery, humor—are also used.

Subliminal advertising is a type of psychological appeal that has also been criticized. It refers to advertising that communicates at a subconscious level beneath our normal, conscious awareness. Vance Packard was one of the first popular writers to address the technological manipulation that can result from subliminal advertising. In his enormously popular book, *The Hidden Persuaders,* he explained that it was about

> *. . . the way many of us are being influenced and manipulated—far more than we realize—in the patterns of our everyday lives. Large-scale efforts are being made, often with impressive success, to channel our unthinking habits, our purchasing decisions, and our thought processes by the use of insights gleaned from psychiatry and the social sciences. Typically, these efforts take place beneath our level of awareness.[47]*

Packard suggested that consumers were becoming creatures of conditioned reflex rather than rational thought and that much of this manipulation was done at a subconscious level. Wilson Bryan Key carried this line of thought further, arguing that subliminal messages can be and are concealed within advertisements themselves. For example, he claims to have found the word "sex" baked into the surfaces of Ritz crackers.[48]

Recent research casts serious doubt on both the effectiveness and use of subliminal advertising. Charles Trappey conducted a meta-analysis of the studies conducted thus far and found subliminal advertising to have very little effect on consumer's decisions.[49] Responding to a national survey, advertising practitioners and their clients indicated that they do not use subliminal advertising even though 75 to 80 percent of the U.S. population believe that they do.[50]

Specific Controversial Advertising Issues

We have considered four major kinds of deceptive advertising—ambiguous advertising, concealed facts, exaggerated claims, and psychological appeals. There are many other variations on these themes, but these are sufficient to make our point. Later in this chapter we will discuss the FTC's attempts to keep advertising honest. But even there we will see that the whole issue of what constitutes deceptive advertising is an evolving and amorphous concept, particularly when it comes to the task of proving deception and recommending appropriate remedial action. This is why the role of business responsibility is so crucial as business sincerely attempts to deal with its consumer stakeholders in a fair and honest manner.

Let us now consider six specific advertising issues that have become particularly controversial in recent years: comparative advertising, use of sex and women in advertising, advertising to children, advertising of alcoholic beverages, cigarette advertising, and health and environmental claims.

Comparative Advertising.   One advertising technique that has become controversial and threatens to affect advertising negatively, in general, is *comparative advertising.* This refers to the practice of directly comparing a firm's product with the product of a competitor. Some examples are AT&T long-distance service versus MCI or Sprint, Coke versus Pepsi, Whopper versus Big Mac, Sprite versus 7-Up, and Avis versus Hertz. A recent example is the fierce battle raging between Pizza Hut and Papa John's as they attack and counterattack each other.[51] When Pizza Hut ran an ad daring the customer to find a better pizza, Papa John's ran taste tests. When Papa John's ran ads claiming to have the freshest sauce, Pizza Hut ran a full-page ad describing Papa John's sauce as cooked, concentrated, and canned and extolling the popularity of its own pan pizza. When Pizza Hut sent its employees punching bags with a Papa John's logo, Papa John's ran TV commercials ridiculing the move. Most recently, Papa John's brought out Frank Carney, one of the founders of Pizza Hut but a current owner of 53 Papa John's franchises, to declare he found a better pizza at Papa John's. One of the difficulties with comparative ad campaigns is determining how to de-escalate the conflict. This war is unlikely to end any time soon.

At one time the idea of naming your competitor or competitor's product in an ad was taboo. For years the television networks did not allow it, so companies had to be content with referring to their competition as "the other leading brand" or "Brand X." In about 1972, the FTC began to accept the direct comparison approach, because it thought this approach would provide more and better information to the consumer. The networks cooperated by lifting their ban. Thus, we entered the new era of comparative advertising.

Some companies and large advertising agencies were reluctant to use this new form of advertising, because they predicted that the temptation for name-calling and mudslinging would be high. The networks were not happy, because they had to make the decisions about which ads to air. They saw this trend leading to larger legal staffs and other costly experts. In retrospect, we must say that these fears were not unfounded. Comparative advertising has led to considerable litigation and negative publicity.[52]

Comparative ads have become so popular that they now account for a sizable proportion of all television commercials. This has resulted in stiff competition between traditional rivals. How would you feel about Ford's claim of "the best-built American cars and trucks" if you were Chrysler or GM? This is a case where specific competitors are not named; this may be thought of as a backhanded way of engaging in comparative advertising. One reason companies have gone to these more vague approaches is because of the litigation they have gotten into and the responses they have evoked by naming competitors.

Whether out of pride or general business interest, more and more companies are fighting back when they think the competition has gone too far. Companies may take their adversaries to court, before the FTC, or before voluntary associations, such as the National Advertising Division of the Council of Better Business Bureaus, that attempt to resolve these kinds of disputes.[53]

The weapons used in comparative ad battles have gotten increasingly sophisticated. Companies are turning to elaborate scientific tests and consumer surveys to prove their assertions. For example, to challenge Mars, Inc.'s, claim that Three Musketeers candy bars offer "more of what you buy chocolate for," another candy company provided the Better Business Bureau with a perception test showing that most people interpret the Mars phrase to mean that Three Musketeers has more chocolate than other products—which it does not. Mars agreed to discontinue using the slogan. AMF Inc. ran television ads declaring that an independent study proved that tennis players "overwhelmingly preferred" its new Head racket. Chesebrough-Pond's challenged the test, claiming that its Prince rackets had not been strung to the correct tension for the test. AMF denied the charge but withdrew the ads before the case was settled.[54]

It is unclear what the future of comparative advertising will be. However, it has become one of a few controversial advertising issues that have the potential for more detrimental effects. Any practice that is likely to evoke more criticism from consumer stakeholders, as well as from competitors, should be carefully examined by management to determine if it is a legitimate practice that should be used in the future.

Bruce Buchanan suggests that there are several questions that should be asked by both those who are victims of comparative ads and those who are contemplating using them. For example, were consumers actually asked to compare one brand with another? Was the sample of consumers representative of product users? Could the consumers in the study really discriminate between the products being compared?[55] Questions such as these are essential if companies are to develop sound research methods on which to base comparative ads. To do otherwise is to invite criticism from the public and competitors alike.

A general problem with so much product (as well as advertising) research today, moreover, is that researchers can prove or disprove just about any product claim through the manipulation of facts. In 1994, Cynthia Crossen published an enlightening book, *Tainted Truth: The Manipulation of Fact in America,* in which she developed this argument. Crossen cites case after case in which companies or associations manipulated research studies to dress up the arguments advanced by the researchers or sponsors. She even cites cases where, reviewing the same data, researchers reached opposite conclusions about products' effectiveness. Thus, it is evident that *caveat emptor* remains a key rule in reviewing and judging research on product claims.[56]

Use of Sex and Women in Advertising.   The use versus abuse of sex and women in advertising has been an issue that has essentially grown in importance as the women's movement has grown in power and influence. Although it does not seem to be a burning issue with women in general today, women's special-interest groups increasingly have taken it on as a concern.

Perhaps the first time the use of sex in advertising became a prominent ethical issue was in the early 1970s when several women's groups were offended by a series of television commercials sponsored by National Airlines. In 1971, National introduced its provocative "I'm Cheryl, Fly Me" advertising campaign. After that ad, National enjoyed a reported 23 percent increase in passengers, nearly twice the increase for the industry as a whole. This commercial was so successful that National followed it with even more suggestive ones. One commercial showed female flight attendants looking seductively at the viewers, saying "I'm going to *fly* you like you've never been flown before." The viewer easily might think that the message had a double meaning. It was reported in *Time* magazine that the flight attendants were coached "to say it like you're standing there stark naked."[57]

Professor Lee Reed's analysis of the National Airlines ads explains how these ads also illustrate the subliminal effect we described earlier. In the ad, the *unconditional* stimulus (sexual invitation) evokes the response (heightened excitement, desire, and so on). This is paired with the *conditional* stimulus (National Airlines) and evokes a response. After repeated showings of the "Fly Me" commercial, the advertiser gets its payoff when the businessman goes into the travel agent's office, sees the National Airlines ad, and decides to fly National (Cheryl) instead of Eastern or United. At the conscious level, the consumer is not likely to consider that sex would be the end product of his choice. At the unconscious or subliminal level, however, the National ad influences his choice of airlines. This effect has been called "learning without awareness."[58]

Sexual references and innuendos in advertising today have become increasingly blatant and are being used by a growing number of companies. Marketers have begun some questionable steamy sexual experimentations in recent years. Timex promoted its glow-in-the-dark wristwatch with ads that claimed it would "make your husband glow in the dark" and went on to suggest that "now your hubby can even use his Ironman Triathlon between the sheets." Hyundai made sly anatomical references about men in its ads. In one, the owner of a modest-looking Hyundai drives up and one woman observer purrs, "I wonder what he's got under the hood."[59] There are countless examples similar to these. The fast-food industry has targeted its heavy user group, 18- to 34-year-old males, with ads that mimic the sex and violence of the movies favored by that group.[60] Even the diet-snack-food industry has used ads to convince women that Snackwell treats are better than Prince Charming or sex on the beach.[61]

It is an understatement to observe that the use of sex in advertising has become commonplace. The beautiful woman perched on the hood of the sports car suggests at a minimum that your sex life will improve if you buy this car. At an office building, women employees leer out a window while a handsome hunk of a construction worker takes off his shirt and pops open a Coke. Handsome members of both sexes promote shaving cream, cologne, lipstick, and other cosmetics. Product names and shapes add to the allure. Interestingly, the FTC, which is the principal regulatory body for advertising, does not seem to be concerned about the use of sex or the exploitation of women in ads. However, the major television networks have made an effort to screen commercials for taste and deceptiveness, although the results of this effort may not be readily apparent to viewers. Product ads are carefully screened for sexual innuendos, offensive words, or risqué camera angles. Network editors sift through thousands of commercials a week, searching for the swimsuit that is too brief or the ad that is otherwise too seductive.

Whether sex and the role of women (and, increasingly, men) will become major advertising issues with staying power remains to be seen. However, it is interesting to note that we live in a day and age when exploitation of people as sex objects is rampant in television commercials and other advertisements, and yet at the same time there is very little public response to the issue outside of the efforts of a few women's organizations. The irony of this is that, although there is significant opposition to stereotyping of women or even to subtle forms of sex discrimination or sexual harassment in the workplace, exploitation of women and men as sex objects remains relatively unabated in advertisements. Astute companies that want to be sensitive to their stakeholders will monitor this situation very carefully so that they do not step across the line separating the appropriate from the unacceptable.

Advertising to Children.   A hotly debated issue over the past several decades has been advertising to children, specifically on television. A typical weekday afternoon or Saturday morning in America finds millions of kids sprawled on the floor, glued to the TV. It is estimated that children aged 6 to 11 watch an average of 27 hours of TV a week, or a total of 1,400 hours a year. Preschoolers watch more.[62] A National Science Foundation Study estimated that, on average, children are exposed to about 20,000 commercials per year, mostly for toys, cereals, candies, and fast-food restaurants. The report goes on to say that children under 8 years old have great difficulty in differentiating between commercials and programs.[63] This problem became more severe when several companies began making full-length programs based on toy characters that they promoted for sale. Examples of this included Teenage Mutant Ninja Turtles, Masters of the Universe, Muppet Babies, and Super Mario Brothers.

Recently, that promotion trend was taken to a new level when merchandisers began to instill brand loyalty in the adults children would eventually become. "Cool Shopping Barbie" has her own personal toy Mastercard, with a cash register that has the Mastercard logo and a terminal through which Barbie can swipe her card to make a purchase. According to William F. Keenan of Creative Solutions, an advertising and marketing agency, "M&M says that [if you] set the brand by age seven, they will favor the brand into adulthood. One of the smartest places to plant marketing seeds in the consumer consciousness is with kids."[64]

A question can be raised as to how much harm is done to children by commercials that arc aimed at selling them food products packed with sugar or that present products (mostly toys) in contexts that misrepresent what they actually are or what they actually do. Over the years this issue has been the subject of considerable debate as to what is fair and ethical. It even resulted in the creation by parents of a special-interest group in the early 1970s known as Action for Children's Television (ACT).

The investigations by the FTC into the controversial children's advertising issue in the mid-1970s became known as "kid-vid." One of the early issues that ACT and other groups were concerned about was the prevalence of advertisements promoting sugared cereals. All kinds of attractive characters—elves, Easter bunnies, and the like—sang the praises of products that had doubtful nutritional value and may have been potentially harmful. Experts testified to the numbers of cases of dental problems, heart disease, high blood pressure, and diabetes that were likely to result from regular use of sugared snacks and cereals. Today, a major concern is the promotion of fast foods.

On the other side of the issue, it was easy for broadcasters and companies to turn the kid-vid issue into a question involving the abridgment of the first amendment. If advertising to children were censored, where else would the federal government encroach on citizen rights? Meanwhile, the FTC was being ridiculed for trying to be the "national nanny," usurping the parental role of monitoring and controlling what children see and hear on TV.[65]

Early efforts of the FTC to create a kid-vid rule to regulate children's advertising failed. In 1983, the FTC ruled against ACT's longstanding petition for reforms that would have required all stations to broadcast a minimum of 14 hours of children's programming each week and would have banned all advertisements on children's programs.[66] The climate in the Reagan administration and in Congress throughout most of the 1980s was not conducive to moving in a regulatory sense against children's advertisers. But the issue did not go away.

In 1990, the Children's Television Act was passed. This act prohibited the airing of commercials about products or characters during a show about those products or characters and limited the number of commercial minutes in children's shows. Critics say the FCC created weak rules to enforce the act, thereby sending the message that it was not taking the legislation seriously. Part of the act required stations and networks to schedule educational programs for children. However, most of the networks saw this expectation to be an unpleasant "obligation" and found ways to meet the letter of the law but not its spirit.[67]

Two issues that attract debate are marketing of high-fat foods to children and protection of children from the violence that has become so prevalent in videogames. Michael Jacobson, executive director of Center for Science in the Public Interest, argues: "Marketers have done an absolutely pitiful job of controlling themselves." He adds: "Children's TV is filled with junky toys and junky food."[68]

Although government regulations have not addressed the entire range of issues in children's advertising, this does not mean that voluntary actions have not taken place. As far back as 1972, the Council of Better Business Bureaus, a voluntary association, issued Children's Advertising Guidelines designed to encourage truthful and accurate advertising that is sensitive to the special nature of children. In 1974, a Children's Advertising Review Unit (CARU) of the National Advertising Division of the Council of Better Business Bureaus was established to respond to public concerns. CARU revised its "Self-Regulatory Guidelines for Children's Advertising" in 1997. Figure 9–3 summarizes the six basic principles from those guidelines.

The function of the CARU guidelines is to delineate those areas that need particular attention to help avoid deceptive advertising messages to children. The basic activity of CARU is the review and evaluation of child-directed advertising in all media. When advertising to children is found to be misleading, inaccurate, or inconsistent with the guidelines, CARU seeks changes through the voluntary cooperation of advertisers. CARU's current focus is on guidelines for Web sites that are targeted to children. In 1989, CARU developed voluntary "Guidelines for the Advertising of 900/976 Teleprograms to Children," and in 1997 it developed guidelines

---

FIGURE 9–3   Principles of Advertising to Children

Six basic principles underlie these guidelines for advertising directed to children:

1. Advertisers should always take into account the level of knowledge, sophistication, and maturity of the audience to which their message is primarily directed. Younger children have a limited capability for evaluating the credibility of information they receive. Advertisers, therefore, have a special responsibility to protect children from their own susceptibilities.

2. Realizing that children are imaginative and that make-believe play constitutes an important part of the growing-up process, advertisers should exercise care not to exploit unfairly the imaginative quality of children. Unreasonable expectations of product quality or performance should not be stimulated either directly or indirectly by advertising.

3. Recognizing that advertising may play an important part in educating the child, information advertisers should communicate in a truthful and accurate manner and in language understandable to young children, with full recognition that the child may learn practices from advertising that can affect her or his health and well-being.

4. Advertisers are urged to capitalize on the potential of advertising to influence behavior by developing advertising that, wherever possible, addresses itself to positive and beneficial social behavior, such as friendship, kindness, honesty, justice, generosity, and respect for others.

5. Care should be taken to incorporate minority and other groups in advertisements in order to present positive and prosocial roles and role models wherever possible. Social stereotyping and appeals to prejudice should be avoided.

6. Although many influences affect a child's personal and social development, it remains the prime responsibility of the parents to provide guidance for children. Advertisers should contribute to this parent-child relationship in a constructive manner.

SOURCE: *Self-Regulatory Guidelines for Children's Advertising, Third Edition.* Children's Advertising Review Unit, National Advertising Division, Council of Better Business Bureaus, Inc. (1997).

---

for Interactive Electronic Media (e.g., Internet and online services). These guidelines were developed with the cooperation and input of teleprogram producers, television representatives, telephone companies, and government agencies, together with the CARU Academic Advisory Panel and the CARU Business Advisory Panel.[69] We will consider further the activities of the National Advertising Division later in this chapter.

Advertising of Alcoholic Beverages.   Special issues about advertising to adults also exist. One that has become quite controversial in recent years is advertising of alcoholic beverages (specifically beer and wine) on television. This issue got its most significant attention beginning in 1985, when a coalition was formed operating under the banner of Project SMART (Stop Marketing Alcohol on Radio and Television). The coalition was spearheaded by the Washington-based Center for Science in the Public Interest, a Nader-style health advocacy group. Other members of the coalition included the 5.5 million members of the National Parent-Teacher Association, the National Council on Alcoholism, and scores of other civic and religious organizations.[70]

These members mounted a lobbying campaign in Congress and planned to gather 1 million signatures on a petition demanding that Congress either ban advertisements of alcoholic beverages or allow equal time for countermessages on the dangers of alcohol. The group cited as its cause for alarm the statistics that over 25,000 traffic deaths per year and half of all homicides are alcohol related.[71] It has been estimated that alcohol contributes to over 100,000 deaths and $120 billion in economic losses each year.[72] Furthermore, a *Business Week*/Harris Poll found that 57 percent of Americans wanted beer and wine ads banned from the airwaves.[73] This is because of the coalition's major fear that these types of promoters glamorize alcohol to youths. Project SMART claimed some credit for Congress's decision to withhold federal highway funds from states that had not raised their drinking age to 21 by 1986.[74]

A study commissioned by the alcoholic beverage industry group known as the Century Council found that despite the industry's efforts to improve its image, "the vast majority of Americans still believe the booze business is irresponsible and unethical and that its ads encourage teenagers to drink." The study also found that the public holds the industry in low esteem and believes that it is moving in the wrong direction. A finding that was particularly troubling to the industry was that 73 percent of the people polled either "strongly" or "somewhat" agreed that alcohol advertising is "a major contributor" to underage drinking.[75]

The brewing industry has not been sitting idly by. Beer and wine companies spend over $750 million a year for advertising. The networks are concerned because they receive the majority of the advertising money, and major sports organizations such as the National Football League get well over half as much as the networks receive. And all these groups are aware that a ban on advertising is not without precedent. In 1971, cigarette ads were banned from television, and the ban was upheld by the courts.[76]

The president of the U.S. Brewers Association said, "We take this threat seriously."[77] Determined to stave off government regulations, beverage industry officials and nervous broadcasters have been taking actions to tighten standards on their own. Their first line of defense has been the claim that advertising just enhances market share; it does not convert or encourage new drinkers.

Specific actions have been taken voluntarily, however. For example, NBC strengthened its standards for beer and wine commercials, and ABC and CBS argued that they were more stringently applying and adhering to existing standards. NBC rejected a wine commercial that featured a Michael Jackson look-alike because of its blatant appeal to the youth market. Adolph Coors pulled an ad for its light beer that contained the refrain "beer after beer," fearing it could be misinterpreted as encouraging excessive use. The U.S. Brewers Association revised its voluntary code to warn members not to include scenes involving inebriation or denigration of academic study. The Wine Institute, a trade association of California growers, barred the use of athletes and other youth heroes from its wine ads.[78]

The recently created Century Council, which claims to be an independent antialcohol-abuse organization even though it was founded and funded by alcohol companies, believes that its new code of conduct for advertising would help the problem. The code dictated that alcoholic beverages not be "actively promoted" at events where most of the audience was underage. A footnote to the code exempted professional sports events and signs already in place in stadiums and arenas. Marketing to underage drinkers at college events was also prohibited, but campus marketing was considered acceptable if it did not violate the college's rules. The Council further asserted that perceptions would change because of the code, even though it argued that "most" alcohol companies were already working within the guidelines.[79]

In 1996, Seagram and Sons broke the voluntary ban on liquor advertisements by placing TV ads in the Texas and Boston markets. The company argued that a standard serving of hard liquor contained the same amount of alcohol as beer or wine.[80] Although networks and cable TV moved quickly to ban the ads, the Seagram decision created a groundswell for change in all possible directions. Beer and wine sellers tried to distance themselves from the distilled-spirits industry in the hope of returning to the old arrangement. Advertisers are positioned between the two industries, hoping simply to avoid a ban. Public interest groups (such as Mothers Against Drunk Driving and the National Council on Alcoholism) are pushing for a ban. Debate began on Capitol Hill in 1997 and has not yet been resolved.[81]

Like the issues of comparative ads, use of sex, and ads for children, the advertising of alcoholic beverages serves as a constant reminder to the business community that it cannot generalize about consumer stakeholders. Rather, consumer stakeholders are composed of many special interests, each having the capacity to change the rules of the game for business if it is not responsive. Business's challenge is to monitor and be sensitive to these threats and expectations and must do so if it is to prosper and survive.

Cigarette Advertising.   No industry has been under greater attack recently than the cigarette industry for its products and its marketing and advertising practices. As a *Time* magazine article concluded, cigarette makers are "under fire from all sides."[82] Two particularly important issues dominate the current debate about cigarette advertising. First, there is the general opposition to promotion of a dangerous product. As Louis Sullivan, former U.S. Secretary of Health and Human Services, put it, "Cigarettes are the only legal product that when used as intended cause death."[83] According to the Centers for Disease Control and Prevention in Atlanta, lung cancer and other smoking-related diseases kill 434,000 people a year.[84] In the past couple of years, the FTC has argued that the tobacco companies have secretly manipulated the nicotine content of cigarettes and that cigarettes may need to be regulated as a drug because of the addictive qualities of nicotine. As a result of offensive and dangerous secondary smoke, cigarette smoking is now severely restricted in workplaces, in government buildings, in restaurants, and on airline flights.

The second issue concerns the ethics of the tobacco industry's advertising to young people and, in particular, to less-educated consumer markets. An example of this has been the industry's target marketing of specific groups. Two examples illustrate this latter concern. R.J. Reynolds (RJR) was publicly taken to task by several consumer groups for its advertising of Dakota, a new cigarette aimed at women, and Uptown, a new cigarette targeted at African Americans. The Advocacy Institute, an antismoking group, released copies of an RJR marketing plan to target Dakota (known in the company documents as Project VF, for "virile female") to a specific group of young women. The prototype woman was characterized as an entry-level factory worker, 18 to 20 years old, who enjoys drag racing and tractor pulls and aspires to get married in her early 20s and raise a family. Women's groups and health experts criticized RJR for exploiting uninformed young women and targeting them for death. It was pointed out that lung cancer among women now surpasses breast cancer as the leading cause of death. Over the past 20 years, lung cancer among women has increased over five times and the percentage of women smoking has only decreased from about 40 percent to 30 percent over the period 1965 to 1988, whereas the rate for men has decreased from 60 percent to 30 percent over the same period.[85]

Louis Sullivan was also instrumental in condemning RJR for its promotion of Uptown cigarettes, which were targeted at African Americans. Sullivan called for "an all-out effort to resist the attempts of tobacco merchants to earn profits at the expense of the health and well-being of our poor and minority citizens." Uptown billboards in the inner city were also the target of a shadowy figure, known only as "Mandrake," who secretly stalked the inner city of Chicago and whitewashed billboards that promoted cigarettes and beer to young people. Mandrake was reportedly a middle-aged black professional who had had enough of ads that encouraged youth to smoke and drink. The efforts of Sullivan, Mandrake, and a host of other grassroots supporters were undoubtedly instrumental in RJR's decision to cease its test marketing of Uptown cigarettes.[86]

In a related issue, the director of Consumer Affairs for New York City, Mark Greene, strongly argued that RJR should discontinue its "Smooth Dude" Joe Camel cigarette advertisements, which he asserted were a thinly veiled attempt to lure children to start smoking.[87] Critics as well as the FTC argued that RJR target marketed youth with its "smooth character" campaign. One Camel ad was a four-page, full-color fold-out ad featuring Joe's Place, a happening duplex bar, crowded with male and female camels shooting pool, playing darts and cards, schmoozing, and smoking or holding lit cigarettes. The ads depicted a stable of female smokers—"Josephine Camels"—using the cigarettes.[88]

Studies have documented the popularity and awareness of Joe Camel among today's youth. One frequently cited study appeared in the *Journal of the American Medical Association.* In this study, it was found that more than half the children aged 3 to 6 were able to match the Joe Camel logo with a photograph of a cigarette. Six-year-olds were almost as familiar with Joe Camel as they were with a Mickey Mouse logo.[89]

Perhaps one of the strongest indicators of the success of the Joe Camel ad campaign was the statistic of smoking among the youth market. Since the Joe Camel mascot was introduced in 1987, Camel's share of the under-18 market soared from 0.5 to 33 percent, according to data supplied by a coalition of health groups. The market share among smokers aged 18 to 24 increased from 4.4 to 7.9 percent.

In 1997, the FTC ruled 3–2 that the Joe Camel ads violated the law by targeting children under 18, and asked RJR to remove the cartoon from any venue where a child might see it. RJR canceled the ad campaign.[90] Shortly after that, the government asked Philip Morris to retire the Marlboro man.[91]

The manufacture and advertising of cigarettes and other tobacco products, such as "smokeless tobacco," raise several important ethical issues worth contemplating. Is it fair to criticize a company that is promoting a legal product? Should these products remain legal given that we know they are addictive and are linked to serious health problems and death-causing diseases? Are some of the companies' marketing practices appropriate whereas others are questionable? Is it fair to criticize tobacco companies for target marketing when all business school students know that market segmentation is taught as a way of business life? Would discontinuing the advertising of cigarettes and alcoholic beverages be an acceptable and desirable solution to current problems? Given the health consciousness trends of the 1990s and the political strength of the manufacturers of these products, these issues will likely be with us for some time.

The future of the tobacco industry was thrown into a state of turmoil in 1995, when two important court rulings were handed down. In one ruling, the nation's first national class-action lawsuit seeking damages on behalf of tens of millions of smokers and their heirs was given the "green light" to move forward in federal court in New Orleans. In a second but related 1995 lawsuit, the state of Florida was planning to sue tobacco companies for $1.43 billion in an attempt to recover the costs of treating welfare recipients who have gotten sick from smoking. The state of Florida passed a law in 1994 that would make it easier for the state to win such a court victory over the tobacco companies.

Tobacco companies paid about $11 billion to settle the Florida suit and negotiated a national settlement with 40 state attorneys general. In return for an end to class-action suits, the tobacco companies agreed to pay about $370 billion over 25 years to settle lawsuits brought by states. Critics argued that as much as one-third of the money would come from taxpayers, because the settlement allowed businesses to consider the payments "ordinary and necessary business expenses." The critics also questioned whether Congress would be effective at taking the punitive action for which the settlement gave them responsibility.[92] In response to these and other criticisms, Senator John McCain (R-Arizona) and his Commerce Committee drafted a tougher bill that would cost tobacco companies $516 billion over 25 years, increase penalties if teen smoking did not decline, and grant far fewer legal protections than the original settlement.

The tobacco companies walked out of the settlement vowing to fight in the courts. The tobacco industry mounted a $40 million advertising campaign against the settlement, painting it as a big tax increase for big government. The campaign was a success. Sensing that the bill no longer had broad public support, Senate Republicans killed the antismoking legislation. "When people call in, they parrot the ads," said Senator McCain.[93] As of this writing, all parties were in limbo. Senate Republicans hope their vote will have no election-year ramifications, as Democrats vow to make it a campaign issue. Tobacco companies face a slew of lawsuits as plaintiffs' attorneys now have access to hundreds of damaging documents that were disclosed as part of the settlement process.[94]

Health and Environmental Claims.   Currently under criticism are an assortment of advertising and labeling practices that entail product claims related to health and environmental safety. One major reason that these issues have come to the forefront is the renewed enforcement activities of the Food and Drug Administration (FDA), the Federal Trade Commission (FTC), and state attorneys general in cracking down on misleading claims. In the health- and environmentally conscious 1990s, these issues have taken on major importance. Given consumers' desires for products that are healthy and protect the environment, it is not too surprising that these issues have gained so much attention.

John Calfee claims that the modern era of using health claims to promote foods actually began in 1984, when ads and labels for Kellogg's All-Bran recounted the National Cancer Institute's message on fiber and cancer. Health claims spread quickly to ingredients such as saturated fats, calcium, and beta carotene and their effects on the incidence of such illnesses as heart disease, osteoporosis, and gum disease. One major positive outcome of the All-Bran high-fiber cereal example is that the competitors quickly brought out their own versions of the product and, in a short 3 years, the breakfast market was transformed into one in which cereals were much higher in fiber yet lower in fat and salt.[95]

By 1991, the FDA was again on the attack against companies that it claimed "misled" consumers with untrue or deceptive advertising health claims. A *Time* magazine cover story asserted that "by launching a holy war against misleading claims, the government could clear up some of the confusion on supermarket shelves and help Americans become healthier consumers." *Time* cited the following as illustrations of how shoppers are shamelessly deceived:[96]

- There is no real fruit—just fruit flavors—in Post Fruity Pebbles.

- Honey Nut Cheerios provides more sugar than honey and more salt than nuts.

- Mrs. Smith's Natural Juice Apple Pie contains preservatives. The word "natural" refers to the fruit juice used to make the pie.

- Diet Coke contains more than the one heavily advertised calorie per can (and so does Diet Pepsi).

Several high-profile incidents have communicated to the business community that the FDA is serious. The FDA wrote letters to Procter and Gamble (P&G) about its advertising use of the word "fresh" on Citrus Hill packages, because the orange juice is made from concentrate. Despite long meetings between the agency and the company, P&G would not voluntarily back down and remove the offending word. The meetings apparently ended with P&G convinced that the FDA would not take action. They were wrong. Within days, the FDA seized a shipment of Citrus Hill, and an embarrassed P&G quickly agreed to alter its labels. Weeks later, P&G was forced to remove the words "no cholesterol" and a small heart insignia from its packaging for Crisco corn oil. For its part, P&G set up a new worldwide organization for handling regulatory issues, and it believes it will have some success in Washington.[97]

The FDA has been in the process of developing new guidelines for health and nutritional advertising and labeling. Three major areas of label and advertising abuse have been targeted: deceptive definitions, hazy health claims, and shrinking serving sizes. The FDA has been developing standard definitions to be used in each of these three areas.[98] Regulating the claims of dietary supplements and homeopathic drugs is the FDA's current focus.[99]

In addition to the FDA, the states have also begun to crack down on misleading health and food claims. Examples of the states' successes include the following: Nine states got Nestlé's Carnation unit to stop claiming that its Good Start formula was hypoallergenic; Campbell Soup was pressured by state officials to stop broad ads that promoted its soups as sources of calcium and fiber; and Texas sued Quaker Oats over a claim that some of its cereals significantly reduced the risk of heart attacks. In the late 1980s, a task force of attorneys general from 10 states formed a joint effort to protect consumers from misleading food ads and claims.[100]

Another major controversial advertising practice in the 1990s is companies claiming that their products and/or their product packages are environmentally friendly or safe. As recently as 1989, studies found that consumers balked at environmentally friendly packaging and advertisements. Convenience seemed to win out over environmentalism.[101] By 1991, what had come to be known as "green marketing" seemed destined to dominate the near future. *Fortune* magazine captured the new trend well: "Manufacturers eager to appear ecologically correct are frantically relabeling, repackaging, and repositioning products, often in the face of fast-changing and inconsistent state laws." One research study found that in 1990, 26 percent of all new household items advertised that they were ozone friendly, recyclable, biodegradable, compostable, or some other form of "green." At the same time, another research firm found that nearly 47 percent of consumers dismiss environmental claims as mere gimmickry.[102]

Many of the companies that have sold their products by claiming that they were more socially responsible (natural, "environmentally friendly") are now finding that there are limits beyond which consumers will not go to purchase their products, particularly with respect to price. Thus, many of these cause-driven companies are having to reduce their prices and focus more on company profits. Although the health and environmental claims of companies have opened up new market segments, it is becoming apparent that these product claims must be balanced against competitive pricing. Some critics claim that the so-called socially responsible companies are paying less attention to their core customers. The companies claim that they are just better balancing their idealism with business pragmatism and that their customers will benefit from the new balance.[103]

Because of the ease with which environmental claims might deceive or be misunderstood, it is not surprising that in 1991 state attorneys general from 10 states issued a report entitled "The Green Report II: Recommendations for Responsible Environmental Advertising," which was intended to identify how "environmental claims can be made in a manner that is most likely to be consistent with state laws." The Green Report was built on the basic premise that "as more and more manufacturers turn to environmental claims to market their products, the need for federal standards to control and regulate these claims is more important than ever."[104] In 1998, as part of its mandate to prohibit unfair or deceptive advertising, the FTC issued guidelines on the proper use of the terms "compostable," "recyclable," and "recycled content."[105]

The realms of health claims and environmental claims, when added to the controversial topics of alcohol- and tobacco-related advertising, create a growth field in terms of potential advertising abuses. Consumer groups are likely to continue their attacks where they seem warranted, and federal and state regulators are expected to assume ever-larger roles if companies do not initiate reforms on their own. The subject of businesses' responsibilities to consumers and stakeholders remains a vital topic of concern.

Warranties

From the glamorous realm of advertising, we now proceed to the less glamorous issues of warranties. Although *warranties* were initially used by manufacturers to limit the length of time they were expressly responsible for products, they came to be viewed by consumers as devices to protect the buyer against faulty or defective products. Most consumers have had the experience of buying a hair dryer, a stereo, a computer, a refrigerator, an automobile, a washing machine, a chain saw, or any of thousands of other products only to find that it did not work properly or did not work at all. Then, when the buyer read the fine print on the warranty, it was found to include so many qualifications and exceptions that it made useless the manufacturer's promise to remedy the defect. Thus, the topic of warranties is an important product information issue.

Much of this was changed with the passage of the Magnuson-Moss Warranty Act of 1975. This act was aimed at clearing up some misunderstandings about manufacturers' warranties—especially whether a *full warranty* was in effect or whether certain parts of the product or certain types of defects were excluded from coverage. Also at issue was whether or not the buyer had to pay shipping charges when a product was sent to and from the factory for servicing of a defect.[106]

The warranty law sets standards for what must be contained in a warranty and the ease with which consumers must be able to understand it. If a company, for example, claims that its product has a full warranty, it must contain certain features, including repair "within a reasonable time and without charge."[107] The law holds that anything less than this unconditional assurance must be promoted as a *limited warranty*.

There was some speculation in the business community that calling attention to an unwillingness to offer a full warranty might scare off buyers. A midwestern producer of auto replacement parts, for example, was so afraid that a warranty labeled "limited" would be counterproductive that it dropped warranties from its entire product line.[108] Similarly, Fisher-Price dropped written warranties on toy music boxes rather than use the word "limited."[109] Many products, on the other hand, need the warranty as an aid to sales (as in the case of big-ticket items), and thus companies such as General Electric and Whirlpool continue to offer full warranties.

Catalog companies, in particular, find that warranties or guarantees are essential when marketing by mail. Few companies, however, go to the lengths to which L. L. Bean has gone with its "100% guarantee." L. L. Bean asserts, "All our products are guaranteed to give 100% satisfaction in every way. Return anything purchased from us at any time if it proves otherwise. We will replace it, refund your purchase price or credit your credit card, as you wish. We do not want you to have anything from L. L. Bean that is not completely satisfactory."[110]

Warranties continue to be an important product information issue to consumer stakeholders, even though many consumers believe they are not adequate.[111] Warranties and guarantees are not at the top of the list of consumer concerns, but they have been an enduring issue. The public wants warranties to be both understandable and adequate. This concern has had an impact on the marketplace and is likely to be the focus of increased consumer demands if business does not remain responsive to this consumer expectation.

Packaging and Labeling

Like warranties, packaging and labeling have not, until recently, been leading issues. Abuses in the packaging and labeling areas were fairly frequent until the passage of the Federal Packaging and Labeling Act of 1967. The purpose of this act was to prohibit deceptive labeling of certain consumer products and to require disclosure of certain important information. This act, which is administered by the Federal Trade Commission, requires the FTC to issue regulations regarding net contents disclosures, identity of commodity, and name and place of manufacturer, packer, or distributor. The act authorizes additional regulations when necessary to prevent consumer deception or to facilitate value comparisons with respect to declaration of ingredients, slack filling of packages, "downsizing" of packaging, and use of "cents off" designations. The act gives the FTC responsibility for consumer commodities and cosmetics, which are regulated by the Food and Drug Administration.[112] As we mentioned in an earlier section, the packaging and labeling issue is drawing renewed interest because of health and environmental claims.

Other Product Information Issues

It is difficult to catalog all the consumer issues in which product information is a key factor. Certainly, advertising, warranties, packaging, and labeling constitute the bulk of the issues. In addition to these, however, we must briefly mention several others. Sales techniques in which direct sellers use deceptive information must be mentioned. Other laws that address information disclosure issues include the following:

1. *Equal Credit Opportunity Act,* which prohibits discrimination in the extension of consumer credit

2. *Truth-in-Lending Act,* which requires all suppliers of consumer credit to fully disclose all credit terms and to permit a 3-day right of rescission in any transaction involving a security interest in the consumer's residence (for example, in the case of home equity loans)

3. *Fair Credit Reporting Act,* which ensures that consumer reporting agencies provide information in a manner that is fair and equitable to the consumer

4. *Fair Debt Collection Practices Act,* which regulates the practices of third-party debt-collection agencies

THE FEDERAL TRADE COMMISSION

We have discussed three main areas of product information—advertising, warranties, and packaging/labeling. Both the FTC and the FDA are actively involved in these issues. It is important now to look more closely at the federal government's major instrument, the FTC, for ensuring that business lives up to its responsibilities in these areas. Actually, the FTC has broad and sweeping powers, and it delves into several other areas that we will refer to throughout the book. The Consumer Product Safety Commission and the Food and Drug Administration are major regulatory agencies, too, but we will consider them more carefully in the next chapter, where we discuss products and services more specifically.

Some history and evolution of the FTC will be helpful in gaining a better appreciation of government activism and its relationship to the political parties in power in Washington at various points in time. The FTC is one of the oldest of the federal agencies charged with responsibility for overseeing commercial acts and practices. It was created in 1914, originally as an antitrust weapon, and was broadened in 1938 to permit the agency to pursue "unfair or deceptive acts or practices in commerce."[113]

Two major activities of the FTC are (1) to maintain free and fair competition in the economy, and (2) to protect consumers from unfair or misleading practices. The FTC may issue cease and desist orders against companies it believes to be engaging in unlawful practices. The firms must then stop such practices unless a court decision sets aside the order. The FTC also issues trade regulation guides for business and conducts a wide variety of consumer-protection activities.[114] In the arena of possible deceptive advertising practices, the FTC monitors advertising and may ask advertisers for proof of their claims. If the FTC decides an ad is false or misleading, it may order the advertiser to withdraw the ad or run "corrective" advertising to inform the public that the former ads were deceptive. Advertisers also may be fined for violating an FTC order.[115]

Over the years, Congress has given the FTC enforcement responsibility in a variety of consumer-related fields, including the important Truth-in-Lending, Fair Packaging and Labeling, Fair Credit Reporting, and Equal Credit Opportunity Acts. Congress gave the FTC broad powers out of fear that any specification of a list of prohibitions might lead business to reason that it could do anything *not* on the list. Figure 9–4 presents an overview statement of the vision, mission, and goals of the FTC. The FTC's Bureau of Consumer Protection has the following major divisions: advertising practices, credit practices, enforcement, marketing practices, and service industry practices.

Early Activism of the FTC

The FTC actually did relatively little from 1941 to 1969, a period Thomas G. Krattenmaker called the "decades of neglect." But 1970 to 1973 were the "years of promise" for the FTC.[116] The agency became "activist" when President Richard Nixon appointed Miles Kirkpatrick chairman. Kirkpatrick and his staff of eager young lawyers put the FTC on the map, so to speak, and the agency became so aggressive that it created "an escalating struggle" between itself and business.[117] The

---

FIGURE 9–4   Role of the FTC

Vision, Mission, and Goals

The Federal Trade Commission enforces a variety of federal antitrust and consumer-protection laws. The Commission seeks to ensure that the nation's markets function competitively and are vigorous, efficient, and free of undue restrictions. The Commission also works to enhance the smooth operation of the marketplace by eliminating acts or practices that are unfair or deceptive. In general, the Commission's efforts are directed toward stopping actions that threaten consumers' opportunities to exercise informed choice. Finally, the Commission undertakes economic analysis to support its law enforcement efforts and to contribute to the policy deliberations of the Congress, the Executive Branch, other independent agencies, and state and local governments, when requested.

In addition to carrying out its statutory enforcement responsibilities, the Commission advances the policies underlying the congressional mandates through cost-effective, nonenforcement activities, such as consumer education.

SOURCE: Federal Trade Commission, *www.ftc.gov.*

source of the struggle was the FTC's zealousness, its fuzzy and broad powers, its lack of consistency in its own administration, and its concept of what constitutes proper business conduct.

The FTC's activism continued when Michael Pertschuk became chairman in 1977. His directorship spanned the late 1970s and early 1980s and encompassed the "kid-vid" period that we discussed earlier in this chapter. Although many of the controversial initiatives preceded his appointment, he became identified with all of them. Yet Pertschuk was accurately identified with the initiatives, because for 12 years prior to his chairmanship he was staff director and chief counsel for the Senate Commerce Committee. He had nurtured and drafted practically all the major consumer legislation that was passed, including the Magnuson-Moss Warranty Act. Unfortunately, Pertschuk developed a reputation for being antibusiness. This hurt his relationship with the business community so much that he never overcame it.[118]

Less Active Years of the FTC

Succeeding Pertschuk as chairman was James C. Miller III, appointed by President Reagan. As do so many agencies upon the election of a new administration, the FTC shifted its focus to the Reagan approach to regulation. Miller was dubbed by some in the press as Reagan's "deregulation czar," and he took the FTC off into another, less active direction. Miller characterized the FTC's activism on behalf of consumers during the 1970s as "excesses" and embarked on a course that was much more in keeping with the Reagan doctrine.[119] The same general approach to regulation continued under Miller's successor, Daniel Oliver. Miller and Oliver gained reputations as deregulators who willingly slashed the FTC's budget and staff.

The FTC Reasserts Itself

After almost a decade of Reagan-era deregulation that saw the FTC's work force cut in half and its enforcement efforts greatly reduced or redirected, the FTC began reasserting itself in the early 1990s. Its chairperson became Janet D. Steiger, and under Steiger the FTC came back to life. It did not return to its heyday of the 1970s, but through a series of highly visible cases it reasserted itself. According to one observer, the FTC started looking more like the FTC of the pre-Reagan administration rather than the seemingly toothless agency it became in the 1980s.[120]

Among the high-profile cases the FTC has pursued in the 1990s, it has won headlines by cracking down on Nintendo, the videogame maker, for price fixing; moving in on "900" telephone numbers for advertisements aimed at children; and accusing major colleges and Capital Cities-ABC for conspiring to limit the market for televised college football games.[121]

In another initiative, the FTC took action against shoemakers who claim their shoes are "Made in USA" when, in fact, some are "assembled" in the United States but include some imported components and materials. This was a significant action against New Balance and Hyde Athletic Industries, who had touted the "Made in USA" claim. Although most would agree that the integrity of a "Made in USA" label is important, many agree that the increasingly global economy makes 100 percent U.S. content unreachable. A spokesman for Toyota Motor Sales USA, Inc., has said,

"If you applied the FTC standard to our industry, there's no such thing as an American car."[122]

In April 1995, Robert Pitofsky, a specialist on trade regulation and antitrust law, became the new chairman of the FTC. Pitofsky's appointment signals a shift in focus for the agency. Although advertising and other marketing issues are still pursued, antitrust battles have moved to the front burner. In June 1998, the FTC issued an antitrust complaint against Intel Corporation, alleging that the company withheld important technology information from competing vendors.[123] Coupled with the Microsoft case described in the previous chapter, and assessed in the light of the speeches Pitofsky has given since his appointment, the complaint against Intel points to a new direction for the FTC. Only time will tell what the "new" FTC will accomplish.

In addition to the FTC, the state attorneys general have been quite aggressive and successful in prosecuting misleading advertising, and they should be acknowledged as a significant source of consumer regulation. While we are giving credit to groups other than the FTC, we would be remiss if we did not also mention the renewed activism at the FDA. According to New York City Consumer Affairs Commissioner Mark Green, the FDA has "metamorphosed from a lap dog into a watchdog." The FDA's early successes in cracking down on food advertisers have brought applause from consumer groups and Capitol Hill.[124]

SELF-REGULATION IN ADVERTISING

Cases of deceptive or unfair advertising in the United States are handled primarily by the FTC. In addition to this regulatory approach, however, self-regulation of advertising has become an important business response, primarily in the past two decades. Under the regulatory approach, advertising behavior is controlled through various governmental rules that are backed by the use of penalties. *Self-regulation*, on the other hand, refers to the control of business conduct and performance by business itself rather than by government or by market forces.[125]

Types of Self-Regulation

Business self-regulation of advertising may take on various forms. One is *self-discipline*, where the *firm* itself controls its own advertising. Another is *pure self-regulation*, where the *industry* (one's peers) controls advertising. A third type is *co-opted self-regulation*, where the industry, of its own volition, involves nonindustry people (for example, consumer or public representatives) in the development, application, and enforcement of norms. A fourth type is *negotiated self-regulation*, where the industry voluntarily negotiates the development, use, and enforcement of norms with some outside body (for example, a government department or a consumer association). Finally, a fifth type is *mandated self-regulation* (which may sound like a contradiction of terms), where the industry is ordered or designated by the government to develop, use, and enforce norms, whether alone or in concert with other bodies.[126]

The National Advertising Division's Program

The most prominent instance of self-regulation in the advertising industry is the program sponsored by the National Advertising Division (NAD) of the Council of Better Business Bureaus, Inc. The NAD and the National Advertising Review Board (NARB) were created in 1971 by the American Advertising Federation, the American Association of Advertising Agencies, the Association of National Advertisers, and the Council of Better Business Bureaus to help sustain high standards of truth and accuracy in national advertising.

The NAD initiates investigations, determines issues, collects and evaluates data, and makes the initial decision whether it can agree that an advertiser's claims are substantiated. When the NAD is unable to agree that substantiation is satisfactory, the advertiser is asked to undertake modification or permanent discontinuance of the advertising. If the NAD fails to resolve a controversy, appeal can be made to the NARB, which has a reservoir of over 50 men and women representing national advertisers, advertising agencies, and the public sector. The chairman of the NARB selects an impartial panel of five members for each appeal. The parties involved submit briefs expressing their views for discussion at an oral hearing, after which the panel issues a public report.[127]

It is useful to conclude this chapter by providing insights into how the three types of moral manager models, introduced in Chapter 4, would view consumer stakeholders. Therefore, Figure 9–5 presents a brief statement as to the likely orientations of immoral, amoral, and moral managers to this vital stakeholder group.

FIGURE 9–5   Three Moral Management Models and Their Orientations Toward Consumer Stakeholders

Model of Management Morality	Orientation To Consumer Stakeholders
Immoral Management	Customers are viewed as opportunities to be exploited for personal or organizational gain. Ethical standards in dealings do not prevail; indeed, an active intent to cheat, deceive, and/or mislead is present. In all marketing decisions—advertising, pricing, packaging, distribution—the customer is taken advantage of to the fullest extent.
Amoral Management	Management does not think through the ethical consequences of its decisions and actions. It simply makes decisions with profitability within the letter of the law as a guide. Management is not focused on what is fair from the perspective of the customer. The focus is on management's rights. No consideration is given to ethical implications of interactions with customers.
Moral Management	Customers are viewed as equal partners in transactions. The customer brings needs/expectations to the exchange transaction and is treated fairly. Managerial focus is on giving the customer fair value, full information, fair guarantee, and satisfaction. Consumer rights are liberally interpreted and honored.

SUMMARY

Among stakeholder groups, consumers rank at the top. In a consumption-driven society, business must be especially attentive to the issues that arise in its relationships with consumers. It is a paradox that consumerism arose during the very period that the business community discovered the centrality of the marketing concept to business success. The consumer's Magna Carta includes the rights to safety, to be informed, to choose, and to be heard. Consumers expect more than this, however, and thus the consumer movement, or consumerism, was born. Ralph Nader was the father of this movement and made consumer complaining respectable.

Product information issues compose a major area in the business/consumer stakeholder relationship. Foremost among these is advertising. Many issues have arisen because of perceived advertising abuses, such as ambiguity, concealed facts, exaggerations, and psychological appeals. Specific controversial spheres have included, but are not limited to, comparative advertising, use of sex and women in advertising, advertising to children, advertising of alcoholic beverages, advertising of cigarettes, and health and environmental claims. Other product information issues include warranties, packaging, and labeling. The major body for regulating product information issues has been the FTC. The FDA and the state attorneys general have become especially active recently. On its own behalf, however, business has initiated a variety of forms of self-regulation.

KEY TERMS

accurate information (page 280)

adequate information (page 280)

ambiguous advertising (page 280)

clear information (page 280)

concealing facts (page 281)

consumerism (page 274)

co-opted self-regulation (page 300)

exaggerated claims (page 281)

mandated self-regulation (page 300)

negotiated self-regulation (page 300)

product information (page 277)

psychological appeals (page 283)

puffery (page 282)

pure self-regulation (page 300)

right to be heard (page 273)

right to be informed (page 273)

right to choose (page 273)

right to safety (page 273)

self-discipline (page 300)

self-regulation (page 300)

subliminal advertising (page 283)

the product itself (page 277)

warranties (page 295)

weasel words (page 280)

DISCUSSION QUESTIONS

1. In addition to the basic consumer rights expressed in the consumer's Magna Carta, what other expectations do you think consumer stakeholders have of business?

2. What is your opinion of the consumerism movement? Is it "alive and well" or is it dead? Provide evidence for your observations.
3. Give an example of a major abuse of advertising from your own observations and experiences. How do you feel about this as a consumer?
4. With which of the kinds of controversial advertising issues are you most concerned? Explain.

ENDNOTES

1. Peter F. Drucker, *Management: Tasks, Responsibilities, Practices* (New York: Harper & Row, 1973), 61.
2. Steven N. Brenner and Earl A. Molander, "Is the Ethics of Business Changing?" *Harvard Business Review* (January–February, 1977), 57–71.
3. Vincent Alonzo, "Consumer Complaints Rise with Employment Rate," *Incentive* (September, 1997), 10.
4. "Customers Turned Off by Poor Service Levels," *Marketing Week* (March 5, 1998), 11.
5. Robert J. Keith, "The Marketing Revolution," *Journal of Marketing* (January, 1960).
6. *Ibid.*
7. Regis McKenna, "Marketing Is Everything," *Harvard Business Review* (January–February, 1991), 65.
8. "The Tough New Consumer," *Fortune* (Autumn/Winter, 1993), 6–88.
9. Martin L. Bell and C. William Emory, "The Faltering Marketing Concept," *Journal of Marketing* (October, 1971).
10. "Business Responds to Consumerism," *Business Week* (September 4, 1969), 95.
11. Robert J. Holloway and Robert S. Hancock, *Marketing in a Changing Environment,* 2nd ed. (New York: John Wiley & Sons, 1973), 558–565. For additional discussion, see Robert M. Estes, "Consumerism and Business," *California Management Review* (Winter, 1971), 5–12.
12. *Ibid.*, 565–566.
13. Robert O. Herrmann, "Consumerism: Its Goals, Organizations, and Future," *Journal of Marketing* (October, 1970), 55–60.
14. Ruth Simon, "You're Losing Your Consumer Rights," *Money* (Vol. 25, No. 3, 1996), 100–111.
15. Philip Kotler, "What Consumerism Means for Marketers," *Harvard Business Review* (May–June, 1972), 48–57.
16. Henry Assael, *Consumer Behavior and Marketing Action,* 3rd ed. (Boston: Kent, 1987), 667.
17. Ralph Nader, *Unsafe at Any Speed* (New York: Grossman Publishers, 1965).
18. Kotler, 50. Kotler states that these conditions were proposed by Neil J. Smelser, *Theory of Collective Behavior* (New York: The Free Press, 1963).
19. Robert J. Samuelson, "The Aging of Ralph Nader," *Newsweek* (December 16, 1985), 57.
20. Rich Thomas, "Safe at This Speed," *Business Week* (August 22, 1994), 40; and Douglas Harbrecht and Ronald Grover, "The Second Coming of Ralph Nader," *Business Week* (March 6, 1989), 28.
21. Alicia Mundy, "Nader at the Nadir," *Mediaweek* (October 30, 1995), 22–24.

22. Jeffrey H. Birnbaum, "Washington's Power 25," *Fortune* (December 8, 1997), 145–158.

23. Owen Ullman and Catherine Yang, "The Regulators Are Back in Business," *Business Week* (January 20, 1997), 41.

24. Ronald Grover, "Fighting Back: The Resurgence of Social Activism," *Business Week* (May 22, 1989), 34–35.

25. *Ibid.*

26. Christine Gorman, "Listen Here, Mr. Big!" *Time* (July 3, 1989), 38–40.

27. "The Customer Is King," *Chief Executive* (1998 CEO Brief Supplement), 8–9. For a comprehensive study of mass customization, see Suresh Kotha, "Mass Customization: Implementing the Emerging Paradigm for Competitive Advantage," *Strategic Management Journal* (Summer, 1995), 21–42, special issue.

28. *Ibid.*

29. *Ibid.*

30. "Upon Closer Look," *Consumer Reports* (August, 1986), 551.

31. "Patriot Games," *Consumer Reports* (March, 1998), 67.

32. "This Offer Is All Wet," *Consumer Reports* (June, 1986), 423.

33. "Make That 'Tree of Darkness,'" *Consumer Reports* (March, 1998), 67.

34. "Dept. of Doublespeak," *Consumer Reports* (August, 1986), 551.

35. William Leiss, Stephen Kline, and Sut Jhally, *Social Communication in Advertising* (Toronto: Methuen, 1986), 13.

36. *Ibid.*

37. Rob Norton, "How Uninformative Advertising Tells Consumers Quite a Bit," *Fortune* (December 26, 1994), 37.

38. William Shaw and Vincent Barry, *Moral Issues in Business,* 4th ed. (Belmont, CA: Wadsworth, 1989), 389–414.

39. *Ibid.,* 403.

40. *Ibid.,* 404.

41. *Ibid.*

42. *Ibid.,* 405.

43. John Koten, "More Firms File Challenges to Rivals' Comparative Ads," *The Wall Street Journal* (January 12, 1984), 27.

44. Eli P. Cox, "Deflating the Puffer," *MSU Business Topics* (Summer, 1973), 29.

45. Shaw and Barry, 406–407.

46. O. Lee Reed, "The Next 25 Years of Advertising Regulations," *Collegiate Forum* (Fall, 1981), 2.

47. Vance Packard, *The Hidden Persuaders* (New York: D. McKay, 1957), 1.

48. Wilson Bryan Key, *Subliminal Seduction* (New York: Signet, 1972) and *Media Sexploitation* (New York: Signet, 1976).

49. Charles Trappey, "A Meta-Analysis of Consumer Choice and Subliminal Advertising," *Psychology and Marketing* (August, 1996), 517–530.

50. Martha Rogers and Christine A. Seiler, "The Answer Is No: A National Survey of Advertising Industry Practitioners and Their Clients About Whether They Use Subliminal Advertising," *Journal of Advertising Research* (March/April, 1994), 36–45.

51. Dennis Berman and Robert McNatt, "Louisville's Pizza Sluggers," *Business Week* (May 4, 1998), 6.

52. Bruce Buchanan, "Can You Pass the Comparative Ad Challenge?" *Harvard Business Review* (July–August, 1985), 109.

53. Koten, 27.

54. *Ibid.*

55. Buchanan, 106.

56. Cynthia Crossen, *Tainted Truth: The Manipulation of Fact in America* (New York: Simon & Schuster, 1994), reviewed in Joseph Weber, "Lies, Damn Lies, and Product Research," *Business Week* (August 1, 1994), 13.

57. *Time* (June 24, 1974), 76.

58. O. Lee Reed, Jr., "The Psychological Impact of TV Advertising and the Need for FTC Regulation," *American Business Law Journal* (Vol. 13, 1975), 176–177.

59. Eben Shapiro, "In the Safe-Sex Society, Advertisers Lose Inhibitions About How Much Sex is Safe," *The Wall Street Journal* (December 3, 1993), B1. See also Kevin Goldman, "Sexy Sony Ad Riles a Network of Women," *The Wall Street Journal* (August 23, 1994), B5.

60. Richard Martin, "Sex, Fries, and Videotape: New Ads Aim to Lure Heavy Users," *Nation's Restaurant News* (November 10, 1997), 3.

61. Jennifer Comiteau, "Snackwell's New Ads by Foote, Coone, and Belding Abandon the Cookie Man but Keep the Humor," *Adweek* (September 8, 1997), 5.

62. Claudia Mills, "Children's Television," *Report from the Center for Philosophy and Public Policy* (College Park, MD: University of Maryland, Summer, 1986), 11. Also see David Walsh, *Selling Out America's Children* (Minneapolis: Deaconess Press, 1994).

63. Marie Winn, *The Plug-in-Drug,* rev. ed. (Middlesex: Penguin, 1985).

64. "Barbie Gets Her First Credit Card," *Credit Card Management* (January, 1998), 6–8.

65. Susan J. Tolchin and Martin Tolchin, *Dismantling America: The Rush to Deregulate* (Boston: Houghton-Mifflin, 1983), 153–161.

66. Mills, 14.

67. Ellen Edwards, "Television's Problem Child," *The Washington Post National Weekly Edition* (June 20–26, 1994), 22.

68. Emily DeNitto, "Fast-Food Ads Come Under Fire," *Advertising Age* (February 14, 1994), 5–14.

69. For information on the Better Business Bureau (BBB) and its programs, refer to *http://www.bbb.org.* The BBB's Web site contains the complete text of the self-regulatory guidelines.

70. Michael F. Jacobsen and Ronald Collins, "Blitz Against Beer Commercials: Ads Glamorize Alcohol, Hide Dangers," *The New York Times* (April 21, 1985), 2F.

71. Robert Friedman, "Beer and Wine Industry Girds for Battle as Campaign to Ban Ads Gathers Steam," *The Wall Street Journal* (January 30, 1985), 9.

72. Jacobsen and Collins, 21.

73. Brenton Welling, "What If the Airwaves Can't Hold Their Beer?" *Business Week* (March 11, 1985), 112.

74. *Fortune* (January 21, 1985), 84.

75. Joanne Lipman, "Sobering View: Alcohol Firms Put Off Public," *The Wall Street Journal* (August 21, 1991), B1.

76. Friedman, 9.

77. *Fortune,* 84.
78. Friedman, 9.
79. John E. Gallagher, "Under Fire From All Sides," *Time* (March 5, 1990), 41.
80. Kirk Davidson, "Look for Abundance of Opposition to TV Ads," *Marketing News* (January 6, 1997), 26–28.
81. Alicia Mundy, "The Bar Will Soon Open," *Mediaweek* (January 27, 1997), 26–28.
82. Gallagher, 41. Also see "Tobacco: Does It Have a Future?" *Business Week* (July 4, 1994), 24–29.
83. Gallagher, *ibid.*
84. Eben Shapiro, "FTC Staff Recommends Ban of Joe Camel Campaign," *The Wall Street Journal* (August 11, 1993), B1.
85. Mark Greene, "Luring Kids to Light Up," *Business and Society Review* (Spring, 1990, No. 73), 22–26.
86. Marcus Mabry, "Fighting Ads in the Inner City," *Newsweek* (February 5, 1990), 46; and Ben Wildavsky, "Tilting at Billboards," *The New Republic* (August 20 and 27, 1990), 19.
87. Mabry, 46.
88. Kevin Goldman, "A Stable of Females Has Joined Joe Camel in Controversial Cigarette Ad Campaign," *The Wall Street Journal* (February 18, 1994), B1.
89. Shapiro, B1.
90. Ira Teinowitz, "FTC's Camel Case Hinges on Ad's Power Over Kids," *Advertising Age* (June 2, 1997), 4, 45.
91. Judann Pollack and Ira Teinowitz, "With Joe Camel Out, Government Wants the Marlboro Man Down," *Advertising Age* (July 14, 1997), 3, 34.
92. Paul Raeburn, John Carey, Susan Garland, Amy Barrett, and Mike France, "Smoke and Mirrors?," *Business Week* (August 25, 1997), 36–37.
93. Allison Mitchell, "The Tobacco Bill: News Analysis: High Risk on Tobacco," *New York Times* (June 18, 1998), Section A, 1.
94. *Ibid.*
95. John E. Calfee, "FDA Underestimates Food Shoppers," *The Wall Street Journal* (May 29, 1991), A10.
96. Christine Gorman, "The Fight Over Food Labels," *Time* (July 15, 1991), 52–53; and Zachary Schillar and John Carey, "Procter & Gamble: On a Short Leash," *Business Week* (July 22, 1991), 76, 78.
97. Gorman, 55–56.
98. John Carey, "Snap, Crackle, Stop: States Crack Down on Misleading Food Claims," *Business Week* (September 25, 1989), 42–43.
99. Elizabeth Smith, "FDA to Clarify Claims for Diet Supplements," *Drug Topics* (June 1, 1998), 42. See also Christine Blank, "Some Homeopathy Suits Settled: Others Pending" (September 16, 1997), 65–66.
100. Alecia Swasy, "For Consumers, Ecology Comes Second," *The Wall Street Journal* (August 23, 1989), B1.
101. Jerry Taylor, "Bossy States Censor Green Ads," *The Wall Street Journal* (August 8, 1991), A12.
102. Jaclyn Fierman, "The Big Muddle in Green Marketing," *Fortune* (June 3, 1991), 91.

103. Udayan Gupta, "Cause-Driven Companies' New Cause: Profits," *The Wall Street Journal* (November 8, 1994), B1.

104. Taylor, A12.

105. "FTC Finalizes Green Marketing Guides," *Environmental Manager* (July, 1998), 14–15.

106. "The Guesswork on Warranties," *Business Week* (July 15, 1975), 51; "Marketing: Anti-Lemon Aid," *Time* (February, 1976), 76.

107. *Ibid.*

108. "Marketing: Anti-Lemon Aid," *Time* (February, 1976), 76.

109. *Ibid.*

110. *L.L. Bean Catalog* (Freeport, ME: Fall, 1991), 3.

111. For a good discussion of warranties, see James R. Brennan, *Warranties: Planning, Analysis and Implementation* (New York: McGraw-Hill, Inc.), 1994.

112. Federal Trade Commission, *Fiscal Year 1988 Budget* (Washington, DC: Federal Trade Commission, 1987), B-6.

113. "The Escalating Struggle Between the FTC and Business," *Business Week* (December 13, 1976), 52.

114. "Federal Trade Commission," *The World Book Encyclopedia,* Vol. 7 (Chicago: World Book, Inc., 1988), 68.

115. "Advertising," *The World Book Encyclopedia,* Vol. 1 (Chicago: World Book, Inc., 1988), 78.

116. Thomas G. Krattenmaker, "The Federal Trade Commission and Consumer Protection," *California Management Review* (Summer, 1976), 94–95.

117. *Business Week* (December 13, 1976), 52–59.

118. Tolchin and Tolchin, 147–149.

119. James C. Miller III, "Revamping the Federal Trade Commission" (St. Louis: Center for the Study of American Business, December, 1984), 3.

120. Mark Potts, "What's Gotten into the FTC?" *The Washington Post National Weekly Edition* (June 17–23, 1991), 32.

121. *Ibid.*

122. Michael Oneal, "Does New Balance Have an American Soul?" *Business Week* (December 12, 1994), 86–87.

123. Detailed information on FTC activities is available on the FTC's Web site at *www.ftc.gov.*

124. Malcolm Gladwell, "A Fresh Approach at the FDA," *The Washington Post Weekly Edition* (May 13–19, 1991), 32.

125. J. F. Pickering and D. C. Cousins, *The Economic Implications of Codes of Practice* (Manchester, England: University of Manchester Institute of Science and Technology, Department of Management Sciences, 1980), 17. See also J. J. Boddewyn, "Advertising Self-Regulation: Private Government and Agent of Public Policy," *Journal of Public Policy and Marketing* (1985), 129.

126. *Ibid.,* 135.

127. *NAD Guide for Advertisers and Advertising Agencies* (New York: Council of Better Business Bureaus, 1985), 1–2.

10 Consumer Stakeholders: Product and Service Issues

CHAPTER OBJECTIVES

After studying this chapter, you should be able to:

1 Describe and discuss the two major product issues: quality and safety.

2 Explain the role and functions of the Consumer Product Safety Commission and the Food and Drug Administration.

3 Enumerate and discuss the reasons for the growing concern about product liability and differentiate strict liability, absolute liability, and market share liability.

4 Outline business's responses to consumer stakeholders to include consumer affairs offices, product safety offices, total quality management (TQM) programs, and consumer satisfaction measurement (CSM).

If product information has historically been a pivotal issue between business and consumer stakeholders, more recently product and service issues such as *quality* and *safety* have occupied center stage. It is not so much that product information issues have declined in importance as that quality and safety have risen in significance.

In recent years, the quest to improve product and service quality has been driven by the international competitiveness of business. American firms have had no choice but to emphasize quality, because more and more foreign manufacturers have been producing better products. In addition, consumers have been insisting on better quality as a natural evolution in the scheme of societal advancement.

The same has been true of product safety. With product safety, however, the driving force has become the threat of huge product liability lawsuits and judgments. Notable product liability judgments have escalated the product safety issue into a national obsession. Recent examples include the multimillion-dollar judgment against GM for having gas tanks of an unsafe design on its pickup trucks, litigation against manufacturers of defective silicone breast implants, and the now-famous multimillion-dollar judgment against McDonald's involving an elderly woman who was burned because the fast-food chain's coffee, which she spilled on herself, was served too hot. A state court awarded the plaintiff $2.7 million in punitive damages and $160,000 in compensatory damages, although the judge later reduced that award significantly.

In this chapter, we will limit our discussion to product quality and safety issues. In connection with safety, we consider the product liability issue and the calls for tort reform. The Consumer Product Safety Commission and the Food and Drug

Administration are also discussed. Finally, we will discuss business's response to consumer stakeholders regarding the issues introduced both in Chapter 9 and in this chapter.

TWO CENTRAL ISSUES: QUALITY AND SAFETY

The two central issues we are concerned with in this chapter represent the overwhelming attention that has been given to product and service issues over the past decade: *quality* and *safety*.

The Issue of Quality

There are several particularly important reasons for the current obsession with product quality. First, a concern for quality has been driven by the fact that the average consumer household has experienced a rise in family income and consequently demands more. As more and more American homes are characterized by both adults working outside the home, they become more demanding of a higher lifestyle. In addition, no one has surplus time to hang around repair shops or wait at home all day for service representatives to show up. This results in a need for products to work as they should, to be durable and long lasting, and to be easy to maintain and fix. A *Time*/CNN survey showed that consumers were less interested in technical innovation and attractive designs than they were in the product's ability to function as promised, its durability, and its ease of maintenance and repair.[1] A survey of households by Walker Research found that quality ranked first, price ranked second, and service ranked third among a list of factors consumers felt impacted a firm's reputation and their own purchasing decisions.[2]

Closely related to rising household expectations is the global competitiveness issue. American manufacturers had found themselves taking second or third place, in terms of quality, behind European, Japanese, or other competitors. Throughout most of the 1980s and well into the 1990s, U.S. firms have been struggling to match the quality that has come from other countries just so they could remain competitive in world markets. The evidence suggests that U.S. efforts have paid off. By 1990, the United States was ranked first among foreign competitors for its major appliances, clothing, telephones, and small appliances.[3] A Gallup Poll also found that 51 percent of those surveyed thought the United States has gained ground relative to competitors such as Japan, South Korea, Taiwan, and Hong Kong.[4] Although the struggle remains for international competitiveness, it is encouraging to see that U.S. efforts have had some positive effects.

Consideration of a specific case helps us to see how payoffs can be achieved when firms redirect their efforts to consumers and quality. Xerox was in serious jeopardy in the early 1980s. Xerox, whose name is synonymous with copying machines, began losing business to Japan's Ricoh, Canon, and other competitors. The company's world market share plummeted from 86 percent in 1974 to just 16.6 percent in 1984. A careful study of its competition made it clear that Japan's secret was close adherence to quality standards. Xerox chairman David Kearns was appalled at his firm's sloppiness and inefficiency and in 1983 launched a quality program. Using employee teams to encourage problem solving and innovation and tough new standards for every phase of its operations, Xerox cut manufacturing costs and product defects in half. Customer satisfaction increased 38 percent. Xerox recaptured the lead in moderately priced copiers. Kearns observed, "At Xerox we define quality as meeting customer requirements. It's an axiom as old as business itself. Yet much of American business lost sight of that. Xerox was one of those companies. But by focusing on quality, we have turned that around." In 1989, President Bush singled out Xerox's copier division for one of two Malcolm Baldridge National Quality Awards, named after the former secretary of commerce who died in 1987. The awards were created by Congress to recognize U.S. companies. They have become highly sought-after prizes in American industry.[5] It should come as no surprise that a cartoon appeared in *The New Yorker* magazine in 1983 depicting an executive commenting to several other executives sitting around a conference table: "Unless I'm misinterpreting the signs, gentlemen, we are approaching the end of the golden age of shoddy merchandise." This cartoon is an excellent summary of what had been happening in the world of product and service quality.

It should be emphasized that our discussion of quality here includes *service* as well as products. We have clearly become a service economy in the United States, and poor quality of service has become one of the great consumer frustrations of all time. This is shown in the *Fortune* 1998 American Customer Satisfaction Index, wherein personal computers posted a 4-year, 10 percent decline. This was surprising given that the industry created rapidly and vastly improved products, with plummeting prices during that same period. *Fortune* noted that these improvements apparently meant little to customers who could not get through to help lines.[6]

It has been argued that on the front line of the new economy, service—bold, fast, imaginative, and customized—is now the ultimate strategic business imperative. This is little surprise when it is considered that service-producing industries contribute almost three times as much as goods-producing industries in terms of share of GNP. Further, it is projected that all net job creation through the year 2005 will come from services.[7]

Consumers today seem to swap horror stories about poor service as a kind of ritualistic, cathartic exercise. Consider the following examples: repeated trips to the car dealer; poor installation of refrigerator ice makers, resulting in several visits from repair people; returned food to the supermarket, resulting in brusque treatment; fouled-up travel reservations; poorly installed carpeting; no clerk at the shoe department of your favorite department store—and on and on. Shoddy service comes at a price. In a 1998 study, 54 percent of the people interviewed indicated that they would lose all loyalty to a company that had rude or unhelpful staff. One in ten said they would walk away if a company did not seem to listen.[8]

There is evidence that U.S. firms are now becoming increasingly sensitive to service quality. In the 1990s it became clear that service companies were attempting to satisfy consumers through service guarantees. If you were unhappy with your hotel room, Hampton Inn would refund your money. If you were transferred from phone to phone while seeking an answer to an insurance question, Delta Dental Plan of Massachusetts would send you $50. If your luncheon pizza took more than 5 minutes to be served, Pizza Hut would give you a free one. Banks, auto service outlets, restaurants, and other service firms have embraced a quality emphasis as market growth has slowed.[9]

The rising clamor about service quality suggests that there has been something fundamentally wrong in the U.S. service sector. Sloppy service has the potential to become more than just a consumer annoyance. Some economists warn that diminishing quality standards could cost the United States more of its international competitive standing in services and thus worsen existing trade problems.[10]

With respect to quality, it is not clear whether American business has fully appreciated the spectrum of meanings that quality takes on for the consumer stakeholder. As David Garvin has expressed, there are at least eight critical dimensions of product or service quality that must be understood if business is to respond strategically to this factor.[11] These eight dimensions include (1) performance, (2) features, (3) reliability, (4) conformance, (5) durability, (6) serviceability, (7) aesthetics, and (8) perceived quality.

Performance refers to a product's primary operating characteristics. For an automobile, this would include such items as handling, steering, and comfort. *Features* are the "bells and whistles" of products that supplement their basic functioning. *Reliability* reflects the probability of a product malfunctioning or failing. *Conformance* is the extent to which the product or service meets established standards. *Durability* is a measure of product life. *Serviceability* refers to the speed, courtesy, competence, and ease of repair. *Aesthetics* is a subjective factor that refers to how the product looks, feels, tastes, and so on. Finally, *perceived quality* is a subjective inference that the consumer makes on the basis of a variety of tangible and intangible product characteristics. To address the issue of product or service quality, a manager must be astute enough to appreciate these different dimensions of quality and the subtle and dynamic interplays among them.

An important question is whether quality is a social or an ethical issue or just a competitive factor that business needs to emphasize to be successful in the marketplace. Business must be attentive to the competitive factor for economic reasons. Beyond this, firms are expected to do what is fair and right in terms of consumer expectations, and this is where the ethical dimension enters the picture. In the preceding chapter we noted that consumers expect *fair value* for money spent, a product that will satisfy *reasonable expectations,* and a product that reflects the representations that were made for it in advertising. Each of these considerations embodies notions of fairness. Perhaps most important here is that consumers expect and deserve quality that is at least commensurate with the price paid for the product. Thus, a Sears Craftsman spark-plug wrench that sells for $8.95 is expected to be of proportionally higher quality than a spark-plug wrench sold at Wal-Mart for $3.95. Quality, therefore, should definitely be thought of as a concept embodying ethical norms.

The Issue of Safety

Business clearly has a responsibility to consumer stakeholders to sell them safe products and services. The concept of safety, in a definitional sense, means "free from harm or risk" or "secure from threat of danger, harm, or loss." In reality, however, the use of virtually any consumer product or service entails some degree of risk or some chance that the consumer may be harmed by the product or service.

In the 1800s, the legal view that prevailed was *caveat emptor* ("let the buyer beware"). The basic idea behind this concept was that the buyer had as much knowledge of what she or he wanted as the seller and, in any event, the marketplace would punish any violators. In the 1900s, *caveat emptor* gradually lost its favor and rationale, because it was frequently impossible for the consumer to have complete knowledge about manufactured goods. Today, manufacturers are held responsible for all products placed on the market.[12]

Through a series of legal developments as well as changing societal values, business has become significantly responsible for product safety. Court cases and legal doctrine now hold companies financially liable for harm to consumers. Yet this still does not answer the difficult question, "How safe are manufacturers obligated to make products?" It is not possible to make products totally "risk free"; experience has shown that consumers seem to have an uncanny ability to injure themselves in novel and creative ways, many of which cannot be anticipated. The challenge to management, therefore, is to make products as safe as possible while at the same time making them affordable and useful to consumers.

Today the public is concerned, perhaps even to the point of paranoia, about a variety of hazards, such as pesticide residues in food, the dangers of living near toxic waste dumps or nuclear plants, and so on. In some states (for example, California and New York), supermarkets now compete by advertising that their produce is free of pesticides. In 1989, many consumers halted their consumption of red apples, apple juice, and other apple products for fear of residues from the chemical Alar. During this same period, all importing of fruit from Chile was suspended because two grapes were found to have been injected with cyanide.[13]

In response to these food scares, several states passed "vegetable disparagement" laws that impose penalties on anyone who makes negative comments about produce that cannot be backed by scientific evidence. In 1998, a group of Texas cattle barons used these laws to sue Oprah Winfrey. On the show in question, Winfrey had commented that she would not eat any more hamburgers because of health issues, including the threat of "mad cow" or BSE disease. Winfrey responded to the lawsuit by bringing her show to Amarillo for the duration of the trial, winning both the trial and the support of the media.[14]

Manufactured products create hazards of harm not only because of unsafe product design but also as a result of consumers being given inadequate information regarding the hazards associated with using the products. Consequently, it is not surprising in product liability claims to find that the charges are based on one or more of several allegations. First, it may be charged that the product was *improperly manufactured*. Here the producer failed to exercise due care in the product's production, and this failure contributed directly to the accident or injury. Second, if the product was manufactured properly, its *design* could have been defective in that alternative designs or devices, if used at the time of manufacture, may have prevented the accident. Third, it may be charged that the producer failed to provide *satisfactory instructions and/or warnings* and that the accident or injury could have been prevented if such information had been provided. Fourth, it may be charged that the producer *failed to foresee a reasonable and anticipated misuse* of the product and warn against such misuse.[15]

To appreciate the "big picture" of dangerous products, it should be noted that the Consumer Product Safety Commission keeps track of injuries treated in hospital emergency rooms and has identified the following categories of consumer products as being the most frequently associated with hospital-treated injuries:

ETHICS IN PRACTICE

To Check or Not to Check the Chicken?

Over the Christmas break of 1994/95, I went back to work at a fast-food restaurant where I had been working since high school. The restaurant sold lots of chicken sandwiches. We were supposed to measure the temperature of the chicken every hour to make sure that it was below 40 degrees (I assume in response to the incident in which a few people died as a result of bacteria formed in warm meat). That responsibility was assigned to whoever was battering the chicken at the time. All that the person had to do was stick a thermometer in the chicken, measuring the bottom, middle, and top until the digital read stayed at a single temperature for about 10 to 15 seconds. The whole process took a few minutes at most. This information was then sent to the restaurant's home office every day.

Unfortunately, not everyone would keep up with taking the temperatures. As an assistant manager, I was responsible for making sure the temperatures were checked, but it was difficult when I had other things to do. For instance, if I were at the register, I could not leave the customers to go back and make sure the batterer was taking the temperatures. At the end of the shift, I would sometimes see a sheet of paper with few or no temperatures noted on it. The store manager would have been upset had he known that I was making up temperatures I did not know to be true, but he would have been even more upset if there had been no temperatures on the sheet at all. He would just make up the numbers himself before he sent them off to the home office, with all the temperatures, of course, below 40 degrees. I have even seen the store manager make up temperatures when he was battering chicken and had forgotten to check the temperatures on the hour.

1. What is the ethical issue in this case? Is it product quality, product safety, or deceptive practices?

2. What responsibilities does the restaurant have to consumers in this situation?

3. As an assistant manager, what should I have done about this situation?

Contributed by Jason Greene

- Sports and recreational activities and equipment
- Home structures and construction materials
- Home furnishings and fixtures
- Housewares
- Home workshop apparatus, tools, and attachments
- Packaging and containers for household products
- Personal use items
- Toys

Whether we are dealing with consumer products, where there is potential for harm as a result of accidents or misuse, or with food products, where not-so-visible threats to human health may exist, the field of product safety is a significant responsibility and a growing challenge for the business community. It seems that no matter how careful business is with respect to these issues, the threat of product liability lawsuits has become an industry unto itself and becomes intimately linked with discussions of product safety. Therefore, we will now turn our attention to this vital topic.

Product Liability

Product liability has become a monumental consumer issue in the United States for several reasons.

Reasons for the Growing Concern About Product Liability. First, product liability has become such a major issue because of the *sheer number of cases* where products have resulted in illness, harm, or death. Second, we have become an *increasingly litigious society.* More and more citizens are responding "I'll sue!" when faced with situations they are unhappy about. Lawsuits of all shapes and sizes have been piling up in the nation's courts. More than 20 million civil and criminal cases are filed each year in state and local courts. Furthermore, many of the lawsuits are for unusual reasons.[16] The overall litigation explosion in the United States has definitely affected the number of product liability suits filed.

Closely paralleling the rise in the number of lawsuits in the United States has been the *growing size of the financial awards* given by the courts. Perhaps the path-breaking award in the product liability category was the $128.5 million awarded in 1978 in the case of a 19-year-old who at age 13 was severely injured. He was riding with a friend in a Ford Pinto that was struck from behind. The Pinto's gas tank ruptured, and the passenger compartment was filled with flames that killed his friend and severely burned him over 90 percent of his body. The badly scarred teenager underwent more than 50 operations. Ford was required by the jury to pay $666,280 to the dead driver's family and to pay the survivor $2.8 million in compensatory damages and $125 million in punitive damages.[17] It has been estimated that each year over $130 billion flows through the liability system from companies to claimants and lawyers. This additional cost to companies represents approximately 30 percent of a stepladder's price, 50 percent of a football helmet, and 95 percent of the price of a childhood vaccine. The problem is largely confined to the United States. In 1995, Dupont had nearly 5,000 personal injury lawsuits inside the United States but fewer than 20 outside the United States. Although half the company's sales come from overseas, 95 percent of the company's legal costs come from the United States.[18]

Since the Pinto case, multimillion-dollar lawsuits have become commonplace. Some major companies have been hit so hard by lawsuits that they have filed for protection under Chapter 11 of the federal bankruptcy law. One example of this is the Johns Manville Corporation, which faced an avalanche of asbestos-related lawsuits that totaled 16,500 suits demanding over $12 billion. Manville sought Chapter 11 protection in 1982.[19] A second example is that of A. H. Robins, which filed for protection in 1985. Robins faced over 5,000 product liability lawsuits in which women charged that its Dalkon Shield, an intrauterine contraceptive device, had injured them.[20] Other companies encountering large lawsuits have included Union Carbide, with its poison gas explosion in Bhopal, India; Dow Chemical, with its Agent Orange defoliant; and Merrill Dow, with its Bendectin morning sickness drug, which allegedly caused birth defects.[21] In discussions aimed at settling the dispute between Union Carbide and the country of India, a figure in excess of $500 million has been most commonly mentioned as the final settlement.

In the 1990s, one of the industries most significantly affected has been the silicone breast implant industry. In July 1998, Dow Chemical, the principal manufacturer of silicone breast implants, reached a tentative agreement to pay a $3.2 billion settlement. The agreement, which at this writing had yet to be finalized, would allow Dow Corning to rise from the Chapter 11 bankruptcy it entered in 1995.[22]

Our final reason for product liability becoming such an issue is the *doctrine of strict liability* and the expansion of this concept in the courts. In many ways, the doctrine of strict liability is behind the issues we have discussed up to this point. In its most general form, the doctrine of strict liability holds that anyone in the chain of distribution of a product is liable for harm caused to the user if the product as sold was unreasonably dangerous because of its defective condition. This applies to anyone involved in the design, manufacture, or sale of a defective product. Beyond manufacturing, courts have ruled against plaintiffs from a broad array of functions, such as selling, advertising, promotion, and distribution. Organizations such as retailers, wholesalers, assemblers, and component-parts suppliers have been found liable for defective products.[23] In other words, there is no legal defense for placing on the market a product that is dangerous to a consumer because of a known or knowable defect.

Extensions of the Strict-Liability Rule.   Courts in several states have established a standard that is much more demanding than strict liability. This concept is called *absolute liability*. The ruling that established this new concept was handed down by the New Jersey Supreme Court in *Beshada v. Johns Manville Corporation* (1982). The plaintiffs in the Beshada case were employees of Johns Manville and other companies who had developed asbestos-related diseases as a result of exposure in the workplace.[24] The court ruled in this case that a manufacturer could be held strictly liable for failure to warn of a product hazard, even if the hazard was *scientifically unknowable* at the time of manufacture and sale. Therefore, a company cannot use as its defense the assurance that it did its best according to the state-of-the-art in the industry at that time. Under this ruling, the manufacturer is liable for damages even if it had no way of knowing that the product might cause a problem later.

The absolute-liability rule frequently involves cases involving chemicals or drugs. For example, a drug producer might put a drug on the market (with government approval) thinking that it is safe based on current knowledge. Under the doctrine of absolute liability, the firm could be held liable for side effects or health problems that develop years, or even decades, later. The result is that a large amount of uncertainty is injected into the production process.[25]

Another extension of strict liability is known as *market share liability*. This concept evolved from *delayed manifestation cases*—situations in which delayed reactions to such products as asbestos, drugs, Agent Orange, and formaldehyde appear years later after consumption of, or exposure to, the product.[26] An example of market share liability is the California case in which a group of women with birth defects claimed that the defects had been caused by the drug DES, which their mothers had taken while pregnant years earlier. The women could not name the company that had made the pills their mothers had taken. But in 1980 the California Supreme Court upheld a ruling that the six drug firms that made DES would be held responsible in proportion to their market shares of DES sales unless they could prove that they had not made the actual doses the women had taken.[27]

Product Tampering and Product Extortion

Two other concerns that have contributed to the product liability discussion are *product tampering* and *product extortion*. Consider the Tylenol cases—first in 1982, when seven Chicago people died from taking tainted Extra Strength Tylenol capsules, and again in 1986, when cyanide-laced bottles of Tylenol were found in New York and one woman died. James Burke, chairman of Johnson & Johnson, characterized the case as "terrorism, pure and simple."[28] In 1991, two people died after taking some Sudafed that had been poisoned. We earlier mentioned the discovery of Chilean grapes that had been poisoned, apparently en route to the United States. Adulterated and poisoned products stretch beyond such national brands as Tylenol, and the targets include more than national drug companies.

Product extortion schemes emerged in the late 1970s and at first received only local publicity. In a typical situation, an adulterated product was sent to the manufacturer along with a note demanding money, in exchange for disclosure of other locations where poisoned or drugged products had been put on retail shelves. A variation of this scheme was the Vlasic pickles case in 1980, when retail stores in Atlanta were told of the location of one adulterated product and warned that they would not be told of other similarly poisoned products if they did not pay. On several occasions in the 1970s, the national press investigated and decided not to publish stories on the growing extortion menace. The Tylenol disaster in 1982 highlighted the problem, however.[29] Product tampering and product extortion have had significant implications for product packaging as well as product liability.

Product Liability Reform

The problems discussed up to this point have combined to generate calls from many groups for *product liability reform*. Experts of all persuasions are attempting to pinpoint blame for the problems we now have and identify the guilty parties. Some experts point to corporations that produce dangerous products. But other reasons are singled out, too: for example, abuses by lawyers, activist liberal judges, overly generous juries, the insurance industry, and the "system" itself. It is a complex issue, and there seems to be blame enough to spread around to everyone.

However, not everyone agrees that reform is needed. On one side are business groups, medical associations, local and state governments, and insurance companies that want to change the system that they claim gives costly and unfair advantage to plaintiffs in liability suits. On the other side are consumer groups and trial lawyers who defend the present system as one that protects the constitutional rights of wrongfully injured parties.[30]

The business community's criticisms of the current system illustrate some of the aspects of the controversy. Currently, we have a patchwork of state laws. Business wants a uniform federal code. Currently, there are no statutory limits on punitive damages in most states. Business argues for no punitive damages unless the plaintiff meets tougher standards of proof. Currently, meeting government standards is no defense in most states. Business thinks it should have an absolute shield against punitive damages for drugs, medical devices, and aircraft that meet government regulations. Currently, victorious plaintiffs in about 30 states can collect full damages from any defendant, even if the company is only partly at fault. Business wants victorious plaintiffs to be able to recover damages to the extent that defendants are liable.[31]

On the other side of the issue are consumer and citizen groups and others who support the current system and say the critics of the product liability laws have exaggerated the problems. These supporters of the current system say that the product liability costs to business are not $100 billion annually but more like $4 billion annually. One writer puts this in perspective by saying that this is less than Americans spend annually on dog food. It is also argued that the proportion of personal injury cases won by plaintiffs dropped from 63 percent in 1989 to 52 percent in 1992 and that product liability premiums dropped 45 percent between 1987 and 1993. Thus, runaway juries are not increasingly siding with consumers. Supporters of the current system also point out that some of the most infamous injuries inflicted on consumers were remedied mainly through lawsuits, not regulatory action. Examples include the Dalkon Shield, a contraceptive device that made thousands of women infertile; the Pinto's exploding gas tank; the damage to workers exposed to asbestos; and many lesser-known cases.[32]

The law governing liability for injury is known as *tort law,* and it has traditionally been left to the courts and to the states. In the past 25 years, product liability law has become a separate branch of tort law according to Dorsey Ellis, dean of the Washington University School of Law. According to Dean Ellis, this separate branch possesses unique characteristics. The most salient feature of product liability is "strict liability," as contrasted with the fault-based liability concept found in other areas of tort law. The "litigation explosion," the "insurance crisis," and the skyrocketing monetary awards from juries have all combined to focus attention on product liability law. Consequently, in the past decade we have seen almost every state legislature consider, and some adopt, tort reforms. In addition, bills have been introduced in Congress to reform product liability laws.[33]

A product liability reform law almost passed in the summer of 1994. At the last minute, lobbyists on both sides of the issue went to work and the proposed tort reform failed.[34] In 1995, it once again was expected that the system would be revised by the Republican-led Congress. Many in the new Congress sensed that the public mood was now behind tort reform. A postelection Gallup Poll in 1994 revealed that 58 percent of the public favored legal reform, whereas 28 percent opposed it.

Although product liability reform has been enacted in a few states, two decades of effort to enact a federal reform bill have been unsuccessful. There are indications now, however, that the time for federal reform may have arrived. Members of Congress and President Clinton have reached agreement on a modest reform bill. The bill caps punitive damages for small firms (fewer than 25 employees and less than $5 million in annual revenues). There is no cap for larger firms, but the bill does strengthen the standards for proving punitive damages are warranted. Plaintiffs must provide clear and convincing evidence, which is more stringent than the current requirement. Companies would be held accountable for only 18 years after the product left the manufacturer's facility, a change from the perpetual liability that is in place now. Although the bill is supported by President Clinton and a bipartisan group, a legislative battle is likely.[35] A vote was originally scheduled for July 1998, but it was postponed. With individual members of Congress adding amendments to the bill, the bill became bogged down in politics.[36]

The debate over product liability law is likely to continue unabated. Business claims the current system is inherently inefficient, raises the costs of litigation, and imposes a hidden tax on consumers because it inhibits innovation and dampens competitiveness. Consumer groups argue that the current system has forced companies to make safer products. Recent studies show that both sides have valid arguments: The laws have spurred some safety improvements, but they have also hampered innovation.[37] It is expected that product liability will remain a vital issue and that as businesses increasingly internalize the notion of product safety, the entire business/consumer relationship will be well served.

We now consider two major government agencies that are dedicated to product safety: the Consumer Product Safety Commission and the Food and Drug Administration.

CONSUMER PRODUCT SAFETY COMMISSION

The Consumer Product Safety Commission (CPSC) is an independent regulatory agency that was created by the Consumer Product Safety Act of 1972. The statutory purposes of the CPSC[38] are as follows:

1. Protect the public against unreasonable risks of injury associated with consumer products.

2. Assist consumers in evaluating the comparative safety of consumer products.

3. Develop uniform safety standards for consumer products and minimize conflicts between state and local regulations.

4. Promote research and investigations into the causes and prevention of product-related deaths, illnesses, and injuries.

The CPSC was created at the zenith of the consumer movement as a result of initiatives taken in the late 1960s. President Lyndon Johnson established a National Commission on Product Safety in 1968, and this commission recommended the creation of a permanent agency. The commission justified its recommendation by its finding that an estimated 20 million Americans were injured annually by consumer products. President Richard Nixon, who took office while the proposed agency was still being debated, supported the agency's creation, but not as an independent agency. Congress gave the agency an unusually high degree of independence and required that it open its proceedings to the public to address the often-heard criticism of regulatory agencies that they become captives of the industries they regulate. Congress's intent was to keep business at arm's length and to involve consumers as primary participants in the agency's decision making.[39]

The CPSC experienced ups and downs as various administrations came into office. The agency grew in the 1970s, became controversial in the late 1970s, and was significantly reduced in power after the 1980 election of Ronald Reagan as president. The Reagan years of the CPSC (1980–1988) were marked by drastic budget cuts, massive staff reductions, and eventual paralysis of the agency. The agency survived several attempts to dismantle it. As one indication of the downturn it took during the Reagan years, its budget steadily declined from $40.6 million in 1980 to $32.6 million in 1988 before experiencing an upturn.[40]

Like most of the regulatory agencies in the post-Reagan environment, the CPSC has been demonstrating renewed activism. For its part, the CPSC claims it protects the public against unreasonable risks of injury associated with consumer products. In 1997, the CPSC negotiated 362 recalls involving more than 76 million individual consumer products that were deemed significant risks to the public. Products that were the subjects of recent investigations and actions include bunk beds, handheld hair dryers, playpens, portable cribs, lawn chairs, attic stairways, lawn darts, and halogen floor lamps. The CPSC also conducted public-information campaigns regarding the safe use of such items as fireworks and residential pools, and it served as a resource center for small-business and individual inquiries. In 1998, the CPSC instituted new bike helmet safety standards, convened a roundtable on mattress and bedding fires, and began a new "fast-track" recall program.[41]

Despite these accomplishments, criticism of the agency has continued unabated. *Consumer's Research Magazine* judged 1997 to be "not a good year" for CPSC. The magazine cited a U.S. Government Accounting Office (GAO) report that derided the commission for poor data-gathering techniques that resulted in sketchy information that makes it difficult for the commission to make informed decisions or to monitor and evaluate results. The magazine also called the CPSC Chairman's Award the "biggest lowlight of 1997." For example, the Playskool 1-2-3 Highchair received the award and was hailed as a "creative safety innovation." Later, the chair was involved in more than 40 child injuries. In another instance cited by the magazine, Lowe's, a chain of home-improvement stores, was granted a CPSC safety award a few months after a Lowe's hot tub had been cited by the Centers for Disease Control as the cause of a deadly outbreak of Legionnaire's disease.[42]

Consumer-group critics of the CPSC think the agency is doing an inadequate job of regulating product safety and that the agency could be doing much better if it had more money and more power. Others have argued that the agency takes on products and companies that represent only a very limited set of hazards or trivial risks. Some economists think that simply providing information to the public about hidden product hazards may be a more useful role for the commission to assume given the difficulty of taking on major product standards with so many technical issues involved.[43]

Whatever its future, the CPSC is certain to continue to play an important role in protecting consumers from unsafe products. The CPSC remains the only clearinghouse available for consumers who have safety concerns with the 15,000 products under its care, and it is the only mechanism available for recalling unsafe products. One year after entering the position, CPSC Chairman Ann Brown received a "Hammer" award from Vice President Al Gore for her initiative in transforming the CPSC hotline.[44] Brown's background as a consumer advocate and her expressed commitment to working with rather than against business to develop voluntary standards have won her supporters from the ranks of both industry and consumer advocacy. However, only time will tell whether her tenure will improve the CPSC's ability to fulfill its consumer-protection mandate.

Figure 10–1 provides examples of the CPSC's development of standards.

FIGURE 10–1   CPSC: Development of Voluntary Standards

Voluntary Safety Standards

Indoor Air Quality Hazards	Children's Product Hazards	Fire/Electrical Hazards	Other Hazards
Carbon Monoxide (CO) Detectors. Includes new alarm requirements based on both CO concentration and exposure time.	Bunk Beds. Includes provisions to prevent the collapse of the mattress and its foundation, as well as provisions to prevent entrapment or strangulation in the bunk bed's structure.	National Electrical Code (1992 edition). Provides added GFCI protection around household sinks, requires GFCI protection for spas and hot tubs, and adds a requirement that heat tapes be safety certified.	Automatic Garage Door Openers (two revisions). Includes cautionary labeling on the risk of entrapment.
Formaldehyde in Particleboard and Formaldehyde in Hardwood and Decorative Plywood (two standards). Specifies allowable formaldehyde emissions.	Drawstrings on Children's Clothing. Four months after CPSC presented evidence of dangers to children, manufacturers voluntarily removed drawstrings from existing children's clothing and promised that new clothing would be manufactured with safer alternatives, such as Velcro and snaps.	Handheld Hair Dryers. Includes requirements for polarized plugs, cautionary labeling on the risk of use near water, and protections from electrocution when immersed, whether the unit is turned on or off.	Above Ground/Onground Swimming Pools. Provides recommended barrier requirements (within an appendix to the standard) to prevent child drownings.

SOURCE: U.S. Consumer Product Safety Commission, www.cpsc.gov.

FOOD AND DRUG ADMINISTRATION

The health and food safety concerns of Americans reached new heights in the late 1980s as a result of two incidents. First, an apparent terrorist injected Chilean grapes with cyanide, and an anonymous phone call in 1989 warned that the grapes were en route to the United States. Food and Drug Administration (FDA) Commissioner James S. Young decided to impose a controversial embargo on all fruit imports from Chile after inspectors discovered two cyanide-tainted grapes. The embargo was suspended after 5 days, but by then consumer worries had already been firmly established.

During the same period as the grape incident, a private Washington, DC, environmental group, the National Resources Defense Council (NRDC), stirred up a massive public outcry with a report on Alar, a crop preservative frequently sprayed on apples. Alar was branded a carcinogen by the Environmental Protection Agency (EPA). The Food and Drug Administration got involved when Commissioner Young joined with other top government officials to assure the public that U.S.-grown apples were safe to eat. By then, public outcry over Alar forced its maker to withdraw it from the market, and the EPA banned it.[45]

As a result of the two tainted grapes and the Alar threat triggering a panic about what we eat, along with a slowly growing public concern about food and drug safety, it is not surprising that *Newsweek* and *Time* solidified public concern with their March 27, 1989, cover stories: "How Safe Is Your Food?" and "Is Anything Safe?"[46] It is against this backdrop that we describe briefly the Food and Drug Administration, an agency that has become much more high profile and controversial in the past 5 to 10 years.

The FDA grew out of experiments with food safety by one man—Harvey W. Wiley—chief chemist for the Agricultural Department in the late 1800s. Wiley's most famous experiments involved feeding small doses of poisons to human volunteers. The substances fed to the volunteers were similar to those found in food preservatives at the time. The volunteers became known as the "Poison Squad," and their publicity generated a public awareness of the dangers of eating adulterated foods. The Food and Drug Act of 1906 was a direct result of the publicity created by Wiley's experiments. The act was administered by Wiley's Bureau of Chemistry until 1931, when the name "Food and Drug Administration" first was used. The Food and Drug Act called for the protection of the public from potential health hazards presented by adulterated or mislabeled foods, drugs, cosmetics, and medical devices. Later laws for which the FDA became responsible included the Food, Drug, and Cosmetic Act of 1938; the Public Health Service Act of 1944; the 1968 Radiation Control for Health & Safety Act; the Fair Packaging and Labeling Act of 1966; and the 1984 Drug Price Competition and Patent Restoration Act. In response to these and other major laws, the FDA regulates foods, drugs, cosmetics, and medical devices found in interstate commerce.[47] Figure 10–2 summarizes some of the major responsibilities of the FDA.

The powers of the FDA were expanded as a result of other laws and amendments. The 1958 *Delaney Amendment* to the Food, Drug, and Cosmetic Act was especially notable. The Delaney Amendment requires the FDA to ban any food or color additive that has been shown to cause cancer in laboratory test animals. In 1962, amendments were passed to require drug manufacturers to prove the effectiveness as well as the safety of their products before marketing them. In addition, the FDA was authorized to order the withdrawal of dangerous products from the market. In 1976, Congress passed legislation requiring the regulation of complex medical products and diagnostic devices.

The FDA is composed of a commissioner and seven associate commissioners and resides within the Health and Human Services Department. The FDA engages in three broad categories of activity: analysis, surveillance, and correction. Under President Reagan throughout most of the 1980s, the themes emphasized were the cutting of bureaucratic delays and red tape, the speeding up of agency decisions, and the elimination of unnecessary regulation. A major blow to the agency occurred during the 1980s, when it was disclosed that four FDA employees were accused of taking cash payoffs and illegal gifts from a major generic drug company in return for favored treatment. Major challenges the FDA faced early in the Bush administration included the AIDS epidemic, regulation of medical devices, food safety, fat substitutes, nutritional labeling, and over-the-counter drug review.[48] Today, the average consumer encounters the FDA through the new nutritional food labels that were created and are now required on food products. The new labels, as depicted in Figure 10–3, were the result of the FDA's implementation of the Nutrition Labeling and Education Act of 1990.[49]

FIGURE 10-2   Major Responsibilities of the Food and Drug Administration

- Regulates the composition, quality, safety, and labeling of foods, food additives, food colors, and cosmetics and carries out research in these areas

- Monitors and enforces regulations through the inspection of food and cosmetic producers' facilities, surveillance of advertising and media reports, and researching of consumer complaints

- Regulates the composition, quality, safety, efficacy, and labeling of all drugs for human use and establishes, in part through research, scientific standards for this purpose

- Requires premarket testing of new drugs and evaluates new drug applications and requests to approve drugs for experimental use

- Develops standards for the safety and effectiveness of over-the-counter drugs

- Develops guidelines on good drug manufacturing practices and makes periodic inspections of drug manufacturing facilities in the United States and overseas

- Monitors the quality of marketed drugs through product testing, surveillance, and compliance and adverse reaction reporting programs

- Conducts recalls or seizure actions of products found to violate federal laws and pose hazards to human health

- Conducts research and establishes scientific standards for the development, manufacture, testing, and use of biological products

- Inspects and licenses manufacturers of biological products

- Requires premarket testing of new biological products and evaluates the claims for new drugs that are biologics

- Tests biological products, often on a lot-by-lot basis

- Collects data on medical device experience and sets standards for medical devices

- Regulates the safety, efficacy, and labeling of medical devices and requires premarket testing of medical devices categorized as potentially hazardous

SOURCE: Food and Drug Administration, 1995.

In 1991, under a new commissioner, David Kessler, the FDA embarked on an aggressive crackdown on deceptive product labels, which created a fair amount of controversy. In early 1991, the FDA targeted two highly visible products and companies to make its point. It seized Procter and Gamble's Citrus Hill "Fresh Choice" orange juice and, a few days later, Ragu "Fresh Italian" pasta sauce, the nation's leading tomato sauce brand. In both cases, the FDA forced the companies to remove the term "fresh" from their products because they thought the companies were inaccurately applying that term to their products.

The point of the FDA was clear. It was no longer going to pursue the practice, which had become commonplace throughout the 1980s, of companies suspected of violations stretching out negotiations with the agency for years while engaging in an endless back-and-forth exchange of proposals and counterproposals. The FDA was reasserting itself as an agency that was planning to take swift action against violators. In addition to the two cases cited, the FDA sent warning letters to the manufacturers of Listerine, Plax, and Viadent mouthwash brands; Weight Watchers and Kraft brands cholesterol-free mayonnaise; and Fleischmann's reduced-calorie margarine,

FIGURE 10–3   The New FDA Food label

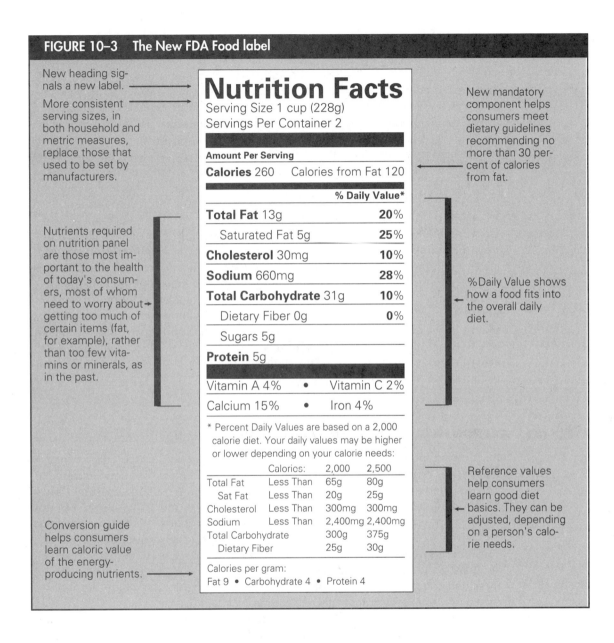

New heading signals a new label. ⟶

More consistent serving sizes, in both household and metric measures, replace those that used to be set by manufacturers.

Nutrients required on nutrition panel are those most important to the health of today's consumers, most of whom need to worry about → getting too much of certain items (fat, for example), rather than too few vitamins or minerals, as in the past.

Conversion guide helps consumers learn caloric value of the energy-producing nutrients. ⟶

New mandatory component helps consumers meet dietary guidelines recommending no more than 30 percent of calories from fat.

%Daily Value shows how a food fits into the overall daily diet.

Reference values help consumers learn good diet basics. They can be adjusted, depending on a person's calorie needs.

Nutrition Facts
Serving Size 1 cup (228g)
Servings Per Container 2

Amount Per Serving

Calories 260   Calories from Fat 120

% Daily Value*

Total Fat 13g	**20**%
Saturated Fat 5g	**25**%
Cholesterol 30mg	**10**%
Sodium 660mg	**28**%
Total Carbohydrate 31g	**10**%
Dietary Fiber 0g	**0**%
Sugars 5g	
Protein 5g	

Vitamin A 4%   •   Vitamin C 2%

Calcium 15%   •   Iron 4%

* Percent Daily Values are based on a 2,000 calorie diet. Your daily values may be higher or lower depending on your calorie needs:

		Calories:	2,000	2,500
Total Fat	Less Than		65g	80g
Sat Fat	Less Than		20g	25g
Cholesterol	Less Than		300mg	300mg
Sodium	Less Than		2,400mg	2,400mg
Total Carbohydrate			300g	375g
Dietary Fiber			25g	30g

Calories per gram:
Fat 9 • Carbohydrate 4 • Protein 4

among other products. The agency thought that these manufacturers had made claims that misrepresented the features of their products.[50]

There is perhaps no other regulatory body that has become more controversial in recent years than the FDA. Under David Kessler's leadership, the FDA has aggressively and zealously pursued companies it felt were out of compliance with government regulations or were taking advantage of consumers. Supporters of the FDA have applauded it for relentlessly pursuing violators. In 1997, Dr. Kessler resigned and Dr. Michael Friedman was appointed as the interim commissioner. Dr. Jane Henney, vice president of research for the University of New Mexico, has been proposed as his successor.[51] Analysts expect Congress's interrogation of Henney to be far more rigorous than that experienced by Kessler because of the kind of controversy Kessler subsequently attracted. Having served under both Bush and Clinton, Henney enjoys bipartisan credentials. However, her tenure as deputy to Dr. Kessler is likely to raise red flags for Senate Republicans who found Kessler overly quick to regulate and overly slow to approve treatments and devices. A further source of controversy will be the abortion pill, which the FDA will soon be asked to approve.[52]

The new commissioner will inherit a host of challenges at the FDA. One of the first responsibilities will be to put into effect legislation Congress adopted in 1997 to speed the review of new medicines. Another challenge will be to balance the demands of a Congress that is pushing for the FDA to streamline its operations and an administration that is proposing expanded activities in food safety and tobacco. On July 4, 1998, President Clinton announced a sweeping array of food-safety initiatives, including an Institute of Food Research, labeling requirements for fresh juices, and food-safety legislation that would expand the authority of the FDA over imported foods. These initiatives will add to the new commissioner's challenges.

In summary, the FDA continues to be a controversial agency. Journalist Herbert Burkholz, author of *The FDA Follies,* captured the situation well: Industry grouses that the FDA overregulates. Consumers complain that it underprotects. Victims of unsafe drugs and medical devices howl that it approves products willy-nilly. AIDS activists agonize over its testing procedures. It is little wonder that the FDA has become a target for bashing.[53]

BUSINESS'S RESPONSE TO CONSUMER STAKEHOLDERS

Business's response to consumerism and consumer stakeholders has varied over the years. It has ranged from poorly conceived public relations ploys at one extreme to well-designed and implemented departments of consumer affairs, consumer satisfaction measurement, and total quality programs at the other. The history of business's response to consumers parallels its perceptions of the seriousness, pervasiveness, effectiveness, and longevity of the consumer movement. When the consumer movement first began, business's response was casual, perhaps symbolic, and hardly effective. An early study of the communication systems between management and consumers, for example, showed that although such communication did exist, it was not used for managerial decision-making purposes.[54]

Today the consumer movement has matured, and formal interactions with consumer stakeholders have become more and more institutionalized. Business has realized that consumers today are more persistent than in the past, more assertive, and more likely to use or exhaust all appeal channels before being satisfied. Armed with considerable power, consumer activists have been a major stimulus to more sincere responses on behalf of business. These responses have included the creation of toll-free hot lines and consumer service representatives, the integration of consumer input into marketing decisions, the designation of specific consumer affairs officers, extensive efforts to monitor and measure consumer satisfaction, and the creation of specific company departments to handle consumer affairs.

Early attempts to be responsive to consumer stakeholders involved the creation of organizational units such as *consumer affairs offices* and *product safety offices.* Today, these kinds of responses have become an institutionalized part of business's response to consumers. More recently, *total quality management* programs and sophisticated attempts at *consumer satisfaction measurement* have become the strategic responses. These four kinds of responses merit brief consideration.

Consumer Affairs Offices

There are various ways of organizing the corporate response to consumers. A company might appoint a consumer affairs officer or create a consumer affairs task force or committee, but a more sophisticated way is to establish a *consumer affairs office* or department. To be sure, the establishment of such a formalized unit is not a substitute for a consumer-stakeholder focus on the part of all members of the organization. But it does provide a hub around which a dedicated consumer-stakeholder thrust might be built.

Basic Mission

The basic mission of a consumer affairs office is to heighten management responsiveness to consumer stakeholders. In accomplishing this mission, consumer affairs professionals have to execute two key roles: one is the role of consumer advocate in the company, and the other is the role of consumer specialist making managerial recommendations about corporate practices that mesh well with the needs of both consumers and the company. Some companies take one or the other of these two postures, whereas other companies use both approaches and/or additional approaches. There are potential conflicts between the two roles, but they need not create conflicts if consumer affairs professionals and management have a sympathetic understanding of each other's goals.[55]

Essential Functions

Mary Gardner Jones, former vice president for consumer affairs at Western Union Telegraph and former federal trade commissioner, has suggested that there are four essential functions of an effective consumer affairs office:[56]

- *Establish a comprehensive, complete, and accurate database* that assesses the levels of consumer satisfaction and dissatisfaction with the company's products and services in all important areas involving consumers, such as billing and collection practices, repair services, guarantee policy and practice, handling of complaints, quality of products and services, and pricing.

- *Audit the company's programs* to determine how adequate they are in responding to consumer complaints and interests. Use company records, special task forces, outside consultants, and consumer groups.

- *Recommend specific consumer programs, policies, and practices* in all areas where needed.

- *Establish programs to ensure effective communication* between the company and consumers to build public confidence and understanding of company policy and practice.

Jones goes on to argue that there are four principal factors that determine the success or failure of consumer affairs offices.[57] These factors, which are essential if the office is to be able to accomplish its two central objectives of raising consumer satisfaction and improving long-term company profitability, are as follows:

- The office should be located close to that of the chief executive of the company.

- The office should have access to all relevant information in the company about consumers and must be given authority to create effective mechanisms to get it.

- Information about consumers should be quantified to the extent feasible. This is necessary to make intelligent decisions/trade-offs.

- These managers should be skilled in designing effective performance measurement tools with which to evaluate what people throughout the company are doing. (Cliché: People will do what is inspected, not expected.)

In general, the appropriate response of a company to consumer stakeholders is to ensure an understanding of the consumer movement throughout the organization, especially at top management levels, where it is easy for executives to get isolated from company activities.

Product Safety Offices

Obviously, a consumer affairs office could be divided into units, one of which might focus on product safety. In a growing number of firms, however, *product safety offices* are being established independently. This is quite logical, given what we documented earlier as the product safety and product liability problems.

Three particular factors contribute to the need for greater organization in handling the product safety issue. First, there is the *complexity of most current products.* Products today may be made of exotic materials and incorporate complex and sensitive control devices. They are often built up from subsystems that themselves are quite complex—for example, the modern automobile. Second, there is the *subtlety of the hazards that can be generated during product use.* People often use products in novel and strange ways, not for their intended purposes. Complexity contributes to an impatience with reading the instructions, and this can lead to additional hazards, too. Third, there are *coordination problems in large, multidivision manufacturing organizations* that inhibit communications among departments, and structures are frequently set up wherein top management is insulated from safety problems. The net effect of these three factors working together is to create a need for some sort of product safety organization.[58]

Levels at Which to Locate Product Safety Offices

The most important locations for product safety offices in organizations, according to a study by George Eads and Peter Reuter, are the divisional level and the corporate level. The division responsible for the product is a logical location, because the interactions among processes such as manufacturing, quality control, and packaging can best be monitored at this level. The division is also likely to know the most about the product's basic technology and conditions for use. Finally, the division's financial performance might be directly linked to the product's success, and, therefore, the division has the strongest incentive to ensure the product's safety.

Whereas a product safety office at the divisional level would have the greatest operational responsibility, one at the corporate level could also be critical. At the corporate level, the product safety officer would most likely serve in a liaison role with the divisions. Activities that the product safety officer might perform include supervision of safety education and training, auditing of corporate design and safety policies, transmitting and reinforcing top management's commitment to safety, and acting as a court of appeals when safety issues arise. A corporate-level product safety officer has greater organizational access to key decision makers, and this is an important factor, also.[59]

Other Functions of a Product Safety Office

Other important functions of a product safety office include the following:

- Setting the tone for the firm's product safety effort
- Structuring and helping to enforce financial and nonfinancial rewards and penalties
- Developing links to other safety- and quality-related activities in the firm
- Helping with product safety litigation
- Helping with regulatory liaison[60]
- Setting up product safety committees
- Performing periodic safety audits and tests
- Designing a contingency plan for product recalls[61]

Of all the product issues management faces, product safety has become one of the most important. Some companies produce high-hazard products and might need to incorporate all the ideas we have discussed, plus more. Other companies produce products in which the hazards are much lower. In any event, the product safety issue has become a "front burner" consumer issue, and there is no sign of it abating. Because human health and safety are involved, product safety is justified as a central concern on its own merit. Trends in litigation, jury awards, and insurance premiums offer other practical reasons why the consumer stakeholder must be carefully considered when management is planning its responsiveness efforts with the groups with which it interacts.

Total Quality Management Programs

In the late 1980s and the 1990s, companies have adopted total quality management (TQM) programs at an accelerating rate. Undoubtedly, this has been a response to the rapidly escalating global competitiveness and the continuous allegations that U.S. products cannot compete in world markets. In its essence, TQM represents a paradigm shift away from the mode of thought that heretofore characterized American business.[62]

Total quality management has many different characteristics, but it essentially means that all of the functions of the business are blended into a holistic, integrated philosophy built around the concepts of quality, teamwork,

SEARCH THE WEB

The American Society for Quality (ASQ) has a Web site (**www.asq.org**) with an array of information on such quality topics as standards and certification, process improvements, teamwork, and certification. Web site visitors can track trends in the American Customer Satisfaction Index, an economic indicator that measures customer satisfaction with goods and services purchased in the United States.

FIGURE 10-4   Principles, Practices, and Techniques of Total Quality Management

	Customer Focus	Continuous Improvement	Teamwork
Principles	• Paramount importance of customers • Providing products and services that fulfill customer needs; requires organizationwide focus on customers	• Consistent customer satisfaction can be attained only through relentless improvement of processes that create products and services	• Customer focus and continuous improvement are best achieved by collaboration throughout an organization as well as with customers and suppliers
Practices	• Direct customer contact • Collecting information about customer needs • Using information to design and deliver products and services	• Process analysis • Reengineering • Problem solving • Plan/do/check/act	• Search for arrangements that benefit all units involved in a process • Formation of various types of teams • Group skills training
Techniques	• Customer surveys and focus groups • Quality function deployment (translates customer information into product specifications)	• Flowcharts • Pareto analysis • Statistical process control • Fishbone diagrams	• Organizational development methods, such as the nominal group technique • Team-building methods (e.g., role clarification and group feedback)

SOURCE: James W. Dean, Jr., and David E. Bowen, "Management Theory and Total Quality: Improving Research and Practice Through Theory Development," *Academy of Management Review* (Vol. 19, No. 3, July, 1994), 395.

productivity, and customer understanding and satisfaction.[63] Figure 10–4 depicts one useful view of the principles, practices, and techniques of TQM. It should be noted that the customer, or consumer stakeholder, is the focus of the process.

A vital assumption and premise of TQM is that the customer is the final judge of quality. Therefore, the first part of the TQM process is to define quality in terms of customer expectations and requirements. Figure 10–5 presents several different popular definitions of quality and their strengths and weaknesses.

Customer expectations and requirements are then converted to standards and specifications. Finally, the entire organization is realigned to ensure that both conformance quality (adherence to standards and specifications) and perceived quality (meeting or exceeding customer expectations) are achieved.[64] It is clear in TQM that "delighted customers" is the overarching goal of management's efforts.[65]

A significant impetus for improved quality at the national level began in 1987, when the Malcolm Baldridge National Quality Improvement Act was passed by President Reagan. This act created the Malcolm Baldridge Award, which has come to be regarded as a badge of honor among the manufacturing, service, and small businesses that have won it. Key selection criteria for the Baldridge Award include quality and operational results and customer focus and satisfaction.[66] Winners of Baldridge Awards have included Federal Express, Xerox, and the Ritz-Carlton Hotel Company.

FIGURE 10–5   Strengths and Weaknesses of Quality Definitions

Definition	Strengths	Weaknesses
Excellence	• Strong marketing and human resource benefits • Universally recognizable—mark of uncompromising standards and high achievement	• Provides little practical guidance to practitioners • Measurement difficulties • Attributes of excellence may change dramatically and rapidly • Sufficient number of customers must be willing to pay for excellence
Value	• Concept of value incorporates multiple attributes • Focuses attention on a firm's internal efficiency and external effectiveness • Allows for comparisons across disparate objects and experiences	• Difficulty extracting individual components of value judgment • Questionable inclusiveness • Quality and value are different constructs
Conformance to Specifications	• Facilitates precise measurement • Leads to increased efficiency • Necessary for global strategy • Should force disaggregation of consumer needs • Most parsimonious and appropriate definition for some customers	• Consumers do not know or care about internal specifications • Inappropriate for services • Potentially reduces organizational adaptability • Specifications may quickly become obsolete in rapidly changing markets • Internally focused
Meeting and/or Exceeding Expectations	• Evaluates from customer's perspective • Applicable across industries • Responsive to market changes • All-encompassing definition	• Most complex definition • Difficult to measure • Customers may not know expectations • Idiosyncratic reactions • Prepurchase attitudes affect subsequent judgments • Short-term and long-term evaluations may differ • Confusion between customer service and customer satisfaction

SOURCE: Carol. A. Reeves and David A. Bednar, "Defining Quality: Alternatives and Implications," *Academy of Management Review* (Vol. 19, No. 3, July, 1994), 437.

Customer Satisfaction Measurement

One vital component of many quality programs is customer satisfaction measurement (CSM). Lawrence Crosby, an expert in this area, has argued: "Clearly, there is a potentially large role for customer satisfaction measurement in facilitating the TQM process.[67] Figure 10–6 depicts in a rather general way the relationships between product and service quality and consumer satisfaction and its outcomes.

FIGURE 10-6 A Consumer-Stakeholder Satisfaction Model

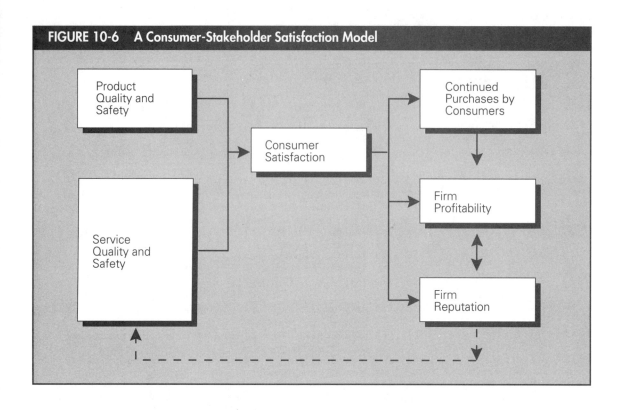

ETHICS IN PRACTICE

Should a Company Stop This Deviant Consumer Behavior?

During my senior year, I was working for a major retail store. What struck me the most about this experience was how easily customers could bring back used merchandise and get refunds. A good example might be "Super Bowl Fever." People came to the store and bought the largest TV sets just to watch the Super Bowl on the weekend. Then, they returned and requested full refunds for the TV sets on the following Monday morning. Furthermore, I was amazed by the fact that some customers asked the store for full refunds without receipts, and the merchandise not only was used but in some cases had been used for several months. However, on many occasions the customers got their money back right away, or checks would be sent to them if they didn't have their receipts with them.

1. What exactly do businesses owe consumers? Is this not an example of taking consumer satisfaction to ridiculous lengths?

2. Is this an ethical practice on the part of consumers? Does a company "owe" customers this degree of satisfaction?

3. What actions, if any, should such a retail store take to control this practice?

Anonymously contributed

Crosby observes that the growth and popularity of CSM has spread as TQM has spread. Today, it is a global movement. In Western Europe, quality award programs similar to the U.S. Baldridge Award have begun. Practically all of these award programs place a heavy emphasis on customer satisfaction measurement. In addition, CSM is making inroads in Japan, Australia, and Southeast Asia.[68]

All of the initiatives we have discussed—consumer affairs offices, product safety offices, TQM, and CSM—have one major theme in common: They all are symptoms of the growing belief on the part of business that the interests of the consumer stakeholder are supreme. These initiatives have multiple objectives: to make money for the companies involved and to bring customers back; to obey the letter and spirit of consumer-related laws and regulations; and, finally, to treat these vital stakeholders fairly and ethically. It is little wonder that the concept of "relationship marketing" developed when it became apparent to business executives that a relationship rather than an ad hoc acquaintance is what is needed for the mutual satisfaction of all parties.

SUMMARY

In the 1990s, consumer stakeholders have become obsessed with product quality and safety. On the quality front, U.S. firms have declined from a position of world leadership to one of competing to survive with other world producers. The situation has been no different with services. Although we are now a service-dominated economy, consumer dissatisfaction with service quality has continued. One major challenge has been to identify and understand all the different dimensions of the quality issue. Today, quality may mean performance, features, reliability, conformance, durability, serviceability, aesthetics, perceived quality, or some combination of these dimensions.

An extremely important legal and ethical issue has been the consumer's right to safety. Product safety has become one of the most crucial consumer issues for firms. The product liability crisis has been an outgrowth of business's lack of attention to this issue. Other factors contributing to the product liability crisis have been the sheer number of harmful-product cases, our increasingly litigious society, the growing size of financial awards given by the courts, and rising insurance rates. A major consequence of these phenomena has been cries for tort reform. Product tampering and product extortion have also become safety-related issues. In recent years, the health and safety issues related to foods, drugs, and medical devices have propelled the Consumer Product Safety Commission and the Food and Drug Administration into prominent roles.

Major responses to consumer-stakeholder issues have been the creation of consumer affairs offices, product safety offices, total quality management programs, and consumer satisfaction measurement. Although these institutional responses have not solved all the problems, they have the potential for addressing the problems in a significant way if they are properly formulated and implemented. In addition to these specific responses, a consumer focus and orientation needs to permeate management decision making if consumer affairs are to be handled effectively. In today's business environment, consumers have many choices. Consequently, companies have no alternative but to internalize the consumer focus if they are to succeed.

KEY TERMS

absolute liability (page 315)

doctrine of strict liability (page 315)

product liability reform (page 316)

delayed manifestation cases (page 315)

market share liability (page 315)

DISCUSSION QUESTIONS

1. Identify the eight dimensions of quality. Give an example of a product or service in which each of these characteristics is important.
2. Identify the principal reasons why we have a product liability crisis. Have any reasons been omitted? Discuss.
3. Differentiate the doctrine of strict liability from the doctrine of absolute liability. What implications do these views have for the business community and for future products and services that might be offered?
4. What type of company would most need a product safety office? Explain.
5. Given the current business and consumer climate, what do you anticipate the future to be for the CPSC and the FDA? What role does politics play in your answer?

ENDNOTES

1. Janice Castro, "Making It Better," *Time* (November 13, 1989), 78–80. Also see "Quality: How to Make It Pay," *Business Week* (August 8, 1994), 54ff.
2. Walker Research, "Reputation and Social Performance Assessment Study" (Indianapolis: Walker Research, August, 1994), 17.
3. Castro, 80.
4. Jay Schmiedeskamp, "Most Americans Optimistic That Product Quality Will Be Improved," *The Gallup Poll Monthly* (November, 1990), 32–33.
5. Castro, 78–79.
6. Ronald B. Lieber, "Now Are You Satisfied? The 1998 Customer Satisfaction Index" (February 16, 1998), 161–164.
7. Ronald Henkoff, "Service Is Everybody's Business," *Fortune* (June 27, 1994), 48–60.
8. "Customers Turned Off by Poor Service Levels," *Marketing Week* (March 5, 1998), 11.
9. Daniel Pearl, "More Firms Pledge Guaranteed Service," *The Wall Street Journal* (July 17, 1991), B1.
10. Stephen Koepp, "Pul-eese! Will Somebody Help Me?" *Time* (February, 1987), 50.
11. David A. Garvin, "Competing on the Eight Dimensions of Quality," *Harvard Business Review* (November–December, 1987), 101–109.
12. Yair Aharoni, *The No Risk Society* (Chatham, NJ: Chatham House Publishers, 1981), 62–63.
13. Lester B. Lave, *How Safe Is Safe Enough? Setting Safety Goals* (St. Louis: Center for the Study of American Business, Washington University, January, 1990), 1.

14. "United States: No Beef with Oprah," *The Economist* (March 7, 1998), 29.

15. E. Patrick McGuire, "Product Liability: Evolution and Reform" (New York: The Conference Board, 1989), 6.

16. Ted Gest, "Order in the Court—And Weirdness, Too," *U.S. News & World Report* (March 2, 1987), 24.

17. "Ford's $128.5 Million Headache," *Time* (February 10, 1978), 65.

18. Earnest W. Deavenport, Jr., "Profound Opportunities: Profound Threats," *Vital Speeches of the Day* (May 1, 1997), 428–430.

19. Andrew Hacker, "The Asbestos Nightmare," *Fortune* (January 20, 1986), 121.

20. Francine Schwadel, "Robins and Plaintiffs Face Uncertain Future," *The Wall Street Journal* (August 23, 1985), 4.

21. Clemens P. Work, "Why It Isn't Easy to Settle Huge Claims," *U.S. News & World Report* (April 7, 1986), 52.

22. David J. Morrow, "Implant Maker Reaches Accord on Damage Suits," *New York Times* (July 9, 1998), A1.

23. Fred W. Morgan and Karl A. Boedecker, "A Historical View of Strict Liability for Product-Related Injuries," *Journal of Macromarketing* (Spring, 1996), 103–117.

24. Terry Morehead Dworkin and Mary Jane Sheffet, "Product Liability in the 1980s," *Journal of Public Policy and Marketing* (1985), 71.

25. Roger Leroy Miller, "Drawing Limits on Liability," *The Wall Street Journal* (April 4, 1984), 28.

26. Dworkin and Sheffet, 69.

27. Clemens P. Work, "Product Safety: A New Hot Potato for Congress," *U.S. News & World Report* (June 14, 1982), 62.

28. "Tampering with Buyers' Confidence," *U.S. News & World Report* (March 3, 1986), 46.

29. Priscilla S. Meyer and Jay Gissen, "The Poison Problem," *Forbes* (December 20, 1982), 34.

30. Peter Waldman and Eileen White, "Battle Rages Over Damages, Insurance Rates: States Are Debating Sweeping Changes in Tort Laws," *The Wall Street Journal* (April 15, 1986), 5. Also see R.J. Samuelson, "Lawyer Heaven," *The Washington Post National Weekly Edition* (June 27–July 3, 1994), 28.

31. Michele Galen, "The Class Action Against Product Liability Laws," *Business Week* (July 29, 1997), 74.

32. Richard D. Haley, "Don't Let the Rogues Off the Hook," *ENR* (May 4, 1998), 89; Robert Kuttner, "How Tort Reform Will Hurt Consumers," San Diego Union Tribune (June 24, 1994), B7. Also see Jerry Phillips, "Attacks on the Legal System: Fallacy of Tort Reform Arguments," Trial (February, 1992), 106–110.

33. Dorsey D. Ellis, Jr., "Introduction," in Kenneth Chilton (ed.), *Product Liability Reform: Debating the Issues* (St. Louis: Center for the Study of American Business, Washington University, April, 1990), 1.

34. Catherine Yang, "Product Liability: Snatching Defeat from the Jaws of Victory," *Business Week* (August 1, 1994), 76–77.

35. Rory FitzPatrick, "Product Liability: Product Liability Reform Set for 1998," *International Commercial Litigation* (March, 1998), 39–40.

36. Neil A. Lewis, "Lott Tries to Avert Amendments to Bill; Then He Adds One," *New York Times* (July 9, 1998), A1.

37. "The Defects in Product-Liability Laws," *Business Week* (July 29, 1991), 88.
38. "Consumer Product Safety Commission," *Federal Regulatory Directory*, 6th ed. (Washington, DC: Congressional Quarterly, 1990), 46. Information about the Consumer Product Safety Commission is available at the Web site *www.cpsc.gov.*
39. *Ibid.*, 46–47.
40. *Ibid.*, 48–54.
41. Consumer Product Safety Commission Overview, *www.cpsc.gov.*
42. Rich Zipperer, "'97 Not a Good Year at CPSC," *Consumer's Research Magazine* (December, 1997), 34–35.
43. Carolyn Lochhead, "A Risky Walk on the Safe Side," Insight (December 18, 1989), 8–17.
44. Chairman Brown's biography is available at *www.cpsc.gov.*
45. "Food and Drug Administration," *Federal Regulatory Directory* (Washington, DC: Congressional Quarterly, 1990), 297.
46. "How Safe Is Your Food? A Newsweek Guide," *Newsweek* (March 27, 1989); and "Is Anything Safe?" *Time* (March 27, 1989).
47. *Federal Regulatory Directory*, 290–292.
48. *Ibid.*, 292.
49. "The New Food Label," *FDA Backgrounder* (April, 1994), 1.
50. Malcolm Gladwell, "A Fresh Approach at the FDA," *The Washington Post Weekly Edition* (May 13–19, 1991), 32.
51. "Woman in the News: Jean Ellen Henney: For FDA an Old Hand," *New York Times* (June 24, 1998), A16.
52. Richard S. Dunham, "New Trials at the FDA," *Business Week* (June 1, 1998), 50.
53. Herbert Burkholz, *The FDA Follies* (New York: Basic Books, 1994), as reviewed by Andrew E. Serwer, "SOS for the FDA," *Fortune* (April 14, 1994), 142.
54. D. Cohen (ed.), *Communication Systems Between Management and the Consumer in Selected Industries* (Hofstra University Yearbook of Business, 1969).
55. Mary Gardner Jones, "The Consumer Affairs Office: Essential Element in Corporate Policy and Planning," *California Management Review* (Summer, 1978), 63.
56. *Ibid.*, 64–69.
57. *Ibid.*, 70–72.
58. George Eads and Peter Reuter, "Designing Safer Products: Corporate Response to Product Liability Law and Regulation," *Journal of Products Liability* (Vol. 7, 1984), 265–267.
59. *Ibid.*, 268–271.
60. *Ibid.*, 285–289.
61. Rajan Chandran and Robert Linneman, "Planning to Minimize Product Liability," *Sloan Management Review* (Fall, 1978), 36.
62. E.C. Hughes, *Total Quality: An Executive's Guide for the 1990s* (Homewood, IL: Dow-Jones-Irwin, 1990). See also Colin G. Armistead and Graham Clark, *Outstanding Customer Service* (Homewood, IL: Richard D. Irwin, Inc., 1994).
63. K. Ishikawa, *What Is Total Quality Control?* (Milwaukee, WI: Quality Press, 1985).
64. Lawrence A. Crosby, "Measuring Customer Satisfaction," in E.E. Scheuing and W.F. Christopher (eds.), *The Service Quality Handbook* (New York, AMACOM, 1993), 392.

65. A. Blanton Godfrey and E.G. Kammerer, "Service Quality vs. Manufacturing Quality: Five Myths Exploded," in *The Service Quality Handbook,* ibid., 5.

66. David A. Garvin, "How the Baldridge Award Really Works," *Harvard Business Review* (November–December, 1991), 80–96.

67. Lawrence A. Crosby, "Integrating Customer Satisfaction Measurement (CSM) with Total Quality Management (TQM)," Managing Service Quality (Vol. 1, No. 3, March, 1991), 137–140.

68. *Ibid.,* 404. Also see Roland T. Rust and Richard L. Oliver, *Service Quality: New Directions in Theory and Practice* (Thousand Oaks, CA: Sage Publications, Inc., 1994).

11

The Natural Environment as Stakeholder: Issues and Challenges

---

CHAPTER OBJECTIVES

After studying this chapter, you should be able to:

1 Identify what comprises the natural environment.

2 Discuss why natural environment issues are complex.

3 Describe eight major natural environment issues.

4 Recognize the causes of environmental problems.

5 Characterize two differing perspectives on these issues.

The ecological perspective begins with a view of the whole, an understanding of how the various parts of nature interact in patterns that tend toward balance and persist over time. But this perspective cannot treat the earth as something separate from human civilization; we are part of the whole too, and looking at it means ultimately also looking at ourselves.[1]

—Vice President Al Gore

There is something fundamentally wrong in treating the Earth as if it were a business in liquidation.[2]

—Herman Daly, Economist

A BRIEF INTRODUCTION TO THE NATURAL ENVIRONMENT

Similar to other broad terms, "environment" means many things to many people—trees in the backyard, a family's favorite vacation spot, a mare and her colt in a pasture, a trout stream in the mountains, earth and the other planets and space objects in our solar system. This and the following chapter focus on the natural environment—specifically, what it is, why it is important, how it has become a major concern, and what businesses and other organizations have done both to and for it. This chapter identifies what we mean when we use the term "environment" and why it has become one of the most significant societal issues of our time. The next chapter describes the variety of responses human organizations, including businesses, have developed to address this issue. Throughout both chapters, we will emphasize

This chapter was contributed by Professor Mark Starik of George Washington University.

two themes: that humans are a part of their natural environment and that the environment itself, as well as the issues and human responses related to it, are extremely complex, defying simple analyses.

To assist you in making business environmental decisions in the future, we will present facts and figures, some of which will be technical and scientific, related to environmental issues and responses. These facts and figures are included to help you understand the complexities involved in the business and public environmental issues of today. Ten years ago, for instance, most students and business executives had never heard of the words "chlorofluorocarbon" or "entropy." Yet today, because of the influence of business, government, and environmental interest groups and individuals, these and many other technical terms and concepts are discussed in the media and, increasingly, in business and society texts. Environmental literacy, whether for wise business, government, or individual decision making, requires, at minimum, some rudimentary knowledge. Without at least some basic technical information, would-be stakeholder managers abdicate their responsibility to make prudent choices potentially crucial to the survival of their organizations, as well as to the survival of humans and other species in the natural environment.

We present this technical information not only to support the claims and conclusions we make throughout these chapters, but also to increase your GPA—that is, your *Green Point Average*. A mid-1997 Roper poll found that nearly three-quarters of Americans did not know that the leading cause of water pollution is water running off farmland, parking lots, city streets, and lawns, and one-half of those surveyed erroneously believed that most U.S. electricity is produced by hydropower, when only about 12 percent is so generated.[3] Although two chapters on a topic this broad and deep will not make you an environmental expert, we hope that the environmental issues and responses presented here will prompt you to think twice about how you interact with your environment and will pique your interest so that you explore these topics further in future courses and throughout your career.

Concern about the current and future states of the world's natural environment is evident in nearly every aspect of organizational life. Businesses are forming environmental associations, holding environmental conferences, supporting environmental organizations, publishing environmental newsletters, creating pollution prevention and cleanup programs, and including environmental concerns in their advertising. Business schools and other educational institutions are increasingly focusing on the natural environment as an important subject for preparing students to succeed in their careers. Growing out of a cooperative effort among several major U.S. businesses and a large U.S. environmental group, the Management Institute for Environment and Business was established in 1990 (and later incorporated within the World Resources Institute) to develop curriculum materials for business school faculty to begin to incorporate environmental issues into courses as diverse as accounting, strategic management, production and operations, marketing, and finance. Political parties (including "green" political parties in the United States and elsewhere), governments, unions, civic groups, religious institutions, health centers, and athletic organizations all have recently intensified their efforts to contribute to resolving perceived environmental problems. The evidence appears overwhelming that, as we move into the next millennium, many organizations, including businesses and many societies, both developed and developing, are vitally interested and involved in natural environment topics.

Although some jaded business students might think this particular business and society topic is less serious than others presented in this text, the U.S. federal government for one is treating business environmental violations more seriously than ever. For instance, in 1992, for "the fourth straight year, the value of civil, administrative, and judicial (federal environmental) enforcement efforts exceeded $1 billion, with the figure for 1992 approaching $2 billion; a record number of criminal indictments, 174, were handed down; [and] of jail time imposed, 91 percent was served."[4] The aspiring and prudent business executive would do well not to ignore this increasingly important subject.

On the more positive side, opportunistic businesses have identified the recent concern for the environment as good for business. In 1996 in the United States alone, 14 environmental industry segments, ranging from environmental consulting to monitoring of equipment manufacturers, earned $184.3 billion in revenue, compared with 1990 revenues of $146.4 billion. Worldwide, firms in these environmental businesses brought in $288 billion in business in 1993, with 1998 projections nearing $400 billion. The environmentally sensitive entrepreneurial manager is advised to treat each complaint by a polluting business about the high costs of complying with environmental regulations as an advertisement of yet another opportunity to "clean up."[5]

The Natural Environment

As busy people, we often take nature for granted. For instance, just before reading it, did you consider that this page you are reading required various natural resources for its production, as did production of the energy for the light that allows you to read this page, and of the chair and building in which you are sitting? The problem with taking nature for granted is that we have a tendency not to appreciate the amazing complexity of the world around us. One amazing but typically forgotten characteristic about the natural world is that we *interact* with it every minute of every day of our lives. From this point of view, earth and everything else in the universe comprise our environment and can be considered our continuous, ever-present stakeholders (and we theirs).

For our purposes, we will consider the planets and other objects in our solar system, together with the energy and matter they receive from and return to outer space, as our relevant environment. Earth is a water planet, that is, two-thirds of its surface is covered by water, which can be found in oceans, lakes, glaciers, aquifers, rivers, bays, creeks, human-made containers, the air, and all plants and animals. The earth's core is a mixture of molten metals, which the closer to the surface from the core, the more likely these metals will have formed crusts on ocean bottoms and land masses, such as continents and islands. Surrounding both land and water is the atmosphere, layered gases of mostly nitrogen and oxygen that circulate around the globe. Finally, on the land and in the water are plants and animals so numerous that, after centuries of doing and developing natural science, we are still trying to identify and count them all. A recent estimate puts the overall number of earth species—plants, animals, and microbes—somewhere between 2 and 20 million.[6]

Whereas such a listing of earthian components is a useful start to an understanding of our environment, those who study and appreciate ecology go well beyond list making. They wonder, they are in awe of, the ". . . extraordinary motion, complexity, and interaction of the ecosphere. A confusion of birth and death, sex and violence, organic construction and decay, . . . a perception of the ecosphere as a scene of almost incredible living activity in contrast to the staticness that abounds [in the rest of the universe]."[7] The *interacting* of species under certain time, place, chemical, and physical conditions is what drives this complexity. Consider just one aspect of nature, the habitat, or the location where a species spends most of its life. Habitats can be hundreds of miles up in the atmosphere, deep within the ocean, several inches below the surface of the soil, or in the intestines of human beings. Some species' habitats, such as those of various shorebirds, bacteria, and insects, include the interfaces between or among two or more of these environments.

Interaction can, but does not always, take place among these and other species, adding the element of chance to the complex webs we call ecosystems. Further, consider the intricacy of just two, perhaps adjoining, habitats: a meadow and a pond. Any number of rooted meadow plants from short grasses to towering trees and their surrounding soil could provide habitats for a vast variety of microorganisms, insects, reptiles, birds, and mammals. By contrast, although ponds also contain some rooted aquatic plants, numerous types of algae, green bacteria, and green protozoa and their surroundings might provide shelter and food energy for an entirely different set of animals, including amphibians and fish. This tremendous variety of habitats and inhabitants, and their *interactions,* are but a minute fraction of all that continues to astound ecologists about the natural environment.

The ongoing attempts of ecologists to unravel nature's many perplexing mysteries also produce findings that are surprising and potentially very useful. For instance, comparing once again the meadow and the pond, while land masses such as meadows appear to be prolific producers of plant and animal mass, watery environments such as ponds have been found to produce 2,000 times more "bio-mass" than meadows, because of differences in the metabolisms of the plants and animals found in each.[8] This fact may have significant implications for how a hungry human world, running out of good topsoil, can be fed most efficiently in the future. As we mentioned earlier, the topic of the environment is so all-encompassing and potentially overwhelming that we are only introducing it here. In addition, we call your attention to Figure 11–1, which presents definitions of a few of the most important environmental terms that might be helpful to you now and in the future.

The Human/Environment Interface

Humans interact with the rest of their natural environments in numerous ways. The air we breathe, the water we drink, and the food we eat all originate in nature, and eventually all return to nature. Other significant human needs provided by the natural environment include materials for shelter, clothing and energy for temperature control, and transportation. In fact, nature's materials, whether in liquid, solid, or gaseous form, provide the base of every human product and service. Indeed, every human activity has its beginnings and ends in the natural environment, which

FIGURE 11–1	Glossary of Important and Helpful Environmental Terms
Environment	Broadly, anything that is external or internal to an entity. For humans, the environment can include external living, working, and playing spaces and natural resources, as well as internal physical, mental, and emotional states.
Carrying Capacity	The volume of and intensity of use by organisms that can be sustained in a particular place and at a particular time without degrading the environment's future suitability for that use. A resource's carrying capacity has limits that need to be respected for continued use.
Entropy	A measure of disorder of energy, indicating its unavailability for recycling for the same use. Energy tends to break down into lower quality with each use. For instance, a kilowatt of electricity, once it is produced and consumed, can never be used as electricity again, and, if stored, will allow far less than 1 kilowatt to be consumed.
Ecosystem	All living and nonliving substances present in a particular place, often interacting with others.
Niche	The role an organism plays in its natural community, including what it eats and the conditions it requires for survival. Habitats and niches are interrelated concepts.
Cycle	The continuous looplike movement of water, air, and various nutrients, such as nitrogen, phosphorous, and sulfur, through the environment. Such cycles can be impaired in performing their evolutionary roles, such as purification and sustenance, by excessive human-caused pollution and depletion.
Threshold	The point at which a particular phenomenon, previously suppressed, suddenly begins to be activated. For instance, when a population's carrying capacity threshold is exceeded, the population tends to decrease or even crash as a result of increased morbidity and mortality.
Pollution	The existence of material or energy that has gone through a transformation process and is perceived as unwanted or devalued in a particular place at a particular time.
Irreversibility	The inability of humans and nature to restore environmental conditions to a previous state within relevant timeframes. Human environment-related actions that appear irreversible are the destruction of a rainforest or wilderness area and the extinction of a species.
Sustainability	The characteristic of an entity, such as an economic or environmental system, that is related to its ability to exist and flourish over an acceptably long period of time.

is a very strong argument for including nature as a consideration in human organizational decisions and actions.

Why are humans and the natural environment so intricately connected? Mainly because *humans are part of nature.* As biological entities composed of organic and inorganic natural substances, humans, as individuals and as collections in organizations, depend on nature's physical resources and processes for survival and development. As we mentioned, we humans often take this dependency for granted. However, by continuously reminding ourselves that we, too, are part of nature, individuals and organizations, including businesses, might begin to develop a closer conceptual connection with the natural environment. Environmental protection could then be thought of as human protection, a concept most of us can easily support. One perspective on considering that humans are part of nature is that the ways we *interact* with one another may be an important aspect of our overall environmental sensitivity. In this view, ensuring that human stakeholders, such as employees and customers, and even competitors, are treated with respect is one way to advance natural environment goals.

Unfortunately, that businesses have played a major role in contributing to natural environment pollution and depletion is beyond debate. Virtually every sector of business in every country is responsible for consuming significant amounts of materials and energy and causing waste accumulation and resource degradation. For instance, companies that process raw materials, such as uranium, coal, oil, and forestry firms, have caused major air, water, and land pollution problems in their extraction, transportation, and processing stages. Manufacturing firms, such as those in steel, petrochemicals, and paper products, have long been identified as major sources of air and water pollution.

Figure 11–2 illustrates that most major industry sectors contribute significant levels of pollution, identifying the top ten polluting manufacturing industry categories in 1996, which were responsible for more than 90 percent of the total reported releases of some 2.4 billion pounds of more than 500 chemicals and compounds into the air, water, and land, both surface and underground.

Figure 11–3 identifies those U.S. companies that released the greatest amounts of these polluting substances in 1993. Even service businesses, such as dry cleaners, grocery and retail stores, and auto repair shops, use nonnegligible amounts of energy and materials that can be associated with hazardous wastes and urban sprawl.

FIGURE 11–2	Toxics Release Inventory by Industry, 1996: Top 10 U.S. Industries		
Industry	*Rank*	*Pounds*	*Percent of Total*
Chemicals	1	785,178,163	32.3
Primary Metals	2	564,535,183	23.2
Paper	3	227,563,372	9.4
Multiple Industries	4	120,779,018	5.0
Plastics	5	116,409,291	4.8
Transportation	6	111,352,769	4.6
Fabrication Metals	7	90,254,367	3.7
Food	8	83,303,395	3.4
Petroleum	9	68,887,258	2.8
Electrical	10	41,765,377	1.7

SOURCE: Environmental Protection Agency, *Toxics Release Inventory: Public Data Release* (1998), 159.

FIGURE 11–3	Ten Companies with the Largest Toxics Release Inventory, Total Releases, 1993		
Company	*Rank*	*Pounds*	*Percent of Total*
Du Pont	1	206,025,321	7.3
Freeport-McMoran	2	193,760,607	6.7
American Cyanamid	3	124,640,754	4.4
Renco Holdings	4	74,507,492	2.7
Asanco	5	57,057,182	2.0
Monsanto	6	55,032,422	2.0
Eastman Kodak Co.	7	49,926,822	1.8
BP America	8	44,534,370	1.6
Courtaulds U.S.	9	43,728,541	1.6
General Motors	10	36,319,810	1.3

SOURCE: Environmental Protection Agency, *Toxics Release Inventory: Public Data Release* (Washington, DC: USGPO, 1993), 40.

As a major consumer of the world's energy and materials, and as a large producer of waste and degraded ecosystems, business definitely affects the natural environment. Therefore, businesses that profess to practice good stakeholder management need to play a leading role in finding and implementing solutions to our environmental problems.

Although manufacturing and operations processes are the most visible contributors to air, water, and land pollution, virtually every other department within a business potentially plays some role in affecting the natural environment. Research labs and engineering departments, for instance, could be producing their own nonnegligible amounts of environmental contaminants and often forwarding to their manufacturing departments products they have designed that are toxic and nonrecyclable. Finance departments, using inadequate accounting department data, could be recommending decisions based on short-term criteria that have not incorporated the full costs to the environment of potentially damaging projects. Human resources departments could be neglecting to incorporate environmental concerns in their personnel recruitment, selection, and development decisions, potentially advancing individuals within the organization who do not share the organization's environmental values. Finally, marketing departments could be advertising and selling environmentally dubious products and services, with or without their customers' knowledge of this fact.

NATURAL ENVIRONMENT ISSUES

The latest wave of environmentalism has paralleled a growing public perception that global environmental problems are severe and worsening with time.[9] The UN has identified the following eight key global natural environment problems:

- Ozone depletion
- Global warming
- Solid and hazardous wastes
- Degradation of marine environments
- Freshwater quality and quantity
- Deforestation
- Land degradation
- Endangerment of biological diversity

We will discuss each of these environmental problems briefly to give the reader a sense of the complexity and urgency with which these issues are increasingly viewed.

SEARCH THE WEB

To interact effectively with environmental stakeholders, managers must educate themselves about environmental movement issues. Hundreds of organizations and Web sites deal with the natural environment. One particularly valuable Web site is EnviroLink Network, a grassroots environmental community located at **www.envirolink.org/**. EnviroLink is a nonprofit organization that unites hundreds of organizations and volunteers around the world with millions of people in more than 150 countries. EnviroLink states that it "is dedicated to providing you with the most comprehensive, up-to-date environmental resources available." To learn more about EnviroLink's purposes, news, library, services, and awards, and such topics as sustainable business, animal rights, the green marketplace, and green living, visit this interesting and comprehensive Web site.

Ozone Depletion

Ozone is an oxygen-related gas that is harmful to life near the earth's surface but is vital in the stratosphere in blocking dangerous ultraviolet radiation from the sun. Every spring in the southern hemisphere, a "hole" that has grown as large as the North American continent opens over Antarctica. This area, which in 1993 had 50 to 70 percent less ozone than in the 1960s, is growing annually and is thought to be caused by human-produced chemicals—chlorofluorocarbons (CFCs), used in refrigeration, and halons, used in fire extinguisher systems. The northern hemisphere ozone layer is also thinning by several percent per decade, and populated areas in 1993 underwent wintertime ozone depletion rates of up to 25 percent. These ozone reductions may be putting at risk thousands of humans and uncounted numbers of other animals to blinding cataracts and increases in skin cancer. Ozone depletion has also been identified as a potential cause of plant stunting, including food crops, and widespread killing of phytoplankton, which are the base of ocean food chains.[10]

Global Warming

According to a number of reputable sources, the earth's atmosphere is in danger of heating up. Human production of carbon dioxide, primarily through the burning of fossil fuels in power plants and automobile engines, has been identified as a probable contributor to this "greenhouse effect"—that is, the prevention of solar heat absorbed by our atmosphere from returning to space. One estimate has been made that the amount of global carbon dioxide has increased by 25 percent since the

Industrial Revolution[11] and continues to increase at a rate of 0.4 percent per year.[12] Several researchers estimate that this increased carbon dioxide production has raised the global average air temperature at the earth's surface by 1 degree Fahrenheit over the last century.[13] Global sea surface temperature increased about the same amount just from 1982 to 1989.[14]

These recent temperature increases are about half of the entire warming of the earth that has occurred in the last 10,000 years. Some atmospheric prediction models indicate that, with continued global warming of from 2 to 9 degrees Fahrenheit by the middle of the next century, coastal flooding from glacial melting might result and that forests, farm belts, wildlife habitats, and deserts might shift significantly. Both the severity and the effects of these shifts are unknown, as are the adaptability of ecosystems and living species, including humans, to these effects.[15, 16] We do not yet know if we have crossed a threshold beyond which many of these projected effects will begin to be more substantially, perhaps threateningly, realized. Figure 11–4 identifies the gases and countries that are the primary contributors to global warming.

Solid and Hazardous Wastes

The most visible evidence that much of the world has become a garbage-making machine can be found at the local dump, landfill, or incinerator. These disposal

FIGURE 11–4 Global Warming Gases and Producer Countries

Greenhouse Gas	Percentage Contribution
Carbon Dioxide	49
Methane	18
Chlorofluorocarbons	14
Nitrous Oxide	6
Other Gases	13
Total	100

Country Producer	Percentage Contribution
United States	21
Former Soviet Union	14
Europe	14
China	7
Brazil	4
India	4
Rest of the World	36
Total	100

SOURCE: Environmental Protection Agency, *Meeting the Environmental Challenge* (Washington, DC: USGPO, December, 1990), 12.

sites, which in some countries are quickly being outstripped by the sheer volume of primarily the "developed" world's garbage, annually accumulate billions of tons of wastes of all kinds. However, because record keeping of waste is inadequate, no one knows exactly how much trash is produced by people every day. Estimates have been made for Western "developed" nations, however. The United States produces about 10 billion metric tons of solid waste each year, with about two-thirds of this categorized as nonhazardous. While U.S. households create about 140 million metric tons of municipal solid waste each year (or 3.5 pounds per person daily), the overwhelming bulk of solid waste in the United States is generated by industry.[17] Because these industrial wastes are primarily disposed of in private facilities, little is known about their content. Figure 11–5, however, identifies the composition of U.S. municipal waste by source. Every year Americans discard about 1 billion foil-lined fruit-juice boxes, 25 billion styrofoam cups, 1.6 billion disposable pens, and 16 billion disposable diapers.[18] In comparison to the United States, the European community discards an estimated 2 billion metric tons of waste each year, or about 20 percent as much.

The production of global wastes considered hazardous—that is, those requiring special handling to protect humans and the environment—has been estimated at between 375 and 500 million tons,[19] about 90 percent of which is produced in industrialized countries. These hazardous wastes include pesticides, petrochemicals, other organic chemicals such as dioxin and PCBs, and heavy metals. The United States produces more than a ton of these hazardous wastes per person per year. Unfortunately, many of these substances were not identified as hazardous until the 1970s and, consequently, their disposal up to that point is cause for great concern today, because many of these older disposal sites are unlined and are located within leaching distance of various bodies of water, especially underground aquifers.[20] In addition, as a result of tightening site controls in some areas, hazardous wastes are being transported away from their sources with greater frequency in recent years, both within countries and between countries, often to sites with weaker controls. For instance, in 1983, Western European countries sent Eastern European countries

FIGURE 11–5 Composition of U.S. Municipal Wastes	
Waste Category	**Percentage of Composition**
Paper/Paperboard	38
Yard Waste	18
Metals	8
Plastics	8
Glass	7
Food Waste	7
Wood	6
Other	8

SOURCE: Environmental Protection Agency, *Guide to Environmental Issues* (April, 1995), 29.

between 200,000 and 300,000 metric tons of hazardous waste.[21] One report suggests that this amount tripled in just a few years.[22]

Degradation of Marine Environments

Water is both literally and figuratively our lifeblood. We evolved from it, we are made of it, we need it for drink and food. Yet humans often treat this precious resource as just another garbage dump. Municipal sewage, industrial wastes, urban runoff, agricultural runoff, atmospheric fallout, and overharvesting all contribute to the degradation of the world's oceans and their most productive areas, the coastal waters within 700 miles of land. Although the marine environment problem is global, consider just the effects of businesses and cities in the United States. Each year, roughly 4 trillion gallons of American sewage and 5 trillion gallons of industrial waste are dumped into marine waters. These and other pollutants, such as oil and plastics, have been associated with significant damage to a number of coastal ecosystems, including salt marshes, mangrove swamps, estuaries, and coral reefs. The result has been local and regional shellfish bed closures, declining fish populations, seafood-related illnesses, and reduced shoreline protection from floods and storms.[23] The U.S. Council on Environmental Quality (CEQ) reports that over 4 million acres of shellfish beds off the East Coast and the Gulf of Mexico were closed in 1990, about the same total amount as in 1985.[24]

Freshwater Quality and Quantity

Although three-quarters of the earth's surface is water, 97.4 percent is salt water, and most of the remaining fresh water is inaccessible because of its underground or polar locations. Although so little fresh water is available, humans have acted as though the supply is limitless by overusing, polluting, or otherwise mismanaging this vital resource. Fresh water is used for numerous important human activities, including drinking, bathing, agriculture, manufacturing, transportation, recreation, and waste disposal.

Because global fresh water is unequally distributed, supplies are already overtaxed in shortage areas. Dam sedimentation, deforestation, overgrazing, overirrigation, and various sources of pollution are reducing the quality of fresh water available for necessary human purposes. The associated results have been drought, desertification, and water-borne diseases in the developing world, as well as river, lake, bay, and accessible groundwater contamination on a large scale in developed countries. For instance, one EPA study estimated that 10 percent of the U.S. surface waters were significantly polluted,[25] while another study estimated groundwater contamination at 2 5 percent of the total U.S. ground water available for human consumption.[26]

One organization known for its global environmental studies has identified several large areas around the world where water scarcity has become a health-threatening problem. These water-shortage areas include rapidly shrinking water tables in China, the loss of two-thirds of the Aral Sea in the former Soviet Union, and the overappropriation of about half the rivers in the American West.[27] However, the U.S. Council on Environmental Quality reported that the trend in the United States was toward decreasing water demand, greater wastewater treatment, and greater water quality control efforts.[28] This discrepancy in information is a common condition in the discussion of environmental issues, contributing further complexity to the environmental manager's task.

Deforestation

In a previous era, environmentalists were derided as "treehuggers," referring to their concern for forests and other woodlands. After the decimation of the world's tree species in the 1980s—an era that has been called "The Decade of Destruction"—such concern appears justified. Although humans depend on forests for building materials, fuel, medicines, chemicals, food, employment, and recreation, the world's forests are quickly being depleted by a variety of human factors. More than 50 million acres of trees fall each year worldwide, most of which are in tropical rain forests. Two-thirds of Western Europe's natural forests and 95 percent of the virgin forests in the United States have been felled,[29] leaving less than 1 percent of the world's original (precivilization) forests still standing.[30]

If human activities, such as overharvesting, land clearing, and the production of tree-weakening air pollution, do not change, forests could continue to diminish, to the extent that the developing world's remaining forests may be gone within a matter of decades.[31] Whereas the impact on humans of forest depletion would likely be tragic, the effect on other species and on ecosystems could be devastating. Forests are homes to millions of animal and plant species. Tropical rain forests in particular are prolific habitats, but thousands of their species may soon be doomed to extinction, because these forests are being cut down at the rate of 85 acres per minute.[32]

In addition, deforestation adds to soil erosion problems and is a major cause of the greenhouse effect, because felled trees are no longer able to absorb carbon dioxide and are sometimes burned for land clearing and charcoal, thereby releasing rather than absorbing carbon dioxide. Moisture and nutrient ecosystem cycles can also be severely damaged in deforesting activities, negatively affecting adjacent land and water ecosystems.

Land Degradation

Another disturbing environmental issue human populations face in the 1990s is the continuing and increasing problem of soil erosion and spoilage. Every year the world has about 90 million "more mouths to feed and over 20 billion tons less topsoil on which to grow food."[33] Productive, nutrient-rich soil is blown away by winds and carried away by rains when unprotected. Deforestation, acid rain, waterlogging, ozone depletion, and overgrazing all contributed to a loss of 240 billion tons of topsoil in the 1980s.[34] World grain production has fallen 14 percent since 1984, and famine, drought, and overpopulation and distribution inequities have annually been responsible for 40 to 60 million human deaths from hunger and hunger-related disease.[35] Although many of these land degradation problems are regionalized in Third World countries, developed nations, too, have experienced land productivity difficulties. The United States may be losing more than 3 billion tons of topsoil each year,[36] stripping 170 million acres annually.[37] Loss of topsoil productivity costs Canada an estimated $1 billion per year.

Endangerment of Biological Diversity

Of all the environmental issues related to human individual and organizational activity, protecting and preserving the plant and animal species with which we share this planet is perhaps the most pressing. The reason why protection of biological diversity is so important is that many ecosystems are very fragile webs of interconnected and interdependent plant and animal species, so that affecting one species can set off a kind of chain reaction requiring too-quick adaptations by other species with which it interacts. The irony is that several traditionally important human activities, such as hunting, fishing, agriculture, and livestock raising, as well as construction for human settlements, have seriously threatened many of these species. Their endangerment now threatens humans, either as individuals or as a species, through global warming, soil erosion, and the loss of botanical medicines upon which many humans depend.

To put the problem in perspective, of the some 20 million species on earth today, perhaps 100 are lost every single day, a rate of extinction many times greater than the rate thought to have been in effect before the Industrial Revolution.[38] In addition to the depletion of large mammal species, such as the elephants and black rhinos of Africa, and birds such as the California condor and mosquito-catcher, there are some 20,000 endangered species of animals around the world, many of which are in trouble because of overhunting and poaching. Ecosystem and habitat destruction through agricultural and urban development activities, and, of course, pollution, have put at risk not only wildlife, but many species of very beneficial plants as well. Up to half of all human medicines are derived from plants, and yet, in especially productive areas such as the world's rain forests, excesses in individual and organizational activities are responsible for significant and tragic ecosystem and species degradation.

Other Environmental Issues

In addition to these eight major environmental issues identified by the UN, other concerns have arisen around the world that appear to threaten human health and other aspects of the natural environment. *Air pollution,* both outdoors and indoors, often rates high in concern according to public opinion polls. Although several industrialized countries have achieved decreases in several outdoor, or ambient, air pollutants in the past two decades, many metropolitan areas in these nations still face severe problems with sulfur dioxides, nitrogen oxides, and particulates. The burning of some fossil fuels for energy production, car and truck emissions, and a combination of these two sources are the main culprits responsible for ambient air problems, which are increasing in many urban areas.[39] In Mexico City, for instance, nearly 3 million motor vehicles making nearly 30 million trips every day are being blamed for the city's worsening ozone smog problem, contributing to the unfortunate fact that 125 days each year the city's air quality is considered dangerous to people's health.[40] In the former Soviet Union, 68 cities were said to have the highest degrees of atmospheric pollution in 1988, with the capitals of the republics having the most trouble meeting the maximum permissible concentrations of air pollutants.[41] Figure 11–6 identifies these and other air pollutants and their associated human health concerns.

FIGURE 11–6   Health Effects of Several Air Pollutants

Pollutants	Health Concerns
Ozone	Respiratory tract problems such as difficult breathing and reduced lung function. Asthma, eye irritation, nasal congestion, reduced resistance to infection, and possible premature aging of lung tissue.
Particulates	Eye and throat irritation, bronchitis, lung damage, and impaired vision.
Carbon Monoxide	Impairment of the blood's ability to carry oxygen and effects on cardiovascular, nervous, and pulmonary systems.
Sulfur Dioxide	Respiratory tract problems, permanent harm to lung tissue.
Lead	Retardation and brain damage, especially in children.
Nitrogen Dioxide	Respiratory illness and lung damage.

SOURCE: Environmental Protection Agency, *Meeting the Environmental Challenge* (Washington, DC: USGPO, December, 1990), 10.

FIGURE 11–7   Definition and Effects of Acid Rain

"Acid rain" refers to all acid deposition that occurs in the form of rain, snow, fog, dust, or gas. Human-made emissions of SO_2 and NOX are transformed into acids in the atmosphere, where they may travel hundreds of miles before falling as acid rain. Acid rain has been measured with a pH of less than 2.0—more acidic than lemon juice. The political implications of this problem are important because the pollutants may originate in one jurisdiction but affect another.

EPA research has increased scientific understanding of the effects of acid rain, including the sterilization of lakes and streams, reproductive effects on fish and amphibians, possible forest dieback, and deterioration of human-made structures. These effects have been most obvious in the eastern United States and Canada and in western and eastern Europe.

SOURCE: Environmental Protection Agency, "Progress and Challenges: Looking at EPA Today," *EPA Journal* (September/October, 1990), 17.

In addition to causing human health problems, ambient air pollution is also responsible for a condition called *acid rain*, which has caused a variety of significant negative impacts on the natural environments of several countries. Figure 11–7 defines this condition and lists some of its effects. To date, the damage from this fossil fuel–caused problem appears to have hit Europe the hardest, being blamed for sterilizing up to 80 percent of the lakes and streams in Norway, damaging 64 percent of British forests, and destroying more than 40 percent of the coniferous forests in central Switzerland.[42] Acid rain has caused significant deterioration of both the natural environment and human structures in other areas of the world, including Pennsylvania; Nova Scotia; Agra, India; Tokyo; Central Africa; and Sao Paulo, Brazil.[43]

Indoor air pollution is another environmental problem that is becoming an increasing concern, primarily in industrialized countries. Asbestos was used as an insulator in schools and other buildings in the United States for many years but has been identified as causing asbestosis, an incurable lung disease afflicting those who inhale asbestos fibers. Other serious indoor air pollutants include radon, tobacco smoke, formaldehyde, pesticide residues, and perchloroethylene (associated with dry cleaning). Certain construction materials and other household products, such as some paints, carpeting, and gas furnaces, are primarily responsible for these contaminants, which are associated with a variety of human health problems from nausea to cancer.[44]

A third environmental problem, one that received significant attention in the 1970s and is once again garnering major interest in the 1990s, is *energy inefficiency*, or the wasting of precious nonrenewable sources of energy. Nonrenewable energy sources, such as coal, oil, and natural gas, were formed millions of years ago under unique conditions of temperature, pressure, and biological phenomena (hence the term "fossil" fuels). Once these are used up, they will apparently be gone forever. Not only does overreliance on these nonrenewable energy sources cause them to be consumed faster than they otherwise would be, but, because of their hydrocarbon nature, fossil fuels cause a variety of pollution and depletion problems, which are identified later in this chapter. In addition, because these fuels are not equally distributed around the world, they are the cause of significant power imbalances worldwide, with associated armed conflicts that are typically disastrous for both humans and the natural environment in general.[45]

Although none of the environmental problems mentioned above appears easy to resolve (with the possible exception of the cessation of tobacco smoking), part of the answer to the nonrenewability problem is to use as little as possible of these energy sources through implementation of sound energy conservation practices. In addition, shifting to renewable energy sources, such as solar, wind, hydroelectric, and biomass forms of energy, is an increasingly attractive option for both industrial and agricultural societies. Several technologies for tapping these renewable, low-polluting energy sources are becoming economically competitive with nonrenewable sources,[46, 47] but continued subsidies and systems promoting nonrenewable energy development continue to hamper this transition.[48]

Another environmental problem, which is interconnected with those mentioned above, deserves special attention because of its potential for harm: the production of toxic substances, whether as constituents of intended end-products or as unwanted by-products. Toxic substances, defined by the EPA as chemicals or mixtures that may present unreasonable risks of injury to health or to the environment,[49] can include pesticides, herbicides, solvents, fuels, radioactive substances, and many other potential candidates. Whether or not they are considered waste materials, toxic substances can have significant negative impacts on humans and on the natural environment in general. The problem with materials such as benzyl chloride, hydrogen cyanide, and methyl isocyanate is that very small amounts are incompatible with living tissue, destroy cell functions, and eventually cause total system shutdown.[50]

Although extreme care may be exercised if society decides it needs to manufacture such substances, which is a questionable prospect, two problems remain. First, we are not always aware of the effects, especially the long-term and *interactive* effects, of exposure to the thousands of chemicals that are produced each year. The U.S.

EPA, for instance, has no long-term health effects information on most of the 70,000 chemicals it has listed. "Of greatest concern are 10,000 to 14,000 high volume chemicals for which little to no data exists."[51] Even in those instances where the toxicity of a chemical is known and the chemical is banned for sale in a country, such as the pesticide DDT in the United States, the substance can still be manufactured in that country and exported, only to return when products that have been exposed to these substances are imported.

Second, toxic substances can be associated with industrial accidents, causing unforeseen widespread biological damage. The 1984 Bhopal, India, chemical plant leak; the 1986 Chernobyl nuclear power plant meltdown in the former Soviet Union; and the 1989 Exxon *Valdez* 11-million-gallon oil spill in Alaska are three well-known environmental disasters involving toxic substances. Not so well known are the 20,000 toxic chemical accidents that occurred in the United States between 1980 and 1985, the more than 30,000 nuclear power plant mishaps that occurred in the United States between the 1979 Three Mile Island disaster and 1989, or the 91 million gallons of oil that were spilled in U.S. waters between 1980 and 1986.[52] Consider, for example, that just one oil storage tank farm and pipeline complex in New York State, run by Amoco and Mobil, was responsible for leaking an estimated 17 million gallons of fuel into the surrounding ground water.[53] The world seems awash in toxic substances, and this and the other environmental issues mentioned in this section lead us to ask about the core causes of this perceived crisis.

Three types of pollution that recently have received less attention than they once did are *radon, noise pollution,* and *aesthetic pollution.* Radon is a radioactive gas that has been found in an increasing number of residential structures resulting from the natural radioactive decay of certain substances either found in the soil or used in construction materials. After tobacco smoking, radon has been identified as the leading cause of lung cancer in the United States.[54] Noise pollution can exist anywhere unwanted sounds are heard, but it most often results from operation of heavy machinery within limited areas. Factories, construction sites, and airports are frequently identified as noise pollution areas. Severe noise pollution can cause hearing impairment in humans and habitat disruption for other species. Aesthetic pollution occurs when visual tastes are violated and typically center around construction, signage, and land appearance. Commercial building facades, outdoor billboards, and litter were significant local issues in the past. We mention these pollution sources to illustrate that environmental issues change with time and can vary from place to place, arguing for a flexible approach to environmental management.

CAUSES OF THE ENVIRONMENTAL CRISIS

Nonhuman Natural Pollution and Depletion

In assessing environmental quality, one needs to start with the fact that not even nature is perfect. That is, the natural environment is responsible for a significant amount of pollution and degradation itself. Sometimes called "background" or "natural" levels of destructive materials and processes, these pollution and depletion sources are numerous and significant. For instance, every day and everywhere on earth, our planet's surface receives a huge dose of various forms of harmful radiation from the earth's subsurface, our sun, and the rest of the cosmos. "Natural disasters" here on earth can be considered environmental problems, as was evidenced by the Mount St. Helen's volcanic eruption and resulting air pollution in Washington State in 1980. The earth's core is continuously polluting many bodies of water and airsheds with a full range of toxic heavy metals, some of which, such as uranium 238, are especially toxic because they are radioactive.

Viral and bacterial diseases, whether plant or animal, are also considered to be forms of natural pollution or degradation. Species have been going extinct since life first evolved, and ecosystems such as lakes, streams, and glaciers die "natural" deaths continuously. Overpopulation of species (such as locusts and other insects) has led to pollution and habitat degradation, necessitating huge die-offs and mass migrations. Nature, indeed, acts as its own destroyer, in a continuous cycle of birth and death, of creation and destruction of life.

Human-Caused Natural Pollution and Depletion

So, if nature is a big polluter and humans have survived as a species for thousands of years while nature has been destroying itself, what's the problem? Won't humans continue to survive as a species for thousands of more years as nature continues to degrade? The problem answer to these questions is that humans have "put the pedal to the metal" in drastically increasing the levels and kinds of pollution and depletion, threatening numerous ecosystems and many species. This human intensification of pollution and depletion, if not immediately endangering *Homo sapiens* as a species, has at least contributed to a lowering of the quality of life for many individuals worldwide, both now and in the future.

Consider, for instance, that, prior to the Industrial Revolution, one plant or animal species went extinct every 300 years. Since that time, the rate of species extinction has increased to perhaps 100 species a day. In category after category, human-caused environmental pollution and degradation have increased manyfold in the past 200 years, and at a constantly increasing rate. Human population, settlements, production, consumption, and waste are continuing to rise and are increasingly identified as causes of environmental destruction. Rain forests and other wilderness areas around the world are fast disappearing, directly as a result of this increased human activity.

The difference between natural and human-caused destruction is that nature has evolved over billions of years, blending its destruction with creation or construction and proceeding at a pace much slower than the comparatively frenetic pace of most human activity. Natural pollution and depletion allow habitats and niches time to reemerge and cycles to regenerate.

However, human-caused pollution and depletion can occur with such swiftness, destruction, and staying power that their additions to the natural or background levels can overwhelm nature's capacity to adapt to this heightened pace of degradation. Nowhere is this more the case than in the world's rain forests, which take hundreds of years to grow back and less than a fraction of that to burn or chop down. Once destroyed, rain forests have been planted with crops, harvested, and grazed until little if any life-giving nutrients remain in the soil. A second obvious example is long-half-life radioactive waste, which can be manufactured in seconds and yet take thousands of years to decay to safe biological levels.

Although the scope of this text does not allow us to discuss all of the ways humans contribute to environmental deterioration, we can focus on one critical resource that illustrates the human (and mostly business) potential for environmental destruction—*energy*. Humans need energy as much as water for their existence. We need food energy, typically produced by our agricultural systems, to maintain our internal life support functions, and we need energy to provide heat and light for most human shelters and to prepare some foods. In addition, we humans use energy to transport ourselves and our goods at high speeds, to cool our living spaces and perishable food supplies, to run labor-saving household devices, and to manufacture many goods and provide many services desired by human society.

The problem with current energy use by humans at home and in business is that all of these benefits, whether physically necessary or simply desirable, have environmental costs. Much of our current agricultural production is based on increasing usage of petroleum-based herbicides and pesticides and petroleum-based, on-farm fuel usage. For instance, the world used nearly 2 billion barrels of oil equivalent of energy for agriculture in 1985, up 3.4 percent from 1980.[55] Food processing, both before and after sale, currently utilizes significant amounts of energy—especially natural gas and electricity. Residential, commercial, and industrial buildings consume large amounts of these same fossil fuels for space and water heating and cooling. Power plants that produce electricity using fossil fuels do so with an efficiency rate of only about one-third, illustrating the entropy idea that energy with a high capacity for work is capable of doing much less work each time it is transformed. In the United States, about a quarter of the energy consumed in the 1990s was used in transportation,[56] with about three-eighths being used in the industrial sector for the production of goods and services. Overall, the per capita use of energy is once again increasing in the United States, nearing pre-energy-crisis levels.[57]

What happens when all this primarily fossil fuel energy is consumed? More fossil fuel burning releases more carbon dioxide (up worldwide more than 120 percent since 1960[58]). Increased use of herbicides and pesticides typically results in more water pollution and soil degradation. More utility-generated electricity may mean more acid rain, smog, and airborne heavy metals.[59] Increasing numbers of gasoline-burning passenger and freight vehicles also exacerbate acid rain, smog, and carbon dioxide problems. One fossil fuel—petroleum—is also the base material for a variety of consumer products, and, as illustrated in Figure 11–8, the manufacture and consumption of these products also produce negative environmental impacts.

Human settlement patterns, too, play a role in energy consumption. The current approach to organization used in most developed countries, and increasingly adopted by cities in developing countries, requires significant amounts of energy to transport people and goods into the city and people, goods, and wastes out of the city.[60] In addition, the quest for dispersed single-family housing, the development of strip shopping malls, and the never-ending building of highways and car parking lots encourage even greater use of fossil fuels.[61] Indeed, considering just this one natural resource—energy—it is clear that human activity, mostly business-related activity, is a current major factor in environmental degradation.

The keys to ecosystem protection and the halting or slowing of the deterioration in human quality of life are to reduce the negative impacts of individual and organizational human activities and to ensure that any necessary impacts are as

FIGURE 11–8 Selected Petroleum Products and Associated Hazardous Wastes	
Petroleum Product	**Associated Hazardous Wastes**
Plastics	Organic chlorine compounds; organic solvents
Pesticides	Organic chlorine compounds; organic phosphate compounds
Paints	Heavy metals; pigments; solvents; organic residues
Oil, gasoline, and other petroleum products	Oils, phenols, and other organic compounds; heavy metals; ammonia; salt acids; caustics

SOURCE: Environmental Protection Agency, *Meeting the Environmental Challenge* (Washington, DC: USGPO, December, 1990), 10.

environmentally benign as possible. The human species' strategy needs to allow nature to return to its role as environmental purifier, creator, and destroyer—that is, to ensure that human activity does not harm nature's beneficial stable systems or worsen its turbulent, chaotic characteristics.

ENVIRONMENTAL PERSPECTIVES

In the mid-1970s, a small paperback book called *Ecotopia*[62] appeared in bookstores throughout the United States, offering a vision of a modern society based on ecological values. This novel, which has received renewed interest in recent years, describes a nation in which the norm is for people to "walk lightly on the land" and in which recycling, renewable (solar, wind, hydroelectric, and biomass) energy development, and nonautomobile transport are commonplace. However, even in this idealized econation, issues related to how humans interact with their environment are continuously debated. In our world, environmental issues, similar to other issues that capture the public's attention, have generated their share of heated disputes and multiple perspectives. Questions such as those regarding how serious environmental issues are; who is responsible for taking action to reduce the negative effects of air, water, and land pollution; and what should be done to preserve endangered species, have arisen once again with the resurgence of environmentalism in the late 1980s and early 1990s, with no overwhelming consensus on the appropriate answers. However, as with other highly visible public issues, viewpoints have tended to polarize into at least two camps: the optimists and the pessimists. This chapter closes with these two alternative perceptions of the current situation and the probable futures of these environmental issues and whether or not these perspectives can be reconciled.

The Optimistic Perspective

One view of environmental issues takes a decidedly optimistic approach and is widely supported by traditional business interests. This view holds, first, that environmental problems may not be as bad as environmentalists have made them out to be. Global warming and other ecological issues are not a significant, current reality in this perspective, but require further study and measured action, if absolutely necessary. According to this perspective, technology will be developed in time to handle many air, land, and water pollution problems. Capitalist economies will, if allowed, allocate capital, labor, entrepreneurship, information, and natural resources efficiently to develop the demand and supply for these technologies (at the right times, places, and levels). These technologically oriented "free" economies will also simultaneously provide a high material standard of living. In this view, human demands on natural resources are not significant problems; rather, these phenomena are identified as central solutions to problems of economic development and environmental improvement.

One proponent of this view has proposed a perspective that looks ". . . optimistically upon people as a resource rather than as a burden—a vision of receding limits, increasing resources and possibilities, a game in which everyone can win . . . [A perspective in which] creation, building excitement, and the belief that persons and firms, acting spontaneously in the search of their individual welfare, regulated only by rules of a fair game, will produce enough to maintain and increase economic progress and liberty. [This] view leads to hope and progress, in the reasonable expectation that the energetic efforts of humankind will prevail in the future, as they have in the past to increase worldwide our numbers, our health, our wealth, and our opportunities."[63]

The Pessimistic Perspective

A completely different perspective has been advanced in both of the more recent waves of environmentalism in the West. This view is far less optimistic about either the near- or long-term prospect that humans and their organizations will deal effectively with what are perceived by these environmental advocates as intractable, urgent issues of survivability and quality of life. Here the argument is made either that the full extent of our environmental problems is not known because of their complexity and our current limits of understanding or that what we do know reveals a daunting, global problem whose resolution will require unprecedented levels of human individual and organizational effort and cooperation. Proponents of these arguments tend to focus on nonhuman aspects of the natural environment and on the problems of air, land, and water degradation and species endangerment to a far greater extent than do the optimists. Population growth and human material and energy production, consumption, and waste are often identified as the sources of the ecological crises that pessimists perceive, and, therefore, their calls for resolution of these dilemmas usually entail significant decreases in either population growth rates or material and energy demands, or both.

After describing his position on several population and production issues, one advocate of this view stated, "We have wasted two critical decades. If we miss this chance, we face unprecedented peril. The processes of environmental abuse are as destructive as nuclear war and far less easy to avert—for they are already well advanced and gaining momentum. A gigantic task looms ahead."[64]

A Realistic Perspective?

How can these two contrasting views of human interaction with the natural environment be reconciled? Again, perhaps there are two answers to this question. The first is that we can find a middle ground and adopt the moderate view that humans, through their businesses and other institutions, can design systems that advance both material (and energy) growth and protection of the environment. This view is advanced by some progressive business organizations and the more conservative environmental groups. If these "middle-ground" advocates are correct, environmental issues will become just administrative details that will be worked out over time. Although some species will be lost and some level of pollution will need to be tolerated, this view would not require either wondrous technologies or radical social changes.[65]

The second answer to the question of how the optimistic and pessimistic perspectives on human/natural environment issues can be reconciled is that they cannot be. Advocates in both camps would likely argue that the rosy technological solution and the stark social change solution are mutually exclusive. Society needs to decide to go down one path or the other, because, the respective advocates might argue, technological creativity can be hamstrung by "excessive" regulation, and significant social change toward greater environmental consciousness can be hindered by the belief that a savior technology is just around the corner." As with most business and society issues, the individual manager may need to devote considerable amounts of time, energy, and concern to resolving these complex environmental issues to develop her or his own "realistic perspective."

A third potentially achievable approach, called the Ecotrek Hypothesis by this chapter's author, advances the thesis that, on the one hand, human beings have caused some significant and complex environmental problems in their evolution but that, on the other hand, they not only have the need and capacity to solve these problems but also the need and capacity to be more than environmental problem solvers. That is, our species apparently has the need and capacity to be environmental opportunity developers as well, exploring both less-accessible places on earth, like oceans, and places beyond earth's atmosphere, like neighboring planets, moons, and asteroids. Under this hypothesis, humans are learning, sometimes painfully, both through rigorously protecting natural places and through continuing and expanding the codevelopment of environmental and space technologies. The advantage of this perspective is that it combines a respect for sensitive natural areas and species with significant doses of hope, adventure, and fun. The disadvantage is that this approach may distract attention from and promote allocation of resources to programs that do not address the most pressing environmental problems of our time.

SUMMARY

The natural environment can be considered to be all of the natural, physical phenomena that surround us every day. This all-encompassing concept is one that we as humans can appreciate but typically do not understand and often take for granted. A variety of environmental issues have captured our attention recently, and we are just beginning to become aware of their scope and interrelatedness and our role in contributing to them. These issues include ozone depletion, global warming, solid and hazardous wastes, degradation of marine environments, freshwater quality and quantity, deforestation, land degradation, and endangerment of biological diversity.

Other environmental issues, such as ambient and indoor air quality, acid rain, energy inefficiency, and toxic substances, also apparently need to be addressed. Although we know that nature itself plays some role in these conditions, human activity, including agricultural, sylvicultural, manufacturing, transportation, and consumption activities, appear to be exaggerating these problems, which is leading to widespread concern about the future of our environment. At least three perspectives on environmental issues have been identified, and students of business are advised to be alert to, collect, and attempt to process information from a variety of sources to help them decide which of these three perspectives, or some other, is appropriate for their future environmental management decisions.

KEY TERMS

acid rain (page 349)

air pollution (page 348)

energy inefficiency page 350)

Green Point Average (page 337)

DISCUSSION QUESTIONS

1. What is the natural environment?
2. Should businesses be concerned about the natural environment? Why or why not?
3. What are several of the most important environmental issues now receiving worldwide attention?
4. What are some of the causes of environmental pollution and depletion?
5. What is the future outlook for the natural environment?

ENDNOTES

1. A. Gore, *Earth in the Balance: Ecology and the Human Spirit* (New York: Houghton-Mifflin, 1992), 2.
2. Editors, "A Heretic Amid Economic Orthodoxy," *Science* (June 17, 1988), 1611.
3. National Environmental Education and Training Foundation. "Two Out of Three Adults Flunk Simple Test on Environmental Knowledge" (Washington, DC, 1997).
4. The Council on Environmental Quality, *Environmental Quality*, 23rd Annual Report of the Council on Environmental Quality, USGPO (Washington, DC: 1993), 82.
5. G. Ferrier, "Environmental Business Segments," *EPA Journal* (Vol. 20), 13.
6. W. Arthur, *The Green Machine* (Oxford, UK: Basil Blackwell, 1990), 13.
7. *Ibid.*, 5–6.
8. E.P. Odum, *Ecology and Our Endangered Life-Support Systems* (Sunderland, MA: Sinauer Associates, 1990), 44.
9. *UNEP Profile* (Nairobi, Kenya: United Nations Environment Programme, 1990), 2.

10. Council on Environmental Quality, *Twenty-Fourth Annual Report* (Washington, DC: USGPO), 42–43.
11. *UNEP Profile,* 6.
12. L.R. Brown, "The New World Order," in L.R. Brown et al., *State of the World, 1991* (New York: Norton, 1991), 7.
13. J. Hansen, "I'm Not Being an Alarmist About the Greenhouse Effect," *The Washington Post* (February 11, 1989), A23.
14. L.R. Brown, C. Flavin, and S. Postel, "Outlining a Global Action Plan," in L.R. Brown et al., *State of the World, 1989* (New York: Norton, 1989), 178.
15. *UNEP Profile,* 6, 7.
16. W. H. Corson (ed.), *The Global Ecology Handbook* (Boston: Beacon Press), 231–233.
17. *Ibid.,* 267.
18. J.S. Hirschhorn and K.U. Oldenburg, *Prosperity without Pollution* (New York: Van Nostrand Reinhold, 1991), 14.
19. Corson, 247.
20. *UNEP Profile,* 8.
21. *Ibid.*
22. United Nations Environment Programme, *UNEP North American News* (April, 1989), reporting on a GreenPeace study.
23. Corson, 137.
24. Council on Environmental Quality, *Environmental Quality* (Washington, DC: USGPO, 1990), 303.
25. International Rivers Network, *World Rivers Review* (July/August, 1989), 4.
26. E. Draper, "Groundwater Protection," *Clean Water Action News* (Fall, 1987), 4.
27. S. Postel, "Saving Water for Agriculture" in L.R. Brown et al., *State of the World, 1990* (New York: Norton, 1990), 49.
28. Council on Environmental Quality, 303.
29. United Nations Environment Programme, 16.
30. Postel, 75.
31. United Nations Environment Programme, 17.
32. *Ibid.*
33. United Nations Environment Programme, 14.
34. Postel, 60.
35. Corson, 68.
36. *Ibid.*
37. Council on Environmental Quality, 338.
38. United Nations Environment Programme, 18.
39. J. Seager (ed.), *The State of the Earth Atlas* (New York: Simon & Schuster, 1990), 110.
40. E. Cody, "In Mexico City, There's Fear in the Air," *The Washington Post* (November 24, 1991), A27.
41. B. Richman, "The Changing Face of Environmentalism in the Soviet Union," *Environment* (Vol. 32, No. 2, 1990), 28.
42. Seager, 116.
43. J. Naar, *Design for a Livable Planet* (New York: Harper & Row, 1990), 101.

44. Environmental Protection Agency, *Meeting the Environmental Challenge* (Washington, DC: USGPO, December, 1990), 11.

45. J. Mathews, "Acts of War and the Environment," *The Washington Post* (April 8, 1991), A17.

46. T.W. Lippman, "Future of Wind Power Gets a Lift," *The Washington Post* (November 17, 1991), H1.

47. T. Coffin (ed.), "A Look at Alternative Energy," *The Washington Spectator* (Vol. 16, No. 18, 1991), 1–3.

48. M. Brower, "Energy Favoritism: Why Renewable Sources Are Not Being Developed Fast Enough," *Nucleus* (Union of Concerned Scientists) (Vol. 11, No. 3, 1989), 3.

49. Environmental Protection Agency, *Glossary of Environmental Terms and Acronym List* (Washington, DC: U.S. EPA, 1989), 18.

50. Naar, 38.

51. Naar, 39.

52. Environmental Protection Agency, *Guide to Environmental Issues* (Washington, DC: USGPO, 1995), 4.

53. R.B. Rackleff, "The Oozing of America," *The Washington Post* (September 15, 1991), C5.

54. Environmental Protection Agency, 1990, 10.

55. L.R. Brown, "Sustaining World Agriculture," in L.R. Brown et al., State of the World, 1987 (New York: Norton, 1987), 131.

56. Council on Environmental Quality, 287.

57. Council on Environmental Quality, 298.

58. C. Flavin, "Slowing Global Warming," in L.R. Brown, *State of the World, 1990* (New York: Norton, 1990), 19.

59. S. Postel, "Stabilizing Chemical Cycles," in L.R. Brown et al., *State of the World, 1987* (New York: Norton, 1987), 170.

60. L.R. Brown, and J. Jacobsen, "Assessing the Future of Urbanization," in L.R. Brown et al., *State of the World, 1987* (New York: Norton, 1987), 51.

61. T. Cook, "Sprawl vs. Greenbelt," in *Land Use Patterns,* presented at the First International Ecology City Conference (Berkeley, CA: March, 1990).

62. E. Callenbach, *Ecotopia* (New York: Bantam Press, 1975).

63. J.L. Simon, "Population Growth Is Not Bad," *Phi Kappa Phi Journal* (Winter, 1990), 12–16.

64. M.K. Tolba, "Introduction," *UNEP Profile* (1990), 2–3.

65. R.L. Olson, "The Greening of High Tech," *The Futurist* (Vol. 25, No. 3, 1990), 29.

12

Business and Stakeholder Responses to Environmental Challenges

---

CHAPTER OBJECTIVES

After studying this chapter, you should be able to:

1 Describe the NIMBY environmental problem.

2 Explain the concept of environmental ethics.

3 Discuss the roles governments play in environmental issues.

4 Identify various environmental stakeholders and their impacts.

5 Catalog a variety of business responses to these stakeholders.

6 Examine business eco-responses with several decision models.

7 Focus on the root causes of environmental dilemmas.

Behind all the studies, the figures, and the debates, the environment is a moral issue. We can and should be nature's advocate.[1]

—Former President George Bush

Green consumers . . . will be looking for products which hurt no one, which damage nothing and which are produced by companies espousing the gentler values that they themselves espouse.[2]

—Anita Roddick, Founder, The Body Shop Ltd.

The preceding chapter identified the nature of the environmental challenge. Air, water, land, ecosystem, and species devastation appear to be both ubiquitous and, in many cases, increasing. Around the world, environmental damage apparently continues unabated day after day, gradually but inexorably deteriorating the quality of life for us, for future generations of humans, and for the rest of nature. Should something be done, and, if so, what, who, how, how much, and when? Although these questions are being asked with increasing frequency, the answers are less than clear and no consensus has emerged. Is the environment the responsibility of governments? If so, which ones and to what extent? Is the environment the responsibility of environmental groups and the general public? What responsibilities do

This chapter was contributed by Professor Mark Starik of George Washington University.

businesses and other organizations have in addressing the environmental challenge? If there is no consensus on the answers to these questions, what should "society" do to prevent serious deterioration of the quality of human life and of the health and robustness of the natural environment?

RESPONSIBILITY FOR ENVIRONMENTAL ISSUES

Problems such as smog, toxic waste, and acid rain can be described as "wicked problems"—that is, problems with characteristics such as interconnectedness, complexity, uncertainty, ambiguity, conflict, and societal constraints.[3] Affixing responsibility for such messy situations is problematic, because solutions to wicked problems are seldom complete and final and, therefore, credit for these solutions is seldom given or taken. Chlorofluorocarbons, or CFCs, for example, were once thought to be safe alternatives to other, more toxic refrigerants, which is why these ozone destroyers are so ubiquitous in our society's technologies.

The NIMBY Problem

One example of this question of responsibility has arisen recently in a variety of environmental areas and has been labeled the *NIMBY,* or "Not In My Back Yard," phenomenon. This acronym, which can be found on bumper stickers and conference agendas and in newspaper articles, college courses, and many other communication vehicles, is the human denial of responsibility for the misuse of the environment. One example of NIMBY is the community that uses ever-increasing amounts of electricity but decides it does not want a power plant that produces electricity to locate nearby. Another is a company that generates increasing amounts of waste but is unwilling to pay the full cost of proper disposal. Essentially, NIMBY is an attitude/behavior set based on avoidance or denial of responsibility. When applied to the field of environmental management, NIMBY spells big trouble.

The obvious difficulty with the NIMBY syndrome is that the entities (human individuals, organizations, or both) causing environmental pollution or degradation are not identified as the sources of the problem, and therefore no action is taken to reduce the problem. The NIMBY phenomenon avoids or denies the root cause of the damage and addresses only the symptoms with an attitude of nonresponsibility characterized by an approach of "I'll create an environmental problem, but I want to have as little as possible to do with solving it." One popular cartoon characterizing the NIMBY problem pictures a stream of polluting, honking cars passing along a highway in front of a huge billboard that reads "Honk if you love the environment!"

Environmental Ethics

Another way to view business/environment issues is through the perspective of ethics, which, as you will recall from Chapter 4, is "an act, decision, or behavior [which] . . . is consonant [in agreement] with prevailing norms or standards of society." Environmental ethics, then, might be considered to be those acts, decisions, and behaviors related to the natural environment that agree with society's norms. In addition, the principles of justice, rights, and utilitarianism serve as moral anchors for society's norms, as discussed in Chapter 5. This definition of environmental ethics brings up issues similar to those raised in Chapter 4: (1) whether these norms are absolute or relative and (2) who it is that sets these norms.

As discussed in Chapter 11, nature itself is a polluter and destroyer. Given this fact, what does *absolute* human environmental sensitivity mean? Humans must consume at least some plants and water to survive. If humans and their organizations need to pollute and destroy at least some of nature for their survival, what is the *relative* level of degradation that is ethical? Do nonhuman species have any "rights," and, if so, what are they, and how can they be reconciled with human rights? Concerning human rights and the environment, how do we assess the claims of indigenous cultures to the use of their respective environments? Is there any connection between the domination of humans by humans (for example, the domination of one nation, race, or gender by another) and the domination of nature by humans? This latter question is especially central to several schools of environmental ethical thought, including social ecology, ecofeminism, and environmental justice.

The second problem with ethics in general, and environmental ethics in particular, is the question of whose standards will determine what is or is not ethical. Numerous public opinion polls taken in the late 1980s and throughout the 1990s have indicated that most citizens in many countries (such as the United States) support the concept of environmental protection,[4] but how much the public will do itself or insist that governments and businesses do to protect the environment is still an unanswered question. How clean do the air and water need to be, and how much is the public willing to pay to meet these standards? As in our earlier discussion of business ethics, values play a major role and can be highly variable in breadth and depth across perspectives, situations, and time.

What are some environmental values (or *"green" values*)? According to one source associated with the "green" movement, many environmentalists hold four beliefs as fundamental values: (1) life on earth should continue; (2) human life on earth should continue; (3) natural justice should be done; and (4) nonmaterial qualities of life are worth pursuing.[5] These four principles form the basis of the 12 integrated attitudes and behaviors identified in Figure 12–1. They are summed up in the statement: "Overall the Green goal is to allow everyone the opportunity to live a fulfilling life, caring and sharing with each other, future generations and other species, while living sustainably within the capacities of a limited world."[6]

Another attempt at defining environmental values was undertaken by a pair of sociologists from Washington State University. In 1978, these researchers developed a 12-question scale to measure the strength of what they called the "New Environmental Paradigm," or NEP. This scale contains eight questions (actually, statements to be agreed or disagreed with) that are intended to indicate environmental sensitivity, such as "Mankind is severely abusing the environment," and four questions that are reverse scored and are associated with what the authors call the "Dominant Social Paradigm," or DSP—a set of values, beliefs, and attitudes that are more traditional perspectives of humans and nature—such as, "Mankind was created to rule over the rest of nature." This questionnaire has been administered many times to numerous groups since its development. In general, these researchers have found a surprisingly high level of agreement among the general public on the NEP, and, as might be expected, an even higher level among individuals associated with environmental interest groups.[7]

FIGURE 12–1   One Listing of "Green" Values

Put earth first: respect nature's life support systems.

Live within limits: unlimited expansion is self-defeating.

Think in terms of sufficiency: "enough" must replace "more."

Tread lightly: seek productive coexistence, not domination.

Defend diversity: promote variety of environment and culture.

Respect our descendants' rights: save for future generations.

Design with nature: respect long-term, stable patterns.

Keep things in proportion: human scale for human-made systems.

Balance rights and responsibilities: society has value.

Decentralize and democratize: localism and participation.

Tread carefully: technology can have unforeseen results.

Bad means produce bad ends: how is as important as what.

SOURCE: S. Irvine and A. Pouton, *A Green Manifesto* (London: Optima, 1988), 14–16.

Following the ethical models discussed in Chapters 4 and 5, other environmental issues can be added to develop a better idea of what environmental ethics is and how it can be practiced. Kohlberg's model of moral development, for instance, can be used to identify environment-related attitudes and behaviors by developmental level. At the preconventional (infant) level in environmental ethics, humans and human organizations can be perceived as being concerned only with self or with their own species and habitats. A conventional (adolescent) level might entail some appreciation of nature, but only when and where such appreciation is common-place or "in." A postconventional (adult) environmental ethic might include more mature attitudes and behaviors that are more universal (including all species and habitats), of greater duration (including unborn generations), and more consistent (if we humans have a right to survive as a species, why don't all species have that right?). Similarly, the moral principle of utilitarianism—the greatest good for the greatest number—could be expanded in environmental ethics to the greatest good for the greatest numbers of species and ecosystems. The Golden Rule could read, "Do unto other species as you would have them do unto you." Finally, the "Best Self" ethical test could include the question, "Is this action or decision related to the natural environment compatible not only with my concept of myself at my best but also with my concept of myself as a human representing my species at its best?"

Environmental ethics is an important and intriguing subtopic of business ethics and is gaining attention in both academics and business. However, the prudent business environmentalist is advised to guard against becoming self-righteous in terms of either personal or organizational environmental ethics. The concept of "ecological correctness" is a very slippery issue (because both nature and humans and their technology are so varied around the planet and are constantly changing), and it can even be an obstacle to those who might wish to become more environmentally sensitive but are put off by a "more-ecological-than-thou" attitude.

To return to the question of who sets environmental norms, the answer may be similar to the question of who sets society's norms—We all do, in part. This analysis implies that, as in ethical questions in general, the best approach to environmental ethics may be to practice tolerance, to see the world through others' perspectives, and to continue to question one's own environmental values as well as those of others.

THE ROLE OF GOVERNMENTS IN ENVIRONMENTAL ISSUES

As we mentioned earlier, governments have played major roles in environmental issues since the inception of such issues. Governments have procured, distributed, and developed habitable lands and other resources; protected, taxed, and zoned natural environment–based areas; and, more recently, exercised regulatory control over how those environments could be used. In this section, we'll look at how governments in the United States have dealt with environmental challenges and then identify what has been done in several other countries and at the international level.

Responses of Governments in the United States

Although the U.S. federal government has influenced environmental policy since at least 1899, with its permit requirement for discharge of hazardous materials into navigable waters, the major entrance of the U.S. government into environmental issues occurred in 1970 with the signing of PL 91-190, the National Environmental Policy Act (NEPA). The second section of this act spells out its purposes: "To declare a national policy which will encourage productive and enjoyable harmony between man and his environment; to promote efforts which will prevent or eliminate damage to the environment and biosphere and stimulate the health and welfare of man; and to enrich the understanding of the ecological systems and natural resources important to the Nation."[8]

In addition to establishing these broad policy goals, this legislation requires federal agencies to prepare environmental impact statements (EISs) for any "proposals for legislation and other major federal action significantly affecting the quality of the human environment." Environmental impact statements are reports of studies explaining and estimating the environmental impacts of questionable practices and irreversible uses of resources and proposing detailed, reasonable alternatives to these practices and uses.

Business is affected by the NEPA in several ways. First, the federal government pays private consultants to conduct over $40 billion worth of EISs each year. Second, because the federal government is the largest landholder in the United States, private businesses wishing to secure licenses and permits to conduct timber, grazing, mining, and highway dam and nuclear construction operations likely will be parties to the preparation of EISs. Third, private businesses working under federal government contracts are typically obliged to participate in EIS preparation. Fourth, the NEPA has been used as a model by many state governments, and therefore busi-

SEARCH THE WEB

Laws and regulations are major tools for protecting the environment. The U.S. Environmental Protection Agency (EPA) is the primary regulatory body in the United States with responsibility for administering the country's major environmental laws. The mission of the U.S. EPA is to protect human health and to safeguard the natural environment—air, water, and land—upon which life depends. For a review of the latest information on regulations and proposed rules, codified regulations, laws, and current legislation, visit the EPA's Web site at **www.epa.gov**.

Not all scientists believe that EPA regulations are based on good science. In fact, some scientists at the EPA believe and have argued that bad science is involved in many environmental regulations. One EPA scientist, Dr. David L. Lewis, was awarded Accuracy in Media honors for whistle-blowing in 1998 for his efforts to inform the public of a dramatic turn for the worse with regard to politics versus science at the EPA. To check out Dr. Lewis's claims, visit his Web site at **http://members.aol.com/LewisDaveL/**.

nesses heavily involved in significant state and local government contracts are likely to be involved in the EIS process.

Also in 1970, the U.S. Environmental Protection Agency (EPA) was created as an independent agency to research pollution problems, aid state and local government environmental efforts, and administer many of the federal environmental laws. These laws can be categorized into three areas—air, water, and land—even though a specific problem of pollution and/or degradation, such as acid rain, often involves two or more of these categories.

Air Quality Legislation

The key piece of federal air quality legislation, called the Clean Air Act, was significantly amended in 1990. The overall approach of this act is similar to that used in other areas of federal regulation, such as safety and health legislation, in that standards are set and timetables for implementation are established. In the Clean Air Act, there are two kinds of standards: primary standards, which are designed to protect human health, and secondary standards, which are intended to protect property, vegetation, climate, and aesthetic values. As of this writing, the EPA has set primary and secondary standards for a variety of air pollutants, including lead, particulates, hydrocarbons, sulfur dioxide, and nitrogen oxide. Businesses that directly produce these substances (such as electric utilities), and those whose products when used cause these substances to be produced, such as automobiles, must reduce their emissions to these standard levels within a certain time frame.[9, 10]

State governments are responsible for filing plans with the EPA on how these standards will be met. Depending on the business and the pollution emitted, firms invest in various state-of-the-art control technologies to meet these standards. For instance, the 1990 Clean Air Act requires coal-burning electric power plants to cut their acid rain–related sulfur dioxide emissions roughly in half by the year 2000, and so many utilities are installing new scrubbers and electrostatic precipitators or are using lower-sulfur coal.

One emerging but controversial concept that has recently been included in the Clean Air Act is the *bubble concept*. This approach is intended to reduce a particular pollutant over an entire industrial region by treating all emission sources as if they were under one bubble. Thus, a business can increase its emissions of sulfur dioxide in one part of a plant or region if it reduces its sulfur dioxide pollution by as much or more in another part of the plant or region. In addition, and as an extension of this bubble concept, businesses that reduce their emissions can trade these rights to other businesses that want to increase their emissions. Proponents of the bubble concept and emissions credit trading hail these policies as "free market environmentalism," whereas opponents ridicule them as "licenses to pollute." Early returns indicate mixed success for this new policy tool, with some firms (especially utilities) taking advantage of the concepts and others (such as 3M) refusing to use their credits to pollute further and, in effect, "retiring" their credits so that no other firm can use their credits to produce more pollution.

One type of air pollution that is increasing in importance is indoor air pollution, but it is not yet regulated by the Clean Air Act. Tobacco smoke, paints, fumes, furnace exhaust, and outgassing products of many kinds have been identified as potential indoor air pollutants, causing business employees and housing residents to complain about a variety of health problems. Apparently, businesses are left to regulate themselves in this area, unless state law and/or local ordinances establish restrictions. Many businesses and other organizations have decided, for instance, to establish no-smoking areas on their premises.

Water Quality Legislation

U.S. government involvement in water quality issues has followed a pattern similar to that of air quality issues. The Clean Water Act (also known as the Federal Water Pollution Control Act) was passed in the early 1970s with broad environmental quality goals and an implementation system, involving both the federal and state governments, designed to attain those goals. The ultimate purpose of the Clean Water Act was to achieve water quality consistent with protection of fish, shellfish, and wildlife and with safe conditions for human recreation in and on the water. The more tangible goal was to eliminate discharges of pollutants into navigable waters, which include most U.S. rivers, streams, and lakes. These goals were to be accomplished through a pollution permit system, called the National Pollutant Discharge Elimination System, which specifies maximum permissible discharge levels, and often timetables for installation of state-of-the-art pollution control equipment. Another act—the Marine Protection, Research, and Sanctuaries Act of 1972—sets up a similar system for control of discharges into coastal ocean waters within U.S. territory. A third water quality law administered by the EPA, the Safe Drinking Water Act of 1974, establishes maximum contaminant levels for drinking water.[11, 12]

One significant water quality problem is virtually unregulated—nonpoint-source water pollution. Runoff from city streets, construction sites, farmlands and rangelands, and animal feedlots can cause significant nutrient and toxic substance buildup in the bodies of water receiving these pollutants, thereby damaging the usability of those water resouces for plants, animals, and humans alike. Again, as with the indoor air quality issue, businesses can regulate their own nonpoint-source pollution. Many farmers, for instance, have adopted voluntary planting and tillage practices that limit soil erosion and runoff and the use of harmful chemical herbicides and pesticides.

Land-Related Legislation

Land pollution and degradation issues differ from air and water quality issues, because land by definition is far less fluid and therefore somewhat more visible than air and water and is more amenable to local or regional problem-solving approaches. Consequently, the U.S. federal government, in the Solid Waste Disposal Act of 1965, recognized that regional, state, and local governments should have the main responsibility for nontoxic waste management. The EPA's role in this area is limited to research and provision of technical and financial assistance to these other government levels. However, a 1976 amendment to this act, called the Resource Conservation and Recovery Act, set up a federal regulatory system for tracking and reporting the generation, transportation, and eventual disposal of hazardous wastes by businesses responsible for creating these wastes.

Concerning *toxic* wastes, however, the U.S. government has staked out a much larger role for itself. The 1976 Toxic Substances Control Act requires manufacturing and distribution businesses in the chemical industry to identify any chemicals that pose "substantial risks" of human or other natural environment harm. This act also requires chemical testing before commercialization and the possible halting of manufacture if the associated risks are unreasonable. Because there are over 70,000 chemicals already in use in the United States and more than 1,000 new chemicals introduced every year, the EPA has prioritized the substances that must be tested to focus on those that might cause cancer, birth defects, or gene mutations.

The other major U.S. government activity in toxic wastes is known as Superfund, or, more formally, the Comprehensive Environmental Response, Compensation, and Liability Act of 1980 (CERCLA). Superfund is an effort to clean up over 2,000 hazardous waste dumps and spills around the country, some dating back to the previous century. Funded by taxes on chemicals and petroleum, this program has established a National Priorities List to focus on the most hazardous sites, and places legal and financial responsibility for the proper remediation of these sites on the appropriate parties. In addition, CERCLA also requires that unauthorized hazardous waste spills be reported and can order those responsible to clean up the sites.

One of the most recent and perhaps most important amendments to the Superfund law, the Emergency Planning and Community Right-to-Know Act of 1986, requires manufacturing companies to report to the federal government annually all of their releases into the environment of any of more than 500 toxic chemicals and chemical compounds. These reports are accumulated and made available to the public, with the intention that an informed public will pressure manufacturers to reduce these toxic releases.[13, 14]

Other Environment-Related Legislation in the United States

The U.S. government's role in the natural environment is not restricted to activities of the EPA. Although this agency and the major laws it administers are the most visible, nearly every major department in the federal government has some actual or potential impact on environmental quality. Figure 12–2 is a brief list of these departments and assessments of their actual or potential environment-related activities.

One particular legislative effort of national governments worthy of the attention of business managers is the protection of endangered species by law. Costa Rica, for

FIGURE 12-2   U.S. Government Departments and Actual or Potential Environment-Related Activities

Department	Environment-Related Activities
Agriculture	• Forest management, wilderness preservation, soil and water conservation
	• Water bank (wetlands) management
	• Range (livestock grazing) management
Commerce (NOAA)	• Monitoring of radioactive ocean dumping
	• Environmental monitoring
Defense (Corps of Engineers)	• Inland waterways dredging/pollution
	• Dam building
	• Toxic waste sites
Energy	• Energy efficiency, renewable energy, fossil fuels, nuclear power development
Nuclear Regulatory Commission	• Radioactive waste, nuclear reactor regulation
Interior	• Endangered species, oil and gas leases, mining reclamation, national parks, wildlife refuges, fish hatcheries, dam building, livestock grazing, coastal protection
Justice	• Environmental law enforcement
State	• Global environmental negotiations
	• Debt for nature swaps
	• Ocean protection
Transportation	• Energy efficiency, air pollution control
Treasury	• Debt for nature swaps

SOURCE: T. A. Comp (ed.), *Blueprint for the Environment* (Salt Lake City: Howe Brothers, 1989).

instance, has restricted industrial development in fully one-quarter of its territory and 80 percent of the wilderness outside of this area. Although wilderness areas are also set aside in the United States through several programs, the U.S. federal legislation that perhaps most directly affects business activity is the Endangered Species Act. This federal law assigns the responsibility of preventing harm to species considered "endangered" (that is, facing extinction) or "threatened" (likely to become endangered). Since the law was passed in 1973, more than 800 species have been so listed, and another 3,500 animals and plants are being considered.[15] Whereas protection of species sometimes means moving them to safe areas when their original habitats have been destroyed by human activities, it often involves prevention of these activities, such as mining, construction, and fishing, before such habitat deprivation occurs. This restriction of business activities can be expected to continue as the extinction rate for nonhuman species climbs, resulting in sometimes intense political conflicts between business interests and environmental groups.

One recent Endangered Species Act case involved the protection of the northern spotted owl, a hornless, nocturnal bird native to the ancient forests of the Pacific Northwest, whose numbers had been reduced by human logging activity to 2,000 known pairs. In 1990, the U.S. Department of the Interior declared the owl "threatened." The Department estimated that the subsequent restriction of logging by forestry firms in the region, whose heavy cutting activities had involved 70,000 acres per year, would jeopardize 28,000 timber and related jobs by the year 2000.[16] Forestry firms complained that this action would entail $1 billion in lost wages for the U.S. Northwest economy and force unnecessary hardship on smaller loggers, whereas environmentalists argued that more jobs would be lost through the forestry industry's ongoing efforts to replace labor with technology and that the owl was an "indicator" species that needed to be protected so that the entire ancient forest ecosystem in the region could be conserved.

In the United States, state governments have been given increased responsibility for environmental protection since the "New Federalism" effort of the Reagan administration, which attempted to decentralize nondefense domestic programs. One independent organization that tracks state government environmental activities, Renew America, published several "State of the States" reports in the late 1980s, assessing and ranking state governments on various environmental criteria. Although this study found some excellent state programs in areas such as air, water, and land quality protection, the overall level of federal funding assistance for many of these programs fell precipitously during the 1980s, and many states experienced cutbacks of their own. The result of this greater state burden for environmental protection with diminishing financial resources, according to Renew America, was fragmented, inconsistent, inadequate, and waste-producing institutional policies. For instance, although water consumption had increased by 51 percent in the United States since 1960, contributing to significant local and regional shortages, only six states had water conservation programs.[17] Figure 12–3 identifies eight of the areas of environmental concern, identifying the state government programs perceived as model programs in those particular areas.

With the U.S. Congressional elections of 1994, and the resulting Republican majority, some observers believed U.S. environmental policy was to undergo significant change. The Republican majority apparently favored a less-activist orientation toward government protection of the natural environment, supporting proposals that reduce the ability of the federal government to require local governments to make investments in such environmental projects as water treatment facilities and to restrict the use of private property for environmental purposes without compensation. In addition, this view favors an increased use by the government environmental agencies of cost-benefit and risk-management analyses (described below) before environmental actions are taken.[18]

While the Republican assumption of control of the U.S. Congress in 1994, which portended major changes in U.S. environmental policy, was not significantly altered in 1996, the major victory of the Clinton presidential campaign that year indicated that major changes would not be forthcoming in the late 1990s. Because the

FIGURE 12–3   Environmental Areas of Concern for U.S. State Governments and Model Programs

Environmental Area	State Government Program
Forest Management	• Washington's cooperative agreement among many parties, including timber producers, to lengthen the application comment period and identify critical environmental priority areas for special attention.
Solid Waste	• Oregon's Opportunity to Recycle Recycling Act, requiring community drop-off centers or curbside recycling programs. Programs to encourage market development through tax credits.
Drinking Water	• Maine's use of computer tracking and training and certification for maintaining water quality and monitoring schedules.
Land-Use Planning	• Oregon's integrated land-use planning program, requiring establishment of urban boundaries and zones for environmental protection.
Surface Water	• North Carolina's significant efforts at controlling agricultural and urban runoff, using in part a cost-sharing program with farmers.
Pesticides	• California's Birth Defects Prevention Act, allowing the state to refuse to register pesticides for which a less environmentally damaging alternative is available.
Indoor Air	• New Jersey's protection of areas by prohibiting smoking in restaurants, workplaces, government buildings, public transportation, and health facilities.
Energy Efficiency	• Massachusetts' policies promoting energy conservation, least-cost electricity planning, appliance efficiency standards, and building code upgrades.

SOURCE: Renew America, *The State of the States, 1989* (Washington, DC: Renew America, 1989).

president, with his environmentally oriented running mate, Vice President Al Gore, campaigned on the slogan of "Medicare, Medicaid, education, and the environment," and the congressional Republicans received most of the blame for the late-1995 U.S. federal government shutdown, including the closing of the very popular U.S. National Parks System, many observers predicted that most changes in environmental policy would subsequently continue at an incremental pace. For example, one of the Clinton administration's main programs in its second term was attempting to improve the EPA regulatory approach through the greater use of voluntary and "market-based" programs. One Clinton administration program that exemplified several of these latter approaches was called the Common Sense Initiative, a multistakeholder, industry-by-industry, multimedia, voluntary program designed to find more effective and efficient approaches to environmental protection (such as toxic pollution prevention) in six sectors: automotive assembly, computers and electronics, iron and steel, metal finishing, petroleum refining, and printing.[19]

International Government Environmental Responses

Although the United States is the focus of many environmental issues as a result of its high profile in causing and responding to environmental problems, the global nature of many natural environment issues has meant that international institutions have also played important roles. Certainly, one international institution that has led the way in identifying global environmental problems and in working toward their resolution has been the United Nations Environment Programme (UNEP). Since its creation in 1972, this agency has been at the forefront in each of eight major environmental areas mentioned in the preceding chapter. As early as 1977, UNEP was studying the ozone problem and began to lay the groundwork for the 1987 Montreal Protocol, in which most of the CFC (chlorofluorocarbon) producing and consuming nations around the world agreed to a quick phase-out of these ozone-destroying substances. UNEP is also conducting research and assisting in information exchange on global warming problems through its Intergovernmental Panel on Climate Change, and at its Rio Earth Summit in 1992, it secured the signatures of the leaders of 153 countries on a plan to work toward reduction of greenhouse gas emissions. In 1995, a UN conference on this topic produced a compromise plan to establish a 2-year, target-setting process for emission reductions and to employ a "joint implementation" principle in which industrial nations would reduce their own reduction quotas by investing in emission reduction technologies in developing nations.[20]

Concerning wastes, UNEP has been instrumental in encouraging countries to reduce the amounts and toxicities of their wastes and to dispose of them in environmentally sound ways. Its Office on Industry and the Environment has been promoting waste-reduction technology since 1977. This pattern of UNEP research, information sharing, and negotiation networking has also been used in addressing marine environment, water and land quality, forest, and biological diversity problems with some success.[21]

Another major UN effort directed at dealing with global environmental problems was the United Nations Conference on the Environment and Development (UNCED), held in Rio de Janeiro in June 1992. This conference was the official worldwide environmental summit, following up on the 1972 UN Conference on the Human Environment, the first UN meeting explicitly recognizing that environmental protection was a global issue. UNCED's six-point agenda included a charter of principles, sustainable development in the twenty-first century, climate change, technology transfer, financial mechanisms, and institutions.

Although several controversial issues had arisen in each of these areas well before the conference began, one particular area of disagreement seemed an especially serious business environmentalism problem—the international trade in hazardous and toxic wastes. The transport and disposal of municipal wastes, including sewage and industrial wastes containing heavy metals such as mercury and lead, are generally supported by waste-producing industrialized nations, but the receipt of such wastes is being stringently regulated and banned outright by an increasing number of less-industrialized nations. For instance, since 1986, 83 nations have prevented the import of wastes, and the European Economic Community has banned the export of hazardous wastes to 67 African, Caribbean, and Pacific nations. The conference made progress on negotiating several treaties on various environmental topics, and a report, called Agenda 21, was drafted to lay out a multipoint global plan for sustainability. However, 5 years after UNCED, few of Agenda 21's many implementation measures had been put into effect.

Other international institutions involved in business environmentalism issues include the World Bank, the Inter-American Development Bank, the Asian Development Bank, and the African Development Bank, sometimes categorized together under the title Multilateral Development Banks, or MDBs. These institutions make low-interest loans to countries interested in further developing their respective economies. MDBs have been charged by some environmentalists as being insensitive, at best, to ecological problems in their borrowing client countries, and as contributing to the environmental problems in those nations, at worst. Protests by GreenPeace and others have centered on MDB loans made to rain-forest nations, which have been used for development projects potentially contributing to deforestation in those countries. In 1982, for example, the World Bank lent money to a company owned and managed by the Brazilian government to finance two dozen industrial projects dependent on charcoal for heat in one region of Eastern Amazonia. The required 1.1 million tons of charcoal per year was produced using a significant portion of the region's virgin tropical rain forest reserves. In addition to financing these forest-denigrating projects, MDBs have been charged with favoring energy supply rather than energy efficiency projects, with neglecting conservation-oriented efforts such as low-pesticide agriculture and solar cookstove and bicycle manufacturing, and with not including local communities adequately in the formulation and implementation of the projects financed by their loans.[22–24]

OTHER ENVIRONMENTAL STAKEHOLDERS

Environmental Interest Groups

Perhaps no force in today's society is more responsible for the "greening" of nations around the world than the many *environmental interest groups* making up what has come to be known as "the environmental movement." This collection of nonprofit membership and think-tank organizations, such as GreenPeace and the World Resources Institute, has been credited with moving the world's governments and businesses, as well as publics, in the direction of environmental responsibility through a host of activities, including demonstrations, boycotts, public education, lobbying, and research.

The history of the environmental movement is instructive. Whereas a few U.S. groups (The National Audubon Society, the Izaak Walton League, and the Sierra Club) were formed in the early 1900s during the first green wave of the century, many of the largest national and international environmental groups, such as the Environmental Defense Fund (EDF), GreenPeace, and the National Resources Defense Council (NRDC), were created during the second environmental wave, during the late 1960s and early 1970s. Since that time, all of the groups mentioned above and hundreds of other smaller, more locally focused environmental organizations have grown in size and clout. It was the century's third wave of environmentalism, beginning in the late 1980s, however, that gave many of these groups the power and legitimacy to become credible players in environmental policy making around the globe.

That environmental interest groups have grown in size and resources in the past decade is undisputed. Since 1988, the memberships and revenues of the largest groups have increased significantly, with some doubling or even tripling in just three years. GreenPeace, one of the more "radical" environmental groups, was one of the fastest-growing organizations in the early 1990s, with received information requests increasing from 1,000 per month to 1,000 per day during that time period[25] and with membership increasing from 600,000 in 1987 to more than 1.8 million in 1989.[26] Another indication of the popularity of environmental groups is the subscription base and revenue generation capacity of the periodicals published by those groups involved in public education campaigns. Even in the face of new entrants in the environmental publications field, environmental group publications were one of the few periodical segments to weather the recession of 1990–1991,[27] although several of them folded or merged in subsequent years.

That environmental interest groups had significant clout in the past decade or so is also difficult to dispute. For example, the former president of the Conservation Law Foundation and World Wildlife Fund, William Reilly, became the Environmental Protection Agency administrator in the Bush administration. Much of the Environmental Defense Fund's work on emissions trading was incorporated into the 1990 Clean Air Act. GreenPeace has scored several international environmental victories, including stopping French nuclear testing in the atmosphere, reducing toxic waste dumping and illegal whaling, and advancing the Antarctica protection cause.[28] The National Resources Defense Council forced the EPA, through a lawsuit settlement, to work for the Montreal Protocol, the international accord to phase out the use of CFCs, sooner than the administration originally had planned.[29]

Environmental interest groups have also been instrumental in significantly influencing business environmental policy in this third wave. EDF has coresearched and coplanned a comprehensive waste reduction plan with McDonald's Corporation, with the ultimate goal of reducing corporate waste by 80 percent. The Conservation Law Foundation has worked with the Massachusetts-based Northeast Utilities to develop a far-reaching energy conservation program, and this has inspired dozens of state and local environmental organizations to become involved in what has become known as "least cost utility planning" efforts, which are multiparty negotiations at the state level that typically encourage utility energy conservation programs.

Other outcomes of relationships between environmental interest groups and business stakeholders have included corporate selection of environmental group representatives for corporate boards and top management positions, mutual participation in environmental "cleanup" projects, and corporate donations of time and money to environmental groups for their environmental conservation programs. This trend toward cooperation between otherwise adversarial groups is a characteristic of the third environmental or green wave that sets this wave apart from the two previous environmental eras. The chairman of the Sierra Club has identified three types of major U.S. environmental organizations based on this criterion of cooperation with business. He has labeled groups characterized by confrontational behaviors as "radicals," groups that seek pragmatic reform through a combination of confrontation and cooperation as "mainstreamers," and groups that avoid confrontation and are more trusting of corporations as "accommodators." These categories, and details of several of the groups in each of them, are listed in Figure 12–4.

During the first 2 years of the Clinton administration, many environmental organizations saw drops in both membership and revenue, and several environmental

FIGURE 12–4   One View of U.S. Environmental Groups

Group Name	Founding Year	Number of Members	Budget (in Millions)
Radicals			
Environmental Action	1970	20,000	$1.2
Friends of the Earth	1969	50,000	$3.2
GreenPeace USA	1971	1,800,000	$50.1
Mainstreamers			
Environmental Defense Fund	1967	150,000	$15.0
National Resources Defense Fund	1970	160,000	$13.5
Sierra Club	1892	545,000	$28.0
National Wildlife Federation	1936	5,800,000	$79.0
Accommodators			
Nature Conservancy	1951	550,000	$109.0
World Wildlife Fund	1961	1,000,000	$50.0

SOURCE: M. E. Kriz, "Shades of Green," *National Journal* (July 28, 1990), 1828.

magazines suffered decreases in readership or were scaled back for budgetary reasons. GreenPeace, for example, lost over 30 percent of its supporters and about 15 percent of its revenue between 1990 and 1995.[30] Apparently, after the Clinton-Gore victory in the 1992 election, many members of the American public believed that, with Al Gore, an acknowledged environmentalist, as vice president, and with many former environmental leaders working throughout the Clinton-Gore administration, environmental problems would be managed without the need for extensive external lobbying and education. However, after the 103rd Congress failed to address a number of important environmental issues, and with the Republican takeover of the U.S. Congress in 1995, many environmental groups predicted that these membership and revenue losses would be reversed. Indeed, Earth Day 1995, which was the twenty-fifth anniversary of the original U.S. celebration of the natural environment, was one of the most successful environmental events in recent years.

Whatever the exact levels of support and resources the environmental movement now commands, businesses and governments may want to consider that decisions to avoid engaging in cooperative negotiations with environmental groups in the 1990s risk involvement in unproductive adversarial relationships with these organizations and their dedicated constituencies. Toxic and hazardous waste producers, such as the nuclear power and petrochemical industries, respectively, appear especially vulnerable to "direct action" and other potentially embarrassing and costly situations, as do mineral and forest products companies and waste management firms. Managers in these high-environmental-exposure firms may want to consider improving their stakeholder relationships with environmental organizations.

Green Consumers, Employees, and Investors

In addition to environmental groups, businesses are paying more attention to the latest green wave because of at least three other stakeholder groups: green consumers, green employees, and green investors. So-called "green" consumers are actual and potential customers of retail firms, usually in the industrialized countries, who express preferences for products, services, and companies that are perceived to be more "environment friendly" than other competitive products, services, and firms. Marketing research firms in these countries have identified a range of green consumerism, often segmenting these consumers into four or five roughly equal groups on the basis of the strengths of these preferences and reported consumer purchases. These studies show that nearly half of all consumers surveyed say they purchase products specifically because the products or the companies are perceived to be "green."[31] Based on these survey results and the evidence that the media have picked up on this trend with increasing frequency, prudent business managers are advised not to ignore the fact that many of their current and potential customers prefer "environment-friendly" products, service, and companies. The popularity of books such as *The Green Consumer,* the development of ecolabeling programs such as Blue Angel in Germany and Green Seal and Scientific Certification Systems in the United States, and a flurry of new environmental catalogs, led by the Vermont firm Harmony (formerly Seventh Generation), attest to the emerging business reality that green consumerism is an important economic and social trend.

A second stakeholder group with which most businesses are concerned is "green" employees. Although the popular press has not focused as much attention on "green" employees as it has on "green" consumers, there is some evidence that employees are playing a major role in promoting environmentalism at work. In addition to union and general employee environmental concerns with plant, warehouse, and office safety and health, employees in many companies have assisted management in going beyond these traditional concerns into areas such as pollution prevention, recycling, energy and environmental audits, and community environmental projects. Successful "Green Teams" have been operating at such diverse businesses as Goldman Sachs, Ace Hardware, Eastman Kodak, and Apple Computer.[32]

In 1991, the 3M Company rewarded several employees for environmental projects, including the establishment of a public park for the preservation of a northern Minnesota waterfall and the development of a system to track hazardous solvent inventories in its St. Paul laboratories. Gail Mayville, an employee of Ben & Jerry's Homemade, Inc., a Vermont-based frozen dessert company, was recognized with a Business Enterprise Trust award for beginning recycling programs in most departments throughout the company. Of course, employees in environmental units, which are increasing in number in major Western corporations, play a vital role in transforming their respective organizations into "greener" firms. In 1991, a corporation-wide 3M Technical Forum on Environmentally Compatible Products and Processes was initiated not by management but by technical specialists throughout the company. Environmental specialists of this kind are in very high demand, especially in the United States, with entry-level salaries far higher in the early 1990s than they were in the late 1980s.[33]

Alliances between organized labor and environmental groups are receiving increasing attention in the third green wave. Ecolabor coalitions have been forged in two areas especially—in proposals for a workers' superfund and in environmentally oriented international trade agreements. Both groups support the general idea of a workers' superfund, which would encourage corporations to fund a pool of money to finance workers who need to be retrained or relocated because of company responses to environmental regulations. The second issue, international trade, revolves around the question of whether high environmental standards are considered barriers to free trade. Both unions and environmental groups want to see high standards maintained in all international trade agreements (such as GATT and the North American Free Trade Agreement) to prevent job flight and cross-border pollution.[34]

Another important business stakeholder involved in environmental issues is the "green" investor. Similar to investors interested in advancing social causes, individuals and organizations sometimes want to "put their money where their environmental values are" by identifying and utilizing financial instruments that are associated with environmentally oriented companies. For instance, in 1995, there were at least 14 mutual funds in the United States that had some type of environmental characteristics, eight of which dealt exclusively with this issue. In addition, a growing number of stock and bond offerings, as well as money market funds and other financial instruments, have included environmental components in recent years. Each of these investment options offered its clients the opportunity to advance one or more environmental interests (e.g., recycling or solar energy development) without being penalized with below-average financial returns.

In addition, about 150 leading Western companies issued environmental progress reports in 1994, a fivefold increase over 1993, and these reports have begun to include more quantitative measures of performance.[35] Although this growing trend appears to be the perfect combination of ideals and practicality, there are problems with these reports and instruments. First of all, about 1,000 firms that are signatories to the International Chamber of Commerce's Business Charter for Sustainable Development have yet to issue environmental performance reports,[36] and thus determining whether or not these companies are good environmental investments is problematic. Moreover, a survey of 41 North American and European companies found that these firms had very different types of environmental reports and that only about a third of these companies mentioned environmental prosecutions and fines. Second, no commonly acceptable set of criteria yet exists for establishing whether a company financed by these investments is or is not environmentally beneficial. For example, some environmental mutual funds invest in Waste Management, Inc., because this firm is the largest collector of recyclables in the United States, whereas others shun Waste Management because of its millions of dollars of environmental, criminal, and antitrust violations.[37]

After the Exxon *Valdez* oil spill, several environmental, labor, and social investor groups, which formed an organization called CERES, developed a preamble and a set of 10 policy statements called the Valdez Principles (later renamed the **CERES Principles**), which have been advanced as models for businesses to express and practice environmental sensitivity. Excerpts from these principles are listed in Figure 12–5 and have been adopted by such companies as Sun Oil Company, Ben & Jerry's Home-made, Inc., and the Herman Miller Company.

The Role of Women in Environmental Issues

Women, both as individuals and as organization leaders and members, have the opportunity to play significant roles in advancing global environmental values. This opportunity gained significant attention just before, during, and after the UNEP World Women's Congress for a Healthy Planet held in Miami in November 1991. This conference identified more than 200 important and successful environmental projects initiated by women around the globe. The projects included the establishment of scientifically trained ecocounselors throughout Europe, ecotourism coops in Greece, an environmental literacy campaign in Mexico, and an organic gardening project in the San Francisco County Jail. In addition, several women environmental entrepreneurs have distinguished themselves in leading the "green business" movement through their successful environmental products and services, including Anita Roddick of The Body Shop, Suzy Tompkins of Esprit, and Sally Fox of Fox Fibre.

Several writers on the environment have suggested that women are more environmentally sensitive than men and that this characteristic can be accounted for by both biological and socioeconomic factors. Regarding the former, as a gender, women are more deeply affected by environmental contaminants, such as radiation and toxic chemicals, which affect their ability to bear and nurse healthy children. Concerning social and economic factors, women in industrialized countries are still more likely to have family responsibilities for consumer purchasing and for maintaining hygienic and safe home environments, whereas women in the less-industrialized world often must gather food and fuel for heating and cooking and pump water for drinking and cleaning purposes. Whatever the rationale, most polls taken during the third green wave have shown that women generally surpass men in being environmentally conscious and in favoring safety- and health-oriented government, business, and individual practices.[38, 39]

BUSINESS ENVIRONMENTALISM

Coping with environmental challenges is nothing new to businesses and other organizations in both the industrialized and less-industrialized worlds. Indeed, if agriculture and agricultural product trading are seen as early human business activities, one could argue that human organizations have needed to develop and implement responses to environmental challenges since very early in their evolution. Sun, wind, rain, soil, and pests posed significant environmental demands on early human organizations. Unwise farming practices and overgrazing of livestock were two early business-caused environmental challenges. The industrial and postindustrial revolutions, however, wrought manifold increases in human-related pollution and degradation. In addition, the pressures of human population and urbanization, the latter associated with real estate, commercial, and financial organizations, increased the challenges of natural disasters through human settlements of floodplains, along

FIGURE 12–5   CERES Principles, Adopted April 28, 1992

By adopting these principles, we publicly affirm our belief that corporations have a responsibility for the environment by operating in a manner that protects the earth. We believe that corporations must not compromise the ability of future generations to sustain themselves. We will update our practices constantly in light of advances in technology and new understandings in health and environmental science. In collaboration with CERES, we will promote a dynamic process to ensure that the Principles are interpreted in a way that accommodates changing technologies and environmental realities. We intend to make consistent, measurable progress in implementing these Principles and to apply them to all aspects of our operations throughout the world.

1. Protection of the Biosphere: We will reduce and make continual progress toward eliminating the release of any substance that may cause environmental damage to the air, water, or earth or its inhabitants. We will safeguard all habitats affected by our operations and will protect open spaces and wilderness, while preserving biodiversity.

2. Sustainable Use of Natural Resources: We will make sustainable use of renewable natural resources, such as water, soils, and forests. We will conserve nonrenewable natural resources through efficient use and careful planning.

3. Reduction and Disposal of Waste: We will reduce and where possible eliminate waste, through source reduction and recycling. All waste will be handled and disposed of through safe and responsible methods.

4. Energy Conservation: We will conserve energy and improve the energy efficiency of our internal operations and of the goods and services we sell. We will make every effort to use environmentally safe and sustainable energy sources.

5. Risk Reduction: We will strive to minimize the environmental, health, and safety risks to our employees and the communities in which we operate through safe technologies, facilities, and operating procedures, and by being prepared for emergencies.

6. Safe Products and Services: We will reduce and where possible eliminate the use, manufacture, or sale of products and services that cause environmental damage or health or safety hazards. We will inform our customers of the environmental impacts of our products or services and try to correct unsafe use.

7. Environmental Restoration: We will promptly and responsibly correct conditions we have caused that endanger health, safety, or the environment. To the extent feasible, we will redress injuries we have caused to persons or damage we have caused to the environment and will restore the environment.

8. Informing the Public: We will inform in a timely manner everyone who may be affected by conditions caused by our company that might endanger health, safety, or the environment. We will regularly seek advice and counsel through dialogue with persons in communities near our facilities. We will not take any action against employees for reporting dangerous incidents or conditions to management or to appropriate authorities.

9. Management Commitment: We will implement these Principles and sustain a process that ensures that the Board of Directors and Chief Executive Officer are fully informed about pertinent environmental issues and are fully responsible for environmental policy. In selecting our Board of Directors, we will consider demonstrated environmental commitment as a factor.

10. Audits and Reports: We will conduct an annual self-evaluation of our progress in implementing these Principles. We will support the timely creation of generally accepted environmental audit procedures. We will annually complete the CERES Report, which will be made available to the public.

SOURCE: CERES, *CERES Principles* (Boston: The Social Investment Forum, 1992). Reprinted with permission.

hurricane and volcanic eruption paths, in structures ill equipped to withstand tornados and other dangerous weather conditions, and, generally, in localities encroaching on "wild" wilderness areas.

The responses to these environmental challenges by businesses and related organizations were initially relatively limited. In the United States before 1970, most of these responses were either voluntary, characterized by participation in antilittering campaigns and support for a limited number of "outdoors" organizations such as the Boy Scouts, or mandated by court cases originating out of nuisance and tort common law. With the enactment of the National Environmental Policy Act and similar legislation at the state level, regulation and the threat of regulation became increasingly important as motivations for business responses. In 1975, 3M became one of the first large U.S.-based businesses to adopt an environmental policy and program.

Examples of Business Environmentalism

With the third and latest wave of environmentalism to wash over the industrialized world in this century, the dam of *business environmentalism* burst asunder. By late 1991, it was common for multinational corporations at least to appear to be involved in some voluntary environment-related activity. Of course, many businesses in the United States and other developed nations need to comply with a variety of laws at various levels designed to protect the natural environment. In addition, however, several business organizations have developed programs that have progressed well beyond mere compliance with environmental regulation.

The 3M Company is perhaps the best known multinational company to have adopted a comprehensive, beyond-compliance, environmental policy and program. Begun in 1975, 3M's Pollution Prevention Pays program is a multiproduct, multiprocess approach to manufacturing that has reportedly saved more than $700 million for the company by reducing various pollutants at their sources. Through product reformulation, process modification, equipment redesign, and waste recycling, 3M has prevented thousands of tons of air, water, and land pollutants from being produced and subsequently discharged. The company gives the credit (and financial rewards) for these environmental successes to its employees, who have developed more than 4,500 subprojects under this program. In 3M's innovative fashion, the firm has begun a new program—3P-Plus—that has set the new goals of reducing its hazardous and nonhazardous air, water, and land releases by an additional 90 percent and its waste generation by an additional 50 percent by the year 2000. In addition to being on target for meeting these objectives, 3M set and achieved in 1993 the interim goal of a 70 percent reduction in air pollutants, 3M's most common pollution problem.[40]

Other good examples of business environmentalism have been identified by four awards programs focusing on outstanding environmental efforts by business. The first of these awards programs, The Business Enterprise Trust, is an organization that recognizes businesses and individuals in businesses who have made substantial social contributions and are selected as examples for the business community to follow. In 1991, two of the several Business Enterprise Trust awards were presented to Merck & Co., for donating one of its drugs to combat an African blindness disease caused by insects, and to an employee at Ben & Jerry's Homemade, Inc., who single-handedly started a companywide recycling program for this frozen dessert maker and its franchisees.[41]

The second awards program, designed and implemented by Renew America, makes annual announcement awards to both profit and not-for-profit organizations. The 1994 awardees included Martin Marietta Corp., which had reduced its toxic chemical releases by 83 percent since the late 1980s, mostly through materials substitution, and the Recycled Paper Coalition, a group of 145 large-volume paper-using companies, which in 2 years recycled more than 17,000 tons of paper that otherwise would have gone to landfills.[42] The 1997 awardees included Central & South West Corporation, the Tulsa, Oklahoma, utility that invested $17 million in wind and solar technologies, and Springs Industries, Inc., of Fort Mill, South Carolina, whose waste minimization program achieved an 80 percent reduction in landfill use by its facilities.

A third business environmentalism awards program, the Better Environment Awards for Industry program, promoted by the Confederation of British Industry and the *Financial Times,* gave recognition in 1991 to Imperial Chemicals Industries for its development of water pollution technology for handling chlorine discharges, British Petroleum Chemicals for its development of an environment-friendly airport runway de-icer, and the Body Shop for its incorporation of environmental concern throughout its personal care products operations.[43]

In addition to the companies recognized by these awards programs, the list of organizations identified as "green businesses" is an ever-lengthening one. Paul Shrivastava, an authority on business environmentalism, identified GM's efforts at fuel efficiency and auto pollution control, DuPont's 35 percent waste reduction, McDonald's intention to use recycled products in restaurant construction and remodeling, and Chevron's industry-leading low oil spill rate as further examples of this movement toward addressing the environmental challenge by big business.[44]

The Green Lights program, a voluntary, nonregulatory program administered by the EPA to encourage major U.S. corporations to install energy-efficient lighting, had, by the middle of 1998, enlisted more than 2,500 companies and other organizations, including Amoco, Eli Lilly, and Polaroid. Industry associations as diverse as the American Bakers Association and the American Paper Institute have begun working with, rather than against, the U.S. EPA in developing environmental legislation and regulations.[45] One association, the Chemical Manufacturers' Association of America, has developed a set of 10 environmental principles, called the Responsible Care program, that have been adopted by a number of large chemical firms. Although this set of environmental policies falls somewhat short of the CERES Principles in scope and specificity, it does include an affirmation to "participate with government and others in creating responsible laws, regulations and standards to safeguard the community, workplace and environment."[46]

Small businesses, too, are promoting "green" products and services. Bodywares, a personal care products company based in Washington, DC, mixes and sells skin moisturizers and cleansers that are made from nonsynthetic bases and are not tested on animals. In addition, this retailer encourages its customers to return its plastic product bottles for refills and discounts. Another environmental entrepreneurial effort, Ecotech Autoworks in McLean, Virginia, offers one of the few "green" auto repair shops in the United States. Ecotech recycles all car fluids, especially CFC-containing air-conditioning fluid, and uses recycled auto parts at customer request. In addition, this innovative service uses recycled-tire shop floor mats and carbon monoxide-absorbing hanging spider plants, and offers a full range of environmental magazines in the customer waiting room.[47]

The "greening of business" has certainly not been limited to corporations based in the United States and Great Britain. Japanese and continental European firms, too, have begun to preach and practice a more environmentally conscious attitude in the third green wave. In 1991, more than 300 large Japanese corporations had environmental planning departments, and a network of 40 Japanese companies, the Nippon Eco Life Center, was formed to facilitate the exchange of information on the natural environment and on green businesses.

In addition to Toyota's campaign to produce a solar-powered car and Mitsubishi's Malaysian rain forest reforestation effort, one prominent environmental program established by a Japanese firm is the environmental credit card of the Daiei Supermarket Group. This program, which was designed by two well-known Japanese environmental groups, allows grocery consumers who use these cards to direct 0.5 percent of their grocery bills to any of 20 different environmental causes.[48] Other examples of Japanese business environmentalism programs include the plans of Sanyo and other firms to use recycled paper instead of plastic foam as packing material and the Japanese Automobile Manufacturers' Association's establishment of standards to mark plastic car parts for easy classification and dismantling for later recycling.[49]

Business environmentalism is also blossoming on the European continent. In Germany, a multi-industry recycling association made up of 95 companies and trade associations has been formed to accept and recycle a variety of packages that will be returned for deposit. The Swiss chemical company Ciba-Geigy has adopted an environmental policy statement, called Vision 2000, that gives equal weight to economic, social, and environmental responsibilities and has put into practice its Oekogenda (Eco-Agenda), providing environmental goals for each department and individual supervisor. The French steel company Usinor Sacilor S.A. is studying the environmental effects of steel cans and car bodies. Several European carmakers are attempting to design their cars for easy recyclability.

Environmental and Financial Performance

The prudent future business manager will likely ask, "Although protecting the earth may be a good reason to practice environmental management, will it pay off on the bottom line?" There are many anecdotes about firms making money from their environmental programs. One example is the experience of Lightolier, Inc., a Massachusetts lighting fixture manufacturer, which retrofitted its gas boiler to use 20,000 gallons of its otherwise-wasted hydraulic oil, saving $40,000, which paid for the investment in less than 1 year.[50] A few research studies exploring the systematic relationship between environmental and financial performance had been conducted by the mid-1990s, and although the results were not conclusive, many found this relationship to be positive. For example, a 1991 study comparing the financial performance of 84 companies with their environmental ratings by a nonprofit consumer group found that those firms with the highest environmental ratings had a 2.24 percent higher return on assets than those with lower environmental ratings.[51] Another study employing a different set of investor environmental ratings found that both return on assets and return on equity were higher for Fortune 500 firms with the highest environmental ratings.[52]

Systematic Business Responses to the Environmental Challenge

Business, as the major economic sector in most developed economies, has begun to address environmental issues in a variety of ways. These responses have been categorized by several business-environment writers. As shown in Figure 12–6, two of these response classification schemes are similar to that used on the corporate social responsiveness axis of the three-dimensional corporate social performance model presented in Chapter 2. This figure indicates that businesses can be categorized on environmental responsiveness dimensions, and so the prudent business manager is advised to determine how she or he wants her or his business to be perceived by others before selecting an environmental management strategy.

Various management tools are available for use in selecting or constructing an environmental strategy. These include several management approaches that will be discussed in more general terms in other chapters and a few that are specific to natural environment issues. In the first group are crisis management, issues management, and stakeholder management. Because these topics are addressed more fully in other chapters, only their applicability to environmental management will be discussed here. In the second group of decision-making tools are cost-benefit analysis, risk management, and strategic environmental management, which will be discussed more fully in this chapter.

Generic Management Decision-Making Tools

Managers can use crisis management in the environmental area by focusing on two factors: prevention and contingency plans. As can be seen in the Exxon *Valdez* case, Exxon, Alyeska, and the federal and state governments apparently did not pay

FIGURE 12–6	Environmental Management Classification Schemes	
Wilson's Social Responsiveness Categories	*Mathews's Green, Inc.*	*Hunt and Auster's Environmental Management*
Reactive management	Exploit the Green Fad While It Lasts	Beginner: Environmental management is unnecessary
		Fire Fighter: Address environmental issues only as necessary
Defensive	Environmentalism Can Sometimes Be Good for Business	Concerned Citizen: Environmental management is a worthwhile function
Accommodative	Environmentalism Is Here to Stay	Pragmatist: Environmental management is an important business function
Proactive	The Environment Is a Strategic Business Opportunity	Proactivist: Environmental management is a priority item

SOURCES: I. Wilson, "What One Company Is Doing About Today's Demands on Business," in G. Steiner (ed.), *UCLA Conference on Changing Business-Society Relationships* (Los Angeles: Graduate School of Management, 1975); J. Mathews, "Green, Inc.," *The Washington Post* (March 15, 1991), A23; and C. B. Hunt and E. R. Auster, "Proactive Environmental Management: Avoiding the Toxic Trap," *Sloan Management Review* (Winter, 1990), 9.

enough attention to preventing the 1989 Alaskan oil spill disaster or to implementing the inadequate contingency plan to recover the oil once it had been spilled. Although some attention had been paid to the vulnerability of the Alaskan natural environment to a small oil spill, this appears to have been understated and generally ignored. That either Exxon or Alyeska assessed its own vulnerability to a spill of any size appears doubtful. Finally, the lack of coordination between the two companies in immediately addressing the spill indicated a response plan that was only a paper tiger, never really put into practice. Had the businesses and governments followed basic crisis management principles, including vulnerability assessments and simulation drills, the outcome may have been different for both of these organizations and for Prince William Sound.

Issues management can be employed to track public interest in natural environment issues and to develop and implement plans to attempt to ensure that the scope of environmental problems is minimized and that the firm develops effective responses at each stage in the life cycles of environmental issues. Environmental issues can be developed as part of the environmental impact statement process or as part of the strategic planning macroenvironmental analysis process.

Similarly, stakeholder management applies to environmental management in that environmental stakeholders and their stakes can be identified, including the environmental public, environmental regulators, environmental groups, and various entities (human and nonhuman) across the entire natural environment. The follow-up stages of stakeholder management—that is, planning for and interacting with stakeholders—can then be conducted, so that each important environmental stakeholder is given adequate attention after it is identified.

Although crisis management, issues management, and stakeholder management can be used as generic approaches to environmental management, there are other, more traditional management approaches that have been used in the past specifically to decide natural environment issues. Two of these approaches are cost-benefit analysis and risk management.

Cost-Benefit Analysis

Although *cost-benefit analysis* has been used in other areas, especially those related to public and private capital budgeting and investment, it has also received an extraordinary amount of attention in natural environmental policy decisions. For instance, most environmental impact statements, which are required by the National Environmental Policy Act, have one or more cost-benefit analyses as the basis for many of the environmental decisions resulting from these studies. The idea behind cost-benefit analysis is that, in a rational planning situation, an organization wants to ensure that an environmental project is worth the investment. Costs are totaled and compared with overall benefits. If benefits are sufficiently greater than costs, the project is given the go-ahead; if not, it is shelved, revised, or scrapped. Decision makers in many dam projects, other water reclamation projects, and land development projects in the United States have utilized cost-benefit analysis to determine the value of these environment-oriented projects.

Although cost-benefit analysis sounds straightforward, several problems have been identified with this environmental decision-making approach. First, measuring all costs and all benefits of a proposed action is often very difficult. What will the costs be to an ecosystem if a species is pressured into extinction? What is the benefit or value of a wilderness area? Second, comparing costs and benefits can be problematic, because these factors are not always measured in the same units. How does one compare the advantages of a commercial or light industrial development project with the loss of scenic beauty and wildlife habitats? Finally, costs can accrue to one party, whereas another party receives the benefits. For instance, a real estate firm wishing to develop residential property may be prevented from earning profits (an opportunity cost) while an ecosystem and its species accrue the benefit of continued existence. One typical way to handle this generic inequality has been through side payments to correct the balance. However, humans have not yet developed a consensus on whether, how, and how much to "pay back" the natural environment for problems they have caused.

Given these significant weaknesses, how can the prudent manager use cost-benefit analysis as a tool in addressing the environmental challenge? First, attempting to identify and measure costs and benefits can be helpful in using other decision methodologies (for instance, stakeholder management). In such cases, costs and benefits can be thought of as negative and positive stakes. Second, if any costs and benefits can be compared, the trade-offs between them can in some cases serve to simplify the often complex decisions involved in environmental management. However, the shortcomings of cost-benefit analysis appear to warrant continuous attention and require the use of additional environmental decision-making methods.

Risk Management

Risk management is a second managerial decision-making tool currently being employed by organizations attempting to address the environmental challenge. This approach is similar to cost-benefit analysis in that quantified trade-offs are evaluted in deciding whether or not an environmental project or program is worth developing and implementing. The difference with this method, however, is that the risk of environmental damage (to ecosystems, nonhuman species, or humans) is substituted for either costs or benefits. In this scheme, the relevant decision-making factor is either the amount that should be invested to reduce the risk of environmental damage resulting from the business activity or the amount of environmental risk that is acceptable in relation to the benefits of the economic development activity. The difficulties of this technique are similar to those of cost-benefit analyses—that is, how can risks (especially long-term risks) be measured, and how can they be appropriately compared with costs or benefits? For instance, even if the risk of a nuclear meltdown could be measured and found to be statistically insignificant, would this assessment of the risk be convincing to community residents who would be neighbors of the proposed nuclear power plant? Again, it is suggested that the disadvantages of using this method in environmental decisions be kept in mind and that additional criteria be incorporated into decision-making frameworks involving the natural environment.

Because they are quantification-oriented methodologies, both cost-benefit analysis and risk management appear to be inappropriate for many environmental decisions. Science often lacks the quantified data that would allow us to estimate carrying capacities, thresholds, and cyclical and long-term effects to work into our cost-benefit or risk calculations. Wicked problems, such as the effects of global warming or the adequacy of nuclear waste storage, often require qualitative data from a wide spectrum of perspectives for their "resolution." Exclusive reliance on either approach, quantitative or qualitative, appears unwise in environmental decision making.

Strategic Environmental Management

The final managerial approach to addressing the business environmental challenge presented here is a well-known organization effectiveness tool that has been adapted by the authors to assist managers in developing and implementing overall approaches to natural environment issues. This model is called *Strategic Environmental Management (SEM)* and is presented as one way in which organizations can readily respond to their environmental challenges and integrate a wide range of responses for environmental effectiveness.

As can be seen in Figure 12–7, this method uses the McKinsey 7S framework, in which seven typical organizational components necessary for success are identified and integrated, and several "green" suggestions are given for each "S." Businesses can build environmental components into their superordinate goals, strategies, structures, and so on, in order to develop an overall organizational environmental response. Superordinate goals can include an emphasis on environmental protection in a company's mission statement, for instance, whereas one of its strategies can be developing or acquiring environmentally sensitive businesses. The key to using this model is for managers to identify opportunities for developing environmental responses in each of the S categories and to ensure that each of these responses is compatible with the others.

Using this approach, the environmental manager can incorporate concern for the environment and take environmentally sensitive actions in all organization departments and at all organizational levels. For instance, the *shared value* of waste minimization can translate into the low-cost *strategy*, enhanced by environmental quality circles *structures*, energy-conservation *systems* in manufacturing facilities, and environmentally *skilled staff* personnel who are motivated by incentives for meeting personal environmental objectives and by managers exhibiting an environmentally sensitive *style*. As mentioned in the previous chapters, each organizational department can play a role in the organization's interaction with the natural environment. Research and development departments can work with manufacturing personnel to alter their products and processes to limit pollution and depletion. Finance and accounting personnel can develop effective environmental auditing systems and cost out the potential for environmentally damaging projects, with the aim of reducing this cost as much as possible. Human resources managers can begin to incorporate environmental concerns in their recruitment and training programs, attempting to build an "environmental culture" in the organization. Marketers can identify their customers' "real needs," as opposed to their frivolous (and potentially environmentally damaging) desires for products and services, and adjust their distribution systems in transportation, packaging, and labeling so as to promote environmental sensitivity. This strategic environmental management approach is similar to both the concept of industrial ecology, which "requires that an industrial system be viewed not in isolation from its surrounding systems, but in concert with them,"[53] and the emerging international environmental management standard called ISO 14000, which includes organizational environmental objectives, issues, policies, systems,

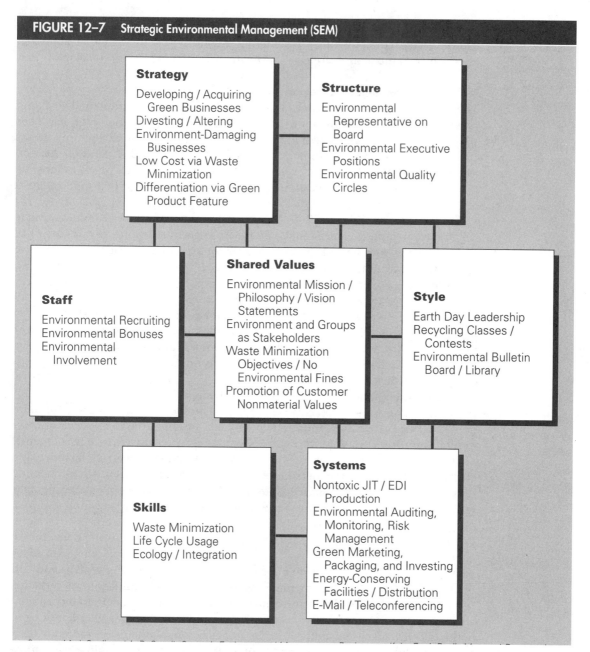

FIGURE 12–7   Strategic Environmental Management (SEM)

Strategy

Developing / Acquiring
    Green Businesses
Divesting / Altering
Environment-Damaging
    Businesses
Low Cost via Waste
    Minimization
Differentiation via Green
    Product Feature

Structure

Environmental
    Representative on
    Board
Environmental Executive
    Positions
Environmental Quality
    Circles

Staff

Environmental Recruiting
Environmental Bonuses
Environmental
    Involvement

Shared Values

Environmental Mission /
    Philosophy / Vision
    Statements
Environment and Groups
    as Stakeholders
Waste Minimization
    Objectives / No
    Environmental Fines
Promotion of Customer
    Nonmaterial Values

Style

Earth Day Leadership
Recycling Classes /
    Contests
Environmental Bulletin
    Board / Library

Skills

Waste Minimization
Life Cycle Usage
Ecology / Integration

Systems

Nontoxic JIT / EDI
    Production
Environmental Auditing,
    Monitoring, Risk
    Management
Green Marketing,
    Packaging, and Investing
Energy-Conserving
    Facilities / Distribution
E-Mail / Teleconferencing

SOURCE: M. Starik and A. B. Carroll, "Strategic Environmental Management: Business As If the Earth Really Mattered," *Proceedings of 1991 International Association for Business and Society,* Sundance, UT (March 22–24, 1991), 28.

and documentation aimed at "continued improvement of the environmental management process, leading to improvement in environmental performance."[54]

We previously identified two well-known organizations that appear to have come closest to developing this strategic view of the environmental challenge: 3M, with its

3P-Plus policy statement and programs mentioned earlier in this chapter, and The Body Shop, which has promoted a business self-concept that includes environmental protection and conservation—using bicycles for delivery, allowing employees to volunteer for environmental projects on company time, and employing a wind farm to produce the equivalent of more that half of its electricity needs. The limitations of the SEM approach are similar to those of the McKinsey 7S model itself, including a decidedly internal orientation (nonorganization stakeholders and forces are not explicitly emphasized) and a potential for much complexity. The prudent manager, once again, is advised to remember these weaknesses and to supplement this method with others mentioned in this section. The stakeholder management approach, with its external focus, might be a good match for the more internal SEM focus. Indeed, an eighth "S" that could be added to this model is "stakeholders," which could include environmentally oriented suppliers, customers, investors, and regulators, as well as the natural environment itself. Figure 12–8 matches some of Xerox Corporation's strategic environmental management features with these "green 7S" categories.

THE FUTURE OF BUSINESS: GREENING AND/OR GROWING?

Although the movie *Wall Street* focused on the ethical problem of insider trading, it also highlighted the salient environmental question we all may need to address in the future: "How much is enough?" A common business and, indeed, public policy goal in most human societies has been economic growth. Typically, businesses and societies have needed increasing amounts of either materials or energy, or both, to achieve that economic growth. Limits on growth, similar to limits on human reproduction, at either the macro or micro level, have not been widely popular. One potential problem with unrestrained economic growth worldwide is that, unless

FIGURE 12–8 Strategic Environmental Management at Xerox	
SEM Characteristics	**Xerox Corporation Reported Feature**
Shared Values	Comprehensive corporate environmental policy
Strategy	Movement beyond compliance toward environmental leadership both to increase revenue and reduce costs
Structure	Environment, Health & Safety (EH&S) Department, an Environmental Leadership Steering Committee, and EH&S Management Teams
Skills	Environmental information collection and dissemination
Staff (Stakeholders)	Employees, customers, nature, and neighbors highlighted in environmental report
Systems	Environmental management system, third-party audits, toner recycling programs
Style	"Earth Day Is Everyday" T-shirts distributed among stakeholders

SOURCE: *Xerox Corporation Environmental Report,* 1997, and discussions with Xerox EH&S.

technology or people change significantly within a generation, environmental problems can change in degree from significant to severe.

World population is projected to continue to increase, potentially requiring greater demands on food and fuel resources. Both industrialized and less-industrialized nations may contribute to this dilemma. The West and Japan continue to use increasing amounts of materials and energy to maintain highly consumptive lifestyles, whereas the rest of the world continues to use these developed nations as models for their own development. Given that the typical resident of an industrialized country uses 15 times more paper, 10 times more steel, and 12 times as much fuel as a typical Third World resident,[55] one can see the problem looming on the horizon. Combined with the Third World's population increase (approximately 1 billion more humans by the end of this decade), this quest for economic growth is responsible for the recent increase in commercial energy consumption among less-industrialized nations (up 4 percent since 1973) and the projected increase (of another 17 percent) by the year 2020.[56] Two pressing questions are whether the earth can support a high-consumption Western lifestyle for an increasing world population and, if not, what the implications will be for business and how business managers should respond.

Businesses might help resolve the human population problem in a number of direct and indirect ways. Businesses could allocate significant resources toward increasing the number and quality of career opportunities for women and educational options for girls, which would provide those of childbearing age with alternatives to raising large families. Businesses could also ensure personnel policies that promote high quality-of-life standards for their employees and communities, given the positive, direct relationship of enriched lives and limited family size. These and other business approaches, such as lobbying for increased attention and other resources devoted to family planning, could help ease the current and future population strain on the earth's limited resources. In addition and alternatively, businesses could support the redirection of less earth-damaging human population growth on the earth's oceans in the short term, and, perhaps in the not-too-distant future, above and beyond Planet Earth.

SUMMARY

In this chapter and the preceding chapter, we have explored a variety of environmental challenges and several actual and potential responses to these challenges. What themes appear to be woven throughout these chapters that can be especially helpful to prospective managers? First, many scientists, policy makers, public-interest groups, individuals, and businesses recognize that the natural environment is crucial for human survival and that a number of complex and interconnected human-induced activities may be threatening this environment. Problems such as human deforestation, pollution, and expanding populations are potentially endangering nonhuman species and ecosystems and reducing the quality of human life. Individuals and their organizations, including businesses, have been found to be directly or indirectly responsible for this situation.

Second, there are significant differences of opinion on how these problems will develop in the future and, of course, what should be done to resolve them. The facts that nature continues to evolve and human knowledge and actions regarding nature also continuously change argue against an "ecological correctness" approach. Instead, individuals and organizations, including businesses, concerned about reducing environmental degradation might adopt a flexible and prudent approach to keeping themselves informed and taking actions, no matter how small, in the direction of "walking lightly on the earth." A minimum baseline of not increasing human-caused pollution and depletion may be a potential starting point for consensus building and environmental consciousness.

This chapter began with a discussion of environmental responsibility, identifying the NIMBY problem of nonresponsibility as a significant factor in human individual and organizational decision making. We discussed the meaning of environmental ethics and several different sets of environmental values. The roles of governments in the United States and elsewhere regarding environmental problems were explored, and the necessity for involving other environmental stakeholders, such as environmental interest groups, consumers, employees, and investors, was advised. We presented numerous examples of business environmentalism and several generic and specific models that managers might use in making more effective environmental management decisions. Finally, the issue of continued economic growth was raised, and it was suggested that managers continue to explore environmental issues and to consider reducing negative environmental impacts related to their organizations.

KEY TERMS

business environmental-ism (page 379)

CERES Principles (page 376)

cost-benefit analysis (page 383)

environmental interest groups (page 372)

"green" values (page 362)

NIMBY (page 361)

risk management (page 384)

Strategic Environmental Management (SEM) (page 385)

DISCUSSION QUESTIONS

1. Who has responsibility for addressing environmental issues?
2. How can ethics be applied in response to environmental issues?
3. How have nonbusiness organizations responded to environmental challenges?
4. What are some examples of business environmentalism and decision models for addressing environmental concerns?
5. Should businesses and societies continue to focus on unlimited economic growth?

ENDNOTES

1. Council on Environmental Quality, *Environmental Quality* (Washington, DC: USGPO, 1990), XV.
2. A. Roddick, *Body and Soul* (New York: Crown Publishers, 1991), 248.

3. R.O. Mason and I.I. Mitroff, *Challenging Strategic Planning Assumptions* (New York: Wiley, 1981), 12–13.

4. R.E. Dunlap, "Public Opinion in the 1980s: Clear Consensus, Ambiguous Commitment," *Environment* (Vol. 33, No. 8, 1991), 10–15, 32–37.

5. S. Irvine and A. Pouton, *A Green Manifesto* (London: Optima, 1988), 14–16.

6. *Ibid.*, 16.

7. R.E. Dunlap and K.D. VanLiere, "The 'New Environmental Paradigm,'" *The Journal of Environmental Education* (Vol. 9, No. 4, 1978), 10–19.

8. Public Law 91-190 (1969), 42 U.S.C. Section 4331 et seq.

9. T. McAdams, *Law, Business, and Society*, 3rd ed. (Homewood, IL: Irwin, 1992), 779–783.

10. O.L. Reed, *The Legal Environment of Business* (New York: McGraw-Hill, 1987), 697–703.

11. McAdams, 784–787.

12. Reed, 704–706.

13. McAdams, 788–792.

14. Reed, 709–712.

15. Environmental Protection Agency, *Guide to Environmental Issues* (Washington, DC: USGPO, April, 1995), 74.

16. T. Egan, "U.S. Declares Owl to Be Threatened by Heavy Logging," *The New York Times* (June 23, 1990), 10.

17. Renew America, *The State of the States, 1989* (Washington, DC: Renew America, 1989), 2, 29.

18. "GOP Will Reform EHS Landscape," *Environment Today* (Vol. 6, No. 1, 1995), 1, 7.

19. A.B. Graham, "Using Common Sense," *Tomorrow* (Vol. 5, No. 1, 1995), 34.

20. R. Atkinson, "Greenhouse Gas Cutback Goals Left Up in Air," *The Washington Post* (April 8, 1995), A24.

21. United Nations Environment Programme, *UNEP Profile* (Nairobi, Kenya: United Nations Environment Programme, 1990), 4–20.

22. S. Postel and C. Flavin, "Reshaping the Global Economy," in L.R. Brown et al., *State of the World, 1991* (New York: Norton, 1991), 75.

23. E.H. Corson (ed.), *The Global Ecology Handbook* (Boston: Beacon Press, 1990), 58.

24. B.M. Rich, "The 'Greening' of the Development Banks: Rhetoric and Reality," *The Ecologist* (Vol. 19, No. 2, 1989), 44–52.

25. M. Weisskopf, "From Fringe to Political Mainstream," *The Washington Post* (April 19, 1990), A1.

26. D. Sterne, "Many Environmental Groups Slow to React to Growth, Some Critics Say," *The NonProfit Times* (Vol. 4, No. 1, 1990), 1, 16–17.

27. A. Thompson, "Environmental Magazines Defy Slump," *The Wall Street Journal* (September 10, 1991), B1, 4.

28. J. Naar, *Design for a Livable Planet* (New York: Harper & Row, 1990), 264–265.

29. Weisskopf, A16.

30. C. Frankel, "GreenPeace Chooses Double," *Tomorrow* (Vol. 5, No. 1, 1995), 22.

31. R. Gutfeld, "Eight of 10 Americans are Environmentalists, At Least They Say So," *The Wall Street Journal* (Vol. 228, No. 24, 1991), A1.

32. J. Makower, "Green Teams," *The Green Business Letter* (November 6, 1991), 1.

33. S.L. Nazario, "Green Field: Environmental Engineers Command High Pay, Choice Assignments," *The Wall Street Journal* (October 21, 1991), B1.

34. B. Ahlberg, "Green Around the Blue Collar?" *Utne Reader* (July/August, 1991). 44–45.

35. T. Browder, "Corporate Environmental Reporting—Evolving Fast," *Investor's Environmental Report* (January/February, 1995), 1.

36. *Ibid.*

37. R.A. Rose, "Environmental Investing," *Garbage* (September/October, 1990), 48–53.

38. P. DiPerna, "Truth vs. 'Facts,'" *Ms.* (Vol. 11, No. 2, 1991), 21–26.

39. T. Dean, "Environment: Global Assembly of Women Offers Success Stories," *Inter Press Service* (November 4, 1991).

40. *3M's Pollution Prevention Pays: An Initiative for a Cleaner Tomorrow* (St. Paul, MN: 3M Company, 1991).

41. James O'Toole, "Do Good, Do Well: The Business Enterprise Trust Awards," *California Management Review* (Spring, 1991), 9–24.

42. "Environmental Excellence Honored by Renew America," *Environment Today* (Vol. 6, No. 2, 1995), 5.

43. J. Hunt, "Winners Announced Today," *Financial Times* (March 13, 1991), IV.

44. P. Shrivastava, "Corporate Self-Greenweal: Strategic Responses to Environmentalism," presented at the Eleventh Annual International Strategic Management Society Conference, Toronto (October 23–26, 1991).

45. K. Staroba, "Environment: Truth, Outrage, and the American Way," *Association Management* (September, 1991), 39–41.

46. Chemical Manufacturers' Association, *Responsible Care: Guiding Principles* (Washington, DC: CMA, 1991).

47. J. Saddler, "Going for the Green," *The Wall Street Journal* (November 22, 1991), R13.

48. D. Porter, "A Greening Corporate Image—Japan Business Survey," advertising supplement to *The Wall Street Journal* (September 23, 1991), B12.

49. D. Porter, "Recycling Is a New Resource," advertising supplement to *The Wall Street Journal* (September 23, 1991), B12.

50. M.M. Hamilton, "Generating Profit from the Waste Up," *The Washington Post* (April 12, 1995), F1.

51. J. Makower, "From Greed to Green," *The Green Business Letter* (December, 1991), 8.

52. M.V. Russo and P.A. Fouts, "The Green Carrot: Do Markets Reward Corporate Environmentalism?" presented at the Academy of Management Annual Meetings, Atlanta, GA (August, 1993).

53. T.E. Graedel and B.R. Allenby, *Industrial Ecology* (Englewood Cliffs, NJ: Prentice Hall, 1995), 9.

54. J.B. Charm, "Joel Charm on ISO 14000," *Environment Today* (Vol. 6, No. 1, 1995), 22.

55. A. Durning, "Asking How Much Is Enough," in L.R. Brown, *State of the World, 1991* (New York: Norton, 1991), 161.

56. T.W. Lippman, "Energy That Both Develops and Depletes the World," *Washington Post National Weekly Edition* (January 28, 1991), 18.

13

Business and Community Stakeholders

CHAPTER OBJECTIVES

After studying this chapter, you should be able to:

1 Identify and discuss two basic ways of business giving.

2 Discuss reasons for community involvement, various types of community projects, and management of community stakeholders.

3 Explain the pros and cons of corporate philanthropy, provide a brief history of corporate philanthropy, and explain why and to whom companies give.

4 Differentiate between strategic philanthropy and cause-related marketing.

5 Characterize the nature of, magnitude of, and reasons for the plant-closing issue.

6 Address steps that a business might take before a plant-closing decision is made.

7 Identify strategies that a business might employ after a plant-closing decision has been made.

When we speak of a community, we usually mean the immediate locale—the town, city, or state—in which a business resides. In our modern age of global business, instantaneous communication, and speedy travel, however, the region, the nation, or even the world can become the relevant community. After Union Carbide suffered its 1984 Bhopal disaster, corporate executives felt that Bhopal had suddenly become part of their world, and this feeling has lingered for years. As global competition increasingly characterizes the nature of business activities, the corporate stake in community involvement will broaden and intensify. Traditional geographic boundaries will be eclipsed by communications technology and high-speed travel, and the community of the near future will encompass the entire world.

When we think of business and its community stakeholders, two major kinds of relationships come to mind. One is the positive contributions business can make to the community. Examples of these positive contributions include volunteerism, company contributions, and support of programs in education, culture, urban development, the arts, civic activities, and other health and welfare endeavors. On the other hand, business can also cause harm to community stakeholders. It can pollute the environment, put people out of work by closing a plant, abuse its power, and exploit consumers and employees.

In this chapter we will concentrate on community involvement and corporate philanthropy as community stakeholder issues. In addition, we will discuss the topic of business and plant closings as a community stakeholder concern. This discussion should provide us with an opportunity to explore both the positive and the detrimental effects that characterize business/community relationships.

In addition to being profitable, obeying the law, and being ethical, a company may create a positive impact in the community by giving in basically two ways: (1) donating the time and talents of its managers and employees and (2) making financial contributions. The first category manifests itself in a wide array of voluntary activities in the community. The second category involves corporate philanthropy or business giving. We should note that there is significant overlap between these two categories, because companies quite frequently donate their time and talents and give financial aid to the same general projects. First, we will discuss community involvement and the various ways in which companies enhance the quality of life in their communities.

COMMUNITY INVOLVEMENT

Perhaps one of the most compelling arguments for increased corporate involvement in community affairs is offered by J. Michael Cook. In addition to his position as chairman and chief executive officer (CEO) of Deloitte & Touche, Cook serves as the volunteer chair of the board of governors of the United Way of Alexandria, Virginia:

> *We have an absolutely enormous stake in the communities where our people live and work. If we have good educational systems, good safety, and good activity programs for young people, we're going to be much more effective in attracting and retaining quality people.*[1]

Therefore, business must—not only for a healthier society, but also for its own well-being—be willing to give the same serious consideration to human needs that it gives to its own needs for production and profits. Robert Cushman, former president of the Norton Company, enumerates six reasons for business involvement in the community:[2]

1. Businesspeople are efficient problem solvers.

2. Employees gain satisfaction and improved morale from involvement in community programs.

3. A positive image in the community facilitates hiring.

4. Often a company gains prestige and greater acceptance in a community when it gets actively involved.

5. Social responsibility in business is the alternative to government regulation.

6. Business helps itself by supporting those institutions that are essential to the continuation of business.

Obviously, it is practical for business to be involved in the community. It is quite appropriate for business to help itself in the process of helping others. This dual objective of business clearly illustrates that making profits and addressing social concerns are not mutually exclusive endeavors. Other rationales for business involvement in community affairs provide moral justification, beyond that of enlightened self-interest. For example, utilitarianism has been used to support corporate giving, with arguments that improvement of the social fabric creates the greatest good for the greatest number. This need not contradict the mandates of self-interest, because the corporation is a community member that will benefit.[3] Although justifications for corporate involvement in the community can be made from various perspectives, one thing is clear: Business has a public responsibility to build a relationship with the community and to be sensitive to its impacts on the world around it.

This point is driven home by the introduction to Eli Lilly's 1998 Corporate Citizenship Report:

> *As Lilly touches the lives of people worldwide, we recognize that we have a particular responsibility to be a good corporate citizen of the communities in which we operate and to help preserve the environment for the generations to come.*[4]

Various Community Projects

To provide an appreciation of the kinds of community projects that businesses get involved in, Figure 13–1 summarizes the wide spectrum of activities reported as being most frequently pursued by firms in the insurance industry. It is difficult to gather this kind of information from business in general. Thus, we report what insurance companies are doing because they have for years systematically gathered these kinds of statistics through the Center for Corporate Public Involvement, sponsored by the American Council of Life Insurance and the Health Insurance Association of America. We will gain a better appreciation of what business, in general, is doing when we later examine discussions and statistics on business giving that closely parallels community projects. It is worth noting in Figure 13–1 that, in the types of projects reported, there is a remarkable stability over a period of years.

Volunteer Programs

One of the most pervasive examples of business involvement in communities is volunteer programs. Corporate volunteer programs reflect the resourcefulness and responsiveness of business to communities in need of increasing services. A survey of 454 U.S. corporations conducted by The Conference Board and the Points of Light Foundation revealed that 92 percent of respondents encourage their employees to become involved in volunteer activities in communities.[5] The activities (and their frequencies) used by companies to encourage employee volunteerism include:

- Recognition through articles, awards, and commendations (91 percent)
- Publicity about community volunteer opportunities (87 percent)
- Board membership (encouraging executives to serve on boards) (86 percent)
- Company-sponsored projects involving multiple volunteers (83 percent)
- Ongoing endorsement of programs by CEOs (72 percent)

FIGURE 13–1	Types of Community Programs Supported by Insurance Companies and Percentages of Reporting Companies Involved

Types of Programs	Percentage
Education	87
Arts and Cultural Programs	78
Youth Activities	73
Local Health Programs	72
Neighborhood Improvement Programs	61
Minority Affairs	58
AIDS Education/Treatment	57
Drug or Alcohol Abuse Programs	53
Programs for the Handicapped	51
Hunger/Homeless Programs	50
Activities for Senior Citizens and Retired Persons	44
Safety Programs	34
Day-Care Programs	32
Housing Programs	32
Environmental Programs	31
Hard-to-Employ Programs	29
Crime Prevention	28
Prenatal and Well-Baby Care	25
Health Promotion: Low-Income and Minority Populations	16
Transportation Programs	16
Others	17
Number of Companies Reporting:167	

SOURCE: *1991 Social Report of the Life and Health Insurance Business* (Washington, DC: Center for Corporate Public Involvement, 1991), 4.

Two companies involved in volunteer programs include Tenneco in Houston and Allstate Insurance Co. Tenneco's Volunteers in Assistance (VIA) program started over 15 years ago in response to the needs of Houston, the site of its corporate offices. Tenneco saw in this program an opportunity to respond to the city's rapid growth and the associated problems. The Tenneco program, which is administered by a volunteer committee, has earned recognition from the city, state, and federal governments.

Allstate Insurance Co. has made urban issues a special focus. In addition to offering urban insurance for over 60 years, Allstate has committed itself to volunteer efforts in U.S. cities. The following list gives examples of some of the projects All-state supports:[6]

- The Lewis Street Center (Rochester, NY), a neighborhood settlement house that provides day care, foster parent/grandparent, and after-school tutoring programs.

- The Neighborhood Housing Services (Bridgeport, CT), which sponsors "Christmas in April," a 1-day-a-year neighborhood renovation blitz involving volunteer teams.

- Fire center demonstration houses (Miami, Chicago, Milwaukee), which teach children about fire safety through planned scenarios in which the "trapped" children effect their own rescues.

Communities obviously benefit from such volunteer programs, but how do companies benefit from employee volunteerism? The surveys cited above revealed that company executives thought they received a variety of benefits,[7] as follows:

- *Indirect community benefits*
  Creation of "healthier" communities
  Improved corporate public image
  Enhanced impact of monetary contributions

- *Employee benefits*
  Building of teamwork skills
  Improved morale
  Attraction of better employees

- *Bottom-line benefits*
  Facilitation of attainment of strategic corporate goals
  Increased employee productivity
  Positive impacts on company productivity

America's Promise

In a 1997 *Newsweek*/NBC News Poll, 74 percent of respondents felt that young people without viable job prospects were a greater threat to the United States than any foreign enemy.[8] When General Colin Powell, retired chairman of the Joint Chiefs of Staff, was asked what represented the greatest threat to the United States, he said, "the threat is young people who are disengaged from American life, who don't believe in the American dream."[9]

While Powell's words relate to the United States, the same situation is playing out in economically developed countries throughout the world. For this reason, service to youth has always been a priority for business. However, the profile of that service has never been higher than when President Clinton and General Powell convened an all-star "Summit on Service" to attack the problem of disadvantaged and disenchanted youth. The guest list included President and Mrs. Clinton; Vice President Gore; all the living former presidents, except Ronald Reagan (who was represented by his wife, Nancy); celebrities like Oprah Winfrey and John Travolta; governors; mayors; clergy; and scores of CEOs. The purpose of the summit was to secure commitments from corporations and civic leaders to work together to save an additional 2 million young people by the year 2000. The price of admission to this summit was a specific commitment to help at-risk youth.[10] Figure 13–2 presents a selection of the commitments received and illustrates the range of activities in which companies can become involved.

Less than 1 year after the Summit, General Powell has received 350,000 corporate commitments.[11] Having obtained significant commitments from Corporate America, Powell now focuses on securing commitments from small businesses, explaining to groups how "mom and pop" establishments are well positioned to serve the community. In a 1998 *Nation's Business* interview, General Powell was asked why he felt small business also had a significant contribution to make. He replied:

> *[They are] . . . more important than the major corporations because they live in these communities; they are out there in the field. Every small business out there that can hire a youngster for an afternoon job, a Saturday job, a summer job, or a holiday job is providing a safe place for a youngster, putting that youngster in the presence of adults who care about the person, teaching the person responsibility, structure, discipline, math and how to interact with customers or others in the work environment.*
>
> *But they have to do more than hire their partner's kid or their neighbor's kid. They have got to find a kid who might not look like too much right away, who might need a little bit of coaching and training, who might need a little bit of instruction in how to show up on time, dress for the job, and interact with customers. . . .*
>
> *There are other roles for small business to play. A small-business manager, a CEO, a boss, can let people off from the workplace for a few hours to go to a school on the other side of town, to spend a few hours with a child, to mentor, to read. What corporations have found is: We're not losing a thing by doing this. We gain in employee satisfaction; we gain in employee productivity at the end of the day; and we gain in what it says to the community about the responsibility of that corporation in the community.*[12]

It is too early to know whether "America's Promise," the umbrella organization formed to continue the work of the Summit, will achieve its ambitious goal of bringing business and nonprofits together to help at-risk youth. Corporate community involvement has been on the decline since the 1980s, when hostile takeovers created a corporate culture that devalued corporate giving due to pressures to cut costs. One example is San Francisco, where Crown-Zellerbach was acquired by Sir James Goldsmith, a corporate raider. Goldsmith placed Al Dunlap in charge of cutting costs, which he accomplished by cutting everything he could. According to William Zellerbach, who was on Crown-Zellerbach's top management team before the acquisition, "We would give employees time off to go out and volunteer. Business leaders would get together and allocate what each company had to give. And that's not going on anymore."[13] If America's Promise is to meet its goals, it needs a concerted effort from the business community. Whatever the outcome, the specific and measurable commitments that came out of the Summit represent a promising start. Examples of those commitments are given in Figure 13–2.

Resource-Based Giving
The increasingly competitive global environment has heightened pressure for efficiency in all areas, including community service. A key goal of corporate community

FIGURE 13–2	Examples of Commitments Made to America's Promise
Company	**Community Service Commitment**
Bank of Boston	Will deploy 500 volunteers to give inner-city youth mentors and jobs
Timberland	Will pay each employee for 40 hours of community service each year and will ask suppliers to do the same
Coca-Cola	Will train teen mentors in 90 schools
Everen Securities	Will bus employees to inner-city schools on company time to tutor in 10 cities
K-Mart	Will provide safe havens for kids in 2,150 stores
LensCrafters	Will provide 1 million children with free eye exams
Pillsbury	Will partner with Big Brothers/Big Sisters to do "School-Plus" mentoring in 10 cities
First Union Corp.	Will provide 4 hours of paid literacy training per month
AT&T	Will spend $30 million to link schools to the Internet
Shell Oil	Will involve 25 percent of its employees in corporate volunteering programs
KaBoom!	Will serve 1 million children by building 1,000 playgrounds in underserved communities
Kellogg	Will carry volunteerism literature on its boxes
Taco Bell	Will open six centers to provide after-school activities and job training for teenagers
VH1	Will expand New York City music-education program across the nation

SOURCE: Jonathan Alter, "Powell's New War," *Newsweek* (April 28, 1997), 28–37; Julian E. Barnes and Michael J. Gerson, "Powell Volunteers His Ideas on Helping," *U.S. News & World Report* (December 8, 1997), 7; and Fran Spielman, "Powell on Kid Crusade: Retired General Speaks at Conference of Mayors," *Chicago Sun-Times* (April 28, 1998), 13.

service is to get the most good possible from each dollar spent on giving. Companies often find that they can achieve the greatest good by providing services that fit their resources and competencies. Several of the America's Promise commitments listed in Figure 13–2 fit into this category. For example, LensCrafters can provide eyeglasses to children more efficiently and effectively than can a business that does not specialize in eye care. KaBoom! already has the expertise and materials needed to build quality playgrounds. K-Mart already owns the buildings needed for safe havens, and Kellogg already manufactures and distributes cereal boxes.

Resource-based giving involves assessing a firm's resources and competencies and determining where sharing those resources and competencies would accomplish the most good. For example, Aerial Communications of Minneapolis and St. Paul has donated wireless phones and air time to crime-prevention block clubs throughout the twin cities.[14] Wireless communications companies have contributed to public safety and education throughout the country by donating the equipment and air time nonprofit organizations cannot afford. Information technology (IT) firms have found their capabilities to be in great demand. Because many nonprofits are technologically behind, the skills and resources of technology-based firms can make significant differences in nonprofit operations. IT workers have given their time to causes as diverse as the Mount Washington weather observatory in New Hampshire, the Berkeley Symphony in California, and the Edmondson Youth Outreach Center in Omaha, Nebraska.[15]

Drug companies have also found they can accomplish more by drawing on their specific resources. In conjunction with the World Health Organization (WHO), SmithKline Beecham has launched a 20-year, $1.7 billion program to eradicate elephantiasis, a disease that affects about 120 million people in Asia, South America, and Africa. The plan is to give annual doses of albendazole to the 1.1 billion people worldwide who are at risk of infection by the disease. To accomplish its goal, SmithKline will donate several billion doses of the drug, as well as technical assistance and health-education support. Similarly, Merck has worked with WHO to provide free ivermectin to treat patients with river blindness in Africa, and it will help support the elephantiasis project by donating ivermectin for clinical trials to determine the drug's ability to treat elephantiasis when used jointly with albendazole.[16]

Managing Community Involvement

For discussion purposes, we are separating our treatment of managing community involvement from that of managing corporate philanthropy. It should be kept in mind, however, that in reality this separation is impossible to achieve. There are significant overlaps between these two areas. Corporate philanthropy involves primarily the giving of financial resources. Community involvement focuses on other issues in the business/community relationship, especially the contribution of managerial and employee time and talent. This section addresses these broader community issues; a later section of this chapter deals with the more specific issue of managing corporate philanthropy.

Business Stake in the Community

When one speaks with corporate executives in the fields of community and civic affairs and examines community affairs manuals and other corporate publications, one sees a broad array of reasons why companies need to keep abreast of the issues, problems, and changes expressed as community needs. One central reason is directly related to *self-interest* and *self-preservation*. For example, companies usually have a significant physical presence in the community and want to protect that investment. Issues of interest to them are zoning regulations, the threat of neighborhood deterioration, corporate property taxes, the community tax base, and the availability of an adequately trained work force.[17]

A second major reason companies need to stay abreast of community needs and problems is that certain issues involve *direct* or *indirect* benefits to them. Examples of such issues include health services, social services, community services, the physical environment, the appearance of the community, and the overall quality of life. A third reason has to do with the company's *reputation* and *image* in the community. For example, companies want to be thought of as responsible corporate citizens by residents, employees, and competitors. Companies may have expertise that can help solve community problems, and they want to build a reserve of community goodwill.[18]

Development of a Community Action Program

The motivation for developing a community action program is evident when one considers the stake a firm has in the community. Likewise, the community represents a major stakeholder of business. Therefore, business has an added incentive to be systematic about its relationship with the community. The four steps in developing a community action program, as articulated by the Norton Company, provide a useful framework for approaching the community from a managerial frame of reference. These four steps are:

1. Knowing the community

2. Knowing the company's resources

3. Selecting projects

4. Monitoring projects

These steps may be beneficial whether the company is considering specific community projects or is attempting to build a strong, long-term relationship with community stakeholders.

Knowing the Community.   A key to developing worthwhile community involvement programs is knowing the community in which the business resides. This is a research step that requires management to assess the characteristics of the local area. Every locale has particular characteristics that can help shape social programs of involvement. Who lives in the community? What is its ethnic composition? What is its unemployment level? Are there inner-city problems or pockets of poverty? What are other organizations doing? What are the really pressing social needs of the area? What is the community's morale?

Knowledge of community leadership is another factor. Is the leadership progressive? Is the leadership cohesive and unified, or is it fragmented? If it is fragmented, the company may have to make difficult choices about the groups with which it wants to work. If the community's present approach to social issues is well led, "jumping on the bandwagon" may be all that is necessary. If the community's leadership is not well organized, the company may want to provide an impetus and an agenda for restructuring or revitalizing the leadership. Figure 13–3 presents a checklist of items that companies might include in conducting an assessment of a community's needs.

Knowing the Company's Resources.   Effective addressing of various community needs requires an inventory and assessment of the company's resources and competencies. What is the variety, mix, and range of resources—personnel, money, meeting space, equipment, and supplies? Many companies are willing to give employees time to engage in and support community projects. This involvement may be in the form of managerial assistance, technical assistance, or personnel. Wide spectra of abilities, skills, interests, potentials, and experience exist in most organizations. To put any of these resources to work, however, it is necessary to know what is available, to what extent it is available, on what terms it is available, and over what period of time it is available.

FIGURE 13–3　A Checklist of Items Companies Might Include in a Community Needs Assessment

Demographics
- Basic descriptions (sex, level of education)
- Racial mix
- Poverty and unemployment
- Neighborhood characteristics
- Implications of the above for crime rate, percent elderly, racial discrimination, and so on

Environment and Land Use
- Housing stock (including restoration and preservation)
- Commercial and industrial space
- Open space planning; recreation
- Quality of water, air, and land

Infrastructure and Physical Services
- Condition of roads and bridges
- Traffic patterns and parking space
- Utilities
- Sanitation
- Communications

Leadership
- Business
- Government
- Civic groups
- Community groups

Leisure
- Parks and indoor recreational facilities
- Cultural and art facilities (museums, libraries, galleries)
- Shopping facilities
- Restaurants

Local Economy
- Tax base and rates
- Cost of living
- Economic development plans and agenda
- Employment and labor-force characteristics
- Aid to small business

Local Education
- Primary and secondary
- Vocational
- Colleges and universities

Local Government
- Structure (e.g., mayor or city manager)
- Municipal finance
- Crime and safety capabilities

Local Health and Human Services
- Social- and family-service capabilities
- Hospitals, ambulance service, emergency care facilities
- Degree of community problems relating to above (e.g., alcohol and drug abuse)

SOURCE: Kathryn Troy, *Studying and Addressing Community Needs: A Corporate Case Book* (New York: The Conference Board, 1985), 8. Reproduced with permission.

Selecting Projects.   The selection of community projects for company involvement grows out of the matching of community stakeholders' needs with company resources. Frequently, because there are many such matches, the company must be selective in choosing among them. Sometimes companies develop and refine policies or guidelines to help in the selection process. These policies are extremely useful, because they further delineate areas in which the company may be involved and provide perspective for channeling the organization's energies.

George Steiner identified several social policies that could be extremely useful to management in its attempts to inject rationality into its selection of community projects.[19] The following policies are illustrative of those an organization might develop.

- It is the policy of this company to concentrate action programs on areas strategically related to the present and prospective economic functions of the business.

- It is the policy of this company to begin action programs close to home before spreading out to far distant regions.

- It is the policy of this company to facilitate employee actions that employees can take as individuals rather than as representatives of the company.

Frank Koch has spelled out guidelines for developing a strategy for community involvement.[20] The following list summarizes some of these guidelines.

- Community involvement must be planned and organized with the same care and energy that are devoted to other parts of the business.

- Community projects should meet the same measure of cost-effectiveness as that applied to investments in research, marketing, production, or administration.

- The corporation should capitalize on its talents and resources. Those responsible should get involved in things they understand. The company should look at social problems that affect its realm of operations.

- Employees should be involved in community programs. The programs should focus on some of the things that affect and interest those employees.

- The corporation should get involved in the communities it knows, the people it knows best, and the needs that have the best chance of being fulfilled and are important goals of the community.

- Not all actions should originate in company headquarters. Effective programs should be initiated wherever business is done.

- Corporate policy should allow continuing support of established causes while new initiatives are being sought.

- The best kind of support is that which helps others help themselves.

Policies and guidelines such as those just presented go a long way toward rationalizing and systematizing business involvement in the community. Such policy statements should be developed and articulated throughout the organization to help provide a unified focus for company efforts.

An excellent example of a community project that was carefully chosen and is likely to meet most of the guidelines discussed above is the Ronald McDonald Houses sponsored by McDonald's Corporation. These houses, which annually provide shelter and solace for half a million people whose children are seriously ill, were begun in 1974. By 1998, there were 190 such houses in 14 countries. McDonald's employs the same pattern in all the communities in which the houses are located. Each is operated by a nonprofit corporation and is staffed by volunteers, except for a paid manager. Each house is located near a hospital that treats children, and families are charged a nominal amount if they can afford it and nothing if they cannot. The families may remain for as long as their children are undergoing treatment.

Another interesting example of community involvement is the attempt of Amoco, the petroleum giant, to pump life into needy neighborhoods. The hands-on program that Amoco initiated in downtown neighborhoods in Atlanta in the early 1990s is illustrative. Amoco created the Amoco Fund for Neighborhood Economies, in which it works closely with community leaders. In one neighborhood, Amoco funded a $6,000 feasibility study for converting a dilapidated school into a community center. In another neighborhood, Amoco helped to organize resources to build and renovate homes, acquire school property, establish a neighborhood crime watch, and implement a program for teens. In an area near the planned Olympic Village for the 1996 Olympics, Amoco helped fund and develop a master plan for neighborhood revitalization. Amoco has held workshops with community leaders in which it has outlined its approach, which includes (1) candidly diagnosing the strengths and weaknesses of neighborhoods, (2) organizing short-term projects that will involve many people and will have an excellent chance for success, (3) finding themes for targeted neighborhoods (for example, one theme was "Together We're Strong"), and (4) tailoring long-range plans to meet neighborhood needs. An Atlanta City Council member boasted about Amoco: "Many corporations in their well-intentioned philanthropy give money and don't see it through. Amoco's involvement is structured so that they get the most bang for the buck."[21]

Monitoring Projects.   Monitoring company projects involves review and control. Follow-up is necessary to ensure that the projects are being executed according to plans and on schedule. Feedback from the various steps in the process provides the information management needs to monitor progress. In later chapters we will elaborate on the managerial approach to dealing with various social issues. The guidelines previously listed, however, provide some insights into the development of business/community stakeholder relationships. As we stated earlier, community involvement is a discretionary or philanthropic activity in our corporate social performance model. It is also an extremely costly area of endeavor. Our stance is that it should be carefully managed, just as other business functions are, so that rationality and effectiveness can be maintained in what otherwise might become just an expensive arena of corporate "do-goodism."

Community Involvement of Foreign-Based Firms

Another indication of the growing sophistication with which companies are developing relationships with communities is the community involvement policies and practices of foreign-based business firms that have located in the United States. It has been extensively documented that foreign direct investing in the United States and its communities is a growing phenomenon.[22] Some observers have questioned the social consequences of foreign direct investment. It is not surprising, therefore, that researchers have sought to ascertain the extent to which these firms are becoming good "corporate citizens."

Foreign-owned companies doing business in the United States were surveyed in 1994 to discover their community involvement perspectives and practices.[23] Among this group of firms it was found that:

- Eighty-one percent had community involvement policies.

- Seventy-one percent reported that community expectations were a "very important" or "moderately important" part of their business plans.

- Their corporate giving levels and patterns approximated those of domestic companies.

- Over half reported being satisfied with their companies' community programs, but a significant number—39 percent—felt they should be more involved in their communities.

In terms of their motivations for community involvement, the foreign direct investors gave reasons very similar to those of U.S. executives[24]—namely:

- They felt a moral obligation to be involved (61 percent).

- They were responding to community expectations (56 percent).

- They felt that community involvement strengthened their corporate image (56 percent).

- They felt they were acting in enlightened self-interest (50 percent).

In interviews, these executives stated that if community involvement was done well, it allowed the business to become an accepted and valued member of society, which was good for its image with customers, employees, governments, and the wider community. Although their involvement was dominated by cash giving, the foreign-based companies had initiated other community programs, such as employee volunteerism and sponsorship (e.g., arts or sports events).[25]

In another 1994 study of the "corporate citizenship" practices and viewpoints of foreign direct investors, Pinkston and Carroll reported that these investors had "corporate citizenship orientations" that were quite similar to those of U.S.-based firms. They concluded that, based on these findings, there was little cause for concern over the increasing foreign presence in the United States. Foreign direct investors want to "fit in," and they perceive involvement with community stakeholders as a vital and integral part of that process.[26]

Joint Community Involvement Efforts

One final type of community involvement initiative that merits mention is the joint effort of several companies working collaboratively on philanthropic community projects. An interesting case study of this kind of endeavor is The Atlanta Project. The Atlanta Project (TAP) was the brainchild of former president Jimmy Carter. In 1991, Mr. Carter announced that he would initiate and lead a campaign in Atlanta to address the devastating social problems associated with urban poverty. TAP was to be one of the largest coalitions of business, government, and community leadership ever formed. The project was launched in 1992, and, in seemingly unprecedented fashion, the Atlanta business community came forward with more resources than were originally budgeted for the program. By mid-1993, TAP's business sector contributions had topped $32 million.[27]

Businesses' involvement with TAP turned out to be a combination of financial donations and community volunteerism. The targeted area—the inner city of Atlanta—was divided into 20 cluster communities, or "clusters." Each cluster had a corporate sponsor from the Atlanta business community. Cluster sponsors included firms such as Georgia Power Co., Sprint, Coca-Cola, NationsBank, UPS, Turner Broadcasting Systems, Andersen Consulting, Equifax, and others. Some of the projects initiated in the clusters and facilitated by the corporate sponsors included a financial aid seminar for high school seniors, donations of computer equipment, technical training in computing and in heating/air conditioning, employment assistance for cluster residents, sponsorship of cluster athletic teams, and development of a resource list of literacy service providers.

There were several primary differences between TAP and traditional community involvement efforts. First, TAP was a cooperative venture of 20 corporate partners rather than an effort of a single firm acting alone. Second, each TAP sponsor assigned a full-time executive to work on site for as long as 5 years. Third, TAP involved large financial commitments—for some of the corporate sponsors, the largest single grant they had ever made.

More than 300 companies from around the United States have visited TAP to learn about the program and its corporate involvement. Some of these visits will likely result in similar initiatives in other major metropolitan areas. Two other community megaprograms are already underway in Los Angeles (in response to the riots several years ago) and in Miami (in response to Hurricane Andrew). Historical antecedents to TAP included a series of 2,000 programs held in other cities (Dallas, Cleveland, San Diego).[28]

The future of mega-CSR projects such as TAP is uncertain. Although the first phase of TAP drew criticism for a lack of resident involvement, communications, and funding, the second phase is moving ahead, according to Douglas Greenwell, the new program director appointed in March 1998. Four collaboration centers and four new programs, providing prekindergarten, after-school, welfare-to-work, and health/immunization services, have begun.[29] TAP, which is slated to phase out in late 1999, still has many challenges ahead. Foremost among these will be to phase out in a way that ensures the continuation of corporate commitments.

Community projects with multiple corporate and governmental sponsors require expensive and complex coordination mechanisms and are not replacements for the efforts of individual firms. To be successful, it helps to have a first-mover such as Jimmy Carter to spearhead the initiative. Without such highly visible, prestigious leadership, it is doubtful that companies would undertake such enormous programs.

CORPORATE PHILANTHROPY OR BUSINESS GIVING

> ### SEARCH THE WEB
>
> The Foundation Center is an independent, nonprofit information clearinghouse that collects, organizes, analyzes, and disseminates information on foundations, corporate giving, and related subjects. The Center publishes the *National Directory of Corporate Giving*, which provides information on more than 2,900 corporate philanthropic programs, detailing more than 1,900 corporate foundations and more than 990 direct-giving programs. A wealth of information on corporate philanthropy and related topics can be found on the Foundation Center's Web site (**www.fdncenter.org**).

The dictionary defines *philanthropy* as "a desire to help mankind as indicated by acts of charity; love of mankind."[30] Robert Payton, an expert on philanthropy, argues that philanthropy is defined as three related activities: voluntary service, voluntary association, and voluntary giving for public purposes.[31] He goes on to state that it includes "acts of community to enhance the quality of life and to ensure a better future."[32] These definitions of philanthropy suggest a broad range of activities.

One more restricted contemporary usage of the word "philanthropy" is "business giving." In this section we will concentrate on the voluntary giving of financial resources by business. One problem with the dictionary definition is that the motive for the giving is characterized as charitable, benevolent, or generous. In actual practice, it is difficult to assess the true motives behind businesses'—or anyone's—giving of themselves or their financial resources.

To be sure, Americans value the philanthropy of the business sector. In a 1995 survey by Boston College's Center for Corporate Community Relations, Richard Barnes reported that more than three out of four Americans take a company's philanthropic record into account when deciding to do business with it. Not only did 80 percent of the respondents say they had decided to do business with a company because of its involvement in community improvement activities, but 74 percent reported that they had chosen not to patronize certain companies because they felt the companies had failed to act in the best interests of communities.[33]

A Brief History of Corporate Philanthropy

Business philanthropy of one kind or another can be traced back many decades. It was in the 1920s that the most significant effort to "translate the new social consciousness of management into action" emerged in the form of organized corporate philanthropy.[34] Before World War I, steps had been taken toward establishing systematic, federated fund-raising for community services. The early successes of the YMCA, the war chests, welfare federations, Community Chests, colleges and universities, and hospitals provided impetus for these groups to organize their solicitations. The business response to the opportunity to help community needs was varied. At one extreme, large enterprises such as the Bell Telephone system, with branches, offices, and subsidiaries in thousands of communities, contributed to literally thousands of civic and social organizations. Smaller firms, such as the companies in small mill towns of North Carolina, supported schools, housing projects, religious activities, and community welfare agencies with a degree of enthusiasm that exceeded most nineteenth-century paternalism.

Corporate giving in the period from 1918 to 1929 was dominated by the Community Chest movement. In the period from 1929 to 1935, there was an attempt to allow business to deduct up to 5 percent of its pretax net income for its community donations. The years 1935 to 1945, marked by the Great Depression and World War II, did not show an expansion of business giving. The period from 1945 to 1960 saw new horizons of corporate responsibility, and the period since about 1960 can truly be called a period in which social responsibility has flourished and gone beyond simple corporate giving. But because we are focusing on corporate contributions to the community, we will exclude those broader endeavors that began in the 1960s. The debate continues about whether businesses should give away money and, if so, how much they should give.

Recently, concern has arisen over proposed federal legislation that would require companies to disclose which charities they support and how much money they give. Although companies are required to disclose the money they give through foundations because of the tax benefits derived from the foundation's tax-exempt status, companies need not disclose direct donations. This has renewed the age-old debate about the role of business in society. Proponents of disclosure contend that the money belongs to the shareholders and they alone have the right to determine where it will go. Representative Paul Gillmor (R-Ohio) said that he introduced the disclosure bill, which was co-sponsored by Representative Michael G. Oxley (R-Ohio) and Representative Thomas Manton (D-New York), because he had sat on corporate boards and observed executives distributing corporate assets to their pet charities while ignoring shareholders. Gillmor's concern is shared by law professors such as Charles M. Elson of Stetson University, who argues that philanthropy often only serves to glorify corporate managers and that, unless the philanthropy clearly benefits the company, it represents a waste of corporate assets. A few nonprofits, such as the American Red Cross, also agree that disclosure would be good public policy. Surprisingly, the National Society of Fundraising Executives even support disclosure, arguing that it would help the image of philanthropy, which has been hurt by scandals in recent years.

This broad-based support notwithstanding, most corporations and nonprofits have expressed concern that disclosure would have a chilling effect on corporate donations. Their arguments include that charitable giving is a business decision, that it would provide competitors with information about a firm's strategy, that it might incite controversy with special-interest groups, and that the paperwork would become an administrative burden. As of this writing, the Securities and Exchange Commission (SEC) was taking testimony and considering modifications to the legislation, such as a lower bound for smaller donations and an exemption for donations to local charities. The SEC is also considering another bill introduced by Gillmor, which would require corporations to let shareholders choose to which charities their share of corporate donations would go. This second bill has received less support and been sharply criticized by industry as being unworkable for large corporations with many shareholders.[35] At this writing, testimony was being collected, but no vote had been held. Whatever the outcome of this proposed legislation, the debate over corporate philanthropy is certain to continue.

Giving to the "Third Sector"—The Nonprofits

Philanthropist John D. Rockefeller III has argued that business giving is necessary to support what has been called the *third sector*—the nonprofit sector. The first two sectors—business and government—receive support through profits and taxes. But the third sector (which includes hundreds of thousands of churches, museums, hospitals, libraries, private colleges and universities, and performing arts groups) depends on philanthropy for support. Philanthropy gives these institutions the crucial margin that assures them of their most precious asset—their independence.[36]

In the past decade, business giving has increased, but not at the same rate as corporate profits. In constant dollars, the real value of philanthropy grew from $5 billion in 1987 to $8.5 billion in 1996, a 70 percent increase that pales in comparison to the 120 percent increase in annual profits during the same period. From 1986 to 1996, the percent of profits designated for corporate philanthropy fell by nearly half; while pretax profits increased from $218 billion to $850 billion, corporate giving, as a percentage of profits, fell from 2.3 to 1.3 percent.[37] It is difficult to know the true impact of these numbers, because some of the corporate proceeds that go to nonprofits are not included in philanthropy figures. For example, cause-related marketing, such as Walt Disney's multimillion-dollar merchandising agreements with the American Society for the Prevention of Cruelty to Animals (ASPCA), is generally deemed a marketing expense and so does not necessarily contribute to the official tally of a company's charitable giving.[38]

Figure 13–4 ranks the firms that were the top givers in 1996 in five categories of giving.

Why Do Companies Give?

Perhaps it would be more worthwhile to know why companies give to charitable causes rather than to know *how much* they give. There are several ways to approach this question. We get initial insights when we consider the five categories of corporate contributions programs identified by the *National Directory of Corporate Charity,* as shown in Figure 13–5.[39] The motivations that are reflected in these categories range from pure self-interest to a desire to practice good corporate citizenship by supporting both traditional and innovative programs in the community.

A more straightforward assessment of the reasons for undertaking contribution activities was provided in a survey conducted by the Conference Board. This study of Fortune 500 companies, with 417 chairpeople and presidents responding, identified the reasons for which corporations support specific contribution activities, as reported in Figure 13–6.

From the data in Figure 13–6, we see that the major reasons for undertaking the specific activities varied slightly but indicated an identifiable overall pattern. In surveys of this kind, altruistic motives for corporate contributions are often indicated. Several studies have been conducted, however, that suggest a profit motive for corporate contributions. Block and Goodman, for example, designed two fund-gathering strategies to ascertain why companies give. One strategy was aimed at the motive of giving to the less fortunate in the community (altruism), and the other was aimed at self-interest of the firms. The conclusion was that the approach appealing to the givers' self-interest was more effective in motivating the giving than the approach

FIGURE 13–4	Top Corporate Givers in 1996 (Rank and Approximate Contribution in Millions of Dollars by Category)									
Firm Name	**Education**		**Social Services**		**Civic Affairs**		**Arts**		**Health**	
Intel	#1	$47								
IBM	#2	43.9	#2	$17.4	#5	$6.4	#1	$10.2	#9	$63.1
Hewlett-Packard	#3	43							#7	7.5
General Motors	#4	34			#6	6.3			#4	12.4
Exxon	#5	23.3								
General Electric	#6	22.7	#3	10	#7	6	#4	6.8		
Procter & Gamble	#7	19							#3	21.3
Microsoft	#8	18.7	#1	17.9						
Merck	#9	13								
Ford	#10	12.3			#10	4.9	#8	5	#10	6.4
Pfizer, Inc.									#1	75.2
Johnson & Johnson					#9	4.9			#2	63.1
AT&T Corp.					#1	14.4				
Sara Lee Corp.							#10	4.5	#5	12
Fannie Mae Corp.					#2	11.6				
Dayton Hudson			#6	8.3			#3	9.6		
Citibank, N.A.					#3	9.3	#9	4.8		
J. C. Penney			#4	8.5						
Boeing			#5	8.4			#6	6		
Mobil Oil Corp.					#4	7.2	#2	10.2		
Chrysler Corp.							#5	6.5		

SOURCE: Taft Corporate Giving Watch/Top 10 Supplement (February, 1998). Figures are approximate and are for 1996 giving.

emphasizing the interests of others.[40] In another study, Fry, Keim, and Meiners found that corporate contributions are motivated by profit considerations that influence both advertising expenditures and corporate giving. They concluded that corporate giving is a complement to advertising and is, therefore, a profit-motivated expense.[41]

As economic pressures and increased international competitiveness force companies to be more careful with their earnings, we should not be surprised to see the profit motive coexisting with loftier goals in corporate contributions programs. Indeed, in a subsequent section of this chapter, we argue that philanthropy *should* be "strategic," which means that corporate giving should be aligned with the firm's economic or profitability objectives.

FIGURE 13–5   Categories of Corporate Contributions Programs

1. *The Nondonor*—This is a firm for which no evidence of charitable giving was found.

2. *The "What's in It for Us" Donor*—With this firm, most contributions relate to the company's direct interest or to the welfare of its employees.

3. *The "Company President Believes in Art Support" Donor*—With this firm, most contributions relate to the company's direct interest, employees' welfare, or management's interest.

4. *The "We Are a Good Citizen" Donor*—Here a substantial portion of the company's giving provides support for traditional nonprofit institutions.

5. *The "We Care" Donor*—Here some funds go to newer organizations and established organizations that deal with nontraditional issues.

FIGURE 13–6   Reasons for Undertaking Contribution Activities (responses of 417 Chairpeople and Presidents)

Possible Reasons for Undertaking Contribution Activities	Specific Activities[a]		
	United Funds	*Higher Education*	*The Arts*
Corporate citizenship: practice good corporate citizenship	74%	49%	48%
Business environment: protect and improve environment in which to live, work, and do business	68%	46%	43%
Employee benefits: realize benefits for company employees (normally in areas where company operates)	47%	31%	31%
Public relations: realize good public relations value	34%	20%	32%
Pluralism: preserve a pluralistic society by maintaining choices between government and private-sector alternatives	28%	40%	10%
Commitment: of directors or senior officers to particular causes, involvement	23%	31%	28%
Pressure: from business peers, customers, and/or suppliers	12%	8%	17%
Altruism: practice altruism with little or no direct or indirect company self-interest	10%	8%	16%
Manpower supply: increase the pool of trained manpower or untrained manpower or access to minority recruiting	5%	63%	2%
No contributions or activities in this area	2%	2%	7%

[a]Totals exceed 100 percent because multiple responses were requested.
SOURCE: James F. Harris and Anne Klepper, *Corporate Philanthropic Public Service Activities* (New York: The Conference Board, 1976), 16. Reproduced with permission.

To Whom Do Companies Give?

During the course of any budget year, companies receive numerous requests for contributions from a wide variety of applicants. Companies must then weigh both quantitative and qualitative factors to arrive at decisions regarding the recipients of their gifts. By looking at the beneficiaries of corporate contributions, we can estimate the value business places on various societal needs in the community.

Data on corporate contributions show that business giving is distributed among the five major categories of recipients in the following approximate proportions: (1) education, 34.9 percent; (2) health and human services, 27.1 percent; (3) civic and community activities, 11.3 percent; (4) culture and the arts, 11.8 percent; and (5) other or unspecified, 14.9 percent. This data, which the Conference Board gathers on a regular basis, shows a remarkable stability over time.[42] A brief discussion of each of these five categories will help explain the nature of business's involvement in philanthropy.

Education. Most of the corporate contributions in this category have gone to higher education—colleges and universities. The major educational recipients have been capital grants (including endowments), unrestricted operating grants, departmental and research grants, scholarships and fellowships, and employee matching gifts. Also included in this category are contributions to educational groups (for example, the United Negro College Fund and the Council for Financial Aid to Education) and to primary and secondary schools.

As we noted earlier, business's most frequently reported reason for supporting higher education has been to increase the pool of trained personnel. This has obvious credibility, because higher education institutions do, indeed, form the resource base from which business fills its managerial and professional positions.

Although contributions to educational institutions rank high in business giving, companies do not always give blindly and expect nothing in return. Over the years, there has been some controversy about whether business should give to educational institutions that do not support the free enterprise values so important to business. The basic issue has been whether support of education should be "with strings attached" or "without strings attached."

Those who argue that business should give to education without strings attached think that attempts to dictate to educational institutions will create conflict between the institutions and industry. Louis W. Cabot, former chairman of the board of Cabot Corporation, argued that it is neither wise nor advantageous for business to limit its gifts to institutions that support free enterprise. His belief is that the corporate self-interest criterion is both illusory and dangerous. It is illusory in that it calls for sweeping generalizations about faculty members; it is dangerous because it tends to discourage all educational giving. He believes, in addition, that if a company genuinely wants to help education function with maximum effectiveness, it should support schools as a whole rather than try to control the use of its funds. Cabot summarized his view as follows: "It is in the corporate community's self-interest to step up its level of financial support. At the same time, it is *not* in the corporate interest to dilute this effort by burdening it with uncalled-for constraints."[43]

On the other side of the issue have been those who think business ought to be more selective in its giving. Robert H. Malott, former chairman of the board of FMC Corporation, argued that corporate self-interest ought to serve as a guide for business giving to education. Malott is especially concerned about corporations giving financial support to schools and colleges that teach the views of radical economists and others who want government to grow at the expense of free enterprise.[44]

Irving Kristol also argues forcefully that business has a responsibility to be discerning in its corporate contributions. He maintains that although universities believe they have a right to business's money, "they have no such right." His position is that if educational institutions want money from a particular segment of the population, they must earn the good opinion of that segment. If educational institutions are indifferent to that good opinion, they also will have to learn to be indifferent to the money. Kristol has argued against business giving money to support educational organizations whose views are "inimical to corporate survival." He summarizes his feelings as follows: "Your philanthropy must serve the longer-term interests of the corporation. Corporate philanthropy should not be, cannot be, disinterested."[45]

Unfortunately, there is no data to tell us which of these extreme positions is the most effective; they represent opposite philosophical postures. A philosophy tempered with the belief that managers should exercise some discretion over their corporate giving to education and at the same time serve the company's self-interest would achieve economic and social goals simultaneously.

Health and Human Services.   The major reason that health and welfare is one of the largest categories of business giving is the huge amount donated to such federated drives as the United Way. Dating back to the Community Chest movement, business has traditionally cooperated with federated giving mechanisms. Money given to federated drives usually goes directly to assist various agencies in a local community. Great public pressure is placed on businesses to support actively such federated campaigns, and so it is not surprising that this category is one of the largest beneficiaries. Business hopes, just as the community does, that such consolidated efforts will lend some order to the requests of major recipients in the community that business has chosen to support.[46]

In addition to federated drives, major recipients in this category include hospitals, youth agencies, and other local health and welfare agencies. Hospitals represent an obviously important need in most communities. They receive financial support for capital investments (new buildings and equipment), operating funds, and matching employee gifts. Youth agencies include such groups as the YMCA, YWCA, Boy Scouts, Girl Scouts, and Boys and Girls Clubs. Because a great part of the turmoil in the United States during the late 1960s and early 1970s had its source in the dissatisfaction of young people, many of whom were antagonistic toward large corporations, it is quite logical for business to include youth as a prominent part of its health and welfare contributions. Dreyer's Grand Ice Cream, Inc., focuses its philanthropic activities on youth to enable those youth to "develop individual initiative and talent in order for them to become contributing members of their communities and caretakers of the communities' values for the next generation."[47]

Civic and Community Activities. This category of business giving represents a wide variety of philanthropic activities in the community. The dominant contributions in this category are those given in support of community improvement activities, environment and ecology, nonacademic research organizations (for example, the Brookings Institute, the Committee for Economic Development, and the Urban League), and neighborhood renewal.

Eli Lilly and Company's education-oriented programs exemplify civic involvement with youth as the focus. For example, in Lilly's Junior Achievement programs, employees serve as business consultants to the local schools. Subjects such as applied economics, global learning, and personal economics are learned by children from kindergarten through twelfth grade. Lilly's "Partners in Education" is a mentoring program that pairs employees with children with special needs. The Minority Engineering Program of Indianapolis (MEPI) exposes minority students to career opportunities in engineering and computer science through mentoring, hands-on exercises, computer presentations, and field trips. In other Eli Lilly programs, employees promote interest in and awareness of science careers.[48]

Corning, Inc., is more than the biggest employer in Corning, New York. It is also a benefactor, landlord, and, some say, social engineer. In the past, Corning, New York, has been a company town, with Corning, Inc., being involved in providing affordable housing, day-care facilities, and new business development. Now, its efforts are more focused. The company plans to convert a remote, insular town into a place that will appeal to professionals. Its goal is to turn Corning into a town that offers social options for young singles, support for new families, and cultural diversity for minorities. Among its activities, Corning bought the run-down bars in one section of town because they did not fit in with the company's redevelopment plans. Employing a $5,000 payment and continuous lobbying, the firm got the dump owner to move. Corning is even trying to develop a region that will be less dependent on its company headquarters and its 15 factories. The company also purchased and revitalized an auto racetrack and convinced a supermarket chain to locate there. Corning continuously works to attract new business to the region, and it built the local Hilton Hotel, the local museum, and the city library.[49]

Culture and the Arts. Support for culture and the arts has been a favorite and prestigious outlet for business philanthropy for decades. Of the various cultural beneficiaries of business support, museums tend to be the most frequent, followed in order by radio and television (especially public broadcasting), music (symphony orchestras, for example), arts funds and councils, and theaters. But as the data show, culture and the arts rank behind health and welfare, civic and community activities, and education in total business giving.

One of the most prominent organized efforts on the part of business to support the arts is the Business Committee for the Arts (BCA). Formed in the mid-1960s, the BCA is a private nationwide group that was designed to "unite corporate money with artistic need." According to BCA data, when the group was formed, corporate giving to the arts amounted to $22 million. This figure grew to $90 million in 1968 and $110 million in 1970.[50] By the 1990s, it exceeded $200 million.

In the late 1990s, philanthropy has placed new emphasis on concrete results, leading to less interest in funding the arts as philanthropy is directed toward environmental, educational, and technological causes.[51] Despite this move away from funding the arts, substantial art donations continue. In 1998, Sara Lee donated about 40 pieces of Impressionist and early modern work, worth an estimated $100 million, to 20 U.S. art museums. This record-setting donation came from paintings that had once hung in the corporation's main offices.[52]

It is interesting to consider why business gives to the arts. Companies seem to gain none of the direct benefits that they receive from their donations to education. As with other philanthropic categories, businesses claim various motives for their giving. There are those who argue altruistically that the reason for business's largesse is that it recognizes that art contributes to the kinds of vitality and creativity that are important to society. The object of the BCA awards, which are given each year to companies that support the arts, is to "stimulate and encourage independent assistance of the arts" by businesspeople.[53]

On the other hand, there are business executives who say openly that their support for the arts has been at least in part a reflection of self-interest. Paul H. Eliker, former president of SCM Corporation, argues that companies should give to the arts in order to gain recognition or visibility and for general image building.[54] He claims that the great patrons of the Renaissance—the Medicis and Pope Julius II—supported culture and the arts for much the same reason: to associate themselves with the grandeur of the times.

Eliker told the story of a reporter who once asked George Weissman, vice chairman of Phillip Morris, why his company supported such exhibitions as American Folk Art. Mr. Weissman is reported to have responded, "It's a lot cheaper than taking out ads saying how great we think we are."[55]

Although no one can peer into the minds of business executives to find out why business really gives to the arts, at least one sociologist suggests that the motive is really self-interest, not altruism and social responsibility. This may not sound very startling, given the public admission of some executives that it is true. But M. David Ermann sees the giving efforts as part of an extremely selfish scenario. Citing gifts from major corporations totaling $12 million per year to the Public Broadcasting System (PBS), Ermann argues that such contributions are intended to create a less hostile social climate and thus mute the critics of business. In his words, the purpose of the corporate charity was to favorably "influence the social milieu . . . to ensure rewards and reduce penalties and uncertainty for the company."[56]

Recipients of business donations to the arts are not likely to turn down such contributions because the givers' motives may not be purely altruistic. Business giving, whatever the intent, does benefit the giver and the receiver, as well as the general public.

Giving to Antibusiness Causes

A recent study conducted by the Capital Research Center (CRC), a nonprofit group that monitors corporate philanthropy, has generated considerable discussion in the business community. This group, which is chaired by Terrence Scanlon, former chairman (1985–1989) of the Consumer Product Safety Commission, has concluded, on the basis of corporate giving patterns, that businesses are giving more money to antibusiness groups than to probusiness groups. The CRC studied 125 corporations and their 1991 contributions and found that for every dollar the companies gave to groups favoring lower taxes and less government intervention, they gave $3.35 to groups backing policies adverse to business. According to Scanlon, companies have been giving money to groups whose political success would mean less after-tax income for the companies and their shareholders.[57]

Foundation professionals have raised questions about the methodology used in this study. To arrive at their findings, CRC staffers labeled grant recipients as left, right, or centrist based on their impressions of the recipients' organizations. No outside experts or independent evaluators were used to validate the staffers' impressions. Further, all analyzed grants were for advocacy and policy work, which represent only 5 to 7 percent of corporate donations. Peter Frumkin, an independent program evaluator, uses the Atlanta-based BellSouth to illustrate his concerns with the study. BellSouth received a grade of "D" from the CRC for giving two grants to public affairs organizations—$240,000 to the National Foundation for the Improvement of Education (NFIE) and $40,000 to the American Council on Education (ACE). However, the former grant was directed at improving the education-related technology at 11 schools, and the latter was restricted to a fellowship program for students. According to Frumpkin, these two grants were used as the sole basis of CRC's judgment of BellSouth, and neither was devoted to advocacy.[58]

Although this issue is interesting to watch, it is likely to become less prominent as firms design their giving programs to maximize their positive impact on the bottom line. In the next section, we will explore the strategic management of corporate philanthropy.

Managing Corporate Philanthropy

As performance pressures on business have continued and intensified, companies more and more have had to turn their attention to managing corporate philanthropy. Despite increasing corporate expenditures on charity and the growing acceptance of corporate philanthropy as a legitimate corporate activity by shareholders, managers have been slow to subject their contributions to the same kinds of rigorous analysis given to expenditures for plants and equipment, inventory, product development, marketing, and a host of other budgetary items.

About a decade ago, all this began to change. Because of cutbacks in federal spending on charitable causes in the early 1980s, there was an increasing need for contributions by business. At the same time, however, the economy was struggling through its worst recession in 50 years. Demands that business become more competitive became the authoritative view on corporate survival. It became increasingly clear that business had to reconcile its economic and social goals, both of which were essential.[59]

Public Purpose Partnerships

As a broad response to this growing need to reconcile financial and social goals, both of which were deemed by business to be desirable and necessary, the concept of public purpose partnerships evolved.[60] A *public purpose partnership* occurs when a for-profit business enters into a cooperative arrangement with a nonprofit organization for their mutual advantage. Businesses see in public purpose partnerships the opportunity for simultaneous achievement of economic and philanthropic objectives. An example of a public purpose partnership is the one between 3M Company and the University of Minnesota. The 3M Company gave $1 million to the MBA program at Minnesota in 1994. Rather than just give the money and run, 3M officials formed a committee with university officials to discuss how the two organizations could work together. This was seen as a smart move on 3M's part, because about 15 percent of its employees are alumni/alumnae of the university.[61]

Another major example of a public purpose partnership was the decision in 1995 on the part of McDonald's Corporation and Georgia Institute of Technology (Georgia Tech) to enter into a multimillion-dollar sponsorship and marketing partnership. The arrangement called for McDonald's to give Georgia Tech $5.5 million to complete the financing of the $12.5 million renovation of its Alexander Memorial Coliseum. As part of the agreement, McDonalds will get to build two restaurants on the Georgia Tech campus, and the building in which Georgia Tech basketball games are played will be named the McDonald's Center. In addition, the McDonald's name will be placed on the basketball court and on tickets and program covers for all coliseum events. The deal also includes other signage, advertising, and promotional elements. Although the partnership was actually formed between McDonald's and the Georgia Tech athletic association, McDonald's representatives said they thought it could lead to other interactions and arrangements in academic and research-related activities.[62]

Public purpose partnerships take on many different forms. Two of the most important are strategic philanthropy and cause-related marketing. Other partnership options include sponsorships, vendor relationships, licensing agreements, and in-kind donations.[63] We will consider strategic philanthropy and cause-related marketing in detail.

Strategic Philanthropy

We should make it clear that strategic philanthropy was not *discovered* in the mid-1980s. For at least a decade, and perhaps longer, the idea has been evolving that business should apply its management knowledge to aligning its economic and social thrusts. In the mid-1980s it became clear that the need for this alignment was urgent. This need, combined with the experiments and experiences of several leading companies, brought this issue to a head.

How might we explain strategic philanthropy? *Strategic philanthropy* is an approach by which corporate giving and other philanthropic endeavors of a firm are designed in a way that best fits with the firm's overall mission, goals, or objectives. This implies that the firm has some idea of what its overall strategy is and that it is able to articulate its missions, goals, or objectives. One goal of all firms is profitability. Therefore, one requirement of strategic philanthropy is to make as direct a contribution as possible to the financial goals of the firm. Philanthropy has long been thought to be in the long-range economic interest of the firm. Strategic philanthropy, moreover, presses for a more direct or immediate contribution of philanthropy to the firm's economic success.

Another important way in which philanthropy can be made strategic is to bring contribution programs into sharper alignment with business endeavors. This means that each firm should pursue those social programs that have a direct rather than an indirect bearing on its success. Thus, a local bank should logically pursue people-oriented projects in the community in which it resides, whereas a manufacturer might pursue programs having to do with environmental protection or technological advancement.

A third way to make philanthropy strategic is to ensure that it is well planned and managed rather than handled haphazardly and without direction. When a program is planned, this implies that it has clearly delineated goals, is properly organized and staffed, and is administered in accordance with certain established policies. Figure 13–7 presents one company's views on what constitutes an effective strategic corporate contributions program.

Timothy Mescon and Donn Tilson elaborate on the need for managing the philanthropic function:

> *A professionally run contributions program requires a set of strategic plans, goals, and objectives which are reviewed regularly; a set of guidelines for determining how much money will be allocated to it; criteria for making and evaluating grants; and either an in-house staff or access to competent consultants.*[64]

An example of a firm that turned its philanthropic program around by making it more strategic is Burger King. For years, Burger King was an average corporate good citizen, quietly dribbling out $200,000 to the United Way along with small contributions to arts organizations and a scattering of other causes. At the same time, McDonald's, its major competitor, was gaining a reputation for strong social programs through its strategically focused Ronald McDonald Houses for children with

---

FIGURE 13–7   Characteristics of an Effective Strategic Corporate Contributions Program

An effective strategic corporate contributions program will have most of the following characteristics:

1. It will be based on the longer-term, strategic self-interest of the company.

2. It will have a clearly stated strategy, agreed to by top management.

3. It will have clear, well-defined guidelines.

4. By definition, it will be planned. (But not all planned giving programs are necessarily strategic.)

5. It will be based on objective criteria understood by all concerned.

6. It will be actively managed and evaluated for results.

7. It will focus on programs, not on capital or endowments. (Strategies change.)

8. It will be recognized as another function or tool in the entire public affairs process—not simply as a measure of corporate conscience.

SOURCES: Gerald S. Gendell, Manager, Public Affairs Division, Procter & Gamble. Excerpted from his talk at the Public Affairs Council's conference on strategic uses of philanthropy in public affairs. Diane R. Shayon, "Strategic Philanthropy Beginning to Take Hold," *Impact* (October, 1984), 2. Reproduced with permission.

terminal cancer. Then, suddenly, Burger King woke up and turned its corporate image around with a contributions strategy that sought to make a social statement. This Pillsbury subsidiary began pumping $4 million a year into highly focused programs to help students, teachers, and schools. Much of Burger King's philanthropy began to consist of scholarships to its own teen work force, designed to reduce the high turnover rate among those workers. As one direct result of the firm's education focus, its turnover rate dropped by more than half during the first 6 months of its national effort.[65]

Another example of strategic philanthropy was the decision of *People* magazine to promote charities that have particular significance to its readers. Thus, the magazine planned to give up more than $3 million worth of advertising space in 1994 to charities that represent such causes as women with ovarian cancer, children with AIDS, and homeless children. The magazine planned to go even further. It decided to experiment with a program whereby it would eliminate many of the usual "perks" offered to its best advertisers—golf outings, expensive dinners, Broadway theater tickets—and, instead, invite these companies' executives to engage in charitable activities themselves.[66]

In recent years, popular social causes adopted by corporate America have included hunger (General Mills, Grand Metropolitan, Sara Lee), community and economic development (Bank of America, Chase Manhattan, Citicorp), literacy (McGraw-Hill, Prentice-Hall, *The Washington Post*), school reform, AIDS, and environmentalism. With corporate support, several of these causes have become national movements.[67]

In a new book entitled *Corporate Social Investing*, Curt Weeden details the importance of selecting the right corporate giving manager to oversee philanthropic activities. First, the giving manager should be no more than one executive away from the CEO or chief operating officer (COO), with both a title and a level of compensation that reflect her or his position in the hierarchy. That person should have basic business skills as well as a solid knowledge of the profit-and-loss activities of the company. In addition, the giving manager should be aware of and interested in the nonprofit sector. Last, the giving manager must have the respect of fellow executives and the ability to be an effective company representative.[68]

Richard Morris and Daniel Biederman provide further recommendations on "how to give away money intelligently."[69] Some of their suggestions, all illustrative of the strategic thrust we have been discussing, include:

- Align your gifts with your product and goals.
- Choose the right organizational structure for your needs.
- Pick a manager to give money away.
- Treat grant seekers like customers.
- Set a long-term budget for contributions.
- Do not run your contributions program as a public relations exercise.
- Do not try to please everyone.
- Take a chance on an unconventional cause.

Finally, Craig Smith has identified six steps companies and their executives can take to implement strategic philanthropy.[70] These steps, which are listed below, help companies institutionalize strategic philanthropy.

1. Appoint and empower a philanthropy czar.

2. Support the czar's efforts to find the company's "natural" causes.

3. Promote and oversee a feisty dialogue between business functions and philanthropy.

4. Decentralize the philanthropic function.

5. Make the parts add up to more than the whole.

6. Continue research, testing, evaluation, and revision of corporate philanthropy.

All of these recommendations have one purpose in common—professionalizing the corporate contributions function so that it is more effective and more efficient. Now let us turn our attention to a special kind of strategic philanthropy that has become quite prevalent in recent years: cause-related marketing.

Cause-Related Marketing
There is some debate as to whether or not cause-related marketing is really philanthropy, but it does represent the closest of linkages between a firm's financial objectives and corporate contributions. Therefore, we will treat it here as one form of strategic philanthropy. Cause-related marketing represents a unique joining of business and charity with the potential for great benefit to each. Stated in its simplest form, *cause-related marketing* is the direct linking of a business's product or service to a specified charity. Each time a consumer uses the service or buys the product, a donation is given to the charity by the business.[71] Cause-related marketing has therefore sometimes been referred to as *quid pro quo* strategic philanthropy.

The term "cause-related marketing" was coined by the American Express Company to describe a program it began in 1983 in which it agreed to contribute a penny to the restoration of the Statue of Liberty every time one of its credit cards was used to make a purchase. The project generated $1.7 million for the statue restoration and a substantial increase in usage of the American Express card.[72] Since that time, American Express has employed this same approach to raise millions of dollars for a wide variety of local and national causes.

In 1985, American Express began "Project Hometown America" with a goal of raising $3 million as seed money for new kinds of hometown projects initiated and run by local volunteers. American Express agreed to make a specific contribution to this fund each time one of its cardholders used the cards, purchased American Express Travelers Cheques, or purchased a travel package worth more than $500 at one of its travel service offices. The money would then be administered by major charitable organizations, such as the United Way, the National Urban League, and the Girl Scouts.[73]

Cause-related marketing has been used by General Foods, Scott Paper, and many other large firms. One of General Foods' major campaigns linked the interest group Mothers Against Drunk Driving (MADD) with the promotion of Tang, a powdered, orange-flavored breakfast drink. In promoting Tang, General Foods staged a 4-month walk across America that raised $100,000 for MADD. The company spurred its own sales by distributing cents-off coupons to consumers and promising to give 10 cents to MADD for every Tang proof-of-purchase seal that consumers sent in. Cause-related marketing has received its most visible publicity in recent years as companies have attached themselves to fund-raising extravaganzas such as Hands Across America and Live Aid, the glitzy bicontinental rock concert that raised $83 million for famine-stricken Africa.[74]

Other notable examples of cause-related marketing have been conducted by Reebok, Nike, and Ralston Purina. Reebok created the Reebok Foundation to underwrite the Human Rights Now! tour, a world concert tour organized by Amnesty International. Nike has been concerned with inner-city issues because its products are coveted by inner-city youth. The company funds programs that deal with drug and gang problems and donates its proceeds to inner-city youth. For example, in one program Nike donated $1,000 to the Boys Club for every point scored by Michael Jordan during an NBA All-Star Game. Ralston Purina sponsored a program called Pets for People that helped senior citizens adopt pets. For each coupon redeemed, the company donated $0.20, for a total of about $1 million, to the Humane Society.[75]

In the 1990s, cause-related marketing has been used by business to achieve a variety of objectives. Listed below are four different, but related, purposes to which the approach has been directed.[76]

- *Global marketing.* Avon, Inc., promotes various causes in its several international markets. These causes include efforts to combat violence against women in Malaysia, child malnourishment in China, and AIDS in Thailand.

- *Short-term promotion.* American Express offered to give 2 cents per transaction to the antihunger organization Share Our Strength. The campaign raised $5 million.

- *Image building.* Coors Brewing Co. pledged to spend $40 million over 5 years for funding literacy organizations and causes.

- *Marketing to women.* Midas courted women drivers with its Project Baby Safe program. Every driver who bought a $42 car seat got a certificate worth that amount in Midas services.

Proponents of cause-related marketing argue that everyone involved in it comes out a winner. Business enhances its public image by being associated with a worthy cause and increases its sales at the same time. Nonprofit organizations get cash for their programs as well as enhanced marketing and public visibility made possible by business's expertise.

Critics of cause-related marketing suggest that there are issues that make the approach controversial. For nonprofit organizations who participate, one issue is the "taint of commercialism" that cause-related marketing may bring. The direct link between the nonprofit organization and the product being marketed may appear to be a promotional effort on the part of the nonprofit organization, and some may see this as compromising the organization's altruistic image. Other critics fear that if cause-related marketing becomes widespread, it could undermine the very basis of philanthropy. Still others fear that some corporations may use cause-related marketing as a substitute for, rather than a supplement to, regular corporate contributions. The consequence of this would be a zero net increase in the amount of funds available.[77]

From the corporate perspective, cause-related marketing looks attractive. Indeed, it is often viewed as a marketing strategy, not as a strategy for corporate giving. Quite often, in fact, funds for these programs are drawn from advertising and marketing budgets. For many businesses, increasing sales is the primary purpose of this approach, and providing resources for charity is secondary.[78] Nevertheless, we continue to see companies basking in the recognition they inevitably receive from supporting charity. From the corporate perspective, we can expect cause-related marketing to increase, although a saturation point may eventually be reached.

Global Philanthropy

Recent additions to corporate contributions programs are formal international philanthropy efforts initiated as part of global business strategies. In the past decade, U.S. companies have increased their contributions to foreign countries by more than 500 percent. Although contributions flattened somewhat in the 1990s, as did domestic contributions, U.S. businesses are now into global philanthropy in a big way.[79]

DuPont sent 1.4 million water-jug filters to eight nations in Africa. The fabric in the filters removes debilitating parasitic worms from drinking water. The cost to DuPont was $400,000. Alcoa teamed up with local authorities in Brazil to build a $112,000 sewage plant to serve 15,000 rural residents. H. J. Heinz spent $94,000 to fund infant nutrition studies in China and Thailand. IBM donated $60,000 in computer equipment and expertise to Costa Rica's National Parks Foundation to develop strategies for preserving rain forests.[80]

Companies among the top ten global contributors state that their contributions go where they have operations as well as a strong presence. In general, giving programs tend to focus on infrastructure needs, education, the environment and health care. Some companies, such as IBM and Merck & Co., donate large quantities of product, especially to undeveloped countries.

Executives claim several advantages of global contributions programs,[81] including:

- An improved corporate image
- A boost in market penetration
- Improved personal relations
- Improved government relations

Executives also note, however, that it can be difficult to administer programs in some cultures that do not place a high priority on voluntary activity. In addition, getting information about the impacts of their programs is difficult.

It is expected that global philanthropy will continue to be an integral and growing part of corporate contributions programs. As long as companies continue to generate revenues and profits abroad, involvement in these countries and their communities will continue.[82]

BUSINESS AND PLANT CLOSINGS

We now shift our focus to business and plant closings. In the preceding sections, we considered the ways in which business firms might have positive, constructive, and creative impacts on community stakeholders. Firms can also have detrimental impacts on communities. We see a most pervasive example of such negative effects when a business or plant closes and its management does not carefully consider the community stakeholders affected.

In the remainder of this chapter, we will examine the nature of the plant-closing problem, identify some reasons for these occurrences, and consider some actions and strategies that businesses might employ to minimize their negative impacts on community stakeholders. We will also consider the status of plant-closing legislation and the role of public action groups and researchers in helping us to understand this problem.

Reasons for Plant Closings

There is no single reason why so many businesses and plants closed over the past 20 years, although the recession of the early 1980s provided a major catalyst for these shutdowns. Some of the affected companies were in declining industries, some had outdated facilities or technology, some moved to less unionized regions of the country, some sought access to new markets, some were victims of the merger/acquisition frenzy, and many were victims of global competition. Although plant closings are not as prevalent in the late 1990s, they continue to occur and to profoundly impact the employees and the community. Therefore, it is important to understand why they happen.

In the mid-1980s, when plant closings were rampant, a major survey was conducted among public affairs executives to ascertain why they thought business closings were occurring. Figure 13–8 summarizes the reasons that were cited. The major reasons included economic recession, consolidation of company operations, outmoded technology/facilities, changes in corporate strategy, and unmet corporate objectives.[83] In later years, foreign competition became a vital factor. It is clear from these findings and other studies that the primary reasons for companies deciding to close down plants have been related to economics.[84]

What Should Business Do?

Although the right to close a business or plant has long been regarded as a management prerogative, the business shutdowns of the past two decades—especially their dramatic effects—have called attention to the question of what rights and responsibilities business has in relation to employee and community stakeholders. The literature of business social responsibility and policy has documented corporate concern with the detrimental impact of its actions. Indeed, business's social response patterns over the past 20 years have borne this out. Management expert

FIGURE 13-8   Reasons Cited for Business/Plant Closings

Reason	Frequency of Mention	Percent
Economic recession	67	48.9
Consolidation of company operations	64	46.7
Outmoded technology/facilities	41	29.9
Changes in corporate strategy	39	28.5
Unmet corporate objectives	39	28.5
Firms in declining industry	32	23.4
Foreign competition	31	22.6
Domestic competition	20	14.6
Search for lower labor costs	18	13.1
State/local attitudes toward business	11	8.0
Costly regulations	10	7.3
Other	8	5.8
Automation	6	4.4
Poor long-term planning	5	3.6
Inadequate capital investment	4	2.9
Quality of life	1	0.7

Note: This survey was answered by executives of 137 firms that had experienced shutdowns in the preceding 5 years. Frequency of mention indicates the number of times the reason was cited as one of the top four factors. It also includes instances in which multiple reasons were cited.
SOURCE: Archie B. Carroll, Elizabeth I. Gatewood, and James J. Chrisman, "Plant Closings: PAOs Respond to a Survey on an Increasingly Troublesome Issue," *Public Affairs Review,* Copyright © 1984, Public Affairs Council, 64. Reproduced with permission.

Peter Drucker has suggested the following business position regarding social impacts of management decisions:

> *Because one is responsible for one's impacts, one minimizes them. The fewer impacts an institution has outside of its own specific purpose and mission, the better does it conduct itself, the more responsibly does it act, and the more acceptable a citizen, neighbor, and contributor it is.*[85]

The question is raised, therefore, whether business's responsibilities in the realm of plant closings and their impacts on employees and communities are any different from the host of responsibilities that have already been assumed in areas such as employment discrimination, employee privacy and safety, honesty in advertising, product safety, and concern for the environment. From the perspective of the employees affected, their role in plant and business closings might be considered an extension of the numerous employee rights issues that many corporate social policy experts think will dominate employer/employee relations throughout the next decade.

Of the executives who have spoken out on this issue, several have indicated that there is an obligation to employees and to the community when a business opens or decides to close. As D. Kenneth Patten, former president of the Real Estate Board of New York, once stated:

> *A corporation has a responsibility not only to its employees but to the community involved. It's a simple question of corporate citizenship. Just as an individual must conduct himself in a way relating to the community, so must a corporation. As a matter of fact, a corporation has an even larger responsibility since it has been afforded even greater advantages than the individual. Just as a golfer must replace divots, a corporation must be prepared at all times to deal with hardships it may create when it moves or closes down.[86]*

Others have also argued that there is a moral obligation at stake in the business-closing issue. In an extensive consideration of plant closings, philosopher John Kavanagh has asserted that companies are not morally free to ignore the impact of a closing on employees and the community. His argument is similar to those that have been given on many other social issues—namely, that business should minimize the negative externalities (unintended side effects) of its actions.[87]

Business essentially has two opportunities to be responsive to employee and community stakeholders in shutdown situations. It can take certain actions *before* the decision to close is made and other actions *after* the decision to close has been made.

Before the Decision to Close Is Made

Before a company makes a decision to close down, it has a responsibility to itself, its employees, and its community to thoroughly and diligently study whether the closing is the only option available. A decision to leave should be preceded by in-depth discussions with community leaders (to test their willingness to cooperate in meeting the resulting difficulties) and by critical and realistic investigations of economic alternatives. Such investigations should include studies of long-term productivity and cost estimates, of the employee base and the nature of the available skills, and of the likelihood that identical problems might recur in a different location.

After a careful study has been made, it may be concluded that finding new ownership for the plant or business is the only feasible alternative. Two basic options exist at this point: (1) find a new owner or (2) explore the possibility of employee ownership.[88]

New Ownership.   Malcolm Baldrige, former chairman of Scoville Manufacturing Co., argued that the first obligation a company has to its employees and the community is to try to sell the business as a going unit instead of shutting down. This may not always be possible, but it is an avenue that should be explored to its fullest extent.[89] Quite often, the most promising new buyers of a firm are residents of the state who have a long-term stake in the community and are willing to make a strong commitment.

For example, when Viner Brothers, a shoe manufacturer in Bangor, Maine, filed for bankruptcy, its three plants presented an attractive investment opportunity for area shoe companies. Within several weeks, Wolverine, the maker of Hush Puppies, was the new owner. Part of the multimillion-dollar sale agreement was that Wolverine hire at least 60 percent of the laid-off workers. About 90 percent of the 900 workers who were laid off were eventually rehired.[90]

Employee Ownership.   The idea of a company selling a plant to the employees as a way of avoiding a closedown is appealing at first glance. Hundreds of U.S. companies with at least 10 workers are employee owned. Most of these arrangements are the results of last-ditch efforts to stay in business. According to the National Center for Employee Ownership, over 50,000 workers have saved their jobs by taking over companies. In the past two decades, such national firms as General Motors, National Steel, Sperry Rand, and Rath Packing Co. have sold plants to employees—plants that otherwise would have been closed.

The experiences of many of these firms have not been extremely favorable, however.[91] In numerous cases, employees have been forced to take significant wage and benefit reductions to make the business profitable. In other cases, morale and working conditions have not been satisfactory under the new method of ownership and management.

In a rather dramatic case, negotiators worked out an agreement whereby the employees of National Steel's Weirton, West Virginia, mill would purchase the mill. The new company, Weirton Steel, became what was then the nation's largest employee-owned enterprise, as well as its eighth-largest producer of steel. Experts gave the mill a surprisingly good chance of succeeding, although Weirton's workers had to take a pay cut of about 32 percent. The mill's union president argued, "32 percent less of $25 an hour is a whole lot better than 100 percent of nothing."[92]

In 1990, however, as demand sank for the steel sheet it produced, Weirton Steel found itself in the unenviable position of actually having to lay off some of its employee-owners. By 1991, Weirton had eliminated 1,000 of its 8,200 jobs, had furloughed another 200 workers, and had plans to cut 700 more jobs. After a decade as owners of the company, Weirton employees became extremely frustrated and angry that employee ownership did not guarantee them that they would not lose their jobs. One employee posed the question many were asking: "How can we be laid off if we own the company?" The reality of the situation, however, is that even an employee-owned company must take whatever actions are necessary if it is to remain solvent and profitable. One of the major pitfalls of worker ownership is that it does not rewrite the laws of capitalism—The bottom line is still the bottom line.[93]

In 1994, United Airlines became America's largest employee-owned corporation. In one of the nastiest and most prolonged corporate battles ever, shareholders of UAL Corp., the parent of United Airlines, awarded employee groups 55 percent of the company's stock in exchange for a $4.9 billion bundle of wage and productivity concessions. U.S. labor leaders have hailed this new arrangement in worker control as a model alternative to the way companies usually battle to control costs. Labor Secretary Robert Reich, whose department facilitated the deal, asserted: "If United is successful, this will be a major landmark in American business history." But the success of the new firm is by no means ensured, because the airline has been buffeted for over a decade by infighting among employee groups, repeated forays by outside potential buyers, and takeover attempts. Opinions vary as to whether United will be successful.[94]

For the employee ownership option to have a chance, a long lead time between the announcement and the actual closing is needed to organize employees while they are still on the site. In addition, time is necessary to conduct complete and detailed feasibility studies. These studies need to assess several factors,[95] such as:

- Employee readiness for ownership
- Union attitudes
- Management/entrepreneurial skills present among employees
- The company's products and markets
- Technology
- Proposed organization structure
- Potential funding sources

After the Decision to Close Is Made

There are a multitude of actions that a business can take once the decision has been made that a closedown or relocation is unavoidable. The overriding concern should be that the company seriously attempt to mitigate the social and economic impacts of its actions on employees and the community. Regardless of the circumstances of the move, some basic planning can help alleviate the disruptions felt by those affected. There are several possible actions that management can take,[96] including:

- Conducting a community-impact analysis
- Providing advance notice to the employees/community
- Providing transfer, relocation, and outplacement benefits
- Phasing out the business gradually
- Helping the community attract replacement industry

Community-Impact Analysis. If management is responsible for its impacts on employees and the community, as Drucker stated, a thorough community-impact analysis of a decision to close down or move is in order. The initial action should be to identify realistically those aspects of the community that would be affected by the company's plans. This would entail asking several questions,[97] such as:

- What groups will be affected?
- How will they be affected?
- What is the timing of initial and later effects?
- What is the magnitude of the effect?
- What is the duration of the impact?
- To what extent will the impact be diffused in the community?

Once these questions have been answered, management is better equipped to modify its plans so that negative impacts can be minimized and favorable impacts, if any, can be maximized.

A community-impact analysis was proposed as part of the Corporate Democracy bill introduced in Congress by Representative Benjamin Rosenthal (D-New York) in 1980. This bill was the outgrowth of some of the work inspired by Ralph Nader and Mark Green. Although it failed to pass, it provides further evidence of the kinds of considerations that have been discussed in an effort to increase corporate accountability.[98] It seems much more reasonable for companies to conduct such impact analyses on their own volition than to have government involved in yet another aspect of business.

Because it is inevitable that management is going to be drawn into economic action teams that will be formed in the community, initiatives should convey a spirit of cooperation in facilitating community action. For example, once National Steel decided it had to close its Weirton mill, its attempt to assess community impact led to management joining with union members, local businesspeople, and government leaders to raise the money needed for the expensive studies and sophisticated investment advice that eventually led to employee ownership.

Advance Notice.   One of the most often discussed responsibilities in business- or plant-closing situations is the provision of advance notice to workers and communities. As discussed earlier, political pressures have been mounting for a law that would mandate such notice before firms close down.

Finally, a national advance-notice law was passed in 1988. It was called the Worker Adjustment and Retraining Notification Act (WARN), and it went into effect in February 1989. WARN requires those firms employing 100 or more workers to provide 60 days advance notice to employees before shutting down or conducting substantial layoffs. A major problem is that most businesses are not large enough to be affected by the law. With WARN, the United States joined many other nations in mandating advance notice of shutdowns. Canada requires 1 to 16 weeks, depending on the case. Great Britain requires 60 to 90 days, depending on the case, and Japan requires "sufficient advance notice."[99]

The advantages of advance notice accrue primarily to the affected employees and their communities. Workers are given time to prepare for the shutdown both emotionally and financially. Advance notice makes it easier for employees to find new jobs, because research has shown that employees have an improved chance at reemployment while they are still employed. Advance notice is motivational in that, once one joins the ranks of the unemployed, there is a tendency to coast until benefits start to be exhausted. Also, the company is in a better position to provide references, retraining, or counseling during the advance-notice period.[100]

The disadvantages of advance notice—particularly long-term advance notice—accrue principally to the business firm. Once word leaks out in the community, financial institutions may be reluctant to grant credit, customers may become worried about items purchased or promised, and the overall level of business activity may decline rapidly. One of the major disadvantages of a lengthy notice is the task of motivating workers who know they are going to lose their jobs. Declines in employee morale, pride in work, and productivity can be expected. Absenteeism may increase as workers begin to seek other employment. In addition, there is the likelihood of vandalism, pilferage, and neglect of property as employees lose interest or attempt to strike back against the employer.[101]

Transfer, Relocation, and Outplacement Benefits.   Enlightened companies are increasingly recognizing that the provision of separation or outplacement benefits is in the long-range best interest of all parties concerned. Everyone is better off if disruptions are minimized in the lives of the firm's management, the displaced workers, and the community. Outplacement benefits have been used for years as companies have attempted to remove redundant or marginal personnel with minimum disruption and cost to the company and maximum benefit to the individuals involved. Increasingly these same benefits are beginning to be used in plant shutdowns.

Gradual Phase-Outs.   Another management action that can significantly ameliorate the effects of a business shutdown is the gradual phasing out of the business. A gradual phase-out buys time for employees and the community to adjust to the new situation and to solve some of their problems.

The American Hospital Supply (AHS) Company provides a useful model of a socially responsive firm. One year, AHS announced its intent to sell its medical manufacturing company of about 275 employees.[102] A meeting of all employees was held to explain the rationale for the decision. Although AHS received numerous inquiries from outside firms, the business did not sell. In preparing for this possible outcome, department heads prepared termination lists specifying those employees essential to the phase-out. Two months later, another all-employee meeting was held, and it was announced that the business would be gradually phased out. A retention/outplacement program was prepared and explained in detail immediately following the meeting.

At AHS, terminated employees with no specific skills or with unique situations (such as illnesses) were identified early so that special outplacement support could be provided. The first group of terminated employees included all of the sales department, half of research and development, all of marketing, and various others not crucial to the wind-down. The outplacement activities resembled those of a college placement office. Over 25 firms visited to conduct on-site interviews. Resumés were drafted by the employees, reviewed and proofed by the personnel department, and typed on the company's word-processing equipment. The volume of outplacement correspondence was so high that additional word-processing capability and clerical support had to be acquired. Final survey results showed that one-fourth of the outplaced employees received "similar" compensation packages and another 65 percent received "superior" compensation packages as compared with those of their previous positions.

In addition, severance pay was offered, and a benefits plan was created for the employees. The benefits plan provided for 100 percent vesting in the company incentive program, retirement and profit-sharing plans, 3 months' basic benefit coverage (medical, dental, life insurance) beyond the date of termination, and various other extensions (maternity, orthodontia) as considered necessary.[103]

Helping to Attract Replacement Industry.   The principal responsibility for attracting new industry falls on the community, but the management of the closing firm can provide cooperation and assistance. The closing company can help by providing inside information on building and equipment characteristics and capabilities, transportation options based on its experience, and contacts with other firms in its industry that may be seeking facilities. Helping the community attract replacement industry has the overwhelming advantage of rapidly replacing large numbers of lost jobs. Also, because attracted businesses tend to be smaller than those that closed, this strategy enables the community to diversify its economic base while regaining jobs.[104]

Decision Factors in a Plant-Closing Situation

Several factors may go into a business's decision regarding the extent to which it should assist displaced employees and the community. These factors include:

- The general size of the negative impact the closedown is creating

- The extent of commitment to the firm displayed over the years by its employees and the community

- How large an employer the firm was in relation to the total economic base

- The length of time the firm was in the community

- The length of time employees had worked for the firm

- The economic options available to the firm for use in providing assistance

- The firm's overall sense of corporate responsibility or corporate social policy

Any one or several of these factors, along with other issues, may assume a major role in dictating the responses of management and the firm.

One recent example of a socially responsible firm undertaking massive layoffs shows the influence of these factors. In 1998, Levi Strauss & Co. began to close 11 U.S. plants, eliminating 6,395 manufacturing positions and more than one-third of its U.S. manufacturing capacity. Long recognized as a leader in employee/community relations, Levi took several measures to lessen the impact of the closures. First, it announced that no jobs would be moving overseas: The closures were needed to deal with excess capacity in the United States.[105] It also announced an unprecedented $200 million employee benefits plan to help laid-off workers make successful transitions back into the work force. Three weeks of severance pay for each year of service was given to each laid-off worker, even if that worker immediately found another job. In addition, 8 months' pay from the date of the announcement, along with outplacement and career counseling services, were provided to everyone. The company also paid up to 18 months' of health care benefits and up to $6,000 in education, job training, or moving expenses for each worker. For the communities affected, the Levi Strauss foundation provided up to $8 million in grants to ease the impact of the plant closings.[106]

Community Lawsuits

To this point we have been focusing on affirmative and socially responsible actions a company might take before or after a decision to close a plant has been made. One of the most recent trends in the business-closings arena is for communities to file lawsuits against companies that are not being as responsible as the communities believe they should be.

One landmark case occurred in 1993 when General Motors announced it was planning to close its plant in Ypsilanti, Michigan, and shift production to Arlington, Texas. In that case, Michigan Circuit Court Judge Donald Shelton enjoined GM from moving its operation. Judge Shelton wrote:

> *There would have been a gross inequity and patent unfairness if General Motors, having lulled the people of Ypsilanti into giving up millions of dollars which they so desperately need to educate their children and provide basic governmental services, is allowed to simply decide that it will desert 4,500 workers and their families because it thinks it can make these same cars a little cheaper somewhere else.*[107]

Judge Shelton's ruling was overturned by a higher court, and the plant did close soon thereafter. The township went back into court trying to win back the $14 million property tax savings it had given GM.[108]

Another lawsuit was filed by the city of Elkhart, Indiana, against Whitehall Laboratories (maker of Dristan, Anacin, and Preparation-H) at its Elkhart plant. The plant closed down in 1991, putting 800 employees out of work. The community decided to fight back. It sued the plant's owner, American Home Products, in federal court, using a law originally intended to snare mobsters—the RICO statute. The lawsuit alleged that American Home Products had unlawfully transferred Elkhart jobs to Puerto Rico, where it had opened a plant in 1988, to obtain local and federal tax benefits. To earn the tax shelter status in Puerto Rico, a firm must declare that no jobs have been displaced on the mainland. The lawsuit maintained that, because hundreds of Elkhart jobs, as well as jobs at other Whitehall plants, had been affected, the firm had misled Puerto Rican authorities.

In its defense, Whitehall rejected the allegations and claimed the shutdown was necessitated by an overcapacity problem following its acquisition of A. H. Robins in 1989. Before it went to trial, the lawsuit was settled out of court in 1993, with the company admitting no liability. The company agreed to a $24 million settlement. Employees, as well as the community, were expected to share in the settlement. The mayor of the city also went on the offensive and pressured the company into giving it the $7 million Whitehall plant and $400,000 to help subsidize the search for a new buyer. The mayor asserted that the negotiating was like ending a marriage: "You say, 'Okay go, but leave the furniture, leave the dog. I think you're wrong, but leave the car.'" At last notice, the city was still looking for a buyer for the plant.[109]

It is likely that lawsuits by communities against employers who plan to close down will remain a threat in the future. This is all the more reason why it is in a company's best long-term interest to arrange for an equitable departure before it ends up facing litigation. Communities today expect more of businesses than they once did, and are not likely to settle for what they perceive to be unfair plant closings.

We are only just beginning to define the stakes and stakeholders involved in the plant-closing issue, the impacts that business closings have on employees and communities, the public's reaction to the problem, and types of corresponding actions that management might take. From observations of other social issues that have received the kind and degree of attention that business closings have, it seems to be necessary for businesses to take positive steps if they are to be responsive to their employees and communities and if further state and federal legislation is to be avoided. It appears that business closings and their adverse consequences is an issue that business will be well advised to address in the future, lest yet another public problem culminate in new laws or another knotty regulatory apparatus.[110]

SUMMARY

Community stakeholders are extremely important to companies. Companies may have positive impacts on their communities in two basic ways: donating the time and talents of managers and employees (volunteerism) and making financial contributions. Because business has a vital stake in the community, it engages in a variety of community projects. Examples include literacy programs and executive loan programs. Community action programs are a key part of managing community involvement. Important components of such efforts include knowing the company's resources, selecting projects to pursue, and monitoring corporate efforts.

Business also contributes to community stakeholders through philanthropy. The third sector, or nonprofit sector, depends on business's support. Companies give for a variety of reasons—some altruistic, some self-interested. Major recipients of business giving include education, health and welfare, civic activities, and culture and the arts. As companies have attempted to manage their philanthropy, two major types of public purpose partnerships have been emphasized: (1) strategic philanthropy, which seeks to improve the overall fit between corporate needs and charitable programs, and (2) cause-related marketing, which tightens the linkage between a firm's profits and its contributions. Cause-related marketing represents a unique joining of business and charity with the potential for great benefit to each. Global philanthropy has recently become an important trend.

Just as firms have beneficial effects on community stakeholders, they can have detrimental effects as well. Business or plant closings are a prime example of these detrimental effects. Plant closings have a pervasive influence in the sense that a multitude of community stakeholders—employees, local government, other businesses, and the general citizenry—are affected. There is no single reason why these closings have occurred, but among the major reasons are economic conditions, consolidation of company operations, outmoded technology or facilities, changes in corporate strategy, and international competition.

Before management makes the decision to close a facility, it has a responsibility to itself, its employees, and the community to study thoroughly whether closing is the only or the best option. Finding a new owner for the business and pursuing the possibility of employee ownership are reasonable and desirable alternatives. After the decision to close has been made, possible actions include community-impact analysis; giving advance notice; providing transfer, relocation, or outplacement benefits; phasing out operations gradually; and helping the community attract replacement industry. Companies have an added incentive to be responsive to the business-closing issue, because state and federal governments are closely watching the manner in which firms are handling this problem. Companies that are sensitive to community stakeholders will want to fashion socially responsive postures in dealing with their stakeholders.

KEY TERMS

cause-related marketing (page 419)   **strategic philanthropy** (page 416)   **third sector** (page 408)

DISCUSSION QUESTIONS

1. Outline the essential steps involved in developing a community action program.
2. Take the social policies attributed to George Steiner and explain how a firm with which you are familiar might apply them in a community.
3. Differentiate among public purpose partnerships, strategic philanthropy, and cause-related marketing, and provide an example of each that is not discussed in the text.
4. In your opinion, why does a business have a responsibility to community stakeholders in a business-closing decision? Enumerate what you think are the major reasons.
5. Identify and discuss briefly what you think are the major trade-offs that firms face as they think about possible plant closings and their responsibility to their employees and their communities.
6. Describe what you think are a firm's social responsibilities in a plant- or business-closing situation and what factors influence the degree of those responsibilities.

ENDNOTES

1. Carole Schweitzer, "Corporate Assets," *Association Management* (January, 1998), 30–37.
2. "Community Action Manual" (Worcester, MA: Norton Company, April, 1978), 1–2.
3. Bill Shaw and Frederick Post, "A Moral Basis for Corporate Philanthropy," *Journal of Business Ethics* (October, 1993), 745–751.
4. Lilly 1998 Corporate Citizenship Report, *www.lilly.com/company/citizenship/index.html.*
5. Cathleen Wild, *Corporate Volunteer Programs: Benefits to Business* (New York: The Conference Board, 1993), 35.
6. *Ibid.,* 23.
7. *Ibid.,* 37.
8. Jonathan Alter, "Powell's New War," *Newsweek* (April 28, 1997), 28–34.
9. *Ibid.,* 28.
10. *Ibid.*
11. George J. Church, "The Corporate Crusaders," *Time* (April 28, 1997), 56–58.
12. "Colin Powell Tells How You Can Help," *Nation's Business* (June, 1998), 25.
13. Allan Sloan, "Can Need Trump Greed?," *Newsweek* (April 28, 1977), 34–35.
14. "Safety First," *Wireless Review* (March 15, 1998), 14.
15. Loretta W. Prencipe, "Volunteer for Adventure," *Network World* (June 8, 1998), 62.

16. Clive Cookson, "Drug Group in Bid to Wipe Out Elephantiasis," *Financial Times* (January 27, 1998), 5.

17. Kathryn Troy, *Studying and Addressing Community Needs: A Corporate Case Book* (New York: The Conference Board, 1985), 1.

18. *Ibid.*

19. George A. Steiner, "Social Policies for Business," *California Management Review* (Winter, 1972), 22–23.

20. Frank Koch, "A Strategy for Corporate Giving and Community Involvement," *Management Review* (December, 1977), 7–13.

21. John A. Conway, "Giving a Hand: The Eagles Score a Touchdown with Ronald McDonald Houses," *The Wall Street Journal* (April 26, 1990), B-2; and Michelle Hiskey, "Amoco Pumps Life into Needy Neighborhoods," *The Atlanta Constitution* (September 9, 1991), B1, B6.

22. Tammie S. Pinkston and Archie B. Carroll, "Corporate Citizenship Perspectives and Foreign Direct Investment in the U.S.," *Journal of Business Ethics* (Vol. 13, 1994), 157–169.

23. David Logan, *Community Involvement of Foreign-Owned Companies* (New York: The Conference Board, 1994), 7.

24. *Ibid.*, 16.

25. *Ibid.*, 15.

26. Pinkston and Carroll, 168–169.

27. For a brief description of TAP, see Archie B. Carroll and Gerald T. Horton, "Do Joint Corporate Social Responsibility Programs Work?" *Business and Society Review* (Summer, 1994), 24–28.

28. *Ibid.*

29. Regina M. Roberts, "New TAP Official Confident About Phaseout," *The Atlanta Journal and Constitution* (March 5, 1998), 2.

30. *Webster's New World Dictionary* (Cleveland: World Publishing Company, 1964), 1098.

31. Robert L. Payton, *Philanthropy: Voluntary Action for the Public Good* (New York: Macmillan, 1988), 32.

32. Robert L. Payton, "Philanthropy in Action," in Robert L. Payton, Michael Novak, Brian O'Connell, and Peter Dobkin Hall, *Philanthropy: Four Views* (New Brunswick: Transaction Books, Inc.), 1.

33. "Americans Value Businesses' Philanthropic Performance, Study Finds," *The Chronicle of Philanthropy* (January 12, 1995), 13.

34. Morrell Heald, *The Social Responsibilities of Business: Company and Community 1900–1960* (Cleveland: Case Western Reserve University Press, 1970), 112.

35. Adam Bryant, "Companies Oppose Disclosure of Details on Gifts to Charity," *New York Times* (April 3, 1998), A1.

36. John D. Rockfeller III, "In Defense of Philanthropy," *Business and Society Review* (Spring, 1978), 26–29.

37. Curt Weeden, *Corporate Social Investing* (San Francisco: Berret Koehler, Inc., 1998), 4–6.

38. *Ibid.*, 3–4.

39. Sam Sternberg, *National Directory of Corporate Charity* (San Francisco: Regional Young Adult Project, 1984), 14.

40. J. R. Block and Norman Goodman, "Why Companies Give," *Journal of Advertising Research* (October, 1976), 59–63.

41. Louis W. Fry, Gerald D. Keim, and Roger E. Meiners, "Corporate Contributions: Altruistic or For-Profit?" *Academy of Management Journal* (March, 1982), 94–106.

42. Anne Klepper, *Corporate Contributions, 1991* (New York: The Conference Board, 1992), 6, 9, 14.

43. Louis W. Cabot, "Corporate Support of Education: No Strings Attached," *Harvard Business Review* (July–August, 1978), 139–144.

44. Robert H. Malott, "Corporate Support of Education: Some Strings Attached," *Harvard Business Review* (July–August, 1978), 133–138.

45. Irving Kristol, "On Corporate Philanthropy," *The Wall Street Journal* (March 21, 1977), 18.

46. For an interesting study of workplace giving, see Melissa A. Berman, *The Future of Workplace Giving* (New York: The Conference Board, 1994).

47. Dreyer's Philanthropy Mission Statement, *www.dreyers.com/corporate/charity.html.*

48. Lilly 1998 Corporate Citizenship Report, *www.lilly.com/company/citizenship/index.html.*

49. Keith H. Hammonds, "Corning's Class Act," *Business Week* (May 13, 1991), 68–76. See also Leslie Goff, "Corning: Those Who Live in Glass Houses . . . ," *Computerworld* (May 25, 1998), S9–S10.

50. John B. Forbes, "Corporate America Giving More to the Arts," *The New York Times* (May 15, 1977), F-19.

51. "The Glories of Philanthropy," *Business Week* (October 6, 1997), 182.

52. "Sara Lee Makes Huge Art Donation," *Fund Raising Management* (July, 1998), 10.

53. "Where Art and Business Meet," *Forbes* (February 1, 1977), 6.

54. Paul H. Eliker, "Why Corporations Give Money to the Arts," *The Wall Street Journal* (March 31, 1978), 15.

55. *Ibid.*

56. Cited in Robert Toth, "PBS Corporate Gifts Selfish?" *The Atlanta Journal* (September 11, 1977), F-7.

57. Terrence Scanlon, "Business Feeds the Hand That Bites It," *The New York Times* (May 8, 1994), F-11.

58. Peter Frumkin, "A Distorted Portrait of Corporate Philanthropy," *Foundation News and Commentary* (March/April, 1996), 22–25.

59. James J. Chrisman and Archie B. Carroll, "Corporate Responsibility: Reconciling Economic and Social Goals," *Sloan Management Review* (Winter, 1984), 59–65.

60. Public purpose partnerships are discussed in Richard Steckel and Robin Simons, *Doing Best by Doing Good* (New York: Dutton Publishers, 1992).

61. Andrew E. Serwer, "Company Givers Get Smart," *Fortune* (August 22, 1994), 16.

62. "Happy Deal for Tech: McDonald's Sponsorship to Finance Coliseum Facelift," *The Atlanta Journal* (January 19, 1995), C1–C2.

63. Steckel and Simons.

64. Timothy S. Mescon and Donn J. Tilson, "Corporate Philanthropy: A Strategic Approach to the Bottom Line," *California Management Review* (Winter, 1987), 50.

65. Avery Hunt, "Strategic Philanthropy," *Across the Board* (July/August, 1986), 27.

66. Deirdre Carmody, "For People Magazine, A New Charity Program May Be Good Business Too," *The New York Times* (February 14, 1994), C6.

67. Craig Smith, "The New Corporate Philanthropy," *Harvard Business Review* (May–June, 1994), 106.

68. Weeden, 1998, 202–205.

69. Richard J. Morris and Daniel A. Biederman, "How to Give Away Money Intelligently," *Harvard Business Review* (November–December, 1985), 151–159.

70. Smith, 115.

71. Patricia Caesar, "Cause-Related Marketing: The New Face of Corporate Philanthropy," *Business and Society Review* (Fall, 1986), 16.

72. Martin Gottlieb, "Cashing in on a Higher Cause," *The New York Times* (July 6, 1986), 6-F.

73. *For Members Only: A Newsletter for American Express Cardmembers* (October, 1985), 1–2.

74. Monci Jo Williams, "How to Cash in on Do-Good Pitches," *Fortune* (June 9, 1986), 76.

75. Cynthia D. Giroud, "Cause-Related Marketing: Potential Dangers and Benefits," in James P. Shannon (ed.), *The Corporate Contributions Handbook* (San Francisco: Jossey-Bass, 1991), 144–146.

76. Geoffrey Smith and Ron Stodghill, "Are Good Causes Good Marketing?" *Business Week* (March 21, 1994), 64.

77. Caesar, 17–18. Also see Steckel and Simons, Chapter 6, "Cause-Related Marketing."

78. *Ibid.,* 18–19.

79. Anne Klepper, *Global Contributions of U.S. Corporations* (New York: The Conference Board, 1993), 6–7.

80. Michael Schroeder and Jonathan Kapstein, "Charity Doesn't Begin at Home Anymore: Multinationals Are Discovering the Value of Global Philanthropy," *Business Week* (February 25, 1991), 91.

81. Klepper, 1993, 6–7.

82. *Ibid.*

83. Archie B. Carroll, Elizabeth J. Gatewood, and James J. Chrisman, "Plant Closings: PAOs Respond to a Survey on an Increasingly Troublesome Issue," *Public Affairs Review* (1984), 64.

84. Cooper and Lybrand, *Closing Plants: Planning and Implementing Strategies* (Morristown, NJ: Financial Executives Research Foundation, 1986), 2.

85. Peter F. Drucker, *Management: Tasks, Responsibilities, Practices* (New York: Harper & Row, 1974), 327–328.

86. Quoted in "A Firm's Obligations: To Employees, Community," *The Atlanta Journal* (September 19, 1977), 4-C.

87. John P. Kavanagh, "Ethical Issues in Plant Relocation," *Business and Professional Ethics Journal* (Winter, 1982), 21–33.

88. Archie B. Carroll, "When Business Closes Down: Social Responsibilities and Management Actions," *California Management Review* (Winter, 1984), 131.

89. Quoted in *The Atlanta Journal* (September 19, 1977), 4-C.

90. Jeff Strout, "Viner Shoe Expected to Be in Full Swing Soon," *Bangor News* (January 21, 1981), 9.

91. Terri Minsky, "Gripes of Rath: Workers Who Bought Iowa Slaughterhouse Regret That They Did," *The Wall Street Journal* (December 2, 1981), 1.
92. "A Steel Town's Fight for Life," *Newsweek* (March 28, 1983), 49.
93. Maria Mallary, "How Can We Be Laid Off If We Own the Company?" *Business Week* (September 9, 1991), 66.
94. Kenneth Labich, "Will United Fly?" *Fortune* (August 22, 1994), 70–78.
95. Cornell University Workshop Report, *The Economic Crisis and Self-Managed Alternatives* (Ithaca, NY: Cornell University, June 6–8, 1980), 8, cited in *Shutdown: A Guide for Communities Facing Plant Closings* (Washington, DC: Northeast-Midwest Institute, 1981), 17.
96. Carroll, 132.
97. Grover Starling, *The Changing Environment of Business* (Boston: Kent, 1980), 319–320.
98. Mark Green, "The Case for Corporate Democracy," *Regulation* (May/June, 1980), 23–24.
99. Paul D. Staudohar, "New Plant Closing Law Aids Workers in Transition," *Personnel Journal* (January, 1989), 87–90.
100. Robert B. McKersie, "Advance Notice," *The Wall Street Journal* (February 25, 1980), 20.
101. *Ibid.*
102. Philip D. Johnston, "Personnel Planning for a Plant Shutdown," *Personnel Administrator* (August, 1981), 53–57.
103. *Ibid.*
104. Cornell University Workshop Report, 28–30.
105. Kathleen DesMarteau, "Levi Closes 11 U.S. Plants," *Bobbin* (January, 1998), 14–16.
106. Mike Verespej, "How to Manage Diversity," *Industry Week* (January 19, 1998), 24.
107. David Moberg, "Flight Cancelled: A Michigan Judge Halts GM from Fleeing Ypsilanti," *In These Times* (March 8, 1993), 8.
108. Benjamin Weiser, "When the Plant Closes," The Washington Post Weekly Edition (January 10–16, 1994), 6.
109. *Ibid.*, 6–7.
110. Carroll, Gatewood, and Chrisman, 71–72.

Internal Stakeholder Issues

14

Employee Stakeholders and Workplace Issues

CHAPTER OBJECTIVES

After studying this chapter, you should be able to:

1 Identify the major changes that are occurring in the work force today.

2 Outline the characteristics of the new social contract between employers and employees.

3 Explain the employee rights movement and its underlying principles.

4 Describe and discuss the employment-at-will doctrine and its role in the employee's right to a job or not to be fired.

5 Discuss the right to due process and fair treatment.

6 Describe the actions companies are taking to make the workplace friendlier.

7 Elaborate on the freedom-of-speech issue and whistle-blowing.

Society's changing values are having a great impact on the workplace. Although external stakeholders such as government, consumers, the environment, and the community continue to be major facets of business's concern for the social environment, considerable attention is now being given to employee stakeholders—their status, their treatment, their rights, and their satisfaction. This should come as no surprise when it is considered that most adult Americans spend the bulk of their daytime hours at work. It was only a matter of time until citizens as employees would express the same kind of concern for their work lives as they had expressed for external, more remote social issues.

The development of employee stakeholder rights has been a direct outgrowth of the kinds of social changes that have brought other societal issues into focus. The history of work has been one of steadily improving conditions for employees. In recent years, however, issues have emerged that are quite unlike the old bread-and-butter concerns advocated by labor unions—higher pay, shorter hours, more job security, and better working conditions. These expectations still exist, but they have given way to other, more complex workplace trends and issues.

In the late 1990s, two major themes or trends seem to be characterizing the modern relationship between employees and their employers. First, we will discuss the dramatic changes that have been occurring in the workplace. Prominent here will be our discussion of a newly evolving social contract between organizations and workers that is quite different from any such contract of the past. This new social contract is being driven by global competition. Second, we will consider a continuation of a trend toward more expansive employee rights. These two trends are interrelated, and we will describe how the changes in the workplace have precipitated a renewal in the employee rights movement.

Because these topics are so extensive, we dedicate two chapters to employee stakeholders and workplace issues. In this chapter, we discuss some of the workplace changes that have been taking place, the emerging social contract, and the employee rights movement. Three employee rights issues, in particular, are treated here: the right to a job (or at least the right not to be fired without just cause), the right to due process and fair treatment, and the right to freedom of speech in the workplace. In Chapter 15, we will continue our discussion of employee rights by examining the related issues of the rights of employees to privacy, safety, and health. These two chapters should be considered a continuous discussion of employee stakeholders wherein economic, legal, and ethical responsibilities are all involved in the treatment.

The quest for employee rights should be viewed as just one part of today's employees' expectations of fair treatment. A study conducted by Walker Research asked the general public to allocate 100 points across 11 business factors to reflect what is most important to them in deciding where to work. Employee treatment was ranked first, followed by business practices, another very important work-related factor. Figure 14–1 summarizes the work-related factors and their rankings.

CHANGES IN THE WORKPLACE

The 1980s represented a turning point for the relationship between employees and employers. Many of the societal changes we described earlier in this book—education, awareness, affluence, rising expectations, the rights movement, and so on—directly affected this issue. These changes caused employees to be more assertive about their treatment and what is owed them as employees. Other, more specific developments occurred as well, and, because these developments have had a more focused effect on the workplace, it is worthwhile discussing them. According to David W. Ewing,[1] a noted authority on workplace issues, four trends, in particular, occurred in the workplace:

1. An increase in technological hazards to employees

2. The invasion of the workplace by the computer

3. The divided loyalties of professionals

4. The increased mobility of employees

Increased Technological Hazards

Over the past 30 years, employees have been subjected to an increasing number and variety of new technologies, chemicals, and hazards in the workplace, including nuclear power, complex electronic control devices, and chemicals such as polychlorinated biphenyls (PCBs). Productivity has been enhanced by the new technologies,

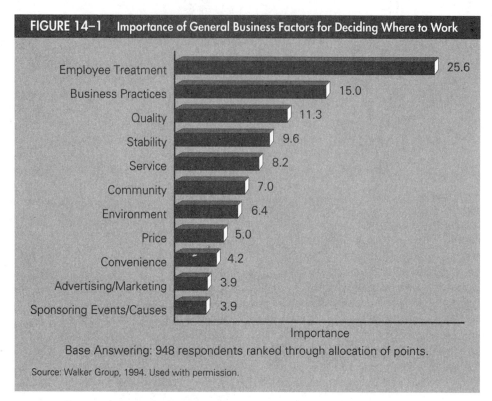

FIGURE 14-1   Importance of General Business Factors for Deciding Where to Work

	Importance
Employee Treatment	25.6
Business Practices	15.0
Quality	11.3
Stability	9.6
Service	8.2
Community	7.0
Environment	6.4
Price	5.0
Convenience	4.2
Advertising/Marketing	3.9
Sponsoring Events/Causes	3.9

Base Answering: 948 respondents ranked through allocation of points.

Source: Walker Group, 1994. Used with permission.

SOURCE: Walker Group, 1994. Used with permission.

but so have employee hazards. A control failure can cause an automated subway train to crash. Careless packaging can result in toxic hazards. Signs of the latent perils of modern chemistry—emergency showers in corridors, "Danger" signs, masks, and protective clothing—have become evident in many manufacturing operations.[2] Technological hazards in the workplace create a constant low-level anxiety among employees, who find it difficult to avoid thoughts of how the next workplace disaster might somehow affect them.

The Computer Invasion

The computer invasion not only has contributed to workplace anxiety but also has turned the classic balance of privacy upside down. There was a time when privacy invasion was restricted to what a supervisor could see or hear or what information could be collected by personnel offices. In the 1980s, a whole new array of computer-based and other electronic devices that monitor employees entered the work environment. Examples include listening devices, polygraphs, closed-circuit television monitors, computer-based information systems, and drug-testing devices. Most companies have been careful about this newly found power, but employees still worry about abuses and invasions of privacy.[3] We will discuss this issue more fully in the next chapter.

Professionals with Divided Loyalties

One of the most significant trends now occurring in the workplace is the dramatic growth in the number of professional and technical employees. According to the Census Bureau, the number of professional and technical employees in the work force doubled from 1960 to 1980.[4]

The increased number of professionals has improved organizations, but it has also altered attitudes and values in the workplace. Especially affected has been loyalty to the employer. Professionals such as scientists, engineers, accountants, computer specialists, and others find it hard to subscribe to the traditional philosophy, "my corporation, right or wrong." Their codes of conduct require that they use their knowledge and skill for the public welfare. In fact, it is a growing conviction among professionals that acts of dissidence, honestly and thoughtfully taken in the public interest, are not only permissible but obligatory.[5]

Conventional management wisdom used to be that, once management had reached a decision, all employees were to assume that the decision was right and were to support it fully. Today's professionals, on the other hand, feel a compulsion to question what they think is wrong because of their duty to their professional codes. More and more, this brings them into conflict with their employers.[6]

There is evidence that loyalty to employers is diminishing for other reasons as well. Younger workers, who are generally better educated, have higher expectations about their jobs and are more likely to feel dissatisfied when their ambitions are not fulfilled. Also, the wave of mergers, acquisitions, reorganizations, and downsizing that has resulted in significant reductions in professional and managerial jobs over the past decade has convinced many employees that companies will no longer return their loyalty. Cutbacks and closings, as well as general cynicism about the workplace, have also resulted in diminished employee loyalty and an increase in concern about employee rights.[7]

A recent book describes how job security (particularly among white-collar professional jobs), which was so prevalent in the 1950s, has disappeared. Amanda Bennett's book *The Death of the Organization Man* describes how the perk-padded paradise for executives described in William H. Whyte's 1956 bestseller *The Organization Man* "went to hell in the 1980s." Managers who had staked everything on their loyalty to a major corporation suddenly found themselves out on their own. Their jobs and their loyalty were sacrificed to meet cutback quotas forced by global competition, postraid reorganizations, and other such unexpected events.[8] Consequently, the loyalty that corporate management routinely expected from professionals was gone, and a new era of workers with divided loyalties had begun. This new era has continued through the 1990s, and we will discuss it more broadly in our treatment of the new social contract.

Increased Mobility of Employees

Another drift of the past several decades has been an increase in employee mobility. At one time, people lived in one or a very few places all their lives. This is no longer the case. Today we live in a corporate society in which transfers from one city to another and career moves from one employer to another to get quick raises and promotions have become commonplace.

As regional lines continue to diminish, one is as likely to find a New Englander living in the Southeast as a Midwesterner living on the West Coast. Employees move geographically, between functions, and between levels of responsibility. One major unintended result of this interchange is an uncertainty in employer/employee relationships. Employees no longer know exactly what to expect from their employers or supervisors. Anxiety, tension, and even conflict can arise as employment relationships become less stable and more transient. Employees in this kind of environment feel vulnerable.[9]

*   *   *

These four kinds of basic changes in workplace relationships have enhanced the professional environment in business organizations. Improvements in productivity have followed, but for employees these changes have had significant downside consequences. These conditions have created an environment in which employees feel more anxious and less secure—indeed, vulnerable to real or perceived detrimental management decisions. In this kind of environment, it should not be surprising to find employees becoming increasingly sensitive and attentive to what rights they have in their employment roles.

THE NEW SOCIAL CONTRACT

The workplace trends just described have contributed not only to a desire for enhanced employee rights but also to a newly emerging social contract between employers and employees. Although the new social contract—or set of reciprocal understandings and expectations regarding each party's role and responsibilities—has been unfolding for at least a decade, it has been only in the mid-1990s that formal descriptions of this new "contract," or "compact," have become commonplace. As a 1994 *Business Week* editorial conveyed it, the change represents a "revolution in America's workplace."[10] The revolution is basically this: The get-along-to-get-ahead culture of the past is being displaced by a high-risk environment in which Americans are being asked to give up the employment security they once took for granted for opportunities that are no longer clearly defined or guaranteed. In short, the workplace once considered to be a stable, protected habitat offering a measure of prosperity and security in exchange for a lifetime of dedicated work and loyalty is now viewed as a dangerous place.[11]

As *Business Week* appropriately observed, there are "no villains at work, just the inexorable forces of economic and technological change." But if there are no villains, there are certainly victims. Workers are being impacted

SEARCH THE WEB

The U.S. Department of Labor maintains an online Corporate Citizenship Resource Center (**www.ttrc.doleta.gov/citizen**) to provide the public with information on workplace practices that promote the principles of corporate citizenship. As defined on the Web page, "corporate citizenship is about treating employees as important assets to be developed and as partners on the road to profitability." The principles that embody a commitment to corporate citizenship are a family-friendly workplace, economic security, investment in employees, partnership with employees, and a safe and secure workplace. The Web site's offerings include profiles of companies that exemplify corporate citizenship, a list of not-for-profit organizations that offer resources to help companies become better corporate citizens, bibliographies and abstracts of related reference materials, and links to other, related Web sites.

as companies have had to reorganize, slim down, "reengineer" and "reinvent" themselves. Downsizing and restructuring have significantly altered pay compensation systems. Pay based on longevity and status is being replaced with rewards based on performance, contributions, and value added.[12]

What is driving the collapse of the old social contract and the emergence of the new? We have touched upon several factors already—most notably, global competition. Chilton and Weidenbaum, in their discussions of the new social contract, pinpoint three sweeping forces that began in the 1970s, grew in salience in the 1980s, and became dominant drivers in the 1990s.[13] These three forces are:

1. *Global competition*

2. *Technology advances* (especially in computers and telecommunications)

3. *Deregulation* (especially of transportation and telecommunications)

As a result of these forces and others in the workplace, we have witnessed the destabilization of organizations and an old social contract. The old social contract between companies and workers was clearer than the new social contract will be. The old, traditional arrangement was predicated on a security-loyalty-paternalism pact. Attributes of the old social contract included lifetime employment, steady advancement, and loyalty.[14] It is easy to see how this arrangement engendered an entitlement mentality on the part of employees.

The new social contract places on employees more responsibility for their own success and prosperity in the employment relationship. Job security, compensation, and advancement depend more on what the employee is contributing to the organization's mission. The notion of "adding value" to the organization has become a crucial factor. In exchange, companies are expected to provide learning opportunities, meaningful work, and honest communication.[15] Figure 14–2 presents some of the characteristics of the old and new social contracts.

An outline of the features of the new social contract between employers and employees has been provided by Chilton and Weidenbaum. This outline is presented in Figure 14–3.

It is challenging to say whether the new social contract will be bad or good. More than anything else, it represents an adaptation to the changing world and changing business circumstances. In some respects, workers may prefer the new model. Whatever turns out to be the case, it is clear that employee stakeholders' expectations of fair treatment will continue to rise. We will continue to see the employee rights movement that has characterized business for decades, but it will grow in the new environment. Employee rights will be moderated by employer expectations that are being driven by uncontrollable economic, social, and technological forces.

The moderating impact of these forces became apparent in 1998, when a booming economy combined with shifting demographics to create an unemployment rate of 4.7 percent, the lowest in 25 years. In this environment, highly trained young knowledge workers were in great demand. A *Fortune* article on "The New Organization Man" described the lengths to which companies were going to attract the best of Generation X (i.e., those born between 1965 and 1977). In addition to generous salaries and bonuses, enticements include flexible working conditions, the right to

FIGURE 14–2 The Changing Social Contract Between Employers and Employees

Old Social Contract	New Social Contract
Job security; long, stable career and employment relationships	Few tenure arrangements; jobs constantly "at risk"; employment as long as you "add value" to the organization
Life careers with one employer	Fewer life careers; employer changes common; careers more dynamic
Stable positions/job assignments	Temporary project assignments
Loyalty to employer; identification with employer	Loyalty to self and profession; diminished identification with employer
Paternalism; family-type relationships	Relationships far less warm and familial; no more parent-child relationships
Employee sense of entitlement	Personal responsibility for one's own career/job future
Stable, rising income	Pay that reflects contributions; pay for "value added"
Job-related skill training	Learning opportunities; employees in charge of their own education and updating
Focus on individual job accomplishments	Focus on team building and projects

bring pets to work, sumptuous offices, casual attire, music festivals, and parties. Having learned from their parents' experience that companies were no longer loyal to them, these young employees are comfortable changing jobs frequently to improve their work situations.[16] After completing a study on the changing U.S. work force, David Friedman, a partner at McKinsey & Co., had the following comment:

> The stereotype is that Generation X thinks it's entitled. But the people who sound like they have an entitlement mentality are the companies. They think they are entitled to have a work force that works like their parents did.[17]

Of course, the economic boom will not last, and unemployment will eventually rise. As these forces shift, so will the social contract between employers and employees. It is within this context, therefore, that we consider further the employee rights movement.

THE EMPLOYEE RIGHTS MOVEMENT

To appreciate the background of employee rights issues (especially the rights of freedom of speech and due process), it is useful to consider the underlying public sector/ private sector dichotomy that organizations in society face. The public sector is subject to constitutional control of its power. The private sector generally has not been subject to constitutional control because of the concept of private prop-

**FIGURE 14–3   One View of the New Social Contract
Between Employers and Employees**

Outline for A New Social Contract

Employer Expectations of Employees	*Employee Expectations of Employers*
• Performance to the best of one's ability	• "Fair" pay and benefits proportionate to contribution to company success
• Commitment to the objectives of the firm	• Security tied to fortunes of the company and ability to perform
• Participation (suggestions)	• Respect, recognition, and participation
• Willingness to take training to improve productivity	• Opportunities for growth
• Ethical and honest behavior	• Access to timely information and openness by candid leaders
	• Safe and healthy workplace

Joint Expectations

- Partnering replaces paternalism
- Employees are value-adding resources, not merely costs to be cut
- Employee and employer must focus on customer needs and desires

SOURCE: Kenneth Chilton and Murray Weidenbaum, *A New Social Contract for the American Workplace: From Paternalism to Partnering* (St. Louis: Center for the Study of American Business, Washington University, 1994), 43. Used with permission.

erty. The ***private property*** notion holds that individuals and private organizations are free to use their property as they desire. As a result, private corporations historically and traditionally have not had to recognize employee rights because society honored the corporation's private property rights. The underlying issues then become *why* and *to what extent* the private property rights of business should be changed or diluted.

Although Americans have enjoyed civil liberties for nearly two centuries, these same rights have not always been afforded by many companies, government agencies, and other organizations where Americans work. David W. Ewing states the matter quite strongly:

> *Once a U.S. citizen steps through the plant or office door at 9 a.m., he or she is nearly rightless until 5 p.m., Monday through Friday. The employee continues to have political freedoms, of course, but these are not the significant ones now. While at work, the important relationships are with bosses, associates, and subordinates. Inequalities in dealing with these people are what really count for an employee.*[18]

Although there are growing exceptions to Ewing's rather strong statement, it does call attention to the importance of the issue. Ewing goes on to state, "The employee sector of our civil liberties universe is more like a black hole, with rights so

ETHICS IN PRACTICE

Manager's Makeshift Rules

It is Holland Flowers's mission to deliver fresh and innovative floral designs. To achieve this, Holland Flowers hires creative university students from the local area. The company feels it is important to make every possible attempt to work around the students' schedules.

John Smith was a delivery driver for Holland Flowers and a university student. Before accepting the position with Holland Flowers in August 1994, John requested several days off the week prior to Christmas. December is a very busy time at Holland Flowers. To accommodate the increase in business, Holland Flowers hires seasonal employees. That year, the owner's son, Bob, was one of the seasonal employees. Bob was to work with John and the other drivers. The week prior to Christmas, the owner informed John that Bob was sick and unable to work. Subsequently, the owner told John he was to work that week, even though, before John was hired, they had agreed that John would be off. Reluctantly, John agreed to work.

The following night, John was downtown when he saw Bob with a drink in his hand and appearing quite healthy. John approached Bob, questioning his sickness and absence from work. Bob denied his illness, acting as if being the owner's son meant he could be off when he wanted.

John was furious, because the owner had previously stressed that Holland Flowers was built on honest working relationships. John felt that this incident went against the principles on which the company was founded. John no longer felt respect for the owner or Holland Flowers; instead, he felt lied to and betrayed. John called the owner that night and informed him of his feelings. Because the owner offered no defense, John felt he could no longer work for Holland Flowers, and he resigned.

1. Did the management of Holland Flowers behave unethically with respect to employee treatment in this case?

2. Was John right in questioning the owner's employee practices?

3. If you were John, what action would you have taken in this dilemma?

Contributed by Christopher Lockett

compacted, so imploded by the gravitational forces of legal tradition, that, like the giant black stars in the physical universe, light can scarcely escape."[19]

A brief comment on the role of labor unions is appropriate here. In general, although labor unions have been quite successful in improving the material conditions of life at work—pay, fringe benefits, and working conditions—they have not been as interested in pursuing civil liberties. Unions must be given credit, however, for the gains they have made in converting what were typically regarded as management's rights or prerogatives into issues in which labor could participate. It should be noted, moreover, that labor unions are disappearing from the business scene. In 1953, union representation reached its highest proportion of the private employment workforce, at 36 percent. Labor unions represented about 11 percent of the private workforce in the mid-1990s, and one estimate is that this would fall to 7 percent by the year 2000.

Although public sector unionism is growing, it is not expected to have a significant impact on the kinds of employee rights we are discussing here.[20] For nonunion workers, however, the employee rights issue continues to be a problem.

Many managers find the movement for employee rights to be disturbing. Management prerogatives are being challenged at an unprecedented rate, and the traditional model of employee loyalty and conformity to the wishes of management is rapidly fading from the scene. Some have observed that the traditional model seems to be disappearing more as a concept than as a reality, however. Although managers indicate strong support for wider employee rights when responding to questionnaires, practice does not show employee rights prevailing extensively in business today. Indeed, although managers support the concept in principle, they sometimes express an ambivalence about employee rights and their costs. One survey of managers showed a higher concern for instability in our society (confusion about sexual standards, attitudes toward drugs, treatment of criminals, respect for the family and authority, breakdown of law and order, and disintegration of the work ethic) than for obstacles to individuality in the workplace.[21] Thus, although managers sympathize with the need for privacy, due process, and free speech in the workplace, they seem to be more concerned with general social trends and their impacts.

The Meaning of Employee Rights

Before we consider specific employee rights issues, it is useful to discuss briefly what the term "employee rights" means. A lawyer might look at employee rights as claims that may be enforced in a court of law. To many economists as well, rights are only creations of the law. More generally, however, employee rights might refer to legitimate and enforceable claims or privileges obtained by workers through group membership that entitle or protect them in specific ways from the prevailing system of governance. In this light, employee rights are seen as individuals' legitimate and enforceable claims to some desired treatment, situation, or resource.[22]

Richard Edwards has argued that employee or workplace rights serve to provide workers with either (1) desired outcomes or (2) protection from unwanted outcomes. He also asserts that these rights find their source in *law, union contracts,* or *employers' promises.* Rights provided by law are called statutory rights. These rights include, for example, those rights established by The Civil Rights Act of 1964 (at a national level), or by Massachusetts' "right-to-know" law (at the state level), which grants production workers the right to be notified of specific toxic substances they may be exposed to in the workplace. Union contracts, by contrast, provide workers with rights established through the process of collective bargaining. Examples of these rights are seniority preferences, job security mechanisms, and grievance procedures.[23]

Employer promises are the third source of employees' rights categorized by Edwards. He calls these employer grants or promises *enterprise rights.* Typical examples of such enterprise rights might include the right to petition beyond one's immediate supervisor, the right to be free from physical intimidation, the right to a grievance or complaint system, the right to due process in discipline, the right to have express standards for personnel evaluation, the right to have one's job clearly defined, the right to a "just-cause" standard for dismissal, the right to be free from nepotism and unfair favoritism, and so on.[24]

It is clear that these enterprise rights, as construed by Edwards, are provided and justified by management on the basis of several different criteria. In some cases, these rights simply extend beyond what the organization is required to do by law. In other situations, they address issues that are not covered by law. In either case, these rights are sometimes justified on the basis of customs and practices that may be necessary for the firm to remain competitive (and thus are economically justified). In addition, the rights are sometimes afforded on the basis of some normative ethical principle or reasoning (for example, "This is the way workers *ought* to be treated"). In this situation, the ethical principles of justice, rights, and utilitarianism, as well as notions of virtue ethics, may be employed as rationales.

In this connection, management may provide the employee rights as part of an effort to display moral management, as discussed in Chapter 4. To illustrate this point further, Figure 14–4 characterizes how moral managers, as well as amoral and immoral managers, might view employee stakeholders.

To summarize, employee rights may be afforded on the basis of economic, legal, or ethical sources of justification. In a limited number of cases, companies even use philanthropic arguments as the bases for providing employee rights or benefits. For example, some companies have justified day-care rights and benefits to employees on philanthropic grounds. For purposes of our discussion here, however, we will concentrate on legal and ethical bases for considering employee rights. In all these discussions, moreover, we take the perspective of organizations blending ethical wisdom with management wisdom.

The job-related rights that are mentioned often enough to merit further discussion here include: (1) the *right to a job,* or at least the right *not to be fired without just*

FIGURE 14–4	Three Models of Management Morality and Their Orientations Toward Employee Stakeholders
Model of Management Morality	**Orientation Toward Employee Stakeholders**
Moral Management	Employees are a human resource that must be treated with dignity and respect. Employees' rights to due process, privacy, freedom of speech, and safety are maximally considered in all decisions. Management seeks fair dealings with employees. The goal is to use a leadership style, such as consultative/participative, that will result in mutual confidence and trust. Commitment is a recurring theme.
Amoral Management	Employees are treated as the law requires. Attempts to motivate focus on increasing productivity rather than satisfying employees' growing maturity needs. Employees are still seen as factors of production, but a remunerative approach is used. The organization sees self-interest in treating employees with minimal respect. Organization structure, pay incentives, and rewards are all geared toward short- and medium-term productivity.
Immoral Management	Employees are viewed as factors of production to be used, exploited, and manipulated for gain of individual manager or company. No concern is shown for employees' needs/rights/expectations. Short-term focus. Coercive, controlling, alienating environment.

cause; (2) the *right to due process and fair treatment;* and (3) the *right to freedom,* particularly freedom of expression and freedom of speech. In Chapter 15 we will consider the rights to privacy, safety, and health in the workplace.

THE RIGHT TO A JOB/NOT TO BE FIRED WITHOUT CAUSE

We are not suggesting by the title of this section that employees have a *right* to a job. We are attempting, however, to assert that current trends in employment practices, if extended to their logical conclusion, may be signaling a belief on the part of workers that they have such a right. Given the entitlement mentality that prevails in our country today, and in spite of tough global competition, a significant proportion of Americans may think they are entitled to jobs. Our discussion, however, addresses this issue from another direction. There is growing evidence that Americans think they have a right *not to be fired without just cause.* Depending on how one defines "just cause," we may be seeing a trend toward a right to keep a job once one has it, or perhaps even a right to a job. If this occurs, it will surely spell the death of the common-law principle known as the employment-at-will doctrine.

Employment-at-Will Doctrine

The central issue in the movement to protect workers' jobs surrounds changing views of the *employment-at-will doctrine.* This doctrine is the longstanding, common-law principle that the relationship between employer and employee is a voluntary one and can be terminated at any time by either party. Just as employees are free to quit a company any time they choose, this doctrine holds that employers can discharge employees for any reason, or no reason, as long as they do not violate federal discrimination laws, state laws, or union contracts. What this doctrine means is that if you are not protected by a union contract (about 80 to 90 percent of the work force is not) or by one of the discrimination laws, your employer is free to let you go anytime, for any reason.

The employment-at-will doctrine is being eroded by court decisions, however. The courts have ruled with increasing frequency that employers have responsibilities to employees that, from the standpoint of fairness, restrict management's former prerogative to fire at will. Terms that have been added to the vocabulary of employment relationships include *unjust dismissals* and *wrongful discharge.*

Three broad categories of issues that illustrate the legal challenges now arising in regard to employment-at-will discharges are (1) public policy exceptions, (2) contractual actions, and (3) breach of good faith actions.

Public Policy Exceptions

For a wide variety of reasons, the courts are beginning to hold that employees who previously were unprotected from unjust firings are now so protected. One emerging major exception to the longstanding employment-at-will doctrine is known as the *public policy exception.* This exception protects employees from being fired because they refuse to commit crimes or because they try to take advantage of privileges to which they are entitled by law.[25] The courts have held that management may not discharge an employee who refuses to commit an illegal act (participation in a price-fixing scheme, for example). In one case, a company had to reinstate an x-ray technician who had been fired for refusing to perform a medical procedure that, under state law, could be performed only by a physician or registered nurse. Another public policy exception is that employees cannot be dismissed for performing public obligations, such as serving on a jury or supplying information to the police. Increasingly, the courts are protecting whistle-blowers—those who report company wrongdoings—from being fired. We will further discuss the case of whistle-blowers later in the chapter.

There have been so many claims of public policy exceptions in recent years that most courts have had to establish standards for employee plaintiffs. A plaintiff is a person who brings a lawsuit before a court of law. For example, a fired employee must specify a "clear public policy mandate," embodied in a statute, regulation, or court decision, that allegedly has been violated by her or his discharge. In addition, the employee plaintiff must show a direct causal linkage between that public policy and the discharge.[26] However, the *implied* existence of public policy actions is increasingly being accepted by state courts as a basis for successful employee lawsuits.[27]

Contractual Actions

The courts are also more frequently protecting workers who they believe have **contracts** or **implied contracts** with their employers. The courts are holding employers to promises they do not even realize they have made. For example, statements in employee handbooks or personnel manuals, job-offer letters, and even oral assurances about job security are now being frequently interpreted as implied contracts that management is not at liberty to violate.[28] One employee was protected because he proved in court that he was told, "Nobody gets fired around here without a good reason." Another quoted a line in an employee handbook that read, "You will not be fired without just cause."[29] Still another employee successfully argued that, when the company had used the term "permanent employee" to mean an employee who had worked beyond the 6-month probationary period, it had implied *continuous employment*.

Breach of Good Faith Actions

The courts also recognize that employers are expected to hold themselves to a standard of fairness and good faith dealings with employees. This concept is probably the broadest restraint on employment-at-will terminations. The good faith principle suggests that employers may run the risk of losing lawsuits to former employees if they fail to show that unsatisfactory employees had every reasonable opportunity to improve their performance before being fired. The major implication for companies is that they may need to introduce systems of disciplinary measures or grievance-type review procedures for employees.[30] We will discuss such due-process mechanisms later in the chapter.

Management's Response to Employees' Job Claims

With respect to employees' job claims, management needs to be aware of two important points: (1) it is now appropriate stakeholder management policy to treat workers fairly and to dismiss them only for justifiable cause, and (2) the law today increasingly protects workers who do not get fair treatment. Therefore, management has an added incentive not to get embroiled in complex legal entanglements over wrongful discharges. Four specific actions that management might consider in dealing with this issue[31] include the following:

1. *Stay on the right side of the law.* It is management's responsibility to know the law and to obey it. This is the clearest, best, and most effective position to take. The company that conducts itself honestly and legally has the least to fear from disgruntled employees.

2. *Investigate any complaints fully and in good faith.* Well-motivated complainers in organizations are likely to report problems or concerns to someone within the company first. Therefore, employee complaints about company activities should be checked out. If there is substance to the problem, management has time to make corrections internally, with a minimum of adverse publicity.

3. *Deal in good faith with your employees.* Honor commitments, including those made in writing and those that employees have a reasonable right to expect as matters of normal policy, behavior, and good faith. Employees continue to win court cases when it is determined that their companies have acted in bad faith.

4. When you fire someone, make sure it is for a good reason. This is the best advice possible. Also make sure that the reason is supported by sound records and documentation. Effective performance appraisals, disciplinary procedures, dispute-handling procedures, and employee communications are all keys to justifiable discharges. Management needs to be attentive to abusive or retaliatory firings that are supported by thin technicalities. If the need arises to fire someone, it should not be difficult to document sound reasons for doing so.

Before an employee is terminated, wisdom suggests that management should ask the supervisor, "If you had to appear before a jury, why would you say the employee should be discharged?" Management should also ask the supervisor if the action being taken is consistent with other actions and whether the employee was aware that certain conduct would result in discharge. Finally, management should assume that litigation might result from the firing and that the supervisor making the decision to fire might not be with the company when the case goes to court. Therefore, documentation for each event leading to the termination should be assembled immediately.[32]

Effective stakeholder management suggests that organizations seriously consider their obligations to employee stakeholders and their rights and expectations with respect to their jobs. Not only are the courts increasingly affording employees greater job protection, but evolving notions of ethical treatment are increasingly expanding employees' job rights as well. Companies that are aspiring to emulate the tenets of the moral management model will need to reexamine continuously their attitudes, perceptions, practices, and policies with respect to this issue.

THE RIGHT TO DUE PROCESS AND FAIR TREATMENT

One of the most frequently proclaimed employee rights issues of the past decade has been the right to due process. Basically, *due process* is the right to receive an impartial review of one's complaints and to be dealt with fairly. In the context of the workplace, due process is thought to be the right of employees to have decisions that adversely affect them be reviewed by objective, impartial third parties.

One major obstacle to the due-process idea is that to some extent it is seen to be contrary to the employment-at-will principle discussed earlier. It is argued, however, that due process is consistent with the democratic ideal that undergirds the universal right to fair treatment. It could be argued that without due process employees do not receive fair treatment in the workplace. Furthermore, the fact that the employment-at-will principle is being eroded by the courts might be taken as an indication that this principle is basically unfair. If this is true, the due-process concept makes more sense.

Patricia Werhane, a leading business ethicist, contends that, procedurally, due process extends beyond simple fair treatment and should state, "Every employee has a right to a public hearing, peer evaluation, outside arbitration, or some other open and mutually agreed-upon grievance procedure before being demoted, unwillingly transferred, or fired."[33] Thus, we see due process ranging from the expectation that employees be treated fairly to the position that employees deserve a fair system of decision making.

Sometimes the employee is treated unfairly in such a subtle way that it is difficult to know that unfair treatment has taken place. What do you do, for example, if your supervisor refuses to recommend you for promotion or permit you to transfer because she or he considers you to be exceptionally good at your job and doesn't want to lose you? How do you prove that a manager has given you a low performance appraisal because you resisted sexual advances? The issues over which due-process questions may arise can be quite difficult and subtle.

Only in the past 30 years have some leading companies given special consideration to employees' rights to due process. Historically, managers have had almost unlimited freedom to deal with employees as they wished. In many cases, unfair treatment was not intentional but was the result of inept or distracted supervisors inflicting needless harm on subordinates.[34] It can also be easily seen how amoral managers may have failed to provide employees with acceptable due process and fair treatment. By failing to institute alternative ways to resolve disputes, the managers lost an opportunity to avoid the time, energy, and money that is often lost in protracted administrative and judicial processes.[35]

Employee Constitutionalism

David Ewing, an authority on the question of employee civil liberties, has argued that employee due process should be regarded as but one part of employee constitutionalism. He suggests that *employee constitutionalism* "consists of a set of clearly defined rights, and a means of protecting employees from discharge, demotion, or other penalties imposed when they assert their rights." He goes on[36] to enumerate the main requirements of a due-process system in an organization:

1. It must be a procedure; it must follow rules. It must not be arbitrary.

2. It must be sufficiently visible and well known that potential violators of employee rights and victims of abuse are aware of it.

3. It must be predictably effective.

ETHICS IN PRACTICE

"How Ethical Values Vary"

During my Christmas break, I was employed at ABC Company, a caulk manufactory located in a small town. Jim Wilson, who had little or no education, was employed in the shipping department at ABC. He was also trained as a blender in case someone in the Blending Department quit, went on vacation, or was fired. Luis Alberto, who was about 58 years old, was also employed at ABC Company, as a packer. Basically, a packer operates a machine that fills the cartridges with caulk, seals the tubes, and finally places either 12 or 24 10-ounce cartridges in a box. Luis's education did not range beyond an eighth-grade level. Luis's daughter-in-law was also employed at ABC, as a chemist in the lab. She spoke up when Luis's employment situation was on the line. She even told management when it was time to consider giving Luis an increase in his earnings.

Prior to the Christmas holiday break, the hired blender quit. Knowing how hard the position was to fill, Jim was told it was a permanent position. Jim was told by his supervisor, "Jim, you can't get another job anywhere in town because you don't have a high school diploma and you can't read, so you are up the creek if you don't take this position." Nothing was mentioned to Luis about the position. Luis's daughter-in-law made sure that the supervisor kept the opening notice out of Luis's sight. Knowing the dangers of that particular job, she thought it was in his best interest not to be made aware of it. It seems as if Jim Wilson had to do all the dirty work in the plant without being able to say anything.

1. How is ethics involved in this situation at the ABC Company?

2. If ethics is involved, what procedures should be implemented?

3. What are Jim's alternatives? What should he do? Why?

4. If you observed the above situation with respect to employees as stakeholders, what would you do? Why?

Contributed by Mystro Whatley

---

4. It must be institutionalized—a relatively permanent fixture in the organization.

5. It must be perceived as equitable.

6. It must be easy to use.

7. It must apply to all employees.

Ewing has gone on to define *corporate due process* in the following way:

> *A fair hearing procedure by a power mediator, investigator, or board with the complaining employee having the right to be represented by another employee, to present evidence, to rebut the other side's charges, to have an objective and impartial hearing, to have the wrong corrected if proved, to be free from retaliation for using the procedure, to enjoy reasonable confidentiality, to be heard reasonably soon after lodging the complaint, to get a timely decision, and so forth.*[37]

Ewing's concept of corporate due process represents a formal ideal, and it is doubtful that many corporate due-process systems meet all his requirements. However, there are many due-process systems or mechanisms in use by companies today as they strive to treat their employees fairly. In the next section we will briefly discuss some of these approaches.

Alternative Dispute Resolution

There are several ways companies can and do provide due process for their employees. The approaches described below represent some of the alternative dispute resolution (ADR) methods that have been employed over the past 30 years.

Common Approaches

One of the most often-used mechanisms is the ***open-door policy***. This approach typically relies on a senior-level executive who asserts that her or his "door is always open" for those who think they have been treated unfairly. Another approach has been to assign to a *human resources department executive* the responsibility for investigating employee grievances and either handling them or reporting them to higher management. Closely related to this technique is the assignment of this same responsibility to an *assistant to the president*.[38] From the employee's standpoint, the major problems with these approaches are that (1) the process is closed, (2) one person is reviewing what happened, and (3) there is a tendency in organizations for one manager to support another manager's decisions. The process is opened up somewhat by companies that use a ***hearing procedure***, which permits employees to be represented by an attorney or another person, with a neutral company executive deciding the outcome based on the evidence. Similar to this approach is the use of a ***management grievance committee***, which may involve multiple executives in the decision process.

The Ombudsperson

An innovative due-process mechanism that has become popular in the past decade for dealing with employee problems is the use of a corporate ***ombudsperson***. "*Ombudsman*," the word from which *ombudsperson* is derived, is a Swedish word that refers to one who investigates reported complaints and helps to achieve equitable settlements. The ombudsperson approach has been used in Sweden since 1809 to curb abuses by government against individuals. In the United States, the corporate version of the ombudsperson was first experimented with in 1972, when the Xerox Corporation named an ombudsperson for its largest division. General Electric and the Boeing Vertol division of Boeing were quick to follow.[39] The ombudsperson is also known as a "troubleshooter."[40]

The operation of the ombudsperson program at Xerox is generally representative of ombudsperson programs. The ombudsperson began as an *employee relations manager* on the organization chart in Xerox's Information Technology Group (ITG). Everyone soon knew that the ombudsperson's function was to ensure fair treatment of employees. This person reported directly to the ITG president, who was the only one who could reverse the ombudsperson's decisions. During the early years of the program, none of the ombudsperson's decisions was overturned—a point signifying the power and effectiveness of the one holding the job.

Under the Xerox system, the employee was expected to try to solve her or his problem through an immediate supervisor or the personnel department before submitting a complaint to the ombudsperson. At this point, the ombudsperson studied the complaint and the company file on the case. Then the ombudsperson discussed both items with a personnel department representative and then with the employee. Subsequently, the ombudsperson's recommended solution was passed on to the personnel department, which presented it as its own idea to the manager involved. Only if the manager declined to go along did the ombudsperson reveal her or his identity and put her or his authority behind the recommendation.[41]

Another recent example of the use of the ombudsperson is provided by Sony Electronics, Inc. In about 1993, Sony named an ombudsman to function as a clearinghouse for employee concerns. The position was intended especially to handle matters regarding illegal or unethical behavior observed within the company. The goal was early identification of legal or ethical violations.

The ombudsman at Sony also acts as a neutral third party in resolving employee complaints and as one who listens to and handles employee and manager complaints and concerns. As an independent third party, the ombudsman functions as a reporting link between employees and management. The ombudsman functions as a confidential assistant, counselor, mediator, fact finder, and upward-feedback facilitator.

At Sony, the ombudsman endeavors to protect the rights of all employees and managers involved in any matter under consideration. In addition, the ombudsman plays a key role in all business ethics matters, including the company's business ethics committee, ethics training, and implementation of the company's code of conduct.[42]

The ombudsperson approach to ensuring due process is not without problems. Managers may feel threatened when employees go to the ombudsperson, who must be willing to anger executives in order to get the job done. There is also the fear that employees might experience retribution for going to the ombudsperson in the first place. Despite these potential problems, once in place and understood, the system has worked. A positive and unexpected result of the Xerox experience was that even supervisors went to the ombudsperson for advice on personnel problems. Thus, in some cases, issues were referred to the ombudsperson even before managerial decisions were made.[43]

The Peer Review Panel

The *peer review panel* is another innovative due-process mechanism presently under experimentation at several large companies. Control Data Corporation (CDC) was one of the pioneers in the use of the peer review process. Over 30 years ago, Control Data was one of the first nonunion companies in the United States to introduce an employee grievance system. It was a system whereby an aggrieved employee could appeal all the way up the chain of authority through six management levels. The company tried to make the system work, but many times the grievance either died because of the cumbersome process or was "kicked upstairs" for some higher level of management to handle. Rulings in favor of the worker were rare. The company determined that this approach was not fair, and in 1983 it added a peer review process to the system.[44]

The peer review process at CDC required the same initial steps as had the traditional grievance system. The employee was to talk first with her or his manager, then to the human resources manager, and then to one higher executive in the management chain. If the employee was still not satisfied that due process had prevailed, she or he was entitled to request a peer review board. The central feature of a peer review board is a panel of two randomly chosen "peers" of the aggrieved employee, along with one disinterested executive from a different division. *Peers* were defined as fellow workers in the same job family at a grade level equal to or higher than that of the grievant.[45]

Managers on the losing side sometimes complain because they think that outsiders are deciding on local issues about which they are not intimately knowledgeable. The company's position is that a manager not only has to convince herself or himself and local superiors that a personnel action is right but also must have it deemed as right against a companywide policy. The success of the system depends on (1) its having the clear support of top management for fair treatment of employees and (2) its being seen as a permanent fixture. The people who operate the peer review system must have sufficient respect and stature to make the process credible in the eyes of even the most authoritarian line manager.[46]

The trend toward using ADR is growing with no end in sight. In 1998, the American Arbitration Association estimated that over 400 employers were using alternative methods to resolve disputes and predicted that 10,000 employers would use such methods by the year 2000. This growth is spurred partly by the time and money saved by avoiding costly litigation. Brown & Root, a Houston-based construction and engineering firm, estimates that its legal fees have dropped 30 to 50 percent since employing ADR, and 70 to 80 percent of the firm's cases are now settled within 8 weeks (40 percent within a month). Further, the proportion of adverse settlements and the size of the judgments are no different from when they went through the court system.[47] A 1997 survey conducted by Cornell University, the Foundation for the Prevention and Resolution of Conflict, and Price Waterhouse, LLP, showed that most Fortune 1000 corporations have used some form of ADR. Of these, 81 percent found ADR to be "a more satisfactory process" than litigation, while 59 percent indicated that ADR "preserves good relationships."[48]

Concerns have recently been expressed that employers are beginning to require new hires to sign contracts waiving their right to sue the firm and accepting mandatory arbitration as the alternative. Critics of this practice argue that this robs employees of their right to due process; supporters contend that the arbitration process is just as fair as a jury trial while costing much less in time and money. At this writing, the courts appear to have generally upheld mandatory arbitration, but Congress is considering bills to ban it.[49]

It is unclear what the future holds for employee due process. As Ewing has indicated, "Due process is a way of fighting institutionalized indifference to the individual—the indifference that says that productivity and efficiency are the goals of the organization, and any person who stands in the way must be sacrificed."[50] Increasingly, companies are learning they must acknowledge due process to be not only an employee right but also a sound and ethical management practice in keeping with the wishes and expectations of employees.

FREEDOM OF SPEECH IN THE WORKPLACE

In the 1980s, Henry Boisvert was a testing supervisor at FMC Corp., makers of the Bradley Fighting Vehicle. The Bradley was designed to transport soldiers around battlefields and, when necessary, "swim" through rivers and lakes. When Boisvert tested the Bradley's ability to move through a pond, he found it filled quickly with water. He wrote the Army a report of his findings but was told by FMC supervisors that the report would never be sent. When Boisvert refused to sign a falsified report of his test results, he was fired.[51]

About the same time that Boisvert was discovering the Bradley's inability to swim, Air Force Lieutenant Colonel James Burton found additional problems with the fighting machine. When hit by enemy fire, the Bradley's aluminum armor melted and filled the inside of the vehicle with poisonous fumes. After 17 years of development and $14 billion for research and prototypes, the Bradley was unfit for warfare. Burton uncovered tests of the Bradley that were rigged by filling the gas tanks with water and the ammunition with noncombustible sand, making it impossible for the Bradley to explode. He also fought an attempt to transfer him to Alaska. After persevering to successfully force changes in the Bradley, Burton was forced to take early retirement as the officers who tried to stop his investigation were promoted.[52]

For most whistle-blowers, the story ends here, but Boisvert and Burton prevailed in their fights to fix the Bradley. In 1998, after a 12-year legal battle, Boisvert received one of the largest damage awards ever seen in a federal case, well over $300 million. During the trial, evidence emerged about employees using putty to fix cracks in the machine while vehicles to be selected for random inspection were marked with "X"s and worked on more carefully than the rest.[53] Burton's story also ends happily. Congress mandated that the Bradley be tested under the supervision of the National Academy of Sciences, using conditions that resembled true battlefield combat. As a result of these tests, the Bradley was redesigned and used successfully during the 1991 Persian Gulf War. Burton wrote a successful book about his experiences, *The Pentagon Wars,* which subsequently became a 1998 HBO movie.[54] It is impossible to estimate how many soldiers' lives were saved by the courage and persistence of these two men.

Unfortunately for employees who believe they have a legitimate right to speak out against a company engaging in an illegal or unethical practice, most whistle-blowers' stories lack happy endings. Studies of whistle-blowers have found that as many as 90 percent experience negative outcomes, and more than half lose their jobs. Many end up taking prescription medicine to ease the stress, while others even contemplate suicide.[55] Nevertheless, the willingness to challenge management by speaking out is typical of a growing number of employees today, and these individuals are receiving increasing amounts of protection from the courts.

Whistle-Blowing

As stated earlier, the current generation of employees has a different concept of loyalty to and acceptance of authority than that of past generations. The result is an unprecedented number of employees "blowing the whistle" on their employers. A whistle-blower has been called a "muckraker from within, who exposes what he [or she] considers the unconscionable practices of his [or her] own organization."[56]

What constitutes whistle-blowing? For our purposes, we define a *whistle-blower* as "an individual who reports to some outside party [for example, media, government agency] some wrongdoing [illegal or unethical act] that he or she knows or suspects his or her employer of committing." An alternative but similar definition of whistle-blowing is provided by Miceli and Near, two experts on the subject, who characterize it as "the disclosure by organization members [former or current] of illegal, immoral, or illegitimate practices under the control of their employers, to persons or organizations that may be able to effect action."[57]

Thus, there are four key elements in the whistle-blowing process: the whistle-blower, the act or complaint the whistle-blower is concerned about, the party to whom the complaint or report is made, and the organization against which the complaint is made.[58] Although our definition indicates that whistle-blowing is done to some outside party, there have been many cases where "internal whistle-blowers" have simply reported their concerns to members of management and yet have been treated as though they had gone to outside parties.

What is at stake is the employee's right to speak out in cases where she or he thinks the company or management is engaging in an unacceptable practice. Whistle-blowing is contrary to our cultural tradition that an employee does not question a superior's decisions and acts, especially not in public. The traditional view holds that loyalty, obedience, and confidentiality are owed solely to the corporate employer. The emerging view of employee responsibility holds that the employee has a duty not only to the employer but also to the public and to her or his own conscience. Whistle-blowing, in this latter situation, becomes a viable option for the employee should management not be responsive to expressed concerns. Figure 14–5 depicts these two views of employee responsibility.

Most whistle-blowers seem to be engaging in these acts out of a genuine or legitimate belief that the actions of their organizations are wrong and that they are doing the right thing by reporting them. They may have learned of the wrongful acts by being requested or coerced to participate in them, or they may have gained knowledge of them through observation or examination of company records. The genuinely concerned employee may initially express concern to a superior or to someone else within the organization.[59] Other potential whistle-blowers may be planning to make their reports for the purpose of striking out or retaliating against the company or a specific manager for some reason. This motive is illegitimate. One recent survey of 233 whistle-blowers disclosed that the average whistle-blower is not an oddball, "loose cannon," or disgruntled employee. The average whistle-blower turns out to be a family man, in his mid-40s, who was motivated by conscience, or what might be termed "universal moral values."[60]

Consequences of Whistle-Blowing

What happens to employees after they blow the whistle? Unfortunately, whistle-blowers are seldom rewarded for their perceived contributions to the public interest. Although they are now more likely to get some form of protection from state courts, whistle-blowers in general have paid dearly for their lack of company loyalty. Short of firings, various types of corporate retaliation have been taken against whistle-blowers,[61] including:

• More stringent criticism of work

• Less desirable work assignments

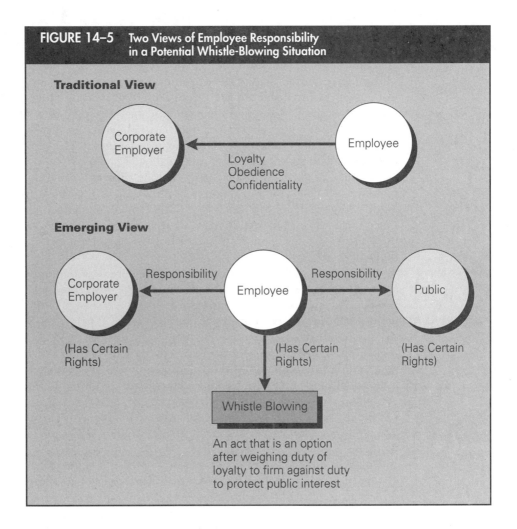

FIGURE 14–5 Two Views of Employee Responsibility in a Potential Whistle-Blowing Situation

Traditional View

Corporate Employer ← Loyalty / Obedience / Confidentiality — Employee

Emerging View

Corporate Employer ← Responsibility — Employee — Responsibility → Public

(Has Certain Rights)   (Has Certain Rights)   (Has Certain Rights)

Whistle Blowing

An act that is an option after weighing duty of loyalty to firm against duty to protect public interest

- Pressure to drop charges against the company
- Heavier workloads
- Lost perquisites (for example, telephone and parking privileges)
- Exclusion from meetings previously attended

One example of what can happen to whistle-blowers as a consequence of their actions is the case of Charles Atchison. At age 40, Atchison stood up before regulators and told them about numerous safety violations at the Commanche Peak Nuclear Plant in Glen Rose, Texas. Atchison was a quality control inspector for Brown & Root, the construction company that built the plant for the Texas Utilities Electric Company. Atchison claimed he couldn't get anyone to fix the problems. Atchison lost his job and ended up in debt. Although Atchison was proud of the stance he had taken, he indicated that he often felt psychic scars from the experience. "The whistle-blower today is probably the most discriminated against individual in the country," Atchison exclaimed.[62]

Another example is the case of Anne Livengood, a 51-year-old medical office worker who claimed she was fired from a physical therapy clinic in Fremont, California, after she had notified management that its accounting system was billing insurance companies for services that had not been performed. Livengood was escorted out of her building by the company accountant. Her response to the experience was, "You feel so alone and intimidated."[63]

Famous cases of whistle-blowing include Ernest Fitzgerald, the Air Force employee who blew the whistle on billions of dollars in cost overruns at Lockheed, and the Morton Thiokol engineers who tried to halt the launch of the space shuttle *Challenger* because of frozen O-rings. All of these whistle-blowers were fired.[64]

Figure 14–6 identifies a pattern that Donald Soeken refers to as the seven stages of life of a typical whistle-blower.

Although whistle-blowers frequently do get fired, as public policy increasingly sides with them and their courageous stances, other corporate actions are becoming possible. An encouraging episode from 1994 is the case of Mark Jorgensen, who was employed at Prudential Insurance Co. of America.[65] Jorgensen was a manager of real estate funds for Prudential. He thought he was just being an honest guy when he exposed fraud he saw occurring in his company. His world then began to fall apart. He was abandoned by his boss, who had once been his friend. His colleagues at work began to shun him. Company lawyers accused him of breaking the law. Jorgensen, who was once a powerful and respected executive in the firm, began to hide out at the local library because he had been forbidden to return to his office. His long and successful career appeared to be dwindling to a pathetic end. Finally, he was fired.

Unlike most whistle-blowers, however, Jorgensen received a phone call from the company chairman, Robert Winters, who wanted to meet with Jorgensen to tell him some startling news: The company now believed him and wanted to reinstate him. Further, the company wanted to force out the boss he had accused of falsely inflating the values of funds that he managed. The turnabout was attributed to Jorgensen's persistence in fighting all odds in his quest to justify his convictions. Coming to the realization that Jorgensen had been right in his allegations all along, Prudential found itself in an unusual situation in business today—siding with the whistle-blower it had fought for months and eventually had fired. The company offered to reinstate Jorgensen in his job, but he elected instead to move on to another company. Prudential paid him a sizable amount to settle his lawsuit.[66] Although we do not read about many stories that end this way, it is encouraging to know that there are some stories that have good endings.

Government's Protection of Whistle-Blowers

Just as employees are beginning to get some protection from the courts through the public policy exception to the employment-at-will doctrine, the same is true for whistle-blowers. The federal government was one of the first organizations to attempt to protect its own whistle-blowers. A highlight of the 1978 *Civil Service Reform Act* was protection for federal employees who expose illegal, corrupt, or

---

FIGURE 14–6   The Seven Stages of Life of a Typical Whistle-Blower

Based on extensive research into the life experiences of whistle-blowers, Donald Soeken has identified a pattern that he calls the "seven stages of life" of a typical whistle-blower. The seven stages are as follows:

1. Discovery of the organizational abuse

2. Reflection on what action to take

3. Confrontation with superiors

4. Retaliation (against the whistle-blower)

5. Long haul of legal action

6. Termination of the case

7. Going on to a new life

In terms of *personal effects,* Soeken found in a survey of 233 whistle-blowers that 90 percent of them had lost their jobs or been demoted, 26 percent had sought psychiatric and medical care, 15 percent had divorced in the aftermath of the episode, 10 percent had attempted suicide, and 8 percent had gone bankrupt.

SOURCE: Cited in Ana Radelat, "When Blowing the Whistle Ruins Your Life," *Public Citizen* (September/October, 1991), 18–19.

wasteful government activities. Unfortunately, this effort has had only mixed results.[67] It is difficult to protect whistle-blowers against retaliation because so often the reprisals are subtle. An added boost for federal employees came in 1989, when Congress passed the *Whistle-Blower Protection Act* and President Bush signed it into law. The effect of this act was to reform the Merit System Protection Board and the Office of General Counsel, the two offices that protect federal employees. Early results show that about one-third of the whistle-blowers had their complaints upheld, whereas less than 5 percent were being upheld prior to the new legislation.[68]

Most state courts recognize a public policy exception and therefore whistle-blowers have some limited protection. The normal remedy for wrongful discharge of employees is reinstatement with back pay, with some sympathetic juries adding compensatory damages for physical suffering.[69]

The problem with most laws intended to protect whistle-blowers is that they are quite spotty. Some state and federal laws, such as environmental, transportation, health, safety, and civil rights statutes, have provisions that protect whistle-blowers from retaliation, but relatively few states have provisions that protect private-sector employees, and these provisions vary widely in their nature and protection coverage. Another obstacle to effective whistle-blowing stems from the recent move toward mandatory arbitration, discussed earlier in the chapter. Because mandatory arbitration is an in-house process, it can deny a whistle-blower the public forum that is one of the whistle-blower's most effective tools for creating change.[70]

Protection is intended to mean that employers are prohibited from firing or otherwise retaliating against employees, but, practically speaking, it typically means that the employee may file suit for harassment or wrongful discharge. Currently, private-sector employees are not protected by federal whistle-blowing laws, but the Government Accountability Project, an independent, nonprofit organization in Washington, DC, is working to promote legislation that would protect private sector jobs.[71] Their challenge will be to get cooperation and action from Congress.

The Whistle-Blowers Protection Act of Michigan

Few states have gone as far as Michigan did by actually creating specific whistle-blower protection. The *Michigan Whistle-Blowers Protection Act of 1981* became the first state law designed to protect any employee in private industry against unjust reprisals for reporting alleged violations of federal, state, or local laws to public authorities. The burden is placed on the employer to show that questionable treatment is justified on the basis of proper personnel standards or valid business reasons.[72]

When the bill was proposed in Michigan, employer groups were opposed to it because they feared it would result in a flood of litigation and harassing actions by employees who were fired for valid reasons. The bill was amended to address employer concerns, and the final law[73] carried the following requirements for employees to be protected under the law:

1. Employees must prove they have filed or are about to file a complaint at the time of dismissal.

2. The complaint must be made to public authorities, not to the media.

3. Reports must not be found to be false or malicious.

Alan Westin thinks that a major flaw in the bill is that it does not require the whistle-blower, before going public, to use the company's own internal procedures for complaints.[74] Generally speaking, when a court is attempting to decide whether a whistle-blower should be protected, it is interested in (1) the whistle-blower's motives, (2) whether internal channels have been used, (3) whether the whistle-blower's allegations are true or false, and (4) the degree of care exercised by the whistle-blower in gathering the information on which the charges are based. These requirements are reasonable safeguards to protect companies against negligent dissenters.

The Michigan act has spurred similar laws in other states. Another likely impact of such laws will be on company personnel practices and policies. Well-managed companies will need to be sure they have effective and fair procedures or systems for dealing with whistle-blowers. Time has shown, however, that few states have followed Michigan's aggressive lead. Many states now insist that a company be given a reasonable opportunity to correct a violation or condition before making a disclosure to a public body.[75]

Although we see more and more cases of employees wanting the right to question management and to speak out, David Ewing[76] argues that there are some forms of speech that should not be protected:

- Employees should not have the right to divulge information about legal and ethical plans, practices, operations, inventions, and other matters that must be kept confidential if the organization is to do its job in an efficient manner.

- Employees should not have the right to make personal accusations or slurs that are irrelevant to questions about policies and actions that seem illegal or irresponsible.

- Employees should not be entitled to disrupt an organization or damage its morale by making accusations that do not reflect a conviction that wrong is being done.

- Employees should not be entitled to rail against the competence of a manager to make everyday work decisions that have nothing to do with the legality, morality, or responsibility of management actions.

- Employees should not be entitled to object to discharge, transfer, or demotion, no matter what they have said about the organization or how they have said it, if management can demonstrate that unsatisfactory performance or violation of a code of conduct was the reason for its actions.

In the final analysis, an employee should have a right to dissent, but this right may be constrained or limited by the kinds of reasons just given, and perhaps others as well.

False Claims Act of 1986

A provocative piece of federal legislation that was passed to add an incentive for whistle-blowers in the public interest is the False Claims Act of 1986. The False Claims Act was originally passed over 100 years ago in 1863 in response to contractors who had cheated the government. The law was revised in 1986 to make recoveries easier and more generous and thereby encourage whistle-blowing against government contractor fraud.[77] The 1986 act grew out of outrage in the mid-1980s over reports of fraud and abuse on the part of military contractors, such as $600 toilet seats and country club memberships billed to the government.[78]

The 1986 amendments were an effort on the part of Congress to put teeth into its efforts to curb contracting fraud. The False Claims Act has *qui tam* (Latin shorthand for "he who sues for the king as well as himself") provisions that allow employees to blow the whistle about contractor fraud and share with the government in any financial recoveries realized by their efforts.

What is particularly controversial about the False Claims Act of 1986 is the magnitude of the financial incentives that individual employees may earn as a result of their whistle-blowing efforts. The law allows individuals to be awarded as much as 15 to 25 percent of the proceeds in cases where the government joins in the action, and from 25 to 30 percent of the proceeds in actions that the government does not join.[79] Thus, there are millions or even tens of millions of dollars of incentives available to whistle-blowers who successfully win their suits against private contractors, thus allowing the government to get back huge sums, too. In 1997, as the result of a whistle-blower's actions, SmithKline Beecham Clinical Laboratories was ordered to pay a record $325 million fraud settlement to the Justice Department.[80]

As a result of the False Claims Act, whistle-blowing against abuse of government by private companies is enjoying a renaissance. The Justice Department is recovering record sums, and whistle-blowers are becoming millionaires. John Phillips, a prominent public-interest lawyer in Los Angeles who helped persuade Congress to strengthen the False Claims Act in 1986, is enjoying a bustling law practice. His target companies have included GE, Teledyne, and National Health Laboratories. His first seven cases brought about $380 million back into the U.S. Treasury.[81]

As of this writing, the False Claims Act has returned nearly $2 billion to the federal government. The Act continues to evolve as it is tested by legislation and the court. Proposed legislative changes have included setting a minimum threshold for claims, excluding discrepancies that result from "unintentional" mistakes, and blocking suits in which there had been "prior disclosure" of the same allegations. In the courts, a federal judge in Houston declared the Act was unconstitutional because the right to prosecute cases belongs to the Executive Branch, not Congress. In 1998, a federal judge ruled that states and municipalities cannot be sued under the Act, because they do not qualify as people under the Civil War–era law. To date, three federal appeals courts have upheld the law's constitutionality, and the Supreme Court has declined to hear challenges.[82]

Whatever the outcome of the challenges to the False Claims Act, it is clear that whistle-blowing will remain a major concern for the private sector. This necessitates careful thought and action on the part of company management as they contemplate how to respond to whistle-blowers and to whistle-blowing situations.

Management Responsiveness to Potential Whistle-Blowing Situations

How can an organization work with its employees to reduce their need to blow the whistle? Kenneth Walters[83] has suggested five considerations that might be kept in mind:

1. The company should assure employees that the organization will not interfere with their basic political freedoms.

2. The organization's grievance procedures should be streamlined so that employees can obtain direct and sympathetic hearings for issues on which they are likely to blow the whistle if their complaints are not heard quickly and fairly.

3. The organization's concept of social responsibility should be reviewed to make sure that it is not being construed merely as corporate giving to charity.

4. The organization should formally recognize and communicate respect for the individual consciences of employees.

5. The organization should realize that dealing harshly with a whistle-blowing employee could result in needless adverse public reaction.

Companies are learning that whistle-blowing can be averted if visible efforts are made on the part of management to listen and be responsive to employees' concerns. One specific approach is the use of an ombudsperson, which we discussed earlier, as a due-process mechanism. The ombudsperson can also be used to deal with employee grievances against the company. The Corporate Ombudsman Association, which includes such firms as Anheuser-Busch, Control Data, McDonald's, and Upjohn, even goes so far as to prepare training materials that include likely whistle-blowing scenarios. According to one report, the national grapevine among corporate ombudspersons is constantly buzzing with rumors of front-page scandals that they have averted. The companies that have put money into such programs say they are well worth the investment.[84]

Whether or not an ombudsperson is used, management should respond in a positive way to employee objectors and dissenters. At a minimum, companies that want to be responsive to such employees[85] should engage in the following four actions:

1. *Listen.* Management must listen very carefully to the employee's concern. Be particularly attentive to the employee's valid points, and acknowledge them and show that you have a genuine respect for the employee's concerns. It is recommended that you attempt to "draw out the objector's personal concerns."

2. *Delve into why the employee is pursuing the complaint or issue.* Determining the objector's motives may give you important insights into the legitimacy of the complaint and how it should best be handled.

3. *Look for solutions that will address the interests of both the objector and the company.*

4. *Attempt to establish an equitable means of judging future actions.* Objective tests or criteria that are agreeable to both sides are superior to perseverance or negotiation as a means of resolving an impasse.

In a related set of recommendations, *Business Week* and The Conference Board have set forth four key components of a model whistle-blower policy.[86] These four recommended actions are as follows:

1. *Shout it from the rooftops.* The company should aggressively publicize a reporting policy that encourages employees to bring forward valid complaints of wrongdoing.

2. *Face the fear factor.* Employee fear may be defused by directing complaints to someone outside the whistle-blower's chain of command.

3. *Get right on it.* The complaint should be investigated immediately by an independent group, either within or outside the company.

4. *Go public.* The outcomes of investigations should be publicized whenever possible so that employees can see that complaints are taken seriously.

The desire of employees to speak out is increasingly becoming a right in their eyes and in the eyes of the courts as well. Although the courts differ from state to state, it is likely that whistle-blowers and employees' rights to free expression will increasingly be protected in the future. This being the case, management needs to assess carefully where it stands on this vital issue. It is becoming more and more apparent that respecting an employee's right to publicly differ with management may indeed serve the longer-term interests of the organization. We should also remember, however, that companies need and deserve protection from employees who do not perform as they should. Thus, "in the end, nothing could be more contrary to public policy than providing judicially imposed job tenure for those who least deserve it."[87]

SUMMARY

Employee stakeholders today are more sensitive about employee rights issues for a variety of reasons. Underlying this new concern are changes in the social contract between employers and employees. Four other changes that have occurred in the workplace are increased technological hazards, the computer invasion, professionals with divided loyalties, and increased mobility of employees. Central among the growing employee rights issues that are treated in this chapter are the right to a job or the right not to be fired without just cause, the right to due process and fair treatment, and the right to freedom of speech.

The basis for the argument that we may be moving toward an employee's right to a job, or not to be fired, is the erosion by the courts of the employment-at-will doctrine. More and more the courts are making exceptions to this longstanding common-law principle. Three major exceptions are the public policy exception, the idea of an implied contract, and breach of good faith. Society's concept of what represents fair treatment to employees is also changing.

The right to due process is concerned primarily with fair treatment. Common approaches for management responding to this concern include the open-door policy, human resource specialists, grievance committees, and hearing procedures. The ombudsperson approach is becoming more prevalent, and recently the peer review panel seems to have become a popular due-process mechanism. A special case in which due process is needed is the employee who chooses to speak out against management or blow the whistle on unethical or illegal actions. In spite of government efforts to protect whistle-blowers, these individuals face severe reprisals for taking actions against their employers. Managers should be genuinely attentive to employees' rights in this realm if they wish to avert major scandals and prolonged litigation. A stakeholder approach that emphasizes ethical relationships with employees would ordain this attention and concern.

KEY TERMS

contracts (page 450)

due process (page 451)

employee constitutionalism (page 452)

employment-at-will doctrine (page 449)

hearing procedure (page 454)

implied contracts (page 450)

management grievance committee (page 454)

ombudsperson (page 454)

open-door policy (page 454)

peer review panel (page 455)

peers (page 456)

private property (page 445)

public policy exception (page 449)

whistle-blower (page 457)

DISCUSSION QUESTIONS

1. Rank the various changes that are occurring in the workplace in terms of their importance to the growth of the employee rights movement. Briefly explain your ranking.

2. Explain the employment-at-will doctrine, and describe why it is being eroded. Do you think its erosion is leading to a healthy or an unhealthy employment environment in the United States? Justify your reasoning.

3. In your own words, explain the right to due process. What are some of the major ways management is attempting to ensure due process in the workplace?

4. If you could choose only one, would the ombudsperson approach or the peer review panel be your choice as the most effective approach to employee due process? Explain.

5. How do you feel about whistle-blowing now that you have read about it? Are you now more sympathetic or less sympathetic to whistle-blowers? Explain.

6. What is your assessment of the value of the 1986 False Claims Act?

ENDNOTES

1. David W. Ewing, "Due Process: Will Business Default?" *Harvard Business Review* (November–December, 1982), 115–116.

2. *Ibid.*, 115.

3. Ewing, 115.

4. *Ibid.*

5. *Ibid.*, 116.

6. *Ibid.*

7. Thomas F. O'Boyle, "Loyalty Ebbs at Many Companies as Employees Grow Disillusioned," *The Wall Street Journal* (July 16, 1985), 27.

8. Amanda Bennett, *The Death of the Organization Man* (Morrow, 1990); and Raymond Sokolov, "Troubles in the Corporation and on Campus," *The Wall Street Journal* (April 16, 1990), A11.

9. Ewing, 116.

10. "Revolution in America's Workplace," *Business Week* (October 17, 1994), 252.

11. *Ibid.*

12. *Ibid.*

13. Kenneth Chilton and Murray Weidenbaum, *A New Social Contract for the American Workplace: From Paternalism to Partnering* (St. Louis: Center for the Study of American Business, Washington University, November, 1994), 2.

14. John Wyatt, "The New Deal: What Companies and Employees Owe One Another," *Fortune* (June 13, 1994), 44–52.

15. Hal Lancaster, "A New Social Contract to Benefit Employer and Employee," *The Wall Street Journal* (November 29, 1994), B1.

16. Nina Munk, "The New Organization Man," *Fortune* (March 16, 1998), 62–74.

17. *Ibid.*, 73–74.

18. David W. Ewing, *Freedom Inside the Organization: Bringing Civil Liberties to the Workplace* (New York: McGraw-Hill, 1977), 3.

19. *Ibid.*, 5.

20. Leo Troy, *The End of Unionism: An Appraisal* (St. Louis: Center for the Study of American Business, Washington University, September, 1994), 1–2.

21. David W. Ewing, "What Business Thinks About Employee Rights," *Harvard Business Review* (September–October, 1977), 81–94.

22. Richard Edwards, *Rights at Work* (Washington, DC: The Brookings Institution, 1993), 25–26.
23. *Ibid.*, 31–33.
24. *Ibid.*, 33–35.
25. T. J. Condon, "Fire Me and I'll Sue: A Manager's Guide to Employee Rights," (Alexander Hamilton Institute, 1984–1985), 4. Also see John D. Rapoport and Brian L. P. Zevnik, *The Employee Strikes Back!* (New York: Collier Books, 1994).
26. Linda D. McGill, "Public Policy Claims in Employee Termination Disputes," *Employment Relations Today* (Spring, 1988), 46–47.
27. Axel R. Granholm, *Handbook of Employee Termination* (New York: John Wiley & Sons, 1991), 21. Also see Ronald M. Green, *The Ethical Manager* (NY: Macmillan, 1994), Chapter 5, "Employee Rights."
28. Andrew M. Kramer, "The Hazards of Firing at Will," *The Wall Street Journal* (March 9, 1987), 22. Also see Rapoport and Zevnik.
29. Richard Greene, "Don't Panic," *Forbes* (August 29, 1983), 122.
30. Granholm, 24–25.
31. Condon, 12.
32. Kramer, 22.
33. Patricia H. Werhane, *Persons, Rights and Corporations* (Englewood Cliffs, NJ: Prentice Hall, 1985), 110.
34. Ewing, *Freedom Inside the Organization* (1977), 10.
35. Kay O. Wilburn, "Employment Disputes: Solving Them Out of Court," *Management Review* (March, 1998), 17–21. See also Marc Lampe, "Mediation as an Ethical Adjunct of Stakeholder Theory," working paper, University of San Diego.
36. Ewing, *Freedom Inside the Organization* (1977), 11.
37. David W. Ewing, *Justice on the Job: Resolving Grievances in the Nonunion Workplace* (Boston: Harvard Business School Press, 1989), 324.
38. Ewing, *Harvard Business Review,* 1977.
39. "Where Ombudsmen Work Out," *Business Week* (May 3, 1976), 114–116.
40. John T. Ziegenfuss, Jr., *Organizational Troubleshooters: Resolving Problems with Customers and Employees* (San Francisco: Jossey-Bass Publishers, 1988).
41. "How the Xerox Ombudsman Helps Xerox," *Business Week* (May 12, 1973), 188–190.
42. "Pathway to Excellence: A Guide to Ethical Business Conduct," (Sony Electronics, April, 1994), company handouts.
43. *Ibid.*, 190.
44. Fred C. Olson, "How Peer Review Works at Control Data," *Harvard Business Review* (November–December, 1984), 58.
45. *Ibid.*, 58–59.
46. *Ibid.*, 58, 64.
47. Wilburn, 17–21.
48. Elaine McShulski, "ADR Gains Overwhelming Acceptance," *HR Magazine* (November, 1997), 22.
49. Leslie Kaufman and Anne Underwood, "Sign or Hit the Street," *Newsweek* (June 30, 1997), 48–49.
50. Ewing, *Freedom Inside the Organization* (1977), 172–173.

51. Lee Gomes, "A Whistle-Blower Finds Jackpot at the End of His Quest," *Wall Street Journal* (April 27, 1998), B1.
52. Robert P. Lawrence, "Go Ahead, Laugh at Army's Expense," *The San Diego Union-Tribune* (February 27, 1998), E12.
53. Gomes, B1.
54. Lawrence, E12.
55. Marcy Mason, "The Curse of Whistleblowing," *Wall Street Journal* (March 14, 1994), A14.
56. Charles Peters and Taylor Branch (eds.), *Blowing the Whistle: Dissent in the Public Interest* (New York: Praeger, 1972), 4.
57. Marcia P. Miceli and Janet P. Near, *Blowing the Whistle: The Organizational and Legal Implications for Companies and Employees* (New York: Lexington Books, 1992), 15.
58. Janet P. Near and Marcia P. Miceli, *The Whistle-Blowing Process and Its Outcomes: A Preliminary Model* (Columbus, OH: The Ohio State University, College of Administrative Science, Working Paper Series 83-55, September, 1983), 2. See also Miceli and Near, 1992.
59. Nancy R. Hauserman, "Whistle-Blowing: Individual Morality in a Corporate Society," *Business Horizons* (March–April, 1986), 5.
60. Ana Radelat, "When Blowing the Whistle Ruins Your Life," *Public Citizen* (September/October, 1991), 16–20.
61. Janet P. Near, Marcia P. Miceli, and Tamila C. Jensen, "Variables Associated with the Whistle-Blowing Process," (Columbus, OH: The Ohio State University, College of Administrative Science, Working Paper Series 83-11, March, 1983), 5.
62. N. R. Kleinfield, "The Whistle-Blower's Morning After," *The New York Times* (November 9, 1986), 1-F.
63. Joan Hamilton, "Blowing the Whistle without Paying the Piper," *Business Week* (June 3, 1991), 139.
64. *Ibid.*, 138.
65. Kurt Eichenwald, "He Told. He Suffered. Now He's a Hero." *The New York Times* (May 29, 1994), 1-F.
66. *Ibid.*
67. Joann S. Lublin, "Watchdog Has Hard Time Hearing Whistles," *The Wall Street Journal* (October 17, 1980), 30.
68. Radelat, 20.
69. Michael W. Sculnick, "Disciplinary Whistle-Blowers," *Employment Relations Today* (Fall, 1986), 194.
70. Margaret A. Jacobs, "Arbitration Policies Are Muting Whistleblower Claims," *Wall Street Journal* (August 6, 1998), B1.
71. Hamilton, 138–139.
72. Alan F. Westin, "Michigan's Law to Protect the Whistle Blowers," *The Wall Street Journal* (April 13, 1981), 18. Also see Daniel P. Westman, *Whistle Blowing: The Law of Retaliatory Discharge* (Washington, DC: The Bureau of National Affairs, 1991); Robert L. Brady, "Blowing the Whistle," *HR Focus* (February, 1996), 20. Additional information on whistle-blowing is available at the Government Accountability Web site at *www.whistleblower.org.*

73. Westin, *ibid.*
74. Westin, *ibid.*
75. Rapoport and Zevnik, 27–31.
76. Ewing, *Freedom Inside the Organization* (1977), 109–110.
77. Miceli and Near (1992), 247.
78. Andrew W. Singer, "The Whistle-Blower: Patriot or Bounty Hunter?" *Across the Board* (November, 1992), 16–22.
79. Alfred G. Feliu, *Primer on Individual Employee Rights* (Washington, DC: The Bureau of National Affairs, Inc., 1992), 194–195.
80. Scott Hensley, "Settling Fraud Charges," *Modern Healthcare* (March 3, 1997), 28.
81. Richard B. Schmitt, "Honesty Pays Off: John Phillips Fosters a Growing Industry of Whistle-Blowing," *The Wall Street Journal* (January 11, 1995), A1.
82. Dean Starkman, "Whistle-Blowers Can't File Fraud Suits for Government, Federal Judge Rules," *Wall Street Journal* (November 3, 1997), 12; Joan R. Rose, "A Safe Harbor for Doctors Who Are Falsely Accused?," *Medical Economics* (May 26, 1998), 32; Catherine Yang and Mike France, "Whistleblowers on Trial," *Business Week* (March 24, 1997), 172–178; and Kristen Hallam, "Ruling Endangers Fraud Probes," *Modern Healthcare* (June 22, 1998), 8.
83. Kenneth D. Walters, "Your Employees' Right to Blow the Whistle," *Harvard Business Review* (July–August, 1975), 161–162.
84. Michael Brody, "Listen to Your Whistle-Blower," *Fortune* (November 24, 1986), 77–78.
85. David W. Ewing, "How to Negotiate with Employee Objectors," *Harvard Business Review* (January–February, 1983), 104.
86. Lisa Driscoll, "A Better Way to Handle Whistle-Blowers: Let Them Speak," *Business Week* (July 27, 1992), 36.
87. Charles C. Bakaly, Jr. and Joel M. Grossman, "Does First Amendment Let Employees Thwart the Boss?" *The Wall Street Journal* (December 8, 1983), 30.

15

Employee Stakeholders: Privacy, Safety, and Health

CHAPTER OBJECTIVES

After studying this chapter, you should be able to:

1   Articulate the concerns surrounding the employee's right to privacy in the workplace.

2   Identify the advantages and disadvantages of polygraphs, honesty tests, and drug testing as management instruments for decision making.

3   Discuss the right to safety in the workplace, and summarize the role and responsibilities of OSHA.

4   Explain right-to-know laws, and identify the status of workplace threats to reproductive health.

5   Elaborate on the right to health in the workplace, with particular reference to the recent concerns about smoking in the office and AIDS.

Employee stakeholders are concerned not only with the issues we discussed in the preceding chapter but also with several other issues. These other issues should be thought of as extensions of the concept of employee rights developed in Chapter 14. In this chapter we are concerned with the employee's rights to privacy, safety, and a healthy work environment.

The right to privacy primarily addresses the psychological dimension, whereas the rights to health and safety primarily address the physical dimension. The status of an employee's right to privacy in the workplace today is ill defined at best. Constitutional protection of privacy, such as the prohibition of unreasonable searches and seizures, applies only to the actions of government, not to those of private sector employers. From a legal standpoint, privacy protection, as with so many employee rights, is a collection of diverse statutes that vary from issue to issue and from state to state. Hence, there is a genuine need for management groups to impose ethical thinking and standards in this increasingly important area.

Employee rights to safety and health are issues of rising intensity, too. In today's workplace, whether it be a manufacturing facility or an office complex, workers are exposed to hazards or risks of accidents or occupational diseases. If the normal hazards of work were not enough, the recent phenomenon of violence in the workplace should cause management to pay serious attention to this threat to workplace peace and stability. Recent Labor Department statistics suggest a spectacle of workplace violence that has captured corporate America's attention: attacks on workers at company offices, law firms, and shopping malls.[1] Two crucial health issues today are smoking in the workplace and the implications of AIDS. Management also has to be aware of what legal rights employees have today under the recently passed Family and Medical Leave Act of 1993, a piece of legislation designed to make life easier for employees with health or family problems.

To reiterate a point we made in the preceding chapter, the distinction between the issues discussed there and those discussed here is made for discussion purposes. With that in mind, let us continue our consideration of social and ethical issues that have become important to employee stakeholders in recent years. If managers are to be successful in dealing with employees' needs and treating them fairly as stakeholders, they must address these concerns now and in the future.

RIGHT TO PRIVACY IN THE WORKPLACE

In New York, an employee returned to work after a prolonged illness. His supervisor was concerned about the possibility of a relapse, so the supervisor asked the company physician to talk with the employee's doctor. When the employee found out about this, he filed an invasion of privacy suit. During the same year, managers at a New Mexico newspaper got a tip from undercover investigators that members of the night production crew were using drugs. Complete with roaring cars and whirring helicopters, the company's security force moved in. They lined up 27 employees for urine tests. Later, 17 were fired for failing the test or refusing to take it. Several privacy invasion suits were filed.[2]

Both of these cases typify the escalating number of privacy suits being filed against employers. In the first case, a federal court upheld the employer's action, saying that the supervisor was legitimately interested in the employee's health and, therefore, did not commit "an outrageous act of privacy invasion." In the second case, a lower court also found in favor of the employer's action because reasonable cause for suspicion existed.[3] In this age of increased sensitivity to invasion of privacy, however, the outcomes of such cases are not always in the employer's favor. The number of cases of privacy invasion has been increasing in recent years and is expected to continue.[4]

Figure 15–1 summarizes some recent court cases in which workplace privacy invasion allegations were both upheld and denied.[5]

There are no clear legal definitions of what constitutes privacy or invasion of privacy, but everyone seems to have an opinion on when it has happened to them. Most experts say that *privacy* means the right to keep personal affairs to oneself and to know how information about one is being used.[6] Patricia Werhane, a business ethicist, opts for a broader definition. She says that privacy includes (1) the right to be left alone, (2) the related right to autonomy, and (3) the claim of individuals and groups to determine for themselves when, how, and to what extent information about them is communicated to others.[7]

Defining privacy in this way, however, does not settle the issue. In today's world, achieving these ideals is extremely difficult and fraught with judgment calls about our own privacy rights versus other people's rights. This problem is exacerbated by the increasingly computerized, technological world in which we live. We gain great

---

FIGURE 15–1   Examples of Workplace Privacy Invasion Claims

Employers *invaded privacy* in these cases, say the courts:

- The officer of a company opened and read the private mail of another company officer (*Vernars v. Young*).

- A manager made offensive remarks, offers, threats, and demands to an employee, including inquiries concerning the nature of the sexual relationship between the employee and her spouse (*Phillips v. Smalley Maintenance*).

- An employer improperly pressured an employee into taking a lie-detector test based on rumors of off-the-job drug use (*O'Brien v. Papa Gino's*).

- To investigate the theft of a watch, a manager broke into an employee's personal locker and went through the employee's personal belongings, including a purse (*K-Mart v. Trotti*).

Employers *did not invade privacy* in these cases, say the courts:

- An employer investigated allegations by coworkers that a supervisor had an inappropriate relationship with a subordinate. The investigation involved interviews of employees and examination of company records (*Rogers v. IBM*).

- An employer requested that an employee disclose the medications the employee was taking prior to a drug test (*Mares v. Conagra Poultry Co.*).

- While an employee was on medical leave, the employer wrote to a doctor asking for information about the employee's condition and ability to return to work (*Saldana v. Kelsey-Hayes Co.*).

---

efficiencies from computers and new technologies, but we also pay a price. Part of the price we pay is that information about us is stored in dozens of places, including federal agencies (the Internal Revenue Service and the Social Security Administration), state agencies (courts and motor vehicle departments), and many local departments and businesses (school systems, credit bureaus, banks, life insurance companies, and direct-mail companies).

According to a recent survey conducted by Louis Harris and Associates and Dr. Alan Westin, more than half of the Americans polled (55.5 percent) were "very concerned" about threats to their privacy.[8] These results nearly double the 31 percent who were "very concerned" in 1978.[9] Clearly, the increase in the ease with which personal information can be collected has been accompanied by an increase in concern over how that information will be gathered and used.

In the realm of employee privacy, which is our central concern here, the following five important issues stand out as representative of the major workplace privacy issues of the past decade:

1. Collection and use of employee information in personnel files

2. Use of the polygraph, or lie detector, in making employee decisions

3. Honesty testing

4. Drug testing

5. Monitoring of employee work and conversations by electronic means

There are other issues that involve protection or invasion of privacy, but the five listed above account for the majority of today's concerns. Therefore, they merit separate consideration.

Collection and Use of Employee Information by Employers

Although our focus here is not a global or societal one, the collection, use, and possible abuse of employee information is a serious public policy issue that warrants scrutiny. Today's government databases, with some 15 agencies mixing and matching data, form a cohesive web of information on individual citizens. Ostensibly, we are protected as citizens by laws such as the Privacy Act of 1974, which requires the consent of individuals before federal agencies can collect and use data for purposes other than those for which the data was originally intended.[10] In the private sector, however, there are very few laws that protect individuals in this regard.

According to privacy expert David F. Linowes, "Most Americans have no idea of the scope of record-keeping by corporations."[11] Linowes, who has conducted major studies on the privacy issue, warns that information collected by employers is being used to decide job promotions, grant credit, sell insurance, and help marketers and political groups tailor commercial or political solicitations. For example, Linowes cites a case where an executive was passed over for promotion because his personnel file reported "larcenous tendencies." It turns out that his file had been poorly summarized, and the report referred to a ninth-grade prank. In another instance, an executive was denied a promotion because his file included an investigator's report of marijuana use years earlier and because of a report that he and his wife had seen a marriage counselor.

The overriding principle that should guide corporate decision making in regard to the collection and use of employee information is that companies should only collect that information from employees that is absolutely necessary and only use it in ways that are appropriate. Companies should be careful not to misuse this information by employing it for purposes for which it was not intended. For example, information collected during a medical exam for insurance purposes should not be used by a supervisor in making an evaluation for a promotion. In 1989, a troubling study revealed that over 60 Fortune 500 companies used medical data in making "employment-related" decisions. The companies defended this practice by referring to high medical costs and substance-abuse problems.[12] The Americans with Disabilities Act now makes it illegal to base employment decisions on a medical condition that does not affect the employee's ability to perform the essential functions of the job. However, it remains very difficult for employees to know, or to be able to prove, when medical information is used to make employment decisions.

Another important principle is that the employer should understand that information collected from employees is not a commodity to be exchanged, sold, or released in the marketplace.[13] Thus, the release of information to a landlord, credit grantor, or any other third party without the employee's consent may be seen as an invasion of privacy.

A final important principle pertains to employees' access to information about themselves in company personnel files or other recordkeeping systems. Employees should have some way of knowing what information is being stored about them, and they should have the opportunity to correct or amend inaccurate information. A study by David Linowes revealed that 87 percent of companies allowed employees to look at their personnel files, but only 27 percent gave the employees access to their supervisors' files, which often contain the most subjective information.[14]

Use of the Polygraph

In the invasion-of-privacy arena, few topics have generated as much controversy as the use of the polygraph, or lie detector, in business. The following brief scenario typifies the type of employee experience that led up to the Employee Polygraph Protection Act (EPPA) of 1988, which banned most private sector uses of the lie detector. A polygraph machine was perched on a makeshift table in a tiny storage area. The examiner, hired by the employer, connected electrodes to 28-year-old Sandra Kwasniewski and then started interrogating her. "Have you ever shoplifted anything? Whom do you live with? Where does your boyfriend live? What are your dating practices? Do you drink?" Ms. Kwasniewski, manager of a gas station convenience store in the eastern United States, maintained that nothing had been stolen or even reported missing, but 2 days after the lie detector test she was fired.[15]

The notion of a "lie detector," historians tell us, is nothing new. The Bedouins of Arabia knew that certain physiological changes, triggered by guilt and fear, occurred when a person lied. The outstanding change they observed was that a liar would stop salivating. They developed a simple test in which a heated blade was passed across the tongue of a suspected liar. If innocent, the suspect would be salivating normally and the tongue would not be burned; if the person was lying, the tongue would be scorched. The ancient Chinese used dry rice powder. Someone suspected of lying was forced to keep a handful of rice powder in the mouth. If the powder was soggy when it was spat out, the truth was being told; if it was dry, the person was lying.[16]

Critics of today's lie detectors may well argue that the modern devices are not much more advanced than these ancient techniques. The polygraph machine, as it is known today, was developed by John Larson in 1929, although others trace it to an earlier date. It measures changes in blood pressure, respiration, and perspiration, sometimes called galvanic skin response. The theory behind polygraphy is that the act of lying causes stress, which in turn is manifested by observable physiological changes. The examiner, or machine operator, then interprets the subject's physiological responses to specific questions and makes inferences about whether or not the subject's answers indicate deception.[17]

Although the 1988 Employee Polygraph Protection Act banned most uses of the lie detector by private employers, it is easy to sympathize with the desire of businesses to protect themselves against serious losses. A striking figure is that companies suffer annual losses from employee theft in excess of $40 billion. Other studies have shown that 75 percent of employees who handle money steal some of it. In addition, one must add to these numbers the large losses that result from employee sabotage, industrial espionage, and other types of misconduct.[18]

It is little wonder, therefore, that businesses turned to the polygraph as a method of screening out dishonest employees or catching employees suspected of theft. Prior to the 1988 law, companies used the lie detector primarily in three types of situations: (1) to examine current employees concerning specific incidences of theft or misconduct, (2) to periodically examine current employees concerning

ETHICS IN PRACTICE

Give Me What I Want or I'll Tell the President!

Place yourself in the role of a personnel director for a bank. It is company policy that neither personnel files nor copies of files are to leave the personnel office. The director of accounting and computer services is due to give his employees their yearly employee evaluations and has sent a memo to your secretary requesting copies of his employees' evaluations from the previous year. Your secretary shows you the memo. You are upset that the director would send such a memo to your secretary, because he should be aware of the policy concerning employee files.

So, you decide to call the director and inform him that he is welcome to read the evaluations of his employees from the previous year in the personnel office. He tells you that he does not have the time to come to personnel and read the files and that he will speak to the president of the bank about this issue. The working relationship between you and the director has been addressed by the president before, and she has informed the two of you that you need to be able to work out problems such as this between the two of you.

The dilemma is whether you should go against company policy in an effort to avoid another lecture from the president, and let the director take the copies of the evaluations to his office, or adhere to the bank's policy on protection of employee privacy.

1. What are the main ethical dilemmas in this situation?

2. Should you report the director's threat to step over you to the president?

3. What would you do in this situation?

Contributed by Leah Herrin

nonspecific conduct, and (3) to screen potential employees in a preemployment situation.[19]

Because lie detectors are still legal in very restricted circumstances, it is useful to note what are seen as their strengths and weaknesses. Proponents of lie detectors argue that employers have a right to protect their property and that lie detectors are more reliable and less expensive than alternatives. They cite the polygraph industry's claim of 95 to 100 percent accuracy in detecting deception. Proponents further argue that although employees and job applicants may sacrifice some privacy, a properly administered test gathers only information the company has a legitimate right to know.[20] Critics of lie detectors cite studies indicating inaccurate diagnoses in 50 percent of the cases. Critics also object to testing that entails broad probes into certain zones of privacy that are strictly personal and not related to the job. Examples of these personal zones include workers' sexual practices, union sympathies, finances, and political and religious beliefs.[21]

Regulations on Use of Polygraphs

Because of the escalating number of complaints about polygraph abuse and the growing patchwork of state restrictions on polygraph use, Congress passed the Employee Polygraph Protection Act (EPPA) of 1988. This legislation reflected, in part, Congress's concern over the scientific evidence supporting the validity of lie detectors and the sometimes demeaning tactics employed during administration of lie detector tests.[22]

In general, the 1988 EPPA law prohibited all use of lie detector tests by private employers to examine current or prospective employees. There are two major exceptions. First, tests may be administered to current employees in the course of an employer's ongoing investigation of economic loss. Second, under certain circumstances, employers in the private security and drug manufacturing industries may conduct preemployment polygraph examinations of applicants. Except in these restricted situations, employers may not directly or indirectly require, request, suggest, or cause any employee or applicant to take a polygraph test. Nor may they use, accept, refer to, or inquire concerning the results of any polygraph test that an employee or an applicant may have taken.[23]

The 1988 act defined the term "lie detector" to include "a polygraph, deceptograph, voice stress analyzer, psychological stress analyzer, or any similar device (whether mechanical or electrical) that is used, or the results of which are used, for the purpose of rendering a diagnostic opinion regarding the honesty or dishonesty of an individual." Because the EPPA was intended to cover mechanical or electronic devices, it does not apply to written psychological tests intended to reveal dishonesty.[24]

Honesty Testing

As criticism grew concerning the use of lie detectors, many companies anticipated an eventual elimination of lie detector use and began experimenting with paper-and-pencil honesty tests, sometimes called "integrity" tests. David Nye, a former human resources executive and now a college professor, dubbed this type of test the "son of the polygraph."[25] There is a certain irony in this title, because honesty tests are already being subjected to the same kinds of criticisms that led to severe restriction of lie detector testing.

A study by the U.S. Office of Technology Assessment was conducted and the findings were reported in a report entitled *Truth and Honesty Testing*. The study said that it was not possible to determine the validity of honesty tests in accurately predicting dishonesty. However, the report[26] did suggest four reasons why employers were using honesty tests:

1. To stem employee theft

2. To avoid "negligent hiring" suits

3. To screen employees cost-effectively

4. To replace polygraphs, which were banned by the EPPA

An honesty-type test typically poses 80 to 90 statements with which the employee or applicant is asked to agree or disagree. Some test questions are framed as yes-or-no and multiple-choice options. Examples include, "Would you tell your boss if you knew of another employee stealing from the company?" and "What percent of employee thieves are never caught?" and "What is the dollar value of cash or merchandise you have stolen from past employers?"[27]

Honesty tests are quick to administer, easy to grade, and cost only $6 to $15 each. This compares favorably with lie detector tests, which cost $25 to $75 each. Perhaps honesty tests have attracted less attention than polygraphs because they come across as less intrusive or intimidating than lie detector tests, in which the examinee is hooked up to wires and sensors. The honesty test comes across more as a red-tape item or a job application to be filled out than as an interrogation.[28]

In 1993, it was estimated that 2 to 5 million honesty tests were given by some 5,000 U.S. companies, and the number was growing.[29] Faced with the elimination of the polygraph, companies wanted to find a substitute, and honesty tests seemed to be a convenient alternative. Critics of honesty tests claim they are intrusive and invade privacy by the nature of their inquiries. Critics also say that they are unreliable and that employers use them as the sole measure of the fitness of an applicant. Even when these tests are properly administered, opponents charge that employers end up rejecting many honest applicants in their efforts to screen out the dishonest ones. Management and testing companies claim the tests are very useful in weeding out potentially dishonest applicants. They claim that each question asked has a specific purpose.

Psychologists disagree widely on the validity and effectiveness of honesty tests. The American Psychological Association issued a report accepting the concept of integrity testing as superior to most other preemployment tests but noting that test publishers' accountability and documentation needed serious improvement.[30] Much of the recent research has been done by the test publishers themselves. The future of honesty tests is uncertain, but it is anticipated that they will probably grow in use but face the same kinds of legal and ethical hurdles that affected polygraph and drug tests.[31]

Drug Testing

"Drug testing" is an umbrella term intended to embrace drug and alcohol testing and employer testing for any suspected substance abuse. The issue of drug testing in the workplace has many of the same characteristics as the lie detector and honesty test issues. Companies say they need to do such testing to protect themselves and the public, but opponents claim that drug tests are not accurate and invade the employee's privacy.

For many years, companies did not conduct widespread testing of workers or job applicants for drug abuse. The reported reasons for their reluctance[32] included the following:

- Moral issue/privacy

- Inaccuracy of tests

- Negative impact on employee morale

- Tests show use, not abuse

- High cost

- Management, employee, and union opposition

In the past decade, however, all this has changed. In 1987, fewer than 25 percent of employers surveyed had drug-testing programs. By 1993, 85 percent of the companies surveyed by the American Management Association reported having drug-testing programs.[33] In 1998, SmithKline Beecham Clinical Laboratories reported that the rate of positive drug tests had dropped to an 11-year low of 5 percent.[34] Despite this promising sign, problems with drugs in the workplace continue to plague corporate America, and so drug testing continues to be an important tool companies can use to address those problems.

Arguments for Drug Testing

Proponents of drug testing argue that the costs of drug abuse on the job are staggering. The consequences range from accidents and injuries to theft, bad decisions, and ruined lives. According to one estimate, drug abuse costs the U.S. economy in excess of $60 billion.[35] More recent estimates are significantly higher but difficult to pin down. The greatest concern is in industries where mistakes can cost lives—for example, the railroad, airline, aerospace, nuclear power, and hazardous equipment and chemicals industries. Edwin Weihenmayer, vice president at Kidder, Peabody, a New York–based investment banking firm, believes that drug testing is essential in his industry, "where the financial security of billions of dollars is entrusted to us by clients."[36] Thus, the primary ethical argument for employers conducting drug tests is the responsibility they have to their own employees and to the general public to provide safe workplaces, secure asset protection, and safe places in which to transact business.

Arguments Against Drug Testing

Opponents of drug testing see it as both a due-process issue and an invasion-of-privacy issue. The due-process issue relates to the questionable accuracy of drug tests. Although one test manufacturer claims a 95 percent accuracy rate, some doctors disagree. For example, Dr. David Greenblatt, chief of clinical pharmacology at Tufts New England Medical Center, claims that "false positives can range up to 25 percent or higher. The test is essentially worthless."[37] In addition, some legal experts argue that, even if the tests were foolproof, they would still be an invasion of employee privacy. They claim that tests represent an unconstitutional attempt on the part of companies to control employees' behavior at home, because the tests can yield positive results days and even weeks after at-home drug use.[38]

Many legitimate questions arise in the drug-testing issue. Do employers have a right to know if their employees use drugs? Are employees performing on the job satisfactorily? Obviously, some delicate balance is needed, because employers and employees alike have legitimate interests that must be protected. This issue is a fairly new one for business, but it is apparent that it will not go away. Therefore, if companies are going to engage in some form of drug testing, they should think carefully about developing policies that not only will achieve their intended goals but also will be fair to the employees and minimize invasions of privacy. Such a balance will not be easy to achieve but must be sought. To do otherwise will guarantee decreased employee morale, more and more lawsuits, and new government regulations.

Guidelines for Drug Testing

If management perceives the need to conduct a drug-testing program to protect other stakeholders, it should carefully design and structure the program so that it will be minimally intrusive of employees' privacy rights. The following guidelines[39] may be helpful.

- Management should not discipline or fire someone for refusing to take a drug test because the results of such tests are inconclusive.

- Drug tests should typically be used only when there is legitimate suspicion of abuse by an employee or work group.

- The focus of testing should be on-the-job performance rather than off-the-job conduct.

- Employees should be informed of methods used and results obtained and given the chance to rebut the test findings.

- If an employee's status is going to be affected by the outcome of a drug test, a confirmatory test should be conducted.

- All tests should be conducted in such a way that the dignity and privacy of the employee are respected and honored.

Obviously, there are exceptions to these guidelines, and there are other guidelines that might be used. The major point is that management needs to think through its policies and their consequences very carefully when designing and conducting drug-testing programs.

State and Federal Legislation

Some states and cities have enacted or are considering laws to restrict workplace drug testing. Generally, these laws restrict the scope of testing by private and public employers and establish privacy protections and procedural safeguards. The laws do not completely ban drug testing but typically restrict the circumstances (for reasonable cause, for example) under which it may be used. States that have passed drug-testing laws include Florida, Vermont, Iowa, Minnesota, Montana, Maine, Connecticut, Rhode Island, and North Carolina. These states restrict drug testing to reasonable suspicion and place limits on the disciplinary actions employers may take. Other states are considering such legislation.[40]

At the federal level, the Americans with Disabilities Act (ADA) must be considered, because the definition of disability applies to drug and alcohol addiction. The ADA prohibits companies from giving applicants medical exams before they extend those applicants conditional offers of employment. Prehire drug tests, however, are permitted. Philadelphia employment lawyer Jonathan Segal advises employers to extend conditional offers before drug testing, because an innocent question on a drug test could easily become a medical question. He recommends conducting the drug test immediately after making the conditional offer and then waiting until the test results are back before beginning employment. An employer who wishes to fire or refuse to hire someone with an alcohol or a drug addiction must show that the employee poses a direct threat to others. Furthermore, if a person loses a job opportunity because of an inaccurate failed drug test, the company has committed an ADA offense by basing an action on the perception of a disability.[41]

It is worth noting some of the categories of employees that the federal government now requires be tested for on-the-job drug and alcohol use. The government, as of 1994, requires both random alcohol and drug tests each year for 25 percent of transportation workers in such safety-sensitive jobs as trucking, aviation, railroads, and pipelines. Before, only random drug testing was required. In addition, the federal government now requires drug and alcohol testing on mass-transit workers and expanded testing on intrastate truckers and bus drivers.[42]

Employee Assistance Programs

One of the most significant strategies undertaken by corporate America to deal with the growing alcohol- and drug-abuse problem in the workplace has been *Employee Assistance Programs (EAPs)*. EAPs originated, for the most part, in the 1940s, 1950s, and 1960s to deal with alcoholism on the job.[43] By the 1990s, EAPs had extended into other employee problem areas as well, such as compulsive gambling, financial stress, emotional stress, marital difficulties, aging, legal problems, AIDs, and other psychological, emotional, and social difficulties.

EAPs are employer-provided programs that are operated either by in-house corporate staff or by an outside contractor. Generally, they are designed for two major objectives: to prevent problems that interfere with employees' ability to do their jobs and to rehabilitate those employees who are experiencing problems that are interfering with their job performance.[44]

In spite of the serious alcohol, drug, and other problems employers must deal with, EAPs represent a positive and proactive step companies can take to deal with these serious problems. EAPs are designed to be confidential and nonpunitive, and they affirm three important propositions: (1) Employees are valuable members of the organization, (2) it is better to help troubled employees than to discipline or discharge them, and (3) recovered employees are better employees.[45] It is encouraging that in an era when employees are increasingly exerting their workplace rights, enlightened companies are offering EAPs in an effort to help solve their mutual problems.

Monitoring Employees on the Job

In the old days, supervisors monitored employees' work activities by peeking over their shoulders and judging how things were going. Next came cameras and listening devices whereby management could keep track of what was going on from remote locations. With the advent of computers, workers and civil liberties activists are concerned about the use of technology to gather information about workers on the job. These concerns are well founded. In a 1997 survey, the American Management Association (AMA) found that 63 percent of mid- to large-sized firms participate in some type of employee electronic surveillance. In many cases, the method is as benign as video cameras in a lobby. However, about 35 percent of firms used more invasive means of monitoring their workers, such as recording their phone calls or voice mail, reading their computer files, or videotaping them. Of these firms, about 23 percent did not inform workers of their practices. An industry has developed around employee monitoring, with an estimated one-third of the Fortune 500 shopping for surveillance devices.[46]

Employer monitoring of employees may take on any of three different forms: *visual, voice,* or *computer based (electronic)*. In each of these cases, we might argue that the key factor in determining the legality, and perhaps the ethics, of the practice is the employee's reasonable expectation of privacy under the particular circumstances.[47]

Balanced against the employee's expectation of privacy might be the employer's need to know information for legitimate business-related, decision-making purposes.

Visual surveillance by employers may be as simple as the observation of employees by a supervisor or security guard or by a video camera. A lawful surveillance might be a security guard monitoring potential theft at a warehouse or distribution center. A questionable surveillance might be video cameras in rest rooms, locker rooms, or employee lounges. Voice monitoring is accomplished primarily through the recording of telephone messages. The federal Omnibus Crime Control and Safe Streets Act of 1968 made it unlawful to intentionally intercept wire, oral, or electronic communications. However, there are exceptions. For example, the "telephone extension" exception permits employers to monitor employee phone calls "in the ordinary course of business." Once it is clear that a call is personal in nature, however, the purposeful listening to it is no longer permitted.[48]

Computer-based or electronic surveillance is now possible with new and expanded technologies. Such technologies allow careful monitoring of employee production and performance.

In response to abuses, the Electronic Communications Privacy Act of 1986 was signed into law by President Reagan, and for the first time restrictions were placed on government's right to intrude on individual privacy by technological means. This law, among other things, made it illegal to eavesdrop on electronic mail, computer-to-computer transmissions, private video conferences, and cellular car phones.[49] It is immediately obvious how difficult it would be to enforce this legislation.

Civil liberties groups have asserted that the use of computers to monitor the efficiency and productivity of workers raises a growing concern related to privacy invasion.[50] In virtually any job in which computer terminals are used by workers today, the machines have the capability of monitoring worker productivity. The consequence is that millions of workers are laboring under the relentless gaze of electronic supervision.[51]

What Can Be Monitored?

It has been estimated that over 50 million Americans use computer terminals in their jobs and that as many as one-third of these people are being scrutinized as they work. Monitoring requires the installation of special software (called AUDIT by one firm) in the central computer to which terminals are attached. The programs are able to measure, record, and tabulate dozens of kinds of information about workers: how slow or fast they are, when they take breaks, how long phone calls take, how much time passes before a next order is processed, what number is called, how many keystrokes per hour an operator is typing, when machines are idle, and so on.

In addition to monitoring those at computer terminals, there is increasing surveillance by management of employees in other work settings. Monitoring of telephone conversations is a significant arena for electronic eavesdropping. Workers in telecommunications, mail-order houses, airline reservations, and brokerage firms are especially hard hit. Not only do supervisors frequently listen in on their conversations, but computers also gather and analyze data about their work habits. One major firm also claims that it uses tiny fisheye lenses installed behind pinholes in walls and ceilings to watch employees suspected of crimes. Another firm actually uses special chairs for their employees that measure wiggling. The assumption is that employees who wiggle too much are not working. Other firms use long-distance cameras to monitor employees around the clock. It is little wonder that some privacy experts are likening the current situation of high-tech snooping to an "electronic sweatshop."[52]

Effects of Being Monitored

Invasion of privacy is one major consequence of employee monitoring. Another is unfair treatment. Employees working under such systems complain about stress and tension resulting from their being expected and pressured to be more productive now that their efforts can be measured. The pressure of being constantly monitored is also producing low morale in a variety of places. The director of a national group of working women declares that, "The potential for corporate abuse is staggering. It puts you under the gun in the short run and drives you crazy in the long run." *The New York Times* installed a software program to track the performance of its clerks who were taking classified ads over the phone. Some of the employees started wearing buttons that read, "BIG BROTHER IS WATCHING."[53]

As with the lie detector issue, the controversy over technology and its use seems to bring employers' rights into conflict with employees' rights. Given the impact that the employee monitoring issue is having on employee morale, wise managers may want to consider it carefully from the standpoint of a desirable management practice, as well as from the perspective of protecting worker privacy. This issue currently is not as controversial as lie detectors or drug testing, but the potential is definitely there as technology continues to outpace our ability to effectively monitor its social consequences.

Legislative Momentum

Since about the mid-1980s, employee advocacy groups have been pushing for legislation that would restrict snooping on workers by employers. Although several states have various restrictions, little has happened at the federal level to protect private sector employees. In 1987, the telemarketing industry lobbied heavily against and defeated a bill that would have mandated an audible beep when employers were listening in on employees. In 1990, two federal bills that were once considered dead began to receive renewed interest. One bill would ban phone bugging without a warrant unless all parties to the call consented, and the other would require employers to notify workers with a visual or an aural signal when they were being monitored with computers, cameras, or taping machines.[54] In 1991, Senate hearings were held on legislation to restrict employers from electronically monitoring employees.[55]

In 1993, worker privacy bills were introduced into each house of the Congress. The "Privacy for Consumers and Workers Act" (H.R. 1218 and S. 516) would have required that employers notify employees of monitoring and limited the way in which the monitoring could be conducted and the information could be used. A massive lobbying effort by the insurance industry resulted in an amended bill that never passed Congress. The following year, reintroduced bills also failed to pass Congress. At this writing, worker privacy legislation is not high on the congressional agenda, but with the exponential growth in new technologies, it is certain to resurface.

Policy Guidelines on the Issue of Privacy

As we have discussed various privacy issues, we have indicated steps that management might consider taking in an attempt to be responsive to employee stakeholders. As a final recommendation, we set forth four policy guidelines that touch on several of the issues we have discussed. Robert Goldstein and Richard Nolan[56] assert that organizations should:

1. *Prepare a "privacy impact statement."* This would require the firm to analyze the potential privacy implications that all systems (especially computerized ones) should be subjected to.

2. *Construct a comprehensive privacy plan.* The purpose of such planning would be to ensure that the necessary privacy controls are integrated into the design of a system at the very beginning.

3. *Train employees who handle personal information.* Be sure they are aware of the importance of protecting privacy and the specific procedures and policies to be followed.

4. *Make privacy a part of social responsibility programs.* Companies need to acknowledge that they have an internal responsibility to their employees and not fail to consider this when designing and implementing corporate social efforts.

Business's concern for protection of the privacy of its employees, customers, and other stakeholders is a growing business. It was not surprising, therefore, when the major newsletter *Privacy and American Business* appeared on the scene in 1993. Alan F. Westin, an expert on privacy issues in the workplace, was one of the cofounders of this newsletter. By 1994, the newsletter was going out to 3,300 business and government subscribers. Company efforts to develop policies and guidelines to protect privacy are at such an embryonic stage that the need for such a newsletter to chronicle what are the best practices is evident.[57]

WORKPLACE SAFETY

The workplace safety issue has grown up like so many other issues we have discussed, complete with the creation in 1970 of a federal agency—the Occupational Safety and Health Administration (OSHA). From the beginning, OSHA has been one of the most controversial and, some would argue, most ineffectual of the federal regulatory agencies. With increasing emphasis on the quality of life, workplace health and safety have been, and continue to be, legitimate concerns of employees. OSHA's goals seemed quite appropriate: inspections in the workplace; development of safety standards, especially those relating to health; training of employers and

---

SEARCH THE WEB

The Occupational Safety and Health Administration (OSHA) has a Web site that serves as a clearinghouse for information about employee safety and health on the job (**www.osha.gov**). On this site are OSHA manuals, continually updated statistics and inspection data, hazard information bulletins, OSHA directives, and a Freedom of Information Act (FOIA) Reading Room.

FIGURE 15–2   OSHA's Purpose

Under the Act, the Occupational Safety and Health Administration (OSHA) was created within the Department of Labor to:

- Encourage employers and employees to reduce workplace hazards and to implement new or improve existing safety and health programs;

- Provide for research in occupational safety and health to develop innovative ways of dealing with occupational safety and health problems;

- Establish "separate but dependent responsibilities and rights" for employers and employees for the achievement of better safety and health conditions;

- Maintain a reporting and recordkeeping system to monitor job-related injuries and illnesses;

- Establish training programs to increase the number and competence of occupational safety and health personnel;

- Develop mandatory job safety and health standards and enforce them effectively; and

- Provide for the development, analysis, evaluation, and approval of state occupational safety and health programs.

Although OSHA continually reviews and redefines specific standards and practices, its basic purposes remain constant. OSHA strives to implement its mandate fully and firmly with fairness to all concerned. In all its procedures, from standards development through implementation and enforcement, OSHA guarantees employers and employees the right to be fully informed, to participate actively, and to appeal actions.

SOURCE: *All About OSHA* (Washington, DC: Department of Labor, OSHA, 1992, Revised), 2.

---

employees to develop self-inspection programs; approval of state plans to provide job safety and health; and administration of programs for federal employees.[58] Figure 15–2 summarizes OSHA's purpose.

The Workplace Safety Problem

Two events, among many, stand out in the past decade or so as symbols of the workplace safety problem. One was the dramatic and catastrophic poisonous gas leak at the Union Carbide plant in Bhopal, India, in 1984. The death toll topped 2,000, and tens of thousands more were injured. People around the globe were startled and shocked at what the results of one major industrial accident could be. The company is still reeling today from the aftermath of this industrial accident, in which lawsuits seeking damages quickly exceeded the net worth of the company.[59] In 1991, India's Supreme Court upheld a $470 million settlement that Union Carbide had already paid, and it lifted the immunity from criminal prosecution that it had granted the company in 1989.

The second event was considerably less publicized but nevertheless ranks among the landmark cases on job safety. In Elk Grove Village, Illinois, Film Recovery Systems operated out of a single plant that extracted silver from used hospital x-ray and photographic film. To extract the silver, the employees first had to dump the film into open vats of sodium cyanide and then transfer the leached remnants to another tank. On February 10, 1983, employee Stefan Golab staggered outside and collapsed, unconscious. Efforts to revive him failed, and he was soon pronounced dead from what the local medical examiner labeled "acute cyanide toxicity."[60]

An intensive investigation by attorneys in Cook County, Illinois, revealed a long list of incriminating details: (1) Film Recovery workers seldom wore even the most rudimentary safety equipment, (2) workers were laboring in what amounted to an industrial gas chamber, and (3) company executives played down the dangers of cyanide poisoning and removed labeling that identified it as poisonous. The prosecutors took action under an Illinois homicide statute that targets anyone who knowingly commits acts that "create a strong probability of death or serious bodily harm."[61] In 1985, three executives at Film Recovery Systems—the president, the plant manager, and the foreman—were convicted of the murder of Stefan Golab and sentenced to 25 years in prison. Their convictions marked the first time that managers had been convicted of homicide in a corporate matter such as an industrial accident.[62] The Film Recovery Systems case marked a new era in managerial responsibility for job safety.

A variety of other prosecutions of managers have followed the Film Recovery Systems case. What this clearly signals is not only that employees have a moral right to a safe working environment but also that managers face prosecution if they do not ensure that employees are protected.

Right-to-Know Laws

Prompted by the Union Carbide tragedy in Bhopal and other, less dramatic industrial accidents, workers have been demanding to know more about the thousands of chemicals and hazardous substances they are being exposed to daily in the workplace. Experts are now arguing that employers have a duty to provide employees with information on the hazards of workplace chemicals *and* to make sure that workers understand what the information means in practical terms. Since the early 1980s, many states have passed *right-to-know laws* and expanded public access to this kind of information by employees and even communities.[63] Since that time, several other states have passed such laws. One point of view is that the states have moved in and taken such actions because of federal nonenforcement of occupational safety and environmental laws.[64]

Although the states have taken the initiative on the right-to-know front, it is inaccurate to say that OSHA has done nothing. In 1983, OSHA created a Hazard Communication Standard that took effect in 1985. This standard requires covered employers to identify hazardous chemicals in their workplaces and to provide employees with specified forms of information on such substances and their hazards. Specifically, manufacturers, whether they are chemical manufacturers or users of chemicals, must take certain steps to achieve compliance with the standard.[65] These steps include the following:

1. Update inventories of hazardous chemicals present in the workplace.

2. Assemble material safety data sheets (MSDSs) for all hazardous chemicals.

3. Ensure that all containers and hazardous chemicals are properly labeled.

4. Provide workers with training on the use of hazardous chemicals.

5. Prepare and maintain a written description of the company's hazard communication program.

6. Consider any problems with trade secrets that may be raised by the standard's disclosure requirements.

7. Review state requirements for hazard disclosure.

Some managers have scoffed at the new state and federal right-to-know laws, arguing either that they will not work or that they will cost too much. It appears clear, however, that legal and regulatory pressures for the disclosure of workplace hazard information will not abate in the near future. Employees as well as the general public want more, not less, information about, disclosure of, and rules governing the use of hazardous substances in the work environment. A 1985 *Business Week* editorial argued that the costs to industry of $600 million to bring its operations into line with the OSHA standard and $160 million in annual compliance costs would be greatly exceeded by the benefits. Furthermore, this editorial provided the following advice for companies:

> They would be well advised to comply with the spirit as well as the letter of the regulations. Tell people the hazards, and tell them simply, in plain English. The point is to save lives and preserve health, and any effort is worth making that will encourage workers to use respirators and protective clothing, for example. In matters such as these, playing it straight is the only way to play it.[66]

In addition to the right-to-know laws, it is also important to note that employees have certain workplace rights with respect to safety and health on the job that OSHA provides by law. As in our discussion of the public policy exceptions to the employment-at-will doctrine in the preceding chapter, it should be clear that workers have a right to seek safety and health on the job without fear of punishment or recrimination. Figure 15–3 spells out OSHA's policies regarding these workplace rights.

Troubles at OSHA

The time was right for an occupational, safety, and health agency such as OSHA, but the effort that followed was not exactly what OSHA or its designers had in mind. OSHA was troubled from the very beginning by the sheer size of its task—to monitor workplace safety and health in millions of workplaces with only several thousand inspectors.[67]

Nitpicking Rules

In its early years, OSHA added to its troubles by promulgating rules and standards that seemed quite trivial when compared with the larger issues of health and safety. It was not until 1978 that OSHA decided to purge itself of some of these nitpicking rules. Some of its standards were senseless, such as the one that said, "Piping located inside or outside of buildings may be placed above or below the ground." This, of course, covered just about every possibility. Consider also a standard that went too far in specifying product design: "Every water closet (toilet) should have a hinged

> **FIGURE 15–3   Employee Rights to Safety and Health Provided by OSHA**
>
> Employees have a right to seek safety and health on the job without fear of punishment. That right is spelled out in Section 11(c) of the Act.
>
> The law says employers shall not punish or discriminate against workers for exercising rights such as:
>
> - Complaining to an employer, union, OSHA, or any other government agency about job safety and health hazards;
>
> - Filing safety or health grievances;
>
> - Participating on a workplace safety and health committee or in union activities concerning job safety and health; and
>
> - Participating in OSHA inspections, conferences, hearings, or other OSHA-related activities.
>
> If an employee is exercising these or other OSHA rights, the employer is not allowed to discriminate against that worker in any way, such as through firing, demotion, taking away seniority or other earned benefits, transferring the worker to an undesirable job or shift, or threatening or harassing the worker.
>
> If the employer has knowingly allowed the employee to do something in the past (such as leaving work early), he or she may be violating the law by punishing the worker for doing the same thing following a protest of hazardous conditions. If the employer knows that a number of workers are doing the same thing wrong, he or she cannot legally single out for punishment the worker who has taken part in safety and health activities.
>
> Workers believing they have been punished for exercising safety and health rights must contact the nearest OSHA office within 30 days of the time they learn of the alleged discrimination. A union representative can file the 11(c) complaint for the worker.
>
> The worker does not have to complete any forms. An OSHA staff member will complete the forms, asking what happened and who was involved.
>
> Following a complaint, OSHA investigates. If an employee has been illegally punished for exercising safety and health rights, OSHA asks the employer to restore that worker's job earnings and benefits. If necessary, and if it can prove discrimination, OSHA takes the employer to court. In such cases the worker does not pay any legal fees.
>
> If a state agency has an OSHA-approved state program, employees may file their complaints with either federal OSHA or the state agency under its laws.

SOURCE: *All About OSHA* (Washington, DC: U.S. Department of Labor, OSHA, 1992, Revised), 37–38.

seat made of substantial material, having a nonabsorbent finish. Seats installed or replaced shall be of the open front type."[68]

In another example, a telephone company was instructed that it could only provide linemen with "belts that have pocket tabs that extend at least 1½ inches down and 3 inches back of the inside of the circle of each D-ring for riveting on plier or tool pockets. . . . There may be no more than four tool loops on any belt."[69] Such nuisance rules and standards created serious credibility problems for OSHA. Although at least 928 such rules were rescinded in 1978, many times that number are still on the books.

In the mid-1990s, it became evident that OSHA's nitpicking rules had not been adequately eliminated or that perhaps there were more of them than initially thought. A 1995 revelation that caused much discussion occurred in Boise, Idaho, where a plumbing company was fined $7,875 by OSHA when company workers rescued a fellow worker from a collapsed trench. The workers had failed to shore up the trench or put on safety hats before pulling the endangered worker to safety. In the face of public outrage, OSHA rescinded the fine.[70]

In *The Death of Common Sense: How Law Is Suffocating America,* author Philip K. Howard pokes fun at OSHA's classification of ordinary beach sand. He asserts:

> *OSHA categorizes sand as poison because sand, including the beach sand you and I sunbathe on, includes silica. Some scientists believe that silica, in conditions found nowhere except in certain grinding operations, might cause cancer.*[71]

Howard goes on to observe that OSHA still has over 4,000 detailed regulations, dictating everything from the height of railings (42 inches) to how much of a plank can stick out from a temporary scaffold (no more than 12 inches). In spite of OSHA's 2,000 safety inspectors in the field and the several hundred billion dollars that U.S. business has spent on compliance with OSHA's rules, Howard thinks that safety in American workplaces in the mid-1990s is about like it was in 1970.[72]

In spite of Howard's observations, there are others who think OSHA has done a better job. In its own defense, OSHA presents statistics about its overall effectiveness. In the 28 years from OSHA's creation in 1970 to 1998, the workplace death rate had been cut in half. Injury and illness rates have declined in the industries on which OSHA has focused, while rates have remained unchanged in those industries in which OSHA has been less involved. According to OSHA, in the 3 years following an OSHA inspection, injuries and illness drop by an average of 22 percent.[73]

Spotty Record

Although OSHA made a serious effort to impact health and injury statistics, over the years its record has been spotty. In 1 year in the mid-1980s, injuries, illnesses, and deaths in the workplace began to climb again after several years of decline.[74] There were numerous reasons for this reversal, and not all of them could be attributed to OSHA. During the recession of the early 1980s, companies sharply reduced their spending on health and safety. With the economic recovery, many employers hired inexperienced workers, which further contributed to rising accident statistics. The Reagan administration deemphasized the writing and enforcement of safety rules, and employers put greater emphasis on competitiveness, often at the expense of safety and health.[75]

A Rejuvenated OSHA

Like so many of the federal agencies we have discussed (FTC, FDA, CPSC), OSHA experienced a new boost of energy and enthusiasm in the post-Reagan period of the late 1980s and early 1990s. The renewed energy came at an appropriate time, because in 1988 the Bureau of Labor Statistics announced that injury rates had been increasing since about 1983. Officials admitted that a part of this increase could be attributed to more accurate reporting.

With a new administrator and an increased budget, OSHA began taking significant actions against high-visibility employers. For example, in 1989 it hit USX Corporation with a $7.3 million fine, which was the largest ever. It charged USX with

58 "willful" hazards it claimed the company knew about but did not address. The company appealed.[76]

OSHA continued to suffer from what it claimed to be a budget and staff that were inadequate for the job that Congress and the public expected it to do. One observer pointed out that the EPA's budget was more than 21 times that of OSHA. In some states, too, there are conflicts between OSHA and state inspectors as to who has responsibility for workplace safety. In 1991, a major accident in North Carolina illustrated this point. A major fire in a poultry processing plant led to the deaths of 25 workers. This occurred because the plant's management kept the emergency exits padlocked to deter pilfering. Employees said there were no fire exits, no sprinkler system, and no fire drills. It was discovered that no government agency had conducted a safety inspection at that plant for 11 years. Some blamed state authorities; others blamed OSHA.[77] In any event, there simply are not enough inspectors to handle all businesses, and therefore a heavy responsibility falls on business for safety in the workplace.

In the mid-1990s, Secretary of Labor Robert Reich began efforts to revitalize OSHA once again. A landmark case occurred in 1994, when Reich phoned the CEO of Bridgestone/Firestone, Inc., to say that it was being charged by OSHA with 107 safety violations and slapped with a $7.5 million fine because one of its plants in Oklahoma City was declared to be an "imminent danger" to workers. This action was symbolic of the Clinton administration's determination to reinvigorate OSHA. Reich declared, "American workers are not going to be sacrificed at the altar of profits."[78] Critics of this move by Reich admit that workplace safety is a problem but claim that in this particular case it was not as severe as Reich judged. In fact, in Reich's eagerness to show the administration's new zeal and aggressiveness, he moved to cite the plant even though he didn't have the support of most of the safety inspectors who had recently walked through the plant. In subsequent depositions, three of the four inspectors admitted that they hadn't discerned any imminent danger.[79]

An important issue for OSHA is repeated trauma disorders, which now account for 60 percent of all occupational illnesses. One major variation of this class of disorders is known as repetitive stress injury (RSI). RSI results from the strain of repetitive motion, such as that resulting from keyboard use in offices. RSI has become the fastest-growing workplace illness in the United States, having increased an astonishing 770 percent over the past decade. While the government is working on ergonomics standards to address the problem of repeated trauma disorders, RSI lawsuits are mounting. In an interesting turn of events, the defendants in these cases are not only employers of afflicted workers, but also manufacturers of computer keyboards, who are being sued for selling flawed products and not warning users of their potential risks. Such blue-chip corporate giants as IBM, AT&T, and Digital Equipment have become ensnared in the resulting legal morass. A 1995 *Business Week* article observed that the scope of worker-injury litigation on this issue could become so vast that RSI could be the nightmare for corporate America in the 1990s that asbestos was in the 1980s.[80]

While technology brings new challenges, the old problems of OSHA remain. In 1995, OSHA turned to negotiated rulemaking to develop standards for industry. Efforts at conciliation continued as Charles Jeffress, a former OSHA administrator

---

ETHICS IN PRACTICE

OSHA's Surprise Visit

During the summers, Mark Price worked at a local caulk manufactory located in Red-dog, Georgia. One hot and busy July day, Willie Truit and Mark received a call from the plant manager's secretary authorizing them to dispose of a batch of monomers, which are a type of hazardous waste. The order was to remove them from the inspector's sight. Willie and Mark bagged them up and threw them in the dumpster, but Mark kept asking why they were doing this. Improper disposal of hazardous materials usually results in heavy fines. This violation would have resulted in a fine of about $20,000.

Mark asked Willie what he thought would happen if they decided not to do what they were told. Willie said that they were working in an employment-at-will state and failure to do what they were authorized to do would definitely result in termination. The OSHA inspector asked Mark if he had been trained in handling hazardous waste. He also asked if Mark had been told to do things that he normally didn't engage in while working. Not wearing the proper clothing and disposing of the material improp-erly could result in danger to both Willie and Mark. It could also endanger whoever comes into contact with the material not disposed of properly.

1. If Mark chose not to perform the task he was told, how could he have protected his job? Could he have lost his job because he was working in an employment-at-will situation?

2. What would you have done if caught in this ethical dilemma?

3. How would you have responded to the OSHA inspector's questions?

Contributed by Mystro Whatley

---

who was known as an effective conciliator, took over the agency. OSHA's efforts at reform have been criticized by labor leaders who feel that OSHA is more concerned with its own operation than with the safety and health of workers. Even the Chamber of Commerce has expressed concern that OSHA is putting more energy into improving its tarnished image than in reducing injuries and illness. While the need for OSHA is evident, the way in which OSHA can meet that need most effectively has yet to be found.[81]

Threats to Reproductive Health

Another important issue on the job safety front is how companies ought to respond to threats to workers' ability to reproduce brought about by exposure to hazards in the workplace. In 1983, pregnant women working at a Digital Equipment Corpora-tion plant in Massachusetts suffered an unusual number of miscarriages. The com-pany commissioned a study, which found that the miscarriage rate for women working in so-called "clean rooms" where computer chips were etched with acids and gases was 39 percent, nearly twice the national average.[82]

The initial corporate responses to the discovery that exposure to workplace hazards might be affecting reproductive processes were varied. AT&T removed all pregnant women from several computer-chip-production jobs. Digital Equipment Corporation "strongly urged" pregnant women to leave such positions. National Semiconductor Corporation and others expressed no opinion on the report, leaving decisions about job transfers to the women themselves. These different responses highlight the dilemma companies face today with one of the most sensitive job safety issues. It has been estimated that many employers put "fetal protection" policies in place to protect against this problem.

Some evidence has shown that exposure to a variety of chemicals and even to video display terminals may be posing health risks, but this evidence is not conclusive and there has been little corporate consensus on what action to take. Some companies have designed policies to address the problem, such as banning pregnant or fertile women from certain jobs, but the results have been controversy and discrimination lawsuits.[83] Some women's groups, in particular, have claimed that these schemes were designed simply to displace women.

The controversy over corporate "fetal protection" policies raged throughout the 1980s. In 1991, however, a case known as *Automobile Workers v. Johnson Controls, Inc.*, reached the U.S. Supreme Court. The Supreme Court ruled that fetal protection policies, which exclude women from certain high-risk jobs because of the potential harm to unborn babies, were illegal. The high court concluded that such fetal protection policies were tantamount to sex discrimination and therefore were contrary to Title VII of the Civil Rights Act of 1964.[84] We will discuss this case further in Chapter 16 under the topic of sex discrimination.

For employers who continue to be concerned about the safety of their female employees, a dilemma still remains. Two equally unpleasant choices are (1) to comply with the law and permit women to continue to be exposed to potentially harmful substances, risking lawsuits over damage to unborn babies, and (2) to reduce the use of dangerous chemicals in the workplace, thus driving up costs and incurring an international competitive disadvantage. One of the major problems facing business is that scientists have not yet been able to figure out what a safe fetal exposure level is.[85]

Workplace Violence

Before we leave our discussion of workplace safety, one other issue that is becoming a major problem and posing challenges to management is that of escalating violence in the workplace. The statistics are difficult to analyze. However, a major Justice Department report recently concluded that "one-sixth of all violent crimes in America occur in the workplace." Estimates are that 8 percent of all rapes, 7 percent of all robberies, and 16 percent of all assaults occur at work.[86] A major Labor Department study concluded that murder in the workplace is an increasingly important death-on-the-job statistic.[87]

A representative case of workplace violence occurred when a middle-aged mortgage banker became angry about a real estate deal he had hired a firm to handle years before. He went into a San Francisco law firm and opened fire. When it was over, eight people were dead and six were wounded. The tragedy ended when he shot himself.[88]

As one writer astutely observed, "Violence has crept from city to suburb, from dim alley to sunny schoolyard. It was only a matter of time before its malevolent shadow darkened the workplace."[89] Another observer concluded that "Workplace violence is the new poison of corporate America."[90]

Companies Respond

How are companies responding to this new kind of workplace hazard? Experts on workplace violence emphasize the importance of anticipating these crises and formulating specific procedures through which employees can report potential trouble so companies can respond. Some firms have decided to fold workplace violence into an already existing department that oversees other personnel matters. Others have decided to take a more proactive strategy. The Postal Service, for example, has trained a nine-person intervention team to be deployed to post offices if tensions get high. It is also striving to screen potential employees more carefully and encourage existing employees to use a hotline to report hot-tempered workers they perceive to be dangerous.[91]

DuPont launched its Personal Safety Program for employees in 1986. This program has evolved into a comprehensive workplace protection program that includes counselors, workshops, and a 24-hour hotline. Both DuPont and the Postal Service claim success with their programs.[92]

Effective stakeholder management necessitates that companies address the growing problem of workplace violence. Companies have only recently started to put safety measures into place, but such measures will become more important in the future. Programs that deal with crises, and long-range efforts to bring about safer workplace environments, will be essential.

THE RIGHT TO HEALTH IN THE WORKPLACE

In the health-conscious 1990s, it was not surprising that companies in the United States became much more sensitive about health issues. In efforts to control runaway health costs, which are rising an estimated 10 percent per year, these companies took drastic steps, some of which have become controversial. Two controversial issues of health in the workplace—smoking and AIDS—merit special attention. Like other issues we have examined, these issues have employee-rights, privacy, and due-process ramifications.

Smoking in the Workplace

The issue of smoking in the workplace grew out of the 1980s, especially in the second half of the decade. The idea that smoking ought to be curtailed or restricted in the workplace is a direct result of the growing antismoking sentiment in society in general. Much of the antismoking sentiment crystallized in 1984, when U.S. Surgeon General C. Everett Koop called for a smoke-free society. In 1986, he proclaimed that smokers were hurting not only themselves but also the nonsmoking people around them, who were being harmed by secondary, or passive, smoke in the air they breathed. Koop argued that the evidence "clearly documents that nonsmokers are placed at increased risks for developing disease as the result of exposure to environmental tobacco smoke."[93] To substantiate his point, a National Academy of Science study estimated that in 1 year, passive smoke was responsible for

2,400 lung cancer deaths in the United States.[94] This finding has been bolstered by public opinion. A Gallup Poll found that 96 percent of the population think that cigarette smoking is harmful to your health.[95]

As a result of the public's view on smoking, it should not be surprising to find comic strips increasingly emphasizing this theme. For example, a comic strip in *The Wall Street Journal* shows a manager interviewing a prospective employee. The manager proclaims, "It's your choice, Ms. Durbin. You can work in the no-smoking area or accept a smoking section hazardous pay increase of 25%."

As the antismoking fervor has hit the nation, effects are being felt everywhere in society. Most states have now restricted smoking in public places; most prohibit it outright in trains, buses, streetcars, and subways; and growing numbers forbid it in offices and other workplaces. There are also an estimated 800 local ordinances against smoking. This number is growing. In 1994, OSHA began hearings that are leading up to a planned ban on all smoking in the workplace.[96]

In 1998, OSHA Administrator Charles Jeffress appeared before the Senate Committee on Labor and Human Resources to urge Congress to take the lead on banning smoking in the workplace. While Congress could initiate a total ban on workplace smoking within months, the rulemaking process within OSHA may take as long as 8 years. Jeffress told legislators that OSHA was ready to enforce any workplace smoking ban legislated by Congress but that the ban would strain the agency's resources.[97]

Corporate Responses

Although companies did not act until considerable public sentiment against smoking had developed, they have quickly begun to adopt policies that restrict smoking. The majority of businesses now restrict smoking in some way, and an increasing number have banned it outright. Others are still studying the issue. Firms are becoming increasingly aware of the costs—higher insurance expenses and higher absenteeism—of having smokers on staff.

Companies were initially slow to restrict workplace smoking. One explanation for this pattern was offered by the executive director of New Jersey's chapter of GASP (Group Against Smoking Pollution), a nonprofit advocacy organization. She said that there are three stages in most smoking policies. First, managers are very apprehensive at the start. Second, the program goes over more smoothly than they anticipated. Finally, managers are flooded with positive responses from their employees.[98]

Companies that have developed smoking policies have generally tried to do so without alienating smokers. (Smokers represent about 26 percent of the population.) Such policies are aimed at restricting smoking to designated areas. Initially there were objections in the workplace to such policies, but much of this opposition has dissipated.

Other, more serious policies, however, have created more controversy. One company adopted the policy that employees may be dismissed if they do not stop smoking. Newspaper classified ads now frequently specify "nonsmokers only." One of the first questions asked of job applicants in one firm is, "Do you smoke?" If the answer is yes, the interview is over. This course of action is legal as long as the employer does not break any of the federal discrimination laws.[99] It has also been found that smoking is growing more and more hazardous to careers in business, with some employees believing that nonsmokers are being favored in selection and promotion decisions.[100]

The USG Ban

The corporate smoking policy debate grew more heated in 1987 when the USG Corporation announced a ban on employee smoking at work *and* at home. The company claimed that the protection of the company against future disability claims was at issue. Critics say this is a preposterous policy and that it represents a serious invasion of privacy. A spokesperson for the Tobacco Institute asserted, "The idea that any corporation has the right to reach beyond company gates, to what you could even describe as the bedroom of the employee, is ridiculous."[101] So far, no one has successfully challenged the USG ban. Attorneys say that constitutional rights to privacy apply only to actions by the state and not to actions by the private sector. On legal grounds, firms may face more of a threat from nonsmokers.

In 1998, *Management Today* declared passive smoking to be the year's big health and safety issue for employers because of the mounting threat of litigation. John Melville Williams QC, in a legal opinion obtained by Action on Smoking and Health (ASH), argues that employers have a responsibility to protect employees from tobacco smoke because, as a hazardous substance, tobacco smoke is covered under the Health and Safety Act of 1974. Williams believes that the level of current knowledge prohibits employers from using either ignorance or uncertainty as an excuse. The leading barrister's opinion is supported by various recent cases, which have been decided in favor of the nonsmoking employee.[102]

One kind of response that companies have made to the smoking issue and other "unhealthy lifestyle conditions" that may cause their health care costs to rise has been the creation of what are being called "lifestyle policies." In general, these policies require that employees who participate in unhealthy activities, such as smoking, substance abuse, skydiving, mountain climbing, or excessive eating (as monitored by weight guidelines), be assessed monthly surcharges on their health insurance or have their activities otherwise restricted. In 1991, for example, Texas Instruments invoked a $10 health insurance surcharge for employees who smoked, and ICH invoked a $15-a-month discount on medical contributions for employees who had not smoked in 90 days and who met a weight guideline. U-Haul International invoked a biweekly surcharge on health insurance for employees who smoked, chewed tobacco, or exceeded weight guidelines. Privacy expert Alan F. Westin worries that if such lifestyle discrimination continues, we could become a two-class society—"one that is perceived as fit and healthy and the [unhealthy] rest who would be unemployed or marginally employed."[103] Companies defend their policies on the basis of the illnesses, chronic diseases, health costs, and adverse impacts on performance caused by certain lifestyle conditions and practices. The companies continue to support their decisions by citing the significant cost savings, running into millions of dollars, that have been generated by the policies and wellness programs they have instituted.[104]

The smoking-in-the-workplace issue and related concerns are bound to stir debates for years to come as conflicts between company rights and individual rights continue to arise. The most reasonable course of action seems to be for managers to consider carefully all employee stakeholders' claims in this issue and then develop reasonable policies that are gradually introduced, while employee feedback is continually monitored. Indeed, some companies have gotten employees themselves involved in the development of such policies. This democratizes the decision-making process and provides management with a more solid foundation for taking particular policy stances.

AIDS in the Workplace

Few public issues have as much potential to create severe problems for business as the widespread incidence of acquired immune deficiency syndrome (AIDS) in the United States. About 343,000 Americans have died of AIDS since its introduction in the mid-1980s; another 900,000 are infected with human immunodeficiency virus (HIV).[105] The Centers for Disease Control and Prevention (CDC) reported recently that 1 in 6 large companies and 1 in 15 small companies knew they had an employee with HIV/AIDS.[106] However, in a 1997 Caravan Opinion Research Corporation study, almost one-third of workers surveyed believed their companies would fire or put on disability a person who was HIV positive. Furthermore, 21 percent indicated they would agree with that action. This latter response is particularly troubling, because either action directly violates the ADA.[107] Considerable effort has been expended on AIDS education programs but, despite these efforts, the American worker remains frightened by the disease. Figure 15–4 is an ad the American Red Cross placed in major magazines as a public service announcement.

Three groups of employees must be considered when developing policies and educational programs about AIDS and HIV. First are the employees who have been diagnosed with the disease. They need clear policies and procedures that comply with the spirit of the ADA and its interpretations by the EEOC. The second group includes those people who come into contact with bodily fluids. This group includes physicians, nurses, lab workers, paramedics, and police officers. The third group includes all other employees who may have fears and prejudices that will affect their morale and productivity if not assuaged.[108] AIDS is clearly more than a health and safety issue. It also has due-process, fair-treatment, and privacy implications.

Corporate Responses

When AIDS first appeared in the early 1980s, the business community was unsure of its responsibilities to employees who were diagnosed with the disease. In 1986, the Justice Department ruled that some employers could legally fire employees diagnosed with AIDS if the employers' motive was to protect other workers.[109] In March 1987, however, that judgment was reversed when the Supreme Court ruled that people with contagious diseases were protected by the same law that protected handicapped workers from workplace discrimination, the Rehabilitation Act of 1973.[110] With the passage of the ADA, AIDS became a recognized and covered disability.[111]

Some evidence exists that corporate AIDS programs are on the decline. In a 1997 survey by the National AIDS Fund (NAF), 18 percent of companies indicated they had AIDS awareness programs, down 10 percent from the 28 percent who had programs in 1992.[112] This apparent complacency may come at a cost as more lawsuits are filed. In one of the first lawsuits to be filed by the EEOC on behalf of a person

---

FIGURE 15–4   An Informative Ad on AIDS

The American Red Cross addresses the most often asked questions about AIDS and the workplace:

CAN AN EMPLOYEE WITH AIDS INFECT OTHER EMPLOYEES?

The AIDS virus cannot be spread by normal everyday contact in the workplace.

CAN THE AIDS VIRUS BE SPREAD BY USING A TELEPHONE OR WATER FOUNTAIN?

No. The AIDS virus is not spread through air, water, or on surfaces, such as telephones, door knobs, or office machines. The virus is spread mainly through an exchange of body fluids during sexual activity, or the exchange of blood as occurs through sharing contaminated IV drug needles.

SHOULD I PROVIDE OR DESIGNATE SEPARATE BATHROOM FACILITIES FOR EMPLOYEES WITH AIDS?

There is no need to. The AIDS virus is not spread through ordinary use of toilets, sinks, or other bathroom facilities.

CAN I TELL IF SOMEONE IS INFECTED WITH THE AIDS VIRUS?

There are many *carriers* of the virus who do not have the symptoms or signs of the disease and may or may not develop the disease. A carrier of the AIDS

SHOULD YOU WORRY ABOUT AIDS AND THE WORK-PLACE?

virus can infect other people but not through ordinary workplace contact.

WHAT IF I TOUCH A COWORKER WITH AIDS WHO HAS A BLEEDING CUT?

All blood and other body fluids should be considered potentially infectious. Whether a person has AIDS or not, all open, bleeding cuts should be taken care of by observing good health and hygiene practices.

HOW SHOULD EMPLOYEES WITH AIDS BE TREATED?

On a day-to-day basis, treat them normally. You and your employees should learn about AIDS, and when dealing with their problem, use compassion and understanding.

Above all, remember...

AIDS IS HARD TO CATCH.

This information is based upon data from the U.S. Public Health Service. For more information, call your local health department, the National AIDS Hotline (1-800-342-AIDS) or your local Red Cross chapter.

Or, if you're interested in an educational program about AIDS for your company, call your local health department or your local Red Cross chapter.

WE WANT YOU TO KNOW AS MUCH ABOUT AIDS AS WE DO.

 American Red Cross

© AMERICAN RED CROSS 6-4-97

SOURCE: Developed by J. Walter Thompson for the American Red Cross. Used with permission of the American Red Cross.

with AIDS, in 1998 a Chicago man successfully sued his employer, Nippon Express, for AIDS discrimination. The company was accused of giving meaningless work to the employee with AIDS, taking away his telephone and forbidding coworkers from speaking with him. According to the 6-year Nippon employee, workers belittled him and made cruel comments about his condition. The settlement called for Nippon Express to pay $160,000 in damages, to donate $25,000 to AIDS research, and to provide management employees with training as to how to deal with a person who has been diagnosed with AIDS or HIV.[113]

As new and more effective drug therapies extend the lives and the productivity of HIV-positive employees, companies face new challenges. From 1992 to 1996, AIDS was the leading cause of death among 25- to 44-year-olds. By 1998, accidents were the leading cause; AIDS fell to second. After receiving new treatments, such as protease inhibitors, HIV-infected workers can often return to work and be productive again.[114] Many employers have helped their HIV-infected employees transition back to work. American Airlines corporate medical director, David McKenas, MD, said, "Many people are on the new medications. They are very successful. We are putting them back to work and they are doing great things for America."[115] Recently, American Airlines worked with the Federal Aviation Administration (FAA) to recertify an HIV-infected pilot. In the words of Dr. McKenas, "We checked him out and he is OK. The FAA has strict policies of people on medication flying commercially." Dr. McKenas went on to say that the pilot "runs marathons and is more muscular than I am. He is doing very well."[116] American's AIDS education program was developed in response to a well-publicized 1992 incident in which flight attendants requested new pillows and blankets after a flight on which many of the passengers were AIDS activists returning from an HIV/AIDS rally in Washington, DC.[117]

Eastman Kodak is another company with an effective HIV/AIDS policy. Since 1988, the company has offered general HIV/AIDS education and awareness programs, as well as specific training for managers who must deal directly with HIV-related issues. Joseph Laymon, vice president of human resources at Eastman Kodak, says the company will tolerate no discrimination in its workplace and will terminate an employee who violates the company's HIV/AIDS policy. Following is a quote from an Eastman Kodak employee who was diagnosed with HIV/AIDS. The quote was taken from the company's training manual, as reported in a February 1998 *HR Magazine* article by Jay Greene.

> *At first I was shaken, scared, afraid that my whole life had come apart. The stigma of HIV/AIDS was on my life and I didn't know what to do or who to tell or even who to trust. . . . My mind was a mess. But I met a lady, Lydia Casiano, who I felt very comfortable with. She works in the Human Relations Department at Kodak. She assured me of Kodak's policy of privacy and told me my job is still secure! . . . This year I've received a raise and have been given opportunities to improve myself and my workplace. We have given training classes to all [division] employees and I've told everyone about this condition. Today I work in an HIV friendly atmosphere because of the efforts made by the management and workforce of Kodak.[118]*

Other organizations known for their HIV/AIDS programs include IBM, Levi Strauss & Co., the National Basketball Association (NBA), and Polaroid.[119]

A cooperative program called Business Responds to AIDS (BRTA) was established as a joint initiative of the U.S. Centers for Disease Control and the business sector. BRTA recommends that, at minimum, organizations develop comprehensive programs that contain five key components,[120] as follows:

1. Workplace policy
2. Training (for managers, supervisors, and union leaders)
3. Employee education
4. Family education
5. Community involvement

What should be the corporate response to employee stakeholders on the AIDS issue? Companies should be sensitive to the needs of their employees who develop AIDS. In addition, companies should sponsor educational programs so that all workers can understand that AIDS cannot be transmitted by casual contact. Management will never be able to overcome fear and hostility if it does not engage in a thorough and ongoing educational program.[121]

Companies also need to be extremely sensitive to the privacy and due-process aspects of AIDS, and thus it is very important that companies adopt policies for dealing with AIDS cases *before* they arise. Managers need to be trained and educated in how to handle AIDS cases. Policies on AIDS should not be developed in an ad hoc, spur-of-the-moment fashion but as part of an overall strategy for dealing with workplace health and safety, privacy, and employee rights.

The Family-Friendly Workplace

One of the rationales that companies have given in recent years for having become more family friendly is that they are looking out for the mental and psychological health of their employees. Whether it be for altruistic or business reasons, workplaces today are becoming more family friendly. By using this term we are repeating a catch-all phrase that refers to a whole host of policies and programs that today's companies have been putting into place.

A special report in *The Wall Street Journal* characterizes this trend:

> *The message from Corporate America is clear and unmistakable. We are attuned to your families. The evidence is everywhere. Corporate child care centers are popping up around the country. "Work-family managers" appear on organization charts, and "flextime" has become a buzzword.*[122]

Although not everyone thinks that companies are becoming as family friendly as they are espousing to be, it is clear that workers are talking more and more about the importance of family-friendly policies, and many leading companies are responding. With the growth in the numbers of women, single parents, and two-paycheck couples in the workforce, it seems that corporate support for families, many of whom are stressed out from their busy lives, is on the growth curve. New issues are being raised: Family-support programs may be developing resentment among childless couples, family feuds at work are occurring more frequently, men want to be sure they are treated as well as women, and corporate cultures are changing. Into the vocabulary of managers have emerged new terms for dealing with employee stakeholders: *employee assistance, parenting workshops, dependent-care spending accounts, flexible scheduling, family-care leave,* and so on.[123]

It is in the context of organizations becoming more "friendly" on their own that we want to discuss one of the most recent laws aimed at health-related issues in the workplace—the Family and Medical Leave Act.

Family and Medical Leave Act

The Family and Medical Leave Act (FMLA) was made into law in 1993. This act was designed to make life easier for employees with family or health problems.

Under the FMLA,[124] employees are granted the following rights:

- An employee may take up to 12 weeks of unpaid leave in any 12-month period for the birth or adoption of a child, or for the care of a child, spouse, or parent with a serious health condition that limits the employee's performance.

- Employees must be reinstated in their old jobs or be given equivalent jobs upon returning to work; the employer does not have to allow employees to accrue seniority or other benefits during the leave periods.

- Employers must provide employees with health benefits during leave periods.

- Employees are protected from retaliation in the same way as under other employment laws; an employee cannot be discriminated against for complaining to other people (even the newspapers) about an employer's family leave policy.

Employers also have rights under the FMLA.[125] These rights include the following:

- Companies with fewer than 50 workers are exempt.

- Employers may demand that employees obtain medical opinions and certifications regarding their needs for leave and may require second or third opinions.

- Employers do not have to pay employees during leave periods, but they must continue health benefits.

- If an employee and a spouse are employed at the same firm and are entitled to leave, the total leave for both may be limited to 12 weeks.

The FMLA will not necessarily be easy to implement, however, because of special and technical key definitions of such terms as "serious health condition," "medical certification," "reasonable prior notice," and "equivalent position."[126]

Many contentious issues will be faced by employers as they attempt to implement the FMLA. A few of these issues are as follows: Can employees substitute accrued sick leave for unpaid leave? Just what constitutes an "equivalent" job when a leave-taker returns and her or his own job has been taken? What sorts of employee illnesses are "serious" enough to justify leave?

The FMLA institutionalizes at the federal level the employee's right to unpaid leave for health and family reasons. However, more than 35 states had their own leave laws before the FMLA was passed. Therefore, many companies have had experience in facing some of the difficult cases that could arise from the implementation of this law. In addition to the complex legal environment for employee issues that many companies already face, the FMLA promises to bring new challenges on a continuing basis.[127]

Early indications are that many employers are not complying with the FMLA. In a 1994 study of 300 employers, it was found that 4 in 10 were failing to allow the 12 weeks of leave and to guarantee jobs or continue benefits during leave—the most basic requirements of the law. In this same study,[128] it was found that many companies, in the percentages indicated, employed the following policies or practices that mitigate against the FMLA's full implementation:

- Companies don't develop an appeals process to resolve disputes (53 percent)
- Companies don't train supervisors to comply with the law (22 percent)
- Companies don't communicate with employees about the law (20 percent)
- Companies don't have formal policies on length of family leave (15 percent)
- Companies don't continue health plans as required (10 percent)
- Companies don't guarantee jobs of employees on leave (9 percent)

In summary, many companies are being slow to comply with the FMLA, and thus employees are on their own in pursuing their rights under the law. If past records of response to law are any indication, businesses will be slow to respond, but they will learn to comply at an accelerating rate as lawsuits begin to impact them. At this writing, various efforts to pass additional family-friendly workplace legislation have been stymied by partisan conflict. The eventual outcome of these efforts is certain to influence the direction corporate policies will take.

SUMMARY

Critical employee stakeholder issues include the rights to privacy, safety, and health. These issues should be seen as extensions of the issues and rights outlined in Chapter 14.

With the development of new technologies, workplace privacy has increasingly become a serious workplace issue. The level of concern surrounding workplace privacy is evidenced by the frequency with which it has been a topic in the print and broadcast media. As Barbara Walters warned employees in a January 12, 1998, segment of ABC News's "20/20," "Your time is theirs and what you do on their computer or their phone is their business." The news magazine showed examples of truck drivers being monitored by satellite so closely that the company knew when, where, and how fast they drove, as well as how much gas they still had in their tanks. In another segment, companies were shown hiring undercover operators to watch and sometimes test their employees. Last, the news magazine explained why e-mail and voice mail can be monitored, even after messages are deleted. This wealth of available technology presents new challenges for companies as they weigh the importance of knowing their workers' activities against the importance of maintaining trust and morale.

Of equal, if not more, importance to employee stakeholders are the issues of workplace safety and health. The workplace safety problem led to the creation of OSHA. In spite of its difficulties, OSHA is still the federal government's major instrument for protecting workers on the job. State-promulgated right-to-know laws, as well as federal statutes, have been passed in recent years to provide employees with an added measure of protection, especially against harmful effects of exposure to chemicals and toxic substances. The Supreme Court's 1991 decision to ban corporate fetal protection policies created continuing challenges for business.

Two major health issues in the current business/employee relationship are smoking in the workplace and AIDS. The smoking issue, although less critical than AIDS, is currently the more pervasive problem. AIDS has become the most serious health issue that business or our society has ever faced. Wise managers will now begin to develop policies for dealing with these issues, both of which have privacy and due-process implications. One of the latest challenges to employers is the Family and Medical Leave Act of 1993.

KEY TERMS

Employee Assistance Programs (EAPs) (page 481)

family-friendly workplace (page 499)

privacy (page 472)

right-to-know laws (page 486)

DISCUSSION QUESTIONS

1. In your own words, describe what privacy means and what privacy protection companies should give employees.
2. Enumerate the strengths and weaknesses of the polygraph as a management tool for decision making. What polygraph uses are legitimate? What uses of the polygraph are illegitimate?
3. What are the two major arguments for and against honesty testing by employers? Under what circumstances could management most legitimately argue that honesty testing is necessary?
4. Which two of the four guidelines on the issue of privacy presented in this chapter do you think are the most important? Why?
5. Identify the privacy, health, and due-process ramifications of both the workplace smoking issue and the AIDS issue.

ENDNOTES

1. Asra Q. Nomani, "Murder in Workplace Is a Major Part of the Latest Death-on-the-Job Statistics," *The Wall Street Journal* (August 11, 1994), A4.
2. Barbara Wagner, "Privacy in the Workplace," *World* (April/June, 1987), 48.
3. *Ibid.*
4. Jeffrey Rothfeder and Michele Galen, "Is Your Boss Spying on You?" *Business Week* (January 15, 1990), 74.

5. Cited in Alfred G. Feliu, *Primer on Individual Employee Rights* (Washington, DC: The Bureau of National Affairs, 1992), 211–212.

6. "Big Brother, Inc. May Be Closer than You Think," *Business Week* (February 9, 1987), 84.

7. Patricia H. Werhane, *Persons, Rights, and Corporations* (Englewood Cliffs, NJ: Prentice Hall, 1985), 118.

8. Laura Pincus Hartman, "The Rights and Wrongs of Workplace Snooping," *Journal of Business Strategy* (May/June, 1998), 16–19.

9. Tiana Harrison, "Privacy in Workplace Called Growing Concern," *The Atlanta Journal* (October 4, 1994), F2.

10. "Big Brother, Inc. May Be Closer than You Think," *Business Week* (February 9, 1987), 84.

11. Cited in Jolie Solomon, "As Firms' Personnel Files Grow, Worker Privacy Falls," *The Wall Street Journal* (April 19, 1989), B1.

12. *Ibid.*

13. Joseph R. DesJardins, "Privacy in Employment," in Gertrude Ezorsky (ed.), *Moral Rights in the Workplace* (Albany, NY: State University of New York Press, 1987), 133.

14. Solomon, B1.

15. Raymond Bonner, "Lie Detectors as Corporate Tools," *The New York Times* (February 13, 1983), 4F.

16. Kenneth F. Englade, "The Business of the Polygraph," *Across the Board* (October, 1982), 21–22.

17. James H. Coil III and Barbara Jo Call, "Congress Targets Employers' Use of Polygraphs," *Employment Relations Today* (Spring, 1986), 23.

18. James H. Coil III, "The Polygraph Protection Act Becomes Law," *Employment Relations Today* (Autumn, 1988), 181.

19. Coil and Call, 24.

20. *Ibid.*, 25. Also see Kenneth A. Kovach, "The Truth About Employers' Use of Lie Detectors," *Business and Society Review* (Spring, 1995), 65–69.

21. Benjamin Kleinmuntz, "Lie Detectors Fail the Truth Test," *Harvard Business Review* (July–August, 1985), 36–42.

22. Coil, 181.

23. *Ibid.*, 184. Also see Feliu, 151–154; and William E. Lissy, "Lie Detector Tests," *Supervision* (October, 1995), 20–21.

24. *Ibid.*

25. David Nye, "Son of the Polygraph," *Across the Board* (June, 1989), 21.

26. Feliu, 154.

27. *Ibid.*

28. Ed Bean, "More Firms Use Attitude Tests to Keep Thieves off the Payroll," *The Wall Street Journal* (January 27, 1987), 41.

29. Matthew Budman, "The Honesty Business," *Across the Board* (November/December, 1993), 34–37.

30. *Ibid.*, 36.

31. Elizabeth M. Cosin, "Tests to Spot the Pinocchios May Fail the Honest Abes," *Insight* (July 30, 1990), 42–43.

32. "Why Firms Don't Test for Drugs," *USA Today* (February 18, 1987), 7B.

33. Anne Newman, "Drug-Testing Firms Face Pluses, Minuses in New Rules," *The Wall Street Journal* (March 15, 1994), B4.

34. Leon Rubis, "Positive Drug Tests Hit 11-Year Low," *HR Magazine* (June, 1998), 20.

35. "Battling the Enemy Within: Companies Fight to Drive Illegal Drugs Out of the Workplace," *Time* (March 17, 1986), 53.

36. Michael Waldholz, "Drug Testing in the Workplace: Whose Rights Take Precedence?" *The Wall Street Journal* (November 11, 1986), 39.

37. "The Many Tests for Drug Abuse," *The New York Times* (February 24, 1985), F17.

38. *Ibid.*

39. Curtis J. Sitomer, "Privacy and Personal Freedom: Balancing the Trade-Offs," *The Christian Science Monitor* (December 3, 1986), 33.

40. John Fay, *Drug Testing* (Boston: Butterworth-Heinemann, 1991), 22. Also see John D. Rapoport and Brian L.P. Zevnik, *The Employee Strikes Back!* (New York: Collier Books, 1994), 91–93.

41. Jane Easter Bahls, "Dealing with Drugs: Keep It Legal," *HR Magazine* (March, 1998), 104–116.

42. Newman, B4.

43. Sarah F. Mulladay, "The Champion Paper Company EAP and Major Issues for Employee Assistance Programs in the 1990s—Managed Care and Aging," *Employee Assistance Quarterly* (Vol. 6, No. 3, 1991), 37–50.

44. *Employee Assistance Programs: Drug, Alcohol and Other Problems* (Chicago: Commerce Clearing House, 1986), 7.

45. Fay, 20.

46. Hartman, 16.

47. Feliu, 100.

48. *Ibid.*, 101.

49. Curtis J. Sitomer, "Privacy and Personal Freedoms: The Impact of Technology," *The Christian Science Monitor* (December 5, 1986), 1.

50. *Ibid.*

51. *Time,* "The Boss That Never Blinks," 46.

52. Rothfeder and Galen, 74.

53. *Ibid.*

54. Rothfeder and Galen, 75.

55. Michael Allen, "Legislation Could Restrict Bosses from Snooping on Their Workers," *The Wall Street Journal* (September 24, 1991), B1.

56. Robert C. Goldstein and Richard L. Nolan, "Personal Privacy versus the Corporate Computer," *Harvard Business Review* (March–April, 1975), 62–70.

57. Barbara Presley Noble, "Tracking Big Brother in the Office," *The New York Times* (October 30, 1994), F23.

58. John L. Paluszek, *Will the Corporation Survive?* (Reston, VA: Reston Publishing Company, 1977), 120.

59. "Union Carbide Fights for Its Life," *Business Week* (December 24, 1984), 52–56.

60. Joseph P. Kahn, "When Bad Management Becomes Criminal," *Inc.* (March, 1987), 47.

61. *Ibid.*

62. David R. Spiegel, "Enforcing Safety Laws Locally," *The New York Times* (March 23, 1986), 11F.
63. James T. O'Reilly, "What's Wrong with the Right to Know?" *Across the Board* (April, 1985), 24.
64. Elizabeth Holtzman, "States Step in Where OSHA Fails to Tread," *The Wall Street Journal* (March 31, 1987), 36.
65. Peter A. Susser, "Chemical Hazard Disclosure Obligations," *Employment Relations Today* (Winter, 1986–1987), 301–302.
66. "Talk Straight on Chemical Hazards," *Business Week* (December 9, 1985), 142.
67. "Now OSHA Must Justify Its Inspection Targets," *Business Week* (April 9, 1979), 64.
68. "OSHA's Nitpicking Rules Die," *Athens Banner Herald* (November 24, 1978), 5.
69. *Ibid.*
70. Walter Williams, "OSHA Looking Out for You," *Conservative Chronicle* (January 25, 1995), 1.
71. Philip K. Howard, *The Death of Common Sense: How Law Is Suffocating America* (New York: Random House, 1994).
72. *Ibid.*, 12.
73. Information on OSHA and its activities is available on the OSHA Web site at *www.osha.gov.*
74. Robert L. Simison, "Job Deaths and Injuries Seem to Be Increasing After Years of Decline," *The Wall Street Journal* (March 18, 1986), 1, 25.
75. *Ibid.*, 1.
76. Steven Waldman, "Danger on the Job," *Newsweek* (December 11, 1989), 44.
77. Scott Bronstein, "They Treated Us Like Dogs, Say Workers at Plant Where 25 Died," *The Atlanta Journal* (September 5, 1991), A6.
78. Cited in Asra Q. Nomani, "Labor Secretary's Bid to Push Plant Safety Runs into Skepticism," *Wall Street Journal* (August 19, 1994), A1.
79. *Ibid.*, A4.
80. Linda Himelstein, "Repetitive Stress Injuries: The Asbestos Case of the 1990s," *Business Week* (January 16, 1995), 82–83.
81. Lisa Finnegan, "Reform and Reinvention," *Occupational Hazards* (July, 1998), 67–68.
82. Barry Meier, "Companies Wrestle with Threats to Workers' Reproductive Health," *The Wall Street Journal* (February 5, 1987), 23.
83. *Ibid.*
84. Marc Hequet and Julie Johnson, "Weighing Some Heavy Metal," *Time* (April 1, 1991), 60.
85. Joann S. Lublin, "Decision Poses Dilemma for Employers," *The Wall Street Journal* (March 21, 1991), B1.
86. "U.S. Workplace Often a Crime Scene," *The Atlanta Journal* (July 25, 1994), A6.
87. Asra Q. Nomani, "Murder in Workplace Is a Major Part of the Latest Death-on-the-Job Statistics," *The Wall Street Journal* (August 11, 1994), A4.
88. Tom Dunkel, "Hazardous Duty," *The Atlanta Journal* (October 2, 1994), Q1, Q3.
89. *Ibid.*, Q1.
90. *Ibid.*, Q1.

91. *Ibid.*, Q3.

92. *Ibid.*, Q3.

93. Otto Friedrich, "Where There's Smoke," *Time* (February 23, 1987), 23.

94. Lois Therrien, "Warning: In More and More Places, Smoking Causes Fines," *Business Week* (December 29, 1986), 40.

95. George Gallup, Jr., and Dr. Frank Newport, "Many Americans Favor Restrictions on Smoking in Public Places," *The Gallup Monthly* (July, 1990), 20.

96. Frank Swoboda and Martha M. Hamilton, "The Smoke Police Eye the Workplace," *The Washington Post National Weekly Edition* (September 26–October 2, 1994), 20.

97. Lisa Finnegan, "Jeffress to Congress: Ban Workplace Smoking," *Occupational Hazards* (April, 1998), 12.

98. Dexter Hutchins, "The Drive to Kick Smoking at Work," *Fortune* (September 15, 1986), 43.

99. Barbara Rudolph, "Thou Shalt Not Smoke: Companies Restrict the Use of Tobacco in the Workplace," *Time* (May 18, 1987), 56.

100. Alix M. Freedman, "Cigarette Smoking Is Growing Hazardous to Careers in Business," *The Wall Street Journal* (April 23, 1987), 1.

101. Carolyn Lochhead, "Banning Employee Smoking Beyond the Company Gates," *Insight* (March 2, 1987), 40–41.

102. "Passive Employers Can't Dodge the Smoking Debate," *Management Today* (May, 1998), 14.

103. Cited in Zachary Schiller and Walecia Konrad, "Lifestyles: If You Light Up on Sunday, Don't Come to Work on Monday," *Business Week* (August 26, 1991), 68–72.

104. Sheri Caudron, "The Wellness Payoff," *Personnel Journal* (July, 1990), 55–60.

105. Jay Greene, "Employers Learn to Live with AIDS," *HR Magazine* (February, 1998), 96–101.

106. *Ibid.*

107. John S. McClenahon, "Working with AIDS," *Management Today* (November 17, 1997), 51–52.

108. Donald Klingner and Nancy G. O'Neill, *Workplace Drug Abuse and AIDS: A Guide to Human Resource Management Policy and Practice* (New York: Quorem Books, 1991), 100.

109. "AIDS in the Workplace," *Newsweek* (July 7, 1986), 62.

110. "A Victory for AIDS Victims," *Newsweek* (March 16, 1987), 33.

111. Susan K. Adler, "HIV/AIDS in the Workplace," *Occupational Health and Safety* (May, 1995), 79–80.

112. Greene, 96–101.

113. David Mendell, "Settlement Is Reached in AIDS Bias Lawsuit," *Chicago Tribune* (July 30, 1998), 8.

114. Greene, 96–101.

115. *Ibid.*, 96.

116. *Ibid.*

117. *Ibid.*, 96–101.

118. *Ibid.*

119. *Ibid.* For additional information on HIV/AIDS, visit the Society for Human Resource Management (SHRM) Web site at *www.shrm.org.*

120. Cited in Romuald A. Stone, "AIDS in the Workplace: An Executive Update," *Academy of Management Executive* (August, 1994), 57.

121. "Business Should Help Battle AIDS," *Business Week* (March 23, 1987), 174; "Why AIDS Policy Must Be a Special Policy," *Business Week* (February 1, 1993), 53–54; and "Managing AIDS," *Business Week* (February 1, 1993), 48–52.

122. Sue Shellenbarger, "Work and Family: So Much Talk, So Little Action," *The Wall Street Journal* (June 21, 1993), R1.

123. Robert L. Rose, "Small Steps," *The Wall Street Journal* (June 21, 1993), R10.

124. Rapoport and Zevnik, 229–230.

125. *Ibid.*, 230–232.

126. *Ibid.*

127. Michele Galen, "Sure, 'Unpaid Leave' Sounds Simple, But . . . ," *Business Week* (August 9, 1993), 32–33.

128. Sue Shellenbarger, "Many Employers Flout Family and Medical Leave Law," *The Wall Street Journal* (July 26, 1994), B1.

16

Employment Discrimination and Affirmative Action

CHAPTER OBJECTIVES

After studying this chapter, you should be able to:

1 Chronicle the civil rights movement and minority progress for the past 35 years.

2 Outline the essentials of the federal discrimination laws, particularly Title VII of the Civil Rights Act of 1964.

3 Provide two different meanings of discrimination and give examples of how each might be committed.

4 Elaborate on issues in employment discrimination relating to race, color, national origin, sex, age, religion, and disability.

5 Identify different postures with respect to affirmative action, explain the concept of reverse discrimination, and provide an overview of the Supreme Court's decisions on affirmative action.

6 Articulate the corporate view on affirmative action.

A particular subgroup of employee stakeholders are those whose job rights are protected by federal, state, and local laws against discrimination. In the previous two chapters we considered employee rights issues that affect virtually everyone in the workplace. In this chapter we concentrate on that group of stakeholders whose rights are protected by discrimination laws. In general, these *protected groups* include minorities, women, older people, people with disabilities, and people with religious affiliations that might affect their conditions of employment. Many of the issues we treat in this chapter have grown out of the general notion that employees have certain workplace rights that ought to be protected.

To complicate matters, there is a growing group of observers who think that legitimate protective status is giving way to victim status as increasing numbers of people set forth their claims that they too should have their rights as employees protected by law. Charles Sykes, author of *A Nation of Victims: The Decay of the American Character* (1992), articulates this most vigorously as he presents a strong argument that we have become a "society of victims" with growing numbers of employees asserting claims for protected status.[1] Sykes is not alone, however. Paul Hollander has argued that "the ideology of victimhood is so strong in the United States today that not only does it induce people to claim victimhood where none exists, it has created a climate in which such inventions, no matter how false, are seen as true on a higher level than 'mere' facts." Thus, he argues, if we add up the spectacular expansion of people claiming protected status over the past 25 years, it may emerge that not more than 15 percent of the U.S. population is now free from the injuries of victimhood, a major form of which is claimed to be employment discrimination.[2]

It is within this context in which claims to be protected by law are proliferating that we embark on this discussion of employment discrimination and affirmative action. We must work hard to remember that the civil rights movement, which effectively started it all, was quite legitimate and long overdue.

Upon reflection, it is difficult to believe that our country is over 200 years old but has only made a serious and concerted effort to protect employees' legitimate rights against employment discrimination for about 30 years. On the other hand, some would argue that we have come a long way in the past three decades. Actually, federal antidiscrimination laws date back to the U.S. Constitution—in particular, the First, Fifth, and Fourteenth Amendments, which were designed to forbid religious discrimination and deprivation of employment rights without due process. There were also the Civil Rights Acts of 1866, 1870, and 1871, which were based on these amendments. None of these acts was ever effective, however. Most authorities agree that the Civil Rights Act of 1964 was the effective beginning of the employee protection movement, particularly for those special groups that we will be discussing in this chapter.

Civil rights issues among protected groups are highly debated and controversial. Although there is basic acceptance of the idea of groups' workplace rights being protected, the extent of this protection and the degree to which governmental policy should go to accelerate the infusion of minorities, women, and others into the work force and into higher-paying jobs remains a topic of considerable debate, even in the 1990s. To explore these and related issues, we will cover the following major topics in this chapter: the civil rights movement and minority progress; federal laws that protect against employment discrimination; the meaning of discrimination; a variety of issues related to employment discrimination; and, finally, affirmative action in the workplace.

THE CIVIL RIGHTS MOVEMENT AND MINORITY PROGRESS

It would take volumes to trace thoroughly the historical events that led ultimately to passage of the first significant piece of civil rights legislation in the modern period—the Civil Rights Act of 1964. William Glueck and James Ledvinka have provided a brief analysis of these events. They have argued that the act grew out of conflict that had been apparent for years but that erupted in the 1950s and 1960s in the form of protests and boycotts.[3]

Civil Rights in the 1950s and 1960s

Behind the American dream had historically been the belief that merit rather than privilege was the means of getting ahead. Equal opportunity was everyone's birthright. Blacks and other minorities, however, had not shared fully in this American dream. In the 1950s and 1960s, the disparity between American ideals and American realities became quite pronounced and evident for minorities. Americans became aware of it, not because they suddenly awoke to the realization that equal opportunity was not available to everyone, but because of individuals who had the courage to stand up for what they believed were their rights as U.S. citizens.

It began on December 1, 1955, when Mrs. Rosa Parks, a black department store worker, was arrested for refusing to yield her bus seat to a white man. Out of that previously unthinkable act grew yet another—a bus boycott by blacks. One of the leaders of the boycott was a young minister, Dr. Martin Luther King, Jr. After the bus boycott came years of demonstrations, marches, and battles with police. Television coverage depicted scenes of civil rights demonstrators being attacked by officials with cattle prods, dogs, and fire hoses. Along with the violence that grew out of confrontations between protestors and authorities came the stark awareness of the *economic inequality* between the races that existed in the United States at that time.[4]

In the voluminous data gathered by the Bureau of the Census, a few notable statistics documented the point quite well. Unemployment figures for blacks were double those for whites and higher still among nonwhite youth. Blacks accounted for only 10 percent of the labor force but represented 20 percent of total unemployed and nearly 30 percent of long-term unemployed. In 1961, only about one-half of black men worked steadily at full-time jobs, whereas nearly two-thirds of white men did so. Against this backdrop of blacks and other minorities being denied their share in the American ideal of equal opportunity in employment, it should have been no surprise that Congress finally acted in a dramatic way in 1964.

The 1970s: The Women's Movement Begins

As we entered the 1970s, blacks were making strong gains in employment and earnings. From the 1973–1975 recession on, however, rampant unemployment among blacks was discouraging. As the decade of the 1970s ended, the following statistics[5] profiled the situation blacks faced:

- The unemployment rate was about 12 percent for blacks, compared with 5 percent for whites.

- Black men were dropping out of the labor force at record rates; many could not get jobs.

- Real weekly earnings rose faster for blacks than for whites until 1973 and then stalled for both groups.

The women's movement began in the 1970s. Women's groups began to see that the workplace situation was little better for women than for blacks and other minorities. Despite the fact that the labor participation rate for women was growing, women were still occupying low-paying jobs. Women were making some small inroads into managerial and professional jobs, but progress was very slow. Women, for the most part, were still in the lower-paying "women's jobs," such as bank teller, secretary, waitress, and laundry worker.[6]

The 1980s: Gains Are Made

In the 1980s, the plights of blacks and women improved, but women, in general, made greater progress in the workplace than blacks. From 1983 to 1986, the unemployment rate for all whites fell from 8.4 percent to 6.1 percent. During this same time, the unemployment rate for blacks fell from 19.5 percent to 15.1 percent. For women, it fell from 6.9 percent to 5.4 percent.[7] From these statistics we can see that unemployment represented a major problem for blacks but was not a major problem for women. Indeed, the unemployment rate for blacks remained more than twice that of whites.

As the mid- to late 1980s arrived, inequality in the work force remained a serious problem. Blacks continued to have lower participation rates in the work force, and undoubtedly some of this was traceable to racial discrimination. Women did not have the labor participation rate problem of blacks but continued to sense that they were being excluded from higher-paying managerial jobs. Also problematic were pay inequities between men and women, and between whites and blacks, performing essentially the same jobs.

Employment discrimination began essentially as a racial issue, but it soon became apparent that sex or gender discrimination was a significant problem, too. We have focused on these two issues because they have historically constituted the bulk of the problem. The civil rights movement was aimed primarily at improving the status of blacks, although it later openly embraced the causes of other minorities and of women. Out of this movement grew a concern for fair treatment irrespective of age, disability, or religion.

By the end of the 1980s, the progress of blacks—or, as many people prefer to be called, African Americans—was mixed. There were notable gains on the education front, but the incomes of blacks continued to trail those of whites. In 1990, nearly 80 percent of blacks aged 35 to 44 had completed 4 years of high school, compared with 63 percent in 1980. For the same period, 89 percent of whites completed high school, compared with 80 percent in 1980. In terms of college attendance, the rate for black females steadily increased from 24 percent in 1970 to 31 percent in 1988. For black males, the percent attending college declined from 29 percent in 1970 to 25 percent in 1988. The poverty rate for black Americans in 1990 remained virtually the same as it had been for the past 20 years—nearly one-third.[8]

The 1990s: Some Progress, But Problems Remain

As we near the millennium, 28 percent of blacks still live in poverty, compared to 11 percent of whites.[9] While 12.9 percent of the employees in private companies are African American, only 5.3 percent hold managerial jobs.[10] Despite these problems, gains are being made at the highest levels of the corporate sector. According to Richard Parsons, president of Time Warner and one of the United States' most powerful black executives:

> *People of color are achieving corporate positions that their parents could never have dreamed of reaching, and in unprecedented numbers. Is this trend sweeping the land? No. Are there still problems? Yes. But there's no question that the group of black leaders in business is stronger than ever.*[11]

The following incident illustrates the irony inherent in the experiences of African Americans in the workplace. In 1994, six Texaco employees filed a class-action lawsuit charging racial discrimination in hiring practices and workplace treatment. In 1996, when a tape of Texaco executives surfaced containing racial slurs directed at employees, as well as evidence that the executives were planning to shred incriminating documents and withhold information from the plaintiff's lawyers, they settled the suit for $115 million.[12] When news of the tape became public, an activist friend called New York State Comptroller Carl McCall, the first African American to be elected to statewide office in New York, and asked him to join a picket line at the company's headquarters. McCall replied, "When you own 1 million shares of stock, you don't have to picket." McCall oversees a public pension fund that is one of the largest in the country and one of the few that is managed by an individual rather than by a committee. He simply called Texaco Chairman Peter Bijur to express his concern. Since then, Bijur has continued to update McCall regularly on the progress of Texaco's diversity plan.[13]

One of the most significant issues coming to a head in the 1990s has been the changing work-force composition. From reading most headlines, one would think that the public debate is exclusively about the role and progress of blacks. However, today's discrimination laws and affirmative action policies also cover more than 48 million white women, 10 million Hispanics, and 3 million Asians, in addition to 13 million blacks. Combined, they make up 54 percent of the labor force. From 1980 to 1990, the percentage of the work force composed of women grew from 42 to 45 percent; for blacks, from 9.4 to 10.1 percent; for Hispanics, from 5.6 to 7.5 percent; and for Asians, from 1.0 to 2.6 percent. The black, Hispanic, and Asian populations are all growing much more quickly than the white population. As competition for jobs grows, affirmative action policies sometimes pit these groups against each other.[14]

As the numbers and percentages of workers protected by discrimination laws continue to increase, following present trends, it is expected that civil rights issues will continue to be front-burner topics. Operating against these trends has been a growing sentiment against affirmative action. The challenge for business will be to assimilate an increasingly diverse work force while adopting a posture on affirmative action that does not engender additional resentful reactions on the part of the majority.

An indispensable way to understand the changing public policy with respect to employment discrimination is to examine the evolution of federal laws prohibiting discrimination. Once we have a better appreciation of the legal status of protected groups, we can more completely understand the complex issues that have arisen with respect to the evolving meaning of discrimination and its relationship to related work-force issues—in particular, affirmative action.

FEDERAL LAWS PROHIBITING DISCRIMINATION

This section provides an overview of the major laws that have been passed to protect workers against discrimination. We will concentrate our treatment on legislation at the federal level that has been created since the 1960s. We will discuss issues arising

SEARCH THE WEB

The Web site of the U.S. Equal Employment Opportunity Commission (EEOC) is a good source for updated information about employment discrimination and litigation (**www.eeoc.gov**). Visitors can find enforcement statistics, a technical assistance program, and information on how to file a charge of discrimination.

from the various forms of discrimination in more detail later in this chapter. We should keep in mind that there are a host of state and local laws that address many of these same topics, but space does not permit their consideration here. Our purpose in this section is to provide an overview of antidiscrimination laws and the major federal agencies that enforce those laws.

Title VII of the Civil Rights Act of 1964

Title VII of the Civil Rights Act of 1964, as amended, *prohibits discrimination* in hiring, promotion, discharge, pay, fringe benefits, and other aspects of employment on the basis of *race, color, religion, sex, or national origin.* Title VII was extended to cover federal, state, and local employers and educational institutions by the Equal Employment Opportunity Act of 1972. This amendment to Title VII also gave the Equal Employment Opportunity Commission (EEOC) the authority to file suits in federal district court against employers in the private sector on behalf of individuals whose charges had not been successfully conciliated. In 1978, Title VII was amended to include the Pregnancy Discrimination Act, which requires employers to treat pregnancy and pregnancy-related medical conditions the same as any other medical disability with respect to all terms and conditions of employment, including employee health benefits.[15] Figure 16–1 presents an overview of Title VII's coverage.

Age Discrimination in Employment Act of 1967

This law protects workers 40 years old and older from arbitrary age discrimination in hiring, discharge, pay, promotions, fringe benefits, and other aspects of employment. It is designed to promote employment of older people on the basis of ability rather than age and to help employers and workers find ways to meet problems arising from the impact of age on employment.[16]

Like the provisions of Title VII, the Age Discrimination in Employment Act does not apply where age is a ***bona fide occupational qualification (BFOQ)***—a qualification that might ordinarily be argued as being a basis for discrimination but for which a company can legitimately argue that it is job related and necessary. Neither does the act bar employers from differentiating among employees based on reasonable factors other than age.[17]

Equal Pay Act of 1963

As amended, this act prohibits sex discrimination in payment of wages to women and men who perform substantially equal work in the same establishment. Passage of this landmark law marked a significant milestone in helping women, who were the chief victims of unequal pay, to achieve equality in their paychecks.[18] Figure 16–2 summarizes other details of the Equal Pay Act of 1963.

Rehabilitation Act of 1973, Section 503

This law, as amended, prohibits job discrimination on the basis of a handicap. It applies to employers holding federal contracts or subcontracts. In addition, it

FIGURE 16–1   Title VII of the Civil Rights Act of 1964

EMPLOYMENT discrimination based on race, color, religion, sex, or national origin is prohibited by Title VII of the Civil Rights Act of 1964.

Title VII covers private employers, state and local governments, and educational institutions that have 15 or more employees. The federal government, private and public employment agencies, labor organizations, and joint labor–management committees for apprenticeship and training also must abide by the law.

It is illegal under Title VII to discriminate in:

- Hiring and firing;
- Compensation, assignment, or classification of employees;
- Transfer, promotion, layoff, or recall;
- Job advertisements;
- Recruitment;
- Testing;
- Use of company facilities;
- Training and apprenticeship programs;
- Fringe benefits;
- Pay, retirement plans, and disability leave; or
- Other terms and conditions of employment.

Under the law, pregnancy, childbirth, and related medical conditions must be treated the same as any other nonpregnancy-related illness or disability.

Title VII prohibits retaliation against a person who files a charge of discrimination, participates in an investigation, or opposes an unlawful employment practice.

Employment agencies may not discriminate in receiving, classifying, or referring applications for employment or in their job advertisements.

Labor unions may not discriminate in: accepting applications for membership; classifying members; referrals; training and apprenticeship programs; and in advertising for jobs. It is illegal for a labor union to cause or try to cause an employer to discriminate. It is also illegal for an employer to cause or try to cause a union to discriminate.

SOURCE: *Information for the Private Sector and State and Local Governments: EEOC* (Washington: Equal Employment Opportunity Commission), 6–7.

requires these employers to engage in affirmative action to employ the handicapped, a concept we will discuss later in this chapter. Related to this act is the Vietnam Era Veterans Readjustment Assistance Act of 1974, which also prohibits discrimination and requires affirmative action among federal contractors or subcontractors.[19]

Americans with Disabilities Act of 1990

The most significant labor and employment statute to be enacted in 15 years was the 1990 Americans with Disabilities Act (ADA). Although it was passed in July 1990, this act became effective for most businesses in July 1992, after the Equal Employment

---

FIGURE 16–2   Equal Pay Act of 1963

The EQUAL PAY ACT prohibits employers from discriminating between men and women on the basis of sex in the payment of wages where they perform substantially equal work under similar working conditions in the same establishment. The law also prohibits employers from reducing the wages of either sex to comply with the law.

A violation may exist where a different wage is paid to a predecessor or successor employee of the opposite sex. Labor organizations may not cause employers to violate the law.

Retaliation against a person who files a charge of equal pay discrimination, participates in an investigation, or opposes an unlawful employment practice also is illegal.

The law protects virtually all private employees, including executive, administrative, professional, and outside sales employees who are exempt from minimum wage and overtime laws. Most federal, state, and local government workers also are covered.

The law does not apply to pay differences based on factors other than sex, such as seniority, merit, or systems that determine wages based upon the quantity or quality of items produced or processed.

Many EPA violations may be violations of Title VII of the Civil Rights Act of 1964, which also prohibits sex-based wage discrimination. Such charges may be filed under both statutes.

SOURCE: *Information for the Private Sector and State and Local Governments: EEOC* (Washington: Equal Employment Opportunity Commission), 9.

Opportunity Commission had published preliminary regulations for its implementation. The ADA prohibits discrimination based on physical or mental disabilities in private places of employment and public accommodation, in addition to requiring transportation systems and communication systems to facilitate access for the disabled. The ADA is modeled after the Rehabilitation Act of 1973, which applies to federal contractors and grantees.[20]

Essentially, the ADA gives individuals with disabilities civil rights protections similar to those provided to individuals on the basis of race, sex, national origin, and religion. ADA applies not only to private employers but also to state and local governments, employment agencies, and labor unions. In July 1992, when the act went into effect, employers of 25 or more employees were covered. In 1995, the act began applying to employers of 15 to 24 employees as well.[21]

The ADA prohibits discrimination in all employment practices, including job application procedures, hiring, firing, advancement, compensation, training, and other terms, conditions, and privileges of employment. Under the act, employment discrimination against "qualified individuals with disabilities" is prohibited. This includes people who have physical or mental impairments that substantially limit one or more major life activities, such as seeing, hearing, speaking, walking, breathing, performing manual tasks, learning, caring for oneself, and working.[22] Uncertainty over the definition of "disability" sent the ADA to the courts for clarification. In June 1998, the Supreme Court decided that the definition of "disability" included both major and minor impairments. Under this ruling, the ADA applies to disabilities as diverse as HIV, diabetes, cancer, dyslexia, and bad backs.[23] Figure 16–3 provides a brief overview of the Americans with Disabilities Act.

FIGURE 16–3   The Americans with Disabilities Act

Title I of the Americans with Disabilities Act of 1990, which took effect July 26, 1992, prohibits private employers, state and local governments, employment agencies, and labor unions from discriminating against qualified individuals with disabilities in job application procedures, hiring, firing, advancement, compensation, job training, and other terms, conditions, and privileges of employment. An individual with a disability is a person who:

- Has a physical or mental impairment that substantially limits one or more major life activities;

- Has a record of such an impairment; or

- Is regarded as having such an impairment.

A qualified employee or applicant with a disability is an individual who, with or without reasonable accommodation, can perform the essential functions of the job in question. Reasonable accommodation may include, but is not limited to:

- Making existing facilities used by employees readily accessible to and usable by persons with disabilities;

- Job restructuring, modifying work schedules, reassignment to a vacant position;

- Acquiring or modifying equipment or devices; adjusting or modifying examinations, training materials, or policies; and providing qualified readers or interpreters.

An employer is required to make an accommodation to the known disability of a qualified applicant or employee if it would not impose an "undue hardship" on the operation of the employer's business. Undue hardship is defined as an action requiring significant difficulty or expense when considered in light of factors such as an employer's size, its financial resources, and the nature and structure of its operation.

An employer is not required to lower quality or production standards to make an accommodation, nor is an employer obligated to provide personal use items such as glasses or hearing aids.

SOURCE: EEOC Fact Sheet (Washington: Equal Employment Opportunity Commission).

The ADA has quickly become a controversial law. In the early years following the act's passage, news reports were filled with stories of frivolous lawsuits and outrageous abuses of the protections offered by the ADA. Many fear these abuses created a backlash against people with disabilities. Kathi Wolfe, a Virginia writer with a visual handicap, recalls having an able-bodied writer tell her, "With the ADA, I'll bet editors are scared to reject your stuff. They'd be afraid you'd sue them." In another instance, a drugstore clerk said to Wolfe, "Please don't sue us because we don't have Braille signs." Knowing that two-thirds of severely disabled individuals remain unemployed despite the ADA, Wolfe wonders if the ADA has made employers more hesitant than ever to hire individuals with disabilities.[24]

Although the stories of ADA excess remain, the evidence supporting them is thin. In a 1998 "Dateline" report for NBC News, John Hockenberry tracked down several well-known "legends of the ADA," including a 400-pound subway worker who sued for being denied a conductor's position because he could not fit in the cab, a man who had a deep-seated need to bring a gun to work, and a dentist whose disability would not let him stop grabbing women. Hockenberry found that the first two cases were thrown out by the EEOC and that, in the third case, the dentist never actually sued because he was self-employed and so was never fired. The difficulty these cases had in getting past the EEOC appears to be typical. Of the 90,000 complaints received by the EEOC, only 250 have been filed in court.[25] Of the cases that make it to court, few are won by the plaintiffs. In a 1998 study, the American Bar Association (ABA), which reviewed more than 1,200 ADA cases filed since 1992, found that employers won 92 percent of the cases decided by a judge and 86 percent of the cases decided by the EEOC. Don Donaldson, risk manager at the Jacksonville (FL) Port Authority, said "The survey findings to me are not surprising because I've been monitoring developments and trends on this issue . . . if employers make reasonable accommodations to disabled workers, then the courts would likely rely on common sense and rule in the employer's favor."[26]

Donaldson's remarks help to explain why the ADA found a high level of support in a 1995 Louis Harris survey of corporate employers. These corporate executives, 81 percent of whom had modified their offices since the ADA went into effect, estimated the average cost of accommodation as $223 per disabled employee. About half of the executives (48 percent) said the ADA increased their costs a little, 82 percent reported no change in costs, and 7 percent reported that their costs increased "a lot." Most of the executives said the ADA should be strengthened or kept as it is, while only 12 percent felt it should be weakened or repealed.[27]

Civil Rights Act of 1991

In 1990 and 1991, civil rights bills were debated in Congress. The proposed bills were aimed primarily at restoring and strengthening civil rights laws and interpretations that banned discrimination in employment, many of which had been overturned by earlier U.S. Supreme Court rulings.

Finally, a bill, with some modifications, was introduced as the Civil Rights Act of 1991. Throughout 1991, a partisan debate between Democrats and Republicans continued on the proposed civil rights legislation. Supporters of the legislation argued that it would not mandate hiring quotas, but detractors believed that quotas would be necessitated in its implementation.

The Civil Rights Act of 1991 was passed. The primary objective of the 1991 Civil Rights Act was to provide increased financial damages and jury trials in cases of intentional discrimination relating to sex, religion, race, disability, and national origin. Under Title VII, monetary awards were limited to such items as back pay, lost benefits, and attorney fees and costs. The new act permitted both compensatory and punitive damages to be awarded. In addition, charges of unintentional discrimination will be more difficult for employers to defend, because the act shifts the burden of proof back to the employer. Initial amounts of compensatory and punitive damages an employee could receive were set at $50,000 to $300,000. The 1991 act also altered parts of several Supreme Court decisions that had once been considered to be management victories.[28]

The laws we have just discussed constitute the backbone of federal efforts to prevent employment discrimination. Several executive orders issued by the president of the United States also prohibit discrimination. However, because these executive orders also contain provisions for affirmative action, we will discuss them during our treatment of affirmative action later in this chapter.

Equal Employment Opportunity Commission

As the major federal body created to administer and enforce job bias laws, the Equal Employment Opportunity Commission (EEOC) deserves special consideration. Several other federal agencies also are charged with enforcing certain aspects of the discrimination laws and executive orders, but we will restrict our discussion to the EEOC because it is the major agency.

The EEOC has five commissioners and a general counsel appointed by the president and confirmed by the Senate. The five-member commission is responsible for making equal employment opportunity policy and approving all litigation the commission undertakes. The EEOC staff receives and investigates employment discrimination charges/complaints. If the commission finds reasonable cause to believe that unlawful discrimination has occurred, its staff attempts to conciliate the charges/ complaints. When conciliation is not achieved, the EEOC may file lawsuits in federal district court against employers. Private employers may be sued under Title VII, but only the Justice Department may sue a state or local government for a violation of Title VII.[29]

To provide some appreciation of the kinds of discrimination cases handled by the EEOC, Figure 16–4 presents a breakdown of the job-bias claims filed with the EEOC from 1991 to 1997. The increase in disability claims reflects the implementation of the Americans with Disabilities Act in July 1992.

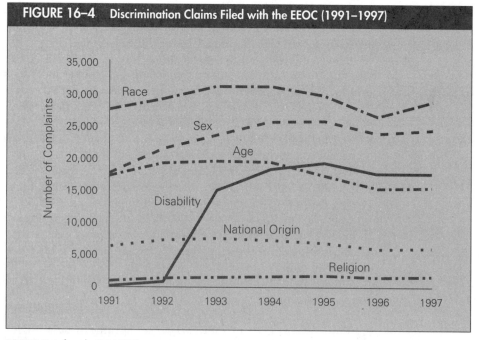

FIGURE 16–4   Discrimination Claims Filed with the EEOC (1991–1997)

SOURCE: Data from the U.S. EEOC.

Like other federal regulatory bodies we have discussed, such as the EPA, FTC, and OSHA, the EEOC has had mixed success over the years. Its fortunes, successes, and failures have been somewhat dictated by the times, the administration in office, and the philosophy and zeal of its chairperson. Over the course of its existence, the EEOC has at various times been criticized for mismanagement, overspending, leniency, zealousness, ineptness, inefficiency, and an assortment of other charges. During the late 1970s it was thought that the EEOC was on a "witch hunt," looking for violations so it could punish business for its past wrongs. Business thought this was unfair, because it believed it had made more progress on the EEO front than in any other sector in which federal regulations existed.[30]

In the 1980s, the Reagan administration set a new course for the EEOC. By 1990, the agency had (1) eliminated the use of minority hiring goals and timetables used by employers to correct racial and ethnic disparities, (2) largely abandoned class-action lawsuits that relied on statistical evidence to prove widespread discrimination at large companies, and (3) yielded the EEOC's once-dominant role on civil rights initiatives to the Justice Department. The prevailing philosophy was to direct and support lawsuits on behalf of only those individuals who could show that they had been personally hurt by discrimination.[31]

When President Clinton took office in 1992, he brought with him a revitalized concept of what the EEOC and the Justice Department ought to be doing in their crackdown against employment discrimination. All the nation's civil rights enforcers—the Justice Department, the U.S. Commission on Civil Rights, and the Labor Department—joined efforts with the EEOC to step up enforcement of business discrimination laws. Among the crackdown's targets were unsettled discrimination lawsuits against major employers, polluters who dump their muck in minority neighborhoods, banks whose loan departments redline poor areas, and other forms of day-to-day discrimination.[32]

The renewed effort, combined with a broadened mandate, resulted in an upsurge of cases. In fiscal year 1991, there were 63,898 new cases. By fiscal year 1994, there were 91,189 new cases. This increase in the number of new cases coincided with a reduction in staffing levels, which were at an all-time low. These combined trends resulted in a backlog of cases, which peaked at 110,000.

Through an influx of capital from Congress, overall efficiency improvements, and efforts to use alternative dispute resolution (ADR), the backlog decreased by 45 percent and stood at a little over 61,000 in 1998.[33] In 1998, President Clinton nominated Ida L. Castro to be the new EEOC commissioner. At this writing, the appointment had not been confirmed, leaving the EEOC with acting commissioner Paul Igasaki, who was active in instituting the EEOC reforms that lessened the backlog, and two other commissioners. In the Senate confirmation/oversight hearing, Senator Barbara Mikulski (D-Maryland) argued for quick action, because three commissioners is the bare minimum of a quorum for the EEOC. Senator Mikulski warned, "If the commission loses its quorum of three members, it will be a travesty. The commission will not be able to hear new litigation, enter new contracts, or adopt new regulations or guidelines. Much of its work will come to a grinding halt."[34] At this writing, no new commissioners have been confirmed.

The EEOC continues to attract controversy. Considerable criticism arose over a recent decision regarding the Exxon Corporation. After the Valdez disaster, in which a tanker captain ran aground and spilled 11 million gallons of crude oil into the Prince William Sound, Exxon instituted a policy that declared tanker captain positions off limits for anyone with a history of any form of substance abuse. In 1997, the EEOC sued the company under the ADA, claiming that the company's policy discriminated against about 50 employees who once had drug or alcohol problems but were since rehabilitated. In *Forbes,* David Price said, "Big companies like Exxon can afford to pay these fines and put up with expensive red tape and legal costs. Owners of small businesses cannot. Talk about discrimination."[35]

Despite the criticism and the lack of a full complement of commissioners, the work of the EEOC continues and appears slated for growth. In 1998 alone, the EEOC broadened its scope by extending equal employment rights to temporary workers and ruling that qualified individuals with psychiatric disabilities were protected under the ADA.[36] The courts and Congress also opened new arenas for the EEOC. In March 1998, the Supreme Court ruled that same-sex sexual harassment is covered under Title VII of the Civil Rights Act.[37] Also, in response to an increasing number of complaints of religious bias at work, Congress is considering the Workplace Religious Freedom Act, which would make it more difficult for companies to assert that accommodation of a religion would present an undue hardship.[38] Each of these developments will add new cases to an already overburdened system.

In fiscal year 1990, the EEOC had 62,135 claims, but by fiscal year 1997 that number had risen to over 80,000. In 1980, EEOC staffing was at an all-time full-time equivalent (FTE)[39] high of 3,390, but by 1998 that number had dropped to 2,586 (a 20-year low).[40] President Clinton proposed a $37 million increase in the EEOC budget for 1999. The GOP leadership placed two conditions on the approval of the increase: (1) The increase must be used to clean up the backlog of cases rather than seek out new investigations, and (2) the EEOC must drop its proposal to start using "testers" (decoy job applicants) to determine if a firm discriminates in employment.[41] As of this writing, no action on the proposal has been taken.

EXPANDED MEANINGS OF DISCRIMINATION

Over the years, it has been left to the courts to define the word "discrimination," because it was not defined in Title VII. Over time, it has become apparent that two specific kinds of discrimination have been identified. These two kinds are known as disparate treatment and disparate impact.

Disparate Treatment

Initially, the word "discrimination" meant the use of race, color, religion, sex, or national origin as a basis for treating people differently or unequally. This form of discrimination became known as *unequal treatment,* or **disparate treatment**. Examples of disparate treatment might include refusing to consider blacks for a job, paying women less than men for the same work, or supporting any decision rule with a racial or sexual premise or cause.[42] According to this common-sense view of discrimination, the employer was allowed to impose any criteria so long as they were imposed on all groups alike.[43] This view of discrimination equated nondiscrimination with color-blind decision making. In other words, to avoid this kind of discrimination, it meant that all groups or individuals had to be treated equally, without regard for color, sex, or other characteristics.[44]

Disparate Impact

Congress's intent in prohibiting discrimination was to eliminate practices that contributed to economic inequality. What it found was that, although companies could adhere to the disparate treatment definition of discrimination, this did not eliminate all of the economic inequalities it was intended to address. For example, a company could use two neutral, color-blind criteria for selection: a high school diploma and a standardized ability test. Blacks and whites could be treated the same under the criteria, but the problem arose when it became apparent that the policy of equal treatment resulted in *unequal consequences* for blacks and whites. Blacks were less likely to have high school diplomas, and blacks who took the test were less likely than whites to pass it. Therefore, a second, more expanded idea of what constituted discrimination was thought to be needed.

The Supreme Court had to decide whether an action was discriminatory if it resulted in unequal consequences in the *Griggs v. Duke Power Company* case in 1971.[45] In this case, the court concluded that it was the *consequences* of an employer's actions, not the employer's intentions, that determined whether discrimination had taken place. If any employment practice or test had an adverse or differential effect on minorities, then it was a discriminatory practice. An unequal impact, or ***disparate impact***, as this new kind of discrimination came to be known, simply meant that fewer minorities were included in the outcome of the test or the hiring or promotion practice than would be expected by their numerical proportion. The court also held that a policy or procedure with a disparate impact would be permissible if the employer could demonstrate that it was a business- or job-related necessity. In the Duke Power case, for example, a high school diploma and good scores on a general intelligence test were *not* shown to have a clearly demonstrable relationship to successful performance on the job under consideration.[46]

The concept of "unequal impact" is quite significant, because it runs counter to so many traditional employment practices. There are many other examples. The minimum height and weight requirements of some police departments have unequal impact and have been struck down by courts because they tend to disproportionately screen out women, Orientals, and Hispanics.[47] The practice of discharging employees who have had their wages garnished to pay off debts has also been struck down, because it falls heavily on minorities.[48] Several Supreme Court rulings have addressed the issue of the kind of evidence needed to document or prove discrimination.

With at least two different ways in which to commit discrimination, managers have had to be extremely careful, because practically any action they take may possibly have discriminatory effects. Figure 16–5 summarizes the characteristics of disparate treatment and disparate impact.

FIGURE 16–5 Two Kinds of Employment Discrimination	
Definition 1 **Disparate Treatment**	**Definition 2** **Disparate Impact**
Direct discrimination	Indirect discrimination
Unequal treatment	Unequal consequences or results
Decision rules with a racial/sexual premise or cause	Decision rules with racial/sexual consequences or results
Intentional discrimination	Unintentional discrimination
Prejudiced actions	Neutral, color-blind actions
Different standards for different groups	Same standards, but different consequences for different groups

SOURCE: James Ledvinka and Vida G. Scarpello, *Federal Regulation of Personnel and Human Resources Management,* 2nd ed. (Boston: PWS-Kent, 1991), 48.

ISSUES IN EMPLOYMENT DISCRIMINATION

We have identified the essentials of the major laws on discrimination and traced the evolution of the concept of discrimination. Now it is useful to discuss briefly the different issues that are related to the types of discrimination we have discussed. It is also important to indicate some of the particular problems that have arisen with respect to each of the different issues.

The Two Nations of Black America

In a 1998 essay for the *Brookings Review,* Henry Louis Gates, Jr., describes the present day as the "best of times and the worst of times" for the African American community. Gates, the W. E. B. Dubois Professor of the Humanities and chairman of the Department of Afro-American Studies at Harvard University, profiles the "two nations of Black America" that are separated by money, power, and education:

> We have the largest black, middle class in our history and the largest black underclass. In 1990, 2,280,000 black men were in prison, or probation, or parole, while 23,000 earned a college degree. That's a ratio of 99 to 1 compared with a ratio of 6 to 1 for white men.[49]

The two nations are reflected in the attitudes of black professionals toward corporate America. In a 1998 *Fortune* poll, most blacks indicated that they felt discrimination was still common in the workplace. However, more than two-thirds felt optimistic about the future of their careers. *Fortune* called the combination of optimism and skepticism a "post-Texaco hangover."[50]

There is no shortage of statistics to support Gates's argument that these are the "worst of times." To commemorate the thirtieth anniversary of the Kerner Commission Report, which warned that the nation was "moving toward two societies, one black and one white—separate and unequal," the Eisenhower Foundation prepared a 1998 update, "The Millennium Breach." In it, the authors decried the economic status and racial divide of the inner city. They found that in a time of "full employment," unemployment in the inner city is at crisis levels. Racial minorities were shown to suffer disproportionately from child poverty, which increased more than 20 percent during the 1980s. In fact, in 1998 the U.S. child poverty rate stood at four times the average of most Western European countries.[51]

What is surprising to many people is the wealth of statistics that support Gates's arguments that these are the "best of times." The number of blacks going to college grew from 14.2 percent in 1970 to 44.2 percent in 1990. Black men in technical jobs earn almost as much as white men, while college-educated black women earn more than their college-educated white counterparts. College-educated black men are about equally likely as college-educated white men to hold managerial positions, and college-educated black female managers and executives earn 10 percent more than their white counterparts. The trends among youth also show more promise for the future. In 1970, the work force contained five times as many black high-school dropouts as black college graduates. Now, the percentage of black students dropping out is only 5 percent, not far from the 4 percent reported for white students. Smoking among black high-school seniors has dropped precipitously, from 24.9 percent in 1977 to 4.1 percent in 1993. In comparison, white high-school seniors had only a 7.5 percent decline during the same period (from 28.9 to 21.4 percent).[52]

The two nations can exist simultaneously, because the same glass may be half-full or half-empty, depending on your perspective. For example, the educational achievements of black students provide both good and bad news. In 1990, the good news was that the number of 17-year-old blacks who were able to read at an adept level had doubled from 1970 figures. The bad news was that only 20 percent were able to read at that level in 1990, while 48 percent of all American students measured could.[53] Why does the public assume the bad news is true and find the good news surprising? Although most poor people in the United States are white, the media has tended to focus on blacks when covering stories about poverty. Martin Gilens, a political scientist, studied 4 years of stories from major magazines and 5 years of news-show broadcasts on the major networks. Of the poor people in the United States, 29 percent were black, but all the news magazines portrayed the majority of the poor as black, ranging from 53 percent at *U.S. News & World Report* to 66 percent at *Newsweek*. At the three major television networks, 65.2 percent of the people portrayed as poor in the news were black. The only time blacks were underrepresented was when stories were about the more sympathetic working poor or elderly. Although 42 percent of poor African Americans work, only 12 percent were portrayed as "working poor" in the media. Similarly, 8 percent of poor black Americans are elderly, but less than 1 percent of the people portrayed as elderly poor were black.[54]

In summary, although many blacks are succeeding and moving ahead, poverty hangs over many others and much media coverage gives the appearance that progress is not being made. Civil rights leaders, politicians, and academics debate fiercely the causes of and possible solutions to the problem. Even black leadership is fractured into at least two camps—those who hold that lingering racism and cramped economic opportunities are the problem and those who say that racism is not the only critical factor. People in this camp point also to the valorization of the ghetto culture and the need for blacks to take the initiative and break the cycle of poverty. The role that business could and should play remains at the forefront of this debate and is likely to be there for the foreseeable future.[55]

The Case of Hispanics

The growth rate among Hispanics in the United States exceeds the growth rate among blacks. Hispanics now account for about 7 to 8 percent of the U.S. work force, and this number is increasing. Hispanics hold only about 4 percent of white-collar jobs and frequently tend to be found in agricultural, janitorial, and other types of menial labor. Hispanics face a different set of problems than blacks. For many Hispanics, language is a barrier to good jobs. Another problem is employers' fear of hiring illegal immigrants. Although affirmative action has given Hispanics a higher profile, discrimination against them is still considered to be a critical problem. In some states, such as California, tensions among Hispanics and blacks over jobs is an increasingly frequent problem.[56]

Statistics from the U.S. Census Bureau point to Hispanics becoming the largest minority category within the next decade. Already, the nation's Hispanic preschoolers outnumber African Americans under age 5, making them the leading edge of the trend. From 1990 to 1994, the Hispanic population grew 17 percent while the black population grew 7 percent. The Census Bureau projects that high birth rates combined with a continuing influx of immigrants will close the gap between Hispanics and blacks by the year 2006, if present trends continue.[57]

Asian Image of Model Minority

Asian Americans have a problem that is unique to U.S. minority groups: a stereotype that may be too positive. Aggregate data about educational achievement, occupational distribution, annual household income, and other indicators of success show that Asian Americans, particularly East Asian Americans and Asian Indian immigrants and descendants of immigrants from Confucian countries like China, Japan, or Korea, have outperformed other minority groups and achieved a level of success comparable to that of white workers. As a result, the popular press, many pundits, and various policy makers have argued that Asian Americans represent an ideal that should be emulated by other minorities (i.e., Asian Americans are the "Model Minority").[58]

Recently, scholars in various disciplines, including Asian American studies, have refuted this characterization. They argue that aggregated data hide the impact of such critical factors as highly selective immigration policies, high numbers of hours worked, and high numbers of individuals per household. When these critics have disaggregated the data used to support the Model Minority characterization, they have found a bimodal distribution: One group of well-educated, higher paid Asian American professionals do well until they reach the glass ceiling; the other group is low skilled, low paid, and generally disadvantaged.[59]

A major report by the Commission on Civil Rights concluded, "Anti-Asian activity in the form of violence, vandalism, harassment, and intimidation continues to occur across the nation."[60] In the 1990s, Asian Americans started relying more on the courts to battle discrimination and hate crimes. This seems to signal a growing realization by Asian Americans that their past reluctance to apply pressure through the legal system has placed them at a disadvantage.[61] It has been argued that many of the problems of Asian Americans stem from their image as a model minority, which embraces discipline, hard work, and education. This image has a downside, because quiet achievement can be interpreted as passivity. The Asian American response to this has been to avoid confrontation and simply work harder. It is estimated that the presence of Asian Americans will double to 10 million by the end of the century, and so their treatment in the workplace will continue to be an issue for years to come.

Issues of Sex Discrimination

Issues surrounding sex discrimination are quite different from issues involving race, color, and national origin. Statistics show that women are flooding the job market, boosting economic growth, and helping to reshape the economy dramatically. In 1973, women earned about 57 percent of what men earned. This figure had grown to 60 percent by 1980 and to about 64 percent by 1985.[62] By 1994, women earned approximately 77 percent of men's annual income, but the pay gap then widened a bit in 1998, when women's median income lowered to 75 percent of men's. Throughout the 1990s, women's pay remained relatively constant, at approximately three-fourths that of men's.[63]

The major issues for women today include (1) getting into professional and managerial positions and out of traditional female-dominated positions, (2) achieving pay commensurate with that of men, (3) eliminating sexual harassment, and (4) being able to take maternity leave without losing their jobs. Significant progress is being made on most of these fronts.

Moving into Professional/Managerial Positions

Statistics show that women are moving quickly into formerly male-dominated professional and managerial jobs. They are making inroads into professional jobs for which education is a major prerequisite. In 1972, only about 4 percent of MBA graduates were women. This figure now exceeds 33 percent. Similarly, in 1972, women occupied about 20 percent of nonclerical white-collar jobs. This figure grew to more than 46 percent in 1994.[64] In 1972, 17 percent of the managerial jobs were held by women, but by 1995, that number had increased to 42.7 percent. Although women have flooded the managerial pipeline, concerns remain about a "glass ceiling" that prohibits women from reaching the top levels of corporate management. In 1995, less than 3 percent of women had reached the highest levels of corporate leadership and less than 2 percent held the most highly compensated officer positions in Fortune 500 companies. Only four of the Fortune 1000 CEO positions are held by women.[65]

A recent study asked Fortune 1000 male CEOs and senior-level female executives for their views on why glass ceilings exist. Their views differed. The male CEOs blamed the glass ceiling on the women's lack of experience and time "in the pipeline." The female executives disagreed sharply, citing an exclusionary corporate culture as the reason for women's lack of advancement to senior positions. They described a corporate playing field that was not level due to negative preconceptions and stereotypes. Despite their differences about the causes of the glass ceiling, the male CEOs and female executives agreed that both individuals and the organization are responsible for creating positive organizational changes.[66]

Comparable Worth

Pay equity can be approached from two directions: equal pay and comparable worth. Equal pay argues that workers doing the same job should receive the same pay, irrespective of gender. Comparable worth presents a more controversial solution: Workers doing different jobs should receive the same pay if those different jobs contribute equally to the firm's performance. As previously discussed, the Equal Pay Act requires that people holding equal positions receive equal compensation. Despite the Act's existence, however, the pay of men and women remains disparate, due largely to the wage effects of labor market segregation, whereby jobs traditionally held by women pay less than their requirements or contributions might indicate. The persistent disparity between men's and women's median incomes has led some legal scholars and women's advocates to recommend comparable worth.[67]

The idea of comparable worth was born in the public sector. Advocates of comparable worth argue that differences in seniority and education cannot explain the fact that women generally earn only about three-fourths of what men do. They argue that certain jobs are paid less just because they are traditionally held by women. Opponents of comparable worth counter that comparable worth would mean replacing market forces with regulation by government wage-setting boards.[68] These opponents argue that it is not pragmatic to apply comparable worth to the private sector, because the private sector lacks the public sector's civil service categories, which are fixed by legislation.[69]

The current state of comparable worth in the United States suggests very limited growth and acceptance. The progress that has been made has been restricted to the public sector and has been more in the form of pay equity adjustments than of full-blown comparable-worth programs. The states of Washington and Minnesota have experienced some success with efforts to close the salary gap between male and female jobs. One expert points to the state of Minnesota as the most successful institution of pay equity in state and local government. Minnesota not only was among the first to achieve pay equity for its own employees, but it then adopted legislation requiring all jurisdictions within the state—cities, counties, school boards—to report plans for implementation by 1985 and to have completed implementation by 1991. Some localities, such as San Jose and Alameda counties in California and also San Francisco, have been successful with pay equity plans, but their route to success required a coalition of women's organizations combined with a powerful labor union to achieve results. Such efforts have failed to penetrate the private sector as state and federal laws have relied on more traditional means to achieve equity.[70]

Sexual Harassment

A 1998 nationwide survey showed that 4 out of every 10 employees have seen ethical or legal problems at work in the past 2 years. The most common problem was sexual harassment; nineteen percent of the respondents reported that they had seen it.[71]

It is difficult to document fully the extent to which *sexual harassment* has become a major issue in American business today. With the increasing number of women in the work force, however, it is understandable why sexual harassment has become a much-debated issue. Sexual harassment has been a high-profile issue ever since 1991, when Supreme Court nominee Clarence Thomas was accused of sexual harass-

What Constitutes Harassment?

Last spring, I had a part-time job at a newly opened local gift store. Approximately 2 months after I started working there, a new manager was hired. This manager took the store by surprise. Up until she was hired, the store was run by the owners in a very informal but efficient way. Once the new manager came to work, normal work duties that were often fun became regimented and hectic. The new manager had a militaristic style of management, as opposed to the "laid-back" attitude of the owners. Since I was working for extra cash and did not have the option of quitting my job, I quickly adjusted to the new manager's style. Shortly after the manager began, our store's inventory/computer manager quit. The manager said that the inventory/computer manager quit because she could not handle the work. Somehow, I knew that this was not true, because the inventory manager had been at the store since it had opened and the owners relied on her implicitly.

After this first lie of the manager came others. Soon, I had the owners asking me why I did not check in certain inventories when I had been told to do so. Incidentally, I had done these tasks, but the store manager had misplaced the inventory list. In the meantime, while these manager/employee problems were occurring, the store manager was having difficulties in dealing with one of the owners. The owner, a domineering male with a heart of gold, was having trouble communicating with the new manager. Every suggestion or comment that he made was construed by her as threatening. She would say this to me and the other employees as well. Since I was good friends with the other part-time employees, I knew that we all respected this particular owner and had never felt threatened by him, but we all saw him get upset with the store manager and perhaps give her a hard time about the way she was running his store. After about 2 months, the store manager was fired. Within the next week, our owner was slapped with a sexual harassment suit. Over the next month, all employees had to give testimonies of their perspectives on the situation. When the affidavits came back for us to sign, we all said that we had not witnessed the owner harassing the store manager. My dilemma is this: A signature on an affidavit indicates that everything stated in the document is true, but I felt that I had seen the owner harass the manager. In retrospect, I felt that the harassment was justified. I felt that the store manager deserved what she got and did not feel that the owner was out of line. Should I have signed an affidavit that may not have been completely true?

1. Does it sound as though sexual harassment has occurred in this case?

2. How would you respond to the request to sign the affidavit? Explain.

Contributed Anonymously

ment by Anita Hill, a former employee of the EEOC. The country witnessed days of televised hearings over the issue, and the event created a springboard for many women to come forward and publicly claim that they had been sexually harassed by coworkers in the past. The country was divided in its opinion of whether Hill had actually been sexually harassed by Thomas 10 years earlier, and Thomas was eventually confirmed to a seat on the highest court. The Thomas Hearings were a watershed event for sexual harassment. The hearings catapulted sexual harassment into the limelight, just as the explosion at the Union Carbide plant in Bhopal, India, and the massive oil spill from the Exxon Valdez made workplace safety and environmental issues, respectively, national concerns.

Since 1991, allegations of sexual harassment against other public figures, including Senator Bob Packwood and President Clinton, have kept the issue on the front burner. Adding to the fuel of debate was the 1994 book by Michael Crichton entitled *Disclosure,* which was also made into a major motion picture. In *Disclosure,* there was a twist of events as a male executive charged his female boss with sexual harassment. This movie staked claim to the view that sexual harassment can be perpetrated by men or women, although typically it is carried out by men against women.

Data from the EEOC report an escalating number of sexual harassment complaints. In 1988, about 5,500 complaints were filed. By 1992, this number had risen to 10,000.[72] With this background, let us now consider what Title VII and the EEOC have to say about sexual harassment as a type of sex discrimination.

The EEOC defines sexual harassment in the following way:

> *Unwelcome sexual advances, requests for sexual favors, and other verbal or physical conduct of a sexual nature constitute sexual harassment when submission to or rejection of this conduct explicitly or implicitly affects an individual's employment, unreasonably interferes with an individual's work performance, or creates an intimidating, hostile, or offensive work environment.*

Implicit in this definition are two broad types of sexual harassment. First is what has been called *quid pro quo* harassment. This is a situation where something is given or received for something else. For example, a boss may make it explicit or implicit that a sexual favor is expected if the employee wants a pay raise or a promotion. Second is what has been referred to as *hostile work environment* harassment. In this type, nothing is given or received, but the employee perceives a hostile or offensive work environment by virtue of uninvited sexually oriented behaviors or materials being present in the workplace. Examples of this might include sexual teasing or jokes or sexual materials, such as pictures or cartoons, being present in the workplace.

Figure 16–6 lists the kinds of experiences women are typically talking about when they say they have been sexually harassed.

Meritor Savings Bank v. Vinson.   Prior to 1986, sexual harassment was not a specific violation of federal law. In a landmark case, however, the Supreme Court ruled in 1986 in *Meritor Savings Bank v. Vinson* that sexual harassment was a violation of Title VII. In this case, the court ruled that the creation of a "hostile environment" through sexual harassment violates Title VII, even in the absence of economic harm to the employee or a demand for sexual favors in exchange for promotions, raises, or the like. Remedies made available to the victims at that time included back pay, damages for emotional stress, and attorney fees.[73] We should reiterate that sexual harassment can be committed by women against men or by individuals of the same sex.

Harris v. Forklift Systems.   The stage was set for another major Supreme Court ruling (*Harris v. Forklift Systems*) in 1993 in what many were hoping would more clearly define what constituted sexual harassment. The court agreed to hear the case of a Tennessee woman, Teresa Harris, who claimed her boss (at Forklift Systems) made

---

FIGURE 16–6   Examples of Sexual Harassment Complaints

- Being subjected to sexually suggestive remarks and propositions
- Being sent on unnecessary errands through work areas where men have an added opportunity to stare
- Being subjected to sexual innuendo and joking
- Being touched by a boss while working
- Coworkers' "remarks" about a person sexually cooperating with the boss
- Suggestive looks and gestures
- Deliberate touching and "cornering"
- Suggestive body movements
- Sexually oriented materials being circulated around the office
- Pornographic cartoons and pictures posted or present in work areas
- Pressure for dates and sexual favors
- Boss's cruelty after sexual advances are resisted
- A boss rubbing employee's back while she is typing

Note: It should be noted that these are "complaints." Whether each item turns out to be sexual harassment or not in the eyes of the law is determined in an official hearing or trial.

---

sexual remarks about her clothing, asked her to retrieve coins from his pants pockets, and once joked about going to a motel "to negotiate your raise." The lower courts had thrown out her lawsuit, arguing that she had only been offended and had not suffered any "severe psychological injury."[74]

The Supreme Court overturned the lower courts and ruled that employers can be forced to pay damages even if the workers suffered no proven psychological harm. Justice Sandra Day O'Connor, who wrote the court's unanimous decision, said that employees can be awarded damages as long as their work "environment would reasonably be perceived, and is perceived, as hostile or abusive."[75]

Another key part of the Supreme Court's ruling addressed the question of "from whose perspective is sexual harassment to be judged?" Historically, the courts had used the common-law concept of a "reasonable man." A 1991 appeals court ruling had argued that the standards of a "reasonable woman" should prevail when women charged harassment. In *Harris v. Forklift Systems*, however, the Supreme Court argued that a "reasonable *person*" standard would prevail and that it would more appropriately focus on the conduct, not the victim.

Finally, the Supreme Court's ruling on the question of "what constitutes sexual harassment" was less than definitive. Again, Justice O'Connor wrote:

> *Whether an environment is "hostile" or "abusive" can be determined only by looking at all the circumstances. These may include the frequency of the discriminatory conduct; its severity; whether it is physically threatening or humiliating, or a mere offensive utterance; and whether it unreasonably interferes with an employee's work performance.*[76]

ETHICS IN PRACTICE

Matters of the Heart

During a recent summer, I worked at the liquor store of my best friend's stepfather. Sometimes during work hours there would be just the two of us in the store. On numerous occasions he made sexual comments to me about my body. He would also "accidentally" brush up against the front of me. Once he called me into his office to show me graphic pictures of girls in a pornographic magazine and asked why I had not posed for one. He seemed consumed with the female anatomy. The obvious ethical question forced me to choose between my friendship with the girl I had grown up with and my self-respect, which was severely restricted at that job. A temporary hold on my ideas won out over losing the best friend I had ever had.

1. Has sexual harassment taken place in this case, or is it just my imagination?

2. What would you have done in this situation?

    a. Continued this job without confronting the owner.

    b. Quit and acted as if nothing had happened.

    c. Confronted the owner to see if anything changed.

    d. Other. (Describe.)

Contributed Anonymously

Corporate Responses to Sexual Harassment.   It is clear that sexual harassment is legally and ethically wrong. Most major companies have already begun taking steps to raise the corporate consciousness about sexual harassment. These efforts include, but are not limited to, letters from the CEO, workshops and training as to what constitutes sexual harassment, policies highlighted in company handbooks, worker orientation programs, films, and role-playing exercises.[77] Other companies are employing sexual harassment audits, which pose a series of questions designed to root out discriminatory practices.[78] Following are some other suggested guidelines:[79]

- Educate employees as to prohibited conduct.

- Reexamine, revise, and reissue written policy statements on the subject.

- Make employees aware of how to obtain redress if harassed.

- Introduce, or update, training programs.

- Make certain that environmental harassment ("hostile environment") is absent from the workplace.

- Get input from women employees and union leaders.

In 1998, Mitsubishi Motors agreed to make a record $34 million payment to settle a sexual harassment case involving female factory workers at a plant in Illinois. In

1997, Mitsubishi made a reported $9.5 million payment to settle a separate lawsuit with similar charges.[80] It is not surprising, therefore, that a 1998 survey by the National Association of Independent Insurers found that insurers offering sexual harassment coverage have been writing more policies and seeing more claims over the past 5 years.[81] Clearly, companies are taking a two-pronged approach to sexual harassment, adopting policies that discourage harassment while protecting themselves from the financial costs that can result from sexual harassment lawsuits.

The huge surge in sexual harassment claims that took place in the early 1990s has slowed, but the number of claims remains high: About 15,500 cases have been filed each year for the past 3 years.[82] Twenty-five years ago, sexual harassment was generally considered nothing more than a "radical-fringe by-product of feminist theory."[83] Today, it is a permanent fixture in the corporate landscape. Recent Supreme Court rulings underscore the importance of companies' being diligent in their efforts to discourage harassing behavior. In June 1998, the Supreme Court ruled that employers may be held liable even if they did not know about the harassment or their supervisors never carried out any threatened job actions.[84] Clearly, employers must develop comprehensive programs to protect their employees from harassment.

Eliminating sexual harassment is a noble and worthy objective and should be actively pursued. In today's culture, however, it will be difficult to make much headway until the root causes of such practices are exposed and addressed. Respecting women's and men's worth and dignity as people, and not just as sexual objects, will require, at a societal level, attacks on today's cultural conditions. We should not be surprised that sexual harassment exists and has become a serious problem. It has grown in a societal incubator in which it has been planted and nourished, and now we are reaping the harvest.[85] Against this backdrop, managers in all organizations have a responsibility to do all they can to eliminate this practice.

Maternity Leave

For some time, maternity leave has been an issue for women. In 1987, the Supreme Court upheld a California law that granted pregnant workers 4 months of unpaid maternity leave and guaranteed that their jobs would be waiting for them when they returned. Justice Thurgood Marshall argued, "By taking pregnancy into account, California's statute allows women, as well as men, to have families without losing their jobs."[86] The Pregnancy Discrimination Act of 1978, an amendment to Title VII, requires employers to treat pregnancy and pregnancy-related medical conditions the same as any other medical disability with respect to all terms and conditions of employment. Until recently, however, few women felt protected by this law. Although the EEOC had been empowered to protect women against discrimination in pregnancy, it was not until 1991 that it won a significant case that caught the public's attention. In 1991, after 13 years of litigation, the EEOC announced a $66 million settlement by which AT&T would compensate 13,000 employees for job discrimination during pregnancy. The settlement came as a result of AT&T discriminating against women by restricting their maternity leaves beyond that permitted by law.[87]

Pregnancy discrimination continues to be a present-day problem. According to EEOC statistics, the number of pregnancy discrimination complaints increased 48 percent between 1990 and 1994. It is speculated that some of the surge may be demographics, with aging baby boomers starting families while a majority of them work. Another cause may be corporate downsizing as employers are forced to get more work out of fewer people. They may see pregnant employees as unreliable—no longer able to work long hours and, after the child is born, the first to run home when baby gets sick.[88] The 1993 Family and Medical Leave Act has helped, but pregnancy discrimination charges continue to increase.

Fetal Protection Policies

In 1991, a new form of sex discrimination was identified as the Supreme Court ruled that fetal protection policies constituted sex discrimination. The decisive case was *UAW v. Johnson Controls, Inc.* Johnson Controls, like a number of other major firms, developed a policy of barring women of child-bearing age from working in sites in which they, and their developing fetuses, might be exposed to such harmful chemicals as lead. Johnson Controls believed it was taking an appropriate action in protecting the women and their unborn children from exposure to chemicals. In 1984, a class-action lawsuit was brought against Johnson Controls by eight current and former employees and the United Auto Workers (UAW) union, who argued that the policy was discriminatory and illegal under Title VII of the Civil Rights Act. A U.S. District Court ruled in the company's favor, and the Chicago-based U.S. Court of Appeals for the Seventh Circuit affirmed that decision. In 1991, however, the U.S. Supreme Court reversed the appellate court, arguing that the policy was on its face discriminatory and that the company had not shown that women were more likely than men to suffer reproductive damage from lead.[89]

Even though the Supreme Court ruled that injured children, once born, would not be able to bring lawsuits against the company, several experts think it likely that such lawsuits will indeed be filed in the future. One expert said, "A mother can waive her own right to sue, but she can't waive the right of a child to bring suit. So, 5 or 10 years down the line you might see children born with cognitive disabilities, and they could independently sue businesses." The UAW does not dispute this possibility and asserts that it should provide a major impetus for companies to make workplaces safer.[90]

Issues of Age and Religion

Issues surrounding discrimination on the basis of age or religion are increasing with each year. In the case of age discrimination, the aging of 76 million baby boomers caused a rise in the cost of age discrimination lawsuits. Although race, sex and, more recently, disability discrimination result in a greater number of lawsuits (see Figure 16–4), the settlement costs and jury awards for age discrimination suits have been substantially higher. Between 1985 and 1995, age discrimination plaintiffs were awarded an average of $219,000, compared to $147,799 for race discrimination, $106,728 for sex discrimination, and $100,345 for disability discrimination.[91]

Although the awards for age discrimination have been higher on average, they are not obtained easily. One typical type of age discrimination involves older workers, some only in their 40s, being laid off to save money because younger workers can be paid less. Many companies get around this by requiring workers, to receive

ETHICS IN PRACTICE

Is Religion Allowed in the Workplace?

For 6 months I worked as a receptionist at a local doctor's office that employed about 30 people. The owner and head practitioner was a member of a religious cult. During business hours, everything seemed normal for a doctor's office of this size, but during the 2-hour lunch break, all of the employees had to go upstairs and go "on course." These mandatory courses encompassed everything from communication skills to office efficiency. They were all designed by a man who founded the religious cult of which my boss was a member. Granted that they were business teachings, other staff members and I felt that these teachings were heavily weighted with religious undertones.

For example, one of the most important keys to these lessons was that you had to understand every word. After every exercise we were individually tested to make sure that we knew all of the words. Most of the words that I didn't understand could not be found in the dictionary, because they came straight from the man's religious teachings. Whenever I questioned my boss about a word, it usually led into a long discussion about the cult leader's works and I would have to read paragraphs out of the religious teachings to "fully understand" the meaning. To me, it felt as though I was being brainwashed, and from then on I scheduled my university classes during this course time.

My dilemma was this: Did the doctor have the right to insist that we submit to such "teachings," which made us uncomfortable?

1. Is any form of discrimination or harassment taking place in this case?

2. What ethical issues arise in this case?

3. If you were faced with this dilemma, what action would you take?

Contributed by Allison Grice

---

severance packages, to sign waivers of their right to sue. Although a 1998 Supreme Court decision protected older workers by setting some conditions on those waivers, a 1993 Supreme Court decision made it much more difficult to prove that age discrimination was the cause of a layoff. One employment law attorney is quoted as saying that his firm is agreeing to take fewer age bias cases, not because there is less bias occurring but because age discrimination cases are notoriously hard to win.[92] After a review of age discrimination in the workplace, Sheldon Steinhauser concluded:

> *American firms can no longer afford to tolerate cultures of negativity toward older workers. Nearly 16 million Americans age 55 and over are working or seeking work. This number will increase drastically as the baby boomer generation ages. Further, trends in pension benefits, potential changes in Social Security, better health and fitness, and higher education levels will keep many of these people working longer. And they will all be covered by workplace laws banning age discrimination. Employers that fail to wake up to age discrimination and age bias in the workplace could collectively spend millions, perhaps even billions, of dollars in court-imposed fines, punitive damages, and legal fees. Executives need to take action now to minimize wrongful termination complaints and lawsuits in the future.[93]*

In the case of religion, relatively few discrimination cases have occurred, but the EEOC is seeing a steady increase in complaints about religion discrimination in the workplace. At this writing, the Workplace Religious Freedom Act is working its way through Congress. Backed by a broad-based coalition of religious groups, this legislation is designed to respond to the increase in incidents of religious bias by requiring employers to do more to accommodate religious beliefs. According to the Title VII law, employers must make reasonable accommodations unless doing so represents an undue hardship. In 1977, the Supreme Court ruled that anything more than minimal effort or expense could be considered undue hardship. The proposed legislation would raise the definition of undue hardship to "significant difficulty or expense."[94]

The nature of religious bias incidents varies widely. In 1993, a woman who was a practicing Jehovah's Witness sued a restaurant chain because she could not wait tables unless she agreed to join in the singing of "Happy Birthday," a practice that would conflict with her religious beliefs. She settled for $53,000 and a new religious accommodation policy. In two other cases, a restaurant did not have to relax its grooming policy to allow a Sikh man to keep his beard, and a public school did not have to allow a Muslim teacher to wear religious garb. Still another lawsuit, which has not yet been tried, was filed by a public health nurse who was fired for telling an AIDS patient that homosexuality is not an acceptable lifestyle according to her religious beliefs. Future lawsuits are certain to break new ground as companies, the courts, and Congress determine how to deal with religious discrimination in the workplace.[95]

AFFIRMATIVE ACTION IN THE WORKPLACE

Affirmative action is the taking of positive steps to hire and promote people from groups previously discriminated against. The concept of affirmative action was formally introduced to the business world in 1965, when President Lyndon B. Johnson signed Executive Order 11246. The purpose of this order was to require all firms doing business with the federal government to engage in affirmative actions to accelerate the movement of minorities into the work force. Many companies today have affirmative action programs because they do business with the government, have begun the plans voluntarily, or have entered into them through collective bargaining agreements with labor unions.

The Range of Affirmative Action Postures

The meaning of affirmative action has changed since it was first introduced. It originally referred only to special efforts to ensure *equal opportunity* for members of groups that had been subject to discrimination. More recently, the term has come to refer to programs in which members of such groups are given some degree of *definite preference* in determining access to positions from which they were formerly excluded.[96]

Daniel Seligman[97] identified four postures in two groupings that define the range that affirmative action may take. He categorized the following affirmative action postures as "soft" or "weak":

1. *Passive nondiscrimination.* This posture involves a willingness in hiring, promotion, and pay decisions to *treat the races and the sexes alike.* This stance fails to recognize that past discrimination leaves many prospective employees unaware of or unprepared for present opportunities.

2. *Pure affirmative action.* This posture involves a *concerted effort to enlarge the pool of applicants* so that no one is excluded because of past or present discrimination. At the point of decision to hire or promote, however, the company selects the most qualified applicant without regard to sex or race.

Postures that Seligman termed "hard" or "strong" were as follows:

3. *Affirmative action with preferential hiring.* Here, the company not only enlarges the labor pool but *systematically favors minorities and women in the actual decisions.* This could be thought of as a "soft" quota system.

4. *Hard quotas.* In this posture, the company *specifies numbers or proportions of minority group members that must be hired.*

Over the past 30 years, much confusion has surrounded the concept of affirmative action, because it was never clear which of the aforementioned views was being advocated by the government. In hindsight, we can now see that the government was advocating positions based on whichever posture it thought would work, or based on the particular candidate and political party in office at the time. Early on, "soft" or "weak" affirmative action (Postures 1 and 2) was advocated. It became apparent, however, that these postures were not as effective in getting the results desired. Therefore, "hard" or "strong" affirmative action (Postures 3 and 4) was later advocated. The real controversy over affirmative action began with the use of soft quotas and "preferential hiring" (Posture 3) and "hard quotas" (Posture 4). Today, when people speak of affirmative action, they are typically referring to some degree of preferential hiring, as in Postures 3 and 4. Figure 16–7 summarizes the key Supreme Court decisions on affirmative action.

The Concept of Preferential Treatment

Let us briefly consider some of the arguments that have been set forth both for and against the concept of preferential treatment, which undergirds affirmative action. The underlying rationale for **preferential treatment** is the *principle of compensatory justice,* which holds that whenever an injustice is done, just compensation or reparation is owed to the injured party or parties.[98] Many people believe that groups discriminated against in the past (for example, women, blacks, Native North Americans, and Mexican Americans) should be recompensed for these injustices by positive affirmative action. Over the years, deliberate barriers were placed on opportunities for minorities—especially blacks. These groups were prevented from participating in business, law, universities, and other desirable professions and institutions. Additionally, when official barriers were finally dropped, matters frequently did not improve. Inequalities became built into the system, and although mechanisms for screening and promotion did not intentionally discriminate *against* certain groups, they did *favor* other groups. Thus, the view that we can and should restore the

FIGURE 16–7	Key Supreme Court Decisions on Affirmative Action		
Date	**Case**	**Setting**	**General Finding**
1978	*Bakke*	Admission to university medical school	Mildly supportive affirmative action (AA)
1979	*Weber*	Quota-based training program of private employer (Kaiser)	Supportive of AA
1984	*Shotts*	City fire department (Memphis)	Minor setback for AA; qualified seniority plans OK for layoffs
1986	*Wygant*	Jackson, Michigan, Board of Education–school teachers	Mixed finding; seniority system upheld, preferential treatment not always wrong
1986	*Firefighters*	Municipality (City of Cleveland Fire Department)	Supportive of AA; minorities may be given hiring preferences
1986	*Sheet Metal Workers*	Labor union	Strongly supportive of AA; court can order AA for those who were not specific victims of discrimination
1987	*Alabama State Police*	State police force	Strongly supportive of AA; court can order promotion quotas
1987	*Johnson*	County transportation department (Santa Clara)	Strongly supportive of AA; AA can promote women to remedy their historical exclusion from certain job categories
1989	*Richmond v. Crosen*	City government	Mild limitation of AA
1989	*Martin v. Wilkes*	Setting unknown	Supportive of reverse discrimination charges
1995	*Adarand Constructors*	Federal contractors	Instituted strict scrutiny standards; set-asides did not pass test
1996	*Hopwood*	University of Texas Law School	Race-based admission did not pass strict scrutiny test

balance of justice by showing preferential treatment became established as a viable option for moving more quickly toward economic equality in the workplace and in our society.[99]

The Concept of Reverse Discrimination

The principal objection to affirmative action and the reason it has become and remained controversial is that it leads to *reverse discrimination*. This concept holds that when any sort of preference is given to minorities and women, discrimination may occur against those in the majority—usually white males. For well over a decade now, white males who have been passed over because of preferences for minorities or women have been filing reverse discrimination suits.[100] They argue that Title VII prohibits discrimination based on race, color, or sex and that this includes reverse discrimination as well. All of this has created an intensely controversial public policy dilemma: How can we show preferential treatment for minorities and women and at the same time not discriminate against white males? This is very difficult, if not impossible, to do. The next question then becomes a matter of public priority: Should we as a nation pursue affirmative action, even if it means that some opportunities for white males will have to be sacrificed in the process? There are strong opinions on both sides.

Minority Opposition to Affirmative Action

Although it is clear that affirmative action is one of the major pillars of the mainstream civil rights agenda, during the past decade a growing and more visible number of blacks have begun to speak out against such policies.

Two prominent African-American critics of affirmative action are Dr. Thomas Sowell and Professor Stephen L. Carter. Dr. Sowell has argued that blacks would be better served in the long run if affirmative action programs as we now know them were abolished.[101] Stephen L. Carter, a law professor at Yale University, who admits that his race helped him get into college, wrote a widely read and reported book entitled *Reflections of an Affirmative Action Baby* (1991).[102] Professor Carter's concern seems to be with the effects of affirmative action on those whom the policy was intended to help. According to Carter, affirmative action sets up a dichotomy between "best" and "best black." Carter recalls how, over and over, his teachers told him he was the "best black" they had enrolled. The "best black" syndrome holds that, however accomplished a black person might be, she or he is likely to be categorized as "first black," "only black," or "best black" or measured by a different, most likely inferior, standard.[103] Carter apparently does not want to eliminate all types of affirmative action immediately. He supports some degree of racial consciousness, particularly in admissions to colleges and professional schools, but thinks that at some point the preferences must fall away entirely. He is against turning affirmative action into a tool for representing the "points of view" of excluded groups.[104]

The Adarand Decision and Strict Scrutiny

The 1995 case of *Adarand Constructors Inc. v. Pena* (115 S. Ct. 2097) was a turning point in affirmative action. In it, the Supreme Court ruled 5 to 4 that all government action based on race must meet the "strict scrutiny" standard of judicial review. Strict scrutiny has two components: (1) The program or policy must meet a compelling government interest and (2) the program or policy must be tailored narrowly to meet the program or policy objectives. Although the ruling does not declare affirmative action to be unconstitutional, it sets extremely tough standards for any program to pass.[105]

The effects of the Adarand decision are still being felt. An intense round of court cases followed the decision, as affirmative action programs were put to the strict scrutiny test. These cases resulted in some landmark decisions, such as *Hopwood v. the State of Texas,* in which the Fifth Circuit Court held that using race as a consideration in University of Texas Law School admissions did not pass the strict scrutiny test. In June 1995, President Clinton issued a memorandum to all programs that use race, ethnicity, or gender as a consideration in decisions. The directive said that any program must be eliminated if it creates a quota or a preference, causes reverse discrimination, or continues after the goal of equal opportunity has been achieved. Although the Adarand decision applies to federal programs only, its effect is being felt in the private sector, because it sheds light on the actions the courts may take.[106]

The Corporate View

It is not easy to generalize on how the corporate community feels about affirmative action. Initially, business was opposed to the idea. As time passed, however, and as business leaders gained experience with affirmative action programs, their views changed somewhat. The corporate sector does not appear to be adamantly opposed to affirmative action. However, it is also clear that business would prefer to be free of government mandates.

In a 1991 survey of business leaders by *Business Week* magazine gives us an opportunity to see how corporate America felt about these issues.[107] In this survey, 65 percent of the senior executives responded that business, on its own, would hire and train minorities and women and give them the chance to get ahead without affirmative action laws. Thirty-one percent of the executives thought that such laws were needed. The reason given for the majority viewpoint was that the marketplace was already forcing companies to end discrimination. The executives pointed to the shifting composition of the labor supply and the benefits of a diverse work force as more effective spurs to affirmative action than fears of government enforcement or private lawsuits.

The survey also revealed that 53 percent of the respondents thought that business needed to do a better job of hiring, training, and promoting minorities, and 44 percent were not satisfied with their progress in hiring, training, and promoting women. Another interesting finding was that 53 percent of those surveyed thought that the whole issue of affirmative action had posed "not much trouble" for their companies, whereas 39 percent said that it had caused "some but not a lot" of trouble.[108]

In 1998, a survey of 3,200 employers in Atlanta, Boston, Detroit, and Los Angeles showed that affirmative action has little if any negative effect on worker productivity. The results indicated that when companies stress affirmative action in their recruiting, they are more likely to follow it with appropriate training and careful evaluation. Proactive companies have found that the qualifications and work performances of the female and minority employees they hire through these efforts equal those of their other workers. Firms that put no effort into outreach tend to hire less qualified female and minority candidates. However, the study found that even these workers' performances did not suffer.[109]

The business community seems to have accepted affirmative action programs as "good business policy." Some executives see goals and timetables simply as good ways of measuring progress, and others see them as ways to stave off expensive discrimination suits. For some employers, affirmative action has practical business value in customer relations, especially for makers of consumer goods and providers of consumer services. Most large companies have entrenched affirmative action programs, and they think that tinkering with these programs now might draw wrath from women and minorities. Many executives think that if affirmative action is necessary and government requires it, a systematic program that has the government's approval is an effective way of going about it.[110]

The Future of Affirmative Action

As we approach the new millennium, challenges to affirmative action continue to mount. From the courts to Congress and state legislatures to the Oval Office, affirmative action defenders have been difficult to find, and the system of law developed on affirmative action has continued to unravel.[111] The United States is split evenly; in a 1998 WSJ/NBC survey, 51 percent of adults indicated they favor affirmative action. However, 82 percent of African Americans surveyed favored affirmative action. It is not surprising, therefore, that the beginning of a coordinated effort to restore affirmative action is coming from a coalition of organizations in the black community.[112]

An important affirmative action battleground is certain to be university campuses, because much of the recent activity for and against affirmative action has been directed at college admissions. When California voters approved Proposition 209 in 1996, affirmative action in state programs and state schools ended. That same year, the Fifth Circuit Court of Appeals ruled that the University of Texas cannot use race as a factor in admissions. In May 1998, the House defeated an amendment that would eliminate race- or gender-based preferences in admission to colleges that receive federal funds, but that fight has moved to the voting booth. In November 1998, Washington state voters cast ballots on Initiative-200 (I-200), which is modeled after California's Proposition 209.

Coinciding with this landmark vote is the publication of a new book that addresses the issue of preference in college admission, *The Shape of the River* by William Bowen, former president of Princeton, and Derek Bok, former president of Harvard.[113] In this book, Bowen and Bok present a major study that analyzes the performance of 45,000 students at 28 selective colleges and universities over 20 years. The authors draw on student data and lengthy follow-up questionnaires to chart the progress of white and black students (they focus on black because of the wealth of data available). Compared to whites, blacks entered with lower grades and lower test scores and subsequently had lower degree-completion rates. However, 20 years later, more blacks had obtained professional or doctoral degrees. In addition, blacks were more active in community service and more likely to lead civic groups. According to Bowen and Bok, blacks became the backbone of the middle class. Black and white students felt that the diversity they experienced on campus improved their college experience and subsequently helped them adjust to the workplace.[114]

Of course, as the authors allow, statistics do not tell the whole story. No statistics were available about the white students who were not admitted because of affirmative action and the opportunities they may have lost. Whatever the subsequent decisions regarding affirmative action in university admissions, there will be a reaction. In the wake of Proposition 209, minority enrollment at the University of California has dropped sharply, creating a "brain drain" in graduate programs. The problem is that fewer minority students are applying: Schools have taken advantage of Proposition 209 to recruit bright minority students away from California campuses.[115]

The future of affirmative action in the United States is more uncertain than it has ever been. Business must wait until the dust settles on this issue before committing to any radical positions. In the meantime, it is expected that businesses will continue their diversity programs as demographic changes in the work-force composition continue and as they realize their ongoing responsibility—both legally and ethically—to address race, gender, age, disability, and family issues in a socially responsible manner.

Companies are increasingly recognizing that their diversity programs may constitute a competitive advantage or may be used as competitive weapons and that this strategic incentive is an added reason for them to stay on track. It is somewhat ironic to note that some firms are realizing that the civil rights laws cover white males as well as minorities and women and that some companies are even taking special care to be sure they reach out to white males and gain their support as part of their diversity programs.[116]

SUMMARY

This chapter addresses several subgroups of employee stakeholders whose job rights are protected by law. The United States got serious about the problem of discrimination by enacting the Civil Rights Act of 1964, which prohibited discrimination on the basis of race, color, religion, sex, or national origin. Laws covering age and disabilities were passed later. The EEOC was created to assume the major responsibility for enforcing the discrimination laws. Like other federal agencies, the EEOC has had problems. However, on balance it has done a reasonable job of monitoring the two major forms of discrimination: disparate treatment and disparate impact. Discrimination issues discussed in this chapter include the movement from civil rights to social benefits; the plights of African Americans, Asian Americans, Hispanics, and women moving into professional/managerial positions; comparable worth; sexual harassment; and fetal protection policies.

Affirmative action was one of the government's answers to the problem of discrimination. Although originally intended simply to broaden the applicant pool so that everyone would have equal employment opportunity, affirmative action quickly became a form of preferential treatment, up to and including actual numerical goals and quotas. Considerable controversy has surrounded the question of how far affirmative action should go. There is considerable evidence that opposition to affirmative action is growing, however. Corporations have undertaken affirmative action by building their human resource management policies on affirmative action principles, and they will likely continue these practices in the future. To do otherwise at this point might evoke criticism from minorities, women, and others. Furthermore, sound stakeholder management requires companies to continue to be fair in their employment practices.

KEY TERMS

affirmative action
(page 534)

bona fide occupational qualification (BFOQ)
(page 513)

disparate impact
(page 521)

disparate treatment
(page 520)

preferential treatment
(page 535)

protected groups
(page 508)

reverse discrimination
(page 536)

sexual harassment
(page 526)

DISCUSSION QUESTIONS

1. List the major federal discrimination laws and indicate what they prohibit. Which agency is primarily responsible for enforcing these laws?
2. Give two different definitions of discrimination, and provide an example of each.
3. Do you think the Americans with Disabilities Act (ADA) is turning out to be productive or counterproductive? Comment.
4. Explain the dilemma of affirmative action versus reverse discrimination. Do you think the Supreme Court is headed in the right direction for handling this issue? Explain.
5. Do you think preferential treatment should be given in university admissions? Explain.

ENDNOTES

1. Charles J. Sykes, *A Nation of Victims: The Decay of the American Character* (New York: St. Martin's Press, 1992).
2. Paul Hollander, "We Are All (Sniffle, Sniffle) Victims Now," *The Wall Street Journal* (January 18, 1995), A14.
3. William F. Glueck and James Ledvinka, "Equal Employment Opportunity Programs," in William F. Glueck, *Personnel: A Diagnostic Approach,* rev. ed. (Dallas, TX: Business Publications, 1978), 593–633.
4. *Ibid.,* 597–599.
5. "Equal Opportunity: A Scorecard," *Dun's Review* (November, 1979), 107.
6. *Ibid.,* 108.
7. *The World Almanac and Book of Facts 1987* (New York: World Almanac, 1986), 129.
8. McKay Jenkins, "Despite Education Gains, Blacks Still Trailing Whites in Income," *The Atlanta Journal* (September 20, 1991), A16.
9. Isabelle dePomereau, "United States: Why Black Financial Progress Is Running into Speed Bumps," *The Christian Science Monitor* (February 4, 1998), 5.
10. "Black Hole," *Economist* (November 16, 1996), 67–68.
11. Roy S. Johnson, "The New Black Power," *Fortune* (August 4, 1997), 47.
12. *Ibid.*

13. Eileen P. Gunn, "The Money Men," *Fortune* (August 4, 1997), 75.

14. Paula Dwyer, "The 'Other Minorities' Demand Their Due," *Business Week* (July 8, 1991), 62. Also see Jonathan Tilove, "Blacks, Immigrants Vie for Affirmative Action," *The Huntsville Times* (December 26, 1993), F1, F3.

15. EEOC, "Title VII: Enforces Job Rights" (Washington, DC: The U.S. Equal Employment Opportunity Commission, Office of Communications, October, 1988), 1.

16. EEOC, "Age Discrimination Is Against the Law" (Washington, DC: The U.S. Equal Employment Opportunity Commission, Office of Communications, April, 1988), 1.

17. *Ibid.*, 2.

18. EEOC, "Equal Work, Equal Pay" (Washington, DC: The U.S. Equal Employment Opportunity Commission, Office of Communications, October, 1988), 1.

19. EEOC, "Equal Employment Opportunity is . . . the Law" (Washington, DC: The U.S. Equal Employment Opportunity Commission, Office of Communications, 1986), 1.

20. Henry H. Perritt, Jr., *Americans with Disabilities Act Handbook* (New York: John Wiley & Sons, 1990), vii.

21. U.S. Department of Justice, Office on the Americans with Disabilities Act, *The Americans with Disabilities Act: Questions and Answers* (Washington, DC: Government Printing Office, 1991), 1. Also see "Disabilities Act to Cover 500,000 More Firms," *The Atlanta Journal* (July 25, 1994), E1.

22. *Ibid.*

23. Ron Lent, "Employers Usually Win Disability Cases," *Journal of Commerce* (July 9, 1998), 5A.

24. Kathi Wolfe, "Handicapped by a Law That Helps," *The Washington Post* (July 26, 1998), C1.

25. John Hockenberry, "A Just Cause; Americans with Disabilities Act Helped Disabled People Get Fair Treatment, Despite Rumors of Frivolous Lawsuits," *NBC News Transcripts: Dateline NBC* (August 24, 1998).

26. Lent, 5A.

27. Jay Matthews, "Most Corporate Leaders Support Disabilities Act; Poll Reveals Little Increase in Actual Hiring," *The Washington Post* (July 14, 1995), B3.

28. John D. Rapoport and Brian L.P. Zevnik, *The Employee Strikes Back* (New York: Collier Books, 1994), 233–234.

29. EEOC, "Commission Enforces EEO Laws" (Washington, DC: The U.S. Equal Employment Opportunity Commission, Office of Communications, November, 1988), 1.

30. Bob Tarmarkin, "Is Equal Opportunity Turning into a Witch Hunt?" *Forbes* (May 29, 1978), 29–31.

31. Bill McAllister, "Civil Rights: What Happened at the EEOC When Thomas Was There?" *The Washington Post Weekly Edition* (September 16–22, 1991), 31.

32. "Quiet Crackdown: The Quarry—Corporate Civil Rights Violators," *Business Week* (September 26, 1994), 52.

33. This and other information about the EEOC is available on the EEOC's Web site at *www.eeoc.gov.*

34. Testimony of Senator Barbara Mikulski before the Senate Labor and Human Resources Committee. Subject—Confirmation/Oversight Hearing, *Federal News Service* (July 23, 1998).

35. David A. Price, "Kafka Wasn't Kidding," *Forbes* (June 2, 1997), 160.

36. Susan Meltsner, "Psych Disabilities: What's Real, What's Protected," *Business and Health* (June, 1998), 46–53.

37. Roy Whitehead, Jr., Kenneth Griffin, and Pamela Spikes, "Preparing for Same-Sex Harassment Claims," *CPA Journal* (June, 1998), 54–55.

38. Mark Hansen, "Suing Bosses Over Beliefs," *ABA Journal* (April, 1998), 30–32.

39. FTEs make it possible to compare staffing levels by converting a part-time or temporary employee to a fraction of a full-time employee.

40. This and other information about the EEOC is available on the EEOC's Web site at *www.eeoc.gov*.

41. Larry Reynolds, "Monitoring EEOC Spending," *HR Focus* (May, 1998), 15.

42. James Ledvinka, *Federal Regulation of Personnel and Human Resource Management* (Boston: Kent, 1982), 37. Also see W.N. Outten, R.J. Rabin, and L.R. Lipman, *The Rights of Employees and Union Members* (Carbondale, IL: Southern Illinois University Press, 1994), Chapter VIII, 154–156.

43. Glueck and Ledvinka, 304.

44. Ledvinka, 37–38.

45. *Griggs v. Duke Power Company*, 401 U.S. 424, 1971.

46. Theodore Purcell, "Minorities, Management of and Equal Employment Opportunity," in L.R. Bittel (ed.), *Encyclopedia of Professional Management* (New York: McGraw-Hill, 1978), 744–745.

47. *Smith v. City of East Cleveland*, 502 F. 2d 492, 1975.

48. *Wallace v. Debron Corp.*, 494 F. 2d 674, 8th Cir., 1974.

49. Henry Louis Gates, Jr., "The Two Nations of Black America," *Brookings Review* (Spring, 1998), 4–7.

50. Shelley Branch, "What Blacks Think of Corporate America," *Fortune* (July 6, 1998), 140–143.

51. Eisenhower Foundation, "Kerner Commission's Separate and Unequal Societies Exist Today: Report," *Jet* (March 23, 1998), 4–6.

52. "Blacks: A Cheerier Picture," *The Economist* (July 8, 1995), 27.

53. *Ibid.*

54. Martin Gilens, "Race and Poverty in America: Public Misconceptions and the American News Media," *Public Opinion Quarterly* (Winter, 1996), 515–541. See also Mark Fitzgerald, "Media Perpetuate a Myth," *Editor and Publisher* (August 16, 1977); and Abigail Thernstrom and Stephan Thernstrom, "Black Progress: How Far We've Come—and How Far We Have to Go," *Brookings Review* (Spring, 1998), 12–16.

55. Gates, 4–7.

56. Dwyer, 62.

57. Carrie Teegardin, "Hispanics Emerging as Top Minority," *The Atlanta Journal* (March 1, 1995), A3.

58. Anthony Ramirez, "America's Super Minority," *Fortune* (November 24, 1986), 148–164.

59. Cliff Cheng, "Are Asian American Employees a Model Minority or Just a Minority?," *Journal of Applied Behavioral Science* (September, 1997), 277–290. See also Joyce Taing, "The Model Minority Revisited," *Journal of Applied Behavioral Science* (September, 1997), 291–315. Some popular press articles have also questioned the Model Minority characterization of Asian Americans. For examples, see James Walsh, "The Perils of Success," *Time* (Fall, 1993), 55–56; and Chris Peacock, "The Asian American Success Myth," *Utne Reader* (March, 1988), 22–23.

60. "A Superminority Tops Out," *Newsweek* (May 11, 1987), 48.

61. Arthur S. Hayes, "Asian Americans Go to Court to Fight Bias," *The Wall Street Journal* (September 3, 1991), B5.

62. "Women at Work," *Business Week* (January 28, 1985), 80.

63. Teresa Brady, "How Equal Is Equal Pay?," *Management Review* (March, 1998), 59–61.

64. Rochelle Sharpe, "Women Make Strides, But Men Stay Firmly in Top Company Jobs," *The Wall Street Journal* (March 29, 1994), A1.

65. Belle Rose Ragins, Bickley Townsend, and Mary Mattis, "Gender Gap in the Executive Suite: CEOs and Female Executives Report on Breaking the Glass Ceiling," *Academy of Management Executive* (February, 1998), 28–42.

66. Regina Fazio Maruca, "Says Who?," *Harvard Business Review* (November/December, 1997), 15–17.

67. Laura Pincus and Bill Shaw, "Comparable Worth: An Economic and Ethical Analysis," *Journal of Business Ethics* (April, 1998), 455–470.

68. Cathy Trost, "Pay Equity, Born in Public Sector, Emerges as an Issue in Private Firms," *The Wall Street Journal* (July 8, 1985), 15.

69. Lee Smith, "The EEOC's Bold Foray into Job Evaluation," *Fortune* (September 11, 1978), 58.

70. Alice H. Cook, "Current State of Comparable Worth in the United States," *Labor Law Journal* (August, 1990), 525–531.

71. Louisa Wah, "Workplace Conscience Needs a Boost," *American Management Association International* (July/August, 1998), 6.

72. Cited in "Getting Serious About Sexual Harassment," *Business Week* (November 9, 1992), 82.

73. Marilyn Machlowitz and David Machlowitz, "Hug by the Boss Could Lead to a Slap from the Judge," *The Wall Street Journal* (September 25, 1986), 20.

74. "Ruling to Define Sex Harassment in the Workplace," *The Atlanta Journal* (March 2, 1993), A4.

75. Lisa Genasci, "What Does High Court's Harassment Ruling Mean?" *Athens Banner-Herald* (November 10, 1993), 21.

76. Quoted in Genasci.

77. "Ending Sexual Harassment: Business Is Getting the Message," *Business Week* (March 18, 1991), 98–99.

78. Rapoport and Zevnik, 86–87.

79. Machlowitz and Machlowitz, 20.

80. "Mitsubishi Harassment Settlement Approved," *The New York Times* (June 26, 1998), D20.

81. Dan Lonkevich, "Demand Growing for Harassment Coverage," *National Underwriter (Property and Casualty/Risk and Benefits Management)* (August 10, 1998), 26.

82. John Cloud, "Sex and the Law," *Time* (March 23, 1998), 48–54.

83. *Ibid.*

84. Susan B. Garland, "Finally, A Corporate Tip Sheet on Sexual Harassment," *Business Week* (July 13, 1998), 39.

85. Archie B. Carroll, "Sex Harassment a Natural Part of Our Culture," *Athens Daily News* (February 26, 1995), 7D.

86. Beth Brophy, "Supreme Court Gives Motherhood Its Legal Due," *U.S. News & World Report* (January 26, 1987), 12.

87. Isabel Wilkerson, "AT&T Settles Bias Suit for $66 Million," *The New York Times* (July 18, 1991), A16.

88. Mary Lord, "Pregnant—And Now Without a Job," *U.S. News & World Report* (January 23, 1995), 66.

89. "Under a Civil Rights Cloud, Fetal Protection Looks Dismal," *Insight* (April 15, 1991), 40–41.

90. *Ibid.*

91. Sheldon Steinhauser, "Age Bias: Is Your Corporate Culture in Need of an Overhaul?," *HR Magazine* (July, 1998), 86–88.

92. George J. Church, "Unmasking Age Bias," *Time* (September 7, 1998), H3.

93. Steinhauser, 86–88.

94. Mark Hansen, "Suing Bosses Over Beliefs," *ABA Journal* (April, 1998), 30–32.

95. *Ibid.*

96. Thomas Nagel, "A Defense of Affirmative Action," *Report from the Center for Philosophy and Public Policy* (College Park, MD: University of Maryland, Fall, 1981), 6–9.

97. Daniel Seligman, "How 'Equal Opportunity' Turned into Employment Quotas," *Fortune* (March, 1973), 160–168.

98. Tom L. Beauchamp and Norman E. Bowie (eds.), *Ethical Theory and Business,* 2nd ed. (Englewood Cliffs, NJ: Prentice Hall, 1983), 477–478.

99. *Ibid.,* 478.

100. "White, Male and Worried," *Business Week* (January 31, 1994), 50–55.

101. Tony Mecia, "Sowell Blasts Affirmative Action's Harmful Effects," *Campus* (Fall, 1991), 6–7.

102. Stephen L. Carter, *Reflections of an Affirmative Action Baby* (New York: Basic Books, 1991).

103. Ernest Holsendolph, "Affirmative Action: Books Take a Hard Look," *The Atlanta Journal* (September/20, 1991), 1G, book review.

104. Linda Chavez, "An Insider's Account of Affirmative Action," *The Wall Street Journal* (September 6, 1991), A7, book review. See also James E. Ellis, "Up from Affirmative Action," *Business Week* (September 23, 1997), 20.

105. Mitchell F. Rice and Maurice Mongkuo, "Did Adarand Kill Minority Set-Asides?" *Public Administration Review* (January/February, 1998), 82–86.

106. *Ibid.*

107. "*Business Week*/Harris Executive Poll: Corporate America Grades Its Efforts," *Business Week* (July 8, 1991), 63.

108. *Ibid.*

109. "Does Hiring Minorities Hurt?," *Business Week* (September 14, 1998), 26.

110. "*Business Week*/Harris Executive Poll," 26–30.

111. Norma M. Riccucci, "The Legal Status of Affirmative Action: Past Developments, Future Prospects," *Review of Public Personnel Administration* (Fall, 1997), 22–37.

112. Dorothy J. Gaiter, "Blacks Mobilize Politically to Defeat Enemies of Affirmative Action," *The Wall Street Journal* (June 8, 1998), A24.

113. William G. Bowen and Derek C. Bok, *The Shape of the River: Long-Term Consequences of Considering Race in College and University Admissions* (Princeton: Princeton University Press, 1998).

114. Ethan Bronner, "Study Strongly Supports Affirmative Action in Admissions to Elite Colleges," *New York Times* (September 9, 1998), B10.

115. Laura Hamburg, "UC Graduate Programs See Fewer Blacks," *San Francisco Chronicle* (September 18, 1998), A19.

116. "Taking Adversity Out of Diversity," *Business Week* (January 31, 1994), 54–55.

17

Owner Stakeholders and Corporate Governance

CHAPTER OBJECTIVES

After studying this chapter, you should be able to:

1 Link the issue of legitimacy to corporate governance.

2 Identify the major criticisms of boards of directors.

3 Describe the general problems with greenmail, golden parachutes, and insider trading.

4 Identify the major changes in boards of directors that are being employed to improve corporate governance.

5 Discuss the principal ways in which shareholder activism is exerting pressure on corporate management groups to improve governance.

6 Summarize what companies are doing to become more responsive to owner stakeholders.

The giant corporation in the United States is in trouble. Indeed, it could be said that the American system of doing business is in trouble. When companies receive severe and unrelenting criticism from a group that historically has been their number one stakeholder (corporate owners or shareholders), it is time to assess how American industry got to this point and what needs to be done to correct the problem.

What are some of the manifestations of the problem? The one that stands out above the rest is the increased shareholder activism of the past 20 years, especially in the 1980s and 1990s. Shareholder groups have become increasingly critical of how management groups and boards of directors run their firms. They complain about management's lack of accountability, ineffective and complacent boards, excessive managerial compensation, and a general lack of focus on the importance of shareholders relative to management. This latter criticism suggests that managers are looking out for number one, but the number one they are protecting frequently is themselves, not their owners.

One possible view is that management groups have gotten so caught up in addressing the needs of other stakeholder groups—employees, customers, communities, and vocal activist groups—that the owner/stakeholder has been neglected. Another view is that management has become so preoccupied with its own status, position, and rewards that it is no longer making corporate decisions in the interests of owners and other stakeholders but rather in its own interests. There may be some truth in each of these views. Whatever the actual nature of the problem, one point is clear: Corporate governance has become a major issue as shareholders, legal experts, and others are asking, "Who governs the giant corporation, and for whom is it governed? The shareholders? The management? The directors? Special-interest groups? Others?"

To address these concerns and explore recommendations that have been set forth, we need to cover two broad issues. First, we need to examine the components of the corporate governance problem. How have we gotten to the point where we are today? Second, we need to discuss what actions are being taken and may be taken to address these problems.

LEGITIMACY AND THE CORPORATE GOVERNANCE PROBLEM

To understand corporate governance, it is useful to understand the idea of *legitimacy*. Legitimacy is a somewhat abstract concept, but it is vital in that it helps explain the importance of the relative roles of a corporation's charter, shareholders, board of directors, management, and employees—all of which are components of the modern corporate governance system.

Let us start with a slightly modified version of Talcott Parsons's definition of legitimacy. He argued that "organizations are legitimate to the extent that their activities are congruent with the goals and values of the social system within which they function."[1] From this definition, we may see **legitimacy** as a *condition* that prevails when there is a congruence between the organizations' activities and society's expectations. Thus, whereas legitimacy is a condition, **legitimation** is a dynamic process by which business seeks to perpetuate its acceptance. The dynamic process aspect should be emphasized, because society's norms and values change, and business must change if its legitimacy is to continue. It is also useful to consider legitimacy at both the *micro,* or company, level and the *macro,* or business institution, level.

At the *micro* level, we refer to individual business firms achieving and maintaining legitimacy by conforming with societal expectations. According to Epstein and Votaw, companies seek legitimacy in several ways. First, a company may adapt its methods of operating to conform to what it perceives to be the prevailing standard. For example, a company may discontinue door-to-door selling if that marketing approach comes to be viewed in the public mind as a shoddy sales technique,[2] or a pharmaceutical company may discontinue offering free drug samples to medical students if this practice begins to take on the aura of a bribe. Second, a company may try to change the public's values and norms to conform to its own practices by advertising and other techniques. Amazon.com was successful at this with its marketing through the Internet.

Finally, an organization may seek to enhance its legitimacy by identifying itself with other organizations, people, values, or symbols that have a powerful legitimate base in society.[3] This occurs at several levels. At the national level, companies proudly announce appointments of celebrities, former politicians, or other famous people to managerial positions or board directorships. At the community level, the winning local football coach may be asked to endorse a company by sitting on its board or promoting its products.

The *macro* level of legitimacy is the level with which we are most concerned in this chapter. The macro level refers to the corporate system—the totality of business enterprises. It is difficult to talk about the legitimacy of business in pragmatic terms at this level. American business is such a potpourri of institutions of different shapes, sizes, and industries that saying anything conclusive about it is difficult. Yet this is an important level at which business needs to be concerned about its legitimacy. What is at stake is the existence, acceptance, and form of business as an institution in our society. William Dill has suggested that business's social (or societal) legitimacy is a fragile thing:

> *Business has evolved by initiative and experiment. It never had an overwhelmingly clear endorsement as a social institution [emphasis added]. The idea of allowing individuals to joust with one another in pursuit of personal profit was an exciting and romantic one when it was first proposed as a way of correcting other problems in society; but over time, its ugly side and potential for abuse became apparent.*[4]

Quite a bit of the excitement and romanticism has long since worn off; business must accept that it has a fragile mandate. It must realize that its legitimacy is constantly subject to ratification. And it must realize that it has no inherent right to exist—It exists solely because society has given it that right.

In comparing the micro view of legitimacy with the macro view, one may observe that, although specific business organizations try to perpetuate their own legitimacy, the corporate or business system as a whole rarely addresses the issue at all. This is unfortunate because the spectrum of powerful issues regarding business conduct clearly indicates that such institutional introspection is needed if business is to survive and prosper. If business is to continue to justify its right to exist, the question of legitimacy and its operational ramifications cannot be ignored.

SEARCH THE WEB

The Internet has various Web sites devoted to corporate governance, each with its own political standpoint. The two following sites, while different in their viewpoints, offer a thorough, relatively balanced set of resources for exploring corporate governance and related issues. The Corporate Governance Web site (**www.corpgov.net**) is dedicated to "enhancing the return on capital through increased accountability" and, as such, focuses on issues from the perspective of the shareholder. Taking a broader view of accountability, the Business for Social Responsibility (BSR) Web site (**www.bsr.org**), which includes a global responsibility resource center with information on such corporate governance topics as board diversity, board accountability, CEO compensation, and shareholder resolutions, is dedicated to helping "companies be commercially successful in ways that demonstrate respect for ethical values, people, communities, and the environment." BSR member companies range from corporate giants like Coca-Cola and Ford to medium- and small-sized companies like Stonyfield Yogurt and Tom's of Maine.

The Issue of Corporate Governance

The issue of corporate governance is a direct outgrowth of the question of legitimacy. For business to be legitimate and to maintain its legitimacy in the eyes of the public, its governance must correspond to the will of the people.

Corporate governance refers to the method by which a firm is being governed, directed, administered, or controlled and to the goals for which it is being governed. Corporate governance is concerned with the relative roles, rights, and accountability of such stakeholder groups as owners, boards of directors, managers, employees, and others who assert to be stakeholders. Not since the early days of the New Deal has the field of corporation law been so astir with proposals to reform the corporation.[5] Indeed, the subject has become a favorite preoccupation of congresspeople, SEC commissioners, legal scholars, shareholders, and Naderites.[6]

This issue has not arisen in a vacuum. Questions about how corporations govern themselves and to whom they are accountable are direct consequences of their failure to perform to society's satisfaction—or at least to the satisfaction of many of society's most vocal activists and opinion leaders, including owners/stakeholders. Business corporations have grown large and powerful, and so have the people who manage them. We do not argue that their power is irreparably socially destructive. Yet, despite the many economic and financial successes of modern business, several incidents have raised questions about management's performance in noneconomic spheres. Because many corporate giants have been tarnished by charges of malfeasance, there are demands for closer scrutiny of business and for more accountability for their actions. As the public learns of corporate directors who claim to have no knowledge of admitted bribes, unlawful political contributions, and other chicanery, the question being raised time and again is, "Who governs the corporation?"

The issue of corporate governance is framed by some in this way: "Is corporate management really responsible to anyone except itself?"[7] As company executives have become insulated from effective control by directors and shareholders—to whom they are legally responsible—they have become even further removed from the influence of customers, employees, community groups, and others who have an interest in how the company performs.[8] The corporate governance issue, then, comes back to the questions, "Who governs the giant corporation, and for whom is it governed? The shareholders? The management group? The directors? Other stakeholders? The government?"

Components of Corporate Governance

To appreciate fully the legitimacy and corporate governance issues, it is important that we understand the major groups that make up the corporate form of business organization, because it is only by so doing that we can appreciate how the system has failed to work according to its intended design.

Roles of Four Major Groups

The four major groups we need to mention in setting the stage are the shareholders (owners/stakeholders), the board of directors, the managers, and the employees. Overarching these groups is the *charter* issued by the state, giving the corporation the right to exist and stipulating the basic terms of its existence. Figure 17–1 presents these four groups, along with the state charter, in a hierarchy of corporate governance authority.

Under American corporate law, *shareholders* are the owners of a corporation. As owners, they should have ultimate control over the corporation. This control is manifested primarily in the right to select the board of directors of the company. The degree of each shareholder's right is determined by the number of shares of stock owned. The individual who owns 100 shares of Apple Computer, for example, has 100 "votes" when electing the board of directors. By contrast, the large public pension fund that owns 10 million shares has 10 million "votes."

Because large organizations may have hundreds of thousands of shareholders, they elect a smaller group, known as the *board of directors*, to govern and oversee the management of the business. Traditionally, boards have been composed of individuals whose principal employment was with some other company. In the twentieth

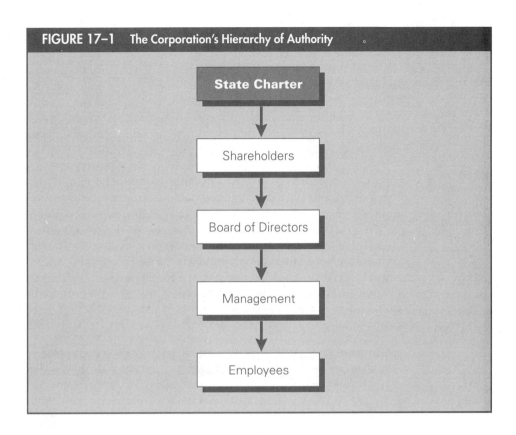

FIGURE 17–1   The Corporation's Hierarchy of Authority

State Charter

Shareholders

Board of Directors

Management

Employees

century, however, the practice of appointing *inside directors*—individuals serving as managers of the very companies that employ them—became prevalent. Current trends are reverting toward more outside directors.

The third major group in the authority hierarchy is *management*—the group of individuals hired by the board to run the company and manage it on a daily basis. Along with the board, top management establishes overall policy. Middle- and lower-level managers carry out this policy and conduct the daily supervision of the operative employees. *Employees* are those hired by the company to perform the actual operational work. Managers are employees, too, but in this discussion we use the term *employees* to refer to nonmanagerial employees.

Separation of Ownership from Control

The social and ethical issues that have evolved in recent years focus on the *intended* versus *actual* roles, rights, responsibilities, and accountability of these four major groups. The major condition embedded in the structure of modern corporations that has contributed to the corporate governance problem has been *the separation of ownership from control.* In the precorporate period, owners were typically the managers themselves. Thus, the system worked the way it was intended; the owners also controlled the business. Even when firms grew larger and managers were hired, the owners often were on the scene to hold the management group accountable. For example, if a company got in trouble, the Carnegies or Mellons or Morgans were always there to fire the president.[9]

As the public corporation grew and stock ownership became widely dispersed, a separation of ownership from control became the prevalent condition. Figure 17–2 illustrates the precorporate and corporate periods and the separation of ownership from control problem. The dispersion of ownership into hundreds of thousands or millions of shares meant that essentially no one or no one group owned enough shares to exercise control. This being the case, the most effective control that owners could exercise was the election of the board of directors. As we will see in the next section, boards of directors became groups beholden to management, not to the owners, and thus management came to control the board of directors rather than vice versa.

The upshot of this evolution was that authority, power, and control rested with the group that had the most concentrated interest at stake—management. The corporation did not function according to its designed plan with effective authority, power, and control flowing *downward* from the owners. The shareholders were owners in a technical sense, but most of them perceived themselves as *investors* rather than owners. If you owned 100 shares of Walt Disney Co. and there were 10 million

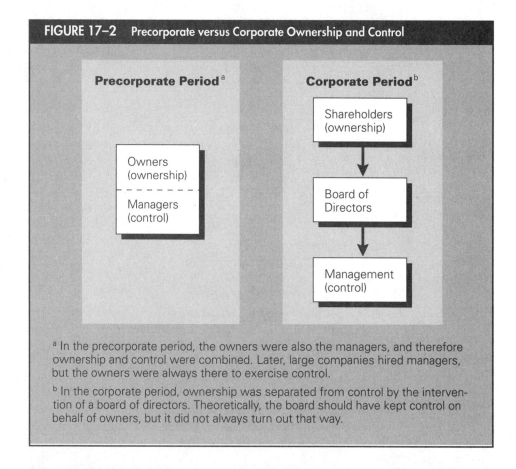

FIGURE 17–2   Precorporate versus Corporate Ownership and Control

Precorporate Period[a]

Owners (ownership)
- - - - - - -
Managers (control)

Corporate Period[b]

Shareholders (ownership)
↓
Board of Directors
↓
Management (control)

[a] In the precorporate period, the owners were also the managers, and therefore ownership and control were combined. Later, large companies hired managers, but the owners were always there to exercise control.

[b] In the corporate period, ownership was separated from control by the intervention of a board of directors. Theoretically, the board should have kept control on behalf of owners, but it did not always turn out that way.

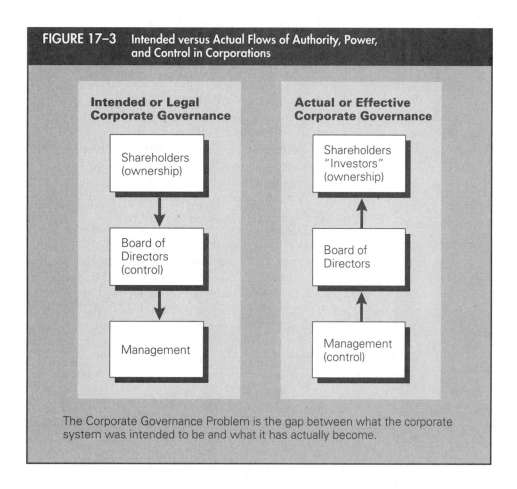

FIGURE 17–3   Intended versus Actual Flows of Authority, Power, and Control in Corporations

Intended or Legal Corporate Governance

Shareholders (ownership)

Board of Directors (control)

Management

Actual or Effective Corporate Governance

Shareholders "Investors" (ownership)

Board of Directors

Management (control)

The Corporate Governance Problem is the gap between what the corporate system was intended to be and what it has actually become.

shares outstanding, you likely would see yourself as an investor rather than an owner. With just a telephone call issuing a sell order to your stockbroker, your "ownership" stake could be gone. Furthermore, with stock ownership so dispersed, no conscious, intended supervision of corporate boards was possible.

The other factors that added to management's power were the corporate laws and traditions that gave the management group control over the *proxy process*—the method by which the shareholders elected boards of directors. Over time, it was not difficult for management groups to create boards of directors of like-minded executives who would simply collect their fees and defer to management on whatever it wanted. The result of this process was that power, authority, and control began to flow *upward from management* rather than downward from the shareholders (owners). Figure 17–3 contrasts the traditional, intended, legal flow of authority and control with what has become the actual, or extant, flow of authority or control.

Ineffective Boards of Directors

It is clear from the preceding discussion that a potential governance problem is built into the corporate system because of the separation of ownership from control.

It is equally clear that the board of directors is intended to oversee management on behalf of the shareholders. However, this is where the system often has broken down, and it could well be argued that for corporate governance to function as it was originally intended, the board of directors must be an effective, potent body carrying out its roles and responsibilities in the supervision of management.

Murray Weidenbaum approaches this problem by saying that we need to contrast what directors are *supposed to do* with what they *actually do* or have done.[10] This is a useful approach worth developing. First, what *should* directors do? From a formal or legal standpoint, corporate boards exist to fulfill the legal requirements imposed by state chartering authorities. Boards are given the authority and responsibility to direct and oversee management. This is quite a broad charge, and attempts have been made to flesh out that role by focusing on the board's primary function. The American Bar Association has asserted that the board's primary function is as follows: "The fundamental responsibility of the individual corporate director is to represent the interests of the shareholders as a group, as the owners of the enterprise, in dealing with the business and affairs of the corporation within the law."[11]

Others have attempted to state more completely what all this means, as shown in Figure 17–4. It is clear that the purpose of boards of directors is to oversee management and to ensure that the shareholders' interests are represented and protected.

Are boards doing what they are supposed to be doing? The evidence is mixed. In 1998, Ram Charan published his findings from observations of and interviews with CEOs, directors, and senior executives of major U.S. corporations. He concluded:

> *Everyone knows about boards that don't work. At GM, IBM, Westinghouse, K-Mart, Digital Equipment Corporation, and other corporate giants, the board seemed to stand idle as billions of dollars in market value went down the drain. The public failure of those boards triggered widespread cynicism about whether corporate boards would ever be more than rubber stamps.*
>
> *But some boards do work. They listen, probe, debate, and become engaged in the company's most pressing issues. Directors share their expertise and wisdom as a matter of course. As they do, management and the board learn together, a collective wisdom emerges, and managerial judgment improves. The on-site coaching and counseling expand the mental capacity of the CEO and the top management team and give the company a competitive edge out there in the marketplace.[12]*

The mixed record of corporate boards has kept them at the forefront of public concern. There have been three major, interrelated criticisms of boards: (1) The board is a rubber stamp of management's decisions, (2) the board is dominated by the CEO, and (3) the board is plagued with conflicts of interest.[13] These three criticisms are not applicable for every firm, but they do represent the historical problems associated with most boards.

The Board Is a Rubber Stamp

This longstanding criticism of boards of directors probably evolved from the fact that managements have historically controlled the proxy machinery by which directors to the board are elected. Furthermore, boards were for many years dominated by *inside* directors. So, if boards had been composed primarily of members of management along with carefully chosen outsiders, it is not surprising that they had begun to be seen as a "rubber stamp" of management's decisions.

FIGURE 17–5   What Boards of Directors Ought to Do: Three Viewpoints

The American Assembly[a]

Boards should:

- Appraise management performance and provide for management/board succession.
- Determine significant policies and actions and future profitability and the strategic direction of the enterprise.
- Determine policies and procedures to obtain compliance with the law.
- Monitor the totality of corporate performance.
- Interpret for management society's expectations and standards.

Peter Drucker[b]

Boards should:

- Ask crucial questions.
- Act as a conscience, a keeper of human and moral values.
- Give advice and counsel to top management.
- Serve as a window on the outside world.
- Help the corporation be understood by its constituencies and by the outside community.
- Ensure management competence.

George A. Steiner[c]

Boards should:

- Provide for management succession.
- Consider decisions and actions having major economic impacts.
- Establish policies and procedures for compliance with the law.
- Make sure that there is an appropriate flow of information to the board and that internal policies and procedures are capable of responding to board decisions.

SOURCES: [a]*Corporate Governance in America* (New York: The American Assembly, 1978), 6. [b]Peter Drucker, "The Bored Board," *Wharton Magazine* (Fall, 1976), 31. [c]George A. Steiner, *The New CEO* (New York: Macmillan, 1984), 69.

Historically, board memberships have been cushy, well-paid positions with lots of perks, embedded in a country-club atmosphere where nobody rocks the boat. As Frederick Sturdivant characterized them, boards were cozy groups of insiders— "members of top management, an attorney from the corporation's outside law firm, the president of the company's bank, and a few of the chief executive officer's personal friends."[14] Can anyone imagine such a board challenging top management?

The Board Is Dominated by the CEO

This criticism[15] is closely related to the first. In one survey, it was found that in only 20 percent of the corporations responding the chairman of the board was also the firm's CEO.[16] What this means is that the board chairman/CEO controls both the agenda of the board meetings and the daily performance of the company. On the positive side, this dual appointment provides the CEO with the discretion and flexibility to respond quickly to dynamic changes in the environment. The downside is a decrease in independent monitoring. One cannot help but recall the old saying about the "fox guarding the chicken coop." In an environment in which the board chair is also held by the CEO, over whom the board is ostensibly exercising direction, it is not surprising that allegations of nonaccountability have been leveled against boards of directors.

CEO domination can also stem from inside directors. Having inside directors is also a double-edged sword. Inside directors have a greater knowledge of the company, and so they have much to offer in terms of advice and counsel. However, the inside director is a subordinate of the CEO, who controls the director's salary, career, and future in the company. Courtney Brown, an experienced director who served on many boards, said that he never saw a subordinate officer serving on a board dissent from the position taken by the CEO.[17]

The Board Is Plagued with Conflicts of Interest

Another realm in which a conflict of interest is manifested is the process of deciding on executive compensation. A board committee typically sets the CEO's salary. One researcher claims to have found an interesting correlation. Apparently, the higher the fees paid to directors, the higher the CEO's pay. The researcher's implication is that CEOs, who typically recruit board members (who get elected because management controls the proxy process), buy loyalty with high fees for directors. An example often cited is the case in which the ITT Corporation board doubled the pay of its chairman despite the company's ragged financial performance. The board members got $51,000 in basic fees that year, plus $40,000 in extras.[18]

There are also conflict-of-interest situations created by outside directors of companies who do business with the companies on whose boards they serve.[19] For example, a commercial banker/director may expect the company on whose board she or he is serving to restrict itself to using the services of her or his own firm. Another example is the "back scratching" that may be done by board members serving on the compensation committee when they are determining the compensation packages for the CEO and other top management officials.

An Alternative View

We have touched on some of the traditional criticisms of boards of directors. Fortunately, those criticisms do not always hold. While some boards fail in their responsibilities, others conscientiously provide solid governance. Examples of both extremes can be seen in *Business Week*'s annual list of the best and worst boards of America. In 1997, Walt Disney Co. was named the worst board because of boardroom members' long ties to CEO Michael Eisner or the company. Observers worried that this board was handpicked and would be detached and weak. The best boards included governance pioneers like Campbell Soup Co., which not only avoided the problems that have plagued boards in the past but broke new ground as a corporate governance pioneer.[20] There is evidence too that the good boards are not necessarily limited to a few exemplars. Recent research has shown that, in general, boards often serve as the watchdogs they were intended to be.[21]

As we examine other issues that have contributed to the corporate governance problem today, we find that they all come back to the role and effectiveness of the board of directors. The board of directors has the principal oversight responsibility on these issues. And if the board is falling prey to the rubber-stamp role, to subordinates of the CEO/board chairman, or to conflicts of interest, it cannot effectively address governance issues. Later in this chapter we will discuss changes that could strengthen such boards.

Executive Compensation

The issue of executive pay has become a lightning rod for the concern that managers place their own interests over those of their shareholders. Historically, many executives have gotten staggering salaries, irrespective of their companies' financial performances. Since about 1992–1993, however, corporate boards have been looking more closely at their firms' performances and have been trying to link CEO compensation to performance. After years of resisting pressure from shareholders to reduce excessive pay for executives, boards are finally attempting to link pay to performance. They are being assisted in this effort by stricter disclosure requirements from the Securities and Exchange Commission (SEC).[22] The new compensation disclosure rule, adopted by the SEC in 1992, has had the desired impact. Since the rule's implementation, compensation committees have met more frequently, had significantly fewer insiders as members, and have become moderate sizes. More important, CEO pay is more closely aligned with accounting and market performance measures than it was before the rule's implementation.[23]

In spite of the fact that boards have been attempting to link pay to performance, criticism of executive compensation continues because of its absolute levels and its relationship to the compensation of other workers. Fueled largely by a bull stock market, CEO pay rose 30 percent from 1996 to 1997. Topping the list of a William M. Mercer executive compensation survey was Sandy Weill of Travelers, who earned $230.5 million in 1997.[24] John Byrne observed that there is a "yawning gap" between salaries in the executive suite and wages on the shop floor. This gap began to widen most dramatically in 1980, when the average CEO made 42 times the pay of the average factory worker. By 1990, CEOs were earning 85 times what the average factory worker was earning.[25] By 1998, that gap had risen to 182 to 1.[26] Serious questions are still being raised as to how this growing gap can be justified. As a *Business Week* editorial so aptly commented:

> *But meanwhile, many CEOs are reaping a disproportionate share of the rewards. . . . Taking home tens of millions of dollars as tens of thousands of employees are laid off and the "survivors" shoulder heavier workloads builds a wall of resentment against CEOs. It's a time bomb ticking.*[27]

It was suggested earlier that there may be some link between CEO and executive compensation and board members. Therefore, it should not be surprising that directors' pay is becoming an issue, too. According to a survey by Executive Compensation Reports, the average annual compensation for a 1996 nonexecutive board member was $73,473, with an additional fee of $1,284 for each meeting attended. In addition, 94 percent of the companies surveyed gave their directors stock.[28] Paying board members is a relatively recent idea. Eighty years ago it was illegal to pay nonexecutive board members. The logic was that because board members represented the shareholders, paying them out of the company's (i.e., shareholders') funds would be self-dealing.[29]

Companies claim they pay directors well in order to secure the best available people. For their part, however, CEOs know that good pay and perks help to buy director loyalty. A prime example of this expectation was the free-spending F. Ross Johnson, former CEO of RJR Nabisco. Concerning the lavish care of his directors, Johnson once said, "If I'm there for them, they'll be there for me." They were there for him until his greed got out of hand and he tried to buy the company through a leveraged buyout.[30]

Managerial Self-Interest or Managerial Stewardship?

The governance of corporations is complex, and so are the issues surrounding it. For decades, both scholarly research and the popular press have focused on the problems that can result from the separation of ownership and management. Recently, however, research has shown that attempts to tightly control the actions of CEOs can have dysfunctional consequences. Too much monitoring can lessen a CEO's desire to take the risks that must be taken to thrive in hypercompetitive markets.[31] Furthermore, pay that is too tightly linked to shareholder returns can encourage a managerial myopia that ignores long-term concerns. In addition, in large U.S. companies, nearly 80 percent of CEO pay is set to vary with stock-market performance.[32]

Walt Disney Co. provides a good example of the paradox in corporate governance. As we mentioned previously, *Business Week* dubbed the company's board the worst in America. It received this dubious distinction because its members are largely handpicked by CEO Michael Eisner, and most have ties to Eisner or the company. Despite a board many would consider weak, the company has outperformed the S&P 500 by far. In the 14 years between Eisner's arrival in 1984 and June 1998, the wealth of Disney shareholders increased more than $80 billion.[33] How can a CEO with a weak board perform so well? Like other people, many CEOs are driven by an intrinsic desire to succeed. Research has shown that the best financial performance comes when both boards and CEOs are powerful and they share that power in participative decision making.[34] Determining how to monitor CEOs' performances without destroying their discretion is the challenge facing corporate governance in the new millennium.

Consequences of the Merger, Acquisition, and Takeover Craze

The merger, acquisition, and hostile takeover craze of the 1980s brought out many issues related to corporate organization, the separation of ownership from control, the functioning of boards of directors, and managerial self-interest. These factors had been around for years, but the economic prosperity of the 1980s, coupled with other factors, brought these issues out like never before in recent times. In the 1980s, complacent companies with undervalued assets became the targets for "takeover artists" or "corporate raiders," as they were variously called. The most notable of these raiders were T. Boone Pickens, Carl Icahn, and Saul Steinberg. The mere mention of these names could strike fear in the hearts of most CEOs. These corporate raiders became the business celebrities of the 1980s, and their names were more well known than the names of the corporate giants such as IBM, AT&T, GM, and GE.

The merger, acquisition, and takeover frenzy of the 1980s was characterized by hostile takeovers, financed with junk bonds, and LBOs (leveraged buyouts). Many corporate CEOs and boards went to great lengths to protect themselves from these takeovers. One major criticism of CEOs and boards during this period was that they were overly obsessed with self-preservation rather than making optimal decisions on behalf of their owners/stakeholders. The takeover era generated a colorful vocabulary of its own—*raiders, poison pills, shark repellents, white knights, junk bonds, insider trading, greenmail,* and *golden parachutes.*[35]

Two of the most questionable top management practices to emerge from the hostile takeover wave were greenmail and golden parachutes. We will briefly consider each of these and see how they fit into the corporate governance problem we have been discussing. Then, we will examine the outburst of insider trading scandals that flourished during the takeover period.

Greenmail

Named after blackmail, *greenmail* is the repurchase of stock from an unwanted suitor at a higher-than-market price. Companies pay the greenmail to end the threat of a takeover.[36] For example, assume that Corporate Raider A quietly purchases a 5 percent stake in the ABC Corporation. It threatens to launch an all-out hostile takeover of ABC. ABC's management sees this as a threat to their jobs and agree to pay greenmail for (buy back) the shares from Corporate Raider A at a premium price. This example is somewhat simplified, but it basically describes the process.

Two classic cases of greenmail are worth mentioning. First, consider Saul Steinberg's pass at Walt Disney Co. Steinberg quickly earned $59 million when Disney bought back his 11.1 percent share of the company for $12 a share more than ordinary stockholders could get at the time. Second, consider the Bass brothers' run on Texaco Co. The Bass brothers earned $280 million for holding just under 10 percent of the oil company for 49 days. The corporate raider wins big in these transactions, and management gets to keep its jobs and perks. The shareholders of the target company are left sitting with shares whose underlying value has been eroded.[37] However, some companies have now passed corporate bylaws that prohibit greenmail.

Another popular action has been for companies to adopt a "poison pill" defense. A *poison pill* is a shareholder rights plan aimed at discouraging or preventing a hostile takeover. Typically the poison pill provides that when a hostile suitor acquires more than a certain percentage of a company's stock, other shareholders receive share purchase rights designed to dilute the suitor's holdings and make the acquisition prohibitively expensive. Some poison pills adopted by companies, however, have been ruled illegal by the courts.[38] A recent District Court decision has now limited the tax deductibility of greenmail payments.[39]

Golden Parachutes

Whereas greenmail is designed to prevent hostile takeovers and help a firm's top executives keep their jobs, golden parachutes are a key instrument in providing the executives with financial security should they lose their jobs. A *golden parachute* may be defined as a contract in which a corporation agrees to make payments to key officers in the event of a change in the control of the corporation.[40] In the past decade, golden parachutes have become extremely controversial and have been assailed by shareholders and others as totally unfair and a "flagrant waste of corporate assets." Some acquiring companies are refusing to honor them, and the battle over their validity continues to be fought in the courts.

An alarming trend is the extent to which offers of golden parachutes have been made down the management hierarchy. Union Carbide, which successfully defeated a hostile takeover attack by GAF, provided $28 million worth of "silver parachutes" for 42 managers. Beneficial Corporation extended "tin parachutes," to 500 of its 8,000 employees. These offers clearly were not in keeping with the original intent of golden parachutes.[41]

The original intent of golden parachutes was to prevent top executives involved in takeover battles from putting themselves before their shareholders. With the huge flurry of hostile takeovers in the mid-1980s, corporate boards hoped golden parachutes would keep managers from resisting shareholder wealth-maximizing takeover attempts. However, in a study of over 400 tender offers (i.e., takeover attempts in which the acquirers offered shareholders premiums to sell their shares), golden parachutes showed no effect on takeover resistance. Neither the existence of the parachute, nor the magnitude of the potential parachute payout, influenced CEO reactions to takeover attempts.[42]

Cochran and Wartick offer several arguments against golden parachutes. They argue that executives are already being paid well to represent their companies and that their getting additional rewards constitutes "double dipping." They also argue that these executives are, in essence, being rewarded for failure. The logic here is that if the executives have managed their companies in such a way that the companies' stock prices are low enough to make the firms attractive to takeover specialists, the executives are being rewarded for failure. Another argument is that executives, to the extent that they control their own boards, are giving themselves the golden parachutes. This represents a conflict of interest.[43]

Insider Trading Scandals

The insider trading scandals of the late 1980s were a direct outgrowth of the takeover flurry that characterized U.S. business during that decade. Trading on inside information was not discovered just then, but in the merger and acquisition frenzy of the mid- to late 1980s it was raised to new and unprecedented heights. We could just as easily have treated the insider trading scandals in the chapters on business ethics, but it seemed appropriate here because it is entwined with the debate over corporate governance. Although it does not illustrate managerial selfishness as do greenmail and golden parachutes, it is a direct outgrowth of the accelerated takeover activity. In the environment of takeover and buyout, of offer and counteroffer, insider trading of astounding magnitude took place. The American public still remembers this period well, so a brief coverage of these events is useful. Furthermore, recent data suggests that insider trading has once again been on the rise since 1991.[44]

Insider trading refers to the practice of obtaining critical information from someone inside a company and then using that information for one's own personal financial gain. For example, an individual may hear from a corporate insider that the insider's firm is about to sell out to another firm at $10 per share above current market price; the individual then buys stock at the current price and later sells it for a profit at the higher price. The 1987 movie "Wall Street" had insider trading as one of its major themes, and the public became much more aware of this practice when the movie became popular.

Insider trading was once thought of as a minor problem that often resulted from someone casually picking up information at lunch or a cocktail party and then buying or selling stock at a profit based on that information. The 1980s scandal began in 1986 when the Securities and Exchange Commission (SEC) filed a civil complaint against Dennis B. Levine, a former managing partner of the Drexel Burnham Lambert investment banking firm, and charged him with illegally trading in 54 stocks. Levine then pleaded guilty to four criminal charges and gave up $10.6 million in illegal profits—the biggest insider trading penalty up to that point.[45] He also spent 17 months in prison.

Levine's downfall set off a chain reaction on Wall Street. His testimony led directly to the SEC's $100 million judgment against Ivan Boesky, one of Wall Street's most frenetically active individual speculators. In a *consent decree,* Boesky agreed to pay $100 million, which was then described as by far the largest settlement ever obtained by the SEC in an insider trading case. Boesky, it turns out, had made a career of the high-rolling financial game known as *risk arbitrage*—the opportunistic buying and selling of companies that appear on the verge of being taken over by other firms.[46] The Boesky settlement set off a flurry of litigation as dozens of private and corporate lawsuits were filed in response to these disclosures.[47]

Ivan Boesky then fingered Martin Siegel, one of America's most respected investment bankers, at Kidder Peabody. Apparently Siegel and Boesky began conspiring in 1982, and over the next 2 years Siegel leaked information about upcoming takeovers to Boesky in exchange for $700,000 cash. Siegel pleaded guilty and began cooperating with investigators, and then he himself proceeded to finger two former executives at Kidder Peabody and one at Goldman Sachs.[48]

The insider trading scandals rocked Wall Street as accusations reached the upper levels of the financial industry's power and salary structure. New arrests seemed to occur weekly, and one of the most frequently asked questions was "Who's next?"[49]

In 1987, Ivan Boesky was sentenced to 3 years in prison. However, Boesky helped prosecutors reel in the biggest fish of all—junk bond king Michael Milkin. The Securities and Exchange Commission accused Milkin and his employer, Drexel Burnham, of insider trading, stock manipulation, and other violations of federal securities laws. Drexel Burnham agreed in 1988 to plead guilty to six felonies, settle SEC charges, and pay a record fine of $650 million. A year later, the junk bond market crashed and Drexel Burnham filed for bankruptcy. In 1990, Milkin agreed to plead guilty to six felony counts of securities fraud, market manipulation, and tax fraud. He agreed to pay a personal fine of $600 million and later was sentenced to 10 years in prison.[50] He served only 2 years in prison before being released.

In a 1991 book, *Inside Out: An Insider's Account of Wall Street,* Dennis Levine made it clear that the insider trading scandals had grown out of the takeover craze of the 1980s. Without question, the takeover period provided the opportunity. What took over next was human greed. Levine's legitimate income rose to $2 million a year, but he kept breaking the law. He rationalized his crimes by asserting that everyone was doing it and that he really didn't think he would get caught. Levine called himself an "insider trading junkie" who couldn't stop.[51]

In the 1990s, hostile takeovers have diminished greatly. Replacing them have been a growing number of legitimate mergers and consolidations that are free of the junk bond financing of the 1980s.[52] Only time will tell whether the consolidations, mergers, and strategic alliances that characterized the 1990s will succeed.

Although merger and acquisition activity reached a record level in 1988 and then declined until 1991, the period 1991–1994 saw mergers roaring back. This time, the merger activity was being driven by technological change, international competition, deregulation, and the incessant demand to cut costs.[53] Once again, however, insider trading statistics reveal a similar pattern of growth with the increasing merger and acquisition pattern. A *Business Week* analysis of 100 of the largest 1994 merger or takeover deals revealed that 34 were preceded by unexplained stock-price runups or volume surges—the telltale signs of insider trading. So, nearly a decade after the Wall Street scandals, insider trading seems to be alive and well. This time, however, the insider trading is not taking place on Wall Street as much as it is among corporate executives and their friends and relatives.[54] In 1997, the Supreme Court ruled that corporate outsiders can also be charged with insider trading if they trade on the basis of material, nonpublic information.[55]

Without question, the revelations and repercussions of the Wall Street scandal will be with us for years. The scandal was a direct outgrowth of takeover activity, which raised anew the corporate governance problem. The issues are quite complex, and solutions are not easily forthcoming. Unfortunately, the scandal has given the financial industry on Wall Street the biggest "black eye" it has had in over 50 years. Not only are shareholders suspicious of what has been going on unbeknownst to them, but also the small investors and the general public have lost faith in what they thought was the stable and secure financial industry.

Many groups in the United States are concerned about the breakdown of the accountability of management groups and boards of directors to owners/stakeholders. Obviously, the owners themselves are most concerned, and their activism has reached unprecedented levels. We will discuss their actions in more detail shortly when we consider the strengthened role of shareholders. Even legislators, lawyers, educators, and other general social activist groups must be concerned. Although this breakdown in accountability has been discussed ever since Adolph Berle and Gardiner Means first wrote about the problem in 1932,[56] the height of this debate has come in the past 10 years. At this point, it is appropriate to consider some of the actions that have been or should be made to improve management's accountability to its owners and, hence, the overall status of corporate governance. Managements are responsible to a host of stakeholder groups in today's society, but it is clear that their relationships with shareholders have never been worse.

IMPROVING CORPORATE GOVERNANCE

Efforts to improve corporate governance may be classified into three major categories for discussion purposes. First, changes could be made in the structure and functioning of boards of directors. Second, shareholders—on their own initiative or on the initiative of management or the board—could assume a more active role in governance. Third, changes in the chartering of corporations could be made at the state level, or federal chartering of corporations could be instituted. Each of these broad groupings deserves closer examination.

Changes in Boards of Directors

It is quite logical that boards of directors be the initial focus for improving corporate governance. Boards are the specific groups assigned the responsibility of holding management groups accountable, and, therefore, more changes have been made and proposed here than anywhere else. As we indicated earlier, boards have historically been ineffective bodies composed of individuals who have attended meetings; enjoyed the honor, distinction, and perquisites of being board members; collected handsome fees; and hoped to be appointed to other such cushy positions. One board member expressed it well: "If you get five of them (board memberships), it is total heaven, like having a permanent hot bath."[57] Another outside director of a large corporation, recalling his introduction to the boardroom in the 1960s, said that the following rules were explained to him by the senior director: "After 10 years you can second a motion. After 15 years, you can make a motion. But you never get to vote 'no.'"[58]

Board memberships were once positions that everyone wanted. It was not uncommon for senior executives, CEOs, lawyers, bank presidents, or retired government officials to sit on 5 to 10 such boards and enjoy the accumulated benefits of all of them. However, in the past decade or so, changes have begun to be made in boards of directors. These changes have occurred because of the growing belief that CEOs and executive teams need to be made more accountable to shareholders and other stakeholders. Here we will discuss several of these changes and some other recommendations that have been set forth for improving board functioning.

Composition of the Board

Prior to the 1960s, boards were composed primarily of inside directors. It was not until the 1960s that pressure from Washington and Wall Street began to emphasize the concept of *outside directors*—individuals who were not currently members of management. Examples of the occupations of outside directors are CEOs or executives of other firms, academicians, retired executives of other firms, attorneys, and former government officials. Some boards use major shareholders, investment bankers, or "professional" directors.[59] By the 1970s, outsiders had become the majorities on the boards of many, if not most, corporations.

This trend toward outside directors dominating boards has long been a recommendation for improving corporate governance. It was believed that outside directors would be more likely to monitor management carefully than would inside directors. Since about the mid-1970s, the trend has been toward an even greater increase in the proportion of outsiders on boards.[60] It was estimated that by 1980, 87 percent of boards had outside directors.[61] The percentage of boards of major corporations that are now comprised of outsiders is much higher. A 1991 study of 100 major firms confirmed that only 5 percent still had majorities of inside directors. The study concluded that these changes came about because of pressure from large institutional investors and from a belief that the turbulent business environment that confronts directors today—from stiff global competition to takeover threats to difficult restructurings—necessitates these changes.[62]

It has been recommended not only that outside directors be appointed to boards but also that they be *independent* outside directors—individuals who have no business relationship to the companies they serve. Examples of independent outside directors include executives of unrelated companies, former government officials, college professors, "professional" directors, and representatives of consumer, environmental, and civil rights groups. Unfortunately, many of today's outside directors are not very independent. An outside director may be the company's banker, lawyer, or management consultant, or a close friend of the CEO.[63]

In addition to a move toward independent outside directors, it also has been recommended that companies create boards with a broader diversity of backgrounds.[64] In the 1970s, there started a trend toward appointing minority members, women, and academics to boards.[65] We should note, however, that most boards have very few representatives of these groups, if any at all. A major executive search firm, Heidrick and Struggles, Inc., reported that among all boards the composition was as follows: 82.2 percent white males, 6.9 percent white females, 3.1 percent black females, 2.6 percent black males, 2.6 percent Hispanic females, 2.0 percent Asian/other males, 0.5 percent Hispanic males, and 0.1 percent Asian/other females.[66]

Among the nation's largest corporations, the Fortune 500, a 1994 survey showed that 52 percent of these firms now have at least one woman director. One female corporate president observed that CEOs tend to look to their peers to fill spots on corporate boards and that left out women because only three were chief executives of Fortune 1000 firms as of 1994.[67]

The compositions of corporate boards have been made more diverse not only by the addition of women and minorities but also by the addition of *environmentalists* and other stakeholder-interest groups (e.g., labor representatives) and the appointment of international outside directors. During the late 1980s and early 1990s it became popular for corporations to place environmentalists on their boards. A prominent example of this was Exxon, which placed an environmentalist on its board soon after its 1989 Alaskan oil spill. By 1994, about 20 companies had added environmentalists to their boards, including Atlantic Richfield, Dow Chemical, International Paper Co., Monsanto, DuPont, Cummins Engine Co., and Chevron Corp.[68] The purposes of such appointments ranged from a genuine concern for the environmental perspective to the appeasement of vocal special-interest groups.

With the increasing advent of global competition, it should not be surprising that companies are also adding international outside directors to their boards. A 1992 survey showed that 22 of the largest 100 corporations surveyed had a total of 27 directors from other countries.[69] Related to this trend, Heidrick and Struggles, the executive search firm, has reported on an emerging trend—the *global outside director.* The role of the global outside director is to inject the board with a different perspective so that all directors may begin to expand their thinking and alter their posture on a range of global issues. Distinguishing attributes of global outside directors include global experience, global outlook, ease in working with several cultures, stature in their home universes, and diverse life experiences (e.g., exposure to different educational systems, values, beliefs, and cultures).[70]

In the mid- to late 1980s, not many individuals wanted board director positions. Concerned about increasing legal hassles emanating from stockholder, customer, and employee lawsuits, directors were quitting such positions or refusing to accept them in the first place. Although courts rarely hold directors personally liable in the hundreds of shareholder suits filed every year, over the past several years there have been a few cases in which directors have been held personally and financially liable for their decisions. The Trans Union Corporation case involved an agreement among the directors to sell the company for a price the owners later decided was too low. A suit was filed, and the court ordered that the board members be held personally responsible for the difference between the price the company was sold for and a later-determined "fair value" for the deal.[71] In addition to the Trans Union case, Cincinnati Gas and Electric reached a $14 million settlement in a shareholder suit that charged directors and officers with improper disclosure concerning a nuclear power plant.[72]

The recent Caremark case has heightened directors' concerns about personal liability. Caremark, a home health care company, paid substantial civil and criminal fines for submitting false claims and making illegal payments to doctors and other health care providers. The Caremark board of directors was then sued for breach of fiduciary duties because the board members had failed in their responsibility to monitor effectively the Caremark employees who violated various state and federal laws. In late 1996, the Delaware Chancery Court ruled that it is the duty of the board of directors to ensure that a company has an effective reporting and monitoring system in place. If the board fails to do this, individual directors can be held personally liable for losses that are caused by their failure to meet appropriate standards.[73]

Use of Stronger Board Committees

When the American Assembly studied the corporate governance problem in the late 1970s, it not only recommended that a majority of board members be true outsiders but also concluded that boards make more use of committees. In particular, the American Assembly recommended that the following four strong committees be established: audit, nominating, compensation, and public issues.[74] In the past decade or so, the use of such committees has become a definite trend, although not all corporations have used them effectively. By 1992, almost 100 percent of boards surveyed had audit committees, 91 percent had compensation committees, and 64 percent had nominating committees.[75]

The *audit committee* is typically responsible for assessing the adequacy of internal control systems and the integrity of financial statements. Recent scandals, like the July 1998 revelation that Cendant Corporation booked almost $300 million in fake revenues, underscore the importance of a strong audit committee. Commenting on the Cendant Corporation situation, the *Wall Street Journal* opined, "Too many audit committees are turning out to be toothless tigers."[76] To lessen the occurrence of such scandals, the Securities and Exchange Commission has placed much emphasis on audit committees, and the New York Stock Exchange mandates such committees, composed of independent outside directors, for the firms listed with it. Charles Anderson and Robert Anthony, authors of *The New Corporate Directors: Insights for*

Board Members and Executives,[77] argue that the principal responsibilities of an audit committee are as follows:

1. To ensure that published financial statements are not misleading
2. To ensure that internal controls are adequate
3. To follow up on allegations of material, financial, ethical, and legal irregularities
4. To ratify the selection of the external auditor

A major report by the Conference Board concluded that the audit committee should also have a broader mandate. The report argued that audit committees should have more authority and responsibility, should have more impact in improving financial controls reporting, should play a growing role in strengthening auditors' independence, and should become a major force in boosting board effectiveness.[78]

According to Arjay Miller, a board member and former president of Ford Motor Company, there should be at least one meeting per year between the audit committee and the firm's *internal auditor.*[79] The internal auditor should be scheduled to meet alone with the committee and always be instructed to speak out whenever she or he believes something should be brought to the committee's attention. The committee should also meet with the *outside auditor* in a setting in which members of management are not present. Three major questions should be asked of the outside auditor by the audit committee:

1. Is there anything more that you think we should know?
2. What is your biggest area of concern?
3. In what area did you have the largest difference of opinion with company accounting personnel?

The ***nominating committee***, which should be composed of outside directors, or at least a majority of outside directors, has the responsibility of ensuring that competent, objective board members are selected. The American Assembly recommended that this committee be composed entirely of independent outside directors. The function of the nominating committee is to nominate candidates for the board and for senior management positions. In spite of the suggested role and responsibility of this committee, in most companies the CEO continues to exercise a powerful role in the selection of board members.

The ***compensation committee*** has the responsibility of evaluating executive performance and recommending terms and conditions of employment. Ideally, this committee is composed of outside directors, or at least a majority of outsiders. Although most large companies have compensation committees, one might ask how objective these board members are when the CEO has played a significant role in their being elected to the board.

Finally, the American Assembly recommended that each board have a ***public issues committee***, or public policy committee. Although it is recognized that most management structures have some sort of formal mechanism for responding to public or social issues, this area is important enough to warrant a board committee that would become sensitive to these issues, provide policy leadership, and monitor management's performance on these issues. Most major companies today have public issues committees that typically deal with such issues as affirmative action, equal employment opportunity, environmental affairs, employee health and safety, consumer affairs, political action, and other areas in which public or ethical issues are present. Debate continues over the extent to which large firms really use such committees, but the fact that they have institutionalized such concerns by way of formal corporate committees is encouraging. The American Assembly recommended that firms develop evaluation systems to help them monitor the social performance of their corporate executives, but the evidence does not show that companies are doing this.[80]

Changing the composition of the board of directors to make it more independent and using strong committees are the two most often-mentioned suggestions for improving corporate governance. Other suggestions have also been set forth. For example, it has been suggested that the CEO should not simultaneously occupy the position of chairman of the board. Another suggestion is that boards be smaller and better paid.[81] Still another suggestion is that boards be given more authority and that directors be chosen from among major constituencies, such as consumers, civil rights activists, environmentalists, and so on.[82]

Different Roles for Board Members

The changes in boards just discussed must continue to be analyzed and effected if the issues of corporate governance and responsiveness to stakeholders are to be effectively and responsibly addressed. A broader view is that boards need to alter the fundamental roles that they assume in the corporation. William R. Boulton[83] has suggested that corporate boards typically move through three stages in which they assume different roles:

1. *The legitimizing stage.* At the legitimizing stage, boards do the minimum—sign papers and adopt resolutions required by law. At this stage, the board is truly a rubber stamp and has no role in decision making.

2. *The auditing stage.* At this stage, the board recommends specific actions to improve the functioning of the management control or auditing process. The appearance of audit committees assumes an important role in the transition to the auditing stage. The auditing role, however, must not be seen as the final role but rather as just a steppingstone in the transition of the board to an even more active stage—that of directing.

3. *The directing stage.* Here the board ensures that executive functions are carried out over time in an appropriate and ethical manner. In this final stage, boards actively assert their leadership. They do not just wait for management to make a decision and then react to it.

The boards of many companies seem stalled in the legitimizing stage. It seems clear from our discussion, however, that the auditing stage is the minimum that is acceptable and that, ideally, boards should aim for the directing stage. The complexities of today's business environment demands this broader view of an active board of directors.

An example of a board taking on the *directing* role has been provided by the board of directors at General Motors. Led primarily by its outside directors, the GM board has produced a new model for corporate governance at GM. The six-page, 28-point document has been called a corporate Magna Carta. The document tries to spell out the way things ought to be if directors are going to do their job of making management accountable to shareholders. GM's guidelines are designed to ensure the board's independence and are mostly common sense.[84]

In 1992, the GM board fired CEO Robert Stempl and hired a new CEO, the hard-driving John F. Smith, Jr. Then they appointed John Smale, retired CEO of Procter & Gamble, to the position of nonexecutive chairman. Smale attempted to bring about reform by writing the new boardroom code in consultation with the company's other outside directors. The key provisions of the new board guidelines[85] included the following:

- The board, not the CEO, would choose new board members "in fact as well as in procedure."

- A "lead director" would be chosen by the outside director anytime the roles of CEO and chairman was not split.

- The board would employ a "Director Affairs Committee" to assign members to working committees, assess lacking board skills, and assess the board's performance annually.

- Board members would have "complete access" to GM's management.

- Management would distribute to board members before each meeting its planned presentations on specific subjects.

- All decisions about corporate governance would be made by GM's outside directors.

Only time will tell whether GM's new model of corporate governance will work. On the surface, however, it appears to be a significant step forward in establishing how boards ought to function so as to achieve accountability.

Getting Tough with CEOs

It has always been a major responsibility of board directors to monitor CEO performance and to get tough if the situation dictates. Historically, however, chief executives have been pampered and protected. Changes are now occurring that are resulting in CEOs being taken to task, or even fired, for reasons that heretofore did not create a stir in the boardroom. These changes include the tough, competitive economic times; the rising vigilance of outside directors; and the increasing power of large institutional investors.

Examples of recently fired CEOs include Tom Barrett, former chairman and CEO of Goodyear Tire and Rubber. Barrett quit under the pressure of his directors' increased dissatisfaction with how he was managing the troubled tiremaker. The board of General Public Utilities forced out its CEO after it learned that he was having an affair with a married vice president. The CEO of Greyhound was ousted partly because of his differences with some creditors. Other companies that recently ousted CEOs include IBM, Westinghouse, American Express, Compaq,[86] and K-Mart.[87] Most recently, the Sunbeam Corporation board of directors ousted "Chainsaw Al" Dunlap, who received his nickname from the many workers he laid off in the course of numerous turnarounds. Because the Sunbeam directors had large shareholdings in the company, the company's continued losses directly impacted their wallets.[88]

Although there is no wholesale move against CEOs, their jobs are not as insulated as they once were. Many boards are getting tougher and are taking the actions they should take against CEOs. Jay Lorsch, a Harvard Business School professor, argues that boards take too long to act and that there are too many impediments in their way. Critics also contend that directors act only when they are under intense heat from regulators, shareholders, or the media.[89]

Other suggestions have been proposed for creating effective boards of directors and for improving board members' abilities to monitor executive teams to ensure that crises do not occur undetected. Figure 17–5 summarizes some of these recommendations.

Increased Role of Shareholders

Prior to the 1980s, civil rights activists, consumer groups, and other social activist pressure groups insisted that companies join their causes. The typical corporate response was, "Our job is to maximize returns to the legal owners of our corporation, the shareholders. We have no right to use their assets to promote social goals, no matter how worthy." Today, however, the typical corporate response is similar to that of the chairman of Avon Products, Inc., Hicks B. Waldron: "We have 40,000 employees and 1.3 million representatives around the world. We have a number of suppliers, institutions, customers, and communities. They have much deeper and much more important stakes in our company than our shareholders."[90]

The situation described above appears to be an innocent shift in perspective from viewing shareholders as the sole stakeholders to viewing shareholders as just one group among many stakeholders and not necessarily the most important one. This change reflects the fact that companies are increasingly understanding the stakeholder perspective. However, it has created a new dilemma for companies as they deal with two broad types of shareholders. First, there are the traditional shareholder groups that are primarily interested in the firm's financial performance. Examples of such groups include the large institutional investors, such as pension funds. Second, there are growing numbers of social activist shareholders. These groups are typically pressuring firms to adopt their desired postures on social causes, such as Third World employment practices, animal testing, affirmative action, and environmental protection.

A major problem seems to be that both groups of shareholders feel like neglected constituencies. They are attempting to rectify this condition through a variety of means. They are demanding effective power. They want to hold management groups accountable. They want to make changes, including changes in management if necessary. Like companies' earlier responses to other stakeholder activist groups, many managements are resisting. The result is a battle between managers and shareholders for corporate control.[91]

FIGURE 17–5   Improving Boards and Board Members

Building a Better Board[a]

- Don't overload it with too many members.
- Don't meet too often.
- Don't think you need high-profile CEOs or famous academics.
- Keep directors on for at least 5 years.
- Encourage directors to buy large quantities of stock.
- Pay directors with stock options, not with restricted stock.

Sharpening the Board's Sensors[b]

- Insist that board members become educated about their company.
- Insist that information-gathering systems deliver quickly the right information from the bottom to the top.
- Insist that board members understand board decision-making processes and not operate by consensus.
- Insist that the company undergo periodic audits of corporate activities and results.

Board Actions[c]

- Directors should evaluate regularly the CEO's performance against established goals and strategies.
- Evaluations of the CEO should be done by "outside directors."
- Outside directors should meet alone at least once a year.
- Directors should set qualifications for board members and communicate these expectations to shareholders.
- Outside directors should screen and recommend board candidates who meet the established qualifications.

Keep Directors' Eyes on CEO[d]

- CEOs need written job descriptions and annual report cards.
- Boards should measure their own performance as well as assess individual members.
- Board nominating committees should exclude the company's major suppliers, officials of non-profit organizations that receive substantial donations from the corporation, and the CEO's close friends.
- A chief executive should hold only one outside board seat.

SOURCES: [a]Graef S. Crystal, "Do Directors Earn Their Keep?" *Fortune* (May 6, 1991), 79. [b]Richard O. Jacobs, "Why Boards Miss Black Holes," *Across the Board* (June, 1991), 54. [c]The Working Group on Corporate Governance, "A New Compact for Owners and Directors," *Harvard Business Review* (July–August, 1991), 142–143. [d]Joann S. Lublin, "How to Keep Directors' Eyes on the CEO," *The Wall Street Journal* (July 20, 1994), B1.

Recent examples of this battle between managers and shareholders include experiences at Time Warner and at Sears. At Time Warner, the world's largest communications company, a shareholder revolt against management led to the firm dropping a plan to issue 34.5 million new shares of stock.[92] At Sears, the battle took place between the company's management and shareholder activist Robert A. G. Monks, who was vying for a seat on the Sears board. Edward A. Brennan, chairman and CEO of Sears, spent $5.6 million to make sure Monks did not win the seat on the Sears board.[93]

A recent trend has been for shareholder activists to pressure corporate boards to hold CEOs more accountable for the firm's performance. A prime example of this was when shareholder activists pressured the K-Mart board to take away from CEO and Chairman Joseph Antonini his position as board chairman. Soon thereafter, in 1995, these same shareholder groups claimed that "Joe has to go," and he was forced out completely. The new chairman cited the unrelenting pressure from large institutional shareholders for the board's unanimous decision to force Antonini out.[94] Now the pressure is on board members to improve their performance or be ousted. Institutional Shareholder Services has encouraged its members to vote against board members who miss 25 percent of board meetings.[95]

Our discussion of an increased role for shareholders centers around two perspectives: (1) the perspective of shareholders themselves asserting their rights on their own initiative and (2) initiatives being taken by companies to make shareholders a true constituency. The shareholder initiatives will dominate our discussion, because they clearly constitute the bulk of the activity underway.

Shareholder Initiatives

These initiatives may be classified into three major, overlapping areas: (1) the rise of shareholder activist groups, (2) the filing of shareholder resolutions and activism at annual meetings, and (3) the filing of shareholder lawsuits.

Rise of Shareholder Activist Groups. One major reason that relations between management groups and shareholders have heated up is that shareholders have discovered the benefits of organizing and wielding power. Shareholder activism is not a new phenomenon. It goes back over 60 years to 1932, when Lewis Gilbert, then a young owner of 10 shares, was appalled by the absence of communication between New York–based Consolidated Gas Company's management and its owners. Supported by a family inheritance, Gilbert decided to quit his job as a newspaper reporter and "fight this silent dictatorship over other people's money." He resolved to devote himself "to the cause of the public shareholder."[96]

The history of shareholder activism is too detailed to report fully here, but Gilbert's efforts planted a seed that grew, albeit slowly. The major impetus for the movement came in the 1960s and early 1970s. The early shareholder activists were an unlikely conglomeration—corporate gadflies, political radicals, young lawyers, an assortment of church groups, and a group of physicians.[97] The movement grew out of a period of political and social upheaval—civil rights, the Vietnam War, pollution, and consumerism.

The watershed event for shareholder activism was *Campaign GM* in the early 1970s, also known as the Campaign to Make General Motors Responsible. Among those involved with this effort was, not surprisingly, Ralph Nader. The shareholder group did not achieve all its objectives, but it won enough to demonstrate that shareholder groups could wield power if they worked hard enough at it. Two of Campaign GM's most notable early accomplishments were that (1) the company created a public policy committee of the board, composed of five outside directors, to monitor social performance, and (2) GM appointed the Reverend Leon Sullivan as its first black director.[98]

One direct consequence of the success of Campaign GM was the growth of *church activism*. Church groups were the early mainstay of the corporate social responsibility movement and were among the first shareholder groups to adopt Campaign GM's strategy of raising social issues with corporations. Church groups began examining the relationship between their portfolios and corporate practices, such as minority hiring and companies' presence in South Africa. Church groups remain among the largest groups of institutional stockholders willing to take on management and press for what they think is right. Many churches' activist efforts are coordinated by the Interfaith Center on Corporate Responsibility (ICCR), which coordinates the shareholder advocacy of about 275 religious orders with about $90 billion in investments. The ICCR was instrumental in convincing Kimberly-Clark to divest the cigarette paper business and pressuring PepsiCo to move out of Burma. It is now taking on such issues as global warming, environmental pollution, and the practice of using sweatshops to manufacture garments and shoes.[99]

In December 1972, the Investor Responsibility Research Center (IRRC) was formed "to provide timely and impartial analysis concerning corporate social responsibility issues."[100] The IRRC became a central organization that served as a resource center for shareholder activism.

From the mid-1980s to the mid-1990s, two groups characterized the new breed of shareholder activism. One was the Council of Institutional Investors (CII). Institutional investors (pension funds, church groups, foundations) now dominate the marketplace and thus wield considerable power because of their enormous stock holdings. This influence continues to grow. By the end of 1997, institutional investors controlled 60 percent of the stock in the 1,000 largest U.S. companies, compared to 46.6 percent in 1987.[101]

Filing of Shareholder Resolutions and Activism at Annual Meetings.   One of the major vehicles by which shareholder activists communicate their concerns to management groups is through the filing of *shareholder resolutions*, or shareholder proposals. An example of such a resolution is, "The company should name women and minorities to the board of directors." To file a resolution, a shareholder or a shareholder group must obtain a stated number of signatures to require management to place the resolution on the proxy statement so that it can be voted on by all the shareholders. Resolutions that are defeated (fail to get majority votes) may be resubmitted provided that they meet certain SEC requirements for such resubmission.

The shareholder groups behind these shareholder proposals are usually socially oriented—that is, they want to exert pressure to make the companies in which they own stock more socially responsive. Although an individual could initiate a shareholder resolution, she or he probably would not have the resources or means to obtain the required signatures to have the resolution placed on the proxy. Thus, most resolutions are initiated by large institutional investors that own large blocks of stock or by other activist groups that own few shares of stock but have financial backing. Foundations, religious groups, universities, and other such large shareholders are in an ideal position to initiate resolutions. Religious groups prominent in this endeavor include the Episcopal Church, the United Church of Christ, the Lutheran Church in America, the United Methodists, the United Presbyterian Church, and the American Jewish Congress.

The issues on which shareholder resolutions are filed vary widely, but they typically concern some aspect of a firm's social performance. For example, Mobil, Pfizer, and Union Camp were asked to study the safety of tobacco additives produced and sold by them and combusted and inhaled by humans. Several firms, including American Brands, Kimberly-Clark, Philip Morris, and RJR Nabisco, were asked to spin off their tobacco units from the rest of their operations. Wendy's and PepsiCo (Kentucky Fried Chicken, Taco Bell, Pizza Hut) were asked again to make all their restaurants smoke-free. Other popular resolutions have dealt with environmental issues, use of the McBride Principles in doing business in Northern Ireland, and board diversity (naming more women and minorities to corporate boards).[102] The 1998 proxy season saw an unprecedented number of shareholder resolutions from organized labor, focusing on issues such as multiemployer trusts and labor retirement plans.[103]

The past several years have seen boards cracking down on executive compensation and perks, as discussed earlier. In an interesting turn of events, however, shareholders are now beginning to take aim at directors' lavish benefits. According to the Investors Rights Association, shareholder resolutions were filed at over 20 companies in 1995 with the goal of bringing board members' benefits under control. In addition to annual retainers, board members typically receive meeting fees, stock options, stock grants, and pensions. Companies argue that the large financial packages are needed to attract and keep good directors; however, shareholder groups are not as sympathetic as they once were.[104]

Because most shareholder resolutions never pass, one might ask why groups pursue them. The main reason is that they gain national publicity, which is part of what protesting groups are out to achieve. Increasingly, companies are negotiating with groups to settle issues before resolutions ever come up for a vote. Several years ago, in a rare reversal of attitude, Exxon Corporation's management recommended that shareholders vote in favor of a resolution calling for the company to provide reams of data on its strip-mining operations. Exxon had agreed ahead of time to the request of the United Presbyterian Church and several Catholic groups, which sponsored the resolution, but the groups wanted the resolution to go all the way to a vote, and the company acquiesced. What happened at Exxon reflects subtle changes as management groups, increasingly sensitive to public criticism, are more willing to sit down before annual meetings and work out agreements on shareholder resolutions. In 1995, resolution requests were withdrawn from Pfizer, Inc., and Union Camp after Pfizer agreed to draft a written policy banning sales of its products to tobacco makers and Union Camp agreed to cease promoting flavors it generates for tobacco products.[105]

Closely related to the surge in shareholder resolutions has been the increased activism at *corporate annual meetings* in the past decade. Professional "corporate gadflies" purchase small numbers of shares of a company's stock and then attend its annual meetings to put pressure on managers to explain themselves. An example of the kind of social activism that can occur during an annual meeting was the case in which GM shareholders sought explanations for a series of embarrassing controversies surrounding the automaker. Some shareholders wanted to know why the company substituted Chevrolet engines in cars sold by some of its other divisions, a move that infuriated many consumers who were not notified of the changes.[106] More recently, corporate executives have been asked to explain high executive compensation packages, positions on hostile takeover attempts, plant closings, greenmail, golden parachutes, and environmental issues.

The motives for bringing up these issues at annual meetings are similar to those for filing shareholder resolutions: to put management "on the spot" and publicly demand some explanation or corrective action. Activism at annual meetings is one of the few methods shareholders have of demanding explanations and obtaining accountability from top management.

Being able to defend a company at annual meetings has become such an important task of top management that several consulting firms now publish annual booklets of shareholder questions that are likely to be asked. These booklets are intended to help management and directors anticipate and plan for what they might be quizzed on at annual meetings.

In 1997, the SEC proposed amendments to its rules on shareholder proposals. Some of these amendments would have made it more difficult for shareholders to resubmit proposals after they had been voted down. A 340-group coalition, including the Episcopal Church, the Methodist Church Pension Fund, the National Association for the Advancement of Colored People (NAACP), the Sierra Club, and the AFL-CIO, converged on Washington to protest the proposal. A study by the Social Investment Forum showed that 80 percent of past resolutions would have been barred after their third year if the original proposals had been accepted. Bowing to "considerable public controversy," the SEC took only one action—reversing the "Cracker Barrel" decision. In 1991, when Cracker Barrel Old Country Store decided to fire, and no longer hire, gay employees, shareholders sought to have that policy overturned. The SEC ruled that hiring falls under the category of "ordinary business" decisions and thus was entirely the province of corporate directors and officers. In 1998, the SEC reversed that ruling and returned to its earlier policy of deciding on a case-by-case basis.[107]

Filing of Shareholder Lawsuits.   We earlier made reference to the Trans Union case wherein shareholders sued the board of directors for approving a buyout offer that the shareholders argued should have had a higher price tag. Their suit charged that the directors had been negligent in failing to secure a third-party opinion from experienced investment bankers. The case went to trial and resulted in a $23.5 million judgment against the directors.[108] The Trans Union case may be one of the largest successful shareholder suits, but it does not stand alone. One estimate was that the number of shareholder rights suits quadrupled over the decade from 1977 to 1987.[109] The large number of shareholder suits being filed today makes one think that almost every decision a company makes is subject to a shareholder suit. As these suits proliferate, many wonder whose interests are really being served. Quite often, the shareholders' attorneys walk away with more money than the protesting shareholders receive.

Shareholder suits are easy to file but difficult to defend. One study estimated that 70 percent of the suits are settled out of court. Therefore, charges of corporate wrongdoing are seldom resolved. Quite often, these lawsuits are seen as legitimate protests by shareholders against management actions, and the threat of litigation does deter corporate misbehavior. From the company's viewpoint, however, such lawsuits are an expensive nuisance. Some experts argue that management's quick willingness to settle before going to trial invites more suits. In spite of this, companies give in because the downside risks of trials and adverse publicity are too great.[110]

In 1995, Congress sought to stem the growing tide of shareholder lawsuits by passing the Private Securities Litigation Reform Act of 1995. The law made it more difficult for companies to bring class-action lawsuits to federal court.[111] However, rather than stemming the tide of lawsuits, the Act simply prompted shareholders to change their venue. Suits filed in federal court decreased, while suits filed in state courts increased. The Securities Litigation Uniform Standards Act of 1997 is designed to plug that loophole. In 1998, slightly different versions of the bill were passed by the House and the Senate and passage of a compromise bill appeared likely.[112]

Company Initiatives

The need for companies to reestablish a relationship with their owners/stakeholders is somewhat akin to parents having to reestablish relations with their children once the children have grown up. Over the years, the evidence suggests that corporate managements have neglected their owners rather than making them a genuine part of the family. As share ownership has dispersed, there are several legitimate reasons why this separation has taken place. But there is also evidence that management groups have been too preoccupied with their own self-interests. In either case, corporations are beginning to realize that they have a responsibility to their shareholders that cannot be further neglected. Owners are demanding accountability, and it appears that they will be tenacious until they get it.

Public corporations have obligations to their shareholders and to potential shareholders. Full disclosure is one of these responsibilities. Disclosure should be made at regular and frequent intervals and should contain information that might affect the investment decisions of shareholders. This information might include the nature and activities of the business, financial and policy matters, tender offers, and special problems and opportunities in the near future and in the longer term.[113] Of paramount importance are the interests of the investing public, not the interests of the incumbent management team. Board members should avoid conflicts between personal interests and the interests of shareholders. Company executives and directors have an obligation to avoid taking personal advantage of information that is not disclosed to the investing public and to avoid any personal use of corporation assets and influence.

With regard to corporate takeovers, fair treatment of shareholders necessitates special safeguards, including (1) candor in public statements on the offer made, (2) full disclosure of all information, (3) absence of undue pressure, and (4) sufficient time for shareholders to make considered decisions. A constructive purpose, not a predatory one, should be served by takeovers. The firm's major stakeholders are its owners. They are interdependent with other stakeholders, and, therefore, management should carry out its obligations to other constituency groups within the context of shareholder concern.[114]

Part of management's challenge is to have and maintain a constructive attitude toward shareholders. Some firms view shareholders with scorn, whereas others view them with sensitivity. Sun Company has illustrated the latter position. According to one Sun Company executive, "Shareholders are our business partners. It's helpful to us if management gets an insight on what they think of us." Sun is concerned about getting its point across, even to the smallest stockholder. Each new stockholder gets a welcoming note from the chairman. Each dividend check contains a folksy newsletter prepared by the shareholder relations department. The department randomly selects about 100 shareholders six or eight times a year and invites them to a dinner at which a top company executive speaks. Sun makes company news available to shareholders on a toll-free telephone line. Shareholders are invited to call the shareholder relations department whenever they have questions or something bothers them. The whole focus is one of active interest rather than the ambivalence or bare tolerance shown by some corporate management groups.[115]

Another way some companies are attempting to integrate shareholders into the corporate family is by getting them involved in political activities on behalf of the firm. One study found that shareholders often agree with company views on political issues. To the extent that this is true, companies can form grassroots networks of shareholders to call or write congressional representatives. Not everyone agrees with the strategy of using shareholders in this way, but it works for some firms. Sun Company has allowed shareholders to contribute to its PAC by automatically withholding part of their quarterly dividends, and this has been a successful program for them.[116]

Berkshire Hathaway Inc. has set up a program whereby shareholders are allowed to determine the recipients of the several million dollars in charitable contributions the firm gives each year. For each share owned, a shareholder can instruct the firm to send $3 to a designated charity. Warren E. Buffett, chairman, told shareholders: "Your charitable preferences are as good as mine." Shareholders have sent Mr. Buffett many letters praising this idea. Buffett hopes that the shareholder designation program will foster what he calls "an owner mentality" in the shareholders and that it will strengthen shareholder loyalty.[117]

None of these shareholder programs is a substitute for keeping shareholders foremost in the minds of managements and boards when economic decisions are being made. However, the programs do demonstrate an attempt by managements to give serious consideration to corporate/shareholder relations. Taken together, these programs help the corporate governance problem because they show the shareholders that they matter and that they are important to the firm.

SUMMARY

To remain legitimate, corporations must be governed according to the intended and legal pattern. However, corporations are not always being governed the way they were intended to be. One of the major criticisms is that managements have taken effective control away from boards of directors and are running the corporations in their own self-interests. Another, related criticism is that corporate boards have been remiss and have not functioned the way they should. It has been claimed that boards are rubber stamps for management groups, that they are dominated by the CEOs, and that they are riddled with conflicts of interest. The wave of mergers, acquisitions, and hostile takeovers that occurred in the 1980s brought to light other major problems—for example, greenmail, golden parachutes, and insider trading.

Over the past decade, several suggestions for improving corporate governance have been made. Most of them have centered on the role, composition, and functioning of the board of directors. It has been recommended that boards (1) be recomposed to include more independent, outside directors; (2) use stronger committees; and (3) assume more active roles in governance and direction. In addition to board changes, suggestions for reform have focused on an increased role for shareholders and federal chartering of corporations. Increased shareholder activism has become a reality as groups speak out at annual meetings, file and negotiate shareholder resolutions, and file lawsuits. For their part, company managements have taken the initiative on several fronts to reestablish relations with owners/stakeholders.

KEY TERMS

audit committee (page 565)

board of directors (page 550)

charter (page 550)

compensation committee (page 566)

corporate governance (page 549)

employees (page 551)

golden parachute (page 559)

greenmail (page 559)

inside directors (page 551)

insider trading (page 560)

legitimacy (page 548)

legitimation (page 548)

management (page 551)

nominating committee (page 566)

poison pill (page 559)

proxy process (page 553)

public issues committee (page 566)

risk arbitrage (page 561)

shareholders (page 550)

DISCUSSION QUESTIONS

1. Explain the corporate governance problem. Why has it occurred?
2. What are the major criticisms of boards of directors? Which single criticism do you find to be the most important? Why?
3. Explain how mergers, acquisitions, takeovers, greenmail, golden parachutes, and insider trading are related to the corporate governance issue.
4. Outline the major suggestions that have been set forth for improving corporate governance. In your opinion, which suggestions have the greatest chance of being effective? Why?
5. In what ways have companies taken the initiative in becoming more responsive to owners/stakeholders? Discuss.

ENDNOTES

1. Cited in Edwin M. Epstein and Dow Votaw (eds.), *Rationality, Legitimacy, Responsibility: Search for New Directions in Business and Society* (Santa Monica, CA: Goodyear Publishing Co., 1978), 72.
2. *Ibid.*, 73.
3. *Ibid.*
4. William R. Dill (ed.), *Running the American Corporation* (Englewood Cliffs, NJ: Prentice-Hall, 1978), 11.
5. Sumner Marcus and Kenneth Walters, "Assault on Managerial Autonomy," *Harvard Business Review* (January–February, 1978), 56–66.
6. Victor H. Palmieri, "Officers of the Board?" *The Wall Street Journal* (August 14, 1978). Also see "The Fight for Good Governance," *Harvard Business Review* (January–February, 1993), 76–83.
7. "Corporate Governance—New Heat on Outside Directors?" *Forbes* (October 1, 1977), 33.
8. Dill, 2.
9. Carl Icahn, "What Ails Corporate America—And What Should Be Done," *Business Week* (October 17, 1986), 101.
10. Murray L. Weidenbaum, *Strengthening the Corporate Board: A Constructive Response to Hostile Takeovers* (St. Louis: Washington University, Center for the Study of American Business, September, 1985), 4–5.
11. *Corporate Director's Guidebook* (Chicago: American Bar Association, 1978), 12. Also see Dawn-Marie Driscoll and W. Michael Hoffman, "Doing the Right Thing: Business Ethics and the Board of Directors," *Director's Monthly* (November, 1994).
12. Ram Charan, *Boards That Work: How Corporate Boards Create Competitive Advantage* (San Francisco: Jossey Bass, 1998), 3–4.
13. Weidenbaum, 11–16. Also see Murray Weidenbaum, *The Evolving Corporate Board* (St. Louis: Washington University, Center for the Study of American Business, May, 1994), 2–5.
14. Frederick D. Sturdivant, *Business and Society* (Homewood, IL: Richard D. Irwin, Inc., 1981), 341.
15. Weidenbaum (1985), 13; and Weidenbaum (1994), 3.
16. Judith H. Dobrzynski, "Corporate Boards May Finally Be Shaping Up," *Business Week* (August 9, 1993), 26.
17. Weidenbaum (1985), 15–16.
18. Rich Thomas and Larry Reibstein, "The Pay Police," *Newsweek* (June 17, 1991), 45.
19. Linda Himelstein, "Boardrooms: The Ties That Blind," *Business Week* (May 2, 1994), 112–114.
20. John A. Byrne, Ronald Grover, and Richard A. Melcher, "The Best and Worst Boards," *Business Week* (December 8, 1997), 90–98.
21. Ann Buchholtz, Michael Young, and Gary Powell, "Are Board Members Pawns or Watchdogs? The Link Between CEO Pay and Firm Performance," *Group and Organization Management* (March, 1998), 6–26.
22. John A. Byrne, "Executive Pay: Deliver—Or Else," *Business Week* (March 27, 1995), 36–38.

23. Nikos Vafeas and Zaharoulla Afxentiou, "The Association Between the SEC's 1992 Compensation Disclosure Rule and Executive Compensation Policy Changes," *Journal of Accounting and Public Policy* (Spring, 1998), 27–54.

24. Bethany McLean, "Where's the Loot Coming From?" *Fortune* (September 7, 1998), 128–130.

25. John A. Byrne, "The Flap Over Executive Pay," *Business Week* (May 6, 1994), 95.

26. Anne Fisher, "Readers on CEO Pay: Many Are Angry, A Few Really Think the Big Guy Is Worth It," *Fortune* (June 8, 1998), 296.

27. "CEO Pay: A Skyrocket That Could Backfire," *Business Week* (April 25, 1994), 146.

28. Tracey Grant, "Big Bucks on Board," *The Washington Post* (September 29, 1997), F3.

29. Geoffrey Colvin, "Is the Board Too Cushy?" *Director* (February, 1997), 64–65.

30. Judith H. Dobrzynski, "Directors' Pay Is Becoming an Issue Too," *Business Week* (May 6, 1991), 94.

31. Edward J. Zajac and James D. Westphal, "The Costs and Benefits of Managerial Incentives and Monitoring in Large U.S. Corporations: When Is More Not Better?" *Strategic Management Journal* (Winter, 1994), 121–142, special issue.

32. Thomas A. Steven, "CEO Pay: Mom Wouldn't Approve," *Fortune* (March 31, 1997), 119–120.

33. "This is Not Michael Eisner's Pay Stub," *Fortune* (June 8, 1998), 294.

34. John A. Pearce and Shaker A. Zahra, "The relative Power of CEOs and Boards of Directors: Associations with Corporate Performance," *Strategic Management Journal* (February, 1991), 135–153.

35. Ed Leefeldt, "Greenmail, Far from Disappearing, Is Doing Quite Well in Disguised Forms," *The Wall Street Journal* (December 4, 1984), 15.

36. *Ibid.*

37. Ruth Simon, "Needed: A Generic Remedy," *Forbes* (November 5, 1984), 40.

38. James B. Stewart and Daniel Hertzberg, "Life Becomes Easier for Corporate Raiders," *The Wall Street Journal* (August 22, 1986), 6.

39. Craig W. Friedrich, "Recent Developments," *Journal of Corporate Taxation* (Winter, 1998), 422–425.

40. Philip L. Cochran and Steven L. Wartick, "Golden Parachutes: Good for Management and Society?" in S. Prakash Sethi and Cecilia M. Falbe (eds.), *Business and Society: Dimensions of Conflict and Cooperation* (Lexington, MA: Lexington Books, 1987), 321.

41. Steven E. Prokesch, "Too Much Gold in the Parachutes?" *The New York Times* (January 26, 1986), 3–1, 28F.

42. Ann K. Buchholtz and Barbara A. Ribbens, "Role of Chief Executive Officers in Takeover Resistance: Effects of CEO Incentives and Individual Characteristics," *Academy of Management Journal* (June, 1994), 554–579.

43. Cochran and Wartick, 325–326.

44. Amy Barrett, "Insider Trading," *Business Week* (December 12, 1994), 71.

45. George Russell, "The Fall of a Wall Street Superstar," *Time* (November 24, 1986), 71.

46. *Ibid.*

47. Donald Baer, "Getting Even with Ivan and Company," *U.S. News & World Report* (March 2, 1987), 46.

48. Anthony Bianco and Gary Weiss, "Suddenly the Fish Get Bigger," *Business Week* (March 2, 1987), 29–30.

49. "New Arrests on Wall Street: Who's Next in the Insider Trading Scandal?" *Newsweek* (February 23, 1987), 48–50.

50. James B. Stewart, "Scenes from a Scandal: The Secret World of Michael Milkin and Ivan Boesky," *The Wall Street Journal* (October 2, 1991), B1.

51. Dennis B. Levine with William Hoffer, *Inside Out: An Insider's Account of Wall Street* (Putnam, 1991), reviewed by John Greenwald, "Bad Trades," *Time* (September 23, 1991). Also see Joe Queenan, "Wall Street Scoundrel," *The Wall Street Journal* (September 10, 1991), A18.

52. "The Age of Consolidation," *Business Week* (October 14, 1991), 86–93. See also "The Dealers Return," *Time* (September 16, 1991), 46–47.

53. Amy Borrus, "Mergers Today, Trouble Tomorrow?" *Business Week* (September 12, 1994), 30.

54. "Wanted: Clearer Laws on Insider Trading," *Business Week* (December 12, 1994), 126.

55. Richard W. Painter, Kimberly D. Krawiec, and Cynthia A. Williams, "Don't Ask, Just Tell: Insider Trading After *United States v. O'Hagan,*" *Virginia Law Review* (March, 1998), 153–228.

56. Adolph Berle and Gardiner Means, *The Modern Corporation and Private Property* (New York: Macmillan, 1932).

57. Leo Herzel, Richard W. Shepro, and Leo Katz, "Next-to-Last Word on Endangered Directors," *Harvard Business Review* (January–February, 1987), 38.

58. Neil Budde, "Shareholders and Raiders Stir Directors," *USA Today* (June 12, 1987), 1B.

59. "Who Sits on America's Corporate Boards?" *The Atlanta Journal* (April 14, 1991), P1.

60. Leslie Wayne, "Who's Playing the Board Game?" *The New York Times* (October 9, 1983), 18F.

61. Lawrence Ingrassia, "Outsider-Dominated Boards Grow, Spurred by Calls for Independence," *The Wall Street Journal* (November 3, 1980), 33.

62. Timothy D. Schellhardt, "More Directors Are Recruited from Outside," *The Wall Street Journal* (March 20, 1991), B1.

63. *Ibid.*, 56.

64. Weidenbaum (1985), 20.

65. Wayne, 18F.

66. "Who Sits on America's Corporate Boards?" P1.

67. "Fortune 500 Boards Adding More Women," *The Atlanta Journal* (November 15, 1994), F6.

68. Howard Muson, "Winds of Change: Who Are These Environmentalists Who Sit on Corporate Boards?" *Across the Board* (June, 1994), 16–23.

69. Weidenbaum (1994), 11.

70. John Viney and Theodore Jadick, *The Global Outside Director* (Chicago: Heidrick and Struggles, Inc., 1993), 2–3.

71. "A Landmark Ruling That Puts Board Members in Peril," *Business Week* (March 18, 1985), 56–57.

72. Laurie Baum and John A. Byrne, "The Job Nobody Wants: Outside Directors Find That the Risks and Hassles Just Aren't Worth It," *Business Week* (September 8, 1986), 57.

73. Paul E. Fiorella, "Why Comply? Directors Face Heightened Personal Liability After Caremark," *Business Horizons* (July/August, 1998), 49–52.

74. Donald E. Schwartz, "Corporate Governance," in Thorton Bradshaw and David Vogel (eds.), *Corporations and Their Critics* (New York: McGraw-Hill, 1981), 227–228.

75. Preston Townley, "Accountable—But to Whom?" *Across the Board* (October, 1993), 11.

76. Joann S. Lublin and Elizabeth MacDonald, "Scandals Signal Laxity of Audit Panels," *The Wall Street Journal* (July 17, 1998), B1.

77. Charles A. Anderson and Robert N. Anthony, *The New Corporate Directors: Insights for Board Members and Executives* (New York: John Wiley & Sons, 1986), 141.

78. Jeremy Bacon, *The Audit Committee: A Broader Mandate* (New York: The Conference Board, Research Report No. 914, 1988).

79. Arjay Miller, "A Director's Questions," *The Wall Street Journal* (August 18, 1980), 10.

80. Schwartz, 228.

81. David J. Dunn, "Directors Aren't Doing Their Jobs," *Fortune* (March 16, 1987), 118.

82. Weidenbaum (1985), 24, 31.

83. William R. Boulton, "The Evolving Board: A Look at the Board's Changing Roles and Information Needs," *Academy of Management Review* (October, 1978), 827–836.

84. Judith H. Dobrzynski, "At GM, A Magna Carta for Directors," *Business Week* (April 4, 1994), 37.

85. *Ibid.*

86. Thomas McCarroll, "Board Games," *Time* (February 8, 1993), 54.

87. Christina Duff, John Dorfman, and Joann Lublin, "Kmart's Embattled CEO Resigns Post Under Pressure from Key Shareholders," *The Wall Street Journal* (March 22, 1995), A3.

88. John A. Byrne, "At Least Chainsaw Al Knew How to Hire a Board," *Business Week* (June 29, 1998), 40.

89. Jay Lorsch, cited in Duff, Dorfman, and Lublin.

90. "Shareholders Should Exercise Their Rights," *Business Week* (May 18, 1987), 168.

91. Bruce Nussbaum and Judith Dobrzynski, "The Battle for Corporate Control," *Business Week* (May 18, 1987), 102–109.

92. "Time Warner Feels the Force of Shareholder Power," *Business Week* (July 29, 1991), 58.

93. "Bolting the Boardroom Door at Sears," *Business Week* (May 13, 1991), 86.

94. Duff, Dorfman, and Lublin, A3.

95. "Why Not Sack a Few Directors?" *Business Week* (December 8, 1997), 134.

96. Lauren Tainer, *The Origins of Shareholder Activism* (Washington, DC: Investor Responsibility Research Center, July, 1983), 2.

97. *Ibid.*, 1.

98. *Ibid.*, 12–22.

99. "Religious Activists Raise Cain with Corporations," *Chicago Tribune* (June 7, 1998), Business Section, 8.

100. *Ibid.*, 28–44. Also see the IRRC Web site at *www.irrc.org.*

101. Phyllis Feinberg, "Report Shows Growing Share for Institutions," *Pensions and Investments* (September 21, 1998), 25.

102. Dale Kurschner, "Tobacco Taboo: How Affirmative Action Are You?" *Business Ethics* (March/April, 1995), 14–15. Also see Robert C. Pozen, "Institutional Investors: The Reluctant Activists," *Harvard Business Review* (January–February, 1994), 140–149.

103. Richard C. Ferlauto, "Labor's Growing Shareholder Activism Agenda," *Pensions and Investments* (March 23, 1998), 12.

104. John A. Byrne, "How Much Should It Take to Keep the Board on Board?" *Business Week* (April 17, 1995), 41.

105. *Ibid.*

106. Leonard Apcar and Terry Brown, "GM Reputation Is Defended by Chairman Under Barrage of Shareholder Questions," *The Wall Street Journal* (May 23, 1977), 17.

107. "Shareholders and Corporate Hiring," *The New York Times* (May 23, 1998), A14. Information is also available on the SEC Web site (*www.sec.gov*) and the Social Investment Forum Web site (*www.socialinvest.org*).

108. Thomas J. Neff, "Liability Panic in the Board Room," *The Wall Street Journal* (November 10, 1986), 22.

109. Julie Amparano, "A Lawyer Flourishes by Suing Corporations for Their Shareholders," *The Wall Street Journal* (April 28, 1987), 1.

110. Richard B. Schmitt, "Attorneys Are Often Big Winners When Shareholders Sue Companies," *The Wall Street Journal* (June 12, 1986), 31.

111. Steven M. Schatz and Douglas J. Clark, "Securities Litigation," *International Financial Law Review* (June, 1998), 27.

112. Susanne Sclafane, "Securities Act Impact May Be Overstated," *National Underwriter* (August 3, 1998), 5, 46.

113. "The Responsibility of a Corporation to Its Shareholders," *Criteria for Decision Making* (C.W. Post Center, Long Island University, 1979), 14.

114. *Ibid.*, 14–15.

115. "Executives' View of Small Holders Ranges from Sensitivity to Scorn," *The Wall Street Journal* (April 8, 1981), 31.

116. Paul A. Gigot, "Some Corporations Trying to Turn Shareholders into a Political Force," *The Wall Street Journal* (January 19, 1982), 31.

117. Bill Richards, "Berkshire Hathaway Pleases Shareholders by Letting Them Earmark Corporate Gifts," *The Wall Street Journal* (April 26, 1983), 26.

P A R T 5

Strategic Management
for Social Responsiveness

18

Strategic Management and Corporate Public Policy

CHAPTER OBJECTIVES

After studying this chapter, you should be able to:

1 Explain the concept of corporate public policy and relate it to strategic management.

2 Articulate the four major strategy levels and explain enterprise-level strategy.

3 Enumerate and briefly describe how a concern for social and ethical issues fits into the strategic management process.

4 Relate the notion of social audits to strategic control.

5 Identify and discuss the four major stages in environmental analysis.

Understanding the multitude of external and internal social and public issues that impinge on business is not enough. Nor is it enough to appreciate the evolution of business's changing social role; the notions of corporate social responsibility and responsiveness, business ethics, and stakeholder management; and the intricacies of the complex business/government relationship. This knowledge primarily provides a frame of reference for the formulation of corporate public policy and the implementation of corporate social action.

In this chapter and the next two, we more closely examine how management has responded and should respond, in a managerial sense, to the kinds of social and ethical issues we have been discussing up to this point. Although we have mentioned in previous chapters how business has or should respond to stakeholder groups with various efforts and programs, we now want to consider how the traditional processes of management have been affected by business's acceptance of the social environment as a legitimate influence in decision making and corporate action.

In this chapter, we provide a broad overview of how social, ethical, and public issues fit into the general strategic management processes of the organization. We use the term "corporate public policy" to describe that component part of management decision making that embraces these issues. The overriding goal of this chapter is to focus on planning for the turbulent social or stakeholder environment, and this encompasses the strategic management process and environmental analysis.

UNDERSTANDING THE CONCEPT OF CORPORATE PUBLIC POLICY

The impact of the social-ethical-public environment on business organizations is becoming more pronounced each year. It is an understatement to suggest that this complex environment has become tumultuous, and brief reminders of a few actual cases points out the validity of this claim quite dramatically. Procter & Gamble and its Rely Tampon recall, Firestone and its radial tire debacle, Ford Motor Company and its disastrous Pinto gas tank problem, and Johnson & Johnson and its Tylenol capsules are reminders of how social issues can directly affect a firm's product offerings. In addition, there are many examples in which social issues have had major impacts on firms at the general management level.[1] Bank of Boston's involvement in money laundering, E. F. Hutton's high-level check-kiting scheme, General Electric's and General Dynamics' fraudulent overcharges on defense contracts, Exxon's catastrophic *Valdez* oil spill, Drexel Burnham's involvement with junk bonds and securities fraud, and Dow Corning's ill-fated silicone breast implants are all examples of the impacts of top-level decisions that entail ethical ramifications.

What started as an awareness of social issues and social responsibility in the 1960s matured into a focus on the management of social responsiveness in the 1970s. Now it looms on the horizon as an emphasis, if not a preoccupation, with ethics, stakeholders, and corporate public policy as we approach the millennium. The term "corporate public policy" is an outgrowth of an earlier term, "corporate social policy," which has been in general usage for over 20 years. The two concepts have essentially the same meaning, but we will use "corporate public policy" because it is more in keeping with terminology used in business today. Apparently, the word "social" has connotations that the business community wants to get away from; therefore, we will use the language that is more applicable to actual business practice.

Corporate Public Policy Defined

What is meant by corporate public policy? Let us set forth and use the following definition. *Corporate public policy* is a firm's posture, stance, or position regarding the public, social, and ethical aspects of stakeholders and corporate functioning. Businesses encounter many situations in their daily operations that involve highly visible public and ethical issues. Some of these issues are subject to intensive public debate for specific periods of time before they become institutionalized. Examples of such issues include sexual harassment, AIDS in the workplace, affirmative action, product safety, and employee privacy. Other issues are more basic, more enduring, and more philosophical.

SEARCH THE WEB

One of the best ways to appreciate a company's corporate public policy or enterprise level strategy is to examine the company's posture on social/ethical issues. A company that was recognized recently for its corporate public policy was SmithKline Beecham, one of the world's leading health care companies. With corporate headquarters in London and U.S. headquarters in Philadelphia, SmithKline employs 58,000 people worldwide.

In January 1998, SmithKline announced one of the largest global disease-elimination programs ever undertaken. In its 10th Annual Business Ethics awards in 1998, *Business Ethics* magazine honored SmithKline for its path-breaking, $1 billion worldwide commitment to eradicating lymphatic filariasis, the second largest cause of disability in the world. The disease affects 120 million people in 73 countries.

For insights into SmithKline Beecham and its corporate public policy, visit its Web site at **www.sb.com**. To learn more about the company's path-breaking and award-winning Global Programme to Eliminate Lymphatic Filariasis, visit the following Web page: **www.sb.com/company/community/gpe_main.htm**.

Reference: Skip Kaltenheuser, "10th Annual Business Ethics Awards," *Business Ethics* (November–December, 1998), 10–11.

These issues might include the broad role of business in society, the corporate governance question, and the relative balance of business versus government direction that is best for our society.

The idea behind corporate public policy is that a firm must give specific attention to issues in which basic questions of right, wrong, justice, fairness, or public policy reside. The dynamic stakeholder environment of the past 25 to 30 years has necessitated that management apply a policy perspective to these issues. At one time, the social environment was thought to be a relatively constant backdrop against which the real work of business took place. Today these issues are center stage, and managers at all levels must address them. Corporate public policy is the process by which management addresses these heretofore neglected concerns.

Corporate Public Policy as Part of Strategic Management

Where does corporate public policy fit into a concern for strategic management? First, let us briefly discuss strategic management. *Strategic management* refers to the overall management process that focuses on positioning a firm relative to its environment. A basic way in which the firm relates to its environment is through the products and services it produces and the markets it chooses to address. Strategic management is also thought of as a kind of overall organizational management by the firm's top-level executives. In this sense, it represents the overall executive leadership function in which the sense of direction of the organization is decided on and implemented.

Top management must address many issues as a firm is positioning itself relative to its environment. The more traditional issues involve product/market decisions—the principal decision thrust of most organizations. Other decisions relate to competition, marketing, finance, accounting, personnel, production, research and development, and so on. Corporate public policy is that part of the overall strategic management of the organization that focuses specifically on the public, ethical, and stakeholder issues that are embedded in the functioning and decision processes of the firm. Therefore, just as a firm needs to develop policy on personnel, production, marketing, or finance, it also must develop a corporate public policy to deal with the host of issues we have been discussing throughout this book.

Relationship of Ethics to Strategic Management

Although a consideration of ethics is implicit in corporate public policy discussions, it is useful to make this relationship more explicit by special mention here. Over the years, a growing number of writers have stressed this point. Kenneth R. Andrews, for example, is well known for his emphasis on the moral component of corporate strategy. In particular, he highlights the leadership challenge of determining future strategy in the face of rising moral and ethical standards. He argues that coming to terms with the morality of choice may be the most strenuous undertaking in strategic decision making. This is particularly stressful in the inherently amoral corporation.[2]

The challenge of linking ethics and strategy was moved to center stage by R. Edward Freeman and Daniel R. Gilbert, Jr., in their book *Corporate Strategy and the Search for Ethics*. The authors argued that if business ethics was to have any meaning beyond pompous moralizing, it must be linked to business strategy. Their view is that we can revitalize the concept of corporate strategy by linking ethics to strategy. This linkage permits the most pressing management issues of the day to be addressed in ethical terms. They suggest the concept of enterprise strategy as the idea that best links these two vital notions together, and we will examine this concept in more detail in the next section.[3]

The concept of corporate public policy and the linkage between ethics and strategy are better understood when we think about (1) the four key levels at which strategy decisions arise and (2) the steps in the strategic management process.

FOUR KEY STRATEGY LEVELS

Because organizations are hierarchical, it is not surprising to find that strategic management is hierarchical, too. That is, there are several different levels in the firm at which strategic decisions are made or the strategy process occurs. These levels range from the broadest or highest levels (where missions, goals, decisions, and policies entail higher risks and are characterized by longer time horizons, more subjective values, and greater uncertainty) to the lowest levels (where planning is done for specific functional areas, where time horizons are shorter, where information needs are less complex, and where there is less uncertainty). Four key strategy levels are important to consider: enterprise-level strategy, corporate-level strategy, business-level strategy, and functional-level strategy.

The Four Strategy Levels

The broadest level of strategic management is known as societal-level strategy or **enterprise-level strategy**, as it has come to be known. Enterprise-level strategy is the overarching strategy level that poses the basic question, *"What is the role of the organization in society?"* Enterprise-level strategy, as we will discuss in more detail later, encompasses the development and articulation of corporate public policy. It is the first and most important level at which ethics and strategy are linked. Until fairly recently, **corporate-level strategy** was thought to be the broadest strategy level. In a limited, traditional sense, this is true, because corporate-level strategy addresses what is often posed as the most defining question for a firm, *"What business(es) are we in or should we be in?"* It is easy to see how **business-level strategy** is a natural follow-on because this strategy level is concerned with the question, *"How should we compete in a given business or industry?"* Thus, a company whose products or services take it into many different businesses or industries might need a business-level strategy to define its competitive posture in each of them. A competitive strategy might be based on low cost or a differentiated product. Finally, **functional-level strategy** addresses the question, *"How should a firm integrate its various subfunctional activities and how should these activities be related to changes taking place in the various functional areas (finance, marketing, production)?"*[4]

The purpose of identifying the four strategy levels is to clarify that corporate public policy is primarily a part of enterprise-level strategy, which, in turn, is but one level of strategic decision making that occurs in organizations. Figure 18–1 illustrates that enterprise-level strategy is the broadest level and that the other levels are narrower concepts that flow from it.

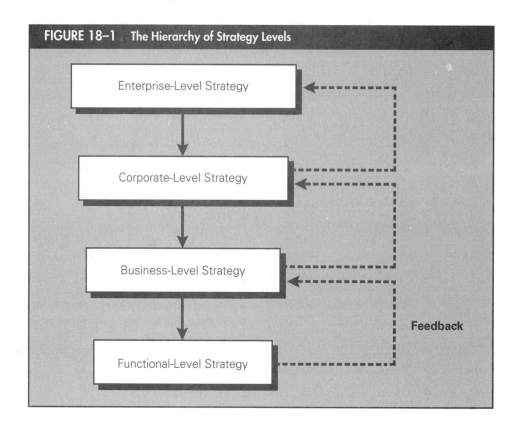

FIGURE 18–1 The Hierarchy of Strategy Levels

Emphasis on Enterprise-Level Strategy

The terms "enterprise-level strategy" and "societal-level strategy" may be used interchangeably. The reader needs to be alerted to the fact that neither of these terms is used with any degree of regularity in the business community. Although many firms address the issues that enterprise-level strategy is concerned with, use of this terminology is restricted primarily to the academic community. This terminology arose in an attempt to describe the level of strategic thinking that an increasing number of observers believe is necessary if firms are to be fully responsive to today's complex and dynamic social environment. Many organizations today convey this enterprise or societal strategy in their missions or values statements. Others embed their enterprise strategies in codes of conduct.

Igor Ansoff visualized the enterprise strategy level as one in which the political legitimacy of the organization is addressed.[5] Ansoff later discussed this same concern for legitimacy using the title "Societal Strategy for the Business Firm."[6] Hofer and others have described the enterprise level as the societal level.

According to Ed Freeman, enterprise-level strategy needs to be thought of in such a way that it more closely aligns "social and ethical concerns" with traditional "business concerns."[7] In setting the direction for a firm, a manager needs to understand the impact of changes in business strategy on the underlying values of the firm and the new stakeholder relations that will emerge and take shape as a result. Freeman proposes that enterprise-level strategy needs to address the overriding question, "What do we stand for?"[8] Thus, at the enterprise level the task of setting strategic direction involves understanding the role of a particular firm as a whole and its relationships to other social institutions. The appropriate questions then become:

- What is the role of our organization in society?

- How is our organization perceived by our stakeholders?

- What principles or values does our organization represent?

- What obligations do we have to society at large?

- What are the implications for our current mix of business and allocation of resources?

Many firms have addressed some of these questions—perhaps only in part, perhaps only in an ad hoc way. The point of enterprise-level strategy, however, is that the firm needs to address these questions intentionally, specifically, and cohesively in such a way that a corporate public policy is articulated.

How have business firms addressed these questions? What are the manifestations of enterprise-level thinking and corporate public policy? The manifestations show up in a variety of ways in different companies—for example, how a firm responds when faced with public crises. Does it respond to its stakeholders in a positive, constructive, and sensitive way or in a negative, defensive, and insensitive way? Corporate actions reveal the presence or absence of soundly developed enterprise-level strategy. Companies also demonstrate the degree of thinking that has gone into public issues by the presence or absence and use or nonuse of codes of ethics, codes of conduct, mission statements, values statements, corporate creeds, vision statements, or other such policy-oriented codes and statements.

One company that has addressed these concerns is Borg-Warner. In a document entitled "Believe It: Managing by Shared Values at Borg-Warner," Chairman James F. Bere posed and then answered these questions:

- What kind of company are we anyway?

- What does Borg-Warner stand for?

- What do we believe?

Figure 18–2 presents "The Beliefs of Borg-Warner," a document that clearly manifests enterprise-level strategy and corporate public policy.

Another example of enterprise-level strategy is the corporate credo of Johnson & Johnson, shown in Figure 18–3. Note that the Johnson & Johnson credo focuses on statements of responsibility by enumerating its stakeholder groups in the following sequence:

- Doctors, nurses, patients, mothers and fathers (consumers)

- Employees

- Communities

- Stockholders

FIGURE 18–2   The Beliefs of Borg-Warner: To Reach Beyond the Minimal

Any business is a member of a social system, entitled to the rights and bound by the responsibilities of that membership. Its freedom to pursue economic goals is constrained by law and channeled by the forces of a free market. But these demands are minimal, requiring only that a business provide wanted goods and services, compete fairly, and cause no obvious harm. For some companies, that is enough. It is not enough for Borg-Warner. We impose upon ourselves an obligation to reach beyond the minimal. We do so convinced that by making a larger contribution to the society that sustains us, we best ensure not only its future vitality, but our own.

This is what we believe.

We believe in the dignity of the individual.

However large and complex a business may be, its work is still done by people dealing with people. Each person involved is a unique human being, with pride, needs, values, and innate personal worth. For Borg-Warner to succeed, we must operate in a climate of openness and trust, in which each of us freely grants others the same respect, cooperation, and decency we seek for ourselves.

We believe in our responsibility to the common good.

Because Borg-Warner is both an economic and social force, our responsibilities to the public are large. The spur of competition and the sanctions of the law give strong guidance to our behavior, but alone do not inspire our best. For that we must heed the voice of our natural concern for others. Our challenge is to supply goods and services that are of superior value to those who use them; to create jobs that provide meaning for those who do them; to honor and enhance human life; and to offer our talents and our wealth to help improve the world we share.

We believe in the endless quest for excellence.

Although we may be better today than we were yesterday, we are not as good as we must become. Borg-Warner chooses to be a leader—in serving our customers, advancing our technologies, and rewarding all who invest in us their time, money, and trust. None of us can settle for doing less than our best, and we can never stop trying to surpass what already has been achieved.

We believe in continuous renewal.

A corporation endures and prospers only by moving forward. The past has given us the present to build on. But to follow our visions to the future, we must see the difference between traditions that give us continuity and strength, and conventions that no longer serve us—and have the courage to act on that knowledge. Most can adapt after change has occurred; we must be among the few who anticipate change, shape it to our purpose, and act as its agents.

We believe in the commonwealth of Borg-Warner and its people.

Borg-Warner is both a federation of businesses and a community of people. Our goal is to preserve the freedom each of us needs to find personal satisfaction while building the strength that comes from unity. True unity is more than a melding of self-interests; it results when values and ideals also are shared. Some of ours are spelled out in these statements of belief. Others include faith in our political, economic, and spiritual heritage; pride in our work and our company; the knowledge that loyalty must flow in many directions; and a conviction that power is strongest when shared. We look to the unifying force of these beliefs as a source of energy to brighten the future of our company and all who depend upon it.

SOURCE: Company document, Borg-Warner Corporation. Reproduced by permission.

FIGURE 18–3   Johnson & Johnson Credo

Our Credo

We believe our first responsibility is to the doctors, nurses and patients,
to mothers and fathers and all others who use our products and services.
In meeting their needs everything we do must be of high quality.
We must constantly strive to reduce our costs.
in order to maintain reasonable prices.
Customers' orders must be serviced promptly and accurately.
Our suppliers and distributors must have an opportunity
to make a fair profit.

We are responsible to our employees,
the men and women who work with us throughout the world.
Everyone must be considered as an individual.
We must respect their dignity and recognize their merit.
They must have a sense of security in their jobs.
Compensation must be fair and adequate,
and working conditions clean, orderly and safe.
We must be mindful of ways to help our employees fulfill
their family responsibilities.
Employees must feel free to make suggestions and complaints.
There must be equal opportunity for employment, development
and advancement for those qualified.
We must provide competent management,
and their actions must be just and ethical.

We are responsible to the communities in which we live and work
and to the world community as well.
We must be good citizens—support good works and charities
and bear our fair share of taxes.
We must encourage civic improvements and better health and education.
We must maintain in good order
the property we are privileged to use,
protecting the environment and natural resources.

Our final responsibility is to our stockholders.
Business must make a sound profit.
We must experiment with new ideas.
Research must be carried on, innovative programs developed
and mistakes paid for.
New equipment must be purchased, new facilities provided
and new products launched.
Reserves must be created to provide for adverse times.
When we operate according to these principles,
the stockholders should realize a fair return.

Johnson & Johnson

SOURCE: Reprinted courtesy of Johnson & Johnson.

The "core values" program implemented at the Aluminum Company of America (Alcoa) by its chairman Paul H. O'Neill is another excellent illustration of an enterprise-level strategy. O'Neill had been chairman of Alcoa for less than 3 months when he began making decisions that seemed to reflect a new way of thinking at Alcoa. Four years later, it became apparent that Alcoa's six "core values" would provide the guiding direction for a new corporate conscience at the firm.[9]

The six "core values" at Alcoa were identified and articulated by O'Neill, then company president C. Fred Fetterolf, and ten senior executives during 100 hours of discussions and reflections. The core values program, known as "Visions, Values, and Milestones," set forth a new ethics agenda built around the following six core values:

1. Integrity

2. Safety and health

3. Quality of work

4. Treatment of people

5. Accountability

6. Profitability

In part, O'Neill and Fetterolf placed values at the center of their corporate culture out of deep personal religious convictions. They argued that biblical principles such as truthfulness, compassion, and stewardship should not stop at the factory gate. On another level, they said they were attempting to reshape the company into the kind of unified, harmonious enterprise that would be needed to survive and compete in the global marketplace of the future.[10]

In terms of implementation, Alcoa first began disseminating the core values to its employees. Follow-up was done with films, training seminars, and departmental meetings. Later, the company began evaluating employees to see how well they had been applying the core values in their work. Although Alcoa, like all large metalmakers, has faced some tough economic times, O'Neill argued that whether business was good or bad, the firm was committed to its ethics program. O'Neill argued, "I don't think it's necessary to compromise your values to succeed economically."[11]

Another illustration of enterprise-level strategic thinking may be seen in the "Commitment to Integrity" statement articulated by The Boeing Company. This statement, presented in Figure 18–4, reflects the company's values and how these values are targeted toward a vision of full customer satisfaction. Merck & Co., Inc., the leading pharmaceutical firm, conveys its enterprise strategy in its values statement, which is part of its mission statement. Herman Miller, maker of office furniture, reflects its enterprise strategy in its "Blueprint for Corporate Community." In 1998, Herman Miller was judged to be *Fortune*'s "most admired" major corporation in the category of social responsibility.[12]

Other manifestations of enterprise-level strategic thinking in corporations include the extent to which firms have established board or senior management committees. Such committees might include the following: public policy/issues committees, ethics committees, social audit committees, corporate philanthropy

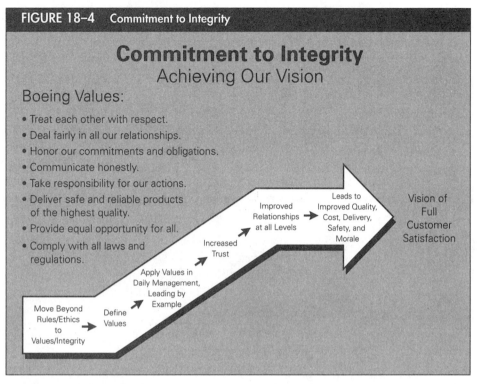

FIGURE 18–4   Commitment to Integrity

Commitment to Integrity
Achieving Our Vision

Boeing Values:

- Treat each other with respect.
- Deal fairly in all our relationships.
- Honor our commitments and obligations.
- Communicate honestly.
- Take responsibility for our actions.
- Deliver safe and reliable products of the highest quality.
- Provide equal opportunity for all.
- Comply with all laws and regulations.

Move Beyond Rules/Ethics to Values/Integrity → Define Values → Apply Values in Daily Management, Leading by Example → Increased Trust → Improved Relationships at all Levels → Leads to Improved Quality, Cost, Delivery, Safety, and Morale → Vision of Full Customer Satisfaction

SOURCE: Reprinted courtesy of Boeing.

committees, and ad hoc committees to address specific public issues. The firm's public affairs function can also indicate enterprise-level thinking. Does the firm have an established public affairs office? To whom does the director of corporate public affairs report? What role does public affairs play in corporate-level decision making? Do public affairs managers play a formal role in the firm's strategic planning?

Another major indicator of enterprise-level strategic thinking is the extent to which the firm attempts to identify social or public issues, analyze them, and integrate them into its strategic management processes. We will now discuss how corporate public policy is integrated into the strategic management process.

THE STRATEGIC MANAGEMENT PROCESS

To understand how corporate public policy is but one part of the larger system of management decision making, it is useful to provide an overview of the major steps that make up the strategic management process. There are several acceptable ways to conceptualize this process, but we will use the six-step process identified by Hofer and Schendel. These six steps are (1) goal formulation, (2) strategy formulation, (3) strategy evaluation, (4) strategy implementation, (5) strategic control, and (6) environmental analysis.[13] Figure 18–5 graphically portrays an expanded view of this

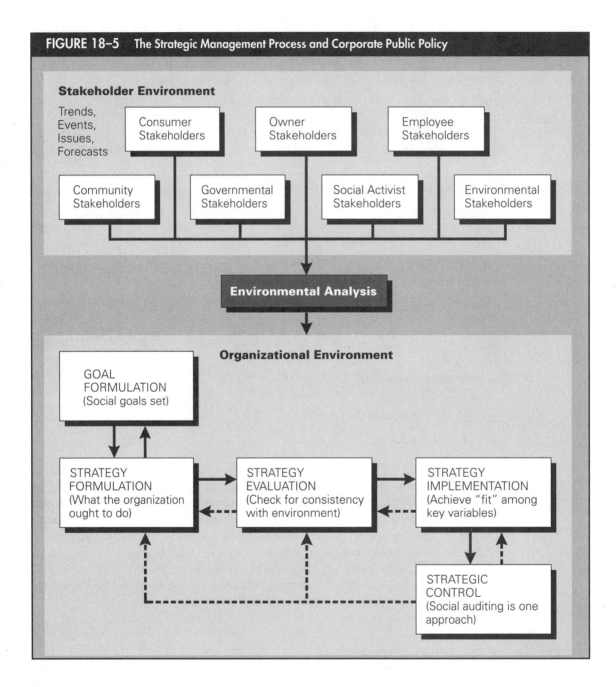

FIGURE 18–5   The Strategic Management Process and Corporate Public Policy

process. Note that the environmental analysis component collects information on trends, events, and issues that are occurring in the stakeholder environment and that this information is then fed into the other steps of the process. Note also that, although the tasks or steps are discussed sequentially in this chapter, they are in fact interactive and do not always occur in a neatly ordered pattern or sequence. We will discuss the first five steps, then consider environmental analysis, which links the stakeholder environment with the organizational environment.

Goal Formulation

The **goal formulation** process of an organization is a complex task. It involves both the establishment of goals and the setting of priorities among goals. Often a politically charged process, goal formulation integrates the personal values, perceptions, attitudes, and power of the managers and owners involved in the process. Economic or financial goals typically dominate the goal formulation process. It is being increasingly recognized, however, that goal setting as it pertains to the public, social, and ethical domains of the firm is in dire need of more attention.[14] Typical areas in which public policy goals might be set include affirmative action, consumer product safety, occupational safety and health, corporate philanthropy, and environmental protection. Furthermore, it has become clear that economic and social goals are not at odds with each other and that the two can be integrated in such a way that the firm's best interests, as well as the best interests of the stakeholders, are simultaneously served.[15]

We should note that the steps in the strategic management process could be activated for each of the four levels of strategy discussed earlier. Therefore, the strategic management process entails a system of decisions in which goals are successively more refined—moving from broad to specific—just as we illustrated in Figure 18–1. The result is a cascading of goals that addresses the various domains that have been identified.

Strategy Formulation

Once goals have been established, the *strategy formulation* process becomes important. It is difficult to neatly factor out the formulation, evaluation, implementation, and control aspects of the process, because in real life they are intimately related and interdependent. For purposes of discussion, however, we will treat them as though they were distinct steps.

As shown in Figure 18–6, Kenneth Andrews suggests that there are four major components of the **strategy formulation** decision: (1) identification and appraisal of the firm's *strengths and weaknesses,* (2) identification and appraisal of *opportunities and threats* in the environment, (3) identification and appraisal of *personal values and aspirations of management,* and (4) identification and appraisal of *acknowledged obligations to society.*[16]

Components 1 and 2 are the most fundamental, because they require a company to examine carefully its own capabilities—its strengths, weaknesses, and resources—and think in terms of matching those capabilities with the opportunities, threats, and risks present in the market environment. Another way of stating this is that management must compare what the firm *can do* with what it *might do.* An analysis of the company's strengths and weaknesses is compatible with the "resource-based view of the firm," which has become quite popular in strategic management theory in the past decade. This view holds that strategic managers must look carefully at the firm's resources to identify critical factors that are likely to contribute to competitive advantage.[17]

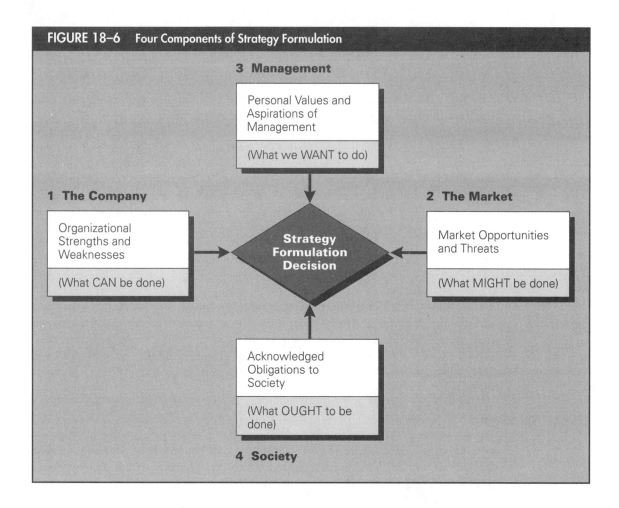

FIGURE 18-6   Four Components of Strategy Formulation

3 Management

Personal Values and Aspirations of Management

(What we WANT to do)

1 The Company

Organizational Strengths and Weaknesses

(What CAN be done)

Strategy Formulation Decision

2 The Market

Market Opportunities and Threats

(What MIGHT be done)

Acknowledged Obligations to Society

(What OUGHT to be done)

4 Society

Components 3 and 4 are also vital. Realistically, attention needs to be paid to the personal values and aspirations of the management group. These subjective influences are real and, therefore, must be factored into the strategy formulation process. Thus, Component 3—what management *wants to do*—is a key factor. Finally, strategic choice has a social or an ethical aspect that can no longer be ignored. Component 4—what the firm *ought to do* in terms of its acknowledged obligations to society—should be factored in as well.[18]

Component 4 is the corporate public policy component in strategy formulation. It is not the most urgent factor, because a firm that does not have an acceptable matching of organizational characteristics with market characteristics (Components 1 and 2) will not survive. However, in today's business environment, the successful firm blends these components in such a way that the needs or issues arising out of each are properly addressed. A careful consideration of how these public or ethical issues should be defined is discussed more fully in the subsection on environmental analysis in this chapter, as well as in the next two chapters.

Strategy Evaluation

In some conceptualizations of the strategic management process, *strategy evaluation* occurs in conjunction with strategic control, after implementation has taken place. We are treating it as the third step in the strategic management process because, in an ongoing organization, it can also be viewed as an integrative process that takes place in conjunction with goal formulation and strategy formulation. In an ongoing organization that already has a strategy, strategy evaluation entails a continuing assessment of the firm's current goals and strategy relative to proposed goals and strategic alternatives. Seymour Tilles[19] has set forth, in question form, six criteria for evaluating strategy:

1. Is the strategy internally consistent?

2. Is the strategy consistent with the environment?

3. Is the strategy appropriate in view of available resources?

4. Does the strategy involve an acceptable degree of risk?

5. Does the strategy have an appropriate time frame?

6. Is the strategy workable?

Each of these criteria is important in strategy evaluation. Perhaps the most important, in terms of corporate public policy, is the strategy's consistency with the environment. The stakeholder environment is complex and dynamic, and the strategy that was once successful may no longer be so. Careful attention to this criterion, then, should be the hallmark of a successful public policy.

Strategy Implementation

No strategy design, however grand, will benefit an organization if it is left on the drawing board. In its simplest form, *strategy implementation* means putting the plans (goals, strategies) that have been developed and evaluated into effect. It means working the plan with the aim of achieving the desired results. At a more complex level, implementation means that many different organizational processes must be activated and coordinated in such a way that the implementation is successful.

The McKinsey 7S framework is a straightforward identification of seven key variables that must be skillfully coordinated in order for successful strategy implementation to occur. These seven variables are strategy, structure, systems, style, staff, skills, and shared values.[20]

The 7S framework was originally conceived as a way of broadly thinking about the problems of effective organizing, but it also provides an excellent vehicle for thinking about the elements that must be successfully coordinated in strategy implementation. Of particular note in terms of corporate public policy is the "shared values" element. Although these shared values did not refer to shared ethical or social responsiveness values in the original 7S framework, we can readily see how they might be expanded to embrace more than "corporate culture" as it has most typically been conceived.

The key to the successful use of the 7S framework is achieving *fit*, or congruence, among all of the elements. *Fit* is a process, as well as a state, in which there is a dynamic search that seeks to align an organization with its environment and to arrange internal resources in such a way that the alignment is supported. It is argued that a "minimal fit" is essential for survival in a competitive environment and that a "tight fit" is needed for long-term effectiveness.[21]

Strategic Control

As a management function, **strategic control** seeks to ensure that the organization stays on track and achieves its goals and strategies. The first three elements we have discussed so far in this section—goal formulation, strategy formulation, and strategy evaluation—are parts of the overall planning that is essential if firms are to succeed. Planning is not complete without control, however, because control aims to keep management activities in conformance with plans.

Traditionally, control has subsumed three essential steps: (1) setting standards against which performance may be compared, (2) comparing actual performance with what was planned (the standard), and (3) taking corrective action to bring the two back into alignment, if needed.[22] It has been argued that a planning system will not achieve its full potential unless at the same time it monitors and assesses the firm's progress along key strategic dimensions. Furthermore, there is a need to control the "strategic momentum" by focusing on a particular strategic direction while at the same time coping with environmental turbulence and change.[23]

Development of the Social Audit

In the context of corporate social performance or corporate public policy, the idea of a **social audit**, or social performance report, as a technique for providing control has been experimented with for a number of years. Although the term "social audit" has been used to describe a wide variety of activities, in this discussion we define it as follows:

> *The social audit is a systematic attempt to identify, measure, monitor, and evaluate an organization's performance with respect to its social efforts, goals, and programs.*

Implicit in this definition is the idea that planning has already taken place. And although we discuss the social audit here as a control mechanism, it could just as easily be thought of as a planning/control technique.[24]

In the context of strategic control, the social audit could assume a role much like that portrayed in Figure 18–7. This figure is similar to the diagram of the strategic management process and corporate public policy shown in Figure 18–5 but is modified somewhat to focus on social goals, corporate social performance, the social audit, and the first three steps in the strategic control process.

Although the corporate social audit is not in widespread use in U.S. industry today, it is worth considering in more detail because of its potential for serving as a planning and control mechanism. Again, the components of the social audit include *identification, measurement, monitoring,* and *evaluation.* The identification function is included as a part of the definition because experience has shown that companies often are not completely aware of all that they are doing in the social or ethics arena. Any serious effort to determine what a company is doing requires the development of measures by which performance can be reported, analyzed, and

FIGURE 18–7   The Social Audit in the Context of Strategic Control

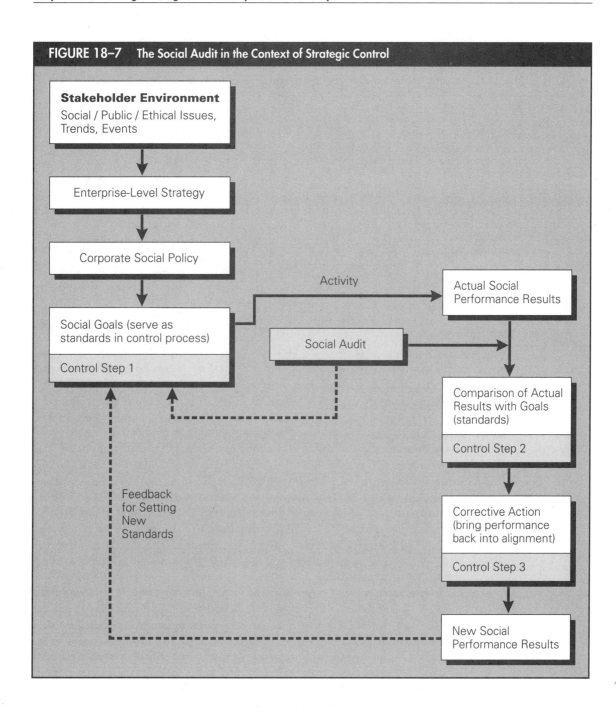

compared. Monitoring and evaluation stress that the effort is continuous and aimed at achieving certain standards or goals the company may have in mind.

The term "social audit" has been subjected to some criticism. The foremost objection has been that it implies an "independent attestation" to the company's social performance, whereas such an independent attestation typically does not exist. The term "audit," as used by accountants, usually means a verification by some outside party that the firm's situation is as it has been reported. Because social audits are typically conducted by people within the organization, it is obvious why this objection is raised. The criticism has also been made that there exist no generally accepted social accounting principles, no professionally recognized independent auditors, and no generally agreed-on criteria against which to measure a firm's social performance.[25] Despite these concerns, the term "social audit" continues to be used. More recently, firms have been using "ethics audits" or "stakeholder audits" to describe efforts to review social performance.

Another term, *social accounting*, is frequently used in reference to social auditing and has been defined as follows: "The measurement and reporting, internal or external, of information concerning the impact of an entity and its activities on society."[26] We can readily see that these definitions are quite similar. The only term for the function we have been describing that has not been severely criticized is "corporate social performance reporting." However, there is some evidence that this term is no longer in vogue. We will, nevertheless, use all these terms interchangeably and urge the reader to keep in mind the points we have made with respect to each. This is especially necessary in regard to social auditing, a term we will use frequently, because it is so much a part of the already existing literature on and experience of social performance measurement and reporting.

The social audit as a concept for monitoring, measuring, and appraising the social performance of business dates back over 50 years to at least 1940.[27] In a 1940 publication of the Temporary National Economic Committee, Theodore J. Kreps presented a monograph entitled *Measurement of the Social Performance of Business*.[28] Not only was the term "social audit" used in 1940 (a remarkable fact considering that a firm's social performance was hardly discussed then), but it was used in a vein similar to that employed today—as a concept for measuring the social performance of business. In fact, Kreps introduced the term "social audit" in a chapter entitled "Tests of Social Performance."[29]

Upon close examination of Kreps's monograph, however, we find that many of what he called "social issues" during this late Depression/pre-World War II period were closer to what we would refer to today as economic issues. For example, the measurements he used were employment, production, payroll, dividends, and interest.[30] In contrast to current social audits, the Kreps audit involved more economic-type issues, represented a governmental evaluation of business's social performance, and was to be used by society to assess business performance.

Another landmark in the development of social audits came in 1953 in a book by Howard R. Bowen.[31] Bowen's concept of the social audit was that of a high-level, independent appraisal conducted about every 5 years by a group of disinterested auditors. The auditors' report would be an evaluation with recommendations intended for internal use by the directors and the management of the firm audited.

Some of the areas that Bowen designated for auditing were similar to those of Kreps, but Bowen also included more socially oriented activities.

In contrast to these earlier landmark models, the social audit as it came of age in the 1970s attempted to focus on such social performance categories as minority employment, pollution/environment, community relations, consumer issues, and philanthropic contributions. Very few companies initially undertook social audits as control mechanisms. To use a device as a control mechanism implied that there were some goals or standards against which to compare actual performance. Initially, social audits were employed by companies to examine what the company was actually doing in selected areas, appraise or evaluate social performance, identify social programs that the company thought it ought to be pursuing, or just inject into the general thinking of managers a social point of view.[32] During this early time, companies had not developed enterprise-level strategy or corporate social policy. As firms began to plan for the social environment and to set social goals, the social audit began to be better used as a control mechanism.

Social auditing fell out of favor in the 1980s. In the 1990s, however, there has been some resurgence in interest in social performance, ethics, and values audits and reports. Several examples illustrate. As part of an ethics program at Dow Corning, for example, six managers serve 3-year terms on a Business Conduct Committee. Dow Corning schedules this committee to conduct an ethics audit of each of its business operations every 3 years. These audits include 3-hour review sessions with employees at the audited location. The committee then reports its findings to the Audit and Social Responsibility Committee of the Dow Corning Board of Directors.[33]

One of the most comprehensive examples of social or ethical auditing is the process conducted by The Body Shop, the skin and hair products company. The Body Shop began its ethics audit process in the early 1990s, and the process yielded several major reports, the most recent of which is the *Values Report 1997*.[34]

This report is a 219-page volume that details the goals, approach, and results of the company's ethical auditing process. The volume contains the following key components of the company's corporate public policy: mission statement, founder's statement, social and ecological milestones 1995–1997, approach to ethical auditing, 1995–2000 targets, performance reports with respect to key stakeholder groups, and other reports.[35] The Body Shop's "Framework for Social Auditing and Disclosure" involves continuous improvement via the implementation of a cyclical audit loop. Steps or stages in the framework include:

- Policy review

- Determination of audit scope

- Agreement of standards and performance indicators

- Stakeholder consultation

- Stakeholder surveys

- Internal audit

- Preparation of accounts and internal reports

- Verification

- Publication of statement
- Stakeholder dialogue

One final indicator of the increasing popularity of social auditing in the 1990s is the appearance of consulting and research firms willing to help companies conduct audits. SmithOBrien Services, for example, offers as a core service the Corporate Responsibility Audit™. The company describes its audit as a "multidisciplinary methodology for identifying and eliminating often-overlooked negative effects of a company's operations on its stakeholders, and thus reducing legal exposure, production inefficiencies, and reputational risk."[36] The research firm Walker Information of Indianapolis, which provides measurement services to companies that want to know more about their impact on key stakeholder groups, also is worthy of mention because its service is similar to social auditing.[37] Walker Information's Reputation and Stakeholder Assessment is a comprehensive tool for measuring and managing stakeholder relationships. Through its assessment process, Walker gathers information from multiple stakeholder groups and provides the company with a "scorecard" summary of how these groups perceive or evaluate the company's reputation. Among other measures, the scorecard shows a company's reputation relative to that of the competition and of world-class leaders in other industries.[38]

As firms develop enterprise-level strategies and corporate public policies, the potential for social and ethical audits remains high. Social auditing is best seen not as an isolated, periodic attempt to assess social performance but rather as an integral part of the overall strategic management process as it has been portrayed here. Because the need to improve planning and control will remain as long as management desires to evaluate its corporate social performance, the need for strategic control through techniques such as the social audit will likely be with us for some time, too. The net result of continued use and refinement should be improved corporate social performance and enhanced credibility of business in the eyes of the public.

Environmental Analysis

To this point, we have described the strategic management process without dwelling on the sources of the information that management uses in its goal formulation, strategy formulation, and other processes. Now we should discuss environmental analysis, the process by which this information is gathered and assembled. ***Environmental analysis*** is the linking pin between the organization, which is the managerial setting for the strategic management process, and the stakeholder environment, from which information is gathered.

Before we describe environmental analysis, let us briefly discuss the idea of the stakeholder environment as portrayed in Figure 18–5. One popular conception is to visualize the environment of business in terms of three levels: (1) the ***task environment***, which is that set of customers, suppliers, competitors, and others with which a firm interacts on an almost daily basis; (2) the ***competitive or industry environment***, which comprises those firms functioning in the same markets or industry; and (3) the ***general environment***, or ***macroenvironment***, which includes everything else "out there" that influences the organization. The macroenvironment is sometimes referred to as the *political economy*.[39]

Another way of thinking about the environment of business is in terms of the *component subsystems,* or *segments,* that compose it. The standard scheme here is that the environment is composed of social, economic, political, and technological components, or subenvironments. Because the environment is complex, these four components are highly interdependent and often indistinguishable from one another. In addition, the environment is seen as having other dimensions that must be acknowledged and recognized. Some of these other dimensions are simplicity-complexity, homogeneity-heterogeneity, and stability-dynamism.[40]

In keeping with our general theme, we will refer to the environment of business, which possesses all of the attributes described above, as the **stakeholder environment**. As a basis or resource for information gathering, we should also observe that this environment is composed of trends, events, issues, and forecasts that may have a bearing on the strategic management process.

One further point needs to be made before we describe the environmental analysis process. In this chapter we are striving to convey the idea that a concern for enterprise-level strategy and corporate public policy is just one part of the more comprehensive strategic management process. Therefore, we are concerned with all four components of the business environment—economic, technological, political, and social. In other words, we are just as interested in such economic and technological trends as interest rates, the balance of payments, international competitiveness, changes in computer technology, and trends in research-and-development expenditures as we are in ethical or other public issues. In the next chapter, however, we will focus on a set of techniques that share a common heritage with environmental analysis but are more concerned with public or ethical issues. These techniques are known as *issues management* and *crisis management*.

Narayanan and Fahey's conceptualization of the environmental analysis stage in the strategic management process is best suited for our purposes. They suggest that the process consists of four analytical stages: (1) *scanning* the environment to detect warning signals, (2) *monitoring* specific environmental trends, (3) *forecasting* the future directions of environmental changes, and (4) *assessing* current and future environmental changes for their organizational implications.[41]

Scanning the Environment

The *environmental scanning stage* focuses on identification of precursors or indicators of potential environmental changes and issues. The purpose of this stage is to alert management to potentially significant events, issues, or trends before they have fully formed or crystallized.[42] Early on, companies did their scanning in an informal, irregular, ad hoc manner. Executives simply read newspapers, magazines, institutional reports, polls, and surveys. As the environment became more turbulent, firms began engaging in periodic or continuous scanning rather than irregular scanning. As companies got more serious about scanning the environment, their techniques became more sophisticated, and a whole industry opened up to supply managers with professionally generated information. Examples include the Yankelovich "Corporate Priorities" service and various newsletters and services provided by John Naisbitt, author of the book *Megatrends*.

Monitoring Environmental Trends

Whereas environmental scanning entails an open-ended viewing of the environment to identify early signals, the *environmental monitoring stage* focuses on the tracking of specific trends and events with an eye toward confirming or disconfirming trends or patterns. Monitoring often involves following up on indicators or signals that were detected during the scanning stage. The goal here is to gather and assemble sufficient data to discern patterns. Three outputs of scanning are useful: (1) specific descriptions of environmental patterns that may then be forecast, (2) the identification of other trends that need to be continually monitored, and (3) the identification of patterns that require future scanning.[43] We should note that many of the sources of information that are employed in scanning, such as the professional services mentioned, are also used in monitoring.

Forecasting Environmental Changes

Scanning and monitoring are restricted to the past and the present. Firms also need to obtain information concerning the likely future states of events, trends, or issues. The *environmental forecasting stage* is the future-oriented stage and is concerned with the development of plausible and realistic projections of the direction, scope, speed, and intensity of environmental change.[44] Forecasts of the economic, technological, social, and political components of the environment are needed, and this information base then forms the premises on which goal formulation, strategy formulation, and other strategic planning activities are developed.

Economic forecasting is the most frequently addressed area in this process. Only in the past two decades or so have firms begun formal attempts to forecast the technological, social, and political environments. A technique known as *sociopolitical forecasting* emerged at General Electric. Ian Wilson, an early proponent of this new technique, was one of the first to call to our attention the need to leave behind our two-sided approach to planning, which dwelt on economic and technological forecasts, and to adopt a "four-sided framework," which also included social and political forecasting.[45]

Assessment for Organizational Implications

Scanning, monitoring, and forecasting are done to enable current and projected environmental information and changes to be used for setting new goals and formulating strategies. The assessment stage of environmental analysis shifts the attention away from gathering and projecting and toward the task of understanding what the information means to management. The central question becomes, "What are the implications of our analysis of the environment for our organization?"[46] The key at this stage is to develop the ability to sift through all the information that has been generated and determine what is relevant to management. Relevance may be thought of in terms of two primary dimensions: (1) the probability that the event, trend, or forecast will occur and (2) the impact that the event, trend, or forecast will have on the organization. These two dimensions make it possible to create what is known as a probability-impact matrix. Such a matrix permits management to categorize issues according to priorities that then can be used as a framework for assessment, comparison, and discussion.

The strategic management process provides an excellent framework for thinking about stakeholder management. The processes of goal formulation, strategy formulation, strategy evaluation, strategy implementation, strategic control, and environmental analysis describe what managers must do in their leadership roles. Furthermore, the strategic management process provides a comprehensive context in which we can better appreciate how enterprise-level strategy and corporate public policy fit into the total array of managerial challenges and responsibilities. Only by seeing public and ethical issues emanating from the stakeholder environment and having to compete with economic, technological, and political factors can we fully appreciate what it means to be a manager in the business climate of the new millennium.

SUMMARY

Corporate public policy is a firm's posture or stance regarding the public, social, or ethical aspects of stakeholders and corporate functioning. It is a part of strategic management, particularly enterprise-level strategy. Enterprise-level strategy is the broadest, overarching level of strategy, and its focus is on the role of the organization in society. Other questions that help to flesh out enterprise-level strategy include the following: How is our organization perceived by our stakeholders? What principles or values does our organization represent? What obligations do we have to society at large? Enterprise-level strategy is manifested by way of mission statements, values statements, corporate creeds, codes of ethics, "core values," public issues committees, and the degree, formalization, and stature of the public affairs function. The other strategy levels include the corporate, business, and functional levels.

The strategic management process entails six stages, and a concern for social, ethical, and public issues may be seen at each stage. The stage at which public issues are most addressed for planning purposes is the environmental analysis stage. Vital components of environmental analysis include scanning, monitoring, forecasting, and assessing. In the overall environmental analysis process, social, ethical, and public issues are considered along with economic, political, and technological factors.

KEY TERMS

business-level strategy (page 587)

competitive or industry environment (page 602)

corporate-level strategy (page 587)

corporate public policy (page 585)

enterprise-level strategy (page 587)

environmental analysis (page 602)

environmental forecasting stage (page 604)

environmental monitoring stage (page 604)

environmental scanning stage (page 603)

fit (page 597)

functional-level strategy (page 587)

general environment (page 602)

goal formulation (page 595)

macroenvironment (page 602)

social accounting (page 600)

social audit (page 598)   strategic control (page 598)   strategy formulation (page 595)

sociopolitical forecasting (page 604)   strategic management (page 586)   strategy implementation (page 597)

stakeholder environment (page 603)   strategy evaluation (page 597)   task environment (page 602)

DISCUSSION QUESTIONS

1. Explain the relationship between corporate public policy and strategic management.
2. Which of the four strategy levels is most concerned with social, ethical, or public issues? Discuss the characteristics of this level.
3. Identify the steps involved in the strategic management process. In which step is a concern for social issues planning most evident? Explain.
4. What is a social audit? Describe how it may be seen as a tool for strategic control.
5. What are the four stages in environmental analysis? Briefly explain each stage.

ENDNOTES

1. Charles Alexander, "Crime in the Suites," *Time* (June 10, 1985), 56–57.
2. Kenneth R. Andrews, *The Concept of Corporate Strategy,* 3rd ed. (Homewood, IL: Irwin, 1987), 68–69.
3. R. Edward Freeman and Daniel R. Gilbert, Jr., *Corporate Strategy and the Search for Ethics* (Englewood Cliffs, NJ: Prentice-Hall, 1988), 20. Also see R. Edward Freeman, Daniel R. Gilbert, Jr., and Edwin Hartman, "Values and the Foundations of Strategic Management," *Journal of Business Ethics* (Vol. 7, 1988), 821–834; and Daniel R. Gilbert, Jr., "Strategy and Ethics," in *The Blackwell Encyclopedic Dictionary of Business Ethics* (Malden, MA: Blackwell Publishers Ltd., 1997), 609–611.
4. Charles W. Hofer, Edwin A. Murray, Jr., Ram Charan, and Robert A. Pitts, *Strategic Management: A Casebook in Policy and Planning,* 2nd ed. (St. Paul, MN: West Publishing Co., 1984), 27–29. Also see Gary Hamel and C. K. Prahalad, *Competing for the Future* (Boston: Harvard Business School Press, 1994).
5. H. Igor Ansoff, "The Changing Shape of the Strategic Problem," paper presented at a Special Conference on Business Policy and Planning Research: The State of the Art (Pittsburgh: May, 1977).
6. H. Igor Ansoff, *Implanting Strategic Management* (Englewood Cliffs, NJ: Prentice-Hall, International, 1984), 129–151.
7. R. Edward Freeman, *Strategic Management: A Stakeholder Approach* (Boston: Pitman, 1984), 90.
8. *Ibid.,* 90–91. For further discussion, see Martin B. Meznar, James J. Chrisman, and Archie B. Carroll, "Social Responsibility and Strategic Management: Toward an Enterprise Strategy Classification," *Business & Professional Ethics Journal* (Vol. 10, No. 1, Spring, 1991), 47–66. Also see William Q. Judge, Jr., and Hema Krishnan, "An Empirical Examination of the Scope of a Firm's Enterprise Strategy," *Business & Society* (Vol. 33, No. 2, August, 1994), 167–190.

9. Laura Sessions Stepp, "Industrial-Strength Ethics, Being Tested in the Crucible of Reality," *The Washington Post National Weekly Edition* (April 8–14, 1991), 22–23.

10. *Ibid.*, 22–23.

11. *Ibid.*, 23.

12. Edward A. Robinson, "The Ups and Downs of the Industry Leaders," *Fortune* (March 2, 1998), 87.

13. C.W. Hofer and D.E. Schendel, *Strategy Formulation: Analytial Concepts* (St. Paul: West, 1978), 52–55. Also see J. David Hunger and Thomas L. Wheelen, *Essentials of Strategic Management* (Reading, MA: Addison-Wesley, 1997), 13–16; 18–33.

14. Archie B. Carroll, "Setting Operational Goals for Corporate Social Responsibility," *Long Range Planning* (April, 1978), 35. Also see Joseph A. Petrick and John F. Quinn, *Management Ethics: Integrity at Work* (Thousand Oaks, CA: Sage Publications, 1997), 129–165.

15. James J. Chrisman and Archie B. Carroll, "Corporate Responsibility: Reconciling Economic and Social Goals," *Sloan Management Review* (Winter, 1984), 59–65.

16. Kenneth R. Andrews, *The Concept of Corporate Strategy*, 3rd ed. (Homewood, IL: Irwin, 1987), 18–20.

17. R. M. Grant, "The Resource-Based Theory of Competitive Advantage: Implications for Strategy Formulation," *California Management Review* (Spring, 1991), 114–135.

18. Andrews, 18–20.

19. Seymour Tilles, "How to Evaluate Corporate Strategy," *Harvard Business Review* (July–August, 1963), 111–121. Also see Hunger and Wheelen, 160–162.

20. Robert H. Waterman, Jr., Thomas J. Peters, and Julien R. Phillips, "Structure Is Not Organization," *Business Horizons* (June, 1980), 14–26.

21. R. Miles and C. Snow, *Environmental Strategy and Organization Structure* (New York: McGraw-Hill, 1978), 1. Also see Hamel and Prahalad, 160–161.

22. Archie B. Carroll, *Business and Society: Managing Corporate Social Performance* (Boston: Little, Brown, 1981), 381.

23. Peter Lorange, Michael F. Scott Morton, and Sumantra Ghoshal, *Strategic Control Systems* (St. Paul, MN: West, 1986), 1, 10. Also see Hunger and Wheelen, 161–162.

24. David H. Blake, William C. Frederick, and Mildred S. Myers, *Social Auditing: Evaluating the Impact of Corporate Programs* (New York: Praeger, 1976), 3. Also see Roger Spear, "Social Audit and Social Economy," *www.ny.airnet.ne.jp/ccij/eng/public-e.htm*, August 8, 1998.

25. *Ibid.*

26. Ralph Estes, *Corporate Social Accounting* (New York: John Wiley, 1976), 3.

27. Archie B. Carroll and George W. Beiler, "Landmarks in the Evolution of the Social Audit," *Academy of Management Journal* (September, 1975), 589–599.

28. Theodore J. Kreps, *Measurement of the Social Performance of Business,* Monograph No. 7, "An Investigation of Concentration of Economic Power for the Temporary National Economic Committee" (Washington, DC: U.S. Government Printing Office, 1940).

29. Cited in Carroll and Beiler, 590–591.

30. Kreps, 3–4.

31. Howard R. Bowen, *Social Responsibilities of the Businessman* (New York: Harper & Row, 1953).

32. John J. Corson and George A. Steiner, *Measuring Business's Social Performance: The Corporate Social Audit* (New York: Committee for Economic Development, 1974), 33.

33. J. A. Byrne, "The Best-Laid Ethics Programs," *Business Week* (March 9, 1992), 67–69.

34. The Body Shop, *Values Report 1997* (October, 1997). For more information, visit the Body Shop Internet Web site at *www.the-body-shop.com.*

35. *Ibid.*

36. SmithOBrien Services, *www.smithobrien.com/lServices.html,* August 22, 1998.

37. Walker Information, "Reputation and Stakeholder Assessment" (Indianapolis: Walker Information, undated).

38. *Ibid.,* 2–3.

39. Liam Fahey and V.K. Narayanan, *Macroenvironmental Analysis for Strategic Management* (St. Paul, MN: West, 1986), 25.

40. *Ibid.,* 28–30.

41. V.K. Narayanan and Liam Fahey, "Environmental Analysis for Strategy Formulation," in William R. King and David I. Cleland (eds.), *Strategic Planning and Management Handbook* (New York: Van Nostrand Reinhold, 1987), 156.

42. *Ibid.* Also see John D. Stoffels, *Strategic Issues Management: A Comprehensive Guide to Environmental Scanning* (New York: Pergamon Press, 1994).

43. *Ibid.,* 159–160. Also see Liam Fahey and Robert Randall (eds.), *Learning from the Future: Competitive Foresight Scenarios* (New York: Wiley, 1998).

44. *Ibid.,* 160.

45. Ian H. Wilson, "Socio-Political Forecasting: A New Dimension to Strategic Planning," in Archie B. Carroll (ed.), *Managing Corporate Social Responsibility* (Boston: Little, Brown, 1977), 159–169.

46. Narayanan and Fahey, 162. Also see Frank Vanclay and Daniel Bronstein (eds.), *Environmental and Social Impact Assessment* (Brisbane: Chichester, John Wiley, 1995).

19

Issues Management and Crisis Management

CHAPTER OBJECTIVES

After studying this chapter, you should be able to:

1 Distinguish between the conventional and strategic management approaches to issues management.

2 Identify and briefly explain the stages in the issues management process.

3 Describe the major components in the issues development process and some of the factors that have characterized issues management in actual practice.

4 Define a crisis and identify the four crisis stages.

5 List and discuss the major stages in managing business crises.

Throughout this book we have referred to major social and ethical issues that have become controversies in the public domain. Some have been serious events or crises that continue to serve as recognizable code words for business—Love Canal, Three Mile Island, the Tylenol poisonings, the Pinto gas tank explosions, the insider trading scandals, the Union Carbide Bhopal tragedy, the Exxon *Valdez* oil spill, and the AIDS crisis. Other issues—employee rights, sexual harassment, product safety, workplace safety, smoking in the workplace, affirmative action, deceptive advertising, and so on—have not been characterized as being of crisis proportions. Nevertheless, to business these are formidable social issues that have evolved over time and that must be addressed.

Managerial decision-making processes known as *issues management* and *crisis management* are two ways in which business has responded to these situations. These two approaches symbolize the extent to which the environment has become turbulent and the public has become sensitized to business's responses to the issues that have emerged from this turbulence. In the ideal situation, issues management and crisis management might be seen as the natural and logical by-products of a firm's development of enterprise-level strategy and overall corporate public policy, but this has not always been the case. Some firms have not thought seriously about public and ethical issues; for them, these approaches represent first attempts to come to grips with the practical reality of a threatening social environment. Many of these firms have been fortunate that major crises have not emerged to stun them as they did in the Johnson & Johnson Tylenol poisonings, the Union Carbide Bhopal explosion, the Procter & Gamble Rely tampon crisis, the Dow Corning breast implant probe, the crashes of TWA Flight 800 and ValuJet Flight 592, and the cynanide-tainted Sudafed capsule crisis that led to two deaths. Thus, they have seen what major business crises can do to companies without having experienced such crises themselves. Such firms should now be concerned with issues management and crisis management.

Like all planning processes, issues management and crisis management have many characteristics in common. They also have differences, however, and we have chosen to treat them separately for discussion purposes. One common thread that should be mentioned at the outset is that both processes are focused on improving stakeholder management and enabling the organization to be more ethically responsive to stakeholders' expectations. Issues and crisis management, to be effective, must have as their ultimate objective an increase in the organization's social responsiveness to its stakeholders.

ISSUES MANAGEMENT

Issues management is a process by which organizations identify issues in the stakeholder environment, analyze and prioritize those issues in terms of their relevance to the organization, plan responses to the issues, and then evaluate and monitor the results. It is helpful to think of issues management in connection with concepts introduced in the preceding chapter, such as the strategic management process, enterprise-level strategy, corporate public policy, and environmental analysis. The process of strategic management and environmental analysis requires an overall way of managerial thinking that includes economic, technological, social, and political issues. Enterprise-level strategy and corporate public policy, on the other hand, focus on public or ethical issues. Issues management, then, devolves from these broader concepts.

Approaches to Issues Management

Thinking about the concepts mentioned above requires us to make some distinctions. A central consideration seems to be that issues management has been thought of in two major ways: (1) narrowly, in which public, or social, issues are the primary focus, and (2) broadly, in which strategic issues and the strategic management process are the focus of attention. Liam Fahey provides a useful distinction between these two approaches. He refers to (1) the conventional approach and (2) the strategic management approach.[1] The *conventional approach to issues management* has the following characteristics:[2]

- Issues fall within the domain of public policy or public affairs management.

- Issues typically have a public policy/public affairs orientation or flavor.

- An issue is any trend, event, controversy, or public policy development that might affect the corporation.

- Issues originate in social/political/regulatory/judicial environments.

The *strategic management approach to issues management* has evolved in a small number of companies and is typified by the following:[3]

- Issues management is typically the responsibility of senior line management or strategic planning staff.

- Issues identification is more important than it is in the conventional approach.

- Issues management is seen as an approach to the anticipation and management of external and internal challenges to the company's strategies, plans, and assumptions.

The strategic approach to issues management has also been advocated by such authorities as H. Igor Ansoff[4] and William R. King.[5] Figure 19–1 portrays strategic issues management as depicted by Ansoff. Note the "strategic" characteristics—threats/opportunities and strengths/weaknesses—that we alluded to in the preceding chapter.

At the risk of oversimplification, we will consider the principal distinction between the two approaches to issues management to be that the conventional approach focuses on public/social issues, whereas the strategic approach is inclusive of all issues. In addition, the conventional approach can be used as a "stand-alone" decision-making process, whereas the strategic approach is intimately interconnected with the strategic management process as a whole. Another difference may be whether line managers/strategic planners or public affairs staff members are activating the system. Beyond these distinctions, the two approaches have much in common.

Our discussion in this chapter will emphasize the conventional approach, because this book focuses on public and ethical issues. We should point out, however, that our purpose in the preceding chapter was to convey the notion that social issues ought to be seen as just one part of the strategic management process. We discussed environmental analysis as a broad phenomenon. Now we emphasize social or ethical issues, although it is obvious that a consideration of these issues is embedded in a larger, more strategically focused process, such as that depicted in Figure 19–1. Therefore, we are comfortable with both of these approaches to issues management. We should point out that the conventional approach could be perceived as a subset of the strategic approach, although this is typically not the way companies see it. In a sense, the two approaches are highly inseparable, and it is difficult for organizations to operate effectively unless both are addressed in some way.

The Changing Mix of Issues

The emergence in the past decade of new "company issues management groups" and "issues managers" has been a direct outgrowth of the changing mix of issues that managers have had to handle. Economic and financial issues have always been an inherent part of the business process, although their complexity seems to have increased as international markets have broadened and competitiveness has become such an important issue. The growth of technology has presented business with other issues that need to be addressed. The most dramatic growth has been in social, ethical, and political issues—all public issues that have high visibility, media appeal, and interest among special-interest stakeholder groups. We should further observe that these issues become more interrelated over time.

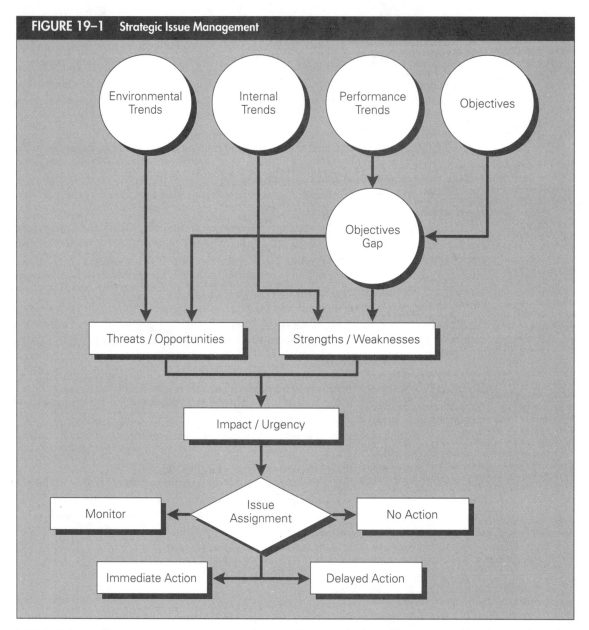

FIGURE 19–1   Strategic Issue Management

SOURCE: H. Igor Ansoff, "Strategic Issue Management," *Strategic Management Journal* (Vol. I, 1980), 137. Reprinted by permission of John Wiley & Sons, Ltd.

For most firms, social, ethical, political, and technological issues are at the same time economic issues, because firms' success in handling them frequently has a direct bearing on their financial statuses and well-being. Over time, there is a changing mix of issues and an escalating challenge that management groups face as these issues create a cumulative effect.

The Issues Management Process

Before explaining the issues management process, we should briefly discuss what constitutes an issue and what assumptions we are making about issues management. An *issue* may be thought of as a matter that is in dispute between two or more parties. The dispute typically evokes debate, controversy, or differences of opinion that need to be resolved. At some point, the organization needs to make a decision on the unresolved matter, but such a decision does not mean that the issue is resolved. Once an issue becomes public and subject to public debate and high-profile media exposure, its resolution becomes increasingly difficult. One of the features of issues, particularly those arising in the social or ethical realm, is that they are ongoing and therefore require ongoing responses.

Joseph Coates, Vary Coates, Jennifer Jarratt, and Lisa Heinz, authors of *Issues Management*,[6] identify the following characteristics of an "emerging issue":

* The terms of the debate are not clearly defined.

* The issue deals with matters of conflicting values and interest.

* The issue does not lend itself to automatic resolution by expert knowledge.

* The issue is often stated in value-laden terms.

* Trade-offs are inherent.

John Mahon describes how complicated the question of issue definition can be in his observation about the multiple viewpoints that come into play when an issue is considered. He has noted that there are multiple stakeholders and motivations in any given management situation. Personal stakes frequently can be important factors but often are ignored or not taken into consideration. For example, some of the participants may be interested in the issue from a deep personal perspective and will not compromise or give up their positions even in the face of concrete evidence that clearly refutes them.[7] Thus, we can see that the resolution of issues in organizations is not easy.

What about the assumptions we make when we choose to use issues management? Coates et al. go on to say that the following assumptions are made:[8]

* Issues can be identified earlier, more completely, and more reliably than in the past.

* Early anticipation widens the organization's range of options.

* Early anticipation permits study and understanding of the full range of issues.

* Early anticipation permits the organization to develop a positive orientation toward the issue.

- The organization will have earlier identification of stakeholders.

- The organization will be able to supply information to influential publics earlier and more positively, thus allowing them to better understand the issue.

These are not only assumptions of issues management but also *benefits* to the extent that they make the organization more effective in its issues management process.

Like the strategic management process or almost any other process that entails a multitude of sequential and interrelated steps or stages, the issues management process has been conceptualized by many different authorities in a variety of ways. Conceptualizations of issues management have been developed by companies, academics, consultants, and associations. The issues management process we will discuss here has been extracted from many of the conceptualizations previously developed. This process represents the elements or stages that seem to be common to most of those conceptualizations and consistent with the stakeholder orientation we have been developing and using.

Figure 19–2 presents a model of the issues management process as we will discuss it. It contains *planning* aspects (identification, analysis, and ranking/prioritization of issues, and formulation of responses) and *implementation* aspects (implementation of responses and evaluation, monitoring, and control of results). Although we will discuss the stages in the issues management process as though they were discrete, we should recognize that in reality they overlap one another.

Identification of Issues

Many names have been given to the process of issue identification. At various times, the terms "social forecasting," "futures research," "environmental scanning," and "public issues scanning" have been used. Similarly, many techniques have been employed. All of these approaches/techniques are similar, but each has its own unique characteristics. Common to all of them, however, is the need to scan the environment and to identify emerging issues that might later be determined to have some relevance to or impact on the organization.

Issue identification, in its most rudimentary form, involves the assignment to some *individual* in the organization the tasks of continuously scanning a variety of publications—newspapers, magazines, specialty publications, the World Wide Web—and developing a comprehensive list of issues. Often this same person is instructed to review public documents, records of congressional hearings, and other such sources of information. One result of this scanning is an internal report or a newsletter that is circulated throughout the organization. The next step in this evolution may be for the company to subscribe to a *trend information service* or *newsletter* that is prepared and published by a private individual or consulting firm that specializes in environmental or issue scanning.[9]

Two popular trend-spotting services have been (1) the Washington-based Naisbitt Group, founded by John Naisbitt, who was thrust into public recognition by his bestseller *Megatrends*, and (2) Yankelovich, Skelly, and White, the New York–based social research firm. For fees that range from $10,000 to $30,000 per year and more, these professionals provide firms with materials they have assembled.[10] Among the

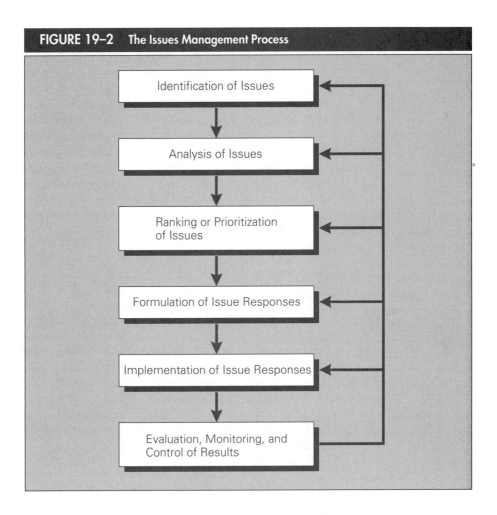

FIGURE 19–2   The Issues Management Process

Identification of Issues

Analysis of Issues

Ranking or Prioritization of Issues

Formulation of Issue Responses

Implementation of Issue Responses

Evaluation, Monitoring, and Control of Results

services they offer are newsletters, short weekly or monthly reports, telephone bulletins, and quarterly visits to discuss what the trends mean. Trend spotters do not claim clairvoyance, but they do say that they have less psychological resistance than their clients to seeing impending change.[11]

The Naisbitt Group has claimed to be different from many trend spotters. The 30 or so professionals in that group do not scan national magazines but rather scan the local news in local newspapers. Their approach, which is controversial, is based on the belief that trends start with isolated local events. As Naisbitt stated, "The really important things that happen always start somewhere in the countryside. Taken together, what's going on locally is what's going on." Thus, according to Naisbitt, it is what people are *doing*, not what they are *saying*, that provides the most reliable pictures of issues. Naisbitt has continued his identification of public issues with *Megatrends 2000: Ten New Directions for the 1990s* (1990),[12] and *Global Paradox* (1995), *Megatrends Asia* (1996), and *High Tech/High Touch*, scheduled for 1999.

Yankelovich, Skelly, and White (YSW), on the other hand, have pursued a diametrically opposed strategy. Years ago, through long interviews, YSW identified 35 widespread social trends, such as rejection of authority and female careerism. They then developed a survey made up of questions that assess the strengths of these trends, and each year they administer the questionnaire to 2,500 people. YSW tracks the waxing and waning of these trends and claims to predict the trends' relative strengths for the next 5 years. For $20,000 or more yearly, each of the service's sponsors gets the survey's results, a videocassette on the meaning of the results, a book discussing the implications of the results, and individual consulting.[13]

T. Graham Molitor, who was also a consultant on social issues, has proposed the following five leading forces as predictors of social change:[14]

- Leading events
- Leading authorities/advocates
- Leading literature
- Leading organizations
- Leading political jurisdictions

If these five forces are monitored closely, impending social change can be identified and, in some cases, predicted. Figure 19–3 presents Molitor's five leading forces, as well as examples that might be thought to illustrate his points.

Companies vary considerably in their willingness to spend thousands of dollars for the kinds of professional services we have described, but some rely almost exclusively on these kinds of sources for issue identification. Others use less costly and more informal means.

Analysis of Issues

In a sense, the next two steps (analysis and ranking of issues) are closely related. To analyze an issue means to carefully study, dissect, break down, group, or engage in any specific process that helps you better understand the nature or characteristics of the issue. An analysis requires that you look beyond the obvious manifestations of the issue and strive to learn more of its history, development, current nature, and potential for future relevance to the organization. William King proposed a series of key questions that focus on stakeholder groups in attempting to analyze issues:[15]

- Who (which stakeholders) are affected by the issue?
- Who has an interest in the issue?
- Who is in a position to exert influence on the issue?
- Who has expressed opinions on the issue?
- Who ought to care about the issue?

In addition to these questions, a consulting firm—Human Resources Network—proposed the following key questions to help with issue analysis:[16]

FIGURE 19–3	Examples of Forces Leading Social Change	
Leading Forces	**Examples**	**Public Issue Realm**
Events	Three Mile Island/Chernobyl nuclear plant explosions	Nuclear plant safety
	Bhopal explosion	Plant safety
	Earth Day	Environment
	Tylenol poisonings	Product tampering
	Love Canal	Toxic waste—environment
	Rely tampons	Product safety
	Ivan Boesky scandal	Insider trading abuses
	Thomas hearings	Sexual harassment
	Valdez oil spill	Environment
Authorities/ Advocates	Ralph Nader	Consumerism
	Rachel Carson	Pesticides—environment
	Rev. Martin Luther King	Civil rights
	Rev. Jesse Jackson	Blacks' rights
	General Colin Powell	Volunteerism
Literature	*Silent Spring* (Rachel Carson)	Pesticides—environment
	Unsafe at Any Speed (Ralph Nader)	Automobile safety
	Megatrends (John Naisbitt)	Issues identification
Organizations	Friends of the Earth	Environment
	Sierra Club	Environment
	Action for Children's Television (ACT)	Children's advertising
	Mothers Against Drunk Driving (MADD)	Highway safety/alcohol abuse
Political jurisdictions	State of Michigan—Whistle-Blower Protection Act	Employee freedom of speech
	State of Delaware	Corporate governance

- Who started the ball rolling? (Historical view)
- Who is now involved? (Contemporary view)
- Who will get involved? (Future view)

Answers to these questions place management in a better position to rank or prioritize the issues so that it will have a better sense of the urgency with which the issues need to be addressed.

Ranking or Prioritization of Issues

Once issues have been carefully analyzed and are well understood, it is necessary to rank them in some form of a hierarchy of importance or relevance to the organization. We should note that some issues management systems place this step before analysis. This is done especially when it is desired to screen out those issues that are obviously not relevant and deserving of further analysis.

The prioritization stage may range from a simple grouping of issues into categories of urgency to a more elaborate or sophisticated scoring system. Two examples will serve to illustrate the grouping technique. Xerox has used a process of categorizing issues into three classifications: (1) *high priority* (issues on which management must be well informed), (2) *nice to know* (issues that are interesting but not critical or urgent), and (3) *questionable* (issues that may not be issues at all unless something else happens). PPG Industries has grouped issues into three priorities: *Priority A* (critical issues that warrant executive action and review), *Priority B* (issues that warrant surveillance by the division general manager or staff), and *Priority C* (issues that have only potential impact and warrant monitoring by the public affairs department).[17]

A somewhat more sophisticated approach uses a probability-impact matrix requiring management to assess the *probability of occurrence* of an issue (high, medium, or low) on one dimension and its *impact on the company* (high, medium, or low) on the other dimension. In using such an approach, management would place each issue in the appropriate cell of the matrix, and the completed matrix would then serve as an aid to prioritization. As a variation on this theme, management could rank issues by considering the mathematical product of each issue's impact (for example, on a scale from 1 to 10) and probability of occurrence (on a scale from 0 to 1).

William R. King has provided a somewhat more elaborate issues-ranking scheme. He recommends that issues be screened on five filter criteria: strategy, relevance, actionability, criticality, and urgency.[18] Once each issue has been scored on a 10-point scale on each criterion, issues are then ranked according to their resulting point totals. Figure 19–4 illustrates this filtering/ranking process. Other techniques that have been used in issues identification, analysis, and prioritization include polls/surveys, expert panels, content analysis, the Delphi technique, trend extrapolation, scenario building, and the use of precursor events or bellwethers.[19]

Earlier we described a simple issues identification process as involving an individual in the organization or a subscription to a newsletter or trend-spotting service. The analysis and ranking stages could be done by an individual, but more often the company has moved up to a next stage of formalization. This next stage involves assignment of the issues management function to a team, often as part of a public affairs department, which begins to specialize in the issues management function. This group of specialists can provide a wide range of issues management activities, depending on the commitment of the company to the process.

Several companies have created issues management units to alert management to emerging trends and controversies and to help mobilize the companies' resources to deal with them. Firms such as Arco, Monsanto, and Sears are among those that have used such units. At Monsanto, an issues manager organized a committee of middle managers to help do the work. At Arco, the group monitored hundreds of publications, opinion polls, and think-tank reports. It then prepared its own daily publication called *Scan,* which summarized considerable data for over 500 company middle managers and top executives. The group tracked over 140 issues in all.[20]

Formulation and Implementation of Responses

These two steps in the issues management process are combined here because we do not discuss them extensively. Also, we should observe that the formulation and implementation stages in the issues management process are quite similar to the

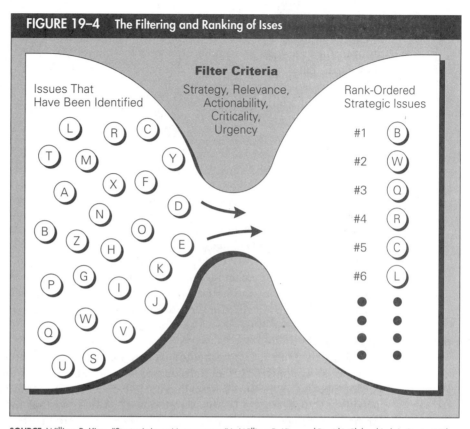

FIGURE 19–4   The Filtering and Ranking of Issues

Filter Criteria

Issues That Have Been Identified

Strategy, Relevance, Actionability, Criticality, Urgency

Rank-Ordered Strategic Issues

SOURCE: William R. King, "Strategic Issue Management," in William R. King and David I. Cleland (eds.), *Strategic Planning and Management Handbook* (New York: Van Nostrand Reinhold, 1987), 257. Reproduced with permission.

corresponding stages we discussed in the preceding chapter, which pertained to the strategic management process as a whole.

Formulation in this case refers to the response design process. Based on the analysis conducted, companies can then identify options that might be pursued in dealing with the issues, in making decisions, and in implementing those decisions. Strategy formulation refers not only to the formulation of the actions that the firm intends to take but also to the creation of the overall strategy, or degree of aggressiveness, employed in carrying out those actions. Options might include aggressive pursuit, gradual pursuit, or selective pursuit of goals, plans, processes, or programs.[21] All of these more detailed plans are part of the strategy formulation process.

Once plans for dealing with issues have been formulated, implementation becomes the focus. There are many organizational aspects that need to be addressed in the implementation process. Some of these include the clarity of the plan itself, resources needed to implement the plan, top management support, organizational structure, technical competence, and timing.[22] For additional implementation considerations, refer to our discussion of the McKinsey 7S framework in Chapter 18.

Evaluation, Monitoring, and Control

These recognizable steps in the issues management process were also treated as steps in the strategic management process in Chapter 18. In the present context, they mean that companies should continually evaluate the results of their responses to the issues and ensure that these actions are kept on track. In particular, this stage requires careful monitoring of stakeholders' opinions. A form of stakeholder audit—something derivative of the social audit discussed in Chapter 18—might be used. The information that is gathered during this final stage in the issues management process is then fed back to the earlier stages in the process so that changes or adjustments might be made as needed. Evaluation information may be useful at each stage in the process.

We have presented the issues management process as a complete system. In actual practice, companies apply the stages in various degrees of formality/ informality as needed. For example, because issues management is more important in some situations than in others, some stages of the process may be truncated to meet the needs of different firms in different industries. In addition, some firms are more committed to issues management than others. Those firms that are committed are probably members of the Issues Management Association, which was founded in 1981. Today, this association has hundreds of member firms.

The Issues Development Process

A vital attribute of issues management is that issues tend to develop according to an evolutionary pattern. This pattern might be thought of as a developmental or growth process or, as some have called it, a life cycle. It is important for managers to have some appreciation of this development process so that they can recognize when something becomes an issue and also because it might affect the strategy that the firm employs in dealing with the issue. Companies may take a variety of courses of action depending on the stage of the issue in the process.

One view has been that issues tend to follow an 8-year curve, although it is very difficult to generalize about the time frame, especially in today's world of instantaneous global communications. For the first 5 years or so, a nascent issue emerges in local newspapers, is enunciated by public-interest organizations, and is detected through public-opinion polling. According to Margaret Stroup, director of corporate responsibility at Monsanto, the issue is low-key and flexible at this stage.[23] During this time, the issue may reflect a felt need, receive media coverage, and attract interest-group development and growth. A typical firm may notice the issue but take no action at this stage. John Mahon's view is that more issues-oriented firms may become more active in their monitoring and in their attempts to shape or help "define the issue."[24] Active firms have the capacity to prevent issues from going any further, through either effective responses to the issues or effective lobbying.

In the fifth or sixth year of the cycle, national media attention and leading political jurisdictions (for example, cities or states) may address the issue. Issues managers have identified several "precursor" or bellwether states where national issues frequently arise first. Many experts think these states include California, Oregon, Florida, Michigan, and Connecticut.[25] Quite often, federal government attention is generated in the form of studies and hearings; legislation, regulation, and litigation

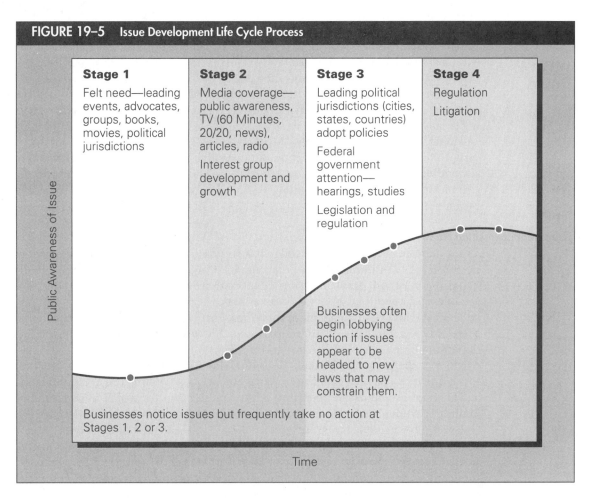

FIGURE 19–5   Issue Development Life Cycle Process

Stage 1
Felt need—leading events, advocates, groups, books, movies, political jurisdictions

Stage 2
Media coverage—public awareness, TV (60 Minutes, 20/20, news), articles, radio

Interest group development and growth

Stage 3
Leading political jurisdictions (cities, states, countries) adopt policies

Federal government attention—hearings, studies

Legislation and regulation

Stage 4
Regulation

Litigation

Businesses often begin lobbying action if issues appear to be headed to new laws that may constrain them.

Businesses notice issues but frequently take no action at Stages 1, 2 or 3.

Public Awareness of Issue

Time

follow. Today, it would not be uncommon for issues to mature much more quickly than the 8-year model just described. Figure 19–5 presents a simplified view of what this issue development life cycle process might look like.

We should note that the stages in the process, especially the early stages, might occur in a different sequence or in an iterative pattern. Further, not all issues complete the process; some are resolved before they reach the stage of legislation or regulation. Thomas G. Marx takes the view that issues go from *social expectations* to *political issues* to *legislation* and finally to *social control.*

Marx illustrates this evolution through two examples. First, consider the issue of environmental protection. The social expectation was manifested in Rachel Carson's book *Silent Spring* (1963); it became a political issue in Eugene McCarthy's political platform (1968); it resulted in legislation in 1971–1972 with the creation of the EPA; and it was reflected in social control by emissions standards, pollution fines, product recalls, and environmental permits in later years. The second example involves product/consumer safety. The social expectation was manifested in Ralph Nader's book *Unsafe at Any Speed* (1964); it became a political issue through the National Traffic Auto Safety Act and Motor Vehicle Safety Hearings (1966); it resulted in legislation in 1966 with the passage of the Motor Vehicle Safety Act and mandatory seat belt usage laws in four states (1984); and it was reflected in social control through the ordering of seat belts in all cars (1967), defects litigation, product recalls, and driver fines.[26]

Finally, we are reminded by Bigelow, Fahey, and Mahon that "issues do not necessarily follow a linear, sequential path, but instead follow paths that reflect the intensity and diversity of the values and interests stakeholders bring to an issue and the complexity of the interaction among . . ." all the variables.[27] This should serve as a warning not to oversimplify the issues development process.

Issues Management in Practice

Issues management in practice today has very much become a subset of activities performed by the public affairs departments of major corporations. Public affairs departments or offices will be discussed more thoroughly in Chapter 20. A 1997 survey of corporate public affairs officers of major corporations revealed that 67 percent engage in issues management functions. Furthermore, the survey revealed that there is now greater use of interdepartmental issues teams, with the public affairs department serving as coordinator and strategist but with appropriate line and staff executives charged with ultimate accountability for implementation. In practice, therefore, it can be seen that issues management does not function as a stand-alone activity but has been subsumed into a host of functions for which modern public affairs departments take responsibility.[28]

Issues management faces a serious challenge in business today. From the standpoint of the turbulence in the stakeholder environment, issues management may be needed. To become a permanent part of the organization, however, issues management will have to continuously prove itself. We can talk conceptually about the process with ease, but the field still remains somewhat nebulous even though it is struggling to become more scientific and legitimate. Managers in the real world want results, and if issues management cannot deliver those results, it will be destined to failure as a management process.

Some companies have claimed specific successes for their issues management programs. S. C. Johnson & Sons, the maker of floor waxes and other chemicals, claims it removed environmentally chancy fluorocarbons from its aerosol sprays 3 years before federal action required the industry to do so. Sears claims it spotted the flammable-nightwear controversy early and got nonflammable goods into its stores before government action mandated it. Bank of America claims it was alerted early by its issues managers about a practice known as "redlining" and took action to change its lending policies 2 years before Congress required banks to disclose whether they were barring all loans in certain parts of a city. According to the bank, its early action reduced its eventual cost of compliance significantly and spared it "a lot of grief and antagonism from cities and public-interest groups."[29] In the final analysis, identifiable successes such as these will be needed to ensure the future of issues management.

CRISIS MANAGEMENT

Crisis management as a management term is largely a product of the past decade and a half. This has been the era of the megacrisis: Union Carbide's Bhopal disaster, which killed over 2,000 people in India; Johnson & Johnson's Tylenol poisonings, which resulted in numerous deaths; and Procter & Gamble's Rely tampon crisis, in which that product was associated with toxic shock syndrome. Other significant crises included the following:

- ValuJet's Flight 592 crashed in the Florida Everglades, killing all 110 people on board.

- Texaco was slammed with a $176 million racial discrimination lawsuit.

- TWA Flight 800 from New York to Paris crashed off the coast of Long Island; CEO Jeffrey Erickson was in London when he received the news.

- Schwan's ice cream company was charged as the responsible party in a salmonella outbreak in 39 states.

- Star-Kist Foods was charged with shipping rancid and decomposing tuna.

- Dow Corning was targeted in an FDA silicone breast implant probe.

- Chrysler Corporation was indicted for disconnecting odometer cables on new cars, using the cars, and then selling them as new.

- Sudafed capsules were tainted with cyanide, leading to two deaths.

- Perrier Water's benzene incident led to product recalls.

- Hurricane Andrew devastated businesses in south Florida.

- Twenty-four customers of Luby's Cafeteria in Killeen, Texas, were shot to death during a lunch-hour massacre.

- Intel's distribution of flawed Pentium chips in computers created a nightmare for the company.

- A federal building in Oklahoma City was bombed in 1995, resulting in the deaths of well over 100 persons.

It should be apparent from this list of crises that there is a major distinction between issues management, discussed in the preceding section, and crisis management, the subject of this section. Issues typically evolve over a period of time. Issues management is a process of identifying and preparing to respond to potential issues. Crises, on the other hand, occur abruptly. They cannot always be anticipated or forecast. Some crises occur within an issue category considered; many do not. Issues and crisis management are related, however, in that they both are concerned about organizations becoming prepared for uncertainty in the stakeholder environment.

The Nature of Crises

There are many kinds of crises. Those we have just mentioned have all been associated with major stakeholder groups and have achieved high-visibility status. Hurt or killed customers, hurt employees, hurt stockholders, and unfair practices are the concerns of modern crisis management. Not all crises involve such public or ethical issues, but these kinds of crises almost always ensure front-page status. Major companies can be seriously damaged by such episodes, especially if the episodes are poorly handled.

What is a crisis? Dictionaries state that a *crisis* is a "turning point for better or worse," an "emotionally significant event," or a "decisive moment." We all think of crises as being emotion charged, but we do *not* always think of them as turning points for *better* or for *worse*. The implication here is that a crisis is a decisive moment that, if managed one way, could make things worse but, if managed another way, could make things better. Choice is present, and how the crisis is managed *can* make a difference.

From a managerial point of view, a line needs to be drawn between a problem and a crisis. Problems, of course, are common in business. A crisis, however, is not as common. A useful way to think about a crisis is with a definition set forth by Laurence Barton:

> *A crisis is a major, unpredictable event that has potentially negative results. The event and its aftermath may significantly damage an organization and its employees, products, services, financial condition, and reputation.*[30]

Another definition set forth by Pearson and Clair is also helpful in understanding the critical aspects of a crisis:

> *An organizational crisis is a low-probability, high-impact event that threatens the viability of the organization and is characterized by ambiguity of cause, effect, and means of resolution, as well as by a belief that decisions must be made swiftly.*[31]

Consider, for a moment, the case referred to earlier wherein Star-Kist Foods, a subsidiary of H. J. Heinz Co., faced a management crisis. Gerald Clay was appointed general manager of the Canadian subsidiary and was given the mandate to develop a 5-year business strategy for the firm. Just after his arrival in Canada, the crisis hit: The Canadian Broadcasting Corporation accused his company of shipping 1 million cans of rancid and decomposing tuna. Dubbed "Tunagate" by the media, the

---

SEARCH THE WEB

An article in *Time* magazine called "crisis management" the "new corporate discipline." Every company today, large or small, runs the risk of a crisis. Forward-looking companies practice crisis management and either develop their own in-house crisis management programs or avail themselves of the many consulting firms that provide crisis management consulting. One consulting firm that specializes in crisis management is Lexicon Communications Corporation. Among its many services Lexicon provides crisis management training seminars, workshops, and full-blown crisis simulations to help executives hone the skills they may need to serve on crisis management teams or to respond to the media in a crisis-filled atmosphere. To learn more about which topics might be covered in such seminars, check out the Lexicon Web site at **www.crisismanagement.com**.

Another major consulting firm that specializes in crisis management is The Wilson Group. Whether it's a chemical spill, a plant explosion, a plant closing, or another crisis. The Wilson Group offers personalized crisis management and media training workshops, crisis communication plans, community relations programs, and on-the-scene counsel. Part of the group's intense training includes on-camera media training for executives in a mock disaster context. To learn more about crisis management, visit The Wilson Group Web site at **www.wilson-group.com**.

crisis dragged on for weeks. With guidance from Heinz, Clay chose to keep quiet, even as the Canadian prime minister ordered the tuna seized. The silence cost plenty. According to Clay's boss, "We were massacred in the press." The company, which used to have half the Canadian tuna market, watched revenues plunge by 90 percent. Clay's boss observed that the company's future was in doubt.[32]

Being prepared for crises has become a primary activity in a growing number of companies. Part of being prepared entails knowing something about the nature of crises. Steven Fink conducted a major survey of Fortune 500 firms on the subject and wrote one of the first books on crisis management. Fink's survey disclosed that a staggering 89 percent of those who responded agreed that "a crisis in business today is as inevitable as death and taxes," but 50 percent of the executive respondents admitted that they did not have prepared crisis plans.[33] Today, more companies may be prepared for crises, but their degree of preparedness varies widely.

Situations in which the executives surveyed by Fink felt they were vulnerable to crises included industrial accidents, environmental problems, union problems/ strikes, product recalls, investor relations, hostile takeovers, proxy fights, rumors/ media leaks, government regulatory problems, acts of terrorism, and embezzlement.[34] Other common crises include product tampering, executive kidnapping, work-related homicides, malicious rumors, and natural disasters that destroy corporate offices or information bases.[35] We have discussed many of these situations in this book. The majority of them emanate from the major stakeholder groups: consumers, employees, communities, and shareholders. Of the major crises that had recently occurred, the majority of the companies reported the following outcomes: The crises escalated in intensity, were subjected to media and government scrutiny, interfered with normal business operations, and damaged the company's bottom line.[36]

The Four Crisis Stages

According to Steven Fink, a crisis may consist of as many as four distinct stages: (1) a prodromal crisis stage, (2) an acute crisis stage, (3) a chronic crisis stage, and (4) a crisis resolution stage.[37]

The *prodromal crisis stage* is the warning stage. ("Prodromal" is a medical term that refers to a previous notice or warning.) This warning stage could also be thought of as a symptom stage. Although it could be called a "precrisis" stage, this presupposes that one knows that a crisis is coming. Perhaps management should adopt this perspective: *Watch each situation with the thought that it could be a crisis in the making.* Early symptoms may be quite obvious, such as in the case where a social activist group tells management it will boycott the company if a certain problem is not addressed. On the other hand, symptoms may be more subtle, as in the case where defect rates for a particular product a company makes start edging up over time.

The *acute crisis stage* is the stage at which the crisis actually occurs. There is no turning back; the incident has occurred. Damage has been done at this point, and it is now up to management to handle or contain the damage. If the prodromal stage is the precrisis stage, the acute stage is the actual *crisis* stage. The crucial decision point at which things may get worse or better has been reached.

The *chronic crisis stage* is the lingering period. It may be the period of investigations, audits, or in-depth news stories. Management may see it as a period of recovery, self-analysis, or self-doubt. In Fink's survey of major companies, he found that crises tended to linger as much as two and a half times longer in firms without crisis management plans than in firms with such plans.

The *crisis resolution stage* is the final stage—the goal of all crisis management efforts. Fink argues that when an early warning sign of a crisis is noted, the manager should seize control swiftly and determine the most direct and expedient route to resolution. If the warning signs are missed in the first stage, the goal is to speed up all phases and reach the final stage as soon as possible.

Figure 19–6 presents one way in which these four stages might be depicted. It should be noted that the phases may overlap and that each phase varies in intensity and duration. It is hoped that management will learn from the crisis and thus will be better prepared for, and better able to handle, any future crisis.

Other views of crises and crisis management may be taken. Gerald C. Meyers, former chairman of American Motors Corporation and a consultant on crisis management, and others lay out the scenario for a *poorly managed crisis,* which typically follows a predictable pattern.[38] The pattern is as follows:

* Early indications that trouble is brewing occur.

* Warnings are ignored/played down.

* Warnings build to a climax.

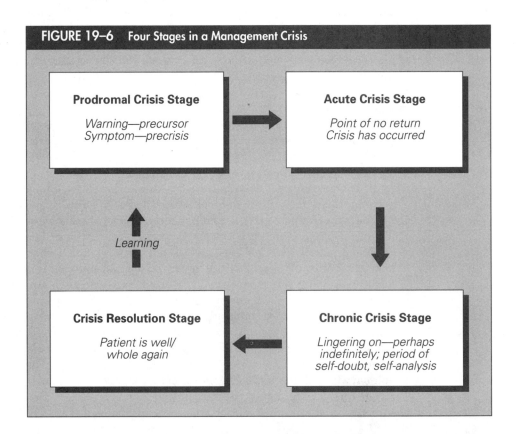

FIGURE 19–6   Four Stages in a Management Crisis

Prodromal Crisis Stage

Warning—precursor Symptom—precrisis

Acute Crisis Stage

Point of no return Crisis has occurred

Learning

Crisis Resolution Stage

Patient is well/ whole again

Chronic Crisis Stage

Lingering on—perhaps indefinitely; period of self-doubt, self-analysis

- Pressure mounts.
- Executives are often overwhelmed or can't cope effectively.
- Quick-fix alternatives look appealing. Hasty moves create trouble.
- Clamming-up versus opening-up options present themselves.
- Most firms choose the former.
- A siege mentality prevails.

Visualizing the attributes or pattern of a poorly managed crisis is valuable because it illustrates how *not* to do it—a lesson that many managers may find quite valuable.

Managing Business Crises

There are many suggestions for managing a crisis, although they cannot be reduced to a cookbook recipe. Fink argues that there are three vital stages in crisis management: identifying the crisis, isolating the crisis, and managing the crisis. All should be done *quickly.*[39] Another view on crisis management is that a series of five steps must be taken. These steps are discussed next and are summarized in Figure 19–7.

Identifying Areas of Vulnerability

In this first step, some areas of vulnerability are obvious, such as potential chemical spills, whereas others are more subtle. The key seems to be in developing a greater consciousness of how things can go wrong and get out of hand. At Heinz, after the

---

FIGURE 19–7   Steps in Crisis Management

1. Identifying areas of vulnerability
   A. Obvious areas
   B. Subtle areas
2. Developing a plan for dealing with threats
   A. Communications planning is vital
   B. Training executives in product dangers and dealing with media
3. Forming crisis teams
   A. Vital to successful crisis management
   B. Identifying executives who can work well under stress
4. Simulating crisis drills
   A. Experience/practice is helpful
   B. "War rooms" serve as gathering places for team members
5. Learning from experience
   A. Assess effectiveness of crisis strategies
   B. Move from reaction to proaction

"Tunagate" incident, a vice president set up brainstorming sessions. He said, "We're brainstorming about how we would be affected by everything from a competitor who had a serious quality problem to a scandal involving a Heinz executive.[40]

Developing a Plan for Dealing with Threats

A plan for dealing with the most serious crisis threats is a logical next step. One of the most crucial issues is *communications planning*. After a Dow Chemical railroad car derailed near Toronto, forcing the evacuation of 250,000 people, Dow Canada prepared information kits on the hazards of its products so that executives would be knowledgeable enough to respond properly if a similar crisis were to arise in the future. Dow Canada also trained executives in interviewing techniques. This effort paid off several years later when an accident caused a chemical spill into a river that supplied drinking water for several nearby towns. The company's emergency response team arrived at the site almost immediately and established a press center that distributed information about the chemicals. In addition, the company recruited a neutral expert to speak on the hazards and how to deal with them. Officials praised Dow for its handling of this crisis.[41]

Richard J. Mahoney, CEO of Monsanto Company from 1983–1995, has offered the following 10 "Rs" for the effective handling of public policy crises. He recommends these steps as part of an overall crisis plan:[42]

- Respond early.
- Recruit a credible spokesperson.
- Reply truthfully.
- Respect the opposition's concerns.
- Revisit the issue with follow-up.
- Retreat early if it's a loser.
- Redouble efforts early if it's a critical company issue.
- Reply with visible top management.
- Refuse to press for what is not good public policy.
- Repeat the prior statement regularly.

Some of these steps may not apply to every crisis situation, but many may be useful as part of a crisis management plan. Mahoney notes that getting an entire organization trained to deal with crises is difficult and expensive, but he paraphrases what a car repairman said in a TV commercial: "You can pay now or pay a lot more later." Mahoney thinks that *now* is infinitely better for everyone.[43]

Forming Crisis Teams

Another step that can be taken as part of an overall planning effort is the formation of *crisis teams*. Such teams have played key roles in many well-managed disasters. A good example is the team formed at Procter & Gamble when its Rely tampon products were linked with the dreaded disease toxic shock syndrome. The team was quickly assembled, a vice president was appointed to head it, and after 1 week the decision was made to remove Rely from marketplace shelves. The quick action earned the firm praise, and it paid off for P&G in the long run.

Another task in assembling crisis teams is identifying managers who can cope effectively with stress. Not every executive can handle the fast-moving, high-pressured, ambiguous decision environment that is created by a crisis, and early identification of executives who can is important. We should also note that it is not always the CEO who can best perform in such a crisis atmosphere.

Despite the careful use of crisis teams, crises can often overwhelm a carefully constructed plan. When ValuJet's Flight 592 crashed in the Florida Everglades in 1996, for example, ValuJet flawlessly executed a three-pronged, team-based crisis management plan calling for the company to (1) show compassion, (2) take responsibility, and (3) demonstrate that the airline learned from the crisis. Experts have said that the company handled the crisis well. However, a close look at the tragedy revealed that a series of complicating factors turned the crisis into something even more difficult than a well-scripted, perfectly executed crisis management plan could handle.[44]

Crisis Drills

Some companies have gone so far as to run crisis drills in which highly stressful situations are simulated so that managers can "practice" what they might do in a real crisis. As a basis for conducting crisis drills and experiential exercises, a number of companies have adopted a software package known as Crisis Plan wRiter (CPR). This software allows companies to centralize and maintain up-to-date crisis management information and allows company leaders to assign responsibilities to their crisis team, target key audiences, identify and monitor potential issues, and create crisis-response processes.[45]

Learning from Experience

The final stage in crisis management is learning from experience. At this point, managers need to ask themselves exactly what they have learned from past crises and how that knowledge can be used to advantage in the future. Part of this stage entails an assessment of the effectiveness of the firm's crisis-handling strategies and identification of areas where improvements in capabilities need to be made. Without a crisis management system of some kind in place, the organization will find itself reacting to crises after they have occurred. If learning and preparation for the future are occurring, however, the firm may engage in more proactive behavior.[46]

We should note that Pearson and Mitroff have accurately observed that effective crisis management requires a program that is tailored to a firm's specific industry, business environment, and crisis management experience. Effective crisis managers will understand that there are major crisis management factors that may vary from situation to situation, such as the type of crisis (e.g., natural disaster or human induced), the phase of the crisis, the systems affected (e.g., humans, technology, culture), and the stakeholders affected. Managers cannot eliminate crises. However, they can become keenly aware of their vulnerabilities and make concerted efforts to understand and reduce these vulnerabilities through continuous crisis management programs.[47]

Successful Crisis Management

It is informative to conclude this chapter with an illustration of a successful crisis management case study. This case study started with the kind of phone call every company dreads—"Your product is injuring people; we're announcing it at a press conference today." Schwan's Sales Enterprises, Inc., got the call from the Minnesota Department of Health at about noon on October 7, 1994. The Health Department reported that it had found a statistical link between Schwan's ice cream and confirmed cases of salmonella. Thousands of people in at least 39 states became ill with salmonella after eating tainted Schwan's ice cream, potentially setting the company up for a decade's worth of litigation. Instead, in a little more than a year after the outbreak, the vast majority of claims had been handled outside the legal system through direct settlements or as part of a class action in Minneapolis.[48]

Schwan's knew that its image of the smiling man in the sunshine-yellow Schwan's truck (with a Swan on the side) busily hand-delivering ice cream to grateful consumers was one of its major assets. Before the company was sure of the Health Department's findings, it halted sales and production, shut down, and invited the state health department, the Department of Agriculture, and the FDA into the plant to investigate. It also notified all its sales offices nationwide. Also, within the first 24 hours of the crisis, the company set up a hotline to answer consumer questions, contacted employees and managers to staff the hotline, prepared for a product recall, and began working with its insurer.[49]

By placing consumer safety as its number one priority, Schwan's was able to resolve the crisis much more quickly than ever would have been possible without a carefully designed crisis management plan. Whether by coincidence or preparedness, the manager of public affairs and the company's general counsel had completed a review and rewriting of the company's crisis management manual just 2 months before the outbreak. One vital component of the plan was a crisis management team, which went to work immediately when the news came. The crisis management team quickly set up a process for handling consumers who had been affected. The team, working with its insurance company, quickly helped customers get medical treatment and get their bills paid. Settlements to customers who suffered from salmonella symptoms included financial damages, medical expenses, and other costs, such as reimbursement for work days missed.[50]

How did the ice cream get contaminated with salmonella? After a month's investigation that kept the Marshall, Minnesota, plant closed, it was determined that the ice cream mix supplied by a few vendors was the culprit. The mix of cream, sugar, and milk had been shipped in a tanker truck that had previously held raw, unpasteurized eggs that had the bacteria. Schwan's quietly sought and received legal damages from the suppliers but stayed focused on its customers throughout the crisis.

What did Schwan's learn from this crisis? Previously, Schwan's did not repasteurize its ice cream mix once the mix arrived at the Marshall plant. Within a few weeks of the outbreak, however, the company had broken ground to build its own repasteurization plant. The company also leased a dedicated fleet of tanker trucks to deliver the ice cream mix from the suppliers to the plant, set up a system for testing each shipment, and delayed shipping the final product until the test results were known. In summary, Schwan's planning, quick response, and customer-oriented strategy combined to retain customer loyalty and minimize the company's legal exposure.[51] It was a case of good crisis management.

SUMMARY

Crisis management, like issues management, is not a panacea for organizations. In spite of well-intended efforts by management, not all crises will be resolved in the company's favor. Nevertheless, being prepared for the inevitable makes sense, especially in today's world of instantaneous worldwide communications and obsessive media coverage. Whether we are thinking about the long term, the intermediate term, or the short term, managers need to be prepared to handle the turbulent public-social-ethical stakeholder environment.

A range of management approaches can be used to impose some order on these decision processes. At the macro level, enterprise-level strategy and corporate public policy are essential underpinnings. Environmental analysis is a vital component of the strategic management process, and issues management helps a firm deal with those current issues that affect the firm's immediate and future stakeholder environments. Finally, crisis management is there standing ready for those traumatic "surprises" that firms now inevitably face. Taken together, these processes provide a bundle of approaches that all managers should be acquainted with for dealing with the turbid and fluid stakeholder environment. Effective management does not simply recommend these kinds of approaches but mandates them. Failure to employ such practices is failure to live up to a sound code of stakeholder management professionalism.

KEY TERMS

acute crisis stage (page 625)

chronic crisis stage (page 625)

conventional approach to issues management (page 610)

crisis management (page 623)

crisis resolution stage (page 626)

crisis teams (page 628)

issue (page 613)

issues management (page 610)

prodromal crisis stage (page 625)

strategic management approach to issues management (page 610)

DISCUSSION QUESTIONS

1. Which of the major stages in the issues management process do you think is the most important? Why?
2. What is your opinion of Naisbitt's belief that the major public issues start as isolated, local events? Give an example you are aware of that appears to support or refute his hypothesis.

3. Identify one example, other than those listed in Figure 19–3, of each of the leading force categories: events, authorities/advocates, literature, organizations, and political jurisdictions.

4. Identify a crisis that has occurred in your life or in the life of someone you know, and briefly explain it in terms of the four crisis stages: prodromal, acute, chronic, and resolution.

5. One of the steps suggested in the discussion of crisis management is the development of a crisis management team. List the kinds of personal and managerial characteristics you think are important in someone who might effectively serve on such a team.

ENDNOTES

1. Liam Fahey, "Issues Management: Two Approaches," *Strategic Planning Management* (November, 1986), 81, 85–96.

2. *Ibid.*, 81.

3. *Ibid.*, 86.

4. H. Igor Ansoff, "Strategic Issue Management," *Strategic Management Journal* (Vol. I, 1980), 131–148.

5. William R. King, "Strategic Issue Management," in William R. King and David I. Cleland (eds.), *Strategic Planning and Management Handbook* (New York: Van Nostrand Reinhold, 1987), 252–264.

6. Joseph F. Coates, Vary T. Coates, Jennifer Jarratt, and Lisa Heinz, *Issues Management* (Mt. Airy, MD: Lomond Publications, 1986), 19–20.

7. John Mahon, "Issues Management: The Issue of Definition," *Strategic Planning Management* (November, 1986), 81–82. For further discussion on what constitutes an issue, see Steven L. Wartick and John F. Mahon, "Toward a Substantive Definition of the Corporate Issue Construct," *Business & Society* (Vol. 33, No. 3, December, 1994), 293–311.

8. Coates et al., 18.

9. *Ibid.*, 32.

10. Myron Magnet, "Who Needs a Trend-Spotter?" *Fortune* (December 9, 1985), 51–56. Also see Gary Hamel and C. K. Prahalad, "Seeing the Future First," *Fortune* (September 5, 1994), 64–70.

11. Magnet, 52.

12. John Naisbitt, *Megatrends 2000: Ten New Directions for the 1990s* (New York, Morrow, 1990); *Global Paradox* (New York: Avon Books, 1995); *Megatrends Asia: Eight Asian Megatrends That Are Reshaping Our World* (New York: Simon and Schuster, 1996); and *High Tech/High Touch* (scheduled for 1999).

13. Magnet, 56.

14. T. Graham Molitor, "How to Anticipate Public Policy Changes," SAM *Advanced Management Journal* (Vol. 42, No. 3, Summer, 1977), 4.

15. King, 259.

16. James K. Brown, *This Business of Issues: Coping with the Company's Environment* (New York: The Conference Board, 1979), 45.

17. *Ibid.*, 33.

18. King, 257.

19. Coates et al., 46.

20. Earl C. Gottschalk, Jr., "Firms Hiring New Type of Manager to Study Issues, Emerging Troubles," *The Wall Street Journal* (June 10, 1982), 33, 36.

21. I. C. MacMillan and P. E. Jones, "Designing Organizations to Compete," *Journal of Business Strategy* (Vol. 4, No. 4, Spring, 1984), 13.

22. Roy Wernham, "Implementation: The Things That Matter," in King and Cleland, 453.

23. Gottschalk, 3.

24. Mahon, 81–82.

25. Gottschalk, 33.

26. Thomas G. Marx, "Integrating Public Affairs and Strategic Planning," *California Management Review* (Fall, 1986), 145.

27. Barbara Bigelow, Liam Fahey, and John Mahon, "A Typology of Issue Evolution," *Business & Society* (Spring, 1993), 28. For another useful perspective, see John F. Mahon and Sandra A. Waddock, "Strategic Issues Management: An Integration of Issue Life Cycle Perspectives," *Business & Society* (Spring, 1992), 19–32. Also see Steven L. Wartick and Robert E. Rude, "Issues Management: Fad or Function," *California Management Review* (Fall, 1986), 134–140.

28. Public Affairs Council, "Public Affairs: Its Origins, Its Present, and Its Trends," *www.pac.org/whatis/index.htm*, September 16, 1998.

29. Gottschalk, 21.

30. Laurence Barton, *Crisis in Organizations: Managing and Communicating in the Heat of Chaos* (Cincinnati: South-Western Publishing Co., 1993), 2.

31. Christine M. Pearson and Judith Clair, "Reframing Crisis Management," *Academy of Management Review* (Vol. 23, No. 1, 1998), 60.

32. "How Companies Are Learning to Prepare for the Worst," *Business Week* (December 23, 1985), 74.

33. Steven Fink, *Crisis Management: Planning for the Inevitable* (New York: Amacom, 1986).

34. *Ibid.*, 68. For further discussion of types of crises, see Ian Mitroff, "Crisis Management and Environmentalism: A Natural Fit," *California Management Review* (Winter, 1994), 101–113.

35. Pearson and Clair, 60.

36. Fink, 69. Also see Sharon H. Garrison, *The Financial Impact of Corporate Events on Corporate Stakeholders* (New York: Quorem Books, 1990); and Joe Marconi, *Crisis Marketing: When Bad Things Happen to Good Companies* (Chicago: NTC Business Books, 1997).

37. Fink, 20.

38. "How Companies Are Learning to Prepare for the Worst," *Business Week* (December 23, 1985), 74–75.

39. Fink, 70. Norman R. Augustine distinguishes six stages of crisis management in "Managing the Crisis You Tried to Prevent," *Harvard Business Review* (November–December, 1995), 147–158.

40. "How Companies Are Learning to Prepare for the Worst," *Business Week* (December 23, 1985), 76.

41. *Ibid.*

42. Richard J. Mahoney, "The Anatomy of a Public Policy Crisis," The CEO Series, Center for the Study of American Business (May 1996), 7.
43. *Ibid.*
44. Greg Jaffe, "How Florida Crash Overwhelmed ValuJet's Skillful Crisis Control," *Wall Street Journal* (June 5, 1996), S1.
45. Melissa Master, "Keyword: Crisis," *Across the Board* (September, 1998), 62.
46. Ian Mitroff, Paul Shrivastava, and Firdaus Udwadia, "Effective Crisis Management," *Academy of Management Executive* (November, 1987), 285.
47. Christine M. Pearson and Ian I. Mitroff, "From Crisis Prone to Crisis Prepared: A Framework for Crisis Management," *Academy of Management Executive* (Vol. VII, No. 1, February, 1993), 58–59. Also see Ian Mitroff, Christine M. Pearson, and L. Katherine Harrington, *The Essential Guide to Managing Corporate Crises* (New York: Oxford University Press, 1996).
48. Bruce Rubenstein, "Salmonella-Tainted Ice Cream: How Schwan's Recovered," Corporate Legal Times Corp., untitled Web page, June, 1998.
49. *Ibid.*
50. *Ibid.*
51. *Ibid.*

20 Public Affairs Management

CHAPTER OBJECTIVES

After studying this chapter, you should be able to:

1 Describe the evolution of the public affairs function in organizations.

2 Identify the major functions of public affairs departments.

3 Highlight trends that have been identified with respect to the public affairs function.

4 Characterize the elements of an international public affairs effort.

5 Link public affairs strategy with organizational characteristics.

6 Indicate how public affairs might be incorporated into every manager's job.

"Corporate public affairs" and *"public affairs management"* are umbrella terms used by companies to describe the management process we have been discussing in Part 5 of this book. The public affairs function is a logical and increasingly prevalent component of the overall strategic management process, which we introduced in Chapter 18. As an overall concept, public affairs management embraces corporate public policy, which we also introduced in Chapter 18, and issues management, which we discussed in Chapter 19. Indeed, many issues management and crisis management programs are housed in public affairs departments or intimately involve public affairs professionals.

It is easy to get confused at this point by all the different terms that are used to describe management's efforts to address the stakeholder environment. Part of the confusion arises from the fact that companies use different titles for the same functions. For example, terms that are often used interchangeably by firms are "public affairs/external affairs," "public policy/corporate social responsibility," "corporate communications," and "public issues management/public affairs management." Some companies create stand-alone public affairs departments without even addressing the strategic management issue or enterprise-level strategy.

In a comprehensive management system, which we have been describing in Part 5 of this book, the overall flow of activity would be as follows. A firm engages in *strategic management,* part of which includes the development of *enterprise-level strategy,* which poses the question, "What do we stand for?" The answers to this question should help the organization to form a *corporate public policy,* which is a more specific posture on the public, social, or stakeholder environment or specific issues within this environment. Some firms call this a ***public affairs strategy***. Two important planning aspects of corporate public policy are *issues management* and, often, *crisis management*. These two planning aspects frequently derive from or are related to environmental analysis, which we covered in Chapter 18. Some companies embrace these processes as part of the ***corporate public affairs*** function. These processes are typically housed, from a departmental perspective, in a public affairs department. ***Public affairs management*** is a term that often describes all these components. Figure 20–1 helps illustrate likely relationships among these processes.

Our focus in this chapter will be on the organizational aspects of the public affairs management function or process within businesses. We will consider how public affairs has evolved in business firms, what issues public affairs departments currently face, and how public affairs thinking might be incorporated into the operating manager's job. This last issue is crucial, because public affairs management, to be most effective, is best thought of as an indispensable part of every manager's job, not as an isolated function or department that alone is responsible for the public issues and stakeholder environment of the firm.

EVOLUTION OF THE CORPORATE PUBLIC AFFAIRS FUNCTION

A comprehensive history of the public affairs function is not needed for our purposes, but it is helpful to appreciate some of its beginnings. One report traces a public affairs department back to a company organization chart in the early 1950s, but

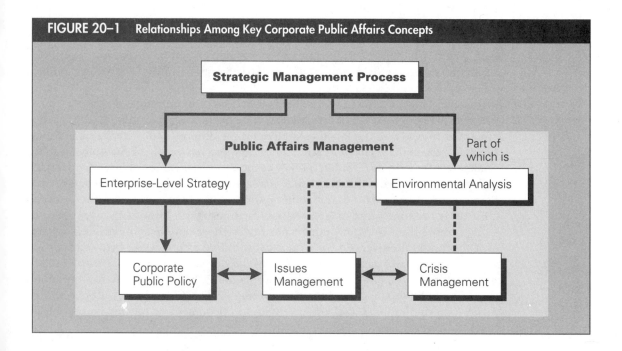

FIGURE 20–1 Relationships Among Key Corporate Public Affairs Concepts

that was not an isolated case. A 1980 study found that 60 percent of 400 large companies that then had public affairs departments had created them within the previous decade.[1] According to former Public Affairs Council President Richard Armstrong, public affairs blossomed in the United States in the 1960s because of four primary reasons: (a) the growing magnitude and impact of government; (b) the changing nature of the political system, especially its progression from a patronage orientation to an issues orientation; (c) the growing recognition by business that it was being outflanked by interests that were counter to its own on a number of policy matters; and (d) the need to be more active in politics outside the traditional community-related aspects, such as the symphony and art museums.[2]

Thus, the public affairs function as we know it today was an outgrowth of the social activism of the 1960s. Just as significant federal laws were passed in the early 1970s to address such issues as discrimination, environmental protection, occupational health and safety, and consumer safety, corporations responded with a surge of public affairs activities and creation of public affairs departments. Corporate public affairs, therefore, is clearly a product of the 1970s and 1980s.

Public affairs as a management function evolved out of isolated company initiatives designed to handle such diverse activities as community relations, corporate philanthropy and contributions, governmental affairs, lobbying, grassroots programs, corporate responsibility, and public relations. In some firms, the public relations staff handled issues involving communication with external publics, so it is not surprising that public affairs often evolved from public relations. Part of the confusion between public relations and public affairs is traceable to the fact that some corporate public relations executives changed their *titles*, but not their *functions*, to public affairs.

Richard Armstrong, former president of the Public Affairs Council, addressed the distinctions between **public relations (PR)** and **public affairs (PA)** in terms of their relative emphases, interests, and directions. He submits that the terminology is very important. The principal distinctions he has made are as follows: (1) whereas PR deals with government as one of many publics, PA professionals are *experts* on government, and (2) whereas PR has many communication responsibilities, PA deals with issues management and serves as a corporate conscience.[3]

Though modern public affairs may have evolved from early public relations efforts and company activities, today public affairs embraces public relations as one of its many functions. According to the latest major survey of corporate public affairs, 64 percent of the companies surveyed included public relations in the list of activities they performed.[4]

SEARCH THE WEB

To learn more about the public affairs function within major companies, visit the Public Affairs Council Web site at **www.pac.org**. The Public Affairs Council is the national organization of and for public affairs officers, based in Washington, DC. The Council defines public affairs as the external, noncommercial activities of an organization. These activities include government relations, community involvement, philanthropy, political education, and public relations. The Public Affairs Council comprises more than 530 organizational entities (approximately 420 corporations, 57 associations, and 55 consulting firms and nonprofit organizations).

MODERN PERSPECTIVES OF CORPORATE PUBLIC AFFAIRS

The Public Affairs Council, a major Washington-based professional association, has defined corporate public affairs as follows:

> *The management function responsible for monitoring and interpreting the corporation's non-commercial environment and managing the company's response to those factors.*[5]

This definition is quite broad and encompasses a wide assortment of activities. To appreciate what specific activities are typically included in this definition, it is useful to consider the results of a survey on the state of public affairs conducted in 1996 and published in 1997. This survey asked corporate respondents to indicate whether they included certain activities as parts of their public affairs function. Figure 20–2 lists the activities and the percentages of firms indicating they engaged in those activities. Government relations—federal, state, and local—heads the list, along with community relations and corporate contributions/philanthropy.[6]

James E. Post and Patricia C. Kelley provide an excellent perspective on the public affairs function in organizations today. They state:

> *The public affairs function serves as a window: Looking out, the organization can observe the changing environment. Looking in, the stakeholders in that environment can observe, try to understand, and interact with the organization.*[7]

When the public affairs function is viewed in this way, it is easy to understand how Post and Kelley can conclude that the "product" of the public affairs department is the smoothing of relationships with external stakeholders and the management of company-specific issues.

Martin Meznar and Douglas Nigh have provided another modern perspective on public affairs that is also useful. They suggest that corporate public affairs activities can be broken into two types: activities that "buffer" the organization from the social and political environment and activities that "bridge" with that environment. Meznar and Nigh found that as organizations experienced increased environmental uncertainty, buffering and bridging increased as well. They concluded that building bridges with external environmental uncertainty was positively related to top management's philosophy.[8] Bridging is a proactive stance that is most likely to be undertaken by companies with a stakeholder orientation.

A significant challenge today for public affairs professionals is to conduct their functions in an ethical fashion. There are many opportunities for questionable practices, especially in such arenas as political action, government relations, and communications. Therefore, it is encouraging to know that a code of conduct or set of ethical guidelines has been established for individuals working in public affairs. These ethical guidelines are set forth in Figure 20–3. They deserve scrutiny.

International Public Affairs as a Growth Area

It is important at this point to provide some additional comments on international public affairs. In 1983, the Public Affairs Council identified international PA as a new corporate function and formed a task force to investigate it. Three points

FIGURE 20-2 Current Public Affairs Activities	
Activity	*Percent of Firms*
Federal Government Relations	75
State Government Relations	75
Community Relations	71
Local Government Relations	69
Contributions/Philanthropy	69
Grassroots	68
Issues Management	67
Media Relations	66
Political Action Committee	66
Public Relations	64
Employee Communications	58
Public Interest Group Relations	51
Educational Affairs/Outreach	44
Regulatory Affairs	43
Volunteer Program	41
Advertising	39
International Public Affairs	35
Environmental Affairs	29
Stockholder Relations	24
Institutional Investor	23
Consumer Affairs	17

SOURCE: James E. Post and Jennifer J. Griffin, *The State of Corporate Public Affairs*, Foundation for Public Affairs and Boston University School of Management, 1997, Figure 3.1.

seemed to emerge time and again. First, it became obvious that more and more significant public affairs challenges and problems were occurring in the international arena, with greater impact on the company. Second, the number of firms with effective international PA capacities was small and growing very slowly. Third, the task force found that serious internal and external challenges often made an international PA program more difficult than a domestic program.[9]

International public affairs, to function properly, must balance externally and internally focused activities. Externally, the central challenge is to manage the company's relations with various host countries where business is conducted. Requirements here include understanding and meeting host-country needs and dealing with diverse local constituencies, audiences, and governments. Internally, international PA programs must establish and coordinate external programs, educate company

---

FIGURE 20–3   Ethical Guidelines for Public Affairs Professionals

The public affairs professional . . .
. . . maintains professional relationships based on honesty and reliable information, and therefore:

1. Represents accurately his or her organization's policies on economic and political matters to government, employees, shareholders, community interests, and others.

2. Serves always as a source of reliable information, discussing the varied aspects of complex public issues within the context and constraints of the advocacy role.

3. Recognizes the diverse viewpoints within the public policy process, knowing that disagreement on issues is both inevitable and healthy.

The public affairs professional . . .
. . . seeks to protect the integrity of the public policy process and the political system, and he or she therefore:

1. Publicly acknowledges his or her role as a legitimate participant in the public policy process and discloses whatever work-related information the law requires.

2. Knows, respects, and abides by federal and state laws that apply to lobbying and related public affairs activities.

3. Knows and respects the laws governing campaign finance and other political activities, and abides by the letter and intent of those laws.

The public affairs professional . . .
. . . understands the interrelation of business interests with the larger public interests, and therefore:

1. Endeavors to ensure that responsible and diverse external interests and views concerning the needs of society are considered within the corporate decision-making process.

2. Bears the responsibility for management review of public policies that may bring corporate interests into conflict with other interests.

3. Acknowledges dual obligations—to advocate the interests of his or her employer, and to preserve the openness and integrity of the democratic process.

4. Presents to his or her employer an accurate assessment of the political and social realities that may affect corporate operations.

SOURCE: The Public Affairs Council (Washington, DC), *1998 Annual Report,* 32. Reprinted with permission.

---

officials on PA techniques, and assist wherever possible the company's efforts to improve operations, activities, and image.[10] Companies that have been noted for having well-developed international public affairs programs include IBM, Avon, Standard Oil of California, and Dow Corning Corporation. According to Post and Griffin's recent survey of corporate public affairs, international public affairs was found to be one of the fastest-growing new areas of public affairs activities.[11]

Public Affairs in the 1990s

A survey on the state of corporate public affairs was conducted in 1992 by the Foundation for Public Affairs, and its findings were reported by James Post.[12] This survey of public affairs departments essentially supported the findings of Post's 1985 survey but yielded a few additional trends worthy of mention.

In terms of the activities being emphasized by public affairs departments of major corporations, environmental affairs, education affairs, and grassroots activities were among the fastest-growing areas of new PA responsibility. Another important trend revealed by the survey was the reorganization of public affairs responsibilities within companies. The trend was toward more centralization of the PA function. Regarding involvement in political affairs, it had become apparent that companies were concentrating on three specific forms of corporate political involvement: visits to political officials, use of political action committees (PACs), and meetings with political candidates.[13]

The survey showed that corporate communication with various stakeholders on public policy issues had grown in recent years. It also had become apparent that there had been a shift in the past decade from separate political analysis and political action specialties within organizations toward more integrated approaches to issues management. In fact, the rise of issues management as an organizing concept in PA departments was confirmed in this survey. The growing importance of international public affairs was documented, and it was confirmed that many companies preferred to treat international public affairs as country-specific political matters that were best managed by local managers in the respective countries. Finally, it was apparent that measurement and evaluation of PA activities now were occurring in most companies surveyed.[14]

As organizations have become more sensitive to their investments in and expenditures on public affairs activities, the evaluation and measurement of public affairs management have increased. In a comprehensive study of this topic, Craig S. Fleisher found quite different approaches to evaluation and measurement taking place. He concluded that in common use were three evaluation archetypes based primarily on three factors: (1) the nature of PA evaluation *policies/systems,* where evaluations ranged from none to highly formalized; (2) the nature of the *evaluation methods* used, with methods ranging from mostly intuitive to mostly analytical; and (3) the nature of the *information* utilized, with information ranging from mostly objective to mostly subjective. An increasing trend toward evaluation and measurement was disclosed.[15]

Out of the focus on evaluation and measurement of public affairs activities has arisen the concept of public affairs *benchmarking.* Fleisher defines this as "an ongoing, systematic approach by which a public affairs unit measures and compares itself with higher performing and world-class units in order to generate knowledge and action about public affairs roles, practices, processes, products, services, and strategic issues that will lead to improvement in performance."[16] The concept of benchmarking had its origins in the total quality management (TQM) movement.

To update what has been going on in the area of corporate public affairs, it is useful to look at some of the major findings of the Post and Griffin 1996 survey of public affairs management. The researchers found that various forces, perhaps most notably restructuring and downsizing driven by competitive pressures, have produced important changes. They found that there is a sharpened and expanded use of benchmarking. The 1996 study found that nearly half the companies responding had undertaken benchmarking in the previous year. The rationales offered for this trend included mandates from the CEO and continuous self-improvement. The activities studied by way of benchmarking were most often PAC operations, issues management processes, Washington office operations, and philanthropy.[17]

The study also revealed that a large number of public affairs officers had reorganized their departments, partially or across the board, in recent years. Key trends seem to be (1) changes in organizational relationships, often caused by retirement and nonreplacement of previous senior public affairs staff; (2) new linkages to internal customers (e.g., in one company each business unit has a specific PA executive assigned to service all its public affairs needs; and (3) contradictory trends in consolidation versus "disaggregation" of external public affairs functions.[18]

Other trends include use of the profit-center concept and increased attempts to measure the costs-benefits of PA efforts. PA has been seeking to contribute more to the "bottom line" by more deliberately and aggressively looking for marketing opportunities in government relations work (e.g., modifications in legislation or regulations that would increase the likelihood of government purchase of company products or services). Other trends in the use of technology include greater use of the Internet, using e-mail for company-wide alerts on breaking legislation, requiring lobbyists to use networked laptop computers, and using interactive computer systems to manage all aspects of public policy work.[19]

As a result of changes taking place in the environment of the late 1990s, Craig S. Fleisher, an expert on corporate public affairs, has proposed a "new public affairs model."[20] Fleisher proposes the new public affairs organization as one that:

1. Manages public affairs as an ongoing, year-round process, internally and externally

2. Cultivates and harvests the capability to build, develop, and maintain enduring stakeholder relationships

3. Recognizes the importance of managing the grassroots

4. Communicates in an integrated manner

5. Continuously aligns its values and strategies with the public's interests

6. Is systematically and proactively focused on helping the organization to compete

It is interesting to note that Fleisher names several nonprofit organizations as examples of organizations that have most effectively embraced these characteristics: The American Association of Retired Persons (AARP), the National Education Association, the American Medical Association (AMA), and the Christian Coalition. He says that all these organizations have achieved excellent levels of performance in the public policy marketplace through their practice of the new public affairs model.

It is becoming clear that public affairs management professionals in the 1990s are keenly interested in making sure that their function continues to add value to the bottom lines of corporations. In an era of corporate downsizings and reorganizations, staff functions such as PA are quite susceptible to budget cuts by higher executives who do not see clearly how PA's performance, effectiveness, and efficiency contribute to the company's profitability and success. In keeping with this theme, it should be noted that one of the Public Affairs Council's most important handbooks is a collection of quality-oriented readings entitled *Adding Value to the Public Affairs Function: Using Quality to Improve Performance* (1994) by Peter Shafer.[21] Figure 20–4 depicts how a quality improvement program might be implemented in

FIGURE 20–4   Initiating a Quality Improvement Program in Public Affairs

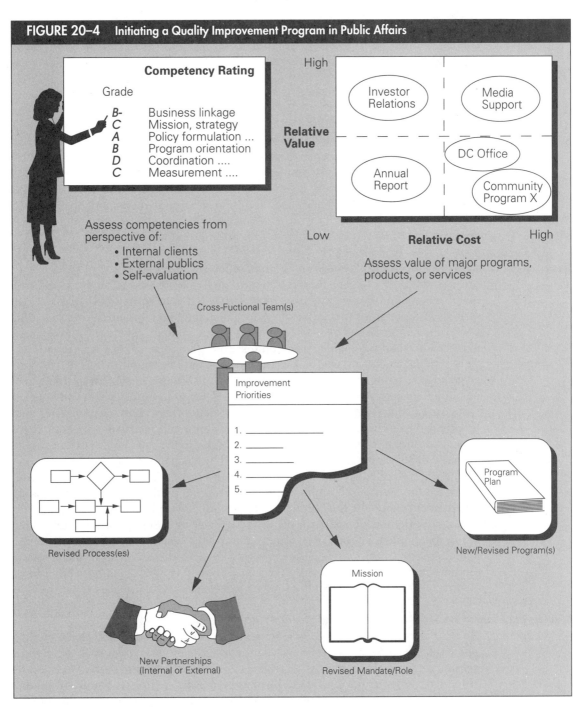

Competency Rating

Grade

B-   Business linkage
C   Mission, strategy
A   Policy formulation ...
B   Program orientation
D   Coordination ....
C   Measurement ....

Assess competencies from perspective of:
- Internal clients
- External publics
- Self-evaluation

High

Investor Relations   Media Support

Relative Value

Annual Report   DC Office   Community Program X

Low   **Relative Cost**   High

Assess value of major programs, products, or services

Cross-Fuctional Team(s)

Improvement Priorities

1. _____
2. _____
3. _____
4. _____
5. _____

Revised Process(es)

Program Plan

New/Revised Program(s)

New Partnerships (Internal or External)

Mission

Revised Mandate/Role

SOURCE: Peter Shafer, *Adding Value to the Public Affairs Function: Using Quality to Improve Performance* (Washington, DC: Public Affairs Council, 1994), 44.

corporate public affairs. This theme and others are carried forward in the Public Affairs Council's handbook entitled *Assessing, Managing and Maximizing Public Affairs Performance* (1997) by Craig Fleisher.[22]

PUBLIC AFFAIRS STRATEGY

We will not discuss the issue of public affairs strategy extensively, but we want to report the findings of a major research project that was undertaken by Robert H. Miles and resulted in a book entitled *Managing the Corporate Social Environment: A Grounded Theory*. Because very little work has been done on public affairs strategy, Miles's work deserves reference even though we cannot do it complete justice here. Miles's study focused on the insurance industry, but many of his findings may be applicable to other businesses. A few of his findings follow.[23]

Design of the Corporate External Affairs Function and Corporate Social Performance

Miles studied the external affairs strategies (also called public affairs strategies) of major insurance firms in an effort to see what relationships existed between the strategy and design of the corporate external affairs function and corporate social performance. He found that the companies that ranked best in corporate social performance had top management philosophies that were *institution oriented*. That is, top management saw the corporation as a social institution that had a duty to adapt to a changing society and thus needed a collaborative/problem-solving external affairs strategy. The **collaborative/problem-solving strategy** was one in which firms emphasized long-term relationships with a variety of external constituencies and broad problem-solving perspectives on the resolution of social issues affecting their businesses and industries.[24] Note how similar this is to the stakeholder management view and the bridge-building activity identified by Meznar and Nigh.

Miles also found that the companies with the worst social performance records employed top management philosophies based on operation of the company as an independent economic franchise. Such philosophies were in sharp contrast with the institution-oriented perspectives of the best social performers. In addition, Miles found that these worst social performers employed an **individual/adversarial external affairs strategy**. In this posture, the executives denied the legitimacy of social claims on their businesses and minimized the significance of challenges they received from external critics. Therefore, they tended to be adversarial and legalistic.[25]

Business Exposure to the Social Environment and External Affairs Design

On the subject of the external affairs units within firms, Miles found that a contingency relationship existed between what he called *business exposure to the social environment* and four dimensions of the external affairs design: breadth, depth, influence, and integration. High business exposure to the social environment means that the firm produces products that move them into the public arena because of such issues as their availability, affordability, reliability, and safety. In general, consumer products tend to be more exposed to the social environment than do commercial or industrial products.[26]

Breadth, depth, influence, and integration refer to dimensions of the external affairs unit that provide a measure of *sophistication* versus *simplicity*. Units that are high on these dimensions are sophisticated, whereas units low on these dimensions are simple. Miles found that firms with high business exposure to the social environment require more sophisticated units, whereas firms with low business exposure to the social environment could manage reasonably well with simple units.[27]

It is tempting to overgeneralize Miles's study, but we must note it as a significant advance in the realm of public affairs strategy and organizational design research. The important conclusion seems to be that a firm's corporate social performance (as well as its industry legitimacy and viability and economic performance) is a function of business exposure, top management philosophy, external affairs strategy, and external affairs design. Figure 20–5 presents Miles's theory of corporate social performance.

Other initiatives in public relations strategy include integrating public affairs into corporate strategic planning, using strategic management audits for public affairs,

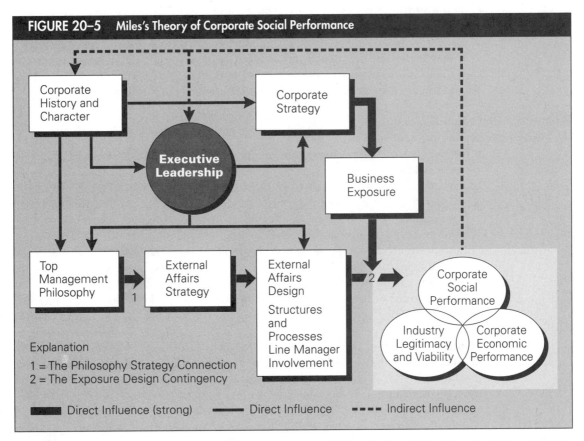

FIGURE 20–5 Miles's Theory of Corporate Social Performance

Explanation
1 = The Philosophy Strategy Connection
2 = The Exposure Design Contingency

Direct Influence (strong) ——— Direct Influence ---- Indirect Influence

SOURCE: Robert H. Miles, *Managing the Corporate Social Environment: A Grounded Theory* (Englewood Cliffs, NJ: Prentice-Hall, Inc., 1987), 274. Reprinted with permission.

building a balanced performance scorecard for public affairs, managing the corporation's reputation, and using core competencies to manage performance.[28]

INCORPORATING PUBLIC AFFAIRS THINKING INTO EVERY MANAGER'S JOB

In today's highly specialized business world, it is easy for line managers or operating managers to let public affairs departments worry about government affairs, community relations, issues management, or any of the numerous other PA functions. Public affairs managers are concerned about this attitude. PA departments have the central leadership role in getting their functions accomplished; in most cases, however, it is essential that line managers or operating managers develop sensitivities or skills that can be useful to the public affairs function.

David H. Blake has taken the position that organizations ought to incorporate public affairs, or what we would call public affairs thinking, into every operating manager's job. He argues that operating managers are vital to a successful PA function, especially if they can identify the public affairs consequences of their actions, be sensitive to the concerns of external groups, act to defuse or avoid crisis situations, and know well in advance when to seek the help of the PA experts. There are no simple ways to achieve these goals, but Blake proposes four specific strategies that may be helpful: (1) make public affairs truly relevant, (2) develop a sense of ownership of success, (3) make it easy for operating managers, and (4) show how public affairs makes a difference.[29] Each of these strategies is discussed below.

Make Public Affairs Truly Relevant

Operating managers often need help in seeing how external factors can and do affect them. A useful mechanism is *analysis of the manager's job* in terms of the likely or potential impacts that her or his decisions may have on the stakeholder environment and possible developments in the environment that may affect the company or the decision maker. One procedure for doing this might be to list the manager's various impacts, the interested or affected strategic stakeholder groups, the potential actions of the groups, and the effects of the groups on jobs or the company.

Another mechanism is *linking achievement of the manager's goals to public affairs*. A plant manager, for example, can be shown how failure to pay attention to community groups can hinder plant expansion, increased output, and product delivery. Failure to address the affected stakeholders can be shown to be related to extensive delays as these neglected groups seek media attention or pressure local officials.

A third way to make PA relevant is to *use the language of the operating manager*. Instead of using the jargon of public affairs, every effort should be made to employ language and terms with which the manager is familiar. Thus, terms such as *environment* to mean local community and *stakeholder* to mean employees and residents must be used cautiously, because operating managers may not be able to fully comprehend them.[30]

Still another way to make public affairs relevant is to demonstrate to operating managers that several operations areas are affected by public affairs issues. John E. Fleming has argued that some of these key areas include marketing, manufacturing, and human resources. Some of the specifics he identifies in the manufacturing arena are product safety and quality, energy conservation, water pollution, air pollution, transportation, and raw materials. Fleming goes on to suggest that public affairs should be linked with corporate planning. If such a linkage is made, the operating manager should see more clearly how these issues are relevant to management decision making.[31]

Develop a Sense of Ownership of Success

It is helpful for operating managers to have participated in planning and goal setting and thus to have had an opportunity to develop a sense of ownership of the public affairs endeavor. Operating managers may be formally or informally enlisted in these planning efforts. At PPG Industries, Inc., operating managers have been given the responsibility for coordinating all actions concerning specific issues. As issue managers, they are asked to see to it that issue and environmental monitoring occurs, that strategy is developed, and that actions are implemented at various governmental levels.[32]

At Kroger, Inc., regional public affairs executives have worked with the individual operating divisions as they have developed their business plans. A public affairs section has been included in each operating *division's* plan, and it is the *division's* plan, not the PA department's plan. As a result of these efforts, the divisions have begun to feel that *they* have "ownership" of the PA goals in *their* plans.[33] This approach seems to work much better than having PA executives simply impose goals or expectations on the operating units.

Make It Easy for Operating Managers

Operating managers have experience in meeting goals and timetables in their own realms. The PA area, however, can often appear nebulous, fuzzy, or inconclusive. Further, operating managers have neither the time for nor the interest in setting up systems or strategies for PA initiatives. This is where the PA professionals can assist them by making their tasks easier. Any procedures, data collection systems, or strategies that PA can supply should be used.

Training in public affairs can be helpful, too. Operating managers can better see the relevance and importance of PA work if carefully chosen topics are put on the agendas of their periodic training sessions. If PA effectiveness is to be monitored, measured, and made a part of performance evaluation systems, care must be taken to make sure that such systems are fair and straightforward, or at least understandable. If PA does not make a careful effort to ensure that its expectations are reasonably met, resistance, resentment, and failure will surely follow.

Show How Public Affairs Makes a Difference

Part of what professional PA staff members need to do is to keep track of public affairs successes in such a way that operating managers can see that their specific actions or efforts have led to identifiable successes for the company. A scorecard approach, whereby operating managers can see that their efforts have helped to avoid problems or prevent serious problems, is useful. The scorecard may be used to reinforce managers' efforts and to help other managers see the potential of the PA function. The scorecard should explicitly state the objectives that have been achieved, the problems that have been avoided, and the friends that have been made for the company.

Obviously, such a scorecard would be of a qualitative nature, but this is necessary in order to describe clearly what has been accomplished. Operating managers need to be shown that there are specific payoffs to be enjoyed from their public affairs efforts. It is up to the PA professionals to document these achievements. If no payoff is demonstrable from PA efforts, operating managers are likely to invest their time elsewhere.[34]

Public affairs is not just a specialized set of management functions to be performed by a designated staff. The nature of the tasks and challenges that characterize public affairs work is such that participation by operating managers is essential. To be sure, PA departments will continue to serve as the backbones of corporate systems, but true effectiveness will require that operating managers be integrated into the accomplishment of these tasks. The mutual interdependence of these two groups—professionals and line managers—will produce optimal results.

SUMMARY

Public affairs might be described as the management function that is responsible for monitoring and interpreting a corporation's noncommercial environment and managing its response to that environment. Public affairs is intimately linked to corporate public policy, environmental analysis, issues management, and crisis management. The major functions of public affairs departments today include the following: government relations, political action, community involvement/responsibility, issues management, international public affairs, and corporate philanthropy. Public affairs has gained widespread acceptance, and there is a vital concern with the productivity of this function. A major growth area is international public affairs.

In terms of public affairs strategy, a collaborative/problem-solving strategy has been shown to be more effective than one that is individualistic/adversarial. Research has shown that a firm's corporate social performance, as well as its industry legitimacy, viability, and economic performance, is a function of business exposure, top management's philosophy, external affairs strategy, and external affairs design. In addition to being viewed as a staff function, public affairs is important for line managers. Four specific strategies are set forth for incorporating public affairs into operating managers' jobs: make it relevant, develop a sense of ownership, make it easy, and show how it can make a difference.

KEY TERMS

benchmarking (page 641)

collaborative/problem-solving strategy (page 644)

corporate public affairs (page 636)

individual/adversarial external affairs strategy (page 644)

public affairs (PA) (page 637)

public affairs management (page 636)

public affairs strategy (page 636)

public relations (PR) (page 637)

DISCUSSION QUESTIONS

1. What is the difference between public relations and public affairs? Why has there been confusion regarding these two concepts?
2. Why do you think international public affairs is a major growth area? Give specific reasons for your answer.
3. What factors will influence the growth of the public affairs function in the future? Briefly discuss.
4. Differentiate between a collaborative/problem-solving strategy and an individual/adversarial strategy. Which seems to be more effective in corporate public affairs?
5. What are the major ways in which public affairs might be incorporated into every manager's job? Rank them in terms of what you think their impact might be.

ENDNOTES

1. James C. Bowling, "Managing Public Affairs: New Dimensions" (Remarks before Public Affairs Conference of The Conference Board, January 15, 1981), 2.
2. Craig S. Fleisher, "Evaluating Your Existing Public Affairs Management System," in Craig S. Fleisher (ed.) *Assessing, Managing and Maximizing Public Affairs Performance* (Washington, DC: Public Affairs Council, 1997), 4.
3. Richard A. Armstrong, "Public Affairs vs. Public Relations," *Public Relations Quarterly* (Fall, 1981), 26. Also see Craig S. Fleisher and Natasha M. Blair, "Tracing the Parallel Evolution of Public Affairs and Public Relations: An Examination of Practice, Scholarship, and Teaching" (Paper presented at The Fifth International Public Relations Research Symposium, Lake Bled, Slovenia, July, 1998).
4. James E. Post and Jennifer J. Griffin, *The State of Corporate Public Affairs: Final Report* (Washington, DC, and Boston: Foundation for Public Affairs, 1997), Figure 3.1.
5. *Public Affairs Council* (Washington, DC: Public Affairs Council, 1983), 5.
6. Post and Griffin.
7. James E. Post and Patricia C. Kelley, "Lessons from the Learning Curve: The Past, Present and Future of Issues Management," in Robert L. Heath and Associates, *Strategic Issues Management* (San Francisco: Jossey-Bass, 1988), 352.
8. Martin B. Meznar and Douglas Nigh, "Buffer or Bridge? Environmental and Organizational Determinants of Public Affairs Activities in American Firms," *Academy of Management Journal* (August, 1995), 975–996.
9. The Public Affairs Council, "International Public Affairs: A Preliminary Report by a PAC Task Force" (Washington, DC: Public Affairs Council, April, 1983), 2. For further perspectives on international public affairs, see D. Jeffrey Lenn, Steven N. Brenner, Lee Burke, Diane Dodd-McCue, Craig S. Fleisher, Lawrence J. Lad, David R. Palmer, Kathryn S. Rogers, Sandra S. Waddock, and Richard E. Wokutch, "Managing Corporate Public Affairs and Government Relations: U.S. Multinational Corporations in Europe," in James E. Post (ed.), *Research in Corporate Social Performance and Policy*, Vol. 14 (Greenwich, CT: JAI Press, 1993), 103–108.
10. The Public Affairs Council, "Effective Management of International Public Affairs," (Washington, DC: Public Affairs Council, April, 1985), 1.

11. Post and Griffin, Figure 3.2.

12. James E. Post and the Foundation for Public Affairs, "The State of Corporate Public Affairs in the United States: Results of a National Survey," in James E. Post (ed.), *Research in Corporate Social Performance and Policy*, Vol. 14 (Greenwich, CT: JAI Press, 1993), 79–89.

13. *Ibid.*, 81–85.

14. *Ibid.*, 85–88.

15. Craig S. Fleisher, "Public Affairs Management Performance: An Empirical Analysis of Evaluation and Measurement," in James E. Post (ed.), *Research in Corporate Social Performance and Policy*, Vol. 14 (Greenwich, CT: JAI Press, 1993), 139–163.

16. Quoted in Peter Shafer, "Benchmarking: Here's a Management Fad You Could Learn to Love," *Impact* (July/August, 1994), 1–3. Also see Craig S. Fleisher, *Public Affairs Benchmarking: A Comprehensive Guide* (Washington, DC: Public Affairs Council, 1995).

17. Post and Griffin. Also see "Public Affairs: Its Origins, Its Present and Its Trends," *www.pac.org/whatis/index.htm.*

18. *Ibid.*

19. *Ibid.*

20. Craig S. Fleisher, "The New Public Affairs," *Impact* (July/August, 1998), 1–3.

21. Peter Shafer, *Adding Value to the Public Affairs Function: Using Quality to Improve Performance* (Washington, DC: Public Affairs Council, 1994).

22. Fleisher, 1997.

23. Robert H. Miles, *Managing the Corporate Social Environment: A Grounded Theory* (Englewood Cliffs, NJ: Prentice-Hall, Inc., 1987).

24. *Ibid.*, 8.

25. *Ibid.*, 9–10, 111.

26. *Ibid.*, 2–3.

27. *Ibid.*, 11, 113.

28. Fleisher (ed.), 1997, 139–196.

29. David H. Blake, "How to Incorporate Public Affairs into the Operating Manager's Job," *Public Affairs Review* (1984), 35.

30. *Ibid.*, 36–38.

31. John E. Fleming, "Linking Public Affairs with Corporate Planning," *California Management Review* (Winter, 1980), 42.

32. Blake, 38–39.

33. Jack W. Partridge, "Making Line Managers Part of the Public Affairs Team: Innovative Ideas at Kroger," in Wesley Pederson (ed.), *Cost-Effective Management for Today's Public Affairs* (Washington, DC: Public Affairs Council, 1987), 67. Also see Fleisher, 1997.

34. *Ibid.*, 40–41. Also see Craig Fleisher and Darren Mahaffy, "Building the Balanced Performance Scorecard for Public Affairs," in Fleisher, 1997, 152–156.

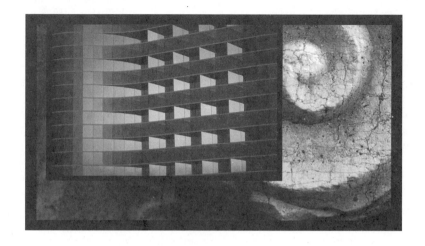

Cases

Case Analysis

The guidelines presented below have been designed to help the student analyze the cases. They are not, however, intended to be a rigid format. Each question is intended to bring out information that will be helpful in analyzing and resolving the case. Each case is different, and some parts of the guidelines may not apply in every case. Also, the student should be attentive to the questions for discussion at the end of each case. These questions should be answered in any complete case analysis. The heart of any case analysis is the recommendations that are made. The Problem/Issue Identification and Analysis/Evaluation steps should be focused on generating and defending the most effective set of recommendations possible.

GUIDELINES FOR ANALYZING CASES

Problem/Issue Identification

1. What are the *central facts of the case* and the *assumptions* you are making on the basis of these facts?

2. What is the *major overriding issue* in this case? (What major questions/issue does this case address that merit(s) their/its study in this course and in connection with the chapter/material you are now covering?)

3. What *subissues or related issues* are present in the case that merit consideration and discussion?

Analysis/Evaluation

4. Who are the *stakeholders* in this case, and what are their *stakes*? (Create a stakeholder map if this is helpful.) What challenges/threats/opportunities are posed by these stakeholders?

5. What *economic/legal/ethical/philanthropic responsibilities* does the company have, and what exactly are the nature and extent of these responsibilities?

6. If the case involves a company's action, *evaluate what the company did or did not do* in handling the issue affecting it.

Recommendations

7. What recommendations would you make in this case? If a company's strategies or actions are involved, should the company have acted the way it did? What actions should the company take now, and why? Be as specific as possible, and include a discussion of *alternatives* you have considered but decided not to pursue. Mention and discuss any important *implementation considerations*.

The Main Street Merchant of Doom

1

The small town was in need of a hired gun. The people were tired of dealing with the local price-fixing merchant scum who ran the town like a company store. This lowlife bunch held the people of the town in a death grip and were perceived by the townspeople to overcharge on every purchase. In spite of what appeared to be a case of collusion, the law was powerless to do anything. What competition there was had been effectively eliminated.

Suddenly, coming over the rise and wearing white, their hired man came riding. The women and children buzzed with excitement. The men were happy. Although his methods of getting the job done turned some people's stomachs, the local watering hole buzzed with tales of how this hired gun would change their world for the better, how some day soon they would have the benefits long afforded the big city. But, others asked, at what price?

THE 1990S VERSION OF THE "HIRED GUN"

In his final days, the man appeared to be somewhat too frail to handle the enormous job. Yet, the courage and self-confidence that he instilled in his associates radiated a belief in low prices and good value for all to see. As his associates rode into town, that radiance put to rest the people's fears that things had changed. Sam's spirit, the Wal-Mart Way, had come to town.

Sam Walton, founder, owner, and mastermind of Wal-Mart, passed away on April 5, 1992, leaving behind his spirit to ride herd on the massive Wal-Mart organization. To the consumer in the small community, his store, Wal-Mart, was seen as a friend. On the flip side, many a small-town merchant had been the victim of Sam's blazing merchandising tactics. So what is Wal-Mart to the communities it services? Is Wal-Mart the consumer's best friend, the purveyor of the free enterprise system, the "Mother of All Discount Stores," or, conversely, is it really "The Main Street Merchant of Doom"?

This case was prepared by William T. Rupp of the College of Management at Robert Morris College. It was revised for the fourth edition by Archie B. Carroll.

THE MAN NAMED SAM

Samuel Moore Walton was born March 29, 1918, near Kingfisher, Kansas. His father was a salesman in the insurance, real estate, and mortgage businesses. The family moved often. Sam was a strong, lean boy who learned to work hard in order to help the family. He attended the University of Missouri starting in the fall of 1936 and graduated with a degree in business administration. During his time there, he was a member of the Beta Theta Phi fraternity, was president of the senior class, played various sports, and taught what was believed to be the largest Sunday school class in the world, numbering over 1,200 Missouri students.[1]

At age 22, Sam joined J. C. Penney. One of his first tasks was to memorize and practice the "Penney Idea." Adopted in 1913, this credo exhorts the associate to serve the public; not to demand all the profit the traffic will bear; to pack the customer's dollar full of value, quality, and satisfaction; to continue to be trained; to reward men and women in the organization through participation in what the business produces; and to test every policy, method, and act against the question: "Does it square with what is right and just?"[2]

In 1962, at 44 years of age, Sam Walton opened his first Wal-Mart store. He took all the money and expertise he could gather and applied the J. C. Penney Idea to Middle America. Sam first targeted small, underserved rural towns with populations of no more than 10,000 people. The people responded, and Wal-Mart soon developed a core of loyal customers who loved the fast, friendly service coupled with consistently low prices.

THE STORE THAT SAM BUILT

By 1981, Wal-Mart's rapid growth was evident to all and especially disturbing to Sears, J. C. Penney, Target, and K-Mart, because Wal-Mart had become America's largest retailer. The most telling figures are those of overhead expenses and sales per employee. The overhead expenses of Sears and K-Mart ran 29 and 23 percent of sales, respectively, whereas Wal-Mart's overhead expenses ran 16 percent of sales. The average Sears employee generated $85,000 in sales per year, whereas the average Wal-Mart employee generated $95,000.[3]

By August 1998, Wal-Mart Company operated 2,374 Wal-Mart stores, including 479 Wal-Mart Supercenters, 446 Sam's Clubs (membership warehouse clubs), and numerous Bud's Discount City deep-discount warehouse outlets. Wal-Mart, as America's largest retailer, had 1998 sales of $117.9 million. The company employed more than 720,000 associates in the United States and more than 115,000 associates internationally. The company served more than 90 million customers weekly in 50 states, Puerto Rico, Canada, and several other countries.[4]

Sam, the motivational wizard and cheerleader, promoted the associate—the hourly employee—to a new level of participation within the organization. He offered profit sharing, incentive bonuses, and stock options in an effort to have his Wal-Mart associates share in the wealth. Sam, as the head cheerleader, saw his job as the chief proponent of the "Wal-Mart Way."

Sam, the courageous, borrowed and borrowed, sometimes just to pay other creditors. Arkansas banks that at one time had turned him down now competed with banks that Sam himself owned.

Sam, the CEO, hired the best managers he could find. He let them talk him into buying an extensive computer network system. This network corporate satellite system enabled Sam to use round-the-clock inventory control and credit card sales control and provided him with information on total sales of which products where and when. This computer control center is about the size of a football field and uses a Hughes satellite for uplinking and downlinking to each store.

In 1992, Sam, the mortal, died of incurable bone cancer. At age 73, Sam Walton said that if he had to do it over again he would not change a thing. He said, "This is still the most important thing I do, going around to the stores, and I'd rather do it than anything I know of. I know I'm helping our folks when I get out to the stores. I learn a lot about who's doing good things in the office, and I also see things that need fixing, and I help fix them. Any good management person in retail has got to do what I do in order to keep his finger on what's going on. You've got to have the right chemistry and the right attitude on the part of the folks who deal with the customers."[5]

Sam, the innovator, developed the "store within a store" concept of training people to be merchants, not just employees. These "store within a store" managers have all the numbers for their departments—breakdowns of how they are doing in relation to the store and the company as a whole. This concept provides big opportunities by providing big responsibilities. Sam set the goal of visiting every Wal-Mart store every year. To do this, he flew his own twin-prop Cessna and visited up to five or six stores per day. Two early social responsibility programs were Wal-Mart's "Buy American" plan and its "Environmental Awareness" campaign.

SAM AND SOCIAL AWARENESS: THE "BUY AMERICAN" PLAN

The "Buy American" program was a result of a 1984 telephone conversation with then Arkansas Governor Bill Clinton. The program was a response to Sam's own enlightenment: He learned that Wal-Mart was adding to the loss of American jobs by buying cheaper foreign goods. Everything Sam stood for came out of his heartfelt obligation to supply the customer with low-cost quality goods, but running counter to this inner driving force was the realization that he was responsible for the loss of American jobs. This contradiction and dilemma drove him to find a solution. The conversation with Governor Clinton inspired Sam to do something about the problem. The following story describes Sam's actions in regard to the Farris Borroughs Corporation.

Farris Borroughs operated Farris Fashions, a clothing manufacturer in Brinkley, Arkansas (population 5,000). The plant employed 90 people and had been making flannel shirts for Van Heusen. The shirts had been distributed through J. C. Penney and Sears, but now, because of the cost advantages enjoyed by foreign competitors, Farris Fashions had lost the ability to be competitive. The factory would probably close, and 90 Arkansas people would be out of work. Sam listened to Governor Clinton's story and replied, "I'd hate to see an Arkansas plant shut down. I'll call you back." He knew he had to try to save Farris Fashions. It seemed the "Buy American" bug had infected Sam's decision-making mindset, and it was full steam ahead.

Farris Borroughs and Farris Fashions needed help. Financing problems and a lack of "American-made" flannel material had to be overcome. Sam called in representatives from big textile firms to discuss the "American-made" problem. However, there was no answer to the raw flannel manufacturing problem. It was explained that American companies simply could not make a profit producing the flannel material. A compromise allowed Farris Fashions to buy foreign flannel material if all construction of the shirts would be done at the Brinkley factory. Sam also guaranteed Farris Fashions a $612,000 order, scheduling help, and a fast payment arrangement.[6]

Sam wanted other manufacturers to join him in the "Buy American" plan. He wrote to 3,000 American manufacturers and solicited them to sell to Wal-Mart items that Wal-Mart was currently buying from overseas suppliers. Wal-Mart's competitors did not meet the challenge to "Buy American." K-Mart stated that it would rather buy American-made goods but that it was looking for the best deal for the customer. Target said it was for free trade and that as the customer's representative it just wanted the best deal for the customer. Wall Street analysts responded positively, saying that Wal-Mart's plan was possibly the beginning of a change of direction for American retailers.[7]

In February 1986, about 12 months after the "Buy American" plan had begun, Sam held a press conference. He showed off all the merchandise Wal-Mart was now buying domestically. He estimated that Wal-Mart's "Buy American" plan had restored 4,538 jobs to the American economy and its people.[8]

SAM AND SOCIAL CONCERNS: THE "ENVIRONMENTAL AWARENESS" CAMPAIGN

As awareness of the environment was on the rise, Sam looked for a way to involve Wal-Mart in the environmental movement. In August 1989, an ad in *The Wall Street Journal* proclaimed Wal-Mart's "commitment to our land, air and water." Sam envisioned Wal-Mart as a leader among American companies in the struggle to clean up the environment. John Lowne, corporate vice president and division manager for Reynolds Metals Company, stated, "Wal-Mart's move will indeed set a precedent for the entire retail industry. I'm surprised it has taken other retailers this long to follow suit."[9]

Wal-Mart wanted to use its tremendous buying power to aid in the implementation of the campaign. Wal-Mart sent a booklet to manufacturers stating the following:

At Wal-Mart we're committed to help improve our environment. Our customers are concerned about the quality of our land, air and water, and want the opportunity to do something positive. We believe it is our responsibility to step up to their challenge.[10]

In the stores, shelf tags made from 100 percent recycled paper inform customers as to the environmental friendliness of the highlighted product. As a result of these shelf tags and Wal-Mart's advertising, customer awareness has increased and some environmentally safe product manufacturers are reaping the rewards of increased Wal-Mart orders. Linda Downs, administrative manager of Duraflame/California, said that Duraflame logs have been proven to burn cleaner than wood and that Wal-Mart's campaign has helped Duraflame to deliver this message. She goes on to say, "Wal-Mart has helped drive home the message we have been trying to promote for years. They have really given us great publicity."[11]

In the *Wal-Mart Associates Handbook,* new associates are indoctrinated with the "Wal-Mart spirit." The section entitled "Our Commitments" begins with this statement: "We feel a moral obligation not only to our customers, but to our communities in which our stores are located." A personal comment from Sam states:

We live in such a great country, this land of ours, and I'm afraid we all take our freedoms, opportunities and many blessings for granted at times. All of us in our Wal-Mart family should count our blessings daily and do all we can to help others, both within our company and outside, who are less fortunate and in need. Our associates have done just that in our communities. They have shown their willingness to share so generously in 100,000 instances and more. I'm so proud of all you hardworking, dedicated, loyal Wal-Mart associate-partners. You personify, most of all, our Wal-Mart spirit because you care about others![12]

The section on the environment says:

As a responsible member of the community, Wal-Mart's commitments go beyond simply selling merchandise. With environmental concerns mounting world-wide, Wal-Mart has taken action. Home office and store associates are taking decisive steps to help the environment by making community recycling bins available on our facility parking lots. Other action plans include "Adopt-a-Highway" and

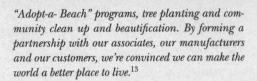

"Adopt-a- Beach" programs, tree planting and community clean up and beautification. By forming a partnership with our associates, our manufacturers and our customers, we're convinced we can make the world a better place to live.[13]

SAM AND THE MERCHANTS OF MAIN STREET

Not everyone has been excited to see Sam and his mechanized Wal-Mart army succeed. Small merchants across America shudder when the winds of the "Wal-Mart Way" begin to blow. Kennedy Smith of the National Main Street Center in Washington, DC, says, "The first thing towns usually do is panic." Once Wal-Mart comes to town, Smith says, "Downtowns will never again be the providers of basic consumer goods and services they once were."[14]

Some towns have learned to "just say 'no'" to Wal-Mart's overtures. Steamboat Springs, Colorado, is one such city. Colorado newspapers called it the "Shootout at Steamboat Springs." Wal-Mart was denied permission to build on a 9-acre parcel along U.S. Route 40. Owners of upscale shops and condos were very concerned with the image of their resort community and Wal-Mart, with its low-cost reputation, just did not fit. The shootout lasted for 2 years, and finally Wal-Mart filed a damage suit against the city. Countersuits followed. A petition was circulated to hold a referendum on the matter. This was the shot that made Wal-Mart blink and back down. Just before the election in April 1989, Don Shinkle, corporate affairs vice president, said, "A vote would not be good for Steamboat Springs, and it would not be good for Wal-Mart. I truly believe Wal-Mart is a kinder, gentler company, and, while we have the votes to win, an election would only split the town more."[15]

In Iowa City, Iowa (population 50,000+), Wal-Mart was planning an 87,000-square-foot store on the out-skirts of town. A group of citizens gathered enough signatures during a petition drive to put a referendum on the ballot to block Wal-Mart and the city council from building the new store (the city council had approved the rezoning of the land Wal-Mart wanted). Jim Clayton, a downtown merchant, said, "Wal-Mart is a freight train going full steam in the opposite direction of this town's philosophy." If businesses wind up going down, Clayton says, "you lose their involvement in the community, involvement I promise you won't get with some assistant manager over at Wal-Mart."[16] Wal-Mart spokesperson Brenda Lockhart commented that downtown merchants can only benefit from the increase in customer traffic provided "they offer superior service and aren't gouging their customers."[17] Efforts to stop Wal-Mart and the Iowa City Council were not successful. Wal-Mart opened its Iowa City store on November 5, 1991.

Meanwhile, in Pawhuska, Oklahoma, as a result of Wal-Mart's entry in 1983 and other local factors, the local "five-and-dime," J. C. Penney, Western Auto, and a whole block of other stores closed their doors. In 1987, Dave Story, general manager of the local *Pawhuska Daily Journal Capital,* wrote that Wal-Mart was a "billion-dollar parasite" and a "national retail ogre."[18]

Wal-Mart managers have become very active in Pawhuska and surrounding communities since 1987. A conversation with the editor of the Pawhuska paper, Jody Smith, and her advertising editor, Suzy Burns, revealed that Wal-Mart sponsored the local rodeo, gave gloves to the local coat drive, and was involved with the local cerebral palsy and multiple sclerosis fund-raisers. On the other hand, Fred Wright, former owner of a TV and record store, said, "Wal-Mart really craters a little town's downtown."[19]

Shift to Kinder, Louisiana (population 2,608). Wal-Mart moved into this small Louisiana town in 1981. On December 31, 1990, the store was closed. During the time Wal-Mart operated in Kinder, one-third of the downtown stores closed. The downtown became three blocks of mostly run-down, red-brick buildings. The closest place to buy shoes or sewing thread is 30 miles away in Oakdale, Louisiana—another Wal-Mart. Moreover, Kinder lost $5,500 in annual tax revenues, which represented 10 percent of the total revenues for the city.

The tactics Wal-Mart employed during its 10 years in Kinder left a bad taste in the mouths of some small retailers. Soon after Wal-Mart's arrival, a price war broke out between Wal-Mart and the downtown retailers. The retailers told *The Atlanta Journal-Constitution* in November 1990, "Wal-Mart sent employees, wearing name tags and smocks, into their stores to scribble down prices and list merchandise." Lou Pearl, owner of Kinder Jewelry and Gifts, stated that Wal-Mart associates came to her store and noted the type of art supplies she was carrying. Shortly thereafter, Wal-Mart began carrying the same merchandise at a discount. Sales at Kinder Jewelry and Gifts dropped drastically, and Pearl dropped the merchandise line. Within several weeks, so did Wal-Mart.[20] Perhaps Troy Marcantel, a 29-year-old downtown clothing merchant, said it best: "What really rankled me was that they used people we have known all our lives. I still don't understand how our own people could do that to us."[21]

THE MAIN STREET MERCHANTS ORGANIZE A WELCOMING COMMITTEE

There are now dozens of organized groups actively opposing Wal-Mart's expansion.[22] Some of these groups are run by activists left over from the 1960s and 1970s. Instead of protesting the Vietnam War, nuclear proliferation, or the destruction of the environment, they have turned their efforts to Wal-Mart specifically and capitalism in general. One of these activists, Paul Glover, who was an antiwar organizer, has defined Wal-Mart as the epitome of capitalism, which he despises. For Mr. Glover and others, Wal-Mart stands for "everything they dislike about American society—mindless consumerism, paved landscapes, and homogenization of community identity."[23]

In Boulder, Colorado, Wal-Mart tried to counter these allegations by proposing a "green" store. Steven Lane, Wal-Mart's real estate manager, said that a "green store" would be built that would be environmentally friendly, with a solar-powered sign out front and everything. His efforts were trumped by Spencer Havlick, an organizer of the first Earth Day in 1970, suggesting that the entire store be powered by solar energy. Mr. Lane did not respond.[24]

Protest organizers united against the spread of the "Wal-Mart Way" differ from the downtown merchants in that these protesters have no financial stake. Hence, these activists are attacking on a higher plane, a philosophical plane. The accusations ring with a tone of argument that were made by other activists protesting polluting industries (e.g., the coal, nuclear, and chemical industries). These activists accuse Wal-Mart of "strip-mining" towns and communities of their culture and values.

One possible root of this culture clash may be attributed to the unique facets of the internal corporate culture at Wal-Mart's headquarters. This is a place where competition for the reputation as the "cheapest" is practiced. An example is the competition among employees in procuring the cheapest haircut, shoes, or necktie. Wal-Mart is a place where playacting as a backwoods "hick" has been an acceptable behavior within the organization. Consequently,

as a result of the internal culture of Wal-Mart and the external environment, some analysts believe that a clash of priorities was inevitable as Wal-Mart moved into larger, more urban settings.

Some of the greatest opposition to Wal-Mart's growth has come from the New England area. This area holds great promise for Wal-Mart because of the large population and the many underserved towns. These towns are typically underserved in three ways: in variety of product choices, in value, and in convenience. The opposition to Wal-Mart entering these New England markets includes some high-profile names, such as Jerry Greenfield, cofounder of Ben & Jerry's Homemade ice cream, and Arthur Frommer, a well-known travel writer.[25]

Al Norman, a lobbyist and media consultant, has turned opposition to Wal-Mart into a cottage industry. Mr. Norman publishes a monthly newsletter called *Sprawl-Busters Alert*. He has also developed a Web site (*www.sprawl-busters.com*) that has vast information for citizens who are fighting to prevent Wal-Mart or other "big box" stores from locating in their cities or neighborhoods. Norman achieved national attention in 1993, when he stopped Wal-Mart from locating in his hometown of Greenfield, Massachusetts. Since then, he has appeared on "60 Minutes," which called him "the guru of the anti-Wal-Mart movement," and has gained widespread media attention. Today Norman continues to serve as a consultant and travels throughout the United States helping dozens of coalitions fight Wal-Mart.

RECENT TRENDS

Opposing Wal-Mart continues to be big business, spurred by activists like Mr. Norman and citizen-leaders who do not want big box stores in their communities. The successes and failures of Wal-Mart opposition are chronicled on the "Sprawl-Busters" Web page.[26]

For its part, Wal-Mart continues its aggressive diversification and growth pattern. In October 1998, Wal-Mart announced plans for 40 new discount stores and 150 new Supercenters. When Wal-Mart replaces regular stores with Supercenters, communities face a new problem: what to do with the vacant Wal-Mart locations, which leave empty buildings as well as other merchants who built near them to capitalize on Wal-Mart's heavy traffic.

In addition to diversifying, Wal-Mart plans to continue growing internationally. It plans to develop 75 to 80 new retail units outside the United States. New stores are planned for Argentina, Brazil, Canada, China, Korea, Mexico, and Puerto Rico.[27] In 1998, Wal-Mart announced plans for three "experimental" grocery stores in Arkansas to be known as Wal-Mart "Neighborhood Markets." By leveraging its distribution and buying strengths, Wal-Mart is hoping its new grocery stores will be able to beat conventional grocery stores with lower everyday prices and more conveniences than its Supercenters. Grocery store industry executives are already shuddering at the prospects of Wal-Mart growing into their industry, where margins are already razor thin.[28]

Wal-Mart has millions of supporters, 90 million of them weekly customers. Many consider the company to be socially responsible in addition to a provider of thousands of jobs, low prices, and high value and service. As we enter the millennium, Wal-Mart has numerous corporate citizenship initiatives at the local and national levels. Locally, Wal-Mart stores underwrite college scholarships for high school seniors, raise funds for children's hospitals through The Children's Miracle Network Telethon, provide local fund-raisers money and manpower, and educate the public about recycling and other environmental topics with the help of "Green Coordinators."[29] On October 6, 1998, the Walton Family Charitable Support Foundation, the charitable program created by Sam Walton's family, announced the largest ever single gift made to an American business school: $50 million to the College of Business Administration of the University of Arkansas. Helen R. Walton, the "first lady" of Wal-Mart, said that she and her husband established the Foundation to support specific charities, including the University.[30]

Nationally, Wal-Mart provides industrial development grants to cities and towns trying to bolster their economic bases; encourages American companies to bring offshore manufacturing operations "back home" through its Buy American program; underwrites Support American Manufacturing (SAM), a program administered by Southwest Missouri State University that shows small companies how to improve their operations; and sponsors the American Hometown Leadership Award, which salutes small-town government leaders who are mapping long-term goals for their communities.[31]

EPILOGUE

Sam, the hired gun, learned his lessons well. The people who bought at his stores were well satisfied. The downtown merchants who survived learned to coexist with the hired gun's associates. But things would never be the same. The changes had come rapidly. The social fabric of the small town was changed forever.

The hired gun rode on, searching for that next town that needed to be liberated from the downtown price-fixing bad guys. The search has become more complicated as the opposition has risen, but the spirit of Sam rides on.

QUESTIONS FOR DISCUSSION

1. What are the major issues in this case? Assess Wal-Mart's corporate social responsibility using the four-part CSR model. Is Wal-Mart socially responsible for its devastating impact on small merchants? What responsibility, if any, does the company have to these merchants or to the communities it enters?

2. Most of Wal-Mart's success has come at the expense of the small merchant. What should Wal-Mart do, if anything, to help other vital businesses in the community survive? Why?

3. Sam Walton has been called a motivational genius. After reading this case and with what you have observed at your local Wal-Mart store, explain how this motivational genius empowered the employee. What is the "Wal-Mart Way"? Explain its impact on the associate and on the community. What will happen now that Sam is no longer the motivational leader?

4. Some regard Wal-Mart as a leader in the area of corporate social responsibility. How do the "Buy American" program and the "Environmental Awareness" campaign illustrate this? Are these programs really examples of corporate social responsibility or are they gimmicks to entice customers into the stores? Are the benefits of these programs offset by the company's devastating impact on merchants?

5. Wal-Mart has closed five stores in its short history. What responsibility, if any, does Wal-Mart have to the employees who are let go? What about its loyal customers and the community?

6. In the case of Kinder, Louisiana, Wal-Mart left town without any type of reciprocity. Given Wal-Mart's commitment statements, did the company owe a debt to the city of Kinder? Why or why not?

7. Wal-Mart is finding severe resistance to its expansion into New England. From Wal-Mart's perspective, draw the stakeholder map. Define the true goals of the opponents of Wal-Mart. Include a consideration of the following: (a) stopping Wal-Mart's expansion, (b) preserving the status quo (e.g., downtown community, social fabric), (c) developing a cause that will pay their bills, (d) fighting for an ideology, or (e) something else. What should Wal-Mart do?

CASE ENDNOTES

1. Vance H. Trimble, *Sam Walton: The Inside Story of America's Richest Man* (New York: Penguin Books, 1990), 30. Also see Bob Ortega, *In Sam We Trust* (New York: Times Business, 1998).

2. *Ibid.*, 34.

3. Janice Castro, "Mr. Sam Stuns Goliath," *Time* (February 25, 1991), 62.

4. Wal-Mart's Web page, "Data Sheet," *wal-mart.com/*; Also see Lorrie Grant, "They Still Cheer at Company Meetings," *USA Today* (November 6, 1998), B1.

5. John Huey, "America's Most Successful Merchant," *Fortune* (September 23, 1991), 50.

6. Trimble, 259.

7. *Ibid.*, 260.

8. *Ibid.*, 261.

9. Richard Turcsik, "A New Environment Evolves at Wal-Mart," *Supermarket News* (January 15, 1990), 10.

10. *Ibid.*, 10.

11. *Ibid.*, 11.

12. Wal-Mart Corporation, *Wal-Mart Associates Handbook* (July, 1991), 14.

13. *Ibid.*, 14.

14. Dan Koeppel, "Wal-Mart Finds New Rivals on Main Street," *Adweek's Marketing Week* (November 10, 1990), 5.

15. Trimble, 255.

16. "Just Saying No to Wal-Mart," *Newsweek* (November 13, 1989), 65.

17. *Ibid.*, 65.

18. Karen Blumenthal, "Arrival of Discounter Tears the Civic Fabric of Small-Town Life," *The Wall Street Journal* (April 14, 1987), 1, 23.

19. *Ibid.*, 23.

20. Charles Haddad, "Wal-Mart Leaves Town 'High, Dry,'" *The Atlanta Journal-Constitution* (November 26, 1990), A4.

21. *Ibid.*, A4.

22. Bob Ortega, "Aging Activists Turn, Turn, Turn Attention to Wal-Mart Protests," *The Wall Street Journal* (October 11, 1994), A1, A8.

23. *Ibid.*, A1.

24. *Ibid.*, A8.

25. Joseph Pereira and Bob Ortega, "Once Easily Turned Away by Local Foes, Wal-Mart Gets Tough in New England," *The Wall Street Journal* (September 7, 1994), B1.

26. "Sprawl-Busters," *www.sprawl-busters.com.*

27. Wal-Mart Web page, "Wal-Mart Announces Expansion Plans," *wal-mart.com/corporate/wm_story.shtml* (October 28, 1998).

28. Emily Nelson, "Why Wal-Mart Sings, 'Yes, We Have Bananas!'" *The Wall Street Journal,* October 6, 1998, B1; and Wendy Zellner, "Look Out, Supermarkets—Wal-Mart Is Hungry," *Business Week* (September 14, 1998), 98–100.

29. Wal-Mart Web page, *wal-mart.com/corporate/wm_story.shtml.*

30. University of Arkansas Web page, *www.uark.edu* (October 6, 1998), press release.

31. Wal-Mart Web page.

The Body Shop International PLC (1991) 2A

When North American consumers are asked to describe the cosmetics industry, they often respond with words such as "glamour" and "beauty." Beginning in 1976, The Body Shop provided a contrast to this image by selling a range of 400 products designed to "cleanse and polish the skin and hair." The product line included such items as "Honeyed Beeswax, Almond, and Jojoba Oil Cleanser" and "Carrot Facial Oil." Women's cosmetics and men's toiletries were also available. They were all produced without the use of animal testing and were packaged in plain-looking, recyclable packages.[1] The primary channel of distribution was a network of over 600 franchised retail outlets in Europe, Australia, Asia, and North America.[2] The company enjoyed annual growth rates of approximately 50 percent until 1990, when net income began to level off. Few questions were raised in the media about this decline in performance, because the firm's social agenda and exotic product line captured most of the public's interest.

Managing director and founder Anita Roddick was responsible for creating and maintaining much of the company's marketing strategy and product development.[3] Roddick believed that The Body Shop was fundamentally different from other firms in the cosmetics industry because "we don't claim that our products will make you look younger, we say they will only help you look your best."[4] She regularly assailed her competitors: "We loathe the cosmetic industry with a passion. It's run by men who create needs that don't exist."[5] During the 1980s, Anita Roddick became one of the richest women in the United Kingdom by challenging the well-established firms and rewriting the rules of the cosmetics industry.

Anita Roddick became admired within the business community for the conviction of her beliefs and the success of her company. She received many honors and awards, including U.K. Businesswoman of the Year in 1985, British Retailer of the Year in 1989,

and the Order of the British Empire.[6] The firm's customers included several celebrities, including Princess Diana of Wales, Sting, and Bob Weir of the Grateful Dead. Ben Cohen, cofounder and chairman of Ben and Jerry's, described her as:

> an incredibly dynamic, passionate, humorous and intelligent individual who believes it's the responsibility of a business to give back to the community . . . she understands that a business has the power to influence the world in a positive way.[7]

Mrs. Roddick opened the first Body Shop store in Brighton, England, as a means of supporting her family while her husband was taking a year-long sabbatical in America. Her husband, Gordon Roddick, a chartered accountant by trade, was using much of their savings to finance his trip. Anita Roddick had little money to open a store, much less to develop products or purchase packaging materials.[8]

She called upon her previous experience as a resource. Having been a United Nations researcher for several years in the 1960s, she had had many opportunities during field expeditions to see how men and women in Africa, Asia, and Australia used locally grown plants and extracts, such as beeswax, rice grains, almonds, bananas, and jojoba, as grooming products. Roddick knew that these materials were inexpensive and readily obtainable. With some library research, she found several recipes, some of which were centuries old, that used these same ingredients to make cosmetics and skin cleansers. With the addition of inexpensive bottles and handwritten labels, Roddick quickly developed a line of products for sale in her first Body Shop. She soon opened a second store in a nearby town. When Gordon Roddick returned to the United Kingdom in 1977, The Body Shop was recording sizable profits. At Anita's request, he joined the company as its chief executive officer.[9]

The Body Shop's strategy grew out of the company's early reliance on cost containment. Roddick was able to afford only 600 bottles when she opened her first store. Customers were offered a small discount to encourage the return of empty bottles for

This case was prepared by William A. Sodeman using publicly available information.

product refills. This offer was extended to both retail and mail-order customers.[10] The Body Shop could not afford advertising, so Roddick resolved to do without it.[11]

The Body Shop's retail stores were somewhat different from the cosmetic salons and counters familiar to shoppers in highly industrialized nations. The typical retail sales-counter relied on high-pressure tactics that included promotions, makeovers, and an unspoken contract with the customer that virtually required a purchase in order for the customer to receive any advice or consultation from a sales-counter employee.[12] Body Shop employees were taught to wait for the customer to ask questions, be forthright and helpful, and not to press for sales.[13]

Store employees were paid a half-day's wages every week to perform community service activities. At the company headquarters in Littlehampton, England, The Body Shop employed an anthropologist, six herbalists, and a variety of others in similar fields. There was nothing that resembled a marketing department. Husbands and wives frequently worked together and could visit their children during the workday at the on-site day-care center.[14] The company's hiring procedures included questions about the applicant's personal heroes and literary tastes, as well as their individual beliefs on certain social issues. At one time, Roddick was ready to hire a retail director, but refused to do so when he professed his fondness for hunting, a sport that Roddick despised because of her support for animal rights.[15]

As the company prospered, Anita Roddick used her enthusiasm and growing influence on her suppliers and customers. The Body Shop began to produce products in the country of origin when it was feasible and paid the workers wages that were comparable to those in the European Community.[16] Customers were asked to sign petitions and join activist groups that The Body Shop endorsed, mostly in the areas of animal rights and environmental causes. The Body Shop contributed significant portions of its earnings to these groups, including Amnesty International and People for the Ethical Treatment of Animals (PETA). Roddick was careful to choose causes that were "easy to understand"[17] and could be communicated quickly to a customer during a visit to a Body Shop store.

An example of this corporate activism was The Body Shop's opposition to a practice that had become common in the cosmetics industry. Cosmetics firms were not required to perform animal test-

ing of their products to comply with product safety and health regulations. Rather, companies voluntarily adopted animal-based testing procedures to guard against product liability lawsuits.[18]

The Body Shop was not worried about such lawsuits, because the product ingredients Roddick chose had been used safely for centuries. In addition, the older recipes had been used for many decades without incident. These circumstances led to the company's rejection of animal-based product testing. Any supplier wishing to do business with The Body Shop had to sign a statement guaranteeing that it had done no animal testing for the previous 5 years and would never do such testing in the future. The Body Shop used human volunteers from its own staff and the University Hospital of Wales to test new and current products under normal use. The Body Shop also volunteered to share the results of its tests on individual ingredients with other cosmetics manufacturers.[19]

Most other cosmetics firms used a variety of procedures to determine the safety of cosmetics products, with two animal-based tests becoming the standard procedures. The Draize test involved dripping the substance in question, such as shampoo or a detergent paste, into the eyes of conscious, restrained rabbits, and measuring the resultant damage over the course of several days. Rabbits cannot cry, which allowed researchers to complete the tests quickly. Another test required researchers to force-feed large quantities of a substance to a sample of laboratory animals. The substance could be a solid (such as lipstick or shaving cream), a paste, or a liquid. The lethal dose of a substance was determined by the amount that had been ingested by an individual surviving animal when 50 percent of the sample had died, hence the name of the test, LD50.[20] Beginning in the 1970s, animal rights groups such as the Humane Society and PETA began protesting the use of these tests by the cosmetics industry. The Body Shop lent its support to these groups' efforts, labeling all animal testing as "cruel and unnecessary." By 1991, alternative procedures that involved far less cruelty to animals had already been developed but were yet to be approved for industry use.[21]

In the United States, The Body Shop's market share was limited by two factors. First, its prices were significantly higher than those charged for mass-marketed products in drug stores, although they were generally comparable to the prices charged for cosmetics and cleansers at department store sales counters. Second, The Body Shop was constrained by the number of stores it had opened in the United States. By 1991, only 40 stores had been opened in a dozen metropolitan areas across the country. A mail-order catalog and a telephone order line were used to supplement the American retail stores, but they were inadequate substitutes for the product sampling and advice that were readily available at The Body Shop's stores. Roddick maintained that those consumers who sampled Body Shop products became loyal customers: "Once they walk into one of our stores or buy from our catalogue, they're hooked."[22]

The Body Shop was taken public in 1984, with the Roddicks owning a combined 30 percent of the outstanding stock. The firm's subsequent sales and net income figures are as follows (figures for 1988 were not available):[23]

Year	Sales Revenue (millions)	Net Income (millions)
1985	$15.3	$1.4
1986	28.4	3.4
1987	46.4	6.2
1989	119.0	14.6
1990	137.7	14.7

Without The Body Shop's monetary donations to various social causes, all of these net income figures would be higher than reported in the financial statements. Estimates of the company's annual contributions to outside organizations varied from several hundred thousand to several million dollars.

Industry analysts considered The Body Shop to be a strong performer with the potential to prosper even in an economic downturn. The exotic nature of its products, such as hair conditioner made with 10 percent real bananas and a peppermint foot lotion, would attract consumers who desired affordable luxuries. Analysts regarded the public's desire for personal care products as "insatiable," especially in North America.[24] The addition of the strong emotional appeal of social issues formed the basis for one of the most successful marketing concepts in the cosmetics industry in decades.

The twentieth anniversary of Earth Day, celebrated in 1990, focused media attention on many of the environmental issues that Roddick and The Body Shop regularly addressed. Further, it spurred interest in environmental issues in the commercial sector.

Several new entrants and existing competitors challenged The Body Shop in the United States and Europe. Among the largest of these firms were Estee Lauder and Revlon. The Limited had opened 50 Bath & Body Works stores, patterned after The Body Shop's outlets and located in shopping malls across the United States. In addition, an English competitor, Crabtree & Evelyn, had held a significant presence in North America and Europe since the mid-1970s.

By 1991, The Body Shop was a successful and profitable firm that had attracted a variety of well-financed competitors. The company faced a real threat from these firms because they were all well financed and had a broad range of experience in marketing cosmetics. Each of these firms was well established in the United States, yet no one firm dominated the new product segment that The Body Shop had helped create.

In addition, there were indications that the environmental concerns that attracted customers to The Body Shop might not have permanent drawing power. Roddick had vowed never to sell anything but environmentally friendly cosmetics and grooming products in her stores, but the industry was growing and changing faster than anyone had anticipated. It seemed that The Body Shop needed to take action to ensure its long-term survival.

When asked about her role in the company, Anita Roddick stated:

> The purpose of a business isn't just to generate profits to create an ever-larger empire. It's to have the power to affect social change, to make the world a better place. I have always been an activist, I have always been incredibly impassioned about human rights and environmental issues. The Body Shop is simply my stage.[25]

QUESTIONS FOR DISCUSSION

1. How does The Body Shop address the four components of corporate social responsibility?
2. Anita Roddick claims that her firm does not advertise, yet it receives free media exposure and publicity through the social causes it champions. Is this an appropriate approach for a business to follow?
3. What are The Body Shop's long-term goals? Are they realistic, given the nature of the cosmetics industry?
4. What is your assessment of Anita Roddick's philosophy regarding the "purpose of a business"?

5. What are Anita Roddick's strengths and weaknesses as a leader? Should she stay on in a managing role or step aside and allow a more experienced person to run the marketing operations?

6. Should The Body Shop enter the mass market and retail its products in drug stores and supermarkets? How would this affect its operations and direction?

7. The Body Shop asks potential employees questions about "personal heroes" and individual beliefs. Is it ethical to ask such questions of applicants? Are these questions legitimate ones to ask in the first place? Are such questions fair to the applicants?

CASE ENDNOTES

1. Catalog, The Body Shop (Fall, 1990).
2. Laura Zinn, "Whales, Human Rights, Rain Forests—and the Heady Smell of Profits," *Business Week* (July 15, 1991), 114.
3. *Ibid.*, 114.
4. Samuel Greengard, "Face Values," *USAir Magazine* (November, 1990), 89.
5. Zinn, 114.
6. Greengard, 93.
7. Greengard, 97.
8. Zinn, 115.
9. Greengard, 94.
10. Greengard, 94.
11. Zinn, 114.
12. Greengard, 90.
13. Maria Koklanaris, "Trio of Retailers Finds Soap and Social Concern an Easy Sell," *The Washington Post* (April 27, 1991).
14. Greengard, 90.
15. Zinn, 115.
16. The Body Shop promotional literature, 1991.
17. Zinn, 115.
18. The Body Shop promotional literature, 1991.
19. The Body Shop promotional literature, 1991.
20. Peter Singer, *Animal Liberation: A New Ethics for Treatment of Animals* (New York: Avon Books, 1975), 48.
21. The Body Shop promotional literature, 1991.
22. Greengard, 89.
23. Compact Disclosure database, 1991.
24. Koklanaris.
25. Greengard, 97.

2B The Body Shop International PLC (1993)[1]

The first appearance by Anita Roddick in a U.S. television commercial was seen in 1993. This came as something of a surprise to long-time Body Shop (BSI) customers and her competitors in the cosmetics industry. These people believed that Roddick abhorred advertising as a wasteful practice that creates needs. The company did promote certain nonprofit groups in its stores and catalogs, including Greenpeace, People for the Ethical Treatment of Animals, and Amnesty International. However, The Body Shop had a policy of not advertising directly to consumers.

Roddick agreed to lend her endorsement to an American Express marketing campaign that featured founders of fast-growing retail firms such as BSI and Crate & Barrel. Not coincidentally, all of the firms featured in the campaign accepted the American Express charge card as a payment method. The main message of the campaign was that customers of these stores preferred to use the American Express card and that the store founders also found the card useful in their day-to-day business.

Roddick appeared in three commercials and a series of print advertisements as part of this advertising campaign. The advertisements included Roddick's brief description of the company's purpose and sourcing practices and used film footage and photographs of her travels in search of exotic new ingredients.

This case was prepared by William A. Sodeman.

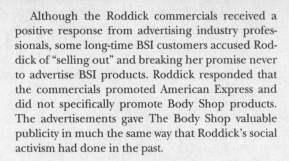

Although the Roddick commercials received a positive response from advertising industry professionals, some long-time BSI customers accused Roddick of "selling out" and breaking her promise never to advertise BSI products. Roddick responded that the commercials promoted American Express and did not specifically promote Body Shop products. The advertisements gave The Body Shop valuable publicity in much the same way that Roddick's social activism had done in the past.

QUESTIONS FOR DISCUSSION

1. What is your opinion on The Body Shop/American Express advertising campaign? Was it a sound business decision on Roddick's part?

2. What does the American Express campaign imply about The Body Shop and its customers? Is this different from the image of the nonprofit organizations that The Body Shop endorses?

3. What (if any) conflicts exist between the images and public reputations of The Body Shop and American Express?

CASE ENDNOTE

1. The materials used in this case are based on Jennifer Conlin, "Survival of the Fittest," *Working Woman* (February, 1994).

The Body Shop International PLC (1995)   3A

Between 1991 and 1995, The Body Shop continued to expand its operations. The Body Shop had opened 1,200 stores by early 1995.[1] Over 100 company-owned and franchised stores were operating in U.S. shopping malls and downtown shopping districts. Selected financial results include the following:

Year	Sales Revenue (millions)	Net Income (millions)
1991	$231	$41
1992	252	33
1993	298	45
1994	330	47

The Body Shop had moved its U.S. headquarters from Cedar Knolls, New Jersey, to a less expensive and more central location—Raleigh, North Carolina. The original location worked well when The Body Shop opened its initial U.S. stores in New York City and Washington, DC, but soon proved to be a logistical problem. Roddick was frustrated that the New Jersey hires did not seem as creative or impulsive as her English staff. In retrospect, she realized that having some of her U.K. staff help train the first U.S. managers and employees or even setting up her headquarters in a college town such as Boulder, Colorado, or a city such as San Francisco would have been a better choice than starting from scratch in New Jersey.[2]

LIMITATIONS

The Body Shop had bigger problems to deal with than the location of its national headquarters. The Limited continued to open its chain of Bath & Body Works stores on a nationwide scale. Placement of a Bath & Body Works store in a mall usually precluded The Body Shop from entering the same mall. (There were some exceptions, most notably very large shopping malls such as the Mall of America in Bloomington, Minnesota.) All of The Limited's stores, from Express and Victoria's Secret to Structure and Lerner's, were company owned. This allowed a greater degree of flexibility and speed than The Body Shop's franchising system. Further, The Limited had started grouping its stores in malls to create its own version of the department store. During the holidays, Express and Structure stores carried special selections of Bath & Body Works products to induce customer trial and develop brand awareness. The Limited's size and power as one of the major retailers in the United States made the company a strong threat to The Body Shop's continued presence in the U.S. retail market. In an alarming move,

This case was prepared by William A. Sodeman.

The Limited began opening Bath & Body Works stores in the United Kingdom, which presented a direct threat to The Body Shop on the company's home soil.

The similarities between The Body Shop and Bath & Body Works stores also created some confusion. Some less-observant customers of The Body Shop were bringing empty Bath & Body Works bottles to The Body Shop to be refilled because Bath & Body Works did not have its own refill policy and the products seemed similar in some cases. The Body Shop protected its slogans, territory, and franchises with an aggressive legal strategy that included an out-of-court settlement with The Limited in 1993.[3]

Other companies had successfully introduced organic or natural beauty products in discount and drug stores, a market segment that The Body Shop had completely ignored in its global operations. Traditional retailers including Woolworth's and K-Mart had also entered what had come to be known as the minimalist segment of the personal care products industry. Woolworth's entry was an expanded selection of organic bath and body case products in its deep discount R_x Place chain. K-Mart's line of Naturalistic cosmetics was sold in over 1,800 stores.[4] Other new companies included H_2O Plus, which sold its products in its own retail stores but did not make claims about animal testing as had The Body Shop and Bath & Body Works.

GOOD PRESS

The Body Shop continued to receive new accolades and to hit new heights of prosperity. Anita Roddick published her autobiography, *Body and Soul*, in late 1991. Roddick donated her portion of the royalties to several groups, including the Unrepresented Nations and Peoples Organization, a self-governing group that spoke for Kurds, Tibetans, and Native Americans; the Medical Foundation, which treated victims of torture; and a variety of individual political prisoners. The 256-page book, which was written and designed by Roddick, Body Shop staff, and an outside group, resembled a mixture of catalog and personal memoir: Hundreds of pictures and headlines were used throughout to emphasize and clarify particular points of interest. On the final page of the book, where one would expect to see the last page of the index, is the coda of the final chapter. The last line of text, printed in large boldface letters, reads "Make no mistake about it—I'm doing this for me."[5]

Partly as a result of the book's publication, The Body Shop received a great deal of flattering media attention. *Inc.*[6] and *Working Woman*[7] ran cover stories featuring Anita Roddick. *Fortune*[8] and *Business Week*[9] published shorter articles that focused on Anita Roddick and the company's performance. *Time* began its article with a story on Anita's fact-finding mission to Oman, where she obtained a perfume recipe from a local tribe only after dropping her pants and showing the Bedouin women her pubic hair—Bedouin women pluck theirs every day.[10]

BAD PRESS

In 1992, some members of the media began to criticize The Body Shop and the Roddicks. The *Financial Times* gave The Body Shop the dubious honor of headlining its 1992 list of top ten corporate losers after the price of Body Shop stock dipped from $5.20 to $2.70 during September.[11] Stock analysts had reacted to a disappointing earnings report, and the news set some minds to wondering if the company could indeed grow quickly enough to capture a leadership position in the minimalist market, or if there was a minimalist market at all.

Around this time, The Body Shop invested $5 million in a ten-part documentary series called *Millennium.* This series, which was shown around the world on television networks including PBS and the BBC, was meant to celebrate the wisdom and history of native cultures. The director quit the project during filming, accusing the Roddicks of distorting the tribal rituals depicted in the film to suit various new-age ideals.[12] The Body Shop sold a book version of *Millennium* in its stores to help promote the series and raise funds for donations.

In 1993, a British television news magazine telecast a report on The Body Shop. The show alleged that The Body Shop knowingly sourced materials from suppliers that had recently performed animal testing. The Body Shop sued the TV station and the production company for libel and won a significant financial award after a 6-week court battle. Anita Roddick sat in the courtroom every day and compared the experience to confinement in a "mahogany coffin." The Body Shop won the suit and a £276,000 settlement by proving to the British court that the company had never intentionally misled consumers about the animal testing policy, which encouraged manufacturers to give up animal testing but did not claim that ingredients had never been tested on animals.[13]

In 1994, *Business Ethics* magazine, a well-respected U.S. publication, published a cover story on The Body Shop that built upon many of the allegations that others had presented over the years. The resulting controversy engulfed the journalist, the magazine, and The Body Shop in a new wave of controversy that threatened The Body Shop's slow expansion into the U.S. market.

In June of 1993, Jon Entine had first been approached by disgruntled current and former Body Shop staffers about several of the company's practices. After overcoming his initial skepticism and doing some preliminary investigations in Littlehampton, The Body Shop's headquarters, Entine was convinced he had a sound basis on which to develop a story for his current employer, the ABC news magazine "Primetime Live." When ABC decided not to renew the contract and to drop The Body Shop story, Entine began his own investigation, which eventually resulted in the *Business Ethics* article.[14] In the preface to the article, magazine editor and publisher Marjorie Kelly wrote:

> Long-time readers will note that the following article represents a distinct departure from our typical editorial style. It has not been part of our mission to publish the exploits of companies that fall short of their stated social goals. But we believe the story of The Body Shop must be told, chiefly for the lessons it provides those of us who seek to promote ethical business practices. Still, we bring this story to you with mixed emotions. We have been ardent admirers of Anita Roddick and her company for many years; two years ago this month [September 1992] we featured her on our cover. But, after weeks of debate, including several conversations with Body Shop representatives, we concluded the greater good would be served by raising these issues in print. We earnestly hope this dialogue will be a constructive one.

In the article, Entine made several claims:

- Anita Roddick had stolen the concept of The Body Shop, including the store name, recycling of bottles, store design, catalogs, and products, from a similar store she had visited in Berkeley, California, in 1971, several years before she opened her first Body Shop in Brighton in 1976.
- Roddick had not discovered exotic recipes for some of her products as she had previously claimed: Some were outdated, off-the-shelf formulas that had been used by other manufacturers,

whereas others featured unusual ingredients around, which Roddick and company employees had woven fanciful tales of her travels of discovery.

- Many Body Shop products were full of petrochemicals, artificial colors and fragrances, and synthetic preservatives and contained only small amounts of naturally sourced ingredients.
- Quality control was a continuing problem with instances of mold, formaldehyde, and *E. coli* contamination reported around the world, thus requiring the use of large amounts of preservatives to give the products stable shelf lives.
- The U.S. Federal Trade Commission had launched a probe into The Body Shop's franchising practices, including deceptive financial data, unfair competition, and misleading company representation. One husband-and-wife franchising team compared the company to the Gambino crime family.
- The Body Shop's "Trade Not Aid" program was a sham, providing only a small portion of The Body Shop's raw materials while failing to fulfill the company's promises to suppliers.
- Between 1986 and 1993, The Body Shop contributed far less than the average annual pretax charitable donations for U.S. companies, according to the Council on Economic Priorities.

Entine published a similar article in a trade magazine, *Drug and Cosmetic Industry,* in February of 1995.[15] In this article, he discussed The Body Shop's policies regarding animal testing, citing an internal memo from May 1992. At that time, 46.5 percent of The Body Shop's ingredients had been tested on animals by the ingredients' manufacturers, which was an increase from 34 percent the previous year. This and other practices raised new concerns about the company's slogan "Against Animal Testing" and tainted the company's 1993 victory in its libel suit against the TV program.[16]

The response to Entine's *Business Ethics* article was swift and furious. In June, well before the article's publication, Franklin Development and Consulting, a leading U.S.-based provider of social investment services, had sold 50,000 shares of The Body Shop because of "financial concerns."[17] With rumors spreading about the article in early August, the stock fell from $3.75 to $3.33 per share. Ben Cohen, cofounder of Ben & Jerry's and a *Business Ethics* advisory board member, severed his ties with the magazine. The U.S. and British press ran numerous pieces on the article and its allegations. These articles appeared in newspapers and magazines such as *USA Today*,[18] *The Economist*,[19] *The New York Post*,[20] and *The San Francisco Chronicle*.[21] The London *Daily Mail* secured an exclusive interview with one of the founders of the California Body Shop, who described the company's early years and how they eventually came to legal terms with the Roddicks over the rights to The Body Shop trademark.[22]

Entine was interviewed by a small newsletter, the *Corporate Crime Reporter*, in which he defended and explained his research and the article.[23] One point of interest was Entine's claim that Body Shop products were of "drug store quality," which he based on the company's use of obsolete ingredients and formulas and a *Consumer Reports* ranking that placed Body Shop Dewberry perfume last out of 66 tested.[24] Dewberry is The Body Shop's trademark scent and is used in all of its stores as part of the "atmosphere." *Corporate Crime Reporter* also noted that another reporter, David Moberg, had brought similar allegations against The Body Shop in a separate article published the same month as Entine's.[25]

In January of 1995, *Utne Reader* published a forum including commentaries by Anita Roddick, Entine, Moberg, and Franklin Research founder Joan Bavaria. The forum was remarkable in the sense that it presented a structured set of responses to the charges. Editor Eric Utne noted the rift that the article had caused in the progressive business community and described how the Roddicks, Marjorie Kelly, and other parties had begun holding face-to-face meetings to mend their relationships.[26] Entine described the same meetings as "a family gathering a few days after everyone's favorite uncle was found molesting a neighbor's child. The scandal was on everyone's mind, few would openly talk about it, and most hoped that ignoring it would make it fade away. It didn't."[27] Moberg encouraged consumer watchdog groups to do their jobs more carefully, citing the case of the British group New Consumer, which had previously given The Body Shop high ratings.[28] Roddick maintained that the truth had been sacrificed in a rush to judgment but that she had managed to cope with and learn from the experience.[29]

GORDON RODDICK: DEFENDER OF THE REALM

Anita Roddick has been known to ask her employees what irritates them about their store.[30] Gordon, Anita's husband, is a bit more philosophical in his approach, yet he also speaks out on issues that concern him. After their entry into the U.S. market, the Roddicks became frustrated with the amount of regulatory barriers. Most of the problems that The Body Shop encountered were small. However, The Body Shop had two full-time employees and one lawyer devoted exclusively to regulatory compliance in the United States. Gordon Roddick estimated that it cost The Body Shop an additional 5 percent of its revenues to do business in the United States, thus supporting his claim that the American free market economy was anything but free.[31]

Entine's *Business Ethics* article aroused Gordon to new heights of anger according to those who knew him. Body Shop lawyers had successfully persuaded *Vanity Fair* to refrain from publishing a different version of the article earlier in the year. *Vanity Fair* compensated Entine for his work, paying him $15,000 plus an additional $18,000 to cover his expenses in writing and researching the article. Entine was paid only $750 by *Business Ethics* magazine for the article.[32]

Early in Entine's investigation, The Body Shop had hired the international public relations firm of Hill & Knowlton (H&K) to launch a counterattack on Entine's credibility and motives. H&K vice president Frank Mankiewicz, who was a former president of National Public Radio (NPR), sent letters to ABC requesting that it drop its Body Shop story.[33] He also used his Contacts at NPR to place an interview with Entine and a follow-up story that included comments from Body Shop supporters on NPR news programs such as *All Things Considered*. Further attempts to intimidate *Business Ethics* magazine failed. The editor and pub] her, Marjorie Kelly, knew that publishing the article was a risk, but she had checked and rechecked Entine's sources and was satisfied that his charges were sound. However, if The Body Shop chose to sue the magazine, she also knew that the cost of getting to the summary/judgment phase of the trial could put the small magazine out of business.[34]

Gordon Roddick responded to the *Business Ethics* article within a month of its publication by sending a 10-page letter on Body Shop letterhead to all *Business Ethics* subscribers. In this letter, he denied many of the charges made in the article. The letter offered statements by several people that appeared to contradict their own quotations in the article.

Several staff members at *Business Ethics* magazine were not pleased with the letter, which they had received in the mail because they were included as decoys on the subscriber mailing list. This is a common practice in the mailing-list industry to help prevent the misuse of subscriber addresses. The publisher of *Business Ethics* magazine could not recall authorizing the magazine's mailing-list service to rent the list to The Body Shop. It did not take long for the mailing-list company to discover that The Body Shop had obtained the magazine's subscriber list through a third party. Said Ralph Stevens, president of the mailing-list firm, "The Body Shop duped a prominent and legitimate list-brokerage company, a respected magazine, and they duped us. . . . If this is any indication of the way [The Body Stop does] business, of their regard for honesty and integrity, I give them a failing mark on all counts."[35] In late 1994, The Body Shop hired a business ethics expert to lead a social audit of the company.[36]

THE AFTERMATH AND THE FUTURE OF THE BODY SHOP

By July of 1995, Anita Roddick was already considering the possibility of opening Body Shop stores in Cuba, hoping to beat her competitors to that market and at the same time convert the Cubans' social revolution into a profitable yet honorable business revolution.[37] The company was also considering opening retail stores in Eastern European countries. At the same time, the media attention on the company had raised serious concerns among customers, among Body Shop supporters, and within the financial community. Since August 1994, the company's stock price had plummeted by almost 50 percent to 120p, an all-time low. The Roddicks took millions of dollars in paper losses on their holdings, despite having sold a portion of their stock in July 1994.[38] The company faced increased competition from several larger firms, including Procter & Gamble, Avon, K-Mart, The Limited, L'Oreal, Crabtree & Evelyn, and Marks & Spencer. Other companies, such as H_2O Plus, were making progress in their efforts to open retail stores that featured products similar to those of The Body Shop. The company had hired Chiat/Day to develop advertising campaigns for worldwide use and conduct a marketing study in the United States.[39] There was at least one report that the company was looking for a U.S. advertising agency.[40] The questions that had been raised as a result of media investigations and The Body Shop's

responses left some observers wondering what principles the company espoused and if the company could regain its earlier level of success.

QUESTIONS FOR DISCUSSION

1. How has The Body Shop continued to address the four components of corporate social responsibility?
2. How well has The Body Shop handled the challenges from its competition, especially Bath & Body Works?
3. What is your assessment of The Body Shop's response to the *Business Ethics* article? Has The Body Shop misrepresented itself to stakeholders, and if so, how?
4. Jon Entine and others have accused The Body Shop of using intimidation to stifle critics. Does this appear to be a valid criticism? Was The Body Shop justified in hiring Hill & Knowlton to conduct a public relations campaign?
5. Has The Body Shop's reputation been damaged by the incidents in this case? How might the company improve its reputation? Do you believe the steps described in this case, including the hiring of an advertising agency, will help or hinder these efforts?
6. Describe the roles you believe Gordon and Anita Roddick should play in The Body Shop's operations. How might a stockholder, a customer, a supplier, and an employee assess the roles that the Roddicks should play?

CASE ENDNOTES

1. *Body Language—The Body Shop World Wide Web Site, www.the-body-shop.com* (May, 1995).
2. Anita Roddick, *Body and Soul: Profits with Principles, The Amazing Success Story of Anita Roddick & The Body Shop* (New York: Crown, 1991), 135–136.
3. Jennifer Conlin, "Survival of the Fittest," *Working Woman* (February, 1994).
4. Faye Brookman, "Prototypes Debut," *Stores* (April, 1994), 20–22.
5. Roddick, 1991.
6. Bo Burlingame, "This Woman Has Changed Business Forever," *Inc.* (June, 1990).
7. Conlin, 29.
8. Andrew Erdman, "Body Shop Gets into Ink," *Fortune* (October 7, 1991), 166.

9. Laura Zinn, "Whales, Human Rights, Rain Forests—And the Heady Smell of Profits." *Business Week* (July 15, 1991), 114–115.

10. Philip Elmer-Dewitt, "Anita the Agitator," *Time* (January 25, 1993), 52–54.

11. *Ibid.*, 54.

12. *Ibid.*, 54.

13. Conlin, 30–31.

14. Jon Entine, "Shattered Image," *Business Ethics* (October, 1994), 23–28.

15. Jon Entine, "The Body Shop: Truth & Consequences," *Drug and Cosmetic Industry* (February, 1995), 54–64.

16. Entine, 1995, 62.

17. Judith Valente, "Body Shop Shares Plunge on Reports of Sales by Funds and FTC Inquiry," *The Wall Street Journal* (August 24, 1994).

18. Ellen Neuborne, "Body Shop in a Lather over Ethics Criticism," *USA Today* (August 29, 1995), B1.

19. "Storm in a Bubble Bath," *The Economist* (September 3, 1994), 56.

20. Martin Peers, "Journalist's Probe Hits Body Shop," *New York Post* (August 25, 1994), 33.

21. Dirk Beveridge, "Uproar Threatens Body Shop Stock," *The San Francisco Chronicle* (August 25, 1994), D1.

22. Rebecca Hardy, "American Woman recalls the Heady Days of Her Hippy Perfume Store . . . And a £2.3m Deal with the Roddicks," *London Daily Mail* (August 28, 1994).

23. "Interview with Jon Entine," *Corporate Crime Reporter* (September 19, 1994), 13–18.

24. "Interview with Jon Entine," 17.

25. David Moberg, "The Beauty Myth," *In These Times* (September 19–October 2, 1994).

26. Eric Utne, "Beyond The Body Shop Brouhaha," *Utne Reader* (January–February, 1995), 101–102.

27. Jon Entine, "Exploiting Idealism," *Utne Reader* (January–February, 1995), 108–109.

28. David Moberg, "Call in the Watchdogs!" *Utne Reader* (January–February, 1995), 101–102.

29. Anita Roddick, "Who Judges the Judges?" *Utne Reader* (January–February, 1995), 104.

30. Elmer-Dewitt, 52.

31. "Regulation Time: 60 Seconds with . . . Gordon Roddick," *Inc.* (June, 1993), 16.

32. Ruth G. Davis, "The Body Shop Plays Hardball," *New York Magazine* (September 19, 1994), 16.

33. *Ibid.*

34. Maureen Clark, "Socially Responsible Business Brawl," *The Progressive* (March, 1995), 14.

35. *Ibid.*

36. "Ethics Study for Body Shop," *The New York Times* (October 31, 1994), C7.

37. Conlin, 73.

38. "Stake Reduced in Body Shop," *The New York Times* (July 11, 1994), C7.

39. James Fallon, "Body Shop Regroups to Meet Competition in Crowded U.S. Arena," *Women's Wear Daily* (October 21, 1994), 1.

40. Anthony Ramirez, "Body Shop Seeks Its First U.S. Agency," *The New York Times* (June 27, 1995), D7.

The Body Shop International PLC (1998) 3B

By 1998, The Body Shop International had grown into a multinational enterprise with almost 1,600 stores and 5,000 employees in 47 countries.[1] That year, after several years of lackluster financial performance, Anita Roddick gave the company's CEO post to a professional manager and became executive cochairman with her husband, Gordon. Anita maintained that job titles were meaningless, anyway.[2]

This case was written by Archie B. Carroll.

Despite the change, the company's financial performance between 1995 and 1997 continued to be unimpressive:[3]

Year	Worldwide Sales Revenue (millions)	Operating Profits (millions)
1995	$303	$21
1996	350	20
1997	377	19

In 1995 to 1996, The Body Shop began to experiment with advertising in North American markets. According to one observer, the Body Shop originally thought that its brands and human-rights agenda would create valuable word-of-mouth promotion among socially conscious consumers and that advertising would not be needed. The Body Shop's anti-advertising strategy largely paid off in the United Kingdom and other European nations, where human rights activism and commerce blended more seamlessly and consumers had fewer brands and retailers than in the United States. The strategy has not worked effectively in the United States, where brand differentiation is crucial. In 1997, for example, The Body Shop's same-stores sales in the United States plunged 6 percent, the company's worst performance since entering the U.S. market 10 years earlier.[4]

Since it has begun, U.S. advertising has been piecemeal, often targeted toward the Christmastime holiday sales push. In addition, it has been quirky. For example, Anita Roddick taped a radio spot that slammed the cosmetics industry. In the radio spot, Roddick said "If more men and more women understood what really makes people beautiful, most cosmetic companies would be out of business."[5]

The Body Shop seems to be trying hard to get its act together in the U.S. market. It hired a new CEO in fall 1998 and created the position of vice president for promotions. These are significant moves for the company, but it may take more than advertising to turn things around. The Body Shop typically plays down product efficacy in favor of hyping product ethicality. A case in point is its Mango Body Butter, whose ingredients the company promotes as from a "woman's cooperative in Ghana." Sean Mehegan, a writer for *Brandweek*, summarizes the company's dilemma this way: "How much American consumers care about such claims lies at the heart of whether The Body Shop can turn itself around here."[6]

THE BODY SHOP'S SOCIAL AUDITS

In 1994, perhaps in response to the *Business Ethics* magazine article by Jon Entine calling its integrity into question and perhaps on its own initiative, The Body Shop began an elaborate program of annual social audits examining, in particular, its environmental, social, and animal protection initiatives. Through the social audit program, which the company based on mission statements and goals in numerous social performance categories, the company established detailed social and ecological milestones for 1995–1997. In its 218-page *Values Report 1997,* the company reported its progress.[7]

The Body Shop set policies in three areas: Human and Civil Rights, Environmental Sustainability, and Animal Protection. In each category, the company set forth a conceptual framework for the auditing process. The auditing process in each category depended heavily on stakeholder interviews. The stakeholders who were interviewed included employees, international franchisees, customers, suppliers, shareholders, and local community/campaigning groups. The company identified the media as a potential stakeholder group for inclusion in future social auditing cycles.[8]

ALLEGATIONS CONTINUE

In 1998, The Body Shop continued to face charges that could threaten its future. The company faced a possible flood of allegations and lawsuits by franchisees charging fraudulent presentations by the company when they bought their franchises. Many U.S. franchisees are angry at what they see as unfair buyback terms if they want to get out of the business. There is talk of group action that could involve claims in the hundreds of millions of dollars.[9]

An example of the kind of lawsuit being filed is that of Jim White, who is asking for $32 million in damages. He is suing The Body Shop for fraud, fraudulent inducement, and inequitable treatment of franchisees. White claims that the company offered rock-bottom buyback prices to franchisees caught in a 5-year spiral of declining U.S. sales. White claimed he was only offered 20 cents on the dollar and that others were offered as low as 5 cents on the dollar.[10]

The future is uncertain for The Body Shop. Journalists like Jon Entine continue to write articles that are critical of The Body Shop.[11] Despite the criticism, the company continues to make management and strategic changes and to pursue social programs and social audits. In the hard, cold world of global competition, founder Anita Roddick has experienced some tough lessons in the past few years. While she may still believe that the purpose of a business is not just to generate profits, it is becoming increasingly apparent that the tension between financial and social performance requires delicate balancing of, and careful attention to, both. At stake

is nothing less than the firm's survival and Roddick's stage for bringing about social change.

QUESTIONS FOR DISCUSSION

1. Has Anita Roddick betrayed her philosophy about advertising by beginning to advertise in U.S. markets? Does this decision have ethical implications? Or, is it just a business decision?
2. Does it seem like The Body Shop will make it in North America? Why or why not?
3. Will the Body Shop's social auditing program save the firm's reputation? Has the firm "snapped back" from the damage done to its reputation in the mid-1990s?
4. Do the low buyback prices offered to U.S. franchisees reflect poor Body Shop ethics or just the economic reality of risky investments?
5. Is The Body Shop regarded today as a socially responsible and ethical firm? Research the answer to this question and be prepared to report your findings.

CASE ENDNOTES

1. "Capitalism and Cocoa Butter," *The Economist* (May 16, 1998), 66–67.
2. *Ibid.* Also see Ernest Beck, "Body Shop Founder Roddick Steps Aside as CEO," *Wall Street Journal* (May 13, 1998), B14.
3. *Values Report 1997,* The Body Shop, (October, 1997), 150.
4. Sean Mehegan, "Not Tested on Humans," *Brandweek* (May 19, 1997), 54.
5. *Ibid.*
6. *Ibid.*
7. *Values Report 1997,* 7–12.
8. *Ibid.,* 10–12.
9. Jan Spooner, "Body Shop Faces U.S. Legal Fights," *Financial Mail* (London) (February 22, 1998).
10. *Ibid.*
11. Jon Entine, "Vivisecting the Anti-Vivisectionist Movement," *Drug & Cosmetic Industry* (January, 1997), 38–41.

To Hire or Not to Hire

4

As a manager in human resources, part of my job is to guide the process by which my company selects new employees. Recently, we selected an applicant to fill a computer analyst position. The supervising manager and a selection panel selected this applicant over a number of others based on her superior qualifications and interview.

However, a routine background check indicated that the applicant had been convicted 18 years earlier for false check writing. The application form has a section where the applicant is asked if he or she has ever been convicted of anything other than a traffic violation. In response to that question, this applicant wrote "no." When informed of this, the supervising manager stated that she would still like to hire the applicant, but asked me for my recommendation. The job does not involve money handling.

This case was prepared by Tim Timmons.

QUESTIONS FOR DISCUSSION

1. If the applicant mistakenly thought that her record had been cleared over time and therefore did not lie intentionally, would that make any difference?
2. Should the fact that the applicant did not tell the truth on one part of the application automatically disqualify her from further consideration?
3. Should the supervising manager be allowed to hire this applicant despite the fact that the applicant lied on her application, provided the manager is willing to take the risk and assume responsibility for the applicant?
4. If the applicant freely admitted the conviction, should she still be considered for the position? Should a minor offense committed 18 years ago, when the applicant was in her early 20s, disqualify her when she is overall the most qualified applicant? What types of convictions, and how recent, should disqualify potential new hires?

5

The Low Bidder

A woman owns an unincorporated small business that sells advertising novelty items. Her husband's company, wishing to buy such items as part of its safety program promotion, solicited bids from vendors known to be in the business, including the woman. The company awarded the woman, who was the low bidder based on a comparison of published catalogs submitted by the vendors, the contract and several purchase orders. The woman's husband was not involved in any way in the bid evaluation or the ordering of goods.

The husband's company's Code of Ethics states, in part, "As an employee, you may not own, either

This case was prepared by Carl Balderson.

directly or indirectly through a close family member, a significant financial interest in any actual or potential vendor or supplier of our company without full disclosure to, and written clearance from, the Ethics Committee."

QUESTIONS FOR DISCUSSION

1. If you were a member of the company's Ethics Committee, how would you deal with the situation?
2. Would your response be different if the vice president of Human Resources (also a member of the Ethics Committee) had approved this situation, subject to your input? If so, how?

6

The High Cost of Principles[1]

Wymodak, a Denver-based firm, acquired 71 7-Eleven convenience stores in the West and Midwest in 1985. Mark Norek was a merchandising manager from the Denver office who visited the various 7-Eleven stores as part of his job. In April 1986, the Southland Corporation, the parent company of most 7-Elevens in the United States, decided to discontinue stocking *Playboy* and *Penthouse* magazines. Wymodak, however, decided to continue stocking the magazines in the stores it owned.

Dean Krych was manager of a Wymodak-owned 7-Eleven in the area of Superior, Wisconsin. In October 1986, Norek fired Krych because Krych refused to sell *Playboy* and *Penthouse* magazines as Wymodak's company policy and Norek had instructed him to. A couple of days later, Krych's assistant manager was also fired for refusing to stock the magazines. Krych's wife, Diane, resigned from her position as store auditor.

This case was written by Archie B. Carroll.

Dean Krych, age 37 at the time of the incident, had served for 7 years as manager. He was a frequent winner of performance awards. He was twice named as his district's manager of the year and won other performance awards as well. Krych noted, after his firing, that "my store had just had the most profitable year it had ever had."

The vice president of Wymodak was Gary Nelson. Nelson noted that refusal to stock certain specified "core items"—such as bread, soft drinks, potato chips, and the two magazines—was grounds for dismissal.

Speaking to an Associated Press reporter in a telephone interview, Krych explained why he had taken the stand that had cost him and his wife their jobs: "We Americans have got to stand up for decency. It's a patriotic cause." Krych explained how he felt about recent trends from soft-porn magazines to X-rated movies and then to X-rated home videos. "If we allow it to continue, the nation will not be a fit place to live." He went on to say, "It's personally not just a religious issue (he is a member of the Assemblies of God Church), but in the interest of community standards." He continued by saying that the philosophy behind the two magazines was "very destructive." "Basically it is that marriage and constancy are not important, that the family is not so important." He added, "It turns women into sex objects. It has begun using children in its cartoons. We're giving up our livelihood in the cause of decency, in the cause of women and children who have suffered abuse, letting them know there are people who care." Diane, Krych's wife, added, "It was something we had to do. Money isn't everything. We're willing to take the consequences."

Christmas of 1986 was tough on the Krych family household. Their income was cut off and so was their medical insurance that covered the $1,000 monthly cost of caring for their infant son, who suffered from cerebral palsy. They felt they could get by for awhile on their savings and the 3 weeks' vacation pay that was owed Dean upon dismissal. He said, "We know in our hearts we did what was right."

QUESTIONS FOR DISCUSSION

1. What is your assessment of Krych's decision to refuse to carry *Playboy* or *Penthouse*? What level of ethical analysis does this decision represent (personal, organizational, or societal)? Do you think Krych really understood the consequences of his actions?

2. In light of all the awards Krych had won for superior performance, assess the firm's decision to fire him. Was it a wise decision? Was it an ethical or socially responsible decision?

3. Can you think of any more creative ways in which Wymodak and Norek might have dealt with this case?

CASE ENDNOTE

1. This case is based on "Man Gives Up His Job, Sticks to His Principles," *Athens Banner-Herald* (December 20, 1986), 13.

Phantom Expenses

7

Jane Adams had just completed a sales training course with her new employer, a major small appliance manufacturer. She was assigned to work as a trainee under Ann Green, one of the firm's most productive sales reps on the East Coast. At the end of the first week, Jane and Ann were sitting in a motel room filling out their expense vouchers for the week.

Jane casually remarked to Ann that the training course had stressed the importance of filling out expense vouchers accurately. Ann immediately launched into a long explanation of how the company's expense reporting resulted in underpayment of actual costs. She claimed that all the sales reps on the East Coast made up the difference by padding

their expenses under $25, which did not require receipts. A rule of thumb used was to inflate total expenses by 25 percent. When Jane questioned whether this was honest, Ann said that even if the reported expenses exceeded actual expenses, the company owed them the extra money, given the long hours and hard work they put in.

Jane said that she did not believe that reporting fictitious expenses was the correct thing to do and that she would simply report her actual expenses. Ann responded in an angry tone, saying that to do so would expose all the sales reps. As long as everyone cooperated, the company would not question the expense vouchers. However, if one person reported only actual expenses, the company would be likely to investigate the discrepancy and all the sales reps could lose their jobs. She appealed to Jane to follow the agreed-upon practice, stating that they would all be better off, that no one would lose his or her job,

This case was written by David J. Fritzsche. Permission to reprint granted by Arthur Andersen & Co., SC.

and that the company did not really need the money because it was very profitable.

QUESTIONS FOR DISCUSSION

1. What are the ethical issues in this case?
2. Given all the factors, what should Jane have done?

3. What would have been the consequences for Jane and the company if she had accurately reported her expenses? What would the consequences have been if she had inflated her expense account as Ann had urged her to do?
4. What ethical principles would be useful here?

Family Business

8

Jane had just been hired as the head of the payroll department at R&S Electronic Service Company, a firm of 75 employees. She had been hired by Eddie, the general manager, who had informed her of the need for maintaining strict confidentiality regarding employee salaries and pay scales. He had also told her that he had fired the previous payroll department head for breaking that confidentiality by discussing employee salaries. She had also been formally introduced to Brad, the owner, who had told her to see him if she had any questions or problems. Both Brad and Eddie had made her feel welcome.

After 3 months of employment, Jane began to wonder why Greg, a service technician and Eddie's brother, made so much more in commissions than the other service technicians. She assumed that he must be highly qualified and must work rapidly because she had overheard Brad commending Greg on his performance on several occasions. She had also noticed Brad, Eddie, and Greg having lunch together frequently.

One day, Eddie gave Jane the stack of work tickets for the service technicians for the upcoming week. The technicians were to take whatever ticket was on top when they finished the job they were working on. After putting the tickets where they belonged, Jane remembered that she had a doctor's appointment the next morning and returned to Eddie's office to tell him she would be reporting late for work. When she entered Eddie's office, she saw Eddie give Greg a separate stack of work tickets. As she stood there, Eddie told her that if she mentioned this to anyone, he would fire her. Jane was upset because she understood that Eddie was giving the easier, high-commission work to his brother. Jane also realized that Eddie had the authority to hire and fire her. Because she had been at the company for only a short time, she was still on probation. This was her first job since college. She wondered what she should do.

QUESTIONS FOR DISCUSSION

1. What are the ethical issues in this case?
2. Is a family business different from other types of businesses with respect to employee treatment?
3. What was Jane's ethical dilemma?
4. What should Jane have done? Why?

This case was written by Dr. Marilyn M. Helms, Associate Professor of Management, University of Tennessee at Chattanooga. Permission to reprint granted by Arthur Andersen & Co., SC.

The Plastichem Corporation

9

BACKGROUND

The Plastichem Corporation is a plastics and chemicals firm, employing about 12,000 people worldwide, with its main headquarters in Chicago. One of the firm's plants produces isocyanate, a reactive component used in the manufacture of polyurethanes. Plastichem's isocyanate production plant is relatively old by industry standards; while it is not considered to be obsolete, neither is it state-of-the-art. This particular plant is located in Termonia, Illinois, a small company town about 85 miles southwest of Chicago.

The plant employs 300 people—about 20 percent of the town's population—and runs on a continuous three-shift basis every day of the year. Although geared primarily for production, the plant is assigned a small technical service group with five professionals (chemists/engineers). The plant is run quite independently of Chicago, and minimal communication exists between Termonia and the home office.

Termonia is a tightly knit community in which everyone seems to know each other. In the past few months, rumors have been circulating around town that the main office is considering closing the Termonia plant and building a larger, more efficient facility somewhere in the South. Termonia's citizens are quite concerned about the likelihood of this closing and its effect on the town's economy. Workers at the plant know very well that they cannot afford any downtime, since the operation is being evaluated for production efficiency (pounds of isocyanate produced per day) by the home office. Plant expenses also must be maintained at the bare minimum to convince the Chicago office of the utility of the plant.

PRECAUTIONS IN THE USE OF ISOCYANATES

The Termonia plant produces TDI, or toluene diisocyanate, which is considered to present the greatest hazard of the commonly used industrial isocyanates.

From John D. Aram, *Managing Business and Public Policy: Concepts, Issues, and Cases,* 2nd ed. (Ballinger Publishing Company, 1986). Reprinted with permission.

If suitable safety measures are applied, no apparent harmful effects should result. Occupational Safety and Health Administration (OSHA) regulations govern the industrial usage of this chemical. The American Conference of Governmental Industrial Hygienists (ACGIH) and the American Standards Association have determined the threshold limit values (TLVs) and maximum acceptable concentrations for isocyanates. OSHA has agreed with these values and is responsible for publishing them. A TLV is the level below which all workers may be continuously exposed without suffering adverse physiological effects. The maximum acceptable concentration is a ceiling level that is not to be surpassed under any circumstances. The TLV for TDI has been set at 0.005 part per million (ppm) for a time-weighted average 8-hour working day, while the maximum acceptable concentration is 0.02 ppm for any continuous 20-minute exposure. Tests have determined that the least detectable odor of TDI occurs at 0.5 ppm, indicating that if a worker smells the TDI, a hazardous condition already exists.

Since the odor cannot be detected at low concentrations, elaborate monitoring systems have been developed by two companies: ADM Scientific and MER Incorporated. These systems are coupled with alarm units that trigger a loud horn when the TLV is exceeded and shut the entire production line down when the maximum acceptable concentration is exceeded for more than 20 continuous minutes. The Plastichem plant has such a monitoring/alarm system.

Inhalation of TDI vapors normally results in severe irritation of the mucous membranes in the respiratory tract. Short exposure at concentrations near the ceiling value can cause progressive disabling illness (analogous to breathlessness or reduced pulmonary functioning). Massive exposure has led to bronchitis, bronchial spasm, and/or pulmonary edema. Liquid TDI splashed directly in the eye can result in irritation of or possible damage to the cornea. Contact with the skin resulting from liquid spills can result in reddening, swelling, and blistering.

Adequate mechanical ventilation is mandatory to control TDI vapor levels. Periodic maintenance of the exhaust system should be done according to OSHA and local air pollution regulations. The Termonia plant has a system that is enclosed and ventilated as specified by OSHA. Termonia also requires that chemical safety goggles and adequate skin protection be used in areas where there is a potential for spills or line ruptures. In addition, the Termonia plant has eyewash fountains and safety showers strategically located about the plant in case of an emergency. Personnel are trained in basic safety procedures.

Finally, TDI is not considered a serious fire hazard, but it can burn in the presence of an open flame or extreme heat. TDI is sensitive to moisture. Uncontrollable isocyanate polymerization can occur in the presence of water, resulting in extreme heat generation and pressure buildup, and possibly an explosion if the TDI is in a sealed container.

SCHNALL'S DILEMMA

Jared Schnall, a chemist in the technical service lab, is well aware of the plant closing rumors. Actually, they are more than rumors. Three months ago, at a meeting attended by Schnall, his supervisor (the head of the lab), a few of the top manufacturing officials, and the liaison from the Chicago office, the corporate liaison explained that the threat of closing down the plant was real. The liaison mentioned that the day-to-day operating data were being monitored carefully so that the main office could make a decision. The key variables were plant expenditures and output rates. The liaison also told them that a decision would be made 8 months from the time of the meeting.

In the 3 months since the meeting with the Chicago liaison, Schnall has become aware of some questionable activities at the production plant. He feels that these activities have resulted directly from the cost-cutting and output-increasing efforts of the production workers. Owing to their fear of the plant closing, the workers have undertaken measures that would be considered questionable under normal operating circumstances.

The first activity noticed by Schnall initially occurred 2 months ago and was repeated on three subsequent occasions. One morning as he was walking back to the technical service lab through the plant control room, the MER monitoring system began to signal, indicating that the TLV had been exceeded. Under normal circumstances, the horn would blow until the TDI leak was found and secured. If the ceiling level was reached during this period and persisted for 20 minutes, the plant would be automatically shut down and evacuated. However, on this occasion and the other three that Schnall witnessed, a worker in the control room "tripped" a circuit to stop the horn's blowing and to prevent the automatic shutdown of the plant, even if the ceiling level was reached. Having been there when the alarm had gone off on a few occasions, Schnall had always heard the continual blowing of the horn, and he had even witnessed a few temporary plant shutdowns. Plant shutdowns are extremely undesirable because it can take anywhere from 2 to 8 hours to locate the leak, to secure the leak, to restart the line, and to reach acceptable equilibrium output conditions.

Wondering why the practice of "tripping" had begun, Schnall asked a friend of his in the control room about it after work. His friend explained to him that this practice had begun when they found out about the possibility of the plant closing. Instead of letting the alarm system shut the plant down temporarily and lower output, the workers in the control room felt it was better to "trip" the circuit and fix the leak while the system continued to run. They believed their jobs were on the line, and they were willing to take the risk. Schnall was not sure if all of the plant workers were aware of the tripping practice.

Schnall asked his friend if he was concerned about the health conditions on the plant floor during these situations. His friend declared, "Sure I'm concerned, but what else can we do? Besides, the worst thing that has happened so far is a few guys coughed a little and a couple of 'em had to step outside and get some fresh air 'cause their eyes were burning. Listen, Jared, our jobs are on the line. Once we get the word from Chicago that they'll keep the plant open, things'll get back to normal. You'll see!"

Another questionable activity that Schnall discovered pertained to inspection and maintenance procedures. In an effort to keep costs down, two inspection practices had been "temporarily" eliminated. The first was the inspection of water lines leading to the safety showers and the eye-washes as well as to the actual showers and washes. Schnall was worried that should these fixtures become unknowingly inoperative, owing to lack of inspection and maintenance, someone could have irreparable harm done to them in an emergency situation.

Inspection and maintenance of the air ventilation and circulation system was the other practice that had been discontinued over the past few months, in an effort to reduce expenses. In this case, Schnall strongly believed that a steady deterioration of the exhaust system could lead to ineffective removal of dangerous vapors in the event of an emergency. In addition, he knew that an inferior exhaust unit would cause the alarm system to be triggered more often than under normal circumstances. In any case, the lack of inspection and maintenance was in direct violation of OSHA regulations and local air pollution standards.

Schnall was not sure if other questionable practices were being carried out besides the ones he knew about, nor was he sure exactly what he should or could do about this situation. He first consulted with his supervisor, the head of the lab, but his boss did not give him a direct answer. By the time he finished talking with his boss, he realized that his boss was already aware of the situation but was willing to "ride it out" like his friend in the control room.

Still confused, Schnall began to weigh his alternatives:

1. Ignore the situation, as his boss was doing.

2. Question or complain to the top management in the production facility. However, Schnall was concerned about how his questions or complaints might affect his permanent working relationship with the production people. His own work schedule was very dependent on the availability of production people and their equipment for trial runs. If they wanted to make work difficult for him, they could. Schnall was especially afraid of confronting the top management because he felt they were probably the ones who had initiated the activities in the first place.

3. Go over the production people's heads and contact the Chicago liaison. In this case, working conditions would probably become unbearable for Schnall. He might simply be transferred, but he still feared being stuck with the label of a "spy" wherever he might go in the company. He could contact the Chicago office anonymously and hope that something would be done about the safety situation.

4. Contact OSHA if alternatives 2 and 3 are undesirable or are proven fruitless. This alternative could be dangerous, too. Schnall knew that, on the one hand, the home office might have to close Termonia if OSHA were brought in and the normal output levels were determined to be unacceptable. On the other hand, even if OSHA decided to keep the plant running, it might be

an uncomfortable working environment for him. Schnall also knew that he was protected by at least three governmental acts. For example, OSHA regulations contain the following statement about employee rights and protection:

No person shall discharge or in any manner discriminate against any employee because such employee has filed any complaint or instituted or caused to be instituted any proceeding under or related to this Act or has testified or is about to testify in any such proceeding or because of the exercise by such employee on behalf of himself or others of any rights afforded by this Act.[1]

The following section goes on to say, "Any employee who believes that he has been discharged or otherwise discriminated against by any person in violation of this subsection may, within thirty days after such violation occurs, file a complaint with the Secretary alleging such discrimination."[2] In a final section, the following statement is made: "Within 90 days of the receipt of a complaint filed under this subsection, the Secretary shall notify the complainant of his determination."[3]

5. Quit. That is, refuse to be a part of these activities but let the workers take the risk if they so desire.

There were a few other items that bothered Schnall. First, he felt that there was no opportunity within the company for someone like himself to question or complain about company practices. He did not feel it was safe for an employee to speak out. In essence, there was no neutral office or third party within the company with whom he could speak.

Second, he knew his job was at stake in more ways than one. Almost no matter what choice he made, other than ignoring the situation, he felt he would end up fired, transferred with a negative label attached to him, laid off, or working under undesirable or uncomfortable conditions. He was not pleased with the choices.

The third question that concerned him was the reality of the threat of closure. Was the Chicago liaison using this threat as a ploy to improve the Termonia plant output and efficiency? Was he trying to scare them into working harder? Was he doing this without his supervisor's knowledge?

A final dilemma that perplexed Schnall regarded what would happen if he remained quiet and the home office decided to keep the plant running. Was it fair for him to withhold information from the main office that would reveal that Termonia people were artificially keeping output high and costs low under potentially dangerous health conditions? Could this false information lead to the home office making the wrong choice? Also, was the home office not responsible for the safety of the Termonia people regardless of whether or not they were aware of the triggering activities? Should Termonia be run so independently of the home office? Should there be more communication than just through the liaison?

QUESTIONS FOR DISCUSSION

1. What actions would you recommend to Jared Schnall, and why? What factors should he weigh in coming to a decision about what to do?

2. What action would you as chief executive officer of Plastichem Corporation want Jared Schnall to take? What is the likelihood that Jared would act in this manner?

3. Is Jared's dilemma likely to be a significant issue in American industry either now or in the future? What lessons can managers of U.S. corporations learn from experiences like Jared's? What reservations might managers have about reacting to such problems?

CASE ENDNOTES

1. "The Occupational Safety and Health Act of 1970, Section 11(c)," *Labor Relations Expediter* (Washington, DC: The Bureau of National Affairs, 1971), 6213.
2. *Ibid.*
3. *Ibid.*

Something's Rotten In Hondo 10

George Mackee thought of himself as bright, energetic, and with lots of potential. "So why is this happening to me?" he thought. George, with his wife Mary and his two children, had moved to Hondo, Texas, from El Paso 4 years earlier and was now the manager of the Ardnak Plastics plant in Hondo, a small plant that manufactured plastic parts for small equipment. The plant employed several hundred workers, which was a substantial portion of the population of Hondo. Ardnak Plastics Inc. had several other small plants the size of Hondo's. George had a good relationship with Bill, his boss, in Austin, Texas.

One of the problems George's plant had was that the smokestack emissions were consistently above EPA guidelines. Several months ago, George got a call from Bill, stating that the EPA had contacted him about the problem and fines would be levied. George admitted the situation was a continual prob-

lem, but because headquarters would not invest in new smokestack scrubbers, he didn't know what to do. Bill replied by saying that margins were at their limits and there was no money for new scrubbers. Besides, Bill commented, other plants were in worse shape than his and they were passing EPA standards.

George ended the conversation by assuring Bill that he would look into the matter. He immediately started calling his contemporaries at other Ardnak plants. He found they were scheduling their heavy emissions work at night so that during the day when the EPA took their sporadic readings they were within standards. George contemplated this option even though it would result in increasing air contamination levels.

A month went by, and George still had not found a solution. The phone rang; it was Bill. Bill expressed his displeasure with the new fines for the month and reminded George that there were very few jobs out in the industry. That's when Bill dropped the whole thing into George's lap. Bill had been speaking to the Mexican government and had received assur-

This case was written by Geoffrey P. Lantos, Associate Professor of Marketing, Stonehill College. Permission to reprint granted by Arthur Andersen & Co., SC.

ances that no such clean air restrictions would be imposed on Ardnak if they relocated 15 miles south of Hondo in Mexico. However, Ardnak must hire Mexican workers. Bill explained that the reason for relocating would be to eliminate the EPA problems. Bill told George he had 1 week to decide whether to eliminate the fines by correcting the current problems or by relocating.

George knew that relocating the plant on the Mexican side would devastate the infrastructure of the city of Hondo and would continue to put contaminants into the air on the U.S. side. When he mentioned the possibility to Mary, she reinforced other concerns.

She did not want him to be responsible for the loss of the jobs of their friends and extended families.

QUESTIONS FOR DISCUSSION

1. Who are the stakeholders in this situation, and what are their stakes?
2. What social responsibility, if any, does Ardnak Plastics Inc. have to the city of Hondo?
3. What are the ethical issues in this case?
4. What should George do? Why?

Multitype Corporation: Doing Business in the Caribbean 11

Like many United States manufacturers saddled with high labor costs, Multitype Corporation, a manufacturer of office equipment, has transferred many of its operations overseas. Yet Multitype finds itself the focus of demonstrations in the United States because of the host country's domestic policies.

In Multitype's case, the host country is a small Caribbean nation, the Swan Island Republic, which consists of one large island and several smaller islets. In the late 1700s, the British began colonizing these small, desolate islands and tried to establish plantation agriculture as they had on Barbados and Jamaica. But the ground was too swampy, and eventually the plantations were abandoned. The British departed, leaving the islands in the hands of the black laborers who had been transported from Africa to work the plantations. The blacks turned to subsistence agriculture, raising barely enough fruits and vegetables to feed themselves.

For over a century, the Swan Islands were a forgotten backwater within the British Empire. Civil servants from Great Britain were used to staff the small administrative office and hospital in the capital town, New Liverpool; and the British willingly carried the expense of maintaining these services. The black Swan Islanders barely managed to scrape by,

living a hand-to-mouth existence generation after generation.

Yet the black Swan Islanders were not alone. In the interior of the island lived about 200 Carib Indians, a tribe related to the Native Americans. The Caribs were content to live in the forested center of the island, and the blacks were content to live along the shore, so the two groups rarely came into contact. In situations where they did meet, violence was the inevitable result. The Caribs, despite their primitive spears and hatchets, had a tradition of militancy and rebellion against outsiders. The Caribs continued the same lifestyle they had before European exploration and settlement, living much the same as they had in the centuries before Columbus. The Caribs and the blacks were tied for the dubious distinction of being the most impoverished people of the Caribbean.

In spite of the islands' poverty and lack of economic development, independence seemed inevitable as other nations pressured Great Britain to dismember its colonial empire. The Swan Islands were not exempt from this pressure. Finally, in 1977, the British flag was lowered in front of Government House in New Liverpool for the last time, and the bright red and green flag of the Swan Island Republic was raised.

John Bailey, the black chief of police under the British, promptly appointed himself president of the Swan Islands and began to seek ways of improving

This case was written by Marc S. Mentzer. Reproduced with permission. *Not to be duplicated without permission of the author and publisher.*

the economy of the new nation. The soil was too wet for commercial agriculture, and the swarms of mosquitoes made tourism impossible.

Thus, when Multitype was seeking a location with cheap labor for a new manufacturing plant, the Swan Islands seemed ideal. The government of John Bailey welcomed Multitype enthusiastically, and the impoverished population of New Liverpool flocked to the new factory in search of jobs. Even at a wage of $5.00 a day (U.S. currency was used in the Swan Islands), Multitype could choose whomever it wanted from the hundreds of eager job seekers. Its local employees, all of them black, spoke English, so communication problems were minimal. And, due to the workers' motivation and enthusiasm, the plant was extremely profitable for Multitype and enabled the firm to maintain its competitive position in the United States.

Back in the United States, Multitype's top management was shocked to find a group of American Indians picketing the company's headquarters one morning, protesting on behalf of the Carib Indians in the Swan Islands. A malaria epidemic was sweeping the Carib community in the interior of the Swan Islands. For some reason, the black population of the Swan Islands seemed to be immune, but the Carib Indians were not. Drugs for both preventing and treating malaria were available, but the government claimed it didn't have the funds to eradicate the disease among the Caribs. As a result, the Caribs were rapidly dying of malaria, and if nothing was done, the small group would be completely wiped out in a few years.

At Multitype's United States headquarters, the initial response was to ignore the pickets, but they didn't go away. Day after day for months, employees were greeted by the protesters' placards, which read "Multitype—Partner in Genocide" and "Get Out of the Swan Islands." Multitype's top management spent more and more of its time discussing the Swan Island situation, especially when it became apparent that the United States demonstrators were hampering Multitype's sales to universities and government agencies.

After doing nothing for 2 months, Multitype's management decided it would pay for a treatment program among the Swan Island Caribs. But the Bailey government in the Swan Islands stonewalled Multitype's efforts at every turn. First, it declared that the Carib areas were quarantined and therefore off limits—even to medical personnel. When Multitype tried to bring in a team of doctors and nurses any-way, the medical team was arrested at the airport and sent back home on the next plane. It was only then that Multitype's management became aware of the deep, centuries-long animosity between the Swan Island blacks and the Caribs and realized what was behind the Swan Island government's stubbornness.

The Swan Island government seemed determined to block any aid effort. Even when Multitype's president, Jean Gardner, made a personal appeal to Bailey and politely reminded him of Multitype's role in the economy, she was curtly told to mind her own business, followed by a lecture from President Bailey on how Americans always like to interfere in the domestic affairs of other nations.

Meanwhile, the United States television networks began to give the story a great deal of attention, and the issue even made the covers of the national news magazines. Like it or not, Multitype was in the limelight.

"Look, we've done all we can," Jean Gardner explained at a meeting of her top management. "Bailey has a point. Who are we to tell him how to run his country? How would we feel if a foreign government started telling us how to deal with the American Indians in our own country? We're here to make office equipment and sell it at a profit. Life is unfair: some of the countries we operate in have serious problems. But does that make it our fault?"

"I couldn't agree more," replied the corporate treasurer. "We have to keep this in perspective. All of Swan Islands have only about 25,000 people. These Carib Indians make up less than 1 percent of the population. And let's not forget the good we've done in that pathetic little country. Five dollars a day isn't much, but it's a lot to those people—enough to make the difference between starving and eating!"

"Absolutely right!" agreed Gardner. "These bleeding heart liberals want us to pull out of the Swan Islands entirely. How does that help anybody?"

"That's all well and fine, but what do I tell my customers?" remarked the vice president of sales, who was normally a quiet fellow but now was visibly agitated. "On every sales call, that's all our reps hear about—those dying Indians in the Swan Islands. I tell you, we're losing sales, and it's going to get worse. We have to do something."

QUESTIONS FOR DISCUSSION

1. Who are the stakeholders in this case, and what are their stakes?

2. What is your appraisal of the attitudes that seem to be developing on the part of Multitype's top management?

3. Identify the ethical issues facing Multitype Corporation.

4. Suppose Multitype had the opportunity of putting together a coup d'etat that would replace Bailey with a leader more compassionate toward the Caribs. Would it be the right thing to do?

5. To fulfill its ethical responsibilities to the parties involved, and also to address its own economic interests, what position and actions should Multitype take?

AndroFit

12

For decades, the U.S. Food and Drug Administration (FDA) has regulated dietary supplements as foods, in most cases to ensure that those supplements are safe and wholesome and that their labeling is truthful and not misleading. An important part of ensuring safety was FDA evaluation of the safety of all new ingredients, including those used in dietary supplements, under the 1958 Food Additive Amendments to the Federal Food, Drug, and Cosmetic Act (FD& C Act).With the passage of the Dietary Supplement Health and Education Act (DSHEA), however, Congress amended the FD& C Act to include several provisions that apply only to dietary supplements and to dietary ingredients of dietary supplements. Because of these provisions, dietary ingredients used in dietary supplements are no longer subject to the premarket safety evaluations required of other new food ingredients or to new uses of old food ingredients.[1]

Dietary supplements have never received the kind of government scrutiny applied to prescription medicines, which undergo a stringent and lengthy series of tests before they are approved and allowed to be marketed. In fact, one purpose of DSHEA was to make dietary supplements more widely and readily available. Most dietary supplements today can be marketed without being reviewed in advance for safety or effectiveness by the FDA.

There are rules to be followed with respect to dietary supplements. However, the industry has grown so large, with an estimated 20,000 dietary supplements on the market in the United States and an annual growth rate of 20 percent, that the $15 billion industry has just grown too big for regulators to monitor. A 1999 report indicated that the FDA had only five employees dedicated to handling dietary supplements. The FDA's Office of Special Nutritionals indicated that it had no systematic process in place for monitoring dietary supplement companies. In 1999, it admitted that it had only taken about 100 actions against companies since the act was passed in 1994 and that in most cases these actions were warning letters.[2]

THE CASE OF ANDROSTENEDIONE

Mr. Wayne Josephson, a graduate of the Wharton School, worked on Wall Street for 20 years before he decided he wanted to start his own company. He left New York for Minneapolis in 1996 seeking a slower-paced life for him and his family, but he couldn't decide what kind of business to start. He began reading about the dietary supplement Mark McGwire had been taking as he was pursuing his baseball home-run record. McGwire had commented publically on his success with androstenedione, also known as "andro," and how it was effective, natural, and legal.

The 49-year-old Josephson began researching andro on the World Wide Web and ran across a number of health professionals who were advocating andro to combat the decline in testosterone levels in older men that is linked with loss of energy and sex drive. Josephson decided to try some himself and immediately felt years younger. He wanted to exercise more, was less sore after his workouts, and convinced himself that older men would clamor to have this supplement if they understood its effects and could order it over the Web.[3] At the time, andro was not widely available in health stores.

Josephson began his adventure into the world of electronic commerce by creating a company he called AndroFit, LLC. He started with what he thought would be the perfect product, andro, and labeled it "The Stud Pill for Men." In the fall of 1998 he began marketing andro over the Web to older men when previously andro had been used only by the body-building crowd. Josephson set up a Web site, issued a press release that declared his product a "safe," "proven," and "FDA legal substance" that increases testosterone levels, "reverses male aging," and "burns fat, builds muscle, and boosts strength, energy, and sex drive." Two months later, Josephson introduced two more products: "The Passion Pill for Women," a low dose of andro, and "Herbal Trim," a dietary supplement he says promotes weight loss. Josephson says that none of his products have side effects.[4]

According to a front-page *Wall Street Journal* article, Josephson has gotten a big boost because he has chosen to market a product for which legislation (the DSHEA) has, in effect, sharply reduced regulatory oversight. He chose products that are protected by scant requirements for substantiating claims and scant resources for policing misdeeds by companies.[5]

Josephson claims that he didn't check into any rules before starting his company and that he has not included any disclaimers that the FDA has not evaluated his claims for his products, as the law requires. He says he has submitted no information to the FDA nor gathered data for the U.S. Federal Trade Commission (FTC). However, he is supposed to be able to substantiate his claims if the FTC so requests. Andro was first sold in the United States in 1996, 2 years after the FDA began requiring safety data on new ingredients. The FDA says it has yet to receive any safety information from companies selling andro, and some experts say there are now over 50 companies selling this product.[6] A Web search shows many companies now selling andro. Some companies have places on their Web pages where customers can share their experiences with andro and other products. Following are some comments posted by andro consumers:[7]

> Andro can cause side-effects you should know about, such as hair loss and pimples on the back. I have taken several different types of andro AND I WOULDN'T WASTE YOUR MONEY. The benefits for me have been zero. Although, it does work for a few select individuals.

> My name is Wade and just about a month ago I started using andro. I was wondering if I will be able to pass a drug test, or will the andro show up on the drug test? If it does show up, could it keep me from getting a job?

> As long as you are not an Olympic athlete, professional football player or basketball player, or play college sports, then it will not matter. The NFL, NBA, NCAA, and IOC have banned andro, but other than that it is a legal substance that can be obtained at any nutritional store. The only concern is that there have not been extensive long-term studies to show the side-effects of andro.

Is andro, and the thousands of other dietary supplements now on the market, safe? Opinions vary, and long-term studies do not exist. Walk into any Wal-Mart, K-Mart, or health-food store and you will face thousands upon thousands of new dietary supplements claiming to fix what ails you. Just remember: These supplements have not had the simple, basic testing that the bottle of aspirin or ibuprofen you have on your shelf has had. In fact, they may have had no testing as to whether they are safe or whether they work. Their claims may have no foundation. Where is government regulation? The regulatory agencies are overworked, understaffed, and underbudgeted. They lack the human resources to enforce the regulations that are on the books.

While the *Wall Street Journal* article may turn the FDA spotlight on Josephson and force him to defend his claims, for now he is delighted with his business and with the increased vigor he has felt since he started taking andro. He says he's going to take andro for the rest of his life.[8]

QUESTIONS FOR DISCUSSION

1. Should the government create legislation that it lacks the resources to enforce? How should government decide which products/services to monitor and which ones to leave to the vagaries of the marketplace?

2. What is your assessment of government regulation and the dietary-supplements industry? Is the industry safe? Does it need more intensive regulatory oversight?

3. What are the social responsibilities of firms doing business in an industry like dietary supplements? Should the companies assume any of the oversight not being provided by government?

4. What is your assessment of the Dietary Supplement Health and Education Act (DSHEA) of 1994? Is it

better to have it than to not have it? What is your assessment of the claim that one effect of the law on dietary supplements is leaner regulation?

CASE ENDNOTES

1. Center for Food Safety and Applied Nutrition, U.S. Food and Drug Administration.
2. Rochelle Sharpe, "One Effect of a Law on Diet Supplements Is Leaner Regulation," *Wall Street Journal* (January 27, 1999), A1–A5.
3. *Ibid.*, A1–A5.
4. *Ibid.*, A1.
5. *Ibid.*
6. *Ibid.*
7. Various Web sites. See also "AndroFit: The Stud Pill," *www.androfit.com/page1.html*; "GQ Magazine Names AndroFit Stud Pill as the 'Get Hard' Alternative to Viagra," *nt.excite.com:80/news/bw/990128/mn-androfit.com*; "Nutritional Supplements.com," *www.nutritionalsupplements.com.*
8. Sharpe, A5.

Telephone Deregulation: The Pricing Controversy 13

The 1996 Telecommunications Act mandated that states allow competition in local telephone service, and it required local telephone providers to lease any or all of their network components to their new competitors at prices to be set by the Federal Communications Commission (FCC). The FCC decided to pursue one national pricing policy, with some state variations to accommodate regional differences in costs. It ruled that the local telephone providers could charge a price for the use of their network components that would just cover the costs that an efficient provider would incur to provide those components for rent. A series of court challenges followed the FCC's decision, but on January 25, 1999, the Supreme Court issued a ruling that the FCC did have the authority to set the pricing.

Reaction to the ruling was decidedly mixed. Proponents of the FCC ruling argued that deregulation would never happen if the local Bells were able to set their own prices. Given that freedom, they would likely overcharge for their networks and possibly deny access to important network components. This seemed particularly unfair because, as long-distance telephone companies were driving hard to enter local markets, local providers were pushing to enter

nationwide long-distance service. Gene Kimmelman of Consumer's Union said, "This decision will help small companies to come into the local market and take on the reigning monopolist."[1]

Opponents of the ruling were less optimistic. They questioned the fairness of charging today's efficiency-based prices for networks that were built at a time of efficiency-suppressing regulation. They also expressed concern that local Bells would not be motivated to upgrade their technologies. Robert W. Crandall of the Brookings Institute opined, "Why should these firms be required to invest in new, often risky technology for delivering advanced high-speed services if they are to be required to offer any such new facilities to their rivals at cost?"[2]

QUESTIONS FOR DISCUSSION

1. How do you balance the property rights of the local Bells against the entry barrier that those networks present?
2. Which is more important: opening a monopoly to competition or encouraging the development of new technology? Do you agree with Mr. Crandall that the pricing procedure designed by the FCC will limit investment in new technology?
3. If you were an FCC commissioner, what would you do?

This case was written by Ann K. Buchholtz.

CASE ENDNOTES

1. Michael M. Weinstein, "Economic Scene: It's Hard to Tell Who Won in the High Court Phone Ruling," *The New York Times* (January 28, 1999), C2.

2. Robert W. Crandall, "The Telecom Act's Phone-y Deregulation," *Wall Street Journal* (January 27, 1999), A22.

Lobbying Ethics

14

One of the United States's most serious environmental problems over the years has been air pollution. After more than a decade of efforts to improve the nation's air quality, it has become apparent that the air pollution problems we have extend beyond what federal legislators envisioned in the early 1970s when the Clean Air Act was passed. Of concern to many has been the increased use of coal. From 1983 to 1984, the use of coal increased 7 percent. It was expected to increase another 5 percent in 1985. Among the problems that arise when coal is burned is the increase in sulfur dioxide and nitrogen dioxide emissions, which are the key ingredients in the formation of acid rain and sulfate haze. Studies in 1985 confirmed that acid rain threatened the purity and life of thousands of streams and lakes all across the nation.[1] Acid rain has become a battleground between those companies that create it and emit it into the atmosphere and environmentalists who think it is one of the nation's most serious ecological hazards and should be strictly regulated.

CITIZENS FOR SENSIBLE CONTROL OF ACID RAIN

For controversial issues such as acid rain, there is considerable lobbying of Congress by the polluting firms that are opposed to additional regulations and by social activist groups that support such legislation. Recently proposed acid rain legislation would require coal-burning power plants to install special equipment or use more expensive low-sulfur coal to reduce pollutants. One of the major lobbying groups that has taken a stand on this issue is "Citizens for Sensible Control of Acid Rain." A recent letter sent

out by this group on its letterhead went to thousands of households warning that Congress is considering legislation against acid rain "that would cost $110 billion" and "would mean up to 30 percent higher electric bills." Recipients of the letter were urged to write their congressional representatives and encourage them to vote down such legislation.[2]

An organization known as the U.S. Public Interest Research Group, which supports acid rain legislation, is outraged by the lobbying efforts of the so-called citizens group. It turns out that "Citizens for Sensible Control of Acid Rain" is not a citizens group at all, at least not in the traditional grassroots sense. The organization is funded by coal and power companies that are major contributors to the acid rain problem.[3] As is the case with many lobbying campaigns, the group is run by a Washington-based public relations firm. Thomas Buckmaster, the public relations executive who runs the campaign, says that his organization generates letters from citizens and, therefore, it is a citizens group. Since the group was founded in 1983, it has spent $4 million sending 800,000 letters to citizens asking them to write their representatives. Buckmaster says that 135,000 people, whom he calls "citizen volunteers," have written letters as a result of the campaign. He goes on to add: "Form letter or not, each letter was signed by an individual citizen who has taken the time to read our letter, decided it accurately reflects their point of view, and took the extraordinary step of signing their name and sending to their elected representatives."

PUBLIC INTEREST RESEARCH GROUP (PIRG)

PIRG, which describes itself as a nonpartisan, nonprofit consumer and environmental advocacy group, has taken the position that the lobbying done by Citi-

This case was written by Archie B. Carroll.

zens for Sensible Control of Acid Rain is misleading and deceptive. Alexandra Allen, a lawyer for PIRG, said that sponsors of the citizens group had a vested interest in the issue.[4] Apparently PIRG is concerned because the citizens group did not communicate to people it wrote to that it was being funded by the power and coal companies. Others in the lobbying business said that they found such efforts questionable. One head of a large public relations firm admitted that he had organized a number of what he called "phony coalitions" but no longer engaged in this practice because he found it to be "personally disturbing." One legislator, Representative James J. Florio (D–New Jersey), said that there is confusion. He cited the case of a constituent who wrote him that he did not realize that the acid rain group was an industry effort. Florio added, "The group purports to be disinterested but clearly is not." Allen, of PIRG, stated, "As Congress considers acid rain legislation this year, we hope that every member is fully aware that Citizens for Sensible Control of Acid Rain is in fact an industry lobby masquerading as a citizens organization."

Buckmaster, from the citizens group, says that what he is doing is not deceptive. He says, "We have been and will continue to be candid about who we are, where our funding comes from, and what the purpose of the organization is." In 1987, the group's stationery was changed to include a line at the bottom indicating that funding for the group was provided by electric, coal, and manufacturing companies.[5]

QUESTIONS FOR DISCUSSION

1. Do you find the practices of Citizens for Sensible Control of Acid Rain to be questionable? Would you go so far as to say that they constituted unethical lobbying practices? Do you find these practices defensible? Explain.
2. If you disapprove of the lobbying practices of this "citizens group," what changes would you recommend it make to improve on these practices? What minimal changes should it implement? What, ideally, should this group do?
3. Because lobbying is frequently seen as a practice of wielding influence or power, is it reasonable to think that certain ethical guidelines should be applied to lobbying? Could and should a code of conduct or ethics be developed for lobbyists?

CASE ENDNOTES

1. *The World Almanac and Book of Facts—1987* (New York: Pharos Books, 1986), 149.
2. Philip Shabecoff, "Corporate Acid Rain Lobbying Deceptive, Foes Say," *The Times-Picayune* (August 9, 1987), F-2.
3. *Ibid.*
4. *Ibid.*
5. *Ibid.*

The Nonuser Celebrity Endorser   15

Amie, a copywriter for Laird & Laird (L&L) Advertising, has just been assigned the Bud's Best (BB) bacon account. She is tickled pink, because she knows that Bud's Best has just signed a 1-year contract to use Lance Willard as a celebrity endorser. Lance is a well-known, well-loved, young, handsome, and vibrant Hollywood movie star who specializes in action drama roles. Victor, president of L&L, tells Amie that she will be writing commercials in which Lance will give product testimonials. Victor explains

to Amie that this endorsement is a testimonial given by a celebrity rather than an average consumer. He tells her that Lance has signed an affidavit swearing that he is a bona fide user of the product, as is legally required. The commercials, explains Victor, should feature Lance testifying as to the quality, value, and tastiness of the bacon. Victor suggests that this will take some good acting on Lance's part, since he has just recently become a vegetarian. Amie wonders whether a testimonial by Lance might not be dishonest, but she says nothing to Victor since she doesn't want to blow her opportunity to meet Lance in person. She figures she can get all of the details later from Lance.

This case was written by Geoffrey P. Lantos, Associate Professor of Marketing, Stonehill College. Permission to reprint granted by Arthur Andersen & Co., SC.

Lance turns out to be as charming in person as he is on the silver screen. After some small talk, Amie decides to query Lance about his experience with Bud's Best. Lance explains that he has had personal experience with the product, as is legally required for a testimonial. He tells her that he has done many celebrity endorsements in the past and knows that the American Advertising Federation's "Advertising Principles of American Business" state that "advertising containing testimonials shall be limited to those of competent witnesses who are reflecting a real and honest opinion or experience" and that as long as the endorser's comments are based on verifiable personal use, the message cannot be challenged as deceptive. In fact, Lance says, Bud's Best has been his favorite brand of bacon ever since he was a small child, and bacon and eggs were his favorite and most frequently consumed breakfast until about a month ago when he became a vegetarian for health reasons. Lance tells Amie that a recent checkup by his physician revealed that his cholesterol level was 200—in the danger zone. His doctor warned Lance to cut down on high-cholesterol foods, such as bacon and eggs. Lance decided to go even further and abstain from eating any meat, since so many meats are high in cholesterol.

Amie asks Lance diplomatically whether he feels comfortable testifying about how much he likes Bud's Best bacon when he no longer uses the product. Lance replies that his conscience is clear. He has discussed the legalities with Victor, who told him that technically it was okay for him to discuss his past enjoyment of the product. After all, Lance reminds Amie, the selling points he would discuss in the commercials would be the bacon's quality, value, and good taste. Lance explains that in his view, as far as bacon goes, Bud's Best is second to none along these criteria. He tells Amie that nothing regarding the bacon's healthiness, or lack thereof, will be mentioned. As long as people are going to eat bacon, Lance asserts, they might as well eat Bud's Best.

Amie thinks that Lance might have a point, but she isn't sure. She doesn't want to rock the boat at this point with either Lance or Victor, for she really wants to work with Lance on the shoot. She thinks she'd better just give it some more thought and prayer for the time being.

QUESTIONS FOR DISCUSSION

1. What are the ethical issues in this case?
2. What is the social responsibility of Laird & Laird Advertising? Of Bud's Best bacon?
3. Put yourself in the role of Amie. What should you do? Why?

Pizza Redlining—Employee Safety or Discrimination? 16

The issue came to a head in March 1996 when William Fobbs, father of three, wanted to order a pepperoni-and-mushroom pizza for his family one night. Much to his surprise, Domino's refused to deliver to his home. Mr. Fobbs then called Mr. Pizza Man, a local restaurant. It also refused to deliver.

Mr. Fobbs, a security guard, lives in a tough, predominantly black neighborhood near Candlestick Park in San Francisco. He was outraged and ended up feeding his kids tuna-fish sandwiches that night instead of the pizza they wanted.

GRANDMOTHER GETS INVOLVED

Exasperated, Mr. Fobbs called his grandmother, Willie Kennedy, then a 72-year-old champion of minority rights who also happened to be a member of San Francisco's Board of Supervisors. Ms. Kennedy's reaction was that her grandson had experienced racism. She said, "It can only be because we are black people." Ms. Kennedy got her friends at City Hall involved, and the result was that San Francisco passed the first law that makes it illegal for a pizza restaurant, or any business, to refuse to deliver to a particular neighborhood that is within its normal delivery area.

Some observers think that a law on pizza redlining is just one more example of the city's propensity to excess. Mr. Fobbs, however, takes the issue seriously. He said, "I felt like I was in Vietnam, somewhere in the far-off jungle."[1]

ACLU SPEAKS OUT

Dorothy Ehrlich, executive director of the American Civil Liberties Union (ACLU) in Northern California, supports the law.[2] She says that it is a blow against discrimination and ought to serve as a model for other communities. Pizza-chain owners and others in the restaurant delivery business say the issue is about crime and safety, not discrimination or race. They point to the fact that several pizza deliverers have been murdered on the job in the past few years. They say that obeying this law puts their employees' safety and lives at risk. Someone pointed out that a Domino's pizza deliveryman was murdered in San Francisco in 1994 in an area designated safe, a so-called "green" zone.[3]

OWNER DEFENDS HIMSELF

Wally Wilcox owns the Domino's restaurant that refused to deliver to Mr. Fobbs. Wilcox owns three restaurants that, like most Domino's restaurants across the country, use a computer system that categorizes neighborhoods as green, yellow, or red. Customers in "green" neighborhoods get delivery without questions. In "yellow" areas, customers must come out to the delivery car to pick up their pizzas. Customers in "red" zones do not get delivery. They are considered dangerous.

Wilcox, who is white, declares that he is not racist and does not discriminate. He pointed out that the Fobbs incident was ironic because it occurred due to error. Mr. Fobbs's street had not been entered into the computer and restaurant workers did not know his address was in their territory. Despite the mistake, Wilcox defends his restaurant's policy of not delivering to dangerous areas, like public housing projects. Wilcox pointed out that the person ordering the pizza could be a good person but that when the deliverer arrives at the address he or she could be attacked by others in the area. Wilcox also pointed out that it was one of his drivers who was shot and killed in 1994 in San Francisco's Excelsior

district, which is not far from where Mr. Fobbs lives. Wilcox said that street toughs "own the area."

THE POSITION OF HEADQUARTERS

Tom McIntyre, spokesman for Domino's Pizza, Inc., which is headquartered in Ann Arbor, Michigan, said that his company has hundreds of outlets with bullet-proof glass because of the threat and the experience of being robbed. The headquarter's office distributes the area classification software the restaurants use to categorize areas as green, yellow, or red. However, the categorization is up to the store owner's discretion.[4]

Other national pizza chains, like Little Caesar Enterprises, Inc., and Pizza Hut, say they have policies similar to Domino's. Pizza Hut, the nation's largest chain, says it uses local crime statistics in each delivery area to determine which areas are safe and which are off limits.

THESE JOBS ARE DANGEROUS

Crime statistics support the conclusion that pizza deliverers are frequently assaulted, robbed, and sometimes killed on the job. The National Institute for Occupational Safety and Health released a study that showed that the riskiest jobs are those in which workers deal with the public, exchange money, and deliver goods and services. In San Francisco, where the Fobbs incident occurred, it has been reported that many pizza drivers, some of them minorities themselves, have been known to carry guns to protect themselves from assaults.

The California Restaurant Association denounced the law in a letter to the Board of Supervisors, pointing out that the requirement violates federal occupational safety and health laws. These laws bar employers from forcing workers into hazardous situations. The Association also pointed out that worker's compensation premiums may escalate due to the new law.

Defenders of the law say it lacks real authority. According to the law, violation is a civil offense that imposes no fines. However, it does make it easier for those who are snubbed to sue for damages.

THE KANSAS CITY EPISODE

In 1997, an episode occurred in Kansas City, Missouri, which was related to the San Francisco case. In this case, Pizza Hut was involved. Paseo Academy in Kansas City phoned in a $450 pizza order 4 days in advance. The pizza was to be for a midday party for honor-roll students. Much to the school's surprise, the Pizza Hut in the area refused to take the order, saying the area was unsafe. A local chain, Westport Pizza, was more than happy to fill the order.

A few days later, Dorothy Shepherd, principal of Paseo Academy, learned that Pizza Hut had recently won a $170,000 contract to deliver pizzas twice a week to 21 Kansas City high schools and junior high schools, including Paseo, a $34 million state-of-the-art school that serves a 70 percent minority student body. Shepherd was outraged. She said, "I respect their wanting to protect their drivers. But how could it be unsafe one day but safe enough for them when it came to that contract? We didn't move the school."

PIZZA HUT ASSERTS SAFETY IS ISSUE

Rob Doughty, a spokesman at Pizza Hut's Dallas headquarters, accused school officials of "reacting to emotion" when they talked about canceling the contract with Pizza Hut. Doughty said, "The sole issue is the safety of our employees." He said that the company works out its "trade area restrictions" based on crime statistics. He pointed out that two Pizza Hut drivers had been killed in the preceding 6 weeks, both in presumably safe areas. One murder occurred in Sacramento, California, and the other in Salt Lake City, Utah.

IS A BOYCOTT APPROPRIATE?

Doughty claimed that regularly scheduled deliveries, like those called for in the school system contract in Kansas City, can be done safely with more than one driver but that the firm does not and cannot afford to do that with spot orders in which one driver is involved, like the order at Paseo Academy. The company may not get a chance to make any deliveries to Paseo on the contract, however, because students were agitating for a Pizza Hut boycott and the school

board was tempted to spruce up menus with pizza from local firms.[5]

QUESTIONS FOR DISCUSSION

1. What are the ethical issues involved in pizza deliveries to dangerous neighborhoods that are often predominantly inhabited by minorities? What tensions exist between economic and ethical issues? Whose interests are dominant—consumer stakeholders or employee stakeholders?

2. Are pizza companies genuinely protecting their employees, for which they should be applauded, or discriminating against minorities, because they "redline" and are unwilling to deliver to areas they consider dangerous?

3. Should San Francisco law, which makes it illegal for a pizza restaurant or any other business to refuse to deliver to a neighborhood that is within its normal service range, be rescinded? What are the ethical as well as the legal issues?

4. Is Pizza Hut in Kansas City engaging in an unethical practice by refusing spot deliveries but agreeing to large-dollar contract deliveries in areas it considers dangerous to its drivers? Is its two-driver versus one-driver explanation reasonable?

CASE ENDNOTES

1. Sewell Chan, "Pizza Redlining: Hot Issue Becomes Law in San Francisco," *The Wall Street Journal* (July 10, 1996), A1.
2. American Civil Liberties Union, "With Liberty and Pizza for All," (1996). Source and date unknown.
3. "The Politics of Pizza Delivery," *Time* (July 22, 1996), 38.
4. Chan, A1.
5. James L. Graff, "The Perils of Pizza Hut," *Time* (January 27, 1997).

Societal Impacts of Marketing

17

Len Quill has been working for Artifacts, Ltd., an importer of ethnic arts, for 4 years. Len was uniquely suited for a position at Artifacts, having majored in marketing and minored in cultural anthropology in college. Len started his career at Artifacts in the importing department of the home office in the United States. He soon became a buyer, traveling through South America and buying native arts from local communities. One of his major sources of artifacts is the Puna Native American tribe. Len became so interested in the tribe that he learned their native language, and now he is the only person from Artifacts who works directly with the Punas.

On a stop back at headquarters, Len's boss, Mary Mathers, has asked Len to join her and a client for lunch. The client is Bob Littman, who owns several art galleries specializing in ethnic arts. Bob is very interested in the arts of the Puna Native Americans. The Puna Native Americans make woven baskets which are very distinctive. The shapes, patterns, and colors of these baskets denote symbols of important events in the tribe's long history. Although Bob is interested in the baskets, he wants to change the patterns and colors to reflect the tastes of his customers. It would be Len's job to market the idea to the Punas. Of course, the Native Americans would receive a good price for their wares. Although the Punas are not poverty stricken, there is certainly room to improve their standard of living. Mary Mathers is very enthusiastic about this opportunity; it will result in a large profit for Artifacts, Ltd.

Len is not sure he wants to convince the Punas to change their artwork. As an anthropology major, Len learned of many societies which weakened when basic cultural symbols were changed. Even if the Punas are eager to enter into the contract to make the new type of baskets, Len is concerned that they are not aware of the damage such changes can do to their society.

Len is leaving in a week for his next trip to South America. He is still unsure about how to handle the

deal with Bob Littman. No contract has been signed, nor will a contract be signed until and unless Len gets an agreement from the Puna tribal council. Just as he is pondering this situation, Mary calls him into her office. Mary informs him that, if the Puna are willing to make baskets according to his specifications, Bob Littman insists on placing a large order that will be due in a short period of time. Len knows that in order to meet the deadline, the Puna would need to have both men and women working on the baskets. Traditionally, however, making the baskets has been women's work.

QUESTIONS FOR DISCUSSION

1. Who are the stakeholders in this case, and what are their stakes? How would you assess the stakeholders' legitimacy and power?
2. What is the social responsibility of Artifacts, Ltd., in this case?
3. What are the ethical issues in this case for Len, for Artifacts, Ltd., and for Littman?
4. Should Len Quill impose his own personal concerns upon a company decision?
5. What should Len do, and why?

This case was written by Judy Cohen, Assistant Professor of Marketing, Rider College, Lawrenceville, New Jersey. Permission to reprint granted by Arthur Andersen & Co., SC.

The Coffee Spill Heard 'Round the World

18

Stella Liebeck and her grandson, Chris Tiano, drove her son, Jim, to the airport 60 miles away in Albuquerque, New Mexico, on the morning of February 27, 1992. Since she had to leave home early, she and Chris missed having breakfast. Upon dropping Jim off at the airport, they proceeded to a McDonald's drive-through for breakfast. Stella, a spry, 79-year-old, retired department-store clerk, ordered a McBreakfast and Chris parked the car so she could add cream and sugar to her coffee.

What occurred next was the coffee spill that has been heard 'round the world. A coffee spill, serious burns, a lawsuit, and an eventual settlement made Stella Liebeck the "poster lady" for the bitter tort reform discussions that dominated Congress during 1995.

According to Liebeck's testimony, she tried to get the coffee lid off. She couldn't find any flat surface in the car so she put the cup between her knees and tried to get it off that way. As she tugged at the lid, scalding coffee spilled into her lap. Chris jumped from the car and tried to help her. She pulled at her sweat suit, squirming as the 170-degree coffee burned her groin, inner thigh, and buttocks. Third-degree burns were evident as she reached an emergency room.

Following the spill, Liebeck spent a week in the hospital and about 3 weeks at home recuperating with her daughter, Nancy Tiano. She was then hospitalized again for skin grafts. Liebeck lost 20 pounds during the ordeal and at times was practically immobilized. Another daughter, Judy Allen, recalled that her mother was in tremendous pain both after the accident and during the skin grafts.

According to a *Newsweek* report, Liebeck wrote to McDonald's in August 1994, asking them to turn down the coffee temperature. Though she wasn't planning to sue, her family thought she was due about $2,000 for out-of-pocket expenses, plus the lost wages of her daughter who stayed at home with her. The family reported that McDonald's offered her $800.

This case was written by Archie B. Carroll.

After this, the family went looking for a lawyer and retained Reed Morgan, a Houston attorney, who had won a $30,000 settlement against McDonald's in 1988 for a woman whose spilled coffee had caused her third-degree burns. Morgan filed a lawsuit on behalf of Liebeck, charging McDonald's with "gross negligence" for selling coffee that was "unreasonably dangerous" and "defectively manufactured." Morgan asked for no less than $100,000 in compensatory damages, including pain and suffering, and triple that amount in punitive damages.

McDonald's moved for summary dismissal of the case, defending the coffee's heat and blaming Liebeck for spilling it. According to the company, she was the "proximate cause" of the injury. With McDonald's motion rejected, a trial date was set for August 1994.

As the trial date approached, no out-of-court settlement occurred. Morgan, the attorney, said that at one point he offered to drop the case for $300,000 and was willing to settle for half that amount, but McDonald's wouldn't budge. Days before the trial, the judge ordered the two parties to attend a mediation session. The mediator, a retired judge, recommended McDonald's settle for $225,000 using the argument that a jury would likely award that amount. Again, McDonald's resisted settlement.

The trial lasted 7 days, with expert witnesses dueling over technical issues, such as the temperature at which coffee causes burns. Initially, the jury was annoyed at having to hear a case about spilled coffee, but the evidence presented by the prosecution grabbed its attention. Photos of Liebeck's charred skin were introduced. A renowned burn expert testified that coffee at 170 degrees would cause second-degree burns within 3.5 seconds of hitting the skin.

Defense witnesses inadvertently helped the prosecution. A quality-assurance supervisor at McDonald's testified that the company didn't lower its coffee heat despite 700 burn complaints over 10 years. A safety consultant argued that 700 complaints—about one in every 24 million cups sold—was basically trivial. An executive for McDonald's testified that the company knew its coffee sometimes caused serious burns but it wasn't planning to go beyond the tiny print warning on the cup that said, "Caution: Contents Hot!" The executive went on to say that McDonald's didn't intend to change any of its coffee policies or procedures, saying, "There are more serious dangers in restaurants."

In the closing arguments, one of the defense attorneys acknowledged that the coffee was hot and that that is how customers wanted it. She went on to insist that Liebeck had only herself to blame as she was unwise to put the cup between her knees. She also noted that Liebeck failed to leap out of the bucket seat in the car after the spill, thus preventing the hot coffee from falling off her. The attorney concluded by saying that the real question in the case is how far society should go to restrict what most of us enjoy and accept.

The jury deliberated about 4 hours and reached a verdict for Liebeck. The jury decided on compensatory damages of $200,000, which it reduced to $160,000 after judging that 20 percent of the fault belonged to Mrs. Liebeck for spilling the coffee. The jury concluded that McDonald's had engaged in willful, reckless, malicious, or wanton conduct, which is the basis for punitive damages. The jury decided upon a figure of $2.7 million in punitive damages.

One juror later said that the facts were overwhelmingly against the company and that the company just was not taking care of its customers. Another juror felt the huge punitive damages were intended to be a stern warning for McDonald's to wake up and realize its customers were getting burned. Another juror said he began to realize that the case was really about the callous disregard for the safety of customers.

Public opinion polls after the jury verdict were squarely on the side of McDonald's. Polls showed that a large majority of Americans—including many who usually support the little guy—were outraged at the verdict.

The judge later slashed the jury award by more than 75 percent to $640,000. Liebeck appealed the reduction and McDonald's continued fighting the award as excessive. In December 1994, it was announced that McDonald's had reached an out-of-court settlement with Liebeck, but the terms of the settlement were not disclosed due to a confidentiality provision. The settlement was reached to end appeals in the case.

Coffee temperature suddenly became a hot topic in the industry. The Specialty Coffee Association of America put coffee safety on its agenda for discussion. A spokesperson for the National Coffee Association said that McDonald's coffee conforms to industry temperature standards. A spokesman for Mr. Coffee, the coffee-machine maker, said that if customer complaints are any indication, industry settings may be too low. Some customers like it hotter. A coffee connoisseur who imported and wholesaled coffee said that 175 degrees is probably the optimum temperature for coffee because that's when aromatics are being released. McDonald's continues to say that it is serving its coffee the way customers like it. As one writer noted, the temperature of McDonald's coffee helps to explain why it sells a billion cups a year.

QUESTIONS FOR DISCUSSION

1. What are the major issues in this case?
2. What are McDonald's social (economic, legal, and ethical) responsibilities toward consumers in this case? What are consumers' responsibilities when they buy a product such as hot coffee? How does a company give consumers what they want and yet protect them at the same time?
3. What are the arguments supporting McDonald's position in the case? What are the arguments supporting Liebeck's position?
4. If you had been a juror in this case, which position would you most likely have supported? Why?
5. What are the implications of this case for future product-related lawsuits? Do we now live in a society where businesses are responsible for customers' accidents or carelessness in using products?

CASE REFERENCES

1. Andrea Gerlin, "A Matter of Degree: How a Jury Decided That a Coffee Spill Is Worth $2.9 Million," *The Wall Street Journal* (September 1, 1994), A1, A4.
2. Theresa Howard, "McDonald's Settles Coffee Suit in Out-of-Court Agreement," *Nation's Restaurant News* (December 12, 1994), 1.
3. "McDonald's Settles Lawsuit Over Burn From Coffee," *The Wall Street Journal* (December 2, 1994), B6.
4. Aric Press and Ginny Carroll, "Are Lawyers Burning America?" *Newsweek* (March 20, 1995), 30–35.

Safety? What Safety? 19

Kirk was a bright individual who was being groomed for the controller's position in a medium-sized manufacturing firm. After Kirk's first year as assistant controller, the officers of the firm started to include him in major company functions. One day, for instance, he was asked to attend the monthly financial statement summary at a prestigious consulting firm. During the meeting, Kirk was intrigued at how the financial data he had accumulated had been transformed by the consultant into revealing charts and graphs.

Kirk was generally optimistic about the session and the company's future until the consultant started talking about the new manufacturing plant the company was adding to the current location and the per-unit costs of the chemically plated products it would produce. At that time, Bob, the president, and John, the chemical engineer, started talking about waste treatment and disposal problems. John mentioned that the current waste treatment facilities could not handle the waste products of the "ultra-modern" new plant in a manner that would meet the industry's fairly high standards, although the plant would still comply with federal standards.

Kirk's boss, Henry, noted that the estimated per-unit costs would increase if the waste treatment facilities were upgraded according to recent industry standards. Industry standards were presently more stringent than federal regulations, and environmentalists were pressuring strongly for stricter regulations at the federal level. Bob mentioned that since their closest competitor did not have the waste treatment facilities that already existed at their firm, he was not in favor of any more expenditures in that area. Most managers at the meeting resoundingly agreed with Bob, and the business of the meeting proceeded to other topics.

Kirk did not hear a word during the rest of the meeting. He kept wondering how the company could possibly have such a casual attitude toward the environment. Yet he did not know if, how, when, or with whom he should share his opinion. Soon he started reflecting on whether this firm was the right one for him.

QUESTIONS FOR DISCUSSION

1. Who are the stakeholders in this case, and what are their stakes?
2. What social responsibility does the firm have for the environment? How would you assess the firm's CSR using the four-part CSR definition presented in Chapter 2?
3. How should Kirk reconcile his own personal thinking with the thinking being presented by the firm's management?
4. What should Kirk do? Why?

This case was written by Donald E. Tidrick, Assistant Professor of Accounting, University of Texas at Austin. Permission to reprint granted by Arthur Andersen & Co., SC.

A Paler Shade of Green

20

Ping Soon watched the advertisement on the television with interest. He used his credit card regularly and felt inclined to give Hongkong Bank (HkB) his business because of its "Care-for-Nature" credit card. The ad said its "Care-for-Nature" Trust Fund had already invested more than 1 million dollars over the past 3 years in environmentally related projects in and around Singapore. Since the Singapore government had initiated the "Green Plan," he had noticed a growing number of products that were labeled "environmentally friendly." These products attracted Ping Soon's attention, but he was often disappointed with the superficial treatment of environmentalism that many of these products represented. Sometimes he felt a product misrepresented itself as "green" when it was simply repackaged and no better than any other. This he felt was "greenwashing," and he would avoid that product in the future.

Ping Soon thought the government's "Green Plan," which tried to encourage levels of pollution control similar to those of the United States, but through voluntary means, was a good idea. He supported a proactive stance on important issues such as the environment. Singapore is a clean and beautiful place to live, and he wanted to keep it that way. He called and had an application sent for the "Care-for-Nature" credit card.

Several days later the application packet arrived. It was appealingly decorated with tropical foliage and a tree frog beautifully printed in full color. The well-written copy in the brochure made Ping Soon feel as though he was making a good choice and that at least in a small way he was helping to create a better environment in which to live. This bank really seemed different from the other banks and appeared to be trying to have a positive impact on the community. As he finished reading the packet of literature, he realized something was missing. The recycled logo was not where he expected it to be. It seemed reasonable to assume that this company, which claimed to care for nature, would want to use recycled paper. Ping

This case was prepared by David H. Saiia.

Soon could not find the emblem. He started thinking about other things that he would expect from a company that claimed to "care for nature." A simple thought occurred to him: This company could have taken the initiative to use soy-based inks, which are much less damaging to the environment. These thoughts unsettled him a bit, so he decided to look into Hongkong Bank a little further.

Ping Soon contacted a friend of his at the National Council on the Environment (NCE), a nongovernmental organization that serves as an umbrella group for other environmental associations in Singapore. He knew that NCE had promoted the use of environmental audits of businesses in Singapore as a way of helping businesses become more conscious of their impact on the environment. He thought they might have had some contact with Hongkong Bank. The Director of NCE knew the Singapore general manager of HkB, Richard Hale, fairly well. They had been allies in various environmental causes. However, she was not aware that HkB practiced environmental auditing as part of its business practice. Ping Soon rationalized that it probably was not very important that a bank should review or audit its environmental practices. After all, banks really were not responsible for much pollution. However, his friend at NCE, Farheen, asked him to think through the issue carefully, to see if he could think of some good reasons why a bank, or any nonmanufacturing firm, should conduct an environmental audit.

The first issue that occurred to Ping Soon was paper. Indeed, paper was the issue that had started him questioning whether Hongkong Bank was truly providing a service or simply marketing to a gullible target market. Farheen also thought paper was a good place to start. She said that manufacture of the bleached white virgin paper that most companies use was a major cause of habitat destruction and environmental pollution around the world. She quickly added that bleached recycled paper also was a major source of organo-chlorine pollution if chlorine bleach was used to whiten the paper. She prodded Ping Soon to think about other issues. Energy was the next issue that came to his mind. How can a bank save energy? Farheen told him that some buildings were more efficient than others and that buildings built with efficiency in mind actually used over 50 percent less energy than conventional buildings. She also said that conventional buildings, when managed properly, could save considerable energy.

Paper and energy—these were the only two issues Ping Soon could think of that a bank might address to become more environmentally sound in its operation. Farheen told him that he was not thinking deeply enough and that this was the problem with most businesses: They stopped thinking about community concerns after they had exhausted the superficial issues. She felt that by addressing the more subtle issues, businesses could have the positive effects they wanted to be associated with in the minds of consumers. Ping Soon did not follow what Farheen was suggesting. Farheen asked him how much paper a bank such as Hongkong Bank used in a year. They both agreed that, because HkB was one of the 30 largest banks in the world, they were talking about a huge amount of paper. Ping Soon said that they had already talked about using recycled paper. Farheen replied that how businesses used paper was often more important than the type of paper they used. Ideally they should use unbleached recycled paper, but the appearance of this type of paper was unacceptable to some people. What they might do was to use unbleached recycled paper internally and a finer grade of recycled paper for correspondence.

A bank also could use a Management Information System to replace written memos with e-mail to reduce the amount of paper it needed internally. It also should institute a company-wide recycling/reuse program to use paper more responsibly within the organization. Did people realize how much demand for recycled paper one firm the size of HkB could generate? Ping Soon was beginning to see her point. Farheen continued that it didn't stop there. What types of businesses did a bank such as HkB finance? What if they made money available to environmentally friendly businesses at a more attractive rate, or encouraged construction of energy- and material-efficient buildings with preferential lending rates?

Ping Soon thought about these things for a while and then asked how many banks were doing all these things? He knew of none. How many were doing any of them? After speaking with the director of NCE, Ping Soon found out that Richard Hale, the general manager of HkB in Singapore, had a history of environmental activism. He also knew that the headquarters of HkB was in Hong Kong and that its management probably was not too concerned about or even aware of the environment in Singapore. Mr. Hale had to balance his personal beliefs regarding Hongkong Bank's role in the environment with his responsibilities of managing the operation of the bank in Singapore profitably. His personal values were not necessarily shared by the whole organization.

After considering the issues, Ping Soon could not decide if he should send in his application for the "Care-for-Nature" credit card. He felt that he should support a company that was making an effort. He agreed that Farheen had brought up some good points but thought that these issues might have more impact coming from a customer. Ping Soon did not want to be "greenwashed" by a marketing program into thinking that his money was supporting an important cause when it was simply increasing the company's sales. He expected more from the companies with whom he chose to do business. He also felt that as a customer he was in a better position to make demands. He knew that the "Care-for-Nature" Fund had done some good things for the environment, but he still wondered whether the Hongkong Bank actually did care for nature.

QUESTIONS FOR DISCUSSION

1. How many products or services have you seen advertised as "environmentally friendly"? What does "environmentally friendly" mean to you? Do these products meet your expectations?

2. What do you assume about a company that makes environmental claims regarding its products? Do you expect a higher level of corporate social performance? What are the risks involved for a corporation that decides on this kind of product positioning or CSR strategy?

3. What do you actually know about businesses that make "environmentally friendly" claims? What would you want to know?

4. Is it important that the routine operation of the firm reflect the position of responsibility presented on its product(s), or is it enough that the company has offered a "responsible" choice for consumers?

5. How much should the values and mores of the general manager of Hongkong Bank, Singapore, affect the operation of his organization?

6. What should Ping Soon do? Why?

Little Enough or Too Much?

21

Bryan was recently hired by a large chemical company to oversee the construction of production facilities to produce a new product. X Chemical developed a new industrial lubricant which it felt it could produce at a price close to those of its competitors. The plant to manufacture the lubricant was built on land adjacent to the East River. X Chemical had already applied for and received the necessary permit to dump waste materials from the process into the river. Several other chemical plants in the near vicinity are also releasing waste materials into the river.

Bryan is concerned because the government agency which oversees the permit process granted X Chemical a permit to release more waste into the river than previously anticipated. An additional stage in the production process which would have reduced the waste and recycled some materials became unnecessary due to the regulatory agency's decision. Because the additional process would have added capital and production costs, it was not built as part of the existing plant. Yet, X Chemical has always stated publicly that it would do all that it could to protect the environment from harmful materials.

The company has had mediocre performance for several quarters, and everyone is anxious to see the new product do well. Tests have shown it to be a top-quality industrial lubricant which can now be produced at a cost significantly below those of their competitors. Orders have been flowing in, and the plant is selling everything it can produce. Morale in the company has increased significantly because of the success of the new product. Due to the success of the new product, all employees are looking forward to sizable bonuses from the company's profit sharing plan.

Bryan is upset that the company failed to build the additional stage on the plant and fears that the excess waste released today will cause problems for the company tomorrow. Bryan approaches Bill Gates, the plant supervisor, with his concerns. Bill replies, "It's up to the government agency to protect the river from excess waste, and the company only had to meet the agency's standards. The amount of waste being released poses no threat to the environment, according to the agency. The engineers and chemists who originally designed the production process must have been too conservative in their estimates. Even if the agency made a mistake, the additional recycling and waste reduction process can be added later when it becomes necessary. At this point, building the additional process would require costly interruptions in the production process and might cause customers to switch to our competitors. Heck, environmental groups might become suspicious if production was stopped to add the additional process—They might see it as an admission of wrongdoing. No one in the company wants to attract any unwarranted attention from the environmental groups. They give us enough trouble as it is. The best thing we can do is make money while the company can and deal with issues as they come up. Don't go trying to cause trouble without any proof. The company doesn't like troublemakers, so watch your step. You're new here, and you wouldn't want to have to find a new job."

Bryan is frustrated and upset. He can see all the benefits of the new product, but inside he is sure the company is making a short-sighted decision which will hurt them in the long run. The vice president of operations will tour the plant next week, and Bryan is considering approaching the officer with his concerns. It might also be possible to contact the government agency and request that the permit be reviewed. Bryan is unsure what to do, but he feels he should do something.

This case was originally developed by Eric Heist, graduate student at Washington University, as a class project in "Ethical Decision Making." Edited and submitted by Dr. Raymond L. Hilgert, Professor of Management and Industrial Relations, Washington University. Permission granted to reprint by Arthur Andersen & Co., SC.

QUESTIONS FOR DISCUSSION

1. What are the social or ethical issues in this case?
2. Are the ethical issues in this case those of the firm or of Bryan?

3. Assess the corporate social responsibility of the firm based on the comments of Bill Gates, the plant supervisor.

4. What ethical responsibility, if any, does Bryan have in this case? What should he do? Why?

Employment-at-Will? 22

Betty Brewer was fired from her position as a nurse's helper at the Watkinsville Nursing Home (WNH) in Birmingham, Alabama. Betty believed that the employee handbook that had been given to her when she was hired constituted a contract of employment. Not only did she feel she was wrongfully discharged, but she also felt that her termination constituted extreme and outrageous conduct that intentionally or recklessly caused her severe emotional distress.

Betty maintained that she was being dismissed for a reason not specifically listed in the employee handbook. Further, she felt that the choice WNH had given her of resigning or being fired caused her severe emotional strain.

In defending its position, the nursing home pointed out that the general common-law rule is that an employee may be terminated at will. It also stated that under Alabama law an employment contract may be terminated by either party for a good reason, a wrong reason, or no reason at all. As for the handbook, WNH presented several excerpts. First, on the inside cover of the handbook was the following statement:

> *This handbook and the policies contained herein do not in any way constitute, and should not be construed as, a contract of employment between the employer and the employee, or a promise of employment.*

WNH went on to argue that there was no evidence anywhere that Betty had been told that she could be terminated only for the reasons listed on page 20 of the handbook. It stated that this must have been Betty's assumption. WNH pointed out that page 20 of the handbook clearly stated that the reasons for dismissal "include, but are not limited to, the follow-

ing . . . " (a list of reasons followed). The company further added, and Betty agreed, that there had been no agreement as to the length or duration of employment and that therefore the term of employment was indefinite.

QUESTIONS FOR DISCUSSION

1. Do you think that Betty was wrongly discharged or that she was legitimately dismissed under the notion of employment-at-will?
2. Do you think, based on the evidence presented, that the company did enough to clearly establish that an employee could be fired for reasons not listed in the employee handbook?
3. In your opinion, did the fact that the nursing home gave Betty the option of resigning or being fired constitute outrageous conduct that intentionally or recklessly caused her severe emotional distress?
4. What implications does this case have for the relationship between employer and employee?

This case was prepared by Archie B. Carroll.

The Letter to the Editor

23

One of the most significant tensions between employers and employees is an employee's freedom or right to speak out. In some extreme cases, the employee "blows the whistle" on his or her employer by going to a government agency or a newspaper and reporting some alleged wrongdoing. One view is that employees have a right to blow the whistle and should be protected against employer retaliation.[1] Many management groups, however, think employees owe loyalty to their employers. Some writers on this subject think that First Amendment rights need to be watched closely and that they do not give employees the right to thwart the boss.[2] Another writer has stated the issue as follows: "Where does a corporate employee's duty to the firm end and his right of free speech as a citizen begin?"[3]

THE INCIDENT

John Cox, a 14-year postal clerk in his mid-30s, was angered by an editorial he read in the newspaper.[4] The editorial was critical of the U.S. Postal Service. Cox was so upset that he sat down and typed out a letter to the editor in which he sought to defend his employer.

His superiors at the Van Nuys, California, postal branch were pleased on reading the letter, which was published, until they got to the last paragraph. Cox concluded his letter as follows: "Despite some of the worst management in industrial society, postal workers move more mail faster and cheaper than anywhere else in the world." This paragraph wiped the smiles off his superiors' faces.[5]

MANAGEMENT'S RESPONSE

Twelve days later, Cox received an official disciplinary letter of warning from his boss. The charge against him was "disloyalty to the Postal Service." The warning letter was placed in his personnel file.

This case was prepared by Archie B. Carroll. Names have been changed, but all other case facts remain the same as they were reported.

This meant that it could affect future promotions or other personnel decisions if he committed other infractions. Other such infractions could eventually result in his being fired. The warning also accused him of violating a Postal Service Code of Ethics that required employees to conduct themselves in a manner that reflects favorably on the Postal Service.[6]

COX FIGHTS BACK

Cox, who had also served as a union shop steward, decided to fight back. He filed a complaint with the National Labor Relations Board. He filed a grievance with his union, the San Fernando Valley local of the American Postal Workers Union, and also with the Equal Employment Opportunity office. In explaining his actions, he said that all he was trying to do was defend the Postal Service because he was tired of people criticizing it and blaming it for rate hikes. Cox thought that the warning letter was in retaliation for his union activities and two previous disputes he had had with his superiors. He added that he was only trying to state what was obvious to him and that he did not refer to any single individual in the letter. He also said he didn't expect *The Los Angeles Times* to publish the letter.

Cox's coworkers seemed almost gleeful about the dispute. One clerk said, "We're all getting a lot of laughs because this is going to come back and hurt management."

QUESTIONS FOR DISCUSSION

1. Do you think Cox went too far in making the statement critical of Postal Service management?
2. In your opinion, was Cox disloyal or did he engage in behavior that violated the Code of Ethics? Was this a reasonable expectation to be placed in a code of ethics?
3. What is your assessment of the supervisor's action in giving Cox an official disciplinary letter of warning?
4. How would you have handled this case if you had been Cox's supervisor?

CASE ENDNOTES

1. Nancy Hauserman, "Whistle-Blowing: Individual Morality in a Corporate Society," *Business Horizons* (March–April, 1986), 4.
2. Charles G. Bakaly, Jr. and Joel M. Grossman, "Does First Amendment Let Employees Thwart the Boss?" *The Wall Street Journal* (December 8, 1983), 30.
3. Alan F. Westin, "Employee Free Speech," *The Wall Street Journal* (November 10, 1980), 28.
4. "'Disloyal' Post Office Worker Reprimanded for Critical Letter," *The Atlanta Journal* (April 23, 1985).
5. *Ibid.*
6. *Ibid.*

The Case of the Fired Waitress 24

Ruth Hatton, a waitress for a Red Lobster restaurant in Pleasant Hills, Pennsylvania, was fired from her job because she had stolen a guest-comment card that had been deposited in the customer comment box by a disgruntled couple. The couple, who happened to be black, had been served by Ms. Hatton and were unhappy with the treatment they perceived they got from her. At the time of her firing, Ms. Hatton, age 53, had been a 19-year veteran employee. She said, "It felt like a knife going through me."

THE INCIDENT

The couple had gone to the Red Lobster restaurant for dinner. According to Hatton, the woman had requested a well-done piece of prime rib. After she was served, she complained that the meat was fatty and undercooked. Hatton then said she politely suggested to the woman that "prime rib always has fat on it." Hatton later explained that, based on her experience with black customers in the working-class area in which the restaurant was located, the customer might have gotten prime rib confused with spare rib.

Upon receiving the complaint, Hatton explained that she returned the meat to the kitchen to be cooked further. When the customer continued to be displeased, Hatton offered the couple a free dessert. The customer continued to be unhappy, doused the prime rib with steak sauce, then pushed it away from her plate. The customer then filled out a restaurant comment card, deposited it in the customer comment box, paid her bill, and left with her husband.

This case was prepared by Archie B. Carroll.

Ms. Hatton explained that she was very curious as to what the woman had written on the comment card, so she went to the hostess and asked for the key to the comment box. She said she then read the card and put it in her pocket with the intention of showing it to her supervisor, Diane Canant, later. Hatton said that Canant, the restaurant's general manager, had commented earlier that the prime rib was overcooked, not undercooked. Apparently, the restaurant had had a problem that day with the cooking equipment and was serving meat that had been cooked the previous day and then was being reheated before being served. Later, Ms. Hatton said that she had forgotten about the comment card and had inadvertently thrown it out. It also came out that it is against Red Lobster's policy to serve reheated meat, and the chain no longer serves prime rib.

Canant said that she fired Ms. Hatton after the angry customer complained to her and to her supervisor. Somehow, the customer had learned later that Ms. Hatton had removed the comment card from the box. Ms. Canant recalled, "The customer felt violated because her card was taken from the box and she felt that her complaint about the food had been ignored." Referring to the company's policy manual, Canant said Ms. Hatton was fired because she violated the restaurant's rule forbidding the removal of company property.

Another person to comment on the incident was the hostess, Dawn Brown, then a 17-year-old student, who had been employed by the restaurant for the summer. Dawn stated, "I didn't think it was a big deal to give her the key (to the comment box). A lot of people would come and get the key from her."

THE PEER REVIEW PROCESS

Ms. Hatton felt she had been unjustly fired for this incident. Rather than filing suit against the restaurant, however, she decided to take advantage of the store's peer review process. The parent company of Red Lobster, Darden Restaurants, had 4 years earlier adopted a peer review program as an alternative dispute resolution mechanism. Many companies across the country have adopted the peer review method as an alternative to lengthy lawsuits and as an avenue of easing workplace tensions.

Executives at Red Lobster observed that the peer review program had been "tremendously successful." It helped to keep valuable employees from unfair dismissals and it had reduced the company's legal bills for employee disputes by $1 million annually. Close to 100 cases have been heard through the peer review process, with only 10 resulting in lawsuits. Executives at the company also said that the process has reduced racial tensions. In some cases, the peer review panels have reversed decisions made by managers who had overreacted to complaints from minority customers and employees.

HATTON'S PEER REVIEW PANEL

The peer review panel chosen to handle Ruth Hatton's case was a small group of Red Lobster employees from the surrounding area. The panel included a general manager, an assistant manager, a hostess, a server, and a bartender, all of whom had volunteered to serve on the panel. The peer review panel members had undergone special peer-review training and were being paid their regular wages and travel expenses. The peer review panel was convened about 3 weeks after Hatton's firing. According to Red Lobster policy, the panel was empowered to hear testimony and to even overturn management decisions and award damages.

The panel met in a conference room at a hotel near Pittsburgh and proceeded to hear testimony from Ruth Hatton, store manager Diane Canant, and hostess Dawn Brown. The three testified as to what had happened in the incident.

Through careful deliberations, the panelists tried to balance the customer's hurt feelings with what Hatton had done and why, and with the fact that a company policy may have been violated. Initially, the panel was split along job category lines, with the hourly workers supporting Ms. Hatton and the managers supporting store management. After an hour and a half of deliberations, however, everyone was finally moving in the same direction and the panel finally came to a unanimous opinion as to what should be done.

QUESTIONS FOR DISCUSSION

1. What are the ethical issues in this case from an employee's point of view? From management's point of view? From a consumer's point of view?
2. Who are the stakeholders, and what are their stakes?
3. As a peer review panel member, how would you judge this case? Do you think Ms. Hatton stole company property? Do you think the discharge should be upheld?
4. Do you think the peer review method of resolving work complaints is a desirable substitute for lawsuits? What are its strengths and weaknesses?
5. If you had been Ms. Hatton, would you be willing to turn your case over to a peer review panel like this and then be willing to live with the results?

CASE REFERENCE

1. Margaret A. Jacobs, "Red Lobster Tale: Peers Decide Fired Waitress's Fate," *The Wall Street Journal* (January 20, 1998), B1, B4.

A Moral Dilemma: Head versus Heart 25

SITUATION

A 42-year-old male suddenly and unexpectedly dies of a brain tumor, leaving behind a wife and small child. During a review of his employee benefits, it was noted that although he was eligible for an additional company-sponsored life insurance plan used for plant decommissioning purposes, his name was not identified on the insurance rolls.

EVALUATION

It was determined that when the employee was promoted to supervisor 3 years before his death, his paperwork had been submitted to the corporate office for inclusion in the program. Coincidentally, the program was under review at the time, and the employee was not entered into the program due to administrative oversight.

LEGAL

A legal department review determined that the program was offered to certain supervisory employees at the discretion of the company. Therefore, there was no legal obligation to pay.

DILEMMA

The death benefit was twice the employee's salary. Because the employee was not enrolled in the life insurance program, if the company were to pay any benefit, it would have to come from the general fund (paid from the business unit's annual operating budget).

DISCUSSION

To pay or not to pay? The company could argue that it must start acting like a business and use its head, not its heart. Existing company programs adequately compensate the individual's family; no additional dollars should be paid. On the other hand, it was an administrative oversight that failed to enter the employee into the program. What would you want the company to do for you if you were the one who suddenly died?

QUESTIONS FOR DISCUSSION

1. As a manager, you are steward of the company's funds. Are you willing to forego departmental improvements and potential salary increases to honor this claim? Remember, there is no legal obligation to pay.
2. Would you feel obligated to pay? Would you be perceived as a weak manager if you do?
3. What are the ethical issues in this case?
4. What would you do?

This case was prepared by David A. Lavigne.

The Case of the Questionable Order 26

Pauline Gossett had been working for Southwestern Color Lithographers for a year and a half and had proved to be a very capable employee. Southwestern specialized in commercial printing and handled many different types of printing jobs, such as booklets, business cards, certificates, church bulletins, labels, letterheads, newsletters, wedding invitations, and so on. Pauline had started out with Southwestern as a secretary, but in the past 9 months she had begun taking on other responsibilities because several other female employees were out due to pregnancies.

The major responsibility she had just taken on was that of providing information about the range of printing services and prices available at Southwestern. It was common in the printing industry for potential customers to seek pricing and service information over the phone. Much to Pauline's dismay, she learned that it had been the practice of her superior, James Smith, to require that such phone inquiries be recorded. His statement to Pauline was, "Do not let customers know that we are recording their phone calls. This information is for our sales and product analyses and there is no need for callers to know about it."

The night that she learned of the recording practice she went home feeling very uneasy. After a short discussion with her husband, Leonard, they both agreed that it wasn't right and that she ought to talk with her boss about it. The next day she tried to bring the topic up gently with Smith, but he obviously did not want to talk about it and quickly retorted, "There is nothing wrong with what we are doing, so don't you worry your little head about it. Anyway, we checked with the state attorney general's office and we were assured that we are not violating either state or federal law with our practice."

Pauline reported her brief discussion with Smith to her husband that evening, and he was not pleased with Smith's reaction. The two discussed her options at this point and concluded that she could not

ignore the issue and should bring it up with Smith's boss, the owner of Southwestern Color Lithographers. The next morning she made an appointment with Mr. Allen Kirby, owner of the company. She explained to Kirby how she was very happy at the company and was especially pleased that her job duties had been expanded to include handling telephone inquiries. She liked this role because she firmly believed that the person explaining services and prices was very influential in landing new accounts. Then she got to her concern about the phone calls being recorded. After briefly explaining why she did not think it was right, she exploded in a burst of tears, "I would rather quit my job than do something I think is wrong!" After the brief outburst, Pauline ran out of the office before Kirby had a chance to respond.

QUESTIONS FOR DISCUSSION

1. Identify the social and/or ethical issues that are present in this case. What was wrong with what Smith was asking Pauline to do?
2. Put yourself in the position of Kirby. What available options do you see at this point? What are the arguments for and against each option?
3. Still in the role of Kirby, what course of action will you take, and why?

This case was prepared by Archie B. Carroll.

Personal Opinion and the Federal Government 27

KARL MERTZ
AND POLICIES AT THE USDA

Karl Mertz's life was going well. He had been an employee of the federal government for 15 years and the senior equal employment manager at the U.S. Department of Agriculture (USDA) in Athens, Georgia, for seven years. In his position as an equal opportunity manager, he enforced the Civil Rights Act, which holds that employee information based on race, sex, age, or religious beliefs is forbidden. He was considered a leader in such areas as racism and sexism, and his experience was backed by a doctorate in race relations.[1]

Inspired by a television program, "The Coral Ridge Hour," that encourages people to speak up for what they believe in, Mertz made a public statement that has changed the direction of his life. He believed that the USDA and other government agencies were being pressured to recognize the homosexual lifestyle as mainstream. He did not believe, however, that it was appropriate to put homosexuals on an equal footing with women and minorities with respect to civil rights.[2]

On March 4, 1994, while on vacation, Karl Mertz told a reporter from WLOX-TV in Biloxi, Mississippi, that the "USDA has had a reputation, rightly or wrongly, of having a plantation mentality, and no one would deny we need to get away from that kind of situation. But we need to be moving toward Camelot, not toward Sodom and Gomorrah. And I'm afraid that that's where our leadership is taking us."[3] His reference to Sodom and Gomorrah was based upon the USDA's decision to add "sexual orientation" to its nondiscrimination policy, which meant that homosexuals could lodge job discrimination claims just as women and minorities could. However, what bothered Mertz the most was a proposal to extend benefits such as health and life insurance to homosexual partners of department personnel. Mertz felt this proposal was "an abomination as well as a waste of taxpayer's money if that was

This case was written by Sarah Wilcox. Used with permission.

ever to be pulled off."[4] He saw that "a policy intended to provide justice for minorities became warped into favoritism for women, blacks and homosexuals."[5] "We're all sinners, but that doesn't mean you have your sins turned into civil rights. There are limits to pluralism. There are limits to tolerance. If this line isn't drawn here, the next debate is going to be about consensual incest and bestiality."[6]

Mertz believed his comments were protected under the First Amendment for freedom of speech. He indicated in the interview that his comments did not represent company policy. Soon after the televised interview, Agriculture Secretary Mike Espy received a multitude of calls from gay rights advocates. Three weeks after his comments, Karl Mertz was transferred without notice or due process.[7] On March 28, 1994, Karl Mertz received a letter indicating that he was being removed from the Equal Employment Opportunity staff because his views stated in the interview "reflect a disagreement with departmental civil rights policy. As a private citizen you have every right to express your opinions freely. . . . However, you must recognize the fact that in publicly disagreeing with an admittedly controversial position of the departmental leadership, you have made it difficult for employees and managers of the agency to accept that you actively support these same policies in your official assignment."[8]

Karl Mertz was transferred to a management analyst position despite his lack of skills or interest. Mertz stated, "In the old USSR, if you spoke out against the party line they sent you to Siberia. . . . In the new USDA, if you speak out against the political correctness, they take your offices and secretary away and put you in a broom closet."[9]

To Mertz, both his freedom of speech and religion were ignored. He also thought that the USDA and the Agricultural Research Service were developing a workplace that was antiheterosexual. His complaint to the Office of Special Counsel claimed that his transfer was without due process and was in retaliation for him exercising his right to free speech. Yet, being a government employee does limit his freedom according to Ruth Larson, a writer for *The*

Washington Times. According to Larson, "Government employees who disclose fraud or abuse are protected under whistle-blower laws. But their rights under the First Amendment must relate to matters of public concern, and their interests are weighed against the government's."[10]

HELMS BACKS MERTZ

The Republican Senator Jesse Helms from North Carolina did not agree with the USDA's handling of Karl Mertz. He believes strongly in the freedom of speech and thinks that Mertz was violated. In a June 27, 1994, personal memo to Mike Espy, Helms wrote, "Neither USDA nor any other federal entity is going to get by with pushing faithful people like Mertz around. I don't know the man, but I have looked into this episode and Mertz does not deserve the treatment he's getting. Put Mertz back on his job and I'll remove my holds from USDA nominations and projects. . . ."[11]

Mike Espy was not so easily swayed. In a July 19, 1994, letter, he supported his department's policies, stating: "There is no gay rights 'agenda' at the department and there will certainly be no seminars or 'sensitivity training' sessions to promote acceptance of alternate 'lifestyles.'" He also wrote, "Dr. Mertz's public statements indicate that he strongly disagrees with and thus cannot faithfully implement current policies in equal employment opportunity."[12]

Helms felt strongly that a government employee should be free to express his personal opinion without fear of being reprimanded. To make his point, in July of 1994 he put a hold on USDA nominations and projects and he proposed amendments directly related to the issue. One amendment from Helms prohibited "the use of taxpayer funds to encourage employees to accept homosexuality as a legitimate or normal lifestyle" and was passed with a definitive majority of 92–8 on July 19, 1994. He proposed another amendment "prohibiting the removal, without public hearings, of employees who make remarks on personal time opposing the USDA's homosexual policies," which passed through the Senate 59–41 on July 20, 1994.[13] The amendment is retroactive, which means that Mertz would be sent back to his old job. Both amendments still needed to be passed through the House of Representatives. On Tuesday, July 19, Senator Helms made the following comment on the Senate floor: "The Clinton administration has launched a concerted effort to extend special rights to homosexuals in the federal workplace—rights not accorded to other groups and individuals. The Department of Agriculture is obviously at the forefront of this effort."[14] A Department of Transportation GLOBE (Gay, Lesbian or Bisexual Employees) representative stated that the amendments proposed by Helms were "blatantly discrimination" and "the message it sends is 'It's open season on gays and lesbians.'"[15]

Helms was upset with many of the activities promoting the gay lifestyle, such as the official sanctioning of GLOBE organizations. He was particularly upset with the creation by the Agriculture Department of the gay, lesbian, and bisexual program manager position in the Foreign Agriculture Service. According to Helms, the purpose of the position is "promoting the gay, lesbian and bisexual employment program and assisting in the recruitment of homosexuals."[16]

BECKETT FUND GETS INVOLVED

The Beckett Fund, a public interest law firm that defends religious freedom, took up Mr. Mertz's cause. It is a bipartisan and ecumenical organization. On Friday, July 22, 1994, the Beckett Fund informed Espy that Mertz would "sue for substantial sums in both compensatory and punitive damages if he was not reinstated immediately with a formal apology and a clear record."[17] Beckett Fund's president and general counsel, Kevin Hasson, expressed to Espy that the lawsuit was for the "bureaucratic retaliation [Mr. Mertz] has suffered at the hands of you and your agency for his religiously based views on the morality of homosexuality."[18] Hasson believed that Mertz's previous actions showed his commitment to equal employment and ability to perform with fairness in his job despite his personal beliefs.[19]

REACTION FROM HOMOSEXUALITY ADVOCACY GROUPS

Gregory King, the spokesman for the Human Rights Campaign Fund, belittled Mr. Mertz's position as he stated, "It undermines the whole concept of the discrimination-free workplace, and it's particularly inappropriate coming from an EEO manager."[20]

Robin Kane, public information manager for the National Gay and Lesbian Task Force, did not believe that Mertz was a victim as she wrote in an article to *The Washington Post:* "In reality, Mertz chose to become a spokesperson by denouncing the USDA antidiscrimination policy and attacking gay people, while maintaining he could conduct himself fairly in his job, in which he was charged with implementing agency policy, including a provision barring discrimination based on sexual orientation. In a March 18, 1994, article in the *Biloxi Sun-Herald*, the reporter wrote that Mertz 'had been granting interviews lately—jeopardizing his career—because he is disturbed over homosexual federal employees who think they should be treated the same as heterosexuals.' The reporter wrote [about Mertz], 'He cringes at the thought of same-sex partners rubbing shoulders with him and his wife . . . Mertz views homosexuals as sex addicts . . . the lifestyle offends Mertz.' Mertz is quoted as saying, 'In my mind, I'm equating these three groups of people to the compulsive-obsessive behavior that's associated with alcoholism. . . . You're not doing them any good by, quote, accepting them for what they are. . . . Abstinence or, eventually, gene therapy, may be the only solution.'" Robin Kane believes that "These are not the statements of a victim."[21]

BECKETT FUND RESPONDS

In response to the accusations by the Gay and Lesbian Task Force, Nathan Forrester, director of appellate litigation for the Beckett Fund for Religious Liberty, said:

> The sincerity of Mertz's commitment to the civil rights of all people, including homosexuals, is beyond reproach. A generation ago, he would frequently appear as the sole counter-protester at local KKK rallies, and he once was fired as the minister of a Mississippi church for preaching against racial segregation. More recently, he hired a black gay secretary, who later died of AIDS. And in the EEO position from which he was transferred, he actively assisted a transsexual employee who was suffering harassment. Mertz's religious convictions lead him to regard the homosexual lifestyle as immoral, but those same convictions also lead him to show its practitioners compassion and love.
>
> Groups like the task force must stop insinuating that sincere religious opposition to homosexual practice is born of ignorance and hate, if we are ever to have fruitful public discourse on this sensitive topic. Silencing the Karl Mertzes of this world will serve only to aggravate the social tensions that the task force purports to denounce.[22]

DID HELMS GET HIS WAY?

After 4 months, on Monday, October 3, 1994, Senator Helms released his procedural hold on USDA nominations. Mike Espy, as he announced his resignation, agreed to reinstate Karl Mertz to his former position. His offer, however, was contingent on the U.S. Office of Special Counsel's declaring that Mertz's constitutional rights were violated.[23]

QUESTIONS FOR DISCUSSION

1. Who are the stakeholders in this case, and what are their stakes?
2. Was Karl Mertz's freedom of speech violated by the USDA's treatment of him?
3. Was Karl Mertz given fair treatment and due process in this case?
4. Is it appropriate, legal, and ethical for an agency, such as the USDA, to adopt a policy that differs from federal law with respect to the treatment of any group?
5. Can Karl Mertz now perform his job in the EEO office fairly considering his expressed opinions?

CASE ENDNOTES

1. *Religious Rights Newsletter.*
2. "Blowing the Whistle on Gay Agenda at USDA," *Coral Ridge Ministries* (Vol. V, No. 12, December, 1994).
3. Ruth Larson, "Man's Opinions Lead to Transfer: He Spoke Against Gay Rights at Agriculture Department," *The Washington Times* (June 13, 1994), A6.
4. *Coral Ridge Ministries.*
5. Mike Christensen, "Helms Holds Up Bill Over Demoted Worker," *Palm Beach Post* (July 23, 1994), 14A.
6. Mike Christensen, "Criticizing Clinton Conservatives Line Up Behind Demoted Worker," *The Atlanta Journal and Constitution* (July 23, 1994), A6.
7. *Coral Ridge Ministries.*
8. "Helms Vs. Espy, Round One, Etc." (Editorial), *The Washington Times* (July 23, 1994), D2.
9. Christensen, *Palm Beach Post,* 14A.
10. Larson, A6.
11. Ruth Larson, "Helms Leads Charge to Return Anti-gay Man to His USDA Post: Employee's Comments to TV Reporter Resulted In Transfer," *The Washington Times* (July 21, 1994), A6.

12. *Ibid.*

13. "Helms vs. Espy, Round One, Etc.," D2.

14. Larson, July 21, 1994, A6.

15. Ruth Larson, "Helms Takes Aim at Pro-gay Programs," *The Washington Times* (January 23, 1995), A10.

16. *Ibid.*

17. Ruth Larson, "Espy Sued by Worker Critical of Gay Policy," *The Washington Times* (July 26, 1994), A6.

18. *Ibid.*

19. *Ibid.*

20. Larson, June 13, 1994.

21. "And the Victim Is . . . " (Editorial), *The Washington Post* (September 3, 1994), A21.

22. "Sincere Religious Opposition" (Editorial), *The Washington Post* (September 10, 1994), A21.

23. Ruth Larson, "Helms Lets 6 Nominations Proceed After Demoted Worker Gets Job Back," *The Washington Times* (October 5, 1994), A8.

True Confessions

28

Joe Smith was an engineer who had been with the company for 11 years. He had always been a dedicated employee as well as a competent, high-producing employee. He often relieved his supervisor, Bob Jones, when Jones was absent from work.

The manager of engineering, Bill Davis, was new in his position and had never worked directly with Joe or Bob. During his first week in the new position, Bob asked Bill to meet and discuss one of Bob's employees. It turns out that Joe confessed to Bob that he had abused some of his privileges over the years and now wanted to reimburse the company. Specifically, Joe said that over the course of his career he had made a few thousand photocopies for personal use on company copy machines. Several years ago, on a few occasions, he also had entered higher amounts for meals on his expense account than he had actually spent. On one occasion, 3 years earlier, Joe said he took home some "scrap" materials from a job site that he said probably had some salvage value. The total Joe felt he owed the company was $2,000. Joe offered to work overtime to compensate the company for its losses.

QUESTIONS FOR DISCUSSION

1. What action should Bill and Bob take? What ethical principles apply?

2. Should this matter be discussed with anyone else?

3. Should the fact that this took place a few years ago influence the decision?

4. Should corporate policies regarding employee theft be followed in this situation? Why? Why not?

Early Retirement: Reward for Whom? 29

Cost reduction is a theme common among electric utilities today as they prepare for competition. Many utilities are finding it necessary to reduce employee numbers to meet their cost-reduction targets. Early retirement programs have become a popular and positive means of reducing employee numbers. Early retirement incentives are often lucrative enough that the demand to participate in the programs is greater than the target reduction. Therefore, employees scrutinize management's process of implementing early retirement programs to ensure they do so fairly.

As the manager of the Southern region of USA Electric, Inc., Dan has determined that he must eliminate one of his supervisory positions to meet his targeted cost reduction. He can offer an early retirement incentive to any employee whose position he eliminates, provided the employee meets certain qualifications, specifically 50 years of age and 10 years of service. The early retirement program is popular among the qualifying members in the organization, and several qualifying supervisors in the Southern region have expressed interest in accepting early retirement. Dan must choose which supervisor should receive the early retirement package.

With 35 years of service, Jack is the most senior supervisor in Dan's organization. Dan characterizes Jack as a typical "old-school" supervisor. He works hard and is an experienced operations man, but he is cynical of many of the changes taking place at USA Electric. Jack has shown little initiative in changing his leadership style, much less trying new approaches to doing business. Jack has decided that he would prefer to retire than to continue to face the new challenges facing his department. He views the early retirement package as "his to turn down" because he is the senior supervisor in the region. Dan would like to see Jack retire because he is doubtful that he will ever change. If Jack does not retire under this program, he will probably be around at least 3 more years until he takes normal retirement.

Bob is another of Dan's supervisors in the Southern region. Bob is an invaluable member of Dan's staff. He has adapted to the fast-changing environment of USA Electric and has been progressive about making changes to reduce costs and improve service. However, Bob is 58 years old, has 33 years of service, and would very much like to accept early retirement. Bob believes he is most deserving of the early retirement package because he has been the best performer among the supervisors in Dan's organization. Dan would hate to lose Bob, because he depends on him greatly to transition his area into a more competitive work unit.

Dan's boss told him that he has complete freedom to select early-retirement candidates as long as they meet the minimum age and years-of-service requirements.

QUESTIONS FOR DISCUSSION

1. Should Dan take advantage of this opportunity to retire Jack, one of his obstacles to change in his organization? After all, Jack is the most senior supervisor in his area.
2. Should Dan reward Bob, his best supervisor, for contributing to the organization?
3. What are the ethical issues that come into play in this case?

This case was prepared by Rusty Harris.

30

Short Shorts

Lucy, a college student, is a waitress at a popular eating and drinking establishment called The Sandtrap, located on the local beach. This restaurant is known for nightly bands and great entertainment. The usual uniform for waitresses is jeans or similar long pants and a "Sandtrap" T-shirt.

Business is always good during the spring and summer months while everyone is vacationing, but during the winter months there is a steady decline. In an effort to improve business during the off-season months, Fred, The Sandtrap's owner, tried a number of new strategies and gimmicks to increase patronage. One plan was to offer extended happy hour specials and complimentary finger foods to customers. His latest successful strategy is to require all waitresses to wear low-cut and tight-fitting shirts and very short shorts.

Sales have improved with the new dress, but there have also been some problems. Many male customers make lewd and abusive remarks to the wait-

resses, particularly after having several drinks. Lucy is tired of being abused by customers' physical and verbal actions, so she consults Don, the manager, and tells him that she will no longer wear the skimpy outfit. Don tells her to wear the revealing attire for the present.

Now, in view of her complaints, Don has to decide what he is going to do. He is reluctant to allow Lucy to go back to the old uniform since he is convinced that the new, revealing clothing is drawing customers that the restaurant badly needs.

This case was written by Dr. Marilyn M. Helms, Associate Professor of Management, University of Tennessee at Chattanooga. Permission to reprint granted by Arthur Andersen & Co., SC.

QUESTIONS FOR DISCUSSION

1. What are the ethical and legal issues in this case?
2. Is it illegal sexual harassment when customers harass a service employee in a restaurant? Discuss what are Lucy's rights? What are Don's rights?
3. Should Don require Lucy to continue wearing the skimpy outfit? If he allows Lucy to discontinue wearing the outfit, must he allow others to do the same if they request it?
4. What should Lucy do if Don requires her to continue wearing the new outfit?

31

Propmore Corporation

OVERVIEW

Don Bradford was on the fast track at the Propmore Corporation. But he wished he could slow things down a bit, given several hard choices he had to make.

Propmore Corporation was a good place to work. It had sales of about $500 million per year, a net profit margin of 5 percent, and a return on equity of

This case was developed by Dr. Peter Madsen and Dr. John Fleming for Arthur Andersen & Co., SC. Used by permission of Arthur Andersen & Co., SC.

15 percent. Propmore made several key components used by the aerospace industry and the consumer goods market. It was a leader in its field. The company was organized by product divisions, each reporting to the executive vice president. Its operations were decentralized, with broad decision-making capability at the divisional level. However, at the corporate level, functional departments (Purchasing, R&D, Personnel, and Marketing) set company policy and coordinated divisional activities in these areas. Propmore was financially successful, and it treated its people well, as Don Bradford's experience had shown.

After earning his M.B.A. from a respected state university, Don had for 4 years quickly risen through the ranks of the Purchasing Department. At age 31, he held the prestigious position of purchasing manager (see organization chart, Figure C-31). Before joining Propmore, Don had earned a B.S. in engineering and had worked for 3 years in the aerospace industry as a design engineer. During his first 3 years at Propmore, Don had been a buyer and had received "excellent" ratings in all his performance appraisals. As purchasing manager, Don enjoyed good working relationships with both superiors and subordinates. He was accountable directly to the division general manager and, functionally, to the corporate vice president of procurement, Mr. Stewart. His dealings with these people were always amiable, and he came to count on them for technical guidance as he learned the role of divisional purchasing manager. Don had several staff assistants who knew the business of buying and were loyal employees. He had done a good job of handling the resentment of those passed over by his promotion to manager, and he had developed a good deal of trust with the buying staff—at least he thought he had until Jane Thompson presented him with the first in a series of dilemmas. Jane Thompson, age 34, had been with Propmore for 10 years. She had a B.A. in English literature and had had 2 years of experience as a material expediter before coming to Propmore. Initially hired as a purchasing assistant, Jane had become a buyer after 2 years. She enjoyed her job and the people she worked with at Propmore. In 4 years of working with Don, Jane had come to admire and respect his approach to management. She appreciated his sensitive yet strong leadership and saw him as an honest person who could be trusted to look after the interests of his subordinates. But the dilemma with which Jane now presented Don made him wonder whether he had the skill to be a manager in a major division.

SITUATION I

A Luncheon Harassment

After a 2-hour purchasing meeting one morning, Bill Smith, an Airgoods Corporation sales representative, had invited Jane Thompson to lunch. They left at noon. An hour and a half later, Jane stormed into Don Bradford's office, obviously upset. When Don asked what was wrong, Jane told him in very strong terms that Bill Smith had sexually harassed her during and after the luncheon.

According to Jane, Bill made some sexual comments and suggestions toward the end of the meal. She considered this behavior to be offensive and unwelcome. Jane, however, told Bill to take her back to the office. He attempted to make light of the situation and said he was only joking, but on the way back he made some further comments and several casual physical contacts to which she objected. When they arrived at the company, Bill was embarrassed and tried to apologize, but Jane entered the office before he could finish.

Jane demanded that the Airgoods Corporation be taken off the bidder list for the raw material contract and that Airgoods' president be informed of the unseemly and illegal behavior of Bill Smith. She said that she was also considering taking legal action against Bill Smith through the Equal Employment Opportunity Commission for sexual harassment and suing the Propmore Corporation for failure to protect her from this form of discrimination while she was performing her duties as an employee of the company. At the end of this outburst, Jane abruptly left Don's office.

Don was significantly troubled. Jane played a critical role in getting bids for the raw material contract. He needed her. Yet, he knew that if he kept Airgoods on the bidder list, it might be difficult for her to view this vendor objectively.

Don was somewhat concerned about Jane's threat to sue Propmore but doubted that she had a very good case. Still, such an action would be costly in legal fees, management time, and damage to the company's image.

Don wasn't sure what to do about the bidder list. Airgoods had an excellent record as a reliable vendor for similar contracts. Propmore might be at a disadvantage if Airgoods was eliminated. On the other hand, Don firmly believed in standing behind his subordinates.

At this point, he needed more information on what constituted sexual harassment and what policy guidelines his company had established. He examined two documents: the EEOC Definition of Sexual Harassment (Appendix 1) and the Propmore Corporation's Policy HR-13, on Sexual Harassment (Appendix 2).

FIGURE C–31 The Propmore Corporation (Partial Organization Chart)

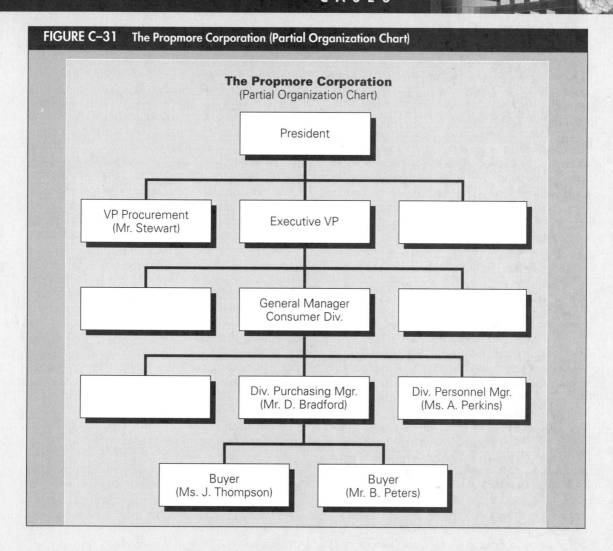

The Propmore Corporation
(Partial Organization Chart)

President

VP Procurement
(Mr. Stewart)

Executive VP

General Manager
Consumer Div.

Div. Purchasing Mgr.
(Mr. D. Bradford)

Div. Personnel Mgr.
(Ms. A. Perkins)

Buyer
(Ms. J. Thompson)

Buyer
(Mr. B. Peters)

QUESTIONS FOR DISCUSSION

1. What are the major issues in this case?
2. How should Don Bradford react to Jane Thompson's emotional allegation against Bill Smith?
3. What should Don do about Jane's threat to sue Propmore and her demand that the Airgoods Corp. be removed from the bidding list? What would be the ethical justification for these actions?
4. According to your interpretation of what constitutes sexual harassment as defined in Appendix 1, has it occurred in this case?

5. How should Don investigate this incident as required by company policy? What additional information does he need?

APPENDIX 1 (SITUATION 1)

Equal Employment Opportunity Commission Definition Of Sexual Harassment

"Unwelcome sexual advances, requests for sexual favors and other verbal or physical contact of a sexual nature constitute sexual harassment when (1) submission to such conduct is made either explicitly or implicitly a term or condition of an individual's employment, (2) submission to or rejection of such conduct by an individual is used as the basis for employment decisions affecting such individual, or (3) such conduct has the purpose or effect of unreasonably interfering with an individual's work performance or creating an intimidating, hostile or offensive working environment."

"Applying general Title VII principles, an employer, employment agency, joint apprenticeship committee or labor organization (hereinafter collectively referred to as 'employer') is responsible for its acts and those of its agents and supervisory employees with respect to sexual harassment regardless of whether the employer knew or should have known of their occurrence."

—EEOC guideline based on the Civil Rights Act of 1964, Title VII

APPENDIX 2 (SITUATION 1)

The Propmore Corporation Policy HR-13

Policy Area: Sexual Harassment

Purpose: The purpose of Policy HR-13 is to inform employees of the company that The Propmore Corporation forbids practices of sexual harassment on the job and that disciplinary action may be taken against those who violate this policy.

Policy Statement: In keeping with its long-standing tradition of abiding by pertinent laws and regulations, The Propmore Corporation forbids practices of sexual harassment on the job which violate Title VII of the Civil Rights Act of 1964. Sexual harassment on the job, regardless of its intent, is against the law. Employees who nevertheless engage in sexual harassment practices face possible disciplinary action which includes dismissal from the company.

Policy Implementation: Those who wish to report violations of Policy HR-13 shall file a written grievance with their immediate supervisors within 2 weeks of the alleged violation. In conjunction with the Legal Department, the supervisor will investigate the alleged violation and issue his or her decision based upon the findings of this investigation within 30 days of receiving the written grievance.

SITUATION II

Gathering More Information

Don Bradford had met Bill Smith, the Airgoods Corporation salesman, on several occasions but did not feel he really knew him. To learn more about Bill,

Don talked with his other key buyer, Bob Peters. Bob had dealt with Bill on many contracts in the past. After Don finished recounting the incident concerning Jane, Bob smiled. In his opinion, it was just a "boys will be boys" situation that got blown out of proportion. It may have been more than a joke, but Bob did not think Bill would do something "too far out." He pointed out that Bill had been selling for 10 years and knew how to treat a customer.

Don's next step was a visit to the division personnel office. In addition to going through Jane's file, he wanted to discuss the matter with Ann Perkins, the division's human resource manager. Fortunately, Ann was in her office and had time to see him immediately.

Don went over the whole situation with Ann. When he had finished his account, Ann was silent for a minute. Then she pointed out that this was a strange sexual harassment situation: It did not happen at the company, and the alleged harasser was not a member of the Propmore organization. The extent of the company's responsibility was not clear.

She had heard of cases in which employees had held their companies responsible for protecting them from sexual harassment by employees of other organizations. But the harassment had taken place on company premises, where some degree of direct supervision and protection could have been expected. Ann filled out a slip authorizing Don to see Jane's personnel file. He took the file to an empty office and went through its contents. There were the expected hiring and annual evaluation forms, which revealed nothing unusual and only confirmed his own high opinion of Jane.

Then Don came to an informal note at the back of the file. It summarized a telephone reference check with the personnel manager of Jane's former employer. The note indicated that Jane had complained of being sexually harassed by her supervisor. The personnel manager had "checked it out" with the supervisor, who claimed "there was nothing to it." The note also indicated that Jane had been terminated 2 months after this incident for "unsatisfactory work."

Don returned to his office and called his functional superior, Mr. Stewart, to inform him of the situation. Mr. Stewart was the corporate vice president of procurement. He had known Bill Smith personally for a number of years. He told Don that Bill's wife had abandoned him and their three children several years ago. Although Bill had a reputation for occasional odd behavior, he was known in the industry as a hard-working salesperson who provided excellent service and follow-through on his accounts.

QUESTIONS FOR DISCUSSION

1. Should Don have talked with Bob Peters about Jane's allegations? What is the ethical justification for doing so? For not doing so?
2. Is the Propmore Corporation responsible in this incident even though Bill Smith is not one of its employees? What moral responsibilities and obligations does the company have in relation to Jane?
3. What is the significance of the "informal note" that Don found in Jane's personnel file? Should he place credence in it? How should this information be used in appraising Jane's current allegation?
4. What significance should Don attach to the information he received from Mr. Stewart? Should he place credence in it? How should Don use this information in appraising Bill Smith?

SITUATION III

A Telephone Call

Don felt he needed more information to make a thorough investigation. He contemplated calling Bill Smith. In fairness to Bill, he felt he should hear Bill's version of what happened during the luncheon. But he knew he was not responsible for the actions of a nonemployee. Furthermore, he wondered if talking to Bill would upset Jane even more if she found out about it. And would it be a proper part of an investigation mandated by company policy?

As Don considered his options, the phone rang. It was Bill Smith's boss, Joe Maxwell. He and Bill had talked about the luncheon, he said, and wanted to know if Jane had reported anything.

"Don, I don't know what you know about that meeting," said Joe, "but Bill has told me all the facts, and I thought we could put our heads together and nip this thing in the bud."

Don wasn't sure if this call was going to help or hinder him in his decision making. At first, he felt Joe was trying to unduly influence him. Also, he wasn't sure if the call was a violation of Jane's right to confidentiality. "Joe, I'm not sure we should be discussing this matter at all," said Don. "We might be jumping the gun. And what if Jane—"

"Wait, wait," Joe interrupted. "This thing can be put to rest if you just hear what really happened. We've been a good supplier for some time now. Give

us the benefit of the doubt. We can talk 'off the record' if you want. But don't close the door on us."

"Okay," said Don, "let's talk off the record. I'll hear Bill's version, but I won't reach a conclusion over the phone. Our policy requires an investigation, and when that's complete, I'll let you know our position."

"Gee, Don," said Joe, "I don't think you even need an investigation. Bill says the only thing that went on at lunch was some innocent flirtation. Jane was giving him the old 'come on,' you know. She was more than friendly to him, smiling a lot and laughing at his jokes. Bill saw all the signals and just responded like a full-blooded male."

"You mean Jane was the cause of his harassing her?" Don asked.

"No, he didn't harass her," Joe said with urgency in his voice. "He only flirted with her because he thought she was flirting with him. It was all very innocent. These things happen every day. He didn't mean any harm. Just the opposite. He thought there was a chance for a nice relationship. He likes her very much and thought the feeling was mutual. No need to make a federal case out of it. These things happen—That's all. Remember when you asked out one of my saleswomen, Don? She said 'no,' but she didn't suggest sexual harassment. Isn't this the same thing?"

"I don't know. Jane was really upset when she came to me. She didn't see it as just flirting," said Don.

"Come on, Don," insisted Joe. "Give her some time to calm down. You know how women can be sometimes. Maybe she has PMS. Why don't you let things just settle down before you do anything rash and start that unnecessary investigation? I bet in a couple of days you can talk to Jane and convince her it was just a misunderstanding. I'll put someone else on this contract, and we'll forget the whole thing ever happened. We've got to think about business first, right?"

Joe Maxwell's phone call put things in a new light for Don. If it was only innocent flirtation, why should good relations between Propmore and Airgoods be damaged? Yet he knew he had an obligation to Jane. He just wasn't sure how far that obligation went.

QUESTIONS FOR DISCUSSION

1. What are Bill Smith's moral rights in this case?
2. In his investigation of the incident, how should Don Bradford regard Bill Smith's rights?
3. Should Don have talked with Joe Maxwell about the case? Why or why not?

4. What is the difference between "flirtation" and "sexual harassment"?

5. How should Don evaluate what Joe told him? What role should this information play in his investigation? What effect should Joe's reminder of the time Don asked out one of Joe's saleswomen have on Don's course of action?

6. What should Don recommend after his investigation is complete? What is your ethical justification for this recommendation? Can all parties be treated fairly?

Greenway Environmental Technologies

32

Greenway Environmental Technologies, an industry leader in hazardous waste cleanup services, specializes in the treatment and disposal of chemical and biological wastes. Due to the wide range of services provided, Greenway employs professionals such as environmental engineers, toxicologists, and certified industrial hygienists, as well as heavy equipment operators and laborers. Over the past 2 years, the company has grown from 65 to 350 employees and revenues have increased from $8 to $20 million. The company employs an ethnically diverse work force and prides itself on its efforts to hire and promote minorities. Although senior management is exclusively comprised of white males, several female and minority employees in middle management are advancing rapidly toward top management. Throughout the company, there is a united spirit aimed at profitably growing the business and rewarding those employees who make outstanding contributions to the effort.

RON DEBITSON

As Greenway's controller, Ron Debitson reports to the CEO and is responsible for all financial and administrative functions. Two years earlier, at the age of 26 and 10 years younger than any other member of senior management, Ron joined the company as controller after practicing as a CPA for 5 years. Ron is very active in the community and serves on the

This case was prepared by Robert B. Carton and Michael D. Meeks. Used with permission. This case is based upon an actual experience. The names of the participants and the company have been changed to maintain confidentiality.

board of directors of a nonprofit bleeding disorders organization. Through this association, Ron has become acquainted with the problems faced by people who are HIV positive, since overwhelming numbers of people with bleeding disorders were the victims of contaminated blood transfusions during the early 1980s. On a regular basis, Ron deals with people with HIV and AIDS and has come to understand the prejudices faced by these people. He has also grown to admire their spirit and determination to lead as normal a life as possible.

Greenway's exceptional growth rate was due, in part, to the changes in financial planning and control that Ron implemented and contracts he negotiated. Consequently, Ron is considered a critical member of the top management team. Still, by virtue of his age, Ron often feels that his views are not always given equal weight with the other senior managers.

HIRING CONFLICT

The rapid growth of the company required Ron to hire several accounting staff members from a local temporary agency. His agreement with the agency was that Greenway could hire the temporary employees without a placement fee if the company would employ them through the agency for a period of 60 days. One of the temporary employees, Paul Carvey, had been working as a project accountant for over 90 days and had proven to be an outstanding worker. He was repeatedly complimented by project managers for his accurate tracking of project costs, timely billings, courteous and timely collections of amounts due the company, and the payment of project vendors.

Due to the nature of the work, Paul only worked with three project managers and with the other members of the accounting department. He had phone contact with customers and vendors on a daily basis, but rarely met with either face-to-face. However, full-time project accountants often were on the project sites, and at those times directly dealt with customers. If the company hired Paul, his contact with customers would increase.

Paul was a quiet young man who was considered by the women in the accounting department to be "sweet," but was considered by some of the men to be rather effeminate. Paul lived at home with his parents and did not talk about his personal life in the office. On several occasions, Paul did mention to Ron or other members of the accounting department that he would like to come to work for the company full time.

When Ron decided to hire a full-time project accountant, he met with Patrick Rush, the head of personnel. Patrick was 20 years older than Ron and had strong religious beliefs. When Ron proposed hiring Paul, Patrick replied that he did not believe that it would be a good idea because he believed that Paul was homosexual. When Ron asked why that should be an issue, Patrick replied that many homosexuals have AIDS, and he was personally uncomfortable using the bathroom or drinking from the water fountain since Paul may have used them. Further, homosexuality was a sin according to his religious beliefs and he did not want to associate with such people.

At this point in the meeting, Sam Sasbe, the executive vice president who was Patrick's age and childhood friend, entered the room. Patrick explained Ron's desire to hire Paul and his reasons for opposing the hire. Sam was not a religious man, but agreed with Patrick on the grounds that the company's customers in the Deep South, where much of the company's business was conducted, would not accept a homosexual. Sam also agreed with Patrick that other men in the company would not be comfortable with using the bathroom or the water fountain after Paul.

Ron was dumbfounded. He could not believe that intelligent people could hold such views. Attempting to reason with the two men, Ron listed several reasons why their fears were unfounded. First, there was no evidence at all that Paul was homosexual. Making such stereotypical categorizations was unconscionable. Second, if Paul was a homosexual, there was no reason to believe that he would be infected with the HIV virus. Third, even if by chance Paul was

HIV positive, the virus cannot be spread by casual contact such as through common toilets and drinking fountains. Fourth, attributing prejudice to customers in the Deep South was once again unfair stereotyping. Fifth, an overt act of prejudice by senior management would destroy much of the effort to date to foster cultural diversity in the company. Sixth, the company's largest customer was the federal government, and such hiring policies were in conflict with the spirit of Equal Employment Opportunity Commission guidelines.

Unmoved by Ron's arguments, Sam informed Ron, "If you hire Paul, I'll fire him." This only served to exacerbate the problem since Ron reported directly to the owner and CEO, and not to Sam. Getting mad, Ron reminded Sam of this point and added that so long as he was controller, he would run his department on his terms unless countermanded by his boss Martin Widdup, the CEO. At this point, Martin was asked to join the meeting.

Martin had a reputation for being a fair boss and was credited with creating a positive atmosphere in the company. He was also a long-time friend of Sam and Patrick. After hearing both sides of the argument, Martin told Ron not to hire Paul. He stated that he had started and still owned the company. Greenway was his, and he would employ whomever he wanted. Martin told Ron to begin looking for another candidate immediately.

Ron left the meeting wondering what to do. He did not agree with the decision of the CEO, and for the first time since joining the company, he had doubts about his future with the organization.

QUESTIONS FOR DISCUSSION

1. What are the ethical issues in this case? From what perspective is each issue being raised?
2. Who are the stakeholders and what are the stakes?
3. Is the proposed decision not to hire Paul an ethical decision?
4. What should Ron do now?

Cracker Barrel Old Country Stores

33

Cracker Barrel Old Country Stores is a popular restaurant chain operating in the southeastern United States. It was founded in 1969 in Lebanon, Tennessee. Travelers on interstate highways are familiar with the stores, which operate in large buildings that look like rural general stores and serve southern-style meals featuring such foods as country ham, turnip greens, fried chicken, cornbread, and grits. Cracker Barrel restaurants are popular with families traveling by car and groups traveling by bus who want quick service and low prices but wish to avoid fast-food franchises. Local residents also enjoy dining at Cracker Barrel after Sunday church services.

Cracker Barrel restaurants are company-owned and feature table service, gift shops, and clean restrooms. Management and employees concentrate on providing the best possible food and service. High-quality ingredients are used; for example, pancakes are served with real maple syrup and butter. "We don't skimp, because you can skimp yourself out of business" says the company's chief financial officer. Employees can be tested on their duties: Even servers and dishwashers have their own sets of tests on sanitation, food preparation, and dish stacking. Those who pass are given raises, cash incentives, and enhanced benefits as they move up the management ranks. Managers can double their incomes by meeting profitability goals.[1]

In February 1991, Cracker Barrel management developed a new employment policy. Local managers were sent a memo instructing them to terminate any employee "whose sexual preferences fail to demonstrate normal heterosexual values." In a press release, the company explained that the new practice was justified because Cracker Barrel was "founded upon a concept of traditional American values."[2] Such employment practices are legal in most states.[3] At least 11 employees were fired as a result of this memo.[4] Some managers noted in the employee files that the terminations were made because the employees were homosexual.[5]

This case was prepared by William A. Sodeman.

The new policy was notable because the restaurant industry employs higher-than-average numbers of gays and lesbians. The flexible schedules, creative atmosphere, easy mobility, and social opportunities that are common in restaurant work are attractive to gays and compatible with the gay lifestyle. According to Wharton entrepreneurship professor Edward Moldt, "There's a heavy preponderance of homosexuals in the restaurant business, and what [Cracker Barrel is] doing is losing a lot of people who could be very good in the jobs they're in. They're missing the business aspect of this."[6]

THE PROTESTS

After 10 days, the termination policy was rescinded by corporate headquarters. Some fired employees claimed that store managers were instructed to hire new employees and to avoid rehiring any employee who had been terminated under the policy.[7]

Over the following 2 years, several external stakeholder groups applied pressure on the company. Queer Nation, a civil disobedience group that advocates gay and lesbian rights, began to picket Cracker Barrel stores in the Atlanta area. Some members staged sit-ins on Sunday afternoons, ordering only beverages as the "after-church crowd" was descending on Cracker Barrel stores. Protesters cooperated with the police and the local media, and when the eventual trespassing arrests were made, Queer Nation members were videotaped by local media and the ABC news magazine "20/20" as they were handcuffed and hauled off to jail.[8]

By this time, Cracker Barrel was expanding its operations to northern, prounion states including Michigan, Ohio, and Wisconsin. The protests in these states were wilder, as they were run by unions and a different gay organization, ACT UP. Both groups became more militant, chanting slogans such as "Shut down the Bigot Barrel" and accusing the company of selling racist merchandise, including Confederate souvenirs and "mammy dolls," in its gift shops. These groups also organized protests on Wall Street to raise awareness of the publicly-traded firm within the investment community.[9]

THE RESOLUTIONS

Investors from various religious organizations and government pension funds filed proxy resolutions with Cracker Barrel to renounce their employment policies that discriminated against homosexuals. This was done because the groups felt the company was continuing its former policies. Cracker Barrel appealed to the Securities and Exchange Commission (SEC), which granted the company permission to exclude these resolutions from its annual meeting. The SEC concluded that employment policies did not require shareholder approval because they were "ordinary business decisions." In early 1998, the SEC reversed its decision, saying that it would review shareholder resolutions on a case-by-case basis.[10]

Cracker Barrel has continued to expand from its southeastern base, opening new facilities in the Midwest and Northeast United States while forming a parent company, CBRL Group, Inc., to make acquisitions, like of the Logan's Roadhouse chain, which it purchased for $179 million in 1998.[11] By 1998, Cracker Barrel Old Country Store had been named "Best Family Dining" by *Restaurants and Institutions* magazine for the eighth year in a row and "Best Restaurant Chain" by *Destinations* magazine for 5 consecutive years.[12] Nevertheless, the controversy continues. In 1998, New York City Comptroller, Alan Hevesi, used the city retirement system's 200,000 shares of stock to propose that Cracker Barrel link executive pay to its ability to recruit new employees "without regard to race, color, creed, gender, age, or sexual orientation."[13] That same year, a protest group picketed the Culinary Institute of America's award dinner because it honored Cracker Barrel president, Ronald N. Magruder.[14] Last, "Out at Work" (an HBO documentary about discrimination in the workplace) featured the story of Cheryl Summerville, a Cracker Barrel cook who had been fired because of her sexual orientation.[15] By 1999, there were nearly 400 Cracker Barrel restaurants throughout the United States.

QUESTIONS FOR DISCUSSION

1. What difficulties do you think Cracker Barrel could have avoided in the implementation of its employment policy? Should the policy have been implemented in the first place?

2. Are special-interest groups justified in holding protests against company policy? How might Cracker Barrel have handled the Queer Nation and ACT UP protests besides calling in the police to arrest the trespassers?

3. How much power should employers have in developing employment policies? What is the proper role of shareholders in defining these policies? What is the proper role of the courts?

4. Despite the controversy described in this case, Cracker Barrel has continued to perform well in a highly competitive environment. Has this performance been achieved in spite of or because of Cracker Barrel's foundation on "traditional American values"?

CASE ENDNOTES

1. Toddi Gutner, "Nostalgia Sells," *Forbes* (April 27, 1992), 102–103.

2. Marlene Givant Star, "SEC Policy Reversal Riles Activist Groups," *Pensions & Investments* (October 2, 1992), 33.

3. Joan Oleck, "Bad Politics," *Restaurant Business* (June 10, 1992), 80, 84, 89.

4. Givant Star, 33.

5. "20/20: Whom Do You Sleep With?" (November 29, 1991).

6. Oleck, 89.

7. Oleck, 84.

8. Oleck, 84; "20/20."

9. Oleck, 84, 89.

10. Abbott A. Leban and Frederick D. Lipman, "Excludability of Shareholder 'Social Responsibility' Proposals from Proxy Statements," *Securities Regulation Law Journal* (Spring, 1994), 78–86.

11. Bill Carlino, "Cracker Barrel to Acquire Logan's Roadhouse in $179M Deal," *Nation's Restaurant News* (December 21, 1998), 3, 141.

12. "Cracker Barrel Old Country Stores Consistently Honored Nationwide as 'Best Family Dining' Restaurant and 'Best Restaurant Chain,'" *PR Newswire* (March 4, 1998).

13. Katia Hetter, "Focus on Cracker Barrel Hiring/ Hevesi Opposes Anti-Gay Policy," *Newsday* (October 16, 1998), A67.

14. "Protest Over Culinary Group's Guest of Honor," *New York Times* (October 15, 1998), B3.

15. Joanne Ostrow, "Out at Work, An Eye-Opener" *Denver Post* (January 6, 1999), F5.

The Betaseron® Decision (A)

34A

On July 23, 1993, the United States Food and Drug Administration (FDA) approved interferon beta-1b (brand name Betaseron®), making it the first multiple sclerosis (MS) treatment to get FDA approval in 25 years. Betaseron was developed by Berlex Laboratories, a U.S. unit of Schering AG, the German pharmaceutical company. Berlex handled the clinical development, trials, and marketing of the drug, while Chiron Corporation, a biotechnology firm based in California, manufactured it. The groundbreaking approval of Betaseron represented not only a great opportunity for Berlex but a dilemma. Supplies were insufficient to meet initial demand, and shortages were forecast until 1996. With insufficient supplies and staggering development costs, how would Berlex allocate and price the drug?

THE CHALLENGE OF MULTIPLE SCLEROSIS

MS is a disease of the central nervous system that interferes with the brain's ability to control such functions as seeing, walking, and talking. The nerve fibers in the brain and spinal cord are surrounded by myelin, a fatty substance that protects the nerve fibers in the same way that insulation protects electrical wires. When the myelin insulation becomes damaged, the ability of the central nervous system to transmit nerve impulses to and from the brain becomes impaired. With MS, there are *sclerosed* (i.e., scarred or hardened) areas in *multiple* parts of the brain and spinal cord when the immune system mistakenly attacks the myelin sheath.

The symptoms of MS depend to some extent on the location and size of the sclerosis. Symptoms may include numbness, slurred speech, blurred vision,

poor coordination, muscle weakness, bladder dysfunction, extreme fatigue, and paralysis. There is no way to know how the disease will progress for any individual, because the nature of the disease can change. Some people will have a relatively benign course of MS with only one or two mild attacks, nearly complete remission, and no permanent disability. Others will have a chronic progressive course resulting in severe disability. A third group displays the most typical pattern, which is periods of *exacerbations,* when the disease is active, and periods of *remission,* when the symptoms recede yet generally leave some damage. People with MS live with an exceptionally high degree of uncertainty, because their disease can change from one day to the next. Dramatic downturns as well as dramatic recoveries are not uncommon.

THE PROMISE OF BETASERON

Interferon beta is a naturally occurring protein that regulates the body's immune system. Betaseron is composed of interferon beta-1b that has been genetically engineered and laboratory manufactured as a recombinant product. Although other interferons (i.e., alpha and gamma) had been tested, only beta interferon had been shown, through large-scale trials, to affect MS. Because it is an immunoregulatory agent, Betaseron was believed to combat the immune problems that make MS worse. However, the exact way in which it works was yet to be determined.

In clinical studies, Betaseron was shown to reduce the frequency and severity of exacerbations in ambulatory MS patients with a relapsing-remitting form of the disease. It did not reverse damage nor did it completely prevent exacerbations. However, Betaseron could dramatically improve the quality of life for the person with MS. For example, people taking Betaseron were shown to have fewer and shorter hospitalizations. Betaseron represented the first and only drug to have an effect on the frequency of exacerbations.

Betaseron is administered subcutaneously (under the skin) every other day by self-injection. To derive the most benefits from the therapy, it was important

This case was written by Ann K. Buchholtz, University of Georgia. It was written from public sources, solely for the purpose of stimulating class discussion. All events are real. The author thanks Dr. Stephen Reingold, Vice President Research and Medical Programs of the National Multiple Sclerosis Society, and Avery Rockwell, Chapter Services Associate of the Greater Connecticut Chapter of the Multiple Sclerosis Society, for their helpful comments. All rights reserved jointly to the author and the North American Case Research Association (NACRA). Published with permission.

that the MS patient maintain a regular schedule of the injections. Some flu-like side-effects, as well as swelling and irritation around the injection, had been noted. However, these side-effects tended to decrease with time on treatment. In addition, one person who received Betaseron committed suicide while three others attempted it. Because MS often leads to depression, there was no way to know whether the administration of Betaseron was a factor. Last, Betaseron was not recommended for use during pregnancy.

THE BETASERON DILEMMA

In July 1993, FDA approval for Betaseron allowed physicians to prescribe the drug to MS patients who were ambulatory and had a relapsing-remitting course of MS. An estimated one-third of the 300,000 people with MS in the United States fell into that category, resulting in a potential client base of 100,000. The expedited FDA approval process for Betaseron took only 1 year instead of the customary 3. As a result, Berlex was unprepared to manufacture and distribute the treatment. Chiron Corporation had been making the drug in small quantities for experimental use and did not have the manufacturing facilities to handle the expected explosion in demand. Chiron estimated that it would have enough of the drug for about 12,000 to 20,000 people by the end of 1993. By the end of 1994, Chiron expected to be able to provide the drug to 40,000 patients. Depending on demand, it might take until about 1996 to provide the drug to all patients who requested it. Chiron's expanded manufacturing represented the only option for Berlex,

because the process required for another company to get FDA approval to manufacture the drug would take even longer.

In addition to availability, price was a concern, because successes must fund the failures that precede them. Betaseron represented years of expensive, risky research by highly trained scientists in modern research facilities. Furthermore, genetically engineered drugs were extremely expensive to manufacture. In the case of Betaseron, a human interferon gene is inserted into bacteria, resulting in a genetically engineered molecule. The stringent quality controls on the procedure take time and are expensive. As a result, the price of Betaseron was expected to be about $10,000 per year for each patient.

Betaseron brought great hope to people with MS and a great quandary to Berlex. How should Berlex handle the supply limitations, the distribution, and the pricing of this drug?

QUESTIONS FOR DISCUSSION

1. What are the ethical issues in this situation? Which issues must Berlex consider first when determining how to distribute Betaseron?
2. Given the shortage of the drug, how should Berlex decide who receives it and who waits?
3. How should Berlex handle the logistics of distribution?
4. How should Berlex determine the drug's relative pricing (assume the drug costs about $12,000 per year)?
5. Who, if anyone, should be involved in the decision making?

34B

The Betaseron® Decision (B)

On August 20, 1993, Berlex announced its distribution and price plan for Betaseron and sent a letter to all U.S. neurologists detailing its pricing and distribution.

- People who have commercial medical insurance or annual family incomes of more than $50,000 would pay $1,000 per month. However, to encourage strict compliance to the treatment regimen, Berlex would give patients 2 months of the drug for free after 10 consecutive months of compliance. Therefore, anyone who adheres to the prescribed treatment regimen would pay $10,000 (annually), the highest price to be paid for the drug.

- People with annual family incomes between $20,000 and $50,000, without medical insurance, would be provided financial assistance by the company to help support the annual costs of the medication.

- People with annual family incomes below $20,000, with no medical insurance, would be provided the medication for free.

To minimize out-of-pocket expenses, Berlex developed the *Betaseron Card*, which would identify patients to prechosen pharmacies and provide information about the patients' payment programs and prices. Qualified patients would receive interest-free deferred payment for up to 55 days. This was intended to enable most patients to pay their bills *after* they received reimbursement. The card was provided through a financial institution and financed by

Berlex. After 55 days, a finance charge of 12 percent would be applied to any unpaid balance. Berlex would receive no portion of the interest payments and would not profit from the card.

Distribution was set to begin in October 1993, with distribution handled by PCS Health Systems, Inc., a nationwide network of affiliated pharmacies. This managed pharmacy network served two purposes. First, it enabled Berlex to cut costs by minimizing handling charges; Berlex estimated that patients would save about $2,000 per year. It also enabled Berlex to provide the drug only to specifically identified patients and to ensure that, once therapy began, the supply of the drug would be continuous.

Initial access to the drug was determined by a lottery, designed to provide equal access to the initially limited supply. Physicians who wished to obtain Betaseron for their patients enrolled them in the program during an open registration period from August 23, 1993, to September 15, 1993. At the conclusion of the registration period, patients were assigned randomly generated numbers. Patients who registered for the drug after registration closed were put at the end of the list on a first-come, first-served basis. Those with numbers under 1,000 were slated to begin receiving the drug immediately. Those with numbers under 12,000 would have the drug by year's end. Those with numbers between 12,001 and 40,000 were expected to have access to the drug by mid- to late 1994, and those with numbers over 40,000 would probably not be supplied Betaseron until late 1994 or early 1995. Berlex placed no restrictions on which MS patients physicians could enroll, despite the FDA indication for ambulatory relapsing-remitting MS.

Patients with MS and their advocates were left with a host of questions. Was the lottery system a fair way to resolve the distribution dilemma? How fair was the pricing structure? Did Berlex do everything possible to guarantee equitable access to the drug? Who were the winners and who were the losers? Last, what problems were likely to result from this solution?

This case was written by Ann K. Buchholtz, University of Georgia. It was written from public sources, solely for the purpose of stimulating class discussion. All events are real. The author thanks Dr. Stephen Reingold, Vice President Research and Medical Programs of the National Multiple Sclerosis Society, and Avery Rockwell, Chapter Services Associate of the Greater Connecticut Chapter of the Multiple Sclerosis Society, for their helpful comments. All rights reserved jointly to the author and the North American Case Research Association (NACRA). Published with permission.

QUESTIONS FOR DISCUSSION

1. What is your assessment of the lottery system? Who wins? Who loses? Is it fair?
2. How fair is the pricing structure?

3. Do you agree with the Betaseron card and the distribution network? Has Berlex done everything possible to guarantee equitable access to the drug?
4. What problems, if any, do you foresee?

35

A Bitter Pill

David Schindler was thinking about his company's entry into Haiti. His firm had been experiencing fierce competition from other garment producers with offshore manufacturing facilities, so he decided to establish his own offshore facility. Haiti was only 3.5 hours from New York and could provide extremely cheap labor. Of course, there were political risks, but the combination of relative proximity to the market compared to the Asian countries that were also providing cheap labor and the U.S. tax benefits for providing jobs to Caribbean neighbors encouraged him to proceed.

A Puerto Rican manager with extensive familiarity with U.S. standards was hired to oversee the work done by a Haitian subcontractor who was hired for a trial period. Clearly, the Haitian standard for work conditions was less than humane, and the Haitian government provided little guidance regarding worker treatment. Despite the working conditions, the work and the attitude of the Haitian workers were excellent. After the contract with the subcontractor expired, Schindler decided to establish his own plant in Port au Prince, Haiti.

The operation started small, with a plant that was built to U.S. specifications in terms of lighting and workspace. The plant provided excellent ventilation and a clean place for workers to have their lunch break. Over several years, the operation grew from 165 to over 900 garment workers. Eventually, about 1,000 Haitians, including support staff, 90 percent of whom were women, worked for the operation. Employee relations were good for over a decade, until the following situation occurred.

From the beginning of the operation, Schindler noticed that the efficiency of the Haitian workers declined dramatically after lunch. A slight decrease in work efficiency is normal as workers get fatigued, but the Haitian workers were getting fatigued more quickly and more dramatically. As other operational issues were resolved, the issue of worker efficiency became a management priority. Schindler felt confident that he could make this already profitable operation into a truly exceptional production facility if he could just resolve this production efficiency problem. From the start he provided the workers with regular access to medical doctors to maintain a healthy work force. Because of the large number of employees, he had a doctor and trained nurses on staff.

In consultation with his medical staff, Schindler concluded that the efficiency problems were related to the local diet. The diet consisted mainly of beans, rice, and plantains (a kind of banana) and seemed to be deficient in protein and vitamins. The first solution was to negotiate with the lunch vendors that supplied meals for the workers. Typical of Haitian plants, there was no kitchen on site. Local businesspeople came each day to cook meals for the workers. To Schindler's great surprise, the local lunch vendors took great offense to the suggestion that they include more meat protein in the food they prepared for the workers. Although Schindler even offered to subsidize the supply of meat, the response was a resounding refusal. The vendors told him in no uncertain terms to mind his own business: They took great pride in their cooking and thought that his interference was an insult to the Haitian lifestyle and culture. After several attempts using different entrées, Schindler abandoned his idea.

For several years, Schindler's wife had been insisting that their family take a vitamin supplement to

This case was prepared by David Saiia. All the events and individuals are real but the names have been disguised.

ensure adequate nutrition, so he thought that this could be an affordable solution to the nutrition problem in the plant. One of his staff identified an appropriate nutritional supplement in conjunction with the staff doctor, and a supply of these pills was brought into the country. When they first introduced these supplements, completely on a voluntary basis, not one worker took advantage of the opportunity. Schindler was dumbfounded. He said, "When these pills were made available for the employees, you would have thought I was asking these people to take cyanide! We had not considered the way the local people would look at taking a pill. The combination of local religion and suspicion of foreigners made the supplements we were offering unappealing."

The doctor visits were popular with the employees, so they decided to go slow and use the good relations with the doctors to advocate the use of the supplements. The doctors and the nurses steadily encouraged and recommended the nutritional supplements. The employees gradually began to accept the supplements and so the company thought it had arrived at a solution to the problem. In fact, it had already started to think about creating an evaluation program to assess the effectiveness of the supplement program. Company staff were very excited to see how this was going to impact production, because everything seemed to be going well.

Though the plant had over 1,000 workers, everyone seemed to know what was going on with everyone else. The Haitian people are very tight knit and community oriented. With so many women on staff, there were quite a few pregnant women at any given time. Just when the company thought the nutrition program was going to take off, disaster struck. One of the pregnant workers had a miscarriage and immediately blamed the nutritional supplement for causing her loss. No matter what the medical staff told her, she was convinced that the supplement had caused the miscarriage. Before the company knew what was happening, news had spread throughout the plant that the nutritional supplement was "bad juju"—bad medicine. Despite management's best efforts, the employees began to view everything they did with increasing suspicion. The supplement program was discontinued as other people started to claim other ailments were associated with taking the supplements.

Schindler was perplexed. He wondered what reason the employees would think he had for poisoning or injuring his workers. None of this made any sense. He was now in worse shape than he was when he started. Not only did he still have an afternoon production slump, he now also had seriously undermined the confidence of his workers.

QUESTIONS FOR DISCUSSION

1. What are the ethical issues that arise when setting up operations overseas?
2. What are the management issues highlighted in this case? What are the social issues? How do they overlap? Does the current situation represent a crisis for the company?
3. What, if anything, could Schindler have done to avoid the problems that developed?
4. What steps should Schindler take to deal with the current situation? Be sure to recommend both short-term and long-term actions.

36

Facing a Fire

Hermann Singer was returning home from his surprise seventieth birthday party when a "not-so-welcome" second surprise occurred. A boiler at his textile firm exploded, injuring 27 people and destroying three buildings. The devastating fire made national news. Suddenly, the future of HFS Corp., the 90-year-old business that his grandfather built, was in doubt.

This case was prepared by Ann K. Buchholtz.

The HFS Corporation was located in a small New England town. Because it employed 2,400 people, it was the one bright light in an economically depressed area. If the plant were to close or move, the impact on the community would be devastating. Furthermore, many of the current workers were the sons, daughters, and even grandchildren of other factory workers: They did high-quality work for which they were well paid. Singer considered his workers to be a part of his extended family, and he considered the community to be his home. While other New England textile manufacturers moved South to find lower wages, HFS Corporation stayed in New England and continued to pay one of the highest wage scales in the business.

Singer had some difficult decisions to make. At 70, he had the option of using the insurance money to retire to Florida. The stock market seemed to be anticipating such a move because, the day after the fire, the price of his main competitor's stock rose sharply. Nevertheless, rebuilding remained an option. Several of HFS's main customers pledged their support of rebuilding and sent checks totaling over $300,000 along with their verbal pledges. Other individuals, moved by the huge loss, sent checks intended to help the now-jobless HFS employees. The money was a help, but nowhere near the estimated $1.5 million per week that would be needed to pay employee salaries. In total, it would cost an estimated $15 million to continue to pay the work force during the rebuilding. Although Singer's personal wealth was sufficient to cover this expense, the potential expenditure was significant.

Singer had two main options: (1) rebuild the factory or (2) retire on the insurance proceeds. If he opted to rebuild, other decisions awaited him. Should he stay in New England or relocate where wages are lower? During rebuilding, should he pay his workers some or all of the wages they would have received, or should he wait until the factory was again operational?

QUESTIONS FOR DISCUSSION

1. What should Hermann Singer do? Why?
2. Should he rebuild the factory or begin retirement?
3. If he rebuilds, should he relocate the firm to an area where wages are lower?
4. What provisions, if any, should Singer make for his employees? for the community?
5. What would you do if you were Singer?

Social Reform or Self-Interest? 37

Raise Hell and Sell Newspapers is the biography of Alden J. Blethen, the man who bought the *Seattle Times* in 1896. It chronicles the ups and downs of Alden's rise from extreme hardship to great success. After a string of business failures, Alden borrowed money from family members to buy a failing newspaper, *The Seattle Daily Times*. When he died in 1915, his wish was that his now-successful newspaper remain in family hands.[1]

Although Frank Blethen became publisher in 1985, he didn't know much about Alden until the biography was published as part of the centennial celebration of Blethen family ownership of the *Seattle Times*. Moved by the book's account of the fiercely independent Alden, Frank Blethen took some family members and *Times* staffers on a pilgrimage to trace Alden's path from Maine to Seattle. Frank returned from the trip saying that it had given him and his family a touchstone they didn't have before, as well as a renewed commitment to family ownership. Since Frank took over as publisher, the *Seattle Times* has won numerous awards, including three Pulitzer Prizes. Frank has rejected numerous offers to buy the paper out.[2]

In the late 1980s and through the 1990s, Frank Blethen took a more active and visible leadership role in promoting issues he felt were important to the community. The paper ran ads supporting the United Way; honoring Dr. Martin Luther King, Jr.; and opposing a ballot measure that would end affirmative action. None of these initiatives, however, caused the kind of controversy that arose when Blethen began a campaign to eliminate the federal inheritance tax. Referred to as the "death tax" by opponents, the inheritance tax rate is as high as 5 percent on estates valued at over $3 million. Proponents of the tax say it brings the federal government

This case was prepared by Ann K. Buchholtz.

$19.8 billion in revenue and that cutting it represents a tax break for the rich. Opponents of the tax point to inheritors who have had to sell off family businesses, like farms and newspapers, to be able to pay their taxes.[3]

The campaign Blethen waged against the inheritance tax was both impassioned and unprecedented. Rather than just writing editorials, the paper published an ad against the tax on its news pages. Larger than a half-page, the ad urged readers to ask their Congresspeople to support the tax's repeal. The ad said that it was sponsored by the "Committee to Repeal the Death Tax," a lobbying group formed by Blethen and Seattle Chamber of Commerce President, George Duff. In small print, the ad said it was "brought to you courtesy of the *Seattle Times*." Readers were referred to a Web site (*www.deathtax.com*) that was created and maintained by the *Seattle Times*.[4]

Critics of Blethen's campaign against the inheritance tax faulted it on several grounds. They argued that creating a public interest group, placing ads in news pages, and maintaining a Web site all went beyond the measures a business like a newspaper should take when supporting a cause. Critics also raised concerns about the role of Blethen's self-interest, citing the millions of dollars that would accrue to Blethen's family if his campaign were successful. They also faulted the Web site for slanted coverage of the issue. For example, the site stated that repeal of the tax would not add to the national deficit and would spur the economy; however, it failed to mention that this view is not supported by Congress's tax estimators. In a 1999 letter to the editor of the *Seattle Times,* Fred Flickinger referred to 1998 as the year journalistic integrity died at the *Seattle Times*.[5]

QUESTIONS FOR DISCUSSION

1. What are Frank Blethen's rights and responsibilities as the publisher of a major regional newspaper?
2. Is Blethen exercising a publisher's right to advance editorial opinion, or is he using the newspaper to promote his own self-interests?
3. Frank Blethen has espoused four core values that guide the activities of the newspaper. The first two are "Remain family-owned, private, and independent" and "Serve the community through quality journalism. " Are these two core values in conflict in this situation? If so, can they be prioritized?
4. If you were advising Blethen, what would you recommend that he do?

CASE ENDNOTES

1. Sherry Boswell and Lorraine McConaghy, *Raise Hell and Sell Newspapers* (Pullman, WA: Washington State University Press, 1996).
2. Michael R. Fancher, "Family Makes Visits to Roots, Reaffirms Commitment to the *Times,*" *The Seattle Times* (October 19, 1997), A27.
3. Danny Westneat, "Publisher Promoting His Causes in *Times* Ads: Blethen May Launch Effort Against I-200," *The Seattle Times* (August 25, 1998), A1.
4. Howard Kurtz, "A Publisher Presses His Point," *The Seattle Times* (August 31, 1998), C1.
5. Fred Flickinger, "Estate Tax Pulled Plug on Journalistic Integrity with Tax Editorial," *The Seattle Times* (January 11, 1999), B5.

URL Appendix

The URLs listed here are current at the time of publication. Should any of these Web sites change, please search under the company's or organization's name for an updated address.

"20/20" www.abcnews.go.com/onair/2020/2020Index.html
3M Company www.3m.com and www.mmm.com
"60 Minutes" www.cbs.com
A. C. Nielsen Company www.acnielsen.com
Abbott Laboratories www.abbott.com
ABC abc.go.com
Ace Hardware www.acehardware.com
Adolph Coors www.coors.com
The Advocacy Institute www.advocacy.org
Aerial Communications www.aerial1.com
AFL-CIO www.aflcio.com
African Development Bank www.afdb.org
All Nippon Airways www.allnipponairways.com
Allis Chalmers www.agcocorp.com/html/agco_allis.html
Allstate Insurance Co. www.allstate.com
Aluminum Company of America (Alcoa) www.alcoa.com
Alyeska www.alyeska-pipe.com
Amazon.com www.amazon.com
American Advertising Federation www.aaf.org
American Airlines www.aa.com
American Arbitration Association www.adr.org
American Association of Advertising Agencies www.aaaa.com
American Association of Retired Persons (AARP) www.aarp.org
American Bar Association www.abanet.org
American Brands www.fortunebrands.com
American Civil Liberties Union (ACLU) www.aclu.org
American Cyanamid www.cyanamid.com
American Express Company www.americanexpress.com
American Home Products www.ahp.com
American Jewish Congress www.ajcongress.org
American Management Association www.amanet.org
American Medical Association www.ama-assn.org
American Motors Corp. www.americanmotors.com

American Psychological Association   **www.apa.org**
American Red Cross   **www.redcross.org**
American Society for Prevention of Cruelty to Animals (ASPCA)   **www.aspca.org**
American Society for Quality   **www.asq.org**
America's Promise   **www.ikan.k12.il.us/ikannews/AP.htm**
Amnesty International   **www.amnesty.org**
Amoco   **www.amoco.com**
Amtrak   **www.amtrack.com**
Andersen Consulting   **www.ac.com/index.html** and **www.andersenconsulting.com**
Anheuser-Busch   **www.anheuser-busch.com**
Apple Computer   **www.apple.com**
Archer Daniels Midland (ADM)   **www.admworld.com**
Arco   **www.arco.com**
Arthur Andersen   **www.arthurandersen.com**
Asian Development Bank   **www.adb.org**
Association of National Advertisers, Inc.   **www.ana.net**
AT&T   **www.att.com**
The Atlanta Project (TAP)   **www.cartercenter.org/atlanta.html**
Atlantic Richfield   **www.arco.com**
Avis   **www.avis.com**
Avon   **www.avon.com**
Bank of America   **www.bankamerica.com** and **www.bofa.com**
BankBoston   **www.bankboston.com**
Bankers Trust   **www.bankerstrust.com**
Bausch & Lomb (B&L)   **www.bausch.com**
Beech-Nut Nutrition Company   **www.beech-nut.com**
BellSouth   **www.bellsouth.com**
Ben & Jerry's Homemade, Inc.   **www.benjerry.com**
Beneficial Corporation   **www.hfc.com**
Berkeley Symphony   **www.berkeleysymphony.org**
Berkshire Hathaway Inc.   **www.berkshirehathaway.com**
Best Practices for Global Competitiveness Initiative (BPI)   **www.efqm.org/satbrief.htm**
Bethlehem Steel Corporation   **www.bethsteel.com**
Better Business Bureau   **www.bbb.com**
The Body Shop   **www.the-body-shop.com**
Boeing   **www.boeing.com**
Borg-Warner   **www.borg-warner.com**
Boston College's Center for Corporate Community Relations   **www.bc.edu/cccr**
Boy Scouts   **www.bsa.scouting.org**
Boys and Girls Clubs   **www.boysandgirlsclub.org**
BP America   **www.bp.com**
Bridgestone/Firestone, Inc.   **www.bridgestone-firestone.com**
Brookings Institute   **www.brook.edu**
Brookings Review   **www.brook.edu/press/review/rev_des.htm**
Bureau of Labor Statistics   **www.bls.gov**
Burger King   **www.burgerking.com**
Business Committee for the Arts (BCA)   **www.bcainc.org**

The Business Enterprise Trust   www.betrust.com
Business for Social Responsibility (BSR)   www.bsr.org
Business Responds to AIDS (BRTA)   www.brta-lrta.org
Business Roundtable   www.brtable.org
Cabot Corporation   www.cabot-corp.com
Campbell Soup   www.campbellsoup.com
Canadian Broadcasting Corporation   www.friendscb.org
Canon Computer Systems   www.ccsi.cannon.com
Capital Research Center   www.capitalresearch.org
Caremark   www.caremark.com
Carter Center   www.cartercenter.org
Caterpillar   www.caterpillar.com
CBS   www.cbs.com
Cendant Corporation   www.cendant.com
Center for Public Integrity   www.publicintegrity.org
Center for Science in the Public Interest   www.cspinet.org
Center for the Study of American Business at Washington University
       www.csab.wustl.edu/home.asp
Central and South West Corporation   www.csw.com
The Century Council   www.centurycouncil.org
Character Education Partnership   www.character.org
Chase Manhattan   www.chasemanhattan.com
Chesebrough-Pond's, USA   www.unilever.com
Chevrolet   www.chevrolet.com
Chevron   www.chevron.com
Christian Coalition   www.cc.org
Chrysler   www1.daimlerchrysler.com
Cincinnati Gas and Electric   www.cincinnatigov.com/cgenf.htm
Circuit City   www.circuitcity.com
Citibank, N.A.   www.citibank.com
Citicorp   www.citicorp.com
Clarkson Centre for Business Ethics   www.mgmt.utoronto.ca/ccbe
CNN   www.cnn.com
Coca-Cola   www.cocacola.com
Colgate-Palmolive   www.colgate.com
Common Cause   www.commoncause.org
Compaq   www.compaq.com
ConAgra   www.conagra.com
Confederation of British Industry   www.cbi.org.uk
The Conference Board   www.conference-board.org
Conrail   www.conrail.com
Consumer Federation of America (CFA)   www.stateandlocal.org
Consumer Product Safety Commission   www.cpsc.gov
Consumers Union   www.consunion.org
Control Data Corporation (CDC)   www.controldata.com
Corning, Inc.   www.corning.com
Corporate Citizenship Resource Center   www.ttrc.doleta.gov/citizen

Corporate Governance   www.corpgov.com
Council of Institutional Investors   www.ciicentral.com
Council of Registrars   www.corenic.org
Council on Economic Priorities (CEP)   www-2.realaudio.com/CEP
Council on Environmental Quality (CEQ)   www.whitehouse.gov/CEQ
Courtaulds Textiles   www.courtaulds-textiles.com
Covenant Investment Management   www.timothyplan.com
Cracker Barrel Old Country Store   www.crackerbarrel.com
Cummins Engine Co.   www.cummins.com
Daiei Supermarket Group   www.daiei.co.jp
"Dallas"   www.members.xoom.com/DallasOnline
Damark International, Inc.   www.damark.com
"Dateline NBC"   www.msnbc.com/news/DATELINE_front.asp
Dayton Hudson   www.dhc.com
Deloitte & Touche   www.dttus.com
Delta Airlines   www.delta-air.com
Delta Dental Plan of Massachusetts   www.deltamass.com
Digital Equipment Corporation   www.digital.com
Disney   www.disney.go.com
Domini 400 Social Index   www.domani.com
Dow Chemical   www.dow.com
Dow Corning   www.dowcorning.com
Dreyer's Grand Ice Cream, Inc.   www.dreyers.com
Drug Enforcement Administration   www.usdoj.gov/dea/
Duke Power Company   www.dukepower.com
DuPont   www.dupont.com
Eastman Kodak Co.   www.kodak.com
Eddie Bauer   www.eddiebauer.com
Edmonton Youth Outreach Center   www.freenet.edmonton.ab.ca/glcce/edmorgs.htm
Eli Lilly   www.lilly.com
EnviroLink Network   www.envirolink.org
Environmental Defense Fund (EDF)   www.edf.org
Environmental Protection Agency (EPA)   www.epa.gov
Episcopal Church   www.ecusa.anglican.org
Equal Employment Opportunity Commission (EEOC)   www.eeoc.gov
Equifax   www.equifax.com
Esprit   www.esprit-intl.com
Ethics Officer Association (EOA)   www.eoa.org
European Foundation for Quality Management (EFQM)   www.efqm.org
Everen Securities   www.everensec.com
Executive Compensation Reports   www.ecronline.com
Exxon   www.exxon.com
Fannie Mae Corp.   www.fanniemae.com
Federal Aviation Administration (FAA)   www.faa.gov
Federal Communications Commission (FCC)   www.fcc.gov
Federal Deposit Insurance Corporation   www.fdic.gov
Federal Election Commission   www.fec.gov

Federal Energy Regulatory Commission   www.ferc.fed.us
Federal Express   www.fedex.com
Federal Highway Administration (FHWA)   www.fhwa.dot.gov
Federal Reserve System   www.bog.frb.fed.us
Federal Trade Commission   www.ftc.gov
Firestone   www.firestone.com
First Union Corp.   www.firstunion.com
Fisher-Price   www.fisher-price.com
FMC Corporation   www.fmc.com
Food and Drug Administration (FDA)   www.fda.gov
Ford   www2.ford.com
Foundation Center   www.fdncenter.org
Freeport-McMoran   www.fcx.com
Friends of the Earth   www.foe.org
GAF   www.gaf.com
Gallup Poll   www.gallup.com
General Dynamics   www.gd.com
General Electric Co. (GE)   www.ge.com
General Foods   www.kraft.com
General Mills   www.generalmills.com
General Motors (GM)   www.gm.com
General Public Utilities   www.paenergycampaign.org/gpu
Georgia Institute of Technology (Georgia Tech)   www.gatech.edu
Georgia Power Co.   www.georgiapower.com
Girl Scouts   www.girlscouts.org
Goldman Sachs   www.gs.com
Good Money, Inc.   www.goodmoney.com
Goodyear   www.goodyear.com
Government Printing Office (GPO)   www.access.gpo.gov
Grand Metropolitan   www.grand-metropolitan.org
Green Seal   www.greenseal.org
GreenPeace   www.greenpeace.org
Greyhound   www.greyhound.com
Gulf Oil   www.gulfoil.com
H. J. Heinz   www.heinz.com
H. B. Fuller Co.   www.hbfuller.com
Hampton Inn and Suites   www.hamptoninnandsuites.com
Harvard Business School   www.hbs.edu
Hasbro   www.hasbro.com
Health Benefits Coalition   www.hbcweb.com
Health Insurance Association of America   www.hiaa.org
Heidrick & Struggles   www.h-s.com
Herman Miller   www.hermanmiller.com
Hertz   www.hertz.com
Hewlett Packard   www.hp.com
Home Depot   www.homedepot.com
Honda   www.honda.com

Honeywell   www.honeywell.com
Human Resources Network   www.ihrim.org
Husqvarna, Inc.   www.husqvarna.com
Hyde Athletic Industries   www.saucony.com
Hydrox   www.keebler.com
Hyundai   www.hyundai.com
IBM   www.ibm.com
Infant Formula Action Coalition (INFACT)   www.infactcanada.ca
Institutional Shareholder Services   www.cda.com/iss
Intel   www.intel.com
Inter-American Development Bank   www.iadb.org
Interfaith Center on Corporate Responsibility (ICCR)   www.domini.com/ICCR.html
Internal Revenue Service (IRS)   www.irs.ustreas.gov
International Labor Organization (ILO)   usa.ilo.org/index.html
International Paper Co.   www.internationalpaper.com
International Standards Organization (ISO)   www.iso.ch
Investor Responsibility Research Center (IRRC)   www.irrc.org
Investors Rights Association   www.iraa.com
Issues Management Association   www.issuesmanagement.com
ITT Industries   www.ittind.com
Izaak Walton League   www.iwla.org
J. C. Penney   www.jcpenny.com
Jacksonville Port Authority   www.jaxport.com
Japanese Automobile Manufacturers' Association   www.japanauto.com
Johns Manville Corporation   www.jm.com and www.johns-manville.com
Johnson & Johnson   www.jnj.com and www.johnsonandjohnson.com
Johnson Controls, Inc.   www.jci.com
Johnson's Wax   www.scjohnsonwax.com
Josephson Institute of Ethics   www.josephsoninstitute.org
K-Mart   www.kmart.com
KaBoom!   www.kaboom.org
Kellogg's   www.kellogs.com
Kinder, Lydenberg, Domini & Co., Inc.   www.kld.com
KPMG   www.kpmg.net
Kraft   www.kraftsimpleanswers.com
Kroger Co.   www.kroger.com
L. L. Bean   www.llbean.com
LensCrafters   www.lenscrafters.com
Levi Strauss & Co.   www.levistrauss.com
Lexicon Communications   www.crisismanagement.com
Lightolier, Inc.   www.lightolier.com
Live Aid   www.herald.co.uk/local_info/live_aid.html
Liz Claiborne   www.lizclaiborne.com
Lockheed Martin   www.lmco.com
Lotus   www.lotus.com
Louis Harris and Associates, Inc.   www.louisharris.com
Luby's Cafeteria   www.lubys.com

Lutheran Church in America   www.elca.org
Management Institute for Environment and Business   www.wri.org/meb
Mars, Incorporated   www.mars.com
Martin Marietta   www.martinmarietta.com
MasterCard   www.mastercard.com
Mattel   www.mattel.com
McDonald's   www.mcdonalds.com
McDonnell Douglas   www.mdc.com
McGraw-Hill   www.mcgraw-hill.com
McKinsey & Company   www.mckinsey.com
MCI   www.mciworldcom.com
McNeil Laboratories   www.jnj.com and www.johnsonandjohnson.com
Medtronic   www.medtronic.com
Merck & Co., Inc.   www.merck.com
Microsoft   www.microsoft.com
Midas   www.midas.com
Miller Brewing   www.millerbrewing.com
The Minority Engineering Program of Indianapolis (MEPI)   www.mepi.org
Mitsubishi   www.mitsubishi.com
Mobil   www.mobil.com
Monsanto Co.   www.monsanto.com
Morton Thiokol   www.mortonthiokol.com
Mothers Against Drunk Driving (MADD)   www.madd.org
Motorola, Inc.   www.mot.com
National Association for the Advancement of Colored People (NAACP)   www.naacp.org
Naisbitt Group   www.naisbitt.com
NASA   www.nasa.gov
National Academy of Sciences   www.nas.edu
National Advertising Division (NAD)   www.bbb.org/advertising/advertiserAssist.html
National Advertising Review Board (NARB)   www.bbb.org/advertising/narb.html
National AIDS Fund (NAF)   www.aidsfund.org
National Association of Home Builders   www.nahb.com
National Association of Independent Insurers   www.naii.org
National Association of Manufacturers   www.nam.org
National Association of Realtors   www.realtor.com
The National Audubon Society   www.audubon.org
National Automobile Dealers Association   www.nada.org
National Basketball Players Association (NBA)   www.nba.com
National Cancer Institute   www.nci.nih.gov
National Center for Employee Ownership   www.nceo.org
National Council of Churches   www.nccusa.org/index.html
National Council on Alcoholism   www.ncadd.org
National Education Association   www.nea.org
National Federation of Independent Businesses (NFIB)   www.nfibonline.com
National Football League   www.nfl.com
National Foundation for the Improvement of Education (NFIE)   www.nfie.org
National Highway Traffic Safety Administration (NHTSA)   www.nhtsa.dot.gov

National Parent-Teacher Association   www.pta.org
National Resources Defense Council (NRDC)   www.nrdc.org
National Science Foundation   www.nsf.gov
National Semiconductor Corporation   www.nsc.com
National Society of Fundraising Executives   www.nsfre.org
National Steel   www.nationalsteel.com
National Telecommunications & Information Administration
National Urban League   www.nul.org
National Wildlife Foundation   www.nwf.org
NationsBank   www.nationsbank.com
Nature Conservancy   www.tnc.org
NBC   www.nbc.com
Nestlé   www.nestle.com
Netscape   www.netscape.com
Network Solutions   www.networksolutions.com
New Balance   www.nbshoes.com
New York Stock Exchange   www.nyse.com
Niagara Falls School Board   www.niagara.k12.ny.us/boardof.htm
Nicole Miller   www.nicolemiller.com
Nike   www.nike.com
Nintendo   www.nintendo.com
Nippon   www.nippon.com
Nordstrom, Inc.   www.nordstrom.com
Northeast Utilities   www.nu.com
Northern Telecom (Nortel)   www.nortel.com
Northrop   www.northgrum.com
Novell   www.novell.com
NYNEX   www.bell-atl.com
Occidental Petroleum Company   www.oxy.com
Occupational Safety and Health Administration (OSHA)   www.osha.gov
Office of Management and Budget (OMB)   www.whitehouse.gov/WH/EOP/omb
OPEC   www.opec.org
Organization for Economic Co-operation and Development (OECD)   www.oecd.org
Otto Versand   www.otto.de/o_index.html
Papa John's   www.papajohns.com
Partnership for a Drug-Free America   www.drugfreeamerica.org
Pennsylvania Department of Environmental Protection   www.dep.state.pa.us
PepsiCo   pepsico.pcy.mci.net
Perrier Water   www.perrier.com
Pfizer   www.pfizer.com
Philip Morris   www.philipmorris.com
Pillsbury   www.pillsbury.com
Pizza Hut   www.pizzahut.com
Points of Light Foundation   www.pointsoflight.org
Polaroid Corporation   www.polaroid.com
Post   www.kraftfoods.com
PPG Industries, Inc   www.ppg.com

Price Waterhouse LLC   www.pwcglobal.com
"Primetime Live"   www.abcnews.go.com/onair/primetimelive/index.html
Procter & Gamble   www.pg.com
Progressive Policy Institute   www.dlcppi.org
Prudential   www.prudential.com
Public Affairs Council   www.pac.org
Public Broadcasting System (PBS)   www.pbs.org
Public Relations Society of America   www.prsa.org/foundation/index.html
Quaker Oats Company   www.quakeroats.com
RJR Nabisco   www.nabisco.com
R. J. Reynolds (RJR) Tobacco Company   www.rjrt.com
Ragu   www.ragu.com
Rainforest Action Network   www.ran.org
Ralston Purina   www.ralstonpurina.com
Real Estate Board of New York   www.hia.com/rebny
Recycled Paper Coalition   www.elpc.org/market/RPC/RPC2.htm
Reebok   www.reebok.com
Renco Holdings   www.renco.com
Renew America   www.solstice.crest.org/environment/renew_america
Rexnord   www.rexnord.com
Ricoh   www.ricoh.co.jp/index_e.html
Ritz-Carlton Hotel Company   www.ritzcarlton.com
Roper Center   www.ropercenter.uconn.edu
Ross Laboratories, Inc.   www.rosslaboratories.com
S. C. Johnson & Sons   www.scjohnsonwax.com
Sabre Foundation, Inc.   www.sabre.com
Sainsbury   www.j-sainsbury.co.uk
The Salomon Brothers   www.sbam.com
Sanyo   www.sanyo.com
Sara Lee   www.saralee.com
Schwan's   www.schwans.com
Scientific Certification Systems   www.scs1.com
Scott Paper   www.kimberly-clark.com
Sears, Roebuck & Co.   www.sears.com
Securities and Exchange Commission (SEC)   www.sec.gov
Seventh Generation   www.seventhgen.com
SGS-ICS   www.sgsicsus.com
Shell Oil   www.shell.com
Sierra Club   www.sierraclub.org
SmithKline-Beecham   www.sb.com
SmithOBrien Services   www.smithobrien.com
Social Investment Forum   www.socialinvest.org
Social Security Administration (SSA)   www.ssa.gov
Society for Human Resource Management (SHRM)   www.shrm.org
Sony   www.sony.com
Sperry Rand   www.unisys.com
Springs Industries, Inc.   www.springs.com

Sprint   www.sprint.com
Standard & Poor's   www.standardandpoors.com
Star-Kist Foods   www.starkist.com
Starbucks Coffee Co.   www.starbucks.com
Stonyfield Farm   www.stonyfield.com
Stride Rite   www.striderite.com
Sun Company   www.sun.com
Sun Microsystems   www.sun.com
Sun Oil Company   www.sunocoinc.com
Sunbeam Corp.   www.sunbeam.com
Sweatshop Watch   www.sweatshopwatch.org
Taco Bell   www.tacobell.com
Teledyne   www.teledyne.com
Tenneco   www.tenneco.com
Tennessee Valley Authority (TVA)   www.tva.gov
Texaco   www.texaco.com
Texas Instruments   www.ti.com
Texas Utilities   www.tu.com
The Timberland Co.   www.timberland.com
Time Warner   www.timewarner.com
Timex   www.timex.com
Tobacco Institute   www.tobaccoinstitute.com
Tom's of Maine   www.toms-of-maine.com
Toyota   www.toyota.com
Toys 'R' Us   www.toysrus.com
Trans Union   www.transunion.com
Transparency International   www.transparency.de
Travelers   www.travelers.com
Tufts New England Medical Center   www.nemc.org
Turner Broadcasting Systems   www.tbssuperstation.com
TWA   www.twa.com
Tyson Foods   www.tyson.com
U-Haul International   www.uhaul.com
U.S. Census Bureau   www.census.gov
U.S. Centers for Disease Control and Prevention   www.cdc.gov
U.S. Chamber of Commerce   www.uschamber.org
U.S. Commission on Civil Rights   www.usccr.gov
U.S. Council on Environmental Quality (CEQ)   www.whitehouse.gov/CEQ
U.S. Department of Agriculture   www.usda.gov
U.S. Department of Commerce   www.doc.gov
U.S. Department of Justice   www.usdoj.gov
U.S. Department of Labor   www.dol.gov
U.S. Department of the Interior   www.doi.gov
U.S. Food and Drug Administration (FDA)   www.fda.gov
U.S. Office of Technology Assessment   www.ota.nap.edu
U.S. Postal Service   www.usps.gov
Union Camp   www.unioncamp.com

Union Carbide   www.unioncarbide.com
Uniroyal   www.uniroyal.com
United Airlines   www.ual.com
United Auto Workers (UAW)   www.uaw.com
United Church of Christ   www.ucc.org
United Methodists   www.umc.org
United Nations Children's Fund (UNICEF)   www.unicef.org
United Nations Environment Programme (UNEP)   www.unep.org
United Negro College Fund   www.uncf.org
United Presbyterian Church   www.pcusa.org
United Way   www.unitedway.org
University of Toronto   www.toronto.edu
Upjohn   www.upjohn.com
UPS   www.ups.com
USG Corporation   www.usg.com
Usinor Sacilor S. A.   www.usinor.com
USX Corporation   www.usx.com
ValuJet   www.valujet.com
VF Corporation   www.vfc.com
VH1   www.vh1.com
Vlasic   www.vlasic.com
Volvo Cars of North America   www.volvo.com
W. R. Grace & Co.   www.grace.com
Wal-Mart   www.wal-mart.com
Walker Research Associates   www.walkerresearch.com
The Washington Post   www.washpostco.com
Weight Watchers   www.weight-watchers.com
Weirton Steel   www.weirton.com
Wendy's   www.wendys.com
Westinghouse   www.westinghouse.com
Whirlpool Corporation   www.whirlpool.com
Whitehall Laboratories   www.healthfront.com
The Wilderness Society   www.wilderness.org
Uncle Wiley's   www.unclewileys.com
The Wilson Group   www.wilson-group.com
The Wine Institute   www.wineinstitute.org
Wolverine World Wide   www.wolverineworldwide.com
The World Bank Group   www.worldbank.org
World Health Organization (WHO)   www.who.org
World Wildlife Fund   www.wwf.org
Xerox Corp.   www.xerox.com
Yankelovich, Skelly, and White (YSW)   www.yankelovich.com
YMCA   www.ymca.net
YWCA   www.ywca.org

Name Index

Subject Index